SCRABBLE
BRAND Crossword Game

WORD
IMPROVER

HarperCollins Publishers
Westerhill Road
Bishopbriggs
Glasgow
G64 2QT
Great Britain

First Edition 2010

Reprint 10 9 8 7 6 5 4 3 2 1 0

© HarperCollins Publishers 2010

ISBN 978-0-00-737467-0

Collins® is a registered trademark of
HarperCollins Publishers Limited

SCRABBLE™ is a registered trademark
of J.W. Spear and Sons Ltd., a subsidiary
of Mattel, Inc., © 2010 Mattel, Inc.
All rights reserved.

www.collinslanguage.com

A catalogue record for this book is
available from the British Library

Typeset by
Davidson Publishing Solutions, Glasgow

Printed in Great Britain by
Clays Ltd, St Ives plc

Acknowledgements
We would like to thank those authors and
publishers who kindly gave permission for
copyright material to be used in the
Collins Word Web. We would also like to
thank Times Newspapers Ltd for providing
valuable data.

SCRABBLE™ CONSULTANT
Allan Simmons

EDITORS
Gerry Breslin
Robert Groves

COMPUTING SUPPORT
Thomas Callan

FOR THE PUBLISHER
Lucy Cooper
Kerry Ferguson
Elaine Higgleton

CONTENTS

Finding New Words for Scrabble

Allan Simmons

Scrabble Word Improver is a unique book for Scrabble fans, whether casual or regular club and tournament players. It focuses on words in the Collins Official Scrabble Wordlist which can be extended by a single letter before or after, termed a 'hook'. Such a play normally occurs when a new word is played at right-angles and at the end of an existing word, thus 'hooking' it.

The most common hook would be playing a word with an **S** so that it pluralizes an existing word. Although any letter could be the hooking letter, the most frequent examples, besides **S**, are **D** and **R**; eg, **TIME** becoming **TIMED** or **TIMER**. Sometimes the new word isn't related to the original word on the board; eg **CAMEO**, **FIRST** and **VINYL** from **CAME**, **FIRS** and **VINY**. These can be more difficult to spot, even if they are common words. This book will help remind you of such extensions as well as introduce you to ones you may never have thought of. Spotting hook possibilities and knowing unusual hooks are fundamental Scrabble skills and this book will extend your knowledge in this area and improve your game.

The book includes all forms of a word, whether plural, verbal inflection, etc, provided it has at least one hook extension. However, words that do not take any hook letters before or after are excluded. These words are called 'blockers', and by leaving blockers out it helps to focus attention on all the useful and interesting hooks available for the game.

For example, these words and their hooks are included:

BIBLES-S
HOMELY-N
MARRIED-S
PIECING-S
I-DEALS
Y-MOLTEN

And these words are excluded because they have no hooks:

LABELS
TIMELY
CARRIED
PEACING
MEALS
BITTEN

Hooks are very useful in Scrabble for increasing your scores, because when you play a word which hooks onto an existing word you score the points for your main play, plus the points for the hooked word. Furthermore, the unusual hooks can help you to squeeze plays onto a tight board, surprise your opponent, and provide selfish access to triple word squares.

For example, if you have the last two I's, and a rack such as **DEIINPV**, perhaps you could play **VIED** to open up, knowing that you have the only I for **IVIED**.

I recommend you use this book in several ways to improve your game. Try and become perfect at knowing all the two-letter words and, if not all, as many as possible the three-letter words that can be formed by front or end-hooking a two-letter word. The last section of this book is all you need to focus on for that exercise.

It can be difficult to remember so many new words, and sometimes an *aide-mémoire* is useful to help you recall them in a game situation. If you look at all the two-letter words which can be extended by adding a letter at the beginning or end to make a new word, you will soon see that some words have many possible hooks. One way to remember these is to use a mnemonic.

Take the word **AH**, for example.

This can be front hooked with any of **A B D F H L N P R Y**

You may conjure up a phrase consisting of words beginning only with those letters to help you remember these, such as:

Always Note Your Rare Hook Letters For Banking Devious Points

The main section of the book lists all words from two to nine letters in length that have at least one hook letter. You can use the main section of the book in various ways. I find it delightful just to flick through and find some interesting hooks that I wouldn't have otherwise known. These are especially useful if the word being extended is a fairly common word or a high probability Scrabble word because then you are more likely to get an opportunity to make use of the hook.

Another approach is to note down any words during a game, that you cannot think of any hooks for at the time, and then check the pages of this book afterwards to see what you might have missed. Don't assume a word is a blocker – you will be surprised by many of the allowable hooks shown in this book. For example, **CATCH**, looks inextensible but both **SCATCH** and **CATCHT** are allowed.

As you become more familiar with useful hooks you need to ensure you remain vigilant during your games. It is all too easy to miss even common extensions if you are not actively looking out for them. Practice looking out for hooking opportunities as the game develops whether they arise from your opponent's plays or your own.

At a first glance the following board looks to be rather blocked but it might surprise you to learn that there are six different triple words that are accessible. Can you find those triple-word plays using the rack supplied? It isn't difficult if you can spot the allowable hooks of existing words. Use the book to help if you are uninspired. (Solutions are given on page 954).

A

FRONT HOOK	ROOT WORD	END HOOK
BAA · CAA · FAA · MAA	**AA**	AAH · AAL · AAS
	AAH	AAHS
BAAL · KAAL · PAAL · TAAL	**AAL**	AALS
	AALII	AALIIS
BAALS · PAALS · TAALS	**AALS**	
	AARDVARK	AARDVARKS
	AARRGH	AARRGHH
	AARTI	AARTIS
BAAS · CAAS · FAAS · KAAS · MAAS	**AAS**	
	AASVOGEL	AASVOGELS
CAB · DAB · FAB · GAB · JAB · KAB · LAB NAB · SAB · TAB · WAB	**AB**	ABA · ABB · ABO (offensive) · ABS · ABY
BABA · CABA · YABA	**ABA**	ABAC · ABAS
	ABAC	ABACA · ABACI · ABACK · ABACS
	ABACA	ABACAS
	ABACTOR	ABACTORS
KABAKA	**ABAKA**	ABAKAS
KABAKAS	**ABAKAS**	
	ABALONE	ABALONES
	ABAMP	ABAMPS
	ABAMPERE	ABAMPERES
	ABAND	ABANDS
	ABANDON	ABANDONS
	ABANDONEE	ABANDONEES
	ABANDONER	ABANDONERS
BABAS · CABAS	**ABAS**	ABASE · ABASH · ABASK
	ABASE	ABASED · ABASER · ABASES
	ABASEMENT	ABASEMENTS
	ABASER	ABASERS
	ABASHMENT	ABASHMENTS
	ABASIA	ABASIAS
	ABATE	ABATED · ABATER · ABATES
	ABATEMENT	ABATEMENTS
	ABATER	ABATERS
	ABATOR	ABATORS
	ABATTOIR	ABATTOIRS
	ABATURE	ABATURES
KABAYA	**ABAYA**	ABAYAS
KABAYAS	**ABAYAS**	
	ABB	ABBA · ABBE · ABBS
DABBA · YABBA	**ABBA**	ABBAS
DABBAS · YABBAS	**ABBAS**	
	ABBE	ABBED · ABBES · ABBEY
CABBED · DABBED · GABBED · JABBED NABBED · SABBED · TABBED	**ABBED**	
	ABBES	ABBESS
	ABBEY	ABBEYS
	ABBOT	ABBOTS
	ABBOTSHIP	ABBOTSHIPS
	ABCEE	ABCEES
	ABCOULOMB	ABCOULOMBS
HABDABS	**ABDABS**	
	ABDICATE	ABDICATED · ABDICATES
	ABDICATOR	ABDICATORS
	ABDOMEN	ABDOMENS
	ABDOMINA	ABDOMINAL
	ABDOMINAL	ABDOMINALS
	ABDUCE	ABDUCED · ABDUCES
	ABDUCT	ABDUCTS
	ABDUCTEE	ABDUCTEES
	ABDUCTION	ABDUCTIONS
	ABDUCTOR	ABDUCTORS
	ABEAR	ABEARS
SABED	**ABED**	
KABELE	**ABELE**	ABELES
KABELES	**ABELES**	

FRONT HOOK	ROOT WORD	END HOOK
	ABELIA	ABELIAN · ABELIAS
	ABELMOSK	ABELMOSKS
	ABERRANCE	ABERRANCES
	ABERRANT	ABERRANTS
	ABERRATE	ABERRATED · ABERRATES
	ABESSIVE	ABESSIVES
	ABET	ABETS
	ABETMENT	ABETMENTS
	ABETTAL	ABETTALS
	ABETTER	ABETTERS
	ABETTOR	ABETTORS
	ABEYANCE	ABEYANCES
	ABFARAD	ABFARADS
	ABHENRY	ABHENRYS
	ABHOR	ABHORS
	ABHORRER	ABHORRERS
	ABHORRING	ABHORRINGS
RABID · TABID	**ABID**	ABIDE
	ABIDANCE	ABIDANCES
	ABIDE	ABIDED · ABIDER · ABIDES
RABIDER	**ABIDER**	ABIDERS
	ABIDING	ABIDINGS
BABIES · GABIES · RABIES	**ABIES**	
RABIETIC	**ABIETIC**	
	ABIGAIL	ABIGAILS
LABILITIES	**ABILITIES**	
LABILITY	**ABILITY**	
	ABJECT	ABJECTS
	ABJECTION	ABJECTIONS
	ABJOINT	ABJOINTS
	ABJURE	ABJURED · ABJURER · ABJURES
	ABJURER	ABJURERS
	ABLATE	ABLATED · ABLATES
	ABLATION	ABLATIONS
	ABLATIVE	ABLATIVES
	ABLATOR	ABLATORS
	ABLAUT	ABLAUTS
CABLE · FABLE · GABLE · HABLE · SABLE · TABLE	**ABLE**	ABLED · ABLER · ABLES · ABLET
CABLED · FABLED · GABLED · SABLED · TABLED	**ABLED**	
	ABLEGATE	ABLEGATES
	ABLEISM	ABLEISMS
	ABLEIST	ABLEISTS
CABLER · FABLER	**ABLER**	
CABLES · FABLES · GABLES · SABLES · TABLES	**ABLES**	ABLEST
CABLET · GABLET · TABLET	**ABLET**	ABLETS
CABLETS · GABLETS · TABLETS	**ABLETS**	
CABLING · FABLING · GABLING · SABLING · TABLING	**ABLING**	ABLINGS
CABLINGS · FABLINGS · TABLINGS	**ABLINGS**	
	ABLUENT	ABLUENTS
	ABLUTION	ABLUTIONS
	ABMHO	ABMHOS
	ABNEGATE	ABNEGATED · ABNEGATES
	ABNEGATOR	ABNEGATORS
	ABNORMAL	ABNORMALS
	ABO	ABOS (offensive)
	ABODE	ABODED · ABODES
	ABODEMENT	ABODEMENTS
	ABOHM	ABOHMS
	ABOIDEAU	ABOIDEAUS · ABOIDEAUX
	ABOITEAU	ABOITEAUS · ABOITEAUX
	ABOLISHER	ABOLISHERS
	ABOLITION	ABOLITIONS
	ABOLLA	ABOLLAE · ABOLLAS
	ABOMA	ABOMAS
	ABOMAS	ABOMASA · ABOMASI

FRONT HOOK	ROOT WORD	END HOOK
	ABOMASA	ABOMASAL
	ABOMINATE	ABOMINATED ▪ ABOMINATES
	ABONDANCE	ABONDANCES
BABOON ▪ GABOON	ABOON	
	ABORD	ABORDS
	ABORIGEN	ABORIGENS
	ABORIGIN	ABORIGINE ▪ ABORIGINS
	ABORIGINE	ABORIGINES
	ABORT	ABORTS
	ABORTEE	ABORTEES
	ABORTER	ABORTERS
	ABORTION	ABORTIONS
	ABOULIA	ABOULIAS
	ABOUND	ABOUNDS
	ABOUT	ABOUTS
	ABOVE	ABOVES
	ABRACHIA	ABRACHIAS
	ABRADANT	ABRADANTS
	ABRADE	ABRADED ▪ ABRADER ▪ ABRADES
	ABRADER	ABRADERS
	ABRAID	ABRAIDS
	ABRASION	ABRASIONS
	ABRASIVE	ABRASIVES
	ABRAY	ABRAYS
	ABRAZO	ABRAZOS
	ABREACT	ABREACTS
	ABREGE	ABREGES
	ABRI	ABRIM ▪ ABRIN ▪ ABRIS
	ABRICOCK	ABRICOCKS
	ABRIDGE	ABRIDGED ▪ ABRIDGER ▪ ABRIDGES
	ABRIDGER	ABRIDGERS
	ABRIN	ABRINS
	ABROAD	ABROADS
	ABROGATE	ABROGATED ▪ ABROGATES
	ABROGATOR	ABROGATORS
	ABROOKE	ABROOKED ▪ ABROOKES
	ABROSIA	ABROSIAS
	ABRUPT	ABRUPTS
	ABRUPTION	ABRUPTIONS
CABS ▪ DABS ▪ FABS ▪ GABS ▪ JABS ▪ KABS LABS ▪ NABS ▪ SABS ▪ TABS ▪ WABS (offensive)	ABS	
	ABSCIND	ABSCINDS
	ABSCISE	ABSCISED ▪ ABSCISES
	ABSCISIN	ABSCISING ▪ ABSCISINS
	ABSCISS	ABSCISSA ▪ ABSCISSE
	ABSCISSA	ABSCISSAE ▪ ABSCISSAS
	ABSCISSE	ABSCISSES
	ABSCISSIN	ABSCISSINS
	ABSCOND	ABSCONDS
	ABSCONDER	ABSCONDERS
	ABSEIL	ABSEILS
	ABSEILING	ABSEILINGS
	ABSENCE	ABSENCES
	ABSENT	ABSENTS
	ABSENTEE	ABSENTEES
	ABSENTER	ABSENTERS
	ABSEY	ABSEYS
	ABSINTH	ABSINTHE ▪ ABSINTHS
	ABSINTHE	ABSINTHES
	ABSIT	ABSITS
	ABSOLUTE	ABSOLUTER ▪ ABSOLUTES
	ABSOLUTES	ABSOLUTEST
	ABSOLVE	ABSOLVED ▪ ABSOLVER ▪ ABSOLVES
	ABSOLVENT	ABSOLVENTS
	ABSOLVER	ABSOLVERS
	ABSORB	ABSORBS
	ABSORBANT	ABSORBANTS
	ABSORBATE	ABSORBATES
	ABSORBENT	ABSORBENTS

FRONT HOOK	ROOT WORD	END HOOK
	ABSORBER	ABSORBERS
	ABSTAIN	ABSTAINS
	ABSTAINER	ABSTAINERS
	ABSTERGE	ABSTERGED ▪ ABSTERGES
	ABSTRACT	ABSTRACTS
	ABSTRICT	ABSTRICTS
	ABSTRUSE	ABSTRUSER
	ABSURD	ABSURDS
	ABSURDISM	ABSURDISMS
	ABSURDIST	ABSURDISTS
	ABTHANE	ABTHANES
	ABULIA	ABULIAS
	ABUNA	ABUNAS
	ABUNDANCE	ABUNDANCES
	ABUSAGE	ABUSAGES
	ABUSE	ABUSED ▪ ABUSER ▪ ABUSES
	ABUSER	ABUSERS
	ABUSION	ABUSIONS
	ABUT	ABUTS
	ABUTILON	ABUTILONS
	ABUTMENT	ABUTMENTS
	ABUTTAL	ABUTTALS
	ABUTTER	ABUTTERS
	ABVOLT	ABVOLTS
	ABWATT	ABWATTS
BABY ▪ GABY	**ABY**	ABYE ▪ ABYS
	ABYE	ABYES
BABYING	**ABYING**	
	ABYS	ABYSM ▪ ABYSS
	ABYSM	ABYSMS
	ACACIA	ACACIAS
	ACADEME	ACADEMES
	ACADEMIA	ACADEMIAS
	ACADEMIC	ACADEMICS
	ACADEMISM	ACADEMISMS
	ACADEMIST	ACADEMISTS
	ACAI	ACAIS
	ACAJOU	ACAJOUS
	ACALCULIA	ACALCULIAS
	ACALEPH	ACALEPHE ▪ ACALEPHS
	ACALEPHAN	ACALEPHANS
	ACALEPHE	ACALEPHES
	ACANTH	ACANTHA ▪ ACANTHI ▪ ACANTHS
	ACANTHA	ACANTHAE ▪ ACANTHAS
	ACANTHI	ACANTHIN
	ACANTHIN	ACANTHINE ▪ ACANTHINS
	ACAPNIA	ACAPNIAS
	ACARBOSE	ACARBOSES
	ACARI	ACARID
	ACARICIDE	ACARICIDES
	ACARID	ACARIDS
	ACARIDAN	ACARIDANS
	ACARIDEAN	ACARIDEANS
	ACARIDIAN	ACARIDIANS
	ACARINE	ACARINES
	ACATER	ACATERS
VACATES	**ACATES**	
	ACATOUR	ACATOURS
BACCA ▪ YACCA	**ACCA**	ACCAS
BACCAS ▪ YACCAS	**ACCAS**	
	ACCEDE	ACCEDED ▪ ACCEDER ▪ ACCEDES
	ACCEDENCE	ACCEDENCES
	ACCEDER	ACCEDERS
	ACCEND	ACCENDS
	ACCENSION	ACCENSIONS
	ACCENT	ACCENTS
	ACCENTOR	ACCENTORS
	ACCEPT	ACCEPTS
	ACCEPTANT	ACCEPTANTS

FRONT HOOK	ROOT WORD	END HOOK
	ACCEPTEE	ACCEPTEES
	ACCEPTER	ACCEPTERS
	ACCEPTOR	ACCEPTORS
	ACCESSION	ACCESSIONS
	ACCIDENCE	ACCIDENCES
	ACCIDENT	ACCIDENTS
	ACCIDIA	ACCIDIAS
	ACCIDIE	ACCIDIES
	ACCINGE	ACCINGED ▪ ACCINGES
	ACCIPITER	ACCIPITERS
	ACCITE	ACCITED ▪ ACCITES
	ACCLAIM	ACCLAIMS
	ACCLAIMER	ACCLAIMERS
	ACCLIMATE	ACCLIMATED ▪ ACCLIMATES
	ACCLOY	ACCLOYS
	ACCOAST	ACCOASTS
	ACCOIL	ACCOILS
	ACCOLADE	ACCOLADED ▪ ACCOLADES
	ACCOMPT	ACCOMPTS
	ACCORAGE	ACCORAGED ▪ ACCORAGES
	ACCORD	ACCORDS
	ACCORDER	ACCORDERS
	ACCORDION	ACCORDIONS
	ACCOST	ACCOSTS
	ACCOUNT	ACCOUNTS
	ACCOURAGE	ACCOURAGED ▪ ACCOURAGES
	ACCOURT	ACCOURTS
	ACCOUTER	ACCOUTERS
	ACCOUTRE	ACCOUTRED ▪ ACCOUTRES
	ACCOY	ACCOYS
	ACCREDIT	ACCREDITS
	ACCRETE	ACCRETED ▪ ACCRETES
	ACCRETION	ACCRETIONS
	ACCREW	ACCREWS
	ACCRUAL	ACCRUALS
	ACCRUE	ACCRUED ▪ ACCRUES
	ACCURSE	ACCURSED ▪ ACCURSES
	ACCUSAL	ACCUSALS
	ACCUSANT	ACCUSANTS
	ACCUSE	ACCUSED ▪ ACCUSER ▪ ACCUSES
	ACCUSER	ACCUSERS
	ACCUSTOM	ACCUSTOMS
DACE ▪ FACE ▪ LACE ▪ MACE ▪ PACE ▪ RACE ▪ TACE	ACE	ACED ▪ ACER ▪ ACES
FACED ▪ LACED ▪ MACED ▪ PACED ▪ RACED	ACED	
	ACEDIA	ACEDIAS
	ACELDAMA	ACELDAMAS
	ACEQUIA	ACEQUIAS
FACER ▪ LACER ▪ MACER ▪ PACER ▪ RACER	ACER	ACERB ▪ ACERS
LACERATE ▪ MACERATE	ACERATE	ACERATED
LACERATED ▪ MACERATED	ACERATED	
	ACERBATE	ACERBATED ▪ ACERBATES
	ACEROLA	ACEROLAS
FACERS ▪ LACERS ▪ MACERS ▪ PACERS ▪ RACERS	ACERS	
DACES ▪ FACES ▪ LACES ▪ MACES ▪ PACES ▪ RACES ▪ TACES	ACES	
	ACESCENCE	ACESCENCES
	ACESCENT	ACESCENTS
	ACETA	ACETAL
	ACETABULA	ACETABULAR
	ACETAL	ACETALS
	ACETAMID	ACETAMIDE ▪ ACETAMIDS
	ACETAMIDE	ACETAMIDES
	ACETATE	ACETATED ▪ ACETATES
	ACETIFIER	ACETIFIERS
	ACETIN	ACETINS
	ACETONE	ACETONES
	ACETOXYL	ACETOXYLS

FRONT HOOK	ROOT WORD	END HOOK
	ACETYL	ACETYLS
	ACETYLATE	ACETYLATED = ACETYLATES
	ACETYLENE	ACETYLENES
	ACETYLIDE	ACETYLIDES
BACH = EACH = MACH = NACH = RACH = TACH	ACH	ACHE = ACHY
	ACHAENIUM	ACHAENIUMS
	ACHAGE	ACHAGES
	ACHALASIA	ACHALASIAS
	ACHARYA	ACHARYAS
CACHE = MACHE = NACHE = RACHE = TACHE	ACHE	ACHED = ACHES
BACHED = CACHED	ACHED	
	ACHENE	ACHENES
	ACHENIA	ACHENIAL
	ACHENIUM	ACHENIUMS
BACHES = CACHES = LACHES = MACHES NACHES = RACHES = TACHES	ACHES	
	ACHIEVE	ACHIEVED = ACHIEVER = ACHIEVES
	ACHIEVER	ACHIEVERS
	ACHILLEA	ACHILLEAS
BACHING = CACHING	ACHING	ACHINGS
	ACHIOTE	ACHIOTES
	ACHKAN	ACHKANS
	ACHOLIA	ACHOLIAS
	ACHROMAT	ACHROMATS
	ACICULA	ACICULAE = ACICULAR = ACICULAS
	ACICULATE	ACICULATED
	ACICULUM	ACICULUMS
	ACID	ACIDS = ACIDY
	ACIDEMIA	ACIDEMIAS
	ACIDFREAK	ACIDFREAKS
	ACIDHEAD	ACIDHEADS
	ACIDIFIER	ACIDIFIERS
	ACIDOPHIL	ACIDOPHILE = ACIDOPHILS
	ACIDULATE	ACIDULATED = ACIDULATES
	ACIDURIA	ACIDURIAS
	ACIERAGE	ACIERAGES
	ACIERATE	ACIERATED = ACIERATES
FACING = LACING = MACING = PACING RACING	ACING	
	ACINI	ACINIC
HACKEE	ACKEE	ACKEES
HACKEES	ACKEES	
BACKER = DACKER = HACKER = JACKER LACKER = PACKER = RACKER = SACKER TACKER = WACKER = YACKER	ACKER	ACKERS
BACKERS = DACKERS = HACKERS = JACKERS LACKERS = PACKERS = RACKERS = SACKERS TACKERS = WACKERS = YACKERS	ACKERS	
	ACKNOW	ACKNOWN = ACKNOWS
	ACKNOWN	ACKNOWNE
	ACME	ACMES
	ACMITE	ACMITES
	ACNE	ACNED = ACNES
TACNODE	ACNODE	ACNODES
TACNODES	ACNODES	
	ACOLYTE	ACOLYTES
	ACOLYTH	ACOLYTHS
TACONITE	ACONITE	ACONITES
TACONITES	ACONITES	
	ACONITINE	ACONITINES
	ACONITUM	ACONITUMS
	ACORN	ACORNS
	ACOSMISM	ACOSMISMS
	ACOSMIST	ACOSMISTS
	ACOUCHI	ACOUCHIS
	ACOUSTIC	ACOUSTICS
	ACQUAINT	ACQUAINTS
	ACQUEST	ACQUESTS
	ACQUIESCE	ACQUIESCED = ACQUIESCES

FRONT HOOK	ROOT WORD	END HOOK
	ACQUIGHT	ACQUIGHTS
	ACQUIRAL	ACQUIRALS
	ACQUIRE	ACQUIRED ▪ ACQUIREE ▪ ACQUIRER ▪ ACQUIRES
	ACQUIREE	ACQUIREES
	ACQUIRER	ACQUIRERS
	ACQUIST	ACQUISTS
	ACQUIT	ACQUITE ▪ ACQUITS
	ACQUITE	ACQUITES
	ACQUITTAL	ACQUITTALS
	ACQUITTER	ACQUITTERS
	ACRASIA	ACRASIAS
	ACRASIN	ACRASINS
NACRE	ACRE	ACRED ▪ ACRES
	ACREAGE	ACREAGES
NACRED ▪ SACRED	ACRED	
NACRES	ACRES	
	ACRIDIN	ACRIDINE ▪ ACRIDINS
	ACRIDINE	ACRIDINES
	ACRITARCH	ACRITARCHS
	ACROBAT	ACROBATS
	ACROBATIC	ACROBATICS
MACRODONT	ACRODONT	ACRODONTS
	ACROGEN	ACROGENS
	ACROLECT	ACROLECTS
	ACROLEIN	ACROLEINS
	ACROLITH	ACROLITHS
	ACROMIA	ACROMIAL
	ACRONYM	ACRONYMS
	ACROPHOBE	ACROPHOBES
	ACROSOME	ACROSOMES
	ACROSPIRE	ACROSPIRES
	ACROSTIC	ACROSTICS
	ACROTER	ACROTERS
	ACROTERIA	ACROTERIAL
	ACROTISM	ACROTISMS
	ACRYLATE	ACRYLATES
	ACRYLIC	ACRYLICS
	ACRYLYL	ACRYLYLS
FACT ▪ PACT ▪ TACT	ACT	ACTA ▪ ACTS
PACTA	ACTA	
	ACTANT	ACTANTS
	ACTIN	ACTING ▪ ACTINS
	ACTING	ACTINGS
	ACTINIA	ACTINIAE ▪ ACTINIAN ▪ ACTINIAS
	ACTINIAN	ACTINIANS
	ACTINIDE	ACTINIDES
	ACTINISM	ACTINISMS
	ACTINIUM	ACTINIUMS
	ACTINOID	ACTINOIDS
	ACTINON	ACTINONS
	ACTINOPOD	ACTINOPODS
FACTION ▪ PACTION ▪ TACTION	ACTION	ACTIONS
PACTIONED	ACTIONED	
	ACTIONER	ACTIONERS
PACTIONING	ACTIONING	
FACTIONIST	ACTIONIST	ACTIONISTS
FACTIONS ▪ PACTIONS ▪ TACTIONS	ACTIONS	
	ACTIVATE	ACTIVATED ▪ ACTIVATES
	ACTIVATOR	ACTIVATORS
FACTIVE	ACTIVE	ACTIVES
	ACTIVISE	ACTIVISED ▪ ACTIVISES
	ACTIVISM	ACTIVISMS
	ACTIVIST	ACTIVISTS
	ACTIVIZE	ACTIVIZED ▪ ACTIVIZES
	ACTON	ACTONS
FACTOR	ACTOR	ACTORS
FACTORS	ACTORS	
	ACTRESS	ACTRESSY
FACTS ▪ PACTS ▪ TACTS	ACTS	

FRONT HOOK	ROOT WORD	END HOOK
FACTUAL · TACTUAL	**ACTUAL**	ACTUALS
	ACTUALISE	ACTUALISED · ACTUALISES
FACTUALIST	**ACTUALIST**	ACTUALISTS
	ACTUALITE	ACTUALITES
FACTUALITY · TACTUALITY	**ACTUALITY**	
	ACTUALIZE	ACTUALIZED · ACTUALIZES
FACTUALLY · TACTUALLY	**ACTUALLY**	
	ACTUATE	ACTUATED · ACTUATES
	ACTUATION	ACTUATIONS
	ACTUATOR	ACTUATORS
FACTURE	**ACTURE**	ACTURES
FACTURES	**ACTURES**	
VACUATE	**ACUATE**	
VACUITIES	**ACUITIES**	
VACUITY	**ACUITY**	
	ACULEATE	ACULEATED
CACUMEN	**ACUMEN**	ACUMENS
	ACUMINATE	ACUMINATED · ACUMINATES
CACUMINOUS	**ACUMINOUS**	
	ACUPOINT	ACUPOINTS
	ACUSHLA	ACUSHLAS
	ACUTANCE	ACUTANCES
	ACUTE	ACUTER · ACUTES
	ACUTES	ACUTEST
	ACYCLOVIR	ACYCLOVIRS
	ACYL	ACYLS
	ACYLATE	ACYLATED · ACYLATES
	ACYLATION	ACYLATIONS
	ACYLOIN	ACYLOINS
BAD · CAD · DAD · FAD · GAD · HAD · LAD MAD · PAD · RAD · SAD · TAD · WAD · YAD	**AD**	ADD · ADO · ADS · ADZ
	ADAGE	ADAGES
	ADAGIO	ADAGIOS
	ADAMANCE	ADAMANCES
	ADAMANT	ADAMANTS
	ADAMSITE	ADAMSITES
	ADAPT	ADAPTS
	ADAPTER	ADAPTERS
	ADAPTION	ADAPTIONS
	ADAPTOGEN	ADAPTOGENS
	ADAPTOR	ADAPTORS
	ADAW	ADAWS
WADD	**ADD**	ADDS · ADDY
DADDED · GADDED · MADDED · PADDED RADDED · SADDED · WADDED	**ADDED**	
	ADDEEM	ADDEEMS
	ADDEND	ADDENDA · ADDENDS
	ADDENDUM	ADDENDUMS
BADDER · GADDER · LADDER · MADDER PADDER · RADDER · SADDER · WADDER	**ADDER**	ADDERS
GADDERS · LADDERS · MADDERS · PADDERS WADDERS	**ADDERS**	
	ADDERWORT	ADDERWORTS
	ADDICT	ADDICTS
	ADDICTION	ADDICTIONS
BADDIES · CADDIES · DADDIES · HADDIES LADDIES · PADDIES · TADDIES · WADDIES	**ADDIES**	
DADDING · GADDING · HADDING · MADDING PADDING · RADDING · SADDING · WADDING	**ADDING**	
	ADDIO	ADDIOS
	ADDITION	ADDITIONS
	ADDITIVE	ADDITIVES
DADDLE · FADDLE · PADDLE · RADDLE SADDLE · WADDLE	**ADDLE**	ADDLED · ADDLES
DADDLED · FADDLED · PADDLED · RADDLED SADDLED · WADDLED	**ADDLED**	
	ADDLEMENT	ADDLEMENTS
DADDLES · FADDLES · PADDLES · RADDLES SADDLES · WADDLES	**ADDLES**	

FRONT HOOK	ROOT WORD	END HOOK
DADDLING ▪ FADDLING ▪ PADDLING RADDLING ▪ SADDLING ▪ WADDLING	**ADDLING**	
	ADDOOM	ADDOOMS
	ADDRESSEE	ADDRESSEES
	ADDRESSER	ADDRESSERS
	ADDRESSOR	ADDRESSORS
WADDS	**ADDS**	
	ADDUCE	ADDUCED ▪ ADDUCER ▪ ADDUCES
	ADDUCER	ADDUCERS
	ADDUCT	ADDUCTS
	ADDUCTION	ADDUCTIONS
	ADDUCTOR	ADDUCTORS
BADDY ▪ CADDY ▪ DADDY ▪ FADDY ▪ PADDY WADDY	**ADDY**	
	ADEEM	ADEEMS
	ADEMPTION	ADEMPTIONS
	ADENINE	ADENINES
	ADENOID	ADENOIDS
	ADENOMA	ADENOMAS
	ADENOSINE	ADENOSINES
	ADENYL	ADENYLS
	ADEPT	ADEPTS
	ADERMIN	ADERMINS
	ADESSIVE	ADESSIVES
	ADHAN	ADHANS
	ADHARMA	ADHARMAS
	ADHERE	ADHERED ▪ ADHERER ▪ ADHERES
	ADHERENCE	ADHERENCES
	ADHEREND	ADHERENDS
	ADHERENT	ADHERENTS
	ADHERER	ADHERERS
	ADHESION	ADHESIONS
	ADHESIVE	ADHESIVES
	ADHIBIT	ADHIBITS
	ADIABATIC	ADIABATICS
	ADIEU	ADIEUS ▪ ADIEUX
RADIOS	**ADIOS**	
	ADIPOCERE	ADIPOCERES
	ADIPOCYTE	ADIPOCYTES
	ADIPOSE	ADIPOSES
	ADIPSIA	ADIPSIAS
	ADIT	ADITS
	ADJACENCE	ADJACENCES
	ADJACENT	ADJACENTS
	ADJECTIVE	ADJECTIVES
	ADJIGO	ADJIGOS
	ADJOIN	ADJOINS ▪ ADJOINT
	ADJOINT	ADJOINTS
	ADJOURN	ADJOURNS
	ADJUDGE	ADJUDGED ▪ ADJUDGES
	ADJUNCT	ADJUNCTS
	ADJURE	ADJURED ▪ ADJURER ▪ ADJURES
	ADJURER	ADJURERS
	ADJUROR	ADJURORS
	ADJUST	ADJUSTS
	ADJUSTER	ADJUSTERS
	ADJUSTOR	ADJUSTORS
	ADJUTAGE	ADJUTAGES
	ADJUTANT	ADJUTANTS
	ADJUVANT	ADJUVANTS
BADLAND	**ADLAND**	ADLANDS
BADLANDS	**ADLANDS**	
BADMAN ▪ MADMAN	**ADMAN**	
	ADMEASURE	ADMEASURED ▪ ADMEASURES
BADMEN ▪ MADMEN	**ADMEN**	
	ADMIN	ADMINS
	ADMINICLE	ADMINICLES
	ADMIRAL	ADMIRALS
	ADMIRANCE	ADMIRANCES

FRONT HOOK	ROOT WORD	END HOOK
	ADMIRE	ADMIRED · ADMIRER · ADMIRES
	ADMIRER	ADMIRERS
	ADMISSION	ADMISSIONS
	ADMIT	ADMITS
	ADMITTEE	ADMITTEES
	ADMITTER	ADMITTERS
	ADMIX	ADMIXT
	ADMIXTURE	ADMIXTURES
	ADMONITOR	ADMONITORS · ADMONITORY
	ADNATION	ADNATIONS
	ADNEXA	ADNEXAL
	ADNOMINAL	ADNOMINALS
	ADNOUN	ADNOUNS
DADO · FADO · SADO	**ADO**	ADOS
	ADOBE	ADOBES
	ADOBO	ADOBOS
	ADONIS	ADONISE
	ADONISE	ADONISED · ADONISES
	ADONIZE	ADONIZED · ADONIZES
	ADOPT	ADOPTS
	ADOPTEE	ADOPTEES
	ADOPTER	ADOPTERS
	ADOPTION	ADOPTIONS
	ADORATION	ADORATIONS
	ADORE	ADORED · ADORER · ADORES
	ADORER	ADORERS
	ADORN	ADORNS
	ADORNER	ADORNERS
	ADORNMENT	ADORNMENTS
DADOS · FADOS · SADOS	**ADOS**	
	ADREAD	ADREADS
	ADRENAL	ADRENALS
	ADRENALIN	ADRENALINE · ADRENALINS
BADS · CADS · DADS · FADS · GADS · HADS LADS · MADS · NADS · PADS · RADS · SADS TADS · WADS · YADS	**ADS**	
	ADSCRIPT	ADSCRIPTS
	ADSORB	ADSORBS
	ADSORBATE	ADSORBATES
	ADSORBENT	ADSORBENTS
	ADSORBER	ADSORBERS
	ADSUKI	ADSUKIS
	ADUKI	ADUKIS
	ADULARIA	ADULARIAS
RADULATE	**ADULATE**	ADULATED · ADULATES
	ADULATION	ADULATIONS
	ADULATOR	ADULATORS · ADULATORY
	ADULT	ADULTS
	ADULTERER	ADULTERERS
	ADULTHOOD	ADULTHOODS
	ADUMBRATE	ADUMBRATED · ADUMBRATES
	ADUNCATE	ADUNCATED
	ADUST	ADUSTS
TADVANCE	**ADVANCE**	ADVANCED · ADVANCER · ADVANCES
	ADVANCER	ADVANCERS
	ADVANTAGE	ADVANTAGED · ADVANTAGES
	ADVECT	ADVECTS
	ADVECTION	ADVECTIONS
	ADVENE	ADVENED · ADVENES
	ADVENT	ADVENTS
	ADVENTIVE	ADVENTIVES
	ADVENTURE	ADVENTURED · ADVENTURER · ADVENTURES
	ADVERB	ADVERBS
	ADVERBIAL	ADVERBIALS
	ADVERSE	ADVERSER
	ADVERT	ADVERTS
	ADVERTISE	ADVERTISED · ADVERTISER · ADVERTISES
	ADVERTIZE	ADVERTIZED · ADVERTIZER · ADVERTIZES
	ADVEW	ADVEWS

FRONT HOOK	ROOT WORD	END HOOK
	ADVICE	ADVICES
	ADVISE	ADVISED ▪ ADVISEE ▪ ADVISER ▪ ADVISES
	ADVISEE	ADVISEES
	ADVISER	ADVISERS
	ADVISING	ADVISINGS
	ADVISOR	ADVISORS ▪ ADVISORY
	ADVOCAAT	ADVOCAATS
	ADVOCATE	ADVOCATED ▪ ADVOCATES
	ADVOCATOR	ADVOCATORS ▪ ADVOCATORY
	ADVOUTRER	ADVOUTRERS
	ADVOWSON	ADVOWSONS
	ADWARD	ADWARDS
	ADWARE	ADWARES
MADWOMAN	**ADWOMAN**	
MADWOMEN	**ADWOMEN**	
	ADYNAMIA	ADYNAMIAS
	ADZ	ADZE
	ADZE	ADZED ▪ ADZES
	ADZUKI	ADZUKIS
DAE ▪ FAE ▪ GAE ▪ HAE ▪ KAE ▪ MAE ▪ NAE SAE ▪ TAE ▪ VAE ▪ WAE ▪ YAE	**AE**	
	AECIA	AECIAL
	AECIDIA	AECIDIAL
	AEDICULE	AEDICULES
	AEDILE	AEDILES
	AEGIRINE	AEGIRINES
	AEGIRITE	AEGIRITES
	AEGLOGUE	AEGLOGUES
	AEGROTAT	AEGROTATS
	AEMULE	AEMULED ▪ AEMULES
	AEOLIPILE	AEOLIPILES
	AEOLIPYLE	AEOLIPYLES
PAEON	**AEON**	AEONS
PAEONIC	**AEONIC**	
PAEONS	**AEONS**	
	AEQUORIN	AEQUORINS
	AERATE	AERATED ▪ AERATES
	AERATION	AERATIONS
	AERATOR	AERATORS
	AERIAL	AERIALS
	AERIALIST	AERIALISTS
FAERIE	**AERIE**	AERIED ▪ AERIER ▪ AERIES
FAERIES	**AERIES**	AERIEST
	AERO	AEROS
	AEROBAT	AEROBATS
	AEROBATIC	AEROBATICS
	AEROBE	AEROBES
	AEROBIC	AEROBICS
	AEROBIONT	AEROBIONTS
	AEROBOMB	AEROBOMBS
	AEROBRAKE	AEROBRAKED ▪ AEROBRAKES
	AERODART	AERODARTS
	AERODROME	AERODROMES
	AERODUCT	AERODUCTS
	AERODYNE	AERODYNES
	AEROFOIL	AEROFOILS
	AEROGEL	AEROGELS
	AEROGRAM	AEROGRAMS
	AEROGRAPH	AEROGRAPHS ▪ AEROGRAPHY
	AEROLITE	AEROLITES
	AEROLITH	AEROLITHS
	AEROMETER	AEROMETERS
	AEROMOTOR	AEROMOTORS
	AERONAUT	AERONAUTS
	AERONOMER	AERONOMERS
	AEROPAUSE	AEROPAUSES
	AEROPHOBE	AEROPHOBES
	AEROPHONE	AEROPHONES
	AEROPHORE	AEROPHORES

FRONT HOOK	ROOT WORD	END HOOK
	AEROPHYTE	AEROPHYTES
	AEROPLANE	AEROPLANES
	AEROPULSE	AEROPULSES
	AEROSAT	AEROSATS
	AEROSCOPE	AEROSCOPES
	AEROSHELL	AEROSHELLS
	AEROSOL	AEROSOLS
	AEROSPACE	AEROSPACES
	AEROSTAT	AEROSTATS
	AEROTONE	AEROTONES
	AEROTRAIN	AEROTRAINS
	AERUGO	AERUGOS
FAERY	AERY	
	AESCULIN	AESCULINS
	AESTHESIA	AESTHESIAS
	AESTHETE	AESTHETES
	AESTHETIC	AESTHETICS
	AESTIVATE	AESTIVATED ▪ AESTIVATES
	AETHER	AETHERS
	AFAR	AFARA ▪ AFARS
	AFARA	AFARAS
	AFEAR	AFEARD ▪ AFEARS
BAFF ▪ CAFF ▪ DAFF ▪ FAFF ▪ GAFF ▪ HAFF NAFF ▪ RAFF ▪ WAFF ▪ YAFF	AFF	AFFY
	AFFAIR	AFFAIRE ▪ AFFAIRS
	AFFAIRE	AFFAIRES
	AFFEAR	AFFEARD ▪ AFFEARE ▪ AFFEARS
	AFFEARE	AFFEARED ▪ AFFEARES
	AFFECT	AFFECTS
	AFFECTER	AFFECTERS
	AFFECTION	AFFECTIONS
	AFFEER	AFFEERS
	AFFERENT	AFFERENTS
	AFFIANCE	AFFIANCED ▪ AFFIANCES
	AFFIANT	AFFIANTS
	AFFICHE	AFFICHES
	AFFIDAVIT	AFFIDAVITS
BAFFIES ▪ DAFFIES ▪ TAFFIES ▪ WAFFIES	AFFIES	
	AFFILIATE	AFFILIATED ▪ AFFILIATES
	AFFINE	AFFINED ▪ AFFINES
	AFFIRM	AFFIRMS
	AFFIRMANT	AFFIRMANTS
	AFFIRMER	AFFIRMERS
	AFFIXER	AFFIXERS
	AFFIXMENT	AFFIXMENTS
	AFFIXTURE	AFFIXTURES
	AFFLATION	AFFLATIONS
	AFFLICT	AFFLICTS
	AFFLICTER	AFFLICTERS
	AFFLUENCE	AFFLUENCES
	AFFLUENT	AFFLUENTS
	AFFLUENZA	AFFLUENZAS
	AFFLUXION	AFFLUXIONS
	AFFOORD	AFFOORDS
	AFFORCE	AFFORCED ▪ AFFORCES
	AFFORD	AFFORDS
	AFFOREST	AFFORESTS
	AFFRAP	AFFRAPS
	AFFRAY	AFFRAYS
	AFFRAYER	AFFRAYERS
	AFFRET	AFFRETS
	AFFRICATE	AFFRICATED ▪ AFFRICATES
	AFFRIGHT	AFFRIGHTS
	AFFRONT	AFFRONTE ▪ AFFRONTS
	AFFRONTE	AFFRONTED ▪ AFFRONTEE
	AFFUSION	AFFUSIONS
BAFFY ▪ DAFFY ▪ TAFFY	AFFY	
	AFGHAN	AFGHANI ▪ AFGHANS
	AFGHANI	AFGHANIS

FRONT HOOK	ROOT WORD	END HOOK
	AFLATOXIN	AFLATOXINS
	AFREET	AFREETS
	AFRIT	AFRITS
	AFRO	AFROS
BAFT ▪ DAFT ▪ HAFT ▪ RAFT ▪ SAFT ▪ WAFT	**AFT**	
DAFTER ▪ HAFTER ▪ RAFTER ▪ SAFTER WAFTER	**AFTER**	AFTERS
	AFTERCARE	AFTERCARES
	AFTERCLAP	AFTERCLAPS
	AFTERDAMP	AFTERDAMPS
	AFTERDECK	AFTERDECKS
	AFTEREYE	AFTEREYED ▪ AFTEREYES
	AFTERGAME	AFTERGAMES
	AFTERGLOW	AFTERGLOWS
	AFTERHEAT	AFTERHEATS
RAFTERINGS	**AFTERINGS**	
	AFTERLIFE	AFTERLIFES
	AFTERMATH	AFTERMATHS
	AFTERNOON	AFTERNOONS
	AFTERPAIN	AFTERPAINS
	AFTERPEAK	AFTERPEAKS
HAFTERS ▪ RAFTERS ▪ WAFTERS	**AFTERS**	
	AFTERSHOW	AFTERSHOWS
	AFTERSUN	AFTERSUNS
	AFTERTIME	AFTERTIMES
	AFTERWARD	AFTERWARDS
	AFTERWORD	AFTERWORDS
	AFTOSA	AFTOSAS
BAG ▪ CAG ▪ DAG ▪ FAG ▪ GAG ▪ HAG ▪ JAG LAG ▪ MAG ▪ NAG ▪ RAG ▪ SAG ▪ TAG ▪ VAG WAG ▪ YAG ▪ ZAG	**AG**	AGA ▪ AGE ▪ AGO ▪ AGS
GAGA ▪ JAGA ▪ NAGA ▪ RAGA ▪ SAGA	**AGA**	AGAR ▪ AGAS
	AGACANT	AGACANTE
	AGACERIE	AGACERIES
	AGALACTIA	AGALACTIAS
	AGALLOCH	AGALLOCHS
	AGALWOOD	AGALWOODS
	AGAMA	AGAMAS
	AGAMETE	AGAMETES
	AGAMI	AGAMIC ▪ AGAMID ▪ AGAMIS
	AGAMID	AGAMIDS
	AGAMOID	AGAMOIDS
	AGAMONT	AGAMONTS
	AGAPE	AGAPES
	AGAR	AGARS
	AGARIC	AGARICS
	AGAROSE	AGAROSES
JAGAS ▪ NAGAS ▪ RAGAS ▪ SAGAS	**AGAS**	AGAST
	AGATE	AGATES
	AGATEWARE	AGATEWARES
	AGATISE	AGATISED ▪ AGATISES
	AGATIZE	AGATIZED ▪ AGATIZES
	AGAVE	AGAVES
	AGAZE	AGAZED
CAGE ▪ GAGE ▪ MAGE ▪ PAGE ▪ RAGE ▪ SAGE WAGE	**AGE**	AGED ▪ AGEE ▪ AGEN ▪ AGER ▪ AGES
CAGED ▪ GAGED ▪ PAGED ▪ RAGED ▪ WAGED RAGEE	**AGED**	
	AGEE	
	AGEING	AGEINGS
	AGEISM	AGEISMS
	AGEIST	AGEISTS
	AGELAST	AGELASTS
WAGELESS	**AGELESS**	
	AGEMATE	AGEMATES
	AGEN	AGENE ▪ AGENT
	AGENDA	AGENDAS
	AGENDUM	AGENDUMS
SAGENE	**AGENE**	AGENES
SAGENES	**AGENES**	

FRONT HOOK	ROOT WORD	END HOOK
	AGENESIA	AGENESIAS
	AGENISE	AGENISED ▪ AGENISES
	AGENIZE	AGENIZED ▪ AGENIZES
	AGENT	AGENTS
	AGENTING	AGENTINGS
	AGENTIVE	AGENTIVES
CAGER ▪ EAGER ▪ GAGER ▪ JAGER ▪ LAGER PAGER ▪ RAGER ▪ SAGER ▪ WAGER ▪ YAGER	AGER	AGERS
	AGERATUM	AGERATUMS
CAGERS ▪ EAGERS ▪ GAGERS ▪ JAGERS LAGERS ▪ PAGERS ▪ RAGERS ▪ WAGERS YAGERS	AGERS	
CAGES ▪ GAGES ▪ MAGES ▪ PAGES ▪ RAGES SAGES ▪ WAGES	AGES	
	AGEUSIA	AGEUSIAS
HAGGADA	AGGADA	AGGADAH ▪ AGGADAS
HAGGADAH	AGGADAH	AGGADAHS
HAGGADAHS	AGGADAHS	
HAGGADAS	AGGADAS	
HAGGADIC	AGGADIC	
HAGGADOT	AGGADOT	AGGADOTH
HAGGADOTH	AGGADOTH	
BAGGER ▪ DAGGER ▪ GAGGER ▪ JAGGER LAGGER ▪ NAGGER ▪ SAGGER ▪ TAGGER WAGGER ▪ YAGGER	AGGER	AGGERS
BAGGERS ▪ DAGGERS ▪ GAGGERS ▪ JAGGERS LAGGERS ▪ NAGGERS ▪ SAGGERS ▪ TAGGERS WAGGERS ▪ YAGGERS	AGGERS	
BAGGIE ▪ MAGGIE	AGGIE	AGGIES
BAGGIES ▪ JAGGIES ▪ MAGGIES ▪ RAGGIES	AGGIES	
	AGGRACE	AGGRACED ▪ AGGRACES
	AGGRADE	AGGRADED ▪ AGGRADES
	AGGRATE	AGGRATED ▪ AGGRATES
	AGGRAVATE	AGGRAVATED ▪ AGGRAVATES
	AGGREGATE	AGGREGATED ▪ AGGREGATES
	AGGRESSOR	AGGRESSORS
	AGGRIEVE	AGGRIEVED ▪ AGGRIEVES
	AGGRO	AGGROS
	AGHA	AGHAS
	AGHAS	AGHAST
	AGILA	AGILAS
VAGILE	AGILE	AGILER
VAGILITIES	AGILITIES	
VAGILITY	AGILITY	
FAGIN	AGIN	AGING
CAGING ▪ GAGING ▪ PAGING ▪ RAGING WAGING	AGING	AGINGS
PAGINGS ▪ RAGINGS	AGINGS	
	AGINNER	AGINNERS
	AGIO	AGIOS
	AGIOTAGE	AGIOTAGES
MAGISM	AGISM	AGISMS
MAGISMS	AGISMS	
	AGIST	AGISTS
MAGISTER	AGISTER	AGISTERS
MAGISTERS	AGISTERS	
	AGISTMENT	AGISTMENTS
	AGISTOR	AGISTORS
	AGITA	AGITAS
	AGITATE	AGITATED ▪ AGITATES
	AGITATION	AGITATIONS
	AGITATO	AGITATOR
	AGITATOR	AGITATORS
	AGITPOP	AGITPOPS
	AGITPROP	AGITPROPS
EAGLET ▪ HAGLET	AGLET	AGLETS
EAGLETS ▪ HAGLETS	AGLETS	
	AGLOO	AGLOOS
	AGLOSSIA	AGLOSSIAS

FRONT HOOK	ROOT WORD	END HOOK
	AGLU	AGLUS
	AGLYCON	AGLYCONE · AGLYCONS
	AGLYCONE	AGLYCONES
MAGMA · TAGMA	**AGMA**	AGMAS
MAGMAS	**AGMAS**	
	AGNAIL	AGNAILS
	AGNAME	AGNAMED · AGNAMES
MAGNATE	**AGNATE**	AGNATES
MAGNATES	**AGNATES**	
	AGNATHAN	AGNATHANS
	AGNATION	AGNATIONS
	AGNISE	AGNISED · AGNISES
	AGNIZE	AGNIZED · AGNIZES
	AGNOMEN	AGNOMENS
	AGNOMINA	AGNOMINAL
	AGNOSIA	AGNOSIAS
	AGNOSTIC	AGNOSTICS
DAGO · KAGO · SAGO	**AGO**	AGOG · AGON
	AGOG	AGOGE
	AGOGE	AGOGES
	AGOGIC	AGOGICS
WAGON	**AGON**	AGONE · AGONS · AGONY
	AGONE	AGONES
	AGONISE	AGONISED · AGONISES
	AGONIST	AGONISTS
	AGONISTIC	AGONISTICS
	AGONIZE	AGONIZED · AGONIZES
WAGONS	**AGONS**	
	AGORA	AGORAE · AGORAS
	AGOROT	AGOROTH
	AGOUTA	AGOUTAS
	AGOUTI	AGOUTIS
	AGRAFE	AGRAFES
	AGRAFFE	AGRAFFES
	AGRAPHIA	AGRAPHIAS
	AGRARIAN	AGRARIANS
	AGREE	AGREED · AGREES
	AGREEMENT	AGREEMENTS
	AGREGE	AGREGES
	AGREMENT	AGREMENTS
	AGRIA	AGRIAS
	AGRISE	AGRISED · AGRISES
	AGRIZE	AGRIZED · AGRIZES
	AGRODOLCE	AGRODOLCES
	AGRONOMIC	AGRONOMICS
	AGRYPNIA	AGRYPNIAS
	AGRYZE	AGRYZED · AGRYZES
BAGS · CAGS · DAGS · FAGS · GAGS · HAGS JAGS · LAGS · MAGS · NAGS · RAGS · SAGS TAGS · VAGS · WAGS · YAGS · ZAGS	**AGS**	
	AGTERSKOT	AGTERSKOTS
	AGUACATE	AGUACATES
VAGUE	**AGUE**	AGUED · AGUES
VAGUED	**AGUED**	
VAGUES	**AGUES**	
	AGUEWEED	AGUEWEEDS
	AGUISE	AGUISED · AGUISES
	AGUIZE	AGUIZED · AGUIZES
	AGUTI	AGUTIS
AAH · BAH · DAH · FAH · HAH · LAH · NAH PAH · RAH · YAH	**AH**	AHA · AHI · AHS
HAHA · TAHA	**AHA**	
AAHED · RAHED	**AHED**	
	AHI	AHIS
	AHIMSA	AHIMSAS
AAHING · RAHING	**AHING**	
	AHOLD	AHOLDS
AAHS · DAHS · FAHS · HAHS · LAHS · PAHS RAHS · YAHS	**AHS**	

FRONT HOOK	ROOT WORD	END HOOK
JAI ▪ KAI ▪ RAI ▪ SAI ▪ TAI ▪ WAI	**AI**	AIA ▪ AID ▪ AIL ▪ AIM ▪ AIN ▪ AIR AIS ▪ AIT
RAIA	**AIA**	AIAS
RAIAS	**AIAS**	
CAID ▪ GAID ▪ KAID ▪ LAID ▪ MAID ▪ PAID QAID ▪ RAID ▪ SAID ▪ WAID	**AID**	AIDE ▪ AIDS
	AIDANCE	AIDANCES
WAIDE	**AIDE**	AIDED ▪ AIDER ▪ AIDES
LAIDED ▪ MAIDED ▪ RAIDED	**AIDED**	
RAIDER	**AIDER**	AIDERS
RAIDERS	**AIDERS**	
LAIDING ▪ MAIDING ▪ RAIDING	**AIDING**	
MAIDLESS	**AIDLESS**	
CAIDS ▪ GAIDS ▪ KAIDS ▪ LAIDS ▪ MAIDS QAIDS ▪ RAIDS ▪ SAIDS	**AIDS**	
SAIGA ▪ TAIGA	**AIGA**	AIGAS
SAIGAS ▪ TAIGAS	**AIGAS**	
	AIGLET	AIGLETS
	AIGRET	AIGRETS
	AIGRETTE	AIGRETTES
	AIGUILLE	AIGUILLES
	AIKIDO	AIKIDOS
BAIL ▪ FAIL ▪ HAIL ▪ JAIL ▪ KAIL ▪ MAIL NAIL ▪ PAIL ▪ RAIL ▪ SAIL ▪ TAIL ▪ VAIL WAIL	**AIL**	AILS
	AILANTO	AILANTOS
BAILED ▪ FAILED ▪ HAILED ▪ JAILED MAILED ▪ NAILED ▪ RAILED ▪ SAILED TAILED ▪ VAILED ▪ WAILED	**AILED**	
TAILERON	**AILERON**	AILERONS
TAILERONS	**AILERONS**	
	AILETTE	AILETTES
BAILING ▪ FAILING ▪ HAILING ▪ JAILING MAILING ▪ NAILING ▪ RAILING ▪ SAILING TAILING ▪ VAILING ▪ WAILING	**AILING**	
BAILMENT	**AILMENT**	AILMENTS
BAILMENTS	**AILMENTS**	
BAILS ▪ FAILS ▪ HAILS ▪ JAILS ▪ KAILS MAILS ▪ NAILS ▪ PAILS ▪ RAILS ▪ SAILS TAILS ▪ VAILS ▪ WAILS	**AILS**	
KAIM ▪ MAIM ▪ SAIM	**AIM**	AIMS
MAIMED	**AIMED**	
MAIMER	**AIMER**	AIMERS
MAIMERS	**AIMERS**	
MAIMING	**AIMING**	
KAIMS ▪ MAIMS ▪ SAIMS	**AIMS**	
CAIN ▪ FAIN ▪ GAIN ▪ HAIN ▪ KAIN ▪ LAIN MAIN ▪ NAIN ▪ PAIN ▪ RAIN ▪ SAIN ▪ TAIN VAIN ▪ WAIN	**AIN**	AINE ▪ AINS
DAINE ▪ FAINE ▪ RAINE ▪ SAINE	**AINE**	AINEE
KAINGA	**AINGA**	AINGAS
KAINGAS	**AINGAS**	
CAINS ▪ FAINS ▪ GAINS ▪ HAINS ▪ KAINS MAINS ▪ PAINS ▪ RAINS ▪ SAINS ▪ TAINS WAINS	**AINS**	
NAINSELL	**AINSELL**	AINSELLS
NAINSELLS	**AINSELLS**	
	AIOLI	AIOLIS
FAIR ▪ GAIR ▪ HAIR ▪ LAIR ▪ MAIR ▪ PAIR SAIR ▪ VAIR ▪ WAIR	**AIR**	AIRN ▪ AIRS ▪ AIRT ▪ AIRY
	AIRBAG	AIRBAGS
	AIRBASE	AIRBASES
	AIRBOAT	AIRBOATS
	AIRBRICK	AIRBRICKS
HAIRBRUSH	**AIRBRUSH**	
	AIRBURST	AIRBURSTS
	AIRCHECK	AIRCHECKS
	AIRCREW	AIRCREWS
	AIRDATE	AIRDATES

FRONT HOOK	ROOT WORD	END HOOK
	AIRDROME	AIRDROMES
	AIRDROP	AIRDROPS
FAIRED ▪ HAIRED ▪ LAIRED ▪ PAIRED SAIRED ▪ WAIRED	**AIRED**	
FAIRER ▪ PAIRER ▪ SAIRER	**AIRER**	AIRERS
FAIREST ▪ PAIREST ▪ SAIREST	**AIREST**	
	AIRFARE	AIRFARES
	AIRFIELD	AIRFIELDS
	AIRFLOW	AIRFLOWS
	AIRFOIL	AIRFOILS
	AIRFRAME	AIRFRAMES
	AIRGAP	AIRGAPS
	AIRGLOW	AIRGLOWS
	AIRGRAPH	AIRGRAPHS
	AIRHEAD	AIRHEADS
	AIRHOLE	AIRHOLES
HAIRIER ▪ LAIRIER ▪ VAIRIER	**AIRIER**	
HAIRIEST ▪ LAIRIEST ▪ VAIRIEST	**AIRIEST**	
FAIRILY	**AIRILY**	
HAIRINESS	**AIRINESS**	
FAIRING ▪ HAIRING ▪ LAIRING ▪ PAIRING SAIRING ▪ WAIRING	**AIRING**	AIRINGS
FAIRINGS ▪ PAIRINGS	**AIRINGS**	
HAIRLESS	**AIRLESS**	
	AIRLIFT	AIRLIFTS
HAIRLIKE	**AIRLIKE**	
HAIRLINE	**AIRLINE**	AIRLINER ▪ AIRLINES
	AIRLINER	AIRLINERS
HAIRLINES	**AIRLINES**	
HAIRLOCK	**AIRLOCK**	AIRLOCKS
HAIRLOCKS	**AIRLOCKS**	
	AIRMAIL	AIRMAILS
BAIRN ▪ CAIRN	**AIRN**	AIRNS
CAIRNED	**AIRNED**	
BAIRNS ▪ CAIRNS	**AIRNS**	
	AIRPARK	AIRPARKS
	AIRPLANE	AIRPLANES
	AIRPLAY	AIRPLAYS
	AIRPORT	AIRPORTS
	AIRPOST	AIRPOSTS
	AIRPOWER	AIRPOWERS
	AIRPROOF	AIRPROOFS
FAIRS ▪ GAIRS ▪ HAIRS ▪ LAIRS ▪ MAIRS PAIRS ▪ SAIRS ▪ VAIRS ▪ WAIRS	**AIRS**	
	AIRSCAPE	AIRSCAPES
	AIRSCREW	AIRSCREWS
	AIRSHAFT	AIRSHAFTS
	AIRSHED	AIRSHEDS
	AIRSHIP	AIRSHIPS
	AIRSHOT	AIRSHOTS
	AIRSHOW	AIRSHOWS
	AIRSIDE	AIRSIDES
	AIRSPACE	AIRSPACES
	AIRSPEED	AIRSPEEDS
	AIRSTOP	AIRSTOPS
	AIRSTREAM	AIRSTREAMS
	AIRSTRIKE	AIRSTRIKES
	AIRSTRIP	AIRSTRIPS
	AIRT	AIRTH ▪ AIRTS
	AIRTH	AIRTHS
	AIRTIME	AIRTIMES
	AIRWARD	AIRWARDS
	AIRWAVE	AIRWAVES
FAIRWAY	**AIRWAY**	AIRWAYS
FAIRWAYS	**AIRWAYS**	
PAIRWISE	**AIRWISE**	
DAIRY ▪ FAIRY ▪ HAIRY ▪ LAIRY ▪ VAIRY	**AIRY**	
DAIS ▪ KAIS ▪ PAIS ▪ RAIS ▪ SAIS ▪ TAIS WAIS	**AIS**	

FRONT HOOK	ROOT WORD	END HOOK
	AISLE	AISLED ▪ AISLES
	AISLEWAY	AISLEWAYS
	AISLING	AISLINGS
BAIT ▪ GAIT ▪ RAIT ▪ TAIT ▪ WAIT	AIT	AITS ▪ AITU
	AITCHBONE	AITCHBONES
BAITS ▪ GAITS ▪ RAITS ▪ TAITS ▪ WAITS	AITS	
	AITU	AITUS
NAIVER ▪ TAIVER ▪ WAIVER	AIVER	AIVERS
TAIVERS ▪ WAIVERS	AIVERS	
	AIZLE	AIZLES
	AJIVA	AJIVAS
	AJOWAN	AJOWANS
	AJUGA	AJUGAS
	AJUTAGE	AJUTAGES
	AJWAN	AJWANS
HAKA ▪ KAKA ▪ TAKA ▪ WAKA	AKA	
	AKARYOTE	AKARYOTES
	AKATHISIA	AKATHISIAS
BAKE ▪ CAKE ▪ FAKE ▪ HAKE ▪ JAKE ▪ LAKE	AKE	AKED ▪ AKEE ▪ AKES
MAKE ▪ RAKE ▪ SAKE ▪ TAKE ▪ WAKE		
	AKEAKE	AKEAKES
BAKED ▪ CAKED ▪ FAKED ▪ LAKED ▪ NAKED	AKED	
OAKED ▪ RAKED ▪ WAKED		
	AKEDAH	AKEDAHS
RAKEE	AKEE	AKEES
RAKEES	AKEES	
	AKELA	AKELAS
	AKENE	AKENES
BAKES ▪ CAKES ▪ FAKES ▪ HAKES ▪ JAKES	AKES	
LAKES ▪ MAKES ▪ RAKES ▪ SAKES ▪ TAKES		
WAKES		
	AKHARA	AKHARAS
LAKIN ▪ TAKIN	AKIN	AKING
	AKINESIA	AKINESIAS
BAKING ▪ CAKING ▪ FAKING ▪ LAKING	AKING	
MAKING ▪ RAKING ▪ TAKING ▪ WAKING		
	AKITA	AKITAS
YAKKAS	AKKAS	
	AKRASIA	AKRASIAS
	AKVAVIT	AKVAVITS
AAL ▪ BAL ▪ DAL ▪ GAL ▪ MAL ▪ PAL ▪ SAL	AL	ALA ▪ ALB ▪ ALE ▪ ALF ▪ ALL ▪ ALP ▪ ALS ▪ ALT
GALA ▪ MALA ▪ NALA ▪ TALA	ALA	ALAE ▪ ALAN ▪ ALAP ▪ ALAR ▪ ALAS ▪ ALAY
	ALAAP	ALAAPS
	ALABAMINE	ALABAMINES
	ALABASTER	ALABASTERS
	ALACHLOR	ALACHLORS
	ALAIMENT	ALAIMENTS
	ALALIA	ALALIAS
	ALAMEDA	ALAMEDAS
	ALAMO	ALAMOS
	ALAMODE	ALAMODES
	ALAN	ALAND ▪ ALANE ▪ ALANG ▪ ALANS ▪ ALANT
	ALAND	ALANDS
LALANG	ALANG	ALANGS
LALANGS	ALANGS	
	ALANIN	ALANINE ▪ ALANINS
	ALANINE	ALANINES
	ALANNAH	ALANNAHS
GALANT ▪ TALANT	ALANT	ALANTS
TALANTS	ALANTS	
	ALANYL	ALANYLS
JALAP	ALAP	ALAPA ▪ ALAPS
PALAPA	ALAPA	ALAPAS
PALAPAS	ALAPAS	
JALAPS	ALAPS	
MALAR ▪ TALAR	ALAR	ALARM ▪ ALARY
	ALARM	ALARMS
	ALARMISM	ALARMISMS
	ALARMIST	ALARMISTS

FRONT HOOK	ROOT WORD	END HOOK
	ALARUM	ALARUMS
SALARY	**ALARY**	
BALAS · GALAS · MALAS · NALAS · PALAS · TALAS	**ALAS**	
	ALASKA	ALASKAS
	ALASTOR	ALASTORS
	ALASTRIM	ALASTRIMS
MALATE · PALATE	**ALATE**	ALATED · ALATES
PALATED	**ALATED**	
MALATES · PALATES	**ALATES**	
HALATION	**ALATION**	ALATIONS
HALATIONS	**ALATIONS**	
PALAY	**ALAY**	ALAYS
PALAYS	**ALAYS**	
	ALB	ALBA · ALBE · ALBS
	ALBA	ALBAS
	ALBACORE	ALBACORES
	ALBARELLO	ALBARELLOS
	ALBATA	ALBATAS
	ALBE	ALBEE
	ALBEDO	ALBEDOS
HALBERT	**ALBERT**	ALBERTS
	ALBERTITE	ALBERTITES
HALBERTS	**ALBERTS**	
	ALBESPINE	ALBESPINES
	ALBESPYNE	ALBESPYNES
	ALBICORE	ALBICORES
	ALBINISM	ALBINISMS
	ALBINO	ALBINOS
	ALBINOISM	ALBINOISMS
	ALBITE	ALBITES
	ALBITISE	ALBITISED · ALBITISES
	ALBITIZE	ALBITIZED · ALBITIZES
	ALBIZIA	ALBIZIAS
	ALBIZZIA	ALBIZZIAS
	ALBUGO	ALBUGOS
	ALBUM	ALBUMS
	ALBUMEN	ALBUMENS
	ALBUMIN	ALBUMINS
	ALBUMOSE	ALBUMOSES
	ALBURNUM	ALBURNUMS
	ALBUTEROL	ALBUTEROLS
FALCADE	**ALCADE**	ALCADES
FALCADES	**ALCADES**	
	ALCAHEST	ALCAHESTS
	ALCAIC	ALCAICS
	ALCAIDE	ALCAIDES
	ALCALDE	ALCALDES
	ALCARRAZA	ALCARRAZAS
	ALCAYDE	ALCAYDES
	ALCAZAR	ALCAZARS
	ALCHEMISE	ALCHEMISED · ALCHEMISES
	ALCHEMIST	ALCHEMISTS
	ALCHEMIZE	ALCHEMIZED · ALCHEMIZES
	ALCHERA	ALCHERAS
	ALCID	ALCIDS
	ALCO	ALCOS
	ALCOHOL	ALCOHOLS
	ALCOHOLIC	ALCOHOLICS
	ALCOLOCK	ALCOLOCKS
	ALCOOL	ALCOOLS
	ALCOPOP	ALCOPOPS
	ALCORZA	ALCORZAS
	ALCOVE	ALCOVED · ALCOVES
	ALDEA	ALDEAS
	ALDEHYDE	ALDEHYDES
BALDER	**ALDER**	ALDERN · ALDERS
	ALDICARB	ALDICARBS
	ALDOL	ALDOLS

FRONT HOOK	ROOT WORD	END HOOK
	ALDOLASE	ALDOLASES
	ALDOSE	ALDOSES
	ALDOXIME	ALDOXIMES
	ALDRIN	ALDRINS
BALE ▪ DALE ▪ EALE ▪ GALE ▪ HALE ▪ KALE MALE ▪ PALE ▪ RALE ▪ SALE ▪ TALE ▪ VALE WALE ▪ YALE	**ALE**	ALEC ▪ ALEE ▪ ALEF ▪ ALES ▪ ALEW
	ALEC	ALECK ▪ ALECS
	ALECK	ALECKS
	ALECOST	ALECOSTS
	ALECTRYON	ALECTRYONS
	ALEF	ALEFS ▪ ALEFT
	ALEGAR	ALEGARS
	ALEGGE	ALEGGED ▪ ALEGGES
	ALEHOUSE	ALEHOUSES
	ALEMBIC	ALEMBICS
	ALEMBROTH	ALEMBROTHS
	ALENCON	ALENCONS
	ALEPH	ALEPHS
	ALEPINE	ALEPINES
	ALERCE	ALERCES
	ALERION	ALERIONS
	ALERT	ALERTS
BALES ▪ DALES ▪ EALES ▪ GALES ▪ HALES KALES ▪ MALES ▪ PALES ▪ RALES ▪ SALES TALES ▪ VALES ▪ WALES ▪ YALES	**ALES**	
	ALEURON	ALEURONE ▪ ALEURONS
	ALEURONE	ALEURONES
	ALEVIN	ALEVINS
	ALEW	ALEWS
KALEWIFE KALEWIVES	**ALEWIFE** **ALEWIVES**	
	ALEXANDER	ALEXANDERS
	ALEXIA	ALEXIAS
	ALEXIN	ALEXINE ▪ ALEXINS
	ALEXINE	ALEXINES
	ALEYE	ALEYED ▪ ALEYES
CALF ▪ HALF HALFA	**ALF**	ALFA ▪ ALFS
	ALFA	ALFAS
	ALFAKI	ALFAKIS
	ALFALFA	ALFALFAS
	ALFAQUI	ALFAQUIN ▪ ALFAQUIS
	ALFAQUIN	ALFAQUINS
HALFAS	**ALFAS**	
	ALFILARIA	ALFILARIAS
	ALFILERIA	ALFILERIAS
	ALFORJA	ALFORJAS
CALFS ▪ HALFS	**ALFS**	
	ALGA	ALGAE ▪ ALGAL ▪ ALGAS
	ALGAECIDE	ALGAECIDES
	ALGAROBA	ALGAROBAS
	ALGARROBA	ALGARROBAS
	ALGARROBO	ALGARROBOS
	ALGATE	ALGATES
	ALGEBRA	ALGEBRAS
	ALGERINE	ALGERINES
	ALGESIA	ALGESIAS
	ALGICIDE	ALGICIDES
	ALGIN	ALGINS
	ALGINATE	ALGINATES
VALGOID	**ALGOID**	
	ALGOMETER	ALGOMETERS
	ALGOR	ALGORS
	ALGORISM	ALGORISMS
	ALGORITHM	ALGORITHMS
	ALGUACIL	ALGUACILS
	ALGUAZIL	ALGUAZILS
	ALGUM	ALGUMS
	ALIASING	ALIASINGS

FRONT HOOK	ROOT WORD	END HOOK
	ALIBI	ALIBIS
	ALICANT	ALICANTS
	ALIDAD	ALIDADE = ALIDADS
	ALIDADE	ALIDADES
	ALIEN	ALIENS
	ALIENAGE	ALIENAGES
	ALIENATE	ALIENATED = ALIENATES
	ALIENATOR	ALIENATORS
	ALIENEE	ALIENEES
	ALIENER	ALIENERS
	ALIENISM	ALIENISMS
	ALIENIST	ALIENISTS
	ALIENOR	ALIENORS
CALIF = KALIF	ALIF	ALIFS
PALIFORM	ALIFORM	
CALIFS = KALIFS	ALIFS	
	ALIGARTA	ALIGARTAS
	ALIGHT	ALIGHTS
MALIGN	ALIGN	ALIGNS
MALIGNED	ALIGNED	
MALIGNER	ALIGNER	ALIGNERS
MALIGNERS	ALIGNERS	
MALIGNING	ALIGNING	
MALIGNMENT	ALIGNMENT	ALIGNMENTS
MALIGNS	ALIGNS	
	ALIMENT	ALIMENTS
PALIMONIES	ALIMONIES	
PALIMONY	ALIMONY	
MALINE = SALINE = VALINE	ALINE	ALINED = ALINER = ALINES
	ALINEMENT	ALINEMENTS
	ALINER	ALINERS
MALINES = SALINES = VALINES	ALINES	
TALIPED	ALIPED	ALIPEDS
TALIPEDS	ALIPEDS	
	ALIQUOT	ALIQUOTS
	ALISMA	ALISMAS
MALISON	ALISON	ALISONS
MALISONS	ALISONS	
MALIST	ALIST	
	ALITERATE	ALITERATES
	ALIYA	ALIYAH = ALIYAS
	ALIYAH	ALIYAHS
	ALIYOT	ALIYOTH
	ALIZARI	ALIZARIN = ALIZARIS
	ALIZARIN	ALIZARINE = ALIZARINS
	ALIZARINE	ALIZARINES
	ALKAHEST	ALKAHESTS
	ALKALI	ALKALIC = ALKALIN = ALKALIS
	ALKALIN	ALKALINE
	ALKALIS	ALKALISE
	ALKALISE	ALKALISED = ALKALISER = ALKALISES
	ALKALISER	ALKALISERS
	ALKALIZE	ALKALIZED = ALKALIZER = ALKALIZES
	ALKALIZER	ALKALIZERS
	ALKALOID	ALKALOIDS
	ALKANE	ALKANES = ALKANET
	ALKANET	ALKANETS
	ALKANNIN	ALKANNINS
	ALKENE	ALKENES
TALKIE	ALKIE	ALKIES
TALKIES	ALKIES	
	ALKINE	ALKINES
	ALKO	ALKOS
	ALKOXIDE	ALKOXIDES
BALKY = TALKY	ALKY	ALKYD = ALKYL
	ALKYD	ALKYDS
	ALKYL	ALKYLS
	ALKYLATE	ALKYLATED = ALKYLATES
	ALKYNE	ALKYNES

FRONT HOOK	ROOT WORD	END HOOK
BALL · CALL · FALL · GALL · HALL · LALL MALL · PALL · SALL · TALL · WALL	**ALL**	ALLS · ALLY
	ALLANITE	ALLANITES
	ALLANTOID	ALLANTOIDS
	ALLANTOIN	ALLANTOINS
	ALLATIVE	ALLATIVES
	ALLAY	ALLAYS
	ALLAYER	ALLAYERS
	ALLAYING	ALLAYINGS
	ALLAYMENT	ALLAYMENTS
	ALLEDGE	ALLEDGED · ALLEDGES
CALLEE · MALLEE · SALLEE	**ALLEE**	ALLEES
CALLEES · MALLEES · SALLEES	**ALLEES**	
	ALLEGE	ALLEGED · ALLEGER · ALLEGES
	ALLEGER	ALLEGERS
	ALLEGGE	ALLEGGED · ALLEGGES
	ALLEGIANT	ALLEGIANTS
	ALLEGRO	ALLEGROS
HALLEL	**ALLEL**	ALLELE · ALLELS
	ALLELE	ALLELES
	ALLELISM	ALLELISMS
HALLELS	**ALLELS**	
	ALLELUIA	ALLELUIAH · ALLELUIAS
HALLELUIAH	**ALLELUIAH**	ALLELUIAHS
	ALLEMANDE	ALLEMANDES
	ALLERGEN	ALLERGENS
	ALLERGIC	ALLERGICS
	ALLERGIN	ALLERGINS
	ALLERGIST	ALLERGISTS
	ALLERION	ALLERIONS
	ALLETHRIN	ALLETHRINS
	ALLEVIANT	ALLEVIANTS
	ALLEVIATE	ALLEVIATED · ALLEVIATES
GALLEY · VALLEY	**ALLEY**	ALLEYS
	ALLEYCAT	ALLEYCATS
VALLEYED · WALLEYED	**ALLEYED**	
GALLEYS · VALLEYS	**ALLEYS**	
	ALLEYWAY	ALLEYWAYS
	ALLHEAL	ALLHEALS
TALLIABLE	**ALLIABLE**	
DALLIANCE	**ALLIANCE**	ALLIANCES
DALLIANCES	**ALLIANCES**	
	ALLICE	ALLICES
	ALLICIN	ALLICINS
DALLIED · GALLIED · RALLIED · SALLIED TALLIED	**ALLIED**	
BALLIES · DALLIES · GALLIES · RALLIES SALLIES · TALLIES · WALLIES	**ALLIES**	
	ALLIGARTA	ALLIGARTAS
	ALLIGATE	ALLIGATED · ALLIGATES
	ALLIGATOR	ALLIGATORS
TALLIS	**ALLIS**	
GALLISES · TALLISES	**ALLISES**	
BALLIUM · GALLIUM · PALLIUM	**ALLIUM**	ALLIUMS
BALLIUMS · GALLIUMS · PALLIUMS	**ALLIUMS**	
TALLNESS	**ALLNESS**	
TALLNESSES	**ALLNESSES**	
	ALLOBAR	ALLOBARS
	ALLOCATE	ALLOCATED · ALLOCATES
	ALLOCATOR	ALLOCATORS
	ALLOD	ALLODS
	ALLODIA	ALLODIAL
	ALLODIUM	ALLODIUMS
	ALLOGRAFT	ALLOGRAFTS
	ALLOGRAPH	ALLOGRAPHS
	ALLOMONE	ALLOMONES
	ALLOMORPH	ALLOMORPHS
	ALLONGE	ALLONGES
BALLONS · GALLONS	**ALLONS**	

FRONT HOOK	ROOT WORD	END HOOK
	ALLONYM	ALLONYMS
	ALLOPATH	ALLOPATHS ▪ ALLOPATHY
	ALLOPHANE	ALLOPHANES
	ALLOPHONE	ALLOPHONES
	ALLOPLASM	ALLOPLASMS
	ALLOSAUR	ALLOSAURS
BALLOT ▪ HALLOT ▪ TALLOT	**ALLOT**	ALLOTS
	ALLOTMENT	ALLOTMENTS
	ALLOTROPE	ALLOTROPES
BALLOTS ▪ TALLOTS	**ALLOTS**	
	ALLOTTEE	ALLOTTEES
	ALLOTTER	ALLOTTERS ▪ ALLOTTERY
	ALLOTYPE	ALLOTYPES
	ALLOVER	ALLOVERS
BALLOW ▪ CALLOW ▪ FALLOW ▪ GALLOW	**ALLOW**	ALLOWS
HALLOW ▪ MALLOW ▪ SALLOW ▪ TALLOW		
WALLOW		
	ALLOWABLE	ALLOWABLES
	ALLOWANCE	ALLOWANCED ▪ ALLOWANCES
FALLOWED ▪ GALLOWED ▪ HALLOWED	**ALLOWED**	
SALLOWED ▪ TALLOWED ▪ WALLOWED		
FALLOWING ▪ GALLOWING ▪ HALLOWING	**ALLOWING**	
SALLOWING ▪ TALLOWING ▪ WALLOWING		
BALLOWS ▪ CALLOWS ▪ FALLOWS ▪ GALLOWS	**ALLOWS**	
HALLOWS ▪ MALLOWS ▪ SALLOWS ▪ TALLOWS		
WALLOWS		
	ALLOXAN	ALLOXANS
	ALLOY	ALLOYS
	ALLOZYME	ALLOZYMES
BALLS ▪ CALLS ▪ FALLS ▪ GALLS ▪ HALLS	**ALLS**	
LALLS ▪ MALLS ▪ PALLS ▪ TALLS ▪ WALLS		
	ALLSEED	ALLSEEDS
	ALLSPICE	ALLSPICES
	ALLUDE	ALLUDED ▪ ALLUDES
	ALLURE	ALLURED ▪ ALLURER ▪ ALLURES
	ALLURER	ALLURERS
	ALLUSION	ALLUSIONS
	ALLUVIA	ALLUVIAL
	ALLUVIAL	ALLUVIALS
	ALLUVION	ALLUVIONS
	ALLUVIUM	ALLUVIUMS
BALLY ▪ DALLY ▪ GALLY ▪ PALLY ▪ RALLY	**ALLY**	ALLYL
SALLY ▪ TALLY ▪ WALLY		
DALLYING ▪ GALLYING ▪ RALLYING	**ALLYING**	
SALLYING ▪ TALLYING		
	ALLYL	ALLYLS
HALMA ▪ TALMA	**ALMA**	ALMAH ▪ ALMAS
	ALMAGEST	ALMAGESTS
	ALMAH	ALMAHS
	ALMAIN	ALMAINS
	ALMANAC	ALMANACK ▪ ALMANACS
	ALMANACK	ALMANACKS
	ALMANDINE	ALMANDINES
	ALMANDITE	ALMANDITES
HALMAS ▪ TALMAS	**ALMAS**	
	ALME	ALMEH ▪ ALMES
	ALMEH	ALMEHS
	ALMEMAR	ALMEMARS
	ALMIRAH	ALMIRAHS
	ALMNER	ALMNERS
	ALMOND	ALMONDS ▪ ALMONDY
	ALMONER	ALMONERS
BALMS ▪ CALMS ▪ HALMS ▪ MALMS ▪ PALMS	**ALMS**	
	ALMSGIVER	ALMSGIVERS
	ALMSHOUSE	ALMSHOUSES
	ALMUCE	ALMUCES
TALMUD	**ALMUD**	ALMUDE ▪ ALMUDS
	ALMUDE	ALMUDES
TALMUDS	**ALMUDS**	

A

FRONT HOOK	ROOT WORD	END HOOK
	ALMUG	ALMUGS
	ALNAGE	ALNAGER ▪ ALNAGES
	ALNAGER	ALNAGERS
	ALNICO	ALNICOS
	ALOCASIA	ALOCASIAS
	ALOD	ALODS
	ALODIA	ALODIAL
	ALODIUM	ALODIUMS
	ALOE	ALOED ▪ ALOES
HALOED	**ALOED**	
HALOES	**ALOES**	
	ALOETIC	ALOETICS
	ALOGIA	ALOGIAS
	ALOHA	ALOHAS
	ALOIN	ALOINS
KALONG	**ALONG**	
	ALOPECIA	ALOPECIAS
	ALOW	ALOWE
CALP ▪ PALP ▪ SALP	**ALP**	ALPS
	ALPACA	ALPACAS
	ALPACCA	ALPACCAS
	ALPARGATA	ALPARGATAS
	ALPEEN	ALPEENS
	ALPENGLOW	ALPENGLOWS
	ALPENHORN	ALPENHORNS
	ALPHA	ALPHAS
	ALPHABET	ALPHABETS
	ALPHASORT	ALPHASORTS
	ALPHORN	ALPHORNS
	ALPHYL	ALPHYLS
	ALPINE	ALPINES
	ALPINISM	ALPINISMS
	ALPINIST	ALPINISTS
CALPS ▪ PALPS ▪ SALPS	**ALPS**	
AALS ▪ BALS ▪ DALS ▪ GALS ▪ MALS ▪ PALS SALS	**ALS**	ALSO
	ALSIKE	ALSIKES
	ALSOON	ALSOONE
DALT ▪ HALT ▪ MALT ▪ SALT	**ALT**	ALTO ▪ ALTS
	ALTAR	ALTARS
	ALTARAGE	ALTARAGES
FALTER ▪ HALTER ▪ PALTER ▪ SALTER	**ALTER**	ALTERN ▪ ALTERS
	ALTERANT	ALTERANTS
	ALTERCATE	ALTERCATED ▪ ALTERCATES
FALTERED ▪ HALTERED ▪ PALTERED	**ALTERED**	
FALTERER ▪ PALTERER	**ALTERER**	ALTERERS
FALTERERS ▪ PALTERERS	**ALTERERS**	
FALTERING ▪ HALTERING ▪ PALTERING	**ALTERING**	
SALTERN	**ALTERN**	ALTERNE
	ALTERNANT	ALTERNANTS
	ALTERNAT	ALTERNATE ▪ ALTERNATS
	ALTERNATE	ALTERNATED ▪ ALTERNATES
	ALTERNE	ALTERNES
FALTERS ▪ HALTERS ▪ PALTERS ▪ SALTERS	**ALTERS**	
	ALTESSE	ALTESSES
	ALTEZA	ALTEZAS
	ALTEZZA	ALTEZZAS
	ALTHAEA	ALTHAEAS
	ALTHEA	ALTHEAS
	ALTHORN	ALTHORNS
	ALTIGRAPH	ALTIGRAPHS
	ALTIMETER	ALTIMETERS
	ALTIPLANO	ALTIPLANOS
	ALTITUDE	ALTITUDES
SALTO	**ALTO**	ALTOS
	ALTOIST	ALTOISTS
SALTOS	**ALTOS**	
	ALTRICIAL	ALTRICIALS
	ALTRUISM	ALTRUISMS

FRONT HOOK	ROOT WORD	END HOOK
	ALTRUIST	ALTRUISTS
DALTS ▪ HALTS ▪ MALTS ▪ SALTS	**ALTS**	
	ALUDEL	ALUDELS
	ALULA	ALULAE ▪ ALULAR
	ALUM	ALUMS
	ALUMIN	ALUMINA ▪ ALUMINE ▪ ALUMINS
	ALUMINA	ALUMINAS
	ALUMINATE	ALUMINATES
	ALUMINE	ALUMINES
	ALUMINISE	ALUMINISED ▪ ALUMINISES
	ALUMINIUM	ALUMINIUMS
	ALUMINIZE	ALUMINIZED ▪ ALUMINIZES
	ALUMINUM	ALUMINUMS
	ALUMIUM	ALUMIUMS
	ALUMNA	ALUMNAE
	ALUMROOT	ALUMROOTS
	ALUMSTONE	ALUMSTONES
	ALUNITE	ALUNITES
	ALURE	ALURES
	ALVEOLAR	ALVEOLARS
	ALVEOLE	ALVEOLES
	ALWAY	ALWAYS
	ALYSSUM	ALYSSUMS
BAM ▪ CAM ▪ DAM ▪ GAM ▪ HAM ▪ JAM ▪ KAM LAM ▪ MAM ▪ NAM ▪ PAM ▪ RAM ▪ SAM ▪ TAM YAM	**AM**	AMA ▪ AMI ▪ AMP ▪ AMU
CAMA ▪ GAMA ▪ KAMA ▪ LAMA ▪ MAMA ▪ SAMA	**AMA**	AMAH ▪ AMAS
	AMADAVAT	AMADAVATS
	AMADOU	AMADOUS
	AMAH	AMAHS
	AMALGAM	AMALGAMS
	AMANDINE	AMANDINES
	AMANDLA	AMANDLAS
	AMANITA	AMANITAS
	AMANITIN	AMANITINS
	AMARANT	AMARANTH ▪ AMARANTS
	AMARANTH	AMARANTHS
	AMARANTIN	AMARANTINE
	AMARELLE	AMARELLES
	AMARETTO	AMARETTOS
	AMARONE	AMARONES
	AMARYLLID	AMARYLLIDS
CAMAS ▪ GAMAS ▪ KAMAS ▪ LAMAS ▪ MAMAS SAMAS	**AMAS**	AMASS
CAMASS	**AMASS**	
	AMASSER	AMASSERS
CAMASSES	**AMASSES**	
	AMASSMENT	AMASSMENTS
HAMATE ▪ RAMATE	**AMATE**	AMATED ▪ AMATES
HAMATES	**AMATES**	
	AMATEUR	AMATEURS
	AMATION	AMATIONS
	AMATOL	AMATOLS
	AMAUT	AMAUTS
	AMAZE	AMAZED ▪ AMAZES
	AMAZEMENT	AMAZEMENTS
	AMAZON	AMAZONS
	AMAZONIAN	AMAZONIANS
	AMAZONITE	AMAZONITES
	AMBAGE	AMBAGES
	AMBAN	AMBANS
	AMBARI	AMBARIS
	AMBASSAGE	AMBASSAGES
	AMBEER	AMBEERS
CAMBER ▪ JAMBER ▪ LAMBER ▪ TAMBER	**AMBER**	AMBERS ▪ AMBERY
CAMBERED	**AMBERED**	
	AMBERINA	AMBERINAS
	AMBERITE	AMBERITES
	AMBERJACK	AMBERJACKS

A

FRONT HOOK	ROOT WORD	END HOOK
	AMBEROID	AMBEROIDS
CAMBERS · JAMBERS · LAMBERS · TAMBERS	AMBERS	
	AMBIANCE	AMBIANCES
	AMBIENCE	AMBIENCES
	AMBIENT	AMBIENTS
GAMBIT	AMBIT	AMBITS
	AMBITION	AMBITIONS
GAMBITS	AMBITS	
	AMBIVERT	AMBIVERTS
GAMBLE · HAMBLE · RAMBLE · WAMBLE	AMBLE	AMBLED · AMBLER · AMBLES
GAMBLED · HAMBLED · RAMBLED · WAMBLED	AMBLED	
GAMBLER · RAMBLER	AMBLER	AMBLERS
GAMBLERS · RAMBLERS	AMBLERS	
GAMBLES · HAMBLES · RAMBLES · WAMBLES	AMBLES	
GAMBLING · HAMBLING · LAMBLING RAMBLING · WAMBLING	AMBLING	AMBLINGS
GAMBLINGS · LAMBLINGS · RAMBLINGS WAMBLINGS	AMBLINGS	
	AMBLYOPIA	AMBLYOPIAS
GAMBO · JAMBO · MAMBO · SAMBO · ZAMBO	AMBO	AMBOS
	AMBOINA	AMBOINAS
HAMBONES · JAMBONES	AMBONES	
GAMBOS · JAMBOS · MAMBOS SAMBOS (offensive) · ZAMBOS (offensive)	AMBOS	
	AMBOYNA	AMBOYNAS
	AMBROID	AMBROIDS
	AMBROSIA	AMBROSIAL · AMBROSIAN · AMBROSIAS
	AMBROTYPE	AMBROTYPES
	AMBSACE	AMBSACES
	AMBULACRA	AMBULACRAL
	AMBULANCE	AMBULANCES
	AMBULANT	AMBULANTS
	AMBULATE	AMBULATED · AMBULATES
	AMBULATOR	AMBULATORS · AMBULATORY
	AMBULETTE	AMBULETTES
	AMBUSCADE	AMBUSCADED · AMBUSCADER · AMBUSCADES
	AMBUSCADO	AMBUSCADOS
	AMBUSHER	AMBUSHERS
	AMEBA	AMEBAE · AMEBAN · AMEBAS
	AMEBOCYTE	AMEBOCYTES
	AMEER	AMEERS
	AMEERATE	AMEERATES
	AMELCORN	AMELCORNS
CAMELIA	AMELIA	AMELIAS
CAMELIAS	AMELIAS	
RAMEN · SAMEN · YAMEN	AMEN	AMEND · AMENE · AMENS · AMENT
	AMENAGE	AMENAGED · AMENAGES
	AMENAUNCE	AMENAUNCES
	AMEND	AMENDE · AMENDS
	AMENDE	AMENDED · AMENDER · AMENDES
	AMENDER	AMENDERS
	AMENDMENT	AMENDMENTS
	AMENE	AMENED
RAMENS · YAMENS	AMENS	
LAMENT	AMENT	AMENTA · AMENTS
RAMENTA	AMENTA	AMENTAL
	AMENTIA	AMENTIAS
LAMENTS	AMENTS	
RAMENTUM	AMENTUM	
	AMERCE	AMERCED · AMERCER · AMERCES
	AMERCER	AMERCERS
	AMERICIUM	AMERICIUMS
	AMESACE	AMESACES
	AMETHYST	AMETHYSTS
	AMETROPIA	AMETROPIAS
KAMI · RAMI	AMI	AMIA · AMID · AMIE · AMIN · AMIR · AMIS
LAMIA · ZAMIA	AMIA	AMIAS
LAMIAS · ZAMIAS	AMIAS	
	AMICE	AMICES

FRONT HOOK	ROOT WORD	END HOOK
	AMID	AMIDE · AMIDO · AMIDS
	AMIDASE	AMIDASES
	AMIDE	AMIDES
	AMIDIN	AMIDINE · AMIDINS
	AMIDINE	AMIDINES
	AMIDO	AMIDOL
	AMIDOGEN	AMIDOGENS
	AMIDOL	AMIDOLS
	AMIDONE	AMIDONES
	AMIDS	AMIDST
	AMIDSHIP	AMIDSHIPS
MAMIE · RAMIE	AMIE	AMIES
MAMIES · RAMIES	AMIES	
	AMIGA	AMIGAS
	AMIGO	AMIGOS
	AMILDAR	AMILDARS
GAMIN · RAMIN · TAMIN	AMIN	AMINE · AMINO · AMINS
FAMINE · GAMINE · TAMINE	AMINE	AMINES
FAMINES · GAMINES · TAMINES	AMINES	
GAMINS · RAMINS · TAMINS	AMINS	
	AMIR	AMIRS
	AMIRATE	AMIRATES
CAMIS · KAMIS · RAMIS · TAMIS	AMIS	AMISS
CAMISES · KAMISES · TAMISES	AMISES	
	AMITROLE	AMITROLES
	AMLA	AMLAS
	AMMAN	AMMANS
	AMMETER	AMMETERS
	AMMINE	AMMINES
	AMMIRAL	AMMIRALS
	AMMO	AMMON · AMMOS
	AMMOCETE	AMMOCETES
	AMMOCOETE	AMMOCOETES
GAMMON · MAMMON	AMMON	AMMONO · AMMONS
	AMMONAL	AMMONALS
	AMMONATE	AMMONATES
	AMMONIA	AMMONIAC · AMMONIAS
	AMMONIAC	AMMONIACS
	AMMONIATE	AMMONIATED · AMMONIATES
MAMMONITE	AMMONITE	AMMONITES
MAMMONITES	AMMONITES	
	AMMONIUM	AMMONIUMS
	AMMONOID	AMMONOIDS
GAMMONS · MAMMONS	AMMONS	
	AMNESIA	AMNESIAC · AMNESIAS
	AMNESIAC	AMNESIACS
	AMNESIC	AMNESICS
	AMNIO	AMNION · AMNIOS
	AMNION	AMNIONS
	AMNIOTE	AMNIOTES
	AMOEBA	AMOEBAE · AMOEBAN · AMOEBAS
	AMOK	AMOKS
	AMOLE	AMOLES
	AMOMUM	AMOMUMS
	AMOOVE	AMOOVED · AMOOVES
	AMORALISM	AMORALISMS
	AMORALIST	AMORALISTS
	AMORANCE	AMORANCES
	AMORCE	AMORCES
	AMORET	AMORETS
	AMORETTO	AMORETTOS
	AMORISM	AMORISMS
	AMORIST	AMORISTS
	AMOROSA	AMOROSAS
	AMOROSO	AMOROSOS
	AMORPHISM	AMORPHISMS
	AMORTISE	AMORTISED · AMORTISES
	AMORTIZE	AMORTIZED · AMORTIZES
	AMOSITE	AMOSITES

FRONT HOOK	ROOT WORD	END HOOK
	AMOTION	AMOTIONS
	AMOUNT	AMOUNTS
	AMOUR	AMOURS
	AMOURETTE	AMOURETTES
	AMOVE	AMOVED ▪ AMOVES
	AMOWT	AMOWTS
CAMP ▪ DAMP ▪ GAMP ▪ LAMP ▪ RAMP ▪ SAMP TAMP ▪ VAMP	**AMP**	AMPS
CAMPED ▪ DAMPED ▪ LAMPED ▪ RAMPED TAMPED ▪ VAMPED	**AMPED**	
	AMPERAGE	AMPERAGES
	AMPERE	AMPERES
	AMPERSAND	AMPERSANDS
	AMPERZAND	AMPERZANDS
	AMPHIBIA	AMPHIBIAN
	AMPHIBIAN	AMPHIBIANS
	AMPHIBOLE	AMPHIBOLES
	AMPHIPOD	AMPHIPODS
	AMPHOLYTE	AMPHOLYTES
	AMPHORA	AMPHORAE ▪ AMPHORAL ▪ AMPHORAS
CAMPHORIC	**AMPHORIC**	
CAMPING ▪ DAMPING ▪ LAMPING ▪ RAMPING TAMPING ▪ VAMPING	**AMPING**	
CAMPLE ▪ SAMPLE SAMPLER	**AMPLE**	AMPLER
	AMPLER	
	AMPLIDYNE	AMPLIDYNES
	AMPLIFIER	AMPLIFIERS
	AMPLITUDE	AMPLITUDES
	AMPLOSOME	AMPLOSOMES
CAMPLY ▪ DAMPLY	**AMPLY**	
	AMPOULE	AMPOULES
CAMPS ▪ DAMPS ▪ GAMPS ▪ LAMPS ▪ RAMPS SAMPS ▪ TAMPS ▪ VAMPS	**AMPS**	
	AMPUL	AMPULE ▪ AMPULS
	AMPULE	AMPULES
	AMPULLA	AMPULLAE ▪ AMPULLAR
	AMPULLAR	AMPULLARY
	AMPUTATE	AMPUTATED ▪ AMPUTATES
	AMPUTATOR	AMPUTATORS
	AMPUTEE	AMPUTEES
	AMREETA	AMREETAS
	AMRIT	AMRITA ▪ AMRITS
	AMRITA	AMRITAS
	AMSINCKIA	AMSINCKIAS
	AMTMAN	AMTMANS
	AMTRAC	AMTRACK ▪ AMTRACS
	AMTRACK	AMTRACKS
NAMU	**AMU**	AMUS
	AMUCK	AMUCKS
	AMULET	AMULETS
CAMUS ▪ RAMUS ▪ WAMUS	**AMUS**	AMUSE
	AMUSE	AMUSED ▪ AMUSER ▪ AMUSES
	AMUSEMENT	AMUSEMENTS
	AMUSER	AMUSERS
CAMUSES ▪ WAMUSES	**AMUSES**	
	AMUSETTE	AMUSETTES
	AMUSIA	AMUSIAS
	AMYGDAL	AMYGDALA ▪ AMYGDALE ▪ AMYGDALS
	AMYGDALA	AMYGDALAE ▪ AMYGDALAS
	AMYGDALE	AMYGDALES
	AMYGDALIN	AMYGDALINE ▪ AMYGDALINS
	AMYGDULE	AMYGDULES
	AMYL	AMYLS
	AMYLASE	AMYLASES
	AMYLENE	AMYLENES
	AMYLOGEN	AMYLOGENS
	AMYLOID	AMYLOIDS
	AMYLOPSIN	AMYLOPSINS
	AMYLOSE	AMYLOSES

A

FRONT HOOK	ROOT WORD	END HOOK
	AMYLUM	AMYLUMS
	AMYOTONIA	AMYOTONIAS
	AMYTAL	AMYTALS
BAN ▪ CAN ▪ DAN ▪ EAN ▪ FAN ▪ GAN ▪ HAN MAN ▪ NAN ▪ PAN ▪ RAN ▪ SAN ▪ TAN ▪ VAN WAN	AN	ANA ▪ AND ▪ ANE ▪ ANI ▪ ANN ▪ ANT ▪ ANY
KANA ▪ LANA ▪ MANA ▪ NANA ▪ RANA ▪ TANA	ANA	ANAL ▪ ANAN ▪ ANAS
	ANABAENA	ANABAENAS
	ANABANTID	ANABANTIDS
	ANABOLISM	ANABOLISMS
	ANABOLITE	ANABOLITES
	ANACONDA	ANACONDAS
	ANADEM	ANADEMS
	ANAEMIA	ANAEMIAS
	ANAEROBE	ANAEROBES
	ANAGLYPH	ANAGLYPHS ▪ ANAGLYPHY
	ANAGOGE	ANAGOGES
	ANAGRAM	ANAGRAMS
BANAL ▪ CANAL ▪ FANAL	ANAL	
	ANALCIME	ANALCIMES
	ANALCITE	ANALCITES
	ANALEMMA	ANALEMMAS
	ANALEPTIC	ANALEPTICS
	ANALGESIA	ANALGESIAS
	ANALGESIC	ANALGESICS
	ANALGETIC	ANALGETICS
	ANALGIA	ANALGIAS
BANALITIES	ANALITIES	
BANALITY	ANALITY	
BANALLY	ANALLY	
	ANALOG	ANALOGA ▪ ANALOGS ▪ ANALOGY
	ANALOGISE	ANALOGISED ▪ ANALOGISES
	ANALOGISM	ANALOGISMS
	ANALOGIST	ANALOGISTS
	ANALOGIZE	ANALOGIZED ▪ ANALOGIZES
	ANALOGON	ANALOGONS
	ANALOGUE	ANALOGUES
	ANALYSAND	ANALYSANDS
	ANALYSE	ANALYSED ▪ ANALYSER ▪ ANALYSES
	ANALYSER	ANALYSERS
	ANALYST	ANALYSTS
	ANALYTE	ANALYTES
	ANALYTIC	ANALYTICS
	ANALYZE	ANALYZED ▪ ANALYZER ▪ ANALYZES
	ANALYZER	ANALYZERS
	ANAMNIOTE	ANAMNIOTES
	ANAN	ANANA
BANANA ▪ MANANA ▪ ZANANA BANANAS ▪ MANANAS ▪ ZANANAS	ANANA	ANANAS
	ANANAS	
	ANANKE	ANANKES
	ANAPAEST	ANAPAESTS
	ANAPEST	ANAPESTS
	ANAPESTIC	ANAPESTICS
	ANAPHASE	ANAPHASES
	ANAPHOR	ANAPHORA ▪ ANAPHORS
	ANAPHORA	ANAPHORAL ▪ ANAPHORAS
	ANAPLASIA	ANAPLASIAS
	ANARCH	ANARCHS ▪ ANARCHY
	ANARCHISE	ANARCHISED ▪ ANARCHISES
	ANARCHISM	ANARCHISMS
	ANARCHIST	ANARCHISTS
	ANARCHIZE	ANARCHIZED ▪ ANARCHIZES
	ANARTHRIA	ANARTHRIAS
KANAS ▪ LANAS ▪ MANAS ▪ NANAS ▪ RANAS TANAS	ANAS	
	ANASARCA	ANASARCAS
	ANATA	ANATAS
	ANATAS	ANATASE
	ANATASE	ANATASES

A

FRONT HOOK	ROOT WORD	END HOOK
	ANATHEMA	ANATHEMAS
	ANATMAN	ANATMANS
	ANATOMISE	ANATOMISED ▪ ANATOMISER ▪ ANATOMISES
	ANATOMIST	ANATOMISTS
	ANATOMIZE	ANATOMIZED ▪ ANATOMIZER ▪ ANATOMIZES
	ANATOXIN	ANATOXINS
	ANATTA	ANATTAS
	ANATTO	ANATTOS
DANCE ▪ HANCE ▪ LANCE ▪ NANCE ▪ PANCE RANCE	ANCE	
	ANCESTOR	ANCESTORS
RANCHO ▪ SANCHO	ANCHO	ANCHOR ▪ ANCHOS
	ANCHOR	ANCHORS
	ANCHORAGE	ANCHORAGES
	ANCHORET	ANCHORETS
	ANCHORITE	ANCHORITES
RANCHOS ▪ SANCHOS	ANCHOS	
	ANCHOVETA	ANCHOVETAS
	ANCHUSA	ANCHUSAS
	ANCHUSIN	ANCHUSINS
	ANCHYLOSE	ANCHYLOSED ▪ ANCHYLOSES
	ANCIENT	ANCIENTS
	ANCILLA	ANCILLAE ▪ ANCILLAS
	ANCLE	ANCLES
	ANCOME	ANCOMES
	ANCON	ANCONE
	ANCONE	ANCONES
BAND ▪ FAND ▪ HAND ▪ LAND ▪ MAND ▪ PAND RAND ▪ SAND ▪ WAND	AND	ANDS
	ANDANTE	ANDANTES
	ANDANTINO	ANDANTINOS
	ANDESINE	ANDESINES
	ANDESITE	ANDESITES
	ANDESYTE	ANDESYTES
	ANDIRON	ANDIRONS
	ANDOUILLE	ANDOUILLES
	ANDRADITE	ANDRADITES
	ANDRO	ANDROS
	ANDROECIA	ANDROECIAL
	ANDROGEN	ANDROGENS
	ANDROGYNE	ANDROGYNES
	ANDROID	ANDROIDS
	ANDROMEDA	ANDROMEDAS
BANDS ▪ FANDS ▪ HANDS ▪ LANDS ▪ PANDS RANDS ▪ SANDS ▪ WANDS	ANDS	
	ANDVILE	ANDVILES
BANE ▪ CANE ▪ FANE ▪ GANE ▪ JANE ▪ KANE LANE ▪ MANE ▪ NANE ▪ PANE ▪ SANE ▪ TANE VANE ▪ WANE	ANE	ANES ▪ ANEW
	ANEAR	ANEARS
	ANECDOTA	ANECDOTAL
	ANECDOTE	ANECDOTES
	ANELACE	ANELACES
	ANELE	ANELED ▪ ANELES
PANELED	ANELED	
PANELING	ANELING	
	ANEMIA	ANEMIAS
	ANEMOGRAM	ANEMOGRAMS
	ANEMONE	ANEMONES
MANENT	ANENT	
	ANERGIA	ANERGIAS
	ANEROID	ANEROIDS
BANES ▪ CANES ▪ FANES ▪ JANES ▪ KANES LANES ▪ MANES ▪ PANES ▪ SANES ▪ VANES WANES	ANES	
	ANETHOL	ANETHOLE ▪ ANETHOLS
	ANETHOLE	ANETHOLES
	ANEUPLOID	ANEUPLOIDS ▪ ANEUPLOIDY
	ANEURIN	ANEURINS

FRONT HOOK	ROOT WORD	END HOOK
	ANEURISM	ANEURISMS
	ANEURYSM	ANEURYSMS
FANGA ▪ KANGA ▪ MANGA ▪ PANGA ▪ SANGA ▪ TANGA	**ANGA**	ANGAS
	ANGAKOK	ANGAKOKS
	ANGARIA	ANGARIAS
FANGAS ▪ KANGAS ▪ MANGAS ▪ PANGAS ▪ SANGAS ▪ TANGAS	**ANGAS**	
	ANGASHORE	ANGASHORES
	ANGEKKOK	ANGEKKOKS
	ANGEKOK	ANGEKOKS
MANGEL	**ANGEL**	ANGELS
	ANGELHOOD	ANGELHOODS
	ANGELIC	ANGELICA
	ANGELICA	ANGELICAL ▪ ANGELICAS
MANGELS	**ANGELS**	
BANGER ▪ DANGER ▪ GANGER ▪ HANGER LANGER (offensive) ▪ MANGER ▪ RANGER ▪ SANGER	**ANGER**	ANGERS
MANGERED ▪ LANGERED	**ANGERED**	
DANGERING	**ANGERING**	
DANGERLESS	**ANGERLESS**	
BANGERS ▪ DANGERS ▪ GANGERS ▪ HANGERS LANGERS (offensive) ▪ MANGERS ▪ RANGERS ▪ SANGERS	**ANGERS**	
	ANGICO	ANGICOS
	ANGINA	ANGINAL ▪ ANGINAS
	ANGIOGRAM	ANGIOGRAMS
	ANGIOMA	ANGIOMAS
	ANGKLUNG	ANGKLUNGS
BANGLE ▪ CANGLE ▪ DANGLE ▪ FANGLE JANGLE ▪ MANGLE ▪ TANGLE ▪ WANGLE	**ANGLE**	ANGLED ▪ ANGLER ▪ ANGLES
BANGLED ▪ CANGLED ▪ DANGLED ▪ FANGLED JANGLED ▪ MANGLED ▪ TANGLED ▪ WANGLED	**ANGLED**	
	ANGLEDUG	ANGLEDUGS
	ANGLEPOD	ANGLEPODS
DANGLER ▪ JANGLER ▪ MANGLER ▪ TANGLER ▪ WANGLER	**ANGLER**	ANGLERS
DANGLERS ▪ JANGLERS ▪ MANGLERS ▪ TANGLERS ▪ WANGLERS	**ANGLERS**	
BANGLES ▪ CANGLES ▪ DANGLES ▪ FANGLES JANGLES ▪ MANGLES ▪ TANGLES ▪ WANGLES	**ANGLES**	
	ANGLESITE	ANGLESITES
	ANGLEWORM	ANGLEWORMS
	ANGLICISE	ANGLICISED ▪ ANGLICISES
	ANGLICISM	ANGLICISMS
	ANGLICIST	ANGLICISTS
	ANGLICIZE	ANGLICIZED ▪ ANGLICIZES
CANGLING ▪ DANGLING ▪ FANGLING GANGLING ▪ JANGLING ▪ MANGLING TANGLING ▪ WANGLING	**ANGLING**	ANGLINGS
DANGLINGS ▪ JANGLINGS ▪ TANGLINGS WANGLINGS	**ANGLINGS**	
	ANGLIST	ANGLISTS
	ANGLO	ANGLOS
	ANGLOPHIL	ANGLOPHILE ▪ ANGLOPHILS
	ANGOPHORA	ANGOPHORAS
	ANGORA	ANGORAS
	ANGOSTURA	ANGOSTURAS
	ANGRIES	ANGRIEST
	ANGST	ANGSTS ▪ ANGSTY
	ANGSTROM	ANGSTROMS
SANGUINE	**ANGUINE**	
	ANGUIPED	ANGUIPEDE
LANGUISH	**ANGUISH**	
LANGUISHED	**ANGUISHED**	
LANGUISHES	**ANGUISHES**	
MANGULATE	**ANGULATE**	ANGULATED ▪ ANGULATES
MANGULATED	**ANGULATED**	

A

FRONT HOOK	ROOT WORD	END HOOK
MANGULATES	ANGULATES	
	ANHEDONIA	ANHEDONIAS
	ANHINGA	ANHINGAS
	ANHYDRASE	ANHYDRASES
	ANHYDRIDE	ANHYDRIDES
	ANHYDRITE	ANHYDRITES
BANI · MANI · RANI	ANI	ANIL · ANIS
	ANICCA	ANICCAS
	ANICONISM	ANICONISMS
	ANICONIST	ANICONISTS
	ANICUT	ANICUTS
	ANIGH	ANIGHT
	ANIL	ANILE · ANILS
	ANILIN	ANILINE · ANILINS
	ANILINE	ANILINES
	ANIMA	ANIMAL · ANIMAS
	ANIMAL	ANIMALS
	ANIMALIER	ANIMALIERS
	ANIMALISE	ANIMALISED · ANIMALISES
	ANIMALISM	ANIMALISMS
	ANIMALIST	ANIMALISTS
	ANIMALIZE	ANIMALIZED · ANIMALIZES
	ANIMATE	ANIMATED · ANIMATER · ANIMATES
	ANIMATER	ANIMATERS
	ANIMATIC	ANIMATICS
	ANIMATION	ANIMATIONS
	ANIMATISM	ANIMATISMS
	ANIMATIST	ANIMATISTS
	ANIMATO	ANIMATOR
	ANIMATOR	ANIMATORS
	ANIME	ANIMES
	ANIMI	ANIMIS
	ANIMIS	ANIMISM · ANIMIST
	ANIMISM	ANIMISMS
	ANIMIST	ANIMISTS
FANION · WANION	ANION	ANIONS
FANIONS · WANIONS	ANIONS	
MANIS · RANIS	ANIS	ANISE
	ANISE	ANISES
	ANISEED	ANISEEDS
	ANISETTE	ANISETTES
	ANISOLE	ANISOLES
BANKER · CANKER · DANKER · HANKER JANKER · LANKER · RANKER · TANKER WANKER · YANKER	ANKER	ANKERS
BANKERS · CANKERS · HANKERS · JANKERS RANKERS · TANKERS · WANKERS *(offensive)* YANKERS	ANKERS	ANKERITES
	ANKERITE	ANKERITES
	ANKH	ANKHS
FANKLE · RANKLE · WANKLE	ANKLE	ANKLED · ANKLES · ANKLET
	ANKLEBONE	ANKLEBONES
FANKLED · RANKLED	ANKLED	
FANKLES · RANKLES	ANKLES	
	ANKLET	ANKLETS
FANKLING · RANKLING	ANKLING	
	ANKLONG	ANKLONGS
	ANKLUNG	ANKLUNGS
	ANKUS	ANKUSH
	ANKYLOSE	ANKYLOSED · ANKYLOSES
	ANLACE	ANLACES
	ANLAGE	ANLAGEN · ANLAGES
CANN · JANN	ANN	ANNA · ANNO · ANNS
CANNA · MANNA · NANNA · TANNA · WANNA	ANNA	ANNAL · ANNAS · ANNAT
	ANNAL	ANNALS
	ANNALISE	ANNALISED · ANNALISES
	ANNALIST	ANNALISTS
	ANNALIZE	ANNALIZED · ANNALIZES
CANNAS · MANNAS · NANNAS · TANNAS	ANNAS	

A

FRONT HOOK	ROOT WORD	END HOOK
	ANNAT	ANNATS
TANNATES	ANNATES	
	ANNATTA	ANNATTAS
	ANNATTO	ANNATTOS
	ANNEAL	ANNEALS
	ANNEALER	ANNEALERS
	ANNEALING	ANNEALINGS
	ANNELID	ANNELIDS
	ANNELIDAN	ANNELIDANS
	ANNEX	ANNEXE
	ANNEXE	ANNEXED = ANNEXES
	ANNEXION	ANNEXIONS
	ANNEXMENT	ANNEXMENTS
	ANNEXURE	ANNEXURES
	ANNICUT	ANNICUTS
	ANNO	ANNOY
	ANNONA	ANNONAS
	ANNOTATE	ANNOTATED = ANNOTATES
	ANNOTATOR	ANNOTATORS
	ANNOUNCE	ANNOUNCED = ANNOUNCER = ANNOUNCES
	ANNOUNCER	ANNOUNCERS
TANNOY	ANNOY	ANNOYS
	ANNOYANCE	ANNOYANCES
TANNOYED	ANNOYED	
	ANNOYER	ANNOYERS
TANNOYING	ANNOYING	
TANNOYS	ANNOYS	
BANNS = CANNS = JANNS	ANNS	
	ANNUAL	ANNUALS
	ANNUALISE	ANNUALISED = ANNUALISES
	ANNUALIZE	ANNUALIZED = ANNUALIZES
	ANNUITANT	ANNUITANTS
	ANNUL	ANNULI = ANNULS
CANNULAR	ANNULAR	ANNULARS
CANNULATE	ANNULATE	ANNULATED = ANNULATES
CANNULATED	ANNULATED	
CANNULATES	ANNULATES	
	ANNULET	ANNULETS
	ANNULMENT	ANNULMENTS
	ANOA	ANOAS
	ANOBIID	ANOBIIDS
	ANODE	ANODES
	ANODISE	ANODISED = ANODISES
	ANODIZE	ANODIZED = ANODIZES
	ANODONTIA	ANODONTIAS
	ANODYNE	ANODYNES
	ANOINT	ANOINTS
	ANOINTER	ANOINTERS
	ANOLE	ANOLES
	ANOLYTE	ANOLYTES
	ANOMIE	ANOMIES
CANON = FANON	ANON	
	ANONYM	ANONYMA = ANONYMS
	ANONYMA	ANONYMAS
	ANONYMISE	ANONYMISED = ANONYMISES
	ANONYMIZE	ANONYMIZED = ANONYMIZES
	ANOOPSIA	ANOOPSIAS
	ANOPIA	ANOPIAS
	ANOPSIA	ANOPSIAS
	ANORAK	ANORAKS
	ANORECTIC	ANORECTICS
	ANORETIC	ANORETICS
	ANOREXIA	ANOREXIAS
	ANOREXIC	ANOREXICS
	ANORTHITE	ANORTHITES
	ANOSMIA	ANOSMIAS
	ANOVULANT	ANOVULANTS
	ANOXAEMIA	ANOXAEMIAS
	ANOXEMIA	ANOXEMIAS

FRONT HOOK	ROOT WORD	END HOOK
	ANOXIA	ANOXIAS
HANSA · SANSA	**ANSA**	ANSAE
	ANSATE	ANSATED
	ANSERINE	ANSERINES
	ANSWER	ANSWERS
	ANSWERER	ANSWERERS
BANT · CANT · DANT · GANT · HANT · KANT LANT · PANT · RANT · SANT · VANT · WANT	**ANT**	ANTA · ANTE · ANTI · ANTS
MANTA	**ANTA**	ANTAE · ANTAR · ANTAS
	ANTACID	ANTACIDS
	ANTALGIC	ANTALGICS
	ANTALKALI	ANTALKALIS
CANTAR · KANTAR	**ANTAR**	ANTARA · ANTARS
TANTARA	**ANTARA**	ANTARAS
TANTARAS	**ANTARAS**	
CANTARS · KANTARS	**ANTARS**	
MANTAS	**ANTAS**	
	ANTBEAR	ANTBEARS
	ANTBIRD	ANTBIRDS
ZANTE	**ANTE**	ANTED · ANTES
	ANTEATER	ANTEATERS
	ANTECEDE	ANTECEDED · ANTECEDES
	ANTECHOIR	ANTECHOIRS
BANTED · CANTED · DANTED · GANTED HANTED · KANTED · PANTED · RANTED WANTED	**ANTED**	
	ANTEDATE	ANTEDATED · ANTEDATES
	ANTEFIX	ANTEFIXA
	ANTEFIXA	ANTEFIXAE · ANTEFIXAL
GANTELOPE	**ANTELOPE**	ANTELOPES
GANTELOPES	**ANTELOPES**	
	ANTENATAL	ANTENATALS
	ANTENNA	ANTENNAE · ANTENNAL · ANTENNAS
	ANTENNULE	ANTENNULES
	ANTEPAST	ANTEPASTS
	ANTEROOM	ANTEROOMS
MANTES · ZANTES	**ANTES**	
	ANTETYPE	ANTETYPES
	ANTEVERT	ANTEVERTS
	ANTHELION	ANTHELIONS
	ANTHEM	ANTHEMS
PANTHER	**ANTHER**	ANTHERS
	ANTHERID	ANTHERIDS
PANTHERS	**ANTHERS**	
WANTHILL	**ANTHILL**	ANTHILLS
WANTHILLS	**ANTHILLS**	
	ANTHOCARP	ANTHOCARPS
	ANTHOCYAN	ANTHOCYANS
	ANTHOZOAN	ANTHOZOANS
	ANTHURIUM	ANTHURIUMS
TANTI	**ANTI**	ANTIC · ANTIS
	ANTIAR	ANTIARS
	ANTIARIN	ANTIARINS
	ANTIATOM	ANTIATOMS
	ANTIAUXIN	ANTIAUXINS
	ANTIBUSER	ANTIBUSERS
CANTIC · MANTIC	**ANTIC**	ANTICK · ANTICS
MANTICALLY	**ANTICALLY**	
	ANTICHLOR	ANTICHLORS
	ANTICISE	ANTICISED · ANTICISES
	ANTICIZE	ANTICIZED · ANTICIZES
	ANTICK	ANTICKE · ANTICKS
	ANTICKE	ANTICKED
	ANTICLINE	ANTICLINES
	ANTICODON	ANTICODONS
	ANTICULT	ANTICULTS
	ANTIDOTE	ANTIDOTED · ANTIDOTES
	ANTIDUNE	ANTIDUNES
	ANTIELITE	ANTIELITES

FRONT HOOK	ROOT WORD	END HOOK
	ANTIENT	ANTIENTS
	ANTIGEN	ANTIGENE ▪ ANTIGENS
	ANTIGENE	ANTIGENES
	ANTIKING	ANTIKINGS
	ANTIKNOCK	ANTIKNOCKS
	ANTILIFE	ANTILIFER
	ANTILIFER	ANTILIFERS
	ANTILOG	ANTILOGS ▪ ANTILOGY
	ANTIMASK	ANTIMASKS
	ANTIMERE	ANTIMERES
	ANTIMONY	ANTIMONYL
	ANTIMONYL	ANTIMONYLS
	ANTIMUON	ANTIMUONS
	ANTIMUSIC	ANTIMUSICS
	ANTIMYCIN	ANTIMYCINS
BANTING ▪ CANTING ▪ DANTING ▪ GANTING HANTING ▪ KANTING ▪ PANTING ▪ RANTING WANTING	**ANTING**	ANTINGS
BANTINGS ▪ CANTINGS ▪ PANTINGS RANTINGS ▪ WANTINGS	**ANTINGS**	
	ANTINODE	ANTINODES
	ANTINOME	ANTINOMES
	ANTINOVEL	ANTINOVELS
	ANTINUKE	ANTINUKER ▪ ANTINUKES
	ANTINUKER	ANTINUKERS
	ANTIPASTO	ANTIPASTOS
	ANTIPHON	ANTIPHONS ▪ ANTIPHONY
	ANTIPODAL	ANTIPODALS
	ANTIPODE	ANTIPODES
RANTIPOLE RANTIPOLES	**ANTIPOLE**	ANTIPOLES
	ANTIPOLES	
	ANTIPOPE	ANTIPOPES
	ANTIPYIC	ANTIPYICS
	ANTIQUARK	ANTIQUARKS
	ANTIQUATE	ANTIQUATED ▪ ANTIQUATES
	ANTIQUE	ANTIQUED ▪ ANTIQUER ▪ ANTIQUES ANTIQUEY
	ANTIQUER	ANTIQUERS
	ANTIRADAR	ANTIRADARS
	ANTIRUST	ANTIRUSTS
MANTIS	**ANTIS**	
	ANTISCIAN	ANTISCIANS
	ANTISERUM	ANTISERUMS
	ANTISHOCK	ANTISHOCKS
	ANTISMOKE	ANTISMOKER
	ANTISNOB	ANTISNOBS
	ANTISPAST	ANTISPASTS
	ANTISTAT	ANTISTATE ▪ ANTISTATS
	ANTISTYLE	ANTISTYLES
	ANTITHET	ANTITHETS
	ANTITOXIN	ANTITOXINS
	ANTITRADE	ANTITRADES
	ANTITUMOR	ANTITUMORS
	ANTITYPE	ANTITYPES
	ANTIVENIN	ANTIVENINS
	ANTIVENOM	ANTIVENOMS
	ANTIWORLD	ANTIWORLDS
PANTLER	**ANTLER**	ANTLERS
PANTLERS	**ANTLERS**	
	ANTLIA	ANTLIAE
	ANTLION	ANTLIONS
	ANTONYM	ANTONYMS ▪ ANTONYMY
MANTRA ▪ TANTRA ▪ YANTRA	**ANTRA**	ANTRAL
	ANTRE	ANTRES
TANTRUM	**ANTRUM**	ANTRUMS
TANTRUMS	**ANTRUMS**	
BANTS ▪ CANTS ▪ DANTS ▪ GANTS ▪ HANTS KANTS ▪ LANTS ▪ PANTS ▪ RANTS ▪ SANTS VANTS ▪ WANTS	**ANTS**	ANTSY

FRONT HOOK	ROOT WORD	END HOOK
	ANUCLEATE	ANUCLEATED
	ANURAN	ANURANS
	ANURIA	ANURIAS
MANUS	ANUS	
	ANVIL	ANVILS
	ANVILTOP	ANVILTOPS
CANY ▪ MANY ▪ WANY ▪ ZANY	ANY	
CANYON	ANYON	ANYONE ▪ ANYONS
	ANYONE	ANYONES
CANYONS	ANYONS	
	ANYTHING	ANYTHINGS
	ANYWAY	ANYWAYS
	ANYWHERE	ANYWHERES
	AORIST	AORISTS
	AORTA	AORTAE ▪ AORTAL ▪ AORTAS
	AOUDAD	AOUDADS
	APACHE	APACHES
	APADANA	APADANAS
	APAGOGE	APAGOGES
	APANAGE	APANAGED ▪ APANAGES
	APAREJO	APAREJOS
	APARTHEID	APARTHEIDS
	APARTMENT	APARTMENTS
	APATHATON	APATHATONS
	APATITE	APATITES
	APATOSAUR	APATOSAURS
	APAY	APAYD ▪ APAYS
CAPE ▪ GAPE ▪ JAPE ▪ NAPE ▪ PAPE ▪ RAPE ▪ TAPE	APE	APED ▪ APER ▪ APES ▪ APEX
CAPED ▪ GAPED ▪ JAPED ▪ NAPED ▪ RAPED ▪ TAPED	APED	
	APEDOM	APEDOMS
	APEHOOD	APEHOODS
TAPELIKE	APELIKE	
	APEPSIA	APEPSIAS
CAPER ▪ GAPER ▪ JAPER ▪ PAPER ▪ RAPER ▪ TAPER	APER	APERS ▪ APERT ▪ APERY
	APERCU	APERCUS
	APERIENT	APERIENTS
JAPERIES ▪ NAPERIES	APERIES	
	APERITIF	APERITIFS
	APERITIVE	APERITIVES
CAPERS ▪ GAPERS ▪ JAPERS ▪ PAPERS ▪ RAPERS ▪ TAPERS	APERS	
	APERTURE	APERTURED ▪ APERTURES
JAPERY ▪ NAPERY ▪ PAPERY	APERY	
CAPES ▪ GAPES ▪ JAPES ▪ NAPES ▪ PAPES ▪ RAPES ▪ TAPES	APES	
	APHAGIA	APHAGIAS
	APHAKIA	APHAKIAS
	APHANITE	APHANITES
	APHASIA	APHASIAC ▪ APHASIAS
	APHASIAC	APHASIACS
	APHASIC	APHASICS
	APHELIA	APHELIAN
	APHELION	APHELIONS
	APHETISE	APHETISED ▪ APHETISES
	APHETIZE	APHETIZED ▪ APHETIZES
	APHICIDE	APHICIDES
	APHID	APHIDS
RAPHIDES	APHIDES	
	APHIDIAN	APHIDIANS
RAPHIS	APHIS	
	APHOLATE	APHOLATES
	APHONIA	APHONIAS
	APHONIC	APHONICS
	APHORISE	APHORISED ▪ APHORISER ▪ APHORISES
	APHORISER	APHORISERS
	APHORISM	APHORISMS

FRONT HOOK	ROOT WORD	END HOOK
	APHORIST	APHORISTS
	APHORIZE	APHORIZED ▪ APHORIZER ▪ APHORIZES
	APHORIZER	APHORIZERS
	APHRODITE	APHRODITES
NAPHTHA	**APHTHA**	APHTHAE
NAPHTHOUS	**APHTHOUS**	
	APIARIAN	APIARIANS
	APIARIST	APIARISTS
	APICAL	APICALS
	APIMANIA	APIMANIAS
CAPING ▪ GAPING ▪ JAPING ▪ NAPING RAPING ▪ TAPING	**APING**	
	APIOL	APIOLS
PAPISH	**APISH**	
PAPISM	**APISM**	APISMS
PAPISMS (offensive)	**APISMS**	
	APLANAT	APLANATS
	APLASIA	APLASIAS
HAPLITE	**APLITE**	APLITES
HAPLITES	**APLITES**	
HAPLITIC	**APLITIC**	
	APLOMB	APLOMBS
	APLUSTRE	APLUSTRES
	APNEA	APNEAL ▪ APNEAS
	APNOEA	APNOEAL ▪ APNOEAS
CAPO ▪ GAPO	**APO**	APOD ▪ APOS
	APOCARP	APOCARPS ▪ APOCARPY
	APOCOPATE	APOCOPATED ▪ APOCOPATES
	APOCOPE	APOCOPES
	APOCRYPHA	APOCRYPHAL
	APOD	APODE ▪ APODS
	APODE	APODES
	APOENZYME	APOENZYMES
	APOGEE	APOGEES
	APOGRAPH	APOGRAPHS
	APOLLO	APOLLOS
	APOLOG	APOLOGS ▪ APOLOGY
	APOLOGIA	APOLOGIAE ▪ APOLOGIAS
	APOLOGISE	APOLOGISED ▪ APOLOGISER ▪ APOLOGISES
	APOLOGIST	APOLOGISTS
	APOLOGIZE	APOLOGIZED ▪ APOLOGIZER ▪ APOLOGIZES
	APOLOGUE	APOLOGUES
	APOLUNE	APOLUNES
	APOMICT	APOMICTS
	APOPHYGE	APOPHYGES
	APOPLAST	APOPLASTS
	APOPLEX	APOPLEXY
	APORIA	APORIAS
CAPOS ▪ GAPOS	**APOS**	
	APOSITIA	APOSITIAS
	APOSTATE	APOSTATES
	APOSTIL	APOSTILS
	APOSTILLE	APOSTILLES
	APOSTLE	APOSTLES
	APOTHECE	APOTHECES
	APOTHECIA	APOTHECIAL
	APOTHEGM	APOTHEGMS
	APOTHEM	APOTHEMS
	APOZEM	APOZEMS
YAPP	**APP**	APPS
	APPAIR	APPAIRS
	APPAL	APPALL ▪ APPALS
	APPALL	APPALLS
	APPALOOSA	APPALOOSAS
	APPANAGE	APPANAGED ▪ APPANAGES
	APPARAT	APPARATS
	APPAREL	APPARELS
	APPARENT	APPARENTS
	APPARITOR	APPARITORS

A

FRONT HOOK	ROOT WORD	END HOOK
	APPAY	APPAYD ▪ APPAYS
	APPEAL	APPEALS
	APPEALER	APPEALERS
	APPEAR	APPEARS
	APPEARER	APPEARERS
	APPEASE	APPEASED ▪ APPEASER ▪ APPEASES
	APPEASER	APPEASERS
LAPPEL ▪ RAPPEL	APPEL	APPELS
	APPELLANT	APPELLANTS
	APPELLEE	APPELLEES
	APPELLOR	APPELLORS
LAPPELS ▪ RAPPELS	APPELS	
WAPPEND	APPEND	APPENDS
	APPENDAGE	APPENDAGES
	APPENDANT	APPENDANTS
	APPENDENT	APPENDENTS
	APPERIL	APPERILL ▪ APPERILS
	APPERILL	APPERILLS
	APPERTAIN	APPERTAINS
	APPESTAT	APPESTATS
	APPETENCE	APPETENCES
	APPETISE	APPETISED ▪ APPETISER ▪ APPETISES
	APPETISER	APPETISERS
	APPETITE	APPETITES
	APPETIZE	APPETIZED ▪ APPETIZER ▪ APPETIZES
	APPETIZER	APPETIZERS
	APPLAUD	APPLAUDS
	APPLAUDER	APPLAUDERS
	APPLAUSE	APPLAUSES
DAPPLE ▪ SAPPLE	APPLE	APPLES ▪ APPLET ▪ APPLEY
	APPLECART	APPLECARTS
	APPLEJACK	APPLEJACKS
DAPPLES ▪ SAPPLES	APPLES	
	APPLET	APPLETS
	APPLIANCE	APPLIANCES
	APPLICANT	APPLICANTS
	APPLIER	APPLIERS
	APPLIQUE	APPLIQUED ▪ APPLIQUES
	APPOINT	APPOINTS
	APPOINTEE	APPOINTEES
	APPOINTER	APPOINTERS
	APPOINTOR	APPOINTORS
RAPPORT	APPORT	APPORTS
	APPORTION	APPORTIONS
RAPPORTS	APPORTS	
PAPPOSE	APPOSE	APPOSED ▪ APPOSER ▪ APPOSES
	APPOSER	APPOSERS
	APPRAISAL	APPRAISALS
	APPRAISE	APPRAISED ▪ APPRAISEE ▪ APPRAISER
		APPRAISES
	APPRAISEE	APPRAISEES
	APPRAISER	APPRAISERS
	APPREHEND	APPREHENDS
	APPRISE	APPRISED ▪ APPRISER ▪ APPRISES
	APPRISER	APPRISERS
	APPRISING	APPRISINGS
	APPRIZE	APPRIZED ▪ APPRIZER ▪ APPRIZES
	APPRIZER	APPRIZERS
	APPRIZING	APPRIZINGS
	APPRO	APPROS
	APPROBATE	APPROBATED ▪ APPROBATES
	APPROOF	APPROOFS
	APPROVAL	APPROVALS
	APPROVE	APPROVED ▪ APPROVER ▪ APPROVES
	APPROVER	APPROVERS
YAPPS	APPS	
	APPUI	APPUIS
	APPULSE	APPULSES
	APPUY	APPUYS

FRONT HOOK	ROOT WORD	END HOOK
	APRAXIA	APRAXIAS
	APRICATE	APRICATED ▪ APRICATES
	APRICOCK	APRICOCKS
	APRICOT	APRICOTS
	APRIORISM	APRIORISMS
	APRIORIST	APRIORISTS
NAPRON	**APRON**	APRONS
	APRONFUL	APRONFULS
NAPRONS	**APRONS**	
LAPSE	**APSE**	APSES
LAPSES	**APSES**	
CAPSIDAL	**APSIDAL**	
	APSIDIOLE	APSIDIOLES
	APSO	APSOS
RAPT	**APT**	APTS
	APTERISM	APTERISMS
	APTITUDE	APTITUDES
RAPTLY	**APTLY**	
RAPTNESS	**APTNESS**	
RAPTNESSES	**APTNESSES**	
	APTOTE	APTOTES
	APYRASE	APYRASES
	APYREXIA	APYREXIAS
	AQUA	AQUAE ▪ AQUAS
	AQUABATIC	AQUABATICS
	AQUABOARD	AQUABOARDS
	AQUACADE	AQUACADES
	AQUADROME	AQUADROMES
	AQUAFARM	AQUAFARMS
	AQUAFER	AQUAFERS
	AQUALUNG	AQUALUNGS
	AQUANAUT	AQUANAUTS
	AQUAPHOBE	AQUAPHOBES
	AQUAPLANE	AQUAPLANED ▪ AQUAPLANER ▪ AQUAPLANES
	AQUAPORIN	AQUAPORINS
	AQUARELLE	AQUARELLES
	AQUARIA	AQUARIAL ▪ AQUARIAN
	AQUARIAN	AQUARIANS
	AQUARIIST	AQUARIISTS
	AQUARIST	AQUARISTS
	AQUARIUM	AQUARIUMS
	AQUAROBIC	AQUAROBICS
	AQUASHOW	AQUASHOWS
	AQUATIC	AQUATICS
	AQUATINT	AQUATINTA ▪ AQUATINTS
	AQUATINTA	AQUATINTAS
	AQUATONE	AQUATONES
	AQUAVIT	AQUAVITS
	AQUEDUCT	AQUEDUCTS
	AQUIFER	AQUIFERS
	AQUILEGIA	AQUILEGIAS
	AQUILON	AQUILONS
BAR ▪ CAR ▪ EAR ▪ FAR ▪ GAR ▪ JAR ▪ LAR MAR ▪ OAR ▪ PAR ▪ SAR ▪ TAR ▪ VAR ▪ WAR YAR	**AR**	ARB ▪ ARC ▪ ARD ▪ ARE ▪ ARF ▪ ARK ▪ ARM ARS ▪ ART ▪ ARY
	ARAARA	ARAARAS
	ARABA	ARABAS
	ARABESK	ARABESKS
	ARABESQUE	ARABESQUED ▪ ARABESQUES
	ARABIC	ARABICA
	ARABICA	ARABICAS
	ARABICISE	ARABICISED ▪ ARABICISES
	ARABICIZE	ARABICIZED ▪ ARABICIZES
CARABIN	**ARABIN**	ARABINS
	ARABINOSE	ARABINOSES
CARABINS	**ARABINS**	
MARABIS	**ARABIS**	ARABISE
	ARABISE	ARABISED ▪ ARABISES
	ARABIZE	ARABIZED ▪ ARABIZES

FRONT HOOK	ROOT WORD	END HOOK
PARABLE	**ARABLE**	ARABLES
PARABLES	**ARABLES**	
	ARACHNID	ARACHNIDS
	ARACHNOID	ARACHNOIDS
PARAGONITE	**ARAGONITE**	ARAGONITES
	ARAISE	ARAISED = ARAISES
	ARAK	ARAKS
	ARALIA	ARALIAS
	ARAME	ARAMES
	ARAMID	ARAMIDS
	ARANEID	ARANEIDS
	ARAPAIMA	ARAPAIMAS
	ARAPONGA	ARAPONGAS
	ARAPUNGA	ARAPUNGAS
	ARAR	ARARS
	ARAROBA	ARAROBAS
	ARAUCARIA	ARAUCARIAN = ARAUCARIAS
	ARAYSE	ARAYSED = ARAYSES
BARB = CARB = DARB = GARB = WARB	**ARB**	ARBA = ARBS
	ARBA	ARBAS
	ARBALEST	ARBALESTS
	ARBALIST	ARBALISTS
	ARBELEST	ARBELESTS
	ARBITER	ARBITERS
	ARBITRAGE	ARBITRAGED = ARBITRAGER = ARBITRAGES
	ARBITRATE	ARBITRATED = ARBITRATES
	ARBITRIUM	ARBITRIUMS
	ARBLAST	ARBLASTS
	ARBLASTER	ARBLASTERS
HARBOR	**ARBOR**	ARBORS
HARBORED	**ARBORED**	
	ARBORET	ARBORETA = ARBORETS
	ARBORETUM	ARBORETUMS
	ARBORISE	ARBORISED = ARBORISES
	ARBORIST	ARBORISTS
	ARBORIZE	ARBORIZED = ARBORIZES
HARBOROUS	**ARBOROUS**	
HARBORS	**ARBORS**	
HARBOUR	**ARBOUR**	ARBOURS
HARBOURED	**ARBOURED**	
HARBOURS	**ARBOURS**	
BARBS = CARBS = DARBS = GARBS = WARBS	**ARBS**	
	ARBUSCLE	ARBUSCLES
	ARBUTE	ARBUTES
MARC = NARC	**ARC**	ARCH = ARCO = ARCS
	ARCADE	ARCADED = ARCADES
	ARCADIA	ARCADIAN = ARCADIAS
	ARCADIAN	ARCADIANS
	ARCADING	ARCADINGS
	ARCANA	ARCANAS
	ARCANIST	ARCANISTS
	ARCANUM	ARCANUMS
	ARCATURE	ARCATURES
	ARCCOSINE	ARCCOSINES
FARCED	**ARCED**	
LARCH = MARCH = PARCH	**ARCH**	
	ARCHAEA	ARCHAEAL = ARCHAEAN
	ARCHAEAN	ARCHAEANS
	ARCHAISE	ARCHAISED = ARCHAISER = ARCHAISES
	ARCHAISER	ARCHAISERS
	ARCHAISM	ARCHAISMS
	ARCHAIST	ARCHAISTS
	ARCHAIZE	ARCHAIZED = ARCHAIZER = ARCHAIZES
	ARCHAIZER	ARCHAIZERS
	ARCHANGEL	ARCHANGELS
	ARCHDUKE	ARCHDUKES
MARCHED = PARCHED	**ARCHED**	
MARCHER	**ARCHER**	ARCHERS = ARCHERY
MARCHERS	**ARCHERS**	

FRONT HOOK	ROOT WORD	END HOOK
LARCHES ▪ MARCHES ▪ PARCHES	**ARCHES**	ARCHEST
	ARCHETYPE	ARCHETYPES
	ARCHFIEND	ARCHFIENDS
	ARCHFOE	ARCHFOES
	ARCHICARP	ARCHICARPS
	ARCHIL	ARCHILS
	ARCHILOWE	ARCHILOWES
	ARCHIMAGE	ARCHIMAGES
	ARCHINE	ARCHINES
MARCHING ▪ PARCHING	**ARCHING**	ARCHINGS
	ARCHITECT	ARCHITECTS
	ARCHITYPE	ARCHITYPES
	ARCHIVE	ARCHIVED ▪ ARCHIVES
	ARCHIVIST	ARCHIVISTS
	ARCHIVOLT	ARCHIVOLTS
	ARCHLET	ARCHLETS
	ARCHLUTE	ARCHLUTES
	ARCHON	ARCHONS
	ARCHOSAUR	ARCHOSAURS
	ARCHRIVAL	ARCHRIVALS
	ARCHWAY	ARCHWAYS
FARCING	**ARCING**	ARCINGS
FARCINGS	**ARCINGS**	
	ARCKING	ARCKINGS
	ARCMIN	ARCMINS
NARCO ▪ YARCO	**ARCO**	
	ARCOGRAPH	ARCOGRAPHS
SARCOLOGY	**ARCOLOGY**	
MARCS ▪ NARCS	**ARCS**	
	ARCSEC	ARCSECS
	ARCSECOND	ARCSECONDS
	ARCSIN	ARCSINE ▪ ARCSINS
	ARCSINE	ARCSINES
	ARCTAN	ARCTANS
	ARCTIC	ARCTICS
	ARCTIID	ARCTIIDS
	ARCTOPHIL	ARCTOPHILE ▪ ARCTOPHILS ▪ ARCTOPHILY
	ARCUATE	ARCUATED
	ARCUATION	ARCUATIONS
BARD ▪ CARD ▪ EARD ▪ FARD ▪ HARD ▪ LARD	**ARD**	ARDS
MARD ▪ NARD ▪ PARD ▪ SARD ▪ WARD ▪ YARD		
	ARDEB	ARDEBS
	ARDOR	ARDORS
	ARDOUR	ARDOURS
	ARDRI	ARDRIS
	ARDRIGH	ARDRIGHS
BARDS ▪ CARDS ▪ EARDS ▪ FARDS ▪ HARDS	**ARDS**	
LARDS ▪ NARDS ▪ PARDS ▪ SARDS ▪ WARDS		
YARDS		
BARE ▪ CARE ▪ DARE ▪ FARE ▪ GARE ▪ HARE	**ARE**	AREA ▪ ARED ▪ AREG ▪ ARES ▪ ARET ▪ AREW
LARE ▪ MARE ▪ NARE ▪ PARE ▪ RARE ▪ TARE		
VARE ▪ WARE ▪ YARE		
	AREA	AREAD ▪ AREAE ▪ AREAL ▪ AREAR ▪ AREAS
	AREAD	AREADS
	AREAWAY	AREAWAYS
	ARECA	ARECAS
	ARECOLINE	ARECOLINES
BARED ▪ CARED ▪ DARED ▪ EARED ▪ FARED	**ARED**	AREDD ▪ AREDE
HARED ▪ OARED ▪ PARED ▪ RARED ▪ SARED		
TARED ▪ WARED		
	AREDE	AREDES
RAREFIED	**AREFIED**	
RAREFIES	**AREFIES**	
RAREFY	**AREFY**	
RAREFYING	**AREFYING**	
	ARENA	ARENAS
	ARENATION	ARENATIONS
	ARENE	ARENES
	ARENITE	ARENITES

FRONT HOOK	ROOT WORD	END HOOK
	AREOLA	AREOLAE · AREOLAR · AREOLAS
	AREOLATE	AREOLATED
	AREOLE	AREOLES
	AREOMETER	AREOMETERS
	AREOSTYLE	AREOSTYLES
	AREPA	AREPAS
BARES · CARES · DARES · FARES · HARES LARES · MARES · NARES · PARES · RARES TARES · VARES · WARES	ARES	
CARET	ARET	ARETE · ARETS · ARETT
	ARETE	ARETES
	ARETHUSA	ARETHUSAS
CARETS	ARETS	
	ARETT	ARETTS
BARF · ZARF	ARF	ARFS
BARFS · ZARFS	ARFS	
	ARGAL	ARGALA · ARGALI · ARGALS
	ARGALA	ARGALAS
	ARGALI	ARGALIS
	ARGAN	ARGAND · ARGANS
	ARGAND	ARGANDS
	ARGEMONE	ARGEMONES
MARGENT	ARGENT	ARGENTS
	ARGENTINE	ARGENTINES
	ARGENTITE	ARGENTITES
MARGENTS	ARGENTS	
	ARGENTUM	ARGENTUMS
	ARGHAN	ARGHANS
	ARGIL	ARGILS
	ARGILLITE	ARGILLITES
	ARGINASE	ARGINASES
	ARGININE	ARGININES
DARGLE · GARGLE	ARGLE	ARGLED · ARGLES
GARGLED	ARGLED	
DARGLES · GARGLES	ARGLES	
GARGLING	ARGLING	
	ARGOL	ARGOLS
JARGON	ARGON	ARGONS
	ARGONAUT	ARGONAUTS
	ARGONON	ARGONONS
JARGONS	ARGONS	
	ARGOT	ARGOTS
	ARGUE	ARGUED · ARGUER · ARGUES
	ARGUER	ARGUERS
	ARGUFIER	ARGUFIERS
	ARGUMENT	ARGUMENTA · ARGUMENTS
SARGUS	ARGUS	
SARGUSES	ARGUSES	
	ARGYLE	ARGYLES
	ARGYLL	ARGYLLS
	ARGYRIA	ARGYRIAS
	ARGYRITE	ARGYRITES
	ARHAT	ARHATS
	ARHATSHIP	ARHATSHIPS
	ARHYTHMIA	ARHYTHMIAS
MARIA · VARIA	ARIA	ARIAS
VARIAS	ARIAS	
MARID	ARID	
	ARIEL	ARIELS
	ARIETTA	ARIETTAS
	ARIETTE	ARIETTES
	ARIL	ARILS
	ARILLATE	ARILLATED
	ARILLODE	ARILLODES
CARIOSE	ARIOSE	
	ARIOSO	ARIOSOS
DARIS · GARIS · LARIS · NARIS · PARIS SARIS	ARIS	ARISE · ARISH
	ARISE	ARISEN · ARISES

FRONT HOOK	ROOT WORD	END HOOK
PARISES	**ARISES**	
BARISH = GARISH = HARISH = MARISH PARISH	**ARISH**	
GARISHES = MARISHES = PARISHES	**ARISHES**	
BARISTA	**ARISTA**	ARISTAE = ARISTAS
BARISTAS	**ARISTAS**	
	ARISTO	ARISTOS
	ARISTOTLE	ARISTOTLES
BARK = CARK = DARK = HARK = JARK = KARK LARK = MARK = NARK = PARK = RARK = SARK WARK = YARK	**ARK**	ARKS
BARKED = CARKED = DARKED = HARKED KARKED = LARKED = MARKED = NARKED PARKED = RARKED = WARKED = YARKED	**ARKED**	
BARKING = CARKING = DARKING = HARKING KARKING = LARKING = MARKING = NARKING PARKING = RARKING = SARKING = WARKING YARKING	**ARKING**	
	ARKITE	ARKITES
	ARKOSE	ARKOSES
BARKS = CARKS = DARKS = HARKS = JARKS KARKS = LARKS = MARKS = NARKS = PARKS RARKS = SARKS = WARKS = YARKS	**ARKS**	
CARLE = FARLE = MARLE = PARLE	**ARLE**	ARLED = ARLES
HARLED = MARLED = PARLED	**ARLED**	
CARLES = FARLES = MARLES = PARLES	**ARLES**	
CARLING = DARLING = HARLING = MARLING PARLING = WARLING	**ARLING**	
BARM = FARM = HARM = MARM = WARM	**ARM**	ARMS = ARMY
	ARMADA	ARMADAS
	ARMADILLO	ARMADILLOS
	ARMAGNAC	ARMAGNACS
	ARMAMENT	ARMAMENTS
	ARMATURE	ARMATURED = ARMATURES
	ARMBAND	ARMBANDS
	ARMCHAIR	ARMCHAIRS
FARMED = HARMED = WARMED	**ARMED**	
FARMER = HARMER = WARMER	**ARMER**	ARMERS
FARMERS = HARMERS = WARMERS	**ARMERS**	
	ARMET	ARMETS
HARMFUL	**ARMFUL**	ARMFULS
	ARMHOLE	ARMHOLES
SARMIES	**ARMIES**	
	ARMIGER	ARMIGERO = ARMIGERS
	ARMIGERO	ARMIGEROS
	ARMIL	ARMILS
	ARMILLA	ARMILLAE = ARMILLAS
FARMING = HARMING = WARMING	**ARMING**	ARMINGS
FARMINGS = WARMINGS	**ARMINGS**	
	ARMISTICE	ARMISTICES
HARMLESS	**ARMLESS**	
	ARMLET	ARMLETS
	ARMLOAD	ARMLOADS
	ARMLOCK	ARMLOCKS
	ARMOIRE	ARMOIRES
HARMONICA	**ARMONICA**	ARMONICAS
HARMONICAS	**ARMONICAS**	
	ARMOR	ARMORS = ARMORY
	ARMORER	ARMORERS
	ARMORIAL	ARMORIALS
	ARMORIST	ARMORISTS
	ARMOUR	ARMOURS = ARMOURY
	ARMOURER	ARMOURERS
	ARMOZEEN	ARMOZEENS
	ARMOZINE	ARMOZINES
	ARMPIT	ARMPITS
	ARMREST	ARMRESTS
BARMS = FARMS = HARMS = MARMS = WARMS	**ARMS**	
	ARMURE	ARMURES

FRONT HOOK	ROOT WORD	END HOOK
BARMY	**ARMY**	
	ARMYWORM	ARMYWORMS
VARNA	**ARNA**	ARNAS
VARNAS	**ARNAS**	
	ARNATTO	ARNATTOS
	ARNICA	ARNICAS
	ARNOTTO	ARNOTTOS
	ARNUT	ARNUTS
	AROBA	AROBAS
	AROHA	AROHAS
LAROID	**AROID**	AROIDS
	AROINT	AROINTS
	AROLLA	AROLLAS
	AROMA	AROMAS
	AROMATASE	AROMATASES
	AROMATIC	AROMATICS
	AROMATISE	AROMATISED · AROMATISES
	AROMATIZE	AROMATIZED · AROMATIZES
CAROUSAL	**AROUSAL**	AROUSALS
CAROUSALS	**AROUSALS**	
CAROUSE	**AROUSE**	AROUSED · AROUSER · AROUSES
CAROUSED	**AROUSED**	
CAROUSER	**AROUSER**	AROUSERS
CAROUSERS	**AROUSERS**	
CAROUSES	**AROUSES**	
CAROUSING	**AROUSING**	
	AROYNT	AROYNTS
	ARPA	ARPAS
	ARPEGGIO	ARPEGGIOS
PARPEN	**ARPEN**	ARPENS · ARPENT
PARPENS	**ARPENS**	
PARPENT	**ARPENT**	ARPENTS
PARPENTS	**ARPENTS**	
	ARPILLERA	ARPILLERAS
HARQUEBUS	**ARQUEBUS**	
	ARRACACHA	ARRACACHAS
BARRACK · CARRACK	**ARRACK**	ARRACKS
BARRACKS · CARRACKS	**ARRACKS**	
JARRAH	**ARRAH**	
DARRAIGN	**ARRAIGN**	ARRAIGNS
DARRAIGNED	**ARRAIGNED**	
	ARRAIGNER	ARRAIGNERS
DARRAIGNS	**ARRAIGNS**	
	ARRANGE	ARRANGED · ARRANGER · ARRANGES
	ARRANGER	ARRANGERS
FARRANT · WARRANT	**ARRANT**	
BARRAS · NARRAS · PARRAS · TARRAS	**ARRAS**	
	ARRASENE	ARRASENES
NARRASES · TARRASES	**ARRASES**	
WARRAY	**ARRAY**	ARRAYS
	ARRAYAL	ARRAYALS
WARRAYED	**ARRAYED**	
	ARRAYER	ARRAYERS
WARRAYING	**ARRAYING**	
	ARRAYMENT	ARRAYMENTS
WARRAYS	**ARRAYS**	
	ARREAR	ARREARS
	ARREARAGE	ARREARAGES
CARRECT	**ARRECT**	
	ARREEDE	ARREEDES
	ARREST	ARRESTS
	ARRESTANT	ARRESTANTS
	ARRESTEE	ARRESTEES
	ARRESTER	ARRESTERS
	ARRESTOR	ARRESTORS
BARRET · GARRET	**ARRET**	ARRETS
BARRETS · GARRETS	**ARRETS**	
CARRIAGE · MARRIAGE	**ARRIAGE**	ARRIAGES
CARRIAGES · MARRIAGES	**ARRIAGES**	

FRONT HOOK	ROOT WORD	END HOOK
	ARRIDE	ARRIDED ▪ ARRIDES
	ARRIERO	ARRIEROS
KARRIS ▪ MARRIS	**ARRIS**	ARRISH
	ARRIVAL	ARRIVALS
	ARRIVANCE	ARRIVANCES
	ARRIVE	ARRIVED ▪ ARRIVER ▪ ARRIVES
	ARRIVER	ARRIVERS
	ARRIVISME	ARRIVISMES
	ARRIVISTE	ARRIVISTES
	ARROBA	ARROBAS
	ARROGANCE	ARROGANCES
	ARROGATE	ARROGATED ▪ ARROGATES
	ARROGATOR	ARROGATORS
BARROW ▪ FARROW ▪ HARROW ▪ MARROW NARROW ▪ TARROW ▪ YARROW	**ARROW**	ARROWS ▪ ARROWY
FARROWED ▪ HARROWED ▪ MARROWED NARROWED ▪ TARROWED	**ARROWED**	
	ARROWHEAD	ARROWHEADS
FARROWING ▪ HARROWING ▪ MARROWING NARROWING ▪ TARROWING	**ARROWING**	
MARROWLESS	**ARROWLESS**	
	ARROWROOT	ARROWROOTS
BARROWS ▪ FARROWS ▪ HARROWS ▪ MARROWS NARROWS ▪ TARROWS ▪ YARROWS	**ARROWS**	
	ARROWWOOD	ARROWWOODS
	ARROWWORM	ARROWWORMS
MARROWY	**ARROWY**	
	ARROYO	ARROYOS
BARS ▪ CARS ▪ EARS ▪ FARS ▪ GARS ▪ JARS LARS ▪ MARS ▪ OARS ▪ PARS ▪ SARS ▪ TARS VARS ▪ WARS	**ARS**	ARSE ▪ ARSY (offensive)
CARSE ▪ FARSE ▪ MARSE ▪ PARSE	**ARSE**	ARSED (offensive) ▪ ARSES (offensive) ▪ ARSEY
FARSED ▪ PARSED	**ARSED**	
	ARSEHOLE	ARSEHOLES (offensive)
	ARSENAL	ARSENALS
	ARSENATE	ARSENATES
	ARSENIATE	ARSENIATES
	ARSENIC	ARSENICS
	ARSENICAL	ARSENICALS
	ARSENIDE	ARSENIDES
	ARSENITE	ARSENITES
CARSES ▪ FARSES ▪ MARSES ▪ PARSES	**ARSES**	
CARSEY ▪ KARSEY	**ARSEY**	
	ARSHEEN	ARSHEENS
	ARSHIN	ARSHINE ▪ ARSHINS
	ARSHINE	ARSHINES
TARSIER	**ARSIER**	
	ARSINE	ARSINES
FARSING ▪ PARSING	**ARSING**	
PARSON	**ARSON**	ARSONS
	ARSONIST	ARSONISTS
	ARSONITE	ARSONITES
PARSONS	**ARSONS**	
KARSY	**ARSY**	
CART ▪ DART ▪ FART ▪ GART ▪ HART ▪ KART MART ▪ PART ▪ TART ▪ WART	**ART**	ARTI ▪ ARTS ▪ ARTY
HARTAL	**ARTAL**	
	ARTEFACT	ARTEFACTS
CARTEL ▪ MARTEL	**ARTEL**	ARTELS
CARTELS ▪ MARTELS	**ARTELS**	
	ARTEMISIA	ARTEMISIAS
	ARTERIAL	ARTERIALS
	ARTERIOLE	ARTERIOLES
CARTFUL	**ARTFUL**	
	ARTHRITIC	ARTHRITICS
	ARTHRODIA	ARTHRODIAE ▪ ARTHRODIAL
	ARTHROPOD	ARTHROPODS
AARTI ▪ PARTI	**ARTI**	ARTIC ▪ ARTIS
	ARTIC	ARTICS

FRONT HOOK	ROOT WORD	END HOOK
	ARTICHOKE	ARTICHOKES
PARTICLE	**ARTICLE**	ARTICLED ▪ ARTICLES
PARTICLES	**ARTICLES**	
PARTICULAR	**ARTICULAR**	
PARTIER ▪ TARTIER ▪ WARTIER	**ARTIER**	
PARTIES	**ARTIES**	ARTIEST
TARTIEST ▪ WARTIEST	**ARTIEST**	
	ARTIFACT	ARTIFACTS
	ARTIFICE	ARTIFICER ▪ ARTIFICES
	ARTIFICER	ARTIFICERS
TARTILY	**ARTILY**	
TARTINESS	**ARTINESS**	
AARTIS ▪ PARTIS	**ARTIS**	ARTIST
BARTISAN ▪ PARTISAN	**ARTISAN**	ARTISANS
BARTISANS ▪ PARTISANS	**ARTISANS**	
	ARTIST	ARTISTE ▪ ARTISTS
	ARTISTE	ARTISTES
	ARTLESS	
WARTLESS	**ARTS**	ARTSY
CARTS ▪ DARTS ▪ FARTS (offensive) ▪ HARTS		
KARTS ▪ MARTS ▪ PARTS ▪ TARTS ▪ WARTS		
	ARTSIES	ARTSIEST
PARTWORK	**ARTWORK**	ARTWORKS
PARTWORKS	**ARTWORKS**	
PARTY ▪ TARTY ▪ WARTY	**ARTY**	
	ARUGOLA	ARUGOLAS
	ARUGULA	ARUGULAS
GARUM ▪ LARUM	**ARUM**	ARUMS
GARUMS ▪ LARUMS	**ARUMS**	
HARUSPEX	**ARUSPEX**	
HARUSPICES	**ARUSPICES**	
LARVAL	**ARVAL**	
	ARVICOLE	ARVICOLES
PARVO	**ARVO**	ARVOS
PARVOS	**ARVOS**	
MARY ▪ NARY ▪ OARY ▪ VARY ▪ WARY	**ARY**	ARYL
	ARYL	ARYLS
	ARYTENOID	ARYTENOIDS
	ARYTHMIA	ARYTHMIAS
AAS ▪ BAS ▪ DAS ▪ EAS ▪ FAS ▪ GAS ▪ HAS	**AS**	ASH ▪ ASK ▪ ASP ▪ ASS
KAS ▪ LAS ▪ MAS ▪ NAS ▪ PAS ▪ RAS ▪ TAS		
VAS ▪ WAS ▪ ZAS		
	ASAFETIDA	ASAFETIDAS
	ASANA	ASANAS
TASAR	**ASAR**	
	ASARUM	ASARUMS
	ASCARID	ASCARIDS
	ASCEND	ASCENDS
	ASCENDANT	ASCENDANTS
	ASCENDENT	ASCENDENTS
	ASCENDER	ASCENDERS
	ASCENDEUR	ASCENDEURS
	ASCENSION	ASCENSIONS
NASCENT	**ASCENT**	ASCENTS
	ASCERTAIN	ASCERTAINS
	ASCETIC	ASCETICS
FASCI	**ASCI**	
	ASCIAN	ASCIANS
	ASCIDIA	ASCIDIAN
	ASCIDIAN	ASCIDIANS
	ASCLEPIAD	ASCLEPIADS
	ASCOCARP	ASCOCARPS
	ASCORBATE	ASCORBATES
	ASCOSPORE	ASCOSPORES
MASCOT	**ASCOT**	ASCOTS
MASCOTS	**ASCOTS**	
	ASCRIBE	ASCRIBED ▪ ASCRIBES
	ASDIC	ASDICS
GASEITIES	**ASEITIES**	
GASEITY	**ASEITY**	

FRONT HOOK	ROOT WORD	END HOOK
	ASEPTIC	ASEPTICS
BASH ▪ CASH ▪ DASH ▪ FASH ▪ GASH ▪ HASH LASH ▪ MASH ▪ PASH ▪ RASH ▪ SASH ▪ TASH WASH	**ASH**	ASHY
	ASHAME	ASHAMED ▪ ASHAMES
	ASHCAKE	ASHCAKES
	ASHCAN	ASHCANS
BASHED ▪ CASHED ▪ DASHED ▪ FASHED GASHED ▪ HASHED ▪ LASHED ▪ MASHED PASHED ▪ RASHED ▪ SASHED ▪ TASHED WASHED	**ASHED**	
WASHEN	**ASHEN**	
FASHERIES ▪ WASHERIES	**ASHERIES**	
FASHERY ▪ WASHERY	**ASHERY**	
BASHES ▪ CASHES ▪ DASHES ▪ FASHES GASHES ▪ HASHES ▪ LASHES ▪ MASHES PASHES ▪ RASHES ▪ SASHES ▪ TASHES WASHES	**ASHES**	
	ASHET	ASHETS
	ASHFALL	ASHFALLS
CASHIER ▪ DASHIER ▪ HASHIER ▪ MASHIER WASHIER	**ASHIER**	
DASHIEST ▪ HASHIEST ▪ MASHIEST ▪ WASHIEST WASHINESS	**ASHIEST**	
	ASHINESS	
BASHING ▪ CASHING ▪ DASHING ▪ FASHING GASHING ▪ HASHING ▪ LASHING ▪ MASHING PASHING ▪ RASHING ▪ SASHING ▪ TASHING WASHING	**ASHING**	
	ASHKEY	ASHKEYS
	ASHLAR	ASHLARS
	ASHLARING	ASHLARINGS
	ASHLER	ASHLERS
	ASHLERING	ASHLERINGS
BASHLESS ▪ CASHLESS ▪ SASHLESS	**ASHLESS**	
MASHMAN	**ASHMAN**	
MASHMEN	**ASHMEN**	
	ASHPLANT	ASHPLANTS
	ASHRAM	ASHRAMA ▪ ASHRAMS
	ASHRAMA	ASHRAMAS
	ASHRAMITE	ASHRAMITES
	ASHTRAY	ASHTRAYS
DASHY ▪ HASHY ▪ MASHY ▪ WASHY	**ASHY**	
	ASIAGO	ASIAGOS
	ASIDE	ASIDES
	ASINICO	ASINICOS
BASK ▪ CASK ▪ HASK ▪ MASK ▪ TASK	**ASK**	ASKS
	ASKANCE	ASKANCED ▪ ASKANCES
	ASKANT	ASKANTS
	ASKARI	ASKARIS
BASKED ▪ CASKED ▪ MASKED ▪ TASKED	**ASKED**	
MASKER ▪ TASKER	**ASKER**	ASKERS
MASKERS ▪ TASKERS	**ASKERS**	
BASKING ▪ CASKING ▪ GASKING ▪ MASKING TASKING	**ASKING**	ASKINGS
GASKINGS ▪ MASKINGS ▪ TASKINGS	**ASKINGS**	
BASKS ▪ CASKS ▪ HASKS ▪ MASKS ▪ TASKS	**ASKS**	
	ASLAKE	ASLAKED ▪ ASLAKES
	ASOCIAL	ASOCIALS
GASP ▪ HASP ▪ JASP ▪ RASP ▪ WASP	**ASP**	ASPS
	ASPARTAME	ASPARTAMES
	ASPARTATE	ASPARTATES
	ASPECT	ASPECTS
	ASPEN	ASPENS
GASPER ▪ JASPER ▪ RASPER	**ASPER**	ASPERS
	ASPERATE	ASPERATED ▪ ASPERATES
	ASPERGE	ASPERGED ▪ ASPERGER ▪ ASPERGES
	ASPERGER	ASPERGERS
	ASPERGILL	ASPERGILLA ▪ ASPERGILLI ▪ ASPERGILLS
	ASPERMIA	ASPERMIAS

FRONT HOOK	ROOT WORD	END HOOK
JASPEROUS	**ASPEROUS**	
GASPERS · JASPERS · RASPERS	**ASPERS**	ASPERSE
	ASPERSE	ASPERSED · ASPERSER · ASPERSES
	ASPERSER	ASPERSERS
	ASPERSION	ASPERSIONS
	ASPERSOIR	ASPERSOIRS
	ASPERSOR	ASPERSORS · ASPERSORY
	ASPHALT	ASPHALTS
	ASPHALTER	ASPHALTERS
	ASPHALTUM	ASPHALTUMS
	ASPHODEL	ASPHODELS
	ASPHYXIA	ASPHYXIAL · ASPHYXIAS
	ASPIC	ASPICK · ASPICS
	ASPICK	ASPICKS
	ASPINE	ASPINES
	ASPIRANT	ASPIRANTS
	ASPIRATA	ASPIRATAE
	ASPIRATE	ASPIRATED · ASPIRATES
	ASPIRATOR	ASPIRATORS · ASPIRATORY
	ASPIRE	ASPIRED · ASPIRER · ASPIRES
	ASPIRER	ASPIRERS
	ASPIRIN	ASPIRING · ASPIRINS
JASPIS	**ASPIS**	ASPISH
JASPISES	**ASPISES**	
RASPISH · WASPISH	**ASPISH**	
	ASPLENIUM	ASPLENIUMS
	ASPORT	ASPORTS
	ASPRO	ASPROS
GASPS · HASPS · JASPS · RASPS · WASPS	**ASPS**	
	ASRAMA	ASRAMAS
BASS · JASS · LASS · MASS · PASS · SASS · TASS	**ASS**	
	ASSAGAI	ASSAGAIS
	ASSAI	ASSAIL · ASSAIS
VASSAIL · WASSAIL	**ASSAIL**	ASSAILS
	ASSAILANT	ASSAILANTS
WASSAILED	**ASSAILED**	
WASSAILER	**ASSAILER**	ASSAILERS
WASSAILERS	**ASSAILERS**	
WASSAILING	**ASSAILING**	
VASSAILS · WASSAILS	**ASSAILS**	
	ASSAM	ASSAMS
	ASSART	ASSARTS
	ASSASSIN	ASSASSINS
	ASSAULT	ASSAULTS
	ASSAULTER	ASSAULTERS
	ASSAY	ASSAYS
	ASSAYER	ASSAYERS
	ASSAYING	ASSAYINGS
	ASSEGAAI	ASSEGAAIS
	ASSEGAI	ASSEGAIS
	ASSEMBLE	ASSEMBLED · ASSEMBLER · ASSEMBLES
	ASSEMBLER	ASSEMBLERS
	ASSENT	ASSENTS
	ASSENTER	ASSENTERS
	ASSENTOR	ASSENTORS
	ASSERT	ASSERTS
	ASSERTER	ASSERTERS
	ASSERTION	ASSERTIONS
	ASSERTOR	ASSERTORS · ASSERTORY
BASSES · GASSES · JASSES · LASSES · MASSES · PASSES · RASSES · SASSES · TASSES	**ASSES**	ASSESS
	ASSESSOR	ASSESSORS
BASSET · TASSET	**ASSET**	ASSETS
BASSETS · TASSETS	**ASSETS**	
	ASSEVER	ASSEVERS
	ASSHOLE	ASSHOLES *(offensive)*
	ASSIEGE	ASSIEGED · ASSIEGES

FRONT HOOK	ROOT WORD	END HOOK
	ASSIENTO	ASSIENTOS
	ASSIGN	ASSIGNS
	ASSIGNAT	ASSIGNATS
	ASSIGNEE	ASSIGNEES
	ASSIGNER	ASSIGNERS
	ASSIGNOR	ASSIGNORS
BASSIST	ASSIST	ASSISTS
	ASSISTANT	ASSISTANTS
	ASSISTER	ASSISTERS
	ASSISTOR	ASSISTORS
BASSISTS	ASSISTS	
	ASSIZE	ASSIZED ▪ ASSIZER ▪ ASSIZES
	ASSIZER	ASSIZERS
	ASSOCIATE	ASSOCIATED ▪ ASSOCIATES
	ASSOIL	ASSOILS
	ASSOILZIE	ASSOILZIED ▪ ASSOILZIES
	ASSONANCE	ASSONANCES
	ASSONANT	ASSONANTS
	ASSONATE	ASSONATED ▪ ASSONATES
	ASSORT	ASSORTS
	ASSORTER	ASSORTERS
	ASSOT	ASSOTS ▪ ASSOTT
	ASSUAGE	ASSUAGED ▪ ASSUAGER ▪ ASSUAGES
	ASSUAGER	ASSUAGERS
	ASSUAGING	ASSUAGINGS
	ASSUETUDE	ASSUETUDES
	ASSUME	ASSUMED ▪ ASSUMER ▪ ASSUMES
	ASSUMER	ASSUMERS
	ASSUMING	ASSUMINGS
	ASSUMPSIT	ASSUMPSITS
	ASSURANCE	ASSURANCES
	ASSURE	ASSURED ▪ ASSURER ▪ ASSURES
	ASSURED	ASSUREDS
	ASSURER	ASSURERS
	ASSUROR	ASSURORS
TASSWAGE	ASSWAGE	ASSWAGED ▪ ASSWAGES
CASTABLE ▪ TASTABLE ▪ WASTABLE	ASTABLE	
	ASTART	ASTARTS
	ASTASIA	ASTASIAS
	ASTATIDE	ASTATIDES
	ASTATINE	ASTATINES
	ASTATKI	ASTATKIS
CASTEISM	ASTEISM	ASTEISMS
CASTEISMS	ASTEISMS	
BASTER ▪ CASTER ▪ EASTER ▪ FASTER GASTER ▪ LASTER ▪ MASTER ▪ PASTER RASTER ▪ TASTER ▪ VASTER ▪ WASTER	ASTER	ASTERN ▪ ASTERS ▪ ASTERT
	ASTERIA	ASTERIAS
	ASTERID	ASTERIDS
	ASTERISK	ASTERISKS
	ASTERISM	ASTERISMS
EASTERN ▪ PASTERN	ASTERN	
	ASTEROID	ASTEROIDS
BASTERS ▪ CASTERS ▪ EASTERS ▪ FASTERS GASTERS ▪ LASTERS ▪ MASTERS ▪ PASTERS RASTERS ▪ TASTERS ▪ WASTERS	ASTERS	
	ASTERT	ASTERTS
	ASTHENIA	ASTHENIAS
	ASTHENIC	ASTHENICS
	ASTHMA	ASTHMAS
	ASTHMATIC	ASTHMATICS
	ASTHORE	ASTHORES
	ASTIGMIA	ASTIGMIAS
	ASTILBE	ASTILBES
	ASTONE	ASTONED ▪ ASTONES
	ASTOUND	ASTOUNDS
	ASTRACHAN	ASTRACHANS
	ASTRAGAL	ASTRAGALI ▪ ASTRAGALS
	ASTRAKHAN	ASTRAKHANS

FRONT HOOK	ROOT WORD	END HOOK
	ASTRAL	ASTRALS
CASTRAL · GASTRAL	**ASTRANTIA**	ASTRANTIAS
	ASTRICT	ASTRICTS
	ASTRINGE	ASTRINGED · ASTRINGER · ASTRINGES
	ASTRINGER	ASTRINGERS
	ASTROCYTE	ASTROCYTES
	ASTRODOME	ASTRODOMES
	ASTROFELL	ASTROFELLS
	ASTROID	ASTROIDS
	ASTROLABE	ASTROLABES
GASTROLOGY	**ASTROLOGY**	
	ASTRONAUT	ASTRONAUTS
GASTRONOMY	**ASTRONOMY**	
	ASTROPHEL	ASTROPHELS
	ASTUN	ASTUNS
	ASTUTE	ASTUTER
	ASYLUM	ASYLUMS
	ASYMPTOTE	ASYMPTOTES
	ASYNDETON	ASYNDETONS
	ASYNERGIA	ASYNERGIAS
	ASYSTOLE	ASYSTOLES
BAT · CAT · EAT · FAT · GAT · HAT · KAT LAT · MAT · NAT · OAT · PAT · QAT · RAT SAT · TAT · VAT · WAT	**AT**	ATE · ATT
	ATAATA	ATAATAS
	ATABAL	ATABALS
	ATABEG	ATABEGS
	ATABEK	ATABEKS
	ATABRIN	ATABRINE · ATABRINS
	ATABRINE	ATABRINES
	ATACAMITE	ATACAMITES
YATAGHAN	**ATAGHAN**	ATAGHANS
YATAGHANS	**ATAGHANS**	
	ATALAYA	ATALAYAS
	ATAMAN	ATAMANS
	ATAMASCO	ATAMASCOS
WATAP	**ATAP**	ATAPS
WATAPS	**ATAPS**	
	ATARACTIC	ATARACTICS
	ATARAXIA	ATARAXIAS
	ATARAXIC	ATARAXICS
	ATAVISM	ATAVISMS
	ATAVIST	ATAVISTS
	ATAXIA	ATAXIAS
	ATAXIC	ATAXICS
	ATCHIEVE	ATCHIEVED · ATCHIEVES
BATE · CATE · DATE · FATE · GATE · HATE LATE · MATE · PATE · RATE · SATE · TATE WATE · YATE	**ATE**	ATES
	ATEBRIN	ATEBRINS
	ATELIER	ATELIERS
	ATEMOYA	ATEMOYAS
	ATENOLOL	ATENOLOLS
BATES · CATES · DATES · FATES · GATES HATES · MATES · NATES · PATES · RATES SATES · TATES · YATES	**ATES**	
	ATHAME	ATHAMES
	ATHANOR	ATHANORS
	ATHEISE	ATHEISED · ATHEISES
	ATHEISM	ATHEISMS
	ATHEIST	ATHEISTS
	ATHEIZE	ATHEIZED · ATHEIZES
	ATHELING	ATHELINGS
MATHEMATIC	**ATHEMATIC**	
	ATHENAEUM	ATHENAEUMS
	ATHENEUM	ATHENEUMS
	ATHERINE	ATHERINES
	ATHEROMA	ATHEROMAS
	ATHETISE	ATHETISED · ATHETISES

FRONT HOOK	ROOT WORD	END HOOK
	ATHETIZE	ATHETIZED ▪ ATHETIZES
	ATHLETA	ATHLETAS
	ATHLETE	ATHLETES
	ATHLETIC	ATHLETICS
	ATHODYD	ATHODYDS
	ATHROCYTE	ATHROCYTES
	ATIGI	ATIGIS
	ATISHOO	ATISHOOS
	ATLATL	ATLATLS
	ATMA	ATMAN ▪ ATMAS
- BATMAN ▪ VATMAN	ATMAN	ATMANS
	ATMOLYSE	ATMOLYSED ▪ ATMOLYSES
	ATMOLYZE	ATMOLYZED ▪ ATMOLYZES
	ATMOMETER	ATMOMETERS
	ATOC	ATOCS
	ATOCIA	ATOCIAS
	ATOK	ATOKE ▪ ATOKS
MATOKE	ATOKE	ATOKES
MATOKES	ATOKES	
	ATOLL	ATOLLS
	ATOM	ATOMS ▪ ATOMY
	ATOMIC	ATOMICS
	ATOMISE	ATOMISED ▪ ATOMISER ▪ ATOMISES
	ATOMISER	ATOMISERS
	ATOMISM	ATOMISMS
	ATOMIST	ATOMISTS
	ATOMIZE	ATOMIZED ▪ ATOMIZER ▪ ATOMIZES
	ATOMIZER	ATOMIZERS
	ATONALISM	ATONALISMS
	ATONALIST	ATONALISTS
	ATONE	ATONED ▪ ATONER ▪ ATONES
BATONED	ATONED	
	ATONEMENT	ATONEMENTS
	ATONER	ATONERS
	ATONIA	ATONIAS
	ATONIC	ATONICS
BATONING	ATONING	
	ATOP	ATOPY
	ATRAMENT	ATRAMENTS
	ATRAZINE	ATRAZINES
	ATRESIA	ATRESIAS
LATRIA	ATRIA	ATRIAL
PATRIAL	ATRIAL	
NATRIUM	ATRIUM	ATRIUMS
NATRIUMS	ATRIUMS	
	ATROPHIA	ATROPHIAS
	ATROPIA	ATROPIAS
	ATROPIN	ATROPINE ▪ ATROPINS
	ATROPINE	ATROPINES
	ATROPISM	ATROPISMS
BATT ▪ MATT ▪ TATT ▪ WATT	ATT	
	ATTACH	ATTACHE
	ATTACHE	ATTACHED ▪ ATTACHER ▪ ATTACHES
	ATTACHER	ATTACHERS
	ATTACK	ATTACKS
	ATTACKER	ATTACKERS
	ATTAIN	ATTAINS ▪ ATTAINT
	ATTAINDER	ATTAINDERS
	ATTAINER	ATTAINERS
	ATTAINT	ATTAINTS
	ATTAP	ATTAPS
	ATTAR	ATTARS
	ATTASK	ATTASKS ▪ ATTASKT
	ATTEMPER	ATTEMPERS
	ATTEMPT	ATTEMPTS
	ATTEMPTER	ATTEMPTERS
	ATTEND	ATTENDS
	ATTENDANT	ATTENDANTS
	ATTENDEE	ATTENDEES

FRONT HOOK	ROOT WORD	END HOOK
	ATTENDER	ATTENDERS
	ATTENDING	ATTENDINGS
	ATTENT	ATTENTS
	ATTENTAT	ATTENTATS
	ATTENTION	ATTENTIONS
	ATTENUANT	ATTENUANTS
	ATTENUATE	ATTENUATED · ATTENUATES
	ATTERCOP	ATTERCOPS
FATTEST · WATTEST	**ATTEST**	ATTESTS
	ATTESTANT	ATTESTANTS
	ATTESTER	ATTESTERS
	ATTESTOR	ATTESTORS
	ATTIC	ATTICS
	ATTICISE	ATTICISED · ATTICISES
	ATTICISM	ATTICISMS
	ATTICIST	ATTICISTS
	ATTICIZE	ATTICIZED · ATTICIZES
	ATTIRE	ATTIRED · ATTIRES
	ATTIRING	ATTIRINGS
	ATTITUDE	ATTITUDES
	ATTOLASER	ATTOLASERS
	ATTOLLENT	ATTOLLENTS
	ATTONE	ATTONES
	ATTORN	ATTORNS
	ATTORNEY	ATTORNEYS
	ATTRACT	ATTRACTS
	ATTRACTER	ATTRACTERS
	ATTRACTOR	ATTRACTORS
	ATTRAHENT	ATTRAHENTS
RATTRAP	**ATTRAP**	ATTRAPS
RATTRAPS	**ATTRAPS**	
	ATTRIBUTE	ATTRIBUTED · ATTRIBUTER · ATTRIBUTES
	ATTRIST	ATTRISTS
	ATTRIT	ATTRITE · ATTRITS
	ATTRITE	ATTRITED · ATTRITES
	ATTRITION	ATTRITIONS
	ATTUITE	ATTUITED · ATTUITES
	ATTUITION	ATTUITIONS
	ATTUNE	ATTUNED · ATTUNES
	ATUA	ATUAS
PAUA	**AUA**	
	AUBADE	AUBADES
	AUBERGE	AUBERGES
	AUBERGINE	AUBERGINES
	AUBRETIA	AUBRETIAS
	AUBRIETA	AUBRIETAS
	AUBRIETIA	AUBRIETIAS
	AUBURN	AUBURNS
	AUCTION	AUCTIONS
	AUCUBA	AUCUBAS
CAUDAD	**AUDAD**	AUDADS
	AUDIBLE	AUDIBLED · AUDIBLES
	AUDIENCE	AUDIENCES
	AUDIENCIA	AUDIENCIAS
	AUDIENT	AUDIENTS
	AUDILE	AUDILES
DAUDING · GAUDING · HAUDING · LAUDING	**AUDING**	AUDINGS
	AUDIO	AUDIOS
	AUDIOBOOK	AUDIOBOOKS
	AUDIOGRAM	AUDIOGRAMS
	AUDIOPHIL	AUDIOPHILE · AUDIOPHILS
	AUDIOTAPE	AUDIOTAPED · AUDIOTAPES
	AUDIPHONE	AUDIPHONES
	AUDIT	AUDITS
	AUDITEE	AUDITEES
	AUDITION	AUDITIONS
	AUDITIVE	AUDITIVES
	AUDITOR	AUDITORS · AUDITORY
	AUDITORIA	AUDITORIAL

FRONT HOOK	ROOT WORD	END HOOK
CAUF = HAUF = LAUF	**AUF**	AUFS
	AUFGABE	AUFGABES
HAUFS = LAUFS	**AUFS**	
	AUGEND	AUGENDS
GAUGER = MAUGER = SAUGER	**AUGER**	AUGERS
GAUGERS = SAUGERS	**AUGERS**	
CAUGHT = HAUGHT = NAUGHT = RAUGHT	**AUGHT**	AUGHTS
TAUGHT = WAUGHT		
NAUGHTS = WAUGHTS	**AUGHTS**	
	AUGITE	AUGITES
	AUGMENT	AUGMENTS
	AUGMENTER	AUGMENTERS
	AUGMENTOR	AUGMENTORS
	AUGUR	AUGURS = AUGURY
	AUGURER	AUGURERS
	AUGURSHIP	AUGURSHIPS
	AUGUST	AUGUSTE = AUGUSTS
	AUGUSTE	AUGUSTER = AUGUSTES
	AUGUSTES	AUGUSTEST
BAUK = CAUK = JAUK = WAUK	**AUK**	AUKS
	AUKLET	AUKLETS
BAUKS = CAUKS = JAUKS = WAUKS	**AUKS**	
	AULA	AULAS
	AULARIAN	AULARIANS
CAULD = FAULD = HAULD = TAULD = YAULD	**AULD**	
CAULDER	**AULDER**	
CAULDEST	**AULDEST**	
	AULNAGE	AULNAGER = AULNAGES
	AULNAGER	AULNAGERS
	AUMAIL	AUMAILS
	AUMIL	AUMILS
	AUNE	AUNES
DAUNT = GAUNT = HAUNT = JAUNT = NAUNT	**AUNT**	AUNTS = AUNTY
SAUNT = TAUNT = VAUNT		
DAUNTER = GAUNTER = HAUNTER = SAUNTER	**AUNTER**	AUNTERS
TAUNTER = VAUNTER		
DAUNTERS = HAUNTERS = SAUNTERS	**AUNTERS**	
TAUNTERS = VAUNTERS		
	AUNTHOOD	AUNTHOODS
JAUNTIE = VAUNTIE	**AUNTIE**	AUNTIES
JAUNTIES	**AUNTIES**	
GAUNTLY	**AUNTLY**	
DAUNTS = GAUNTS = HAUNTS = JAUNTS	**AUNTS**	
NAUNTS = SAUNTS = TAUNTS = VAUNTS		
JAUNTY = VAUNTY	**AUNTY**	
LAURA	**AURA**	AURAE = AURAL = AURAR = AURAS
LAURAE	**AURAE**	
LAURAS	**AURAS**	
	AURATE	AURATED = AURATES
LAUREATE	**AUREATE**	
	AURELIA	AURELIAN = AURELIAS
	AURELIAN	AURELIANS
	AUREOLA	AUREOLAE = AUREOLAS
	AUREOLE	AUREOLED = AUREOLES
LAURIC = TAURIC	**AURIC**	
	AURICLE	AURICLED = AURICLES
	AURICULA	AURICULAE = AURICULAR = AURICULAS
	AURICULAR	AURICULARS
TAURIFORM	**AURIFORM**	
KAURIS = MAURIS	**AURIS**	AURIST
	AURISCOPE	AURISCOPES
	AURIST	AURISTS
	AURORA	AURORAE = AURORAL = AURORAS
	AURUM	AURUMS
	AUSFORM	AUSFORMS
	AUSLANDER	AUSLANDERS
	AUSPICATE	AUSPICATED = AUSPICATES
	AUSPICE	AUSPICES
	AUSTENITE	AUSTENITES

FRONT HOOK	ROOT WORD	END HOOK
	AUSTERE	AUSTERER
	AUSTRAL	AUSTRALS
	AUSUBO	AUSUBOS
	AUTACOID	AUTACOIDS
	AUTARCH	AUTARCHS · AUTARCHY
	AUTARKIST	AUTARKISTS
	AUTECISM	AUTECISMS
HAUTEUR	**AUTEUR**	AUTEURS
	AUTEURISM	AUTEURISMS
	AUTEURIST	AUTEURISTS
HAUTEURS	**AUTEURS**	
	AUTHOR	AUTHORS
	AUTHORING	AUTHORINGS
	AUTHORISE	AUTHORISED · AUTHORISER · AUTHORISES
	AUTHORISM	AUTHORISMS
	AUTHORIZE	AUTHORIZED · AUTHORIZER · AUTHORIZES
	AUTISM	AUTISMS
	AUTIST	AUTISTS
	AUTISTIC	AUTISTICS
	AUTO	AUTOS
	AUTOBAHN	AUTOBAHNS
	AUTOCADE	AUTOCADES
	AUTOCAR	AUTOCARP · AUTOCARS
	AUTOCARP	AUTOCARPS
	AUTOCLAVE	AUTOCLAVED · AUTOCLAVES
	AUTOCOID	AUTOCOIDS
	AUTOCRAT	AUTOCRATS
	AUTOCRIME	AUTOCRIMES
	AUTOCUE	AUTOCUES
	AUTOCUTIE	AUTOCUTIES
	AUTOCYCLE	AUTOCYCLES
	AUTODYNE	AUTODYNES
	AUTOECISM	AUTOECISMS
	AUTOFLARE	AUTOFLARES
	AUTOGENIC	AUTOGENICS
	AUTOGIRO	AUTOGIROS
	AUTOGRAFT	AUTOGRAFTS
	AUTOGRAPH	AUTOGRAPHS · AUTOGRAPHY
	AUTOGUIDE	AUTOGUIDES
	AUTOGYRO	AUTOGYROS
	AUTOHARP	AUTOHARPS
TAUTOLOGY	**AUTOLOGY**	
	AUTOLYSE	AUTOLYSED · AUTOLYSES
	AUTOLYSIN	AUTOLYSING · AUTOLYSINS
	AUTOLYZE	AUTOLYZED · AUTOLYZES
	AUTOMAKER	AUTOMAKERS
	AUTOMAT	AUTOMATA · AUTOMATE · AUTOMATS
	AUTOMATE	AUTOMATED · AUTOMATES
	AUTOMATIC	AUTOMATICS
	AUTOMATON	AUTOMATONS
	AUTOMETER	AUTOMETERS
	AUTONOMIC	AUTONOMICS
TAUTONYM	**AUTONYM**	AUTONYMS
TAUTONYMS	**AUTONYMS**	
	AUTOPEN	AUTOPENS
TAUTOPHONY	**AUTOPHONY**	
	AUTOPHYTE	AUTOPHYTES
	AUTOPILOT	AUTOPILOTS
	AUTOPISTA	AUTOPISTAS
	AUTOPOINT	AUTOPOINTS
	AUTOPSIA	AUTOPSIAS
	AUTOPSIST	AUTOPSISTS
	AUTOPUT	AUTOPUTS
	AUTOROUTE	AUTOROUTES
	AUTOSOME	AUTOSOMES
	AUTOSPORE	AUTOSPORES
	AUTOTIMER	AUTOTIMERS
	AUTOTOXIN	AUTOTOXINS
	AUTOTROPH	AUTOTROPHS · AUTOTROPHY

FRONT HOOK	ROOT WORD	END HOOK
	AUTOTUNE	AUTOTUNES
	AUTOTYPE	AUTOTYPED · AUTOTYPES
	AUTOVAC	AUTOVACS
	AUTUMN	AUTUMNS · AUTUMNY
	AUTUNITE	AUTUNITES
	AUXETIC	AUXETICS
	AUXILIAR	AUXILIARS · AUXILIARY
	AUXIN	AUXINS
	AUXOCYTE	AUXOCYTES
	AUXOMETER	AUXOMETERS
	AUXOSPORE	AUXOSPORES
	AUXOTROPH	AUXOTROPHS · AUXOTROPHY
CAVA · FAVA · JAVA · KAVA · LAVA · TAVA	AVA	AVAL · AVAS
	AVADAVAT	AVADAVATS
	AVAIL	AVAILE · AVAILS
	AVAILE	AVAILED · AVAILES
NAVAL	AVAL	AVALE
	AVALANCHE	AVALANCHED · AVALANCHES
	AVALE	AVALED · AVALES
SAVANT	AVANT	AVANTI
	AVANTIST	AVANTISTS
	AVARICE	AVARICES
CAVAS · FAVAS · JAVAS · KAVAS · LAVAS TAVAS	AVAS	AVAST
	AVATAR	AVATARS
	AVAUNT	AVAUNTS
CAVE · EAVE · FAVE · GAVE · HAVE · LAVE NAVE · PAVE · RAVE · SAVE · WAVE	AVE	AVEL · AVER · AVES
CAVEL · FAVEL · GAVEL · JAVEL · NAVEL RAVEL	AVEL	AVELS
	AVELLAN	AVELLANE
CAVELS · GAVELS · JAVELS · NAVELS RAVELS	AVELS	
	AVENGE	AVENGED · AVENGER · AVENGES
	AVENGER	AVENGERS
	AVENIR	AVENIRS
DAVENS · HAVENS · MAVENS · PAVENS RAVENS	AVENS	
	AVENTAIL	AVENTAILE · AVENTAILS
	AVENTAILE	AVENTAILES
	AVENTRE	AVENTRED · AVENTRES
	AVENTURE	AVENTURES
	AVENTURIN	AVENTURINE · AVENTURINS
	AVENUE	AVENUES
CAVER · FAVER · HAVER · LAVER · PAVER RAVER · SAVER · TAVER · WAVER	AVER	AVERS · AVERT
	AVERAGE	AVERAGED · AVERAGES
	AVERAGING	AVERAGINGS
	AVERMENT	AVERMENTS
CAVERS · HAVERS · LAVERS · PAVERS RAVERS · SAVERS · TAVERS · WAVERS	AVERS	AVERSE
	AVERSION	AVERSIONS
	AVERSIVE	AVERSIVES
TAVERT	AVERT	AVERTS
	AVERTER	AVERTERS
CAVES · EAVES · FAVES · HAVES · LAVES NAVES · OAVES · PAVES · RAVES · SAVES WAVES	AVES	
	AVIAN	AVIANS
	AVIANISE	AVIANISED · AVIANISES
	AVIANIZE	AVIANIZED · AVIANIZES
CAVIARIES	AVIARIES	
	AVIARIST	AVIARISTS
	AVIATE	AVIATED · AVIATES
	AVIATION	AVIATIONS
	AVIATOR	AVIATORS
	AVIATRICE	AVIATRICES
NAVICULAR	AVICULAR	
PAVID	AVID	

FRONT HOOK	ROOT WORD	END HOOK
	AVIDIN	AVIDINS
	AVIETTE	AVIETTES
	AVIFAUNA	AVIFAUNAE · AVIFAUNAL · AVIFAUNAS
NAVIGATOR	**AVIGATOR**	AVIGATORS
NAVIGATORS	**AVIGATORS**	
RAVINE · SAVINE	**AVINE**	
	AVION	AVIONS
	AVIONIC	AVIONICS
	AVISANDUM	AVISANDUMS
PAVISE	**AVISE**	AVISED · AVISES
	AVISEMENT	AVISEMENTS
MAVISES · PAVISES	**AVISES**	
	AVISO	AVISOS
	AVIZANDUM	AVIZANDUMS
	AVIZE	AVIZED · AVIZES
	AVO	AVOS · AVOW
	AVOCADO	AVOCADOS
	AVOCATION	AVOCATIONS
	AVOCET	AVOCETS
	AVODIRE	AVODIRES
	AVOID	AVOIDS
	AVOIDANCE	AVOIDANCES
	AVOIDER	AVOIDERS
	AVOISION	AVOISIONS
	AVOSET	AVOSETS
	AVOUCHER	AVOUCHERS
	AVOURE	AVOURES
	AVOUTERER	AVOUTERERS
	AVOUTRER	AVOUTRERS
	AVOW	AVOWS
	AVOWAL	AVOWALS
	AVOWER	AVOWERS
	AVOYER	AVOYERS
	AVRUGA	AVRUGAS
	AVULSE	AVULSED · AVULSES
	AVULSION	AVULSIONS
	AVYZE	AVYZED · AVYZES
CAW · DAW · FAW · HAW · JAW · KAW · LAW MAW · NAW · PAW · RAW · SAW · TAW · VAW WAW · YAW	**AW**	AWA · AWE · AWL · AWN
KAWA · PAWA · TAWA · WAWA	**AWA**	AWAY
	AWAIT	AWAITS
	AWAITER	AWAITERS
	AWAKE	AWAKED · AWAKEN · AWAKES
	AWAKEN	AWAKENS
	AWAKENER	AWAKENERS
	AWAKENING	AWAKENINGS
	AWAKING	AWAKINGS
VAWARD	**AWARD**	AWARDS
	AWARDEE	AWARDEES
	AWARDER	AWARDERS
VAWARDS	**AWARDS**	
	AWARE	AWARER
	AWARN	AWARNS
	AWAY	AWAYS
	AWAYDAY	AWAYDAYS
	AWDL	AWDLS
WAWE	**AWE**	AWED · AWEE · AWES
CAWED · DAWED · HAWED · JAWED · KAWED LAWED · MAWED · PAWED · SAWED · TAWED YAWED	**AWED**	
	AWEE	AWEEL
WAWES	**AWES**	
	AWESTRIKE	AWESTRIKES
	AWETO	AWETOS
LAWFUL	**AWFUL**	
LAWFULLY	**AWFULLY**	
LAWFULNESS	**AWFULNESS**	
	AWHAPE	AWHAPED · AWHAPES

FRONT HOOK	ROOT WORD	END HOOK
	AWHEEL	AWHEELS
CAWING ▪ DAWING ▪ HAWING ▪ JAWING KAWING ▪ LAWING ▪ MAWING ▪ PAWING RAWING ▪ SAWING ▪ TAWING ▪ YAWING	**AWING**	
BAWL ▪ PAWL ▪ WAWL ▪ YAWL	**AWL**	AWLS
	AWLBIRD	AWLBIRDS
JAWLESS ▪ LAWLESS	**AWLESS**	
BAWLS ▪ PAWLS ▪ WAWLS ▪ YAWLS	**AWLS**	
	AWLWORT	AWLWORTS
	AWMRIE	AWMRIES
BAWN ▪ DAWN ▪ FAWN ▪ LAWN ▪ MAWN ▪ PAWN RAWN ▪ SAWN ▪ YAWN	**AWN**	AWNS ▪ AWNY
DAWNED ▪ FAWNED ▪ PAWNED ▪ YAWNED	**AWNED**	
DAWNER ▪ FAWNER ▪ PAWNER ▪ YAWNER	**AWNER**	AWNERS
DAWNERS ▪ FAWNERS ▪ PAWNERS ▪ YAWNERS	**AWNERS**	
FAWNIER ▪ LAWNIER ▪ TAWNIER ▪ YAWNIER	**AWNIER**	
FAWNIEST ▪ LAWNIEST ▪ TAWNIEST YAWNIEST	**AWNIEST**	
DAWNING ▪ FAWNING ▪ PAWNING ▪ YAWNING	**AWNING**	AWNINGS
DAWNINGS ▪ FAWNINGS ▪ YAWNINGS	**AWNINGS**	
BAWNS ▪ DAWNS ▪ FAWNS ▪ LAWNS ▪ PAWNS RAWNS ▪ YAWNS	**AWNS**	
FAWNY ▪ LAWNY ▪ TAWNY ▪ YAWNY	**AWNY**	
	AWOKE	AWOKEN
	AWOL	AWOLS
FAX ▪ LAX ▪ MAX ▪ PAX ▪ RAX ▪ SAX ▪ TAX WAX ▪ ZAX	**AX**	AXE
SAXE	**AXE**	AXED ▪ AXEL ▪ AXES
	AXEBIRD	AXEBIRDS
FAXED ▪ MAXED ▪ RAXED ▪ TAXED ▪ WAXED	**AXED**	
	AXEL	AXELS
FAXES ▪ LAXES ▪ MAXES ▪ PAXES ▪ RAXES SAXES ▪ TAXES ▪ WAXES ▪ ZAXES	**AXES**	
	AXIL	AXILE ▪ AXILS
	AXILEMMA	AXILEMMAS
MAXILLA	**AXILLA**	AXILLAE ▪ AXILLAR ▪ AXILLAS
MAXILLAE	**AXILLAE**	
MAXILLAR	**AXILLAR**	AXILLARS ▪ AXILLARY
MAXILLARY	**AXILLARY**	
MAXILLAS	**AXILLAS**	
FAXING ▪ MAXING ▪ RAXING ▪ TAXING WAXING	**AXING**	
	AXINITE	AXINITES
	AXIOM	AXIOMS
	AXIOMATIC	AXIOMATICS
	AXION	AXIONS
MAXIS ▪ TAXIS	**AXIS**	
TAXITE	**AXITE**	AXITES
TAXITES	**AXITES**	
	AXLE	AXLED ▪ AXLES
	AXLETREE	AXLETREES
WAXLIKE	**AXLIKE**	
TAXMAN	**AXMAN**	
TAXMEN	**AXMEN**	
	AXOID	AXOIDS
	AXOLEMMA	AXOLEMMAS
	AXOLOTL	AXOLOTLS
CAXON ▪ TAXON	**AXON**	AXONE ▪ AXONS
	AXONE	AXONES
	AXONEME	AXONEMES
CAXONS ▪ TAXONS	**AXONS**	
	AXOPLASM	AXOPLASMS
	AXSEED	AXSEEDS
BAY ▪ CAY ▪ DAY ▪ FAY ▪ GAY ▪ HAY ▪ JAY KAY ▪ LAY ▪ MAY ▪ NAY ▪ PAY ▪ RAY ▪ SAY TAY ▪ WAY ▪ YAY	**AY**	AYE ▪ AYS ▪ AYU
RAYAH	**AYAH**	AYAHS
RAYAHS	**AYAHS**	
	AYAHUASCA	AYAHUASCAS

FRONT HOOK	ROOT WORD	END HOOK
	AYAHUASCO	AYAHUASCOS
	AYATOLLAH	AYATOLLAHS
BAYE	**AYE**	AYES
	AYENBITE	AYENBITES
BAYES	**AYES**	
LAYIN ▪ ZAYIN	**AYIN**	AYINS
LAYINS ▪ ZAYINS	**AYINS**	
FAYRE	**AYRE**	AYRES
FAYRES	**AYRES**	
	AYRIE	AYRIES
BAYS ▪ CAYS ▪ DAYS ▪ FAYS ▪ GAYS ▪ HAYS	**AYS**	
JAYS ▪ KAYS ▪ LAYS ▪ MAYS ▪ NAYS ▪ PAYS		
RAYS ▪ SAYS ▪ TAYS ▪ WAYS ▪ YAYS		
	AYU	AYUS
	AYURVEDA	AYURVEDAS
	AYURVEDIC	AYURVEDICS
NAYWORD	**AYWORD**	AYWORDS
NAYWORDS	**AYWORDS**	
	AZALEA	AZALEAS
HAZAN	**AZAN**	AZANS
HAZANS	**AZANS**	
	AZEDARACH	AZEDARACHS
	AZEOTROPE	AZEOTROPES
	AZIDE	AZIDES
	AZIMUTH	AZIMUTHS
	AZINE	AZINES
	AZIONE	AZIONES
	AZLON	AZLONS
LAZO	**AZO**	AZON
	AZOLE	AZOLES
	AZOLLA	AZOLLAS
GAZON	**AZON**	AZONS
GAZONS	**AZONS**	
	AZOTAEMIA	AZOTAEMIAS
	AZOTE	AZOTED ▪ AZOTES
	AZOTEMIA	AZOTEMIAS
	AZOTH	AZOTHS
	AZOTISE	AZOTISED ▪ AZOTISES
	AZOTIZE	AZOTIZED ▪ AZOTIZES
	AZOTURIA	AZOTURIAS
	AZUKI	AZUKIS
	AZULEJO	AZULEJOS
RAZURE	**AZURE**	AZURES
RAZURES	**AZURES**	
	AZURINE	AZURINES
LAZURITE	**AZURITE**	AZURITES
LAZURITES	**AZURITES**	
	AZYM	AZYME ▪ AZYMS
	AZYME	AZYMES
	AZYMITE	AZYMITES

B

FRONT HOOK	ROOT WORD	END HOOK
ABA · OBA	**BA**	BAA · BAC · BAD · BAG · BAH · BAL · BAM BAN · BAP · BAR · BAS · BAT · BAY
	BAA	BAAL · BAAS
	BAAING	BAAINGS
	BAAL	BAALS
	BAALISM	BAALISMS
	BAASKAAP	BAASKAAPS
	BAASKAP	BAASKAPS
	BAASSKAP	BAASSKAPS
	BABA	BABAS
	BABACO	BABACOS
	BABACOOTE	BABACOOTES
	BABASSU	BABASSUS
	BABBITT	BABBITTS
	BABBLE	BABBLED · BABBLER · BABBLES
	BABBLER	BABBLERS
	BABBLING	BABBLINGS
	BABE	BABEL · BABES
	BABEL	BABELS
	BABELDOM	BABELDOMS
	BABELISM	BABELISMS
	BABESIA	BABESIAS
	BABICHE	BABICHES
	BABIES	BABIEST
	BABIRUSA	BABIRUSAS
	BABIRUSSA	BABIRUSSAS
	BABKA	BABKAS
	BABLAH	BABLAHS
	BABOO	BABOOL · BABOON · BABOOS
	BABOOL	BABOOLS
	BABOON	BABOONS
	BABOOS	BABOOSH
	BABOUCHE	BABOUCHES
	BABU	BABUL · BABUS
	BABUCHE	BABUCHES
	BABUDOM	BABUDOMS
	BABUISM	BABUISMS
	BABUL	BABULS
	BABUSHKA	BABUSHKAS
	BABYDOLL	BABYDOLLS
	BABYFOOD	BABYFOODS
	BABYHOOD	BABYHOODS
	BABYPROOF	BABYPROOFS
	BABYSIT	BABYSITS
ABAC	**BAC**	BACH · BACK · BACS
	BACALAO	BACALAOS
	BACCA	BACCAE · BACCAS
	BACCARA	BACCARAS · BACCARAT
	BACCARAT	BACCARATS
	BACCATE	BACCATED
	BACCHANAL	BACCHANALS
	BACCHANT	BACCHANTE · BACCHANTS
	BACCHANTE	BACCHANTES
	BACCO	BACCOS
	BACH	BACHA · BACHS
	BACHA	BACHAS
	BACHARACH	BACHARACHS
	BACHCHA	BACHCHAS
	BACHELOR	BACHELORS
	BACILLAR	BACILLARY
ABACK	**BACK**	BACKS
	BACKACHE	BACKACHES
	BACKBAND	BACKBANDS
	BACKBEAT	BACKBEATS
	BACKBEND	BACKBENDS
	BACKBIT	BACKBITE

59

B

FRONT HOOK	ROOT WORD	END HOOK
	BACKBITE	BACKBITER ▪ BACKBITES
	BACKBITER	BACKBITERS
	BACKBLOCK	BACKBLOCKS
	BACKBOARD	BACKBOARDS
	BACKBOND	BACKBONDS
	BACKBONE	BACKBONED ▪ BACKBONES
	BACKBURN	BACKBURNS
	BACKCAST	BACKCASTS
	BACKCHAT	BACKCHATS
	BACKCHECK	BACKCHECKS
	BACKCLOTH	BACKCLOTHS
	BACKCOMB	BACKCOMBS
	BACKCOURT	BACKCOURTS
	BACKDATE	BACKDATED ▪ BACKDATES
	BACKDOWN	BACKDOWNS
	BACKDRAFT	BACKDRAFTS
	BACKDROP	BACKDROPS ▪ BACKDROPT
	BACKER	BACKERS
	BACKET	BACKETS
	BACKFALL	BACKFALLS
	BACKFIELD	BACKFIELDS
	BACKFILE	BACKFILES
	BACKFILL	BACKFILLS
	BACKFIRE	BACKFIRED ▪ BACKFIRES
	BACKFIT	BACKFITS
	BACKFLIP	BACKFLIPS
	BACKFLOW	BACKFLOWS
	BACKHAND	BACKHANDS
	BACKHAUL	BACKHAULS
	BACKHOE	BACKHOED ▪ BACKHOES
	BACKHOUSE	BACKHOUSES
	BACKIE	BACKIES
	BACKING	BACKINGS
	BACKLAND	BACKLANDS
	BACKLIFT	BACKLIFTS
	BACKLIGHT	BACKLIGHTS
	BACKLIST	BACKLISTS
	BACKLOAD	BACKLOADS
	BACKLOG	BACKLOGS
	BACKLOT	BACKLOTS
	BACKOUT	BACKOUTS
	BACKPACK	BACKPACKS
	BACKPAY	BACKPAYS
	BACKPEDAL	BACKPEDALS
	BACKPIECE	BACKPIECES
	BACKRA	BACKRAS
	BACKREST	BACKRESTS
	BACKROOM	BACKROOMS
	BACKSAW	BACKSAWS
	BACKSEAT	BACKSEATS
	BACKSET	BACKSETS
	BACKSEY	BACKSEYS
	BACKSHORE	BACKSHORES
	BACKSIDE	BACKSIDES
	BACKSIGHT	BACKSIGHTS
	BACKSLAP	BACKSLAPS
	BACKSLID	BACKSLIDE
	BACKSLIDE	BACKSLIDER ▪ BACKSLIDES
	BACKSPACE	BACKSPACED ▪ BACKSPACER ▪ BACKSPACES
	BACKSPEER	BACKSPEERS
	BACKSPEIR	BACKSPEIRS
	BACKSPIN	BACKSPINS
	BACKSTAB	BACKSTABS
	BACKSTAGE	BACKSTAGES
	BACKSTAIR	BACKSTAIRS
	BACKSTALL	BACKSTALLS
	BACKSTAMP	BACKSTAMPS
	BACKSTAY	BACKSTAYS
	BACKSTOP	BACKSTOPS

FRONT HOOK	ROOT WORD	END HOOK
	BACKSWING	BACKSWINGS
	BACKSWORD	BACKSWORDS
	BACKTRACK	BACKTRACKS
	BACKUP	BACKUPS
	BACKVELD	BACKVELDS
	BACKWARD	BACKWARDS
	BACKWATER	BACKWATERS
	BACKWOOD	BACKWOODS
	BACKWOODS	BACKWOODSY
	BACKWORD	BACKWORDS
	BACKWORK	BACKWORKS
	BACKWRAP	BACKWRAPS
	BACKYARD	BACKYARDS
	BACLAVA	BACLAVAS
	BACLOFEN	BACLOFENS
	BACON	BACONS
	BACONER	BACONERS
ABACS	BACS	
	BACTERIA	BACTERIAL ▪ BACTERIAN ▪ BACTERIAS
ABACTERIAL	BACTERIAL	BACTERIALS
	BACTERIN	BACTERINS
	BACTERISE	BACTERISED ▪ BACTERISES
	BACTERIZE	BACTERIZED ▪ BACTERIZES
	BACTEROID	BACTEROIDS
	BACULITE	BACULITES
	BACULUM	BACULUMS
	BAD	BADE ▪ BADS
	BADDIE	BADDIES
	BADGE	BADGED ▪ BADGER ▪ BADGES
	BADGER	BADGERS
	BADINAGE	BADINAGED ▪ BADINAGES
	BADINERIE	BADINERIES
	BADLAND	BADLANDS
	BADMINTON	BADMINTONS
	BADMOUTH	BADMOUTHS
	BAEL	BAELS
	BAETYL	BAETYLS
	BAFF	BAFFS ▪ BAFFY
	BAFFLE	BAFFLED ▪ BAFFLER ▪ BAFFLES
	BAFFLEGAB	BAFFLEGABS
	BAFFLER	BAFFLERS
ABAFT	BAFT	BAFTS
	BAG	BAGH ▪ BAGS
	BAGARRE	BAGARRES
	BAGASS	BAGASSE
	BAGASSE	BAGASSES
	BAGATELLE	BAGATELLES
	BAGEL	BAGELS
	BAGFUL	BAGFULS
	BAGGAGE	BAGGAGES
	BAGGER	BAGGERS
	BAGGIE	BAGGIER ▪ BAGGIES
	BAGGIES	BAGGIEST
	BAGGING	BAGGINGS
	BAGGIT	BAGGITS
	BAGH	BAGHS
	BAGHOUSE	BAGHOUSES
	BAGIE	BAGIES
	BAGNETTE	BAGNETTES
	BAGNIO	BAGNIOS
	BAGPIPE	BAGPIPED ▪ BAGPIPER ▪ BAGPIPES
	BAGPIPER	BAGPIPERS
	BAGPIPING	BAGPIPINGS
	BAGUET	BAGUETS
	BAGUETTE	BAGUETTES
	BAGUIO	BAGUIOS
	BAGWIG	BAGWIGS
	BAGWORM	BAGWORMS
	BAH	BAHT

B

FRONT HOOK	ROOT WORD	END HOOK
	BAHADA	BAHADAS
	BAHADUR	BAHADURS
	BAHT	BAHTS
	BAHUT	BAHUTS
	BAHUVRIHI	BAHUVRIHIS
	BAIDARKA	BAIDARKAS
	BAIGNOIRE	BAIGNOIRES
	BAIL	BAILS
	BAILBOND	BAILBONDS
	BAILEE	BAILEES
	BAILER	BAILERS
	BAILEY	BAILEYS
	BAILIE	BAILIES
	BAILIFF	BAILIFFS
	BAILIWICK	BAILIWICKS
	BAILLI	BAILLIE · BAILLIS
	BAILLIAGE	BAILLIAGES
	BAILLIE	BAILLIES
	BAILMENT	BAILMENTS
	BAILOR	BAILORS
	BAILOUT	BAILOUTS
	BAININ	BAININS
	BAINITE	BAINITES
	BAIRN	BAIRNS
	BAISEMAIN	BAISEMAINS
	BAIT	BAITH · BAITS
	BAITER	BAITERS
	BAITING	BAITINGS
	BAIZA	BAIZAS
	BAIZE	BAIZED · BAIZES
	BAJADA	BAJADAS
	BAJAN	BAJANS
	BAJRA	BAJRAS
	BAJREE	BAJREES
	BAJRI	BAJRIS
	BAJU	BAJUS
	BAKE	BAKED · BAKEN · BAKER · BAKES
	BAKEAPPLE	BAKEAPPLES
	BAKEBOARD	BAKEBOARDS
	BAKEHOUSE	BAKEHOUSES
	BAKELITE	BAKELITES
	BAKEMEAT	BAKEMEATS
	BAKER	BAKERS · BAKERY
	BAKESHOP	BAKESHOPS
	BAKESTONE	BAKESTONES
	BAKEWARE	BAKEWARES
	BAKING	BAKINGS
	BAKKIE	BAKKIES
	BAKLAVA	BAKLAVAS
	BAKLAWA	BAKLAWAS
	BAKRA	BAKRAS
	BAL	BALD · BALE · BALK · BALL · BALM
		BALS · BALU
	BALACLAVA	BALACLAVAS
	BALADIN	BALADINE · BALADINS
	BALADINE	BALADINES
	BALALAIKA	BALALAIKAS
	BALANCE	BALANCED · BALANCER · BALANCES
	BALANCER	BALANCERS
	BALANCING	BALANCINGS
	BALATA	BALATAS
	BALBOA	BALBOAS
	BALCONET	BALCONETS
	BALD	BALDS · BALDY
	BALDACHIN	BALDACHINO · BALDACHINS
	BALDAQUIN	BALDAQUINS
	BALDHEAD	BALDHEADS
	BALDICOOT	BALDICOOTS
	BALDIES	BALDIEST

FRONT HOOK	ROOT WORD	END HOOK
	BALDMONEY	BALDMONEYS
	BALDPATE	BALDPATED = BALDPATES
	BALDRIC	BALDRICK = BALDRICS
	BALDRICK	BALDRICKS
	BALE	BALED = BALER = BALES
	BALECTION	BALECTIONS
	BALEEN	BALEENS
	BALEFIRE	BALEFIRES
	BALER	BALERS
	BALISAUR	BALISAURS
	BALISTA	BALISTAE = BALISTAS
	BALK	BALKS = BALKY
	BALKANISE	BALKANISED = BALKANISES
	BALKANIZE	BALKANIZED = BALKANIZES
	BALKER	BALKERS
	BALKING	BALKINGS
	BALKLINE	BALKLINES
	BALL	BALLS = BALLY
	BALLABILE	BALLABILES
	BALLAD	BALLADE = BALLADS
	BALLADE	BALLADED = BALLADES
	BALLADEER	BALLADEERS
	BALLADIN	BALLADINE = BALLADING = BALLADINS
	BALLADINE	BALLADINES
	BALLADIST	BALLADISTS
	BALLAN	BALLANS = BALLANT
	BALLANT	BALLANTS
	BALLAST	BALLASTS
	BALLASTER	BALLASTERS
	BALLAT	BALLATS
	BALLCLAY	BALLCLAYS
	BALLCOCK	BALLCOCKS
	BALLER	BALLERS
	BALLERINA	BALLERINAS
	BALLET	BALLETS
	BALLGAME	BALLGAMES
	BALLHAWK	BALLHAWKS
	BALLING	BALLINGS
	BALLISTA	BALLISTAE = BALLISTAS
	BALLISTIC	BALLISTICS
	BALLIUM	BALLIUMS
	BALLON	BALLONS
	BALLONET	BALLONETS
	BALLONNE	BALLONNES
	BALLOON	BALLOONS
	BALLOT	BALLOTS
	BALLOTEE	BALLOTEES
	BALLOTER	BALLOTERS
	BALLOW	BALLOWS
	BALLPARK	BALLPARKS
	BALLPOINT	BALLPOINTS
	BALLROOM	BALLROOMS
	BALLS	BALLSY
	BALLUP	BALLUPS (offensive)
	BALLUTE	BALLUTES
	BALLYARD	BALLYARDS
	BALLYHOO	BALLYHOOS
	BALLYRAG	BALLYRAGS
	BALM	BALMS = BALMY
	BALMACAAN	BALMACAANS
	BALMORAL	BALMORALS
	BALONEY	BALONEYS
	BALOO	BALOOS
	BALS	BALSA
	BALSA	BALSAM = BALSAS
	BALSAM	BALSAMS = BALSAMY
	BALSAWOOD	BALSAWOODS
	BALTHASAR	BALTHASARS
	BALTHAZAR	BALTHAZARS

B

FRONT HOOK	ROOT WORD	END HOOK
	BALTI	BALTIS
	BALU	BALUN ▪ BALUS
	BALUN	BALUNS
	BALUSTER	BALUSTERS
	BALZARINE	BALZARINES
	BAM	BAMS
	BAMBI	BAMBIS
	BAMBINO	BAMBINOS
	BAMBOO	BAMBOOS
	BAMBOOZLE	BAMBOOZLED ▪ BAMBOOZLER ▪ BAMBOOZLES
	BAMMER	BAMMERS
	BAMPOT	BAMPOTS
	BAN	BANC ▪ BAND ▪ BANE ▪ BANG ▪ BANI BANK ▪ BANS ▪ BANT
	BANAK	BANAKS
	BANALISE	BANALISED ▪ BANALISES
	BANALIZE	BANALIZED ▪ BANALIZES
	BANANA	BANANAS
	BANC	BANCO ▪ BANCS
	BANCO	BANCOS
ABAND	BAND	BANDA ▪ BANDH ▪ BANDS ▪ BANDY
	BANDA	BANDAR ▪ BANDAS
	BANDAGE	BANDAGED ▪ BANDAGER ▪ BANDAGES
	BANDAGER	BANDAGERS
	BANDALORE	BANDALORES
	BANDANA	BANDANAS
	BANDANNA	BANDANNAS
	BANDAR	BANDARI ▪ BANDARS
	BANDARI	BANDARIS
	BANDBRAKE	BANDBRAKES
	BANDEAU	BANDEAUS ▪ BANDEAUX
ABANDED	BANDED	
	BANDELET	BANDELETS
	BANDELIER	BANDELIERS
	BANDER	BANDERS
	BANDEROL	BANDEROLE ▪ BANDEROLS
	BANDEROLE	BANDEROLES
	BANDH	BANDHS
	BANDICOOT	BANDICOOTS
	BANDIES	BANDIEST
ABANDING	BANDING	BANDINGS
	BANDIT	BANDITO ▪ BANDITS
	BANDITO	BANDITOS
	BANDITTI	BANDITTIS
	BANDMATE	BANDMATES
	BANDOBAST	BANDOBASTS
	BANDOBUST	BANDOBUSTS
	BANDOG	BANDOGS
	BANDOLEER	BANDOLEERS
	BANDOLEON	BANDOLEONS
	BANDOLERO	BANDOLEROS
	BANDOLIER	BANDOLIERS
	BANDOLINE	BANDOLINED ▪ BANDOLINES
	BANDONEON	BANDONEONS
	BANDONION	BANDONIONS
	BANDOOK	BANDOOKS
	BANDORA	BANDORAS
	BANDORE	BANDORES
	BANDROL	BANDROLS
ABANDS	BANDS	
	BANDSAW	BANDSAWS
	BANDSHELL	BANDSHELLS
	BANDSTAND	BANDSTANDS
	BANDSTER	BANDSTERS
	BANDURA	BANDURAS
	BANDWAGON	BANDWAGONS
	BANDWIDTH	BANDWIDTHS
	BANDYING	BANDYINGS
	BANE	BANED ▪ BANES

FRONT HOOK	ROOT WORD	END HOOK
OBANG	**BANG**	BANGS
	BANGALAY	BANGALAYS
	BANGALOW	BANGALOWS
	BANGER	BANGERS
	BANGING	BANGINGS
	BANGKOK	BANGKOKS
	BANGLE	BANGLED ▪ BANGLES
OBANGS	**BANGS**	
	BANGSRING	BANGSRINGS
	BANGSTER	BANGSTERS
	BANGTAIL	BANGTAILS
	BANI	BANIA
	BANIA	BANIAN ▪ BANIAS
	BANIAN	BANIANS
	BANISHER	BANISHERS
	BANISTER	BANISTERS
	BANJO	BANJOS
	BANJOIST	BANJOISTS
	BANJULELE	BANJULELES
	BANK	BANKS
	BANKBOOK	BANKBOOKS
	BANKCARD	BANKCARDS
	BANKER	BANKERS
	BANKET	BANKETS
	BANKING	BANKINGS
	BANKIT	BANKITS
	BANKNOTE	BANKNOTES
	BANKROLL	BANKROLLS
	BANKRUPT	BANKRUPTS
	BANKSIA	BANKSIAS
	BANKSIDE	BANKSIDES
	BANLIEUE	BANLIEUES
	BANNER	BANNERS
	BANNERALL	BANNERALLS
	BANNERET	BANNERETS
	BANNEROL	BANNEROLS
	BANNET	BANNETS
	BANNISTER	BANNISTERS
	BANNOCK	BANNOCKS
	BANOFFEE	BANOFFEES
	BANOFFI	BANOFFIS
	BANQUET	BANQUETS
	BANQUETER	BANQUETERS
	BANQUETTE	BANQUETTES
	BANSELA	BANSELAS
	BANSHEE	BANSHEES
	BANSHIE	BANSHIES
	BANT	BANTS ▪ BANTU ▪ BANTY
	BANTAM	BANTAMS
	BANTENG	BANTENGS
	BANTER	BANTERS
	BANTERER	BANTERERS
	BANTERING	BANTERINGS
	BANTING	BANTINGS
	BANTLING	BANTLINGS
	BANTU	BANTUS (offensive)
	BANXRING	BANXRINGS
	BANYAN	BANYANS
	BANZAI	BANZAIS
	BAOBAB	BAOBABS
	BAP	BAPS ▪ BAPU
	BAPTISE	BAPTISED ▪ BAPTISER ▪ BAPTISES
	BAPTISER	BAPTISERS
	BAPTISIA	BAPTISIAS
	BAPTISM	BAPTISMS
	BAPTIST	BAPTISTS
	BAPTIZE	BAPTIZED ▪ BAPTIZER ▪ BAPTIZES
	BAPTIZER	BAPTIZERS
	BAPU	BAPUS

B

FRONT HOOK	ROOT WORD	END HOOK
KBAR	**BAR**	BARB ▪ BARD ▪ BARE ▪ BARF ▪ BARK BARM ▪ BARN ▪ BARP ▪ BARS
	BARACAN	BARACANS
	BARAGOUIN	BARAGOUINS
	BARASINGA	BARASINGAS
	BARATHEA	BARATHEAS
	BARATHRUM	BARATHRUMS
	BARAZA	BARAZAS
	BARB	BARBE ▪ BARBS ▪ BARBY
	BARBARIAN	BARBARIANS
	BARBARISE	BARBARISED ▪ BARBARISES
	BARBARISM	BARBARISMS
	BARBARIZE	BARBARIZED ▪ BARBARIZES
	BARBASCO	BARBASCOS
	BARBASTEL	BARBASTELS
	BARBATE	BARBATED
	BARBE	BARBED ▪ BARBEL ▪ BARBER ▪ BARBES BARBET
	BARBECUE	BARBECUED ▪ BARBECUER ▪ BARBECUES
	BARBECUER	BARBECUERS
	BARBEL	BARBELL ▪ BARBELS
	BARBELL	BARBELLS
	BARBEQUE	BARBEQUED ▪ BARBEQUES
	BARBER	BARBERS
	BARBET	BARBETS
	BARBETTE	BARBETTES
	BARBICAN	BARBICANS
	BARBICEL	BARBICELS
	BARBIE	BARBIES
	BARBITAL	BARBITALS
	BARBITONE	BARBITONES
	BARBOLA	BARBOLAS
	BARBOTINE	BARBOTINES
	BARBULE	BARBULES
	BARBUT	BARBUTS
	BARBWIRE	BARBWIRES
	BARCA	BARCAS
	BARCAROLE	BARCAROLES
	BARCHAN	BARCHANE ▪ BARCHANS
	BARCHANE	BARCHANES
	BARD	BARDE ▪ BARDO ▪ BARDS ▪ BARDY
	BARDE	BARDED ▪ BARDES
	BARDIE	BARDIER ▪ BARDIES
	BARDIES	BARDIEST
	BARDISM	BARDISMS
	BARDLING	BARDLINGS
	BARDO	BARDOS
	BARDSHIP	BARDSHIPS
	BARE	BARED ▪ BARER ▪ BARES
	BAREBACK	BAREBACKS
	BAREBOAT	BAREBOATS
	BAREBONE	BAREBONED ▪ BAREBONES
	BAREGE	BAREGES
	BAREGINE	BAREGINES
	BAREHAND	BAREHANDS
	BARES	BAREST
	BARESARK	BARESARKS
	BARF	BARFS
	BARGAIN	BARGAINS
	BARGAINER	BARGAINERS
	BARGANDER	BARGANDERS
	BARGE	BARGED ▪ BARGEE ▪ BARGES
	BARGEE	BARGEES
	BARGEES	BARGEESE
	BARGELLO	BARGELLOS
	BARGEPOLE	BARGEPOLES
	BARGES	BARGEST
	BARGEST	BARGESTS
	BARGHEST	BARGHESTS

FRONT HOOK	ROOT WORD	END HOOK
	BARGOON	BARGOONS
	BARGUEST	BARGUESTS
	BARHOP	BARHOPS
	BARILLA	BARILLAS
	BARISTA	BARISTAS
	BARITE	BARITES
	BARITONE	BARITONES
	BARIUM	BARIUMS
	BARK	BARKS ▪ BARKY
	BARKAN	BARKANS
	BARKEEP	BARKEEPS
	BARKEEPER	BARKEEPERS
	BARKEN	BARKENS
	BARKER	BARKERS
	BARKHAN	BARKHANS
	BARLEDUC	BARLEDUCS
	BARLEY	BARLEYS
	BARLOW	BARLOWS
	BARM	BARMS ▪ BARMY
	BARMAID	BARMAIDS
	BARMBRACK	BARMBRACKS
	BARMIE	BARMIER
	BARMKIN	BARMKINS
	BARN	BARNS ▪ BARNY
	BARNACLE	BARNACLED ▪ BARNACLES
	BARNBRACK	BARNBRACKS
	BARNET	BARNETS
	BARNEY	BARNEYS
	BARNSTORM	BARNSTORMS
	BARNYARD	BARNYARDS
	BAROCCO	BAROCCOS
	BAROCK	BAROCKS
	BAROGRAM	BAROGRAMS
	BAROGRAPH	BAROGRAPHS
	BAROLO	BAROLOS
	BAROMETER	BAROMETERS
	BARON	BARONG ▪ BARONS ▪ BARONY
	BARONAGE	BARONAGES
	BARONET	BARONETS
	BARONG	BARONGS
	BARONNE	BARONNES
	BAROPHILE	BAROPHILES
	BAROQUE	BAROQUES
	BAROSAUR	BAROSAURS
	BAROSCOPE	BAROSCOPES
	BAROSTAT	BAROSTATS
	BAROUCHE	BAROUCHES
	BARP	BARPS
	BARPERSON	BARPERSONS
	BARQUE	BARQUES
	BARQUETTE	BARQUETTES
	BARRA	BARRAS ▪ BARRAT
	BARRACAN	BARRACANS
	BARRACE	BARRACES
	BARRACK	BARRACKS
	BARRACKER	BARRACKERS
	BARRACOON	BARRACOONS
	BARRACUDA	BARRACUDAS
	BARRAGE	BARRAGED ▪ BARRAGES
	BARRANCA	BARRANCAS
	BARRANCO	BARRANCOS
	BARRAT	BARRATS
	BARRATER	BARRATERS
	BARRATOR	BARRATORS
	BARRE	BARRED ▪ BARREL ▪ BARREN ▪ BARRES BARRET
	BARREL	BARRELS
	BARRELAGE	BARRELAGES
	BARRELFUL	BARRELFULS

3

FRONT HOOK	ROOT WORD	END HOOK
	BARREN	BARRENS
	BARRET	BARRETS
	BARRETOR	BARRETORS
	BARRETTE	BARRETTER · BARRETTES
	BARRETTER	BARRETTERS
	BARRICADE	BARRICADED · BARRICADER · BARRICADES
	BARRICADO	BARRICADOS
	BARRICO	BARRICOS
	BARRIE	BARRIER · BARRIES
	BARRIER	BARRIERS
	BARRIES	BARRIEST
	BARRING	BARRINGS
	BARRIO	BARRIOS
	BARRISTER	BARRISTERS
	BARRO	BARROW
	BARROOM	BARROOMS
	BARROW	BARROWS
	BARROWFUL	BARROWFULS
	BARRULET	BARRULETS
KBARS	**BARS**	
	BARSTOOL	BARSTOOLS
	BARTEND	BARTENDS
	BARTENDER	BARTENDERS
	BARTER	BARTERS
	BARTERER	BARTERERS
	BARTISAN	BARTISANS
	BARTIZAN	BARTIZANS
	BARTON	BARTONS
	BARTSIA	BARTSIAS
	BARWARE	BARWARES
	BARWOOD	BARWOODS
	BARYE	BARYES
	BARYON	BARYONS
	BARYTA	BARYTAS
	BARYTE	BARYTES
	BARYTON	BARYTONE · BARYTONS
	BARYTONE	BARYTONES
ABAS · OBAS	**BAS**	BASE · BASH · BASK · BASS · BAST
	BASAL	BASALT
	BASALT	BASALTS
	BASAN	BASANS
	BASANITE	BASANITES
	BASCINET	BASCINETS
	BASCULE	BASCULES
ABASE	**BASE**	BASED · BASER · BASES
	BASEBALL	BASEBALLS
	BASEBAND	BASEBANDS
	BASEBOARD	BASEBOARDS
ABASED	**BASED**	
	BASELARD	BASELARDS
	BASELINE	BASELINER · BASELINES
	BASELINER	BASELINERS
	BASEMEN	BASEMENT
ABASEMENT	**BASEMENT**	BASEMENTS
ABASEMENTS	**BASEMENTS**	
	BASENJI	BASENJIS
	BASEPLATE	BASEPLATES
ABASER	**BASER**	
ABASES	**BASES**	BASEST
ABASH	**BASH**	BASHO
	BASHAW	BASHAWS
	BASHAWISM	BASHAWISMS
ABASHED	**BASHED**	
	BASHER	BASHERS
ABASHES	**BASHES**	
ABASHING	**BASHING**	BASHINGS
ABASHLESS	**BASHLESS**	
	BASHLIK	BASHLIKS
	BASHLYK	BASHLYKS

FRONT HOOK	ROOT WORD	END HOOK
	BASIC	BASICS
	BASIDIA	BASIDIAL
	BASIFIER	BASIFIERS
	BASIL	BASILS
	BASILAR	BASILARY
	BASILECT	BASILECTS
	BASILIC	BASILICA
	BASILICA	BASILICAE ▪ BASILICAL ▪ BASILICAN BASILICAS
	BASILICON	BASILICONS
	BASILISK	BASILISKS
	BASIN	BASING ▪ BASINS
	BASINET	BASINETS
	BASINFUL	BASINFULS
ABASING	BASING	
	BASION	BASIONS
ABASK	BASK	BASKS
	BASKET	BASKETS
	BASKETFUL	BASKETFULS
	BASMATI	BASMATIS
	BASNET	BASNETS
	BASOCHE	BASOCHES
	BASON	BASONS
	BASOPHIL	BASOPHILE ▪ BASOPHILS
	BASOPHILE	BASOPHILES
	BASQUE	BASQUED ▪ BASQUES
	BASQUINE	BASQUINES
	BASS	BASSE ▪ BASSI ▪ BASSO ▪ BASSY
	BASSE	BASSED ▪ BASSER ▪ BASSES ▪ BASSET
	BASSES	BASSEST
	BASSET	BASSETS ▪ BASSETT
	BASSETT	BASSETTS
	BASSINET	BASSINETS
	BASSIST	BASSISTS
	BASSO	BASSOS
	BASSOON	BASSOONS
	BASSWOOD	BASSWOODS
	BAST	BASTA ▪ BASTE ▪ BASTI ▪ BASTO ▪ BASTS
	BASTARD	BASTARDS (offensive) ▪ BASTARDY
	BASTE	BASTED ▪ BASTER ▪ BASTES
	BASTER	BASTERS
	BASTI	BASTIS
	BASTIDE	BASTIDES
	BASTILE	BASTILES
	BASTILLE	BASTILLES
	BASTINADE	BASTINADED ▪ BASTINADES
	BASTING	BASTINGS
	BASTION	BASTIONS
	BASTLE	BASTLES
	BASTO	BASTOS
	BASUCO	BASUCOS
	BAT	BATE ▪ BATH ▪ BATS ▪ BATT
ABATABLE	BATABLE	
	BATATA	BATATAS
	BATAVIA	BATAVIAS
	BATBOY	BATBOYS
	BATCHER	BATCHERS
	BATCHING	BATCHINGS
ABATE	BATE	BATED ▪ BATES
	BATEAU	BATEAUX
ABATED	BATED	
	BATELEUR	BATELEURS
ABATEMENT	BATEMENT	BATEMENTS
ABATEMENTS	BATEMENTS	
ABATES	BATES	
	BATFOWL	BATFOWLS
	BATFOWLER	BATFOWLERS
	BATGIRL	BATGIRLS
	BATH	BATHE ▪ BATHS

FRONT HOOK	ROOT WORD	END HOOK
	BATHCUBE	BATHCUBES
	BATHE	BATHED · BATHER · BATHES
	BATHER	BATHERS
	BATHHOUSE	BATHHOUSES
	BATHMAT	BATHMATS
	BATHMISM	BATHMISMS
	BATHOLITE	BATHOLITES
	BATHOLITH	BATHOLITHS
	BATHORSE	BATHORSES
	BATHROBE	BATHROBES
	BATHROOM	BATHROOMS
	BATHTUB	BATHTUBS
	BATHWATER	BATHWATERS
	BATHYLITE	BATHYLITES
	BATHYLITH	BATHYLITHS
	BATIK	BATIKS
ABATING	BATING	
	BATISTE	BATISTES
	BATLER	BATLERS
	BATLET	BATLETS
	BATON	BATONS
	BATOON	BATOONS
	BATRACHIA	BATRACHIAN
	BATT	BATTA · BATTS · BATTU · BATTY
	BATTA	BATTAS
	BATTALIA	BATTALIAS
	BATTALION	BATTALIONS
	BATTEAU	BATTEAUX
	BATTEL	BATTELS
	BATTELER	BATTELERS
	BATTEMENT	BATTEMENTS
	BATTEN	BATTENS
	BATTENER	BATTENERS
	BATTENING	BATTENINGS
	BATTER	BATTERO · BATTERS · BATTERY
	BATTERER	BATTERERS
	BATTERIE	BATTERIES
	BATTERING	BATTERINGS
	BATTERO	BATTEROS
	BATTIK	BATTIKS
	BATTILL	BATTILLS
	BATTING	BATTINGS
	BATTLE	BATTLED · BATTLER · BATTLES
	BATTLER	BATTLERS
ABATTU	BATTU	BATTUE
	BATTUE	BATTUES
	BATTUTA	BATTUTAS
	BAUBEE	BAUBEES
	BAUBLE	BAUBLES
	BAUCHLE	BAUCHLED · BAUCHLES
	BAUD	BAUDS
	BAUDEKIN	BAUDEKINS
	BAUDRIC	BAUDRICK · BAUDRICS
	BAUDRICK	BAUDRICKE · BAUDRICKS
	BAUDRICKE	BAUDRICKES
	BAUERA	BAUERAS
	BAUHINIA	BAUHINIAS
	BAUK	BAUKS
	BAULK	BAULKS · BAULKY
	BAULKER	BAULKERS
	BAUR	BAURS
	BAUXITE	BAUXITES
	BAVARDAGE	BAVARDAGES
	BAVIN	BAVINS
	BAWBEE	BAWBEES
	BAWBLE	BAWBLES
	BAWCOCK	BAWCOCKS
	BAWD	BAWDS · BAWDY
	BAWDIES	BAWDIEST

FRONT HOOK	ROOT WORD	END HOOK
	BAWDKIN	BAWDKINS
	BAWDRIC	BAWDRICS
	BAWL	BAWLS
	BAWLER	BAWLERS
	BAWLEY	BAWLEYS
	BAWLING	BAWLINGS
	BAWN	BAWNS
	BAWNEEN	BAWNEENS
	BAWR	BAWRS
	BAWTIE	BAWTIES
	BAXTER	BAXTERS
	BAY	BAYE ▪ BAYS ▪ BAYT
	BAYADEER	BAYADEERS
	BAYADERE	BAYADERES
	BAYAMO	BAYAMOS
	BAYARD	BAYARDS
	BAYE	BAYED ▪ BAYES
EBAYING	BAYING	
	BAYLE	BAYLES
	BAYONET	BAYONETS
	BAYOU	BAYOUS
	BAYT	BAYTS
	BAYWOOD	BAYWOODS
	BAYYAN	BAYYANS
	BAZAAR	BAZAARS
	BAZAR	BAZARS
	BAZILLION	BAZILLIONS
	BAZOO	BAZOOS
	BAZOOKA	BAZOOKAS
	BAZOUKI	BAZOUKIS
	BDELLIUM	BDELLIUMS
OBE	BE	BED ▪ BEE ▪ BEG ▪ BEL ▪ BEN ▪ BES ▪ BET BEY ▪ BEZ
	BEACH	BEACHY
	BEACHBALL	BEACHBALLS
	BEACHBOY	BEACHBOYS
	BEACHCOMB	BEACHCOMBS
	BEACHGOER	BEACHGOERS
	BEACHHEAD	BEACHHEADS
	BEACON	BEACONS
	BEAD	BEADS ▪ BEADY
	BEADBLAST	BEADBLASTS
	BEADER	BEADERS
	BEADHOUSE	BEADHOUSES
	BEADING	BEADINGS
	BEADLE	BEADLES
	BEADLEDOM	BEADLEDOMS
	BEADROLL	BEADROLLS
	BEADWORK	BEADWORKS
	BEAGLE	BEAGLED ▪ BEAGLER ▪ BEAGLES
	BEAGLER	BEAGLERS
	BEAGLING	BEAGLINGS
	BEAK	BEAKS ▪ BEAKY
	BEAKER	BEAKERS
ABEAM	BEAM	BEAMS ▪ BEAMY
	BEAMER	BEAMERS
	BEAMING	BEAMINGS
	BEAMLET	BEAMLETS
	BEAN	BEANO ▪ BEANS ▪ BEANY
	BEANBAG	BEANBAGS
	BEANBALL	BEANBALLS
	BEANFEAST	BEANFEASTS
	BEANIE	BEANIES
	BEANO	BEANOS
	BEANPOLE	BEANPOLES
	BEANSTALK	BEANSTALKS
ABEAR	BEAR	BEARD ▪ BEARE ▪ BEARS
	BEARBINE	BEARBINES
	BEARCAT	BEARCATS

71

FRONT HOOK	ROOT WORD	END HOOK
	BEARD	BEARDS = BEARDY
	BEARDIE	BEARDIER = BEARDIES
	BEARDIES	BEARDIEST
	BEARE	BEARED = BEARER = BEARES
	BEARER	BEARERS
	BEARHUG	BEARHUGS
ABEARING	**BEARING**	BEARINGS
	BEARNAISE	BEARNAISES
ABEARS	**BEARS**	
	BEARSKIN	BEARSKINS
	BEARWARD	BEARWARDS
	BEARWOOD	BEARWOODS
	BEAST	BEASTS
	BEASTHOOD	BEASTHOODS
	BEASTIE	BEASTIES
	BEAT	BEATH = BEATS = BEATY
	BEATER	BEATERS
	BEATH	BEATHS
	BEATING	BEATINGS
	BEATITUDE	BEATITUDES
	BEATNIK	BEATNIKS
	BEAU	BEAUS = BEAUT = BEAUX
	BEAUCOUP	BEAUCOUPS
	BEAUFET	BEAUFETS
	BEAUFFET	BEAUFFETS
	BEAUFIN	BEAUFINS
	BEAUT	BEAUTS = BEAUTY
	BEAUXITE	BEAUXITES
	BEAVER	BEAVERS = BEAVERY
	BEBEERINE	BEBEERINES
	BEBEERU	BEBEERUS
	BEBLOOD	BEBLOODS
	BEBOP	BEBOPS
	BEBOPPER	BEBOPPERS
	BEBUNG	BEBUNGS
	BECALL	BECALLS
	BECALM	BECALMS
	BECAP	BECAPS
	BECARPET	BECARPETS
	BECASSE	BECASSES
	BECCACCIA	BECCACCIAS
	BECCAFICO	BECCAFICOS
	BECHALK	BECHALKS
	BECHAMEL	BECHAMELS
	BECHANCE	BECHANCED = BECHANCES
	BECHARM	BECHARMS
	BECK	BECKE = BECKS
	BECKE	BECKED = BECKES = BECKET
	BECKET	BECKETS
	BECKON	BECKONS
	BECKONER	BECKONERS
	BECKONING	BECKONINGS
	BECLAMOR	BECLAMORS
	BECLASP	BECLASPS
	BECLOAK	BECLOAKS
	BECLOG	BECLOGS
	BECLOTHE	BECLOTHED = BECLOTHES
	BECLOUD	BECLOUDS
	BECLOWN	BECLOWNS
	BECOME	BECOMES
	BECOMING	BECOMINGS
	BECOWARD	BECOWARDS
	BECQUEREL	BECQUERELS
	BECRAWL	BECRAWLS
	BECRIME	BECRIMED = BECRIMES
	BECROWD	BECROWDS
	BECRUST	BECRUSTS
	BECUDGEL	BECUDGELS
	BECURL	BECURLS

FRONT HOOK	ROOT WORD	END HOOK
	BECURSE	BECURSED ▪ BECURSES
ABED	BED	BEDE ▪ BEDS ▪ BEDU
	BEDABBLE	BEDABBLED ▪ BEDABBLES
	BEDAGGLE	BEDAGGLED ▪ BEDAGGLES
	BEDAMN	BEDAMNS
	BEDARKEN	BEDARKENS
	BEDAUB	BEDAUBS
	BEDAWIN	BEDAWINS
	BEDAZE	BEDAZED ▪ BEDAZES
	BEDAZZLE	BEDAZZLED ▪ BEDAZZLES
	BEDBOARD	BEDBOARDS
	BEDBUG	BEDBUGS
	BEDCHAIR	BEDCHAIRS
	BEDCOVER	BEDCOVERS
	BEDDER	BEDDERS
	BEDDING	BEDDINGS
	BEDE	BEDEL ▪ BEDES ▪ BEDEW
	BEDEAFEN	BEDEAFENS
	BEDECK	BEDECKS
	BEDEGUAR	BEDEGUARS
	BEDEHOUSE	BEDEHOUSES
	BEDEL	BEDELL ▪ BEDELS
	BEDELL	BEDELLS
	BEDELSHIP	BEDELSHIPS
	BEDERAL	BEDERALS
	BEDEVIL	BEDEVILS
	BEDEW	BEDEWS
	BEDFELLOW	BEDFELLOWS
	BEDFRAME	BEDFRAMES
	BEDGOWN	BEDGOWNS
	BEDIAPER	BEDIAPERS
	BEDIGHT	BEDIGHTS
	BEDIM	BEDIMS
	BEDIMMING	BEDIMMINGS
	BEDIMPLE	BEDIMPLED ▪ BEDIMPLES
	BEDIZEN	BEDIZENS
	BEDLAM	BEDLAMP ▪ BEDLAMS
	BEDLAMISM	BEDLAMISMS
	BEDLAMITE	BEDLAMITES
	BEDLAMP	BEDLAMPS
	BEDMAKER	BEDMAKERS
	BEDMATE	BEDMATES
	BEDOUIN	BEDOUINS
	BEDPAN	BEDPANS
	BEDPLATE	BEDPLATES
	BEDPOST	BEDPOSTS
	BEDQUILT	BEDQUILTS
	BEDRAGGLE	BEDRAGGLED ▪ BEDRAGGLES
	BEDRAIL	BEDRAILS
	BEDRAL	BEDRALS
	BEDRAPE	BEDRAPED ▪ BEDRAPES
	BEDRIGHT	BEDRIGHTS
	BEDRIVEL	BEDRIVELS
	BEDROCK	BEDROCKS
	BEDROLL	BEDROLLS
	BEDROOM	BEDROOMS
	BEDROP	BEDROPS ▪ BEDROPT
	BEDRUG	BEDRUGS
	BEDSHEET	BEDSHEETS
	BEDSIDE	BEDSIDES
	BEDSIT	BEDSITS
	BEDSITTER	BEDSITTERS
	BEDSONIA	BEDSONIAS
	BEDSORE	BEDSORES
	BEDSPREAD	BEDSPREADS
	BEDSPRING	BEDSPRINGS
	BEDSTAND	BEDSTANDS
	BEDSTEAD	BEDSTEADS
	BEDSTRAW	BEDSTRAWS

B

FRONT HOOK	ROOT WORD	END HOOK
	BEDTICK	BEDTICKS
	BEDTIME	BEDTIMES
	BEDUCK	BEDUCKS
	BEDUIN	BEDUINS
	BEDUMB	BEDUMBS
	BEDUNCE	BEDUNCED ▪ BEDUNCES
	BEDUNG	BEDUNGS
	BEDUST	BEDUSTS
	BEDWARD	BEDWARDS
	BEDWARF	BEDWARFS
	BEDWARMER	BEDWARMERS
	BEDWETTER	BEDWETTERS
	BEDYE	BEDYED ▪ BEDYES
	BEE	BEEF ▪ BEEN ▪ BEEP ▪ BEER ▪ BEES ▪ BEET
	BEEBEE	BEEBEES
	BEEBREAD	BEEBREADS
	BEECH	BEECHY
	BEECHMAST	BEECHMASTS
	BEECHNUT	BEECHNUTS
	BEECHWOOD	BEECHWOODS
	BEEF	BEEFS ▪ BEEFY
	BEEFALO	BEEFALOS
	BEEFCAKE	BEEFCAKES
	BEEFEATER	BEEFEATERS
	BEEFSTEAK	BEEFSTEAKS
	BEEFWOOD	BEEFWOODS
	BEEGAH	BEEGAHS
	BEEHIVE	BEEHIVES
	BEEKEEPER	BEEKEEPERS
	BEELINE	BEELINED ▪ BEELINES
	BEENAH	BEENAHS
	BEENTO	BEENTOS
	BEEP	BEEPS
	BEEPER	BEEPERS
	BEER	BEERS ▪ BEERY
	BEERAGE	BEERAGES
	BEERHALL	BEERHALLS
	BEESWING	BEESWINGS
	BEET	BEETS
	BEETLE	BEETLED ▪ BEETLER ▪ BEETLES
	BEETLER	BEETLERS
	BEETROOT	BEETROOTS
	BEEYARD	BEEYARDS
	BEEZER	BEEZERS
	BEFALL	BEFALLS
	BEFANA	BEFANAS
	BEFFANA	BEFFANAS
	BEFINGER	BEFINGERS
	BEFIT	BEFITS
	BEFLAG	BEFLAGS
	BEFLEA	BEFLEAS
	BEFLECK	BEFLECKS
	BEFLOWER	BEFLOWERS
	BEFLUM	BEFLUMS
	BEFOAM	BEFOAMS
	BEFOG	BEFOGS
	BEFOOL	BEFOOLS
	BEFORTUNE	BEFORTUNED ▪ BEFORTUNES
	BEFOUL	BEFOULS
	BEFOULER	BEFOULERS
	BEFRET	BEFRETS
	BEFRIEND	BEFRIENDS
	BEFRINGE	BEFRINGED ▪ BEFRINGES
	BEFUDDLE	BEFUDDLED ▪ BEFUDDLES
	BEG	BEGO ▪ BEGS
	BEGALL	BEGALLS
	BEGAR	BEGARS
	BEGAZE	BEGAZED ▪ BEGAZES
	BEGEM	BEGEMS

FRONT HOOK	ROOT WORD	END HOOK
	BEGET	BEGETS
	BEGETTER	BEGETTERS
	BEGGAR	BEGGARS = BEGGARY
	BEGGARDOM	BEGGARDOMS
ABEGGING	BEGGING	BEGGINGS
	BEGHARD	BEGHARDS
	BEGIFT	BEGIFTS
	BEGILD	BEGILDS
	BEGIN	BEGINS
	BEGINNE	BEGINNER = BEGINNES
	BEGINNER	BEGINNERS
	BEGINNING	BEGINNINGS
	BEGIRD	BEGIRDS
	BEGIRDLE	BEGIRDLED = BEGIRDLES
	BEGLAD	BEGLADS
	BEGLAMOR	BEGLAMORS
	BEGLAMOUR	BEGLAMOURS
	BEGLERBEG	BEGLERBEGS
	BEGLOOM	BEGLOOMS
	BEGNAW	BEGNAWS
	BEGO	BEGOT
	BEGONIA	BEGONIAS
	BEGORRA	BEGORRAH
	BEGRIM	BEGRIME = BEGRIMS
	BEGRIME	BEGRIMED = BEGRIMES
	BEGROAN	BEGROANS
	BEGRUDGE	BEGRUDGED = BEGRUDGER = BEGRUDGES
	BEGRUDGER	BEGRUDGERS = BEGRUDGERY
	BEGUILE	BEGUILED = BEGUILER = BEGUILES
	BEGUILER	BEGUILERS
	BEGUIN	BEGUINE = BEGUINS
	BEGUINAGE	BEGUINAGES
	BEGUINE	BEGUINES
	BEGULF	BEGULFS
	BEGUM	BEGUMS
	BEGUN	BEGUNK
	BEGUNK	BEGUNKS
	BEHAPPEN	BEHAPPENS
	BEHAVE	BEHAVED = BEHAVER = BEHAVES
	BEHAVER	BEHAVERS
	BEHAVIOR	BEHAVIORS
	BEHAVIOUR	BEHAVIOURS
	BEHEAD	BEHEADS
	BEHEADAL	BEHEADALS
	BEHEADER	BEHEADERS
	BEHEADING	BEHEADINGS
	BEHEMOTH	BEHEMOTHS
	BEHEST	BEHESTS
	BEHIGHT	BEHIGHTS
	BEHIND	BEHINDS
	BEHOLD	BEHOLDS
	BEHOLDER	BEHOLDERS
	BEHOLDING	BEHOLDINGS
	BEHOOF	BEHOOFS
	BEHOOVE	BEHOOVED = BEHOOVES
	BEHOTE	BEHOTES
	BEHOVE	BEHOVED = BEHOVES
	BEHOWL	BEHOWLS
	BEIGE	BEIGEL = BEIGES
	BEIGEL	BEIGELS
	BEIGNE	BEIGNES = BEIGNET
	BEIGNET	BEIGNETS
	BEIN	BEING
	BEING	BEINGS
	BEJADE	BEJADED = BEJADES
	BEJANT	BEJANTS
	BEJESUIT	BEJESUITS
	BEJEWEL	BEJEWELS
	BEJUMBLE	BEJUMBLED = BEJUMBLES

B

FRONT HOOK	ROOT WORD	END HOOK
	BEKAH	BEKAHS
	BEKNAVE	BEKNAVED · BEKNAVES
	BEKNIGHT	BEKNIGHTS
	BEKNOT	BEKNOTS
	BEL	BELL · BELS · BELT
	BELABOR	BELABORS
	BELABOUR	BELABOURS
	BELACE	BELACED · BELACES
	BELAH	BELAHS
	BELAMOURE	BELAMOURES
	BELAR	BELARS
	BELATE	BELATED · BELATES
	BELAUD	BELAUDS
	BELAY	BELAYS
	BELAYER	BELAYERS
	BELCHER	BELCHERS
	BELDAM	BELDAME · BELDAMS
	BELDAME	BELDAMES
	BELEAGUER	BELEAGUERS
	BELEAP	BELEAPS · BELEAPT
	BELEE	BELEED · BELEES
	BELEMNITE	BELEMNITES
	BELGA	BELGAS
	BELGARD	BELGARDS
	BELIE	BELIED · BELIEF · BELIER · BELIES
	BELIEF	BELIEFS
	BELIER	BELIERS
	BELIEVE	BELIEVED · BELIEVER · BELIEVES
	BELIEVER	BELIEVERS
	BELIEVING	BELIEVINGS
	BELIQUOR	BELIQUORS
	BELITTLE	BELITTLED · BELITTLER · BELITTLES
	BELITTLER	BELITTLERS
	BELL	BELLE · BELLS · BELLY
	BELLBIND	BELLBINDS
	BELLBIRD	BELLBIRDS
	BELLBOY	BELLBOYS
	BELLCOTE	BELLCOTES
	BELLE	BELLED · BELLES
	BELLEEK	BELLEEKS
	BELLETER	BELLETERS
	BELLHOP	BELLHOPS
	BELLIBONE	BELLIBONES
	BELLING	BELLINGS
	BELLOCK	BELLOCKS
	BELLOW	BELLOWS
	BELLOWER	BELLOWERS
	BELLPULL	BELLPULLS
	BELLWORT	BELLWORTS
	BELLYACHE	BELLYACHED · BELLYACHER · BELLYACHES
	BELLYBAND	BELLYBANDS
	BELLYFUL	BELLYFULS
	BELLYING	BELLYINGS
	BELON	BELONG · BELONS
	BELONG	BELONGS
	BELONGER	BELONGERS
	BELONGING	BELONGINGS
	BELOVE	BELOVED · BELOVES
	BELOVED	BELOVEDS
	BELOW	BELOWS
	BELT	BELTS
	BELTER	BELTERS
	BELTING	BELTINGS
	BELTLINE	BELTLINES
	BELTWAY	BELTWAYS
	BELUGA	BELUGAS
	BELVEDERE	BELVEDERES
	BEMA	BEMAD · BEMAS
	BEMAD	BEMADS

FRONT HOOK	ROOT WORD	END HOOK
	BEMADAM	BEMADAMS
	BEMADDEN	BEMADDENS
	BEMAUL	BEMAULS
	BEMEAN	BEMEANS = BEMEANT
	BEMEDAL	BEMEDALS
	BEMETE	BEMETED = BEMETES
	BEMINGLE	BEMINGLED = BEMINGLES
	BEMIRE	BEMIRED = BEMIRES
	BEMIST	BEMISTS
	BEMIX	BEMIXT
	BEMOAN	BEMOANS
	BEMOANER	BEMOANERS
	BEMOANING	BEMOANINGS
	BEMOCK	BEMOCKS
	BEMOIL	BEMOILS
	BEMONSTER	BEMONSTERS
	BEMOUTH	BEMOUTHS
	BEMUD	BEMUDS
	BEMUDDLE	BEMUDDLED = BEMUDDLES
	BEMUFFLE	BEMUFFLED = BEMUFFLES
	BEMURMUR	BEMURMURS
	BEMUSE	BEMUSED = BEMUSES
	BEMUZZLE	BEMUZZLED = BEMUZZLES
	BEN	BEND = BENE = BENI = BENJ = BENS = BENT
	BENADRYL	BENADRYLS
	BENAME	BENAMED = BENAMES
	BENCH	BENCHY
	BENCHER	BENCHERS
	BENCHLAND	BENCHLANDS
	BENCHMARK	BENCHMARKS
	BEND	BENDS = BENDY
	BENDAY	BENDAYS
	BENDEE	BENDEES
	BENDER	BENDERS
	BENDING	BENDINGS
	BENDLET	BENDLETS
	BENDY	BENDYS
	BENE	BENES = BENET
	BENEDICK	BENEDICKS
	BENEDICT	BENEDICTS
	BENEFACT	BENEFACTS
	BENEFIC	BENEFICE
	BENEFICE	BENEFICED = BENEFICES
	BENEFIT	BENEFITS
	BENEFITER	BENEFITERS
	BENET	BENETS
	BENGALINE	BENGALINES
	BENI	BENIS
	BENIGHT	BENIGHTS
	BENIGHTEN	BENIGHTENS
	BENIGHTER	BENIGHTERS
	BENISEED	BENISEEDS
	BENISON	BENISONS
	BENITIER	BENITIERS
	BENJAMIN	BENJAMINS
	BENNE	BENNES = BENNET
	BENNET	BENNETS
	BENNI	BENNIS
	BENOMYL	BENOMYLS
	BENT	BENTO = BENTS = BENTY
	BENTHON	BENTHONS
OBENTO	BENTO	BENTOS
	BENTONITE	BENTONITES
OBENTOS	BENTOS	
	BENTWOOD	BENTWOODS
	BENUMB	BENUMBS
	BENZAL	BENZALS
	BENZENE	BENZENES
	BENZENOID	BENZENOIDS

B

FRONT HOOK	ROOT WORD	END HOOK
	BENZIDIN	BENZIDINE · BENZIDINS
	BENZIDINE	BENZIDINES
	BENZIL	BENZILS
	BENZIN	BENZINE · BENZINS
	BENZINE	BENZINES
	BENZOATE	BENZOATES
	BENZOIN	BENZOINS
	BENZOL	BENZOLE · BENZOLS
	BENZOLE	BENZOLES
	BENZOLINE	BENZOLINES
	BENZOYL	BENZOYLS
	BENZYL	BENZYLS
	BEPAINT	BEPAINTS
	BEPAT	BEPATS
	BEPEARL	BEPEARLS
	BEPELT	BEPELTS
	BEPEPPER	BEPEPPERS
	BEPESTER	BEPESTERS
	BEPIMPLE	BEPIMPLED · BEPIMPLES
	BEPLASTER	BEPLASTERS
	BEPOMMEL	BEPOMMELS
	BEPOWDER	BEPOWDERS
	BEPRAISE	BEPRAISED · BEPRAISES
	BEPROSE	BEPROSED · BEPROSES
	BEPUFF	BEPUFFS
	BEQUEATH	BEQUEATHS
	BEQUEST	BEQUESTS
	BERAKE	BERAKED · BERAKES
	BERASCAL	BERASCALS
	BERATE	BERATED · BERATES
	BERAY	BERAYS
	BERBERE	BERBERES
	BERBERIN	BERBERINE · BERBERINS
	BERBERINE	BERBERINES
	BERCEAU	BERCEAUX
	BERCEUSE	BERCEUSES
	BERDACHE	BERDACHES
	BERE	BERES · BERET
	BEREAVE	BEREAVED · BEREAVEN · BEREAVER BEREAVES
	BEREAVER	BEREAVERS
	BERET	BERETS
	BERETTA	BERETTAS
	BERG	BERGS
	BERGAMA	BERGAMAS
	BERGAMAS	BERGAMASK
	BERGAMASK	BERGAMASKS
	BERGAMOT	BERGAMOTS
	BERGANDER	BERGANDERS
	BERGEN	BERGENS
	BERGENIA	BERGENIAS
	BERGERE	BERGERES
	BERGFALL	BERGFALLS
	BERGHAAN	BERGHAANS
	BERGMEHL	BERGMEHLS
	BERGOMASK	BERGOMASKS
	BERGYLT	BERGYLTS
	BERHYME	BERHYMED · BERHYMES
	BERIBERI	BERIBERIS
	BERIMBAU	BERIMBAUS
	BERIME	BERIMED · BERIMES
	BERK	BERKO · BERKS
	BERKELIUM	BERKELIUMS
	BERLEY	BERLEYS
	BERLIN	BERLINE · BERLINS
	BERLINE	BERLINES
	BERM	BERME · BERMS
	BERME	BERMED · BERMES
	BERNICLE	BERNICLES

B

FRONT HOOK	ROOT WORD	END HOOK
	BEROB	BEROBS
	BERRET	BERRETS
	BERRETTA	BERRETTAS
	BERRIGAN	BERRIGANS
	BERRYING	BERRYINGS
	BERSEEM	BERSEEMS
	BERSERK	BERSERKS
	BERSERKER	BERSERKERS
	BERTH	BERTHA ▪ BERTHE ▪ BERTHS
	BERTHA	BERTHAS
	BERTHAGE	BERTHAGES
	BERTHE	BERTHED ▪ BERTHES
	BERYL	BERYLS
	BERYLLIA	BERYLLIAS
	BERYLLIUM	BERYLLIUMS
OBES	**BES**	BEST
	BESAINT	BESAINTS
	BESCATTER	BESCATTERS
	BESCOUR	BESCOURS
	BESCRAWL	BESCRAWLS
	BESCREEN	BESCREENS
	BESEE	BESEEM ▪ BESEEN ▪ BESEES
	BESEECHER	BESEECHERS
	BESEEKE	BESEEKES
	BESEEM	BESEEMS
	BESEEMING	BESEEMINGS
	BESET	BESETS
	BESETMENT	BESETMENTS
	BESETTER	BESETTERS
	BESHADOW	BESHADOWS
	BESHAME	BESHAMED ▪ BESHAMES
	BESHINE	BESHINES
	BESHIVER	BESHIVERS
	BESHOUT	BESHOUTS
	BESHREW	BESHREWS
	BESHROUD	BESHROUDS
	BESIDE	BESIDES
	BESIEGE	BESIEGED ▪ BESIEGER ▪ BESIEGES
	BESIEGER	BESIEGERS
	BESIEGING	BESIEGINGS
	BESIGH	BESIGHS
	BESING	BESINGS
	BESIT	BESITS
	BESLAVE	BESLAVED ▪ BESLAVER ▪ BESLAVES
	BESLAVER	BESLAVERS
	BESLIME	BESLIMED ▪ BESLIMES
	BESLOBBER	BESLOBBERS
	BESLUBBER	BESLUBBERS
	BESMEAR	BESMEARS
	BESMEARER	BESMEARERS
	BESMILE	BESMILED ▪ BESMILES
	BESMOKE	BESMOKED ▪ BESMOKES
	BESMOOTH	BESMOOTHS
	BESMUDGE	BESMUDGED ▪ BESMUDGES
	BESMUT	BESMUTS
	BESNOW	BESNOWS
	BESOGNIO	BESOGNIOS
	BESOIN	BESOINS
	BESOM	BESOMS
	BESONIAN	BESONIANS
	BESOOTHE	BESOOTHED ▪ BESOOTHES
	BESORT	BESORTS
	BESOT	BESOTS
	BESPANGLE	BESPANGLED ▪ BESPANGLES
	BESPAT	BESPATE
	BESPATTER	BESPATTERS
	BESPEAK	BESPEAKS
	BESPECKLE	BESPECKLED ▪ BESPECKLES
	BESPEED	BESPEEDS

B

FRONT HOOK	ROOT WORD	END HOOK
	BESPICE	BESPICED = BESPICES
	BESPIT	BESPITS
	BESPOKE	BESPOKEN
	BESPORT	BESPORTS
	BESPOT	BESPOTS
	BESPOUSE	BESPOUSED = BESPOUSES
	BESPOUT	BESPOUTS
	BESPREAD	BESPREADS
	BEST	BESTI = BESTS
	BESTAIN	BESTAINS
	BESTAR	BESTARS
	BESTEAD	BESTEADS
	BESTI	BESTIR = BESTIS
	BESTIAL	BESTIALS
	BESTICK	BESTICKS
	BESTILL	BESTILLS
	BESTIR	BESTIRS
	BESTORM	BESTORMS
	BESTOW	BESTOWS
	BESTOWAL	BESTOWALS
	BESTOWER	BESTOWERS
	BESTREAK	BESTREAKS
	BESTREW	BESTREWN = BESTREWS
	BESTRID	BESTRIDE
	BESTRIDE	BESTRIDES
	BESTROW	BESTROWN = BESTROWS
	BESTUD	BESTUDS
	BESWARM	BESWARMS
ABET = YBET	BET	BETA = BETE = BETH = BETS
	BETA	BETAS
	BETACISM	BETACISMS
	BETAINE	BETAINES
	BETAKE	BETAKEN = BETAKES
	BETATRON	BETATRONS
	BETATTER	BETATTERS
	BETE	BETED = BETEL = BETES
	BETEEM	BETEEME = BETEEMS
	BETEEME	BETEEMED = BETEEMES
	BETEL	BETELS
	BETELNUT	BETELNUTS
	BETH	BETHS
	BETHANK	BETHANKS
	BETHANKIT	BETHANKITS
	BETHEL	BETHELS
	BETHESDA	BETHESDAS
	BETHINK	BETHINKS
	BETHORN	BETHORNS
	BETHRALL	BETHRALLS
	BETHUMB	BETHUMBS
	BETHUMP	BETHUMPS
	BETHWACK	BETHWACKS
	BETID	BETIDE
	BETIDE	BETIDED = BETIDES
	BETIME	BETIMED = BETIMES
	BETISE	BETISES
	BETITLE	BETITLED = BETITLES
	BETOIL	BETOILS
	BETOKEN	BETOKENS
	BETON	BETONS = BETONY
	BETRAY	BETRAYS
	BETRAYAL	BETRAYALS
	BETRAYER	BETRAYERS
	BETREAD	BETREADS
	BETRIM	BETRIMS
	BETROTH	BETROTHS
	BETROTHAL	BETROTHALS
	BETROTHED	BETROTHEDS
ABETS	BETS	
	BETTA	BETTAS

FRONT HOOK	ROOT WORD	END HOOK
ABETTED	BETTED	
ABETTER	BETTER	BETTERS
	BETTERING	BETTERINGS
ABETTERS	BETTERS	
ABETTING	BETTING	BETTINGS
	BETTONG	BETTONGS
ABETTOR	BETTOR	BETTORS
ABETTORS	BETTORS	
	BETWEEN	BETWEENS
	BEURRE	BEURRES
	BEVATRON	BEVATRONS
	BEVEL	BEVELS
	BEVELER	BEVELERS
	BEVELLER	BEVELLERS
	BEVELLING	BEVELLINGS
	BEVELMENT	BEVELMENTS
	BEVER	BEVERS
	BEVERAGE	BEVERAGES
	BEVOMIT	BEVOMITS
	BEVOR	BEVORS
	BEVUE	BEVUES
	BEWAIL	BEWAILS
	BEWAILER	BEWAILERS
	BEWAILING	BEWAILINGS
	BEWARE	BEWARED ▪ BEWARES
	BEWEEP	BEWEEPS
	BEWET	BEWETS
	BEWHORE	BEWHORED ▪ BEWHORES
	BEWIG	BEWIGS
	BEWILDER	BEWILDERS
	BEWITCHER	BEWITCHERS ▪ BEWITCHERY
	BEWORM	BEWORMS
	BEWRAP	BEWRAPS ▪ BEWRAPT
	BEWRAY	BEWRAYS
	BEWRAYER	BEWRAYERS
OBEY	BEY	BEYS
	BEYLIC	BEYLICS
	BEYLIK	BEYLIKS
	BEYOND	BEYONDS
OBEYS	BEYS	
	BEZANT	BEZANTS
	BEZEL	BEZELS
	BEZIL	BEZILS
	BEZIQUE	BEZIQUES
	BEZOAR	BEZOARS
	BEZONIAN	BEZONIANS
	BEZZANT	BEZZANTS
	BEZZLE	BEZZLED ▪ BEZZLES
	BHAGEE	BHAGEES
	BHAJAN	BHAJANS
	BHAJEE	BHAJEES
	BHAJI	BHAJIS
	BHAKTA	BHAKTAS
	BHAKTI	BHAKTIS
	BHANG	BHANGS
	BHANGRA	BHANGRAS
	BHARAL	BHARALS
	BHAVAN	BHAVANS
	BHAWAN	BHAWANS
	BHEESTIE	BHEESTIES
	BHEL	BHELS
	BHIKHU	BHIKHUS
	BHIKKHUNI	BHIKKHUNIS
	BHINDI	BHINDIS
	BHISHTI	BHISHTIS
	BHISTEE	BHISTEES
	BHISTI	BHISTIE ▪ BHISTIS
	BHISTIE	BHISTIES
	BHOOT	BHOOTS

B

81

B

FRONT HOOK	ROOT WORD	END HOOK
	BHUNA	BHUNAS
	BHUT	BHUTS
OBI	**BI**	BIB ▪ BID ▪ BIG ▪ BIN ▪ BIO ▪ BIS ▪ BIT ▪ BIZ
	BIACETYL	BIACETYLS
	BIALI	BIALIS
	BIALY	BIALYS
	BIANNUAL	BIANNUALS
OBIAS	**BIAS**	
	BIASING	BIASINGS
	BIATHLETE	BIATHLETES
	BIATHLON	BIATHLONS
	BIB	BIBB ▪ BIBS
	BIBATION	BIBATIONS
	BIBB	BIBBS
	BIBBER	BIBBERS ▪ BIBBERY
	BIBBLE	BIBBLES
	BIBCOCK	BIBCOCKS
	BIBELOT	BIBELOTS
	BIBLE	BIBLES
	BIBLES	BIBLESS
	BIBLICISM	BIBLICISMS
	BIBLICIST	BIBLICISTS
	BIBLIOTIC	BIBLIOTICS
	BIBLIST	BIBLISTS
	BICARB	BICARBS
	BICE	BICEP ▪ BICES
	BICEP	BICEPS
IBICES	**BICES**	
	BICKER	BICKERS
	BICKERER	BICKERERS
	BICKERING	BICKERINGS
	BICKIE	BICKIES
	BICOLOR	BICOLORS
	BICOLOUR	BICOLOURS
	BICORN	BICORNE ▪ BICORNS
	BICORNE	BICORNES
	BICRON	BICRONS
	BICUSPID	BICUSPIDS
	BICYCLE	BICYCLED ▪ BICYCLER ▪ BICYCLES
	BICYCLER	BICYCLERS
	BICYCLIST	BICYCLISTS
ABID	**BID**	BIDE ▪ BIDI ▪ BIDS
	BIDARKA	BIDARKAS
	BIDARKEE	BIDARKEES
ABIDDEN	**BIDDEN**	
	BIDDER	BIDDERS
	BIDDING	BIDDINGS
ABIDE	**BIDE**	BIDED ▪ BIDER ▪ BIDES ▪ BIDET
ABIDED	**BIDED**	
	BIDENT	BIDENTS
	BIDENTAL	BIDENTALS
	BIDENTATE	BIDENTATED
ABIDER	**BIDER**	BIDERS
ABIDERS	**BIDERS**	
ABIDES	**BIDES**	
	BIDET	BIDETS
	BIDI	BIDIS
ABIDING	**BIDING**	BIDINGS
ABIDINGS	**BIDINGS**	
	BIDON	BIDONS
	BIELD	BIELDS ▪ BIELDY
	BIENNALE	BIENNALES
	BIENNIA	BIENNIAL
	BIENNIAL	BIENNIALS
	BIENNIUM	BIENNIUMS
	BIER	BIERS
	BIFACE	BIFACES
	BIFF	BIFFO ▪ BIFFS ▪ BIFFY

FRONT HOOK	ROOT WORD	END HOOK
	BIFFER	BIFFERS
	BIFFIN	BIFFING · BIFFINS
	BIFFO	BIFFOS
	BIFOCAL	BIFOCALS
	BIFTER	BIFTERS
	BIFURCATE	BIFURCATED · BIFURCATES
	BIG	BIGA · BIGG · BIGS
	BIGA	BIGAE
	BIGAMIST	BIGAMISTS
	BIGARADE	BIGARADES
	BIGAROON	BIGAROONS
	BIGARREAU	BIGARREAUS
	BIGENER	BIGENERS
	BIGEYE	BIGEYES
	BIGFOOT	BIGFOOTS
	BIGG	BIGGS · BIGGY
	BIGGIE	BIGGIES
	BIGGIN	BIGGING · BIGGINS
	BIGGING	BIGGINGS
	BIGGON	BIGGONS
	BIGHA	BIGHAS
	BIGHEAD	BIGHEADS
	BIGHORN	BIGHORNS
	BIGHT	BIGHTS
	BIGMOUTH	BIGMOUTHS
	BIGNONIA	BIGNONIAS
	BIGOT	BIGOTS
	BIGUANIDE	BIGUANIDES
	BIGWIG	BIGWIGS
	BIJECTION	BIJECTIONS
	BIJOU	BIJOUS · BIJOUX
	BIJWONER	BIJWONERS
	BIKE	BIKED · BIKER · BIKES
	BIKER	BIKERS
	BIKEWAY	BIKEWAYS
	BIKIE	BIKIES
	BIKING	BIKINGS
	BIKINI	BIKINIS
	BIKKIE	BIKKIES
	BILABIAL	BILABIALS
	BILANDER	BILANDERS
	BILAYER	BILAYERS
	BILBO	BILBOA · BILBOS
	BILBOA	BILBOAS
	BILE	BILED · BILES
	BILECTION	BILECTIONS
	BILESTONE	BILESTONES
	BILEVEL	BILEVELS
	BILGE	BILGED · BILGES
	BILHARZIA	BILHARZIAL · BILHARZIAS
	BILIAN	BILIANS
	BILIMBI	BILIMBIS
	BILIMBING	BILIMBINGS
	BILINGUAL	BILINGUALS
	BILIRUBIN	BILIRUBINS
	BILK	BILKS
	BILKER	BILKERS
	BILL	BILLS · BILLY
	BILLABONG	BILLABONGS
	BILLBOARD	BILLBOARDS
	BILLBOOK	BILLBOOKS
	BILLBUG	BILLBUGS
	BILLER	BILLERS
	BILLET	BILLETS
	BILLETEE	BILLETEES
	BILLETER	BILLETERS
	BILLFOLD	BILLFOLDS
	BILLHEAD	BILLHEADS
	BILLHOOK	BILLHOOKS

B

FRONT HOOK	ROOT WORD	END HOOK
	BILLIARD	BILLIARDS
	BILLIE	BILLIES
	BILLING	BILLINGS
	BILLION	BILLIONS
	BILLIONTH	BILLIONTHS
	BILLON	BILLONS
	BILLOW	BILLOWS ▪ BILLOWY
	BILLOWING	BILLOWINGS
	BILLY	BILLYO
	BILLYBOY	BILLYBOYS
	BILLYCAN	BILLYCANS
	BILLYCOCK	BILLYCOCKS
	BILLYO	BILLYOH ▪ BILLYOS
	BILLYOH	BILLYOHS
	BILOBATE	BILOBATED
	BILSTED	BILSTEDS
	BILTONG	BILTONGS
	BIMA	BIMAH ▪ BIMAS
	BIMAH	BIMAHS
	BIMBASHI	BIMBASHIS
	BIMBETTE	BIMBETTES *(offensive)*
	BIMBO	BIMBOS *(offensive)*
	BIMESTER	BIMESTERS
	BIMETAL	BIMETALS
	BIMETHYL	BIMETHYLS
	BIMORPH	BIMORPHS
	BIN	BIND ▪ BINE ▪ BING ▪ BINK ▪ BINS ▪ BINT
	BINARISM	BINARISMS
	BIND	BINDI ▪ BINDS
	BINDER	BINDERS ▪ BINDERY
	BINDHI	BINDHIS
	BINDI	BINDIS
	BINDING	BINDINGS
	BINDLE	BINDLES
	BINDWEED	BINDWEEDS
	BINE	BINER ▪ BINES
	BINER	BINERS
	BING	BINGE ▪ BINGO ▪ BINGS ▪ BINGY
	BINGE	BINGED ▪ BINGER ▪ BINGES
	BINGER	BINGERS
	BINGHI	BINGHIS *(offensive)*
	BINGLE	BINGLED ▪ BINGLES
	BINGO	BINGOS
	BINIOU	BINIOUS
	BINIT	BINITS
	BINK	BINKS
	BINNACLE	BINNACLES
	BINOCLE	BINOCLES
	BINOCULAR	BINOCULARS
	BINOMIAL	BINOMIALS
	BINOMINAL	BINOMINALS
	BINT	BINTS *(offensive)*
	BINTURONG	BINTURONGS
	BIO	BIOG ▪ BIOS
	BIOASSAY	BIOASSAYS
	BIOBLAST	BIOBLASTS
	BIOCENOSE	BIOCENOSES
	BIOCHIP	BIOCHIPS
	BIOCIDE	BIOCIDES
	BIOCYCLE	BIOCYCLES
	BIODIESEL	BIODIESELS
	BIODOT	BIODOTS
	BIOETHIC	BIOETHICS
	BIOFACT	BIOFACTS
	BIOFILM	BIOFILMS
	BIOFOULER	BIOFOULERS
	BIOFUEL	BIOFUELS
	BIOG	BIOGS
	BIOGEN	BIOGENS ▪ BIOGENY

B

FRONT HOOK	ROOT WORD	END HOOK
ABIOGENIC	**BIOGENIC**	
	BIOGRAPH	BIOGRAPHS · BIOGRAPHY
	BIOHAZARD	BIOHAZARDS
	BIOHERM	BIOHERMS
	BIOLOGIC	BIOLOGICS
	BIOLOGISM	BIOLOGISMS
	BIOLOGIST	BIOLOGISTS
	BIOMARKER	BIOMARKERS
	BIOME	BIOMES
	BIOMETER	BIOMETERS
	BIOMETRIC	BIOMETRICS
	BIOMINING	BIOMININGS
	BIOMORPH	BIOMORPHS
	BIONIC	BIONICS
	BIONOMIC	BIONOMICS
	BIONOMIST	BIONOMISTS
	BIONT	BIONTS
	BIOPARENT	BIOPARENTS
	BIOPHILIA	BIOPHILIAS
	BIOPHOR	BIOPHORE · BIOPHORS
	BIOPHORE	BIOPHORES
	BIOPIC	BIOPICS
	BIOPIRATE	BIOPIRATES
	BIOPLASM	BIOPLASMS
	BIOPLAST	BIOPLASTS
	BIOREGION	BIOREGIONS
	BIORHYTHM	BIORHYTHMS
	BIOSCOPE	BIOSCOPES
	BIOSENSOR	BIOSENSORS
	BIOSOLID	BIOSOLIDS
	BIOSPHERE	BIOSPHERES
	BIOSTATIC	BIOSTATICS
	BIOSTROME	BIOSTROMES
	BIOTA	BIOTAS
	BIOTECH	BIOTECHS
	BIOTERROR	BIOTERRORS
ABIOTIC	**BIOTIC**	BIOTICS
	BIOTIN	BIOTINS
	BIOTITE	BIOTITES
	BIOTOPE	BIOTOPES
	BIOTOXIN	BIOTOXINS
	BIOTRON	BIOTRONS
	BIOTROPH	BIOTROPHS
	BIOTYPE	BIOTYPES
	BIOWEAPON	BIOWEAPONS
	BIPACK	BIPACKS
	BIPED	BIPEDS
	BIPHENYL	BIPHENYLS
	BIPLANE	BIPLANES
	BIPOD	BIPODS
	BIPRISM	BIPRISMS
	BIPYRAMID	BIPYRAMIDS
	BIRADICAL	BIRADICALS
	BIRD	BIRDS
	BIRDBATH	BIRDBATHS
	BIRDBRAIN	BIRDBRAINS
	BIRDCAGE	BIRDCAGES
	BIRDCALL	BIRDCALLS
	BIRDDOG	BIRDDOGS
	BIRDER	BIRDERS
	BIRDFARM	BIRDFARMS
	BIRDFEED	BIRDFEEDS
	BIRDHOUSE	BIRDHOUSES
	BIRDIE	BIRDIED · BIRDIES
	BIRDING	BIRDINGS
	BIRDLIME	BIRDLIMED · BIRDLIMES
	BIRDSEED	BIRDSEEDS
	BIRDSEYE	BIRDSEYES
	BIRDSHOT	BIRDSHOTS

B

FRONT HOOK	ROOT WORD	END HOOK
	BIRDSONG	BIRDSONGS
	BIRDWING	BIRDWINGS
	BIREME	BIREMES
	BIRETTA	BIRETTAS
	BIRIANI	BIRIANIS
	BIRIYANI	BIRIYANIS
	BIRK	BIRKS
	BIRKIE	BIRKIER ▪ BIRKIES
	BIRKIES	BIRKIEST
	BIRL	BIRLE ▪ BIRLS
	BIRLE	BIRLED ▪ BIRLER ▪ BIRLES
	BIRLER	BIRLERS
	BIRLING	BIRLINGS
	BIRLINN	BIRLINNS
	BIRO	BIROS
	BIRR	BIRRS
	BIRRETTA	BIRRETTAS
	BIRSE	BIRSES
	BIRSLE	BIRSLED ▪ BIRSLES
	BIRTH	BIRTHS
	BIRTHDAY	BIRTHDAYS
	BIRTHDOM	BIRTHDOMS
	BIRTHING	BIRTHINGS
	BIRTHMARK	BIRTHMARKS
	BIRTHNAME	BIRTHNAMES
	BIRTHRATE	BIRTHRATES
	BIRTHROOT	BIRTHROOTS
	BIRTHWORT	BIRTHWORTS
	BIRYANI	BIRYANIS
IBIS ▪ OBIS	**BIS**	BISE ▪ BISH ▪ BISK ▪ BIST
	BISCACHA	BISCACHAS
	BISCUIT	BISCUITS ▪ BISCUITY
	BISE	BISES
	BISECT	BISECTS
	BISECTION	BISECTIONS
	BISECTOR	BISECTORS
IBISES	**BISES**	
	BISEXUAL	BISEXUALS
	BISHOP	BISHOPS
	BISHOPDOM	BISHOPDOMS
	BISHOPRIC	BISHOPRICS
	BISK	BISKS
	BISMAR	BISMARS
	BISMUTH	BISMUTHS
	BISNAGA	BISNAGAS
	BISON	BISONS
	BISQUE	BISQUES
	BISTABLE	BISTABLES
	BISTER	BISTERS
	BISTORT	BISTORTS
	BISTRE	BISTRED ▪ BISTRES
	BISTRO	BISTROS
	BISULFATE	BISULFATES
	BISULFIDE	BISULFIDES
	BISULFITE	BISULFITES
OBIT	**BIT**	BITE ▪ BITO ▪ BITS ▪ BITT
	BITCH	BITCHY
	BITCHFEST	BITCHFESTS
	BITE	BITER ▪ BITES
	BITEPLATE	BITEPLATES
OBITER	**BITER**	BITERS
	BITEWING	BITEWINGS
	BITING	BITINGS
	BITMAP	BITMAPS
	BITO	BITOS ▪ BITOU
OBITS	**BITS**	BITSY
	BITSER	BITSERS
	BITSTOCK	BITSTOCKS
	BITSTREAM	BITSTREAMS

FRONT HOOK	ROOT WORD	END HOOK
	BITT	BITTE · BITTS · BITTY
	BITTACLE	BITTACLES
	BITTE	BITTED · BITTEN · BITTER
	BITTER	BITTERN · BITTERS
	BITTERN	BITTERNS
	BITTERNUT	BITTERNUTS
	BITTIE	BITTIER · BITTIES
	BITTIES	BITTIEST
	BITTING	BITTINGS
	BITTOCK	BITTOCKS
	BITTOR	BITTORS
	BITTOUR	BITTOURS
	BITTUR	BITTURS
	BITUMEN	BITUMENS
	BIVALENCE	BIVALENCES
	BIVALENT	BIVALENTS
	BIVALVE	BIVALVED · BIVALVES
	BIVARIANT	BIVARIANTS
	BIVARIATE	BIVARIATES
	BIVINYL	BIVINYLS
	BIVOUAC	BIVOUACS
	BIZ	BIZE
	BIZARRE	BIZARRES
	BIZARRO	BIZARROS
	BIZCACHA	BIZCACHAS
	BIZE	BIZES
	BIZNAGA	BIZNAGAS
	BIZONE	BIZONES
	BIZZO	BIZZOS
	BLAB	BLABS
	BLABBER	BLABBERS
	BLABBING	BLABBINGS
	BLACK	BLACKS
	BLACKBALL	BLACKBALLS
	BLACKBAND	BLACKBANDS
	BLACKBIRD	BLACKBIRDS
	BLACKBOY	BLACKBOYS
	BLACKBUCK	BLACKBUCKS
	BLACKBUTT	BLACKBUTTS
	BLACKCAP	BLACKCAPS
	BLACKCOCK	BLACKCOCKS
	BLACKDAMP	BLACKDAMPS
	BLACKEN	BLACKENS
	BLACKENER	BLACKENERS
	BLACKFACE	BLACKFACED · BLACKFACES
	BLACKFIN	BLACKFINS
	BLACKGAME	BLACKGAMES
	BLACKGUM	BLACKGUMS
	BLACKHEAD	BLACKHEADS
	BLACKING	BLACKINGS
	BLACKJACK	BLACKJACKS
	BLACKLAND	BLACKLANDS
	BLACKLEAD	BLACKLEADS
	BLACKLEG	BLACKLEGS
	BLACKLIST	BLACKLISTS
	BLACKMAIL	BLACKMAILS
	BLACKOUT	BLACKOUTS
	BLACKPOLL	BLACKPOLLS
	BLACKTAIL	BLACKTAILS
	BLACKTOP	BLACKTOPS
	BLACKWOOD	BLACKWOODS
	BLAD	BLADE · BLADS · BLADY
	BLADDER	BLADDERS · BLADDERY
	BLADE	BLADED · BLADER · BLADES
	BLADER	BLADERS
	BLADEWORK	BLADEWORKS
	BLADING	BLADINGS
	BLAE	BLAER · BLAES
	BLAES	BLAEST

B

FRONT HOOK	ROOT WORD	END HOOK
	BLAFF	BLAFFS
	BLAG	BLAGS
	BLAGGER	BLAGGERS
	BLAGGING	BLAGGINGS
	BLAGUE	BLAGUER · BLAGUES
	BLAGUER	BLAGUERS
	BLAGUEUR	BLAGUEURS
	BLAH	BLAHS
	BLAIN	BLAINS
	BLAM	BLAME · BLAMS
	BLAME	BLAMED · BLAMER · BLAMES
	BLAMER	BLAMERS
	BLANCHER	BLANCHERS
	BLANCO	BLANCOS
	BLAND	BLANDS
	BLANK	BLANKS · BLANKY
	BLANKET	BLANKETS · BLANKETY
	BLANKING	BLANKINGS
	BLANQUET	BLANQUETS
	BLARE	BLARED · BLARES
	BLARNEY	BLARNEYS
	BLART	BLARTS
	BLASH	BLASHY
	BLASPHEME	BLASPHEMED · BLASPHEMER · BLASPHEMES
OBLAST	**BLAST**	BLASTS · BLASTY
	BLASTEMA	BLASTEMAL · BLASTEMAS
	BLASTER	BLASTERS
	BLASTIE	BLASTIER · BLASTIES
	BLASTIES	BLASTIEST
	BLASTING	BLASTINGS
	BLASTMENT	BLASTMENTS
	BLASTOFF	BLASTOFFS
	BLASTOID	BLASTOIDS
	BLASTOMA	BLASTOMAS
	BLASTOPOR	BLASTOPORE · BLASTOPORS
OBLASTS	**BLASTS**	
	BLASTULA	BLASTULAE · BLASTULAR · BLASTULAS
	BLAT	BLATE · BLATS · BLATT
ABLATE · OBLATE	**BLATE**	BLATER
	BLATHER	BLATHERS
	BLATHERER	BLATHERERS
	BLATT	BLATTS
	BLATTER	BLATTERS
	BLAUBOK	BLAUBOKS
	BLAUD	BLAUDS
	BLAW	BLAWN · BLAWS
	BLAWORT	BLAWORTS
	BLAY	BLAYS
ABLAZE	**BLAZE**	BLAZED · BLAZER · BLAZES
	BLAZER	BLAZERS
	BLAZON	BLAZONS
	BLAZONER	BLAZONERS
	BLAZONING	BLAZONINGS
	BLEACHER	BLEACHERS · BLEACHERY
	BLEACHING	BLEACHINGS
	BLEAK	BLEAKS · BLEAKY
	BLEAR	BLEARS · BLEARY
	BLEAT	BLEATS
	BLEATER	BLEATERS
	BLEATING	BLEATINGS
	BLEB	BLEBS
	BLEBBING	BLEBBINGS
ABLED	**BLED**	
	BLEE	BLEED · BLEEP · BLEES
	BLEED	BLEEDS
	BLEEDER	BLEEDERS
	BLEEDING	BLEEDINGS
	BLEEP	BLEEPS
	BLEEPER	BLEEPERS

FRONT HOOK	ROOT WORD	END HOOK
	BLELLUM	BLELLUMS
	BLEMISHER	BLEMISHERS
	BLENCHER	BLENCHERS
	BLEND	BLENDE ▪ BLENDS
	BLENDE	BLENDED ▪ BLENDER ▪ BLENDES
	BLENDER	BLENDERS
	BLENDING	BLENDINGS
	BLENNIOID	BLENNIOIDS
YBLENT	**BLENT**	
	BLERT	BLERTS
	BLESBOK	BLESBOKS
	BLESBUCK	BLESBUCKS
	BLESSER	BLESSERS
	BLESSING	BLESSINGS
ABLEST	**BLEST**	
ABLET	**BLET**	BLETS
	BLETHER	BLETHERS
	BLETHERER	BLETHERERS
ABLETS	**BLETS**	
	BLEWART	BLEWARTS
	BLEY	BLEYS
	BLIGHT	BLIGHTS ▪ BLIGHTY
	BLIGHTER	BLIGHTERS
	BLIGHTING	BLIGHTINGS
	BLIMBING	BLIMBINGS
	BLIMP	BLIMPS
	BLIN	BLIND ▪ BLING ▪ BLINI ▪ BLINK ▪ BLINS
		BLINY
	BLIND	BLINDS
	BLINDAGE	BLINDAGES
	BLINDER	BLINDERS
	BLINDFOLD	BLINDFOLDS
	BLINDGUT	BLINDGUTS
	BLINDING	BLINDINGS
	BLINDSIDE	BLINDSIDED ▪ BLINDSIDES
	BLINDWORM	BLINDWORMS
ABLING	**BLING**	BLINGS
ABLINGS	**BLINGS**	
	BLINI	BLINIS
	BLINK	BLINKS
	BLINKARD	BLINKARDS
	BLINKER	BLINKERS
ABLINS	**BLINS**	
	BLINTZ	BLINTZE
	BLINTZE	BLINTZES
	BLIP	BLIPS
	BLIPVERT	BLIPVERTS
	BLISTER	BLISTERS ▪ BLISTERY
	BLITE	BLITES
	BLITHE	BLITHER
	BLITHER	BLITHERS
	BLITZER	BLITZERS
	BLIZZARD	BLIZZARDS ▪ BLIZZARDY
	BLOAT	BLOATS
	BLOATER	BLOATERS
	BLOATING	BLOATINGS
	BLOATWARE	BLOATWARES
	BLOB	BLOBS
	BLOC	BLOCK ▪ BLOCS
	BLOCK	BLOCKS ▪ BLOCKY
	BLOCKADE	BLOCKADED ▪ BLOCKADER ▪ BLOCKADES
	BLOCKADER	BLOCKADERS
	BLOCKAGE	BLOCKAGES
	BLOCKBUST	BLOCKBUSTS
	BLOCKER	BLOCKERS
	BLOCKHEAD	BLOCKHEADS
	BLOCKHOLE	BLOCKHOLES
	BLOCKIE	BLOCKIER ▪ BLOCKIES
	BLOCKIES	BLOCKIEST

B

FRONT HOOK	ROOT WORD	END HOOK
	BLOCKING	BLOCKINGS
	BLOCKWORK	BLOCKWORKS
	BLOG	BLOGS
	BLOGGER	BLOGGERS
	BLOGGING	BLOGGINGS
	BLOKE	BLOKES = BLOKEY
	BLOKEDOM	BLOKEDOMS
	BLOND	BLONDE = BLONDS
	BLONDE	BLONDER = BLONDES
	BLONDES	BLONDEST
	BLONDINE	BLONDINED = BLONDINES
	BLONDING	BLONDINGS
	BLOOD	BLOODS = BLOODY
	BLOODBATH	BLOODBATHS
	BLOODFIN	BLOODFINS
	BLOODHEAT	BLOODHEATS
	BLOODIES	BLOODIEST
	BLOODING	BLOODINGS
	BLOODLINE	BLOODLINES
	BLOODLUST	BLOODLUSTS
	BLOODROOT	BLOODROOTS
	BLOODSHED	BLOODSHEDS
	BLOODWOOD	BLOODWOODS
	BLOODWORM	BLOODWORMS
	BLOODWORT	BLOODWORTS
ABLOOM	**BLOOM**	BLOOMS = BLOOMY
	BLOOMER	BLOOMERS = BLOOMERY
	BLOOP	BLOOPS
	BLOOPER	BLOOPERS
	BLOOSME	BLOOSMED = BLOOSMES
	BLOQUISTE	BLOQUISTES
	BLORE	BLORES
	BLOSSOM	BLOSSOMS = BLOSSOMY
	BLOT	BLOTS
	BLOTCH	BLOTCHY
	BLOTCHING	BLOTCHINGS
	BLOTTER	BLOTTERS
	BLOTTING	BLOTTINGS
	BLOUBOK	BLOUBOKS
	BLOUSE	BLOUSED = BLOUSES
	BLOUSON	BLOUSONS
	BLOVIATE	BLOVIATED = BLOVIATES
ABLOW	**BLOW**	BLOWN = BLOWS = BLOWY
	BLOWBACK	BLOWBACKS
	BLOWBALL	BLOWBALLS
	BLOWBY	BLOWBYS
	BLOWDOWN	BLOWDOWNS
	BLOWER	BLOWERS
	BLOWGUN	BLOWGUNS
	BLOWHARD	BLOWHARDS
	BLOWHOLE	BLOWHOLES
	BLOWIE	BLOWIER = BLOWIES
	BLOWIES	BLOWIEST
	BLOWJOB	BLOWJOBS *(offensive)*
	BLOWKART	BLOWKARTS
	BLOWLAMP	BLOWLAMPS
	BLOWOFF	BLOWOFFS
	BLOWOUT	BLOWOUTS
	BLOWPIPE	BLOWPIPES
	BLOWS	BLOWSE = BLOWSY
	BLOWSE	BLOWSED = BLOWSES
	BLOWTUBE	BLOWTUBES
	BLOWUP	BLOWUPS
	BLOWZE	BLOWZED = BLOWZES
	BLUB	BLUBS
	BLUBBER	BLUBBERS = BLUBBERY
	BLUBBERER	BLUBBERERS
	BLUCHER	BLUCHERS
	BLUDE	BLUDES

FRONT HOOK	ROOT WORD	END HOOK
	BLUDGE	BLUDGED ▪ BLUDGER ▪ BLUDGES
	BLUDGEON	BLUDGEONS
	BLUDGER	BLUDGERS
	BLUDIE	BLUDIER
	BLUE	BLUED ▪ BLUER ▪ BLUES ▪ BLUET ▪ BLUEY
	BLUEBACK	BLUEBACKS
	BLUEBALL	BLUEBALLS
	BLUEBEARD	BLUEBEARDS
	BLUEBEAT	BLUEBEATS
	BLUEBELL	BLUEBELLS
	BLUEBILL	BLUEBILLS
	BLUEBIRD	BLUEBIRDS
	BLUEBLOOD	BLUEBLOODS
	BLUEBOOK	BLUEBOOKS
	BLUEBUCK	BLUEBUCKS
	BLUECAP	BLUECAPS
	BLUECOAT	BLUECOATS
	BLUEFIN	BLUEFINS
	BLUEGILL	BLUEGILLS
	BLUEGOWN	BLUEGOWNS
	BLUEGUM	BLUEGUMS
	BLUEHEAD	BLUEHEADS
	BLUEING	BLUEINGS
	BLUEJACK	BLUEJACKS
	BLUEJAY	BLUEJAYS
	BLUELINE	BLUELINER ▪ BLUELINES
	BLUELINER	BLUELINERS
	BLUENOSE	BLUENOSED ▪ BLUENOSES
	BLUEPOINT	BLUEPOINTS
	BLUEPRINT	BLUEPRINTS
	BLUES	BLUEST ▪ BLUESY
	BLUESHIFT	BLUESHIFTS
	BLUESTEM	BLUESTEMS
	BLUESTONE	BLUESTONES
	BLUET	BLUETS
	BLUETICK	BLUETICKS
	BLUETIT	BLUETITS
	BLUETTE	BLUETTES
	BLUEWEED	BLUEWEEDS
	BLUEWING	BLUEWINGS
	BLUEWOOD	BLUEWOODS
	BLUEY	BLUEYS
	BLUFF	BLUFFS
	BLUFFER	BLUFFERS
	BLUID	BLUIDS ▪ BLUIDY
	BLUING	BLUINGS
	BLUME	BLUMED ▪ BLUMES
	BLUNDER	BLUNDERS
	BLUNDERER	BLUNDERERS
	BLUNGE	BLUNGED ▪ BLUNGER ▪ BLUNGES
	BLUNGER	BLUNGERS
	BLUNK	BLUNKS
	BLUNKER	BLUNKERS
	BLUNT	BLUNTS
	BLUNTHEAD	BLUNTHEADS
	BLUR	BLURB ▪ BLURS ▪ BLURT
	BLURB	BLURBS
	BLURBIST	BLURBISTS
	BLURT	BLURTS
	BLURTER	BLURTERS
	BLURTING	BLURTINGS
ABLUSH	**BLUSH**	
	BLUSHER	BLUSHERS
	BLUSHET	BLUSHETS
	BLUSHING	BLUSHINGS
	BLUSTER	BLUSTERS ▪ BLUSTERY
	BLUSTERER	BLUSTERERS
	BLUTWURST	BLUTWURSTS
	BLYPE	BLYPES

B

FRONT HOOK	ROOT WORD	END HOOK
ABO (offensive) · OBO	**BO**	BOA · BOB · BOD · BOG · BOH · BOI · BOK BON · BOO · BOP · BOR · BOS · BOT · BOW BOX · BOY
	BOA	BOAB · BOAK · BOAR · BOAS · BOAT
	BOAB	BOABS
	BOAK	BOAKS
	BOAR	BOARD · BOARS · BOART
ABOARD	**BOARD**	BOARDS
	BOARDER	BOARDERS
	BOARDING	BOARDINGS
	BOARDROOM	BOARDROOMS
	BOARDWALK	BOARDWALKS
	BOARHOUND	BOARHOUNDS
	BOART	BOARTS
	BOAS	BOAST
	BOAST	BOASTS
	BOASTER	BOASTERS
	BOASTING	BOASTINGS
	BOAT	BOATS
	BOATBILL	BOATBILLS
	BOATEL	BOATELS
	BOATER	BOATERS
	BOATFUL	BOATFULS
	BOATHOOK	BOATHOOKS
	BOATHOUSE	BOATHOUSES
	BOATIE	BOATIES
	BOATING	BOATINGS
	BOATLIFT	BOATLIFTS
	BOATLOAD	BOATLOADS
	BOATNECK	BOATNECKS
	BOATSWAIN	BOATSWAINS
	BOATTAIL	BOATTAILS
	BOATYARD	BOATYARDS
	BOB	BOBA · BOBS
	BOBA	BOBAC · BOBAK · BOBAS
	BOBAC	BOBACS
	BOBAK	BOBAKS
	BOBBEJAAN	BOBBEJAANS
	BOBBER	BOBBERS · BOBBERY
	BOBBIN	BOBBING · BOBBINS
	BOBBINET	BOBBINETS
	BOBBITT	BOBBITTS
	BOBBLE	BOBBLED · BOBBLES
	BOBBYSOCK	BOBBYSOCKS
	BOBCAT	BOBCATS
	BOBECHE	BOBECHES
	BOBFLOAT	BOBFLOATS
	BOBLET	BOBLETS
	BOBOL	BOBOLS
	BOBOLINK	BOBOLINKS
	BOBOTIE	BOBOTIES
	BOBOWLER	BOBOWLERS
	BOBSLED	BOBSLEDS
	BOBSLEIGH	BOBSLEIGHS
	BOBSTAY	BOBSTAYS
	BOBTAIL	BOBTAILS
	BOBWEIGHT	BOBWEIGHTS
	BOBWHEEL	BOBWHEELS
	BOBWHITE	BOBWHITES
	BOBWIG	BOBWIGS
	BOCACCIO	BOCACCIOS
	BOCAGE	BOCAGES
	BOCCA	BOCCAS
	BOCCE	BOCCES
	BOCCI	BOCCIA · BOCCIE · BOCCIS
	BOCCIA	BOCCIAS
	BOCCIE	BOCCIES
	BOCHE	BOCHES (offensive)
	BOCK	BOCKS

FRONT HOOK	ROOT WORD	END HOOK
	BOCKED	BOCKEDY
	BOD	BODE · BODS · BODY
	BODACH	BODACHS
	BODDLE	BODDLES
ABODE	**BODE**	BODED · BODES
ABODED	**BODED**	
	BODEGA	BODEGAS ·
	BODEGUERO	BODEGUEROS
ABODEMENT	**BODEMENT**	BODEMENTS
ABODEMENTS	**BODEMENTS**	
ABODES	**BODES**	
	BODGE	BODGED · BODGER · BODGES
	BODGER	BODGERS
	BODGIE	BODGIER · BODGIES
	BODGIES	BODGIEST
	BODHRAN	BODHRANS
	BODICE	BODICES
	BODIKIN	BODIKINS
ABODING	**BODING**	BODINGS
	BODKIN	BODKINS
	BODLE	BODLES
	BODRAG	BODRAGS
	BODYBOARD	BODYBOARDS
	BODYCHECK	BODYCHECKS
	BODYGUARD	BODYGUARDS
	BODYLINE	BODYLINES
	BODYSHELL	BODYSHELLS
	BODYSUIT	BODYSUITS
	BODYSURF	BODYSURFS
	BODYWORK	BODYWORKS
	BOEHMITE	BOEHMITES
	BOEP	BOEPS
	BOERBUL	BOERBULS
	BOERTJIE	BOERTJIES
	BOET	BOETS
	BOFF	BOFFO · BOFFS
	BOFFIN	BOFFING · BOFFINS
	BOFFO	BOFFOS
	BOFFOLA	BOFFOLAS
	BOG	BOGS · BOGY
	BOGAN	BOGANS
	BOGART	BOGARTS
	BOGBEAN	BOGBEANS
	BOGEY	BOGEYS
	BOGEYISM	BOGEYISMS
	BOGGARD	BOGGARDS
	BOGGART	BOGGARTS
	BOGGER	BOGGERS
	BOGGLE	BOGGLED · BOGGLER · BOGGLES
	BOGGLER	BOGGLERS
	BOGIE	BOGIED · BOGIES
	BOGLAND	BOGLANDS
	BOGLE	BOGLES
	BOGOAK	BOGOAKS
	BOGONG	BOGONGS
	BOGWOOD	BOGWOODS
	BOGYISM	BOGYISMS
	BOH	BOHO · BOHS
	BOHEA	BOHEAS
	BOHEMIA	BOHEMIAN · BOHEMIAS
	BOHEMIAN	BOHEMIANS
	BOHO	BOHOS
	BOHRIUM	BOHRIUMS
	BOHUNK	BOHUNKS (offensive)
	BOI	BOIL · BOIS
ABOIL	**BOIL**	BOILS
	BOILER	BOILERS · BOILERY
	BOILING	BOILINGS
	BOILOFF	BOILOFFS

93

3

FRONT HOOK	ROOT WORD	END HOOK
	BOILOVER	BOILOVERS
	BOING	BOINGS
	BOINK	BOINKS
	BOISERIE	BOISERIES
	BOITE	BOITES
	BOK	BOKE · BOKO · BOKS
	BOKE	BOKED · BOKES
	BOKO	BOKOS
	BOLA	BOLAR · BOLAS
	BOLD	BOLDS
	BOLDEN	BOLDENS
	BOLDFACE	BOLDFACED · BOLDFACES
OBOLE	**BOLE**	BOLES
	BOLECTION	BOLECTIONS
	BOLERO	BOLEROS
OBOLES	**BOLES**	
	BOLETE	BOLETES
	BOLIDE	BOLIDES
	BOLINE	BOLINES
	BOLIVAR	BOLIVARS
	BOLIVIA	BOLIVIAS
	BOLIVIANO	BOLIVIANOS
	BOLL	BOLLS
	BOLLARD	BOLLARDS
	BOLLETRIE	BOLLETRIES
	BOLLOCK	BOLLOCKS
	BOLLWORM	BOLLWORMS
	BOLO	BOLOS
	BOLOGNA	BOLOGNAS
	BOLOGRAPH	BOLOGRAPHS
	BOLOMETER	BOLOMETERS
	BOLONEY	BOLONEYS
	BOLSHEVIK	BOLSHEVIKI · BOLSHEVIKS
	BOLSHIE	BOLSHIER · BOLSHIES
	BOLSHIES	BOLSHIEST
	BOLSON	BOLSONS
	BOLSTER	BOLSTERS
	BOLSTERER	BOLSTERERS
	BOLT	BOLTS
	BOLTER	BOLTERS
	BOLTHEAD	BOLTHEADS
	BOLTHOLE	BOLTHOLES
	BOLTING	BOLTINGS
	BOLTONIA	BOLTONIAS
	BOLTROPE	BOLTROPES
OBOLUS	**BOLUS**	
ABOMA	**BOMA**	BOMAS
ABOMAS	**BOMAS**	
	BOMB	BOMBE · BOMBO · BOMBS
	BOMBARD	BOMBARDE · BOMBARDS
	BOMBARDE	BOMBARDED · BOMBARDER · BOMBARDES
	BOMBARDER	BOMBARDERS
	BOMBARDON	BOMBARDONS
	BOMBASINE	BOMBASINES
	BOMBAST	BOMBASTS
	BOMBASTER	BOMBASTERS
	BOMBAZINE	BOMBAZINES
	BOMBE	BOMBED · BOMBER · BOMBES
	BOMBER	BOMBERS
	BOMBESIN	BOMBESINS
	BOMBILATE	BOMBILATED · BOMBILATES
	BOMBINATE	BOMBINATED · BOMBINATES
	BOMBING	BOMBINGS
	BOMBLET	BOMBLETS
	BOMBLOAD	BOMBLOADS
	BOMBO	BOMBOS
	BOMBORA	BOMBORAS
	BOMBPROOF	BOMBPROOFS
	BOMBSHELL	BOMBSHELLS

FRONT HOOK	ROOT WORD	END HOOK
	BOMBSIGHT	BOMBSIGHTS
	BOMBSITE	BOMBSITES
	BOMBYCID	BOMBYCIDS
	BOMMIE	BOMMIES
EBON	BON	BONA · BOND · BONE · BONG · BONK · BONY
	BONACI	BONACIS
	BONAMIA	BONAMIAS
	BONANZA	BONANZAS
	BONBON	BONBONS
	BONCE	BONCES
	BOND	BONDS
	BONDAGE	BONDAGER · BONDAGES
	BONDAGER	BONDAGERS
	BONDER	BONDERS
	BONDING	BONDINGS
	BONDMAID	BONDMAIDS
	BONDSTONE	BONDSTONES
	BONDUC	BONDUCS
	BONE	BONED · BONER · BONES · BONEY
	BONEBLACK	BONEBLACKS
	BONEHEAD	BONEHEADS
	BONEMEAL	BONEMEALS
	BONER	BONERS
	BONESET	BONESETS
	BONEYARD	BONEYARDS
	BONFIRE	BONFIRES
	BONG	BONGO · BONGS
	BONGO	BONGOS
	BONGOIST	BONGOISTS
	BONGRACE	BONGRACES
	BONHAM	BONHAMS
	BONHOMIE	BONHOMIES
	BONHOMMIE	BONHOMMIES
	BONIATO	BONIATOS
	BONIBELL	BONIBELLS
	BONIE	BONIER
	BONIFACE	BONIFACES
	BONILASSE	BONILASSES
	BONING	BONINGS
	BONISM	BONISMS
EBONIST	BONIST	BONISTS
EBONISTS	BONISTS	
	BONITA	BONITAS
	BONITO	BONITOS
	BONK	BONKS
	BONKING	BONKINGS
	BONNE	BONNES · BONNET
	BONNET	BONNETS
	BONNIBELL	BONNIBELLS
	BONNIE	BONNIER · BONNIES
	BONNIES	BONNIEST
	BONNOCK	BONNOCKS
	BONOBO	BONOBOS
	BONSAI	BONSAIS
	BONSELA	BONSELAS
	BONSELLA	BONSELLAS
	BONSPELL	BONSPELLS
	BONSPIEL	BONSPIELS
	BONTEBOK	BONTEBOKS
	BONXIE	BONXIES
EBONY	BONY	
	BONZE	BONZER · BONZES
	BOO	BOOB · BOOH · BOOK · BOOL · BOOM · BOON · BOOR · BOOS · BOOT
	BOOB	BOOBS · BOOBY
	BOOBHEAD	BOOBHEADS
	BOOBIALLA	BOOBIALLAS
	BOOBIE	BOOBIES
	BOOBIRD	BOOBIRDS

3

FRONT HOOK	ROOT WORD	END HOOK
	BOOBOISIE	BOOBOISIES
	BOOBOO	BOOBOOK = BOOBOOS
	BOOBOOK	BOOBOOKS
	BOOBYISM	BOOBYISMS
	BOOCOO	BOOCOOS
	BOODIE	BOODIED = BOODIES
	BOODLE	BOODLED = BOODLER = BOODLES
	BOODLER	BOODLERS
	BOOFHEAD	BOOFHEADS
	BOOGER	BOOGERS
	BOOGEY	BOOGEYS
	BOOGIE	BOOGIED = BOOGIES
	BOOH	BOOHS
	BOOHAI	BOOHAIS
	BOOHOO	BOOHOOS
	BOOJUM	BOOJUMS
EBOOK	**BOOK**	BOOKS = BOOKY
	BOOKCASE	BOOKCASES
	BOOKEND	BOOKENDS
	BOOKER	BOOKERS
	BOOKFUL	BOOKFULS
	BOOKIE	BOOKIER = BOOKIES
	BOOKIES	BOOKIEST
	BOOKING	BOOKINGS
	BOOKLAND	BOOKLANDS
	BOOKLET	BOOKLETS
	BOOKLIGHT	BOOKLIGHTS
	BOOKLORE	BOOKLORES
	BOOKMAKER	BOOKMAKERS
	BOOKMARK	BOOKMARKS
	BOOKOO	BOOKOOS
	BOOKPLATE	BOOKPLATES
	BOOKRACK	BOOKRACKS
	BOOKREST	BOOKRESTS
EBOOKS	**BOOKS**	BOOKSY
	BOOKSHOP	BOOKSHOPS
	BOOKSIE	BOOKSIER
	BOOKSTALL	BOOKSTALLS
	BOOKSTAND	BOOKSTANDS
	BOOKSTORE	BOOKSTORES
	BOOKWORK	BOOKWORKS
	BOOKWORM	BOOKWORMS
	BOOL	BOOLS
	BOOM	BOOMS = BOOMY
	BOOMER	BOOMERS
	BOOMERANG	BOOMERANGS
	BOOMING	BOOMINGS
	BOOMKIN	BOOMKINS
	BOOMLET	BOOMLETS
	BOOMSLANG	BOOMSLANGS
	BOOMTOWN	BOOMTOWNS
ABOON	**BOON**	BOONG = BOONS
	BOONDOCK	BOONDOCKS
	BOONER	BOONERS
	BOONG	BOONGA = BOONGS (offensive)
	BOONGA	BOONGAS
	BOOR	BOORD = BOORS
	BOORD	BOORDE = BOORDS
	BOORDE	BOORDES
	BOORKA	BOORKAS
	BOORTREE	BOORTREES
	BOOS	BOOSE = BOOST
	BOOSE	BOOSED = BOOSES
	BOOST	BOOSTS
	BOOSTER	BOOSTERS
	BOOT	BOOTH = BOOTS = BOOTY
	BOOTBLACK	BOOTBLACKS
	BOOTEE	BOOTEES
	BOOTH	BOOTHS

FRONT HOOK	ROOT WORD	END HOOK
	BOOTIE	BOOTIES
	BOOTIKIN	BOOTIKINS
	BOOTJACK	BOOTJACKS
	BOOTLACE	BOOTLACES
	BOOTLAST	BOOTLASTS
	BOOTLEG	BOOTLEGS
	BOOTLICK	BOOTLICKS
	BOOTMAKER	BOOTMAKERS
	BOOTSTRAP	BOOTSTRAPS
	BOOZE	BOOZED ▪ BOOZER ▪ BOOZES ▪ BOOZEY
	BOOZER	BOOZERS
	BOOZING	BOOZINGS
	BOP	BOPS
	BOPEEP	BOPEEPS
	BOPPER	BOPPERS
	BOR	BORA ▪ BORD ▪ BORE ▪ BORK ▪ BORM ▪ BORN ▪ BORS ▪ BORT
	BORA	BORAK ▪ BORAL ▪ BORAS ▪ BORAX
	BORACHIO	BORACHIOS
	BORACITE	BORACITES
	BORAGE	BORAGES
	BORAK	BORAKS
ABORAL	**BORAL**	BORALS
	BORANE	BORANES
	BORATE	BORATED ▪ BORATES
	BORAZON	BORAZONS
ABORD	**BORD**	BORDE ▪ BORDS
	BORDAR	BORDARS
	BORDE	BORDEL ▪ BORDER ▪ BORDES
	BORDEL	BORDELS
	BORDELLO	BORDELLOS
	BORDER	BORDERS
	BORDEREAU	BORDEREAUX
	BORDERER	BORDERERS
ABORDS	**BORDS**	
	BORDURE	BORDURES
ABORE ▪ YBORE	**BORE**	BORED ▪ BOREE ▪ BOREL ▪ BORER ▪ BORES
	BORECOLE	BORECOLES
	BOREDOM	BOREDOMS
	BOREE	BOREEN ▪ BOREES
	BOREEN	BOREENS
	BOREHOLE	BOREHOLES
	BORER	BORERS
	BORESCOPE	BORESCOPES
	BORGHETTO	BORGHETTOS
	BORGO	BORGOS
	BORIDE	BORIDES
	BORING	BORINGS
	BORK	BORKS
	BORM	BORMS
	BORN	BORNA ▪ BORNE
ABORNE	**BORNE**	
	BORNEOL	BORNEOLS
	BORNITE	BORNITES
	BORNYL	BORNYLS
	BORON	BORONS
	BORONIA	BORONIAS
	BOROUGH	BOROUGHS
	BORREL	BORRELL
	BORRELIA	BORRELIAS
	BORROW	BORROWS
	BORROWER	BORROWERS
	BORROWING	BORROWINGS
	BORSCH	BORSCHT
	BORSCHT	BORSCHTS
	BORSHT	BORSHTS
	BORSIC	BORSICS
	BORSTAL	BORSTALL ▪ BORSTALS
	BORSTALL	BORSTALLS

FRONT HOOK	ROOT WORD	END HOOK
ABORT	**BORT**	BORTS ▪ BORTY ▪ BORTZ
ABORTS	**BORTS**	
	BORZOI	BORZOIS
ABOS (*offensive*) ▪ OBOS	**BOS**	BOSH ▪ BOSK ▪ BOSS
	BOSBERAAD	BOSBERAADS
	BOSBOK	BOSBOKS
	BOSCAGE	BOSCAGES
	BOSCHBOK	BOSCHBOKS
	BOSCHE	BOSCHES (*offensive*)
	BOSCHVARK	BOSCHVARKS
	BOSCHVELD	BOSCHVELDS
	BOSHBOK	BOSHBOKS
	BOSHVARK	BOSHVARKS
	BOSK	BOSKS ▪ BOSKY
	BOSKAGE	BOSKAGES
	BOSKET	BOSKETS
	BOSOM	BOSOMS ▪ BOSOMY
	BOSON	BOSONS
	BOSQUE	BOSQUES ▪ BOSQUET
	BOSQUET	BOSQUETS
	BOSS	BOSSY
	BOSSBOY	BOSSBOYS
	BOSSDOM	BOSSDOMS
	BOSSES	BOSSEST
	BOSSET	BOSSETS
	BOSSIES	BOSSIEST
	BOSSISM	BOSSISMS
	BOSTANGI	BOSTANGIS
	BOSTHOON	BOSTHOONS
	BOSTON	BOSTONS
	BOSUN	BOSUNS
	BOT	BOTA ▪ BOTH ▪ BOTS ▪ BOTT
	BOTA	BOTAS
	BOTANIC	BOTANICA ▪ BOTANICS
	BOTANICA	BOTANICAL ▪ BOTANICAS
	BOTANICAL	BOTANICALS
	BOTANISE	BOTANISED ▪ BOTANISER ▪ BOTANISES
	BOTANISER	BOTANISERS
	BOTANIST	BOTANISTS
	BOTANIZE	BOTANIZED ▪ BOTANIZER ▪ BOTANIZES
	BOTANIZER	BOTANIZERS
	BOTARGO	BOTARGOS
	BOTCH	BOTCHY
	BOTCHER	BOTCHERS ▪ BOTCHERY
	BOTCHING	BOTCHINGS
	BOTEL	BOTELS
	BOTH	BOTHY
	BOTHAN	BOTHANS
	BOTHER	BOTHERS
	BOTHIE	BOTHIES
	BOTHOLE	BOTHOLES
	BOTHRIUM	BOTHRIUMS
	BOTNET	BOTNETS
	BOTONE	BOTONEE
	BOTT	BOTTE ▪ BOTTS ▪ BOTTY
	BOTTE	BOTTED ▪ BOTTES
	BOTTEGA	BOTTEGAS
	BOTTINE	BOTTINES
	BOTTLE	BOTTLED ▪ BOTTLER ▪ BOTTLES
	BOTTLEFUL	BOTTLEFULS
	BOTTLER	BOTTLERS
	BOTTLING	BOTTLINGS
	BOTTOM	BOTTOMS
	BOTTOMER	BOTTOMERS
	BOTULIN	BOTULINS
	BOTULINUM	BOTULINUMS
	BOTULISM	BOTULISMS
	BOUBOU	BOUBOUS
	BOUCHE	BOUCHEE ▪ BOUCHES

FRONT HOOK	ROOT WORD	END HOOK
	BOUCHEE	BOUCHEES
	BOUCLE	BOUCLEE ▪ BOUCLES
	BOUCLEE	BOUCLEES
	BOUDERIE	BOUDERIES
	BOUDIN	BOUDINS
	BOUDOIR	BOUDOIRS
	BOUFFANT	BOUFFANTS
	BOUFFE	BOUFFES
	BOUGE	BOUGED ▪ BOUGES ▪ BOUGET
	BOUGET	BOUGETS
	BOUGH	BOUGHS ▪ BOUGHT
	BOUGHPOT	BOUGHPOTS
ABOUGHT	BOUGHT	BOUGHTS
	BOUGIE	BOUGIES
	BOUILLI	BOUILLIS
	BOUILLON	BOUILLONS
	BOUK	BOUKS
	BOULDER	BOULDERS ▪ BOULDERY
	BOULDERER	BOULDERERS
	BOULE	BOULES
	BOULEVARD	BOULEVARDS
	BOULLE	BOULLES
	BOULT	BOULTS
	BOULTER	BOULTERS
	BOULTING	BOULTINGS
	BOUN	BOUND ▪ BOUNS
	BOUNCE	BOUNCED ▪ BOUNCER ▪ BOUNCES
	BOUNCER	BOUNCERS
ABOUND ▪ YBOUND	BOUND	BOUNDS
ABOUNDED	BOUNDED	
YBOUNDEN	BOUNDEN	
	BOUNDER	BOUNDERS
ABOUNDING	BOUNDING	
ABOUNDS	BOUNDS	
	BOUNTREE	BOUNTREES
	BOUNTYHED	BOUNTYHEDS
	BOUQUET	BOUQUETS
	BOURASQUE	BOURASQUES
	BOURBON	BOURBONS
	BOURD	BOURDS
	BOURDER	BOURDERS
	BOURDON	BOURDONS
	BOURG	BOURGS
	BOURGEOIS	BOURGEOISE
	BOURGEON	BOURGEONS
	BOURKHA	BOURKHAS
	BOURLAW	BOURLAWS
	BOURN	BOURNE ▪ BOURNS
	BOURNE	BOURNES
	BOURREE	BOURREES
	BOURRIDE	BOURRIDES
	BOURSE	BOURSES
	BOURSIER	BOURSIERS
	BOURSIN	BOURSINS
	BOURTREE	BOURTREES
	BOUSE	BOUSED ▪ BOUSES
	BOUSOUKI	BOUSOUKIA ▪ BOUSOUKIS
ABOUT	BOUT	BOUTS
	BOUTADE	BOUTADES
	BOUTIQUE	BOUTIQUES ▪ BOUTIQUEY
	BOUTON	BOUTONS
	BOUTONNE	BOUTONNEE
ABOUTS	BOUTS	
	BOUVARDIA	BOUVARDIAS
	BOUVIER	BOUVIERS
	BOUZOUKI	BOUZOUKIA ▪ BOUZOUKIS
OBOVATE	BOVATE	BOVATES
	BOVID	BOVIDS
	BOVINE	BOVINES

FRONT HOOK	ROOT WORD	END HOOK
	BOVVER	BOVVERS
	BOW	BOWL · BOWR · BOWS
	BOWAT	BOWATS
	BOWEL	BOWELS
	BOWER	BOWERS · BOWERY
	BOWERBIRD	BOWERBIRDS
	BOWET	BOWETS
	BOWFIN	BOWFINS
	BOWGET	BOWGETS
	BOWHEAD	BOWHEADS
	BOWHUNTER	BOWHUNTERS
	BOWING	BOWINGS
	BOWKNOT	BOWKNOTS
	BOWL	BOWLS
	BOWLDER	BOWLDERS
	BOWLEG	BOWLEGS
	BOWLER	BOWLERS
	BOWLFUL	BOWLFULS
	BOWLINE	BOWLINES
	BOWLING	BOWLINGS
	BOWNE	BOWNED · BOWNES
	BOWPOT	BOWPOTS
	BOWR	BOWRS
	BOWS	BOWSE
	BOWSAW	BOWSAWS
	BOWSE	BOWSED · BOWSER · BOWSES · BOWSEY
	BOWSER	BOWSERS
	BOWSEY	BOWSEYS
	BOWSHOT	BOWSHOTS
	BOWSIE	BOWSIES
	BOWSPRIT	BOWSPRITS
	BOWSTRING	BOWSTRINGS
	BOWWOW	BOWWOWS
	BOWYANG	BOWYANGS
	BOWYER	BOWYERS
	BOX	BOXY
	BOXBALL	BOXBALLS
	BOXBOARD	BOXBOARDS
	BOXCAR	BOXCARS
	BOXER	BOXERS
	BOXERCISE	BOXERCISES
	BOXFUL	BOXFULS
	BOXHAUL	BOXHAULS
	BOXING	BOXINGS
	BOXKEEPER	BOXKEEPERS
	BOXROOM	BOXROOMS
	BOXTHORN	BOXTHORNS
	BOXWALLAH	BOXWALLAHS
	BOXWOOD	BOXWOODS
	BOY	BOYF · BOYG · BOYO · BOYS
	BOYAR	BOYARD · BOYARS
	BOYARD	BOYARDS
	BOYARISM	BOYARISMS
	BOYAU	BOYAUX
	BOYCHICK	BOYCHICKS
	BOYCHIK	BOYCHIKS
	BOYCOTT	BOYCOTTS
	BOYCOTTER	BOYCOTTERS
	BOYF	BOYFS
	BOYFRIEND	BOYFRIENDS
	BOYG	BOYGS
	BOYHOOD	BOYHOODS
	BOYLA	BOYLAS
	BOYO	BOYOS
	BOYS	BOYSY
	BOZO	BOZOS
	BRA	BRAD · BRAE · BRAG · BRAK · BRAN BRAS · BRAT · BRAW · BRAY
	BRAAI	BRAAIS

FRONT HOOK	ROOT WORD	END HOOK
	BRAATA	BRAATAS
	BRABBLE	BRABBLED ▪ BRABBLER ▪ BRABBLES
	BRABBLER	BRABBLERS
	BRACE	BRACED ▪ BRACER ▪ BRACES
	BRACELET	BRACELETS
	BRACER	BRACERO ▪ BRACERS
	BRACERO	BRACEROS
	BRACH	BRACHS
	BRACHAH	BRACHAHS
	BRACHET	BRACHETS
ABRACHIA	**BRACHIA**	BRACHIAL
	BRACHIAL	BRACHIALS
	BRACHIATE	BRACHIATED ▪ BRACHIATES
	BRACING	BRACINGS
	BRACIOLA	BRACIOLAS
	BRACIOLE	BRACIOLES
	BRACK	BRACKS
	BRACKEN	BRACKENS
	BRACKET	BRACKETS
	BRACONID	BRACONIDS
	BRACT	BRACTS
EBRACTEATE	**BRACTEATE**	BRACTEATES
	BRACTEOLE	BRACTEOLES
	BRACTLET	BRACTLETS
	BRAD	BRADS
	BRADAWL	BRADAWLS
	BRADOON	BRADOONS
	BRAE	BRAES
	BRAEHEID	BRAEHEIDS
	BRAG	BRAGS
	BRAGGART	BRAGGARTS
	BRAGGER	BRAGGERS
	BRAGGING	BRAGGINGS
	BRAHMA	BRAHMAN ▪ BRAHMAS
	BRAHMAN	BRAHMANI ▪ BRAHMANS
	BRAHMANI	BRAHMANIS
	BRAHMANIS	BRAHMANISM ▪ BRAHMANIST
	BRAHMIN	BRAHMINS
ABRAID	**BRAID**	BRAIDE ▪ BRAIDS
	BRAIDE	BRAIDED ▪ BRAIDER
ABRAIDED	**BRAIDED**	
	BRAIDER	BRAIDERS
ABRAIDING	**BRAIDING**	BRAIDINGS
ABRAIDS	**BRAIDS**	
	BRAIL	BRAILS
	BRAILLE	BRAILLED ▪ BRAILLER ▪ BRAILLES
	BRAILLER	BRAILLERS
	BRAILLIST	BRAILLISTS
	BRAIN	BRAINS ▪ BRAINY
	BRAINCASE	BRAINCASES
	BRAINFART	BRAINFARTS
	BRAINIAC	BRAINIACS
	BRAINPAN	BRAINPANS
	BRAINSTEM	BRAINSTEMS
	BRAINWAVE	BRAINWAVES
	BRAIRD	BRAIRDS
	BRAISE	BRAISED ▪ BRAISES
	BRAIZE	BRAIZES
	BRAK	BRAKE ▪ BRAKS ▪ BRAKY
	BRAKE	BRAKED ▪ BRAKES
	BRAKEAGE	BRAKEAGES
	BRAMBLE	BRAMBLED ▪ BRAMBLES
	BRAMBLING	BRAMBLINGS
	BRAME	BRAMES
	BRAN	BRAND ▪ BRANK ▪ BRANS ▪ BRANT
	BRANCARD	BRANCARDS
	BRANCH	BRANCHY
	BRANCHER	BRANCHERS ▪ BRANCHERY
	BRANCHIA	BRANCHIAE ▪ BRANCHIAL

FRONT HOOK	ROOT WORD	END HOOK
ABRANCHIAL	**BRANCHIAL**	
	BRANCHING	BRANCHINGS
	BRANCHLET	BRANCHLETS
	BRAND	BRANDS · BRANDY
	BRANDADE	BRANDADES
	BRANDER	BRANDERS
	BRANDING	BRANDINGS
	BRANDISE	BRANDISES
	BRANDLING	BRANDLINGS
	BRANDRETH	BRANDRETHS
	BRANGLE	BRANGLED · BRANGLES
	BRANGLING	BRANGLINGS
	BRANK	BRANKS · BRANKY
	BRANLE	BRANLES
	BRANNER	BRANNERS
	BRANNIGAN	BRANNIGANS
	BRANSLE	BRANSLES
	BRANT	BRANTS
	BRANTAIL	BRANTAILS
	BRANTLE	BRANTLES
	BRAS	BRASH · BRASS · BRAST
	BRASCO	BRASCOS
	BRASERO	BRASEROS
	BRASH	BRASHY
	BRASHES	BRASHEST
	BRASIER	BRASIERS
	BRASIL	BRASILS
	BRASILEIN	BRASILEINS
	BRASILIN	BRASILINS
	BRASS	BRASSY
	BRASSAGE	BRASSAGES
	BRASSARD	BRASSARDS
	BRASSART	BRASSARTS
	BRASSERIE	BRASSERIES
	BRASSET	BRASSETS
	BRASSICA	BRASSICAS
	BRASSIE	BRASSIER · BRASSIES
	BRASSIER	BRASSIERE
	BRASSIERE	BRASSIERES
	BRASSIES	BRASSIEST
	BRASSWARE	BRASSWARES
	BRAST	BRASTS
	BRAT	BRATS
	BRATCHET	BRATCHETS
	BRATLING	BRATLINGS
	BRATPACK	BRATPACKS
	BRATTICE	BRATTICED · BRATTICES
	BRATTLE	BRATTLED · BRATTLES
	BRATTLING	BRATTLINGS
	BRATWURST	BRATWURSTS
	BRAUNITE	BRAUNITES
	BRAVA	BRAVAS
	BRAVADO	BRAVADOS
	BRAVE	BRAVED · BRAVER · BRAVES
	BRAVER	BRAVERS · BRAVERY
	BRAVES	BRAVEST
	BRAVO	BRAVOS
	BRAVURA	BRAVURAS
	BRAW	BRAWL · BRAWN · BRAWS
	BRAWL	BRAWLS · BRAWLY
	BRAWLER	BRAWLERS
	BRAWLIE	BRAWLIER
	BRAWLING	BRAWLINGS
	BRAWN	BRAWNS · BRAWNY
ABRAY	**BRAY**	BRAYS
ABRAYED	**BRAYED**	
	BRAYER	BRAYERS
ABRAYING	**BRAYING**	
ABRAYS	**BRAYS**	

FRONT HOOK	ROOT WORD	END HOOK
	BRAZA	BRAZAS
	BRAZE	BRAZED ▪ BRAZEN ▪ BRAZER ▪ BRAZES
	BRAZEN	BRAZENS
	BRAZER	BRAZERS
	BRAZIER	BRAZIERS ▪ BRAZIERY
	BRAZIL	BRAZILS
	BRAZILEIN	BRAZILEINS
	BRAZILIN	BRAZILINS
	BREACHER	BREACHERS
	BREAD	BREADS ▪ BREADY
	BREADHEAD	BREADHEADS
	BREADLINE	BREADLINES
	BREADNUT	BREADNUTS
	BREADROOM	BREADROOMS
	BREADROOT	BREADROOTS
	BREADTH	BREADTHS
	BREAK	BREAKS
	BREAKABLE	BREAKABLES
	BREAKAGE	BREAKAGES
	BREAKAWAY	BREAKAWAYS
	BREAKBEAT	BREAKBEATS
	BREAKDOWN	BREAKDOWNS
	BREAKER	BREAKERS
	BREAKEVEN	BREAKEVENS
	BREAKFAST	BREAKFASTS
	BREAKING	BREAKINGS
	BREAKOFF	BREAKOFFS
	BREAKOUT	BREAKOUTS
	BREAKTIME	BREAKTIMES
	BREAKUP	BREAKUPS
	BREAKWALL	BREAKWALLS
	BREAM	BREAMS
	BREARE	BREARES
	BREASKIT	BREASKITS
ABREAST	**BREAST**	BREASTS
	BREASTPIN	BREASTPINS
	BREATH	BREATHE ▪ BREATHS ▪ BREATHY
	BREATHE	BREATHED ▪ BREATHER ▪ BREATHES
	BREATHER	BREATHERS
	BREATHING	BREATHINGS
	BRECCIA	BRECCIAL ▪ BRECCIAS
	BRECCIATE	BRECCIATED ▪ BRECCIATES
	BRECHAM	BRECHAMS
	BRECHAN	BRECHANS
	BRED	BREDE ▪ BREDS
	BREDE	BREDED ▪ BREDES
	BREDIE	BREDIES
	BREE	BREED ▪ BREEM ▪ BREER ▪ BREES
	BREECHING	BREECHINGS
	BREED	BREEDS
	BREEDER	BREEDERS
	BREEDING	BREEDINGS
	BREENGE	BREENGED ▪ BREENGES
	BREER	BREERS
	BREES	BREESE ▪ BREEST
	BREESE	BREESES
	BREEST	BREESTS
	BREEZE	BREEZED ▪ BREEZES
	BREEZEWAY	BREEZEWAYS
	BREHON	BREHONS
	BREI	BREID ▪ BREIS
	BREID	BREIDS
	BREINGE	BREINGED ▪ BREINGES
	BREIS	BREIST
	BREIST	BREISTS
	BRELOQUE	BRELOQUES
	BREN	BRENS ▪ BRENT
	BRENNE	BRENNES
YBRENT	**BRENT**	BRENTS

FRONT HOOK	ROOT WORD	END HOOK
	BRER	BRERE · BRERS
	BRERE	BRERES
	BRETASCHE	BRETASCHES
	BRETESSE	BRETESSES
	BRETON	BRETONS
	BRETTICE	BRETTICED · BRETTICES
	BREVE	BREVES · BREVET
	BREVET	BREVETE · BREVETS
	BREVETE	BREVETED
	BREVIATE	BREVIATES
	BREVIER	BREVIERS
	BREW	BREWS
	BREWAGE	BREWAGES
	BREWER	BREWERS · BREWERY
	BREWING	BREWINGS
	BREWPUB	BREWPUBS
	BREWSKI	BREWSKIS
	BREWSTER	BREWSTERS
	BREY	BREYS
	BRIAR	BRIARD · BRIARS · BRIARY
	BRIARD	BRIARDS
	BRIARROOT	BRIARROOTS
	BRIARWOOD	BRIARWOODS
	BRIBE	BRIBED · BRIBEE · BRIBER · BRIBES
	BRIBEE	BRIBEES
	BRIBER	BRIBERS · BRIBERY
	BRICABRAC	BRICABRACS
	BRICK	BRICKS · BRICKY
	BRICKBAT	BRICKBATS
	BRICKCLAY	BRICKCLAYS
	BRICKIE	BRICKIER · BRICKIES
	BRICKIES	BRICKIEST
	BRICKING	BRICKINGS
	BRICKKILN	BRICKKILNS
	BRICKLE	BRICKLES
	BRICKWALL	BRICKWALLS
	BRICKWORK	BRICKWORKS
	BRICKYARD	BRICKYARDS
	BRICOLAGE	BRICOLAGES
	BRICOLE	BRICOLES
	BRIDAL	BRIDALS
	BRIDE	BRIDED · BRIDES
	BRIDECAKE	BRIDECAKES
	BRIDEMAID	BRIDEMAIDS
	BRIDEWELL	BRIDEWELLS
ABRIDGABLE	**BRIDGABLE**	
ABRIDGE	**BRIDGE**	BRIDGED · BRIDGES
ABRIDGED	**BRIDGED**	
ABRIDGES	**BRIDGES**	
ABRIDGING	**BRIDGING**	BRIDGINGS
	BRIDIE	BRIDIES
	BRIDLE	BRIDLED · BRIDLER · BRIDLES
	BRIDLER	BRIDLERS
	BRIDLEWAY	BRIDLEWAYS
	BRIDOON	BRIDOONS
	BRIE	BRIEF · BRIER · BRIES
	BRIEF	BRIEFS
	BRIEFCASE	BRIEFCASES
	BRIEFER	BRIEFERS
	BRIEFING	BRIEFINGS
	BRIER	BRIERS · BRIERY
	BRIERROOT	BRIERROOTS
	BRIERWOOD	BRIERWOODS
	BRIG	BRIGS
	BRIGADE	BRIGADED · BRIGADES
	BRIGADIER	BRIGADIERS
	BRIGALOW	BRIGALOWS
	BRIGAND	BRIGANDS
	BRIGHT	BRIGHTS

FRONT HOOK	ROOT WORD	END HOOK
	BRIGHTEN	BRIGHTENS
	BRIGUE	BRIGUED • BRIGUES
	BRIGUING	BRIGUINGS
	BRIK	BRIKS
	BRILL	BRILLO • BRILLS
	BRILLIANT	BRILLIANTE • BRILLIANTS
	BRILLO	BRILLOS
ABRIM	BRIM	BRIMS
	BRIMFUL	BRIMFULL
	BRIMFULL	BRIMFULLY
	BRIMING	BRIMINGS
	BRIMMER	BRIMMERS
	BRIMSTONE	BRIMSTONES
ABRIN	BRIN	BRINE • BRING • BRINK • BRINS • BRINY
	BRINDISI	BRINDISIS
	BRINDLE	BRINDLED • BRINDLES
	BRINE	BRINED • BRINER • BRINES
	BRINER	BRINERS
	BRING	BRINGS
	BRINGDOWN	BRINGDOWNS
	BRINGER	BRINGERS
	BRINGING	BRINGINGS
	BRINIES	BRINIEST
	BRINJAL	BRINJALS
	BRINK	BRINKS
ABRINS	BRINS	
	BRIO	BRIOS
	BRIOCHE	BRIOCHES
	BRIOLETTE	BRIOLETTES
	BRIQUET	BRIQUETS
	BRIQUETTE	BRIQUETTED • BRIQUETTES
ABRIS	BRIS	BRISE • BRISK • BRISS
	BRISANCE	BRISANCES
	BRISE	BRISES
	BRISK	BRISKS • BRISKY
	BRISKEN	BRISKENS
	BRISKET	BRISKETS
	BRISLING	BRISLINGS
	BRISTLE	BRISTLED • BRISTLES
	BRISTOL	BRISTOLS
	BRISURE	BRISURES
	BRIT	BRITH • BRITS • BRITT
	BRITANNIA	BRITANNIAS
	BRITH	BRITHS
	BRITSCHKA	BRITSCHKAS
	BRITSKA	BRITSKAS
	BRITT	BRITTS
	BRITTANIA	BRITTANIAS
	BRITTLE	BRITTLED • BRITTLER • BRITTLES
	BRITTLES	BRITTLEST
	BRITZKA	BRITZKAS
	BRITZSKA	BRITZSKAS
	BRIZE	BRIZES
	BRO	BROD • BROG • BROO • BROS • BROW
ABROACH	BROACH	
	BROACHER	BROACHERS
ABROAD	BROAD	BROADS
	BROADAX	BROADAXE
	BROADAXE	BROADAXES
	BROADBAND	BROADBANDS
	BROADBEAN	BROADBEANS
	BROADBILL	BROADBILLS
	BROADBRIM	BROADBRIMS
	BROADCAST	BROADCASTS
	BROADEN	BROADENS
	BROADENER	BROADENERS
	BROADLINE	BROADLINES
	BROADLOOM	BROADLOOMS
ABROADS	BROADS	

FRONT HOOK	ROOT WORD	END HOOK
	BROADSIDE	BROADSIDED · BROADSIDES
	BROADTAIL	BROADTAILS
	BROADWAY	BROADWAYS
	BROCADE	BROCADED · BROCADES
	BROCAGE	BROCAGES
	BROCARD	BROCARDS
	BROCATEL	BROCATELS
	BROCCOLI	BROCCOLIS
	BROCH	BROCHE · BROCHO · BROCHS
	BROCHAN	BROCHANS
	BROCHE	BROCHED · BROCHES
	BROCHETTE	BROCHETTES
	BROCHO	BROCHOS
	BROCHURE	BROCHURES
	BROCK	BROCKS
	BROCKAGE	BROCKAGES
	BROCKET	BROCKETS
	BROCKRAM	BROCKRAMS
	BROCOLI	BROCOLIS
	BROD	BRODS
	BRODDLE	BRODDLED · BRODDLES
	BRODEKIN	BRODEKINS
	BRODKIN	BRODKINS
	BROG	BROGH · BROGS
	BROGAN	BROGANS
	BROGH	BROGHS
	BROGUE	BROGUES
	BROIDER	BROIDERS · BROIDERY
	BROIDERER	BROIDERERS
	BROIL	BROILS
	BROILER	BROILERS
	BROKAGE	BROKAGES
	BROKE	BROKED · BROKEN · BROKER · BROKES
	BROKER	BROKERS · BROKERY
	BROKERAGE	BROKERAGES
	BROKERING	BROKERINGS
	BROKING	BROKINGS
	BROLGA	BROLGAS
	BROMAL	BROMALS
	BROMATE	BROMATED · BROMATES
	BROME	BROMES
	BROMELAIN	BROMELAINS
	BROMELIA	BROMELIAD · BROMELIAS
	BROMELIAD	BROMELIADS
	BROMELIN	BROMELINS
	BROMEOSIN	BROMEOSINS
	BROMID	BROMIDE · BROMIDS
	BROMIDE	BROMIDES
	BROMIN	BROMINE · BROMINS
	BROMINATE	BROMINATED · BROMINATES
	BROMINE	BROMINES
	BROMINISM	BROMINISMS
	BROMISE	BROMISED · BROMISES
	BROMISM	BROMISMS
	BROMIZE	BROMIZED · BROMIZES
	BROMMER	BROMMERS
	BROMO	BROMOS
	BROMOFORM	BROMOFORMS
	BRONC	BRONCO · BRONCS
	BRONCHI	BRONCHIA
	BRONCHIA	BRONCHIAL
	BRONCHO	BRONCHOS
	BRONCO	BRONCOS
	BROND	BRONDS
	BRONDYRON	BRONDYRONS
	BRONZE	BRONZED · BRONZEN · BRONZER · BRONZES
	BRONZER	BRONZERS
	BRONZING	BRONZINGS
	BRONZITE	BRONZITES

FRONT HOOK	ROOT WORD	END HOOK
	BROO	BROOD · BROOK · BROOL · BROOM · BROOS
	BROOD	BROODS · BROODY
	BROODER	BROODERS
	BROODING	BROODINGS
	BROODMARE	BROODMARES
	BROOK	BROOKS
ABROOKED	BROOKED	
	BROOKIE	BROOKIES
ABROOKING	BROOKING	
	BROOKITE	BROOKITES
	BROOKLET	BROOKLETS
	BROOKLIME	BROOKLIMES
	BROOKWEED	BROOKWEEDS
	BROOL	BROOLS
	BROOM	BROOMS · BROOMY
	BROOMBALL	BROOMBALLS
	BROOMCORN	BROOMCORNS
	BROOMRAPE	BROOMRAPES
	BROOS	BROOSE
	BROOSE	BROOSES
	BROS	BROSE · BROSY
	BROSE	BROSES
	BROTH	BROTHS · BROTHY
	BROTHEL	BROTHELS
	BROTHER	BROTHERS
	BROUGH	BROUGHS · BROUGHT
	BROUGHAM	BROUGHAMS
	BROUGHT	BROUGHTA
	BROUGHTA	BROUGHTAS
	BROUHAHA	BROUHAHAS
	BROUZE	BROUZES
	BROW	BROWN · BROWS
	BROWALLIA	BROWALLIAS
	BROWBAND	BROWBANDS
	BROWBEAT	BROWBEATS
	BROWN	BROWNS · BROWNY
	BROWNIE	BROWNIER · BROWNIES
	BROWNIES	BROWNIEST
	BROWNING	BROWNINGS
	BROWNNOSE	BROWNNOSED · BROWNNOSER · BROWNNOSES
	BROWNOUT	BROWNOUTS
	BROWRIDGE	BROWRIDGES
	BROWS	BROWSE · BROWST · BROWSY
	BROWSABLE	BROWSABLES
	BROWSE	BROWSED · BROWSER · BROWSES
	BROWSER	BROWSERS
	BROWSING	BROWSINGS
	BROWST	BROWSTS
	BRR	BRRR
	BRU	BRUS · BRUT · BRUX
	BRUCELLA	BRUCELLAE · BRUCELLAS
	BRUCHID	BRUCHIDS
	BRUCIN	BRUCINE · BRUCINS
	BRUCINE	BRUCINES
	BRUCITE	BRUCITES
	BRUGH	BRUGHS
	BRUHAHA	BRUHAHAS
	BRUILZIE	BRUILZIES
	BRUIN	BRUINS
	BRUISE	BRUISED · BRUISER · BRUISES
	BRUISER	BRUISERS
	BRUISING	BRUISINGS
	BRUIT	BRUITS
	BRUITER	BRUITERS
	BRULE	BRULES
	BRULOT	BRULOTS
	BRULYIE	BRULYIES
	BRULZIE	BRULZIES
	BRUME	BRUMES

B

FRONT HOOK	ROOT WORD	END HOOK
	BRUMMAGEM	BRUMMAGEMS
	BRUMMER	BRUMMERS
	BRUNCHER	BRUNCHERS
	BRUNET	BRUNETS
	BRUNETTE	BRUNETTES
	BRUNIZEM	BRUNIZEMS
	BRUNT	BRUNTS
	BRUS	BRUSH ▪ BRUSK ▪ BRUST
	BRUSH	BRUSHY
	BRUSHBACK	BRUSHBACKS
	BRUSHER	BRUSHERS
	BRUSHFIRE	BRUSHFIRES
	BRUSHING	BRUSHINGS
	BRUSHLAND	BRUSHLANDS
	BRUSHMARK	BRUSHMARKS
	BRUSHOFF	BRUSHOFFS
	BRUSHUP	BRUSHUPS
	BRUSHWOOD	BRUSHWOODS
	BRUSHWORK	BRUSHWORKS
	BRUSQUE	BRUSQUER
	BRUST	BRUSTS
	BRUT	BRUTE ▪ BRUTS
	BRUTALISE	BRUTALISED ▪ BRUTALISES
	BRUTALISM	BRUTALISMS
	BRUTALIST	BRUTALISTS
	BRUTALIZE	BRUTALIZED ▪ BRUTALIZES
	BRUTE	BRUTED ▪ BRUTER ▪ BRUTES
	BRUTER	BRUTERS
	BRUTING	BRUTINGS
	BRUTISM	BRUTISMS
	BRUXISM	BRUXISMS
	BRYOPHYTE	BRYOPHYTES
	BRYOZOAN	BRYOZOANS
	BUAT	BUATS
	BUAZE	BUAZES
	BUB	BUBA ▪ BUBO ▪ BUBS ▪ BUBU
	BUBA	BUBAL ▪ BUBAS
	BUBAL	BUBALE ▪ BUBALS
	BUBALE	BUBALES
	BUBBA	BUBBAS
ABUBBLE	**BUBBLE**	BUBBLED ▪ BUBBLER ▪ BUBBLES
	BUBBLEGUM	BUBBLEGUMS
	BUBBLER	BUBBLERS
	BUBBLIES	BUBBLIEST
	BUBINGA	BUBINGAS
	BUBU	BUBUS
	BUBUKLE	BUBUKLES
	BUCCANEER	BUCCANEERS
	BUCCANIER	BUCCANIERS
	BUCCINA	BUCCINAS
	BUCENTAUR	BUCENTAURS
	BUCHU	BUCHUS
	BUCK	BUCKO ▪ BUCKS ▪ BUCKU
	BUCKAROO	BUCKAROOS
	BUCKAYRO	BUCKAYROS
	BUCKBEAN	BUCKBEANS
	BUCKBOARD	BUCKBOARDS
	BUCKEEN	BUCKEENS
	BUCKER	BUCKERS
	BUCKEROO	BUCKEROOS
	BUCKET	BUCKETS
	BUCKETFUL	BUCKETFULS
	BUCKETING	BUCKETINGS
	BUCKEYE	BUCKEYES
	BUCKHORN	BUCKHORNS
	BUCKHOUND	BUCKHOUNDS
	BUCKIE	BUCKIES
	BUCKING	BUCKINGS
	BUCKLE	BUCKLED ▪ BUCKLER ▪ BUCKLES

FRONT HOOK	ROOT WORD	END HOOK
	BUCKLER	BUCKLERS
	BUCKLING	BUCKLINGS
	BUCKO	BUCKOS
	BUCKRA	BUCKRAM ▪ BUCKRAS (offensive)
	BUCKRAKE	BUCKRAKES
	BUCKRAM	BUCKRAMS
	BUCKSAW	BUCKSAWS
	BUCKSHEE	BUCKSHEES
	BUCKSHOT	BUCKSHOTS
	BUCKSKIN	BUCKSKINS
	BUCKTAIL	BUCKTAILS
	BUCKTHORN	BUCKTHORNS
	BUCKU	BUCKUS
	BUCKWHEAT	BUCKWHEATS
	BUCKYBALL	BUCKYBALLS
	BUCKYTUBE	BUCKYTUBES
	BUCOLIC	BUCOLICS
	BUD	BUDA ▪ BUDI ▪ BUDO ▪ BUDS
	BUDA	BUDAS (offensive)
	BUDDER	BUDDERS
	BUDDHA	BUDDHAS
	BUDDIES	BUDDIEST
	BUDDING	BUDDINGS
	BUDDLE	BUDDLED ▪ BUDDLES
	BUDDLEIA	BUDDLEIAS
	BUDGE	BUDGED ▪ BUDGER ▪ BUDGES ▪ BUDGET
	BUDGER	BUDGERO ▪ BUDGERS
	BUDGERO	BUDGEROS ▪ BUDGEROW
	BUDGEROW	BUDGEROWS
	BUDGET	BUDGETS
	BUDGETEER	BUDGETEERS
	BUDGETER	BUDGETERS
	BUDGIE	BUDGIES
	BUDI	BUDIS (offensive)
	BUDO	BUDOS
	BUDWORM	BUDWORMS
	BUFF	BUFFA ▪ BUFFE ▪ BUFFI ▪ BUFFO ▪ BUFFS ▪ BUFFY
	BUFFALO	BUFFALOS
	BUFFE	BUFFED ▪ BUFFEL ▪ BUFFER ▪ BUFFET
	BUFFER	BUFFERS
	BUFFET	BUFFETS
	BUFFETER	BUFFETERS
	BUFFETING	BUFFETINGS
	BUFFING	BUFFINGS
	BUFFO	BUFFOS
	BUFFOON	BUFFOONS
	BUFO	BUFOS
	BUFOTALIN	BUFOTALINS
	BUG	BUGS
	BUGABOO	BUGABOOS
	BUGBANE	BUGBANES
	BUGBEAR	BUGBEARS
	BUGEYE	BUGEYES
	BUGGAN	BUGGANE ▪ BUGGANS
	BUGGANE	BUGGANES
	BUGGER	BUGGERS (offensive) ▪ BUGGERY
	BUGGIES	BUGGIEST
	BUGGIN	BUGGING ▪ BUGGINS
	BUGGING	BUGGINGS
	BUGHOUSE	BUGHOUSES (offensive)
	BUGLE	BUGLED ▪ BUGLER ▪ BUGLES ▪ BUGLET
	BUGLER	BUGLERS
	BUGLET	BUGLETS
	BUGLEWEED	BUGLEWEEDS
	BUGONG	BUGONGS
	BUGOUT	BUGOUTS
	BUGSEED	BUGSEEDS
	BUGSHA	BUGSHAS

3

FRONT HOOK	ROOT WORD	END HOOK
	BUGWORT	BUGWORTS
	BUHL	BUHLS
	BUHLWORK	BUHLWORKS
	BUHR	BUHRS
	BUHRSTONE	BUHRSTONES
	BUHUND	BUHUNDS
	BUIBUI	BUIBUIS
	BUIK	BUIKS
	BUILD	BUILDS
	BUILDDOWN	BUILDDOWNS
	BUILDER	BUILDERS
ABUILDING	BUILDING	BUILDINGS
	BUILDUP	BUILDUPS
	BUIST	BUISTS
	BUKE	BUKES
	BUKKAKE	BUKKAKES
	BUKSHEE	BUKSHEES
	BUKSHI	BUKSHIS
	BULB	BULBS
	BULBEL	BULBELS
	BULBIL	BULBILS
	BULBLET	BULBLETS
	BULBUL	BULBULS
	BULGE	BULGED · BULGER · BULGES
	BULGER	BULGERS
	BULGHUR	BULGHURS
	BULGINE	BULGINES
	BULGINES	BULGINESS
	BULGUR	BULGURS
	BULIMIA	BULIMIAC · BULIMIAS
	BULIMIC	BULIMICS
	BULK	BULKS · BULKY
	BULKAGE	BULKAGES
	BULKER	BULKERS
	BULKHEAD	BULKHEADS
	BULL	BULLA · BULLS · BULLY
	BULLA	BULLAE
	BULLACE	BULLACES
	BULLBAR	BULLBARS
	BULLBAT	BULLBATS
	BULLBRIER	BULLBRIERS
	BULLDOG	BULLDOGS
	BULLDOZE	BULLDOZED · BULLDOZER · BULLDOZES
	BULLDOZER	BULLDOZERS
	BULLDUST	BULLDUSTS
	BULLDYKE	BULLDYKES
	BULLER	BULLERS
	BULLET	BULLETS
	BULLETIN	BULLETING · BULLETINS
	BULLETRIE	BULLETRIES
	BULLFIGHT	BULLFIGHTS
	BULLFROG	BULLFROGS
	BULLGINE	BULLGINES
	BULLHEAD	BULLHEADS
	BULLHORN	BULLHORNS
	BULLIES	BULLIEST
	BULLING	BULLINGS
	BULLION	BULLIONS
	BULLNECK	BULLNECKS
	BULLNOSE	BULLNOSES
	BULLOCK	BULLOCKS · BULLOCKY
	BULLPEN	BULLPENS
	BULLPOUT	BULLPOUTS
	BULLRING	BULLRINGS
	BULLSHIT	BULLSHITS (offensive)
	BULLSHOT	BULLSHOTS
	BULLSNAKE	BULLSNAKES
	BULLWEED	BULLWEEDS
	BULLWHACK	BULLWHACKS

FRONT HOOK	ROOT WORD	END HOOK
	BULLWHIP	BULLWHIPS
	BULLYBOY	BULLYBOYS
	BULLYISM	BULLYISMS
	BULLYRAG	BULLYRAGS
	BULNBULN	BULNBULNS
	BULRUSH	BULRUSHY
	BULSE	BULSES
	BULWADDEE	BULWADDEES
	BULWARK	BULWARKS
	BUM	BUMF ▪ BUMP ▪ BUMS
	BUMALOTI	BUMALOTIS
	BUMBAG	BUMBAGS
	BUMBAZE	BUMBAZED ▪ BUMBAZES
	BUMBLE	BUMBLED ▪ BUMBLER ▪ BUMBLES
	BUMBLEBEE	BUMBLEBEES
	BUMBLEDOM	BUMBLEDOMS
	BUMBLER	BUMBLERS
	BUMBLING	BUMBLINGS
	BUMBO	BUMBOS
	BUMBOAT	BUMBOATS
	BUMELIA	BUMELIAS
	BUMF	BUMFS
	BUMFLUFF	BUMFLUFFS
	BUMFUZZLE	BUMFUZZLED ▪ BUMFUZZLES
	BUMKIN	BUMKINS
	BUMMALO	BUMMALOS
	BUMMALOTI	BUMMALOTIS
	BUMMAREE	BUMMAREES
	BUMMEL	BUMMELS
	BUMMER	BUMMERS
	BUMMLE	BUMMLED ▪ BUMMLES
	BUMMOCK	BUMMOCKS
	BUMP	BUMPH ▪ BUMPS ▪ BUMPY
	BUMPER	BUMPERS
	BUMPH	BUMPHS
	BUMPING	BUMPINGS
	BUMPKIN	BUMPKINS
	BUMSUCKER	BUMSUCKERS
	BUN	BUNA ▪ BUND ▪ BUNG ▪ BUNK ▪ BUNN ▪ BUNS ▪ BUNT
ABUNA	**BUNA**	BUNAS
ABUNAS	**BUNAS**	
	BUNCE	BUNCED ▪ BUNCES
	BUNCH	BUNCHY
	BUNCHING	BUNCHINGS
	BUNCO	BUNCOS
	BUNCOMBE	BUNCOMBES
	BUND	BUNDE ▪ BUNDH ▪ BUNDS ▪ BUNDT ▪ BUNDU ▪ BUNDY
	BUNDE	BUNDED
	BUNDH	BUNDHS
	BUNDIST	BUNDISTS
	BUNDLE	BUNDLED ▪ BUNDLER ▪ BUNDLES
	BUNDLER	BUNDLERS
	BUNDLING	BUNDLINGS
	BUNDOBUST	BUNDOBUSTS
	BUNDOOK	BUNDOOKS
	BUNDT	BUNDTS
	BUNDU	BUNDUS
	BUNDWALL	BUNDWALLS
	BUNFIGHT	BUNFIGHTS
	BUNG	BUNGS ▪ BUNGY
	BUNGALOID	BUNGALOIDS
	BUNGALOW	BUNGALOWS
	BUNGEE	BUNGEES
	BUNGER	BUNGERS
	BUNGEY	BUNGEYS
	BUNGHOLE	BUNGHOLES
	BUNGIE	BUNGIES

FRONT HOOK	ROOT WORD	END HOOK
	BUNGLE	BUNGLED = BUNGLER = BUNGLES
	BUNGLER	BUNGLERS
	BUNGLING	BUNGLINGS
	BUNGWALL	BUNGWALLS
	BUNIA	BUNIAS
	BUNION	BUNIONS
	BUNJE	BUNJEE = BUNJES
	BUNJEE	BUNJEES
	BUNJIE	BUNJIES
	BUNK	BUNKO = BUNKS
	BUNKER	BUNKERS
	BUNKHOUSE	BUNKHOUSES
	BUNKMATE	BUNKMATES
	BUNKO	BUNKOS
	BUNKUM	BUNKUMS
	BUNN	BUNNS = BUNNY
	BUNNET	BUNNETS
	BUNNIA	BUNNIAS
	BUNRAKU	BUNRAKUS
	BUNSEN	BUNSENS
	BUNT	BUNTS = BUNTY
	BUNTAL	BUNTALS
	BUNTER	BUNTERS
	BUNTING	BUNTINGS
	BUNTLINE	BUNTLINES
	BUNYA	BUNYAS
	BUNYIP	BUNYIPS
	BUOY	BUOYS
	BUOYAGE	BUOYAGES
	BUOYANCE	BUOYANCES
	BUPLEVER	BUPLEVERS
	BUPPIE	BUPPIES
	BUPRESTID	BUPRESTIDS
	BUQSHA	BUQSHAS
	BUR	BURA = BURB = BURD = BURG = BURK
		BURL = BURN = BURP = BURR = BURS = BURY
	BURA	BURAN = BURAS
	BURAN	BURANS
	BURB	BURBS
	BURBLE	BURBLED = BURBLER = BURBLES
	BURBLER	BURBLERS
	BURBLING	BURBLINGS
	BURBOT	BURBOTS
	BURD	BURDS
	BURDEN	BURDENS
	BURDENER	BURDENERS
	BURDIE	BURDIES
	BURDIZZO	BURDIZZOS
	BURDOCK	BURDOCKS
	BUREAU	BUREAUS = BUREAUX
	BURET	BURETS
	BURETTE	BURETTES
	BURG	BURGH = BURGS
	BURGAGE	BURGAGES
	BURGANET	BURGANETS
	BURGEE	BURGEES
	BURGEON	BURGEONS
	BURGER	BURGERS
	BURGH	BURGHS
	BURGHER	BURGHERS
	BURGHUL	BURGHULS
	BURGLAR	BURGLARS = BURGLARY
	BURGLE	BURGLED = BURGLES
	BURGONET	BURGONETS
	BURGOO	BURGOOS
	BURGOUT	BURGOUTS
	BURGRAVE	BURGRAVES
	BURHEL	BURHELS
	BURIAL	BURIALS

FRONT HOOK	ROOT WORD	END HOOK
	BURIER	BURIERS
	BURIN	BURINS
	BURINIST	BURINISTS
	BURITI	BURITIS
	BURK	BURKA · BURKE · BURKS
	BURKA	BURKAS
	BURKE	BURKED · BURKER · BURKES
	BURKER	BURKERS
	BURKITE	BURKITES
	BURL	BURLS · BURLY
	BURLADERO	BURLADEROS
	BURLAP	BURLAPS
	BURLER	BURLERS
	BURLESK	BURLESKS
	BURLESQUE	BURLESQUED · BURLESQUER · BURLESQUES
	BURLETTA	BURLETTAS
	BURLEY	BURLEYS
	BURLEYCUE	BURLEYCUES
	BURN	BURNS · BURNT
	BURNABLE	BURNABLES
	BURNER	BURNERS
	BURNET	BURNETS
	BURNIE	BURNIES
	BURNING	BURNINGS
	BURNISHER	BURNISHERS
	BURNOOSE	BURNOOSED · BURNOOSES
	BURNOUS	BURNOUSE
	BURNOUSE	BURNOUSED · BURNOUSES
	BURNOUT	BURNOUTS
	BURNSIDE	BURNSIDES
	BUROO	BUROOS
	BURP	BURPS
	BURPEE	BURPEES
	BURQA	BURQAS
	BURR	BURRO · BURRS · BURRY
	BURRAWANG	BURRAWANGS
	BURREL	BURRELL · BURRELS
	BURRELL	BURRELLS
	BURRER	BURRERS
	BURRHEL	BURRHELS
	BURRITO	BURRITOS
	BURRO	BURROS · BURROW
	BURROW	BURROWS
	BURROWER	BURROWERS
	BURRSTONE	BURRSTONES
	BURS	BURSA · BURSE · BURST
	BURSA	BURSAE · BURSAL · BURSAR · BURSAS
	BURSAR	BURSARS · BURSARY
	BURSE	BURSES
	BURSEED	BURSEEDS
	BURSICON	BURSICONS
ABURST	BURST	BURSTS
	BURSTER	BURSTERS
	BURSTONE	BURSTONES
	BURTHEN	BURTHENS
	BURTON	BURTONS
	BURWEED	BURWEEDS
	BUS	BUSH · BUSK · BUSS · BUST · BUSY
	BUSBAR	BUSBARS
	BUSBOY	BUSBOYS
ABUSED	BUSED	
	BUSERA	BUSERAS
ABUSES	BUSES	
	BUSGIRL	BUSGIRLS
	BUSH	BUSHY
	BUSHBUCK	BUSHBUCKS
	BUSHCRAFT	BUSHCRAFTS
	BUSHEL	BUSHELS
	BUSHELER	BUSHELERS

3

FRONT HOOK	ROOT WORD	END HOOK
	BUSHELLER	BUSHELLERS
	BUSHER	BUSHERS
	BUSHFIRE	BUSHFIRES
	BUSHGOAT	BUSHGOATS
	BUSHIDO	BUSHIDOS
	BUSHIE	BUSHIER · BUSHIES
	BUSHIES	BUSHIEST
	BUSHING	BUSHINGS
	BUSHLAND	BUSHLANDS
	BUSHMEAT	BUSHMEATS
	BUSHPIG	BUSHPIGS
	BUSHTIT	BUSHTITS
	BUSHVELD	BUSHVELDS
	BUSHWA	BUSHWAH · BUSHWAS
	BUSHWAH	BUSHWAHS
	BUSHWALK	BUSHWALKS
	BUSHWHACK	BUSHWHACKS
	BUSIES	BUSIEST
	BUSINESS	BUSINESSY
ABUSING	**BUSING**	BUSINGS
	BUSK	BUSKS · BUSKY
	BUSKER	BUSKERS
	BUSKET	BUSKETS
	BUSKIN	BUSKING · BUSKINS
	BUSKING	BUSKINGS
	BUSLOAD	BUSLOADS
	BUSS	BUSSU
	BUSSING	BUSSINGS
	BUSSU	BUSSUS
	BUST	BUSTI · BUSTS · BUSTY
	BUSTARD	BUSTARDS
	BUSTEE	BUSTEES
	BUSTER	BUSTERS
	BUSTI	BUSTIC · BUSTIS
	BUSTIC	BUSTICS
	BUSTICATE	BUSTICATED · BUSTICATES
	BUSTIER	BUSTIERS
	BUSTING	BUSTINGS
	BUSTLE	BUSTLED · BUSTLER · BUSTLES
	BUSTLER	BUSTLERS
	BUSTLINE	BUSTLINES
	BUSULFAN	BUSULFANS
	BUSUUTI	BUSUUTIS
	BUSYWORK	BUSYWORKS
ABUT	**BUT**	BUTE · BUTS · BUTT
	BUTADIENE	BUTADIENES
	BUTANE	BUTANES
	BUTANOL	BUTANOLS
	BUTANONE	BUTANONES
	BUTCHER	BUTCHERS · BUTCHERY
	BUTCHERER	BUTCHERERS
	BUTCHES	BUTCHEST
	BUTCHING	BUTCHINGS
	BUTE	BUTEO · BUTES
	BUTENE	BUTENES
	BUTEO	BUTEOS
	BUTEONINE	BUTEONINES
	BUTLE	BUTLED · BUTLER · BUTLES
	BUTLER	BUTLERS · BUTLERY
	BUTLERAGE	BUTLERAGES
ABUTMENT	**BUTMENT**	BUTMENTS
ABUTMENTS	**BUTMENTS**	
ABUTS	**BUTS**	
	BUTSUDAN	BUTSUDANS
	BUTT	BUTTE · BUTTS · BUTTY
ABUTTALS	**BUTTALS**	
	BUTTE	BUTTED · BUTTER · BUTTES
ABUTTED	**BUTTED**	
ABUTTER	**BUTTER**	BUTTERS · BUTTERY

FRONT HOOK	ROOT WORD	END HOOK
	BUTTERBUR	BUTTERBURS
	BUTTERCUP	BUTTERCUPS
	BUTTERFAT	BUTTERFATS
	BUTTERIES	BUTTERIEST
	BUTTERINE	BUTTERINES
	BUTTERNUT	BUTTERNUTS
ABUTTERS	BUTTERS	
	BUTTHEAD	BUTTHEADS
ABUTTING	BUTTING	
	BUTTINSKI	BUTTINSKIS
	BUTTLE	BUTTLED ▪ BUTTLES
	BUTTOCK	BUTTOCKS
	BUTTON	BUTTONS ▪ BUTTONY
	BUTTONER	BUTTONERS
	BUTTSTOCK	BUTTSTOCKS
	BUTUT	BUTUTS
	BUTYL	BUTYLS
	BUTYLATE	BUTYLATED ▪ BUTYLATES
	BUTYLENE	BUTYLENES
	BUTYRAL	BUTYRALS
	BUTYRATE	BUTYRATES
	BUTYRIN	BUTYRINS
	BUTYRYL	BUTYRYLS
	BUVETTE	BUVETTES
	BUY	BUYS
	BUYABLE	BUYABLES
	BUYBACK	BUYBACKS
	BUYER	BUYERS
	BUYOFF	BUYOFFS
	BUYOUT	BUYOUTS
	BUZKASHI	BUZKASHIS
	BUZUKI	BUZUKIA ▪ BUZUKIS
ABUZZ	BUZZ	BUZZY
	BUZZARD	BUZZARDS
	BUZZCUT	BUZZCUTS
	BUZZER	BUZZERS
	BUZZING	BUZZINGS
	BUZZWIG	BUZZWIGS
	BUZZWORD	BUZZWORDS
	BWANA	BWANAS
	BWAZI	BWAZIS
ABY	BY	BYE ▪ BYS
	BYCOKET	BYCOKETS
	BYDE	BYDED ▪ BYDES
ABYE	BYE	BYES
	BYELAW	BYELAWS
ABYES	BYES	
	BYGONE	BYGONES
	BYKE	BYKED ▪ BYKES
	BYLANDER	BYLANDERS
	BYLANE	BYLANES
	BYLAW	BYLAWS
	BYLINE	BYLINED ▪ BYLINER ▪ BYLINES
	BYLINER	BYLINERS
	BYNAME	BYNAMES
	BYPATH	BYPATHS
	BYPLACE	BYPLACES
	BYPLAY	BYPLAYS
	BYPRODUCT	BYPRODUCTS
	BYRE	BYRES
	BYRL	BYRLS
	BYRLAW	BYRLAWS
	BYRNIE	BYRNIES
	BYROAD	BYROADS
	BYROOM	BYROOMS
ABYS	BYS	
ABYSSAL	BYSSAL	
	BYSTANDER	BYSTANDERS
	BYSTREET	BYSTREETS

B

FRONT HOOK	ROOT WORD	END HOOK
	BYTALK	BYTALKS
	BYTE	BYTES
	BYTOWNITE	BYTOWNITES
	BYWAY	BYWAYS
	BYWONER	BYWONERS
	BYWORD	BYWORDS
	BYWORK	BYWORKS
	BYZANT	BYZANTS

C

FRONT HOOK	ROOT WORD	END HOOK
	CAA	CAAS
	CAATINGA	CAATINGAS
SCAB	CAB	CABA = CABS
	CABA	CABAL = CABAS
	CABAL	CABALA = CABALS
	CABALA	CABALAS
	CABALETTA	CABALETTAS
	CABALISM	CABALISMS
	CABALIST	CABALISTS
	CABALLER	CABALLERO = CABALLERS
	CABALLERO	CABALLEROS
	CABANA	CABANAS
	CABARET	CABARETS
	CABBAGE	CABBAGED = CABBAGES = CABBAGEY
	CABBALA	CABBALAH = CABBALAS
	CABBALAH	CABBALAHS
	CABBALISM	CABBALISMS
	CABBALIST	CABBALISTS
SCABBED	CABBED	
	CABBIE	CABBIES
SCABBING	CABBING	
SCABBY	CABBY	
	CABDRIVER	CABDRIVERS
	CABER	CABERS
	CABERNET	CABERNETS
	CABESTRO	CABESTROS
	CABEZON	CABEZONE = CABEZONS
	CABEZONE	CABEZONES
	CABILDO	CABILDOS
	CABIN	CABINS
	CABINET	CABINETS
	CABINMATE	CABINMATES
	CABLE	CABLED = CABLER = CABLES = CABLET
	CABLECAST	CABLECASTS
	CABLEGRAM	CABLEGRAMS
	CABLER	CABLERS
	CABLET	CABLETS
	CABLEWAY	CABLEWAYS
	CABLING	CABLINGS
	CABOB	CABOBS
	CABOC	CABOCS
	CABOCEER	CABOCEERS
	CABOCHON	CABOCHONS
	CABOMBA	CABOMBAS
	CABOODLE	CABOODLES
	CABOOSE	CABOOSES
	CABOTAGE	CABOTAGES
	CABRESTA	CABRESTAS
	CABRESTO	CABRESTOS
	CABRETTA	CABRETTAS
	CABRIE	CABRIES
	CABRILLA	CABRILLAS
	CABRIO	CABRIOS
	CABRIOLE	CABRIOLES = CABRIOLET
	CABRIOLET	CABRIOLETS
	CABRIT	CABRITS
SCABS	CABS	
	CABSTAND	CABSTANDS
	CACA	CACAO = CACAS
	CACAFOGO	CACAFOGOS
	CACAFUEGO	CACAFUEGOS
	CACAO	CACAOS
	CACHAEMIA	CACHAEMIAS
	CACHALOT	CACHALOTS
	CACHE	CACHED = CACHES = CACHET
	CACHEPOT	CACHEPOTS

C

FRONT HOOK	ROOT WORD	END HOOK
	CACHET	CACHETS
	CACHEXIA	CACHEXIAS
	CACHOLONG	CACHOLONGS
	CACHOLOT	CACHOLOTS
	CACHOU	CACHOUS
	CACHUCHA	CACHUCHAS
	CACIQUE	CACIQUES
	CACIQUISM	CACIQUISMS
	CACKLE	CACKLED · CACKLER · CACKLES
	CACKLER	CACKLERS
	CACODEMON	CACODEMONS
	CACODYL	CACODYLS
	CACOGENIC	CACOGENICS
	CACOLET	CACOLETS
	CACOMIXL	CACOMIXLE · CACOMIXLS
	CACOMIXLE	CACOMIXLES
	CACONYM	CACONYMS · CACONYMY
	CACOON	CACOONS
	CACOTOPIA	CACOTOPIAN · CACOTOPIAS
	CACUMINA	CACUMINAL
	CACUMINAL	CACUMINALS
ECAD · SCAD	**CAD**	CADE · CADI · CADS
	CADAGA	CADAGAS
	CADAGI	CADAGIS
	CADASTER	CADASTERS
	CADASTRE	CADASTRES
	CADAVER	CADAVERS
	CADDICE	CADDICES
	CADDIE	CADDIED · CADDIES
	CADDIS	CADDISH
	CADE	CADEE · CADES · CADET
	CADEAU	CADEAUX
	CADEE	CADEES
	CADELLE	CADELLES
	CADENCE	CADENCED · CADENCES
	CADENZA	CADENZAS
	CADET	CADETS
	CADETSHIP	CADETSHIPS
	CADGE	CADGED · CADGER · CADGES
	CADGER	CADGERS
	CADI	CADIE · CADIS
	CADIE	CADIES
	CADMIUM	CADMIUMS
	CADRE	CADRES
ECADS · SCADS	**CADS**	
	CADUAC	CADUACS
	CAECA	CAECAL
	CAECILIAN	CAECILIANS
	CAEOMA	CAEOMAS
	CAESAR	CAESARS
	CAESAREAN	CAESAREANS
	CAESARIAN	CAESARIANS
	CAESARISM	CAESARISMS
	CAESIUM	CAESIUMS
	CAESURA	CAESURAE · CAESURAL · CAESURAS
	CAFARD	CAFARDS
	CAFE	CAFES
	CAFETERIA	CAFETERIAS
	CAFETIERE	CAFETIERES
SCAFF	**CAFF**	CAFFS
	CAFFEIN	CAFFEINE · CAFFEINS
	CAFFEINE	CAFFEINES
	CAFFEISM	CAFFEISMS
	CAFFILA	CAFFILAS
SCAFFS	**CAFFS**	
	CAFILA	CAFILAS
	CAFTAN	CAFTANS
SCAG	**CAG**	CAGE · CAGS · CAGY
	CAGANER	CAGANERS

FRONT HOOK	ROOT WORD	END HOOK
	CAGE	CAGED · CAGER · CAGES · CAGEY
	CAGEBIRD	CAGEBIRDS
	CAGEFUL	CAGEFULS
	CAGELING	CAGELINGS
	CAGER	CAGERS
	CAGEWORK	CAGEWORKS
	CAGMAG	CAGMAGS
	CAGOT	CAGOTS
	CAGOUL	CAGOULE · CAGOULS
	CAGOULE	CAGOULES
SCAGS	CAGS	
	CAHIER	CAHIERS
	CAHOOT	CAHOOTS
	CAHOW	CAHOWS
	CAID	CAIDS
	CAILLACH	CAILLACHS
	CAILLE	CAILLES
	CAILLEACH	CAILLEACHS
	CAILLIACH	CAILLIACHS
	CAIMAC	CAIMACS
	CAIMACAM	CAIMACAMS
	CAIMAN	CAIMANS
	CAIN	CAINS
	CAIQUE	CAIQUES
	CAIRD	CAIRDS
	CAIRN	CAIRNS · CAIRNY
	CAIRNGORM	CAIRNGORMS
	CAISSON	CAISSONS
	CAITIFF	CAITIFFS
	CAITIVE	CAITIVES
	CAJAPUT	CAJAPUTS
	CAJEPUT	CAJEPUTS
	CAJOLE	CAJOLED · CAJOLER · CAJOLES
	CAJOLER	CAJOLERS · CAJOLERY
	CAJUPUT	CAJUPUTS
	CAKE	CAKED · CAKES · CAKEY
	CAKEWALK	CAKEWALKS
	CAKING	CAKINGS
	CALABAZA	CALABAZAS
	CALABOOSE	CALABOOSES
	CALABRESE	CALABRESES
	CALADIUM	CALADIUMS
	CALALOO	CALALOOS
	CALALU	CALALUS
	CALAMANCO	CALAMANCOS
	CALAMAR	CALAMARI · CALAMARS · CALAMARY
	CALAMARI	CALAMARIS
	CALAMATA	CALAMATAS
	CALAMINE	CALAMINED · CALAMINES
	CALAMINT	CALAMINTS
	CALAMITE	CALAMITES
	CALANDRIA	CALANDRIAS
	CALANTHE	CALANTHES
	CALATHEA	CALATHEAS
	CALAVANCE	CALAVANCES
	CALCANEA	CALCANEAL · CALCANEAN
	CALCAR	CALCARS
	CALCEATE	CALCEATED · CALCEATES
	CALCICOLE	CALCICOLES
	CALCIFUGE	CALCIFUGES
	CALCIMINE	CALCIMINED · CALCIMINES
	CALCINE	CALCINED · CALCINES
	CALCITE	CALCITES
	CALCIUM	CALCIUMS
	CALCRETE	CALCRETES
	CALCSPAR	CALCSPARS
	CALCTUFA	CALCTUFAS
	CALCTUFF	CALCTUFFS
	CALCULAR	CALCULARY

C

FRONT HOOK	ROOT WORD	END HOOK
	CALCULATE	CALCULATED · CALCULATES
	CALDERA	CALDERAS
	CALDRON	CALDRONS
	CALECHE	CALECHES
	CALEMBOUR	CALEMBOURS
	CALENDAR	CALENDARS
	CALENDER	CALENDERS
	CALENDRER	CALENDRERS
	CALENDULA	CALENDULAS
	CALENTURE	CALENTURES
	CALESA	CALESAS
	CALF	CALFS
	CALFDOZER	CALFDOZERS
	CALFLICK	CALFLICKS
	CALFSKIN	CALFSKINS
	CALIATOUR	CALIATOURS
	CALIBER	CALIBERS
	CALIBRATE	CALIBRATED · CALIBRATER · CALIBRATES
	CALIBRE	CALIBRED · CALIBRES
	CALICHE	CALICHES
	CALICLE	CALICLES
	CALICO	CALICOS
	CALIF	CALIFS
	CALIFATE	CALIFATES
	CALIFONT	CALIFONTS
	CALIGO	CALIGOS
	CALIMA	CALIMAS
	CALIPEE	CALIPEES
	CALIPER	CALIPERS
	CALIPH	CALIPHS
	CALIPHATE	CALIPHATES
	CALISAYA	CALISAYAS
	CALIVER	CALIVERS
	CALK	CALKS
	CALKER	CALKERS
	CALKIN	CALKING · CALKINS
	CALKING	CALKINGS
SCALL	**CALL**	CALLA · CALLS
	CALLA	CALLAN · CALLAS
	CALLALOO	CALLALOOS
	CALLAN	CALLANS · CALLANT
	CALLANT	CALLANTS
	CALLBACK	CALLBACKS
	CALLBOARD	CALLBOARDS
	CALLBOY	CALLBOYS
SCALLED	**CALLED**	
	CALLEE	CALLEES
	CALLER	CALLERS
	CALLET	CALLETS
	CALLIGRAM	CALLIGRAMS
	CALLING	CALLINGS
	CALLIOPE	CALLIOPES
	CALLIPEE	CALLIPEES
	CALLIPER	CALLIPERS
SCALLOP	**CALLOP**	CALLOPS
SCALLOPS	**CALLOPS**	
	CALLOSE	CALLOSES
	CALLOW	CALLOWS
SCALLS	**CALLS**	
	CALLUNA	CALLUNAS
	CALM	CALMS · CALMY
	CALMANT	CALMANTS
	CALMATIVE	CALMATIVES
	CALMING	CALMINGS
	CALMSTONE	CALMSTONES
	CALO	CALOS
	CALOMEL	CALOMELS
	CALORIC	CALORICS
	CALORIE	CALORIES

FRONT HOOK	ROOT WORD	END HOOK
	CALORISE	CALORISED = CALORISES
	CALORIST	CALORISTS
	CALORIZE	CALORIZED = CALORIZES
	CALOTTE	CALOTTES
	CALOTYPE	CALOTYPES
	CALOYER	CALOYERS
SCALP	CALP	CALPA = CALPS
	CALPA	CALPAC = CALPAS
	CALPAC	CALPACK = CALPACS
	CALPACK	CALPACKS
	CALPAIN	CALPAINS
SCALPS	CALPS	
	CALQUE	CALQUED = CALQUES
	CALTHA	CALTHAS
	CALTHROP	CALTHROPS
	CALTRAP	CALTRAPS
	CALTROP	CALTROPS
	CALUMBA	CALUMBAS
	CALUMET	CALUMETS
	CALUTRON	CALUTRONS
	CALVARIA	CALVARIAL = CALVARIAN = CALVARIAS
	CALVARIUM	CALVARIUMS
	CALVE	CALVED = CALVER = CALVES
	CALVER	CALVERS
	CALYCLE	CALYCLED = CALYCLES
	CALYCULE	CALYCULES
	CALYPSO	CALYPSOS
	CALYPTER	CALYPTERA = CALYPTERS
	CALYPTERA	CALYPTERAS
	CALYPTRA	CALYPTRAS
	CALZONE	CALZONES
SCAM	CAM	CAMA = CAME = CAMO = CAMP = CAMS
	CAMA	CAMAN = CAMAS
	CAMAIEU	CAMAIEUX
	CAMAIL	CAMAILS
	CAMAN	CAMANS
	CAMANACHD	CAMANACHDS
	CAMARILLA	CAMARILLAS
	CAMARON	CAMARONS
	CAMAS	CAMASH = CAMASS
	CAMBER	CAMBERS
	CAMBERING	CAMBERINGS
	CAMBIA	CAMBIAL
	CAMBISM	CAMBISMS
	CAMBIST	CAMBISTS
	CAMBIUM	CAMBIUMS
	CAMBOGE	CAMBOGES
	CAMBOGIA	CAMBOGIAS
	CAMBOOSE	CAMBOOSES
	CAMBREL	CAMBRELS
	CAMBRIC	CAMBRICS
	CAMCORDER	CAMCORDERS
	CAME	CAMEL = CAMEO = CAMES
SCAMEL	CAMEL	CAMELS
	CAMELBACK	CAMELBACKS
	CAMELEER	CAMELEERS
	CAMELEON	CAMELEONS
	CAMELHAIR	CAMELHAIRS
	CAMELIA	CAMELIAS
	CAMELID	CAMELIDS
	CAMELINE	CAMELINES
	CAMELLIA	CAMELLIAS
	CAMELOID	CAMELOIDS
	CAMELOT	CAMELOTS
SCAMELS	CAMELS	
	CAMEO	CAMEOS
	CAMERA	CAMERAE = CAMERAL = CAMERAS
	CAMES	CAMESE
	CAMESE	CAMESES

C

FRONT HOOK	ROOT WORD	END HOOK
	CAMION	CAMIONS
	CAMIS	CAMISA = CAMISE
	CAMISA	CAMISAS
	CAMISADE	CAMISADES
	CAMISADO	CAMISADOS
	CAMISE	CAMISES
	CAMISIA	CAMISIAS
	CAMISOLE	CAMISOLES
	CAMLET	CAMLETS
SCAMMED	CAMMED	
	CAMMIE	CAMMIES
SCAMMING	CAMMING	
	CAMO	CAMOS
	CAMOGIE	CAMOGIES
	CAMOMILE	CAMOMILES
	CAMOODI	CAMOODIS
	CAMORRA	CAMORRAS
	CAMORRIST	CAMORRISTA = CAMORRISTI = CAMORRISTS
	CAMOTE	CAMOTES
	CAMOUFLET	CAMOUFLETS
SCAMP	CAMP	CAMPI = CAMPO = CAMPS = CAMPY
	CAMPAGNA	CAMPAGNAS
	CAMPAIGN	CAMPAIGNS
	CAMPANA	CAMPANAS
	CAMPANERO	CAMPANEROS
	CAMPANILE	CAMPANILES
	CAMPANIST	CAMPANISTS
	CAMPANULA	CAMPANULAR = CAMPANULAS
	CAMPCRAFT	CAMPCRAFTS
	CAMPEADOR	CAMPEADORS
SCAMPED	CAMPED	
SCAMPER	CAMPER	CAMPERS
SCAMPERS	CAMPERS	
	CAMPESINO	CAMPESINOS
	CAMPFIRE	CAMPFIRES
	CAMPHANE	CAMPHANES
	CAMPHENE	CAMPHENES
	CAMPHINE	CAMPHINES
	CAMPHIRE	CAMPHIRES
	CAMPHOL	CAMPHOLS
	CAMPHOR	CAMPHORS
SCAMPI	CAMPI	
SCAMPING	CAMPING	CAMPINGS
SCAMPINGS	CAMPINGS	
	CAMPION	CAMPIONS
	CAMPLE	CAMPLED = CAMPLES
	CAMPO	CAMPOS
	CAMPODEID	CAMPODEIDS
	CAMPONG	CAMPONGS
	CAMPOREE	CAMPOREES
	CAMPOUT	CAMPOUTS
SCAMPS	CAMPS	
	CAMPSHIRT	CAMPSHIRTS
	CAMPSITE	CAMPSITES
	CAMPSTOOL	CAMPSTOOLS
SCAMS	CAMS	
	CAMSHAFT	CAMSHAFTS
	CAMSTANE	CAMSTANES
	CAMSTONE	CAMSTONES
	CAMWOOD	CAMWOODS
SCAN	CAN	CANE = CANG = CANN = CANS = CANT = CANY
	CANADA	CANADAS
	CANAIGRE	CANAIGRES
	CANAILLE	CANAILLES
	CANAKIN	CANAKINS
	CANAL	CANALS
	CANALBOAT	CANALBOATS
	CANALISE	CANALISED = CANALISES
	CANALIZE	CANALIZED = CANALIZES

C

FRONT HOOK	ROOT WORD	END HOOK
	CANALLER	CANALLERS
	CANAPE	CANAPES
	CANARD	CANARDS
	CANASTA	CANASTAS
	CANASTER	CANASTERS
	CANBANK	CANBANKS
	CANCAN	CANCANS
	CANCEL	CANCELS
	CANCELEER	CANCELEERS
	CANCELER	CANCELERS
	CANCELIER	CANCELIERS
	CANCELLER	CANCELLERS
	CANCER	CANCERS
	CANCERATE	CANCERATED · CANCERATES
	CANCHA	CANCHAS
	CANCROID	CANCROIDS
	CANDELA	CANDELAS
SCANDENT	CANDENT	
	CANDID	CANDIDA · CANDIDS
	CANDIDA	CANDIDAL · CANDIDAS
	CANDIDATE	CANDIDATES
	CANDIE	CANDIED · CANDIES
	CANDLE	CANDLED · CANDLER · CANDLES
	CANDLENUT	CANDLENUTS
	CANDLEPIN	CANDLEPINS
	CANDLER	CANDLERS
	CANDOCK	CANDOCKS
	CANDOR	CANDORS
	CANDOUR	CANDOURS
	CANDYGRAM	CANDYGRAMS
	CANDYTUFT	CANDYTUFTS
	CANE	CANED · CANEH · CANER · CANES
	CANEBRAKE	CANEBRAKES
	CANEFRUIT	CANEFRUITS
	CANEH	CANEHS
	CANELLA	CANELLAS
	CANEPHOR	CANEPHORA · CANEPHORE · CANEPHORS
	CANEPHORA	CANEPHORAS
	CANEPHORE	CANEPHORES
	CANER	CANERS
	CANEWARE	CANEWARES
	CANFIELD	CANFIELDS
	CANFUL	CANFULS
	CANG	CANGS
	CANGLE	CANGLED · CANGLES
	CANGUE	CANGUES
	CANID	CANIDS
	CANIKIN	CANIKINS
	CANINE	CANINES
	CANING	CANINGS
	CANISTEL	CANISTELS
	CANISTER	CANISTERS
	CANKER	CANKERS · CANKERY
	CANN	CANNA · CANNS · CANNY
	CANNA	CANNAE · CANNAS
	CANNABIN	CANNABINS
	CANNACH	CANNACHS
SCANNED	CANNED	
	CANNEL	CANNELS
	CANNELON	CANNELONI · CANNELONS
	CANNELURE	CANNELURES
SCANNER	CANNER	CANNERS · CANNERY
SCANNERS	CANNERS	
	CANNIBAL	CANNIBALS
	CANNIE	CANNIER
	CANNIKIN	CANNIKINS
SCANNING	CANNING	CANNINGS
SCANNINGS	CANNINGS	
	CANNISTER	CANNISTERS

C

FRONT HOOK	ROOT WORD	END HOOK
	CANNOLI	CANNOLIS
	CANNON	CANNONS
	CANNONADE	CANNONADED · CANNONADES
	CANNONEER	CANNONEERS
	CANNONIER	CANNONIERS
	CANNULA	CANNULAE · CANNULAR · CANNULAS
	CANNULATE	CANNULATED · CANNULATES
	CANOE	CANOED · CANOER · CANOES
	CANOEING	CANOEINGS
	CANOEIST	CANOEISTS
	CANOER	CANOERS
	CANOEWOOD	CANOEWOODS
	CANOLA	CANOLAS
	CANON	CANONS
	CANONICAL	CANONICALS
	CANONISE	CANONISED · CANONISER · CANONISES
	CANONISER	CANONISERS
	CANONIST	CANONISTS
	CANONIZE	CANONIZED · CANONIZER · CANONIZES
	CANONIZER	CANONIZERS
	CANOODLE	CANOODLED · CANOODLER · CANOODLES
	CANOODLER	CANOODLERS
SCANS	**CANS**	CANSO · CANST,
	CANSO	CANSOS
	CANSTICK	CANSTICKS
SCANT	**CANT**	CANTO · CANTS · CANTY
	CANTABANK	CANTABANKS
	CANTABILE	CANTABILES
	CANTAL	CANTALA · CANTALS
	CANTALA	CANTALAS
	CANTALOUP	CANTALOUPE · CANTALOUPS
	CANTAR	CANTARS
	CANTATA	CANTATAS
	CANTATE	CANTATES
	CANTDOG	CANTDOGS
SCANTED	**CANTED**	
	CANTEEN	CANTEENS
SCANTER	**CANTER**	CANTERS
SCANTEST	**CANTEST**	
	CANTHARI	CANTHARID · CANTHARIS
	CANTHARID	CANTHARIDS
ACANTHI	**CANTHI**	
	CANTHOOK	CANTHOOKS
ACANTHUS	**CANTHUS**	
	CANTIC	CANTICO
	CANTICLE	CANTICLES
	CANTICO	CANTICOS · CANTICOY
	CANTICOY	CANTICOYS
	CANTICUM	CANTICUMS
SCANTIER	**CANTIER**	
SCANTIEST	**CANTIEST**	
	CANTILENA	CANTILENAS
SCANTILY	**CANTILY**	
	CANTINA	CANTINAS
SCANTINESS	**CANTINESS**	
SCANTING	**CANTING**	CANTINGS
	CANTION	CANTIONS
SCANTLE	**CANTLE**	CANTLED · CANTLES · CANTLET
SCANTLED	**CANTLED**	
SCANTLES	**CANTLES**	
	CANTLET	CANTLETS
SCANTLING	**CANTLING**	
	CANTO	CANTON · CANTOR · CANTOS
	CANTON	CANTONS
	CANTONISE	CANTONISED · CANTONISES
	CANTONIZE	CANTONIZED · CANTONIZES
	CANTOR	CANTORS
	CANTRAIP	CANTRAIPS
	CANTRAP	CANTRAPS

FRONT HOOK	ROOT WORD	END HOOK
	CANTRED	CANTREDS
	CANTREF	CANTREFS
	CANTRIP	CANTRIPS
SCANTS	**CANTS**	
SCANTY	**CANTY**	
	CANULA	CANULAE ▪ CANULAR ▪ CANULAS
	CANULATE	CANULATED ▪ CANULATES
	CANVAS	CANVASS
	CANVASER	CANVASERS
	CANVASSER	CANVASSERS
	CANYON	CANYONS
	CANYONEER	CANYONEERS
	CANYONING	CANYONINGS
	CANZONA	CANZONAS
	CANZONE	CANZONES ▪ CANZONET
	CANZONET	CANZONETS
	CAP	CAPA ▪ CAPE ▪ CAPH ▪ CAPI ▪ CAPO ▪ CAPS
SCAPA	**CAPA**	CAPAS
	CAPABLE	CAPABLER
	CAPACITOR	CAPACITORS
	CAPARISON	CAPARISONS
SCAPAS	**CAPAS**	
SCAPE	**CAPE**	CAPED ▪ CAPER ▪ CAPES
SCAPED	**CAPED**	
	CAPELAN	CAPELANS
	CAPELET	CAPELETS
	CAPELIN	CAPELINE ▪ CAPELINS
	CAPELINE	CAPELINES
	CAPELLET	CAPELLETS
	CAPELLINE	CAPELLINES
	CAPER	CAPERS
	CAPERER	CAPERERS
SCAPES	**CAPES**	
	CAPESKIN	CAPESKINS
	CAPEWORK	CAPEWORKS
	CAPFUL	CAPFULS
	CAPH	CAPHS
SCAPI	**CAPI**	CAPIZ
SCAPING	**CAPING**	
	CAPITA	CAPITAL ▪ CAPITAN
	CAPITAL	CAPITALS
	CAPITAN	CAPITANI ▪ CAPITANO ▪ CAPITANS
	CAPITANO	CAPITANOS
	CAPITATE	CAPITATED
	CAPITAYN	CAPITAYNS
	CAPITOL	CAPITOLS
	CAPITULA	CAPITULAR
	CAPITULAR	CAPITULARS ▪ CAPITULARY
	CAPLE	CAPLES ▪ CAPLET
	CAPLES	CAPLESS
	CAPLET	CAPLETS
	CAPLIN	CAPLINS
	CAPMAKER	CAPMAKERS
	CAPO	CAPON ▪ CAPOS ▪ CAPOT
	CAPOCCHIA	CAPOCCHIAS
	CAPOEIRA	CAPOEIRAS
	CAPON	CAPONS
	CAPONATA	CAPONATAS
	CAPONIER	CAPONIERE ▪ CAPONIERS
	CAPONIERE	CAPONIERES
	CAPONISE	CAPONISED ▪ CAPONISES
	CAPONIZE	CAPONIZED ▪ CAPONIZES
	CAPORAL	CAPORALS
	CAPOT	CAPOTE ▪ CAPOTS
	CAPOTASTO	CAPOTASTOS
	CAPOTE	CAPOTES
	CAPPER	CAPPERS
	CAPPING	CAPPINGS
	CAPRATE	CAPRATES

C

FRONT HOOK	ROOT WORD	END HOOK
	CAPRIC	CAPRICE
	CAPRICCI	CAPRICCIO
	CAPRICCIO	CAPRICCIOS
	CAPRICE	CAPRICES
	CAPRID	CAPRIDS
	CAPRIFIG	CAPRIFIGS
	CAPRIFOIL	CAPRIFOILS
	CAPRIFOLE	CAPRIFOLES
	CAPRIOLE	CAPRIOLED ▪ CAPRIOLES
	CAPROATE	CAPROATES
	CAPROCK	CAPROCKS
	CAPRYLATE	CAPRYLATES
	CAPSAICIN	CAPSAICINS
	CAPSICIN	CAPSICINS
	CAPSICUM	CAPSICUMS
	CAPSID	CAPSIDS
	CAPSIZAL	CAPSIZALS
	CAPSIZE	CAPSIZED ▪ CAPSIZES
	CAPSOMER	CAPSOMERE ▪ CAPSOMERS
	CAPSOMERE	CAPSOMERES
	CAPSTAN	CAPSTANS
	CAPSTONE	CAPSTONES
	CAPSULAR	CAPSULARY
	CAPSULATE	CAPSULATED
	CAPSULE	CAPSULED ▪ CAPSULES
	CAPSULISE	CAPSULISED ▪ CAPSULISES
	CAPSULIZE	CAPSULIZED ▪ CAPSULIZES
	CAPTAIN	CAPTAINS
	CAPTAN	CAPTANS
	CAPTION	CAPTIONS
	CAPTIVATE	CAPTIVATED ▪ CAPTIVATES
	CAPTIVE	CAPTIVED ▪ CAPTIVES
	CAPTOPRIL	CAPTOPRILS
	CAPTOR	CAPTORS
	CAPTURE	CAPTURED ▪ CAPTURER ▪ CAPTURES
	CAPTURER	CAPTURERS
	CAPUCCIO	CAPUCCIOS
	CAPUCHE	CAPUCHED ▪ CAPUCHES
	CAPUCHIN	CAPUCHINS
	CAPUERA	CAPUERAS
	CAPUL	CAPULS
	CAPYBARA	CAPYBARAS
SCAR	**CAR**	CARB ▪ CARD ▪ CARE ▪ CARK ▪ CARL CARN ▪ CARP ▪ CARR ▪ CARS ▪ CART
	CARABAO	CARABAOS
	CARABID	CARABIDS
	CARABIN	CARABINE ▪ CARABINS
	CARABINE	CARABINER ▪ CARABINES
	CARABINER	CARABINERO ▪ CARABINERS
	CARACAL	CARACALS
	CARACARA	CARACARAS
	CARACK	CARACKS
	CARACOL	CARACOLE ▪ CARACOLS
	CARACOLE	CARACOLED ▪ CARACOLER ▪ CARACOLES
	CARACOLER	CARACOLERS
	CARACT	CARACTS
	CARACUL	CARACULS
	CARAFE	CARAFES
	CARAGANA	CARAGANAS
	CARAGEEN	CARAGEENS
	CARAMBOLA	CARAMBOLAS
	CARAMBOLE	CARAMBOLED ▪ CARAMBOLES
	CARAMEL	CARAMELS
	CARANGID	CARANGIDS
	CARANGOID	CARANGOIDS
	CARANNA	CARANNAS
	CARAP	CARAPS
	CARAPACE	CARAPACED ▪ CARAPACES
	CARASSOW	CARASSOWS

FRONT HOOK	ROOT WORD	END HOOK
	CARAT	CARATE = CARATS
	CARATE	CARATES
	CARAUNA	CARAUNAS
	CARAVAN	CARAVANS
	CARAVANCE	CARAVANCES
	CARAVANER	CARAVANERS
	CARAVEL	CARAVELS
	CARAVELLE	CARAVELLES
	CARAWAY	CARAWAYS
	CARB	CARBO = CARBS = CARBY
	CARBACHOL	CARBACHOLS
	CARBAMATE	CARBAMATES
	CARBAMIDE	CARBAMIDES
	CARBAMOYL	CARBAMOYLS
	CARBAMYL	CARBAMYLS
	CARBANION	CARBANIONS
	CARBARN	CARBARNS
	CARBARYL	CARBARYLS
	CARBAZOLE	CARBAZOLES
	CARBEEN	CARBEENS
	CARBENE	CARBENES
	CARBIDE	CARBIDES
	CARBINE	CARBINES
	CARBINEER	CARBINEERS
	CARBINIER	CARBINIERS
	CARBINOL	CARBINOLS
	CARBO	CARBON = CARBOS = CARBOY
	CARBOLIC	CARBOLICS
	CARBOLISE	CARBOLISED = CARBOLISES
	CARBOLIZE	CARBOLIZED = CARBOLIZES
	CARBON	CARBONS
	CARBONADE	CARBONADES
	CARBONADO	CARBONADOS
	CARBONARA	CARBONARAS
	CARBONATE	CARBONATED = CARBONATES
	CARBONISE	CARBONISED = CARBONISER = CARBONISES
	CARBONIUM	CARBONIUMS
	CARBONIZE	CARBONIZED = CARBONIZER = CARBONIZES
	CARBONYL	CARBONYLS
	CARBORA	CARBORAS
	CARBOXYL	CARBOXYLS
	CARBOY	CARBOYS
	CARBUNCLE	CARBUNCLED = CARBUNCLES
	CARBURATE	CARBURATED = CARBURATES
	CARBURET	CARBURETS
	CARBURISE	CARBURISED = CARBURISES
	CARBURIZE	CARBURIZED = CARBURIZES
	CARCAJOU	CARCAJOUS
	CARCAKE	CARCAKES
	CARCANET	CARCANETS
	CARCASE	CARCASED = CARCASES
	CARCEL	CARCELS
	CARCINOID	CARCINOIDS
	CARCINOMA	CARCINOMAS
	CARD	CARDI = CARDS = CARDY
	CARDAMINE	CARDAMINES
	CARDAMOM	CARDAMOMS
	CARDAMON	CARDAMONS
	CARDAMUM	CARDAMUMS
	CARDBOARD	CARDBOARDS = CARDBOARDY
	CARDCASE	CARDCASES
	CARDECU	CARDECUE = CARDECUS
	CARDECUE	CARDECUES
	CARDER	CARDERS
	CARDI	CARDIA = CARDIE = CARDIO = CARDIS
	CARDIA	CARDIAC = CARDIAE = CARDIAS
	CARDIAC	CARDIACS
	CARDIE	CARDIES
	CARDIGAN	CARDIGANS

C

FRONT HOOK	ROOT WORD	END HOOK
	CARDINAL	CARDINALS
	CARDING	CARDINGS
	CARDIOID	CARDIOIDS
	CARDON	CARDONS
	CARDOON	CARDOONS
	CARDPHONE	CARDPHONES
	CARDSHARP	CARDSHARPS
SCARE	CARE	CARED · CARER · CARES · CARET · CAREX
SCARED	CARED	
	CAREEN	CAREENS
	CAREENAGE	CAREENAGES
	CAREENER	CAREENERS
	CAREER	CAREERS
	CAREERER	CAREERERS
	CAREERISM	CAREERISMS
	CAREERIST	CAREERISTS
	CAREGIVER	CAREGIVERS
	CARELINE	CARELINES
	CAREME	CAREMES
SCARER	CARER	CARERS
SCARERS	CARERS	
SCARES	CARES	CARESS
	CARESSER	CARESSERS
	CARESSING	CARESSINGS
	CARET	CARETS
	CARETAKE	CARETAKEN · CARETAKER · CARETAKES
	CARETAKER	CARETAKERS
	CARFARE	CARFARES
	CARFUFFLE	CARFUFFLED · CARFUFFLES
	CARFUL	CARFULS
	CARGO	CARGOS
	CARHOP	CARHOPS
	CARIACOU	CARIACOUS
	CARIAMA	CARIAMAS
	CARIBE	CARIBES
	CARIBOU	CARIBOUS
	CARIERE	CARIERES
	CARILLON	CARILLONS
OCARINA	CARINA	CARINAE · CARINAL · CARINAS
OCARINAS	CARINAS	
ECARINATE	CARINATE	CARINATED
SCARING	CARING	
	CARIOCA	CARIOCAS
	CARIOLE	CARIOLES
SCARIOSE	CARIOSE	
SCARIOUS	CARIOUS	
	CARJACK	CARJACKS
	CARJACKER	CARJACKERS
	CARJACOU	CARJACOUS
	CARK	CARKS
	CARL	CARLE · CARLS
	CARLE	CARLES
	CARLES	CARLESS
SCARLESS	CARLESS	
	CARLIN	CARLINE · CARLING · CARLINS
	CARLINE	CARLINES
	CARLING	CARLINGS
	CARLOAD	CARLOADS
	CARLOCK	CARLOCKS
	CARLOT	CARLOTS
	CARMAKER	CARMAKERS
	CARMELITE	CARMELITES
	CARMINE	CARMINES
	CARN	CARNS · CARNY
	CARNAGE	CARNAGES
	CARNAHUBA	CARNAHUBAS
	CARNAL	CARNALS
	CARNALISE	CARNALISED · CARNALISES
	CARNALISM	CARNALISMS

C

FRONT HOOK	ROOT WORD	END HOOK
	CARNALIST	CARNALISTS
	CARNALIZE	CARNALIZED · CARNALIZES
	CARNAROLI	CARNAROLIS
	CARNATION	CARNATIONS
	CARNAUBA	CARNAUBAS
	CARNELIAN	CARNELIANS
	CARNET	CARNETS
	CARNEY	CARNEYS
	CARNIE	CARNIED · CARNIER · CARNIES
	CARNIES	CARNIEST
	CARNITINE	CARNITINES
	CARNIVAL	CARNIVALS
	CARNIVORE	CARNIVORES
	CARNOSAUR	CARNOSAURS
	CARNOTITE	CARNOTITES
	CAROB	CAROBS
	CAROCH	CAROCHE
	CAROCHE	CAROCHES
	CAROL	CAROLI · CAROLS
	CAROLER	CAROLERS
	CAROLING	CAROLINGS
	CAROLLER	CAROLLERS
	CAROLLING	CAROLLINGS
	CAROM	CAROMS
	CAROMEL	CAROMELS
	CAROTENE	CAROTENES
	CAROTID	CAROTIDS
	CAROTIN	CAROTINS
	CAROUSAL	CAROUSALS
	CAROUSE	CAROUSED · CAROUSEL · CAROUSER CAROUSES
	CAROUSEL	CAROUSELS
	CAROUSER	CAROUSERS
SCARP	CARP	CARPI · CARPS
	CARPACCIO	CARPACCIOS
	CARPAL	CARPALE · CARPALS
	CARPALE	CARPALES
	CARPARK	CARPARKS
SCARPED	CARPED	
	CARPEL	CARPELS
	CARPENTER	CARPENTERS
SCARPER	CARPER	CARPERS
SCARPERS	CARPERS	
	CARPET	CARPETS
	CARPETBAG	CARPETBAGS
	CARPETING	CARPETINGS
SCARPING	CARPING	CARPINGS
SCARPINGS	CARPINGS	
	CARPOOL	CARPOOLS
	CARPOOLER	CARPOOLERS
	CARPORT	CARPORTS
SCARPS	CARPS	
	CARR	CARRS · CARRY
	CARRACK	CARRACKS
	CARRACT	CARRACTS
	CARRAGEEN	CARRAGEENS
	CARRAT	CARRATS
	CARRAWAY	CARRAWAYS
	CARRECT	CARRECTS
	CARREFOUR	CARREFOURS
	CARREL	CARRELL · CARRELS
	CARRELL	CARRELLS
	CARRIAGE	CARRIAGES
SCARRIER	CARRIER	CARRIERS
	CARRIOLE	CARRIOLES
	CARRION	CARRIONS
	CARROM	CARROMS
	CARRONADE	CARRONADES
	CARROT	CARROTS · CARROTY

C

FRONT HOOK	ROOT WORD	END HOOK
	CARROTIN	CARROTINS
	CARROTTOP	CARROTTOPS
	CARROUSEL	CARROUSELS
SCARRY	**CARRY**	
	CARRYALL	CARRYALLS
	CARRYBACK	CARRYBACKS
	CARRYCOT	CARRYCOTS
	CARRYON	CARRYONS
	CARRYOUT	CARRYOUTS
	CARRYOVER	CARRYOVERS
	CARRYTALE	CARRYTALES
SCARS	**CARS**	CARSE
	CARSE	CARSES ▪ CARSEY
	CARSEY	CARSEYS
SCART	**CART**	CARTA ▪ CARTE ▪ CARTS
	CARTA	CARTAS
	CARTAGE	CARTAGES
ECARTE	**CARTE**	CARTED ▪ CARTEL ▪ CARTER ▪ CARTES
SCARTED	**CARTED**	
	CARTEL	CARTELS
	CARTELISE	CARTELISED ▪ CARTELISES
	CARTELISM	CARTELISMS
	CARTELIST	CARTELISTS
	CARTELIZE	CARTELIZED ▪ CARTELIZES
	CARTER	CARTERS
ECARTES	**CARTES**	
	CARTFUL	CARTFULS
	CARTHORSE	CARTHORSES
	CARTILAGE	CARTILAGES
SCARTING	**CARTING**	
	CARTLOAD	CARTLOADS
	CARTOGRAM	CARTOGRAMS
	CARTON	CARTONS
	CARTONAGE	CARTONAGES
	CARTOON	CARTOONS ▪ CARTOONY
	CARTOPPER	CARTOPPERS
	CARTOUCH	CARTOUCHE
	CARTOUCHE	CARTOUCHES
	CARTRIDGE	CARTRIDGES
	CARTROAD	CARTROADS
SCARTS	**CARTS**	
	CARTWAY	CARTWAYS
	CARTWHEEL	CARTWHEELS
	CARUCAGE	CARUCAGES
	CARUCATE	CARUCATES
	CARUNCLE	CARUNCLES
	CARVACROL	CARVACROLS
	CARVE	CARVED ▪ CARVEL ▪ CARVEN ▪ CARVER ▪ CARVES
	CARVEL	CARVELS
	CARVER	CARVERS ▪ CARVERY
SCARVES	**CARVES**	
	CARVING	CARVINGS
	CARYATID	CARYATIDS
	CARYOTIN	CARYOTINS
	CASA	CASAS
	CASABA	CASABAS
	CASAVA	CASAVAS
	CASBAH	CASBAHS
	CASCABEL	CASCABELS
	CASCABLE	CASCABLES
	CASCADE	CASCADED ▪ CASCADES
	CASCADURA	CASCADURAS
	CASCARA	CASCARAS
	CASCHROM	CASCHROMS
	CASCO	CASCOS
	CASE	CASED ▪ CASES
	CASEASE	CASEASES
	CASEATE	CASEATED ▪ CASEATES

FRONT HOOK	ROOT WORD	END HOOK
	CASEATION	CASEATIONS
	CASEBOOK	CASEBOOKS
	CASEIN	CASEINS
	CASEINATE	CASEINATES
	CASELOAD	CASELOADS
	CASEMAKER	CASEMAKERS
	CASEMATE	CASEMATED - CASEMATES
	CASEMEN	CASEMENT
	CASEMENT	CASEMENTS
	CASEOSE	CASEOSES
	CASERN	CASERNE - CASERNS
	CASERNE	CASERNES
	CASETTE	CASETTES
	CASEWORK	CASEWORKS
	CASEWORM	CASEWORMS
	CASHAW	CASHAWS
	CASHBACK	CASHBACKS
	CASHBOOK	CASHBOOKS
	CASHEW	CASHEWS
	CASHIER	CASHIERS
	CASHIERER	CASHIERERS
	CASHMERE	CASHMERES
	CASHOO	CASHOOS
	CASHPOINT	CASHPOINTS
	CASIMERE	CASIMERES
	CASIMIRE	CASIMIRES
	CASING	CASINGS
	CASINO	CASINOS
	CASITA	CASITAS
	CASK	CASKS - CASKY
	CASKET	CASKETS
	CASKSTAND	CASKSTANDS
	CASQUE	CASQUED - CASQUES
	CASSABA	CASSABAS
	CASSAREEP	CASSAREEPS
	CASSATA	CASSATAS
	CASSATION	CASSATIONS
	CASSAVA	CASSAVAS
	CASSENA	CASSENAS
	CASSENE	CASSENES
	CASSEROLE	CASSEROLED - CASSEROLES
	CASSETTE	CASSETTES
	CASSIA	CASSIAS
	CASSIMERE	CASSIMERES
	CASSINA	CASSINAS
	CASSINE	CASSINES
	CASSINGLE	CASSINGLES
	CASSINO	CASSINOS
	CASSOCK	CASSOCKS
	CASSONADE	CASSONADES
	CASSONE	CASSONES
	CASSOULET	CASSOULETS
	CASSPIR	CASSPIRS
	CAST	CASTE - CASTS
	CASTANET	CASTANETS
	CASTAWAY	CASTAWAYS
	CASTE	CASTED - CASTER - CASTES
	CASTEISM	CASTEISMS
	CASTELLA	CASTELLAN
	CASTELLAN	CASTELLANS
	CASTELLUM	CASTELLUMS
	CASTER	CASTERS
	CASTIGATE	CASTIGATED - CASTIGATES
	CASTING	CASTINGS
	CASTLE	CASTLED - CASTLES
	CASTOCK	CASTOCKS
	CASTOFF	CASTOFFS
	CASTOR	CASTORS - CASTORY
	CASTOREUM	CASTOREUMS

C

FRONT HOOK	ROOT WORD	END HOOK
	CASTRATE	CASTRATED ▪ CASTRATER ▪ CASTRATES
	CASTRATER	CASTRATERS
	CASTRATO	CASTRATOR ▪ CASTRATOS
	CASTRATOR	CASTRATORS ▪ CASTRATORY
	CASUAL	CASUALS
	CASUALISE	CASUALISED ▪ CASUALISES
	CASUALISM	CASUALISMS
	CASUALIZE	CASUALIZED ▪ CASUALIZES
	CASUARINA	CASUARINAS
	CASUIST	CASUISTS
SCAT	**CAT**	CATE ▪ CATS
	CATACLASM	CATACLASMS
	CATACLYSM	CATACLYSMS
	CATACOMB	CATACOMBS
	CATALASE	CATALASES
ACATALEPSY	**CATALEPSY**	
	CATALO	CATALOG ▪ CATALOS
	CATALOG	CATALOGS
	CATALOGER	CATALOGERS
	CATALOGUE	CATALOGUED ▪ CATALOGUER ▪ CATALOGUES
	CATALPA	CATALPAS
	CATALYSE	CATALYSED ▪ CATALYSER ▪ CATALYSES
	CATALYSER	CATALYSERS
	CATALYST	CATALYSTS
	CATALYZE	CATALYZED ▪ CATALYZER ▪ CATALYZES
	CATALYZER	CATALYZERS
	CATAMARAN	CATAMARANS
	CATAMENIA	CATAMENIAL
	CATAMITE	CATAMITES
	CATAMOUNT	CATAMOUNTS
	CATAPAN	CATAPANS
	CATAPHORA	CATAPHORAS
	CATAPHYLL	CATAPHYLLS
	CATAPLASM	CATAPLASMS
	CATAPULT	CATAPULTS
	CATARACT	CATARACTS
	CATARRH	CATARRHS
	CATASTA	CATASTAS
	CATATONIA	CATATONIAS
	CATATONIC	CATATONICS
	CATAWBA	CATAWBAS
	CATBIRD	CATBIRDS
	CATBOAT	CATBOATS
	CATBRIER	CATBRIERS
	CATCALL	CATCALLS
	CATCALLER	CATCALLERS
SCATCH	**CATCH**	CATCHT ▪ CATCHY
	CATCHALL	CATCHALLS
	CATCHER	CATCHERS
SCATCHES	**CATCHES**	
	CATCHING	CATCHINGS
	CATCHMENT	CATCHMENTS
	CATCHPOLE	CATCHPOLES
	CATCHPOLL	CATCHPOLLS
	CATCHUP	CATCHUPS
	CATCHWEED	CATCHWEEDS
	CATCHWORD	CATCHWORDS
	CATCLAW	CATCLAWS
	CATE	CATER ▪ CATES
	CATECHIN	CATECHINS
	CATECHISE	CATECHISED ▪ CATECHISER ▪ CATECHISES
	CATECHISM	CATECHISMS
	CATECHIST	CATECHISTS
	CATECHIZE	CATECHIZED ▪ CATECHIZER ▪ CATECHIZES
	CATECHOL	CATECHOLS
	CATECHU	CATECHUS
	CATELOG	CATELOGS
	CATENA	CATENAE ▪ CATENAS
	CATENANE	CATENANES

FRONT HOOK	ROOT WORD	END HOOK
	CATENATE	CATENATED · CATENATES
	CATENOID	CATENOIDS
ACATER	**CATER**	CATERS
	CATERAN	CATERANS
	CATERER	CATERERS
	CATERING	CATERINGS
ACATERS	**CATERS**	
	CATERWAUL	CATERWAULS
ACATES	**CATES**	
	CATFACE	CATFACES
	CATFACING	CATFACINGS
	CATFALL	CATFALLS
	CATFIGHT	CATFIGHTS
	CATGUT	CATGUTS
	CATHARISE	CATHARISED · CATHARISES
	CATHARIZE	CATHARIZED · CATHARIZES
	CATHARTIC	CATHARTICS
	CATHEAD	CATHEADS
	CATHECT	CATHECTS
	CATHEDRA	CATHEDRAE · CATHEDRAL · CATHEDRAS
	CATHEDRAL	CATHEDRALS
	CATHEPSIN	CATHEPSINS
	CATHETER	CATHETERS
	CATHISMA	CATHISMAS
	CATHODE	CATHODES
	CATHOLE	CATHOLES
	CATHOLIC	CATHOLICS
	CATHOLYTE	CATHOLYTES
	CATHOOD	CATHOODS
	CATHOUSE	CATHOUSES
	CATION	CATIONS
	CATJANG	CATJANGS
	CATKIN	CATKINS
	CATLIN	CATLING · CATLINS
	CATLING	CATLINGS
	CATMINT	CATMINTS
	CATNAP	CATNAPS
	CATNAPER	CATNAPERS
	CATNAPPER	CATNAPPERS
	CATNEP	CATNEPS
	CATNIP	CATNIPS
	CATOLYTE	CATOLYTES
	CATOPTRIC	CATOPTRICS
SCATS	**CATS**	
	CATSKIN	CATSKINS
	CATSPAW	CATSPAWS
	CATSUIT	CATSUITS
	CATSUP	CATSUPS
	CATTABU	CATTABUS
	CATTAIL	CATTAILS
	CATTALO	CATTALOS
SCATTED	**CATTED**	
SCATTERY	**CATTERY**	
	CATTIE	CATTIER · CATTIES
SCATTIER	**CATTIER**	
	CATTIES	CATTIEST
SCATTIEST	**CATTIEST**	
SCATTILY	**CATTILY**	
SCATTINESS	**CATTINESS**	
SCATTING	**CATTING**	
	CATTLEYA	CATTLEYAS
SCATTY	**CATTY**	
	CATWALK	CATWALKS
	CATWORM	CATWORMS
	CAUCHEMAR	CAUCHEMARS
	CAUDA	CAUDAD · CAUDAE · CAUDAL
ACAUDAL	**CAUDAL**	
ACAUDATE · ECAUDATE	**CAUDATE**	CAUDATED · CAUDATES
	CAUDATION	CAUDATIONS

C

FRONT HOOK	ROOT WORD	END HOOK
	CAUDICLE	CAUDICLES
	CAUDILLO	CAUDILLOS
	CAUDLE	CAUDLED · CAUDLES
	CAUDRON	CAUDRONS
	CAUK	CAUKS
	CAUKER	CAUKERS
	CAUL	CAULD · CAULK · CAULS
	CAULD	CAULDS
	CAULDRON	CAULDRONS
	CAULICLE	CAULICLES
ACAULINE	**CAULINE**	
	CAULK	CAULKS
	CAULKER	CAULKERS
	CAULKING	CAULKINGS
	CAULOME	CAULOMES
	CAUM	CAUMS
	CAUMSTONE	CAUMSTONES
SCAUP	**CAUP**	CAUPS
SCAUPS	**CAUPS**	
	CAUSA	CAUSAE · CAUSAL
	CAUSAL	CAUSALS
	CAUSALGIA	CAUSALGIAS
	CAUSATION	CAUSATIONS
	CAUSATIVE	CAUSATIVES
	CAUSE	CAUSED · CAUSEN · CAUSER · CAUSES · CAUSEY
	CAUSER	CAUSERS
	CAUSERIE	CAUSERIES
	CAUSEWAY	CAUSEWAYS
	CAUSEY	CAUSEYS
	CAUSTIC	CAUSTICS
	CAUTEL	CAUTELS
	CAUTER	CAUTERS · CAUTERY
	CAUTERANT	CAUTERANTS
	CAUTERISE	CAUTERISED · CAUTERISES
	CAUTERISM	CAUTERISMS
	CAUTERIZE	CAUTERIZED · CAUTERIZES
	CAUTION	CAUTIONS
	CAUTIONER	CAUTIONERS
	CAVA	CAVAS
	CAVALCADE	CAVALCADED · CAVALCADES
	CAVALERO	CAVALEROS
	CAVALIER	CAVALIERS
	CAVALLA	CAVALLAS
	CAVAS	CAVASS
	CAVATINA	CAVATINAS
	CAVE	CAVED · CAVEL · CAVER · CAVES
	CAVEAT	CAVEATS
	CAVEATOR	CAVEATORS
	CAVEL	CAVELS
	CAVER	CAVERN · CAVERS
	CAVERN	CAVERNS
	CAVESSON	CAVESSONS
	CAVETTO	CAVETTOS
	CAVIAR	CAVIARE · CAVIARS
	CAVIARE	CAVIARES
	CAVIARIE	CAVIARIES
	CAVICORN	CAVICORNS
	CAVIE	CAVIER · CAVIES
	CAVIER	CAVIERS
	CAVIL	CAVILS
	CAVILER	CAVILERS
	CAVILLER	CAVILLERS
	CAVILLING	CAVILLINGS
	CAVING	CAVINGS
	CAVITATE	CAVITATED · CAVITATES
	CAVORT	CAVORTS
	CAVORTER	CAVORTERS
SCAW	**CAW**	CAWK · CAWS
	CAWING	CAWINGS

FRONT HOOK	ROOT WORD	END HOOK
	CAWK	CAWKS
	CAWKER	CAWKERS
SCAWS	**CAWS**	
	CAXON	CAXONS
	CAY	CAYS
	CAYENNE	CAYENNED · CAYENNES
	CAYMAN	CAYMANS
	CAYUSE	CAYUSES
	CAZIQUE	CAZIQUES
	CEAS	CEASE
	CEASE	CEASED · CEASES
	CEASEFIRE	CEASEFIRES
	CEASING	CEASINGS
	CEAZE	CEAZED · CEAZES
	CEBADILLA	CEBADILLAS
	CEBID	CEBIDS
	CEBOID	CEBOIDS
	CECA	CECAL
	CECROPIA	CECROPIAS
	CEDAR	CEDARN · CEDARS · CEDARY
	CEDARBIRD	CEDARBIRDS
	CEDARWOOD	CEDARWOODS
	CEDE	CEDED · CEDER · CEDES
	CEDER	CEDERS
	CEDI	CEDIS
	CEDILLA	CEDILLAS
	CEDRATE	CEDRATES
	CEDULA	CEDULAS
	CEE	CEES
	CEIBA	CEIBAS
	CEIL	CEILI · CEILS
	CEILER	CEILERS
	CEILI	CEILIS
	CEILIDH	CEILIDHS
	CEILING	CEILINGS
	CEINTURE	CEINTURES
	CEL	CELL · CELS · CELT
	CELADON	CELADONS
	CELANDINE	CELANDINES
	CELEB	CELEBS
	CELEBRANT	CELEBRANTS
	CELEBRATE	CELEBRATED · CELEBRATES
	CELERIAC	CELERIACS
	CELESTA	CELESTAS
	CELESTE	CELESTES
	CELESTIAL	CELESTIALS
	CELESTINE	CELESTINES
	CELESTITE	CELESTITES
	CELIAC	CELIACS
	CELIBATE	CELIBATES
	CELL	CELLA · CELLI · CELLO · CELLS
	CELLA	CELLAE · CELLAR
OCELLAR	**CELLAR**	CELLARS
	CELLARAGE	CELLARAGES
	CELLARER	CELLARERS
	CELLARET	CELLARETS
	CELLARIST	CELLARISTS
	CELLARWAY	CELLARWAYS
	CELLBLOCK	CELLBLOCKS
OCELLI	**CELLI**	
	CELLIST	CELLISTS
	CELLMATE	CELLMATES
	CELLO	CELLOS
	CELLOIDIN	CELLOIDINS
	CELLOSE	CELLOSE
	CELLOSE	CELLOSES
	CELLPHONE	CELLPHONES
ACELLULAR	**CELLULAR**	CELLULARS
	CELLULASE	CELLULASES

C

C

FRONT HOOK	ROOT WORD	END HOOK
	CELLULE	CELLULES
	CELLULITE	CELLULITES
	CELLULOID	CELLULOIDS
	CELLULOSE	CELLULOSES
	CELOM	CELOMS
	CELOSIA	CELOSIAS
	CELSITUDE	CELSITUDES
	CELT	CELTS
	CEMBALIST	CEMBALISTS
	CEMBALO	CEMBALOS
	CEMBRA	CEMBRAS
	CEMENT	CEMENTA ▪ CEMENTS
	CEMENTER	CEMENTERS
	CEMENTITE	CEMENTITES
	CEMENTUM	CEMENTUMS
	CEMITARE	CEMITARES
	CENACLE	CENACLES
	CENOBITE	CENOBITES
	CENOTAPH	CENOTAPHS
	CENOTE	CENOTES
	CENS	CENSE
	CENSE	CENSED ▪ CENSER ▪ CENSES
	CENSER	CENSERS
	CENSOR	CENSORS
	CENSURE	CENSURED ▪ CENSURER ▪ CENSURES
	CENSURER	CENSURERS
SCENT	CENT	CENTO ▪ CENTS ▪ CENTU
	CENTAGE	CENTAGES
	CENTAL	CENTALS
	CENTARE	CENTARES
	CENTAUR	CENTAURS ▪ CENTAURY
	CENTAUREA	CENTAUREAS
	CENTAVO	CENTAVOS
	CENTENIER	CENTENIERS
	CENTER	CENTERS
	CENTERING	CENTERINGS
	CENTESIMO	CENTESIMOS
	CENTIARE	CENTIARES
	CENTIGRAM	CENTIGRAMS
	CENTILE	CENTILES
	CENTIME	CENTIMES
	CENTIMO	CENTIMOS
	CENTINEL	CENTINELL ▪ CENTINELS
	CENTINELL	CENTINELLS
	CENTIPEDE	CENTIPEDES
	CENTNER	CENTNERS
	CENTO	CENTOS
	CENTOIST	CENTOISTS
	CENTONEL	CENTONELL ▪ CENTONELS
	CENTONELL	CENTONELLS
	CENTONIST	CENTONISTS
	CENTRA	CENTRAL
	CENTRAL	CENTRALS
	CENTRE	CENTRED ▪ CENTRES
	CENTREING	CENTREINGS
ACENTRIC	CENTRIC	
	CENTRING	CENTRINGS
	CENTRIOLE	CENTRIOLES
	CENTRISM	CENTRISMS
	CENTRIST	CENTRISTS
	CENTRODE	CENTRODES
	CENTROID	CENTROIDS
	CENTRUM	CENTRUMS
SCENTS	CENTS	
	CENTU	CENTUM
	CENTUM	CENTUMS
	CENTUMVIR	CENTUMVIRI
	CENTUPLE	CENTUPLED ▪ CENTUPLES
	CENTURION	CENTURIONS

FRONT HOOK	ROOT WORD	END HOOK
	CEORL	CEORLS
	CEP	CEPE · CEPS
	CEPE	CEPES
ACEPHALIC	CEPHALIC	CEPHALICS
	CEPHALIN	CEPHALINS
ACEPHALOUS	CEPHALOUS	
	CEPHEID	CEPHEIDS
ACERACEOUS	CERACEOUS	
	CERAMAL	CERAMALS
	CERAMIC	CERAMICS
	CERAMIDE	CERAMIDES
	CERAMIST	CERAMISTS
	CERASIN	CERASINS
	CERASTIUM	CERASTIUMS
ACERATE	CERATE	CERATED · CERATES
ACERATED	CERATED	
	CERATIN	CERATINS
	CERCARIA	CERCARIAE · CERCARIAL · CERCARIAN CERCARIAS
	CERCARIAN	CERCARIANS
	CERCI	CERCIS
	CERE	CERED · CERES
	CEREAL	CEREALS
	CEREALIST	CEREALISTS
	CEREBELLA	CEREBELLAR
	CEREBRA	CEREBRAL
	CEREBRAL	CEREBRALS
	CEREBRATE	CEREBRATED · CEREBRATES
	CEREBRUM	CEREBRUMS
	CERECLOTH	CERECLOTHS
	CEREMENT	CEREMENTS
	CERESIN	CERESINE · CERESINS
	CERESINE	CERESINES
	CERGE	CERGES
	CERIA	CERIAS
	CERIPH	CERIPHS
	CERISE	CERISES
	CERITE	CERITES
	CERIUM	CERIUMS
	CERMET	CERMETS
SCERNE	CERNE	CERNED · CERNES
SCERNED	CERNED	
SCERNES	CERNES	
SCERNING	CERNING	
	CERO	CEROS
	CEROGRAPH	CEROGRAPHS · CEROGRAPHY
	CEROON	CEROONS
	CEROTYPE	CEROTYPES
ACEROUS	CEROUS	
	CERT	CERTS
	CERTIFIER	CERTIFIERS
	CERTITUDE	CERTITUDES
	CERULEAN	CERULEANS
	CERULEIN	CERULEINS
	CERUMEN	CERUMENS
	CERUSE	CERUSES
	CERUSITE	CERUSITES
	CERUSSITE	CERUSSITES
	CERVELAT	CERVELATS
	CERVEZA	CERVEZAS
	CERVICUM	CERVICUMS
	CERVID	CERVIDS
	CESAREAN	CESAREANS
	CESAREVNA	CESAREVNAS
	CESARIAN	CESARIANS
	CESIUM	CESIUMS
	CESS	CESSE
	CESSATION	CESSATIONS
	CESSE	CESSED · CESSER · CESSES

C

FRONT HOOK	ROOT WORD	END HOOK
	CESSER	CESSERS
	CESSION	CESSIONS
	CESSPIT	CESSPITS
	CESSPOOL	CESSPOOLS
	CESTA	CESTAS
	CESTODE	CESTODES
	CESTOI	CESTOID
	CESTOID	CESTOIDS
	CESTUI	CESTUIS
	CESURA	CESURAE · CESURAL · CESURAS
	CESURE	CESURES
	CETACEAN	CETACEANS
	CETANE	CETANES
	CETE	CETES
	CETERACH	CETERACHS
	CETRIMIDE	CETRIMIDES
ACETYL	**CETYL**	CETYLS
ACETYLS	**CETYLS**	
	CETYWALL	CETYWALLS
	CEVADILLA	CEVADILLAS
	CEVICHE	CEVICHES
	CEYLANITE	CEYLANITES
	CEYLONITE	CEYLONITES
ACH · ECH · ICH · OCH	**CH**	CHA · CHE · CHI
	CHA	CHAD · CHAI · CHAL · CHAM · CHAO · CHAP
		CHAR · CHAS · CHAT · CHAV · CHAW · CHAY
	CHABAZITE	CHABAZITES
	CHABOUK	CHABOUKS
	CHABUK	CHABUKS
	CHACE	CHACED · CHACES
	CHACHKA	CHACHKAS
	CHACK	CHACKS
	CHACMA	CHACMAS
	CHACO	CHACOS
	CHACONNE	CHACONNES
	CHAD	CHADO · CHADS
	CHADAR	CHADARS
	CHADDAR	CHADDARS
	CHADDOR	CHADDORS
	CHADO	CHADOR · CHADOS
	CHADOR	CHADORS
	CHAEBOL	CHAEBOLS
	CHAETA	CHAETAE · CHAETAL
	CHAETODON	CHAETODONS
	CHAETOPOD	CHAETOPODS
	CHAFE	CHAFED · CHAFER · CHAFES
	CHAFER	CHAFERS
	CHAFF	CHAFFS · CHAFFY
	CHAFFER	CHAFFERS · CHAFFERY
	CHAFFERER	CHAFFERERS
	CHAFFING	CHAFFINGS
	CHAFFRON	CHAFFRONS
	CHAFT	CHAFTS
	CHAGAN	CHAGANS
	CHAGRIN	CHAGRINS
	CHAI	CHAIN · CHAIR · CHAIS
	CHAIN	CHAINE · CHAINS
	CHAINE	CHAINED · CHAINES
	CHAINFALL	CHAINFALLS
	CHAINLET	CHAINLETS
	CHAINSAW	CHAINSAWS
	CHAINSHOT	CHAINSHOTS
	CHAINWORK	CHAINWORKS
	CHAIR	CHAIRS
	CHAIRLIFT	CHAIRLIFTS
	CHAIRMAN	CHAIRMANS
	CHAIS	CHAISE
	CHAISE	CHAISES
	CHAKALAKA	CHAKALAKAS

FRONT HOOK	ROOT WORD	END HOOK
	CHAKRA	CHAKRAS
	CHAL	CHALK = CHALS
	CHALAH	CHALAHS
	CHALAN	CHALANS
	CHALAZA	CHALAZAE = CHALAZAL = CHALAZAS
	CHALAZION	CHALAZIONS
	CHALCID	CHALCIDS
	CHALCOGEN	CHALCOGENS
	CHALDER	CHALDERS
	CHALDRON	CHALDRONS
	CHALEH	CHALEHS
	CHALET	CHALETS
	CHALICE	CHALICED = CHALICES
	CHALK	CHALKS = CHALKY
	CHALKFACE	CHALKFACES
	CHALKPIT	CHALKPITS
	CHALLA	CHALLAH = CHALLAN = CHALLAS
	CHALLAH	CHALLAHS
	CHALLAN	CHALLANS
	CHALLENGE	CHALLENGED = CHALLENGER = CHALLENGES
	CHALLIE	CHALLIES
	CHALLOT	CHALLOTH
	CHALONE	CHALONES
	CHALOT	CHALOTH
	CHALUMEAU	CHALUMEAUS = CHALUMEAUX
	CHALUPA	CHALUPAS
	CHALYBITE	CHALYBITES
	CHAM	CHAMP = CHAMS
	CHAMADE	CHAMADES
	CHAMBER	CHAMBERS
	CHAMBERER	CHAMBERERS
	CHAMBRAY	CHAMBRAYS
	CHAMELEON	CHAMELEONS
	CHAMELOT	CHAMELOTS
	CHAMFER	CHAMFERS
	CHAMFERER	CHAMFERERS
	CHAMFRAIN	CHAMFRAINS
	CHAMFRON	CHAMFRONS
	CHAMISA	CHAMISAL = CHAMISAS
	CHAMISAL	CHAMISALS
	CHAMISE	CHAMISES
	CHAMISO	CHAMISOS
	CHAMLET	CHAMLETS
	CHAMOMILE	CHAMOMILES
	CHAMP	CHAMPS = CHAMPY
	CHAMPAC	CHAMPACA = CHAMPACS
	CHAMPACA	CHAMPACAS
	CHAMPAGNE	CHAMPAGNES
	CHAMPAIGN	CHAMPAIGNS
	CHAMPAK	CHAMPAKS
	CHAMPART	CHAMPARTS
	CHAMPER	CHAMPERS
	CHAMPION	CHAMPIONS
	CHAMPLEVE	CHAMPLEVES
	CHANCE	CHANCED = CHANCEL = CHANCER = CHANCES CHANCEY
	CHANCEL	CHANCELS
	CHANCER	CHANCERS = CHANCERY
	CHANCRE	CHANCRES
	CHANCROID	CHANCROIDS
	CHANDELLE	CHANDELLED = CHANDELLES
	CHANDLER	CHANDLERS = CHANDLERY
	CHANFRON	CHANFRONS
	CHANG	CHANGA = CHANGE = CHANGS
	CHANGE	CHANGED = CHANGER = CHANGES
	CHANGER	CHANGERS
	CHANGEUP	CHANGEUPS
	CHANK	CHANKS
	CHANNEL	CHANNELS

C

FRONT HOOK	ROOT WORD	END HOOK
	CHANNELER	CHANNELERS
	CHANNER	CHANNERS
	CHANOYO	CHANOYOS
	CHANOYU	CHANOYUS
	CHANSON	CHANSONS
	CHANT	CHANTS · CHANTY
	CHANTAGE	CHANTAGES
	CHANTER	CHANTERS
	CHANTEUSE	CHANTEUSES
	CHANTEY	CHANTEYS
	CHANTIE	CHANTIES
	CHANTOR	CHANTORS
	CHANUKIAH	CHANUKIAHS
	CHAO	CHAOS
	CHAP	CHAPE · CHAPS · CHAPT
	CHAPARRAL	CHAPARRALS
	CHAPATI	CHAPATIS
	CHAPATTI	CHAPATTIS
	CHAPBOOK	CHAPBOOKS
	CHAPE	CHAPEL · CHAPES
	CHAPEAU	CHAPEAUS · CHAPEAUX
	CHAPEL	CHAPELS
	CHAPERON	CHAPERONE · CHAPERONS
	CHAPERONE	CHAPERONED · CHAPERONES
	CHAPES	CHAPESS
	CHAPITER	CHAPITERS
	CHAPKA	CHAPKAS
	CHAPLAIN	CHAPLAINS
	CHAPLET	CHAPLETS
	CHAPPAL	CHAPPALS
	CHAPPATI	CHAPPATIS
SCHAPPED	CHAPPED	
	CHAPPIE	CHAPPIER · CHAPPIES
	CHAPPIES	CHAPPIEST
	CHAPRASSI	CHAPRASSIS
	CHAPSTICK	CHAPSTICKS
	CHAPTER	CHAPTERS
	CHAPTREL	CHAPTRELS
	CHAQUETA	CHAQUETAS
	CHAR	CHARA · CHARD · CHARE · CHARK · CHARM CHARR · CHARS · CHART · CHARY
	CHARA	CHARAS
	CHARABANC	CHARABANCS
	CHARACID	CHARACIDS
	CHARACIN	CHARACINS
	CHARACT	CHARACTS
	CHARACTER	CHARACTERS · CHARACTERY
	CHARADE	CHARADES
	CHARANGA	CHARANGAS
	CHARANGO	CHARANGOS
	CHARBROIL	CHARBROILS
	CHARCOAL	CHARCOALS · CHARCOALY
ECHARD ECHARDS	CHARD	CHARDS
	CHARDS	
	CHARE	CHARED · CHARES · CHARET
	CHARET	CHARETS
	CHARGE	CHARGED · CHARGER · CHARGES
	CHARGER	CHARGERS
	CHARGRILL	CHARGRILLS
	CHARIDEE	CHARIDEES
	CHARIOT	CHARIOTS
	CHARISM	CHARISMA · CHARISMS
	CHARISMA	CHARISMAS
	CHARIVARI	CHARIVARIS
	CHARK	CHARKA · CHARKS
	CHARKA	CHARKAS
	CHARKHA	CHARKHAS
	CHARLATAN	CHARLATANS
	CHARLEY	CHARLEYS

FRONT HOOK	ROOT WORD	END HOOK
	CHARLIE	CHARLIER · CHARLIES
	CHARLOCK	CHARLOCKS
	CHARLOTTE	CHARLOTTES
	CHARM	CHARMS
	CHARMER	CHARMERS
	CHARMEUSE	CHARMEUSES
	CHARNECO	CHARNECOS
	CHARNEL	CHARNELS
	CHAROSET	CHAROSETH · CHAROSETS
	CHAROSETH	CHAROSETHS
	CHARPAI	CHARPAIS
	CHARPIE	CHARPIES
	CHARPOY	CHARPOYS
	CHARQUI	CHARQUID · CHARQUIS
	CHARR	CHARRO · CHARRS · CHARRY
	CHARRO	CHARROS
	CHART	CHARTA · CHARTS
	CHARTA	CHARTAS
	CHARTER	CHARTERS
	CHARTERER	CHARTERERS
	CHARTISM	CHARTISMS
	CHARTIST	CHARTISTS
	CHARVER	CHARVERS (offensive)
	CHAS	CHASE · CHASM
	CHASE	CHASED · CHASER · CHASES
	CHASEPORT	CHASEPORTS
	CHASER	CHASERS
	CHASING	CHASINGS
	CHASM	CHASMS · CHASMY
	CHASSE	CHASSED · CHASSES
	CHASSEPOT	CHASSEPOTS
	CHASSEUR	CHASSEURS
	CHASTE	CHASTEN · CHASTER
	CHASTEN	CHASTENS
	CHASTENER	CHASTENERS
	CHASTISE	CHASTISED · CHASTISER · CHASTISES
	CHASTISER	CHASTISERS
	CHASUBLE	CHASUBLES
	CHAT	CHATS
	CHATBOT	CHATBOTS
	CHATCHKA	CHATCHKAS
	CHATCHKE	CHATCHKES
	CHATEAU	CHATEAUS · CHATEAUX
	CHATELAIN	CHATELAINE · CHATELAINS
	CHATLINE	CHATLINES
	CHATON	CHATONS
	CHATOYANT	CHATOYANTS
	CHATROOM	CHATROOMS
	CHATTA	CHATTAS
	CHATTEL	CHATTELS
	CHATTER	CHATTERS · CHATTERY
	CHATTERER	CHATTERERS
	CHATTI	CHATTIS
	CHATTIES	CHATTIEST
	CHAUFE	CHAUFED · CHAUFER · CHAUFES
	CHAUFER	CHAUFERS
	CHAUFF	CHAUFFS
	CHAUFFER	CHAUFFERS
	CHAUFFEUR	CHAUFFEURS
	CHAUMER	CHAUMERS
	CHAUNCE	CHAUNCED · CHAUNCES
	CHAUNGE	CHAUNGED · CHAUNGES
	CHAUNT	CHAUNTS
	CHAUNTER	CHAUNTERS
	CHAUSSURE	CHAUSSURES
	CHAUVIN	CHAUVINS
SCHAV	CHAV	CHAVE · CHAVS (offensive)
	CHAVENDER	CHAVENDERS
	CHAVETTE	CHAVETTES (offensive)

C

C

FRONT HOOK	ROOT WORD	END HOOK
SCHAVS	**CHAVS**	
	CHAW	CHAWK · CHAWS
	CHAWBACON	CHAWBACONS
	CHAWDRON	CHAWDRONS
	CHAWER	CHAWERS
	CHAWK	CHAWKS
	CHAY	CHAYA · CHAYS
	CHAYA	CHAYAS
	CHAYOTE	CHAYOTES
	CHAYROOT	CHAYROOTS
	CHAZAN	CHAZANS
	CHAZZAN	CHAZZANS
	CHAZZEN	CHAZZENS
ACHE · ECHE · OCHE	**CHE**	CHEF · CHER · CHEW · CHEZ
	CHEAP	CHEAPO · CHEAPS · CHEAPY
	CHEAPEN	CHEAPENS
	CHEAPENER	CHEAPENERS
	CHEAPIE	CHEAPIES
	CHEAPJACK	CHEAPJACKS
	CHEAPO	CHEAPOS
	CHEAT	CHEATS
	CHEATER	CHEATERS · CHEATERY
	CHEATING	CHEATINGS
	CHEBEC	CHEBECS
	CHECHAKO	CHECHAKOS
	CHECHAQUO	CHECHAQUOS
	CHECHIA	CHECHIAS
	CHECK	CHECKS · CHECKY
	CHECKBOOK	CHECKBOOKS
	CHECKER	CHECKERS
	CHECKLIST	CHECKLISTS
	CHECKMARK	CHECKMARKS
	CHECKMATE	CHECKMATED · CHECKMATES
	CHECKOFF	CHECKOFFS
	CHECKOUT	CHECKOUTS
	CHECKRAIL	CHECKRAILS
	CHECKREIN	CHECKREINS
	CHECKROOM	CHECKROOMS
	CHECKROW	CHECKROWS
	CHECKSUM	CHECKSUMS
	CHECKUP	CHECKUPS
	CHEDDAR	CHEDDARS · CHEDDARY
	CHEDDITE	CHEDDITES
	CHEDER	CHEDERS
	CHEDITE	CHEDITES
	CHEECHAKO	CHEECHAKOS
	CHEEK	CHEEKS · CHEEKY
	CHEEKBONE	CHEEKBONES
	CHEEKFUL	CHEEKFULS
	CHEEP	CHEEPS
	CHEEPER	CHEEPERS
	CHEER	CHEERO · CHEERS · CHEERY
	CHEERER	CHEERERS
	CHEERIO	CHEERIOS
	CHEERLEAD	CHEERLEADS
	CHEERO	CHEEROS
	CHEESE	CHEESED · CHEESES
	CHEESEVAT	CHEESEVATS
	CHEETAH	CHEETAHS
	CHEEWINK	CHEEWINKS
	CHEF	CHEFS
	CHEFDOM	CHEFDOMS
	CHEGOE	CHEGOES
	CHEKA	CHEKAS
	CHEKIST	CHEKISTS
	CHELA	CHELAE · CHELAS
	CHELASHIP	CHELASHIPS
	CHELATE	CHELATED · CHELATES
	CHELATION	CHELATIONS

FRONT HOOK	ROOT WORD	END HOOK
	CHELATOR	CHELATORS
	CHELICERA	CHELICERAE · CHELICERAL
	CHELIPED	CHELIPEDS
	CHELLUP	CHELLUPS
	CHELOID	CHELOIDS
	CHELONE	CHELONES
	CHELONIAN	CHELONIANS
	CHELP	CHELPS
	CHEMIC	CHEMICS
	CHEMICAL	CHEMICALS
	CHEMISE	CHEMISES
	CHEMISM	CHEMISMS
	CHEMISORB	CHEMISORBS
	CHEMIST	CHEMISTS
	CHEMITYPE	CHEMITYPES
	CHEMO	CHEMOS
	CHEMOKINE	CHEMOKINES
	CHEMOSORB	CHEMOSORBS
	CHEMOSTAT	CHEMOSTATS
	CHEMPADUK	CHEMPADUKS
	CHENAR	CHENARS
	CHENET	CHENETS
	CHENILLE	CHENILLES
	CHENOPOD	CHENOPODS
	CHEONGSAM	CHEONGSAMS
	CHEQUE	CHEQUER · CHEQUES
	CHEQUER	CHEQUERS
OCHER	CHER	CHERE · CHERT
	CHERALITE	CHERALITES
	CHERIMOYA	CHERIMOYAS
	CHERISHER	CHERISHERS
	CHERNOZEM	CHERNOZEMS
	CHEROOT	CHEROOTS
	CHERRIES	CHERRIEST
	CHERT	CHERTS · CHERTY
	CHERUB	CHERUBS
	CHERUBIM	CHERUBIMS
	CHERUBIN	CHERUBINS
	CHERUP	CHERUPS
	CHERVIL	CHERVILS
	CHESHIRE	CHESHIRES
	CHESIL	CHESILS
	CHESNUT	CHESNUTS
	CHESSEL	CHESSELS
	CHEST	CHESTS · CHESTY
	CHESTFUL	CHESTFULS
	CHESTNUT	CHESTNUTS
	CHETAH	CHETAHS
	CHETH	CHETHS
	CHETNIK	CHETNIKS
	CHETRUM	CHETRUMS
	CHEVALET	CHEVALETS
	CHEVALIER	CHEVALIERS
	CHEVELURE	CHEVELURES
	CHEVEN	CHEVENS
	CHEVEREL	CHEVERELS
	CHEVERIL	CHEVERILS
	CHEVERON	CHEVERONS
	CHEVERYE	CHEVERYES
	CHEVET	CHEVETS
	CHEVILLE	CHEVILLES
	CHEVIN	CHEVINS
	CHEVIOT	CHEVIOTS
	CHEVRE	CHEVRES · CHEVRET
	CHEVRET	CHEVRETS
	CHEVRETTE	CHEVRETTES
	CHEVRON	CHEVRONS · CHEVRONY
	CHEW	CHEWS · CHEWY
	CHEWER	CHEWERS

C

FRONT HOOK	ROOT WORD	END HOOK
	CHEWET	CHEWETS
	CHEWIE	CHEWIER ▪ CHEWIES
	CHEWIES	CHEWIEST
	CHEWINK	CHEWINKS
	CHI	CHIA ▪ CHIB ▪ CHIC ▪ CHID ▪ CHIK ▪ CHIN CHIP ▪ CHIS ▪ CHIT ▪ CHIV ▪ CHIZ
	CHIA	CHIAO ▪ CHIAS
	CHIACK	CHIACKS
	CHIACKING	CHIACKINGS
	CHIANTI	CHIANTIS
	CHIAS	CHIASM
	CHIASM	CHIASMA ▪ CHIASMI ▪ CHIASMS
	CHIASMA	CHIASMAL ▪ CHIASMAS
	CHIASMI	CHIASMIC
	CHIB	CHIBS
	CHIBOL	CHIBOLS
	CHIBOUK	CHIBOUKS
	CHIBOUQUE	CHIBOUQUES
	CHIC	CHICA ▪ CHICH ▪ CHICK ▪ CHICO ▪ CHICS
	CHICA	CHICAS
	CHICALOTE	CHICALOTES
	CHICANA	CHICANAS
	CHICANE	CHICANED ▪ CHICANER ▪ CHICANES
	CHICANER	CHICANERS ▪ CHICANERY
	CHICANING	CHICANINGS
	CHICANO	CHICANOS
	CHICH	CHICHA ▪ CHICHI
	CHICHA	CHICHAS
	CHICHI	CHICHIS
TCHICK	CHICK	CHICKS
	CHICKADEE	CHICKADEES
	CHICKAREE	CHICKAREES
	CHICKEE	CHICKEES
	CHICKEN	CHICKENS
	CHICKLING	CHICKLINGS
	CHICKPEA	CHICKPEAS
TCHICKS	CHICKS	
	CHICKWEED	CHICKWEEDS
	CHICLE	CHICLES
	CHICO	CHICON ▪ CHICOS
	CHICON	CHICONS
	CHID	CHIDE
	CHIDE	CHIDED ▪ CHIDER ▪ CHIDES
	CHIDER	CHIDERS
	CHIDING	CHIDINGS
	CHIEF	CHIEFS
	CHIEFDOM	CHIEFDOMS
	CHIEFER	CHIEFERY
	CHIEFLING	CHIEFLINGS
	CHIEFSHIP	CHIEFSHIPS
	CHIEFTAIN	CHIEFTAINS
	CHIEL	CHIELD ▪ CHIELS
	CHIELD	CHIELDS
	CHIFFON	CHIFFONS ▪ CHIFFONY
	CHIGETAI	CHIGETAIS
	CHIGGA	CHIGGAS (offensive)
	CHIGGER	CHIGGERS
	CHIGNON	CHIGNONS
	CHIGOE	CHIGOES
	CHIGRE	CHIGRES
	CHIHUAHUA	CHIHUAHUAS
	CHIK	CHIKS
	CHIKARA	CHIKARAS
	CHIKHOR	CHIKHORS
	CHIKOR	CHIKORS
	CHILBLAIN	CHILBLAINS
	CHILD	CHILDE ▪ CHILDS
	CHILDBED	CHILDBEDS
	CHILDCARE	CHILDCARES

FRONT HOOK	ROOT WORD	END HOOK
	CHILDE	CHILDED ▪ CHILDER ▪ CHILDES
	CHILDHOOD	CHILDHOODS
	CHILE	CHILES
	CHILI	CHILIS
	CHILIAD	CHILIADS
	CHILIAGON	CHILIAGONS
	CHILIARCH	CHILIARCHS ▪ CHILIARCHY
	CHILIASM	CHILIASMS
	CHILIAST	CHILIASTS
	CHILIDOG	CHILIDOGS
	CHILIOI	CHILIOIS
	CHILL	CHILLI ▪ CHILLS ▪ CHILLY
	CHILLADA	CHILLADAS
SCHILLER SCHILLERS	CHILLER	CHILLERS
	CHILLERS	
	CHILLI	CHILLIS
	CHILLIES	CHILLIEST
SCHILLING SCHILLINGS	CHILLING	CHILLINGS
	CHILLINGS	
	CHILLUM	CHILLUMS
	CHILOPOD	CHILOPODS
	CHILTEPIN	CHILTEPINS
	CHIMAERA	CHIMAERAS
	CHIMAR	CHIMARS
	CHIMB	CHIMBS
	CHIMBLEY	CHIMBLEYS
	CHIME	CHIMED ▪ CHIMER ▪ CHIMES
	CHIMER	CHIMERA ▪ CHIMERE ▪ CHIMERS
	CHIMERA	CHIMERAS
	CHIMERE	CHIMERES
	CHIMERID	CHIMERIDS
	CHIMERISM	CHIMERISMS
	CHIMLA	CHIMLAS
	CHIMLEY	CHIMLEYS
	CHIMNEY	CHIMNEYS
	CHIMP	CHIMPS
	CHIN	CHINA ▪ CHINE ▪ CHINK ▪ CHINO ▪ CHINS
	CHINA	CHINAR ▪ CHINAS
	CHINAMPA	CHINAMPAS
	CHINAR	CHINARS
	CHINAROOT	CHINAROOTS
	CHINAWARE	CHINAWARES
	CHINBONE	CHINBONES
	CHINCAPIN	CHINCAPINS
	CHINCH	CHINCHY
	CHINCOUGH	CHINCOUGHS
	CHINDIT	CHINDITS
	CHINE	CHINED ▪ CHINES
	CHINES	CHINESE
	CHINK	CHINKS ▪ CHINKY
	CHINKAPIN	CHINKAPINS
	CHINKARA	CHINKARAS
	CHINKIE	CHINKIER ▪ CHINKIES (offensive)
	CHINKIES	CHINKIEST
	CHINO	CHINOS
	CHINONE	CHINONES
	CHINOOK	CHINOOKS
	CHINOVNIK	CHINOVNIKS
	CHINSTRAP	CHINSTRAPS
	CHINTZ	CHINTZY
	CHINWAG	CHINWAGS
	CHIP	CHIPS
	CHIPBOARD	CHIPBOARDS
	CHIPMUCK	CHIPMUCKS
	CHIPMUNK	CHIPMUNKS
	CHIPOCHIA	CHIPOCHIAS
	CHIPOLATA	CHIPOLATAS
	CHIPOTLE	CHIPOTLES
	CHIPPER	CHIPPERS

FRONT HOOK	ROOT WORD	END HOOK
	CHIPPIE	CHIPPIER • CHIPPIES
	CHIPPIES	CHIPPIEST
	CHIPPING	CHIPPINGS
	CHIPSET	CHIPSETS
	CHIRAGRA	CHIRAGRAS
ACHIRAL	**CHIRAL**	
	CHIRIMOYA	CHIRIMOYAS
	CHIRK	CHIRKS
	CHIRL	CHIRLS
	CHIRM	CHIRMS
	CHIRO	CHIROS
	CHIROPTER	CHIROPTERS
	CHIRP	CHIRPS • CHIRPY
	CHIRPER	CHIRPERS
	CHIRR	CHIRRE • CHIRRS
	CHIRRE	CHIRRED • CHIRREN • CHIRRES
	CHIRRUP	CHIRRUPS • CHIRRUPY
	CHIRRUPER	CHIRRUPERS
	CHIRT	CHIRTS
	CHIRU	CHIRUS
	CHISEL	CHISELS
	CHISELER	CHISELERS
	CHISELLER	CHISELLERS
	CHIT	CHITS
	CHITAL	CHITALS
	CHITCHAT	CHITCHATS
	CHITIN	CHITINS
	CHITLIN	CHITLING • CHITLINS
	CHITLING	CHITLINGS
	CHITON	CHITONS
	CHITOSAN	CHITOSANS
	CHITTER	CHITTERS
	CHITTIES	CHITTIEST
	CHIV	CHIVE • CHIVS • CHIVY
	CHIVAREE	CHIVAREED • CHIVAREES
	CHIVE	CHIVED • CHIVES
	CHIYOGAMI	CHIYOGAMIS
	CHIZ	CHIZZ
	CHLAMYDIA	CHLAMYDIAE • CHLAMYDIAL • CHLAMYDIAS
	CHLOASMA	CHLOASMAS
	CHLORACNE	CHLORACNES
	CHLORAL	CHLORALS
	CHLORATE	CHLORATES
	CHLORDAN	CHLORDANE • CHLORDANS
	CHLORDANE	CHLORDANES
	CHLORELLA	CHLORELLAS
	CHLORID	CHLORIDE • CHLORIDS
	CHLORIDE	CHLORIDES
	CHLORIN	CHLORINE • CHLORINS
	CHLORINE	CHLORINES
	CHLORITE	CHLORITES
	CHOANA	CHOANAE
	CHOBDAR	CHOBDARS
	CHOC	CHOCK • CHOCO • CHOCS
	CHOCCIES	CHOCCIEST
	CHOCHO	CHOCHOS
	CHOCK	CHOCKO • CHOCKS
	CHOCKFUL	CHOCKFULL
	CHOCKO	CHOCKOS
	CHOCO	CHOCOS
	CHOCOLATE	CHOCOLATES • CHOCOLATEY
	CHOCTAW	CHOCTAWS
	CHOG	CHOGS
	CHOICE	CHOICER • CHOICES
	CHOICES	CHOICEST
	CHOIR	CHOIRS
	CHOIRBOY	CHOIRBOYS
	CHOIRGIRL	CHOIRGIRLS
	CHOKE	CHOKED • CHOKER • CHOKES • CHOKEY

FRONT HOOK	ROOT WORD	END HOOK
	CHOKEBORE	CHOKEBORES
	CHOKECOIL	CHOKECOILS
	CHOKEDAMP	CHOKEDAMPS
	CHOKEHOLD	CHOKEHOLDS
	CHOKER	CHOKERS
	CHOKEY	CHOKEYS
	CHOKIDAR	CHOKIDARS
	CHOKIES	CHOKIEST
	CHOKO	CHOKOS
	CHOKRA	CHOKRAS
	CHOKRI	CHOKRIS
	CHOLA	CHOLAS
	CHOLAEMIA	CHOLAEMIAS
	CHOLATE	CHOLATES
	CHOLECYST	CHOLECYSTS
	CHOLELITH	CHOLELITHS
	CHOLEMIA	CHOLEMIAS
	CHOLENT	CHOLENTS
	CHOLER	CHOLERA ▪ CHOLERS
	CHOLERA	CHOLERAS
	CHOLI	CHOLIC ▪ CHOLIS
	CHOLIAMB	CHOLIAMBS
	CHOLINE	CHOLINES
	CHOLLA	CHOLLAS
	CHOLO	CHOLOS
	CHOMMIE	CHOMMIES
	CHOMP	CHOMPS
	CHOMPER	CHOMPERS
	CHON	CHONS
	CHONDRE	CHONDRES
	CHONDRI	CHONDRIN
	CHONDRIN	CHONDRINS
ACHONDRITE	**CHONDRITE**	CHONDRITES
	CHONDROMA	CHONDROMAS
	CHONDRULE	CHONDRULES
	CHOOF	CHOOFS
	CHOOK	CHOOKS
	CHOOKIE	CHOOKIES
	CHOOM	CHOOMS
	CHOOSE	CHOOSER ▪ CHOOSES ▪ CHOOSEY
	CHOOSER	CHOOSERS
	CHOP	CHOPS
	CHOPHOUSE	CHOPHOUSES
	CHOPIN	CHOPINE ▪ CHOPINS
	CHOPINE	CHOPINES
	CHOPLOGIC	CHOPLOGICS
	CHOPPER	CHOPPERS
	CHOPPING	CHOPPINGS
	CHOPSTICK	CHOPSTICKS
	CHORAGI	CHORAGIC
	CHORAL	CHORALE ▪ CHORALS
	CHORALE	CHORALES
	CHORALIST	CHORALISTS
	CHORD	CHORDA ▪ CHORDS
	CHORDA	CHORDAE ▪ CHORDAL
	CHORDATE	CHORDATES
	CHORDEE	CHORDEES
	CHORDING	CHORDINGS
	CHORE	CHOREA ▪ CHORED ▪ CHOREE ▪ CHORES
	CHOREA	CHOREAL ▪ CHOREAS
	CHOREE	CHOREES
	CHOREGI	CHOREGIC
	CHORIA	CHORIAL
	CHORIAMB	CHORIAMBI ▪ CHORIAMBS
	CHORIAMBI	CHORIAMBIC
	CHORINE	CHORINES
	CHORIOID	CHORIOIDS
	CHORION	CHORIONS
	CHORISM	CHORISMS

FRONT HOOK	ROOT WORD	END HOOK
	CHORIST	CHORISTS
	CHORISTER	CHORISTERS
	CHORIZO	CHORIZOS
	CHORIZONT	CHORIZONTS
	CHOROID	CHOROIDS
	CHORRIE	CHORRIES
	CHORTEN	CHORTENS
	CHORTLE	CHORTLED ▪ CHORTLER ▪ CHORTLES
	CHORTLER	CHORTLERS
	CHOSE	CHOSEN ▪ CHOSES
	CHOTT	CHOTTS
	CHOU	CHOUT ▪ CHOUX
	CHOUGH	CHOUGHS
	CHOUNTER	CHOUNTERS
	CHOUSE	CHOUSED ▪ CHOUSER ▪ CHOUSES
	CHOUSER	CHOUSERS
SCHOUT	**CHOUT**	CHOUTS
SCHOUTS	**CHOUTS**	
	CHOW	CHOWK ▪ CHOWS
	CHOWCHOW	CHOWCHOWS
	CHOWDER	CHOWDERS
	CHOWHOUND	CHOWHOUNDS
	CHOWK	CHOWKS
	CHOWKIDAR	CHOWKIDARS
	CHOWRI	CHOWRIS
	CHOWS	CHOWSE
	CHOWSE	CHOWSED ▪ CHOWSES
	CHOWTIME	CHOWTIMES
	CHRESARD	CHRESARDS
	CHRISM	CHRISMA ▪ CHRISMS
	CHRISMA	CHRISMAL
	CHRISMAL	CHRISMALS
	CHRISMON	CHRISMONS
	CHRISOM	CHRISOMS
	CHRISTEN	CHRISTENS
	CHRISTIAN	CHRISTIANS
	CHRISTIE	CHRISTIES
	CHRISTOM	CHRISTOMS
	CHROMA	CHROMAS
	CHROMAKEY	CHROMAKEYS
	CHROMATE	CHROMATES
ACHROMATIC	**CHROMATIC**	CHROMATICS
	CHROMATID	CHROMATIDS
ACHROMATIN	**CHROMATIN**	CHROMATINS
	CHROME	CHROMED ▪ CHROMEL ▪ CHROMES
	CHROMEL	CHROMELS
	CHROMENE	CHROMENES
ACHROMIC	**CHROMIC**	
	CHROMIDE	CHROMIDES
	CHROMING	CHROMINGS
	CHROMISE	CHROMISED ▪ CHROMISES
	CHROMITE	CHROMITES
	CHROMIUM	CHROMIUMS
	CHROMIZE	CHROMIZED ▪ CHROMIZES
	CHROMO	CHROMOS
	CHROMOGEN	CHROMOGENS
ACHROMOUS	**CHROMOUS**	
	CHROMY	CHROMYL
	CHROMYL	CHROMYLS
	CHRONAXIE	CHRONAXIES
	CHRONIC	CHRONICS
	CHRONICLE	CHRONICLED ▪ CHRONICLER ▪ CHRONICLES
	CHRONON	CHRONONS
	CHRYSALID	CHRYSALIDS
	CHRYSANTH	CHRYSANTHS
	CHUB	CHUBS
	CHUBASCO	CHUBASCOS
	CHUCK	CHUCKS ▪ CHUCKY
	CHUCKER	CHUCKERS

FRONT HOOK	ROOT WORD	END HOOK
	CHUCKHOLE	CHUCKHOLES
	CHUCKIE	CHUCKIES
	CHUCKLE	CHUCKLED · CHUCKLER · CHUCKLES
	CHUCKLER	CHUCKLERS
	CHUCKLING	CHUCKLINGS
	CHUDDAH	CHUDDAHS
	CHUDDAR	CHUDDARS
	CHUDDER	CHUDDERS
	CHUFA	CHUFAS
	CHUFF	CHUFFS · CHUFFY
	CHUG	CHUGS
	CHUGALUG	CHUGALUGS
	CHUGGER	CHUGGERS
	CHUKAR	CHUKARS
	CHUKKA	CHUKKAR · CHUKKAS
	CHUKKAR	CHUKKARS
	CHUKKER	CHUKKERS
	CHUKOR	CHUKORS
	CHUM	CHUMP · CHUMS
	CHUMLEY	CHUMLEYS
	CHUMMAGE	CHUMMAGES
	CHUMMIES	CHUMMIEST
	CHUMP	CHUMPS
	CHUMPING	CHUMPINGS
	CHUMSHIP	CHUMSHIPS
	CHUNDER	CHUNDERS
	CHUNK	CHUNKS · CHUNKY
	CHUNKING	CHUNKINGS
	CHUNNEL	CHUNNELS
	CHUNNER	CHUNNERS
	CHUNTER	CHUNTERS
	CHUPATI	CHUPATIS
	CHUPATTI	CHUPATTIS
	CHUPPA	CHUPPAH · CHUPPAS
	CHUPPAH	CHUPPAHS
	CHURCH	CHURCHY
	CHURCHING	CHURCHINGS
	CHURCHISM	CHURCHISMS
	CHURCHWAY	CHURCHWAYS
	CHURIDAR	CHURIDARS
	CHURINGA	CHURINGAS
	CHURL	CHURLS
	CHURN	CHURNS
	CHURNER	CHURNERS
	CHURNING	CHURNINGS
	CHURNMILK	CHURNMILKS
	CHURR	CHURRO · CHURRS
	CHURRO	CHURROS
	CHUSE	CHUSES
	CHUT	CHUTE
	CHUTE	CHUTED · CHUTES
	CHUTIST	CHUTISTS
	CHUTNEE	CHUTNEES
	CHUTNEY	CHUTNEYS
	CHUTZPA	CHUTZPAH · CHUTZPAS
	CHUTZPAH	CHUTZPAHS
	CHYACK	CHYACKS
	CHYLE	CHYLES
	CHYLURIA	CHYLURIAS
	CHYME	CHYMES
	CHYMIC	CHYMICS
	CHYMIST	CHYMISTS
	CHYMOSIN	CHYMOSINS
	CHYPRE	CHYPRES
	CHYTRID	CHYTRIDS
	CIABATTA	CIABATTAS
	CIAO	CIAOS
	CIBATION	CIBATIONS
	CIBOL	CIBOLS

FRONT HOOK	ROOT WORD	END HOOK
	CIBOULE	CIBOULES
	CICADA	CICADAE · CICADAS
	CICALA	CICALAS
	CICATRICE	CICATRICES
	CICATRISE	CICATRISED · CICATRISER · CICATRISES
	CICATRIZE	CICATRIZED · CICATRIZER · CICATRIZES
	CICERO	CICEROS
	CICERONE	CICERONED · CICERONES
	CICHLID	CICHLIDS
	CICISBEO	CICISBEOS
	CICLATON	CICLATONS
	CICLATOUN	CICLATOUNS
	CICOREE	CICOREES
	CICUTA	CICUTAS
	CICUTINE	CICUTINES
ACID	**CID**	CIDE · CIDS
	CIDE	CIDED · CIDER · CIDES
ACIDER	**CIDER**	CIDERS · CIDERY
	CIDERKIN	CIDERKINS
ACIDS	**CIDS**	
	CIEL	CIELS
	CIELING	CIELINGS
	CIERGE	CIERGES
	CIG	CIGS
	CIGAR	CIGARS
	CIGARET	CIGARETS
	CIGARETTE	CIGARETTES
	CIGARILLO	CIGARILLOS
	CIGGIE	CIGGIES
	CIGUATERA	CIGUATERAS
	CILANTRO	CILANTROS
	CILIATE	CILIATED · CILIATES
	CILIATION	CILIATIONS
	CILICE	CILICES
	CILL	CILLS
	CIMAR	CIMARS
	CIMBALOM	CIMBALOMS
	CIMIER	CIMIERS
	CIMINITE	CIMINITES
	CIMOLITE	CIMOLITES
	CINCHING	CINCHINGS
	CINCHONA	CINCHONAS
	CINCTURE	CINCTURED · CINCTURES
	CINDER	CINDERS · CINDERY
	CINE	CINES
	CINEAST	CINEASTE · CINEASTS
	CINEASTE	CINEASTES
	CINEMA	CINEMAS
	CINEOL	CINEOLE · CINEOLS
	CINEOLE	CINEOLES
	CINEPHILE	CINEPHILES
	CINERARIA	CINERARIAS
	CINERATOR	CINERATORS
	CINEREA	CINEREAL · CINEREAS
	CINERIN	CINERINS
	CINGULA	CINGULAR
	CINGULATE	CINGULATED
	CINNABAR	CINNABARS
	CINNAMON	CINNAMONS · CINNAMONY
	CINNAMYL	CINNAMYLS
	CINQUAIN	CINQUAINS
	CINQUE	CINQUES
SCION	**CION**	CIONS
SCIONS	**CIONS**	
	CIOPPINO	CIOPPINOS
	CIPHER	CIPHERS
	CIPHERER	CIPHERERS
	CIPHERING	CIPHERINGS
	CIPOLIN	CIPOLINS

FRONT HOOK	ROOT WORD	END HOOK
	CIPOLLINO	CIPOLLINOS
	CIRCA	CIRCAR
	CIRCAR	CIRCARS
	CIRCLE	CIRCLED = CIRCLER = CIRCLES = CIRCLET
	CIRCLER	CIRCLERS
	CIRCLET	CIRCLETS
	CIRCLING	CIRCLINGS
	CIRCLIP	CIRCLIPS
	CIRCUIT	CIRCUITS = CIRCUITY
	CIRCULAR	CIRCULARS
	CIRCULATE	CIRCULATED = CIRCULATES
	CIRCUS	CIRCUSY
	CIRE	CIRES
	CIRL	CIRLS
	CIRQUE	CIRQUES
	CIRRHOTIC	CIRRHOTICS
	CIRRIPED	CIRRIPEDE = CIRRIPEDS
	CIRRIPEDE	CIRRIPEDES
	CIS	CIST
	CISCO	CISCOS
	CISELEUR	CISELEURS
	CISELURE	CISELURES
	CISPLATIN	CISPLATINS
	CISSIES	CISSIEST
	CISSING	CISSINGS
	CISSOID	CISSOIDS
	CIST	CISTS
	CISTERN	CISTERNA = CISTERNS
	CISTERNA	CISTERNAE = CISTERNAL
	CISTRON	CISTRONS
	CISTVAEN	CISTVAENS
	CIT	CITE = CITO = CITS = CITY
	CITADEL	CITADELS
	CITAL	CITALS
	CITATION	CITATIONS
	CITATOR	CITATORS = CITATORY
	CITE	CITED = CITER = CITES
	CITER	CITERS
	CITES	CITESS
	CITHARA	CITHARAS
	CITHARIST	CITHARISTS
	CITHER	CITHERN = CITHERS
	CITHERN	CITHERNS
	CITHREN	CITHRENS
	CITIZEN	CITIZENS
	CITOLA	CITOLAS
	CITOLE	CITOLES
	CITRAL	CITRALS
	CITRANGE	CITRANGES
	CITRATE	CITRATED = CITRATES
	CITRIN	CITRINE = CITRINS
	CITRINE	CITRINES
	CITRININ	CITRININS
	CITRON	CITRONS
	CITRUS	CITRUSY
	CITTERN	CITTERNS
	CITYSCAPE	CITYSCAPES
	CIVE	CIVES = CIVET
	CIVET	CIVETS
	CIVIC	CIVICS
	CIVICISM	CIVICISMS
	CIVIE	CIVIES
	CIVILIAN	CIVILIANS
	CIVILISE	CIVILISED = CIVILISER = CIVILISES
	CIVILISER	CIVILISERS
	CIVILIST	CIVILISTS
	CIVILIZE	CIVILIZED = CIVILIZER = CIVILIZES
	CIVILIZER	CIVILIZERS
	CIVISM	CIVISMS

FRONT HOOK	ROOT WORD	END HOOK
	CLABBER	CLABBERS
	CLACH	CLACHS
	CLACHAN	CLACHANS
	CLACK	CLACKS
	CLACKER	CLACKERS
YCLAD	**CLAD**	CLADE · CLADS
	CLADDAGH	CLADDAGHS
	CLADDER	CLADDERS
	CLADDIE	CLADDIES
	CLADDING	CLADDINGS
	CLADE	CLADES
	CLADISM	CLADISMS
	CLADIST	CLADISTS
	CLADISTIC	CLADISTICS
	CLADODE	CLADODES
	CLADOGRAM	CLADOGRAMS
	CLAFOUTI	CLAFOUTIS
	CLAG	CLAGS
	CLAIM	CLAIMS
	CLAIMANT	CLAIMANTS
	CLAIMER	CLAIMERS
	CLAM	CLAME · CLAMP · CLAMS
	CLAMBAKE	CLAMBAKES
	CLAMBE	CLAMBER
	CLAMBER	CLAMBERS
	CLAMBERER	CLAMBERERS
	CLAME	CLAMES
	CLAMMER	CLAMMERS
	CLAMOR	CLAMORS
	CLAMORER	CLAMORERS
	CLAMOUR	CLAMOURS
	CLAMOURER	CLAMOURERS
	CLAMP	CLAMPS
	CLAMPDOWN	CLAMPDOWNS
	CLAMPER	CLAMPERS
	CLAMSHELL	CLAMSHELLS
	CLAMWORM	CLAMWORMS
	CLAN	CLANG · CLANK · CLANS
	CLANG	CLANGS
	CLANGER	CLANGERS
	CLANGING	CLANGINGS
	CLANGOR	CLANGORS
	CLANGOUR	CLANGOURS
	CLANK	CLANKS · CLANKY
	CLANKING	CLANKINGS
	CLANSHIP	CLANSHIPS
	CLAP	CLAPS · CLAPT
	CLAPBOARD	CLAPBOARDS
	CLAPBREAD	CLAPBREADS
	CLAPNET	CLAPNETS
	CLAPPER	CLAPPERS
	CLAPPING	CLAPPINGS
	CLAPTRAP	CLAPTRAPS
	CLAQUE	CLAQUER · CLAQUES
	CLAQUER	CLAQUERS
	CLAQUEUR	CLAQUEURS
	CLARAIN	CLARAINS
	CLARENCE	CLARENCES
	CLARENDON	CLARENDONS
	CLARET	CLARETS
	CLARIFIER	CLARIFIERS
	CLARINET	CLARINETS
	CLARINO	CLARINOS
	CLARION	CLARIONS
	CLARIONET	CLARIONETS
	CLARKIA	CLARKIAS
	CLARO	CLAROS
	CLARSACH	CLARSACHS
	CLART	CLARTS · CLARTY

FRONT HOOK	ROOT WORD	END HOOK
	CLARTHEAD	CLARTHEADS
	CLASHER	CLASHERS
	CLASHING	CLASHINGS
	CLASP	CLASPS · CLASPT
	CLASPER	CLASPERS
	CLASPING	CLASPINGS
	CLASS	CLASSY
	CLASSER	CLASSERS
	CLASSIC	CLASSICO · CLASSICS
	CLASSICAL	CLASSICALS
	CLASSING	CLASSINGS
	CLASSIS	CLASSISM · CLASSIST
	CLASSISM	CLASSISMS
	CLASSIST	CLASSISTS
	CLASSMATE	CLASSMATES
	CLASSON	CLASSONS
	CLASSROOM	CLASSROOMS
	CLASSWORK	CLASSWORKS
	CLAST	CLASTS
	CLASTIC	CLASTICS
ECLAT	**CLAT**	CLATS
	CLATHRATE	CLATHRATES
ECLATS	**CLATS**	
	CLATTER	CLATTERS · CLATTERY
	CLATTERER	CLATTERERS
	CLAUCHT	CLAUCHTS
	CLAUGHT	CLAUGHTS
	CLAUSE	CLAUSES
	CLAUSTRA	CLAUSTRAL
	CLAUSULA	CLAUSULAE · CLAUSULAR
	CLAUT	CLAUTS
	CLAVATE	CLAVATED
	CLAVATION	CLAVATIONS
SCLAVE	**CLAVE**	CLAVER · CLAVES
	CLAVECIN	CLAVECINS
	CLAVER	CLAVERS
SCLAVES	**CLAVES**	
	CLAVI	CLAVIE · CLAVIS
	CLAVICLE	CLAVICLES
	CLAVICORN	CLAVICORNS
	CLAVICULA	CLAVICULAE · CLAVICULAR
	CLAVIE	CLAVIER · CLAVIES
	CLAVIER	CLAVIERS
	CLAVIGER	CLAVIGERS
	CLAW	CLAWS
	CLAWBACK	CLAWBACKS
	CLAWER	CLAWERS
	CLAXON	CLAXONS
	CLAY	CLAYS
	CLAYBANK	CLAYBANKS
	CLAYMORE	CLAYMORES
	CLAYPAN	CLAYPANS
	CLAYSTONE	CLAYSTONES
	CLAYTONIA	CLAYTONIAS
	CLAYWARE	CLAYWARES
	CLEAN	CLEANS
	CLEANER	CLEANERS
	CLEANING	CLEANINGS
	CLEANS	CLEANSE
	CLEANSE	CLEANSED · CLEANSER · CLEANSES
	CLEANSER	CLEANSERS
	CLEANSING	CLEANSINGS
	CLEANSKIN	CLEANSKINS
	CLEANUP	CLEANUPS
	CLEAR	CLEARS
	CLEARAGE	CLEARAGES
	CLEARANCE	CLEARANCES
	CLEARCOLE	CLEARCOLED · CLEARCOLES
	CLEARCUT	CLEARCUTS

FRONT HOOK	ROOT WORD	END HOOK
	CLEARER	CLEARERS
	CLEARING	CLEARINGS
	CLEARSKIN	CLEARSKINS
	CLEARWAY	CLEARWAYS
	CLEARWEED	CLEARWEEDS
	CLEARWING	CLEARWINGS
	CLEAT	CLEATS
	CLEAVAGE	CLEAVAGES
	CLEAVE	CLEAVED ▪ CLEAVER ▪ CLEAVES
	CLEAVER	CLEAVERS
	CLEAVING	CLEAVINGS
	CLECK	CLECKS ▪ CLECKY
	CLECKING	CLECKINGS
	CLEEK	CLEEKS
	CLEEP	CLEEPS
YCLEEPED	**CLEEPED**	
YCLEEPING	**CLEEPING**	
	CLEEVE	CLEEVES
	CLEF	CLEFS ▪ CLEFT
	CLEFT	CLEFTS
	CLEG	CLEGS
	CLEIK	CLEIKS
	CLEM	CLEMS
	CLENCHER	CLENCHERS
	CLEOME	CLEOMES
	CLEOPATRA	CLEOPATRAS
	CLEPE	CLEPED ▪ CLEPES
YCLEPED	**CLEPED**	
	CLEPSYDRA	CLEPSYDRAE ▪ CLEPSYDRAS
YCLEPT	**CLEPT**	
	CLERIC	CLERICS
	CLERICAL	CLERICALS
	CLERICATE	CLERICATES
	CLERID	CLERIDS
	CLERIHEW	CLERIHEWS
	CLERK	CLERKS
	CLERKDOM	CLERKDOMS
	CLERKLING	CLERKLINGS
	CLERKSHIP	CLERKSHIPS
	CLERUCH	CLERUCHS ▪ CLERUCHY
	CLERUCHIA	CLERUCHIAL ▪ CLERUCHIAS
	CLEUCH	CLEUCHS
	CLEUGH	CLEUGHS
	CLEVE	CLEVER ▪ CLEVES
	CLEVEITE	CLEVEITES
	CLEW	CLEWS
	CLICHE	CLICHED ▪ CLICHES
	CLICK	CLICKS
	CLICKER	CLICKERS
	CLICKET	CLICKETS
	CLICKING	CLICKINGS
	CLIENT	CLIENTS
	CLIENTAGE	CLIENTAGES
	CLIENTELE	CLIENTELES
SCLIFF	**CLIFF**	CLIFFS ▪ CLIFFY
	CLIFFHANG	CLIFFHANGS
SCLIFFS	**CLIFFS**	
	CLIFT	CLIFTS ▪ CLIFTY
	CLIMATE	CLIMATED ▪ CLIMATES
	CLIMATISE	CLIMATISED ▪ CLIMATISES
	CLIMATIZE	CLIMATIZED ▪ CLIMATIZES
	CLIMATURE	CLIMATURES
	CLIMB	CLIMBS
	CLIMBDOWN	CLIMBDOWNS
	CLIMBER	CLIMBERS
	CLIMBING	CLIMBINGS
	CLIME	CLIMES
	CLINAMEN	CLINAMENS
	CLINCHER	CLINCHERS

FRONT HOOK	ROOT WORD	END HOOK
	CLINE	CLINES
	CLING	CLINGS · CLINGY
	CLINGER	CLINGERS
	CLINGFILM	CLINGFILMS
ACLINIC	CLINIC	CLINICS
	CLINICIAN	CLINICIANS
	CLINIQUE	CLINIQUES
	CLINK	CLINKS
	CLINKER	CLINKERS
	CLINOSTAT	CLINOSTATS
	CLINQUANT	CLINQUANTS
	CLINT	CLINTS
	CLINTONIA	CLINTONIAS
	CLIP	CLIPE · CLIPS · CLIPT
	CLIPART	CLIPARTS
	CLIPBOARD	CLIPBOARDS
	CLIPE	CLIPED · CLIPES
	CLIPPER	CLIPPERS
	CLIPPIE	CLIPPIES
	CLIPPING	CLIPPINGS
	CLIPSHEAR	CLIPSHEARS
	CLIPSHEET	CLIPSHEETS
	CLIQUE	CLIQUED · CLIQUES · CLIQUEY
	CLIQUISM	CLIQUISMS
	CLITELLA	CLITELLAR
	CLITIC	CLITICS
	CLITICISE	CLITICISED · CLITICISES
	CLITICIZE	CLITICIZED · CLITICIZES
	CLITTER	CLITTERS
	CLIVIA	CLIVIAS
	CLOACA	CLOACAE · CLOACAL · CLOACAS
	CLOAK	CLOAKS
	CLOAKROOM	CLOAKROOMS
	CLOAM	CLOAMS
	CLOBBER	CLOBBERS
	CLOCHARD	CLOCHARDS
	CLOCHE	CLOCHES
	CLOCK	CLOCKS
	CLOCKER	CLOCKERS
	CLOCKING	CLOCKINGS
	CLOCKWORK	CLOCKWORKS
	CLOD	CLODS
	CLODPATE	CLODPATED · CLODPATES
	CLODPOLE	CLODPOLES
	CLODPOLL	CLODPOLLS
	CLOFF	CLOFFS
	CLOG	CLOGS
	CLOGDANCE	CLOGDANCES
	CLOGGER	CLOGGERS
	CLOGGING	CLOGGINGS
	CLOISON	CLOISONS
	CLOISONNE	CLOISONNES
	CLOISTER	CLOISTERS
	CLOKE	CLOKED · CLOKES
	CLOMP	CLOMPS
	CLON	CLONE · CLONK · CLONS
	CLONE	CLONED · CLONER · CLONES
	CLONER	CLONERS
	CLONIDINE	CLONIDINES
	CLONING	CLONINGS
	CLONISM	CLONISMS
	CLONK	CLONKS
	CLOOP	CLOOPS
	CLOOT	CLOOTS
	CLOP	CLOPS
	CLOQUE	CLOQUES
ECLOSE	CLOSE	CLOSED · CLOSER · CLOSES · CLOSET
ECLOSED	CLOSED	
	CLOSEDOWN	CLOSEDOWNS

FRONT HOOK	ROOT WORD	END HOOK
	CLOSEHEAD	CLOSEHEADS
	CLOSEOUT	CLOSEOUTS
	CLOSER	CLOSERS
ECLOSES	**CLOSES**	CLOSEST
	CLOSET	CLOSETS
	CLOSETFUL	CLOSETFULS
	CLOSEUP	CLOSEUPS
ECLOSING	**CLOSING**	CLOSINGS
	CLOSURE	CLOSURED ▪ CLOSURES
	CLOT	CLOTE ▪ CLOTH ▪ CLOTS
	CLOTBUR	CLOTBURS
	CLOTE	CLOTES
	CLOTH	CLOTHE ▪ CLOTHS
	CLOTHE	CLOTHED ▪ CLOTHES
	CLOTHIER	CLOTHIERS
	CLOTHING	CLOTHINGS
	CLOTPOLL	CLOTPOLLS
	CLOTTER	CLOTTERS
	CLOTTING	CLOTTINGS
	CLOTURE	CLOTURED ▪ CLOTURES
	CLOU	CLOUD ▪ CLOUR ▪ CLOUS ▪ CLOUT
	CLOUD	CLOUDS ▪ CLOUDY
	CLOUDAGE	CLOUDAGES
	CLOUDING	CLOUDINGS
	CLOUDLAND	CLOUDLANDS
	CLOUDLET	CLOUDLETS
	CLOUDTOWN	CLOUDTOWNS
	CLOUGH	CLOUGHS
	CLOUR	CLOURS
	CLOUT	CLOUTS
	CLOUTER	CLOUTERS
	CLOVE	CLOVEN ▪ CLOVER ▪ CLOVES
	CLOVEPINK	CLOVEPINKS
	CLOVER	CLOVERS ▪ CLOVERY
	CLOW	CLOWN ▪ CLOWS
	CLOWDER	CLOWDERS
	CLOWN	CLOWNS
	CLOWNING	CLOWNINGS
	CLOY	CLOYE ▪ CLOYS
	CLOYE	CLOYED ▪ CLOYES
	CLOYMENT	CLOYMENTS
	CLOZAPINE	CLOZAPINES
	CLOZE	CLOZES
	CLUB	CLUBS
	CLUBBER	CLUBBERS
	CLUBBING	CLUBBINGS
	CLUBBISM	CLUBBISMS
	CLUBBIST	CLUBBISTS
	CLUBFACE	CLUBFACES
	CLUBHAND	CLUBHANDS
	CLUBHAUL	CLUBHAULS
	CLUBHEAD	CLUBHEADS
	CLUBHOUSE	CLUBHOUSES
	CLUBLAND	CLUBLANDS
	CLUBROOM	CLUBROOMS
	CLUBROOT	CLUBROOTS
	CLUCK	CLUCKS ▪ CLUCKY
	CLUDGIE	CLUDGIES
	CLUE	CLUED ▪ CLUES
	CLUMBER	CLUMBERS
	CLUMP	CLUMPS ▪ CLUMPY
	CLUMPER	CLUMPERS
	CLUNK	CLUNKS ▪ CLUNKY
	CLUNKER	CLUNKERS
	CLUPEID	CLUPEIDS
	CLUPEOID	CLUPEOIDS
	CLUSIA	CLUSIAS
	CLUSTER	CLUSTERS ▪ CLUSTERY
	CLUTCH	CLUTCHY

FRONT HOOK	ROOT WORD	END HOOK
	CLUTTER	CLUTTERS ▪ CLUTTERY
	CLYPE	CLYPED ▪ CLYPEI ▪ CLYPES
	CLYSTER	CLYSTERS
	CNIDA	CNIDAE
	CNIDARIAN	CNIDARIANS
	COACH	COACHY
	COACHDOG	COACHDOGS
	COACHEE	COACHEES
	COACHER	COACHERS
	COACHING	COACHINGS
	COACHLINE	COACHLINES
	COACHLOAD	COACHLOADS
	COACHWHIP	COACHWHIPS
	COACHWOOD	COACHWOODS
	COACHWORK	COACHWORKS
	COACT	COACTS
	COACTION	COACTIONS
	COACTOR	COACTORS
	COADJUTOR	COADJUTORS
	COADMIRE	COADMIRED ▪ COADMIRES
	COADMIT	COADMITS
	COADUNATE	COADUNATED ▪ COADUNATES
	COAEVAL	COAEVALS
	COAGENT	COAGENTS
	COAGULANT	COAGULANTS
	COAGULASE	COAGULASES
	COAGULATE	COAGULATED ▪ COAGULATES
	COAGULUM	COAGULUMS
	COAITA	COAITAS
	COAL	COALA ▪ COALS ▪ COALY
	COALA	COALAS
	COALBALL	COALBALLS
	COALBIN	COALBINS
	COALER	COALERS
	COALESCE	COALESCED ▪ COALESCES
	COALFACE	COALFACES
	COALFIELD	COALFIELDS
	COALHOLE	COALHOLES
	COALHOUSE	COALHOUSES
	COALISE	COALISED ▪ COALISES
	COALITION	COALITIONS
	COALIZE	COALIZED ▪ COALIZES
	COALMINE	COALMINER ▪ COALMINES
	COALMINER	COALMINERS
	COALPIT	COALPITS
	COALSACK	COALSACKS
	COALSHED	COALSHEDS
	COALTAR	COALTARS
	COALYARD	COALYARDS
	COAMING	COAMINGS
	COANCHOR	COANCHORS
	COAPPEAR	COAPPEARS
	COAPT	COAPTS
	COARB	COARBS
	COARCTATE	COARCTATED ▪ COARCTATES
	COARSE	COARSEN ▪ COARSER
	COARSEN	COARSENS
	COASSIST	COASSISTS
	COASSUME	COASSUMED ▪ COASSUMES
	COAST	COASTS
	COASTER	COASTERS
	COASTING	COASTINGS
	COASTLAND	COASTLANDS
	COASTLINE	COASTLINES
	COASTWARD	COASTWARDS
	COAT	COATE ▪ COATI ▪ COATS
	COATE	COATED ▪ COATEE ▪ COATER ▪ COATES
	COATEE	COATEES
	COATER	COATERS

FRONT HOOK	ROOT WORD	END HOOK
	COATI	COATIS
	COATING	COATINGS
	COATRACK	COATRACKS
	COATROOM	COATROOMS
	COATSTAND	COATSTANDS
	COATTAIL	COATTAILS
	COATTEND	COATTENDS
	COATTEST	COATTESTS
	COAUTHOR	COAUTHORS
	COAXER	COAXERS
	COB	COBB = COBS
	COBAEA	COBAEAS
	COBALAMIN	COBALAMINS
	COBALT	COBALTS
	COBALTINE	COBALTINES
	COBALTITE	COBALTITES
	COBB	COBBS = COBBY
	COBBER	COBBERS
	COBBLE	COBBLED = COBBLER = COBBLES
	COBBLER	COBBLERS = COBBLERY
	COBBLING	COBBLINGS
	COBIA	COBIAS
	COBLE	COBLES
	COBNUT	COBNUTS
	COBRA	COBRAS
	COBURG	COBURGS
	COBWEB	COBWEBS
	COBZA	COBZAS
	COCA	COCAS
	COCAIN	COCAINE = COCAINS
	COCAINE	COCAINES
	COCAINISE	COCAINISED = COCAINISES
	COCAINISM	COCAINISMS
	COCAINIST	COCAINISTS
	COCAINIZE	COCAINIZED = COCAINIZES
	COCAPTAIN	COCAPTAINS
	COCCI	COCCIC = COCCID
	COCCID	COCCIDS
	COCCO	COCCOS
	COCCOID	COCCOIDS
	COCCOLITE	COCCOLITES
	COCCOLITH	COCCOLITHS
	COCHAIR	COCHAIRS
	COCHIN	COCHINS
	COCHINEAL	COCHINEALS
	COCHLEA	COCHLEAE = COCHLEAR = COCHLEAS
	COCHLEAR	COCHLEARE = COCHLEARS
	COCHLEARE	COCHLEARES
	COCHLEATE	COCHLEATED
	COCINERA	COCINERAS
ACOCK	**COCK**	COCKS = COCKY
	COCKADE	COCKADED = COCKADES
	COCKAPOO	COCKAPOOS
	COCKATEEL	COCKATEELS
	COCKATIEL	COCKATIELS
	COCKATOO	COCKATOOS
	COCKBILL	COCKBILLS
	COCKBIRD	COCKBIRDS
	COCKBOAT	COCKBOATS
	COCKCROW	COCKCROWS
	COCKER	COCKERS
	COCKEREL	COCKERELS
	COCKET	COCKETS
	COCKEYE	COCKEYED = COCKEYES
	COCKFIGHT	COCKFIGHTS
	COCKHORSE	COCKHORSES
	COCKIES	COCKIEST
	COCKLE	COCKLED = COCKLER = COCKLES
	COCKLEBUR	COCKLEBURS

FRONT HOOK	ROOT WORD	END HOOK
	COCKLEERT	COCKLEERTS
	COCKLER	COCKLERS
	COCKLOFT	COCKLOFTS
	COCKNEY	COCKNEYS
	COCKPIT	COCKPITS
	COCKS	COCKSY
	COCKSCOMB	COCKSCOMBS
	COCKSFOOT	COCKSFOOTS
	COCKSHOT	COCKSHOTS
	COCKSHUT	COCKSHUTS
	COCKSPUR	COCKSPURS
	COCKSWAIN	COCKSWAINS
	COCKTAIL	COCKTAILS
	COCKUP	COCKUPS
	COCO	COCOA ▪ COCOS
	COCOA	COCOAS
	COCOANUT	COCOANUTS
	COCOBOLA	COCOBOLAS
	COCOBOLO	COCOBOLOS
	COCOMAT	COCOMATS
	COCONUT	COCONUTS
	COCOON	COCOONS
	COCOONING	COCOONINGS
	COCOPAN	COCOPANS
	COCOPLUM	COCOPLUMS
	COCOTTE	COCOTTES
	COCOUNSEL	COCOUNSELS
	COCOYAM	COCOYAMS
	COCOZELLE	COCOZELLES
	COCREATE	COCREATED ▪ COCREATES
	COCREATOR	COCREATORS
	COCTION	COCTIONS
	COCULTURE	COCULTURED ▪ COCULTURES
	COCURATOR	COCURATORS
	COCUSWOOD	COCUSWOODS
ECOD	**COD**	CODA ▪ CODE ▪ CODS
	CODA	CODAS
	CODDER	CODDERS
	CODDLE	CODDLED ▪ CODDLER ▪ CODDLES
	CODDLER	CODDLERS
	CODE	CODEC ▪ CODED ▪ CODEN ▪ CODER ▪ CODES CODEX
	CODEBOOK	CODEBOOKS
	CODEBTOR	CODEBTORS
	CODEC	CODECS
	CODEIA	CODEIAS
	CODEIN	CODEINA ▪ CODEINE ▪ CODEINS
	CODEINA	CODEINAS
	CODEINE	CODEINES
	CODEN	CODENS
	CODENAME	CODENAMES
	CODER	CODERS
	CODERIVE	CODERIVED ▪ CODERIVES
	CODESIGN	CODESIGNS
	CODETTA	CODETTAS
	CODEVELOP	CODEVELOPS
	CODEWORD	CODEWORDS
	CODGER	CODGERS
	CODICIL	CODICILS
	CODIFIER	CODIFIERS
	CODILLA	CODILLAS
	CODILLE	CODILLES
	CODING	CODINGS
	CODIRECT	CODIRECTS
	CODIST	CODISTS
	CODLIN	CODLING ▪ CODLINS
	CODLING	CODLINGS
	CODOMAIN	CODOMAINS
	CODON	CODONS

FRONT HOOK	ROOT WORD	END HOOK
	CODPIECE	CODPIECES
	CODRIVE	CODRIVEN · CODRIVER · CODRIVES
	CODRIVER	CODRIVERS
	COED	COEDS
	COEDIT	COEDITS
	COEDITOR	COEDITORS
	COEFFECT	COEFFECTS
	COEHORN	COEHORNS
	COELIAC	COELIACS
	COELOM	COELOME · COELOMS
ACOELOMATE	**COELOMATE**	COELOMATES
	COELOME	COELOMES
	COELOSTAT	COELOSTATS
	COEMPLOY	COEMPLOYS
	COEMPT	COEMPTS
	COEMPTION	COEMPTIONS
	COENACLE	COENACLES
	COENACT	COENACTS
	COENAMOR	COENAMORS
	COENDURE	COENDURED · COENDURES
	COENOBITE	COENOBITES
	COENOCYTE	COENOCYTES
	COENOSARC	COENOSARCS
	COENURE	COENURES
	COENZYME	COENZYMES
	COEQUAL	COEQUALS
	COEQUATE	COEQUATED · COEQUATES
	COERCE	COERCED · COERCER · COERCES
	COERCER	COERCERS
	COERCION	COERCIONS
	COERECT	COERECTS
	COESITE	COESITES
	COEVAL	COEVALS
	COEVOLVE	COEVOLVED · COEVOLVES
	COEXERT	COEXERTS
	COEXIST	COEXISTS
	COEXTEND	COEXTENDS
	COFACTOR	COFACTORS
	COFEATURE	COFEATURED · COFEATURES
SCOFF	**COFF**	COFFS
SCOFFED	**COFFED**	
	COFFEE	COFFEES
	COFFEEPOT	COFFEEPOTS
SCOFFER	**COFFER**	COFFERS
	COFFERDAM	COFFERDAMS
SCOFFERS	**COFFERS**	
	COFFIN	COFFING · COFFINS
SCOFFING	**COFFING**	
	COFFINITE	COFFINITES
	COFFLE	COFFLED · COFFLES
	COFFRET	COFFRETS
SCOFFS	**COFFS**	
	COFINANCE	COFINANCED · COFINANCES
	COFOUND	COFOUNDS
	COFOUNDER	COFOUNDERS
SCOG	**COG**	COGS
	COGENCE	COGENCES
	COGENER	COGENERS
SCOGGED	**COGGED**	
	COGGER	COGGERS
	COGGIE	COGGIES
SCOGGING	**COGGING**	COGGINGS
	COGGLE	COGGLED · COGGLES
	COGIE	COGIES
	COGITATE	COGITATED · COGITATES
	COGITATOR	COGITATORS
	COGITO	COGITOS
	COGNAC	COGNACS
	COGNATE	COGNATES

FRONT HOOK	ROOT WORD	END HOOK
	COGNATION	COGNATIONS
	COGNISE	COGNISED = COGNISER = COGNISES
	COGNISER	COGNISERS
	COGNITION	COGNITIONS
	COGNIZE	COGNIZED = COGNIZER = COGNIZES
	COGNIZER	COGNIZERS
	COGNOMEN	COGNOMENS
	COGNOMINA	COGNOMINAL
	COGNOSCE	COGNOSCED = COGNOSCES
	COGNOVIT	COGNOVITS
	COGON	COGONS
SCOGS	**COGS**	
	COGUE	COGUES
	COGWAY	COGWAYS
	COGWHEEL	COGWHEELS
	COHAB	COHABS
	COHABIT	COHABITS
	COHABITEE	COHABITEES
	COHABITER	COHABITERS
	COHABITOR	COHABITORS
	COHEAD	COHEADS
	COHEIR	COHEIRS
	COHERE	COHERED = COHERER = COHERES
	COHERENCE	COHERENCES
	COHERER	COHERERS
	COHERITOR	COHERITORS
	COHESION	COHESIONS
	COHIBIT	COHIBITS
	COHO	COHOE = COHOG = COHOS
	COHOBATE	COHOBATED = COHOBATES
	COHOE	COHOES
	COHOG	COHOGS
	COHOLDER	COHOLDERS
	COHORN	COHORNS
	COHORT	COHORTS
	COHOS	COHOSH = COHOST
	COHOST	COHOSTS
	COHOUSING	COHOUSINGS
	COHUNE	COHUNES
	COHYPONYM	COHYPONYMS
	COIF	COIFS
	COIFFE	COIFFED = COIFFES
	COIFFEUR	COIFFEURS
	COIFFEUSE	COIFFEUSES
	COIFFURE	COIFFURED = COIFFURES
	COIGN	COIGNE = COIGNS
	COIGNE	COIGNED = COIGNES
	COIL	COILS
	COILER	COILERS
	COIN	COINS
	COINAGE	COINAGES
	COINCIDE	COINCIDED = COINCIDES
	COINER	COINERS
	COINFECT	COINFECTS
	COINFER	COINFERS
	COINHERE	COINHERED = COINHERES
	COINING	COININGS
	COINMATE	COINMATES
	COINSURE	COINSURED = COINSURER = COINSURES
	COINSURER	COINSURERS
	COINTER	COINTERS
	COINTREAU	COINTREAUS
	COINVENT	COINVENTS
	COIR	COIRS
	COISTREL	COISTRELS
	COISTRIL	COISTRILS
	COIT	COITS
	COITION	COITIONS
	COJOIN	COJOINS

C

C

FRONT HOOK	ROOT WORD	END HOOK
	COKE	COKED = COKES
	COKEHEAD	COKEHEADS
	COKERNUT	COKERNUTS
	COL	COLA = COLD = COLE = COLL = COLS
		COLT = COLY
	COLA	COLAS
	COLANDER	COLANDERS
	COLBY	COLBYS
	COLCANNON	COLCANNONS
	COLCHICUM	COLCHICUMS
	COLCOTHAR	COLCOTHARS
ACOLD = SCOLD	**COLD**	COLDS
	COLDBLOOD	COLDBLOODS
	COLDCOCK	COLDCOCKS
SCOLDER	**COLDER**	
	COLDHOUSE	COLDHOUSES
	COLDIE	COLDIES
SCOLDS	**COLDS**	
	COLE	COLED = COLES = COLEY
	COLEAD	COLEADS
	COLEADER	COLEADERS
	COLEOPTER	COLEOPTERA = COLEOPTERS
	COLESEED	COLESEEDS
	COLESLAW	COLESLAWS
	COLESSEE	COLESSEES
	COLESSOR	COLESSORS
	COLETIT	COLETITS
	COLEWORT	COLEWORTS
	COLEY	COLEYS
	COLIBRI	COLIBRIS
	COLIC	COLICS
	COLICIN	COLICINE = COLICINS
	COLICINE	COLICINES
	COLICROOT	COLICROOTS
	COLICWEED	COLICWEEDS
	COLIFORM	COLIFORMS
	COLIN	COLINS
	COLIPHAGE	COLIPHAGES
	COLISEUM	COLISEUMS
	COLISTIN	COLISTINS
	COLL	COLLS = COLLY
	COLLAGE	COLLAGED = COLLAGEN = COLLAGES
	COLLAGEN	COLLAGENS
	COLLAGIST	COLLAGISTS
	COLLAPSAR	COLLAPSARS
	COLLAPSE	COLLAPSED = COLLAPSES
	COLLAR	COLLARD = COLLARS
	COLLARD	COLLARDS
	COLLARET	COLLARETS
	COLLATE	COLLATED = COLLATES
	COLLATION	COLLATIONS
	COLLATOR	COLLATORS
	COLLEAGUE	COLLEAGUED = COLLEAGUES
	COLLECT	COLLECTS
	COLLECTOR	COLLECTORS
	COLLEEN	COLLEENS
	COLLEGE	COLLEGER = COLLEGES
	COLLEGER	COLLEGERS
	COLLEGIA	COLLEGIAL = COLLEGIAN
	COLLEGIAN	COLLEGIANS
	COLLEGIUM	COLLEGIUMS
	COLLET	COLLETS
	COLLIDE	COLLIDED = COLLIDER = COLLIDES
	COLLIDER	COLLIDERS
	COLLIE	COLLIED = COLLIER = COLLIES
	COLLIER	COLLIERS = COLLIERY
	COLLIGATE	COLLIGATED = COLLIGATES
	COLLIMATE	COLLIMATED = COLLIMATES
	COLLING	COLLINGS

FRONT HOOK	ROOT WORD	END HOOK
	COLLINSIA	COLLINSIAS
	COLLISION	COLLISIONS
	COLLOCATE	COLLOCATED ▪ COLLOCATES
	COLLODION	COLLODIONS
	COLLODIUM	COLLODIUMS
	COLLOGUE	COLLOGUED ▪ COLLOGUES
	COLLOID	COLLOIDS
SCOLLOP	**COLLOP**	COLLOPS
SCOLLOPS	**COLLOPS**	
	COLLOQUE	COLLOQUED ▪ COLLOQUES
	COLLOQUIA	COLLOQUIAL
	COLLOTYPE	COLLOTYPES
	COLLUDE	COLLUDED ▪ COLLUDER ▪ COLLUDES
	COLLUDER	COLLUDERS
	COLLUSION	COLLUSIONS
	COLLUVIA	COLLUVIAL
	COLLUVIUM	COLLUVIUMS
	COLLYRIUM	COLLYRIUMS
	COLOBI	COLOBID
	COLOBOMA	COLOBOMAS
	COLOCATE	COLOCATED ▪ COLOCATES
	COLOCYNTH	COLOCYNTHS
	COLOG	COLOGS
	COLOGNE	COLOGNED ▪ COLOGNES
	COLOMBARD	COLOMBARDS
	COLON	COLONE ▪ COLONI ▪ COLONS ▪ COLONY
	COLONE	COLONEL ▪ COLONES
	COLONEL	COLONELS
	COLONI	COLONIC
	COLONIAL	COLONIALS
	COLONIC	COLONICS
	COLONISE	COLONISED ▪ COLONISER ▪ COLONISES
	COLONISER	COLONISERS
	COLONIST	COLONISTS
	COLONIZE	COLONIZED ▪ COLONIZER ▪ COLONIZES
	COLONIZER	COLONIZERS
	COLONNADE	COLONNADED ▪ COLONNADES
	COLOPHON	COLOPHONS ▪ COLOPHONY
	COLOR	COLORS ▪ COLORY
	COLORANT	COLORANTS
	COLORCAST	COLORCASTS
	COLORED	COLOREDS (offensive)
	COLORER	COLORERS
	COLORING	COLORINGS
	COLORISE	COLORISED ▪ COLORISER ▪ COLORISES
	COLORISER	COLORISERS
	COLORISM	COLORISMS
	COLORIST	COLORISTS
	COLORIZE	COLORIZED ▪ COLORIZER ▪ COLORIZES
	COLORIZER	COLORIZERS
	COLORWAY	COLORWAYS
	COLOSSEUM	COLOSSEUMS
	COLOSTRUM	COLOSTRUMS
	COLOUR	COLOURS ▪ COLOURY
	COLOURANT	COLOURANTS
	COLOURED	COLOUREDS
	COLOURER	COLOURERS
	COLOURING	COLOURINGS
	COLOURISE	COLOURISED ▪ COLOURISES
	COLOURIST	COLOURISTS
	COLOURIZE	COLOURIZED ▪ COLOURIZES
	COLOURWAY	COLOURWAYS
	COLT	COLTS
	COLTAN	COLTANS
	COLTER	COLTERS
	COLTSFOOT	COLTSFOOTS
	COLTWOOD	COLTWOODS
	COLUBRIAD	COLUBRIADS
	COLUBRID	COLUBRIDS

FRONT HOOK	ROOT WORD	END HOOK
	COLUGO	COLUGOS
	COLUMBATE	COLUMBATES
	COLUMBINE	COLUMBINES
	COLUMBITE	COLUMBITES
	COLUMBIUM	COLUMBIUMS
	COLUMEL	COLUMELS
	COLUMELLA	COLUMELLAE · COLUMELLAR
	COLUMN	COLUMNS
	COLUMNEA	COLUMNEAS
	COLUMNIST	COLUMNISTS
	COLURE	COLURES
	COLZA	COLZAS
	COMA	COMAE · COMAL · COMAS
	COMAKE	COMAKER · COMAKES
	COMAKER	COMAKERS
	COMANAGE	COMANAGED · COMANAGER · COMANAGES
	COMANAGER	COMANAGERS
	COMARB	COMARBS
	COMART	COMARTS
	COMATE	COMATES
	COMATIK	COMATIKS
	COMATULA	COMATULAE
	COMATULID	COMATULIDS
	COMB	COMBE · COMBI · COMBO · COMBS · COMBY
	COMBAT	COMBATS
	COMBATANT	COMBATANTS
	COMBATER	COMBATERS
	COMBE	COMBED · COMBER · COMBES
	COMBER	COMBERS
	COMBI	COMBIS
	COMBIES	COMBIEST
	COMBINE	COMBINED · COMBINER · COMBINES
	COMBINED	COMBINEDS
	COMBINER	COMBINERS
	COMBING	COMBINGS
	COMBINING	COMBININGS
	COMBLE	COMBLES
	COMBLES	COMBLESS
	COMBO	COMBOS
	COMBRETUM	COMBRETUMS
	COMBUST	COMBUSTS
	COMBUSTOR	COMBUSTORS
	COME	COMER · COMES · COMET
	COMEBACK	COMEBACKS
	COMEDDLE	COMEDDLED · COMEDDLES
	COMEDIAN	COMEDIANS
	COMEDO	COMEDOS
	COMEDOWN	COMEDOWNS
	COMEMBER	COMEMBERS
	COMEOVER	COMEOVERS
	COMER	COMERS
	COMET	COMETH · COMETS
	COMETHER	COMETHERS
	COMFIT	COMFITS
	COMFITURE	COMFITURES
	COMFORT	COMFORTS
	COMFORTER	COMFORTERS
	COMFREY	COMFREYS
	COMIC	COMICE · COMICS
	COMICE	COMICES
	COMING	COMINGS
	COMINGLE	COMINGLED · COMINGLES
	COMIQUE	COMIQUES
	COMITADJI	COMITADJIS
	COMITIA	COMITIAL · COMITIAS
	COMM	COMMA · COMMO · COMMS · COMMY
	COMMA	COMMAS
	COMMAND	COMMANDO · COMMANDS
	COMMANDER	COMMANDERS · COMMANDERY

FRONT HOOK	ROOT WORD	END HOOK
	COMMANDO	COMMANDOS
	COMMENCE	COMMENCED ▪ COMMENCER ▪ COMMENCES
	COMMENCER	COMMENCERS
	COMMEND	COMMENDS
	COMMENDAM	COMMENDAMS
	COMMENDER	COMMENDERS
	COMMENSAL	COMMENSALS
	COMMENT	COMMENTS
	COMMENTER	COMMENTERS
	COMMENTOR	COMMENTORS
	COMMER	COMMERE ▪ COMMERS
ECOMMERCE	**COMMERCE**	COMMERCED ▪ COMMERCES
ECOMMERCES	**COMMERCES**	
	COMMERE	COMMERES
	COMMERGE	COMMERGED ▪ COMMERGES
	COMMIE	COMMIES
	COMMINATE	COMMINATED ▪ COMMINATES
	COMMINGLE	COMMINGLED ▪ COMMINGLES
	COMMINUTE	COMMINUTED ▪ COMMINUTES
	COMMISSAR	COMMISSARS ▪ COMMISSARY
	COMMIT	COMMITS
	COMMITTAL	COMMITTALS
	COMMITTEE	COMMITTEES
	COMMITTER	COMMITTERS
	COMMIX	COMMIXT
	COMMO	COMMON ▪ COMMOS ▪ COMMOT
	COMMODE	COMMODES
	COMMODORE	COMMODORES
	COMMON	COMMONS
	COMMONAGE	COMMONAGES
	COMMONER	COMMONERS
	COMMONEY	COMMONEYS
	COMMONING	COMMONINGS
	COMMORANT	COMMORANTS
	COMMOT	COMMOTE ▪ COMMOTS
	COMMOTE	COMMOTES
	COMMOTION	COMMOTIONS
	COMMOVE	COMMOVED ▪ COMMOVES
	COMMUNARD	COMMUNARDS
	COMMUNE	COMMUNED ▪ COMMUNER ▪ COMMUNES
	COMMUNER	COMMUNERS
	COMMUNING	COMMUNINGS
	COMMUNION	COMMUNIONS
	COMMUNISE	COMMUNISED ▪ COMMUNISES
	COMMUNISM	COMMUNISMS
	COMMUNIST	COMMUNISTS
	COMMUNIZE	COMMUNIZED ▪ COMMUNIZES
	COMMUTATE	COMMUTATED ▪ COMMUTATES
	COMMUTE	COMMUTED ▪ COMMUTER ▪ COMMUTES
	COMMUTER	COMMUTERS
	COMONOMER	COMONOMERS
	COMP	COMPO ▪ COMPS ▪ COMPT
	COMPACT	COMPACTS
	COMPACTER	COMPACTERS
	COMPACTOR	COMPACTORS
	COMPADRE	COMPADRES
	COMPAGE	COMPAGES
	COMPAND	COMPANDS
	COMPANDER	COMPANDERS
	COMPANDOR	COMPANDORS
	COMPANION	COMPANIONS
	COMPARE	COMPARED ▪ COMPARER ▪ COMPARES
	COMPARER	COMPARERS
	COMPART	COMPARTS
	COMPAS	COMPASS ▪ COMPAST
	COMPEAR	COMPEARS
	COMPEER	COMPEERS
	COMPEL	COMPELS
	COMPELLER	COMPELLERS

FRONT HOOK	ROOT WORD	END HOOK
	COMPEND	COMPENDS
	COMPER	COMPERE · COMPERS
	COMPERE	COMPERED · COMPERES
	COMPESCE	COMPESCED · COMPESCES
	COMPETE	COMPETED · COMPETES
	COMPILE	COMPILED · COMPILER · COMPILES
	COMPILER	COMPILERS
	COMPING	COMPINGS
	COMPLAIN	COMPLAINS · COMPLAINT
	COMPLAINT	COMPLAINTS
	COMPLECT	COMPLECTS
	COMPLETE	COMPLETED · COMPLETER · COMPLETES
	COMPLETER	COMPLETERS
	COMPLETES	COMPLETEST
	COMPLEXES	COMPLEXEST
	COMPLICE	COMPLICES
	COMPLICIT	COMPLICITY
	COMPLIER	COMPLIERS
	COMPLIN	COMPLINE · COMPLINS
	COMPLINE	COMPLINES
	COMPLOT	COMPLOTS
	COMPO	COMPOS · COMPOT
	COMPONENT	COMPONENTS
	COMPORT	COMPORTS
	COMPOS	COMPOSE · COMPOST
	COMPOSE	COMPOSED · COMPOSER · COMPOSES
	COMPOSER	COMPOSERS
	COMPOSITE	COMPOSITED · COMPOSITES
	COMPOST	COMPOSTS
	COMPOSTER	COMPOSTERS
	COMPOSURE	COMPOSURES
	COMPOT	COMPOTE · COMPOTS
	COMPOTE	COMPOTES
	COMPOTIER	COMPOTIERS
	COMPOUND	COMPOUNDS
	COMPRADOR	COMPRADORE · COMPRADORS
	COMPRINT	COMPRINTS
	COMPRISAL	COMPRISALS
	COMPRISE	COMPRISED · COMPRISES
	COMPRIZE	COMPRIZED · COMPRIZES
	COMPT	COMPTS
	COMPTER	COMPTERS
	COMPTROLL	COMPTROLLS
	COMPULSE	COMPULSED · COMPULSES
	COMPUTANT	COMPUTANTS
	COMPUTE	COMPUTED · COMPUTER · COMPUTES
	COMPUTER	COMPUTERS
	COMPUTIST	COMPUTISTS
	COMRADE	COMRADES
	COMSYMP	COMSYMPS (offensive)
	COMTE	COMTES
ICON	**CON**	COND · CONE · CONF · CONI · CONK · CONN · CONS · CONY
	CONACRE	CONACRED · CONACRES
	CONARIA	CONARIAL
	CONATION	CONATIONS
	CONCAUSE	CONCAUSES
	CONCAVE	CONCAVED · CONCAVES
	CONCEAL	CONCEALS
	CONCEALER	CONCEALERS
	CONCEDE	CONCEDED · CONCEDER · CONCEDES
	CONCEDER	CONCEDERS
	CONCEIT	CONCEITS · CONCEITY
	CONCEIVE	CONCEIVED · CONCEIVER · CONCEIVES
	CONCEIVER	CONCEIVERS
	CONCENT	CONCENTS
	CONCENTER	CONCENTERS
	CONCENTRE	CONCENTRED · CONCENTRES
	CONCEPT	CONCEPTI · CONCEPTS

C

FRONT HOOK	ROOT WORD	END HOOK
	CONCERN	CONCERNS
	CONCERT	CONCERTI ▪ CONCERTO ▪ CONCERTS
	CONCERTO	CONCERTOS
	CONCH	CONCHA ▪ CONCHE ▪ CONCHO ▪ CONCHS ▪ CONCHY
	CONCHA	CONCHAE ▪ CONCHAL ▪ CONCHAS
	CONCHE	CONCHED ▪ CONCHES
	CONCHIE	CONCHIES
	CONCHO	CONCHOS
	CONCHOID	CONCHOIDS
	CONCIERGE	CONCIERGES
	CONCILIAR	CONCILIARY
	CONCISE	CONCISED ▪ CONCISER ▪ CONCISES
	CONCISES	CONCISEST
	CONCISION	CONCISIONS
	CONCLAVE	CONCLAVES
	CONCLUDE	CONCLUDED ▪ CONCLUDER ▪ CONCLUDES
	CONCLUDER	CONCLUDERS
	CONCOCT	CONCOCTS
	CONCOCTER	CONCOCTERS
	CONCOCTOR	CONCOCTORS
	CONCORD	CONCORDS
	CONCORDAT	CONCORDATS
	CONCOURS	CONCOURSE
	CONCOURSE	CONCOURSES
	CONCREATE	CONCREATED ▪ CONCREATES
	CONCRETE	CONCRETED ▪ CONCRETES
	CONCREW	CONCREWS
	CONCUBINE	CONCUBINES
	CONCUR	CONCURS
YCOND	**COND**	CONDO
	CONDEMN	CONDEMNS
	CONDEMNER	CONDEMNERS
	CONDEMNOR	CONDEMNORS
	CONDENSE	CONDENSED ▪ CONDENSER ▪ CONDENSES
	CONDENSER	CONDENSERS ▪ CONDENSERY
	CONDER	CONDERS
	CONDIDDLE	CONDIDDLED ▪ CONDIDDLES
	CONDIE	CONDIES
	CONDIMENT	CONDIMENTS
	CONDITION	CONDITIONS
	CONDO	CONDOM ▪ CONDOR ▪ CONDOS
	CONDOLE	CONDOLED ▪ CONDOLER ▪ CONDOLES
	CONDOLER	CONDOLERS
	CONDOM	CONDOMS
	CONDONE	CONDONED ▪ CONDONER ▪ CONDONES
	CONDONER	CONDONERS
	CONDOR	CONDORS
	CONDUCE	CONDUCED ▪ CONDUCER ▪ CONDUCES
	CONDUCER	CONDUCERS
	CONDUCT	CONDUCTI ▪ CONDUCTS
	CONDUCTOR	CONDUCTORS
	CONDUIT	CONDUITS
	CONDYLE	CONDYLES
	CONDYLOMA	CONDYLOMAS
SCONE	**CONE**	CONED ▪ CONES ▪ CONEY
	CONELRAD	CONELRADS
	CONENOSE	CONENOSES
	CONEPATE	CONEPATES
	CONEPATL	CONEPATLS
ICONES ▪ SCONES	**CONES**	
	CONEY	CONEYS
	CONF	CONFS
	CONFAB	CONFABS
	CONFECT	CONFECTS
	CONFER	CONFERS
	CONFEREE	CONFEREES
	CONFERRAL	CONFERRALS
	CONFERREE	CONFERREES

C

C

FRONT HOOK	ROOT WORD	END HOOK
	CONFERRER	CONFERRERS
	CONFERVA	CONFERVAE · CONFERVAL · CONFERVAS
	CONFESSOR	CONFESSORS
	CONFIDANT	CONFIDANTE · CONFIDANTS
	CONFIDE	CONFIDED · CONFIDER · CONFIDES
	CONFIDENT	CONFIDENTS
	CONFIDER	CONFIDERS
	CONFIGURE	CONFIGURED · CONFIGURES
	CONFINE	CONFINED · CONFINER · CONFINES
	CONFINER	CONFINERS
	CONFIRM	CONFIRMS
	CONFIRMEE	CONFIRMEES
	CONFIRMER	CONFIRMERS
	CONFIRMOR	CONFIRMORS
	CONFISEUR	CONFISEURS
	CONFIT	CONFITS
	CONFITEOR	CONFITEORS
	CONFITURE	CONFITURES
	CONFLATE	CONFLATED · CONFLATES
	CONFLICT	CONFLICTS
	CONFLUENT	CONFLUENTS
	CONFORM	CONFORMS
	CONFORMER	CONFORMERS
	CONFOUND	CONFOUNDS
	CONFRERE	CONFRERES
	CONFRERIE	CONFRERIES
	CONFRONT	CONFRONTE · CONFRONTS
	CONFRONTE	CONFRONTED · CONFRONTER
	CONFUSE	CONFUSED · CONFUSES
	CONFUSION	CONFUSIONS
	CONFUTE	CONFUTED · CONFUTER · CONFUTES
	CONFUTER	CONFUTERS
	CONGA	CONGAS
	CONGE	CONGED · CONGEE · CONGER · CONGES
	CONGEAL	CONGEALS
	CONGEALER	CONGEALERS
	CONGEE	CONGEED · CONGEES
	CONGENER	CONGENERS
	CONGER	CONGERS
	CONGES	CONGEST
	CONGEST	CONGESTS
	CONGLOBE	CONGLOBED · CONGLOBES
	CONGO	CONGOS · CONGOU
	CONGOU	CONGOUS
	CONGREE	CONGREED · CONGREES · CONGREET
	CONGREET	CONGREETS
	CONGRUE	CONGRUED · CONGRUES
	CONI	CONIA · CONIC · CONIN
	CONIA	CONIAS
ICONIC	**CONIC**	CONICS
ICONICAL	**CONICAL**	
ICONICALLY	**CONICALLY**	
	CONICINE	CONICINES
ICONICITY	**CONICITY**	
	CONIDIA	CONIDIAL · CONIDIAN
	CONIFER	CONIFERS
	CONIINE	CONIINES
	CONIMA	CONIMAS
	CONIN	CONINE · CONING · CONINS
	CONINE	CONINES
	CONIUM	CONIUMS
	CONJECT	CONJECTS
	CONJEE	CONJEED · CONJEES
	CONJOIN	CONJOINS · CONJOINT
	CONJOINER	CONJOINERS
	CONJUGANT	CONJUGANTS
	CONJUGATE	CONJUGATED · CONJUGATES
	CONJUNCT	CONJUNCTS
	CONJUNTO	CONJUNTOS

C

FRONT HOOK	ROOT WORD	END HOOK
	CONJURE	CONJURED ▪ CONJURER ▪ CONJURES
	CONJURER	CONJURERS
	CONJURING	CONJURINGS
	CONJUROR	CONJURORS
	CONK	CONKS ▪ CONKY
	CONKER	CONKERS
	CONN	CONNE ▪ CONNS
	CONNATION	CONNATIONS
	CONNATURE	CONNATURES
	CONNE	CONNED ▪ CONNER ▪ CONNES
	CONNECT	CONNECTS
	CONNECTER	CONNECTERS
	CONNECTOR	CONNECTORS
	CONNER	CONNERS
	CONNEXION	CONNEXIONS
	CONNING	CONNINGS
	CONNIVE	CONNIVED ▪ CONNIVER ▪ CONNIVES
	CONNIVER	CONNIVERS ▪ CONNIVERY
	CONNOTATE	CONNOTATED ▪ CONNOTATES
	CONNOTE	CONNOTED ▪ CONNOTES
	CONODONT	CONODONTS
	CONOID	CONOIDS
	CONOMINEE	CONOMINEES
	CONQUER	CONQUERS
	CONQUERER	CONQUERERS
	CONQUEROR	CONQUERORS
	CONQUEST	CONQUESTS
	CONQUIAN	CONQUIANS
ICONS	**CONS**	
	CONSCRIBE	CONSCRIBED ▪ CONSCRIBES
	CONSCRIPT	CONSCRIPTS
	CONSEIL	CONSEILS
	CONSENT	CONSENTS
	CONSENTER	CONSENTERS
	CONSERVE	CONSERVED ▪ CONSERVER ▪ CONSERVES
	CONSERVER	CONSERVERS
	CONSIDER	CONSIDERS
	CONSIGN	CONSIGNS
	CONSIGNEE	CONSIGNEES
	CONSIGNER	CONSIGNERS
	CONSIGNOR	CONSIGNORS
	CONSIST	CONSISTS
	CONSOL	CONSOLE ▪ CONSOLS
	CONSOLATE	CONSOLATED ▪ CONSOLATES
	CONSOLE	CONSOLED ▪ CONSOLER ▪ CONSOLES
	CONSOLER	CONSOLERS
	CONSOMME	CONSOMMES
	CONSONANT	CONSONANTS
	CONSORT	CONSORTS
	CONSORTER	CONSORTERS
	CONSORTIA	CONSORTIAL
	CONSPIRE	CONSPIRED ▪ CONSPIRER ▪ CONSPIRES
	CONSPIRER	CONSPIRERS
	CONSTABLE	CONSTABLES
	CONSTANT	CONSTANTS
	CONSTATE	CONSTATED ▪ CONSTATES
	CONSTER	CONSTERS
	CONSTRAIN	CONSTRAINS ▪ CONSTRAINT
	CONSTRICT	CONSTRICTS
	CONSTRUAL	CONSTRUALS
	CONSTRUCT	CONSTRUCTS
	CONSTRUE	CONSTRUED ▪ CONSTRUER ▪ CONSTRUES
	CONSTRUER	CONSTRUERS
	CONSUL	CONSULS ▪ CONSULT
	CONSULAGE	CONSULAGES
	CONSULAR	CONSULARS
	CONSULATE	CONSULATES
	CONSULT	CONSULTA ▪ CONSULTS
	CONSULTA	CONSULTAS

C

FRONT HOOK	ROOT WORD	END HOOK
	CONSULTEE	CONSULTEES
	CONSULTER	CONSULTERS
	CONSULTOR	CONSULTORS · CONSULTORY
	CONSUME	CONSUMED · CONSUMER · CONSUMES
	CONSUMER	CONSUMERS
	CONSUMING	CONSUMINGS
	CONSUMPT	CONSUMPTS
	CONTACT	CONTACTS
	CONTACTEE	CONTACTEES
	CONTACTOR	CONTACTORS
	CONTADINA	CONTADINAS
	CONTAGION	CONTAGIONS
	CONTAIN	CONTAINS
	CONTAINER	CONTAINERS
	CONTANGO	CONTANGOS
	CONTE	CONTES
	CONTECK	CONTECKS
	CONTEMN	CONTEMNS
	CONTEMNER	CONTEMNERS
	CONTEMNOR	CONTEMNORS
	CONTEMPER	CONTEMPERS
	CONTEMPT	CONTEMPTS
	CONTEND	CONTENDS
	CONTENDER	CONTENDERS
	CONTENT	CONTENTS
	CONTES	CONTEST
	CONTESSA	CONTESSAS
	CONTEST	CONTESTS
	CONTESTER	CONTESTERS
	CONTEXT	CONTEXTS
	CONTINENT	CONTINENTS
	CONTINUA	CONTINUAL
	CONTINUE	CONTINUED · CONTINUER · CONTINUES
	CONTINUER	CONTINUERS
	CONTINUO	CONTINUOS
	CONTINUUM	CONTINUUMS
	CONTLINE	CONTLINES
	CONTO	CONTOS
	CONTORNO	CONTORNOS
	CONTORT	CONTORTS
	CONTOUR	CONTOURS
	CONTRA	CONTRAS · CONTRAT
	CONTRACT	CONTRACTS
	CONTRAIL	CONTRAILS
	CONTRALTO	CONTRALTOS
	CONTRAS	CONTRAST
	CONTRAST	CONTRASTS · CONTRASTY
	CONTRAT	CONTRATE · CONTRATS
	CONTRIST	CONTRISTS
	CONTRIVE	CONTRIVED · CONTRIVER · CONTRIVES
	CONTRIVER	CONTRIVERS
	CONTROL	CONTROLE · CONTROLS
	CONTROUL	CONTROULS
	CONTUND	CONTUNDS
	CONTUSE	CONTUSED · CONTUSES
	CONTUSION	CONTUSIONS
	CONUNDRUM	CONUNDRUMS
	CONURBIA	CONURBIAS
	CONURE	CONURES
	CONVECT	CONVECTS
	CONVECTOR	CONVECTORS
	CONVENE	CONVENED · CONVENER · CONVENES
	CONVENER	CONVENERS
	CONVENOR	CONVENORS
	CONVENT	CONVENTS
	CONVERGE	CONVERGED · CONVERGES
	CONVERSE	CONVERSED · CONVERSER · CONVERSES
	CONVERSER	CONVERSERS
	CONVERSO	CONVERSOS

FRONT HOOK	ROOT WORD	END HOOK
	CONVERT	CONVERTS
	CONVERTER	CONVERTERS
	CONVERTOR	CONVERTORS
	CONVEY	CONVEYS
	CONVEYAL	CONVEYALS
	CONVEYER	CONVEYERS
	CONVEYOR	CONVEYORS
	CONVICT	CONVICTS
	CONVINCE	CONVINCED ▪ CONVINCER ▪ CONVINCES
	CONVINCER	CONVINCERS
	CONVIVE	CONVIVED ▪ CONVIVES
	CONVO	CONVOS ▪ CONVOY
	CONVOCATE	CONVOCATED ▪ CONVOCATES
	CONVOKE	CONVOKED ▪ CONVOKER ▪ CONVOKES
	CONVOKER	CONVOKERS
	CONVOLUTE	CONVOLUTED ▪ CONVOLUTES
	CONVOLVE	CONVOLVED ▪ CONVOLVES
	CONVOY	CONVOYS
	CONVULSE	CONVULSED ▪ CONVULSES
	COO	COOF ▪ COOK ▪ COOL ▪ COOM ▪ COON
		COOP ▪ COOS ▪ COOT
SCOOCH	**COOCH**	
SCOOCHES	**COOCHES**	
	COOEE	COOEED ▪ COOEES
	COOER	COOERS
	COOEY	COOEYS
	COOF	COOFS
	COOING	COOINGS
	COOK	COOKS ▪ COOKY
	COOKBOOK	COOKBOOKS
	COOKER	COOKERS ▪ COOKERY
	COOKEY	COOKEYS
	COOKHOUSE	COOKHOUSES
	COOKIE	COOKIES
	COOKING	COOKINGS
	COOKMAID	COOKMAIDS
	COOKOFF	COOKOFFS
	COOKOUT	COOKOUTS
	COOKROOM	COOKROOMS
	COOKSHACK	COOKSHACKS
	COOKSHOP	COOKSHOPS
	COOKSTOVE	COOKSTOVES
	COOKTOP	COOKTOPS
	COOKWARE	COOKWARES
	COOL	COOLS ▪ COOLY
	COOLABAH	COOLABAHS
	COOLAMON	COOLAMONS
	COOLANT	COOLANTS
	COOLDOWN	COOLDOWNS
	COOLER	COOLERS
	COOLHOUSE	COOLHOUSES
	COOLIBAH	COOLIBAHS
	COOLIBAR	COOLIBARS
	COOLIE	COOLIES
	COOLTH	COOLTHS
	COOM	COOMB ▪ COOMS ▪ COOMY
	COOMB	COOMBE ▪ COOMBS
	COOMBE	COOMBES
	COON	COONS
	COONCAN	COONCANS
	COONDOG	COONDOGS
	COONHOUND	COONHOUNDS
	COONSKIN	COONSKINS
	COONTIE	COONTIES
SCOOP	**COOP**	COOPS ▪ COOPT
SCOOPED	**COOPED**	
SCOOPER	**COOPER**	COOPERS ▪ COOPERY
	COOPERAGE	COOPERAGES
	COOPERATE	COOPERATED ▪ COOPERATES

C

FRONT HOOK	ROOT WORD	END HOOK
	COOPERING	COOPERINGS
SCOOPERS	**COOPERS**	
SCOOPING	**COOPING**	
SCOOPS	**COOPS**	
	COOPT	COOPTS
	COOPTION	COOPTIONS
	COORIE	COORIED • COORIES
	COOS	COOST
	COOSEN	COOSENS
	COOSER	COOSERS
	COOSIN	COOSINS
SCOOT	**COOT**	COOTS
SCOOTCH	**COOTCH**	
SCOOTCHED	**COOTCHED**	
SCOOTCHES	**COOTCHES**	
SCOOTCHING	**COOTCHING**	
SCOOTER	**COOTER**	COOTERS
SCOOTERS	**COOTERS**	
	COOTIE	COOTIES
	COOTIKIN	COOTIKINS
SCOOTS	**COOTS**	
	COOZE	COOZES (offensive)
SCOP	**COP**	COPE • COPS • COPY
	COPAIBA	COPAIBAS
	COPAIVA	COPAIVAS
	COPAL	COPALM • COPALS
	COPALM	COPALMS
	COPARENT	COPARENTS
	COPARTNER	COPARTNERS • COPARTNERY
	COPASTOR	COPASTORS
	COPATRIOT	COPATRIOTS
	COPATRON	COPATRONS
	COPAY	COPAYS
	COPAYMENT	COPAYMENTS
SCOPE	**COPE**	COPED • COPEN • COPER • COPES
	COPECK	COPECKS
SCOPED	**COPED**	
	COPEMATE	COPEMATES
	COPEN	COPENS
	COPEPOD	COPEPODS
	COPER	COPERS
SCOPES	**COPES**	
	COPESTONE	COPESTONES
	COPIER	COPIERS
	COPIHUE	COPIHUES
	COPILOT	COPILOTS
SCOPING	**COPING**	COPINGS
	COPITA	COPITAS
	COPLOT	COPLOTS
	COPOLYMER	COPOLYMERS
	COPOUT	COPOUTS
	COPPER	COPPERS • COPPERY
	COPPERAH	COPPERAHS
	COPPERING	COPPERINGS
	COPPICE	COPPICED • COPPICES
	COPPICING	COPPICINGS
	COPPIN	COPPING • COPPINS
	COPPLE	COPPLES
	COPPRA	COPPRAS
	COPRA	COPRAH • COPRAS
	COPRAH	COPRAHS
	COPREMIA	COPREMIAS
	COPRESENT	COPRESENTS
	COPRINCE	COPRINCES
	COPRODUCE	COPRODUCED • COPRODUCER • COPRODUCES
	COPRODUCT	COPRODUCTS
	COPROLITE	COPROLITES
	COPROLITH	COPROLITHS
	COPROSMA	COPROSMAS

C

FRONT HOOK	ROOT WORD	END HOOK
SCOPS	**COPS**	COPSE ▪ COPSY
	COPSE	COPSED ▪ COPSES
	COPSEWOOD	COPSEWOODS
	COPSHOP	COPSHOPS
	COPTER	COPTERS
SCOPULA	**COPULA**	COPULAE ▪ COPULAR ▪ COPULAS
SCOPULAE	**COPULAE**	
SCOPULAS	**COPULAS**	
SCOPULATE	**COPULATE**	COPULATED ▪ COPULATES
	COPYBOOK	COPYBOOKS
	COPYBOY	COPYBOYS
	COPYCAT	COPYCATS
	COPYDESK	COPYDESKS
	COPYEDIT	COPYEDITS
	COPYGIRL	COPYGIRLS
	COPYGRAPH	COPYGRAPHS
	COPYHOLD	COPYHOLDS
	COPYISM	COPYISMS
	COPYIST	COPYISTS
	COPYLEFT	COPYLEFTS
	COPYREAD	COPYREADS
	COPYRIGHT	COPYRIGHTS
	COPYTAKER	COPYTAKERS
	COQUET	COQUETS
	COQUETTE	COQUETTED ▪ COQUETTES
	COQUILLA	COQUILLAS
	COQUILLE	COQUILLES
	COQUINA	COQUINAS
	COQUITO	COQUITOS
	COR	CORD ▪ CORE ▪ CORF ▪ CORK ▪ CORM CORN ▪ CORS ▪ CORY
	CORACLE	CORACLES
	CORACOID	CORACOIDS
	CORAGGIO	CORAGGIOS
	CORAL	CORALS
	CORALLINE	CORALLINES
	CORALLITE	CORALLITES
	CORALROOT	CORALROOTS
	CORALWORT	CORALWORTS
	CORAMINE	CORAMINES
	CORANACH	CORANACHS
	CORANTO	CORANTOS
	CORBAN	CORBANS
	CORBE	CORBEL ▪ CORBES
	CORBEAU	CORBEAUS
	CORBEIL	CORBEILS
	CORBEILLE	CORBEILLES
	CORBEL	CORBELS
	CORBELING	CORBELINGS
	CORBICULA	CORBICULAE
	CORBIE	CORBIES
	CORBINA	CORBINAS
	CORD	CORDS
	CORDAGE	CORDAGES
	CORDELLE	CORDELLED ▪ CORDELLES
	CORDER	CORDERS
	CORDIAL	CORDIALS
	CORDINER	CORDINERS
	CORDING	CORDINGS
	CORDITE	CORDITES
	CORDOBA	CORDOBAS
	CORDON	CORDONS
	CORDONNET	CORDONNETS
	CORDOVAN	CORDOVANS
	CORDUROY	CORDUROYS
	CORDWAIN	CORDWAINS
	CORDWOOD	CORDWOODS
	CORDYLINE	CORDYLINES
SCORE	**CORE**	CORED ▪ CORER ▪ CORES ▪ COREY

FRONT HOOK	ROOT WORD	END HOOK
SCORED	**CORED**	
	COREDEEM	COREDEEMS
	COREGENT	COREGENTS
	COREIGN	COREIGNS
	CORELATE	CORELATED · CORELATES
SCORELESS	**CORELESS**	
	CORELLA	CORELLAS
SCORER	**CORER**	CORERS
SCORERS	**CORERS**	
SCORES	**CORES**	
	COREY	COREYS (offensive)
	CORFHOUSE	CORFHOUSES
	CORGI	CORGIS
SCORIA	**CORIA**	
	CORIANDER	CORIANDERS
SCORING	**CORING**	
SCORIOUS	**CORIOUS**	
	CORIUM	CORIUMS
	CORIVAL	CORIVALS
	CORIXID	CORIXIDS
	CORK	CORKS · CORKY
	CORKAGE	CORKAGES
	CORKBOARD	CORKBOARDS
	CORKBORER	CORKBORERS
	CORKER	CORKERS
	CORKIR	CORKIRS
	CORKSCREW	CORKSCREWS
	CORKTREE	CORKTREES
	CORKWING	CORKWINGS
	CORKWOOD	CORKWOODS
	CORM	CORMS
	CORMEL	CORMELS
	CORMORANT	CORMORANTS
ACORN · SCORN	**CORN**	CORNI · CORNO · CORNS · CORNU · CORNY
	CORNACRE	CORNACRES
	CORNAGE	CORNAGES
	CORNBALL	CORNBALLS
	CORNBORER	CORNBORERS
	CORNBRAID	CORNBRAIDS
	CORNBREAD	CORNBREADS
	CORNCAKE	CORNCAKES
	CORNCOB	CORNCOBS
	CORNCRAKE	CORNCRAKES
	CORNCRIB	CORNCRIBS
	CORNEA	CORNEAE · CORNEAL · CORNEAS
ACORNED · SCORNED	**CORNED**	
	CORNEL	CORNELS
	CORNELIAN	CORNELIANS
	CORNEMUSE	CORNEMUSES
SCORNER	**CORNER**	CORNERS
SCORNERS	**CORNERS**	
	CORNET	CORNETS · CORNETT
	CORNETIST	CORNETISTS
	CORNETT	CORNETTI · CORNETTO · CORNETTS
	CORNFIELD	CORNFIELDS
	CORNFLAG	CORNFLAGS
	CORNFLAKE	CORNFLAKES
	CORNFLOUR	CORNFLOURS
	CORNHUSK	CORNHUSKS
	CORNICE	CORNICED · CORNICES
	CORNICHE	CORNICHES
	CORNICHON	CORNICHONS
	CORNICLE	CORNICLES
SCORNING	**CORNING**	
	CORNIST	CORNISTS
	CORNLAND	CORNLANDS
	CORNLOFT	CORNLOFTS
	CORNMEAL	CORNMEALS
	CORNMILL	CORNMILLS

FRONT HOOK	ROOT WORD	END HOOK
	CORNMOTH	CORNMOTHS
	CORNOPEAN	CORNOPEANS
	CORNPIPE	CORNPIPES
	CORNPONE	CORNPONES
	CORNRENT	CORNRENTS
	CORNROW	CORNROWS
ACORNS ▪ SCORNS	**CORNS**	
	CORNSTALK	CORNSTALKS
	CORNSTONE	CORNSTONES
	CORNU	CORNUA ▪ CORNUS
	CORNUA	CORNUAL
	CORNUTE	CORNUTED ▪ CORNUTES
	CORNUTO	CORNUTOS
	CORNWORM	CORNWORMS
	COROCORE	COROCORES
	COROCORO	COROCOROS
	COROLLA	COROLLAS
	CORONA	CORONAE ▪ CORONAL ▪ CORONAS
	CORONACH	CORONACHS
	CORONAL	CORONALS
	CORONATE	CORONATED ▪ CORONATES
	CORONEL	CORONELS
	CORONER	CORONERS
	CORONET	CORONETS
	CORONIUM	CORONIUMS
	COROTATE	COROTATED ▪ COROTATES
	COROZO	COROZOS
	CORPORA	CORPORAL ▪ CORPORAS
	CORPORAL	CORPORALE ▪ CORPORALS
	CORPORALE	CORPORALES
	CORPORATE	CORPORATES
	CORPOSANT	CORPOSANTS
	CORPS	CORPSE
	CORPSE	CORPSED ▪ CORPSES
	CORPUSCLE	CORPUSCLES
	CORRADE	CORRADED ▪ CORRADES
	CORRAL	CORRALS
	CORRASION	CORRASIONS
	CORREA	CORREAS
	CORRECT	CORRECTS
	CORRECTOR	CORRECTORS ▪ CORRECTORY
	CORRELATE	CORRELATED ▪ CORRELATES
	CORRIDA	CORRIDAS
	CORRIDOR	CORRIDORS
	CORRIE	CORRIES
	CORRIGENT	CORRIGENTS
	CORRIVAL	CORRIVALS
	CORRODANT	CORRODANTS
	CORRODE	CORRODED ▪ CORRODER ▪ CORRODES
	CORRODENT	CORRODENTS
	CORRODER	CORRODERS
	CORROSION	CORROSIONS
	CORROSIVE	CORROSIVES
	CORRUGATE	CORRUGATED ▪ CORRUGATES
	CORRUPT	CORRUPTS
	CORRUPTER	CORRUPTERS
	CORRUPTOR	CORRUPTORS
	CORS	CORSE ▪ CORSO
	CORSAC	CORSACS
	CORSAGE	CORSAGES
	CORSAIR	CORSAIRS
SCORSE	**CORSE**	CORSES ▪ CORSET ▪ CORSEY
	CORSELET	CORSELETS
SCORSES	**CORSES**	
	CORSET	CORSETS
	CORSETIER	CORSETIERE ▪ CORSETIERS
	CORSEY	CORSEYS
	CORSIVE	CORSIVES
	CORSLET	CORSLETS

C

FRONT HOOK	ROOT WORD	END HOOK
	CORSNED	CORSNEDS
	CORSO	CORSOS
	CORTEGE	CORTEGES
	CORTICATE	CORTICATED
	CORTICOID	CORTICOIDS
	CORTIN	CORTINA · CORTINS
	CORTINA	CORTINAS
	CORTISOL	CORTISOLS
	CORTISONE	CORTISONES
	CORULER	CORULERS
	CORUNDUM	CORUNDUMS
	CORUSCATE	CORUSCATED · CORUSCATES
	CORVEE	CORVEES
	CORVET	CORVETS
	CORVETTE	CORVETTED · CORVETTES
	CORVID	CORVIDS
	CORVINA	CORVINAS
	CORYBANT	CORYBANTS
	CORYMB	CORYMBS
	CORYPHE	CORYPHEE · CORYPHES
	CORYPHEE	CORYPHEES
	CORYPHENE	CORYPHENES
	CORYZA	CORYZAL · CORYZAS
ECOS	**COS**	COSE · COSH · COSS · COST · COSY
	COSCRIPT	COSCRIPTS
	COSE	COSEC · COSED · COSES · COSET · COSEY
	COSEC	COSECH · COSECS
	COSECANT	COSECANTS
	COSECH	COSECHS
	COSEISMAL	COSEISMALS
	COSEISMIC	COSEISMICS
	COSET	COSETS
	COSEY	COSEYS
	COSHER	COSHERS · COSHERY
	COSHERER	COSHERERS
	COSHERING	COSHERINGS
	COSIE	COSIED · COSIER · COSIES
	COSIER	COSIERS
	COSIES	COSIEST
	COSIGN	COSIGNS
	COSIGNER	COSIGNERS
	COSINE	COSINES
	COSINES	COSINESS
	COSMEA	COSMEAS
	COSMETIC	COSMETICS
	COSMID	COSMIDS
	COSMIN	COSMINE · COSMINS
	COSMINE	COSMINES
ACOSMISM	**COSMISM**	COSMISMS
ACOSMISMS	**COSMISMS**	
ACOSMIST	**COSMIST**	COSMISTS
ACOSMISTS	**COSMISTS**	
	COSMOCRAT	COSMOCRATS
	COSMOLINE	COSMOLINED · COSMOLINES
	COSMONAUT	COSMONAUTS
	COSMORAMA	COSMORAMAS
	COSMOTRON	COSMOTRONS
	COSPONSOR	COSPONSORS
	COSSACK	COSSACKS
	COSSET	COSSETS
	COSSIE	COSSIES
	COST	COSTA · COSTE · COSTS
	COSTA	COSTAE · COSTAL · COSTAR
	COSTAL	COSTALS
	COSTALGIA	COSTALGIAS
	COSTAR	COSTARD · COSTARS
	COSTARD	COSTARDS
ECOSTATE	**COSTATE**	COSTATED
	COSTE	COSTED · COSTER · COSTES

FRONT HOOK	ROOT WORD	END HOOK
	COSTEAN	COSTEANS
	COSTER	COSTERS
	COSTREL	COSTRELS
	COSTUME	COSTUMED ▪ COSTUMER ▪ COSTUMES ▪ COSTUMEY
	COSTUMER	COSTUMERS ▪ COSTUMERY
	COSTUMIER	COSTUMIERS
SCOT	**COT**	COTE ▪ COTH ▪ COTS ▪ COTT
	COTAN	COTANS
	COTANGENT	COTANGENTS
	COTE	COTED ▪ COTES
	COTEAU	COTEAUX
	COTELETTE	COTELETTES
	COTELINE	COTELINES
	COTENANT	COTENANTS
	COTERIE	COTERIES
	COTH	COTHS
	COTHURN	COTHURNI ▪ COTHURNS
	COTILLION	COTILLIONS
	COTILLON	COTILLONS
	COTING	COTINGA
	COTINGA	COTINGAS
	COTININE	COTININES
	COTISE	COTISED ▪ COTISES
	COTLAND	COTLANDS
	COTQUEAN	COTQUEANS
	COTRUSTEE	COTRUSTEES
SCOTS	**COTS**	
	COTT	COTTA ▪ COTTS
	COTTA	COTTAE ▪ COTTAR ▪ COTTAS
	COTTAGE	COTTAGED ▪ COTTAGER ▪ COTTAGES ▪ COTTAGEY
	COTTAGER	COTTAGERS
	COTTAGING	COTTAGINGS
	COTTAR	COTTARS
	COTTER	COTTERS
	COTTID	COTTIDS
	COTTIER	COTTIERS
	COTTISE	COTTISED ▪ COTTISES
	COTTON	COTTONS ▪ COTTONY
	COTTONADE	COTTONADES
	COTTOWN	COTTOWNS
	COTWAL	COTWALS
	COTYLE	COTYLES
ACOTYLEDON	**COTYLEDON**	COTYLEDONS
	COTYLOID	COTYLOIDS
ECOTYPE	**COTYPE**	COTYPES
ECOTYPES	**COTYPES**	
	COUCAL	COUCALS
	COUCH	COUCHE
	COUCHE	COUCHED ▪ COUCHEE ▪ COUCHER ▪ COUCHES
	COUCHEE	COUCHEES
	COUCHER	COUCHERS
	COUCHETTE	COUCHETTES
	COUCHING	COUCHINGS
	COUGAN	COUGANS
	COUGAR	COUGARS
	COUGH	COUGHS
	COUGHER	COUGHERS
	COUGHING	COUGHINGS
	COUGUAR	COUGUARS
	COULEE	COULEES
	COULIBIAC	COULIBIACA ▪ COULIBIACS
	COULISSE	COULISSES
	COULOIR	COULOIRS
	COULOMB	COULOMBS
	COULTER	COULTERS
	COUMARIN	COUMARINS
	COUMARONE	COUMARONES
	COUMAROU	COUMAROUS
	COUNCIL	COUNCILS

C

FRONT HOOK	ROOT WORD	END HOOK
	COUNCILOR	COUNCILORS
	COUNSEL	COUNSELS
	COUNSELEE	COUNSELEES
	COUNSELOR	COUNSELORS
	COUNT	COUNTS ▪ COUNTY
	COUNTBACK	COUNTBACKS
	COUNTDOWN	COUNTDOWNS
	COUNTER	COUNTERS
	COUNTIAN	COUNTIANS
	COUNTLINE	COUNTLINES
	COUNTROL	COUNTROLS
	COUNTSHIP	COUNTSHIPS
SCOUP	**COUP**	COUPE ▪ COUPS
	COUPE	COUPED ▪ COUPEE ▪ COUPER ▪ COUPES
SCOUPED	**COUPED**	
	COUPEE	COUPEES
	COUPER	COUPERS
SCOUPING	**COUPING**	
	COUPLE	COUPLED ▪ COUPLER ▪ COUPLES ▪ COUPLET
	COUPLEDOM	COUPLEDOMS
	COUPLER	COUPLERS
	COUPLET	COUPLETS
	COUPLING	COUPLINGS
	COUPON	COUPONS
	COUPONING	COUPONINGS
SCOUPS	**COUPS**	
	COUPURE	COUPURES
SCOUR	**COUR**	COURB ▪ COURD ▪ COURE ▪ COURS ▪ COURT
	COURAGE	COURAGES
	COURANT	COURANTE ▪ COURANTO ▪ COURANTS
	COURANTE	COURANTES
	COURANTO	COURANTOS
	COURB	COURBS
	COURBARIL	COURBARILS
	COURBETTE	COURBETTES
	COURE	COURED ▪ COURES
SCOURED	**COURED**	
	COURGETTE	COURGETTES
SCOURIE	**COURIE**	COURIED ▪ COURIER ▪ COURIES
	COURIER	COURIERS
SCOURIES	**COURIES**	
SCOURING	**COURING**	
	COURLAN	COURLANS
SCOURS	**COURS**	COURSE
SCOURSE	**COURSE**	COURSED ▪ COURSER ▪ COURSES
SCOURSED	**COURSED**	
	COURSER	COURSERS
SCOURSES	**COURSES**	
SCOURSING	**COURSING**	COURSINGS
	COURT	COURTS
	COURTER	COURTERS
	COURTESAN	COURTESANS
	COURTEZAN	COURTEZANS
	COURTIER	COURTIERS
	COURTING	COURTINGS
	COURTLET	COURTLETS
	COURTLING	COURTLINGS
	COURTROOM	COURTROOMS
	COURTSHIP	COURTSHIPS
	COURTSIDE	COURTSIDES
	COURTYARD	COURTYARDS
	COUSIN	COUSINS
	COUSINAGE	COUSINAGES
	COUTEAU	COUTEAUX
SCOUTER	**COUTER**	COUTERS
SCOUTERS	**COUTERS**	
SCOUTH	**COUTH**	COUTHS ▪ COUTHY
SCOUTHER	**COUTHER**	
	COUTHIE	COUTHIER

FRONT HOOK	ROOT WORD	END HOOK
SCOUTHS	COUTHS	
	COUTIL	COUTILS
	COUTILLE	COUTILLES
	COUTURE	COUTURES
	COUTURIER	COUTURIERE ▪ COUTURIERS
	COUVADE	COUVADES
	COUVERT	COUVERTS
	COUZIN	COUZINS
	COVALENCE	COVALENCES
	COVARIANT	COVARIANTS
	COVARIATE	COVARIATES
	COVE	COVED ▪ COVEN ▪ COVER ▪ COVES ▪ COVET COVEY
	COVELET	COVELETS
	COVELLINE	COVELLINES
	COVELLITE	COVELLITES
	COVEN	COVENS ▪ COVENT
	COVENANT	COVENANTS
	COVENT	COVENTS
	COVER	COVERS ▪ COVERT
	COVERAGE	COVERAGES
	COVERALL	COVERALLS
	COVERER	COVERERS
	COVERING	COVERINGS
	COVERLET	COVERLETS
	COVERLID	COVERLIDS
	COVERSINE	COVERSINES
	COVERSLIP	COVERSLIPS
	COVERT	COVERTS
	COVERTURE	COVERTURES
	COVERUP	COVERUPS
	COVET	COVETS
	COVETER	COVETERS
	COVETISE	COVETISES
	COVEY	COVEYS
	COVIN	COVING ▪ COVINS
	COVING	COVINGS
	COVYNE	COVYNES
SCOW	COW	COWK ▪ COWL ▪ COWP ▪ COWS ▪ COWY
	COWAGE	COWAGES
	COWAL	COWALS
	COWAN	COWANS
	COWARD	COWARDS
	COWARDICE	COWARDICES
	COWBANE	COWBANES
	COWBELL	COWBELLS
	COWBIND	COWBINDS
	COWBIRD	COWBIRDS
	COWBOY	COWBOYS
SCOWED	COWED	
	COWER	COWERS
	COWFEEDER	COWFEEDERS
	COWFLAP	COWFLAPS
	COWFLOP	COWFLOPS
	COWGIRL	COWGIRLS
	COWHAGE	COWHAGES
	COWHAND	COWHANDS
	COWHEARD	COWHEARDS
	COWHEEL	COWHEELS
	COWHERB	COWHERBS
	COWHERD	COWHERDS
	COWHIDE	COWHIDED ▪ COWHIDES
	COWHOUSE	COWHOUSES
SCOWING	COWING	
	COWINNER	COWINNERS
	COWK	COWKS
SCOWL	COWL	COWLS
SCOWLED	COWLED	
	COWLICK	COWLICKS

C

FRONT HOOK	ROOT WORD	END HOOK
SCOWLING	**COWLING**	COWLINGS
SCOWLS	**COWLS**	
	COWLSTAFF	COWLSTAFFS
	COWORKER	COWORKERS
SCOWP	**COWP**	COWPS
	COWPAT	COWPATS
	COWPEA	COWPEAS
SCOWPED	**COWPED**	
	COWPIE	COWPIES
SCOWPING	**COWPING**	
	COWPLOP	COWPLOPS
	COWPOKE	COWPOKES
SCOWPS	**COWPS**	
SCOWRIE	**COWRIE**	COWRIES
SCOWRIES	**COWRIES**	
	COWRITE	COWRITER ▪ COWRITES
	COWRITER	COWRITERS
SCOWS	**COWS**	
	COWSHED	COWSHEDS
	COWSKIN	COWSKINS
	COWSLIP	COWSLIPS
	COWTREE	COWTREES
	COX	COXA ▪ COXY
	COXA	COXAE ▪ COXAL
	COXALGIA	COXALGIAS
	COXCOMB	COXCOMBS
	COXSWAIN	COXSWAINS
	COY	COYS
	COYDOG	COYDOGS
	COYOTE	COYOTES
	COYOTILLO	COYOTILLOS
	COYPOU	COYPOUS
	COYPU	COYPUS
	COYSTREL	COYSTRELS
	COYSTRIL	COYSTRILS
	COZ	COZE ▪ COZY
	COZE	COZED ▪ COZEN ▪ COZES ▪ COZEY
	COZEN	COZENS
	COZENAGE	COZENAGES
	COZENER	COZENERS
	COZEY	COZEYS
	COZIE	COZIED ▪ COZIER ▪ COZIES
	COZIER	COZIERS
	COZIES	COZIEST
	CRAAL	CRAALS
SCRAB	**CRAB**	CRABS
	CRABAPPLE	CRABAPPLES
SCRABBED	**CRABBED**	
	CRABBER	CRABBERS
SCRABBING	**CRABBING**	
	CRABEATER	CRABEATERS
	CRABMEAT	CRABMEATS
SCRABS	**CRABS**	
	CRABSTICK	CRABSTICKS
	CRABWOOD	CRABWOODS
	CRACK	CRACKA ▪ CRACKS ▪ CRACKY
	CRACKA	CRACKAS *(offensive)*
	CRACKBACK	CRACKBACKS
	CRACKDOWN	CRACKDOWNS
	CRACKER	CRACKERS
	CRACKET	CRACKETS
	CRACKHEAD	CRACKHEADS *(offensive)*
	CRACKING	CRACKINGS
	CRACKJAW	CRACKJAWS
	CRACKLE	CRACKLED ▪ CRACKLES
	CRACKLING	CRACKLINGS
	CRACKNEL	CRACKNELS
	CRACKPOT	CRACKPOTS
	CRACKUP	CRACKUPS

FRONT HOOK	ROOT WORD	END HOOK
	CRACOWE	CRACOWES
	CRADLE	CRADLED · CRADLER · CRADLES
	CRADLER	CRADLERS
	CRADLING	CRADLINGS
	CRAFT	CRAFTS · CRAFTY
	CRAFTER	CRAFTERS
	CRAFTWORK	CRAFTWORKS
SCRAG	**CRAG**	CRAGS
SCRAGGED	**CRAGGED**	
SCRAGGIER	**CRAGGIER**	
SCRAGGIEST	**CRAGGIEST**	
SCRAGGILY	**CRAGGILY**	
SCRAGGY	**CRAGGY**	
SCRAGS	**CRAGS**	
	CRAIC	CRAICS
	CRAIG	CRAIGS
	CRAKE	CRAKED · CRAKES
SCRAM	**CRAM**	CRAME · CRAMP · CRAMS
	CRAMBE	CRAMBES
	CRAMBO	CRAMBOS
	CRAME	CRAMES
	CRAMES	CRAMESY
SCRAMMED	**CRAMMED**	
	CRAMMER	CRAMMERS
SCRAMMING	**CRAMMING**	
	CRAMOISIE	CRAMOISIES
	CRAMP	CRAMPS · CRAMPY
	CRAMPBARK	CRAMPBARKS
	CRAMPER	CRAMPERS
	CRAMPET	CRAMPETS
	CRAMPIT	CRAMPITS
	CRAMPON	CRAMPONS
	CRAMPOON	CRAMPOONS
SCRAMS	**CRAMS**	
SCRAN	**CRAN**	CRANE · CRANK · CRANS
	CRANAGE	CRANAGES
SCRANCH	**CRANCH**	
SCRANCHED	**CRANCHED**	
SCRANCHES	**CRANCHES**	
SCRANCHING	**CRANCHING**	
	CRANE	CRANED · CRANES
	CRANIA	CRANIAL
	CRANIATE	CRANIATES
	CRANIUM	CRANIUMS
	CRANK	CRANKS · CRANKY
	CRANKCASE	CRANKCASES
	CRANKLE	CRANKLED · CRANKLES
	CRANKPIN	CRANKPINS
	CRANNOG	CRANNOGE · CRANNOGS
	CRANNOGE	CRANNOGES
SCRANNY	**CRANNY**	
	CRANREUCH	CRANREUCHS
SCRANS	**CRANS**	
SCRAP	**CRAP**	CRAPE · CRAPS · CRAPY
	CRAPAUD	CRAPAUDS
SCRAPE	**CRAPE**	CRAPED · CRAPES
SCRAPED	**CRAPED**	
SCRAPES	**CRAPES**	
SCRAPING	**CRAPING**	
	CRAPLE	CRAPLES
	CRAPOLA	CRAPOLAS
SCRAPPED	**CRAPPED**	
SCRAPPER	**CRAPPER**	CRAPPERS (offensive)
SCRAPPERS	**CRAPPERS**	
	CRAPPIE	CRAPPIER · CRAPPIES
SCRAPPIER	**CRAPPIER**	
	CRAPPIES	CRAPPIEST
SCRAPPIEST	**CRAPPIEST**	
SCRAPPING	**CRAPPING**	

FRONT HOOK	ROOT WORD	END HOOK
SCRAPPY	**CRAPPY**	
SCRAPS	**CRAPS**	
	CRAPSHOOT	CRAPSHOOTS
	CRARE	CRARES
	CRASHER	CRASHERS
	CRASHLAND	CRASHLANDS
	CRASHPAD	CRASHPADS
SCRATCH	**CRATCH**	
SCRATCHES	**CRATCHES**	
	CRATE	CRATED · CRATER · CRATES
	CRATEFUL	CRATEFULS
	CRATER	CRATERS
	CRATERING	CRATERINGS
	CRATERLET	CRATERLETS
	CRATON	CRATONS
	CRATUR	CRATURS
	CRAUNCH	CRAUNCHY
	CRAVAT	CRAVATS
	CRAVE	CRAVED · CRAVEN · CRAVER · CRAVES
	CRAVEN	CRAVENS
	CRAVER	CRAVERS
	CRAVING	CRAVINGS
SCRAW	**CRAW**	CRAWL · CRAWS
	CRAWDAD	CRAWDADS
ACRAWL · SCRAWL	**CRAWL**	CRAWLS · CRAWLY
SCRAWLED	**CRAWLED**	
SCRAWLER	**CRAWLER**	CRAWLERS
SCRAWLERS	**CRAWLERS**	
SCRAWLIER	**CRAWLIER**	
SCRAWLIEST	**CRAWLIEST**	
SCRAWLING	**CRAWLING**	CRAWLINGS
SCRAWLINGS	**CRAWLINGS**	
SCRAWLS	**CRAWLS**	
	CRAWLWAY	CRAWLWAYS
SCRAWLY	**CRAWLY**	
SCRAWS	**CRAWS**	
SCRAY	**CRAY**	CRAYS
	CRAYER	CRAYERS
	CRAYON	CRAYONS
	CRAYONER	CRAYONERS
	CRAYONIST	CRAYONISTS
SCRAYS	**CRAYS**	
	CRAYTHUR	CRAYTHURS
	CRAZE	CRAZED · CRAZES
	CRAZIES	CRAZIEST
	CRAZYWEED	CRAZYWEEDS
	CREACH	CREACHS
	CREAGH	CREAGHS
SCREAK	**CREAK**	CREAKS · CREAKY
SCREAKED	**CREAKED**	
SCREAKIER	**CREAKIER**	
SCREAKIEST	**CREAKIEST**	
SCREAKING	**CREAKING**	
SCREAKS	**CREAKS**	
SCREAKY	**CREAKY**	
SCREAM	**CREAM**	CREAMS · CREAMY
SCREAMED	**CREAMED**	
SCREAMER	**CREAMER**	CREAMERS · CREAMERY
SCREAMERS	**CREAMERS**	
SCREAMING	**CREAMING**	
	CREAMPUFF	CREAMPUFFS
SCREAMS	**CREAMS**	
	CREAMWARE	CREAMWARES
	CREANCE	CREANCES
	CREASE	CREASED · CREASER · CREASES
	CREASER	CREASERS
	CREASOTE	CREASOTED · CREASOTES
OCREATE	**CREATE**	CREATED · CREATES
	CREATIN	CREATINE · CREATING · CREATINS

FRONT HOOK	ROOT WORD	END HOOK
	CREATINE	CREATINES
	CREATION	CREATIONS
	CREATIVE	CREATIVES
	CREATOR	CREATORS
	CREATURE	CREATURES
	CRECHE	CRECHES
ACRED	CRED	CREDO • CREDS
	CREDENCE	CREDENCES
	CREDENZA	CREDENZAS
	CREDIT	CREDITS
	CREDITOR	CREDITORS
	CREDO	CREDOS
SCREE	CREE	CREED • CREEK • CREEL • CREEP • CREES
SCREED	CREED	CREEDS
SCREEDS	CREEDS	
	CREEK	CREEKS • CREEKY
	CREEL	CREELS
	CREEP	CREEPS • CREEPY
	CREEPAGE	CREEPAGES
	CREEPER	CREEPERS
	CREEPIE	CREEPIER • CREEPIES
	CREEPIES	CREEPIEST
SCREES	CREES	CREESE • CREESH
	CREESE	CREESED • CREESES
	CREESH	CREESHY
	CREM	CREME • CREMS
	CREMASTER	CREMASTERS
	CREMATE	CREMATED • CREMATES
	CREMATION	CREMATIONS
	CREMATOR	CREMATORS • CREMATORY
	CREME	CREMES
	CREMINI	CREMINIS
	CREMOCARP	CREMOCARPS
	CREMONA	CREMONAS
	CREMOR	CREMORS
	CREMORNE	CREMORNES
	CRENA	CRENAS
	CRENATE	CRENATED
	CRENATION	CRENATIONS
	CRENATURE	CRENATURES
	CRENEL	CRENELS
	CRENELATE	CRENELATED • CRENELATES
	CRENELLE	CRENELLED • CRENELLES
	CRENSHAW	CRENSHAWS
	CRENULATE	CRENULATED
	CREODONT	CREODONTS
	CREOLE	CREOLES
	CREOLIAN	CREOLIANS
	CREOLISE	CREOLISED • CREOLISES
	CREOLIST	CREOLISTS
	CREOLIZE	CREOLIZED • CREOLIZES
	CREOSOL	CREOSOLS
	CREOSOTE	CREOSOTED • CREOSOTES
	CREPANCE	CREPANCES
	CREPE	CREPED • CREPES • CREPEY
	CREPERIE	CREPERIES
	CREPITATE	CREPITATED • CREPITATES
	CREPOLINE	CREPOLINES
	CREPON	CREPONS
	CREPUSCLE	CREPUSCLES
	CRESCENDO	CRESCENDOS
	CRESCENT	CRESCENTS
	CRESOL	CRESOLS
	CRESS	CRESSY
	CRESSET	CRESSETS
	CREST	CRESTA • CRESTS
	CRESTA	CRESTAL
	CRESTING	CRESTINGS
	CRESTON	CRESTONS

CRESYL → CRINGLE

FRONT HOOK	ROOT WORD	END HOOK
	CRESYL	CRESYLS
	CRETIC	CRETICS
	CRETIN	CRETINS
	CRETINISE	CRETINISED · CRETINISES
	CRETINISM	CRETINISMS
	CRETINIZE	CRETINIZED · CRETINIZES
	CRETINOID	CRETINOIDS
	CRETISM	CRETISMS
	CRETONNE	CRETONNES
	CREUTZER	CREUTZERS
	CREVALLE	CREVALLES
	CREVASSE	CREVASSED · CREVASSES
	CREVETTE	CREVETTES
	CREVICE	CREVICED · CREVICES
SCREW	CREW	CREWE · CREWS
	CREWCUT	CREWCUTS
	CREWE	CREWED · CREWEL · CREWES
SCREWED	CREWED	
	CREWEL	CREWELS
	CREWELIST	CREWELISTS
SCREWING	CREWING	
	CREWMATE	CREWMATES
	CREWNECK	CREWNECKS
SCREWS	CREWS	
	CRIB	CRIBS
	CRIBBAGE	CRIBBAGES
	CRIBBER	CRIBBERS
	CRIBBING	CRIBBINGS
SCRIBBLE	CRIBBLE	CRIBBLED · CRIBBLES
SCRIBBLED	CRIBBLED	
SCRIBBLES	CRIBBLES	
SCRIBBLING	CRIBBLING	
	CRIBELLA	CRIBELLAR
	CRIBWORK	CRIBWORKS
	CRICETID	CRICETIDS
	CRICK	CRICKS · CRICKY
	CRICKET	CRICKETS
	CRICKETER	CRICKETERS
	CRICOID	CRICOIDS
SCRIED	CRIED	
	CRIER	CRIERS
SCRIES	CRIES	
SCRIM	CRIM	CRIME · CRIMP · CRIMS
	CRIME	CRIMED · CRIMEN · CRIMES
	CRIMEWAVE	CRIMEWAVES
	CRIMINA	CRIMINAL
	CRIMINAL	CRIMINALS
	CRIMINATE	CRIMINATED · CRIMINATES
	CRIMINI	CRIMINIS
	CRIMMER	CRIMMERS
SCRIMP	CRIMP	CRIMPS · CRIMPY
SCRIMPED	CRIMPED	
SCRIMPER	CRIMPER	CRIMPERS
SCRIMPERS	CRIMPERS	
SCRIMPIER	CRIMPIER	
SCRIMPIEST	CRIMPIEST	
SCRIMPING	CRIMPING	
	CRIMPLE	CRIMPLED · CRIMPLES
SCRIMPS	CRIMPS	
SCRIMPY	CRIMPY	
SCRIMS	CRIMS	
	CRIMSON	CRIMSONS
	CRINATE	CRINATED
SCRINE	CRINE	CRINED · CRINES
SCRINES	CRINES	
	CRINGE	CRINGED · CRINGER · CRINGES
	CRINGER	CRINGERS
	CRINGING	CRINGINGS
	CRINGLE	CRINGLES

184

FRONT HOOK	ROOT WORD	END HOOK
	CRINITE	CRINITES
	CRINKLE	CRINKLED · CRINKLES
	CRINKLIES	CRINKLIEST
	CRINOID	CRINOIDS
	CRINOLINE	CRINOLINED · CRINOLINES
	CRINUM	CRINUMS
	CRIOLLO	CRIOLLOS
	CRIPE	CRIPES
	CRIPPLE	CRIPPLED · CRIPPLER · CRIPPLES
	CRIPPLER	CRIPPLERS
	CRIPPLING	CRIPPLINGS
	CRIS	CRISE · CRISP
	CRISE	CRISES
	CRISP	CRISPS · CRISPY
	CRISPATE	CRISPATED
	CRISPEN	CRISPENS
	CRISPER	CRISPERS
	CRISPHEAD	CRISPHEADS
	CRISPIN	CRISPING · CRISPINS
	CRISSA	CRISSAL
	CRISTA	CRISTAE
	CRISTATE	CRISTATED
	CRIT	CRITH · CRITS
	CRITERIA	CRITERIAL
	CRITERION	CRITERIONS
	CRITERIUM	CRITERIUMS
	CRITH	CRITHS
	CRITIC	CRITICS
ACRITICAL	**CRITICAL**	
	CRITICISE	CRITICISED · CRITICISER · CRITICISES
	CRITICISM	CRITICISMS
	CRITICIZE	CRITICIZED · CRITICIZER · CRITICIZES
	CRITIQUE	CRITIQUED · CRITIQUES
	CRITTER	CRITTERS
	CRITTUR	CRITTURS
	CROAK	CROAKS · CROAKY
	CROAKER	CROAKERS
	CROAKING	CROAKINGS
	CROC	CROCI · CROCK · CROCS
	CROCEIN	CROCEINE · CROCEINS
	CROCEINE	CROCEINES
	CROCHE	CROCHES · CROCHET
	CROCHET	CROCHETS
	CROCHETER	CROCHETERS
	CROCK	CROCKS
	CROCKET	CROCKETS
	CROCKPOT	CROCKPOTS
	CROCODILE	CROCODILES
	CROCOITE	CROCOITES
	CROCOSMIA	CROCOSMIAS
	CROFT	CROFTS
	CROFTER	CROFTERS
	CROFTING	CROFTINGS
SCROG	**CROG**	CROGS
SCROGGY	**CROGGY**	
SCROGS	**CROGS**	
	CROISSANT	CROISSANTS
	CROJIK	CROJIKS
	CROKINOLE	CROKINOLES
	CROMACK	CROMACKS
	CROMB	CROMBS
	CROMBEC	CROMBECS
SCROME	**CROME**	CROMED · CROMES
SCROMED	**CROMED**	
SCROMES	**CROMES**	
SCROMING	**CROMING**	
	CROMLECH	CROMLECHS
	CROMORNA	CROMORNAS
	CROMORNE	CROMORNES

FRONT HOOK	ROOT WORD	END HOOK
	CRONE	CRONES · CRONET
	CRONET	CRONETS
	CRONYISM	CRONYISMS
	CROODLE	CROODLED · CROODLES
	CROOK	CROOKS
	CROOKBACK	CROOKBACKS
	CROOKER	CROOKERY
	CROOKNECK	CROOKNECKS
	CROOL	CROOLS
	CROON	CROONS
	CROONER	CROONERS
	CROONING	CROONINGS
	CROOVE	CROOVES
	CROP	CROPS
	CROPFUL	CROPFULL · CROPFULS
	CROPLAND	CROPLANDS
	CROPPER	CROPPERS
	CROPPIE	CROPPIES
	CROPPING	CROPPINGS
	CROQUANTE	CROQUANTES
	CROQUET	CROQUETS
	CROQUETTE	CROQUETTES
	CRORE	CRORES
	CROSIER	CROSIERS
ACROSS	**CROSS**	CROSSE
	CROSSARM	CROSSARMS
	CROSSBAND	CROSSBANDS
	CROSSBAR	CROSSBARS
	CROSSBEAM	CROSSBEAMS
	CROSSBILL	CROSSBILLS
	CROSSBIT	CROSSBITE
	CROSSBITE	CROSSBITES
	CROSSBOW	CROSSBOWS
	CROSSBRED	CROSSBREDS
	CROSSBUCK	CROSSBUCKS
	CROSSCUT	CROSSCUTS
	CROSSE	CROSSED · CROSSER · CROSSES
	CROSSER	CROSSERS
	CROSSES	CROSSEST
	CROSSETTE	CROSSETTES
	CROSSFALL	CROSSFALLS
	CROSSFIRE	CROSSFIRES
	CROSSHAIR	CROSSHAIRS
	CROSSHEAD	CROSSHEADS
	CROSSING	CROSSINGS
	CROSSJACK	CROSSJACKS
	CROSSLET	CROSSLETS
	CROSSOVER	CROSSOVERS
	CROSSROAD	CROSSROADS
	CROSSRUFF	CROSSRUFFS
	CROSSTALK	CROSSTALKS
	CROSSTIE	CROSSTIED · CROSSTIES
	CROSSTREE	CROSSTREES
	CROSSWALK	CROSSWALKS
	CROSSWAY	CROSSWAYS
	CROSSWIND	CROSSWINDS
	CROSSWORD	CROSSWORDS
	CROSSWORT	CROSSWORTS
	CROSTINI	CROSTINIS
SCROTAL	**CROTAL**	CROTALA · CROTALS
	CROTALISM	CROTALISMS
	CROTCHET	CROTCHETS · CROTCHETY
	CROTON	CROTONS
	CROTONBUG	CROTONBUGS
	CROTTLE	CROTTLES
	CROUP	CROUPE · CROUPS · CROUPY
	CROUPADE	CROUPADES
	CROUPE	CROUPED · CROUPER · CROUPES
	CROUPER	CROUPERS

FRONT HOOK	ROOT WORD	END HOOK
	CROUPIER	CROUPIERS
	CROUPON	CROUPONS
	CROUSTADE	CROUSTADES
	CROUT	CROUTE ▪ CROUTS
	CROUTE	CROUTES
	CROUTON	CROUTONS
SCROW	CROW	CROWD ▪ CROWN ▪ CROWS
	CROWBAR	CROWBARS
	CROWBOOT	CROWBOOTS
	CROWD	CROWDS ▪ CROWDY
	CROWDER	CROWDERS
	CROWDIE	CROWDIES
	CROWEA	CROWEAS
	CROWER	CROWERS
	CROWFOOT	CROWFOOTS
	CROWN	CROWNS
	CROWNER	CROWNERS
	CROWNET	CROWNETS
	CROWNING	CROWNINGS
	CROWNLAND	CROWNLANDS
	CROWNLET	CROWNLETS
	CROWNWORK	CROWNWORKS
SCROWS	CROWS	
	CROWSTEP	CROWSTEPS
	CROZE	CROZER ▪ CROZES
	CROZER	CROZERS
	CROZIER	CROZIERS
ECRU	CRU	CRUD ▪ CRUE ▪ CRUS ▪ CRUX
	CRUBEEN	CRUBEENS
	CRUCIAN	CRUCIANS
	CRUCIBLE	CRUCIBLES
	CRUCIFER	CRUCIFERS
	CRUCIFIER	CRUCIFIERS
	CRUCIFORM	CRUCIFORMS
	CRUCK	CRUCKS
	CRUD	CRUDE ▪ CRUDS ▪ CRUDY
	CRUDDLE	CRUDDLED ▪ CRUDDLES
	CRUDE	CRUDER ▪ CRUDES
	CRUDES	CRUDEST
	CRUE	CRUEL ▪ CRUES ▪ CRUET
	CRUEL	CRUELS
	CRUET	CRUETS
	CRUISE	CRUISED ▪ CRUISER ▪ CRUISES
	CRUISER	CRUISERS
	CRUISEWAY	CRUISEWAYS
	CRUISIE	CRUISIES
	CRUISING	CRUISINGS
	CRUIVE	CRUIVES
	CRUIZIE	CRUIZIES
	CRULLER	CRULLERS
	CRUMB	CRUMBS ▪ CRUMBY
	CRUMBER	CRUMBERS
	CRUMBLE	CRUMBLED ▪ CRUMBLES
	CRUMBLIES	CRUMBLIEST
	CRUMBLING	CRUMBLINGS
	CRUMBUM	CRUMBUMS
	CRUMEN	CRUMENS
	CRUMENAL	CRUMENALS
	CRUMHORN	CRUMHORNS
	CRUMMACK	CRUMMACKS
SCRUMMIE	CRUMMIE	CRUMMIER ▪ CRUMMIES
SCRUMMIER	CRUMMIER	
SCRUMMIES	CRUMMIES	CRUMMIEST
SCRUMMIEST	CRUMMIEST	
	CRUMMOCK	CRUMMOCKS
SCRUMMY	CRUMMY	
SCRUMP	CRUMP	CRUMPS ▪ CRUMPY
SCRUMPED	CRUMPED	
	CRUMPET	CRUMPETS

FRONT HOOK	ROOT WORD	END HOOK
SCRUMPING	**CRUMPING**	
SCRUMPLE	**CRUMPLE**	CRUMPLED · CRUMPLES
SCRUMPLED	**CRUMPLED**	
SCRUMPLES	**CRUMPLES**	
SCRUMPLING	**CRUMPLING**	CRUMPLINGS
SCRUMPS	**CRUMPS**	
SCRUMPY	**CRUMPY**	
SCRUNCH	**CRUNCH**	CRUNCHY
SCRUNCHED	**CRUNCHED**	
	CRUNCHER	CRUNCHERS
SCRUNCHES	**CRUNCHES**	
SCRUNCHIE	**CRUNCHIE**	CRUNCHIER · CRUNCHIES (offensive)
SCRUNCHIER	**CRUNCHIER**	
SCRUNCHIES	**CRUNCHIES**	CRUNCHIEST
SCRUNCHING	**CRUNCHING**	CRUNCHINGS
SCRUNCHY	**CRUNCHY**	
	CRUNKLE	CRUNKLED · CRUNKLES
	CRUNODE	CRUNODES
	CRUOR	CRUORS
	CRUPPER	CRUPPERS
	CRURA	CRURAL
ECRUS	**CRUS**	CRUSE · CRUSH · CRUST · CRUSY
	CRUSADE	CRUSADED · CRUSADER · CRUSADES
	CRUSADER	CRUSADERS
	CRUSADO	CRUSADOS
	CRUSE	CRUSES · CRUSET
	CRUSET	CRUSETS
	CRUSHER	CRUSHERS
	CRUSIAN	CRUSIANS
	CRUSIE	CRUSIES
	CRUST	CRUSTA · CRUSTS · CRUSTY
	CRUSTA	CRUSTAE · CRUSTAL
	CRUSTACEA	CRUSTACEAN
	CRUSTATE	CRUSTATED
	CRUSTIES	CRUSTIEST
	CRUTCHING	CRUTCHINGS
	CRUVE	CRUVES
	CRUZADO	CRUZADOS
	CRUZEIRO	CRUZEIROS
	CRUZIE	CRUZIES
	CRWTH	CRWTHS
SCRY	**CRY**	
SCRYING	**CRYING**	CRYINGS
SCRYINGS	**CRYINGS**	
	CRYOBANK	CRYOBANKS
	CRYOCABLE	CRYOCABLES
	CRYOGEN	CRYOGENS · CRYOGENY
	CRYOGENIC	CRYOGENICS
	CRYOLITE	CRYOLITES
	CRYOMETER	CRYOMETERS
	CRYONIC	CRYONICS
	CRYOPHYTE	CRYOPHYTES
	CRYOPROBE	CRYOPROBES
	CRYOSCOPE	CRYOSCOPES
	CRYOSTAT	CRYOSTATS
	CRYOTRON	CRYOTRONS
	CRYPT	CRYPTO · CRYPTS
	CRYPTO	CRYPTON · CRYPTOS
	CRYPTOGAM	CRYPTOGAMS · CRYPTOGAMY
	CRYPTON	CRYPTONS
	CRYPTONYM	CRYPTONYMS
	CRYSTAL	CRYSTALS
	CTENE	CTENES
	CUADRILLA	CUADRILLAS
	CUATRO	CUATROS
	CUB	CUBE · CUBS
	CUBAGE	CUBAGES
	CUBANE	CUBANES
	CUBANELLE	CUBANELLES

FRONT HOOK	ROOT WORD	END HOOK
	CUBATURE	CUBATURES
	CUBBING	CUBBINGS
	CUBBYHOLE	CUBBYHOLES
	CUBE	CUBEB · CUBED · CUBER · CUBES
	CUBEB	CUBEBS
	CUBER	CUBERS
	CUBHOOD	CUBHOODS
	CUBIC	CUBICA · CUBICS
	CUBICA	CUBICAL · CUBICAS
	CUBICLE	CUBICLES
	CUBISM	CUBISMS
	CUBIST	CUBISTS
	CUBIT	CUBITI · CUBITS
	CUBOID	CUBOIDS
	CUCKOLD	CUCKOLDS
	CUCKOLDOM	CUCKOLDOMS
	CUCKOO	CUCKOOS
	CUCULLATE	CUCULLATED
	CUCUMBER	CUCUMBERS
	CUCURBIT	CUCURBITS
SCUD	**CUD**	CUDS
	CUDBEAR	CUDBEARS
	CUDDEN	CUDDENS
	CUDDIE	CUDDIES
	CUDDIN	CUDDINS
SCUDDLE	**CUDDLE**	CUDDLED · CUDDLER · CUDDLES
SCUDDLED	**CUDDLED**	
	CUDDLER	CUDDLERS
SCUDDLES	**CUDDLES**	
SCUDDLING	**CUDDLING**	
	CUDGEL	CUDGELS
	CUDGELER	CUDGELERS
	CUDGELLER	CUDGELLERS
	CUDGERIE	CUDGERIES
SCUDS	**CUDS**	
	CUDWEED	CUDWEEDS
	CUE	CUED · CUES
	CUEIST	CUEISTS
	CUESTA	CUESTAS
SCUFF	**CUFF**	CUFFO · CUFFS
SCUFFED	**CUFFED**	
	CUFFIN	CUFFING · CUFFINS
SCUFFING	**CUFFING**	
SCUFFLE	**CUFFLE**	CUFFLED · CUFFLES
SCUFFLED	**CUFFLED**	
SCUFFLES	**CUFFLES**	CUFFLESS
SCUFFLING	**CUFFLING**	
	CUFFLINK	CUFFLINKS
SCUFFS	**CUFFS**	
	CUFFUFFLE	CUFFUFFLES
	CUIF	CUIFS
	CUISINART	CUISINARTS
	CUISINE	CUISINES
	CUISINIER	CUISINIERS
	CUISSE	CUISSER · CUISSES
	CUISSER	CUISSERS
	CUIT	CUITS
	CUITER	CUITERS
	CUITIKIN	CUITIKINS
	CUITTLE	CUITTLED · CUITTLES
	CUKE	CUKES
SCULCH	**CULCH**	
SCULCHES	**CULCHES**	
	CULCHIE	CULCHIES
	CULET	CULETS
	CULICID	CULICIDS
	CULICINE	CULICINES
SCULL	**CULL**	CULLS · CULLY
	CULLAY	CULLAYS

FRONT HOOK	ROOT WORD	END HOOK
SCULLED	**CULLED**	
	CULLENDER	CULLENDERS
SCULLER	**CULLER**	CULLERS
SCULLERS	**CULLERS**	
	CULLET	CULLETS
SCULLING	**CULLING**	CULLINGS
SCULLINGS	**CULLINGS**	
SCULLION	**CULLION**	CULLIONS
SCULLIONS	**CULLIONS**	
	CULLS	
SCULLS		
	CULLYISM	CULLYISMS
	CULM	CULMS
	CULMEN	CULMENS
	CULMINATE	CULMINATED · CULMINATES
	CULOTTE	CULOTTES
	CULPA	CULPAE
	CULPRIT	CULPRITS
	CULT	CULTI · CULTS · CULTY
SCULTCH	**CULTCH**	
SCULTCHES	**CULTCHES**	
	CULTER	CULTERS
	CULTI	CULTIC
	CULTIGEN	CULTIGENS
	CULTISM	CULTISMS
	CULTIST	CULTISTS
	CULTIVAR	CULTIVARS
	CULTIVATE	CULTIVATED · CULTIVATES
	CULTRATE	CULTRATED
	CULTURE	CULTURED · CULTURES
	CULTURIST	CULTURISTS
	CULVER	CULVERS · CULVERT
	CULVERIN	CULVERINS
	CULVERT	CULVERTS
SCUM	**CUM**	
	CUMACEAN	CUMACEANS
	CUMARIN	CUMARINS
	CUMARONE	CUMARONES
SCUMBER	**CUMBER**	CUMBERS
SCUMBERED	**CUMBERED**	
	CUMBERER	CUMBERERS
SCUMBERING	**CUMBERING**	
SCUMBERS	**CUMBERS**	
	CUMBIA	CUMBIAS
	CUMBRANCE	CUMBRANCES
	CUMBUNGI	CUMBUNGIS
	CUMEC	CUMECS
	CUMIN	CUMINS
SCUMMER	**CUMMER**	CUMMERS
SCUMMERS	**CUMMERS**	
	CUMMIN	CUMMINS
	CUMQUAT	CUMQUATS
	CUMSHAW	CUMSHAWS
	CUMULATE	CUMULATED · CUMULATES
	CUMULET	CUMULETS
	CUNCTATOR	CUNCTATORS · CUNCTATORY
	CUNDUM	CUNDUMS
	CUNEATE	CUNEATED
	CUNEIFORM	CUNEIFORMS
	CUNETTE	CUNETTES
	CUNIFORM	CUNIFORMS
	CUNJEVOI	CUNJEVOIS
SCUNNER	**CUNNER**	CUNNERS
SCUNNERS	**CUNNERS**	
	CUNNING	CUNNINGS
	CUNT	CUNTS *(offensive)*
SCUP	**CUP**	CUPS
	CUPBEARER	CUPBEARERS
	CUPBOARD	CUPBOARDS
	CUPCAKE	CUPCAKES

FRONT HOOK	ROOT WORD	END HOOK
	CUPEL	CUPELS
	CUPELER	CUPELERS
	CUPELLER	CUPELLERS
	CUPFERRON	CUPFERRONS
	CUPFUL	CUPFULS
	CUPGALL	CUPGALLS
	CUPHEAD	CUPHEADS
	CUPID	CUPIDS
	CUPOLA	CUPOLAR · CUPOLAS
	CUPPA	CUPPAS
SCUPPER	CUPPER	CUPPERS
SCUPPERS	CUPPERS	
	CUPPING	CUPPINGS
	CUPRITE	CUPRITES
	CUPRUM	CUPRUMS
SCUPS	CUPS	
	CUPULA	CUPULAE · CUPULAR
	CUPULE	CUPULES
SCUR	CUR	CURB · CURD · CURE · CURF · CURL
		CURN · CURR · CURS · CURT
	CURACAO	CURACAOS
	CURACOA	CURACOAS
	CURAGH	CURAGHS
	CURANDERA	CURANDERAS
	CURANDERO	CURANDEROS
	CURARA	CURARAS
	CURARE	CURARES
	CURARI	CURARIS
	CURARINE	CURARINES
	CURARIS	CURARISE
	CURARISE	CURARISED · CURARISES
	CURARIZE	CURARIZED · CURARIZES
	CURASSOW	CURASSOWS
	CURAT	CURATE · CURATS
	CURATE	CURATED · CURATES
	CURATIVE	CURATIVES
	CURATOR	CURATORS · CURATORY
	CURB	CURBS
	CURBER	CURBERS
	CURBING	CURBINGS
	CURBSIDE	CURBSIDES
	CURBSTONE	CURBSTONES
	CURCHEF	CURCHEFS
	CURCULIO	CURCULIOS
	CURCUMA	CURCUMAS
	CURCUMIN	CURCUMINE · CURCUMINS
	CURCUMINE	CURCUMINES
	CURD	CURDS · CURDY
	CURDLE	CURDLED · CURDLER · CURDLES
	CURDLER	CURDLERS
	CURE	CURED · CURER · CURES · CURET
	CURER	CURERS
	CURET	CURETS
	CURETTAGE	CURETTAGES
	CURETTE	CURETTED · CURETTES
SCURF	CURF	CURFS
	CURFEW	CURFEWS
SCURFS	CURFS	
	CURFUFFLE	CURFUFFLED · CURFUFFLES
	CURIA	CURIAE · CURIAL · CURIAS
	CURIALISM	CURIALISMS
	CURIALIST	CURIALISTS
ECURIE	CURIE	CURIES · CURIET
ECURIES	CURIES	
	CURIET	CURIETS
	CURIO	CURIOS
	CURIOS	CURIOSA
	CURITE	CURITES
	CURIUM	CURIUMS

FRONT HOOK	ROOT WORD	END HOOK
	CURL	CURLI · CURLS · CURLY
	CURLER	CURLERS
	CURLEW	CURLEWS
	CURLICUE	CURLICUED · CURLICUES
	CURLIES	CURLIEST
	CURLING	CURLINGS
	CURLPAPER	CURLPAPERS
	CURLYCUE	CURLYCUES
	CURN	CURNS · CURNY
	CURPEL	CURPELS
	CURR	CURRS · CURRY
	CURRACH	CURRACHS
	CURRAGH	CURRAGHS
	CURRAJONG	CURRAJONGS
	CURRAN	CURRANS · CURRANT
	CURRANT	CURRANTS · CURRANTY
	CURRAWONG	CURRAWONGS
SCURRED	**CURRED**	
	CURREJONG	CURREJONGS
	CURRENT	CURRENTS
	CURRICLE	CURRICLES
	CURRICULA	CURRICULAR
	CURRIE	CURRIED · CURRIER · CURRIES
SCURRIED	**CURRIED**	
SCURRIER	**CURRIER**	CURRIERS · CURRIERY
SCURRIERS	**CURRIERS**	
SCURRIES	**CURRIES**	
	CURRIJONG	CURRIJONGS
SCURRING	**CURRING**	
SCURRY	**CURRY**	
	CURRYCOMB	CURRYCOMBS
SCURRYING	**CURRYING**	CURRYINGS
SCURS	**CURS**	CURSE · CURSI · CURST
	CURSE	CURSED · CURSER · CURSES
	CURSER	CURSERS
	CURSING	CURSINGS
	CURSITOR	CURSITORS · CURSITORY
	CURSIVE	CURSIVES
	CURSOR	CURSORS · CURSORY
	CURTAIL	CURTAILS
	CURTAILER	CURTAILERS
	CURTAIN	CURTAINS
	CURTAL	CURTALS
	CURTALAX	CURTALAXE
	CURTALAXE	CURTALAXES
	CURTANA	CURTANAS
	CURTATION	CURTATIONS
	CURTAXE	CURTAXES
	CURTILAGE	CURTILAGES
	CURTSEY	CURTSEYS
	CURVATE	CURVATED
	CURVATION	CURVATIONS
	CURVATURE	CURVATURES
	CURVE	CURVED · CURVES · CURVET · CURVEY
	CURVEBALL	CURVEBALLS
	CURVET	CURVETS
SCURVIER	**CURVIER**	
SCURVIEST	**CURVIEST**	
SCURVY	**CURVY**	
	CUSEC	CUSECS
	CUSH	CUSHY
	CUSHAT	CUSHATS
	CUSHAW	CUSHAWS
	CUSHIE	CUSHIER · CUSHIES
	CUSHIES	CUSHIEST
	CUSHION	CUSHIONS · CUSHIONY
	CUSHIONET	CUSHIONETS
	CUSK	CUSKS
	CUSP	CUSPS

FRONT HOOK	ROOT WORD	END HOOK
	CUSPATE	CUSPATED
	CUSPID	CUSPIDS
	CUSPIDATE	CUSPIDATED
	CUSPIDOR	CUSPIDORE · CUSPIDORS
	CUSPIDORE	CUSPIDORES
	CUSS	CUSSO
	CUSSER	CUSSERS
	CUSSO	CUSSOS
	CUSSWORD	CUSSWORDS
	CUSTARD	CUSTARDS · CUSTARDY
	CUSTOCK	CUSTOCKS
	CUSTODE	CUSTODES
	CUSTODIAN	CUSTODIANS
	CUSTODIER	CUSTODIERS
	CUSTOM	CUSTOMS
	CUSTOMER	CUSTOMERS
	CUSTOMISE	CUSTOMISED · CUSTOMISER · CUSTOMISES
	CUSTOMIZE	CUSTOMIZED · CUSTOMIZER · CUSTOMIZES
	CUSTREL	CUSTRELS
	CUSTUMAL	CUSTUMALS
SCUT	**CUT**	CUTE · CUTS
	CUTAWAY	CUTAWAYS
	CUTBACK	CUTBACKS
	CUTBANK	CUTBANKS
SCUTCH	**CUTCH**	CUTCHA
SCUTCHES	**CUTCHES**	
	CUTDOWN	CUTDOWNS
ACUTE · SCUTE	**CUTE**	CUTER · CUTES · CUTEY
ACUTELY	**CUTELY**	
ACUTENESS	**CUTENESS**	
ACUTER	**CUTER**	
ACUTES · SCUTES	**CUTES**	CUTEST · CUTESY
	CUTESIE	CUTESIER
ACUTEST	**CUTEST**	
	CUTEY	CUTEYS
	CUTICLE	CUTICLES
	CUTICULA	CUTICULAE · CUTICULAR
	CUTIE	CUTIES
	CUTIKIN	CUTIKINS
	CUTIN	CUTINS
	CUTINISE	CUTINISED · CUTINISES
	CUTINIZE	CUTINIZED · CUTINIZES
	CUTLAS	CUTLASS
	CUTLER	CUTLERS · CUTLERY
	CUTLET	CUTLETS
	CUTLINE	CUTLINES
	CUTOFF	CUTOFFS
	CUTOUT	CUTOUTS
	CUTOVER	CUTOVERS
	CUTPURSE	CUTPURSES
SCUTS	**CUTS**	
	CUTTAGE	CUTTAGES
SCUTTER	**CUTTER**	CUTTERS
SCUTTERS	**CUTTERS**	
	CUTTHROAT	CUTTHROATS
	CUTTIES	CUTTIEST
	CUTTING	CUTTINGS
SCUTTLE	**CUTTLE**	CUTTLED · CUTTLES
SCUTTLED	**CUTTLED**	
SCUTTLES	**CUTTLES**	
SCUTTLING	**CUTTLING**	
	CUTTO	CUTTOE
	CUTTOE	CUTTOES
	CUTUP	CUTUPS
	CUTWATER	CUTWATERS
SCUTWORK	**CUTWORK**	CUTWORKS
SCUTWORKS	**CUTWORKS**	
	CUTWORM	CUTWORMS
	CUVEE	CUVEES

FRONT HOOK	ROOT WORD	END HOOK
	CUVETTE	CUVETTES
SCUZZES	**CUZZES**	
	CWM	CWMS
	CYAN	CYANO · CYANS
	CYANAMID	CYANAMIDE · CYANAMIDS
	CYANAMIDE	CYANAMIDES
	CYANATE	CYANATES
	CYANID	CYANIDE · CYANIDS
	CYANIDE	CYANIDED · CYANIDES
	CYANIDING	CYANIDINGS
	CYANIN	CYANINE · CYANINS
	CYANINE	CYANINES
	CYANISE	CYANISED · CYANISES
	CYANITE	CYANITES
	CYANIZE	CYANIZED · CYANIZES
	CYANOGEN	CYANOGENS
	CYANOTYPE	CYANOTYPES
	CYANURATE	CYANURATES
	CYANURET	CYANURETS
	CYATHI	CYATHIA
	CYBERCAFE	CYBERCAFES
	CYBERCAST	CYBERCASTS
	CYBERNATE	CYBERNATED · CYBERNATES
	CYBERNAUT	CYBERNAUTS
	CYBERPET	CYBERPETS
	CYBERPORN	CYBERPORNS
	CYBERPUNK	CYBERPUNKS
	CYBERWAR	CYBERWARS
	CYBORG	CYBORGS
	CYBRARIAN	CYBRARIANS
	CYBRID	CYBRIDS
	CYCAD	CYCADS
	CYCADEOID	CYCADEOIDS
	CYCASIN	CYCASINS
	CYCLAMATE	CYCLAMATES
	CYCLAMEN	CYCLAMENS
	CYCLASE	CYCLASES
	CYCLE	CYCLED · CYCLER · CYCLES
	CYCLECAR	CYCLECARS
	CYCLER	CYCLERS · CYCLERY
	CYCLEWAY	CYCLEWAYS
ACYCLIC	**CYCLIC**	
	CYCLICAL	CYCLICALS
	CYCLICISM	CYCLICISMS
	CYCLIN	CYCLING · CYCLINS
	CYCLING	CYCLINGS
	CYCLISE	CYCLISED · CYCLISES
	CYCLIST	CYCLISTS
	CYCLITOL	CYCLITOLS
	CYCLIZE	CYCLIZED · CYCLIZES
	CYCLIZINE	CYCLIZINES
	CYCLO	CYCLOS
	CYCLOGIRO	CYCLOGIROS
	CYCLOID	CYCLOIDS
	CYCLOLITH	CYCLOLITHS
	CYCLONE	CYCLONES
	CYCLONITE	CYCLONITES
	CYCLORAMA	CYCLORAMAS
	CYCLOTRON	CYCLOTRONS
	CYDER	CYDERS
	CYGNET	CYGNETS
	CYLINDER	CYLINDERS
	CYMA	CYMAE · CYMAR · CYMAS
	CYMAGRAPH	CYMAGRAPHS
	CYMAR	CYMARS
	CYMBAL	CYMBALO · CYMBALS
	CYMBALEER	CYMBALEERS
	CYMBALER	CYMBALERS
	CYMBALIST	CYMBALISTS

FRONT HOOK	ROOT WORD	END HOOK
	CYMBALO	CYMBALOM · CYMBALOS
	CYMBALOM	CYMBALOMS
	CYMBIDIUM	CYMBIDIUMS
	CYMBLING	CYMBLINGS
	CYME	CYMES
	CYMENE	CYMENES
	CYMLIN	CYMLING · CYMLINS
	CYMLING	CYMLINGS
	CYMOGENE	CYMOGENES
	CYMOGRAPH	CYMOGRAPHS
	CYMOL	CYMOLS
	CYMOPHANE	CYMOPHANES
	CYNANCHE	CYNANCHES
	CYNIC	CYNICS
	CYNICISM	CYNICISMS
	CYNODONT	CYNODONTS
	CYNOSURE	CYNOSURES
	CYPHER	CYPHERS
	CYPRES	CYPRESS
	CYPRIAN	CYPRIANS
	CYPRID	CYPRIDS
	CYPRINID	CYPRINIDS
	CYPRINOID	CYPRINOIDS
	CYPSELA	CYPSELAE
	CYST	CYSTS
	CYSTEIN	CYSTEINE · CYSTEINS
	CYSTEINE	CYSTEINES
	CYSTID	CYSTIDS
	CYSTIDEAN	CYSTIDEANS
	CYSTINE	CYSTINES
	CYSTOCARP	CYSTOCARPS
	CYSTOCELE	CYSTOCELES
	CYSTOID	CYSTOIDS
	CYSTOLITH	CYSTOLITHS
	CYTASE	CYTASES
	CYTASTER	CYTASTERS
	CYTE	CYTES
	CYTIDINE	CYTIDINES
	CYTISINE	CYTISINES
	CYTODE	CYTODES
	CYTOKINE	CYTOKINES
	CYTOKININ	CYTOKININS
	CYTOLYSIN	CYTOLYSINS
	CYTOMETER	CYTOMETERS
	CYTON	CYTONS
	CYTOPENIA	CYTOPENIAS
	CYTOPLASM	CYTOPLASMS
	CYTOPLAST	CYTOPLASTS
	CYTOSINE	CYTOSINES
	CYTOSOL	CYTOSOLS
	CYTOSOME	CYTOSOMES
	CYTOTOXIN	CYTOTOXINS
	CZAPKA	CZAPKAS
	CZAR	CZARS
	CZARDOM	CZARDOMS
	CZAREVNA	CZAREVNAS
	CZARINA	CZARINAS
	CZARISM	CZARISMS
	CZARIST	CZARISTS
	CZARITSA	CZARITSAS
	CZARITZA	CZARITZAS

D

FRONT HOOK	ROOT WORD	END HOOK
ODA	**DA**	DAB ▪ DAD ▪ DAE ▪ DAG ▪ DAH ▪ DAK ▪ DAL DAM ▪ DAN ▪ DAP ▪ DAS ▪ DAW ▪ DAY
	DAB	DABS
	DABBA	DABBAS
	DABBER	DABBERS
	DABBLE	DABBLED ▪ DABBLER ▪ DABBLES
	DABBLER	DABBLERS
	DABBLING	DABBLINGS
	DABCHICK	DABCHICKS
	DABSTER	DABSTERS
	DACE	DACES
	DACHA	DACHAS
	DACHSHUND	DACHSHUNDS
	DACITE	DACITES
	DACK	DACKS
	DACKER	DACKERS
	DACOIT	DACOITS ▪ DACOITY
	DACOITAGE	DACOITAGES
	DACQUOISE	DACQUOISES
	DACRON	DACRONS
	DACTYL	DACTYLI ▪ DACTYLS
	DACTYLI	DACTYLIC
	DACTYLIC	DACTYLICS
	DACTYLIST	DACTYLISTS
	DAD	DADA ▪ DADO ▪ DADS
	DADA	DADAH ▪ DADAS
	DADAH	DADAHS
	DADAISM	DADAISMS
	DADAIST	DADAISTS
	DADDLE	DADDLED ▪ DADDLES
	DADDOCK	DADDOCKS
	DADO	DADOS
	DAE	DAES
	DAEMON	DAEMONS
	DAFF	DAFFS ▪ DAFFY
	DAFFIES	DAFFIEST
	DAFFING	DAFFINGS
	DAFFODIL	DAFFODILS
	DAFTAR	DAFTARS
	DAFTIE	DAFTIES
	DAG	DAGO ▪ DAGS
	DAGABA	DAGABAS
	DAGGA	DAGGAS
	DAGGER	DAGGERS
	DAGGING	DAGGINGS
	DAGGLE	DAGGLED ▪ DAGGLES
	DAGLOCK	DAGLOCKS
	DAGO	DAGOS *(offensive)*
	DAGOBA	DAGOBAS
	DAGWOOD	DAGWOODS
ODAH	**DAH**	DAHL ▪ DAHS
	DAHABEAH	DAHABEAHS
	DAHABEEAH	DAHABEEAHS
	DAHABIAH	DAHABIAHS
	DAHABIEH	DAHABIEHS
	DAHABIYA	DAHABIYAH ▪ DAHABIYAS
	DAHABIYAH	DAHABIYAHS
	DAHABIYEH	DAHABIYEHS
	DAHL	DAHLS
	DAHLIA	DAHLIAS
	DAHOON	DAHOONS
ODAHS	**DAHS**	
	DAIDLE	DAIDLED ▪ DAIDLES
	DAIDZEIN	DAIDZEINS
	DAIKER	DAIKERS
	DAIKON	DAIKONS

FRONT HOOK	ROOT WORD	END HOOK
	DAIMIO	DAIMIOS
	DAIMOKU	DAIMOKUS
	DAIMON	DAIMONS
	DAIMYO	DAIMYOS
SDAINE	**DAINE**	DAINED · DAINES
SDAINED	**DAINED**	
SDAINES	**DAINES**	
SDAINING	**DAINING**	
	DAINT	DAINTY
	DAINTIES	DAINTIEST
	DAIQUIRI	DAIQUIRIS
	DAIRYING	DAIRYINGS
	DAIRYMAID	DAIRYMAIDS
	DAIS	DAISY
	DAISHIKI	DAISHIKIS
	DAK	DAKS
	DAKER	DAKERS
	DAKERHEN	DAKERHENS
	DAKOIT	DAKOITI · DAKOITS · DAKOITY
	DAKOITI	DAKOITIS
ODAL · UDAL	**DAL**	DALE · DALI · DALS · DALT
	DALAPON	DALAPONS
	DALASI	DALASIS
	DALE	DALED · DALES
	DALED	DALEDH · DALEDS
	DALEDH	DALEDHS
	DALETH	DALETHS
	DALGYTE	DALGYTES
	DALI	DALIS
	DALLE	DALLES
	DALLIANCE	DALLIANCES
	DALLIER	DALLIERS
	DALLOP	DALLOPS
	DALMAHOY	DALMAHOYS
	DALMATIAN	DALMATIANS
	DALMATIC	DALMATICS
ODALS · UDALS	**DALS**	
	DALT	DALTS
	DALTON	DALTONS
	DALTONISM	DALTONISMS
	DAM	DAME · DAMN · DAMP · DAMS
	DAMAGE	DAMAGED · DAMAGER · DAMAGES
	DAMAGER	DAMAGERS
	DAMAN	DAMANS
	DAMAR	DAMARS
	DAMASCENE	DAMASCENED · DAMASCENES
	DAMASK	DAMASKS
	DAMASKEEN	DAMASKEENS
	DAMASKIN	DAMASKING · DAMASKINS
	DAMASQUIN	DAMASQUINS
	DAMASSIN	DAMASSINS
	DAMBOARD	DAMBOARDS
	DAMBROD	DAMBRODS
	DAME	DAMES
	DAMEWORT	DAMEWORTS
	DAMIANA	DAMIANAS
	DAMMAR	DAMMARS
	DAMME	DAMMED · DAMMER
	DAMMER	DAMMERS
	DAMN	DAMNS
	DAMNATION	DAMNATIONS
	DAMNDEST	DAMNDESTS
	DAMNEDEST	DAMNEDESTS
	DAMNER	DAMNERS
	DAMOISEL	DAMOISELS
	DAMOSEL	DAMOSELS
	DAMOZEL	DAMOZELS
	DAMP	DAMPS · DAMPY
	DAMPEN	DAMPENS

FRONT HOOK	ROOT WORD	END HOOK
	DAMPENER	DAMPENERS
	DAMPER	DAMPERS
	DAMPING	DAMPINGS
	DAMSEL	DAMSELS
	DAMSON	DAMSONS
	DAN	DANG ▪ DANK ▪ DANS ▪ DANT
	DANAZOL	DANAZOLS
	DANCE	DANCED ▪ DANCER ▪ DANCES ▪ DANCEY
	DANCEHALL	DANCEHALLS
	DANCER	DANCERS
	DANCETTE	DANCETTEE ▪ DANCETTES
	DANCING	DANCINGS
	DANDELION	DANDELIONS
	DANDER	DANDERS
	DANDIES	DANDIEST
	DANDIPRAT	DANDIPRATS
	DANDLE	DANDLED ▪ DANDLER ▪ DANDLES
	DANDLER	DANDLERS
	DANDRIFF	DANDRIFFS
	DANDRUFF	DANDRUFFS ▪ DANDRUFFY
	DANDYFUNK	DANDYFUNKS
	DANDYISM	DANDYISMS
	DANDYPRAT	DANDYPRATS
	DANEGELD	DANEGELDS
	DANEGELT	DANEGELTS
	DANELAGH	DANELAGHS
	DANELAW	DANELAWS
	DANEWEED	DANEWEEDS
	DANEWORT	DANEWORTS
	DANG	DANGS
	DANGER	DANGERS
	DANGLE	DANGLED ▪ DANGLER ▪ DANGLES
	DANGLER	DANGLERS
	DANGLING	DANGLINGS
	DANIO	DANIOS
	DANK	DANKS
	DANNEBROG	DANNEBROGS
	DANSEUR	DANSEURS
	DANSEUSE	DANSEUSES
IDANT	**DANT**	DANTS
	DANTHONIA	DANTHONIAS
	DANTON	DANTONS
IDANTS	**DANTS**	
	DAP	DAPS
	DAPHNE	DAPHNES
	DAPHNIA	DAPHNIAS
	DAPHNID	DAPHNIDS
	DAPPER	DAPPERS
	DAPPLE	DAPPLED ▪ DAPPLES
	DAPSONE	DAPSONES
	DAQUIRI	DAQUIRIS
	DARAF	DARAFS
	DARB	DARBS
	DARBAR	DARBARS
	DARCY	DARCYS
	DARE	DARED ▪ DARER ▪ DARES
	DAREDEVIL	DAREDEVILS
	DARER	DARERS
	DARG	DARGA ▪ DARGS
	DARGA	DARGAH ▪ DARGAS
	DARGAH	DARGAHS
	DARGLE	DARGLES
	DARI	DARIC ▪ DARIS
	DARIC	DARICS
	DARING	DARINGS
	DARIOLE	DARIOLES
	DARK	DARKS ▪ DARKY
	DARKEN	DARKENS
	DARKENER	DARKENERS

FRONT HOOK	ROOT WORD	END HOOK
	DARKEY	DARKEYS (offensive)
	DARKIE	DARKIES (offensive)
	DARKLE	DARKLED ▪ DARKLES
	DARKLING	DARKLINGS
	DARKROOM	DARKROOMS
	DARLING	DARLINGS
	DARN	DARNS
	DARNATION	DARNATIONS
	DARNDEST	DARNDESTS
	DARNEDEST	DARNEDESTS
	DARNEL	DARNELS
	DARNER	DARNERS
	DARNING	DARNINGS
	DAROGHA	DAROGHAS
	DARRAIGN	DARRAIGNE ▪ DARRAIGNS
	DARRAIGNE	DARRAIGNED ▪ DARRAIGNES
	DARRAIN	DARRAINE ▪ DARRAINS
	DARRAINE	DARRAINED ▪ DARRAINES
	DARRAYN	DARRAYNS
	DARRE	DARRED ▪ DARRES
	DARSHAN	DARSHANS
	DART	DARTS
	DARTBOARD	DARTBOARDS
	DARTER	DARTERS
	DARTLE	DARTLED ▪ DARTLES
	DARTRE	DARTRES
	DARZI	DARZIS
ODAS	DAS	DASH
	DASH	DASHI ▪ DASHY
	DASHBOARD	DASHBOARDS
	DASHEEN	DASHEENS
	DASHEKI	DASHEKIS
	DASHER	DASHERS
	DASHI	DASHIS
	DASHIKI	DASHIKIS
	DASHPOT	DASHPOTS
	DASSIE	DASSIES
	DASTARD	DASTARDS ▪ DASTARDY
	DASYMETER	DASYMETERS
	DASYPOD	DASYPODS
	DASYURE	DASYURES
	DATA	DATAL
	DATABANK	DATABANKS
	DATABASE	DATABASED ▪ DATABASES
	DATACARD	DATACARDS
	DATAGLOVE	DATAGLOVES
	DATAL	DATALS
	DATALLER	DATALLERS
	DATARIA	DATARIAS
	DATCHA	DATCHAS
	DATE	DATED ▪ DATER ▪ DATES
	DATEBOOK	DATEBOOKS
	DATELINE	DATELINED ▪ DATELINES
	DATER	DATERS
	DATING	DATINGS
	DATIVE	DATIVES
	DATO	DATOS
	DATOLITE	DATOLITES
	DATTO	DATTOS
	DATUM	DATUMS
	DATURA	DATURAS
	DATURINE	DATURINES
	DAUB	DAUBE ▪ DAUBS ▪ DAUBY
	DAUBE	DAUBED ▪ DAUBER ▪ DAUBES
	DAUBER	DAUBERS ▪ DAUBERY
	DAUBING	DAUBINGS
	DAUD	DAUDS
	DAUGHTER	DAUGHTERS
	DAULT	DAULTS

FRONT HOOK	ROOT WORD	END HOOK
	DAUNDER	DAUNDERS
	DAUNER	DAUNERS
	DAUNT	DAUNTS
	DAUNTER	DAUNTERS
	DAUNTON	DAUNTONS
	DAUPHIN	DAUPHINE · DAUPHINS
	DAUPHINE	DAUPHINES
	DAUPHINES	DAUPHINESS
	DAUR	DAURS
	DAUT	DAUTS
	DAUTIE	DAUTIES
	DAVEN	DAVENS
	DAVENPORT	DAVENPORTS
	DAVIDIA	DAVIDIAS
	DAVIT	DAVITS
ADAW	**DAW**	DAWD · DAWK · DAWN · DAWS · DAWT
	DAWAH	DAWAHS
	DAWBAKE	DAWBAKES
	DAWCOCK	DAWCOCKS
	DAWD	DAWDS
	DAWDLE	DAWDLED · DAWDLER · DAWDLES
	DAWDLER	DAWDLERS
ADAWED	**DAWED**	
ADAWING	**DAWING**	
	DAWK	DAWKS
	DAWN	DAWNS
	DAWNER	DAWNERS
	DAWNING	DAWNINGS
ADAWS	**DAWS**	
	DAWSONITE	DAWSONITES
	DAWT	DAWTS
	DAWTIE	DAWTIES
	DAY	DAYS
	DAYAN	DAYANS
	DAYBED	DAYBEDS
	DAYBOOK	DAYBOOKS
	DAYBOY	DAYBOYS
	DAYBREAK	DAYBREAKS
	DAYCARE	DAYCARES
	DAYCENTRE	DAYCENTRES
	DAYDREAM	DAYDREAMS · DAYDREAMT · DAYDREAMY
	DAYFLOWER	DAYFLOWERS
	DAYGLO	DAYGLOW
	DAYGLOW	DAYGLOWS
	DAYLIGHT	DAYLIGHTS
	DAYMARE	DAYMARES
	DAYMARK	DAYMARKS
	DAYROOM	DAYROOMS
ADAYS	**DAYS**	
	DAYSACK	DAYSACKS
	DAYSHELL	DAYSHELLS
	DAYSIDE	DAYSIDES
	DAYSPRING	DAYSPRINGS
	DAYSTAR	DAYSTARS
	DAYTALE	DAYTALER · DAYTALES
	DAYTALER	DAYTALERS
	DAYTIME	DAYTIMES
	DAYWORK	DAYWORKS
	DAYWORKER	DAYWORKERS
	DAZE	DAZED · DAZER · DAZES
	DAZER	DAZERS
	DAZZLE	DAZZLED · DAZZLER · DAZZLES
	DAZZLER	DAZZLERS
	DAZZLING	DAZZLINGS
IDE · ODE	**DE**	DEB · DEE · DEF · DEG · DEI · DEL · DEN DEV · DEW · DEX · DEY
	DEACON	DEACONS
	DEAD	DEADS
	DEADBEAT	DEADBEATS

FRONT HOOK	ROOT WORD	END HOOK
	DEADBOLT	DEADBOLTS
	DEADBOY	DEADBOYS
	DEADEN	DEADENS
	DEADENER	DEADENERS
	DEADENING	DEADENINGS
	DEADER	DEADERS
	DEADEYE	DEADEYES
	DEADFALL	DEADFALLS
	DEADHEAD	DEADHEADS
	DEADHOUSE	DEADHOUSES
	DEADLIFT	DEADLIFTS
	DEADLIGHT	DEADLIGHTS
	DEADLINE	DEADLINED · DEADLINES
	DEADLINES	DEADLINESS
	DEADLOCK	DEADLOCKS
	DEADPAN	DEADPANS
	DEADSTOCK	DEADSTOCKS
	DEADWOOD	DEADWOODS
	DEAERATE	DEAERATED · DEAERATES
	DEAERATOR	DEAERATORS
	DEAFEN	DEAFENS
	DEAFENING	DEAFENINGS
	DEAIR	DEAIRS
IDEAL	**DEAL**	DEALS · DEALT
	DEALATE	DEALATED · DEALATES
	DEALATION	DEALATIONS
	DEALER	DEALERS
	DEALING	DEALINGS
IDEALS	**DEALS**	
	DEAMINASE	DEAMINASES
	DEAMINATE	DEAMINATED · DEAMINATES
	DEAMINISE	DEAMINISED · DEAMINISES
	DEAMINIZE	DEAMINIZED · DEAMINIZES
	DEAN	DEANS
	DEANER	DEANERS · DEANERY
	DEANSHIP	DEANSHIPS
	DEAR.	DEARE · DEARN · DEARS · DEARY
	DEARE	DEARED · DEARER · DEARES
	DEARES	DEAREST
	DEARIE	DEARIES
	DEARLING	DEARLINGS
	DEARN	DEARNS
	DEARTH	DEARTHS
	DEASIL	DEASILS
	DEASIUL	DEASIULS
	DEASOIL	DEASOILS
	DEATH	DEATHS · DEATHY
	DEATHBED	DEATHBEDS
	DEATHBLOW	DEATHBLOWS
	DEATHCUP	DEATHCUPS
	DEATHTRAP	DEATHTRAPS
	DEATHWARD	DEATHWARDS
	DEAVE	DEAVED · DEAVES
	DEAW	DEAWS · DEAWY
	DEB	DEBE · DEBS · DEBT
	DEBACLE	DEBACLES
	DEBAG	DEBAGS
	DEBAGGING	DEBAGGINGS
	DEBAR	DEBARK · DEBARS
	DEBARK	DEBARKS
	DEBARKER	DEBARKERS
	DEBARMENT	DEBARMENTS
	DEBASE	DEBASED · DEBASER · DEBASES
	DEBASER	DEBASERS
	DEBATE	DEBATED · DEBATER · DEBATES
	DEBATER	DEBATERS
	DEBAUCHEE	DEBAUCHEES
	DEBAUCHER	DEBAUCHERS · DEBAUCHERY
	DEBBIES	DEBBIEST

FRONT HOOK	ROOT WORD	END HOOK
	DEBE	DEBEL · DEBES
	DEBEAK	DEBEAKS
	DEBEARD	DEBEARDS
	DEBEL	DEBELS
	DEBENTURE	DEBENTURED · DEBENTURES
	DEBIT	DEBITS
	DEBITOR	DEBITORS
	DEBONAIR	DEBONAIRE
	DEBONE	DEBONED · DEBONER · DEBONES
	DEBONER	DEBONERS
	DEBOUCH	DEBOUCHE
	DEBOUCHE	DEBOUCHED · DEBOUCHES
	DEBRIDE	DEBRIDED · DEBRIDES
	DEBRIEF	DEBRIEFS
	DEBRIEFER	DEBRIEFERS
	DEBRUISE	DEBRUISED · DEBRUISES
	DEBT	DEBTS
	DEBTEE	DEBTEES
	DEBTOR	DEBTORS
	DEBUD	DEBUDS
	DEBUG	DEBUGS
	DEBUGGER	DEBUGGERS
	DEBUNK	DEBUNKS
	DEBUNKER	DEBUNKERS
	DEBURR	DEBURRS
	DEBUT	DEBUTS
	DEBUTANT	DEBUTANTE · DEBUTANTS
	DEBUTANTE	DEBUTANTES
	DEBYE	DEBYES
	DECACHORD	DECACHORDS
	DECAD	DECADE · DECADS
	DECADE	DECADES
	DECADENCE	DECADENCES
	DECADENT	DECADENTS
	DECAF	DECAFF · DECAFS
	DECAFF	DECAFFS
	DECAGON	DECAGONS
	DECAGRAM	DECAGRAMS
	DECAHEDRA	DECAHEDRAL
	DECAL	DECALS
	DECALITER	DECALITERS
	DECALITRE	DECALITRES
	DECALOG	DECALOGS
	DECALOGUE	DECALOGUES
	DECAMETER	DECAMETERS
	DECAMETRE	DECAMETRES
	DECAMP	DECAMPS
	DECANE	DECANES
	DECANT	DECANTS
	DECANTATE	DECANTATED · DECANTATES
	DECANTER	DECANTERS
	DECAPOD	DECAPODS
	DECAPODAN	DECAPODANS
	DECARB	DECARBS
	DECARE	DECARES
	DECASTERE	DECASTERES
	DECASTICH	DECASTICHS
	DECASTYLE	DECASTYLES
	DECATHLON	DECATHLONS
	DECAUDATE	DECAUDATED · DECAUDATES
	DECAY	DECAYS
	DECAYER	DECAYERS
	DECCIE	DECCIES
	DECEASE	DECEASED · DECEASES
	DECEDENT	DECEDENTS
	DECEIT	DECEITS
	DECEIVE	DECEIVED · DECEIVER · DECEIVES
	DECEIVER	DECEIVERS
	DECEIVING	DECEIVINGS

FRONT HOOK	ROOT WORD	END HOOK
	DECELERON	DECELERONS
	DECEMVIR	DECEMVIRI · DECEMVIRS
	DECENNIA	DECENNIAL
	DECENNIAL	DECENNIALS
	DECENNIUM	DECENNIUMS
	DECENTER	DECENTERS
	DECENTRE	DECENTRED · DECENTRES
	DECEPTION	DECEPTIONS
	DECERN	DECERNS
	DECESSION	DECESSIONS
	DECHEANCE	DECHEANCES
	DECIARE	DECIARES
	DECIBEL	DECIBELS
	DECIDE	DECIDED · DECIDER · DECIDES
	DECIDER	DECIDERS
	DECIDUA	DECIDUAE · DECIDUAL · DECIDUAS
	DECIGRAM	DECIGRAMS
	DECILE	DECILES
	DECILITER	DECILITERS
	DECILITRE	DECILITRES
	DECILLION	DECILLIONS
	DECIMAL	DECIMALS
	DECIMATE	DECIMATED · DECIMATES
	DECIMATOR	DECIMATORS
	DECIME	DECIMES
	DECIMETER	DECIMETERS
	DECIMETRE	DECIMETRES
	DECIPHER	DECIPHERS
	DECISION	DECISIONS
	DECISTERE	DECISTERES
	DECK	DECKO · DECKS
	DECKCHAIR	DECKCHAIRS
	DECKEL	DECKELS
	DECKER	DECKERS
	DECKHAND	DECKHANDS
	DECKHOUSE	DECKHOUSES
	DECKING	DECKINGS
	DECKLE	DECKLED · DECKLES
	DECKO	DECKOS
	DECLAIM	DECLAIMS
	DECLAIMER	DECLAIMERS
	DECLARANT	DECLARANTS
	DECLARE	DECLARED · DECLARER · DECLARES
	DECLARER	DECLARERS
	DECLASS	DECLASSE
	DECLASSE	DECLASSED · DECLASSEE · DECLASSES
	DECLAW	DECLAWS
	DECLINE	DECLINED · DECLINER · DECLINES
	DECLINER	DECLINERS
	DECLINIST	DECLINISTS
	DECLUTTER	DECLUTTERS
	DECO	DECOR · DECOS · DECOY
	DECOCT	DECOCTS
	DECOCTION	DECOCTIONS
	DECOCTURE	DECOCTURES
	DECODE	DECODED · DECODER · DECODES
	DECODER	DECODERS
	DECOHERER	DECOHERERS
	DECOKE	DECOKED · DECOKES
	DECOLLATE	DECOLLATED · DECOLLATES
	DECOLLETE	DECOLLETES
	DECOLOR	DECOLORS
	DECOLOUR	DECOLOURS
	DECOMMIT	DECOMMITS
	DECOMPOSE	DECOMPOSED · DECOMPOSER · DECOMPOSES
	DECONGEST	DECONGESTS
	DECONTROL	DECONTROLS
	DECOR	DECORS
	DECORATE	DECORATED · DECORATES

FRONT HOOK	ROOT WORD	END HOOK
	DECORATOR	DECORATORS
	DECORUM	DECORUMS
	DECOUPAGE	DECOUPAGED · DECOUPAGES
	DECOUPLE	DECOUPLED · DECOUPLER · DECOUPLES
	DECOUPLER	DECOUPLERS
	DECOY	DECOYS
	DECOYER	DECOYERS
	DECREASE	DECREASED · DECREASES
	DECREE	DECREED · DECREER · DECREES · DECREET
	DECREER	DECREERS
	DECREET	DECREETS
	DECREMENT	DECREMENTS
	DECRETAL	DECRETALS
	DECRETIST	DECRETISTS
	DECREW	DECREWS
	DECRIAL	DECRIALS
	DECRIER	DECRIERS
	DECROWN	DECROWNS
	DECRYPT	DECRYPTS
	DECTET	DECTETS
	DECUMAN	DECUMANS
	DECUPLE	DECUPLED · DECUPLES
	DECURIA	DECURIAS
	DECURION	DECURIONS
	DECURSION	DECURSIONS
	DECURVE	DECURVED · DECURVES
	DECUSSATE	DECUSSATED · DECUSSATES
	DEDICANT	DEDICANTS
	DEDICATE	DEDICATED · DEDICATEE · DEDICATES
	DEDICATEE	DEDICATEES
	DEDICATOR	DEDICATORS · DEDICATORY
	DEDUCE	DEDUCED · DEDUCES
	DEDUCT	DEDUCTS
	DEDUCTION	DEDUCTIONS
IDEE	**DEE**	DEED · DEEK · DEEM · DEEN · DEEP
		DEER · DEES · DEET · DEEV
	DEED	DEEDS · DEEDY
	DEEJAY	DEEJAYS
ADEEM	**DEEM**	DEEMS
ADEEMED	**DEEMED**	
ADEEMING	**DEEMING**	
ADEEMS	**DEEMS**	
	DEEMSTER	DEEMSTERS
	DEEN	DEENS
	DEEP	DEEPS
	DEEPEN	DEEPENS
	DEEPENER	DEEPENERS
	DEEPFROZE	DEEPFROZEN
	DEEPIE	DEEPIES
	DEER	DEERE · DEERS
	DEERHORN	DEERHORNS
	DEERHOUND	DEERHOUNDS
	DEERLET	DEERLETS
	DEERSKIN	DEERSKINS
	DEERWEED	DEERWEEDS
	DEERYARD	DEERYARDS
IDEES	**DEES**	
	DEET	DEETS
	DEEV	DEEVE · DEEVS
	DEEVE	DEEVED · DEEVES
	DEEWAN	DEEWANS
	DEF	DEFI · DEFT · DEFY
	DEFACE	DEFACED · DEFACER · DEFACES
	DEFACER	DEFACERS
	DEFAECATE	DEFAECATED · DEFAECATES
	DEFALCATE	DEFALCATED · DEFALCATES
	DEFAME	DEFAMED · DEFAMER · DEFAMES
	DEFAMER	DEFAMERS
	DEFAMING	DEFAMINGS

FRONT HOOK	ROOT WORD	END HOOK
	DEFANG	DEFANGS
	DEFAST	DEFASTE
	DEFAT	DEFATS
	DEFAULT	DEFAULTS
	DEFAULTER	DEFAULTERS
	DEFEAT	DEFEATS
	DEFEATER	DEFEATERS
	DEFEATISM	DEFEATISMS
	DEFEATIST	DEFEATISTS
	DEFEATURE	DEFEATURED ▪ DEFEATURES
	DEFECATE	DEFECATED ▪ DEFECATES
	DEFECATOR	DEFECATORS
	DEFECT	DEFECTS
	DEFECTION	DEFECTIONS
	DEFECTIVE	DEFECTIVES
	DEFECTOR	DEFECTORS
	DEFENCE	DEFENCED ▪ DEFENCES
	DEFEND	DEFENDS
	DEFENDANT	DEFENDANTS
	DEFENDER	DEFENDERS
	DEFENSE	DEFENSED ▪ DEFENSES
	DEFENSIVE	DEFENSIVES
	DEFER	DEFERS
	DEFERENCE	DEFERENCES
	DEFERENT	DEFERENTS
	DEFERMENT	DEFERMENTS
	DEFERRAL	DEFERRALS
	DEFERRER	DEFERRERS
	DEFI	DEFIS
	DEFIANCE	DEFIANCES
	DEFICIENT	DEFICIENTS
	DEFICIT	DEFICITS
	DEFIER	DEFIERS
	DEFILADE	DEFILADED ▪ DEFILADES
	DEFILE	DEFILED ▪ DEFILER ▪ DEFILES
	DEFILER	DEFILERS
	DEFINE	DEFINED ▪ DEFINER ▪ DEFINES
	DEFINER	DEFINERS
	DEFLATE	DEFLATED ▪ DEFLATER ▪ DEFLATES
	DEFLATER	DEFLATERS
	DEFLATION	DEFLATIONS
	DEFLATOR	DEFLATORS
	DEFLEA	DEFLEAS
	DEFLECT	DEFLECTS
	DEFLECTOR	DEFLECTORS
	DEFLEXION	DEFLEXIONS
	DEFLEXURE	DEFLEXURES
	DEFLORATE	DEFLORATED ▪ DEFLORATES
	DEFLOWER	DEFLOWERS
	DEFLUXION	DEFLUXIONS
	DEFOAM	DEFOAMS
	DEFOAMER	DEFOAMERS
	DEFOG	DEFOGS
	DEFOGGER	DEFOGGERS
	DEFOLIANT	DEFOLIANTS
	DEFOLIATE	DEFOLIATED ▪ DEFOLIATES
	DEFORCE	DEFORCED ▪ DEFORCER ▪ DEFORCES
	DEFORCER	DEFORCERS
	DEFOREST	DEFORESTS
	DEFORM	DEFORMS
	DEFORMER	DEFORMERS
	DEFOUL	DEFOULS
	DEFRAG	DEFRAGS
	DEFRAGGER	DEFRAGGERS
	DEFRAUD	DEFRAUDS
	DEFRAUDER	DEFRAUDERS
	DEFRAY	DEFRAYS
	DEFRAYAL	DEFRAYALS
	DEFRAYER	DEFRAYERS

FRONT HOOK	ROOT WORD	END HOOK
	DEFREEZE	DEFREEZES
	DEFROCK	DEFROCKS
	DEFROST	DEFROSTS
	DEFROSTER	DEFROSTERS
	DEFROZE	DEFROZEN
	DEFUEL	DEFUELS
	DEFUNCT	DEFUNCTS
	DEFUND	DEFUNDS
	DEFUSE	DEFUSED · DEFUSER · DEFUSES
	DEFUSER	DEFUSERS
	DEFUZE	DEFUZED · DEFUZES
	DEG	DEGS
	DEGAME	DEGAMES
	DEGAMI	DEGAMIS
	DEGASSER	DEGASSERS
	DEGAUSSER	DEGAUSSERS
	DEGEARING	DEGEARINGS
	DEGENDER	DEGENDERS
	DEGERM	DEGERMS
	DEGLAZE	DEGLAZED · DEGLAZES
	DEGOUT	DEGOUTS
	DEGRADE	DEGRADED · DEGRADER · DEGRADES
	DEGRADER	DEGRADERS
	DEGREASE	DEGREASED · DEGREASER · DEGREASES
	DEGREASER	DEGREASERS
	DEGREE	DEGREED · DEGREES
	DEGUM	DEGUMS
	DEGUST	DEGUSTS
	DEGUSTATE	DEGUSTATED · DEGUSTATES
	DEHISCE	DEHISCED · DEHISCES
	DEHORN	DEHORNS
	DEHORNER	DEHORNERS
	DEHORT	DEHORTS
	DEHORTER	DEHORTERS
	DEHYDRATE	DEHYDRATED · DEHYDRATER · DEHYDRATES
	DEI	DEID · DEIF · DEIL
	DEICE	DEICED · DEICER · DEICES
	DEICER	DEICERS
	DEICIDE	DEICIDES
	DEICTIC	DEICTICS
	DEID	DEIDS
	DEIF	DEIFY
	DEIFIER	DEIFIERS
SDEIGN	**DEIGN**	DEIGNS
SDEIGNED	**DEIGNED**	
SDEIGNING	**DEIGNING**	
SDEIGNS	**DEIGNS**	
	DEIL	DEILS
	DEINOSAUR	DEINOSAURS
	DEIONISE	DEIONISED · DEIONISER · DEIONISES
	DEIONISER	DEIONISERS
	DEIONIZE	DEIONIZED · DEIONIZER · DEIONIZES
	DEIONIZER	DEIONIZERS
	DEISEAL	DEISEALS
	DEISHEAL	DEISHEALS
	DEISM	DEISMS
	DEIST	DEISTS
	DEJECT	DEJECTA · DEJECTS
	DEJECTION	DEJECTIONS
	DEJEUNE	DEJEUNER · DEJEUNES
	DEJEUNER	DEJEUNERS
	DEKAGRAM	DEKAGRAMS
	DEKALITER	DEKALITERS
	DEKALITRE	DEKALITRES
	DEKAMETER	DEKAMETERS
	DEKAMETRE	DEKAMETRES
	DEKARE	DEKARES
	DEKE	DEKED · DEKES
	DEKKO	DEKKOS

FRONT HOOK	ROOT WORD	END HOOK
	DEL	DELE · DELF · DELI · DELL · DELO DELS · DELT
	DELAINE	DELAINES
	DELAPSE	DELAPSED · DELAPSES
	DELAPSION	DELAPSIONS
	DELATE	DELATED · DELATES
	DELATION	DELATIONS
	DELATOR	DELATORS
	DELAY	DELAYS
	DELAYER	DELAYERS
	DELE	DELED · DELES
	DELEAD	DELEADS
	DELEAVE	DELEAVED · DELEAVES
	DELECTATE	DELECTATED · DELECTATES
	DELEGATE	DELEGATED · DELEGATEE · DELEGATES
	DELEGATEE	DELEGATEES
	DELEGATOR	DELEGATORS
	DELETE	DELETED · DELETES
	DELETION	DELETIONS
	DELF	DELFS · DELFT
	DELFT	DELFTS
	DELFTWARE	DELFTWARES
	DELI	DELIS
	DELIBATE	DELIBATED · DELIBATES
	DELICATE	DELICATES
	DELICE	DELICES
	DELICT	DELICTS
	DELIGHT	DELIGHTS
	DELIGHTER	DELIGHTERS
	DELIME	DELIMED · DELIMES
	DELIMIT	DELIMITS
	DELIMITER	DELIMITERS
	DELINEATE	DELINEATED · DELINEATES
	DELIQUIUM	DELIQUIUMS
	DELIRIUM	DELIRIUMS
	DELIS	DELISH · DELIST
	DELIST	DELISTS
	DELIVER	DELIVERS · DELIVERY
	DELIVERER	DELIVERERS
	DELL	DELLS · DELLY
	DELO	DELOS
	DELOPE	DELOPED · DELOPES
	DELOUSE	DELOUSED · DELOUSER · DELOUSES
	DELOUSER	DELOUSERS
	DELPH	DELPHS
	DELT	DELTA · DELTS
	DELTA	DELTAS
	DELTOID	DELTOIDS
	DELUBRUM	DELUBRUMS
	DELUDE	DELUDED · DELUDER · DELUDES
	DELUDER	DELUDERS
	DELUGE	DELUGED · DELUGES
	DELUNDUNG	DELUNDUNGS
	DELUSION	DELUSIONS
	DELUSTER	DELUSTERS
	DELVE	DELVED · DELVER · DELVES
	DELVER	DELVERS
	DEMAGOG	DEMAGOGS · DEMAGOGY
	DEMAGOGUE	DEMAGOGUED · DEMAGOGUES
	DEMAIN	DEMAINE · DEMAINS
	DEMAINE	DEMAINES
	DEMAN	DEMAND · DEMANS
	DEMAND	DEMANDS
	DEMANDANT	DEMANDANTS
	DEMANDER	DEMANDERS
	DEMANNING	DEMANNINGS
	DEMANTOID	DEMANTOIDS
	DEMARCATE	DEMARCATED · DEMARCATES
	DEMARCHE	DEMARCHES

FRONT HOOK	ROOT WORD	END HOOK
	DEMARK	DEMARKS
	DEMARKET	DEMARKETS
	DEMAST	DEMASTS
	DEMAYNE	DEMAYNES
	DEME	DEMES
	DEMEAN	DEMEANE · DEMEANS
	DEMEANE	DEMEANED · DEMEANES
	DEMEANOR	DEMEANORS
	DEMEANOUR	DEMEANOURS
	DEMENT	DEMENTI · DEMENTS
	DEMENTATE	DEMENTATED · DEMENTATES
	DEMENTI	DEMENTIA · DEMENTIS
	DEMENTIA	DEMENTIAL · DEMENTIAS
	DEMERARA	DEMERARAN · DEMERARAS
	DEMERGE	DEMERGED · DEMERGER · DEMERGES
	DEMERGER	DEMERGERS
	DEMERIT	DEMERITS
	DEMERSE	DEMERSED · DEMERSES
	DEMERSION	DEMERSIONS
	DEMESNE	DEMESNES
	DEMETON	DEMETONS
	DEMIGOD	DEMIGODS
	DEMIJOHN	DEMIJOHNS
	DEMILUNE	DEMILUNES
	DEMIMONDE	DEMIMONDES
	DEMIPIQUE	DEMIPIQUES
	DEMIREP	DEMIREPS
	DEMISE	DEMISED · DEMISES
	DEMISSION	DEMISSIONS
	DEMIST	DEMISTS
	DEMISTER	DEMISTERS
	DEMIT	DEMITS
	DEMITASSE	DEMITASSES
	DEMIURGE	DEMIURGES
	DEMIVOLT	DEMIVOLTE · DEMIVOLTS
	DEMIVOLTE	DEMIVOLTES
	DEMIWORLD	DEMIWORLDS
	DEMO	DEMOB · DEMON · DEMOS
	DEMOB	DEMOBS
	DEMOCRAT	DEMOCRATS · DEMOCRACY
	DEMODE	DEMODED
	DEMON	DEMONS
	DEMONIAC	DEMONIACS
	DEMONISE	DEMONISED · DEMONISES
	DEMONISM	DEMONISMS
	DEMONIST	DEMONISTS
	DEMONIZE	DEMONIZED · DEMONIZES
	DEMOTE	DEMOTED · DEMOTES
	DEMOTIC	DEMOTICS
	DEMOTION	DEMOTIONS
	DEMOTIST	DEMOTISTS
	DEMOUNT	DEMOUNTS
	DEMPSTER	DEMPSTERS
	DEMULCENT	DEMULCENTS
	DEMUR	DEMURE · DEMURS
	DEMURE	DEMURED · DEMURER · DEMURES
	DEMURES	DEMUREST
	DEMURRAGE	DEMURRAGES
	DEMURRAL	DEMURRALS
	DEMURRER	DEMURRERS
	DEMYSHIP	DEMYSHIPS
	DEN	DENE · DENI · DENS · DENT · DENY
	DENAR	DENARI · DENARS · DENARY
	DENARI	DENARII
	DENATURE	DENATURED · DENATURES
	DENAY	DENAYS
	DENDRIMER	DENDRIMERS
	DENDRITE	DENDRITES
	DENDRON	DENDRONS

FRONT HOOK	ROOT WORD	END HOOK
	DENE	DENES · DENET
	DENERVATE	DENERVATED · DENERVATES
	DENET	DENETS
	DENGUE	DENGUES
	DENI	DENIM · DENIS
	DENIAL	DENIALS
	DENIER	DENIERS
	DENIGRATE	DENIGRATED · DENIGRATES
	DENIM	DENIMS
	DENITRATE	DENITRATED · DENITRATES
	DENIZEN	DENIZENS
	DENNET	DENNETS
	DENOTATE	DENOTATED · DENOTATES
	DENOTE	DENOTED · DENOTES
	DENOUNCE	DENOUNCED · DENOUNCER · DENOUNCES
	DENOUNCER	DENOUNCERS
	DENS	DENSE
	DENSE	DENSER
	DENSIFIER	DENSIFIERS
IDENT	**DENT**	DENTS
EDENTAL	**DENTAL**	DENTALS
	DENTALIUM	DENTALIUMS
	DENTARIA	DENTARIAS
EDENTATE	**DENTATE**	DENTATED
	DENTATION	DENTATIONS
	DENTEL	DENTELS
	DENTELLE	DENTELLES
	DENTICLE	DENTICLES
	DENTIL	DENTILS
	DENTIN	DENTINE · DENTING · DENTINS
	DENTINE	DENTINES
	DENTIST	DENTISTS
	DENTITION	DENTITIONS
IDENTS	**DENTS**	
EDENTULOUS	**DENTULOUS**	
	DENTURE	DENTURES
	DENTURIST	DENTURISTS
	DENUDATE	DENUDATED · DENUDATES
	DENUDE	DENUDED · DENUDER · DENUDES
	DENUDER	DENUDERS
	DEODAND	DEODANDS
	DEODAR	DEODARA · DEODARS
	DEODARA	DEODARAS
	DEODATE	DEODATES
	DEODORANT	DEODORANTS
	DEODORISE	DEODORISED · DEODORISER · DEODORISES
	DEODORIZE	DEODORIZED · DEODORIZER · DEODORIZES
	DEONTIC	DEONTICS
	DEORBIT	DEORBITS
	DEOXIDATE	DEOXIDATED · DEOXIDATES
	DEOXIDISE	DEOXIDISED · DEOXIDISER · DEOXIDISES
	DEOXIDIZE	DEOXIDIZED · DEOXIDIZER · DEOXIDIZES
	DEPAINT	DEPAINTS
	DEPANNEUR	DEPANNEURS
	DEPART	DEPARTS
	DEPARTEE	DEPARTEES
	DEPARTER	DEPARTERS
	DEPARTING	DEPARTINGS
	DEPARTURE	DEPARTURES
	DEPASTURE	DEPASTURED · DEPASTURES
	DEPECHE	DEPECHES
	DEPEINCT	DEPEINCTS
	DEPEND	DEPENDS
	DEPENDANT	DEPENDANTS
	DEPENDENT	DEPENDENTS
	DEPEOPLE	DEPEOPLED · DEPEOPLES
	DEPERM	DEPERMS
	DEPICT	DEPICTS
	DEPICTER	DEPICTERS

FRONT HOOK	ROOT WORD	END HOOK
	DEPICTION	DEPICTIONS
	DEPICTOR	DEPICTORS
	DEPICTURE	DEPICTURED · DEPICTURES
	DEPILATE	DEPILATED · DEPILATES
	DEPILATOR	DEPILATORS · DEPILATORY
	DEPLANE	DEPLANED · DEPLANES
	DEPLETE	DEPLETED · DEPLETER · DEPLETES
	DEPLETER	DEPLETERS
	DEPLETION	DEPLETIONS
	DEPLORE	DEPLORED · DEPLORER · DEPLORES
	DEPLORER	DEPLORERS
	DEPLOY	DEPLOYS
	DEPLOYER	DEPLOYERS
	DEPLUME	DEPLUMED · DEPLUMES
	DEPONE	DEPONED · DEPONES
	DEPONENT	DEPONENTS
	DEPORT	DEPORTS
	DEPORTEE	DEPORTEES
	DEPORTER	DEPORTERS
	DEPOSAL	DEPOSALS
	DEPOSE	DEPOSED · DEPOSER · DEPOSES
	DEPOSER	DEPOSERS
	DEPOSIT	DEPOSITS
	DEPOSITOR	DEPOSITORS · DEPOSITORY
	DEPOT	DEPOTS
	DEPRAVE	DEPRAVED · DEPRAVER · DEPRAVES
	DEPRAVER	DEPRAVERS
	DEPRECATE	DEPRECATED · DEPRECATES
	DEPREDATE	DEPREDATED · DEPREDATES
	DEPREHEND	DEPREHENDS
	DEPRENYL	DEPRENYLS
	DEPRESSOR	DEPRESSORS
	DEPRIVAL	DEPRIVALS
	DEPRIVE	DEPRIVED · DEPRIVER · DEPRIVES
	DEPRIVER	DEPRIVERS
	DEPROGRAM	DEPROGRAMS
	DEPSIDE	DEPSIDES
	DEPTH	DEPTHS
	DEPURANT	DEPURANTS
	DEPURATE	DEPURATED · DEPURATES
	DEPURATOR	DEPURATORS · DEPURATORY
	DEPUTE	DEPUTED · DEPUTES
	DEPUTISE	DEPUTISED · DEPUTISES
	DEPUTIZE	DEPUTIZED · DEPUTIZES
	DERAIGN	DERAIGNS
	DERAIL	DERAILS
	DERAILER	DERAILERS
	DERANGE	DERANGED · DERANGER · DERANGES
	DERANGER	DERANGERS
	DERAT	DERATE · DERATS
	DERATE	DERATED · DERATES
	DERATING	DERATINGS
	DERATION	DERATIONS
	DERAY	DERAYS
	DERE	DERED · DERES
	DERELICT	DERELICTS
	DERHAM	DERHAMS
	DERIDE	DERIDED · DERIDER · DERIDES
	DERIDER	DERIDERS
	DERIG	DERIGS
	DERINGER	DERINGERS
	DERISION	DERISIONS
	DERIVATE	DERIVATES
	DERIVE	DERIVED · DERIVER · DERIVES
	DERIVER	DERIVERS
	DERM	DERMA · DERMS
	DERMA	DERMAL · DERMAS
	DERMATOME	DERMATOMES
	DERMESTID	DERMESTIDS

FRONT HOOK	ROOT WORD	END HOOK
	DERMOID	DERMOIDS
	DERN	DERNS
	DERO	DEROS
	DEROGATE	DEROGATED · DEROGATES
	DERRICK	DERRICKS
	DERRIERE	DERRIERES
	DERRINGER	DERRINGERS
	DERRO	DERROS
	DERTH	DERTHS
	DERV	DERVS
	DESALT	DESALTS
	DESALTER	DESALTERS
	DESALTING	DESALTINGS
	DESAND	DESANDS
	DESCALE	DESCALED · DESCALES
	DESCANT	DESCANTS
	DESCANTER	DESCANTERS
	DESCEND	DESCENDS
	DESCENDER	DESCENDERS
	DESCENT	DESCENTS
	DESCHOOL	DESCHOOLS
	DESCRIBE	DESCRIBED · DESCRIBER · DESCRIBES
	DESCRIBER	DESCRIBERS
	DESCRIER	DESCRIERS
	DESCRIVE	DESCRIVED · DESCRIVES
	DESECRATE	DESECRATED · DESECRATER · DESECRATES
	DESELECT	DESELECTS
	DESERT	DESERTS
	DESERTER	DESERTERS
	DESERTION	DESERTIONS
	DESERVE	DESERVED · DESERVER · DESERVES
	DESERVER	DESERVERS
	DESERVING	DESERVINGS
	DESICCANT	DESICCANTS
	DESICCATE	DESICCATED · DESICCATES
	DESIGN	DESIGNS
	DESIGNATE	DESIGNATED · DESIGNATES
	DESIGNEE	DESIGNEES
	DESIGNER	DESIGNERS
	DESIGNING	DESIGNINGS
	DESILVER	DESILVERS
	DESINE	DESINED · DESINES
	DESINENCE	DESINENCES
	DESIRABLE	DESIRABLES
	DESIRE	DESIRED · DESIRER · DESIRES
	DESIRER	DESIRERS
	DESIST	DESISTS
	DESK	DESKS
	DESKFAST	DESKFASTS
	DESKILL	DESKILLS
	DESKNOTE	DESKNOTES
	DESKTOP	DESKTOPS
	DESMAN	DESMANS
	DESMID	DESMIDS
	DESMINE	DESMINES
	DESMODIUM	DESMODIUMS
	DESMOID	DESMOIDS
	DESMOSOME	DESMOSOMES
	DESNOOD	DESNOODS
	DESOLATE	DESOLATED · DESOLATER · DESOLATES
	DESOLATER	DESOLATERS
	DESOLATOR	DESOLATORS · DESOLATORY
	DESORB	DESORBS
	DESPAIR	DESPAIRS
	DESPAIRER	DESPAIRERS
	DESPERADO	DESPERADOS
	DESPIGHT	DESPIGHTS
	DESPISAL	DESPISALS
	DESPISE	DESPISED · DESPISER · DESPISES

FRONT HOOK	ROOT WORD	END HOOK
	DESPISER	DESPISERS
	DESPITE	DESPITED · DESPITES
	DESPOIL	DESPOILS
	DESPOILER	DESPOILERS
	DESPOND	DESPONDS
	DESPOT	DESPOTS
	DESPOTAT	DESPOTATE · DESPOTATS
	DESPOTATE	DESPOTATES
	DESPOTISM	DESPOTISMS
	DESPUMATE	DESPUMATED · DESPUMATES
	DESSE	DESSES
	DESSERT	DESSERTS
	DESTAIN	DESTAINS
	DESTEMPER	DESTEMPERS
	DESTINATE	DESTINATED · DESTINATES
	DESTINE	DESTINED · DESTINES
	DESTITUTE	DESTITUTED · DESTITUTES
	DESTOCK	DESTOCKS
	DESTRIER	DESTRIERS
	DESTROY	DESTROYS
	DESTROYER	DESTROYERS
	DESTRUCT	DESTRUCTO · DESTRUCTS
	DESTRUCTO	DESTRUCTOR · DESTRUCTOS
	DESUETUDE	DESUETUDES
	DESUGAR	DESUGARS
	DESULFUR	DESULFURS
	DESULPHUR	DESULPHURS
	DESYATIN	DESYATINS
	DESYNE	DESYNED · DESYNES
	DETACHER	DETACHERS
	DETAIL	DETAILS
	DETAILER	DETAILERS
	DETAILING	DETAILINGS
	DETAIN	DETAINS
	DETAINEE	DETAINEES
	DETAINER	DETAINERS
	DETASSEL	DETASSELS
	DETECT	DETECTS
	DETECTER	DETECTERS
	DETECTION	DETECTIONS
	DETECTIVE	DETECTIVES
	DETECTOR	DETECTORS
	DETENT	DETENTE · DETENTS
	DETENTE	DETENTES
	DETENTION	DETENTIONS
	DETENTIST	DETENTISTS
	DETENU	DETENUE · DETENUS
	DETENUE	DETENUES
	DETER	DETERS
	DETERGE	DETERGED · DETERGER · DETERGES
	DETERGENT	DETERGENTS
	DETERGER	DETERGERS
	DETERMENT	DETERMENTS
	DETERMINE	DETERMINED · DETERMINER · DETERMINES
	DETERRENT	DETERRENTS
	DETERRER	DETERRERS
	DETERSION	DETERSIONS
	DETERSIVE	DETERSIVES
	DETEST	DETESTS
	DETESTER	DETESTERS
	DETHRONE	DETHRONED · DETHRONER · DETHRONES
	DETHRONER	DETHRONERS
	DETICK	DETICKS
	DETICKER	DETICKERS
	DETINUE	DETINUES
	DETONATE	DETONATED · DETONATES
	DETONATOR	DETONATORS
	DETORSION	DETORSIONS
	DETORT	DETORTS

FRONT HOOK	ROOT WORD	END HOOK
	DETORTION	DETORTIONS
	DETOUR	DETOURS
	DETRACT	DETRACTS
	DETRACTOR	DETRACTORS ▪ DETRACTORY
	DETRAIN	DETRAINS
	DETRAQUE	DETRAQUEE ▪ DETRAQUES
	DETRAQUEE	DETRAQUEES
	DETRIMENT	DETRIMENTS
	DETRITION	DETRITIONS
	DETRUDE	DETRUDED ▪ DETRUDES
	DETRUSION	DETRUSIONS
	DETUNE	DETUNED ▪ DETUNES
	DEUCE	DEUCED ▪ DEUCES
	DEUDDARN	DEUDDARNS
	DEUTERATE	DEUTERATED ▪ DEUTERATES
	DEUTERIDE	DEUTERIDES
	DEUTERIUM	DEUTERIUMS
	DEUTERON	DEUTERONS
	DEUTON	DEUTONS
	DEUTZIA	DEUTZIAS
	DEV	DEVA ▪ DEVS
	DEVA	DEVAS
	DEVALL	DEVALLS
	DEVALUATE	DEVALUATED ▪ DEVALUATES
	DEVALUE	DEVALUED ▪ DEVALUES
	DEVASTATE	DEVASTATED ▪ DEVASTATES
	DEVEIN	DEVEINS
	DEVEL	DEVELS
	DEVELOP	DEVELOPE ▪ DEVELOPS
	DEVELOPE	DEVELOPED ▪ DEVELOPER ▪ DEVELOPES
	DEVELOPER	DEVELOPERS
	DEVELOPPE	DEVELOPPES
	DEVERBAL	DEVERBALS
	DEVEST	DEVESTS
	DEVIANCE	DEVIANCES
	DEVIANT	DEVIANTS
	DEVIATE	DEVIATED ▪ DEVIATES
	DEVIATION	DEVIATIONS
	DEVIATOR	DEVIATORS ▪ DEVIATORY
	DEVICE	DEVICES
	DEVIL	DEVILS
	DEVILDOM	DEVILDOMS
	DEVILET	DEVILETS
	DEVILING	DEVILINGS
	DEVILISM	DEVILISMS
	DEVILKIN	DEVILKINS
	DEVILMENT	DEVILMENTS
	DEVILSHIP	DEVILSHIPS
	DEVILWOOD	DEVILWOODS
	DEVISAL	DEVISALS
	DEVISE	DEVISED ▪ DEVISEE ▪ DEVISER ▪ DEVISES
	DEVISEE	DEVISEES
	DEVISER	DEVISERS
	DEVISOR	DEVISORS
	DEVLING	DEVLINGS
	DEVOICE	DEVOICED ▪ DEVOICES
	DEVOIR	DEVOIRS
	DEVOLVE	DEVOLVED ▪ DEVOLVES
	DEVON	DEVONS
	DEVONPORT	DEVONPORTS
	DEVORE	DEVORES
	DEVOT	DEVOTE ▪ DEVOTS
	DEVOTE	DEVOTED ▪ DEVOTEE ▪ DEVOTES
	DEVOTEE	DEVOTEES
	DEVOTION	DEVOTIONS
	DEVOUR	DEVOURS
	DEVOURER	DEVOURERS
	DEVVEL	DEVVELS
	DEW	DEWS ▪ DEWY

FRONT HOOK	ROOT WORD	END HOOK
	DEWAN	DEWANI · DEWANS
	DEWANI	DEWANIS
	DEWAR	DEWARS
	DEWATER	DEWATERS
	DEWATERER	DEWATERERS
	DEWCLAW	DEWCLAWS
	DEWDROP	DEWDROPS
	DEWFALL	DEWFALLS
	DEWITT	DEWITTS
	DEWLAP	DEWLAPS · DEWLAPT
	DEWOOL	DEWOOLS
	DEWORM	DEWORMS
	DEWORMER	DEWORMERS
	DEWPOINT	DEWPOINTS
	DEX	DEXY
	DEXIE	DEXIES
	DEXTER	DEXTERS
	DEXTRAN	DEXTRANS
	DEXTRIN	DEXTRINE · DEXTRINS
	DEXTRINE	DEXTRINES
	DEXTROSE	DEXTROSES
	DEY	DEYS
	DEZINC	DEZINCS
	DHAK	DHAKS
	DHAL	DHALS
	DHAMMA	DHAMMAS
	DHANSAK	DHANSAKS
ADHARMA	**DHARMA**	DHARMAS
ADHARMAS	**DHARMAS**	
	DHARMSALA	DHARMSALAS
	DHARNA	DHARNAS
	DHOBI	DHOBIS
	DHOL	DHOLE · DHOLL · DHOLS
	DHOLE	DHOLES
	DHOLL	DHOLLS
	DHOORA	DHOORAS
	DHOOTI	DHOOTIE · DHOOTIS
	DHOOTIE	DHOOTIES
	DHOTI	DHOTIS
	DHOURRA	DHOURRAS
	DHOW	DHOWS
	DHURNA	DHURNAS
	DHURRA	DHURRAS
	DHURRIE	DHURRIES
	DHUTI	DHUTIS
	DI	DIB · DID · DIE · DIF · DIG · DIM · DIN DIP · DIS · DIT · DIV
	DIABASE	DIABASES
	DIABETIC	DIABETICS
	DIABLE	DIABLES
	DIABLERIE	DIABLERIES
	DIABOLISE	DIABOLISED · DIABOLISES
	DIABOLISM	DIABOLISMS
	DIABOLIST	DIABOLISTS
	DIABOLIZE	DIABOLIZED · DIABOLIZES
	DIABOLO	DIABOLOS
	DIACETYL	DIACETYLS
	DIACHYLON	DIACHYLONS
	DIACHYLUM	DIACHYLUMS
	DIACID	DIACIDS
	DIACODION	DIACODIONS
	DIACODIUM	DIACODIUMS
	DIACONATE	DIACONATES
	DIACRITIC	DIACRITICS
ADIACTINIC	**DIACTINIC**	
	DIADEM	DIADEMS
	DIADROM	DIADROMS
	DIAGLYPH	DIAGLYPHS
	DIAGNOSE	DIAGNOSED · DIAGNOSES

FRONT HOOK	ROOT WORD	END HOOK
	DIAGONAL	DIAGONALS
	DIAGRAM	DIAGRAMS
	DIAGRAPH	DIAGRAPHS
	DIAGRID	DIAGRIDS
	DIAL	DIALS
	DIALECT	DIALECTS
	DIALECTIC	DIALECTICS
	DIALER	DIALERS
	DIALING	DIALINGS
	DIALIST	DIALISTS
	DIALLAGE	DIALLAGES
	DIALLER	DIALLERS
	DIALLING	DIALLINGS
	DIALLIST	DIALLISTS
	DIALOG	DIALOGS
	DIALOGER	DIALOGERS
	DIALOGISE	DIALOGISED · DIALOGISES
	DIALOGISM	DIALOGISMS
	DIALOGIST	DIALOGISTS
	DIALOGITE	DIALOGITES
	DIALOGIZE	DIALOGIZED · DIALOGIZES
	DIALOGUE	DIALOGUED · DIALOGUER · DIALOGUES
	DIALOGUER	DIALOGUERS
	DIALYSATE	DIALYSATES
	DIALYSE	DIALYSED · DIALYSER · DIALYSES
	DIALYSER	DIALYSERS
	DIALYZATE	DIALYZATES
	DIALYZE	DIALYZED · DIALYZER · DIALYZES
	DIALYZER	DIALYZERS
	DIAMAGNET	DIAMAGNETS
	DIAMANTE	DIAMANTES
	DIAMETER	DIAMETERS
	DIAMIDE	DIAMIDES
	DIAMIN	DIAMINE · DIAMINS
	DIAMINE	DIAMINES
	DIAMOND	DIAMONDS
	DIANOIA	DIANOIAS
	DIAPASE	DIAPASES
	DIAPASON	DIAPASONS
	DIAPAUSE	DIAPAUSED · DIAPAUSES
	DIAPENTE	DIAPENTES
	DIAPER	DIAPERS
	DIAPERING	DIAPERINGS
	DIAPHONE	DIAPHONES
	DIAPHRAGM	DIAPHRAGMS
	DIAPIR	DIAPIRS
	DIAPIRISM	DIAPIRISMS
	DIAPSID	DIAPSIDS
	DIAPYETIC	DIAPYETICS
	DIARCH	DIARCHY
	DIARISE	DIARISED · DIARISES
	DIARIST	DIARISTS
	DIARIZE	DIARIZED · DIARIZES
	DIARRHEA	DIARRHEAL · DIARRHEAS
	DIARRHOEA	DIARRHOEAL · DIARRHOEAS
	DIASCOPE	DIASCOPES
	DIASPORA	DIASPORAS
	DIASPORE	DIASPORES
	DIASTASE	DIASTASES
	DIASTEM	DIASTEMA · DIASTEMS
	DIASTEMA	DIASTEMAS
	DIASTER	DIASTERS
	DIASTOLE	DIASTOLES
	DIASTYLE	DIASTYLES
	DIATOM	DIATOMS
	DIATOMIST	DIATOMISTS
	DIATOMITE	DIATOMITES
	DIATRETUM	DIATRETUMS
	DIATRIBE	DIATRIBES

D

FRONT HOOK	ROOT WORD	END HOOK
	DIATRON	DIATRONS
	DIAXON	DIAXONS
	DIAZEPAM	DIAZEPAMS
	DIAZIN	DIAZINE ▪ DIAZINS
	DIAZINE	DIAZINES
	DIAZINON	DIAZINONS
	DIAZO	DIAZOS
	DIAZOLE	DIAZOLES
	DIAZONIUM	DIAZONIUMS
	DIAZOTISE	DIAZOTISED ▪ DIAZOTISES
	DIAZOTIZE	DIAZOTIZED ▪ DIAZOTIZES
	DIB	DIBS
	DIBBER	DIBBERS
	DIBBLE	DIBBLED ▪ DIBBLER ▪ DIBBLES
	DIBBLER	DIBBLERS
	DIBBUK	DIBBUKS
	DIBROMIDE	DIBROMIDES
	DICACODYL	DICACODYLS
	DICAMBA	DICAMBAS
	DICAST	DICASTS
	DICE	DICED ▪ DICER ▪ DICES ▪ DICEY
	DICENTRA	DICENTRAS
	DICENTRIC	DICENTRICS
	DICER	DICERS
	DICH	DICHT
	DICHASIA	DICHASIAL
	DICHONDRA	DICHONDRAS
	DICHORD	DICHORDS
	DICHROISM	DICHROISMS
	DICHROITE	DICHROITES
	DICHROMAT	DICHROMATE ▪ DICHROMATS
	DICHT	DICHTS
	DICING	DICINGS
	DICK	DICKS (offensive) ▪ DICKY
	DICKER	DICKERS
	DICKEY	DICKEYS
	DICKHEAD	DICKHEADS (offensive)
	DICKIE	DICKIER ▪ DICKIES
	DICKIES	DICKIEST
	DICKYBIRD	DICKYBIRDS
	DICLINISM	DICLINISMS
	DICOT	DICOTS
	DICOTYL	DICOTYLS
	DICROTISM	DICROTISMS
EDICT	**DICT**	DICTA ▪ DICTS ▪ DICTY
	DICTATE	DICTATED ▪ DICTATES
	DICTATION	DICTATIONS
	DICTATOR	DICTATORS ▪ DICTATORY
	DICTATURE	DICTATURES
	DICTION	DICTIONS
EDICTS	**DICTS**	
	DICTUM	DICTUMS
	DICTYOGEN	DICTYOGENS
	DICUMAROL	DICUMAROLS
	DID	DIDO ▪ DIDY
	DIDACT	DIDACTS
	DIDACTIC	DIDACTICS
	DIDACTYL	DIDACTYLS
	DIDAKAI	DIDAKAIS
	DIDAKEI	DIDAKEIS
	DIDAPPER	DIDAPPERS
	DIDDER	DIDDERS
	DIDDICOY	DIDDICOYS
	DIDDIES	DIDDIEST
	DIDDLE	DIDDLED ▪ DIDDLER ▪ DIDDLES ▪ DIDDLEY
	DIDDLER	DIDDLERS
	DIDDLEY	DIDDLEYS
	DIDELPHID	DIDELPHIDS
	DIDICOI	DIDICOIS

FRONT HOOK	ROOT WORD	END HOOK
	DIDICOY	DIDICOYS
	DIDIE	DIDIES
	DIDJERIDU	DIDJERIDUS
	DIDO	DIDOS
	DIDRACHM	DIDRACHMA ▪ DIDRACHMS
	DIDRACHMA	DIDRACHMAS
	DIDYMIUM	DIDYMIUMS
	DIE	DIEB ▪ DIED ▪ DIEL ▪ DIES ▪ DIET
	DIEB	DIEBS
	DIEBACK	DIEBACKS
	DIEDRAL	DIEDRALS
	DIEDRE	DIEDRES
	DIEHARD	DIEHARDS
	DIELDRIN	DIELDRINS
	DIELYTRA	DIELYTRAS
	DIEMAKER	DIEMAKERS
	DIENE	DIENES
	DIEOFF	DIEOFFS
	DIESEL	DIESELS
	DIESELING	DIESELINGS
	DIESELISE	DIESELISED ▪ DIESELISES
	DIESELIZE	DIESELIZED ▪ DIESELIZES
	DIESINKER	DIESINKERS
	DIESTER	DIESTERS
	DIESTOCK	DIESTOCKS
	DIESTRUM	DIESTRUMS
	DIET	DIETS
	DIETARIAN	DIETARIANS
	DIETER	DIETERS
	DIETETIC	DIETETICS
	DIETHER	DIETHERS
	DIETHYL	DIETHYLS
	DIETICIAN	DIETICIANS
	DIETINE	DIETINES
	DIETING	DIETINGS
	DIETIST	DIETISTS
	DIETITIAN	DIETITIANS
	DIF	DIFF ▪ DIFS
	DIFF	DIFFS
	DIFFER	DIFFERS
	DIFFICULT	DIFFICULTY
	DIFFRACT	DIFFRACTS
	DIFFUSE	DIFFUSED ▪ DIFFUSER ▪ DIFFUSES
	DIFFUSER	DIFFUSERS
	DIFFUSION	DIFFUSIONS
	DIFFUSOR	DIFFUSORS
	DIG	DIGS
	DIGAMIST	DIGAMISTS
	DIGAMMA	DIGAMMAS
	DIGASTRIC	DIGASTRICS
	DIGEST	DIGESTS
	DIGESTANT	DIGESTANTS
	DIGESTER	DIGESTERS
	DIGESTIF	DIGESTIFS
	DIGESTION	DIGESTIONS
	DIGESTIVE	DIGESTIVES
	DIGESTOR	DIGESTORS
	DIGGER	DIGGERS
	DIGGING	DIGGINGS
	DIGHT	DIGHTS
	DIGICAM	DIGICAMS
	DIGIT	DIGITS
	DIGITAL	DIGITALS
	DIGITALIN	DIGITALINS
	DIGITALIS	DIGITALISE ▪ DIGITALISM
	DIGITATE	DIGITATED
	DIGITISE	DIGITISED ▪ DIGITISER ▪ DIGITISES
	DIGITISER	DIGITISERS
	DIGITIZE	DIGITIZED ▪ DIGITIZER ▪ DIGITIZES

D

FRONT HOOK	ROOT WORD	END HOOK
	DIGITIZER	DIGITIZERS
	DIGITONIN	DIGITONINS
	DIGITOXIN	DIGITOXINS
	DIGITRON	DIGITRONS
	DIGITULE	DIGITULES
	DIGLOSSIA	DIGLOSSIAS
	DIGLOT	DIGLOTS
	DIGLYPH	DIGLYPHS
	DIGOXIN	DIGOXINS
	DIGRAPH	DIGRAPHS
	DIGRESSER	DIGRESSERS
	DIHEDRA	DIHEDRAL
	DIHEDRAL	DIHEDRALS
	DIHEDRON	DIHEDRONS
	DIHYBRID	DIHYBRIDS
	DIKA	DIKAS
	DIKAS	DIKAST
	DIKAST	DIKASTS
	DIKDIK	DIKDIKS
	DIKE	DIKED ▪ DIKER ▪ DIKES ▪ DIKEY
	DIKER	DIKERS
	DIKKOP	DIKKOPS
	DIKTAT	DIKTATS
	DILATANT	DILATANTS
	DILATATOR	DILATATORS
	DILATE	DILATED ▪ DILATER ▪ DILATES
	DILATER	DILATERS
	DILATION	DILATIONS
	DILATOR	DILATORS ▪ DILATORY
	DILDO	DILDOE ▪ DILDOS
	DILDOE	DILDOES
	DILEMMA	DILEMMAS
	DILIGENCE	DILIGENCES
	DILL	DILLI ▪ DILLS ▪ DILLY
	DILLI	DILLIS
	DILLIES	DILLIEST
	DILLING	DILLINGS
	DILTIAZEM	DILTIAZEMS
	DILUENT	DILUENTS
	DILUTABLE	DILUTABLES
	DILUTE	DILUTED ▪ DILUTEE ▪ DILUTER ▪ DILUTES
	DILUTEE	DILUTEES
	DILUTER	DILUTERS
	DILUTION	DILUTIONS
	DILUTOR	DILUTORS
	DILUVIA	DILUVIAL ▪ DILUVIAN
	DILUVION	DILUVIONS
	DILUVIUM	DILUVIUMS
	DIM	DIME ▪ DIMP ▪ DIMS
	DIMBLE	DIMBLES
	DIME	DIMER ▪ DIMES
	DIMENSION	DIMENSIONS
	DIMER	DIMERS
	DIMERISE	DIMERISED ▪ DIMERISES
	DIMERISM	DIMERISMS
	DIMERIZE	DIMERIZED ▪ DIMERIZES
	DIMETER	DIMETERS
	DIMETHYL	DIMETHYLS
	DIMIDIATE	DIMIDIATED ▪ DIMIDIATES
	DIMMER	DIMMERS
	DIMORPH	DIMORPHS
	DIMOUT	DIMOUTS
	DIMP	DIMPS
	DIMPLE	DIMPLED ▪ DIMPLES
	DIMPS	DIMPSY
	DIMWIT	DIMWITS
	DIN	DINE ▪ DING ▪ DINK ▪ DINO ▪ DINS ▪ DINT
	DINAR	DINARS
	DINDLE	DINDLED ▪ DINDLES

FRONT HOOK	ROOT WORD	END HOOK
	DINE	DINED · DINER · DINES
	DINER	DINERO · DINERS
	DINERO	DINEROS
	DINETTE	DINETTES
	DING	DINGE · DINGO · DINGS · DINGY
	DINGBAT	DINGBATS
	DINGDONG	DINGDONGS
	DINGE	DINGED · DINGER · DINGES · DINGEY
	DINGER	DINGERS
	DINGEY	DINGEYS
	DINGIES	DINGIEST
	DINGLE	DINGLES
	DINIC	DINICS
	DINK	DINKS · DINKY
	DINKEY	DINKEYS
	DINKIE	DINKIER · DINKIES
	DINKIES	DINKIEST
	DINKUM	DINKUMS
	DINMONT	DINMONTS
	DINNER	DINNERS
	DINNLE	DINNLED · DINNLES
	DINO	DINOS
	DINOMANIA	DINOMANIAS
	DINOSAUR	DINOSAURS
	DINOTHERE	DINOTHERES
	DINT	DINTS
	DIOBOL	DIOBOLS
	DIOBOLON	DIOBOLONS
	DIOCESAN	DIOCESANS
	DIOCESE	DIOCESES
	DIODE	DIODES
	DIOECISM	DIOECISMS
	DIOL	DIOLS
	DIOLEFIN	DIOLEFINS
	DIOPSIDE	DIOPSIDES
	DIOPTASE	DIOPTASES
	DIOPTER	DIOPTERS
	DIOPTRE	DIOPTRES
	DIOPTRIC	DIOPTRICS
	DIORAMA	DIORAMAS
	DIORISM	DIORISMS
	DIORITE	DIORITES
	DIOSGENIN	DIOSGENINS
	DIOTA	DIOTAS
	DIOXAN	DIOXANE · DIOXANS
	DIOXANE	DIOXANES
	DIOXID	DIOXIDE · DIOXIDS
	DIOXIDE	DIOXIDES
	DIOXIN	DIOXINS
	DIP	DIPS · DIPT
	DIPCHICK	DIPCHICKS
	DIPEPTIDE	DIPEPTIDES
	DIPHENYL	DIPHENYLS
	DIPHONE	DIPHONES
	DIPHTHONG	DIPHTHONGS
	DIPHYSITE	DIPHYSITES
	DIPLEGIA	DIPLEGIAS
	DIPLEXER	DIPLEXERS
	DIPLOE	DIPLOES
	DIPLOGEN	DIPLOGENS
	DIPLOID	DIPLOIDS · DIPLOIDY
	DIPLOMA	DIPLOMAS · DIPLOMAT
	DIPLOMAT	DIPLOMATA · DIPLOMATE · DIPLOMATS
	DIPLOMATE	DIPLOMATED · DIPLOMATES
	DIPLON	DIPLONS · DIPLONT
	DIPLONEMA	DIPLONEMAS
	DIPLONT	DIPLONTS
	DIPLOPIA	DIPLOPIAS
	DIPLOPOD	DIPLOPODS

D

FRONT HOOK	ROOT WORD	END HOOK
	DIPLOTENE	DIPLOTENES
	DIPNET	DIPNETS
	DIPNOAN	DIPNOANS
	DIPOLE	DIPOLES
	DIPPER	DIPPERS
	DIPPERFUL	DIPPERFULS
	DIPPING	DIPPINGS
	DIPS	DIPSO
	DIPSHIT	DIPSHITS
	DIPSO	DIPSOS
	DIPSTICK	DIPSTICKS
	DIPTERA	DIPTERAL ▪ DIPTERAN ▪ DIPTERAS
	DIPTERAN	DIPTERANS
	DIPTERIST	DIPTERISTS
	DIPTERON	DIPTERONS
	DIPTYCA	DIPTYCAS
	DIPTYCH	DIPTYCHS
	DIQUARK	DIQUARKS
	DIQUAT	DIQUATS
	DIRAM	DIRAMS
	DIRDAM	DIRDAMS
	DIRDUM	DIRDUMS
	DIRE	DIRER
	DIRECT	DIRECTS
	DIRECTION	DIRECTIONS
	DIRECTIVE	DIRECTIVES
	DIRECTOR	DIRECTORS ▪ DIRECTORY
	DIREMPT	DIREMPTS
	DIRGE	DIRGES
	DIRHAM	DIRHAMS
	DIRHEM	DIRHEMS
	DIRIGE	DIRIGES
	DIRIGIBLE	DIRIGIBLES
	DIRIGISM	DIRIGISME ▪ DIRIGISMS
	DIRIGISME	DIRIGISMES
	DIRK	DIRKE ▪ DIRKS
	DIRKE	DIRKED ▪ DIRKES
	DIRL	DIRLS
	DIRNDL	DIRNDLS
	DIRT	DIRTS ▪ DIRTY
	DIRTBAG	DIRTBAGS
	DIRTIES	DIRTIEST
	DIS	DISA ▪ DISC ▪ DISH ▪ DISK ▪ DISS
	DISA	DISAS
	DISABLE	DISABLED ▪ DISABLER ▪ DISABLES
	DISABLER	DISABLERS
	DISABUSAL	DISABUSALS
	DISABUSE	DISABUSED ▪ DISABUSES
	DISACCORD	DISACCORDS
	DISADORN	DISADORNS
	DISAFFECT	DISAFFECTS
	DISAFFIRM	DISAFFIRMS
	DISAGREE	DISAGREED ▪ DISAGREES
	DISALLOW	DISALLOWS
	DISANCHOR	DISANCHORS
	DISANNUL	DISANNULS
	DISANOINT	DISANOINTS
	DISAPPEAR	DISAPPEARS
	DISARM	DISARMS
	DISARMER	DISARMERS
	DISARRAY	DISARRAYS
	DISASTER	DISASTERS
	DISATTIRE	DISATTIRED ▪ DISATTIRES
	DISATTUNE	DISATTUNED ▪ DISATTUNES
	DISAVOW	DISAVOWS
	DISAVOWAL	DISAVOWALS
	DISAVOWER	DISAVOWERS
	DISBAND	DISBANDS
	DISBAR	DISBARK ▪ DISBARS

FRONT HOOK	ROOT WORD	END HOOK
	DISBARK	DISBARKS
	DISBELIEF	DISBELIEFS
	DISBOSOM	DISBOSOMS
	DISBOWEL	DISBOWELS
	DISBUD	DISBUDS
	DISBURDEN	DISBURDENS
	DISBURSAL	DISBURSALS
	DISBURSE	DISBURSED ▪ DISBURSER ▪ DISBURSES
	DISBURSER	DISBURSERS
	DISC	DISCI ▪ DISCO ▪ DISCS
	DISCAGE	DISCAGED ▪ DISCAGES
	DISCANDIE	DISCANDIED ▪ DISCANDIES
	DISCANT	DISCANTS
	DISCANTER	DISCANTERS
	DISCARD	DISCARDS
	DISCARDER	DISCARDERS
	DISCASE	DISCASED ▪ DISCASES
	DISCEPT	DISCEPTS
	DISCERN	DISCERNS
	DISCERNER	DISCERNERS
	DISCERP	DISCERPS
	DISCHARGE	DISCHARGED ▪ DISCHARGEE ▪ DISCHARGER DISCHARGES
	DISCIDE	DISCIDED ▪ DISCIDES
	DISCIPLE	DISCIPLED ▪ DISCIPLES
	DISCLAIM	DISCLAIMS
	DISCLOSE	DISCLOSED ▪ DISCLOSER ▪ DISCLOSES
	DISCLOSER	DISCLOSERS
	DISCO	DISCOS
	DISCOER	DISCOERS
	DISCOID	DISCOIDS
	DISCOLOR	DISCOLORS
	DISCOLOUR	DISCOLOURS
	DISCOMFIT	DISCOMFITS
	DISCOMMON	DISCOMMONS
	DISCORD	DISCORDS
	DISCOUNT	DISCOUNTS
	DISCOURE	DISCOURED ▪ DISCOURES
	DISCOURSE	DISCOURSED ▪ DISCOURSER ▪ DISCOURSES
	DISCOVER	DISCOVERS ▪ DISCOVERT ▪ DISCOVERY
	DISCREDIT	DISCREDITS
	DISCRETE	DISCRETER
	DISCROWN	DISCROWNS
	DISCUMBER	DISCUMBERS
	DISCURE	DISCURED ▪ DISCURES
	DISCUS	DISCUSS
	DISCUSSER	DISCUSSERS
	DISDAIN	DISDAINS
	DISEASE	DISEASED ▪ DISEASES
	DISEDGE	DISEDGED ▪ DISEDGES
	DISEMBARK	DISEMBARKS
	DISEMPLOY	DISEMPLOYS
	DISENABLE	DISENABLED ▪ DISENABLES
	DISENDOW	DISENDOWS
	DISENGAGE	DISENGAGED ▪ DISENGAGES
	DISENROL	DISENROLS
	DISENTAIL	DISENTAILS
	DISENTOMB	DISENTOMBS
	DISESTEEM	DISESTEEMS
	DISEUR	DISEURS
	DISEUSE	DISEUSES
	DISFAME	DISFAMES
	DISFAVOR	DISFAVORS
	DISFAVOUR	DISFAVOURS
	DISFIGURE	DISFIGURED ▪ DISFIGURER ▪ DISFIGURES
	DISFOREST	DISFORESTS
	DISFORM	DISFORMS
	DISFROCK	DISFROCKS
	DISGAVEL	DISGAVELS

FRONT HOOK	ROOT WORD	END HOOK
	DISGEST	DISGESTS
	DISGORGE	DISGORGED · DISGORGER · DISGORGES
	DISGORGER	DISGORGERS
	DISGOWN	DISGOWNS
	DISGRACE	DISGRACED · DISGRACER · DISGRACES
	DISGRACER	DISGRACERS
	DISGRADE	DISGRADED · DISGRADES
	DISGUISE	DISGUISED · DISGUISER · DISGUISES
	DISGUISER	DISGUISERS
	DISGUST	DISGUSTS
	DISH	DISHY
	DISHABIT	DISHABITS
	DISHABLE	DISHABLED · DISHABLES
	DISHALLOW	DISHALLOWS
	DISHCLOTH	DISHCLOTHS
	DISHCLOUT	DISHCLOUTS
	DISHDASHA	DISHDASHAS
	DISHELM	DISHELMS
	DISHERIT	DISHERITS
	DISHEVEL	DISHEVELS
	DISHFUL	DISHFULS
	DISHING	DISHINGS
	DISHOME	DISHOMED · DISHOMES
	DISHONEST	DISHONESTY
	DISHONOR	DISHONORS
	DISHONOUR	DISHONOURS
	DISHORN	DISHORNS
	DISHORSE	DISHORSED · DISHORSES
	DISHOUSE	DISHOUSED · DISHOUSES
	DISHPAN	DISHPANS
	DISHRAG	DISHRAGS
	DISHTOWEL	DISHTOWELS
	DISHUMOUR	DISHUMOURS
	DISHWARE	DISHWARES
	DISHWATER	DISHWATERS
	DISILLUDE	DISILLUDED · DISILLUDES
	DISIMMURE	DISIMMURED · DISIMMURES
	DISINFECT	DISINFECTS
	DISINFEST	DISINFESTS
	DISINFORM	DISINFORMS
	DISINHUME	DISINHUMED · DISINHUMES
	DISINTER	DISINTERS
	DISINURE	DISINURED · DISINURES
	DISINVEST	DISINVESTS
	DISINVITE	DISINVITED · DISINVITES
	DISJECT	DISJECTS
	DISJOIN	DISJOINS · DISJOINT
	DISJOINT	DISJOINTS
	DISJUNCT	DISJUNCTS
	DISJUNE	DISJUNES
	DISK	DISKS
	DISKETTE	DISKETTES
	DISLEAF	DISLEAFS
	DISLEAVE	DISLEAVED · DISLEAVES
	DISLIKE	DISLIKED · DISLIKEN · DISLIKER · DISLIKES
	DISLIKEN	DISLIKENS
	DISLIKER	DISLIKERS
	DISLIMB	DISLIMBS
	DISLIMN	DISLIMNS
	DISLINK	DISLINKS
	DISLOAD	DISLOADS
	DISLOCATE	DISLOCATED · DISLOCATES
	DISLODGE	DISLODGED · DISLODGES
	DISLOIGN	DISLOIGNS
	DISLUSTRE	DISLUSTRED · DISLUSTRES
	DISMAL	DISMALS
	DISMAN	DISMANS
	DISMANTLE	DISMANTLED · DISMANTLER · DISMANTLES
	DISMASK	DISMASKS

D

FRONT HOOK	ROOT WORD	END HOOK
	DISMAST	DISMASTS
	DISMAY	DISMAYD · DISMAYL · DISMAYS
	DISMAYL	DISMAYLS
	DISME	DISMES
	DISMEMBER	DISMEMBERS
	DISMISSAL	DISMISSALS
	DISMOUNT	DISMOUNTS
	DISNEST	DISNESTS
	DISOBEY	DISOBEYS
	DISOBEYER	DISOBEYERS
	DISOBLIGE	DISOBLIGED · DISOBLIGES
	DISORDER	DISORDERS
	DISORIENT	DISORIENTS
	DISOWN	DISOWNS
	DISOWNER	DISOWNERS
	DISPACE	DISPACED · DISPACES
	DISPARAGE	DISPARAGED · DISPARAGER · DISPARAGES
	DISPARATE	DISPARATES
	DISPARK	DISPARKS
	DISPART	DISPARTS
	DISPAUPER	DISPAUPERS
	DISPEACE	DISPEACES
	DISPEL	DISPELS
	DISPELLER	DISPELLERS
	DISPENCE	DISPENCED · DISPENCES
	DISPEND	DISPENDS
	DISPENSE	DISPENSED · DISPENSER · DISPENSES
	DISPENSER	DISPENSERS
	DISPEOPLE	DISPEOPLED · DISPEOPLES
	DISPERSAL	DISPERSALS
	DISPERSE	DISPERSED · DISPERSER · DISPERSES
	DISPERSER	DISPERSERS
	DISPIRIT	DISPIRITS
	DISPLACE	DISPLACED · DISPLACER · DISPLACES
	DISPLACER	DISPLACERS
	DISPLANT	DISPLANTS
	DISPLAY	DISPLAYS
	DISPLAYER	DISPLAYERS
	DISPLE	DISPLED · DISPLES
	DISPLEASE	DISPLEASED · DISPLEASES
	DISPLODE	DISPLODED · DISPLODES
	DISPLUME	DISPLUMED · DISPLUMES
	DISPONDEE	DISPONDEES
	DISPONE	DISPONED · DISPONEE · DISPONER · DISPONES
	DISPONEE	DISPONEES
	DISPONER	DISPONERS
	DISPONGE	DISPONGED · DISPONGES
	DISPORT	DISPORTS
	DISPOSAL	DISPOSALS
	DISPOSE	DISPOSED · DISPOSER · DISPOSES
	DISPOSER	DISPOSERS
	DISPOSING	DISPOSINGS
	DISPOST	DISPOSTS
	DISPOSURE	DISPOSURES
	DISPRAISE	DISPRAISED · DISPRAISER · DISPRAISES
	DISPREAD	DISPREADS
	DISPRED	DISPREDS
	DISPRISON	DISPRISONS
	DISPRIZE	DISPRIZED · DISPRIZES
	DISPROFIT	DISPROFITS
	DISPROOF	DISPROOFS
	DISPROOVE	DISPROOVED · DISPROOVES
	DISPROVAL	DISPROVALS
	DISPROVE	DISPROVED · DISPROVEN · DISPROVER · DISPROVES
	DISPROVER	DISPROVERS
	DISPUNGE	DISPUNGED · DISPUNGES
	DISPURSE	DISPURSED · DISPURSES
	DISPURVEY	DISPURVEYS

D

FRONT HOOK	ROOT WORD	END HOOK
	DISPUTANT	DISPUTANTS
	DISPUTE	DISPUTED · DISPUTER · DISPUTES
	DISPUTER	DISPUTERS
	DISQUIET	DISQUIETS
	DISRANK	DISRANKS
	DISRATE	DISRATED · DISRATES
	DISREGARD	DISREGARDS
	DISREPAIR	DISREPAIRS
	DISREPUTE	DISREPUTES
	DISROBE	DISROBED · DISROBER · DISROBES
	DISROBER	DISROBERS
	DISROOT	DISROOTS
	DISRUPT	DISRUPTS
	DISRUPTER	DISRUPTERS
	DISRUPTOR	DISRUPTORS
	DISSAVE	DISSAVED · DISSAVES
	DISSAVING	DISSAVINGS
	DISSEAT	DISSEATS
	DISSECT	DISSECTS
	DISSECTOR	DISSECTORS
	DISSEISE	DISSEISED · DISSEISEE · DISSEISES
	DISSEISEE	DISSEISEES
	DISSEISIN	DISSEISING · DISSEISINS
	DISSEISOR	DISSEISORS
	DISSEIZE	DISSEIZED · DISSEIZEE · DISSEIZES
	DISSEIZEE	DISSEIZEES
	DISSEIZIN	DISSEIZING · DISSEIZINS
	DISSEIZOR	DISSEIZORS
	DISSEMBLE	DISSEMBLED · DISSEMBLER · DISSEMBLES
	DISSENT	DISSENTS
	DISSENTER	DISSENTERS
	DISSERT	DISSERTS
	DISSERVE	DISSERVED · DISSERVES
	DISSEVER	DISSEVERS
	DISSHIVER	DISSHIVERS
	DISSIDENT	DISSIDENTS
	DISSIGHT	DISSIGHTS
	DISSIMILE	DISSIMILES
	DISSIPATE	DISSIPATED · DISSIPATER · DISSIPATES
	DISSOLUTE	DISSOLUTES
	DISSOLVE	DISSOLVED · DISSOLVER · DISSOLVES
	DISSOLVER	DISSOLVERS
	DISSUADE	DISSUADED · DISSUADER · DISSUADES
	DISSUADER	DISSUADERS
	DISSUNDER	DISSUNDERS
	DISTAFF	DISTAFFS
	DISTAIN	DISTAINS
	DISTANCE	DISTANCED · DISTANCES
	DISTASTE	DISTASTED · DISTASTES
	DISTEMPER	DISTEMPERS
	DISTEND	DISTENDS
	DISTENDER	DISTENDERS
	DISTHENE	DISTHENES
	DISTHRONE	DISTHRONED · DISTHRONES
	DISTICH	DISTICHS
	DISTIL	DISTILL · DISTILS
	DISTILL	DISTILLS
	DISTILLER	DISTILLERS · DISTILLERY
	DISTINGUE	DISTINGUEE
	DISTOME	DISTOMES
	DISTORT	DISTORTS
	DISTORTER	DISTORTERS
	DISTRACT	DISTRACTS
	DISTRAIL	DISTRAILS
	DISTRAIN	DISTRAINS · DISTRAINT
	DISTRAINT	DISTRAINTS
	DISTRAIT	DISTRAITE
	DISTRICT	DISTRICTS
	DISTRUST	DISTRUSTS

FRONT HOOK	ROOT WORD	END HOOK
	DISTUNE	DISTUNED ▪ DISTUNES
	DISTURB	DISTURBS
	DISTURBER	DISTURBERS
	DISTYLE	DISTYLES
	DISULFATE	DISULFATES
	DISULFID	DISULFIDE ▪ DISULFIDS
	DISULFIDE	DISULFIDES
	DISUNION	DISUNIONS
	DISUNITE	DISUNITED ▪ DISUNITER ▪ DISUNITES
	DISUNITER	DISUNITERS
	DISUSAGE	DISUSAGES
	DISUSE	DISUSED ▪ DISUSES
	DISVALUE	DISVALUED ▪ DISVALUES
	DISYOKE	DISYOKED ▪ DISYOKES
ADIT ▪ EDIT	**DIT**	DITA ▪ DITE ▪ DITS ▪ DITT ▪ DITZ
	DITA	DITAL ▪ DITAS
	DITAL	DITALS
	DITCHER	DITCHERS
	DITE	DITED ▪ DITES
EDITED	**DITED**	
	DITHEISM	DITHEISMS
	DITHEIST	DITHEISTS
	DITHELETE	DITHELETES
	DITHELISM	DITHELISMS
	DITHER	DITHERS ▪ DITHERY
	DITHERER	DITHERERS
	DITHYRAMB	DITHYRAMBS
EDITING	**DITING**	
	DITONE	DITONES
	DITROCHEE	DITROCHEES
ADITS ▪ EDITS	**DITS**	DITSY
	DITT	DITTO ▪ DITTS ▪ DITTY
	DITTANDER	DITTANDERS
	DITTAY	DITTAYS
	DITTO	DITTOS
	DITZ	DITZY
	DIURETIC	DIURETICS
	DIURNAL	DIURNALS
	DIURON	DIURONS
	DIV	DIVA ▪ DIVE ▪ DIVI ▪ DIVS
	DIVA	DIVAN ▪ DIVAS
	DIVAGATE	DIVAGATED ▪ DIVAGATES
	DIVALENCE	DIVALENCES
	DIVALENT	DIVALENTS
	DIVAN	DIVANS
	DIVE	DIVED ▪ DIVER ▪ DIVES
	DIVEBOMB	DIVEBOMBS
	DIVER	DIVERS ▪ DIVERT
	DIVERGE	DIVERGED ▪ DIVERGES
	DIVERS	DIVERSE
	DIVERSE	DIVERSED ▪ DIVERSES
	DIVERSION	DIVERSIONS
	DIVERT	DIVERTS
	DIVERTER	DIVERTERS
	DIVES	DIVEST
	DIVEST	DIVESTS
	DIVESTURE	DIVESTURES
	DIVI	DIVIS
	DIVIDE	DIVIDED ▪ DIVIDER ▪ DIVIDES
	DIVIDEND	DIVIDENDS
	DIVIDER	DIVIDERS
	DIVIDING	DIVIDINGS
	DIVIDIVI	DIVIDIVIS
	DIVINATOR	DIVINATORS ▪ DIVINATORY
	DIVINE	DIVINED ▪ DIVINER ▪ DIVINES
	DIVINER	DIVINERS
	DIVINES	DIVINEST
	DIVING	DIVINGS
	DIVINISE	DIVINISED ▪ DIVINISES

FRONT HOOK	ROOT WORD	END HOOK
	DIVINIZE	DIVINIZED · DIVINIZES
	DIVISION	DIVISIONS
	DIVISOR	DIVISORS
	DIVORCE	DIVORCED · DIVORCEE · DIVORCER DIVORCES
	DIVORCEE	DIVORCEES
	DIVORCER	DIVORCERS
	DIVOT	DIVOTS
	DIVULGATE	DIVULGATED · DIVULGATER · DIVULGATES
	DIVULGE	DIVULGED · DIVULGER · DIVULGES
	DIVULGER	DIVULGERS
	DIVULSE	DIVULSED · DIVULSES
	DIVULSION	DIVULSIONS
	DIWAN	DIWANS
	DIXI	DIXIE · DIXIT
	DIXIE	DIXIES
	DIXIT	DIXITS
	DIZAIN	DIZAINS
	DIZEN	DIZENS
	DIZENMENT	DIZENMENTS
	DIZZARD	DIZZARDS
	DIZZIES	DIZZIEST
	DJEBEL	DJEBELS
	DJELLABA	DJELLABAH · DJELLABAS
	DJELLABAH	DJELLABAHS
	DJEMBE	DJEMBES
	DJIBBAH	DJIBBAHS
	DJIN	DJINN · DJINS
	DJINN	DJINNI · DJINNS · DJINNY
ADO · UDO	**DO**	DOB · DOC · DOD · DOE · DOF · DOG · DOH DOL · DOM · DON · DOO · DOP · DOR · DOS DOT · DOW · DOY
	DOAB	DOABS
	DOAT	DOATS
	DOATER	DOATERS
	DOATING	DOATINGS
	DOB	DOBS · DOBY
	DOBBER	DOBBERS
	DOBBIE	DOBBIES
	DOBBIN	DOBBING · DOBBINS
	DOBCHICK	DOBCHICKS
	DOBIE	DOBIES
	DOBLA	DOBLAS
	DOBLON	DOBLONS
	DOBRA	DOBRAS
	DOBRO	DOBROS
	DOBSON	DOBSONS
	DOC	DOCK · DOCO · DOCS
	DOCENT	DOCENTS
	DOCILE	DOCILER
	DOCK	DOCKS
	DOCKAGE	DOCKAGES
	DOCKEN	DOCKENS
	DOCKER	DOCKERS
	DOCKET	DOCKETS
	DOCKHAND	DOCKHANDS
	DOCKING	DOCKINGS
	DOCKISE	DOCKISED · DOCKISES
	DOCKIZE	DOCKIZED · DOCKIZES
	DOCKLAND	DOCKLANDS
	DOCKSIDE	DOCKSIDES
	DOCKYARD	DOCKYARDS
	DOCO	DOCOS
	DOCQUET	DOCQUETS
	DOCTOR	DOCTORS
	DOCTORAND	DOCTORANDS
	DOCTORATE	DOCTORATED · DOCTORATES
	DOCTRINE	DOCTRINES
	DOCUDRAMA	DOCUDRAMAS

FRONT HOOK	ROOT WORD	END HOOK
	DOCUMENT	DOCUMENTS
	DOD	DODO = DODS
	DODDER	DODDERS = DODDERY
	DODDERER	DODDERERS
	DODDIES	DODDIEST
	DODDIPOLL	DODDIPOLLS
	DODDLE	DODDLES
	DODDYPOLL	DODDYPOLLS
	DODECAGON	DODECAGONS
	DODGE	DODGED = DODGEM = DODGER = DODGES
	DODGEBALL	DODGEBALLS
	DODGEM	DODGEMS
	DODGER	DODGERS = DODGERY
	DODGING	DODGINGS
	DODKIN	DODKINS
	DODMAN	DODMANS
	DODO	DODOS
	DODOISM	DODOISMS
	DOE	DOEK = DOEN = DOER = DOES
	DOEK	DOEKS
	DOER	DOERS
	DOES	DOEST
	DOESKIN	DOESKINS
	DOF	DOFF
	DOFF	DOFFS
	DOFFER	DOFFERS
	DOG	DOGE = DOGS = DOGY
	DOGARESSA	DOGARESSAS
	DOGATE	DOGATES
	DOGBANE	DOGBANES
	DOGBOLT	DOGBOLTS
	DOGCART	DOGCARTS
	DOGDOM	DOGDOMS
	DOGE	DOGES = DOGEY
	DOGEAR	DOGEARS
	DOGEATE	DOGEATES
	DOGEDOM	DOGEDOMS
	DOGESHIP	DOGESHIPS
	DOGEY	DOGEYS
	DOGFACE	DOGFACES
	DOGFIGHT	DOGFIGHTS
	DOGGER	DOGGERS = DOGGERY
	DOGGEREL	DOGGERELS
	DOGGIE	DOGGIER = DOGGIES
	DOGGIES	DOGGIEST
	DOGGING	DOGGINGS
	DOGGONE	DOGGONED = DOGGONER = DOGGONES
	DOGGONES	DOGGONEST
	DOGGREL	DOGGRELS
	DOGHOLE	DOGHOLES
	DOGHOUSE	DOGHOUSES
	DOGIE	DOGIES
	DOGLEG	DOGLEGS
	DOGMA	DOGMAN = DOGMAS
	DOGMATIC	DOGMATICS
	DOGMATISE	DOGMATISED = DOGMATISER = DOGMATISES
	DOGMATISM	DOGMATISMS
	DOGMATIST	DOGMATISTS
	DOGMATIZE	DOGMATIZED = DOGMATIZER = DOGMATIZES
	DOGNAP	DOGNAPS
	DOGNAPER	DOGNAPERS
	DOGNAPING	DOGNAPINGS
	DOGNAPPER	DOGNAPPERS
	DOGROBBER	DOGROBBERS
	DOGSHIP	DOGSHIPS
	DOGSKIN	DOGSKINS
	DOGSLED	DOGSLEDS
	DOGSLEEP	DOGSLEEPS
	DOGTOWN	DOGTOWNS

D

D

FRONT HOOK	ROOT WORD	END HOOK
	DOGTROT	DOGTROTS
	DOGVANE	DOGVANES
	DOGWOOD	DOGWOODS
	DOH	DOHS
	DOHYO	DOHYOS
	DOING	DOINGS
	DOIT	DOITS
	DOITKIN	DOITKINS
	DOJO	DOJOS
IDOL	**DOL**	DOLE · DOLL · DOLS · DOLT
	DOLCE	DOLCES
	DOLCETTO	DOLCETTOS
	DOLE	DOLED · DOLES
	DOLENT	DOLENTE
	DOLERITE	DOLERITES
	DOLINA	DOLINAS
	DOLINE	DOLINES
	DOLL	DOLLS · DOLLY
	DOLLAR	DOLLARS
	DOLLARISE	DOLLARISED · DOLLARISES
	DOLLARIZE	DOLLARIZED · DOLLARIZES
	DOLLDOM	DOLLDOMS
	DOLLHOOD	DOLLHOODS
	DOLLHOUSE	DOLLHOUSES
	DOLLIER	DOLLIERS
	DOLLOP	DOLLOPS
	DOLLYBIRD	DOLLYBIRDS
	DOLMA	DOLMAN · DOLMAS
	DOLMAN	DOLMANS
	DOLMEN	DOLMENS
	DOLOMITE	DOLOMITES
	DOLOR	DOLORS
	DOLOSTONE	DOLOSTONES
	DOLOUR	DOLOURS
	DOLPHIN	DOLPHINS
	DOLPHINET	DOLPHINETS
IDOLS	**DOLS**	
	DOLT	DOLTS
	DOM	DOME · DOMS · DOMY
	DOMAIN	DOMAINE · DOMAINS
	DOMAINE	DOMAINES
	DOME	DOMED · DOMES
	DOMESDAY	DOMESDAYS
	DOMESTIC	DOMESTICS
	DOMETT	DOMETTS
	DOMICIL	DOMICILE · DOMICILS
	DOMICILE	DOMICILED · DOMICILES
	DOMINANCE	DOMINANCES
	DOMINANT	DOMINANTS
	DOMINATE	DOMINATED · DOMINATES
	DOMINATOR	DOMINATORS
	DOMINE	DOMINEE · DOMINES
	DOMINEE	DOMINEER · DOMINEES
	DOMINEER	DOMINEERS
	DOMINICK	DOMINICKS
	DOMINIE	DOMINIES
	DOMINION	DOMINIONS
	DOMINIQUE	DOMINIQUES
	DOMINIUM	DOMINIUMS
	DOMINO	DOMINOS
UDON	**DON**	DONA · DONE · DONG · DONS
	DONA	DONAH · DONAS
	DONAH	DONAHS
ODONATE	**DONATE**	DONATED · DONATES
ODONATES	**DONATES**	
	DONATION	DONATIONS
	DONATISM	DONATISMS
	DONATIVE	DONATIVES
	DONATOR	DONATORS · DONATORY

FRONT HOOK	ROOT WORD	END HOOK
	DONDER	DONDERS
	DONE	DONEE • DONER
	DONEE	DONEES
	DONG	DONGA • DONGS
	DONGA	DONGAS
	DONGLE	DONGLES
	DONGOLA	DONGOLAS
	DONING	DONINGS
	DONJON	DONJONS
	DONKEY	DONKEYS
	DONKO	DONKOS
	DONNA	DONNAS • DONNAT
	DONNAT	DONNATS
	DONNE	DONNED • DONNEE • DONNES
	DONNEE	DONNEES
	DONNICKER	DONNICKERS
	DONNIKER	DONNIKERS
	DONNISM	DONNISMS
	DONNOT	DONNOTS
	DONOR	DONORS
	DONORSHIP	DONORSHIPS
UDONS	DONS	DONSY
	DONSHIP	DONSHIPS
	DONSIE	DONSIER
	DONUT	DONUTS
	DONZEL	DONZELS
	DOO	DOOB • DOOK • DOOL • DOOM • DOON
		DOOR • DOOS
	DOOB	DOOBS
	DOOBIE	DOOBIES
	DOOCOT	DOOCOTS
	DOODAD	DOODADS
	DOODAH	DOODAHS
	DOODLE	DOODLED • DOODLER • DOODLES
	DOODLEBUG	DOODLEBUGS
	DOODLER	DOODLERS
	DOODOO	DOODOOS
	DOOFER	DOOFERS
	DOOHICKEY	DOOHICKEYS
	DOOK	DOOKS
	DOOKET	DOOKETS
	DOOL	DOOLE • DOOLS • DOOLY
	DOOLAN	DOOLANS
	DOOLE	DOOLEE • DOOLES
	DOOLEE	DOOLEES
	DOOLIE	DOOLIES
	DOOM	DOOMS • DOOMY
	DOOMSAYER	DOOMSAYERS
	DOOMSDAY	DOOMSDAYS
	DOOMSTER	DOOMSTERS
	DOON	DOONA
	DOONA	DOONAS
	DOOR	DOORN • DOORS
	DOORBELL	DOORBELLS
	DOORCASE	DOORCASES
	DOORFRAME	DOORFRAMES
	DOORJAMB	DOORJAMBS
	DOORKNOB	DOORKNOBS
	DOORKNOCK	DOORKNOCKS
	DOORMAT	DOORMATS
	DOORN	DOORNS
	DOORNAIL	DOORNAILS
	DOORPLATE	DOORPLATES
	DOORPOST	DOORPOSTS
ADOORS	DOORS	
	DOORSILL	DOORSILLS
	DOORSTEP	DOORSTEPS
	DOORSTONE	DOORSTONES
	DOORSTOP	DOORSTOPS

FRONT HOOK	ROOT WORD	END HOOK
	DOORWAY	DOORWAYS
	DOORYARD	DOORYARDS
	DOOSRA	DOOSRAS
	DOOWOP	DOOWOPS
	DOOZER	DOOZERS
	DOOZIE	DOOZIES
	DOP	DOPA · DOPE · DOPS · DOPY
	DOPA	DOPAS
	DOPAMINE	DOPAMINES
	DOPANT	DOPANTS
	DOPATTA	DOPATTAS
	DOPE	DOPED · DOPER · DOPES · DOPEY
	DOPEHEAD	DOPEHEADS
	DOPER	DOPERS
	DOPESHEET	DOPESHEETS
	DOPESTER	DOPESTERS
	DOPIAZA	DOPIAZAS
	DOPING	DOPINGS
	DOPPER	DOPPERS
	DOPPIE	DOPPIES
	DOPPING	DOPPINGS
	DOPPIO	DOPPIOS
ODOR	**DOR**	DORB · DORE · DORK · DORM · DORP
		DORR · DORS · DORT · DORY
	DORAD	DORADO · DORADS
	DORADO	DORADOS
	DORB	DORBA · DORBS
	DORBA	DORBAS
	DORBEETLE	DORBEETLES
	DORBUG	DORBUGS
ADORE	**DORE**	DOREE
	DOREE	DOREES
	DORHAWK	DORHAWKS
	DORIDOID	DORIDOIDS
	DORIS	DORISE
ODORISE	**DORISE**	DORISED · DORISES
ODORISED	**DORISED**	
ODORISES	**DORISES**	
ODORISING	**DORISING**	
ODORIZE	**DORIZE**	DORIZED · DORIZES
ODORIZED	**DORIZED**	
ODORIZES	**DORIZES**	
ODORIZING	**DORIZING**	
	DORK	DORKS · DORKY
	DORLACH	DORLACHS
	DORM	DORMS · DORMY
	DORMANT	DORMANTS
	DORMER	DORMERS
	DORMIN	DORMINS
	DORMITION	DORMITIONS
	DORMITIVE	DORMITIVES
	DORNECK	DORNECKS
	DORNICK	DORNICKS
	DORNOCK	DORNOCKS
	DORONICUM	DORONICUMS
	DORP	DORPS
	DORPER	DORPERS
	DORR	DORRS
ODORS	**DORS**	DORSA · DORSE
	DORSA	DORSAD · DORSAL
	DORSAL	DORSALS
	DORSE	DORSEL · DORSER · DORSES
	DORSEL	DORSELS
	DORSER	DORSERS
	DORT	DORTS · DORTY
	DORTER	DORTERS
	DORTOUR	DORTOURS
ADOS · UDOS	**DOS**	DOSE · DOSH · DOSS · DOST
	DOSAGE	DOSAGES

D

FRONT HOOK	ROOT WORD	END HOOK
	DOSE	DOSED · DOSEH · DOSER · DOSES
	DOSEH	DOSEHS
	DOSEMETER	DOSEMETERS
	DOSER	DOSERS
	DOSIMETER	DOSIMETERS
	DOSSAL	DOSSALS
	DOSSEL	DOSSELS
	DOSSER	DOSSERS
	DOSSERET	DOSSERETS
	DOSSHOUSE	DOSSHOUSES
	DOSSIER	DOSSIERS
	DOSSIL	DOSSILS
	DOT	DOTE · DOTH · DOTS · DOTY
	DOTAGE	DOTAGES
	DOTANT	DOTANTS
	DOTARD	DOTARDS
	DOTATION	DOTATIONS
	DOTCOM	DOTCOMS
	DOTCOMMER	DOTCOMMERS
	DOTE	DOTED · DOTER · DOTES
	DOTER	DOTERS
	DOTING	DOTINGS
	DOTTEL	DOTTELS
	DOTTER	DOTTERS
	DOTTEREL	DOTTERELS
	DOTTLE	DOTTLED · DOTTLER · DOTTLES
	DOTTLES	DOTTLEST
	DOTTREL	DOTTRELS
	DOUANE	DOUANES
	DOUANIER	DOUANIERS
	DOUAR	DOUARS
	DOUBLE	DOUBLED · DOUBLER · DOUBLES · DOUBLET
	DOUBLER	DOUBLERS
	DOUBLET	DOUBLETS
	DOUBLETON	DOUBLETONS
	DOUBLING	DOUBLINGS
	DOUBLOON	DOUBLOONS
	DOUBLURE	DOUBLURES
	DOUBT	DOUBTS
	DOUBTER	DOUBTERS
	DOUBTFUL	DOUBTFULS
	DOUBTING	DOUBTINGS
	DOUC	DOUCE · DOUCS
	DOUCE	DOUCER · DOUCET
	DOUCEPERE	DOUCEPERES
	DOUCET	DOUCETS
	DOUCEUR	DOUCEURS
	DOUCHE	DOUCHED · DOUCHES
	DOUCHEBAG	DOUCHEBAGS
	DOUCINE	DOUCINES
	DOUGH	DOUGHS · DOUGHT · DOUGHY
	DOUGHBOY	DOUGHBOYS
	DOUGHFACE	DOUGHFACED · DOUGHFACES
	DOUGHNUT	DOUGHNUTS
	DOUGHT	DOUGHTY
	DOUK	DOUKS
	DOULA	DOULAS
	DOULEIA	DOULEIAS
	DOUM	DOUMA · DOUMS
	DOUMA	DOUMAS
	DOUP	DOUPS
	DOUPIONI	DOUPIONIS
	DOUPPIONI	DOUPPIONIS
ODOUR	DOUR	DOURA
	DOURA	DOURAH · DOURAS
	DOURAH	DOURAHS
	DOURINE	DOURINES
	DOUSE	DOUSED · DOUSER · DOUSES
	DOUSER	DOUSERS

231

D

FRONT HOOK	ROOT WORD	END HOOK
	DOUT	DOUTS
	DOUTER	DOUTERS
	DOUZEPER	DOUZEPERS
	DOVE	DOVED · DOVEN · DOVER · DOVES
	DOVECOT	DOVECOTE · DOVECOTS
	DOVECOTE	DOVECOTES
	DOVEKEY	DOVEKEYS
	DOVEKIE	DOVEKIES
	DOVELET	DOVELETS
	DOVEN	DOVENS
	DOVER	DOVERS
	DOVETAIL	DOVETAILS
	DOVIE	DOVIER
	DOW	DOWD · DOWF · DOWL · DOWN · DOWP DOWS · DOWT
	DOWAGER	DOWAGERS
	DOWAR	DOWARS
	DOWD	DOWDS · DOWDY
	DOWDIES	DOWDIEST
	DOWDYISM	DOWDYISMS
	DOWEL	DOWELS
	DOWELLING	DOWELLINGS
	DOWER	DOWERS · DOWERY
	DOWIE	DOWIER
	DOWITCHER	DOWITCHERS
	DOWL	DOWLE · DOWLS · DOWLY
	DOWLE	DOWLES
	DOWLNE	DOWLNES · DOWLNEY
ADOWN	**DOWN**	DOWNA · DOWNS · DOWNY
	DOWNBEAT	DOWNBEATS
	DOWNBOW	DOWNBOWS
	DOWNBURST	DOWNBURSTS
	DOWNCAST	DOWNCASTS
	DOWNCOME	DOWNCOMER · DOWNCOMES
	DOWNCOMER	DOWNCOMERS
	DOWNDRAFT	DOWNDRAFTS
	DOWNER	DOWNERS
	DOWNFALL	DOWNFALLS
	DOWNFLOW	DOWNFLOWS
	DOWNFORCE	DOWNFORCES
	DOWNGRADE	DOWNGRADED · DOWNGRADES
	DOWNHAUL	DOWNHAULS
	DOWNHILL	DOWNHILLS
	DOWNLAND	DOWNLANDS
	DOWNLIGHT	DOWNLIGHTS
	DOWNLINK	DOWNLINKS
	DOWNLOAD	DOWNLOADS
	DOWNPIPE	DOWNPIPES
	DOWNPLAY	DOWNPLAYS
	DOWNPOUR	DOWNPOURS
	DOWNSCALE	DOWNSCALED · DOWNSCALES
	DOWNSHIFT	DOWNSHIFTS
	DOWNSIDE	DOWNSIDES
	DOWNSIZE	DOWNSIZED · DOWNSIZES
	DOWNSLIDE	DOWNSLIDES
	DOWNSPIN	DOWNSPINS
	DOWNSPOUT	DOWNSPOUTS
	DOWNSTAGE	DOWNSTAGES
	DOWNSTAIR	DOWNSTAIRS
	DOWNSTATE	DOWNSTATER · DOWNSTATES
	DOWNSWING	DOWNSWINGS
	DOWNTHROW	DOWNTHROWS
	DOWNTICK	DOWNTICKS
	DOWNTIME	DOWNTIMES
	DOWNTOWN	DOWNTOWNS
	DOWNTREND	DOWNTRENDS
	DOWNTURN	DOWNTURNS
	DOWNWARD	DOWNWARDS
	DOWNZONE	DOWNZONED · DOWNZONES

FRONT HOOK	ROOT WORD	END HOOK
	DOWP	DOWPS
	DOWS	DOWSE
	DOWSABEL	DOWSABELS
	DOWSE	DOWSED ▪ DOWSER ▪ DOWSES ▪ DOWSET
	DOWSER	DOWSERS
	DOWSET	DOWSETS
	DOWT	DOWTS
	DOXIE	DOXIES
	DOY	DOYS
	DOYEN	DOYENS
	DOYENNE	DOYENNES
	DOYLEY	DOYLEYS
ADOZE	**DOZE**	DOZED ▪ DOZEN ▪ DOZER ▪ DOZES
	DOZEN	DOZENS
	DOZENTH	DOZENTHS
	DOZER	DOZERS
	DOZING	DOZINGS
	DRAB	DRABS
	DRABBER	DRABBERS
	DRABBET	DRABBETS
	DRABBLE	DRABBLED ▪ DRABBLER ▪ DRABBLES
	DRABBLER	DRABBLERS
	DRABBLING	DRABBLINGS
	DRABETTE	DRABETTES
	DRABLER	DRABLERS
	DRAC	DRACK ▪ DRACO
	DRACAENA	DRACAENAS
	DRACENA	DRACENAS
	DRACHM	DRACHMA ▪ DRACHMS
	DRACHMA	DRACHMAE ▪ DRACHMAI ▪ DRACHMAS
	DRACONE	DRACONES
	DRACONISM	DRACONISMS
ADRAD ▪ YDRAD	**DRAD**	
	DRAFF	DRAFFS ▪ DRAFFY
	DRAFT	DRAFTS ▪ DRAFTY
	DRAFTEE	DRAFTEES
	DRAFTER	DRAFTERS
	DRAFTING	DRAFTINGS
	DRAG	DRAGS
	DRAGEE	DRAGEES
	DRAGGER	DRAGGERS
	DRAGGLE	DRAGGLED ▪ DRAGGLES
	DRAGHOUND	DRAGHOUNDS
	DRAGLINE	DRAGLINES
	DRAGNET	DRAGNETS
	DRAGOMAN	DRAGOMANS
	DRAGON	DRAGONS
	DRAGONET	DRAGONETS
	DRAGONISE	DRAGONISED ▪ DRAGONISES
	DRAGONISM	DRAGONISMS
	DRAGONIZE	DRAGONIZED ▪ DRAGONIZES
	DRAGOON	DRAGOONS
	DRAGROPE	DRAGROPES
	DRAGSTER	DRAGSTERS
	DRAGSTRIP	DRAGSTRIPS
	DRAIL	DRAILS
	DRAIN	DRAINS
	DRAINAGE	DRAINAGES
	DRAINER	DRAINERS
	DRAINPIPE	DRAINPIPES
	DRAISENE	DRAISENES
	DRAISINE	DRAISINES
	DRAKE	DRAKES
	DRAM	DRAMA ▪ DRAMS
	DRAMA	DRAMAS
	DRAMATIC	DRAMATICS
	DRAMATISE	DRAMATISED ▪ DRAMATISER ▪ DRAMATISES
	DRAMATIST	DRAMATISTS
	DRAMATIZE	DRAMATIZED ▪ DRAMATIZER ▪ DRAMATIZES

D

FRONT HOOK	ROOT WORD	END HOOK
	DRAMATURG	DRAMATURGE ▪ DRAMATURGS ▪ DRAMATURGY
	DRAMMACH	DRAMMACHS
	DRAMMOCK	DRAMMOCKS
	DRAMSHOP	DRAMSHOPS
	DRANGWAY	DRANGWAYS
	DRANT	DRANTS
	DRAP	DRAPE ▪ DRAPS
	DRAPE	DRAPED ▪ DRAPER ▪ DRAPES ▪ DRAPET DRAPEY
	DRAPER	DRAPERS ▪ DRAPERY
	DRAPET	DRAPETS
	DRAPIER	DRAPIERS
	DRAPPIE	DRAPPIES
	DRASTIC	DRASTICS
	DRAT	DRATS
	DRATCHELL	DRATCHELLS
	DRAUGHT	DRAUGHTS ▪ DRAUGHTY
	DRAUGHTER	DRAUGHTERS
	DRAUNT	DRAUNTS
	DRAW	DRAWL ▪ DRAWN ▪ DRAWS
	DRAWBACK	DRAWBACKS
	DRAWBAR	DRAWBARS
	DRAWBORE	DRAWBORES
	DRAWDOWN	DRAWDOWNS
	DRAWEE	DRAWEES
	DRAWER	DRAWERS
	DRAWERFUL	DRAWERFULS
	DRAWING	DRAWINGS
	DRAWL	DRAWLS ▪ DRAWLY
	DRAWLER	DRAWLERS
	DRAWNWORK	DRAWNWORKS
	DRAWPLATE	DRAWPLATES
	DRAWSHAVE	DRAWSHAVES
	DRAWTUBE	DRAWTUBES
	DRAY	DRAYS
	DRAYAGE	DRAYAGES
	DRAYHORSE	DRAYHORSES
	DRAZEL	DRAZELS
ADREAD	**DREAD**	DREADS
ADREADED	**DREADED**	
	DREADER	DREADERS
	DREADFUL	DREADFULS
ADREADING	**DREADING**	
	DREADLOCK	DREADLOCKS
ADREADS	**DREADS**	
	DREAM	DREAMS ▪ DREAMT ▪ DREAMY
	DREAMBOAT	DREAMBOATS
	DREAMER	DREAMERS ▪ DREAMERY
	DREAMHOLE	DREAMHOLES
	DREAMING	DREAMINGS
	DREAMLAND	DREAMLANDS
	DREAMTIME	DREAMTIMES
	DREAR	DREARE ▪ DREARS ▪ DREARY
	DREARE	DREARER ▪ DREARES
	DREARES	DREAREST
	DREARIES	DREARIEST
	DREARING	DREARINGS
	DRECK	DRECKS ▪ DRECKY
	DRECKSILL	DRECKSILLS
	DREDGE	DREDGED ▪ DREDGER ▪ DREDGES
	DREDGER	DREDGERS
	DREDGING	DREDGINGS
	DREE	DREED ▪ DREES
	DREG	DREGS
	DREIDEL	DREIDELS
	DREIDL	DREIDLS
	DREK	DREKS
	DRENCHER	DRENCHERS
	DRENCHING	DRENCHINGS

FRONT HOOK	ROOT WORD	END HOOK
	DREPANID	DREPANIDS
	DREPANIUM	DREPANIUMS
	DRERE	DRERES
	DRERIHEAD	DRERIHEADS
	DRESS	DRESSY
	DRESSAGE	DRESSAGES
	DRESSER	DRESSERS
	DRESSING	DRESSINGS
	DRESSMAKE	DRESSMAKER · DRESSMAKES
	DREVILL	DREVILLS
	DREY	DREYS
	DRIB	DRIBS
	DRIBBER	DRIBBERS
	DRIBBLE	DRIBBLED · DRIBBLER · DRIBBLES DRIBBLET
	DRIBBLER	DRIBBLERS
	DRIBBLET	DRIBBLETS
	DRIBLET	DRIBLETS
	DRICE	DRICES
	DRICKSIE	DRICKSIER
	DRIER	DRIERS
	DRIES	DRIEST
ADRIFT	DRIFT	DRIFTS · DRIFTY
	DRIFTAGE	DRIFTAGES
	DRIFTER	DRIFTERS
	DRIFTPIN	DRIFTPINS
	DRIFTWOOD	DRIFTWOODS
	DRILL	DRILLS
	DRILLER	DRILLERS
	DRILLING	DRILLINGS
	DRILLSHIP	DRILLSHIPS
	DRINK	DRINKS
	DRINKABLE	DRINKABLES
	DRINKER	DRINKERS
	DRINKING	DRINKINGS
	DRIP	DRIPS · DRIPT
	DRIPPER	DRIPPERS
	DRIPPING	DRIPPINGS
	DRIPSTONE	DRIPSTONES
	DRISHEEN	DRISHEENS
	DRIVE	DRIVEL · DRIVEN · DRIVER · DRIVES
	DRIVEL	DRIVELS
	DRIVELER	DRIVELERS
	DRIVELINE	DRIVELINES
	DRIVELLER	DRIVELLERS
	DRIVER	DRIVERS
	DRIVEWAY	DRIVEWAYS
	DRIVING	DRIVINGS
	DRIZZLE	DRIZZLED · DRIZZLES
	DROGER	DROGERS
	DROGHER	DROGHERS
	DROGUE	DROGUES · DROGUET
	DROGUET	DROGUETS
	DROICH	DROICHS · DROICHY
	DROID	DROIDS
	DROIL	DROILS
ADROIT	DROIT	DROITS
	DROLE	DROLER · DROLES
	DROLES	DROLEST
	DROLL	DROLLS · DROLLY
	DROLLER	DROLLERY
	DROLLING	DROLLINGS
	DROME	DROMES
	DROMEDARE	DROMEDARES
	DROMON	DROMOND · DROMONS
	DROMOND	DROMONDS
	DRONE	DRONED · DRONER · DRONES
	DRONER	DRONERS
	DRONGO	DRONGOS

FRONT HOOK	ROOT WORD	END HOOK
	DRONKLAP	DRONKLAPS
	DROOB	DROOBS
	DROOG	DROOGS
	DROOK	DROOKS
	DROOKING	DROOKINGS
	DROOL	DROOLS · DROOLY
	DROOME	DROOMES
	DROOP	DROOPS · DROOPY
	DROP	DROPS · DROPT
	DROPCLOTH	DROPCLOTHS
	DROPFORGE	DROPFORGED · DROPFORGES
	DROPHEAD	DROPHEADS
	DROPKICK	DROPKICKS
	DROPLET	DROPLETS
	DROPLIGHT	DROPLIGHTS
	DROPOUT	DROPOUTS
	DROPPER	DROPPERS
	DROPPING	DROPPINGS
	DROPPLE	DROPPLES
	DROPS	DROPSY
	DROPSHOT	DROPSHOTS
	DROPSONDE	DROPSONDES
	DROPSTONE	DROPSTONES
	DROPWORT	DROPWORTS
	DROSERA	DROSERAS
	DROSS	DROSSY
	DROSTDY	DROSTDYS
	DROUGHT	DROUGHTS · DROUGHTY
	DROUK	DROUKS
	DROUKING	DROUKINGS
	DROUTH	DROUTHS · DROUTHY
	DROVE	DROVED · DROVER · DROVES
	DROVER	DROVERS
	DROVING	DROVINGS
	DROW	DROWN · DROWS
	DROWN	DROWND · DROWNS
	DROWND	DROWNDS
	DROWNER	DROWNERS
	DROWNING	DROWNINGS
	DROWS	DROWSE · DROWSY
	DROWSE	DROWSED · DROWSES
	DROWSIHED	DROWSIHEDS
	DRUB	DRUBS
	DRUBBER	DRUBBERS
	DRUBBING	DRUBBINGS
	DRUDGE	DRUDGED · DRUDGER · DRUDGES
	DRUDGER	DRUDGERS · DRUDGERY
	DRUDGISM	DRUDGISMS
	DRUG	DRUGS
	DRUGGER	DRUGGERS
	DRUGGET	DRUGGETS
	DRUGGIE	DRUGGIER · DRUGGIES
	DRUGGIES	DRUGGIEST
	DRUGGIST	DRUGGISTS
	DRUGLORD	DRUGLORDS
	DRUGMAKER	DRUGMAKERS
	DRUGSTORE	DRUGSTORES
	DRUID	DRUIDS
	DRUIDISM	DRUIDISMS
	DRUM	DRUMS
	DRUMBEAT	DRUMBEATS
	DRUMBLE	DRUMBLED · DRUMBLES
	DRUMFIRE	DRUMFIRES
	DRUMHEAD	DRUMHEADS
	DRUMLIN	DRUMLINS
	DRUMMER	DRUMMERS
	DRUMMOCK	DRUMMOCKS
	DRUMROLL	DRUMROLLS
	DRUMSTICK	DRUMSTICKS

FRONT HOOK	ROOT WORD	END HOOK
	DRUNK	DRUNKS
	DRUNKARD	DRUNKARDS
	DRUPE	DRUPEL · DRUPES
	DRUPEL	DRUPELS
	DRUPELET	DRUPELETS
	DRUSE	DRUSES
ADRY	DRY	DRYS
	DRYAD	DRYADS
	DRYASDUST	DRYASDUSTS
	DRYBEAT	DRYBEATS
	DRYER	DRYERS
	DRYING	DRYINGS
	DRYLOT	DRYLOTS
	DRYMOUTH	DRYMOUTHS
	DRYPOINT	DRYPOINTS
	DRYSALTER	DRYSALTERS · DRYSALTERY
	DRYWALL	DRYWALLS
	DRYWELL	DRYWELLS
ODSO	DSO	DSOS
	DSOBO	DSOBOS
	DSOMO	DSOMOS
ODSOS	DSOS	
	DUAD	DUADS
	DUAL	DUALS
	DUALIN	DUALINS
	DUALISE	DUALISED · DUALISES
	DUALISM	DUALISMS
	DUALIST	DUALISTS
	DUALIZE	DUALIZED · DUALIZES
	DUAN	DUANS
	DUAR	DUARS
	DUATHLON	DUATHLONS
	DUB	DUBS
	DUBBER	DUBBERS
	DUBBIN	DUBBING · DUBBINS
	DUBBING	DUBBINGS
	DUBBO	DUBBOS
	DUBITATE	DUBITATED · DUBITATES
	DUBNIUM	DUBNIUMS
	DUBONNET	DUBONNETS
	DUCAT	DUCATS
	DUCATOON	DUCATOONS
EDUCE	DUCE	DUCES
EDUCES	DUCES	
	DUCHESS	DUCHESSE
	DUCHESSE	DUCHESSED · DUCHESSES
	DUCK	DUCKS · DUCKY
	DUCKBILL	DUCKBILLS
	DUCKBOARD	DUCKBOARDS
	DUCKER	DUCKERS
	DUCKIE	DUCKIER · DUCKIES
	DUCKIES	DUCKIEST
	DUCKING	DUCKINGS
	DUCKLING	DUCKLINGS
	DUCKMOLE	DUCKMOLES
	DUCKPIN	DUCKPINS
	DUCKSHOVE	DUCKSHOVED · DUCKSHOVER · DUCKSHOVES
	DUCKTAIL	DUCKTAILS
	DUCKWALK	DUCKWALKS
	DUCKWEED	DUCKWEEDS
EDUCT	DUCT	DUCTS
	DUCTING	DUCTINGS
EDUCTS	DUCTS	
	DUCTULE	DUCTULES
	DUCTWORK	DUCTWORKS
	DUD	DUDE · DUDS
	DUDDER	DUDDERS · DUDDERY
	DUDDIE	DUDDIER
	DUDE	DUDED · DUDES

FRONT HOOK	ROOT WORD	END HOOK
	DUDEEN	DUDEENS
	DUDGEON	DUDGEONS
	DUDHEEN	DUDHEENS
	DUDISM	DUDISMS
	DUE	DUED · DUEL · DUES · DUET
	DUECENTO	DUECENTOS
	DUEL	DUELS
	DUELER	DUELERS
	DUELIST	DUELISTS
	DUELLER	DUELLERS
	DUELLING	DUELLINGS
	DUELLIST	DUELLISTS
	DUELLO	DUELLOS
	DUENDE	DUENDES
	DUENNA	DUENNAS
	DUET	DUETS · DUETT
	DUETT	DUETTI · DUETTO · DUETTS
	DUETTINO	DUETTINOS
	DUETTIST	DUETTISTS
	DUETTO	DUETTOS
	DUFF	DUFFS
	DUFFEL	DUFFELS
	DUFFER	DUFFERS
	DUFFERDOM	DUFFERDOMS
	DUFFERISM	DUFFERISMS
	DUFFING	DUFFINGS
	DUFFLE	DUFFLES
	DUG	DUGS
	DUGITE	DUGITES
	DUGONG	DUGONGS
	DUGOUT	DUGOUTS
	DUHKHA	DUHKHAS
	DUI	DUIT
	DUIKER	DUIKERS
	DUIKERBOK	DUIKERBOKS
	DUIT	DUITS
	DUKA	DUKAS
	DUKE	DUKED · DUKES
	DUKEDOM	DUKEDOMS
	DUKELING	DUKELINGS
	DUKESHIP	DUKESHIPS
	DUKKA	DUKKAH · DUKKAS
	DUKKAH	DUKKAHS
	DUKKHA	DUKKHAS
	DULCAMARA	DULCAMARAS
	DULCET	DULCETS
	DULCIAN	DULCIANA · DULCIANS
	DULCIANA	DULCIANAS
	DULCIMER	DULCIMERS
	DULCIMORE	DULCIMORES
	DULCINEA	DULCINEAS
	DULCITE	DULCITES
	DULCITOL	DULCITOLS
	DULCITUDE	DULCITUDES
	DULCOSE	DULCOSES
	DULE	DULES
	DULIA	DULIAS
	DULL	DULLS · DULLY
	DULLARD	DULLARDS
	DULSE	DULSES
	DUMA	DUMAS
	DUMAIST	DUMAISTS
	DUMB	DUMBO · DUMBS
	DUMBBELL	DUMBBELLS
	DUMBCANE	DUMBCANES
	DUMBFOUND	DUMBFOUNDS
	DUMBHEAD	DUMBHEADS
	DUMBO	DUMBOS
	DUMBSHIT	DUMBSHITS (offensive)

FRONT HOOK	ROOT WORD	END HOOK
	DUMDUM	DUMDUMS
	DUMFOUND	DUMFOUNDS
	DUMMERER	DUMMERERS
	DUMMIES	DUMMIEST
	DUMMKOPF	DUMMKOPFS
	DUMP	DUMPS · DUMPY
	DUMPBIN	DUMPBINS
	DUMPCART	DUMPCARTS
	DUMPER	DUMPERS
	DUMPIES	DUMPIEST
	DUMPING	DUMPINGS
	DUMPLE	DUMPLED · DUMPLES
	DUMPLING	DUMPLINGS
	DUMPSITE	DUMPSITES
	DUMPSTER	DUMPSTERS
	DUMPTRUCK	DUMPTRUCKS
	DUN	DUNE · DUNG · DUNK · DUNS · DUNT
	DUNAM	DUNAMS
	DUNCE	DUNCES
	DUNCEDOM	DUNCEDOMS
	DUNDER	DUNDERS
	DUNE	DUNES
	DUNELAND	DUNELANDS
	DUNG	DUNGS · DUNGY
	DUNGAREE	DUNGAREED · DUNGAREES
	DUNGEON	DUNGEONS
	DUNGEONER	DUNGEONERS
	DUNGER	DUNGERS
	DUNGHILL	DUNGHILLS
	DUNGMERE	DUNGMERES
	DUNITE	DUNITES
	DUNK	DUNKS
	DUNKER	DUNKERS
	DUNLIN	DUNLINS
	DUNNAGE	DUNNAGES
	DUNNAKIN	DUNNAKINS
	DUNNART	DUNNARTS
	DUNNIES	DUNNIEST
	DUNNING	DUNNINGS
	DUNNITE	DUNNITES
	DUNNOCK	DUNNOCKS
	DUNS	DUNSH
	DUNT	DUNTS
	DUO	DUOS
	DUODECIMO	DUODECIMOS
	DUODENA	DUODENAL
	DUODENUM	DUODENUMS
	DUOLOG	DUOLOGS
	DUOLOGUE	DUOLOGUES
	DUOMO	DUOMOS
	DUOTONE	DUOTONES
	DUP	DUPE · DUPS
	DUPATTA	DUPATTAS
	DUPE	DUPED · DUPER · DUPES
	DUPER	DUPERS · DUPERY
	DUPION	DUPIONS
	DUPLE	DUPLET · DUPLEX
	DUPLET	DUPLETS
	DUPLEXER	DUPLEXERS
	DUPLICAND	DUPLICANDS
	DUPLICATE	DUPLICATED · DUPLICATES
	DURA	DURAL · DURAS
	DURABLE	DURABLES
	DURAL	DURALS
	DURALUMIN	DURALUMINS
	DURAMEN	DURAMENS
	DURANCE	DURANCES
	DURANT	DURANTS
	DURATION	DURATIONS

239

FRONT HOOK	ROOT WORD	END HOOK
	DURATIVE	DURATIVES
	DURBAR	DURBARS
	DURDUM	DURDUMS
	DURE	DURED · DURES
	DURES	DURESS
	DURESS	DURESSE
	DURESSE	DURESSES
	DURGAH	DURGAHS
	DURGAN	DURGANS
	DURIAN	DURIANS
	DURICRUST	DURICRUSTS
	DURION	DURIONS
	DURMAST	DURMASTS
	DURN	DURNS
	DURO	DUROC · DUROS · DUROY
	DUROC	DUROCS
	DUROMETER	DUROMETERS
	DUROY	DUROYS
	DURR	DURRA · DURRS · DURRY
	DURRA	DURRAS
	DURRIE	DURRIES
	DURUKULI	DURUKULIS
	DURUM	DURUMS
	DURZI	DURZIS
	DUSK	DUSKS · DUSKY
	DUSKEN	DUSKENS
ADUST	**DUST**	DUSTS · DUSTY
	DUSTBIN	DUSTBINS
	DUSTCART	DUSTCARTS
	DUSTCOVER	DUSTCOVERS
ADUSTED	**DUSTED**	
	DUSTER	DUSTERS
	DUSTHEAP	DUSTHEAPS
ADUSTING	**DUSTING**	DUSTINGS
	DUSTOFF	DUSTOFFS
	DUSTPAN	DUSTPANS
	DUSTRAG	DUSTRAGS
ADUSTS	**DUSTS**	
	DUSTSHEET	DUSTSHEETS
	DUSTSTORM	DUSTSTORMS
	DUSTUP	DUSTUPS
	DUUMVIR	DUUMVIRI · DUUMVIRS
	DUVET	DUVETS
	DUVETINE	DUVETINES
	DUVETYN	DUVETYNE · DUVETYNS
	DUVETYNE	DUVETYNES
	DUYKER	DUYKERS
	DVANDVA	DVANDVAS
	DVORNIK	DVORNIKS
	DWAAL	DWAALS
	DWALE	DWALES
	DWALM	DWALMS
	DWAM	DWAMS
	DWANG	DWANGS
	DWARF	DWARFS
	DWARFISM	DWARFISMS
	DWAUM	DWAUMS
	DWEEB	DWEEBS · DWEEBY
	DWELL	DWELLS
	DWELLER	DWELLERS
	DWELLING	DWELLINGS
	DWILE	DWILES
	DWINDLE	DWINDLED · DWINDLES
	DWINE	DWINED · DWINES
	DYAD	DYADS
	DYADIC	DYADICS
	DYBBUK	DYBBUKS
	DYE	DYED · DYER · DYES
	DYEING	DYEINGS

FRONT HOOK	ROOT WORD	END HOOK
	DYELINE	DYELINES
	DYER	DYERS
	DYESTER	DYESTERS
	DYESTUFF	DYESTUFFS
	DYEWEED	DYEWEEDS
	DYEWOOD	DYEWOODS
	DYING	DYINGS
	DYKE	DYKED ▪ DYKES ▪ DYKEY (offensive)
	DYNAMETER	DYNAMETERS
ADYNAMIC	DYNAMIC	DYNAMICS
	DYNAMISE	DYNAMISED ▪ DYNAMISES
	DYNAMISM	DYNAMISMS
	DYNAMIST	DYNAMISTS
	DYNAMITE	DYNAMITED ▪ DYNAMITER ▪ DYNAMITES
	DYNAMITER	DYNAMITERS
	DYNAMIZE	DYNAMIZED ▪ DYNAMIZES
	DYNAMO	DYNAMOS
	DYNAMOTOR	DYNAMOTORS
	DYNAST	DYNASTS ▪ DYNASTY
	DYNATRON	DYNATRONS
	DYNE	DYNEL ▪ DYNES
	DYNEIN	DYNEINS
	DYNEL	DYNELS
	DYNODE	DYNODES
	DYNORPHIN	DYNORPHINS
	DYSBINDIN	DYSBINDINS
	DYSCHROA	DYSCHROAS
	DYSCHROIA	DYSCHROIAS
	DYSCRASIA	DYSCRASIAS
	DYSGENIC	DYSGENICS
	DYSLALIA	DYSLALIAS
	DYSLECTIC	DYSLECTICS
	DYSLEXIA	DYSLEXIAS
	DYSLEXIC	DYSLEXICS
	DYSMELIA	DYSMELIAS
	DYSODIL	DYSODILE ▪ DYSODILS
	DYSODILE	DYSODILES
	DYSODYLE	DYSODYLES
	DYSPEPSIA	DYSPEPSIAS
	DYSPEPTIC	DYSPEPTICS
	DYSPHAGIA	DYSPHAGIAS
	DYSPHASIA	DYSPHASIAS
	DYSPHASIC	DYSPHASICS
	DYSPHONIA	DYSPHONIAS
	DYSPHORIA	DYSPHORIAS
	DYSPLASIA	DYSPLASIAS
	DYSPNEA	DYSPNEAL ▪ DYSPNEAS
	DYSPNOEA	DYSPNOEAL ▪ DYSPNOEAS
	DYSPRAXIA	DYSPRAXIAS
	DYSTAXIA	DYSTAXIAS
	DYSTHESIA	DYSTHESIAS
	DYSTHYMIA	DYSTHYMIAC ▪ DYSTHYMIAS
	DYSTHYMIC	DYSTHYMICS
	DYSTOCIA	DYSTOCIAL ▪ DYSTOCIAS
	DYSTONIA	DYSTONIAS
	DYSTOPIA	DYSTOPIAN ▪ DYSTOPIAS
	DYSTOPIAN	DYSTOPIANS
	DYSURIA	DYSURIAS
	DYTISCID	DYTISCIDS
	DYVOUR	DYVOURS ▪ DYVOURY
	DZEREN	DZERENS
	DZHO	DZHOS
	DZIGGETAI	DZIGGETAIS
	DZO	DZOS

E

FRONT HOOK	ROOT WORD	END HOOK
KEA · LEA · PEA · SEA · TEA · YEA · ZEA	**EA**	EAN · EAR · EAS · EAT · EAU
BEACH · LEACH · PEACH · REACH · TEACH	**EACH**	
MEAGER	**EAGER**	EAGERS
MEAGERLY	**EAGERLY**	
MEAGERNESS	**EAGERNESS**	
BEAGLE · TEAGLE	**EAGLE**	EAGLED · EAGLES · EAGLET
BEAGLED · TEAGLED	**EAGLED**	
	EAGLEHAWK	EAGLEHAWKS
BEAGLES · TEAGLES	**EAGLES**	
	EAGLET	EAGLETS
	EAGLEWOOD	EAGLEWOODS
BEAGLING · TEAGLING	**EAGLING**	
MEAGRE	**EAGRE**	EAGRES
MEAGRES	**EAGRES**	
VEALE	**EALE**	EALES
REALES · VEALES	**EALES**	
BEAN · DEAN · GEAN · JEAN · LEAN · MEAN	**EAN**	EANS
PEAN · REAN · SEAN · WEAN · YEAN		
BEANED · DEANED · JEANED · LEANED	**EANED**	
MEANED · PEANED · SEANED · WEANED		
YEANED		
BEANING · DEANING · LEANING · MEANING	**EANING**	
PEANING · SEANING · WEANING · YEANING		
WEANLING · YEANLING	**EANLING**	EANLINGS
WEANLINGS · YEANLINGS	**EANLINGS**	
BEANS · DEANS · GEANS · JEANS · LEANS	**EANS**	
MEANS · PEANS · REANS · SEANS · WEANS		
YEANS		
BEAR · DEAR · FEAR · GEAR · HEAR · LEAR	**EAR**	EARD · EARL · EARN · EARS
NEAR · PEAR · REAR · SEAR · TEAR · WEAR		
YEAR		
	EARACHE	EARACHES
	EARBALL	EARBALLS
	EARBASHER	EARBASHERS
	EARBOB	EARBOBS
	EARBUD	EARBUDS
	EARCON	EARCONS
BEARD · HEARD · YEARD	**EARD**	EARDS
BEARDED · YEARDED	**EARDED**	
BEARDING · YEARDING	**EARDING**	
TEARDROP	**EARDROP**	EARDROPS
TEARDROPS	**EARDROPS**	
	EARDRUM	EARDRUMS
BEARDS · HEARDS · YEARDS	**EARDS**	
BEARED · DEARED · FEARED · GEARED	**EARED**	
LEARED · NEARED · REARED · SEARED		
TEARED · WEARED		
	EARFLAP	EARFLAPS
FEARFUL · TEARFUL	**EARFUL**	EARFULS
BEARING · DEARING · FEARING · GEARING	**EARING**	EARINGS
HEARING · LEARING · MEARING · NEARING		
REARING · SEARING · TEARING · WEARING		
BEARINGS · GEARINGS · HEARINGS	**EARINGS**	
SEARINGS · WEARINGS		
PEARL	**EARL**	EARLS · EARLY
	EARLAP	EARLAPS
	EARLDOM	EARLDOMS
FEARLESS · GEARLESS · TEARLESS	**EARLESS**	
NEARLIER · PEARLIER	**EARLIER**	
PEARLIES · YEARLIES	**EARLIES**	EARLIEST
NEARLIEST · PEARLIEST	**EARLIEST**	
BEARLIKE	**EARLIKE**	
PEARLINESS	**EARLINESS**	
	EARLOBE	EARLOBES
	EARLOCK	EARLOCKS
PEARLS	**EARLS**	

242

FRONT HOOK	ROOT WORD	END HOOK
	EARLSHIP	EARLSHIPS
DEARLY ▪ NEARLY ▪ PEARLY ▪ REARLY ▪ YEARLY	**EARLY**	
	EARLYWOOD	EARLYWOODS
	EARMARK	EARMARKS
	EARMUFF	EARMUFFS
DEARN ▪ LEARN ▪ YEARN	**EARN**	EARNS
LEARNED ▪ YEARNED	**EARNED**	
LEARNER ▪ YEARNER	**EARNER**	EARNERS
LEARNERS ▪ YEARNERS	**EARNERS**	
	EARNEST	EARNESTS
LEARNING ▪ YEARNING	**EARNING**	EARNINGS
LEARNINGS ▪ YEARNINGS	**EARNINGS**	
DEARNS ▪ LEARNS ▪ YEARNS	**EARNS**	
	EARPHONE	EARPHONES
	EARPICK	EARPICKS
	EARPIECE	EARPIECES
	EARPLUG	EARPLUGS
	EARRING	EARRINGS
BEARS ▪ DEARS ▪ FEARS ▪ GEARS ▪ HEARS LEARS ▪ NEARS ▪ PEARS ▪ REARS ▪ SEARS TEARS ▪ WEARS ▪ YEARS	**EARS**	EARST
	EARSHOT	EARSHOTS
PEARST	**EARST**	
	EARSTONE	EARSTONES
DEARTH ▪ HEARTH	**EARTH**	EARTHS ▪ EARTHY
	EARTHFALL	EARTHFALLS
	EARTHLIES	EARTHLIEST
	EARTHLING	EARTHLINGS
	EARTHNUT	EARTHNUTS
	EARTHPEA	EARTHPEAS
	EARTHRISE	EARTHRISES
DEARTHS ▪ HEARTHS	**EARTHS**	
	EARTHSET	EARTHSETS
	EARTHSTAR	EARTHSTARS
	EARTHWARD	EARTHWARDS
	EARTHWORK	EARTHWORKS
	EARTHWORM	EARTHWORMS
	EARWIG	EARWIGS
	EARWORM	EARWORMS
CEAS ▪ KEAS ▪ LEAS ▪ PEAS ▪ SEAS ▪ TEAS YEAS ▪ ZEAS	**EAS**	EASE ▪ EAST ▪ EASY
CEASE ▪ FEASE ▪ LEASE ▪ MEASE ▪ PEASE SEASE ▪ TEASE	**EASE**	EASED ▪ EASEL ▪ EASER ▪ EASES
CEASED ▪ FEASED ▪ LEASED ▪ MEASED PEASED ▪ SEASED ▪ TEASED	**EASED**	
TEASEL ▪ WEASEL	**EASEL**	EASELS
TEASELED ▪ WEASELED	**EASELED**	
CEASELESS	**EASELESS**	
TEASELS ▪ WEASELS	**EASELS**	
	EASEMENT	EASEMENTS
LEASER ▪ TEASER	**EASER**	EASERS
LEASERS ▪ TEASERS	**EASERS**	
CEASES ▪ FEASES ▪ LEASES ▪ MEASES PEASES ▪ SEASES ▪ TEASES	**EASES**	
	EASIES	EASIEST
CEASING ▪ FEASING ▪ LEASING ▪ MEASING PEASING ▪ SEASING ▪ TEASING	**EASING**	
MEASLE	**EASLE**	EASLES
MEASLES	**EASLES**	
BEAST ▪ FEAST ▪ HEAST ▪ LEAST ▪ REAST YEAST	**EAST**	EASTS
FEASTED ▪ REASTED ▪ YEASTED	**EASTED**	
FEASTER	**EASTER**	EASTERN ▪ EASTERS
	EASTERNER	EASTERNERS
FEASTERS	**EASTERS**	
FEASTING ▪ REASTING ▪ YEASTING	**EASTING**	EASTINGS
BEASTINGS ▪ FEASTINGS	**EASTINGS**	
	EASTLIN	EASTLING ▪ EASTLINS

FRONT HOOK	ROOT WORD	END HOOK
BEASTS · FEASTS · HEASTS · LEASTS REASTS · YEASTS	**EASTLING** **EASTS**	EASTLINGS
BEAT · FEAT · GEAT · HEAT · JEAT · LEAT MEAT · NEAT · PEAT · SEAT · TEAT	**EASTWARD** **EAT**	EASTWARDS EATH · EATS
BEATABLE · HEATABLE	**EATABLE**	EATABLES
	EATAGE	EATAGES
	EATCHE	EATCHES
BEATEN · NEATEN	**EATEN**	
BEATER · FEATER · HEATER · NEATER SEATER	**EATER**	EATERS · EATERY
PEATERIES	**EATERIE**	EATERIES
BEATERS · HEATERS · SEATERS	**EATERIES**	
PEATERY	**EATERS**	
	EATERY	
BEATH · DEATH · HEATH · MEATH · NEATH MEATHE	**EATH** **EATHE**	EATHE
DEATHLY	**EATHLY**	
BEATING · FEATING · HEATING · SEATING	**EATING**	EATINGS
BEATINGS · HEATINGS · SEATINGS	**EATINGS**	
BEATS · FEATS · GEATS · HEATS · JEATS LEATS · MEATS · NEATS · PEATS · SEATS TEATS	**EATS**	
BEAU	**EAU**	EAUS · EAUX
BEAUS	**EAUS**	
BEAUX	**EAUX**	
DEAVE · HEAVE · LEAVE · REAVE · WEAVE	**EAVE**	EAVED · EAVES
DEAVED · HEAVED · LEAVED · REAVED WEAVED	**EAVED**	
DEAVES · HEAVES · LEAVES · REAVES WEAVES	**EAVES**	
	EAVESDRIP	EAVESDRIPS
	EAVESDROP	EAVESDROPS
	EBAUCHE	EBAUCHES
DEBAUCHES	**EBAUCHES**	
	EBAYER	EBAYERS
	EBAYING	EBAYINGS
	EBB	EBBS
KEBBED · NEBBED · WEBBED	**EBBED**	
	EBBET	EBBETS
KEBBING · NEBBING · WEBBING	**EBBING**	
	EBBTIDE	EBBTIDES
	EBENEZER	EBENEZERS
	EBENISTE	EBENISTES
	EBIONISE	EBIONISED · EBIONISES
	EBIONISM	EBIONISMS
	EBIONIZE	EBIONIZED · EBIONIZES
	EBON	EBONS · EBONY
	EBONISE	EBONISED · EBONISES
	EBONIST	EBONISTS
	EBONITE	EBONITES
	EBONIZE	EBONIZED · EBONIZES
REBOOK	**EBOOK**	EBOOKS
REBOOKS	**EBOOKS**	
	EBRIATE	EBRIATED
	EBRILLADE	EBRILLADES
DECAD	**ECAD**	ECADS
DECADS	**ECADS**	
	ECARTE	ECARTES
DECAUDATE	**ECAUDATE**	
	ECBOLE	ECBOLES
	ECBOLIC	ECBOLICS
RECCE	**ECCE**	
	ECCENTRIC	ECCENTRICS
	ECCLESIA	ECCLESIAE · ECCLESIAL
RECCO · SECCO	**ECCO**	
	ECCRITIC	ECCRITICS
	ECDYSIAST	ECDYSIASTS

FRONT HOOK	ROOT WORD	END HOOK
	ECDYSON	ECDYSONE · ECDYSONS
	ECDYSONE	ECDYSONES
EECH · HECH · LECH · PECH · SECH · TECH · YECH	**ECH**	ECHE · ECHO · ECHT
	ECHAPPE	ECHAPPES
	ECHARD	ECHARDS
	ECHE	ECHED · ECHES
EECHED · LECHED · PECHED · TECHED	**ECHED**	
	ECHELLE	ECHELLES
	ECHELON	ECHELONS
EECHES · LECHES	**ECHES**	
	ECHEVERIA	ECHEVERIAS
	ECHIDNA	ECHIDNAE · ECHIDNAS
	ECHIDNINE	ECHIDNINES
	ECHINACEA	ECHINACEAS
	ECHINATE	ECHINATED
EECHING · LECHING · PECHING	**ECHING**	
	ECHINOID	ECHINOIDS
	ECHIUM	ECHIUMS
	ECHIUROID	ECHIUROIDS
	ECHO	ECHOS
	ECHOER	ECHOERS
	ECHOGRAM	ECHOGRAMS
	ECHOISE	ECHOISED · ECHOISES
	ECHOISM	ECHOISMS
	ECHOIST	ECHOISTS
	ECHOIZE	ECHOIZED · ECHOIZES
	ECHOLALIA	ECHOLALIAS
FECHT · HECHT · WECHT	**ECHT**	
	ECLAIR	ECLAIRS
	ECLAMPSIA	ECLAMPSIAS
	ECLAT	ECLATS
	ECLECTIC	ECLECTICS
	ECLIPSE	ECLIPSED · ECLIPSER · ECLIPSES
	ECLIPSER	ECLIPSERS
	ECLIPTIC	ECLIPTICS
	ECLOGITE	ECLOGITES
	ECLOGUE	ECLOGUES
RECLOSE	**ECLOSE**	ECLOSED · ECLOSES
RECLOSED	**ECLOSED**	
RECLOSES	**ECLOSES**	
RECLOSING	**ECLOSING**	
	ECLOSION	ECLOSIONS
DECO · SECO	**ECO**	ECOD · ECOS
	ECOCIDE	ECOCIDES
	ECOFREAK	ECOFREAKS
OECOLOGIES	**ECOLOGIES**	
OECOLOGIST	**ECOLOGIST**	ECOLOGISTS
OECOLOGY	**ECOLOGY**	
	ECOMMERCE	ECOMMERCES
	ECONOMIC	ECONOMICS
	ECONOMISE	ECONOMISED · ECONOMISER · ECONOMISES
	ECONOMISM	ECONOMISMS
	ECONOMIST	ECONOMISTS
	ECONOMIZE	ECONOMIZED · ECONOMIZER · ECONOMIZES
	ECONUT	ECONUTS
	ECOPHOBIA	ECOPHOBIAS
	ECORCHE	ECORCHES
	ECOREGION	ECOREGIONS
DECOS	**ECOS**	
	ECOSPHERE	ECOSPHERES
	ECOSSAISE	ECOSSAISES
	ECOSYSTEM	ECOSYSTEMS
	ECOTAGE	ECOTAGES
	ECOTONE	ECOTONES
	ECOTOUR	ECOTOURS
	ECOTYPE	ECOTYPES
	ECRASEUR	ECRASEURS
	ECRITOIRE	ECRITOIRES

FRONT HOOK	ROOT WORD	END HOOK
	ECRU	ECRUS
	ECSTASIS	ECSTASISE
	ECSTASISE	ECSTASISED · ECSTASISES
	ECSTASIZE	ECSTASIZED · ECSTASIZES
	ECSTATIC	ECSTATICS
PECTASES	**ECTASES**	
	ECTASIA	ECTASIAS
	ECTHYMA	ECTHYMAS
	ECTOBLAST	ECTOBLASTS
	ECTOCRINE	ECTOCRINES
	ECTODERM	ECTODERMS
	ECTOMERE	ECTOMERES
	ECTOMORPH	ECTOMORPHS · ECTOMORPHY
	ECTOPHYTE	ECTOPHYTES
	ECTOPIA	ECTOPIAS
	ECTOPLASM	ECTOPLASMS
	ECTOPROCT	ECTOPROCTS
	ECTOSARC	ECTOSARCS
	ECTOTHERM	ECTOTHERMS
	ECTOZOA	ECTOZOAN
	ECTOZOAN	ECTOZOANS
	ECTROPION	ECTROPIONS
	ECTROPIUM	ECTROPIUMS
	ECTYPE	ECTYPES
	ECU	ECUS
	ECUELLE	ECUELLES
OECUMENIC	**ECUMENIC**	ECUMENICS
	ECUMENISM	ECUMENISMS
	ECUMENIST	ECUMENISTS
	ECURIE	ECURIES
DECURIES	**ECURIES**	
	ECZEMA	ECZEMAS
BED · FED · GED · KED · LED · MED · NED PED · RED · SED · TED · WED · ZED	**ED**	EDH · EDS
NEDDIES · TEDDIES	**EDDIES**	
NEDDISH · REDDISH	**EDDISH**	
NEDDY · REDDY · TEDDY	**EDDY**	
OEDEMA	**EDEMA**	EDEMAS
OEDEMAS	**EDEMAS**	
OEDEMATA	**EDEMATA**	
OEDEMATOSE	**EDEMATOSE**	
OEDEMATOUS	**EDEMATOUS**	
	EDENTATE	EDENTATES
HEDGE · KEDGE · LEDGE · SEDGE · WEDGE	**EDGE**	EDGED · EDGER · EDGES
	EDGEBONE	EDGEBONES
HEDGED · KEDGED · LEDGED · SEDGED WEDGED	**EDGED**	
HEDGER · KEDGER · LEDGER	**EDGER**	EDGERS
HEDGERS · KEDGERS · LEDGERS	**EDGERS**	
HEDGES · KEDGES · LEDGES · SEDGES WEDGES	**EDGES**	
WEDGEWISE	**EDGEWISE**	
HEDGIER · KEDGIER · LEDGIER · SEDGIER WEDGIER	**EDGIER**	
HEDGIEST · KEDGIEST · LEDGIEST SEDGIEST · WEDGIEST	**EDGIEST**	
HEDGING · KEDGING · WEDGING	**EDGING**	EDGINGS
HEDGINGS · WEDGINGS	**EDGINGS**	
HEDGY · KEDGY · LEDGY · SEDGY · WEDGY	**EDGY**	
	EDH	EDHS
	EDIBLE	EDIBLES
	EDICT	EDICTS
	EDIFICE	EDIFICES
	EDIFIER	EDIFIERS
AEDILE · SEDILE	**EDILE**	EDILES
AEDILES	**EDILES**	
	EDIT	EDITS
	EDITING	EDITINGS
SEDITION	**EDITION**	EDITIONS

FRONT HOOK	ROOT WORD	END HOOK
SEDITIONS	**EDITIONS**	
	EDITOR	EDITORS
	EDITORIAL	EDITORIALS
BEDS ▪ FEDS ▪ GEDS ▪ KEDS ▪ MEDS	**EDS**	
NEDS *(offensive)* ▪ PEDS ▪ REDS ▪ TEDS		
WEDS ▪ ZEDS		
	EDUCABLE	EDUCABLES
	EDUCATE	EDUCATED ▪ EDUCATES
	EDUCATION	EDUCATIONS
	EDUCATOR	EDUCATORS ▪ EDUCATORY
DEDUCE ▪ REDUCE ▪ SEDUCE	**EDUCE**	EDUCED ▪ EDUCES
DEDUCED ▪ REDUCED ▪ SEDUCED	**EDUCED**	
DEDUCEMENT ▪ SEDUCEMENT	**EDUCEMENT**	EDUCEMENTS
DEDUCES ▪ REDUCES ▪ SEDUCES	**EDUCES**	
DEDUCIBLE ▪ REDUCIBLE ▪ SEDUCIBLE	**EDUCIBLE**	
DEDUCING ▪ REDUCING ▪ SEDUCING	**EDUCING**	
DEDUCT	**EDUCT**	EDUCTS
DEDUCTION ▪ REDUCTION ▪ SEDUCTION	**EDUCTION**	EDUCTIONS
DEDUCTIONS ▪ REDUCTIONS ▪ SEDUCTIONS	**EDUCTIONS**	
DEDUCTIVE ▪ REDUCTIVE ▪ SEDUCTIVE	**EDUCTIVE**	
REDUCTOR ▪ SEDUCTOR	**EDUCTOR**	EDUCTORS
REDUCTORS ▪ SEDUCTORS	**EDUCTORS**	
DEDUCTS	**EDUCTS**	
	EDUSKUNTA	EDUSKUNTAS
BEE ▪ CEE ▪ DEE ▪ FEE ▪ GEE ▪ JEE ▪ LEE	**EE**	EEK ▪ EEL ▪ EEN
MEE ▪ NEE ▪ PEE ▪ REE ▪ SEE ▪ TEE ▪ VEE		
WEE ▪ ZEE		
BEECH ▪ KEECH ▪ LEECH ▪ REECH	**EECH**	
LEECHED ▪ REECHED	**EECHED**	
BEECHES ▪ KEECHES ▪ LEECHES ▪ REECHES	**EECHES**	
LEECHING ▪ REECHING	**EECHING**	
	EEJIT	EEJITS
DEEK ▪ GEEK ▪ KEEK ▪ LEEK ▪ MEEK ▪ PEEK	**EEK**	
REEK ▪ SEEK ▪ TEEK ▪ WEEK		
FEEL ▪ HEEL ▪ JEEL ▪ KEEL ▪ PEEL ▪ REEL	**EEL**	EELS ▪ EELY
SEEL ▪ TEEL ▪ WEEL		
	EELFARE	EELFARES
SEELIER	**EELIER**	
SEELIEST	**EELIEST**	
	EELPOUT	EELPOUTS
FEELS ▪ HEELS ▪ JEELS ▪ KEELS ▪ PEELS	**EELS**	
REELS ▪ SEELS ▪ TEELS ▪ WEELS		
	EELWORM	EELWORMS
	EELWRACK	EELWRACKS
DEELY ▪ JEELY ▪ SEELY	**EELY**	
BEEN ▪ DEEN ▪ FEEN ▪ KEEN ▪ PEEN ▪ REEN	**EEN**	
SEEN ▪ TEEN ▪ WEEN		
FEERIE ▪ PEERIE	**EERIE**	EERIER
BEERIER ▪ LEERIER ▪ PEERIER	**EERIER**	
BEERIEST ▪ LEERIEST ▪ PEERIEST	**EERIEST**	
BEERILY ▪ LEERILY	**EERILY**	
BEERINESS ▪ LEERINESS	**EERINESS**	
BEERY ▪ LEERY ▪ PEERY ▪ VEERY	**EERY**	
	EEVEN	EEVENS
	EEVN	EEVNS
	EEVNING	EEVNINGS
DEF ▪ KEF ▪ NEF ▪ REF ▪ TEF	**EF**	EFF ▪ EFS ▪ EFT
JEFF ▪ MEFF ▪ TEFF	**EFF**	EFFS
	EFFACE	EFFACED ▪ EFFACER ▪ EFFACES
	EFFACER	EFFACERS
	EFFECT	EFFECTS
	EFFECTER	EFFECTERS
	EFFECTIVE	EFFECTIVES
	EFFECTOR	EFFECTORS
JEFFED ▪ REFFED	**EFFED**	
	EFFEIR	EFFEIRS
	EFFENDI	EFFENDIS
	EFFERE	EFFERED ▪ EFFERES
	EFFERENCE	EFFERENCES

247

FRONT HOOK	ROOT WORD	END HOOK
	EFFERENT	EFFERENTS
	EFFICIENT	EFFICIENTS
	EFFIERCE	EFFIERCED · EFFIERCES
JEFFING · REFFING	**EFFING**	EFFINGS
	EFFLUENCE	EFFLUENCES
	EFFLUENT	EFFLUENTS
	EFFLUVIA	EFFLUVIAL
	EFFLUVIUM	EFFLUVIUMS
	EFFLUXION	EFFLUXIONS
	EFFORCE	EFFORCED · EFFORCES
	EFFORT	EFFORTS
	EFFRAY	EFFRAYS
JEFFS · MEFFS · TEFFS	**EFFS**	
	EFFULGE	EFFULGED · EFFULGES
	EFFUSE	EFFUSED · EFFUSES
	EFFUSION	EFFUSIONS
	EFS	
KEFS · NEFS · REFS · TEFS	**EFS**	
DEFT · HEFT · LEFT · REFT · WEFT	**EFT**	EFTS
DEFTEST · LEFTEST	**EFTEST**	
HEFTS · LEFTS · WEFTS	**EFTS**	
	EFTSOON	EFTSOONS
BEGAD	**EGAD**	EGADS
LEGAL · REGAL	**EGAL**	
	EGALITE	EGALITES
LEGALITIES · REGALITIES	**EGALITIES**	
LEGALITY · REGALITY	**EGALITY**	
LEGALLY · REGALLY	**EGALLY**	
	EGAREMENT	EGAREMENTS
REGENCE	**EGENCE**	EGENCES
REGENCES	**EGENCES**	
REGENCIES	**EGENCIES**	
REGENCY	**EGENCY**	
LEGER	**EGER**	EGERS
LEGERS	**EGERS**	
REGEST	**EGEST**	EGESTA · EGESTS
	EGESTION	EGESTIONS
REGESTS	**EGESTS**	
TEGG · YEGG	**EGG**	EGGS · EGGY
BEGGAR · SEGGAR	**EGGAR**	EGGARS
BEGGARS · SEGGARS	**EGGARS**	
	EGGBEATER	EGGBEATERS
	EGGCUP	EGGCUPS
BEGGED · DEGGED · KEGGED · LEGGED PEGGED · VEGGED	**EGGED**	
KEGGER · LEGGER	**EGGER**	EGGERS · EGGERY
KEGGERS · LEGGERS	**EGGERS**	
	EGGFRUIT	EGGFRUITS
	EGGHEAD	EGGHEADS
LEGGIER	**EGGIER**	
LEGGIEST	**EGGIEST**	
BEGGING · DEGGING · KEGGING · LEGGING PEGGING · VEGGING	**EGGING**	
	EGGLER	EGGLERS
	EGGNOG	EGGNOGS
	EGGPLANT	EGGPLANTS
TEGGS · YEGGS	**EGGS**	
	EGGSHELL	EGGSHELLS
	EGGWHISK	EGGWHISKS
LEGGY · PEGGY	**EGGY**	
AEGIS	**EGIS**	
AEGISES	**EGISES**	
	EGLANTINE	EGLANTINES
	EGLATERE	EGLATERES
REGMA	**EGMA**	EGMAS
BEGO · REGO · SEGO · VEGO	**EGO**	EGOS
	EGOISM	EGOISMS
	EGOIST	EGOISTS
	EGOMANIA	EGOMANIAC · EGOMANIAS
	EGOMANIAC	EGOMANIACS

FRONT HOOK	ROOT WORD	END HOOK
REGOS ▪ SEGOS ▪ VEGOS	**EGOS**	
	EGOTHEISM	EGOTHEISMS
	EGOTISE	EGOTISED ▪ EGOTISES
	EGOTISM	EGOTISMS
	EGOTIST	EGOTISTS
	EGOTIZE	EGOTIZED ▪ EGOTIZES
NEGRESS ▪ REGRESS	**EGRESS**	
REGRESSED	**EGRESSED**	
NEGRESSES (offensive) ▪ REGRESSES	**EGRESSES**	
REGRESSING	**EGRESSING**	
DEGRESSION ▪ REGRESSION	**EGRESSION**	EGRESSIONS
REGRET	**EGRET**	EGRETS
REGRETS	**EGRETS**	
	EGYPTIAN	EGYPTIANS
FEH ▪ HEH ▪ PEH ▪ REH ▪ YEH	**EH**	EHS
FEHS ▪ HEHS ▪ PEHS ▪ REHS	**EHS**	
	EIDE	EIDER
DEIDER	**EIDER**	EIDERS
	EIDERDOWN	EIDERDOWNS
	EIDETIC	EIDETICS
	EIDOGRAPH	EIDOGRAPHS
	EIDOLON	EIDOLONS
	EIGENMODE	EIGENMODES
	EIGENTONE	EIGENTONES
HEIGHT ▪ KEIGHT ▪ WEIGHT	**EIGHT**	EIGHTH ▪ EIGHTS ▪ EIGHTY
	EIGHTBALL	EIGHTBALLS
	EIGHTEEN –	EIGHTEENS
	EIGHTFOIL	EIGHTFOILS
HEIGHTH	**EIGHTH**	EIGHTHS
HEIGHTHS	**EIGHTHS**	
	EIGHTIETH	EIGHTIETHS
HEIGHTS ▪ WEIGHTS	**EIGHTS**	
	EIGHTSOME	EIGHTSOMES
	EIGHTVO	EIGHTVOS
WEIGHTY	**EIGHTY**	
BEIGNE	**EIGNE**	
REIK ▪ SEIK	**EIK**	EIKS
	EIKON	EIKONS
REIKS	**EIKS**	
	EILD	EILDS
	EILDING	EILDINGS
SEINE	**EINE**	
	EINKORN	EINKORNS
	EINSTEIN	EINSTEINS
	EIRACK	EIRACKS
	EIRENICON	EIRENICONS
	EISEL	EISELL ▪ EISELS
	EISELL	EISELLS
LEISH	**EISH**	
	EISWEIN	EISWEINS
NEITHER	**EITHER**	
	EJACULATE	EJACULATED ▪ EJACULATES
DEJECT ▪ REJECT	**EJECT**	EJECTA ▪ EJECTS
DEJECTA	**EJECTA**	
REJECTABLE	**EJECTABLE**	
DEJECTED ▪ REJECTED	**EJECTED**	
DEJECTING ▪ REJECTING	**EJECTING**	
DEJECTION ▪ REJECTION	**EJECTION**	EJECTIONS
DEJECTIONS ▪ REJECTIONS	**EJECTIONS**	
REJECTIVE	**EJECTIVE**	EJECTIVES
	EJECTMENT	EJECTMENTS
REJECTOR	**EJECTOR**	EJECTORS
REJECTORS	**EJECTORS**	
DEJECTS ▪ REJECTS	**EJECTS**	
DEKE ▪ LEKE ▪ PEKE ▪ REKE	**EKE**	EKED ▪ EKES
DEKED ▪ REKED	**EKED**	
DEKES ▪ PEKES ▪ REKES	**EKES**	
DEKING ▪ REKING	**EKING**	
	EKISTIC	EKISTICS

FRONT HOOK	ROOT WORD	END HOOK
MEKKA	**EKKA**	EKKAS
MEKKAS	**EKKAS**	
	EKLOGITE	EKLOGITES
	EKPWELE	EKPWELES
	EKTEXINE	EKTEXINES
BEL = CEL = DEL = EEL = GEL = MEL = SEL TEL = ZEL	**EL**	ELD = ELF = ELK = ELL = ELM = ELS = ELT
	ELABORATE	ELABORATED = ELABORATES
	ELAEOLITE	ELAEOLITES
	ELAIN	ELAINS
	ELAIOSOME	ELAIOSOMES
	ELAN	ELAND = ELANS
	ELANCE	ELANCED = ELANCES
RELAND	**ELAND**	ELANDS
RELANDS	**ELANDS**	
	ELANET	ELANETS
	ELAPID	ELAPIDS
DELAPSE = RELAPSE	**ELAPSE**	ELAPSED = ELAPSES
DELAPSED = RELAPSED	**ELAPSED**	
DELAPSES = RELAPSES	**ELAPSES**	
DELAPSING = RELAPSING	**ELAPSING**	
	ELASTANCE	ELASTANCES
	ELASTANE	ELASTANES
	ELASTASE	ELASTASES
GELASTIC	**ELASTIC**	ELASTICS
	ELASTIN	ELASTINS
	ELASTOMER	ELASTOMERS
BELATE = DELATE = GELATE = RELATE = VELATE	**ELATE**	ELATED = ELATER = ELATES
BELATED = DELATED = GELATED = RELATED = VELATED	**ELATED**	
BELATEDLY = RELATEDLY	**ELATEDLY**	
RELATER	**ELATER**	ELATERS
	ELATERID	ELATERIDS
	ELATERIN	ELATERINS
	ELATERITE	ELATERITES
	ELATERIUM	ELATERIUMS
RELATERS	**ELATERS**	
BELATES = DELATES = GELATES = RELATES	**ELATES**	
BELATING = DELATING = GELATING = RELATING	**ELATING**	
DELATION = GELATION = RELATION	**ELATION**	ELATIONS
DELATIONS = GELATIONS = RELATIONS	**ELATIONS**	
RELATIVE	**ELATIVE**	ELATIVES
RELATIVES	**ELATIVES**	
	ELBOW	ELBOWS
	ELBOWROOM	ELBOWROOMS
	ELCHEE	ELCHEES
	ELCHI	ELCHIS
GELD = HELD = MELD = SELD = TELD = VELD WELD = YELD	**ELD**	ELDS
GELDER = MELDER = WELDER	**ELDER**	ELDERS
	ELDERCARE	ELDERCARES
GELDERS = MELDERS = WELDERS	**ELDERS**	
	ELDERSHIP	ELDERSHIPS
	ELDIN	ELDING = ELDINS
GELDING = MELDING = WELDING	**ELDING**	ELDINGS
GELDINGS = WELDINGS	**ELDINGS**	
	ELDORADO	ELDORADOS
GELDS = MELDS = VELDS = WELDS	**ELDS**	
SELECT	**ELECT**	ELECTS
DELECTABLE = SELECTABLE	**ELECTABLE**	
SELECTED	**ELECTED**	
SELECTEE	**ELECTEE**	ELECTEES
SELECTEES	**ELECTEES**	
SELECTING	**ELECTING**	
SELECTION	**ELECTION**	ELECTIONS
SELECTIONS	**ELECTIONS**	
SELECTIVE	**ELECTIVE**	ELECTIVES
SELECTOR	**ELECTOR**	ELECTORS
SELECTORS	**ELECTORS**	
	ELECTRET	ELECTRETS

FRONT HOOK	ROOT WORD	END HOOK
	ELECTRIC	ELECTRICS
	ELECTRISE	ELECTRISED • ELECTRISES
	ELECTRIZE	ELECTRIZED • ELECTRIZES
	ELECTRO	ELECTRON • ELECTROS
	ELECTRODE	ELECTRODES
	ELECTRON	ELECTRONS
	ELECTRUM	ELECTRUMS
SELECTS	**ELECTS**	
	ELEDOISIN	ELEDOISINS
	ELEGANCE	ELEGANCES
	ELEGIAC	ELEGIACS
	ELEGIAST	ELEGIASTS
	ELEGISE	ELEGISED • ELEGISES
	ELEGIST	ELEGISTS
	ELEGIT	ELEGITS
	ELEGIZE	ELEGIZED • ELEGIZES
	ELEMENT	ELEMENTS
	ELEMENTAL	ELEMENTALS
	ELEMI	ELEMIS
	ELENCH	ELENCHI • ELENCHS
	ELENCHI	ELENCHIC
	ELEOPTENE	ELEOPTENES
	ELEPHANT	ELEPHANTS
	ELEVATE	ELEVATED • ELEVATES
	ELEVATED	ELEVATEDS
	ELEVATION	ELEVATIONS
	ELEVATOR	ELEVATORS • ELEVATORY
	ELEVEN	ELEVENS
	ELEVENTH	ELEVENTHS
	ELEVON	ELEVONS
DELF • PELF • SELF	**ELF**	ELFS
SELFED	**ELFED**	
SELFHOOD	**ELFHOOD**	ELFHOODS
SELFHOODS	**ELFHOODS**	
	ELFIN	ELFING • ELFINS
SELFING	**ELFING**	
SELFISH	**ELFISH**	
SELFISHLY	**ELFISHLY**	
	ELFLAND	ELFLANDS
	ELFLOCK	ELFLOCKS
DELFS • PELFS • SELFS	**ELFS**	
	ELIAD	ELIADS
	ELICHE	ELICHES
	ELICIT	ELICITS
	ELICITOR	ELICITORS
RELIDE	**ELIDE**	ELIDED • ELIDES
	ELIGIBLE	ELIGIBLES
	ELIMINANT	ELIMINANTS
	ELIMINATE	ELIMINATED • ELIMINATES
	ELINT	ELINTS
	ELISION	ELISIONS
PELITE	**ELITE**	ELITES
PELITES • VELITES	**ELITES**	
	ELITISM	ELITISMS
	ELITIST	ELITISTS
	ELIXIR	ELIXIRS
WELK • YELK	**ELK**	ELKS
	ELKHOUND	ELKHOUNDS
WELKS • YELKS	**ELKS**	
BELL • CELL • DELL • FELL • HELL • JELL KELL • MELL • PELL • SELL • TELL • VELL WELL • YELL	**ELL**	ELLS
	ELLIPSE	ELLIPSES
	ELLIPSOID	ELLIPSOIDS
BELLS • CELLS • DELLS • FELLS • HELLS JELLS • KELLS • MELLS • PELLS • SELLS TELLS • VELLS • WELLS • YELLS	**ELLS**	
	ELLWAND	ELLWANDS
HELM • YELM	**ELM**	ELMS • ELMY

FRONT HOOK	ROOT WORD	END HOOK
HELMS · YELMS	**ELMS**	
	ELMWOOD	ELMWOODS
	ELOCUTE	ELOCUTED · ELOCUTES
	ELOCUTION	ELOCUTIONS
	ELODEA	ELODEAS
	ELOGE	ELOGES
	ELOGIST	ELOGISTS
	ELOGIUM	ELOGIUMS
	ELOIGN	ELOIGNS
	ELOIGNER	ELOIGNERS
	ELOIN	ELOINS
	ELOINER	ELOINERS
	ELOINMENT	ELOINMENTS
	ELONGATE	ELONGATED · ELONGATES
DELOPE	**ELOPE**	ELOPED · ELOPER · ELOPES
DELOPED	**ELOPED**	
	ELOPEMENT	ELOPEMENTS
	ELOPER	ELOPERS
DELOPES	**ELOPES**	
DELOPING	**ELOPING**	
	ELOQUENCE	ELOQUENCES
	ELPEE	ELPEES
BELS · CELS · DELS · EELS · GELS · MELS	**ELS**	ELSE
SELS · TELS · ZELS		
	ELSHIN	ELSHINS
	ELSIN	ELSINS
BELT · CELT · DELT · FELT · GELT · KELT	**ELT**	ELTS
MELT · PELT · TELT · WELT · YELT		
	ELTCHI	ELTCHIS
BELTS · CELTS · DELTS · FELTS · GELTS	**ELTS**	
KELTS · MELTS · PELTS · WELTS · YELTS		
	ELUANT	ELUANTS
	ELUATE	ELUATES
	ELUCIDATE	ELUCIDATED · ELUCIDATES
DELUDE	**ELUDE**	ELUDED · ELUDER · ELUDES
DELUDED	**ELUDED**	
DELUDER	**ELUDER**	ELUDERS
DELUDERS	**ELUDERS**	
DELUDES	**ELUDES**	
DELUDING	**ELUDING**	
	ELUENT	ELUENTS
DELUSION	**ELUSION**	ELUSIONS
DELUSIONS	**ELUSIONS**	
DELUSIVE	**ELUSIVE**	
DELUSIVELY	**ELUSIVELY**	
DELUSORY	**ELUSORY**	
	ELUTE	ELUTED · ELUTES
	ELUTION	ELUTIONS
	ELUTOR	ELUTORS
	ELUTRIATE	ELUTRIATED · ELUTRIATES
	ELUVIA	ELUVIAL
	ELUVIATE	ELUVIATED · ELUVIATES
	ELUVIUM	ELUVIUMS
	ELVAN	ELVANS
	ELVANITE	ELVANITES
DELVER	**ELVER**	ELVERS
DELVERS	**ELVERS**	
DELVES · HELVES · PELVES · SELVES	**ELVES**	
	ELYTRA	ELYTRAL
FEM · GEM · HEM · MEM · REM · WEM	**EM**	EME · EMO · EMS · EMU
	EMACIATE	EMACIATED · EMACIATES
REMAIL	**EMAIL**	EMAILS
REMAILED	**EMAILED**	
REMAILING	**EMAILING**	
REMAILS	**EMAILS**	
	EMANATE	EMANATED · EMANATES
	EMANATION	EMANATIONS
	EMANATIST	EMANATISTS
	EMANATOR	EMANATORS · EMANATORY

FRONT HOOK	ROOT WORD	END HOOK
	EMBACE	EMBACES
	EMBAIL	EMBAILS
	EMBALE	EMBALED · EMBALES
	EMBALL	EMBALLS
	EMBALLING	EMBALLINGS
	EMBALM	EMBALMS
	EMBALMER	EMBALMERS
	EMBALMING	EMBALMINGS
	EMBANK	EMBANKS
	EMBANKER	EMBANKERS
	EMBAR	EMBARK · EMBARS
	EMBARK	EMBARKS
	EMBARRING	EMBARRINGS
	EMBASE	EMBASED · EMBASES
	EMBASSADE	EMBASSADES
	EMBASSAGE	EMBASSAGES
	EMBATHE	EMBATHED · EMBATHES
	EMBATTLE	EMBATTLED · EMBATTLES
	EMBAY	EMBAYS
	EMBAYMENT	EMBAYMENTS
KEMBED	EMBED	EMBEDS
	EMBEDDING	EMBEDDINGS
	EMBEDMENT	EMBEDMENTS
MEMBER	EMBER	EMBERS
MEMBERS	EMBERS	
	EMBEZZLE	EMBEZZLED · EMBEZZLER · EMBEZZLES
	EMBEZZLER	EMBEZZLERS
	EMBITTER	EMBITTERS
	EMBLAZE	EMBLAZED · EMBLAZER · EMBLAZES
	EMBLAZER	EMBLAZERS
	EMBLAZON	EMBLAZONS
	EMBLEM	EMBLEMA · EMBLEMS
	EMBLEMISE	EMBLEMISED · EMBLEMISES
	EMBLEMIZE	EMBLEMIZED · EMBLEMIZES
	EMBLIC	EMBLICS
	EMBLOOM	EMBLOOMS
	EMBLOSSOM	EMBLOSSOMS
	EMBODIER	EMBODIERS
	EMBOG	EMBOGS
	EMBOGUE	EMBOGUED · EMBOGUES
	EMBOIL	EMBOILS
	EMBOLDEN	EMBOLDENS
	EMBOLI	EMBOLIC
	EMBOLISE	EMBOLISED · EMBOLISES
	EMBOLISM	EMBOLISMS
	EMBOLIZE	EMBOLIZED · EMBOLIZES
	EMBORDER	EMBORDERS
	EMBOSCATA	EMBOSCATAS
	EMBOSK	EMBOSKS
	EMBOSOM	EMBOSOMS
	EMBOSSER	EMBOSSERS
	EMBOUND	EMBOUNDS
	EMBOW	EMBOWS
	EMBOWEL	EMBOWELS
	EMBOWER	EMBOWERS
	EMBOWMENT	EMBOWMENTS
	EMBRACE	EMBRACED · EMBRACER · EMBRACES
	EMBRACEOR	EMBRACEORS
	EMBRACER	EMBRACERS · EMBRACERY
	EMBRAID	EMBRAIDS
	EMBRANGLE	EMBRANGLED · EMBRANGLES
	EMBRASOR	EMBRASORS
	EMBRASURE	EMBRASURED · EMBRASURES
	EMBRAVE	EMBRAVED · EMBRAVES
	EMBRAZURE	EMBRAZURES
	EMBREAD	EMBREADS
	EMBREATHE	EMBREATHED · EMBREATHES
	EMBRITTLE	EMBRITTLED · EMBRITTLES
	EMBROCATE	EMBROCATED · EMBROCATES

FRONT HOOK	ROOT WORD	END HOOK
	EMBROGLIO	EMBROGLIOS
	EMBROIDER	EMBROIDERS · EMBROIDERY
	EMBROIL	EMBROILS
	EMBROILER	EMBROILERS
	EMBROWN	EMBROWNS
	EMBRUE	EMBRUED · EMBRUES
	EMBRUTE	EMBRUTED · EMBRUTES
	EMBRYO	EMBRYON · EMBRYOS
	EMBRYOID	EMBRYOIDS
	EMBRYON	EMBRYONS
	EMBUS	EMBUSY
	EMBUSQUE	EMBUSQUES
	EMCEE	EMCEED · EMCEES
DEME · FEME · HEME · LEME · MEME · SEME · TEME	**EME**	EMES · EMEU
	EMEER	EMEERS
	EMEERATE	EMEERATES
REMEND	**EMEND**	EMENDS
	EMENDATE	EMENDATED · EMENDATES
	EMENDATOR	EMENDATORS · EMENDATORY
REMENDED	**EMENDED**	
	EMENDER	EMENDERS
REMENDING	**EMENDING**	
REMENDS	**EMENDS**	
	EMERALD	EMERALDS
	EMERAUDE	EMERAUDES
DEMERGE · REMERGE	**EMERGE**	EMERGED · EMERGES
DEMERGED · REMERGED	**EMERGED**	
	EMERGENCE	EMERGENCES
	EMERGENT	EMERGENTS
DEMERGES · REMERGES	**EMERGES**	
DEMERGING · REMERGING	**EMERGING**	
	EMERITA	EMERITAE · EMERITAS
	EMEROD	EMERODS
	EMEROID	EMEROIDS
DEMERSED	**EMERSED**	
DEMERSION	**EMERSION**	EMERSIONS
DEMERSIONS	**EMERSIONS**	
DEMES · FEMES · HEMES · LEMES · MEMES · SEMES · TEMES	**EMES**	
NEMESES	**EMESES**	
NEMESIS	**EMESIS**	
	EMETIC	EMETICS
MEMETICS	**EMETICS**	
	EMETIN	EMETINE · EMETINS
	EMETINE/	EMETINES
	EMEU	EMEUS
	EMEUTE	EMEUTES
DEMIC · HEMIC	**EMIC**	
	EMICATE	EMICATED · EMICATES
	EMICATION	EMICATIONS
	EMICTION	EMICTIONS
	EMIGRANT	EMIGRANTS
REMIGRATE	**EMIGRATE**	EMIGRATED · EMIGRATES
REMIGRATED	**EMIGRATED**	
REMIGRATES	**EMIGRATES**	
	EMIGRE	EMIGRES
	EMINENCE	EMINENCES
	EMIR	EMIRS
	EMIRATE	EMIRATES
DEMISSION · REMISSION	**EMISSION**	EMISSIONS
DEMISSIONS · REMISSIONS	**EMISSIONS**	
DEMISSIVE · REMISSIVE	**EMISSIVE**	
DEMIT · REMIT	**EMIT**	EMITS
DEMITS · REMITS	**EMITS**	
REMITTANCE	**EMITTANCE**	EMITTANCES
DEMITTED · REMITTED	**EMITTED**	
REMITTER	**EMITTER**	EMITTERS
REMITTERS	**EMITTERS**	

FRONT HOOK	ROOT WORD	END HOOK
DEMITTING ▪ REMITTING	**EMITTING**	
GEMMA ▪ LEMMA	**EMMA**	EMMAS
	EMMARBLE	EMMARBLED ▪ EMMARBLES
LEMMAS	**EMMAS**	
HEMMER ▪ YEMMER	**EMMER**	EMMERS
HEMMERS ▪ YEMMERS	**EMMERS**	
	EMMET	EMMETS
	EMMETROPE	EMMETROPES
	EMMEW	EMMEWS
	EMMOVE	EMMOVED ▪ EMMOVES
FEMMY ▪ GEMMY ▪ JEMMY	**EMMY**	EMMYS
DEMO ▪ MEMO	**EMO**	EMOS
	EMODIN	EMODINS
	EMOLLIATE	EMOLLIATED ▪ EMOLLIATES
	EMOLLIENT	EMOLLIENTS
	EMOLUMENT	EMOLUMENTS
	EMONGES	EMONGEST
DEMOS ▪ MEMOS	**EMOS**	
DEMOTE ▪ GEMOTE ▪ REMOTE	**EMOTE**	EMOTED ▪ EMOTER ▪ EMOTES
DEMOTED	**EMOTED**	
REMOTER	**EMOTER**	EMOTERS
DEMOTES ▪ GEMOTES ▪ REMOTES	**EMOTES**	
	EMOTICON	EMOTICONS
DEMOTING	**EMOTING**	
DEMOTION ▪ REMOTION	**EMOTION**	EMOTIONS
DEMOTIONS ▪ REMOTIONS	**EMOTIONS**	
	EMOTIVISM	EMOTIVISMS
REMOVE	**EMOVE**	EMOVED ▪ EMOVES
REMOVED	**EMOVED**	
REMOVES	**EMOVES**	
REMOVING	**EMOVING**	
	EMPACKET	EMPACKETS
	EMPAIRE	EMPAIRED ▪ EMPAIRES
	EMPALE	EMPALED ▪ EMPALER ▪ EMPALES
	EMPALER	EMPALERS
	EMPANADA	EMPANADAS
	EMPANEL	EMPANELS
	EMPARE	EMPARED ▪ EMPARES
	EMPARL	EMPARLS
	EMPART	EMPARTS
	EMPATHISE	EMPATHISED ▪ EMPATHISES
	EMPATHIST	EMPATHISTS
	EMPATHIZE	EMPATHIZED ▪ EMPATHIZES
	EMPATRON	EMPATRONS
	EMPAYRE	EMPAYRED ▪ EMPAYRES
	EMPENNAGE	EMPENNAGES
	EMPEOPLE	EMPEOPLED ▪ EMPEOPLES
	EMPERCE	EMPERCED ▪ EMPERCES
	EMPERISE	EMPERISED ▪ EMPERISES
	EMPERIZE	EMPERIZED ▪ EMPERIZES
	EMPEROR	EMPERORS
	EMPHASIS	EMPHASISE
	EMPHASISE	EMPHASISED ▪ EMPHASISES
	EMPHASIZE	EMPHASIZED ▪ EMPHASIZES
	EMPHATIC	EMPHATICS
	EMPHYSEMA	EMPHYSEMAS
	EMPIERCE	EMPIERCED ▪ EMPIERCES
	EMPIRE	EMPIRES
	EMPIRIC	EMPIRICS
	EMPLACE	EMPLACED ▪ EMPLACES
	EMPLANE	EMPLANED ▪ EMPLANES
	EMPLASTER	EMPLASTERS
	EMPLASTIC	EMPLASTICS
	EMPLECTON	EMPLECTONS
	EMPLECTUM	EMPLECTUMS
	EMPLONGE	EMPLONGED ▪ EMPLONGES
	EMPLOY	EMPLOYE ▪ EMPLOYS
	EMPLOYE	EMPLOYED ▪ EMPLOYEE ▪ EMPLOYER EMPLOYES

E

E

FRONT HOOK	ROOT WORD	END HOOK
	EMPLOYEE	EMPLOYEES
	EMPLOYER	EMPLOYERS
	EMPLUME	EMPLUMED ▪ EMPLUMES
	EMPOISON	EMPOISONS
	EMPOLDER	EMPOLDERS
	EMPORIUM	EMPORIUMS
	EMPOWER	EMPOWERS
	EMPRESS	EMPRESSE
	EMPRESSE	EMPRESSES
	EMPRISE	EMPRISES
	EMPRIZE	EMPRIZES
DEMPT ▪ KEMPT ▪ NEMPT ▪ TEMPT ▪ TEMPTED	EMPT	EMPTS ▪ EMPTY
	EMPTED	
	EMPTIER	EMPTIERS
	EMPTIES	EMPTIEST
TEMPTING ▪ TEMPTINGS	EMPTING	EMPTINGS
	EMPTINGS	
	EMPTION	EMPTIONS
TEMPTS	EMPTS	
	EMPTYING	EMPTYINGS
	EMPURPLE	EMPURPLED ▪ EMPURPLES
	EMPUSA	EMPUSAS
	EMPUSE	EMPUSES
	EMPYEMA	EMPYEMAS
	EMPYREAN	EMPYREANS
FEMS ▪ GEMS ▪ HEMS ▪ MEMS ▪ REMS ▪ TEMS ▪ WEMS	EMS	
	EMU	EMUS
	EMULATE	EMULATED ▪ EMULATES
	EMULATION	EMULATIONS
	EMULATOR	EMULATORS
AEMULE	EMULE	EMULED ▪ EMULES
AEMULED	EMULED	
AEMULES	EMULES	
	EMULGE	EMULGED ▪ EMULGES
	EMULGENCE	EMULGENCES
AEMULING	EMULING	
DEMULSIFY	EMULSIFY	
	EMULSIN	EMULSINS
	EMULSION	EMULSIONS
	EMULSOID	EMULSOIDS
	EMULSOR	EMULSORS
	EMUNCTION	EMUNCTIONS
	EMUNGE	EMUNGED ▪ EMUNGES
DEMURE	EMURE	EMURED ▪ EMURES
DEMURED	EMURED	
DEMURES ▪ LEMURES	EMURES	
DEMURING	EMURING	
	EMYD	EMYDE ▪ EMYDS
	EMYDE	EMYDES
BEN ▪ DEN ▪ EEN ▪ FEN ▪ GEN ▪ HEN ▪ KEN ▪ MEN ▪ PEN ▪ REN ▪ SEN ▪ TEN ▪ WEN ▪ YEN	EN	END ▪ ENE ▪ ENG ▪ ENS
TENABLE	ENABLE	ENABLED ▪ ENABLER ▪ ENABLES
	ENABLER	ENABLERS
	ENACT	ENACTS
	ENACTION	ENACTIONS
	ENACTMENT	ENACTMENTS
	ENACTOR	ENACTORS ▪ ENACTORY
	ENACTURE	ENACTURES
	ENALAPRIL	ENALAPRILS
	ENALLAGE	ENALLAGES
	ENAMEL	ENAMELS
	ENAMELER	ENAMELERS
	ENAMELIST	ENAMELISTS
	ENAMELLER	ENAMELLERS
	ENAMINE	ENAMINES
	ENAMOR	ENAMORS
	ENAMORADO	ENAMORADOS
	ENAMOUR	ENAMOURS
MENARCHES	ENARCHES	

FRONT HOOK	ROOT WORD	END HOOK
	ENARM	ENARMS
SENATE	**ENATE**	ENATES
PENATES ▪ SENATES	**ENATES**	
VENATIC	**ENATIC**	
VENATION	**ENATION**	ENATIONS
VENATIONS	**ENATIONS**	
	ENCAENIA	ENCAENIAS
	ENCAGE	ENCAGED ▪ ENCAGES
	ENCALM	ENCALMS
	ENCAMP	ENCAMPS
	ENCAPSULE	ENCAPSULED ▪ ENCAPSULES
	ENCASE	ENCASED ▪ ENCASES
	ENCAUSTIC	ENCAUSTICS
	ENCAVE	ENCAVED ▪ ENCAVES
	ENCEINTE	ENCEINTES
	ENCHAFE	ENCHAFED ▪ ENCHAFES
	ENCHAIN	ENCHAINS
PENCHANT	**ENCHANT**	ENCHANTS
	ENCHANTER	ENCHANTERS
PENCHANTS	**ENCHANTS**	
	ENCHARGE	ENCHARGED ▪ ENCHARGES
	ENCHARM	ENCHARMS
	ENCHASE	ENCHASED ▪ ENCHASER ▪ ENCHASES
	ENCHASER	ENCHASERS
	ENCHEASON	ENCHEASONS
	ENCHEER	ENCHEERS
	ENCHILADA	ENCHILADAS
	ENCIERRO	ENCIERROS
	ENCINA	ENCINAL ▪ ENCINAS
	ENCIPHER	ENCIPHERS
	ENCIRCLE	ENCIRCLED ▪ ENCIRCLES
	ENCLASP	ENCLASPS
	ENCLAVE	ENCLAVED ▪ ENCLAVES
	ENCLITIC	ENCLITICS
	ENCLOSE	ENCLOSED ▪ ENCLOSER ▪ ENCLOSES
	ENCLOSER	ENCLOSERS
	ENCLOSURE	ENCLOSURES
	ENCLOTHE	ENCLOTHED ▪ ENCLOTHES
	ENCLOUD	ENCLOUDS
	ENCODE	ENCODED ▪ ENCODER ▪ ENCODES
	ENCODER	ENCODERS
	ENCOLOUR	ENCOLOURS
	ENCOLPION	ENCOLPIONS
	ENCOLPIUM	ENCOLPIUMS
	ENCOLURE	ENCOLURES
	ENCOMIAST	ENCOMIASTS
	ENCOMIUM	ENCOMIUMS
	ENCORE	ENCORED ▪ ENCORES
RENCOUNTER	**ENCOUNTER**	ENCOUNTERS
	ENCOURAGE	ENCOURAGED ▪ ENCOURAGER ▪ ENCOURAGES
	ENCRADLE	ENCRADLED ▪ ENCRADLES
	ENCREASE	ENCREASED ▪ ENCREASES
	ENCRIMSON	ENCRIMSONS
	ENCRINITE	ENCRINITES
	ENCRUST	ENCRUSTS
	ENCRYPT	ENCRYPTS
	ENCUMBER	ENCUMBERS
	ENCURTAIN	ENCURTAINS
	ENCYCLIC	ENCYCLICS
	ENCYST	ENCYSTS
BEND ▪ FEND ▪ HEND ▪ LEND ▪ MEND ▪ PEND REND ▪ SEND ▪ TEND ▪ VEND ▪ WEND	**END**	ENDS
	ENDAMAGE	ENDAMAGED ▪ ENDAMAGES
	ENDAMEBA	ENDAMEBAE ▪ ENDAMEBAS
	ENDAMOEBA	ENDAMOEBAE ▪ ENDAMOEBAS
	ENDANGER	ENDANGERS
	ENDARCH	ENDARCHY
	ENDART	ENDARTS
	ENDBRAIN	ENDBRAINS

257

FRONT HOOK	ROOT WORD	END HOOK
	ENDEAR	ENDEARS
	ENDEAVOR	ENDEAVORS
	ENDEAVOUR	ENDEAVOURS
HENDECAGON	ENDECAGON	ENDECAGONS
BENDED · FENDED · HENDED · MENDED PENDED · RENDED · SENDED · TENDED VENDED · WENDED	ENDED	
	ENDEMIC	ENDEMICS
	ENDEMISM	ENDEMISMS
	ENDENIZEN	ENDENIZENS
BENDER · FENDER · GENDER · LENDER MENDER · RENDER · SENDER · TENDER VENDER	ENDER	ENDERS
	ENDERON	ENDERONS
BENDERS · FENDERS · GENDERS · LENDERS MENDERS · RENDERS · SENDERS · TENDERS VENDERS	ENDERS	
	ENDEW	ENDEWS
	ENDEXINE	ENDEXINES
	ENDGAME	ENDGAMES
BENDING · FENDING · HENDING · LENDING MENDING · PENDING · RENDING · SENDING TENDING · VENDING · WENDING	ENDING	ENDINGS
BENDINGS · LENDINGS · MENDINGS SENDINGS · VENDINGS	ENDINGS	
	ENDIRON	ENDIRONS
	ENDITE	ENDITED · ENDITES
	ENDIVE	ENDIVES
	ENDLEAF	ENDLEAFS
	ENDNOTE	ENDNOTES
	ENDOBLAST	ENDOBLASTS
	ENDOCARP	ENDOCARPS
	ENDOCAST	ENDOCASTS
	ENDOCRINE	ENDOCRINES
	ENDODERM	ENDODERMS
	ENDOGEN	ENDOGENS · ENDOGENY
	ENDOLYMPH	ENDOLYMPHS
	ENDOMORPH	ENDOMORPHS · ENDOMORPHY
	ENDOPHYTE	ENDOPHYTES
	ENDOPLASM	ENDOPLASMS
	ENDOPOD	ENDOPODS
	ENDOPROCT	ENDOPROCTS
	ENDORPHIN	ENDORPHINS
	ENDORSE	ENDORSED · ENDORSEE · ENDORSER · ENDORSES
	ENDORSEE	ENDORSEES
	ENDORSER	ENDORSERS
	ENDORSOR	ENDORSORS
	ENDOSARC	ENDOSARCS
	ENDOSCOPE	ENDOSCOPES
	ENDOSMOS	ENDOSMOSE
	ENDOSMOSE	ENDOSMOSES
	ENDOSOME	ENDOSOMES
	ENDOSPERM	ENDOSPERMS
	ENDOSPORE	ENDOSPORES
	ENDOSTEA	ENDOSTEAL
	ENDOSTYLE	ENDOSTYLES
	ENDOTHERM	ENDOTHERMS · ENDOTHERMY
	ENDOTOXIN	ENDOTOXINS
	ENDOW	ENDOWS
	ENDOWER	ENDOWERS
	ENDOWMENT	ENDOWMENTS
	ENDPAPER	ENDPAPERS
	ENDPLATE	ENDPLATES
	ENDPLAY	ENDPLAYS
	ENDPOINT	ENDPOINTS
	ENDRIN	ENDRINS
BENDS · FENDS · HENDS · LENDS · MENDS PENDS · RENDS · SENDS · TENDS · VENDS WENDS	ENDS	

FRONT HOOK	ROOT WORD	END HOOK
	ENDSHIP	ENDSHIPS
VENDUE	ENDUE	ENDUED ▪ ENDUES
VENDUES	ENDUES	
	ENDUNGEON	ENDUNGEONS
	ENDURANCE	ENDURANCES
	ENDURE	ENDURED ▪ ENDURER ▪ ENDURES
	ENDURER	ENDURERS
	ENDURO	ENDUROS
BENDWAYS	ENDWAYS	
BENDWISE	ENDWISE	
BENE ▪ DENE ▪ GENE ▪ MENE ▪ NENE ▪ PENE SENE ▪ TENE	ENE	ENES ▪ ENEW
	ENEMA	ENEMAS
	ENERGETIC	ENERGETICS
	ENERGID	ENERGIDS
	ENERGISE	ENERGISED ▪ ENERGISER ▪ ENERGISES
	ENERGISER	ENERGISERS
	ENERGIZE	ENERGIZED ▪ ENERGIZER ▪ ENERGIZES
	ENERGIZER	ENERGIZERS
	ENERGUMEN	ENERGUMENS
DENERVATE	ENERVATE	ENERVATED ▪ ENERVATES
DENERVATED	ENERVATED	
DENERVATES	ENERVATES	
	ENERVATOR	ENERVATORS
	ENERVE	ENERVED ▪ ENERVES
BENES ▪ DENES ▪ GENES ▪ LENES ▪ MENES NENES ▪ PENES ▪ TENES	ENES	
RENEW	ENEW	ENEWS
RENEWED	ENEWED	
RENEWING	ENEWING	
RENEWS	ENEWS	
	ENFACE	ENFACED ▪ ENFACES
	ENFANT	ENFANTS
	ENFEEBLE	ENFEEBLED ▪ ENFEEBLER ▪ ENFEEBLES
	ENFEEBLER	ENFEEBLERS
	ENFELON	ENFELONS
	ENFEOFF	ENFEOFFS
	ENFETTER	ENFETTERS
	ENFEVER	ENFEVERS
	ENFIERCE	ENFIERCED ▪ ENFIERCES
	ENFILADE	ENFILADED ▪ ENFILADES
	ENFIRE	ENFIRED ▪ ENFIRES
	ENFLAME	ENFLAMED ▪ ENFLAMES
	ENFLOWER	ENFLOWERS
PENFOLD ▪ TENFOLD	ENFOLD	ENFOLDS
	ENFOLDER	ENFOLDERS
PENFOLDS ▪ TENFOLDS	ENFOLDS	
RENFORCE	ENFORCE	ENFORCED ▪ ENFORCER ▪ ENFORCES
RENFORCED	ENFORCED	
	ENFORCER	ENFORCERS
RENFORCES	ENFORCES	
RENFORCING	ENFORCING	
	ENFOREST	ENFORESTS
	ENFORM	ENFORMS
	ENFRAME	ENFRAMED ▪ ENFRAMES
	ENFREE	ENFREED ▪ ENFREES
	ENFREEDOM	ENFREEDOMS
	ENFREEZE	ENFREEZES
	ENFROZE	ENFROZEN
LENG ▪ MENG	ENG	ENGS
	ENGAGE	ENGAGED ▪ ENGAGEE ▪ ENGAGER ▪ ENGAGES
	ENGAGER	ENGAGERS
	ENGAOL	ENGAOLS
	ENGARLAND	ENGARLANDS
	ENGENDER	ENGENDERS
	ENGENDURE	ENGENDURES
	ENGILD	ENGILDS
	ENGINE	ENGINED ▪ ENGINER ▪ ENGINES
	ENGINEER	ENGINEERS

FRONT HOOK	ROOT WORD	END HOOK
	ENGINER	ENGINERS · ENGINERY
	ENGIRD	ENGIRDS
	ENGIRDLE	ENGIRDLED · ENGIRDLES
	ENGISCOPE	ENGISCOPES
	ENGLOBE	ENGLOBED · ENGLOBES
	ENGLOOM	ENGLOOMS
	ENGLUT	ENGLUTS
	ENGOBE	ENGOBES
	ENGORE	ENGORED · ENGORES
	ENGORGE	ENGORGED · ENGORGES
	ENGOUMENT	ENGOUMENTS
	ENGRACE	ENGRACED · ENGRACES
	ENGRAFF	ENGRAFFS
	ENGRAFT	ENGRAFTS
	ENGRAIL	ENGRAILS
	ENGRAIN	ENGRAINS
	ENGRAINER	ENGRAINERS
	ENGRAM	ENGRAMS
	ENGRAMMA	ENGRAMMAS
	ENGRAMME	ENGRAMMES
	ENGRASP	ENGRASPS
	ENGRAVE	ENGRAVED · ENGRAVEN · ENGRAVER ENGRAVES
	ENGRAVER	ENGRAVERS · ENGRAVERY
	ENGRAVING	ENGRAVINGS
	ENGRENAGE	ENGRENAGES
	ENGRIEVE	ENGRIEVED · ENGRIEVES
	ENGROOVE	ENGROOVED · ENGROOVES
	ENGROSSER	ENGROSSERS
LENGS · MENGS	**ENGS**	
	ENGUARD	ENGUARDS
	ENGULF	ENGULFS
	ENGULPH	ENGULPHS
	ENGYSCOPE	ENGYSCOPES
	ENHALO	ENHALOS
	ENHANCE	ENHANCED · ENHANCER · ENHANCES
	ENHANCER	ENHANCERS
	ENHEARSE	ENHEARSED · ENHEARSES
	ENHEARTEN	ENHEARTENS
	ENHUNGER	ENHUNGERS
	ENHYDRITE	ENHYDRITES
	ENIAC	ENIACS
	ENIGMA	ENIGMAS
	ENISLE	ENISLED · ENISLES
	ENJAMB	ENJAMBS
	ENJOIN	ENJOINS
	ENJOINDER	ENJOINDERS
	ENJOINER	ENJOINERS
	ENJOY	ENJOYS
	ENJOYER	ENJOYERS
	ENJOYMENT	ENJOYMENTS
	ENKERNEL	ENKERNELS
	ENKINDLE	ENKINDLED · ENKINDLER · ENKINDLES
	ENKINDLER	ENKINDLERS
	ENLACE	ENLACED · ENLACES
	ENLARD	ENLARDS
	ENLARGE	ENLARGED · ENLARGEN · ENLARGER ENLARGES
	ENLARGEN	ENLARGENS
	ENLARGER	ENLARGERS
PENLIGHT	**ENLIGHT**	ENLIGHTS
	ENLIGHTEN	ENLIGHTENS
PENLIGHTS	**ENLIGHTS**	
	ENLINK	ENLINKS
	ENLIST	ENLISTS
	ENLISTEE	ENLISTEES
	ENLISTER	ENLISTERS
	ENLIVEN	ENLIVENS
	ENLIVENER	ENLIVENERS

FRONT HOOK	ROOT WORD	END HOOK
GENLOCK	ENLOCK	ENLOCKS
GENLOCKS	ENLOCKS	
	ENLUMINE	ENLUMINED = ENLUMINES
	ENMEW	ENMEWS
	ENMOVE	ENMOVED = ENMOVES
	ENNAGE	ENNAGES
	ENNEAD	ENNEADS
	ENNEAGON	ENNEAGONS
	ENNOBLE	ENNOBLED = ENNOBLER = ENNOBLES
	ENNOBLER	ENNOBLERS
	ENNOG	ENNOGS
	ENNUI	ENNUIS
	ENNUYE	ENNUYED = ENNUYEE
	ENOKI	ENOKIS
	ENOKIDAKE	ENOKIDAKES
	ENOKITAKE	ENOKITAKES
	ENOL	ENOLS
	ENOLASE	ENOLASES
MENOLOGIES = OENOLOGIES = PENOLOGIES VENOLOGIES	ENOLOGIES	
OENOLOGIST = PENOLOGIST	ENOLOGIST	ENOLOGISTS
MENOLOGY = OENOLOGY = PENOLOGY VENOLOGY	ENOLOGY	
OENOPHILE = XENOPHILE	ENOPHILE	ENOPHILES
OENOPHILES = XENOPHILES	ENOPHILES	
KENOSES	ENOSES	
KENOSIS	ENOSIS	
KENOSISES	ENOSISES	
	ENOUGH	ENOUGHS
DENOUNCE = RENOUNCE	ENOUNCE	ENOUNCED = ENOUNCES
DENOUNCED = RENOUNCED	ENOUNCED	
DENOUNCES = RENOUNCES	ENOUNCES	
DENOUNCING = RENOUNCING	ENOUNCING	
	ENOW	ENOWS
	ENPLANE	ENPLANED = ENPLANES
	ENPRINT	ENPRINTS
	ENQUIRE	ENQUIRED = ENQUIRER = ENQUIRES
	ENQUIRER	ENQUIRERS
	ENRACE	ENRACED = ENRACES
	ENRAGE	ENRAGED = ENRAGES
	ENRANCKLE	ENRANCKLED = ENRANCKLES
	ENRANGE	ENRANGED = ENRANGES
	ENRANK	ENRANKS
	ENRAPTURE	ENRAPTURED = ENRAPTURES
	ENRAUNGE	ENRAUNGED = ENRAUNGES
	ENRHEUM	ENRHEUMS
	ENRICHER	ENRICHERS
	ENRING	ENRINGS
	ENROBE	ENROBED = ENROBER = ENROBES
	ENROBER	ENROBERS
	ENROL	ENROLL = ENROLS
	ENROLL	ENROLLS
	ENROLLEE	ENROLLEES
	ENROLLER	ENROLLERS
	ENROLMENT	ENROLMENTS
	ENROOT	ENROOTS
	ENROUGH	ENROUGHS
	ENROUND	ENROUNDS
BENS = CENS = DENS = FENS = GENS = HENS KENS = LENS = PENS = RENS = SENS = TENS WENS = YENS	ENS	
	ENSAMPLE	ENSAMPLED = ENSAMPLES
SENSATE	ENSATE	
	ENSCONCE	ENSCONCED = ENSCONCES
	ENSCROLL	ENSCROLLS
	ENSEAL	ENSEALS
	ENSEAM	ENSEAMS
	ENSEAR	ENSEARS
	ENSEMBLE	ENSEMBLES

FRONT HOOK	ROOT WORD	END HOOK
	ENSERF	ENSERFS
	ENSEW	ENSEWS
	ENSHEATH	ENSHEATHE · ENSHEATHS
	ENSHEATHE	ENSHEATHED · ENSHEATHES
	ENSHELL	ENSHELLS
	ENSHELTER	ENSHELTERS
	ENSHIELD	ENSHIELDS
	ENSHRINE	ENSHRINED · ENSHRINEE · ENSHRINES
	ENSHRINEE	ENSHRINEES
	ENSHROUD	ENSHROUDS
	ENSIGN	ENSIGNS
	ENSILAGE	ENSILAGED · ENSILAGES
PENSILE · SENSILE · TENSILE	ENSILE	ENSILED · ENSILES
	ENSLAVE	ENSLAVED · ENSLAVER · ENSLAVES
	ENSLAVER	ENSLAVERS
	ENSNARE	ENSNARED · ENSNARER · ENSNARES
	ENSNARER	ENSNARERS
	ENSNARL	ENSNARLS
	ENSORCEL	ENSORCELL · ENSORCELS
	ENSORCELL	ENSORCELLS
	ENSOUL	ENSOULS
	ENSPHERE	ENSPHERED · ENSPHERES
	ENSTAMP	ENSTAMPS
	ENSTATITE	ENSTATITES
	ENSTEEP	ENSTEEPS
	ENSTYLE	ENSTYLED · ENSTYLES
	ENSUE	ENSUED · ENSUES
CENSURE	ENSURE	ENSURED · ENSURER · ENSURES
CENSURED	ENSURED	
CENSURER	ENSURER	ENSURERS
CENSURERS	ENSURERS	
CENSURES	ENSURES	
CENSURING	ENSURING	
	ENSWATHE	ENSWATHED · ENSWATHES
	ENSWEEP	ENSWEEPS
VENTAIL	ENTAIL	ENTAILS
	ENTAILER	ENTAILERS
VENTAILS	ENTAILS	
	ENTAME	ENTAMED · ENTAMES
	ENTAMEBA	ENTAMEBAE · ENTAMEBAS
	ENTAMOEBA	ENTAMOEBAE · ENTAMOEBAS
PENTANGLE	ENTANGLE	ENTANGLED · ENTANGLER · ENTANGLES
	ENTANGLER	ENTANGLERS
PENTANGLES	ENTANGLES	
	ENTASIA	ENTASIAS
VENTAYLE	ENTAYLE	ENTAYLED · ENTAYLES
VENTAYLES	ENTAYLES	
	ENTENDER	ENTENDERS
	ENTENTE	ENTENTES
CENTER · RENTER · TENTER · VENTER	ENTER	ENTERA · ENTERS
	ENTERA	ENTERAL
CENTERED · TENTERED	ENTERED	
	ENTERER	ENTERERS
	ENTERIC	ENTERICS
CENTERING · TENTERING	ENTERING	ENTERINGS
CENTERINGS	ENTERINGS	
	ENTERON	ENTERONS
CENTERS · RENTERS · TENTERS · VENTERS	ENTERS	
	ENTERTAIN	ENTERTAINS
	ENTERTAKE	ENTERTAKEN · ENTERTAKES
	ENTETE	ENTETEE
	ENTHRAL	ENTHRALL · ENTHRALS
	ENTHRALL	ENTHRALLS
	ENTHRONE	ENTHRONED · ENTHRONES
	ENTHUSE	ENTHUSED · ENTHUSES
	ENTHYMEME	ENTHYMEMES
KENTIA	ENTIA	
PENTICE	ENTICE	ENTICED · ENTICER · ENTICES
PENTICED	ENTICED	

FRONT HOOK	ROOT WORD	END HOOK
	ENTICER	ENTICERS
PENTICES	**ENTICES**	
PENTICING	**ENTICING**	ENTICINGS
	ENTIRE	ENTIRES
	ENTITLE	ENTITLED · ENTITLES
	ENTOBLAST	ENTOBLASTS
	ENTODERM	ENTODERMS
	ENTOIL	ENTOILS
	ENTOMB	ENTOMBS
PENTOMIC	**ENTOMIC**	
	ENTOPHYTE	ENTOPHYTES
	ENTOPROCT	ENTOPROCTS
	ENTOPTIC	ENTOPTICS
	ENTOURAGE	ENTOURAGES
	ENTOZOA	ENTOZOAL · ENTOZOAN
	ENTOZOAN	ENTOZOANS
	ENTRAIL	ENTRAILS
	ENTRAIN	ENTRAINS
	ENTRAINER	ENTRAINERS
	ENTRAMMEL	ENTRAMMELS
	ENTRANCE	ENTRANCED · ENTRANCES
	ENTRANT	ENTRANTS
	ENTRAP	ENTRAPS
	ENTRAPPER	ENTRAPPERS
	ENTREAT	ENTREATS · ENTREATY
	ENTRECHAT	ENTRECHATS
	ENTRECOTE	ENTRECOTES
	ENTREE	ENTREES
	ENTREPOT	ENTREPOTS
	ENTRESOL	ENTRESOLS
CENTRIES · GENTRIES · SENTRIES	**ENTRIES**	
CENTRISM	**ENTRISM**	ENTRISMS
CENTRISMS	**ENTRISMS**	
CENTRIST	**ENTRIST**	ENTRISTS
CENTRISTS	**ENTRISTS**	
	ENTROPION	ENTROPIONS
	ENTROPIUM	ENTROPIUMS
	ENTRUST	ENTRUSTS
CENTRY · GENTRY · SENTRY	**ENTRY**	
	ENTRYISM	ENTRYISMS
	ENTRYIST	ENTRYISTS
	ENTRYWAY	ENTRYWAYS
	ENTWINE	ENTWINED · ENTWINES
	ENTWIST	ENTWISTS
	ENUCLEATE	ENUCLEATED · ENUCLEATES
	ENUMERATE	ENUMERATED · ENUMERATES
DENUNCIATE · RENUNCIATE	**ENUNCIATE**	ENUNCIATED · ENUNCIATES
TENURE	**ENURE**	ENURED · ENURES
TENURED	**ENURED**	
	ENUREMENT	ENUREMENTS
TENURES	**ENURES**	
	ENURETIC	ENURETICS
TENURING	**ENURING**	
	ENVASSAL	ENVASSALS
	ENVAULT	ENVAULTS
	ENVEIGLE	ENVEIGLED · ENVEIGLES
	ENVELOP	ENVELOPE · ENVELOPS
	ENVELOPE	ENVELOPED · ENVELOPER · ENVELOPES
	ENVELOPER	ENVELOPERS
	ENVENOM	ENVENOMS
	ENVERMEIL	ENVERMEILS
	ENVIER	ENVIERS
SENVIES	**ENVIES**	
	ENVIRO	ENVIRON · ENVIROS
	ENVIRON	ENVIRONS
	ENVISAGE	ENVISAGED · ENVISAGES
	ENVISION	ENVISIONS
RENVOI	**ENVOI**	ENVOIS
RENVOIS	**ENVOIS**	

FRONT HOOK	ROOT WORD	END HOOK
LENVOY ▪ RENVOY	**ENVOY**	ENVOYS
LENVOYS ▪ RENVOYS	**ENVOYS**	
	ENVOYSHIP	ENVOYSHIPS
SENVY	**ENVY**	
	ENVYING	ENVYINGS
	ENWALL	ENWALLS
	ENWALLOW	ENWALLOWS
	ENWHEEL	ENWHEELS
	ENWIND	ENWINDS
	ENWOMB	ENWOMBS
	ENWRAP	ENWRAPS
	ENWREATH	ENWREATHE ▪ ENWREATHS
	ENWREATHE	ENWREATHED ▪ ENWREATHES
	ENZIAN	ENZIANS
	ENZONE	ENZONED ▪ ENZONES
	ENZOOTIC	ENZOOTICS
	ENZYM	ENZYME ▪ ENZYMS
	ENZYME	ENZYMES
	EOBIONT	EOBIONTS
AEOLIAN	**EOLIAN**	
	EOLIENNE	EOLIENNES
AEOLIPILE	**EOLIPILE**	EOLIPILES
AEOLIPILES	**EOLIPILES**	
NEOLITH	**EOLITH**	EOLITHS
NEOLITHIC	**EOLITHIC**	
NEOLITHS	**EOLITHS**	
	EOLOPILE	EOLOPILES
AEON ▪ JEON ▪ NEON ▪ PEON	**EON**	EONS
AEONIAN	**EONIAN**	
PEONISM	**EONISM**	EONISMS
PEONISMS	**EONISMS**	
AEONS ▪ NEONS ▪ PEONS	**EONS**	
CEORL	**EORL**	EORLS
CEORLS	**EORLS**	
	EOSIN	EOSINE ▪ EOSINS
	EOSINE	EOSINES
	EPACRID	EPACRIDS
	EPACT	EPACTS
	EPAGOGE	EPAGOGES
	EPARCH	EPARCHS ▪ EPARCHY
	EPARCHATE	EPARCHATES
	EPAULE	EPAULES ▪ EPAULET
	EPAULET	EPAULETS
	EPAULETTE	EPAULETTED ▪ EPAULETTES
	EPAZOTE	EPAZOTES
TEPEE	**EPEE**	EPEES
	EPEEIST	EPEEISTS
TEPEES	**EPEES**	
	EPEIRA	EPEIRAS
	EPEIRID	EPEIRIDS
	EPENDYMA	EPENDYMAL ▪ EPENDYMAS
	EPERDU	EPERDUE
	EPERGNE	EPERGNES
	EPHA	EPHAH ▪ EPHAS
	EPHAH	EPHAHS
	EPHEBE	EPHEBES
	EPHEBI	EPHEBIC
	EPHEDRA	EPHEDRAS
	EPHEDRIN	EPHEDRINE ▪ EPHEDRINS
	EPHEDRINE	EPHEDRINES
	EPHEMERA	EPHEMERAE ▪ EPHEMERAL ▪ EPHEMERAS
	EPHEMERAL	EPHEMERALS
	EPHEMERID	EPHEMERIDS
	EPHEMERIS	EPHEMERIST
	EPHEMERON	EPHEMERONS
	EPHOD	EPHODS
	EPHOR	EPHORI ▪ EPHORS
	EPHORATE	EPHORATES
	EPIBLAST	EPIBLASTS

FRONT HOOK	ROOT WORD	END HOOK
	EPIBLEM	EPIBLEMS
SEPIC	**EPIC**	EPICS
	EPICANTHI	EPICANTHIC
	EPICARDIA	EPICARDIAC · EPICARDIAL
	EPICARP	EPICARPS
	EPICEDE	EPICEDES
	EPICEDIA	EPICEDIAL · EPICEDIAN
	EPICENE	EPICENES
	EPICENISM	EPICENISMS
	EPICENTER	EPICENTERS
	EPICENTRA	EPICENTRAL
	EPICENTRE	EPICENTRES
	EPICIER	EPICIERS
	EPICISM	EPICISMS
	EPICIST	EPICISTS
	EPICOTYL	EPICOTYLS
	EPICURE	EPICURES
	EPICUREAN	EPICUREANS
	EPICURISE	EPICURISED · EPICURISES
	EPICURISM	EPICURISMS
	EPICURIZE	EPICURIZED · EPICURIZES
	EPICYCLE	EPICYCLES
	EPIDEMIC	EPIDEMICS
	EPIDERM	EPIDERMS
	EPIDOSITE	EPIDOSITES
LEPIDOTE	**EPIDOTE**	EPIDOTES
LEPIDOTES	**EPIDOTES**	
	EPIDURAL	EPIDURALS
	EPIFAUNA	EPIFAUNAE · EPIFAUNAL · EPIFAUNAS
	EPIGENIST	EPIGENISTS
	EPIGON	EPIGONE · EPIGONI · EPIGONS
	EPIGONE	EPIGONES
	EPIGONI	EPIGONIC
	EPIGONISM	EPIGONISMS
	EPIGRAM	EPIGRAMS
	EPIGRAPH	EPIGRAPHS · EPIGRAPHY
DEPILATE	**EPILATE**	EPILATED · EPILATES
DEPILATED	**EPILATED**	
DEPILATES	**EPILATES**	
DEPILATING	**EPILATING**	
DEPILATION	**EPILATION**	EPILATIONS
DEPILATOR	**EPILATOR**	EPILATORS
DEPILATORS	**EPILATORS**	
	EPILEPTIC	EPILEPTICS
	EPILOBIUM	EPILOBIUMS
	EPILOG	EPILOGS
	EPILOGISE	EPILOGISED · EPILOGISES
	EPILOGIST	EPILOGISTS
	EPILOGIZE	EPILOGIZED · EPILOGIZES
	EPILOGUE	EPILOGUED · EPILOGUES
	EPIMER	EPIMERE · EPIMERS
	EPIMERASE	EPIMERASES
	EPIMERE	EPIMERES
	EPIMERISM	EPIMERISMS
	EPINEURIA	EPINEURIAL
	EPINICION	EPINICIONS
	EPINIKION	EPINIKIONS
	EPIPHRAGM	EPIPHRAGMS
	EPIPHYTE	EPIPHYTES
	EPIPLOON	EPIPLOONS
	EPIPOLISM	EPIPOLISMS
	EPIRRHEMA	EPIRRHEMAS
	EPISCIA	EPISCIAS
	EPISCOPE	EPISCOPES
	EPISEMON	EPISEMONS
	EPISODE	EPISODES
	EPISOME	EPISOMES
	EPISPERM	EPISPERMS
	EPISPORE	EPISPORES

FRONT HOOK	ROOT WORD	END HOOK
	EPISTEMIC	EPISTEMICS
	EPISTERNA	EPISTERNAL
	EPISTLE	EPISTLED · EPISTLER · EPISTLES
	EPISTLER	EPISTLERS
	EPISTOLER	EPISTOLERS
	EPISTOLET	EPISTOLETS
	EPISTOME	EPISTOMES
	EPISTYLE	EPISTYLES
	EPITAPH	EPITAPHS
	EPITAPHER	EPITAPHERS
	EPITHECA	EPITHECAE
	EPITHELIA	EPITHELIAL
	EPITHEM	EPITHEMA · EPITHEMS
	EPITHET	EPITHETS
	EPITHETON	EPITHETONS
	EPITOME	EPITOMES
	EPITOMISE	EPITOMISED · EPITOMISER · EPITOMISES
	EPITOMIST	EPITOMISTS
	EPITOMIZE	EPITOMIZED · EPITOMIZER · EPITOMIZES
	EPITOPE	EPITOPES
	EPITRITE	EPITRITES
	EPIZOA	EPIZOAN
	EPIZOAN	EPIZOANS
	EPIZOISM	EPIZOISMS
	EPIZOITE	EPIZOITES
	EPIZOOTIC	EPIZOOTICS
	EPOCH	EPOCHA · EPOCHS
	EPOCHA	EPOCHAL · EPOCHAS
	EPODE	EPODES
	EPONYM	EPONYMS · EPONYMY
	EPOPEE	EPOPEES
	EPOPOEIA	EPOPOEIAS
	EPOPT	EPOPTS
PEPOS · REPOS	**EPOS**	
DEPOSES · REPOSES	**EPOSES**	
	EPOXIDE	EPOXIDES
	EPOXIDISE	EPOXIDISED · EPOXIDISES
	EPOXIDIZE	EPOXIDIZED · EPOXIDIZES
	EPRIS	EPRISE
REPRISE	**EPRISE**	
	EPROM	EPROMS
	EPSILON	EPSILONS
	EPSOMITE	EPSOMITES
	EPUISE	EPUISEE
	EPULATION	EPULATIONS
	EPULOTIC	EPULOTICS
DEPURATE	**EPURATE**	EPURATED · EPURATES
DEPURATED	**EPURATED**	
DEPURATES	**EPURATES**	
DEPURATING	**EPURATING**	
DEPURATION	**EPURATION**	EPURATIONS
	EPYLLION	EPYLLIONS
	EQUAL	EQUALI · EQUALS
	EQUALISE	EQUALISED · EQUALISER · EQUALISES
	EQUALISER	EQUALISERS
	EQUALIZE	EQUALIZED · EQUALIZER · EQUALIZES
	EQUALIZER	EQUALIZERS
	EQUANT	EQUANTS
	EQUATE	EQUATED · EQUATES
	EQUATION	EQUATIONS
	EQUATOR	EQUATORS
	EQUID	EQUIDS
	EQUINE	EQUINES
	EQUINIA	EQUINIAS
	EQUIP	EQUIPE · EQUIPS
	EQUIPAGE	EQUIPAGED · EQUIPAGES
	EQUIPE	EQUIPES
	EQUIPMENT	EQUIPMENTS
	EQUIPOISE	EQUIPOISED · EQUIPOISES

FRONT HOOK	ROOT WORD	END HOOK
	EQUIPPER	EQUIPPERS
	EQUISETUM	EQUISETUMS
REQUITABLE	**EQUITABLE**	
REQUITES	**EQUITES**	
	EQUIVOKE	EQUIVOKES
	EQUIVOQUE	EQUIVOQUES
FER ▪ HER ▪ PER ▪ SER	**ER**	ERA ▪ ERE ▪ ERF ▪ ERG ▪ ERK ▪ ERN
		ERR ▪ ERS
SERA ▪ VERA	**ERA**	ERAS
RERADIATE	**ERADIATE**	ERADIATED ▪ ERADIATES
RERADIATED	**ERADIATED**	
RERADIATES	**ERADIATES**	
	ERADICANT	ERADICANTS
	ERADICATE	ERADICATED ▪ ERADICATES
TERAS	**ERAS**	ERASE
	ERASE	ERASED ▪ ERASER ▪ ERASES
	ERASEMENT	ERASEMENTS
	ERASER	ERASERS
	ERASION	ERASIONS
	ERASURE	ERASURES
	ERATHEM	ERATHEMS
TERBIA	**ERBIA**	ERBIAS
TERBIAS	**ERBIAS**	
TERBIUM	**ERBIUM**	ERBIUMS
TERBIUMS	**ERBIUMS**	
BERE ▪ CERE ▪ DERE ▪ FERE ▪ GERE ▪ HERE	**ERE**	ERED ▪ ERES ▪ EREV
LERE ▪ MERE ▪ PERE ▪ SERE ▪ WERE		
	ERECT	ERECTS
	ERECTER	ERECTERS
	ERECTION	ERECTIONS
	ERECTOR	ERECTORS
CERED ▪ DERED ▪ LERED ▪ MERED ▪ SERED	**ERED**	
	EREMITE	EREMITES
	EREMITISM	EREMITISMS
	EREPSIN	EREPSINS
BERES ▪ CERES ▪ DERES ▪ FERES ▪ GERES	**ERES**	
HERES ▪ LERES ▪ MERES ▪ PERES ▪ SERES		
TERES		
	ERETHISM	ERETHISMS
	EREV	EREVS
	EREWHILE	EREWHILES
KERF ▪ SERF ▪ TERF	**ERF**	
BERG	**ERG**	ERGO ▪ ERGS
	ERGATANER	ERGATANERS
	ERGATE	ERGATES
	ERGATIVE	ERGATIVES
	ERGO	ERGON ▪ ERGOS ▪ ERGOT
	ERGOGRAM	ERGOGRAMS
	ERGOGRAPH	ERGOGRAPHS
	ERGOMANIA	ERGOMANIAC ▪ ERGOMANIAS
	ERGOMETER	ERGOMETERS
	ERGON	ERGONS
	ERGONOMIC	ERGONOMICS
	ERGOT	ERGOTS
	ERGOTISE	ERGOTISED ▪ ERGOTISES
	ERGOTISM	ERGOTISMS
	ERGOTIZE	ERGOTIZED ▪ ERGOTIZES
BERGS	**ERGS**	
	ERIACH	ERIACHS
CERIC ▪ SERIC ▪ XERIC	**ERIC**	ERICA ▪ ERICK ▪ ERICS
	ERICA	ERICAS
	ERICK	ERICKS
	ERIGERON	ERIGERONS
CERING ▪ DERING ▪ LERING ▪ MERING	**ERING**	ERINGO
SERING		
	ERINGO	ERINGOS
	ERINITE	ERINITES
	ERIOMETER	ERIOMETERS
	ERIONITE	ERIONITES

FRONT HOOK	ROOT WORD	END HOOK
	ERIOPHYID	ERIOPHYIDS
MERISTIC · VERISTIC	**ERISTIC**	ERISTICS
BERK · JERK · MERK · NERK · PERK · SERK YERK · ZERK	**ERK**	ERKS
BERKS · JERKS · MERKS · NERKS · PERKS SERKS · YERKS · ZERKS	**ERKS**	
	ERLANG	ERLANGS
	ERLKING	ERLKINGS
	ERMELIN	ERMELINS
	ERMINE	ERMINED · ERMINES
VERMINED	**ERMINED**	
DERN · FERN · HERN · KERN · PERN · TERN	**ERN**	ERNE · ERNS
CERNE · GERNE · KERNE · TERNE	**ERNE**	ERNED · ERNES
CERNED · GERNED · KERNED · TERNED	**ERNED**	
CERNES · GERNES · KERNES · TERNES	**ERNES**	
CERNING · FERNING · GERNING · KERNING TERNING	**ERNING**	
DERNS · FERNS · HERNS · KERNS · PERNS TERNS	**ERNS**	
	ERODE	ERODED · ERODES
	ERODENT	ERODENTS
	ERODIUM	ERODIUMS
AEROS · CEROS · DERÓS · HEROS · KEROS WEROS · ZEROS	**EROS**	EROSE
REROSE	**EROSE**	EROSES
XEROSES	**EROSES**	
	EROSION	EROSIONS
	EROTEMA	EROTEMAS
	EROTEME	EROTEMES
CEROTIC · XEROTIC	**EROTIC**	EROTICA · EROTICS
	EROTICA	EROTICAL
	EROTICISE	EROTICISED · EROTICISES
	EROTICISM	EROTICISMS
	EROTICIST	EROTICISTS
	EROTICIZE	EROTICIZED · EROTICIZES
	EROTISE	EROTISED · EROTISES
	EROTISM	EROTISMS
	EROTIZE	EROTIZED · EROTIZES
SERR	**ERR**	ERRS
	ERRAND	ERRANDS
	ERRANT	ERRANTS
	ERRATA	ERRATAS
	ERRATIC	ERRATICS
SERRED	**ERRED**	
	ERRHINE	ERRHINES
HERRING · SERRING	**ERRING**	ERRINGS
HERRINGS	**ERRINGS**	
TERROR	**ERROR**	ERRORS
TERRORIST	**ERRORIST**	ERRORISTS
TERRORISTS	**ERRORISTS**	
TERRORLESS	**ERRORLESS**	
TERRORS	**ERRORS**	
SERRS	**ERRS**	
HERS · SERS · VERS	**ERS**	ERST
HERSES · MERSES · PERSES · VERSES PERST · VERST	**ERSES**	
	ERST	
	ERUCT	ERUCTS
	ERUCTATE	ERUCTATED · ERUCTATES
	ERUDITE	ERUDITES
	ERUDITION	ERUDITIONS
AERUGO	**ERUGO**	ERUGOS
AERUGOS	**ERUGOS**	
	ERUPT	ERUPTS
	ERUPTION	ERUPTIONS
	ERUPTIVE	ERUPTIVES
	ERUV	ERUVS
	ERVALENTA	ERVALENTAS
VERVEN	**ERVEN**	
	ERVIL	ERVILS

FRONT HOOK	ROOT WORD	END HOOK
	ERYNGIUM	ERYNGIUMS
	ERYNGO	ERYNGOS
	ERYTHEMA	ERYTHEMAL ERYTHEMAS
	ERYTHRINA	ERYTHRINAS
	ERYTHRISM	ERYTHRISMS
	ERYTHRITE	ERYTHRITES
	ERYTHRON	ERYTHRONS
BES FES HES LES (offensive) MES OES PES RES TES YES	**ES**	ESS EST
	ESCALADE	ESCALADED ESCALADER ESCALADES
	ESCALADER	ESCALADERS
	ESCALATE	ESCALATED ESCALATES
	ESCALATOR	ESCALATORS ESCALATORY
	ESCALIER	ESCALIERS
	ESCALLOP	ESCALLOPS
	ESCALOP	ESCALOPE ESCALOPS
	ESCALOPE	ESCALOPED ESCALOPES
	ESCAPADE	ESCAPADES
	ESCAPE	ESCAPED ESCAPEE ESCAPER ESCAPES
	ESCAPEE	ESCAPEES
	ESCAPER	ESCAPERS
	ESCAPISM	ESCAPISMS
	ESCAPIST	ESCAPISTS
	ESCAR	ESCARP ESCARS
	ESCARGOT	ESCARGOTS
	ESCAROLE	ESCAROLES
	ESCARP	ESCARPS
	ESCHALOT	ESCHALOTS
	ESCHAR	ESCHARS
	ESCHEAT	ESCHEATS
	ESCHEATOR	ESCHEATORS
	ESCHEW	ESCHEWS
	ESCHEWAL	ESCHEWALS
	ESCHEWER	ESCHEWERS
	ESCLANDRE	ESCLANDRES
	ESCOLAR	ESCOLARS
	ESCOPETTE	ESCOPETTES
	ESCORT	ESCORTS
	ESCORTAGE	ESCORTAGES
	ESCOT	ESCOTS
	ESCRIBANO	ESCRIBANOS
DESCRIBE	**ESCRIBE**	ESCRIBED ESCRIBES
DESCRIBED	**ESCRIBED**	
DESCRIBES	**ESCRIBES**	
DESCRIBING	**ESCRIBING**	
	ESCROC	ESCROCS
	ESCROL	ESCROLL ESCROLS
	ESCROLL	ESCROLLS
	ESCROW	ESCROWS
	ESCUAGE	ESCUAGES
	ESCUDO	ESCUDOS
	ESCULENT	ESCULENTS
	ESERINE	ESERINES
BESES LESES (offensive) MESES RESES YESES	**ESES**	
RESILE	**ESILE**	ESILES
RESILES	**ESILES**	
	ESKAR	ESKARS
	ESKER	ESKERS
PESKY	**ESKY**	
	ESLOIN	ESLOINS
	ESLOYNE	ESLOYNED ESLOYNES
MESNE	**ESNE**	ESNES
MESNES	**ESNES**	
OESOPHAGI	**ESOPHAGI**	
OESOPHAGUS	**ESOPHAGUS**	
	ESOTERIC	ESOTERICA
	ESOTERISM	ESOTERISMS
	ESOTROPIA	ESOTROPIAS

FRONT HOOK	ROOT WORD	END HOOK
	ESPADA	ESPADAS
	ESPAGNOLE	ESPAGNOLES
	ESPALIER	ESPALIERS
	ESPARTO	ESPARTOS
	ESPERANCE	ESPERANCES
	ESPIAL	ESPIALS
	ESPIER	ESPIERS
	ESPIONAGE	ESPIONAGES
	ESPLANADE	ESPLANADES
	ESPOUSAL	ESPOUSALS
BESPOUSE	ESPOUSE	ESPOUSED · ESPOUSER · ESPOUSES
BESPOUSED	ESPOUSED	
	ESPOUSER	ESPOUSERS
BESPOUSES	ESPOUSES	
BESPOUSING	ESPOUSING	
	ESPRESSO	ESPRESSOS
	ESPRIT	ESPRITS
	ESPUMOSO	ESPUMOSOS
	ESQUIRE	ESQUIRED · ESQUIRES
	ESQUIRES	ESQUIRESS
	ESQUISSE	ESQUISSES
CESS · FESS · JESS · LESS · MESS · NESS SESS	ESS	ESSE
	ESSAY	ESSAYS
	ESSAYER	ESSAYERS
	ESSAYETTE	ESSAYETTES
	ESSAYIST	ESSAYISTS
CESSE · DESSE · FESSE · GESSE · JESSE	ESSE	ESSES
	ESSENCE	ESSENCES
	ESSENTIAL	ESSENTIALS
CESSES · DESSES · FESSES · GESSES JESSES · LESSES · MESSES · NESSES SESSES · YESSES	ESSES	
	ESSIVE	ESSIVES
	ESSOIN	ESSOINS
	ESSOINER	ESSOINERS
HESSONITE	ESSONITE	ESSONITES
HESSONITES	ESSONITES	
	ESSOYNE	ESSOYNES
BEST · FEST · GEST · HEST · JEST · KEST LEST · NEST · PEST · REST · TEST · VEST WEST · YEST · ZEST	EST	ESTS
	ESTACADE	ESTACADES
	ESTAFETTE	ESTAFETTES
	ESTAMINET	ESTAMINETS
	ESTANCIA	ESTANCIAS
GESTATE · RESTATE · TESTATE	ESTATE	ESTATED · ESTATES
GESTATED · RESTATED	ESTATED	
GESTATES · RESTATES · TESTATES	ESTATES	
GESTATING · RESTATING	ESTATING	
	ESTEEM	ESTEEMS
FESTER · JESTER · MESTER · NESTER PESTER · RESTER · TESTER · WESTER YESTER · ZESTER	ESTER	ESTERS
FESTERS · JESTERS · MESTERS · NESTERS PESTERS · RESTERS · TESTERS · WESTERS ZESTERS	ESTERASE	ESTERASES
	ESTERS	
AESTHESES	ESTHESES	
AESTHESIA	ESTHESIA	ESTHESIAS
AESTHESIAS	ESTHESIAS	
AESTHESIS	ESTHESIS	
AESTHETE	ESTHETE	ESTHETES
AESTHETES	ESTHETES	
AESTHETIC	ESTHETIC	ESTHETICS
AESTHETICS	ESTHETICS	
	ESTIMATE	ESTIMATED · ESTIMATES
	ESTIMATOR	ESTIMATORS
AESTIVAL · FESTIVAL	ESTIVAL	

FRONT HOOK	ROOT WORD	END HOOK
AESTIVATE	**ESTIVATE**	ESTIVATED · ESTIVATES
AESTIVATED	**ESTIVATED**	
AESTIVATES	**ESTIVATES**	
AESTIVATOR	**ESTIVATOR**	ESTIVATORS
	ESTOC	ESTOCS
	ESTOILE	ESTOILES
	ESTOP	ESTOPS
	ESTOPPAGE	ESTOPPAGES
	ESTOPPEL	ESTOPPELS
	ESTOVER	ESTOVERS
	ESTRADE	ESTRADES
OESTRADIOL	**ESTRADIOL**	ESTRADIOLS
	ESTRAGON	ESTRAGONS
OESTRAL · VESTRAL	**ESTRAL**	
	ESTRANGE	ESTRANGED · ESTRANGER · ESTRANGES
	ESTRANGER	ESTRANGERS
	ESTRAPADE	ESTRAPADES
	ESTRAY	ESTRAYS
	ESTREAT	ESTREATS
	ESTREPE	ESTREPED · ESTREPES
	ESTRIDGE	ESTRIDGES
	ESTRILDID	ESTRILDIDS
OESTRIN	**ESTRIN**	ESTRINS
OESTRINS	**ESTRINS**	
OESTRIOL	**ESTRIOL**	ESTRIOLS
OESTRIOLS	**ESTRIOLS**	
	ESTRO	ESTROS
OESTROGEN	**ESTROGEN**	ESTROGENS
OESTROGENS	**ESTROGENS**	
OESTRONE	**ESTRONE**	ESTRONES
OESTRONES	**ESTRONES**	
OESTROUS	**ESTROUS**	
OESTRUM	**ESTRUM**	ESTRUMS
OESTRUMS	**ESTRUMS**	
OESTRUS	**ESTRUS**	
OESTRUSES	**ESTRUSES**	
BESTS · FESTS · GESTS · HESTS · JESTS KESTS · LESTS · NESTS · PESTS · RESTS TESTS · VESTS · WESTS · YESTS · ZESTS	**ESTS**	
	ESURIENCE	ESURIENCES
BET · FET · GET · HET · JET · KET · LET MET · NET · PET · RET · SET · TET · VET WET · YET	**ET**	ETA · ETH
BETA · FETA · GETA · KETA · META · SETA WETA · ZETA	**ETA**	ETAS · ETAT
BETACISM	**ETACISM**	ETACISMS
BETACISMS	**ETACISMS**	
	ETAERIO	ETAERIOS
METAGE	**ETAGE**	ETAGES
	ETAGERE	ETAGERES
METAGES	**ETAGES**	
	ETALAGE	ETALAGES
	ETALON	ETALONS
	ETAMIN	ETAMINE · ETAMINS
KETAMINE	**ETAMINE**	ETAMINES
KETAMINES	**ETAMINES**	
RETAPE	**ETAPE**	ETAPES
RETAPES	**ETAPES**	
BETAS · FETAS · GETAS · KETAS · WETAS ZETAS	**ETAS**	
	ETAT	ETATS
	ETATISM	ETATISME · ETATISMS
	ETATISME	ETATISMES
	ETATIST	ETATISTE
	ETATISTE	ETATISTES
	ETCETERA	ETCETERAS
FETCH · KETCH · LETCH · RETCH · VETCH	**ETCH**	
	ETCHANT	ETCHANTS
FETCHED · LETCHED · RETCHED · TETCHED	**ETCHED**	

FRONT HOOK	ROOT WORD	END HOOK
FETCHER	**ETCHER**	ETCHERS
FETCHERS	**ETCHERS**	
FETCHES · KETCHES · LETCHES · RETCHES	**ETCHES**	
VETCHES		
FETCHING · KETCHING · LETCHING	**ETCHING**	ETCHINGS
RETCHING		
LETCHINGS	**ETCHINGS**	
	ETEN	ETENS
	ETERNAL	ETERNALS
	ETERNISE	ETERNISED · ETERNISES
	ETERNIZE	ETERNIZED · ETERNIZES
	ETESIAN	ETESIANS
BETH · HETH · METH · TETH	**ETH**	ETHE · ETHS
LETHAL	**ETHAL**	ETHALS
LETHALS	**ETHALS**	
METHANAL	**ETHANAL**	ETHANALS
METHANALS	**ETHANALS**	
METHANE	**ETHANE**	ETHANES
METHANES	**ETHANES**	
	ETHANOATE	ETHANOATES
METHANOIC	**ETHANOIC**	
METHANOL	**ETHANOL**	ETHANOLS
METHANOLS	**ETHANOLS**	
	ETHANOYL	ETHANOYLS
LETHE	**ETHE**	ETHER
	ETHENE	ETHENES
	ETHEPHON	ETHEPHONS
AETHER · HETHER · NETHER · PETHER	**ETHER**	ETHERS
TETHER · WETHER		
	ETHERCAP	ETHERCAPS
AETHEREAL	**ETHEREAL**	
AETHERIC	**ETHERIC**	
	ETHERION	ETHERIONS
	ETHERISE	ETHERISED · ETHERISER · ETHERISES
	ETHERISER	ETHERISERS
	ETHERISM	ETHERISMS
	ETHERIST	ETHERISTS
	ETHERIZE	ETHERIZED · ETHERIZER · ETHERIZES
	ETHERIZER	ETHERIZERS
AETHERS · PETHERS · TETHERS · WETHERS	**ETHERS**	
	ETHIC	ETHICS
	ETHICAL	ETHICALS
	ETHICIAN	ETHICIANS
	ETHICISE	ETHICISED · ETHICISES
	ETHICISM	ETHICISMS
	ETHICIST	ETHICISTS
	ETHICIZE	ETHICIZED · ETHICIZES
	ETHINYL	ETHINYLS
	ETHION	ETHIONS
METHIONINE	**ETHIONINE**	ETHIONINES
	ETHMOID	ETHMOIDS
	ETHNARCH	ETHNARCHS · ETHNARCHY
	ETHNIC	ETHNICS
	ETHNICISM	ETHNICISMS
	ETHNOCIDE	ETHNOCIDES
	ETHNONYM	ETHNONYMS
	ETHOGRAM	ETHOGRAMS
	ETHONONE	ETHONONES
METHOS	**ETHOS**	
METHOXIDE	**ETHOXIDE**	ETHOXIDES
METHOXIDES	**ETHOXIDES**	
METHOXY	**ETHOXY**	ETHOXYL
METHOXYL	**ETHOXYL**	ETHOXYLS
BETHS · HETHS · METHS · TETHS	**ETHS**	
METHYL	**ETHYL**	ETHYLS
METHYLATE	**ETHYLATE**	ETHYLATED · ETHYLATES
METHYLATED	**ETHYLATED**	
METHYLATES	**ETHYLATES**	
METHYLENE	**ETHYLENE**	ETHYLENES

E

FRONT HOOK	ROOT WORD	END HOOK
METHYLENES	**ETHYLENES**	
METHYLIC	**ETHYLIC**	
METHYLS	**ETHYLS**	
	ETHYNE	ETHYNES
	ETHYNYL	ETHYNYLS
METIC	**ETIC**	
PETIOLATE	**ETIOLATE**	ETIOLATED ▪ ETIOLATES
PETIOLATED	**ETIOLATED**	
	ETIOLIN	ETIOLINS
AETIOLOGY	**ETIOLOGY**	
NETIQUETTE	**ETIQUETTE**	ETIQUETTES
	ETNA	ETNAS
	ETOILE	ETOILES
	ETOUFFEE	ETOUFFEES
	ETOURDI	ETOURDIE
	ETRANGER	ETRANGERE ▪ ETRANGERS
	ETRANGERE	ETRANGERES
	ETRENNE	ETRENNES
	ETRIER	ETRIERS
	ETTERCAP	ETTERCAPS
	ETTIN	ETTINS
FETTLE ▪ KETTLE ▪ METTLE ▪ NETTLE PETTLE ▪ SETTLE	**ETTLE**	ETTLED ▪ ETTLES
FETTLED ▪ METTLED ▪ NETTLED ▪ PETTLED SETTLED	**ETTLED**	
FETTLES ▪ KETTLES ▪ METTLES ▪ NETTLES PETTLES ▪ SETTLES	**ETTLES**	
FETTLING ▪ NETTLING ▪ PETTLING SETTLING	**ETTLING**	
	ETUDE	ETUDES
	ETUI	ETUIS
	ETWEE	ETWEES
	ETYMON	ETYMONS
	EUCAIN	EUCAINE ▪ EUCAINS
	EUCAINE	EUCAINES
	EUCALYPT	EUCALYPTI ▪ EUCALYPTS
	EUCARYON	EUCARYONS
	EUCARYOT	EUCARYOTE ▪ EUCARYOTS
	EUCARYOTE	EUCARYOTES
	EUCHLORIN	EUCHLORINE ▪ EUCHLORINS
	EUCHRE	EUCHRED ▪ EUCHRES
	EUCLASE	EUCLASES
	EUCRITE	EUCRITES
	EUCRYPHIA	EUCRYPHIAS
	EUDAEMON	EUDAEMONS ▪ EUDAEMONY
	EUDAIMON	EUDAIMONS
	EUDEMON	EUDEMONS
	EUDEMONIA	EUDEMONIAS
	EUDEMONIC	EUDEMONICS
	EUDIALYTE	EUDIALYTES
	EUGARIE	EUGARIES
	EUGENIA	EUGENIAS
	EUGENIC	EUGENICS
	EUGENISM	EUGENISMS
	EUGENIST	EUGENISTS
	EUGENOL	EUGENOLS
HEUGH ▪ LEUGH ▪ TEUGH	**EUGH**	EUGHS
LEUGHEN	**EUGHEN**	
HEUGHS	**EUGHS**	
	EUGLENA	EUGLENAS
	EUGLENID	EUGLENIDS
	EUGLENOID	EUGLENOIDS
NEUK ▪ YEUK	**EUK**	EUKS
	EUKARYON	EUKARYONS
	EUKARYOT	EUKARYOTE ▪ EUKARYOTS
	EUKARYOTE	EUKARYOTES
YEUKED	**EUKED**	
YEUKING	**EUKING**	
NEUKS ▪ YEUKS	**EUKS**	

E

E

FRONT HOOK	ROOT WORD	END HOOK
	EULACHAN	EULACHANS
	EULACHON	EULACHONS
	EULOGIA	EULOGIAE = EULOGIAS
	EULOGISE	EULOGISED = EULOGISER = EULOGISES
	EULOGISER	EULOGISERS
	EULOGIST	EULOGISTS
	EULOGIUM	EULOGIUMS
	EULOGIZE	EULOGIZED = EULOGIZER = EULOGIZES
	EULOGIZER	EULOGIZERS
	EUMELANIN	EUMELANINS
	EUMERISM	EUMERISMS
	EUMONG	EUMONGS
	EUMUNG	EUMUNGS
	EUNUCH	EUNUCHS
	EUNUCHISE	EUNUCHISED = EUNUCHISES
	EUNUCHISM	EUNUCHISMS
	EUNUCHIZE	EUNUCHIZED = EUNUCHIZES
	EUNUCHOID	EUNUCHOIDS
	EUONYMIN	EUONYMINS
	EUOUAE	EUOUAES
	EUPAD	EUPADS
	EUPATRID	EUPATRIDS
	EUPEPSIA	EUPEPSIAS
	EUPHAUSID	EUPHAUSIDS
	EUPHEMISE	EUPHEMISED = EUPHEMISER = EUPHEMISES
	EUPHEMISM	EUPHEMISMS
	EUPHEMIST	EUPHEMISTS
	EUPHEMIZE	EUPHEMIZED = EUPHEMIZER = EUPHEMIZES
	EUPHENIC	EUPHENICS
	EUPHOBIA	EUPHOBIAS
	EUPHON	EUPHONS = EUPHONY
	EUPHONIA	EUPHONIAS
	EUPHONISE	EUPHONISED = EUPHONISES
	EUPHONISM	EUPHONISMS
	EUPHONIUM	EUPHONIUMS
	EUPHONIZE	EUPHONIZED = EUPHONIZES
	EUPHORBIA	EUPHORBIAS
	EUPHORIA	EUPHORIAS
	EUPHROE	EUPHROES
	EUPHUISE	EUPHUISED = EUPHUISES
	EUPHUISM	EUPHUISMS
	EUPHUIST	EUPHUISTS
	EUPHUIZE	EUPHUIZED = EUPHUIZES
	EUPLASTIC	EUPLASTICS
	EUPLOID	EUPLOIDS = EUPLOIDY
	EUPNEA	EUPNEAS
	EUPNOEA	EUPNOEAS
HEUREKA	EUREKA	EUREKAS
HEUREKAS	EUREKAS	
	EURO	EUROS
	EUROBOND	EUROBONDS
	EUROCRAT	EUROCRATS
	EUROCREEP	EUROCREEPS
	EURONOTE	EURONOTES
	EUROPHILE	EUROPHILES
	EUROPIUM	EUROPIUMS
	EURYBATH	EURYBATHS
	EURYTHERM	EURYTHERMS
	EURYTHMIC	EURYTHMICS
	EUSOL	EUSOLS
	EUSTELE	EUSTELES
	EUSTYLE	EUSTYLES
	EUTAXIA	EUTAXIAS
	EUTAXITE	EUTAXITES
	EUTECTIC	EUTECTICS
	EUTECTOID	EUTECTOIDS
	EUTEXIA	EUTEXIAS
	EUTHANISE	EUTHANISED = EUTHANISES
	EUTHANIZE	EUTHANIZED = EUTHANIZES

FRONT HOOK	ROOT WORD	END HOOK
	EUTHENIST	EUTHENISTS
	EUTHERIAN	EUTHERIANS
	EUTHYMIA	EUTHYMIAS
	EUTHYROID	EUTHYROIDS
	EUXENITE	EUXENITES
	EVACUANT	EVACUANTS
	EVACUATE	EVACUATED ▪ EVACUATES
	EVACUATOR	EVACUATORS
	EVACUEE	EVACUEES
	EVADE	EVADED ▪ EVADER ▪ EVADES
	EVADER	EVADERS
	EVAGATION	EVAGATIONS
	EVAGINATE	EVAGINATED ▪ EVAGINATES
DEVALUATE ▪ REVALUATE	EVALUATE	EVALUATED ▪ EVALUATES
DEVALUATED ▪ REVALUATED	EVALUATED	
DEVALUATES ▪ REVALUATES	EVALUATES	
	EVALUATOR	EVALUATORS
	EVANESCE	EVANESCED ▪ EVANESCES
	EVANGEL	EVANGELS ▪ EVANGELY
	EVANITION	EVANITIONS
	EVAPORATE	EVAPORATED ▪ EVAPORATES
	EVAPORITE	EVAPORITES
	EVASION	EVASIONS
LEVE ▪ MEVE ▪ NEVE ▪ YEVE	EVE	EVEN ▪ EVER ▪ EVES ▪ EVET
	EVECTION	EVECTIONS
	EVEJAR	EVEJARS
EEVEN ▪ SEVEN ▪ YEVEN	EVEN	EVENS ▪ EVENT
	EVENEMENT	EVENEMENTS
	EVENER	EVENERS
	EVENFALL	EVENFALLS
	EVENING	EVENINGS
EEVENS ▪ SEVENS	EVENS	
	EVENSONG	EVENSONGS
	EVENT	EVENTS
	EVENTER	EVENTERS
	EVENTIDE	EVENTIDES
	EVENTING	EVENTINGS
	EVENTRATE	EVENTRATED ▪ EVENTRATES
	EVENTUATE	EVENTUATED ▪ EVENTUATES
BEVER ▪ FEVER ▪ LEVER ▪ NEVER ▪ SEVER	EVER	EVERT ▪ EVERY
	EVERGLADE	EVERGLADES
	EVERGREEN	EVERGREENS
NEVERMORE	EVERMORE	
	EVERNET	EVERNETS
REVERSIBLE	EVERSIBLE	
REVERSION	EVERSION	EVERSIONS
REVERSIONS	EVERSIONS	
REVERT	EVERT	EVERTS
REVERTED	EVERTED	
REVERTING	EVERTING	
	EVERTOR	EVERTORS
REVERTS	EVERTS	
REVERY ▪ SEVERY	EVERY	
	EVERYDAY	EVERYDAYS
MEVES ▪ NEVES ▪ YEVES	EVES	
REVET	EVET	EVETS
REVETS	EVETS	
	EVICT	EVICTS
	EVICTEE	EVICTEES
	EVICTION	EVICTIONS
	EVICTOR	EVICTORS
	EVIDENCE	EVIDENCED ▪ EVIDENCES
	EVIDENT	EVIDENTS
DEVIL ▪ KEVIL	EVIL	EVILS
	EVILDOER	EVILDOERS
	EVILDOING	EVILDOINGS
REVILER	EVILER	
DEVILS ▪ KEVILS	EVILS	
	EVINCE	EVINCED ▪ EVINCES

E

E

FRONT HOOK	ROOT WORD	END HOOK
LEVIRATE	**EVIRATE**	EVIRATED · EVIRATES
LEVIRATES	**EVIRATES**	
LEVITATE	**EVITATE**	EVITATED · EVITATES
LEVITATED	**EVITATED**	
LEVITATES	**EVITATES**	
LEVITATING	**EVITATING**	
LEVITATION	**EVITATION**	EVITATIONS
LEVITE	**EVITE**	EVITED · EVITES
LEVITES	**EVITES**	
LEVO	**EVO**	EVOE · EVOS
REVOCABLE	**EVOCABLE**	
	EVOCATE	EVOCATED · EVOCATES
REVOCATION	**EVOCATION**	EVOCATIONS
	EVOCATOR	EVOCATORS · EVOCATORY
REVOCATORY	**EVOCATORY**	
REVOKE	**EVOKE**	EVOKED · EVOKER · EVOKES
REVOKED	**EVOKED**	
REVOKER	**EVOKER**	EVOKERS
REVOKERS	**EVOKERS**	
REVOKES	**EVOKES**	
REVOKING	**EVOKING**	
	EVOLUE	EVOLUES
REVOLUTE	**EVOLUTE**	EVOLUTED · EVOLUTES
DEVOLUTION · REVOLUTION	**EVOLUTION**	EVOLUTIONS
REVOLVABLE	**EVOLVABLE**	
DEVOLVE · REVOLVE	**EVOLVE**	EVOLVED · EVOLVER · EVOLVES
DEVOLVED · REVOLVED	**EVOLVED**	
REVOLVER	**EVOLVER**	EVOLVERS
REVOLVERS	**EVOLVERS**	
DEVOLVES · REVOLVES	**EVOLVES**	
DEVOLVING · REVOLVING	**EVOLVING**	
	EVOVAE	EVOVAES
	EVULGATE	EVULGATED · EVULGATES
	EVULSE	EVULSED · EVULSES
REVULSED	**EVULSED**	
REVULSION	**EVULSION**	EVULSIONS
REVULSIONS	**EVULSIONS**	
	EVZONE	EVZONES
	EWE	EWER · EWES
FEWER · HEWER · NEWER · SEWER	**EWER**	EWERS
HEWERS · SEWERS	**EWERS**	
	EWES	EWEST
FEWEST · NEWEST	**EWEST**	
	EWK	EWKS
NEWT	**EWT**	EWTS
NEWTS	**EWTS**	
DEX · HEX · KEX · LEX · REX · SEX · TEX VEX · WEX · YEX · ZEX	**EX**	EXO
	EXABYTE	EXABYTES
HEXACT	**EXACT**	EXACTA · EXACTS
	EXACTA	EXACTAS
	EXACTER	EXACTERS
	EXACTION	EXACTIONS
	EXACTMENT	EXACTMENTS
	EXACTOR	EXACTORS
HEXACTS	**EXACTS**	
	EXACUM	EXACUMS
	EXALT	EXALTS
	EXALTER	EXALTERS
	EXAM	EXAMS
	EXAMEN	EXAMENS
	EXAMINANT	EXAMINANTS
	EXAMINATE	EXAMINATES
HEXAMINE	**EXAMINE**	EXAMINED · EXAMINEE · EXAMINER EXAMINES
	EXAMINEE	EXAMINEES
	EXAMINER	EXAMINERS
HEXAMINES	**EXAMINES**	
	EXAMPLAR	EXAMPLARS

FRONT HOOK	ROOT WORD	END HOOK
	EXAMPLE	EXAMPLED · EXAMPLES
	EXANTHEM	EXANTHEMA · EXANTHEMS
	EXANTHEMA	EXANTHEMAS
	EXARATION	EXARATIONS
HEXARCH	**EXARCH**	EXARCHS · EXARCHY
	EXARCHATE	EXARCHATES
HEXARCHIES	**EXARCHIES**	
	EXARCHIST	EXARCHISTS
HEXARCHY	**EXARCHY**	
	EXCAMB	EXCAMBS
	EXCAMBION	EXCAMBIONS
	EXCAMBIUM	EXCAMBIUMS
	EXCARNATE	EXCARNATED · EXCARNATES
	EXCAVATE	EXCAVATED · EXCAVATES
	EXCAVATOR	EXCAVATORS
	EXCEED	EXCEEDS
	EXCEEDER	EXCEEDERS
	EXCEL	EXCELS
	EXCELSIOR	EXCELSIORS
	EXCENTRIC	EXCENTRICS
	EXCEPT	EXCEPTS
	EXCEPTANT	EXCEPTANTS
	EXCEPTION	EXCEPTIONS
	EXCEPTOR	EXCEPTORS
	EXCERPT	EXCERPTA · EXCERPTS
	EXCERPTER	EXCERPTERS
	EXCERPTOR	EXCERPTORS
	EXCHANGE	EXCHANGED · EXCHANGER · EXCHANGES
	EXCHANGER	EXCHANGERS
	EXCHEAT	EXCHEATS
	EXCHEQUER	EXCHEQUERS
	EXCIDE	EXCIDED · EXCIDES
	EXCIMER	EXCIMERS
	EXCIPIENT	EXCIPIENTS
	EXCIPLE	EXCIPLES
	EXCISE	EXCISED · EXCISES
	EXCISION	EXCISIONS
	EXCITANT	EXCITANTS
	EXCITE	EXCITED · EXCITER · EXCITES
	EXCITER	EXCITERS
	EXCITON	EXCITONS
	EXCITOR	EXCITORS
	EXCLAIM	EXCLAIMS
	EXCLAIMER	EXCLAIMERS
	EXCLAVE	EXCLAVES
	EXCLOSURE	EXCLOSURES
	EXCLUDE	EXCLUDED · EXCLUDEE · EXCLUDER · EXCLUDES
	EXCLUDEE	EXCLUDEES
	EXCLUDER	EXCLUDERS
	EXCLUSION	EXCLUSIONS
	EXCLUSIVE	EXCLUSIVES
	EXCORIATE	EXCORIATED · EXCORIATES
	EXCREMENT	EXCREMENTA · EXCREMENTS
	EXCRETA	EXCRETAL
	EXCRETE	EXCRETED · EXCRETER · EXCRETES
	EXCRETER	EXCRETERS
	EXCRETION	EXCRETIONS
	EXCULPATE	EXCULPATED · EXCULPATES
	EXCURSE	EXCURSED · EXCURSES
	EXCURSION	EXCURSIONS
	EXCUSAL	EXCUSALS
	EXCUSE	EXCUSED · EXCUSER · EXCUSES
	EXCUSER	EXCUSERS
	EXEAT	EXEATS
	EXEC	EXECS
	EXECRATE	EXECRATED · EXECRATES
	EXECRATOR	EXECRATORS · EXECRATORY
	EXECUTANT	EXECUTANTS

E

E

FRONT HOOK	ROOT WORD	END HOOK
	EXECUTE	EXECUTED · EXECUTER · EXECUTES
	EXECUTER	EXECUTERS
	EXECUTION	EXECUTIONS
	EXECUTIVE	EXECUTIVES
	EXECUTOR	EXECUTORS · EXECUTORY
HEXED · SEXED · VEXED · WEXED · YEXED	**EXED**	
	EXEDRA	EXEDRAE
	EXEEM	EXEEMS
	EXEGETE	EXEGETES
	EXEGETIC	EXEGETICS
	EXEGETIST	EXEGETISTS
LEXEME	**EXEME**	EXEMED · EXEMES
LEXEMES	**EXEMES**	
	EXEMPLA	EXEMPLAR
	EXEMPLAR	EXEMPLARS · EXEMPLARY
	EXEMPLE	EXEMPLES
	EXEMPT	EXEMPTS
	EXEMPTION	EXEMPTIONS
	EXEQUATUR	EXEQUATURS
SEXERCISE	**EXERCISE**	EXERCISED · EXERCISER · EXERCISES
	EXERCISER	EXERCISERS
SEXERCISES	**EXERCISES**	
	EXERCYCLE	EXERCYCLES
	EXERGUE	EXERGUES
	EXERT	EXERTS
	EXERTION	EXERTIONS
DEXES · HEXES · KEXES · LEXES · REXES SEXES · TEXES · VEXES · WEXES · YEXES ZEXES	**EXES**	
	EXFOLIANT	EXFOLIANTS
	EXFOLIATE	EXFOLIATED · EXFOLIATES
	EXHALANT	EXHALANTS
	EXHALE	EXHALED · EXHALES
	EXHALENT	EXHALENTS
	EXHAUST	EXHAUSTS
	EXHAUSTER	EXHAUSTERS
	EXHEDRA	EXHEDRAE
	EXHIBIT	EXHIBITS
	EXHIBITER	EXHIBITERS
	EXHIBITOR	EXHIBITORS · EXHIBITORY
	EXHORT	EXHORTS
	EXHORTER	EXHORTERS
	EXHUMATE	EXHUMATED · EXHUMATES
	EXHUME	EXHUMED · EXHUMER · EXHUMES
	EXHUMER	EXHUMERS
DEXIES	**EXIES**	
	EXIGEANT	EXIGEANTE
	EXIGENCE	EXIGENCES
	EXIGENT	EXIGENTS
	EXILE	EXILED · EXILER · EXILES
	EXILEMENT	EXILEMENTS
	EXILER	EXILERS
REXINE	**EXINE**	EXINES
REXINES	**EXINES**	
HEXING · SEXING · VEXING · WEXING YEXING	**EXING**	
SEXIST	**EXIST**	EXISTS
	EXISTENCE	EXISTENCES
	EXISTENT	EXISTENTS
SEXISTS	**EXISTS**	
	EXIT	EXITS
	EXITANCE	EXITANCES
	EXO	EXON
	EXOCARP	EXOCARPS
	EXOCRINE	EXOCRINES
	EXOCYTOSE	EXOCYTOSED · EXOCYTOSES
	EXODE	EXODES
	EXODERM	EXODERMS
	EXODIST	EXODISTS

FRONT HOOK	ROOT WORD	END HOOK
	EXODONTIA	EXODONTIAS
	EXOENZYME	EXOENZYMES
	EXOGEN	EXOGENS
	EXOGENISM	EXOGENISMS
	EXOMION	EXOMIONS
	EXON	EXONS
	EXONERATE	EXONERATED · EXONERATES
	EXONUMIST	EXONUMISTS
	EXONYM	EXONYMS
	EXOPLANET	EXOPLANETS
	EXOPLASM	EXOPLASMS
	EXOPOD	EXOPODS
	EXOPODITE	EXOPODITES
	EXORATION	EXORATIONS
	EXORCISE	EXORCISED · EXORCISER · EXORCISES
	EXORCISER	EXORCISERS
	EXORCISM	EXORCISMS
	EXORCIST	EXORCISTS
	EXORCIZE	EXORCIZED · EXORCIZER · EXORCIZES
	EXORCIZER	EXORCIZERS
	EXORDIA	EXORDIAL
	EXORDIUM	EXORDIUMS
	EXOSMOSE	EXOSMOSES
	EXOSPHERE	EXOSPHERES
	EXOSPORE	EXOSPORES
	EXOTIC	EXOTICA · EXOTICS
	EXOTICISM	EXOTICISMS
	EXOTICIST	EXOTICISTS
	EXOTISM	EXOTISMS
	EXOTOXIN	EXOTOXINS
	EXOTROPIA	EXOTROPIAS
	EXPAND	EXPANDS
	EXPANDER	EXPANDERS
	EXPANDOR	EXPANDORS
	EXPANSE	EXPANSES
	EXPANSION	EXPANSIONS
	EXPAT	EXPATS
	EXPATIATE	EXPATIATED · EXPATIATES
	EXPECT	EXPECTS
	EXPECTANT	EXPECTANTS
	EXPECTER	EXPECTERS
	EXPECTING	EXPECTINGS
	EXPEDIENT	EXPEDIENTS
	EXPEDITE	EXPEDITED · EXPEDITER · EXPEDITES
	EXPEDITER	EXPEDITERS
	EXPEDITOR	EXPEDITORS
	EXPEL	EXPELS
	EXPELLANT	EXPELLANTS
	EXPELLEE	EXPELLEES
	EXPELLENT	EXPELLENTS
	EXPELLER	EXPELLERS
	EXPEND	EXPENDS
	EXPENDER	EXPENDERS
	EXPENSE	EXPENSED · EXPENSES
SEXPERT	EXPERT	EXPERTS
	EXPERTISE	EXPERTISED · EXPERTISES
	EXPERTISM	EXPERTISMS
	EXPERTIZE	EXPERTIZED · EXPERTIZES
SEXPERTS	EXPERTS	
	EXPIATE	EXPIATED · EXPIATES
	EXPIATION	EXPIATIONS
	EXPIATOR	EXPIATORS · EXPIATORY
	EXPIRANT	EXPIRANTS
	EXPIRE	EXPIRED · EXPIRER · EXPIRES
	EXPIRER	EXPIRERS
	EXPISCATE	EXPISCATED · EXPISCATES
	EXPLAIN	EXPLAINS
	EXPLAINER	EXPLAINERS
	EXPLANT	EXPLANTS

FRONT HOOK	ROOT WORD	END HOOK
	EXPLETIVE	EXPLETIVES
	EXPLICATE	EXPLICATED · EXPLICATES
	EXPLICIT	EXPLICITS
	EXPLODE	EXPLODED · EXPLODER · EXPLODES
	EXPLODER	EXPLODERS
	EXPLOIT	EXPLOITS
	EXPLOITER	EXPLOITERS
	EXPLORE	EXPLORED · EXPLORER · EXPLORES
	EXPLORER	EXPLORERS
	EXPLOSION	EXPLOSIONS
	EXPLOSIVE	EXPLOSIVES
	EXPO	EXPOS
	EXPONENT	EXPONENTS
	EXPORT	EXPORTS
	EXPORTER	EXPORTERS
	EXPOS	EXPOSE
	EXPOSAL	EXPOSALS
	EXPOSE	EXPOSED · EXPOSER · EXPOSES
	EXPOSER	EXPOSERS
	EXPOSIT	EXPOSITS
	EXPOSITOR	EXPOSITORS · EXPOSITORY
	EXPOSTURE	EXPOSTURES
	EXPOSURE	EXPOSURES
	EXPOUND	EXPOUNDS
	EXPOUNDER	EXPOUNDERS
	EXPRESS	EXPRESSO
	EXPRESSER	EXPRESSERS
	EXPRESSO	EXPRESSOS
	EXPUGN	EXPUGNS
	EXPULSE	EXPULSED · EXPULSES
	EXPULSION	EXPULSIONS
	EXPUNCT	EXPUNCTS
	EXPUNGE	EXPUNGED · EXPUNGER · EXPUNGES
	EXPUNGER	EXPUNGERS
	EXPURGATE	EXPURGATED · EXPURGATES
	EXPURGE	EXPURGED · EXPURGES
	EXQUISITE	EXQUISITES
	EXSCIND	EXSCINDS
	EXSECANT	EXSECANTS
	EXSECT	EXSECTS
	EXSECTION	EXSECTIONS
	EXSERT	EXSERTS
	EXSERTION	EXSERTIONS
	EXSICCATE	EXSICCATED · EXSICCATES
SEXTANT	**EXTANT**	
	EXTEMPORE	EXTEMPORES
	EXTEND	EXTENDS
	EXTENDER	EXTENDERS
	EXTENSION	EXTENSIONS
	EXTENSOR	EXTENSORS
	EXTENT	EXTENTS
	EXTENUATE	EXTENUATED · EXTENUATES
	EXTERIOR	EXTERIORS
	EXTERMINE	EXTERMINED · EXTERMINES
	EXTERN	EXTERNE · EXTERNS
	EXTERNAL	EXTERNALS
	EXTERNAT	EXTERNATS
	EXTERNE	EXTERNES
	EXTINCT	EXTINCTS
	EXTINE	EXTINES
	EXTIRP	EXTIRPS
	EXTIRPATE	EXTIRPATED · EXTIRPATES
	EXTOL	EXTOLD · EXTOLL · EXTOLS
	EXTOLL	EXTOLLS
	EXTOLLER	EXTOLLERS
	EXTOLMENT	EXTOLMENTS
	EXTORT	EXTORTS
	EXTORTER	EXTORTERS
	EXTORTION	EXTORTIONS

FRONT HOOK	ROOT WORD	END HOOK
	EXTRA	EXTRAS
	EXTRABOLD	EXTRABOLDS
	EXTRACT	EXTRACTS
	EXTRACTOR	EXTRACTORS
	EXTRADITE	EXTRADITED ▪ EXTRADITES
	EXTRAIT	EXTRAITS
DEXTRALITY	**EXTRALITY**	
	EXTRANET	EXTRANETS
	EXTRAPOSE	EXTRAPOSED ▪ EXTRAPOSES
	EXTRAVERT	EXTRAVERTS
	EXTREAT	EXTREATS
	EXTREMA	EXTREMAL
	EXTREMAL	EXTREMALS
	EXTREME	EXTREMER ▪ EXTREMES
	EXTREMES	EXTREMEST
	EXTREMISM	EXTREMISMS
	EXTREMIST	EXTREMISTS
	EXTRICATE	EXTRICATED ▪ EXTRICATES
DEXTRORSAL	**EXTRORSAL**	
DEXTRORSE	**EXTRORSE**	
	EXTROVERT	EXTROVERTS
	EXTRUDE	EXTRUDED ▪ EXTRUDER ▪ EXTRUDES
	EXTRUDER	EXTRUDERS
	EXTRUSION	EXTRUSIONS
	EXTUBATE	EXTUBATED ▪ EXTUBATES
	EXUBERATE	EXUBERATED ▪ EXUBERATES
	EXUDATE	EXUDATES
	EXUDATION	EXUDATIONS
	EXUDE	EXUDED ▪ EXUDES
	EXUL	EXULS ▪ EXULT
	EXULT	EXULTS
	EXULTANCE	EXULTANCES
	EXURB	EXURBS
	EXURBIA	EXURBIAS
	EXUVIA	EXUVIAE ▪ EXUVIAL
	EXUVIATE	EXUVIATED ▪ EXUVIATES
	EYALET	EYALETS
	EYAS	EYASS
	EYE	EYED ▪ EYEN ▪ EYER ▪ EYES
	EYEBALL	EYEBALLS
	EYEBANK	EYEBANKS
	EYEBAR	EYEBARS
	EYEBATH	EYEBATHS
	EYEBEAM	EYEBEAMS
	EYEBLACK	EYEBLACKS
	EYEBLINK	EYEBLINKS
	EYEBOLT	EYEBOLTS
	EYEBRIGHT	EYEBRIGHTS
	EYEBROW	EYEBROWS
	EYECUP	EYECUPS
FEYED ▪ HEYED ▪ KEYED	**EYED**	
	EYEFOLD	EYEFOLDS
	EYEFUL	EYEFULS
	EYEHOLE	EYEHOLES
	EYEHOOK	EYEHOOKS
	EYELET	EYELETS
	EYELETEER	EYELETEERS
	EYELIAD	EYELIADS
	EYELID	EYELIDS
	EYELIFT	EYELIFTS
	EYELINER	EYELINERS
SEYEN	**EYEN**	
	EYEOPENER	EYEOPENERS
	EYEPIECE	EYEPIECES
	EYEPOINT	EYEPOINTS
	EYEPOPPER	EYEPOPPERS
FEYER ▪ GEYER	**EYER**	EYERS
	EYESHADE	EYESHADES
	EYESHADOW	EYESHADOWS

E

FRONT HOOK	ROOT WORD	END HOOK
	EYESHINE	EYESHINES
	EYESHOT	EYESHOTS
	EYESIGHT	EYESIGHTS
	EYESORE	EYESORES
	EYESPOT	EYESPOTS
	EYESTALK	EYESTALKS
	EYESTONE	EYESTONES
	EYESTRAIN	EYESTRAINS
	EYEWATER	EYEWATERS
	EYEWINK	EYEWINKS
FEYING · HEYING · KEYING	**EYING**	
	EYLIAD	EYLIADS
	EYOT	EYOTS
	EYRA	EYRAS
	EYRE	EYRES
	EYRIE	EYRIES

F

FRONT HOOK	ROOT WORD	END HOOK
	FA	FAA = FAB = FAD = FAE = FAG = FAH = FAN FAP = FAR = FAS = FAT = FAW = FAX = FAY
	FAA	FAAN = FAAS
	FAB	FABS
	FABLE	FABLED = FABLER = FABLES
	FABLER	FABLERS
	FABLIAU	FABLIAUX
	FABLING	FABLINGS
	FABRIC	FABRICS
	FABRICANT	FABRICANTS
	FABRICATE	FABRICATED = FABRICATES
	FABULATE	FABULATED = FABULATES
	FABULATOR	FABULATORS
	FABULISE	FABULISED = FABULISES
	FABULIST	FABULISTS
	FABULIZE	FABULIZED = FABULIZES
	FABURDEN	FABURDENS
	FACADE	FACADES
	FACE	FACED = FACER = FACES = FACET
	FACEBAR	FACEBARS
	FACECLOTH	FACECLOTHS
	FACEDOWN	FACEDOWNS
	FACELIFT	FACELIFTS
	FACEMAIL	FACEMAILS
	FACEMASK	FACEMASKS
	FACEPLATE	FACEPLATES
	FACEPRINT	FACEPRINTS
	FACER	FACERS
	FACET	FACETE = FACETS
	FACETE	FACETED
	FACIA	FACIAE = FACIAL = FACIAS
	FACIAL	FACIALS
	FACIEND	FACIENDS
	FACING	FACINGS
	FACONNE	FACONNES
	FACSIMILE	FACSIMILED = FACSIMILES
	FACT	FACTS
	FACTICE	FACTICES
	FACTION	FACTIONS
	FACTOID	FACTOIDS
	FACTOR	FACTORS = FACTORY
	FACTORAGE	FACTORAGES
	FACTORIAL	FACTORIALS
	FACTORING	FACTORINGS
	FACTORISE	FACTORISED = FACTORISES
	FACTORIZE	FACTORIZED = FACTORIZES
	FACTOTUM	FACTOTUMS
	FACTSHEET	FACTSHEETS
	FACTUM	FACTUMS
	FACTURE	FACTURES
	FACULA	FACULAE = FACULAR
	FAD	FADE = FADO = FADS = FADY
	FADAISE	FADAISES
	FADDISM	FADDISMS
	FADDIST	FADDISTS
	FADDLE	FADDLED = FADDLES
	FADE	FADED = FADER = FADES
	FADEAWAY	FADEAWAYS
	FADEIN	FADEINS
	FADEOUT	FADEOUTS
	FADER	FADERS
	FADEUR	FADEURS
	FADGE	FADGED = FADGES
	FADING	FADINGS
	FADO	FADOS
	FADOMETER	FADOMETERS

F

FRONT HOOK	ROOT WORD	END HOOK
	FAENA	FAENAS
	FAERIE	FAERIES
	FAFF	FAFFS
	FAG	FAGS
	FAGGING	FAGGINGS
	FAGGOT	FAGGOTS = FAGGOTY (offensive)
	FAGGOTING	FAGGOTINGS
	FAGIN	FAGINS
	FAGOT	FAGOTS
	FAGOTER	FAGOTERS
	FAGOTING	FAGOTINGS
	FAGOTTIST	FAGOTTISTS
	FAH	FAHS
	FAHLBAND	FAHLBANDS
	FAHLORE	FAHLORES
	FAIBLE	FAIBLES
	FAIENCE	FAIENCES
	FAIK	FAIKS
	FAIL	FAILS
	FAILING	FAILINGS
	FAILLE	FAILLES
	FAILURE	FAILURES
	FAIN	FAINE = FAINS = FAINT
	FAINE	FAINED = FAINER = FAINES
	FAINEANCE	FAINEANCES
	FAINEANT	FAINEANTS
	FAINES	FAINEST
	FAINNE	FAINNES
	FAINNES	FAINNESS
	FAINT	FAINTS = FAINTY
	FAINTER	FAINTERS
	FAINTING	FAINTINGS
	FAIR	FAIRS = FAIRY
	FAIRGOER	FAIRGOERS
	FAIRING	FAIRINGS
	FAIRLEAD	FAIRLEADS
	FAIRWAY	FAIRWAYS
	FAIRYDOM	FAIRYDOMS
	FAIRYHOOD	FAIRYHOODS
	FAIRYISM	FAIRYISMS
	FAIRYLAND	FAIRYLANDS
	FAIRYTALE	FAIRYTALES
	FAITH	FAITHS
	FAITHCURE	FAITHCURES
	FAITHER	FAITHERS
	FAITHFUL	FAITHFULS
	FAITOR	FAITORS
	FAITOUR	FAITOURS
	FAJITA	FAJITAS
	FAKE	FAKED = FAKER = FAKES = FAKEY
	FAKEER	FAKEERS
	FAKEMENT	FAKEMENTS
	FAKER	FAKERS = FAKERY
	FAKIR	FAKIRS
	FAKIRISM	FAKIRISMS
	FALAFEL	FALAFELS
	FALANGISM	FALANGISMS
	FALANGIST	FALANGISTS
	FALBALA	FALBALAS
	FALCADE	FALCADES
	FALCATE	FALCATED
	FALCATION	FALCATIONS
	FALCHION	FALCHIONS
	FALCON	FALCONS
	FALCONER	FALCONERS
	FALCONET	FALCONETS
	FALCULA	FALCULAE = FALCULAS
	FALDAGE	FALDAGES
	FALDERAL	FALDERALS

FRONT HOOK	ROOT WORD	END HOOK
	FALDEROL	FALDEROLS
	FALDETTA	FALDETTAS
	FALDSTOOL	FALDSTOOLS
	FALL	FALLS
	FALLAL	FALLALS
	FALLAWAY	FALLAWAYS
	FALLBACK	FALLBACKS
	FALLBOARD	FALLBOARDS
	FALLER	FALLERS
	FALLING	FALLINGS
	FALLOFF	FALLOFFS
	FALLOUT	FALLOUTS
	FALLOW	FALLOWS
	FALSE	FALSED ▪ FALSER ▪ FALSES
	FALSEFACE	FALSEFACES
	FALSEHOOD	FALSEHOODS
	FALSER	FALSERS
	FALSES	FALSEST
	FALSETTO	FALSETTOS
	FALSEWORK	FALSEWORKS
	FALSIE	FALSIES
	FALSIFIER	FALSIFIERS
	FALSISM	FALSISMS
	FALTBOAT	FALTBOATS
	FALTER	FALTERS
	FALTERER	FALTERERS
	FALTERING	FALTERINGS
	FAME	FAMED ▪ FAMES
	FAMILIAR	FAMILIARS
	FAMILISM	FAMILISMS
	FAMILLE	FAMILLES
	FAMINE	FAMINES
	FAN	FAND ▪ FANE ▪ FANG ▪ FANK ▪ FANO ▪ FANS
	FANAL	FANALS
	FANATIC	FANATICS
	FANBASE	FANBASES
	FANCIER	FANCIERS
	FANCIES	FANCIEST
	FANCYWORK	FANCYWORKS
	FAND	FANDS
	FANDANGLE	FANDANGLES
	FANDANGO	FANDANGOS
	FANDOM	FANDOMS
	FANE	FANES
	FANEGA	FANEGAS
	FANEGADA	FANEGADAS
	FANFARADE	FANFARADES
	FANFARE	FANFARED ▪ FANFARES
	FANFARON	FANFARONA ▪ FANFARONS
	FANFARONA	FANFARONAS
	FANFIC	FANFICS
	FANFOLD	FANFOLDS
	FANG	FANGA ▪ FANGO ▪ FANGS
	FANGA	FANGAS
	FANGLE	FANGLED ▪ FANGLES
	FANGLES	FANGLESS
	FANGO	FANGOS
	FANION	FANIONS
	FANJET	FANJETS
	FANK	FANKS
	FANKLE	FANKLED ▪ FANKLES
	FANLIGHT	FANLIGHTS
	FANNEL	FANNELL ▪ FANNELS
	FANNELL	FANNELLS
	FANNER	FANNERS
	FANNING	FANNINGS
	FANO	FANON ▪ FANOS
	FANON	FANONS
	FANTAD	FANTADS

F

F

FRONT HOOK	ROOT WORD	END HOOK
	FANTAIL	FANTAILS
	FANTASIA	FANTASIAS
	FANTASIE	FANTASIED · FANTASIES
	FANTASISE	FANTASISED · FANTASISER · FANTASISES
	FANTASIST	FANTASISTS
	FANTASIZE	FANTASIZED · FANTASIZER · FANTASIZES
	FANTASM	FANTASMS
	FANTASQUE	FANTASQUES
	FANTAST	FANTASTS
	FANTASTIC	FANTASTICO · FANTASTICS
	FANTEEG	FANTEEGS
	FANTIGUE	FANTIGUES
	FANTOD	FANTODS
	FANTOM	FANTOMS
	FANUM	FANUMS
	FANWORT	FANWORTS
	FANZINE	FANZINES
	FAQIR	FAQIRS
	FAQUIR	FAQUIRS
AFAR	**FAR**	FARD · FARE · FARL · FARM · FARO FARS · FART
	FARAD	FARADS
	FARADAY	FARADAYS
	FARADISE	FARADISED · FARADISER · FARADISES
	FARADISER	FARADISERS
	FARADISM	FARADISMS
	FARADIZE	FARADIZED · FARADIZER · FARADIZES
	FARADIZER	FARADIZERS
	FARANDINE	FARANDINES
	FARANDOLE	FARANDOLES
	FARAWAY	FARAWAYS
	FARCE	FARCED · FARCER · FARCES
	FARCEMEAT	FARCEMEATS
	FARCER	FARCERS
	FARCEUR	FARCEURS
	FARCEUSE	FARCEUSES
	FARCI	FARCIE · FARCIN
	FARCIE	FARCIED · FARCIES
	FARCIN	FARCING · FARCINS
	FARCING	FARCINGS
	FARD	FARDS
	FARDAGE	FARDAGES
	FARDEL	FARDELS
	FARDEN	FARDENS
	FARDING	FARDINGS
	FARE	FARED · FARER · FARES
	FARER	FARERS
	FAREWELL	FAREWELLS
	FARFAL	FARFALS
	FARFEL	FARFELS
	FARINA	FARINAS
	FARINHA	FARINHAS
	FARL	FARLE · FARLS
	FARLE	FARLES
	FARM	FARMS
	FARMER	FARMERS · FARMERY
	FARMHAND	FARMHANDS
	FARMHOUSE	FARMHOUSES
	FARMING	FARMINGS
	FARMLAND	FARMLANDS
	FARMSTEAD	FARMSTEADS
	FARMWORK	FARMWORKS
	FARMYARD	FARMYARDS
	FARNARKEL	FARNARKELS
	FARNESOL	FARNESOLS
	FARO	FAROS
	FAROLITO	FAROLITOS
	FARRAGO	FARRAGOS
	FARREN	FARRENS

FRONT HOOK	ROOT WORD	END HOOK
	FARRIER	FARRIERS · FARRIERY
	FARROW	FARROWS
	FARRUCA	FARRUCAS
AFARS	FARS	FARSE
	FARSE	FARSED · FARSES
	FARSIDE	FARSIDES
	FART	FARTS (offensive)
	FARTHEL	FARTHELS
	FARTHING	FARTHINGS
	FARTLEK	FARTLEKS
	FAS	FASH · FAST
	FASCI	FASCIA · FASCIO · FASCIS
	FASCIA	FASCIAE · FASCIAL · FASCIAS
	FASCIATE	FASCIATED
	FASCICLE	FASCICLED · FASCICLES
	FASCICULE	FASCICULES
	FASCINATE	FASCINATED · FASCINATES
	FASCINE	FASCINES
	FASCIOLA	FASCIOLAS
	FASCIOLE	FASCIOLES
	FASCIS	FASCISM · FASCIST
	FASCISM	FASCISMI · FASCISMO · FASCISMS
	FASCIST	FASCISTA · FASCISTI · FASCISTS
	FASCISTI	FASCISTIC
	FASHION	FASHIONS · FASHIONY
	FASHIONER	FASHIONERS
	FAST	FASTI · FASTS
	FASTBACK	FASTBACKS
	FASTBALL	FASTBALLS
	FASTEN	FASTENS
	FASTENER	FASTENERS
	FASTENING	FASTENINGS
	FASTER	FASTERS
	FASTI	FASTIE
	FASTIE	FASTIES
	FASTIGIUM	FASTIGIUMS
	FASTING	FASTINGS
	FAT	FATE · FATS
	FATALISM	FATALISMS
	FATALIST	FATALISTS
	FATBACK	FATBACKS
	FATBIRD	FATBIRDS
	FATE	FATED · FATES
	FATHEAD	FATHEADS
	FATHER	FATHERS
	FATHERING	FATHERINGS
	FATHOM	FATHOMS
	FATHOMER	FATHOMERS
	FATIGATE	FATIGATED · FATIGATES
	FATIGUE	FATIGUED · FATIGUES
	FATLING	FATLINGS
	FATS	FATSO
	FATSIA	FATSIAS
	FATSO	FATSOS (offensive)
	FATSTOCK	FATSTOCKS
	FATTEN	FATTENS
	FATTENER	FATTENERS
	FATTENING	FATTENINGS
	FATTIES	FATTIEST
	FATTISM	FATTISMS
	FATTIST	FATTISTS
	FATWA	FATWAH · FATWAS
	FATWAH	FATWAHS
	FATWOOD	FATWOODS
	FAUBOURG	FAUBOURGS
	FAUCAL	FAUCALS
	FAUCET	FAUCETS
	FAUCHION	FAUCHIONS
	FAUCHON	FAUCHONS

FRONT HOOK	ROOT WORD	END HOOK
	FAULCHION	FAULCHIONS
	FAULD	FAULDS
	FAULT	FAULTS ▪ FAULTY
	FAUN	FAUNA ▪ FAUNS
	FAUNA	FAUNAE ▪ FAUNAL ▪ FAUNAS
	FAUNIST	FAUNISTS
	FAUNULA	FAUNULAE
	FAUNULE	FAUNULES
	FAUR	FAURD
	FAUT	FAUTS
	FAUTEUIL	FAUTEUILS
	FAUTOR	FAUTORS
	FAUVE	FAUVES
	FAUVETTE	FAUVETTES
	FAUVISM	FAUVISMS
	FAUVIST	FAUVISTS
	FAVA	FAVAS
	FAVE	FAVEL ▪ FAVER ▪ FAVES
	FAVEL	FAVELA ▪ FAVELL
	FAVELA	FAVELAS
	FAVELL	FAVELLA
	FAVELLA	FAVELLAS
	FAVES	FAVEST
	FAVISM	FAVISMS
	FAVOR	FAVORS
	FAVORER	FAVORERS
	FAVORITE	FAVORITES
	FAVOUR	FAVOURS
	FAVOURER	FAVOURERS
	FAVOURITE	FAVOURITES
	FAVRILE	FAVRILES
	FAW	FAWN ▪ FAWS
	FAWN	FAWNS ▪ FAWNY
	FAWNER	FAWNERS
	FAWNING	FAWNINGS
OFAY	**FAY**	FAYS
	FAYALITE	FAYALITES
	FAYENCE	FAYENCES
	FAYNE	FAYNED ▪ FAYNES
	FAYRE	FAYRES
OFAYS (offensive)	**FAYS**	
	FAZE	FAZED ▪ FAZES
	FAZENDA	FAZENDAS
	FE	FED ▪ FEE ▪ FEG ▪ FEH ▪ FEM ▪ FEN ▪ FER ▪ FES ▪ FET ▪ FEU ▪ FEW ▪ FEY ▪ FEZ
	FEAGUE	FEAGUED ▪ FEAGUES
	FEAL	FEALS
AFEAR	**FEAR**	FEARE ▪ FEARS
	FEARE	FEARED ▪ FEARER ▪ FEARES
AFEARED	**FEARED**	
	FEARER	FEARERS
AFEARING	**FEARING**	
AFEARS	**FEARS**	
	FEASANCE	FEASANCES
	FEASE	FEASED ▪ FEASES
	FEAST	FEASTS
	FEASTER	FEASTERS
	FEASTING	FEASTINGS
	FEAT	FEATS
	FEATHER	FEATHERS ▪ FEATHERY
	FEATURE	FEATURED ▪ FEATURES
	FEAZE	FEAZED ▪ FEAZES
	FEBLESSE	FEBLESSES
	FEBRICULA	FEBRICULAS
	FEBRICULE	FEBRICULES
	FEBRIFUGE	FEBRIFUGES
AFEBRILE	**FEBRILE**	
	FECHT	FECHTS
	FECHTER	FECHTERS

FRONT HOOK	ROOT WORD	END HOOK
	FECIAL	FECIALS
	FECK	FECKS (offensive)
	FECKIN	FECKING (offensive)
	FECULA	FECULAE • FECULAS
	FECULENCE	FECULENCES
	FECUNDATE	FECUNDATED • FECUNDATES
	FED	FEDS
	FEDARIE	FEDARIES
	FEDAYEE	FEDAYEEN
	FEDELINI	FEDELINIS
	FEDERAL	FEDERALS
	FEDERARIE	FEDERARIES
	FEDERATE	FEDERATED • FEDERATES
	FEDERATOR	FEDERATORS
	FEDORA	FEDORAS
	FEE	FEEB • FEED • FEEL • FEEN • FEER FEES • FEET
	FEEB	FEEBS
	FEEBLE	FEEBLED • FEEBLER • FEEBLES
	FEEBLES	FEEBLEST
	FEED	FEEDS
	FEEDBACK	FEEDBACKS
	FEEDBAG	FEEDBAGS
	FEEDER	FEEDERS
	FEEDGRAIN	FEEDGRAINS
	FEEDHOLE	FEEDHOLES
	FEEDING	FEEDINGS
	FEEDLOT	FEEDLOTS
	FEEDSTOCK	FEEDSTOCKS
	FEEDSTUFF	FEEDSTUFFS
	FEEDWATER	FEEDWATERS
	FEEDYARD	FEEDYARDS
	FEEL	FEELS
	FEELBAD	FEELBADS
	FEELER	FEELERS
	FEELGOOD	FEELGOODS
	FEELING	FEELINGS
	FEEN	FEENS
	FEER	FEERS
	FEERIE	FEERIES
	FEERIN	FEERING • FEERINS
	FEERING	FEERINGS
	FEES	FEESE
	FEESE	FEESED • FEESES
	FEEZE	FEEZED • FEEZES
	FEG	FEGS
	FEH	FEHM • FEHS
	FEHM	FEHME
	FEIGN	FEIGNS
	FEIGNER	FEIGNERS
	FEIGNING	FEIGNINGS
	FEIJOA	FEIJOAS
	FEINT	FEINTS
	FEIS	FEIST
	FEIST	FEISTS • FEISTY
	FELAFEL	FELAFELS
	FELDGRAU	FELDGRAUS
	FELDSCHAR	FELDSCHARS
	FELDSCHER	FELDSCHERS
	FELDSHER	FELDSHERS
	FELDSPAR	FELDSPARS
	FELDSPATH	FELDSPATHS
	FELICIA	FELICIAS
	FELID	FELIDS
	FELINE	FELINES
	FELL	FELLA • FELLS • FELLY
	FELLA	FELLAH • FELLAS
	FELLAH	FELLAHS
	FELLATE	FELLATED • FELLATES

FRONT HOOK	ROOT WORD	END HOOK
	FELLATIO	FELLATION · FELLATIOS
	FELLATION	FELLATIONS
	FELLATOR	FELLATORS
	FELLER	FELLERS
	FELLOE	FELLOES
	FELLOW	FELLOWS
	FELON	FELONS · FELONY
	FELSITE	FELSITES
	FELSPAR	FELSPARS
	FELSTONE	FELSTONES
	FELT	FELTS · FELTY
	FELTER	FELTERS
	FELTING	FELTINGS
	FELUCCA	FELUCCAS
	FELWORT	FELWORTS
	FEM	FEME · FEMS
	FEMAL	FEMALE · FEMALS
	FEMALE	FEMALES
	FEME	FEMES
	FEMERALL	FEMERALLS
	FEMINAZI	FEMINAZIS
	FEMININE	FEMININES
	FEMINISE	FEMINISED · FEMINISES
	FEMINISM	FEMINISMS
	FEMINIST	FEMINISTS
	FEMINIZE	FEMINIZED · FEMINIZES
	FEMITER	FEMITERS
	FEMME	FEMMES
	FEMORA	FEMORAL
	FEMUR	FEMURS
	FEN	FEND · FENI · FENS · FENT
	FENAGLE	FENAGLED · FENAGLES
	FENCE	FENCED · FENCER · FENCES
	FENCER	FENCERS
	FENCEROW	FENCEROWS
	FENCIBLE	FENCIBLES
	FENCING	FENCINGS
	FEND	FENDS · FENDY
	FENDER	FENDERS
	FENESTRA	FENESTRAE · FENESTRAL · FENESTRAS
	FENESTRAL	FENESTRALS
	FENI	FENIS
	FENITAR	FENITARS
	FENLAND	FENLANDS
	FENNEC	FENNECS
	FENNEL	FENNELS
	FENNIES	FENNIEST
	FENT	FENTS
	FENTANYL	FENTANYLS
	FENTHION	FENTHIONS
	FENUGREEK	FENUGREEKS
	FENURON	FENURONS
	FEOD	FEODS
	FEOFF	FEOFFS
	FEOFFEE	FEOFFEES
	FEOFFER	FEOFFERS
	FEOFFMENT	FEOFFMENTS
	FEOFFOR	FEOFFORS
	FER	FERE · FERM · FERN
	FERAL	FERALS
	FERBAM	FERBAMS
YFERE	**FERE**	FERER · FERES
	FERES	FEREST
	FERIA	FERIAE · FERIAL · FERIAS
	FERLIE	FERLIED · FERLIER · FERLIES
	FERLIES	FERLIEST
	FERM	FERMI · FERMS
	FERMATA	FERMATAS
	FERMENT	FERMENTS

FRONT HOOK	ROOT WORD	END HOOK
	FERMENTER	FERMENTERS
	FERMENTOR	FERMENTORS
	FERMI	FERMIS
	FERMION	FERMIONS
	FERMIUM	FERMIUMS
	FERN	FERNS ▪ FERNY
	FERNBIRD	FERNBIRDS
	FERNING	FERNINGS
	FERNSHAW	FERNSHAWS
	FERNTICLE	FERNTICLED ▪ FERNTICLES
	FERRATE	FERRATES
	FERREL	FERRELS
	FERRET	FERRETS ▪ FERRETY
	FERRETER	FERRETERS
	FERRETING	FERRETINGS
	FERRIAGE	FERRIAGES
	FERRITE	FERRITES
	FERRITIN	FERRITINS
	FERROCENE	FERROCENES
	FERROTYPE	FERROTYPED ▪ FERROTYPES
	FERRUGO	FERRUGOS
	FERRULE	FERRULED ▪ FERRULES
	FERRUM	FERRUMS
	FERRYBOAT	FERRYBOATS
	FERTIGATE	FERTIGATED ▪ FERTIGATES
	FERTILE	FERTILER
	FERTILISE	FERTILISED ▪ FERTILISER ▪ FERTILISES
	FERTILIZE	FERTILIZED ▪ FERTILIZER ▪ FERTILIZES
	FERULA	FERULAE ▪ FERULAS
	FERULE	FERULED ▪ FERULES
	FERVOR	FERVORS
	FERVOUR	FERVOURS
	FES	FESS ▪ FEST
	FESCUE	FESCUES
	FESS	FESSE
	FESSE	FESSED ▪ FESSES
	FEST	FESTA ▪ FESTS ▪ FESTY
	FESTA	FESTAL ▪ FESTAS
	FESTAL	FESTALS
	FESTER	FESTERS
	FESTINATE	FESTINATED ▪ FESTINATES
	FESTIVAL	FESTIVALS
	FESTOON	FESTOONS
	FET	FETA ▪ FETE ▪ FETS ▪ FETT
	FETA	FETAL ▪ FETAS
	FETATION	FETATIONS
	FETCHER	FETCHERS
	FETE	FETED ▪ FETES
	FETERITA	FETERITAS
	FETIAL	FETIALS
	FETICH	FETICHE
	FETICHE	FETICHES
	FETICHISE	FETICHISED ▪ FETICHISES
	FETICHISM	FETICHISMS
	FETICHIST	FETICHISTS
	FETICHIZE	FETICHIZED ▪ FETICHIZES
	FETICIDE	FETICIDES
	FETISHISE	FETISHISED ▪ FETISHISES
	FETISHISM	FETISHISMS
	FETISHIST	FETISHISTS
	FETISHIZE	FETISHIZED ▪ FETISHIZES
	FETLOCK	FETLOCKS
	FETOR	FETORS
	FETOSCOPE	FETOSCOPES
	FETT	FETTA ▪ FETTS
	FETTA	FETTAS
	FETTER	FETTERS
	FETTERER	FETTERERS
	FETTLE	FETTLED ▪ FETTLER ▪ FETTLES

FRONT HOOK	ROOT WORD	END HOOK
	FETTLER	FETTLERS
	FETTLING	FETTLINGS
	FETTUCINE	FETTUCINES
	FETTUCINI	FETTUCINIS
	FETWA	FETWAS
	FEU	FEUD = FEUS
	FEUAR	FEUARS
	FEUD	FEUDS
	FEUDALISE	FEUDALISED = FEUDALISES
	FEUDALISM	FEUDALISMS
	FEUDALIST	FEUDALISTS
	FEUDALIZE	FEUDALIZED = FEUDALIZES
	FEUDING	FEUDINGS
	FEUDIST	FEUDISTS
	FEUILLETE	FEUILLETES
	FEUTRE	FEUTRED = FEUTRES
	FEVER	FEVERS
	FEVERFEW	FEVERFEWS
	FEVERROOT	FEVERROOTS
	FEVERWEED	FEVERWEEDS
	FEVERWORT	FEVERWORTS
	FEWMET	FEWMETS
	FEWTER	FEWTERS
	FEY	FEYS
	FIACRE	FIACRES
	FIANCE	FIANCEE = FIANCES
	FIANCEE	FIANCEES
	FIAR	FIARS
	FIASCO	FIASCOS
	FIAT	FIATS
	FIAUNT	FIAUNTS
	FIB	FIBS
	FIBBER	FIBBERS = FIBBERY
	FIBER	FIBERS
	FIBERFILL	FIBERFILLS
	FIBERISE	FIBERISED = FIBERISES
	FIBERIZE	FIBERIZED = FIBERIZES
	FIBRANNE	FIBRANNES
	FIBRE	FIBRED = FIBRES
	FIBREFILL	FIBREFILLS
	FIBRIL	FIBRILS
	FIBRILLA	FIBRILLAE = FIBRILLAR
	FIBRILLAR	FIBRILLARY
	FIBRILLIN	FIBRILLINS
	FIBRIN	FIBRINS
	FIBRINOID	FIBRINOIDS
	FIBRO	FIBROS
	FIBROCYTE	FIBROCYTES
	FIBROID	FIBROIDS
	FIBROIN	FIBROINS
	FIBROLINE	FIBROLINES
	FIBROLITE	FIBROLITES
	FIBROMA	FIBROMAS
	FIBROS	FIBROSE
	FIBROSE	FIBROSED = FIBROSES
	FIBSTER	FIBSTERS
	FIBULA	FIBULAE = FIBULAR = FIBULAS
	FICE	FICES
	FICHE	FICHES
	FICHU	FICHUS
	FICIN	FICINS
	FICKLE	FICKLED = FICKLER = FICKLES
	FICKLES	FICKLEST
	FICO	FICOS
	FICTION	FICTIONS
	FICTOR	FICTORS
	FID	FIDO = FIDS
	FIDDLE	FIDDLED = FIDDLER = FIDDLES = FIDDLEY
	FIDDLER	FIDDLERS

FRONT HOOK	ROOT WORD	END HOOK
	FIDDLEY	FIDDLEYS
	FIDEISM	FIDEISMS
	FIDEIST	FIDEISTS
	FIDELISMO	FIDELISMOS
	FIDELISTA	FIDELISTAS
	FIDGE	FIDGED = FIDGES = FIDGET
	FIDGET	FIDGETS = FIDGETY
	FIDGETER	FIDGETERS
	FIDO	FIDOS
	FIE	FIEF = FIER
	FIEF	FIEFS
	FIEFDOM	FIEFDOMS
AFIELD	**FIELD**	FIELDS
	FIELDER	FIELDERS
	FIELDFARE	FIELDFARES
	FIELDING	FIELDINGS
	FIELDVOLE	FIELDVOLES
	FIELDWARD	FIELDWARDS
	FIELDWORK	FIELDWORKS
	FIEND	FIENDS
	FIENT	FIENTS
	FIER	FIERE = FIERS = FIERY
	FIERCE	FIERCER
	FIERE	FIERES
	FIEST	FIESTA
	FIESTA	FIESTAS
	FIFE	FIFED = FIFER = FIFES
	FIFER	FIFERS
	FIFTEEN	FIFTEENS
	FIFTEENER	FIFTEENERS
	FIFTEENTH	FIFTEENTHS
	FIFTH	FIFTHS
	FIFTIETH	FIFTIETHS
	FIG	FIGO = FIGS
	FIGEATER	FIGEATERS
	FIGHT	FIGHTS
	FIGHTBACK	FIGHTBACKS
	FIGHTER	FIGHTERS
	FIGHTING	FIGHTINGS
	FIGJAM	FIGJAMS
	FIGMENT	FIGMENTS
	FIGO	FIGOS
	FIGULINE	FIGULINES
	FIGURANT	FIGURANTE = FIGURANTS
	FIGURANTE	FIGURANTES
	FIGURE	FIGURED = FIGURER = FIGURES
	FIGURER	FIGURERS
	FIGURINE	FIGURINES
	FIGURIST	FIGURISTS
	FIGWORT	FIGWORTS
	FIKE	FIKED = FIKES
	FIL	FILA = FILE = FILL = FILM = FILO = FILS
	FILA	FILAR
	FILABEG	FILABEGS
	FILACER	FILACERS
	FILAGREE	FILAGREED = FILAGREES
	FILAMENT	FILAMENTS
	FILANDER	FILANDERS
	FILAREE	FILAREES
	FILARIA	FILARIAE = FILARIAL = FILARIAN
		FILARIAS
	FILARIID	FILARIIDS
	FILASSE	FILASSES
	FILATURE	FILATURES
	FILAZER	FILAZERS
	FILBERD	FILBERDS
	FILBERT	FILBERTS
	FILCHER	FILCHERS
	FILCHING	FILCHINGS

FRONT HOOK	ROOT WORD	END HOOK
	FILE	FILED · FILER · FILES · FILET
	FILECARD	FILECARDS
	FILEMOT	FILEMOTS
	FILENAME	FILENAMES
	FILER	FILERS
	FILET	FILETS
	FILFOT	FILFOTS
	FILIATE	FILIATED · FILIATES
	FILIATION	FILIATIONS
	FILIBEG	FILIBEGS
	FILICIDE	FILICIDES
	FILIGRAIN	FILIGRAINS
	FILIGRANE	FILIGRANES
	FILIGREE	FILIGREED · FILIGREES
	FILING	FILINGS
	FILIOQUE	FILIOQUES
	FILISTER	FILISTERS
	FILL	FILLE · FILLO · FILLS · FILLY
	FILLAGREE	FILLAGREED · FILLAGREES
	FILLE	FILLED · FILLER · FILLES · FILLET
	FILLER	FILLERS
	FILLESTER	FILLESTERS
	FILLET	FILLETS
	FILLIBEG	FILLIBEGS
	FILLING	FILLINGS
	FILLIP	FILLIPS
	FILLIPEEN	FILLIPEENS
	FILLISTER	FILLISTERS
	FILLO	FILLOS
	FILM	FILMI · FILMS · FILMY
	FILMCARD	FILMCARDS
	FILMDOM	FILMDOMS
	FILMER	FILMERS
	FILMGOER	FILMGOERS
	FILMI	FILMIC · FILMIS
	FILMIS	FILMISH
	FILMLAND	FILMLANDS
	FILMMAKER	FILMMAKERS
	FILMSET	FILMSETS
	FILMSTRIP	FILMSTRIPS
	FILO	FILOS
	FILOPLUME	FILOPLUMES
	FILOS	FILOSE
	FILOSELLE	FILOSELLES
	FILTER	FILTERS
	FILTERER	FILTERERS
	FILTH	FILTHS · FILTHY
	FILTRATE	FILTRATED · FILTRATES
	FIMBLE	FIMBLES
	FIMBRIA	FIMBRIAE · FIMBRIAL
	FIMBRIATE	FIMBRIATED · FIMBRIATES
	FIN	FIND · FINE · FINI · FINK · FINO · FINS
	FINAGLE	FINAGLED · FINAGLER · FINAGLES
	FINAGLER	FINAGLERS
	FINAL	FINALE · FINALS
	FINALE	FINALES
	FINALIS	FINALISE · FINALISM · FINALIST
	FINALISE	FINALISED · FINALISER · FINALISES
	FINALISER	FINALISERS
	FINALISM	FINALISMS
	FINALIST	FINALISTS
	FINALIZE	FINALIZED · FINALIZER · FINALIZES
	FINALIZER	FINALIZERS
	FINANCE	FINANCED · FINANCES
	FINANCIER	FINANCIERS
	FINANCING	FINANCINGS
	FINBACK	FINBACKS
	FINCA	FINCAS
	FIND	FINDS

FRONT HOOK	ROOT WORD	END HOOK
	FINDER	FINDERS
	FINDING	FINDINGS
	FINDRAM	FINDRAMS
	FINE	FINED = FINER = FINES
	FINEER	FINEERS
	FINER	FINERS = FINERY
	FINES	FINEST
	FINESSE	FINESSED = FINESSER = FINESSES
	FINESSER	FINESSERS
	FINESSING	FINESSINGS
	FINFOOT	FINFOOTS
	FINGAN	FINGANS
	FINGER	FINGERS
	FINGERER	FINGERERS
	FINGERING	FINGERINGS
	FINGERTIP	FINGERTIPS
	FINI	FINIS
	FINIAL	FINIALS
	FINICKIN	FINICKING
	FINICKING	FINICKINGS
	FINIKIN	FINIKING
	FINING	FININGS
	FINIS	FINISH
	FINISHER	FINISHERS
	FINISHING	FINISHINGS
	FINITE	FINITES
	FINITISM	FINITISMS
	FINITUDE	FINITUDES
	FINJAN	FINJANS
	FINK	FINKS
	FINMARK	FINMARKS
	FINNAC	FINNACK = FINNACS
	FINNACK	FINNACKS
	FINNAN	FINNANS
	FINNER	FINNERS
	FINNMARK	FINNMARKS
	FINNOCHIO	FINNOCHIOS
	FINNOCK	FINNOCKS
	FINO	FINOS
	FINOCCHIO	FINOCCHIOS
	FINOCHIO	FINOCHIOS
	FIORATURA	FIORATURAE
	FIORD	FIORDS
	FIORIN	FIORINS
	FIPPENCE	FIPPENCES
	FIPPLE	FIPPLES
	FIQUE	FIQUES
	FIR	FIRE = FIRK = FIRM = FIRN = FIRS
AFIRE	FIRE	FIRED = FIRER = FIRES
	FIREARM	FIREARMS
	FIREBACK	FIREBACKS
	FIREBALL	FIREBALLS
	FIREBASE	FIREBASES
	FIREBIRD	FIREBIRDS
	FIREBOARD	FIREBOARDS
	FIREBOAT	FIREBOATS
	FIREBOMB	FIREBOMBS
	FIREBRAND	FIREBRANDS
	FIREBRAT	FIREBRATS
	FIREBREAK	FIREBREAKS
	FIREBRICK	FIREBRICKS
	FIREBUG	FIREBUGS
	FIRECLAY	FIRECLAYS
	FIRECREST	FIRECRESTS
	FIREDAMP	FIREDAMPS
	FIREDOG	FIREDOGS
	FIREDRAKE	FIREDRAKES
	FIREFANG	FIREFANGS
	FIREFIGHT	FIREFIGHTS

FRONT HOOK	ROOT WORD	END HOOK
	FIREFLOAT	FIREFLOATS
	FIREFLOOD	FIREFLOODS
	FIREGUARD	FIREGUARDS
	FIREHALL	FIREHALLS
	FIREHOUSE	FIREHOUSES
	FIRELIGHT	FIRELIGHTS
	FIRELOCK	FIRELOCKS
	FIREMARK	FIREMARKS
	FIREPAN	FIREPANS
	FIREPINK	FIREPINKS
	FIREPLACE	FIREPLACED · FIREPLACES
	FIREPLUG	FIREPLUGS
	FIREPOT	FIREPOTS
	FIREPOWER	FIREPOWERS
	FIREPROOF	FIREPROOFS
	FIRER	FIRERS
	FIREROOM	FIREROOMS
	FIRESHIP	FIRESHIPS
	FIRESIDE	FIRESIDES
	FIRESTONE	FIRESTONES
	FIRESTORM	FIRESTORMS
	FIRETHORN	FIRETHORNS
	FIRETRAP	FIRETRAPS
	FIRETRUCK	FIRETRUCKS
	FIREWALL	FIREWALLS
	FIREWATER	FIREWATERS
	FIREWEED	FIREWEEDS
	FIREWOOD	FIREWOODS
	FIREWORK	FIREWORKS
	FIREWORM	FIREWORMS
	FIRIE	FIRIES
	FIRING	FIRINGS
	FIRK	FIRKS
	FIRKIN	FIRKING · FIRKINS
	FIRLOT	FIRLOTS
	FIRM	FIRMS
	FIRMAMENT	FIRMAMENTS
	FIRMAN	FIRMANS
	FIRMER	FIRMERS
	FIRMWARE	FIRMWARES
	FIRN	FIRNS
	FIRRING	FIRRINGS
	FIRS	FIRST
	FIRST	FIRSTS
	FIRSTBORN	FIRSTBORNS
	FIRSTLING	FIRSTLINGS
	FIRTH	FIRTHS
	FISC	FISCS
	FISCAL	FISCALS
	FISCALIST	FISCALISTS
	FISGIG	FISGIGS
	FISH	FISHY
	FISHBALL	FISHBALLS
	FISHBOLT	FISHBOLTS
	FISHBONE	FISHBONES
	FISHBOWL	FISHBOWLS
	FISHCAKE	FISHCAKES
	FISHER	FISHERS · FISHERY
	FISHEYE	FISHEYES
	FISHGIG	FISHGIGS
	FISHHOOK	FISHHOOKS
	FISHING	FISHINGS
	FISHKILL	FISHKILLS
	FISHLINE	FISHLINES
	FISHMEAL	FISHMEALS
	FISHNET	FISHNETS
	FISHPLATE	FISHPLATES
	FISHPOLE	FISHPOLES
	FISHPOND	FISHPONDS

FRONT HOOK	ROOT WORD	END HOOK
	FISHSKIN	FISHSKINS
	FISHTAIL	FISHTAILS
	FISHWAY	FISHWAYS
	FISHWORM	FISHWORMS
	FISHYBACK	FISHYBACKS
	FISK	FISKS
	FISNOMIE	FISNOMIES
	FISSION	FISSIONS
	FISSIPED	FISSIPEDE · FISSIPEDS
	FISSIPEDE	FISSIPEDES
	FISSLE	FISSLED · FISSLES
	FISSURE	FISSURED · FISSURES
	FIST	FISTS · FISTY
	FISTFIGHT	FISTFIGHTS
	FISTFUL	FISTFULS
	FISTICUFF	FISTICUFFS
	FISTMELE	FISTMELES
	FISTNOTE	FISTNOTES
	FISTULA	FISTULAE · FISTULAR · FISTULAS
	FIT	FITS · FITT
	FITCH	FITCHE · FITCHY
	FITCHE	FITCHEE · FITCHES · FITCHET · FITCHEW
	FITCHET	FITCHETS
	FITCHEW	FITCHEWS
	FITMENT	FITMENTS
	FITNA	FITNAS
	FITT	FITTE · FITTS
	FITTE	FITTED · FITTER · FITTES
	FITTER	FITTERS
	FITTES	FITTEST
	FITTING	FITTINGS
	FIVE	FIVER · FIVES
	FIVEPENCE	FIVEPENCES
	FIVEPIN	FIVEPINS
	FIVER	FIVERS
	FIX	FIXT
	FIXATE	FIXATED · FIXATES
	FIXATIF	FIXATIFS
	FIXATION	FIXATIONS
	FIXATIVE	FIXATIVES
	FIXATURE	FIXATURES
	FIXER	FIXERS
	FIXING	FIXINGS
	FIXIT	FIXITY
	FIXTURE	FIXTURES
	FIXURE	FIXURES
	FIZ	FIZZ
	FIZGIG	FIZGIGS
	FIZZ	FIZZY
	FIZZEN	FIZZENS
	FIZZER	FIZZERS
	FIZZGIG	FIZZGIGS
	FIZZING	FIZZINGS
	FIZZLE	FIZZLED · FIZZLES
	FJELD	FJELDS
	FJORD	FJORDS
	FLAB	FLABS
	FLABELLUM	FLABELLUMS
	FLACK	FLACKS
	FLACKER	FLACKERS · FLACKERY
	FLACKET	FLACKETS
	FLACON	FLACONS
	FLAFF	FLAFFS
	FLAFFER	FLAFFERS
OFLAG	**FLAG**	FLAGS
	FLAGELLA	FLAGELLAR
	FLAGELLIN	FLAGELLINS
	FLAGELLUM	FLAGELLUMS
	FLAGEOLET	FLAGEOLETS

	FRONT HOOK	ROOT WORD	END HOOK
		FLAGGER	FLAGGERS
		FLAGGING	FLAGGINGS
		FLAGITATE	FLAGITATED · FLAGITATES
		FLAGON	FLAGONS
		FLAGPOLE	FLAGPOLES
		FLAGRANCE	FLAGRANCES
	OFLAGS	**FLAGS**	
		FLAGSHIP	FLAGSHIPS
		FLAGSTAFF	FLAGSTAFFS
		FLAGSTICK	FLAGSTICKS
		FLAGSTONE	FLAGSTONES
		FLAIL	FLAILS
		FLAIR	FLAIRS
		FLAK	FLAKE · FLAKS · FLAKY
		FLAKE	FLAKED · FLAKER · FLAKES · FLAKEY
		FLAKER	FLAKERS
		FLAKIES	FLAKIEST
		FLAM	FLAME · FLAMM · FLAMS · FLAMY
		FLAMBE	FLAMBEE · FLAMBES
		FLAMBEAU	FLAMBEAUS · FLAMBEAUX
		FLAMBEE	FLAMBEED · FLAMBEES
	AFLAME	**FLAME**	FLAMED · FLAMEN · FLAMER · FLAMES
		FLAMELET	FLAMELETS
		FLAMEN	FLAMENS
		FLAMENCO	FLAMENCOS
		FLAMEOUT	FLAMEOUTS
		FLAMER	FLAMERS
		FLAMFEW	FLAMFEWS
		FLAMING	FLAMINGO
		FLAMINGO	FLAMINGOS
		FLAMM	FLAMMS
		FLAMMABLE	FLAMMABLES
		FLAMMULE	FLAMMULES
		FLAN	FLANK · FLANS
		FLANCARD	FLANCARDS
		FLANCHING	FLANCHINGS
		FLANERIE	FLANERIES
		FLANEUR	FLANEURS
		FLANGE	FLANGED · FLANGER · FLANGES
		FLANGER	FLANGERS
		FLANK	FLANKS
		FLANKER	FLANKERS
		FLANNEL	FLANNELS
		FLANNELET	FLANNELETS
		FLANNEN	FLANNENS
		FLAP	FLAPS
		FLAPERON	FLAPERONS
		FLAPJACK	FLAPJACKS
		FLAPPER	FLAPPERS
		FLAPPING	FLAPPINGS
		FLAPTRACK	FLAPTRACKS
		FLARE	FLARED · FLARES
		FLAREBACK	FLAREBACKS
		FLAREUP	FLAREUPS
		FLASER	FLASERS
		FLASH	FLASHY
		FLASHBACK	FLASHBACKS
		FLASHBULB	FLASHBULBS
		FLASHCARD	FLASHCARDS
		FLASHCUBE	FLASHCUBES
		FLASHER	FLASHERS
		FLASHES	FLASHEST
		FLASHGUN	FLASHGUNS
		FLASHING	FLASHINGS
		FLASHLAMP	FLASHLAMPS
		FLASHOVER	FLASHOVERS
		FLASHTUBE	FLASHTUBES
		FLASK	FLASKS
		FLASKET	FLASKETS

FRONT HOOK	ROOT WORD	END HOOK
	FLAT	FLATS
	FLATBACK	FLATBACKS
	FLATBED	FLATBEDS
	FLATBOAT	FLATBOATS
	FLATBREAD	FLATBREADS
	FLATCAP	FLATCAPS
	FLATCAR	FLATCARS
	FLATETTE	FLATETTES
	FLATFOOT	FLATFOOTS
	FLATHEAD	FLATHEADS
	FLATIRON	FLATIRONS
	FLATLAND	FLATLANDS
	FLATLET	FLATLETS
	FLATLINE	FLATLINED ▪ FLATLINER ▪ FLATLINES
	FLATLINER	FLATLINERS
	FLATLING	FLATLINGS
	FLATMATE	FLATMATES
	FLATPACK	FLATPACKS
	FLATSHARE	FLATSHARES
	FLATTEN	FLATTENS
	FLATTENER	FLATTENERS
	FLATTER	FLATTERS ▪ FLATTERY
	FLATTERER	FLATTERERS
	FLATTIE	FLATTIES
	FLATTING	FLATTINGS
	FLATTOP	FLATTOPS
	FLATWARE	FLATWARES
	FLATWORK	FLATWORKS
	FLATWORM	FLATWORMS
	FLAUGHT	FLAUGHTS
	FLAUGHTER	FLAUGHTERS
	FLAUNE	FLAUNES
	FLAUNT	FLAUNTS ▪ FLAUNTY
	FLAUNTER	FLAUNTERS
	FLAUTA	FLAUTAS
	FLAUTIST	FLAUTISTS
	FLAVANOL	FLAVANOLS
	FLAVANONE	FLAVANONES
	FLAVIN	FLAVINE ▪ FLAVINS
	FLAVINE	FLAVINES
	FLAVONE	FLAVONES
	FLAVONOID	FLAVONOIDS
	FLAVONOL	FLAVONOLS
	FLAVOR	FLAVORS ▪ FLAVORY
	FLAVORER	FLAVORERS
	FLAVORING	FLAVORINGS
	FLAVORIST	FLAVORISTS
	FLAVOUR	FLAVOURS ▪ FLAVOURY
	FLAVOURER	FLAVOURERS
	FLAW	FLAWN ▪ FLAWS ▪ FLAWY
	FLAWN	FLAWNS
	FLAX	FLAXY
	FLAXSEED	FLAXSEEDS
	FLAY	FLAYS
	FLAYER	FLAYERS
	FLEA	FLEAM ▪ FLEAS
	FLEABAG	FLEABAGS
	FLEABANE	FLEABANES
	FLEABITE	FLEABITES
	FLEAM	FLEAMS
	FLEAPIT	FLEAPITS
	FLEAWORT	FLEAWORTS
	FLECHE	FLECHES
	FLECHETTE	FLECHETTES
	FLECK	FLECKS ▪ FLECKY
	FLECKER	FLECKERS
	FLECTION	FLECTIONS
	FLEDGE	FLEDGED ▪ FLEDGES
	FLEDGLING	FLEDGLINGS

FRONT HOOK	ROOT WORD	END HOOK
	FLEE	FLEER · FLEES · FLEET
	FLEECE	FLEECED · FLEECER · FLEECES
	FLEECER	FLEECERS
	FLEECHING	FLEECHINGS
	FLEECIE	FLEECIER · FLEECIES
	FLEECIES	FLEECIEST
	FLEER	FLEERS
	FLEERER	FLEERERS
	FLEERING	FLEERINGS
	FLEET	FLEETS
	FLEG	FLEGS
	FLEHMEN	FLEHMENS
	FLEME	FLEMES
	FLENCHER	FLENCHERS
	FLENSE	FLENSED · FLENSER · FLENSES
	FLENSER	FLENSERS
	FLESH	FLESHY
	FLESHER	FLESHERS
	FLESHHOOD	FLESHHOODS
	FLESHING	FLESHINGS
	FLESHLING	FLESHLINGS
	FLESHMENT	FLESHMENTS
	FLESHPOT	FLESHPOTS
	FLESHWORM	FLESHWORMS
	FLETCHER	FLETCHERS
	FLETCHING	FLETCHINGS
	FLETTON	FLETTONS
	FLEURET	FLEURETS
	FLEURETTE	FLEURETTES
	FLEURON	FLEURONS
	FLEW	FLEWS
	FLEX	FLEXO
	FLEXAGON	FLEXAGONS
	FLEXION	FLEXIONS
	FLEXITIME	FLEXITIMES
	FLEXO	FLEXOR · FLEXOS
	FLEXOR	FLEXORS
	FLEXTIME	FLEXTIMER · FLEXTIMES
	FLEXTIMER	FLEXTIMERS
	FLEXURE	FLEXURES
	FLEY	FLEYS
	FLIBBERT	FLIBBERTS
	FLIC	FLICK · FLICS
	FLICHTER	FLICHTERS
	FLICK	FLICKS
	FLICKER	FLICKERS · FLICKERY
	FLIER	FLIERS
	FLIES	FLIEST
	FLIGHT	FLIGHTS · FLIGHTY
	FLIM	FLIMP · FLIMS
	FLIMFLAM	FLIMFLAMS
	FLIMP	FLIMPS
	FLIMS	FLIMSY
	FLIMSIES	FLIMSIEST
	FLINCHER	FLINCHERS
	FLINCHING	FLINCHINGS
	FLINDER	FLINDERS
	FLING	FLINGS
	FLINGER	FLINGERS
	FLINKITE	FLINKITES
	FLINT	FLINTS · FLINTY
	FLINTHEAD	FLINTHEADS
	FLINTLOCK	FLINTLOCKS
	FLIP	FLIPS
	FLIPBOOK	FLIPBOOKS
	FLIPFLOP	FLIPFLOPS
	FLIPPER	FLIPPERS
	FLIR	FLIRS · FLIRT
	FLIRT	FLIRTS · FLIRTY

FRONT HOOK	ROOT WORD	END HOOK
	FLIRTER	FLIRTERS
	FLIRTING	FLIRTINGS
	FLISK	FLISKS · FLISKY
	FLIT	FLITE · FLITS · FLITT
	FLITE	FLITED · FLITES
	FLITTER	FLITTERN · FLITTERS
	FLITTERN	FLITTERNS
	FLITTING	FLITTINGS
	FLIVVER	FLIVVERS
AFLOAT	**FLOAT**	FLOATS · FLOATY
	FLOATAGE	FLOATAGES
	FLOATANT	FLOATANTS
	FLOATEL	FLOATELS
	FLOATER	FLOATERS
	FLOATING	FLOATINGS
	FLOC	FLOCK · FLOCS
	FLOCCULE	FLOCCULES
	FLOCK	FLOCKS · FLOCKY
	FLOCKING	FLOCKINGS
	FLOE	FLOES
	FLOG	FLOGS
	FLOGGER	FLOGGERS
	FLOGGING	FLOGGINGS
	FLOKATI	FLOKATIS
	FLONG	FLONGS
	FLOOD	FLOODS
	FLOODER	FLOODERS
	FLOODGATE	FLOODGATES
	FLOODING	FLOODINGS
	FLOODMARK	FLOODMARKS
	FLOODTIDE	FLOODTIDES
	FLOODWALL	FLOODWALLS
	FLOODWAY	FLOODWAYS
	FLOOR	FLOORS
	FLOORAGE	FLOORAGES
	FLOORER	FLOORERS
	FLOORHEAD	FLOORHEADS
	FLOORING	FLOORINGS
	FLOORSHOW	FLOORSHOWS
	FLOOSIE	FLOOSIES
	FLOOZIE	FLOOZIES
	FLOP	FLOPS
	FLOPHOUSE	FLOPHOUSES
	FLOPOVER	FLOPOVERS
	FLOPPER	FLOPPERS
	FLOPPIES	FLOPPIEST
	FLOR	FLORA · FLORS · FLORY
	FLORA	FLORAE · FLORAL · FLORAS
	FLORAL	FLORALS
	FLORENCE	FLORENCES
	FLORET	FLORETS
	FLORICANE	FLORICANES
	FLORIDEAN	FLORIDEANS
	FLORIGEN	FLORIGENS
	FLORIN	FLORINS
	FLORIST	FLORISTS
	FLORISTIC	FLORISTICS
	FLORUIT	FLORUITS
	FLORULA	FLORULAE
	FLORULE	FLORULES
	FLOSCULE	FLOSCULES
	FLOSS	FLOSSY
	FLOSSER	FLOSSERS
	FLOSSIE	FLOSSIER · FLOSSIES
	FLOSSIES	FLOSSIEST
	FLOSSING	FLOSSINGS
	FLOTA	FLOTAS
	FLOTAGE	FLOTAGES
	FLOTATION	FLOTATIONS

FRONT HOOK	ROOT WORD	END HOOK
	FLOTE	FLOTEL · FLOTES
	FLOTEL	FLOTELS
	FLOTILLA	FLOTILLAS
	FLOTSAM	FLOTSAMS
	FLOUNCE	FLOUNCED · FLOUNCES
	FLOUNCING	FLOUNCINGS
	FLOUNDER	FLOUNDERS
	FLOUR	FLOURS · FLOURY
	FLOURISH	FLOURISHY
	FLOUSE	FLOUSED · FLOUSES
	FLOUT	FLOUTS
	FLOUTER	FLOUTERS
	FLOW	FLOWN · FLOWS
	FLOWAGE	FLOWAGES
	FLOWCHART	FLOWCHARTS
	FLOWER	FLOWERS · FLOWERY
	FLOWERAGE	FLOWERAGES
	FLOWERBED	FLOWERBEDS
	FLOWERER	FLOWERERS
	FLOWERET	FLOWERETS
	FLOWERING	FLOWERINGS
	FLOWERPOT	FLOWERPOTS
	FLOWMETER	FLOWMETERS
	FLOWSTONE	FLOWSTONES
	FLU	FLUB · FLUE · FLUS · FLUX
	FLUATE	FLUATES
	FLUB	FLUBS
	FLUBBER	FLUBBERS
	FLUBDUB	FLUBDUBS
	FLUCTUATE	FLUCTUATED · FLUCTUATES
	FLUE	FLUED · FLUES · FLUEY
	FLUELLEN	FLUELLENS
	FLUELLIN	FLUELLINS
	FLUENCE	FLUENCES
	FLUENT	FLUENTS
	FLUERIC	FLUERICS
	FLUEWORK	FLUEWORKS
	FLUFF	FLUFFS · FLUFFY
	FLUFFER	FLUFFERS
	FLUGEL	FLUGELS
	FLUID	FLUIDS
	FLUIDIC	FLUIDICS
	FLUIDISE	FLUIDISED · FLUIDISER · FLUIDISES
	FLUIDISER	FLUIDISERS
	FLUIDIZE	FLUIDIZED · FLUIDIZER · FLUIDIZES
	FLUIDIZER	FLUIDIZERS
	FLUIDRAM	FLUIDRAMS
	FLUKE	FLUKED · FLUKES · FLUKEY
	FLUME	FLUMED · FLUMES
	FLUMP	FLUMPS
	FLUNK	FLUNKS · FLUNKY
	FLUNKER	FLUNKERS
	FLUNKEY	FLUNKEYS
	FLUNKIE	FLUNKIES
	FLUNKYISM	FLUNKYISMS
	FLUOR	FLUORS
	FLUORENE	FLUORENES
	FLUORESCE	FLUORESCED · FLUORESCER · FLUORESCES
	FLUORID	FLUORIDE · FLUORIDS
	FLUORIDE	FLUORIDES
	FLUORIN	FLUORINE · FLUORINS
	FLUORINE	FLUORINES
	FLUORITE	FLUORITES
	FLUORSPAR	FLUORSPARS
	FLURR	FLURRS · FLURRY
	FLUS	FLUSH
	FLUSH	FLUSHY
	FLUSHER	FLUSHERS
	FLUSHES	FLUSHEST

FRONT HOOK	ROOT WORD	END HOOK
	FLUSHING	FLUSHINGS
	FLUSHWORK	FLUSHWORKS
	FLUSTER	FLUSTERS = FLUSTERY
	FLUSTRATE	FLUSTRATED = FLUSTRATES
	FLUTE	FLUTED = FLUTER = FLUTES = FLUTEY
	FLUTER	FLUTERS
	FLUTINA	FLUTINAS
	FLUTING	FLUTINGS
	FLUTIST	FLUTISTS
AFLUTTER	FLUTTER	FLUTTERS = FLUTTERY
	FLUTTERER	FLUTTERERS
	FLUXGATE	FLUXGATES
	FLUXION	FLUXIONS
	FLUXMETER	FLUXMETERS
	FLUYT	FLUYTS
	FLYAWAY	FLYAWAYS
	FLYBACK	FLYBACKS
	FLYBANE	FLYBANES
	FLYBELT	FLYBELTS
	FLYBLOW	FLYBLOWN = FLYBLOWS
	FLYBOAT	FLYBOATS
	FLYBOOK	FLYBOOKS
	FLYBOY	FLYBOYS
	FLYBRIDGE	FLYBRIDGES
	FLYBY	FLYBYS
	FLYER	FLYERS
	FLYHAND	FLYHANDS
	FLYING	FLYINGS
	FLYMAKER	FLYMAKERS
	FLYOFF	FLYOFFS
	FLYOVER	FLYOVERS
	FLYPAPER	FLYPAPERS
	FLYPAST	FLYPASTS
	FLYPE	FLYPED = FLYPES
	FLYRODDER	FLYRODDERS
	FLYSCREEN	FLYSCREENS
	FLYSHEET	FLYSHEETS
	FLYSPECK	FLYSPECKS
	FLYSTRIKE	FLYSTRIKES
	FLYTE	FLYTED = FLYTES
	FLYTIER	FLYTIERS
	FLYTING	FLYTINGS
	FLYTRAP	FLYTRAPS
	FLYWAY	FLYWAYS
	FLYWEIGHT	FLYWEIGHTS
	FLYWHEEL	FLYWHEELS
	FOAL	FOALS
	FOALFOOT	FOALFOOTS
	FOAM	FOAMS = FOAMY
	FOAMER	FOAMERS
	FOAMING	FOAMINGS
	FOB	FOBS
	FOCACCIA	FOCACCIAS
	FOCALISE	FOCALISED = FOCALISES
	FOCALIZE	FOCALIZED = FOCALIZES
	FOCIMETER	FOCIMETERS
	FOCOMETER	FOCOMETERS
	FOCUSER	FOCUSERS
	FOCUSING	FOCUSINGS
	FODDER	FODDERS
	FODDERER	FODDERERS
	FODDERING	FODDERINGS
	FOE	FOEN = FOES
	FOEDARIE	FOEDARIES
	FOEHN	FOEHNS
	FOETATION	FOETATIONS
	FOETICIDE	FOETICIDES
	FOETOR	FOETORS
	FOG	FOGS = FOGY

FRONT HOOK	ROOT WORD	END HOOK
	FOGBOW	FOGBOWS
	FOGDOG	FOGDOGS
	FOGEY	FOGEYS
	FOGEYDOM	FOGEYDOMS
	FOGEYISM	FOGEYISMS
	FOGFRUIT	FOGFRUITS
	FOGGAGE	FOGGAGES
	FOGGER	FOGGERS
	FOGHORN	FOGHORNS
	FOGIE	FOGIES
	FOGLE	FOGLES
	FOGLES	FOGLESS
	FOGRAM	FOGRAMS
	FOGRAMITE	FOGRAMITES
	FOGYDOM	FOGYDOMS
	FOGYISM	FOGYISMS
	FOH	FOHN ▪ FOHS
	FOHN	FOHNS
	FOIBLE	FOIBLES
	FOID	FOIDS
	FOIL	FOILS
	FOILING	FOILINGS
	FOIN	FOINS
	FOISON	FOISONS
	FOIST	FOISTS
	FOISTER	FOISTERS
	FOLACIN	FOLACINS
	FOLATE	FOLATES
	FOLD	FOLDS
	FOLDAWAY	FOLDAWAYS
	FOLDBACK	FOLDBACKS
	FOLDBOAT	FOLDBOATS
	FOLDER	FOLDERS
	FOLDEROL	FOLDEROLS
	FOLDING	FOLDINGS
	FOLDOUT	FOLDOUTS
	FOLDUP	FOLDUPS
	FOLEY	FOLEYS
	FOLIA	FOLIAR
	FOLIAGE	FOLIAGED ▪ FOLIAGES
	FOLIATE	FOLIATED ▪ FOLIATES
	FOLIATION	FOLIATIONS
	FOLIATURE	FOLIATURES
	FOLIE	FOLIES
	FOLIO	FOLIOS
	FOLIOLE	FOLIOLES
	FOLIOS	FOLIOSE
	FOLIUM	FOLIUMS
	FOLK	FOLKS ▪ FOLKY
	FOLKIE	FOLKIER ▪ FOLKIES
	FOLKIES	FOLKIEST
	FOLKLAND	FOLKLANDS
	FOLKLORE	FOLKLORES
	FOLKMOOT	FOLKMOOTS
	FOLKMOT	FOLKMOTE ▪ FOLKMOTS
	FOLKMOTE	FOLKMOTES
	FOLKS	FOLKSY
	FOLKSONG	FOLKSONGS
	FOLKTALE	FOLKTALES
	FOLKWAY	FOLKWAYS
	FOLLICLE	FOLLICLES
	FOLLOW	FOLLOWS
	FOLLOWER	FOLLOWERS
	FOLLOWING	FOLLOWINGS
	FOLLOWUP	FOLLOWUPS
	FOMENT	FOMENTS
	FOMENTER	FOMENTERS
	FOMITE	FOMITES
	FON	FOND ▪ FONE ▪ FONS ▪ FONT

FRONT HOOK	ROOT WORD	END HOOK
	FOND	FONDA · FONDS · FONDU
	FONDA	FONDAS
	FONDANT	FONDANTS
	FONDLE	FONDLED · FONDLER · FONDLES
	FONDLER	FONDLERS
	FONDLING	FONDLINGS
	FONDU	FONDUE · FONDUS
	FONDUE	FONDUED · FONDUES
	FONT	FONTS
	FONTANEL	FONTANELS
	FONTANGE	FONTANGES
	FONTINA	FONTINAS
	FONTLET	FONTLETS
	FOOD	FOODS · FOODY
	FOODIE	FOODIES
	FOODISM	FOODISMS
	FOODSTUFF	FOODSTUFFS
	FOOFARAW	FOOFARAWS
	FOOL	FOOLS
	FOOLING	FOOLINGS
	FOOLSCAP	FOOLSCAPS
	FOOSBALL	FOOSBALLS
AFOOT	FOOT	FOOTS · FOOTY
	FOOTAGE	FOOTAGES
	FOOTBAG	FOOTBAGS
	FOOTBALL	FOOTBALLS
	FOOTBAR	FOOTBARS
	FOOTBATH	FOOTBATHS
	FOOTBOARD	FOOTBOARDS
	FOOTBOY	FOOTBOYS
	FOOTCLOTH	FOOTCLOTHS
	FOOTER	FOOTERS
	FOOTFALL	FOOTFALLS
	FOOTFAULT	FOOTFAULTS
	FOOTGEAR	FOOTGEARS
	FOOTHILL	FOOTHILLS
	FOOTHOLD	FOOTHOLDS
	FOOTIE	FOOTIER · FOOTIES
	FOOTIES	FOOTIEST
	FOOTING	FOOTINGS
	FOOTLE	FOOTLED · FOOTLER · FOOTLES
	FOOTLER	FOOTLERS
	FOOTLES	FOOTLESS
	FOOTLIGHT	FOOTLIGHTS
	FOOTLING	FOOTLINGS
	FOOTMARK	FOOTMARKS
	FOOTMUFF	FOOTMUFFS
	FOOTNOTE	FOOTNOTED · FOOTNOTES
	FOOTPACE	FOOTPACES
	FOOTPAD	FOOTPADS
	FOOTPAGE	FOOTPAGES
	FOOTPATH	FOOTPATHS
	FOOTPLATE	FOOTPLATES
	FOOTPOST	FOOTPOSTS
	FOOTPRINT	FOOTPRINTS
	FOOTRA	FOOTRAS
	FOOTRACE	FOOTRACES
	FOOTREST	FOOTRESTS
	FOOTROPE	FOOTROPES
	FOOTROT	FOOTROTS
	FOOTRULE	FOOTRULES
	FOOTS	FOOTSY
	FOOTSIE	FOOTSIES
	FOOTSLOG	FOOTSLOGS
	FOOTSTALK	FOOTSTALKS
	FOOTSTALL	FOOTSTALLS
	FOOTSTEP	FOOTSTEPS
	FOOTSTOCK	FOOTSTOCKS
	FOOTSTONE	FOOTSTONES

F

FRONT HOOK	ROOT WORD	END HOOK
	FOOTSTOOL	FOOTSTOOLS
	FOOTWALL	FOOTWALLS
	FOOTWAY	FOOTWAYS
	FOOTWEAR	FOOTWEARS · FOOTWEARY
	FOOTWELL	FOOTWELLS
	FOOTWORK	FOOTWORKS
	FOOZLE	FOOZLED · FOOZLER · FOOZLES
	FOOZLER	FOOZLERS
	FOOZLING	FOOZLINGS
	FOP	FOPS
	FOPLING	FOPLINGS
	FOR	FORA · FORB · FORD · FORE · FORK · FORM · FORT
	FORA	FORAM · FORAY
	FORAGE	FORAGED · FORAGER · FORAGES
	FORAGER	FORAGERS
	FORAM	FORAMS
	FORAMEN	FORAMENS
	FORAMINA	FORAMINAL
	FORAY	FORAYS
	FORAYER	FORAYERS
	FORB	FORBS · FORBY
	FORBAD	FORBADE
	FORBEAR	FORBEARS
	FORBEARER	FORBEARERS
	FORBID	FORBIDS
	FORBIDAL	FORBIDALS
	FORBIDDAL	FORBIDDALS
	FORBIDDER	FORBIDDERS
	FORBODE	FORBODED · FORBODES
	FORBY	FORBYE
	FORCAT	FORCATS
	FORCE	FORCED · FORCER · FORCES
	FORCEMEAT	FORCEMEATS
	FORCER	FORCERS
	FORCIPATE	FORCIPATED
	FORD	FORDO · FORDS
AFORE	**FORE**	FOREL · FORES · FOREX
	FOREARM	FOREARMS
	FOREBAY	FOREBAYS
	FOREBEAR	FOREBEARS
	FOREBITT	FOREBITTS
	FOREBODE	FOREBODED · FOREBODER · FOREBODES
	FOREBODER	FOREBODERS
	FOREBOOM	FOREBOOMS
	FOREBRAIN	FOREBRAINS
	FOREBY	FOREBYE
	FORECABIN	FORECABINS
	FORECAR	FORECARS
	FORECAST	FORECASTS
	FORECHECK	FORECHECKS
	FORECLOSE	FORECLOSED · FORECLOSES
	FORECLOTH	FORECLOTHS
	FORECOURT	FORECOURTS
	FOREDATE	FOREDATED · FOREDATES
	FOREDECK	FOREDECKS
	FOREDOOM	FOREDOOMS
	FOREFACE	FOREFACES
	FOREFEEL	FOREFEELS
	FOREFEND	FOREFENDS
	FOREFRONT	FOREFRONTS
	FOREGLEAM	FOREGLEAMS
	FOREGOER	FOREGOERS
	FOREGOING	FOREGOINGS
	FOREGUT	FOREGUTS
AFOREHAND	**FOREHAND**	FOREHANDS
	FOREHEAD	FOREHEADS
	FOREHENT	FOREHENTS
	FOREHOCK	FOREHOCKS

FRONT HOOK	ROOT WORD	END HOOK
	FOREHOOF	FOREHOOFS
	FOREIGNER	FOREIGNERS
	FOREJUDGE	FOREJUDGED · FOREJUDGES
	FOREKING	FOREKINGS
	FOREKNOW	FOREKNOWN · FOREKNOWS
	FOREL	FORELS
	FORELAND	FORELANDS
	FORELAY	FORELAYS
	FORELEG	FORELEGS
	FORELEND	FORELENDS
	FORELIE	FORELIES
	FORELIFT	FORELIFTS
	FORELIMB	FORELIMBS
	FORELOCK	FORELOCKS
	FOREMAST	FOREMASTS
	FOREMEAN	FOREMEANS · FOREMEANT
	FOREMILK	FOREMILKS
	FORENAME	FORENAMED · FORENAMES
	FORENIGHT	FORENIGHTS
	FORENOON	FORENOONS
	FORENSIC	FORENSICS
	FOREPART	FOREPARTS
	FOREPAW	FOREPAWS
	FOREPEAK	FOREPEAKS
	FOREPLAN	FOREPLANS
	FOREPLAY	FOREPLAYS
	FOREPOINT	FOREPOINTS
	FORERAN	FORERANK
	FORERANK	FORERANKS
	FOREREAD	FOREREADS
	FORERUN	FORERUNS
	FORES	FOREST
AFORESAID	FORESAID	
	FORESAIL	FORESAILS
	FORESAY	FORESAYS
	FORESEE	FORESEEN · FORESEER · FORESEES
	FORESEER	FORESEERS
	FORESHANK	FORESHANKS
	FORESHEET	FORESHEETS
	FORESHEW	FORESHEWN · FORESHEWS
	FORESHIP	FORESHIPS
	FORESHOCK	FORESHOCKS
	FORESHORE	FORESHORES
	FORESHOW	FORESHOWN · FORESHOWS
	FORESIDE	FORESIDES
	FORESIGHT	FORESIGHTS
	FORESKIN	FORESKINS
	FORESKIRT	FORESKIRTS
	FORESLACK	FORESLACKS
	FORESLOW	FORESLOWS
	FORESPEAK	FORESPEAKS
	FORESPEND	FORESPENDS
	FORESPOKE	FORESPOKEN
	FOREST	FORESTS
	FORESTAGE	FORESTAGES
	FORESTAIR	FORESTAIRS
	FORESTAL	FORESTALL
	FORESTALL	FORESTALLS
	FORESTAY	FORESTAYS
	FORESTER	FORESTERS
	FORESWEAR	FORESWEARS
	FORETASTE	FORETASTED · FORETASTES
	FORETELL	FORETELLS
	FORETHINK	FORETHINKS
AFORETIME	FORETIME	FORETIMES
	FORETOKEN	FORETOKENS
	FORETOP	FORETOPS
	FOREVER	FOREVERS
	FOREWARD	FOREWARDS

FRONT HOOK	ROOT WORD	END HOOK
	FOREWARN	FOREWARNS
	FOREWEIGH	FOREWEIGHS
	FOREWIND	FOREWINDS
	FOREWING	FOREWINGS
	FOREWORD	FOREWORDS
	FOREYARD	FOREYARDS
	FORFAIR	FORFAIRN · FORFAIRS
	FORFAITER	FORFAITERS
	FORFAULT	FORFAULTS
	FORFEIT	FORFEITS
	FORFEITER	FORFEITERS
	FORFEND	FORFENDS
	FORGATHER	FORGATHERS
	FORGE	FORGED · FORGER · FORGES · FORGET
	FORGER	FORGERS · FORGERY
	FORGET	FORGETS
	FORGETTER	FORGETTERS · FORGETTERY
	FORGING	FORGINGS
	FORGIVE	FORGIVEN · FORGIVER · FORGIVES
	FORGIVER	FORGIVERS
	FORGO	FORGOT
	FORGOER	FORGOERS
	FORHAILE	FORHAILED · FORHAILES
	FORHENT	FORHENTS
	FORHOO	FORHOOS
	FORHOOIE	FORHOOIED · FORHOOIES
	FORHOW	FORHOWS
	FORINT	FORINTS
	FORJUDGE	FORJUDGED · FORJUDGES
	FORK	FORKS · FORKY
	FORKBALL	FORKBALLS
	FORKER	FORKERS
	FORKFUL	FORKFULS
	FORKHEAD	FORKHEADS
	FORKLIFT	FORKLIFTS
	FORKTAIL	FORKTAILS
	FORLANA	FORLANAS
	FORLEND	FORLENDS
	FORLESE	FORLESES
	FORLORN	FORLORNS
	FORM	FORME · FORMS
	FORMAL	FORMALS
	FORMALIN	FORMALINS
	FORMALISE	FORMALISED · FORMALISER · FORMALISES
	FORMALISM	FORMALISMS
	FORMALIST	FORMALISTS
	FORMALIZE	FORMALIZED · FORMALIZER · FORMALIZES
	FORMAMIDE	FORMAMIDES
	FORMANT	FORMANTS
	FORMAT	FORMATE · FORMATS
	FORMATE	FORMATED · FORMATES
	FORMATION	FORMATIONS
	FORMATIVE	FORMATIVES
	FORMATTER	FORMATTERS
	FORME	FORMED · FORMEE · FORMER · FORMES
	FORMER	FORMERS
	FORMIATE	FORMIATES
	FORMIC	FORMICA
	FORMICA	FORMICAS
	FORMICATE	FORMICATED · FORMICATES
	FORMING	FORMINGS
	FORMOL	FORMOLS
	FORMULA	FORMULAE · FORMULAR · FORMULAS
	FORMULAR	FORMULARY
	FORMULATE	FORMULATED · FORMULATES
	FORMULISE	FORMULISED · FORMULISES
	FORMULISM	FORMULISMS
	FORMULIST	FORMULISTS
	FORMULIZE	FORMULIZED · FORMULIZES

FRONT HOOK	ROOT WORD	END HOOK
	FORMWORK	FORMWORKS
	FORMYL	FORMYLS
	FORNICATE	FORNICATED = FORNICATES
	FORPET	FORPETS
	FORPINE	FORPINED = FORPINES
	FORPIT	FORPITS
	FORRAY	FORRAYS
	FORSAKE	FORSAKEN = FORSAKER = FORSAKES
	FORSAKER	FORSAKERS
	FORSAKING	FORSAKINGS
	FORSAY	FORSAYS
	FORSLACK	FORSLACKS
	FORSLOE	FORSLOED = FORSLOES
	FORSLOW	FORSLOWS
	FORSPEAK	FORSPEAKS
	FORSPEND	FORSPENDS
	FORSPOKE	FORSPOKEN
	FORSWEAR	FORSWEARS
	FORSWINK	FORSWINKS
	FORSYTHIA	FORSYTHIAS
	FORT	FORTE = FORTH = FORTS = FORTY
	FORTALICE	FORTALICES
	FORTE	FORTED = FORTES
	FORTH	FORTHY
	FORTHCOME	FORTHCOMES
	FORTHINK	FORTHINKS
	FORTIETH	FORTIETHS
	FORTIFIER	FORTIFIERS
	FORTILAGE	FORTILAGES
	FORTITUDE	FORTITUDES
	FORTLET	FORTLETS
	FORTNIGHT	FORTNIGHTS
	FORTUNATE	FORTUNATES
	FORTUNE	FORTUNED = FORTUNES
	FORTUNISE	FORTUNISED = FORTUNISES
	FORTUNIZE	FORTUNIZED = FORTUNIZES
	FORUM	FORUMS
	FORWANDER	FORWANDERS
	FORWARD	FORWARDS
	FORWARDER	FORWARDERS
	FORWARN	FORWARNS
	FORWASTE	FORWASTED = FORWASTES
SFORZANDI	FORZANDI	
SFORZANDO	FORZANDO	FORZANDOS
SFORZANDOS	FORZANDOS	
SFORZATI	FORZATI	
SFORZATO	FORZATO	FORZATOS
SFORZATOS	FORZATOS	
	FOSCARNET	FOSCARNETS
	FOSS	FOSSA = FOSSE
	FOSSA	FOSSAE = FOSSAS
	FOSSE	FOSSED = FOSSES
	FOSSETTE	FOSSETTES
	FOSSICK	FOSSICKS
	FOSSICKER	FOSSICKERS
	FOSSIL	FOSSILS
	FOSSILISE	FOSSILISED = FOSSILISES
	FOSSILIZE	FOSSILIZED = FOSSILIZES
	FOSSOR	FOSSORS
	FOSSULA	FOSSULAE
	FOSTER	FOSTERS
	FOSTERAGE	FOSTERAGES
	FOSTERER	FOSTERERS
	FOSTERING	FOSTERINGS
	FOTHER	FOTHERS
	FOU	FOUD = FOUL = FOUR = FOUS
	FOUAT	FOUATS
	FOUD	FOUDS
	FOUDRIE	FOUDRIES

F

FRONT HOOK	ROOT WORD	END HOOK
	FOUET	FOUETS
	FOUETTE	FOUETTES
	FOUGADE	FOUGADES
	FOUGASSE	FOUGASSES
	FOUGHT	FOUGHTY
AFOUL	**FOUL**	FOULE · FOULS
	FOULARD	FOULARDS
	FOULBROOD	FOULBROODS
	FOULDER	FOULDERS
	FOULE	FOULED · FOULER · FOULES
	FOULES	FOULEST
	FOULIE	FOULIES
	FOULING	FOULINGS
	FOULMART	FOULMARTS
	FOUMART	FOUMARTS
	FOUND	FOUNDS
	FOUNDER	FOUNDERS
	FOUNDING	FOUNDINGS
	FOUNDLING	FOUNDLINGS
	FOUNT	FOUNTS
	FOUNTAIN	FOUNTAINS
	FOUR	FOURS
	FOURBALL	FOURBALLS
	FOURGON	FOURGONS
	FOURPENCE	FOURPENCES
	FOURSOME	FOURSOMES
	FOURTEEN	FOURTEENS
	FOURTH	FOURTHS
	FOUSSA	FOUSSAS
	FOUTER	FOUTERS
	FOUTH	FOUTHS
	FOUTRA	FOUTRAS
	FOUTRE	FOUTRED · FOUTRES
	FOVEA	FOVEAE · FOVEAL · FOVEAS
	FOVEATE	FOVEATED
	FOVEOLA	FOVEOLAE · FOVEOLAR · FOVEOLAS
	FOVEOLATE	FOVEOLATED
	FOVEOLE	FOVEOLES · FOVEOLET
	FOVEOLET	FOVEOLETS
	FOWL	FOWLS
	FOWLER	FOWLERS
	FOWLING	FOWLINGS
	FOWTH	FOWTHS
	FOX	FOXY
	FOXFIRE	FOXFIRES
	FOXGLOVE	FOXGLOVES
	FOXHOLE	FOXHOLES
	FOXHOUND	FOXHOUNDS
	FOXHUNT	FOXHUNTS
	FOXHUNTER	FOXHUNTERS
	FOXIE	FOXIER · FOXIES
	FOXIES	FOXIEST
	FOXING	FOXINGS
	FOXSHARK	FOXSHARKS
	FOXSHIP	FOXSHIPS
	FOXSKIN	FOXSKINS
	FOXTAIL	FOXTAILS
	FOXTROT	FOXTROTS
	FOY	FOYS
	FOYBOAT	FOYBOATS
	FOYER	FOYERS
	FOYLE	FOYLED · FOYLES
	FOYNE	FOYNED · FOYNES
	FRA	FRAB · FRAE · FRAG · FRAP · FRAS FRAT · FRAU · FRAY
	FRAB	FRABS
	FRACKING	FRACKINGS
	FRACT	FRACTI · FRACTS
	FRACTAL	FRACTALS

FRONT HOOK	ROOT WORD	END HOOK
	FRACTION	FRACTIONS
	FRACTUR	FRACTURE ▪ FRACTURS
	FRACTURE	FRACTURED ▪ FRACTURER ▪ FRACTURES
	FRACTURER	FRACTURERS
	FRAENUM	FRAENUMS
	FRAG	FRAGS
	FRAGGING	FRAGGINGS
	FRAGILE	FRAGILER
	FRAGMENT	FRAGMENTS
	FRAGOR	FRAGORS
	FRAGRANCE	FRAGRANCED ▪ FRAGRANCES
	FRAICHEUR	FRAICHEURS
	FRAIL	FRAILS
	FRAILTEE	FRAILTEES
	FRAIM	FRAIMS
	FRAISE	FRAISED ▪ FRAISES
	FRAKTUR	FRAKTURS
	FRAMBESIA	FRAMBESIAS
	FRAMBOISE	FRAMBOISES
	FRAME	FRAMED ▪ FRAMER ▪ FRAMES
	FRAMER	FRAMERS
	FRAMEWORK	FRAMEWORKS
	FRAMING	FRAMINGS
	FRAMPLER	FRAMPLERS
	FRANC	FRANCO ▪ FRANCS
	FRANCHISE	FRANCHISED ▪ FRANCHISEE ▪ FRANCHISER FRANCHISES
	FRANCISE	FRANCISED ▪ FRANCISES
	FRANCIUM	FRANCIUMS
	FRANCIZE	FRANCIZED ▪ FRANCIZES
	FRANCOLIN	FRANCOLINS
	FRANGER	FRANGERS
	FRANION	FRANIONS
	FRANK	FRANKS
	FRANKER	FRANKERS
	FRANKFORT	FRANKFORTS
	FRANKFURT	FRANKFURTS
	FRANKLIN	FRANKLINS
	FRANSERIA	FRANSERIAS
	FRAP	FRAPE ▪ FRAPS
	FRAPPE	FRAPPED ▪ FRAPPEE ▪ FRAPPES
	FRAS	FRASS
	FRASCATI	FRASCATIS
	FRAT	FRATE ▪ FRATI ▪ FRATS
	FRATCH	FRATCHY
	FRATE	FRATER
	FRATER	FRATERS ▪ FRATERY
	FRAU	FRAUD ▪ FRAUS
	FRAUD	FRAUDS
	FRAUDSTER	FRAUDSTERS
	FRAUGHAN	FRAUGHANS
	FRAUGHT	FRAUGHTS
	FRAULEIN	FRAULEINS
	FRAUTAGE	FRAUTAGES
	FRAWZEY	FRAWZEYS
	FRAY	FRAYS
	FRAYING	FRAYINGS
	FRAZIL	FRAZILS
	FRAZZLE	FRAZZLED ▪ FRAZZLES
	FREAK	FREAKS ▪ FREAKY
	FREAKOUT	FREAKOUTS
	FRECKLE	FRECKLED ▪ FRECKLES
	FRECKLING	FRECKLINGS
	FREDAINE	FREDAINES
	FREE	FREED ▪ FREER ▪ FREES ▪ FREET
	FREEBASE	FREEBASED ▪ FREEBASER ▪ FREEBASES
	FREEBASER	FREEBASERS
	FREEBEE	FREEBEES
	FREEBIE	FREEBIES

FRONT HOOK	ROOT WORD	END HOOK
	FREEBOARD	FREEBOARDS
	FREEBOOT	FREEBOOTS - FREEBOOTY
	FREEDOM	FREEDOMS
	FREEGAN	FREEGANS
	FREEHOLD	FREEHOLDS
	FREELANCE	FREELANCED - FREELANCER - FREELANCES
	FREELOAD	FREELOADS
	FREEMASON	FREEMASONS
	FREEPHONE	FREEPHONES
	FREER	FREERS
	FREES	FREEST
	FREESHEET	FREESHEETS
	FREESIA	FREESIAS
	FREESTONE	FREESTONES
	FREESTYLE	FREESTYLER - FREESTYLES
AFREET	**FREET**	FREETS - FREETY
AFREETS	**FREETS**	
	FREEWARE	FREEWARES
	FREEWAY	FREEWAYS
	FREEWHEEL	FREEWHEELS
	FREEWRITE	FREEWRITES
	FREEZE	FREEZER - FREEZES
	FREEZER	FREEZERS
	FREEZING	FREEZINGS
	FREIGHT	FREIGHTS
	FREIGHTER	FREIGHTERS
	FREIT	FREITS - FREITY
	FREMD	FREMDS
	FREMIT	FREMITS
	FRENETIC	FRENETICS
	FRENULA	FRENULAR
	FRENULUM	FRENULUMS
	FRENUM	FRENUMS
	FREON	FREONS
	FREQUENCE	FREQUENCES
	FREQUENT	FREQUENTS
	FRERE	FRERES
	FRESCADE	FRESCADES
	FRESCO	FRESCOS
	FRESCOER	FRESCOERS
	FRESCOING	FRESCOINGS
	FRESCOIST	FRESCOISTS
AFRESH	**FRESH**	
	FRESHEN	FRESHENS
	FRESHENER	FRESHENERS
	FRESHER	FRESHERS
	FRESHES	FRESHEST
	FRESHET	FRESHETS
	FRESHIE	FRESHIES
	FRESNEL	FRESNELS
	FRET	FRETS
	FRETBOARD	FRETBOARDS
	FRETSAW	FRETSAWS
	FRETTER	FRETTERS
	FRETTING	FRETTINGS
	FRETWORK	FRETWORKS
	FRIAND	FRIANDE - FRIANDS
	FRIANDE	FRIANDES
	FRIAR	FRIARS - FRIARY
	FRIARBIRD	FRIARBIRDS
	FRIB	FRIBS
	FRIBBLE	FRIBBLED - FRIBBLER - FRIBBLES
	FRIBBLER	FRIBBLERS
	FRICADEL	FRICADELS
	FRICASSEE	FRICASSEED - FRICASSEES
	FRICATIVE	FRICATIVES
	FRICHT	FRICHTS
	FRICTION	FRICTIONS
	FRIDGE	FRIDGED - FRIDGES

FRONT HOOK	ROOT WORD	END HOOK
	FRIEDCAKE	FRIEDCAKES
	FRIEND	FRIENDS
	FRIENDING	FRIENDINGS
	FRIER	FRIERS
	FRIEZE	FRIEZED = FRIEZES
	FRIG	FRIGS (offensive)
	FRIGATE	FRIGATES
	FRIGATOON	FRIGATOONS
	FRIGGER	FRIGGERS (offensive)
	FRIGGING	FRIGGINGS (offensive)
	FRIGHT	FRIGHTS
	FRIGHTEN	FRIGHTENS
	FRIGOT	FRIGOTS
	FRIJOL	FRIJOLE
	FRIJOLE	FRIJOLES
	FRIKKADEL	FRIKKADELS
	FRILL	FRILLS = FRILLY
	FRILLER	FRILLERS
	FRILLIES	FRILLIEST
	FRILLING	FRILLINGS
	FRINGE	FRINGED = FRINGES
	FRIPON	FRIPONS
	FRIPPER	FRIPPERS = FRIPPERY
	FRIPPERER	FRIPPERERS
	FRIPPET	FRIPPETS
	FRIS	FRISE = FRISK = FRIST
	FRISBEE	FRISBEES
	FRISE	FRISEE = FRISES
	FRISEE	FRISEES
	FRISETTE	FRISETTES
	FRISEUR	FRISEURS
	FRISK	FRISKA = FRISKS = FRISKY
	FRISKA	FRISKAS
	FRISKER	FRISKERS
	FRISKET	FRISKETS
	FRISKING	FRISKINGS
	FRISSON	FRISSONS
	FRIST	FRISTS
	FRISURE	FRISURES
AFRIT	FRIT	FRITH = FRITS = FRITT = FRITZ
	FRITH	FRITHS
	FRITHBORH	FRITHBORHS
AFRITS	FRITS	
	FRITT	FRITTS
	FRITTATA	FRITTATAS
	FRITTER	FRITTERS
	FRITTERER	FRITTERERS
	FRITURE	FRITURES
	FRIVOL	FRIVOLS
	FRIVOLER	FRIVOLERS
	FRIVOLLER	FRIVOLLERS
	FRIZ	FRIZE = FRIZZ
	FRIZE	FRIZED = FRIZER = FRIZES
	FRIZER	FRIZERS
	FRIZETTE	FRIZETTES
	FRIZZ	FRIZZY
	FRIZZER	FRIZZERS
	FRIZZIES	FRIZZIEST
	FRIZZLE	FRIZZLED = FRIZZLER = FRIZZLES
	FRIZZLER	FRIZZLERS
AFRO	FRO	FROE = FROG = FROM = FROS = FROW
	FROCK	FROCKS
	FROCKING	FROCKINGS
	FROE	FROES
	FROG	FROGS
	FROGBIT	FROGBITS
	FROGEYE	FROGEYED = FROGEYES
	FROGGING	FROGGINGS
	FROGLET	FROGLETS

F

FRONT HOOK	ROOT WORD	END HOOK
	FROGLING	FROGLINGS
	FROGMOUTH	FROGMOUTHS
	FROGSPAWN	FROGSPAWNS
	FROIDEUR	FROIDEURS
	FROING	FROINGS
	FROISE	FROISES
	FROLIC	FROLICS
	FROLICKER	FROLICKERS
	FROMAGE	FROMAGES
	FROND	FRONDS
	FRONDAGE	FRONDAGES
	FRONDEUR	FRONDEURS
AFRONT	**FRONT**	FRONTS
	FRONTAGE	FRONTAGER ▪ FRONTAGES
	FRONTAGER	FRONTAGERS
	FRONTAL	FRONTALS
	FRONTIER	FRONTIERS
	FRONTLET	FRONTLETS
	FRONTLINE	FRONTLINES
	FRONTLIST	FRONTLISTS
	FRONTON	FRONTONS
	FRONTOON	FRONTOONS
	FRONTPAGE	FRONTPAGED ▪ FRONTPAGES
	FRONTWARD	FRONTWARDS
	FRORE	FROREN
	FRORN	FRORNE
AFROS	**FROS**	FROSH ▪ FROST
	FROST	FROSTS ▪ FROSTY
	FROSTBIT	FROSTBITE
	FROSTBITE	FROSTBITES
	FROSTED	FROSTEDS
	FROSTING	FROSTINGS
	FROSTLINE	FROSTLINES
	FROSTNIP	FROSTNIPS
	FROSTWORK	FROSTWORKS
	FROTH	FROTHS ▪ FROTHY
	FROTHER	FROTHERS ▪ FROTHERY
	FROTTAGE	FROTTAGES
	FROTTEUR	FROTTEURS
	FROUFROU	FROUFROUS
	FROUNCE	FROUNCED ▪ FROUNCES
	FROW	FROWN ▪ FROWS ▪ FROWY
	FROWARD	FROWARDS
	FROWIE	FROWIER
	FROWN	FROWNS
	FROWNER	FROWNERS
	FROWS	FROWST ▪ FROWSY
	FROWST	FROWSTS ▪ FROWSTY
	FROWSTER	FROWSTERS
	FROZE	FROZEN
	FRUCTAN	FRUCTANS
	FRUCTOSE	FRUCTOSES
	FRUCTUATE	FRUCTUATED ▪ FRUCTUATES
	FRUG	FRUGS
	FRUGALIST	FRUGALISTS
	FRUGIVORE	FRUGIVORES
	FRUICT	FRUICTS
	FRUIT	FRUITS ▪ FRUITY
	FRUITAGE	FRUITAGES
	FRUITCAKE	FRUITCAKES
	FRUITER	FRUITERS ▪ FRUITERY
	FRUITERER	FRUITERERS
	FRUITING	FRUITINGS
	FRUITION	FRUITIONS
	FRUITLET	FRUITLETS
	FRUITWOOD	FRUITWOODS
	FRUMP	FRUMPS ▪ FRUMPY
	FRUMPLE	FRUMPLED ▪ FRUMPLES
	FRUSEMIDE	FRUSEMIDES

F

FRONT HOOK	ROOT WORD	END HOOK
	FRUST	FRUSTA ▪ FRUSTS
	FRUSTRATE	FRUSTRATED ▪ FRUSTRATER ▪ FRUSTRATES
	FRUSTULE	FRUSTULES
	FRUSTUM	FRUSTUMS
	FRYBREAD	FRYBREADS
	FRYER	FRYERS
	FRYING	FRYINGS
	FRYPAN	FRYPANS
	FUB	FUBS
	FUBS	FUBSY
	FUCHSIA	FUCHSIAS
	FUCHSIN	FUCHSINE ▪ FUCHSINS
	FUCHSINE	FUCHSINES
	FUCHSITE	FUCHSITES
	FUCK	FUCKS (offensive)
	FUCKER	FUCKERS (offensive)
	FUCKING	FUCKINGS (offensive)
	FUCKOFF	FUCKOFFS (offensive)
	FUCKUP	FUCKUPS (offensive)
	FUCKWIT	FUCKWITS (offensive)
	FUCOID	FUCOIDS
	FUCOSE	FUCOSES
	FUD	FUDS
	FUDDLE	FUDDLED ▪ FUDDLER ▪ FUDDLES
	FUDDLER	FUDDLERS
	FUDDLING	FUDDLINGS
	FUDGE	FUDGED ▪ FUDGES
	FUEHRER	FUEHRERS
	FUEL	FUELS
	FUELER	FUELERS
	FUELLER	FUELLERS
	FUELWOOD	FUELWOODS
	FUERO	FUEROS
	FUFF	FUFFS ▪ FUFFY
	FUG	FUGS ▪ FUGU
	FUGATO	FUGATOS
	FUGHETTA	FUGHETTAS
	FUGIE	FUGIES
	FUGIO	FUGIOS
	FUGITIVE	FUGITIVES
	FUGLE	FUGLED ▪ FUGLES
	FUGU	FUGUE ▪ FUGUS
	FUGUE	FUGUED ▪ FUGUES
	FUGUIST	FUGUISTS
	FUHRER	FUHRERS
	FUJI	FUJIS
	FULCRUM	FULCRUMS
	FULFIL	FULFILL ▪ FULFILS
	FULFILL	FULFILLS
	FULFILLER	FULFILLERS
	FULGOR	FULGORS
	FULGOUR	FULGOURS
	FULGURATE	FULGURATED ▪ FULGURATES
	FULGURITE	FULGURITES
	FULHAM	FULHAMS
	FULL	FULLS ▪ FULLY
	FULLAGE	FULLAGES
	FULLAM	FULLAMS
	FULLAN	FULLANS
	FULLBACK	FULLBACKS
	FULLBLOOD	FULLBLOODS
	FULLER	FULLERS ▪ FULLERY
	FULLERENE	FULLERENES
	FULLERIDE	FULLERIDES
	FULLERITE	FULLERITES
	FULLFACE	FULLFACES
	FULMAR	FULMARS
	FULMINANT	FULMINANTS
	FULMINATE	FULMINATED ▪ FULMINATES

F

FRONT HOOK	ROOT WORD	END HOOK
	FULMINE	FULMINED · FULMINES
	FULSOME	FULSOMER
	FUM	FUME · FUMS · FUMY
	FUMADO	FUMADOS
	FUMAGE	FUMAGES
	FUMARASE	FUMARASES
	FUMARATE	FUMARATES
	FUMAROLE	FUMAROLES
	FUMBLE	FUMBLED · FUMBLER · FUMBLES
	FUMBLER	FUMBLERS
	FUME	FUMED · FUMER · FUMES · FUMET
	FUMER	FUMERS
	FUMEROLE	FUMEROLES
	FUMET	FUMETS
	FUMETTE	FUMETTES
	FUMIGANT	FUMIGANTS
	FUMIGATE	FUMIGATED · FUMIGATES
	FUMIGATOR	FUMIGATORS · FUMIGATORY
	FUN	FUND · FUNG · FUNK · FUNS
	FUNBOARD	FUNBOARDS
	FUNCTION	FUNCTIONS
	FUNCTOR	FUNCTORS
	FUND	FUNDI · FUNDS · FUNDY
	FUNDAMENT	FUNDAMENTS
	FUNDER	FUNDERS
	FUNDI	FUNDIC · FUNDIE · FUNDIS
	FUNDIE	FUNDIES
	FUNDING	FUNDINGS
	FUNDRAISE	FUNDRAISED · FUNDRAISER · FUNDRAISES
	FUNERAL	FUNERALS
	FUNFAIR	FUNFAIRS
	FUNFEST	FUNFESTS
	FUNG	FUNGI · FUNGO · FUNGS
	FUNGAL	FUNGALS
	FUNGI	FUNGIC
	FUNGIBLE	FUNGIBLES
	FUNGICIDE	FUNGICIDES
	FUNGISTAT	FUNGISTATS
	FUNGOID	FUNGOIDS
	FUNHOUSE	FUNHOUSES
	FUNICLE	FUNICLES
	FUNICULAR	FUNICULARS
	FUNK	FUNKS · FUNKY
	FUNKER	FUNKERS
	FUNKHOLE	FUNKHOLES
	FUNKIA	FUNKIAS
	FUNKSTER	FUNKSTERS
	FUNNEL	FUNNELS
	FUNNIES	FUNNIEST
	FUNSTER	FUNSTERS
	FUR	FURL · FURR · FURS · FURY
	FURAL	FURALS
	FURAN	FURANE · FURANS
	FURANE	FURANES
	FURANOSE	FURANOSES
	FURBEARER	FURBEARERS
	FURBELOW	FURBELOWS
	FURBISHER	FURBISHERS
	FURCA	FURCAE · FURCAL
	FURCATE	FURCATED · FURCATES
	FURCATION	FURCATIONS
	FURCRAEA	FURCRAEAS
	FURCULA	FURCULAE · FURCULAR
	FUREUR	FUREURS
	FURFAIR	FURFAIRS
	FURFUR	FURFURS
	FURFURAL	FURFURALS
	FURFURAN	FURFURANS
	FURFUROL	FURFUROLE · FURFUROLS

F

FRONT HOOK	ROOT WORD	END HOOK
	FURFUROLE	FURFUROLES
	FURIOSO	FURIOSOS
	FURKID	FURKIDS
	FURL	FURLS
	FURLANA	FURLANAS
	FURLER	FURLERS
	FURLONG	FURLONGS
	FURLOUGH	FURLOUGHS
	FURNACE	FURNACED · FURNACES
	FURNIMENT	FURNIMENTS
	FURNISHER	FURNISHERS
	FURNITURE	FURNITURES
	FUROL	FUROLE · FUROLS
	FUROLE	FUROLES
	FUROR	FURORE · FURORS
	FURORE	FURORES
	FURR	FURRS · FURRY
	FURRIER	FURRIERS · FURRIERY
	FURRIES	FURRIEST
	FURRINER	FURRINERS
	FURRING	FURRINGS
	FURROW	FURROWS · FURROWY
	FURROWER	FURROWERS
	FURTHER	FURTHERS
	FURTHERER	FURTHERERS
	FURUNCLE	FURUNCLES
	FURZE	FURZES
	FUSAIN	FUSAINS
	FUSAROL	FUSAROLE · FUSAROLS
	FUSAROLE	FUSAROLES
	FUSE	FUSED · FUSEE · FUSEL · FUSES
	FUSEE	FUSEES
	FUSEL	FUSELS
	FUSELAGE	FUSELAGES
	FUSHION	FUSHIONS
	FUSIL	FUSILE · FUSILS
	FUSILEER	FUSILEERS
	FUSILIER	FUSILIERS
	FUSILLADE	FUSILLADED · FUSILLADES
	FUSILLI	FUSILLIS
	FUSION	FUSIONS
	FUSIONISM	FUSIONISMS
	FUSIONIST	FUSIONISTS
	FUSS	FUSSY
	FUSSER	FUSSERS
	FUSSPOT	FUSSPOTS
	FUST	FUSTS · FUSTY
	FUSTET	FUSTETS
	FUSTIAN	FUSTIANS
	FUSTIC	FUSTICS
	FUSTIGATE	FUSTIGATED · FUSTIGATES
	FUSTOC	FUSTOCS
	FUSULINID	FUSULINIDS
	FUTCHEL	FUTCHELS
	FUTHARC	FUTHARCS
	FUTHARK	FUTHARKS
	FUTHORC	FUTHORCS
	FUTHORK	FUTHORKS
	FUTILE	FUTILER
	FUTON	FUTONS
	FUTSAL	FUTSALS
	FUTTOCK	FUTTOCKS
	FUTURE	FUTURES
	FUTURISM	FUTURISMS
	FUTURIST	FUTURISTS
	FUZE	FUZED · FUZEE · FUZES
	FUZEE	FUZEES
	FUZIL	FUZILS
	FUZZ	FUZZY

F

	FRONT HOOK	ROOT WORD	END HOOK
		FUZZLE	FUZZLED · FUZZLES
		FUZZTONE	FUZZTONES
		FYCE	FYCES
		FYKE	FYKED · FYKES
		FYLE	FYLES
		FYLFOT	FYLFOTS
		FYRD	FYRDS
		FYTTE	FYTTES

F

G

FRONT HOOK	ROOT WORD	END HOOK
	GAB	GABS = GABY
	GABARDINE	GABARDINES
	GABBARD	GABBARDS
	GABBART	GABBARTS
	GABBER	GABBERS
	GABBLE	GABBLED = GABBLER = GABBLES
	GABBLER	GABBLERS
	GABBLING	GABBLINGS
	GABBRO	GABBROS
	GABELLE	GABELLED = GABELLER = GABELLES
	GABELLER	GABELLERS
	GABERDINE	GABERDINES
	GABFEST	GABFESTS
	GABION	GABIONS
	GABIONADE	GABIONADES
	GABIONAGE	GABIONAGES
	GABLE	GABLED = GABLES = GABLET
	GABLET	GABLETS
	GABOON	GABOONS
EGAD = IGAD	GAD	GADE = GADI = GADS
	GADABOUT	GADABOUTS
	GADDER	GADDERS
	GADDI	GADDIS
	GADE	GADES
	GADGE	GADGES = GADGET
	GADGET	GADGETS = GADGETY
	GADGETEER	GADGETEERS
	GADGIE	GADGIES
	GADI	GADID = GADIS
	GADID	GADIDS
	GADJE	GADJES
	GADLING	GADLINGS
	GADOID	GADOIDS
	GADROON	GADROONS
EGADS	GADS	GADSO
	GADSO	GADSOS
	GADWALL	GADWALLS
	GAE	GAED = GAEN = GAES
	GAELICISE	GAELICISED = GAELICISES
	GAELICISM	GAELICISMS
	GAELICIZE	GAELICIZED = GAELICIZES
	GAFF	GAFFE = GAFFS
	GAFFE	GAFFED = GAFFER = GAFFES
	GAFFER	GAFFERS
	GAFFING	GAFFINGS
	GAFFSAIL	GAFFSAILS
	GAG	GAGA = GAGE = GAGS
	GAGAKU	GAGAKUS
	GAGE	GAGED = GAGER = GAGES
	GAGER	GAGERS
	GAGGER	GAGGERS = GAGGERY
	GAGGLE	GAGGLED = GAGGLES
	GAGGLING	GAGGLINGS
	GAGSTER	GAGSTERS
	GAHNITE	GAHNITES
	GAID	GAIDS
	GAILLARD	GAILLARDE
AGAIN	GAIN	GAINS
	GAINER	GAINERS
	GAINING	GAININGS
	GAINS	GAINST
	GAINSAY	GAINSAYS
	GAINSAYER	GAINSAYERS
AGAINST	GAINST	
	GAIR	GAIRS
	GAIRFOWL	GAIRFOWLS

319

G

FRONT HOOK	ROOT WORD	END HOOK
	GAIT	GAITS · GAITT
	GAITER	GAITERS
	GAITT	GAITTS
	GAJO	GAJOS
EGAL	GAL	GALA · GALE · GALL · GALS
	GALA	GALAH · GALAS · GALAX
	GALABEA	GALABEAH · GALABEAS
	GALABEAH	GALABEAHS
	GALABIA	GALABIAH · GALABIAS
	GALABIAH	GALABIAHS
	GALABIEH	GALABIEHS
	GALABIYA	GALABIYAH · GALABIYAS
	GALABIYAH	GALABIYAHS
	GALACTOSE	GALACTOSES
	GALAGE	GALAGES
	GALAGO	GALAGOS
	GALAH	GALAHS
	GALANGA	GALANGAL · GALANGAS
	GALANGAL	GALANGALS
	GALANT	GALANTY
	GALANTINE	GALANTINES
	GALAPAGO	GALAPAGOS
	GALATEA	GALATEAS
	GALAVANT	GALAVANTS
	GALAX	GALAXY
	GALBANUM	GALBANUMS
	GALDRAGON	GALDRAGONS
	GALE	GALE · GALES
	GALEA	GALEAE · GALEAS
	GALEATE	GALEATED
	GALENA	GALENAS
	GALENGALE	GALENGALES
	GALENICAL	GALENICALS
	GALENITE	GALENITES
	GALERE	GALERES
	GALETTE	GALETTES
	GALILEE	GALILEES
	GALINGALE	GALINGALES
	GALIONGEE	GALIONGEES
	GALIOT	GALIOTS
	GALIPOT	GALIPOTS
	GALIVANT	GALIVANTS
	GALL	GALLS · GALLY
	GALLABEA	GALLABEAH · GALLABEAS
	GALLABEAH	GALLABEAHS
	GALLABIA	GALLABIAH · GALLABIAS
	GALLABIAH	GALLABIAHS
	GALLABIEH	GALLABIEHS
	GALLABIYA	GALLABIYAH · GALLABIYAS
	GALLAMINE	GALLAMINES
	GALLANT	GALLANTS
	GALLATE	GALLATES
	GALLEIN	GALLEINS
	GALLEON	GALLEONS
	GALLERIA	GALLERIAS
	GALLERIST	GALLERISTS
	GALLET	GALLETA · GALLETS
	GALLETA	GALLETAS
	GALLEY	GALLEYS
	GALLIARD	GALLIARDS
	GALLIC	GALLICA
	GALLICA	GALLICAN · GALLICAS
	GALLICISE	GALLICISED · GALLICISES
	GALLICISM	GALLICISMS
	GALLICIZE	GALLICIZED · GALLICIZES
	GALLINAZO	GALLINAZOS
	GALLINULE	GALLINULES
	GALLIOT	GALLIOTS
	GALLIPOT	GALLIPOTS

FRONT HOOK	ROOT WORD	END HOOK
	GALLISE	GALLISED = GALLISES
	GALLISISE	GALLISISED = GALLISISES
	GALLISIZE	GALLISIZED = GALLISIZES
	GALLIUM	GALLIUMS
	GALLIVANT	GALLIVANTS
	GALLIVAT	GALLIVATS
	GALLIWASP	GALLIWASPS
	GALLIZE	GALLIZED = GALLIZES
	GALLNUT	GALLNUTS
	GALLON	GALLONS
	GALLONAGE	GALLONAGES
	GALLOON	GALLOONS
	GALLOOT	GALLOOTS
	GALLOP	GALLOPS
	GALLOPADE	GALLOPADED = GALLOPADES
	GALLOPER	GALLOPERS
	GALLOW	GALLOWS
	GALLSTONE	GALLSTONES
	GALLUMPH	GALLUMPHS
EGALLY	GALLY	
	GALOCHE	GALOCHED = GALOCHES
	GALOOT	GALOOTS
	GALOP	GALOPS
	GALOPADE	GALOPADES
	GALOPIN	GALOPING = GALOPINS
	GALORE	GALORES
	GALOSH	GALOSHE
	GALOSHE	GALOSHED = GALOSHES
	GALRAVAGE	GALRAVAGED = GALRAVAGES
	GALTONIA	GALTONIAS
	GALUMPH	GALUMPHS
	GALUMPHER	GALUMPHERS
	GALUT	GALUTH = GALUTS
	GALUTH	GALUTHS
	GALVANISE	GALVANISED = GALVANISER = GALVANISES
	GALVANISM	GALVANISMS
	GALVANIST	GALVANISTS
	GALVANIZE	GALVANIZED = GALVANIZER = GALVANIZES
	GALVO	GALVOS
	GALYAC	GALYACS
	GALYAK	GALYAKS
OGAM	GAM	GAMA = GAMB = GAME = GAMP = GAMS = GAMY
AGAMA	GAMA	GAMAS = GAMAY
	GAMAHUCHE	GAMAHUCHED (offensive)
		GAMAHUCHES (offensive)
	GAMARUCHE	GAMARUCHED (offensive)
		GAMARUCHES (offensive)
AGAMAS	GAMAS	GAMASH
	GAMAY	GAMAYS
	GAMB	GAMBA = GAMBE = GAMBO = GAMBS
	GAMBA	GAMBAS
	GAMBADE	GAMBADES
	GAMBADO	GAMBADOS
	GAMBE	GAMBES = GAMBET
	GAMBESON	GAMBESONS
	GAMBET	GAMBETS
	GAMBETTA	GAMBETTAS
	GAMBIA	GAMBIAS
	GAMBIER	GAMBIERS
	GAMBIR	GAMBIRS
	GAMBIST	GAMBISTS
	GAMBIT	GAMBITS
	GAMBLE	GAMBLED = GAMBLER = GAMBLES
	GAMBLER	GAMBLERS
	GAMBLING	GAMBLINGS
	GAMBO	GAMBOL = GAMBOS
	GAMBOGE	GAMBOGES
	GAMBOL	GAMBOLS
	GAMBREL	GAMBRELS

G

FRONT HOOK	ROOT WORD	END HOOK
	GAMBROON	GAMBROONS
	GAMBUSIA	GAMBUSIAS
	GAME	GAMED ▪ GAMER ▪ GAMES ▪ GAMEY
	GAMECOCK	GAMECOCKS
	GAMELAN	GAMELANS
	GAMEPLAY	GAMEPLAYS
	GAMER	GAMERS
	GAMES	GAMEST ▪ GAMESY
	GAMESTER	GAMESTERS
AGAMETE	GAMETE	GAMETES
AGAMETES	GAMETES	
AGAMIC ▪ OGAMIC	GAMIC	
	GAMIN	GAMINE ▪ GAMING ▪ GAMINS
	GAMINE	GAMINES
	GAMINERIE	GAMINERIES
	GAMINES	GAMINESS
	GAMING	GAMINGS
	GAMMA	GAMMAS ▪ GAMMAT
	GAMMAT	GAMMATS (offensive)
	GAMME	GAMMED ▪ GAMMER ▪ GAMMES
	GAMMER	GAMMERS (offensive)
	GAMMOCK	GAMMOCKS
	GAMMON	GAMMONS
	GAMMONER	GAMMONERS
	GAMMONING	GAMMONINGS
	GAMODEME	GAMODEMES
	GAMONE	GAMONES
	GAMP	GAMPS
OGAMS	GAMS	
	GAMUT	GAMUTS
	GAN	GANE ▪ GANG ▪ GANS ▪ GANT
	GANACHE	GANACHES
	GANDER	GANDERS
	GANDERISM	GANDERISMS
	GANE	GANEF ▪ GANEV
	GANEF	GANEFS
	GANEV	GANEVS
	GANG	GANGS
	GANGBANG	GANGBANGS (offensive)
	GANGBOARD	GANGBOARDS
	GANGER	GANGERS
	GANGING	GANGINGS
	GANGLAND	GANGLANDS
	GANGLIA	GANGLIAL ▪ GANGLIAR
	GANGLIATE	GANGLIATED
	GANGLION	GANGLIONS
	GANGPLANK	GANGPLANKS
	GANGPLOW	GANGPLOWS
	GANGREL	GANGRELS
	GANGRENE	GANGRENED ▪ GANGRENES
	GANGSHAG	GANGSHAGS
	GANGSTA	GANGSTAS
	GANGSTER	GANGSTERS
	GANGUE	GANGUES
	GANGWAY	GANGWAYS
	GANISTER	GANISTERS
	GANJA	GANJAH ▪ GANJAS
	GANJAH	GANJAHS
	GANNET	GANNETS
	GANNISTER	GANNISTERS
	GANOF	GANOFS
	GANOID	GANOIDS
	GANOIN	GANOINE ▪ GANOINS
	GANOINE	GANOINES
	GANSEY	GANSEYS
	GANT	GANTS
	GANTELOPE	GANTELOPES
	GANTLET	GANTLETS
	GANTLINE	GANTLINES

FRONT HOOK	ROOT WORD	END HOOK
	GANTLOPE	GANTLOPES
	GANYMEDE	GANYMEDES
	GAOL	GAOLS
	GAOLBIRD	GAOLBIRDS
	GAOLBREAK	GAOLBREAKS
	GAOLER	GAOLERS
	GAP	GAPE · GAPO · GAPS · GAPY
AGAPE	GAPE	GAPED · GAPER · GAPES
	GAPER	GAPERS
AGAPES	GAPES	
	GAPESEED	GAPESEEDS
	GAPEWORM	GAPEWORMS
	GAPING	GAPINGS
IGAPO	GAPO	GAPOS
IGAPOS	GAPOS	
	GAPPER	GAPPERS
AGAR	GAR	GARB · GARE · GARI · GARS · GART
	GARAGE	GARAGED · GARAGES
	GARAGING	GARAGINGS
	GARAGIST	GARAGISTE · GARAGISTS
	GARAGISTE	GARAGISTES
	GARB	GARBE · GARBO · GARBS
	GARBAGE	GARBAGES · GARBAGEY
	GARBANZO	GARBANZOS
	GARBE	GARBED · GARBES
	GARBLE	GARBLED · GARBLER · GARBLES
	GARBLER	GARBLERS
	GARBLES	GARBLESS
	GARBLING	GARBLINGS
	GARBO	GARBOS
	GARBOARD	GARBOARDS
	GARBOIL	GARBOILS
	GARBURE	GARBURES
	GARCINIA	GARCINIAS
	GARCON	GARCONS
	GARDA	GARDAI
	GARDANT	GARDANTS
	GARDEN	GARDENS
	GARDENER	GARDENERS
	GARDENFUL	GARDENFULS
	GARDENIA	GARDENIAS
	GARDENING	GARDENINGS
	GARDEROBE	GARDEROBES
	GARDYLOO	GARDYLOOS
	GAREFOWL	GAREFOWLS
	GARGANEY	GARGANEYS
	GARGANTUA	GARGANTUAN · GARGANTUAS
	GARGARISE	GARGARISED · GARGARISES
	GARGARISM	GARGARISMS
	GARGARIZE	GARGARIZED · GARGARIZES
	GARGET	GARGETS · GARGETY
	GARGLE	GARGLED · GARGLER · GARGLES
	GARGLER	GARGLERS
	GARGOYLE	GARGOYLED · GARGOYLES
	GARI	GARIS
	GARIAL	GARIALS
	GARIBALDI	GARIBALDIS
	GARIGUE	GARIGUES
	GARIS	GARISH
	GARJAN	GARJANS
	GARLAND	GARLANDS
	GARLIC	GARLICS
	GARMENT	GARMENTS
	GARNER	GARNERS
	GARNET	GARNETS
	GARNISHEE	GARNISHEED · GARNISHEES
	GARNISHER	GARNISHERS
	GARNITURE	GARNITURES
	GAROTE	GAROTED · GAROTES

C

FRONT HOOK	ROOT WORD	END HOOK
	GAROTTE	GAROTTED · GAROTTER · GAROTTES
	GAROTTER	GAROTTERS
	GAROTTING	GAROTTINGS
	GAROUPA	GAROUPAS
	GARPIKE	GARPIKES
	GARRAN	GARRANS
	GARRE	GARRED · GARRES · GARRET
	GARRET	GARRETS
	GARRETEER	GARRETEERS
	GARRIGUE	GARRIGUES
	GARRISON	GARRISONS
	GARRON	GARRONS
	GARROT	GARROTE · GARROTS
	GARROTE	GARROTED · GARROTER · GARROTES
	GARROTER	GARROTERS
	GARROTTE	GARROTTED · GARROTTER · GARROTTES
	GARROTTER	GARROTTERS
	GARRYA	GARRYAS
	GARRYOWEN	GARRYOWENS
AGARS	**GARS**	
	GART	GARTH
	GARTER	GARTERS
	GARTH	GARTHS
	GARUDA	GARUDAS
	GARUM	GARUMS
	GARVEY	GARVEYS
	GARVIE	GARVIES
	GARVOCK	GARVOCKS
AGAS	**GAS**	GASH · GASP · GAST
	GASAHOL	GASAHOLS
	GASALIER	GASALIERS
	GASBAG	GASBAGS
	GASCON	GASCONS
	GASCONADE	GASCONADED · GASCONADER · GASCONADES
	GASCONISM	GASCONISMS
	GASELIER	GASELIERS
	GASFIELD	GASFIELDS
	GASHES	GASHEST
	GASHOLDER	GASHOLDERS
	GASHOUSE	GASHOUSES
	GASIFIER	GASIFIERS
	GASKET	GASKETS
	GASKIN	GASKING · GASKINS
	GASKING	GASKINGS
	GASLIGHT	GASLIGHTS
	GASOGENE	GASOGENES
	GASOHOL	GASOHOLS
	GASOLENE	GASOLENES
	GASOLIER	GASOLIERS
	GASOLINE	GASOLINES
	GASOMETER	GASOMETERS
	GASP	GASPS · GASPY
	GASPER	GASPERS
	GASPEREAU	GASPEREAUS · GASPEREAUX
	GASPING	GASPINGS
	GASSER	GASSERS
	GASSING	GASSINGS
AGAST	**GAST**	GASTS
	GASTER	GASTERS
	GASTNESS	GASTNESSE
	GASTNESSE	GASTNESSES
	GASTRAEA	GASTRAEAS
	GASTRAEUM	GASTRAEUMS
	GASTREA	GASTREAS
	GASTRIN	GASTRINS
	GASTROPOD	GASTROPODS
	GASTRULA	GASTRULAE · GASTRULAR · GASTRULAS
	GAT	GATE · GATH · GATS
AGATE	**GATE**	GATED · GATER · GATES

FRONT HOOK	ROOT WORD	END HOOK
	GATEAU	GATEAUS ▪ GATEAUX
	GATEFOLD	GATEFOLDS
	GATEHOUSE	GATEHOUSES
	GATEPOST	GATEPOSTS
	GATER	GATERS
AGATES	GATES	
	GATEWAY	GATEWAYS
	GATH	GATHS
	GATHER	GATHERS
	GATHERER	GATHERERS
	GATHERING	GATHERINGS
	GATING	GATINGS
	GATOR	GATORS
	GAU	GAUD ▪ GAUM ▪ GAUN ▪ GAUP ▪ GAUR ▪ GAUS
	GAUCHE	GAUCHER
	GAUCHERIE	GAUCHERIES
	GAUCHO	GAUCHOS
	GAUCIE	GAUCIER
	GAUD	GAUDS ▪ GAUDY
	GAUDGIE	GAUDGIES
	GAUDIES	GAUDIEST
	GAUFER	GAUFERS
	GAUFFER	GAUFFERS
	GAUFRE	GAUFRES
	GAUGE	GAUGED ▪ GAUGER ▪ GAUGES
	GAUGER	GAUGERS
	GAUGING	GAUGINGS
	GAUJE	GAUJES
	GAULEITER	GAULEITERS
	GAULT	GAULTS
	GAULTER	GAULTERS
	GAUM	GAUMS ▪ GAUMY
	GAUN	GAUNT
	GAUNT	GAUNTS
	GAUNTLET	GAUNTLETS
	GAUNTREE	GAUNTREES
	GAUP	GAUPS
	GAUPER	GAUPERS
	GAUR	GAURS
	GAUS	GAUSS
	GAUZE	GAUZES
	GAVAGE	GAVAGES
AGAVE	GAVE	GAVEL
	GAVEL	GAVELS
	GAVELKIND	GAVELKINDS
	GAVELOCK	GAVELOCKS
	GAVIAL	GAVIALS
	GAVOT	GAVOTS
	GAVOTTE	GAVOTTED ▪ GAVOTTES
	GAWD	GAWDS
	GAWK	GAWKS ▪ GAWKY
	GAWKER	GAWKERS
	GAWKIES	GAWKIEST
	GAWKIHOOD	GAWKIHOODS
	GAWP	GAWPS
	GAWPER	GAWPERS
	GAWSIE	GAWSIER
	GAY	GAYS
	GAYAL	GAYALS
	GAYDAR	GAYDARS
	GAZABO	GAZABOS
	GAZAL	GAZALS
	GAZANIA	GAZANIAS
	GAZAR	GAZARS
AGAZE	GAZE	GAZED ▪ GAZER ▪ GAZES
	GAZEBO	GAZEBOS
AGAZED	GAZED	
	GAZEHOUND	GAZEHOUNDS
	GAZELLE	GAZELLES

G

FRONT HOOK	ROOT WORD	END HOOK
	GAZEMENT	GAZEMENTS
	GAZER	GAZERS
	GAZETTE	GAZETTED · GAZETTES
	GAZETTEER	GAZETTEERS
	GAZILLION	GAZILLIONS
	GAZING	GAZINGS
	GAZOGENE	GAZOGENES
	GAZON	GAZONS
	GAZOO	GAZOON · GAZOOS
	GAZOOKA	GAZOOKAS
	GAZOON	GAZOONS
	GAZPACHO	GAZPACHOS
	GAZUMP	GAZUMPS
	GAZUMPER	GAZUMPERS
	GAZUNDER	GAZUNDERS
	GEAL	GEALS
	GEALOUS	GEALOUSY
	GEAN	GEANS
	GEAR	GEARE · GEARS
	GEARCASE	GEARCASES
	GEARE	GEARED · GEARES
	GEARHEAD	GEARHEADS
	GEARING	GEARINGS
	GEARSHIFT	GEARSHIFTS
	GEARWHEEL	GEARWHEELS
	GEAT	GEATS
	GEBUR	GEBURS
	GECK	GECKO · GECKS
	GECKO	GECKOS
AGED	**GED**	GEDS
	GEDACT	GEDACTS
	GEDECKT	GEDECKTS
AGEE · OGEE	**GEE**	GEED · GEEK · GEEP · GEES · GEEZ
	GEEBAG	GEEBAGS *(offensive)*
	GEEBUNG	GEEBUNGS
	GEECHEE	GEECHEES
	GEEGAW	GEEGAWS
	GEEK	GEEKS · GEEKY
	GEEKDOM	GEEKDOMS
	GEEKSPEAK	GEEKSPEAKS
	GEELBEK	GEELBEKS
	GEEP	GEEPS
	GEEPOUND	GEEPOUNDS
OGEES	**GEES**	GEESE · GEEST
	GEEST	GEESTS
	GEEZAH	GEEZAHS
	GEEZER	GEEZERS
	GEFUFFLE	GEFUFFLED · GEFUFFLES
	GEGGIE	GEGGIES
	GEHLENITE	GEHLENITES
	GEISHA	GEISHAS
AGEIST	**GEIST**	GEISTS
AGEISTS	**GEISTS**	
	GEIT	GEITS
	GEL	GELD · GELS · GELT
	GELADA	GELADAS
	GELANT	GELANTS
AGELASTIC	**GELASTIC**	
	GELATE	GELATED · GELATES
	GELATI	GELATIN · GELATIS
	GELATIN	GELATINE · GELATING · GELATINS
	GELATINE	GELATINES
	GELATION	GELATIONS
	GELATO	GELATOS
	GELCAP	GELCAPS
	GELD	GELDS
	GELDER	GELDERS
	GELDING	GELDINGS
	GELEE	GELEES

FRONT HOOK	ROOT WORD	END HOOK
	GELIGNITE	GELIGNITES
	GELLANT	GELLANTS
	GELSEMINE	GELSEMINES
	GELSEMIUM	GELSEMIUMS
	GELT	GELTS
	GEM	GEMS
	GEMATRIA	GEMATRIAS
	GEMCLIP	GEMCLIPS
	GEMEL	GEMELS
	GEMINATE	GEMINATED · GEMINATES
	GEMMA	GEMMAE · GEMMAN
	GEMMATE	GEMMATED · GEMMATES
	GEMMATION	GEMMATIONS
	GEMMULE	GEMMULES
	GEMOT	GEMOTE · GEMOTS
	GEMOTE	GEMOTES
	GEMSBOK	GEMSBOKS
	GEMSBUCK	GEMSBUCKS
	GEMSHORN	GEMSHORNS
	GEMSTONE	GEMSTONES
AGEN	GEN	GENA · GENE · GENS · GENT · GENU
	GENA	GENAL · GENAS
	GENAPPE	GENAPPES
	GENDARME	GENDARMES
	GENDER	GENDERS
	GENDERISE	GENDERISED · GENDERISES
	GENDERIZE	GENDERIZED · GENDERIZES
AGENE	GENE	GENES · GENET
	GENERA	GENERAL
	GENERAL	GENERALE · GENERALS
	GENERANT	GENERANTS
	GENERATE	GENERATED · GENERATES
	GENERATOR	GENERATORS
	GENERIC	GENERICS
AGENES	GENES	
AGENESES	GENESES	
AGENESIS	GENESIS	
	GENET	GENETS
AGENETIC	GENETIC	GENETICS
	GENETTE	GENETTES
	GENEVA	GENEVAS
	GENIALISE	GENIALISED · GENIALISES
	GENIALIZE	GENIALIZED · GENIALIZES
	GENIE	GENIES
	GENIP	GENIPS
	GENIPAP	GENIPAPS
	GENISTA	GENISTAS
	GENISTEIN	GENISTEINS
	GENITAL	GENITALS
	GENITALIA	GENITALIAL
	GENITIVE	GENITIVES
	GENITOR	GENITORS
	GENITURE	GENITURES
	GENIZAH	GENIZAHS
	GENIZOT	GENIZOTH
	GENLOCK	GENLOCKS
	GENNAKER	GENNAKERS
	GENNEL	GENNELS
	GENNET	GENNETS
	GENOA	GENOAS
	GENOCIDE	GENOCIDES
	GENOGRAM	GENOGRAMS
	GENOISE	GENOISES
	GENOM	GENOME · GENOMS
	GENOME	GENOMES
	GENOMIC	GENOMICS
	GENOTYPE	GENOTYPES
	GENRE	GENRES
	GENRO	GENROS

FRONT HOOK	ROOT WORD	END HOOK
	GENSENG	GENSENGS
AGENT	GENT	GENTS · GENTY
	GENTIAN	GENTIANS
	GENTIL	GENTILE
	GENTILE	GENTILES
	GENTILISE	GENTILISED · GENTILISES
	GENTILISM	GENTILISMS
	GENTILIZE	GENTILIZED · GENTILIZES
	GENTLE	GENTLED · GENTLER · GENTLES
	GENTLES	GENTLEST
	GENTOO	GENTOOS
	GENTRICE	GENTRICES
AGENTRIES	GENTRIES	
AGENTRY	GENTRY	
AGENTS	GENTS	
	GENU	GENUA · GENUS
	GENUFLECT	GENUFLECTS
	GEO	GEOS
	GEOCORONA	GEOCORONAE · GEOCORONAS
	GEODE	GEODES
	GEODES	GEODESY
	GEODESIC	GEODESICS
	GEODESIST	GEODESISTS
	GEODETIC	GEODETICS
	GEODUCK	GEODUCKS
	GEOFACT	GEOFACTS
	GEOGNOST	GEOGNOSTS
	GEOID	GEOIDS
	GEOLOGER	GEOLOGERS
	GEOLOGIAN	GEOLOGIANS
	GEOLOGISE	GEOLOGISED · GEOLOGISES
	GEOLOGIST	GEOLOGISTS
	GEOLOGIZE	GEOLOGIZED · GEOLOGIZES
	GEOMANCER	GEOMANCERS
	GEOMANT	GEOMANTS
	GEOMETER	GEOMETERS
	GEOMETRIC	GEOMETRICS
	GEOMETRID	GEOMETRIDS
	GEOPHAGIA	GEOPHAGIAS
	GEOPHONE	GEOPHONES
	GEOPHYTE	GEOPHYTES
	GEOPONIC	GEOPONICS
	GEOPROBE	GEOPROBES
	GEORGETTE	GEORGETTES
	GEORGIC	GEORGICS
	GEOSPHERE	GEOSPHERES
	GEOSTATIC	GEOSTATICS
	GEOTHERM	GEOTHERMS
	GERAH	GERAHS
	GERANIAL	GERANIALS
	GERANIOL	GERANIOLS
	GERANIUM	GERANIUMS
	GERARDIA	GERARDIAS
	GERBE	GERBES
	GERBERA	GERBERAS
	GERBIL	GERBILS
	GERBILLE	GERBILLES
	GERE	GERES
	GERENT	GERENTS
	GERENUK	GERENUKS
	GERFALCON	GERFALCONS
	GERIATRIC	GERIATRICS
	GERLE	GERLES
	GERM	GERMS · GERMY
	GERMAIN	GERMAINE · GERMAINS
	GERMAINE	GERMAINES
	GERMAN	GERMANE · GERMANS
	GERMANDER	GERMANDERS
	GERMANISE	GERMANISED · GERMANISES

FRONT HOOK	ROOT WORD	END HOOK
	GERMANITE	GERMANITES
	GERMANIUM	GERMANIUMS
	GERMANIZE	GERMANIZED ▪ GERMANIZES
	GERMEN	GERMENS
	GERMICIDE	GERMICIDES
	GERMIN	GERMINA ▪ GERMING ▪ GERMINS
	GERMINA	GERMINAL
	GERMINATE	GERMINATED ▪ GERMINATES
	GERMPLASM	GERMPLASMS
	GERNE	GERNED ▪ GERNES
	GEROPIGA	GEROPIGAS
	GERUND	GERUNDS
	GERUNDIVE	GERUNDIVES
	GESNERIA	GESNERIAD ▪ GESNERIAS
	GESNERIAD	GESNERIADS
	GESSAMINE	GESSAMINES
	GESSE	GESSED ▪ GESSES
EGEST	GEST	GESTE ▪ GESTS
	GESTALT	GESTALTS
	GESTAPO	GESTAPOS
	GESTATE	GESTATED ▪ GESTATES
	GESTATION	GESTATIONS
	GESTE	GESTES
EGESTS	GESTS	
	GESTURE	GESTURED ▪ GESTURER ▪ GESTURES
	GESTURER	GESTURERS
	GET	GETA ▪ GETS
	GETA	GETAS
	GETAWAY	GETAWAYS
	GETTER	GETTERS
	GETTERING	GETTERINGS
	GETTING	GETTINGS
	GETUP	GETUPS
	GEUM	GEUMS
	GEWGAW	GEWGAWS
	GEYSER	GEYSERS
	GEYSERITE	GEYSERITES
	GHARIAL	GHARIALS
	GHARRI	GHARRIS
AGHAST	GHAST	GHASTS
	GHAT	GHATS
	GHAUT	GHAUTS
	GHAZAL	GHAZALS
	GHAZEL	GHAZELS
	GHAZI	GHAZIS
	GHEE	GHEES
	GHERAO	GHERAOS
	GHERKIN	GHERKINS
	GHESSE	GHESSED ▪ GHESSES
	GHETTO	GHETTOS
	GHETTOISE	GHETTOISED ▪ GHETTOISES
	GHETTOIZE	GHETTOIZED ▪ GHETTOIZES
	GHI	GHIS
	GHIBLI	GHIBLIS
	GHILGAI	GHILGAIS
	GHILLIE	GHILLIED ▪ GHILLIES
	GHOST	GHOSTS ▪ GHOSTY
	GHOSTING	GHOSTINGS
	GHOUL	GHOULS
	GHOULIE	GHOULIES
	GHYLL	GHYLLS
	GI	GIB ▪ GID ▪ GIE ▪ GIF ▪ GIG ▪ GIN ▪ GIO ▪ GIP ▪ GIS ▪ GIT
	GIANT	GIANTS
	GIANTHOOD	GIANTHOODS
	GIANTISM	GIANTISMS
	GIANTSHIP	GIANTSHIPS
	GIAOUR	GIAOURS (offensive)
	GIARDIA	GIARDIAS

FRONT HOOK	ROOT WORD	END HOOK
	GIB	GIBE ▪ GIBS
	GIBBER	GIBBERS
	GIBBET	GIBBETS
	GIBBON	GIBBONS
	GIBBSITE	GIBBSITES
	GIBE	GIBED ▪ GIBEL ▪ GIBER ▪ GIBES
	GIBEL	GIBELS
	GIBER	GIBERS
	GIBLET	GIBLETS
	GIBLI	GIBLIS
	GIBSON	GIBSONS
	GID	GIDS
	GIDDIES	GIDDIEST
	GIDGEE	GIDGEES
	GIDJEE	GIDJEES
	GIE	GIED ▪ GIEN ▪ GIES
	GIF	GIFT
	GIFT	GIFTS
	GIFTABLE	GIFTABLES
	GIFTEE	GIFTEES
	GIFTSHOP	GIFTSHOPS
	GIFTWARE	GIFTWARES
	GIFTWRAP	GIFTWRAPS
	GIG	GIGA ▪ GIGS
	GIGA	GIGAS
	GIGABIT	GIGABITS
	GIGABYTE	GIGABYTES
	GIGACYCLE	GIGACYCLES
	GIGAFLOP	GIGAFLOPS
	GIGANTISM	GIGANTISMS
	GIGATON	GIGATONS
	GIGAWATT	GIGAWATTS
	GIGGIT	GIGGITS
	GIGGLE	GIGGLED ▪ GIGGLER ▪ GIGGLES
	GIGGLER	GIGGLERS
	GIGGLING	GIGGLINGS
	GIGLET	GIGLETS
	GIGLOT	GIGLOTS
	GIGOLO	GIGOLOS
	GIGOT	GIGOTS
	GIGUE	GIGUES
AGILA	**GILA**	GILAS
AGILAS	**GILAS**	
	GILBERT	GILBERTS
	GILCUP	GILCUPS
	GILD	GILDS
	GILDER	GILDERS
	GILDHALL	GILDHALLS
	GILDING	GILDINGS
	GILET	GILETS
	GILGAI	GILGAIS
	GILGIE	GILGIES
	GILL	GILLS ▪ GILLY
	GILLAROO	GILLAROOS
	GILLER	GILLERS
	GILLET	GILLETS
	GILLFLIRT	GILLFLIRTS
	GILLIE	GILLIED ▪ GILLIES
	GILLION	GILLIONS
	GILLNET	GILLNETS
	GILLYVOR	GILLYVORS
	GILPEY	GILPEYS
	GILRAVAGE	GILRAVAGED ▪ GILRAVAGER ▪ GILRAVAGES
	GILSONITE	GILSONITES
	GILT	GILTS
	GILTCUP	GILTCUPS
	GILTHEAD	GILTHEADS
	GIMBAL	GIMBALS
	GIMCRACK	GIMCRACKS

FRONT HOOK	ROOT WORD	END HOOK
	GIMEL	GIMELS
	GIMLET	GIMLETS
	GIMMAL	GIMMALS
	GIMME	GIMMER = GIMMES
	GIMMER	GIMMERS
	GIMMICK	GIMMICKS = GIMMICKY
	GIMMIE	GIMMIES
	GIMMOR	GIMMORS
	GIMP	GIMPS (offensive) = GIMPY (offensive)
AGIN	GIN	GING = GINK = GINN = GINS
AGING	GING	GINGE = GINGS
	GINGAL	GINGALL = GINGALS
	GINGALL	GINGALLS
	GINGE	GINGER = GINGES
	GINGELEY	GINGELEYS
	GINGELI	GINGELIS
	GINGELLI	GINGELLIS
	GINGER	GINGERS = GINGERY
	GINGERADE	GINGERADES
	GINGHAM	GINGHAMS
	GINGILI	GINGILIS
	GINGILLI	GINGILLIS
	GINGIVA	GINGIVAE = GINGIVAL
	GINGKO	GINGKOS
	GINGLE	GINGLES
AGINGS	GINGS	
	GINHOUSE	GINHOUSES
	GINK	GINKS
	GINKGO	GINKGOS
	GINN	GINNY
	GINNEL	GINNELS
AGINNER	GINNER	GINNERS = GINNERY
AGINNERS	GINNERS	
	GINNING	GINNINGS
	GINSENG	GINSENGS
	GINSHOP	GINSHOPS
AGIO	GIO	GIOS
AGIOS	GIOS	
	GIP	GIPS
	GIPON	GIPONS
	GIPPER	GIPPERS
	GIPPO	GIPPOS
	GIPS	GIPSY
	GIPSEN	GIPSENS
	GIPSYDOM	GIPSYDOMS
	GIPSYHOOD	GIPSYHOODS
	GIPSYWORT	GIPSYWORTS
	GIRAFFE	GIRAFFES
	GIRANDOLA	GIRANDOLAS
	GIRANDOLE	GIRANDOLES
	GIRASOL	GIRASOLE = GIRASOLS
	GIRASOLE	GIRASOLES
	GIRD	GIRDS
	GIRDER	GIRDERS
	GIRDING	GIRDINGS
	GIRDLE	GIRDLED = GIRDLER = GIRDLES
	GIRDLER	GIRDLERS
	GIRKIN	GIRKINS
	GIRL	GIRLS = GIRLY
	GIRLHOOD	GIRLHOODS
	GIRLIE	GIRLIER = GIRLIES
	GIRLIES	GIRLIEST
	GIRLOND	GIRLONDS
	GIRN	GIRNS
	GIRNEL	GIRNELS
	GIRNER	GIRNERS
	GIRNIE	GIRNIER
	GIRO	GIRON = GIROS
	GIROLLE	GIROLLES

FRONT HOOK	ROOT WORD	END HOOK
	GIRON	GIRONS
	GIROSOL	GIROSOLS
	GIRR	GIRRS
	GIRT	GIRTH = GIRTS
	GIRTH	GIRTHS
	GIRTHLINE	GIRTHLINES
	GIRTLINE	GIRTLINES
EGIS	**GIS**	GISM = GIST
	GISARME	GISARMES
AGISM	**GISM**	GISMO = GISMS
	GISMO	GISMOS
AGISMS	**GISMS**	
AGIST	**GIST**	GISTS
AGISTS	**GISTS**	
	GIT	GITE = GITS
	GITANA	GITANAS
	GITANO	GITANOS
	GITE	GITES
	GITTARONE	GITTARONES
	GITTERN	GITTERNS
	GITTIN	GITTING
	GIUST	GIUSTO = GIUSTS
OGIVE	**GIVE**	GIVED = GIVEN = GIVER = GIVES
	GIVEAWAY	GIVEAWAYS
	GIVEBACK	GIVEBACKS
	GIVEN	GIVENS
	GIVER	GIVERS
OGIVES	**GIVES**	
	GIVING	GIVINGS
	GIZMO	GIZMOS
	GIZZARD	GIZZARDS
	GIZZEN	GIZZENS
	GJETOST	GJETOSTS
	GJU	GJUS
	GLABELLA	GLABELLAE = GLABELLAR
	GLACE	GLACES
	GLACIAL	GLACIALS
	GLACIATE	GLACIATED = GLACIATES
	GLACIER	GLACIERS
	GLAD	GLADE = GLADS = GLADY
	GLADDEN	GLADDENS
	GLADDENER	GLADDENERS
	GLADDIE	GLADDIES
	GLADDON	GLADDONS
	GLADE	GLADES
	GLADIATOR	GLADIATORS = GLADIATORY
	GLADIOLA	GLADIOLAR = GLADIOLAS
	GLADIOLE	GLADIOLES
	GLADSOME	GLADSOMER
	GLADSTONE	GLADSTONES
	GLADWRAP	GLADWRAPS
	GLAIK	GLAIKS
	GLAIR	GLAIRE = GLAIRS = GLAIRY
	GLAIRE	GLAIRED = GLAIRES
	GLAIRIN	GLAIRING = GLAIRINS
	GLAIVE	GLAIVED = GLAIVES
	GLAM	GLAMS
	GLAMOR	GLAMORS
	GLAMORISE	GLAMORISED = GLAMORISER = GLAMORISES
	GLAMORIZE	GLAMORIZED = GLAMORIZER = GLAMORIZES
	GLAMOUR	GLAMOURS
	GLANCE	GLANCED = GLANCER = GLANCES
	GLANCER	GLANCERS
	GLANCING	GLANCINGS
	GLAND	GLANDS
EGLANDULAR	**GLANDULAR**	
	GLANDULE	GLANDULES
AGLARE	**GLARE**	GLARED = GLARES
	GLASNOST	GLASNOSTS

FRONT HOOK	ROOT WORD	END HOOK
	GLASS	GLASSY
	GLASSFUL	GLASSFULS
	GLASSIE	GLASSIER · GLASSIES
	GLASSIES	GLASSIEST
	GLASSINE	GLASSINES
	GLASSINES	GLASSINESS
	GLASSWARE	GLASSWARES
	GLASSWORK	GLASSWORKS
	GLASSWORM	GLASSWORMS
	GLASSWORT	GLASSWORTS
	GLAUCOMA	GLAUCOMAS
	GLAUM	GLAUMS
	GLAUR	GLAURS · GLAURY
	GLAZE	GLAZED · GLAZEN · GLAZER · GLAZES
	GLAZER	GLAZERS
	GLAZIER	GLAZIERS · GLAZIERY
	GLAZING	GLAZINGS
AGLEAM	GLEAM	GLEAMS · GLEAMY
	GLEAMER	GLEAMERS
	GLEAMING	GLEAMINGS
	GLEAN	GLEANS
	GLEANER	GLEANERS
	GLEANING	GLEANINGS
	GLEAVE	GLEAVES
	GLEBA	GLEBAE
	GLEBE	GLEBES
OGLED	GLED	GLEDE · GLEDS
	GLEDE	GLEDES
	GLEDGE	GLEDGED · GLEDGES
AGLEE	GLEE	GLEED · GLEEK · GLEES · GLEET
	GLEED	GLEEDS
	GLEEK	GLEEKS
	GLEENIE	GLEENIES
	GLEET	GLEETS · GLEETY
	GLEI	GLEIS
	GLEN	GLENS · GLENT
	GLENOID	GLENOIDS
	GLENT	GLENTS
AGLEY	GLEY	GLEYS
	GLEYING	GLEYINGS
	GLIA	GLIAL · GLIAS
	GLIADIN	GLIADINE · GLIADINS
	GLIADINE	GLIADINES
	GLIB	GLIBS
	GLIBBER	GLIBBERY
	GLID	GLIDE
	GLIDDER	GLIDDERY
	GLIDE	GLIDED · GLIDER · GLIDES
	GLIDEPATH	GLIDEPATHS
	GLIDER	GLIDERS
	GLIDING	GLIDINGS
	GLIFF	GLIFFS
	GLIFFING	GLIFFINGS
	GLIFT	GLIFTS
	GLIKE	GLIKES
	GLIM	GLIME · GLIMS
	GLIME	GLIMED · GLIMES
AGLIMMER	GLIMMER	GLIMMERS · GLIMMERY
	GLIMPSE	GLIMPSED · GLIMPSER · GLIMPSES
	GLIMPSER	GLIMPSERS
	GLINT	GLINTS · GLINTY
	GLIOMA	GLIOMAS
	GLISK	GLISKS
	GLISSADE	GLISSADED · GLISSADER · GLISSADES
	GLISSADER	GLISSADERS
	GLISSANDO	GLISSANDOS
	GLISTEN	GLISTENS
	GLISTER	GLISTERS
	GLIT	GLITS · GLITZ

FRONT HOOK	ROOT WORD	END HOOK
	GLITCH	GLITCHY
AGLITTER	**GLITTER**	GLITTERS · GLITTERY
	GLITZ	GLITZY
	GLOAM	GLOAMS
	GLOAMING	GLOAMINGS
	GLOAT	GLOATS
	GLOATER	GLOATERS
	GLOB	GLOBE · GLOBI · GLOBS · GLOBY
	GLOBALISE	GLOBALISED · GLOBALISES
	GLOBALISM	GLOBALISMS
	GLOBALIST	GLOBALISTS
	GLOBALIZE	GLOBALIZED · GLOBALIZES
	GLOBATE	GLOBATED
	GLOBE	GLOBED · GLOBES
	GLOBETROT	GLOBETROTS
	GLOBI	GLOBIN
	GLOBIN	GLOBING · GLOBINS
	GLOBOID	GLOBOIDS
	GLOBOSE	GLOBOSES
	GLOBULAR	GLOBULARS
	GLOBULE	GLOBULES · GLOBULET
	GLOBULET	GLOBULETS
	GLOBULIN	GLOBULINS
	GLOBULITE	GLOBULITES
	GLOCHID	GLOCHIDS
	GLOGG	GLOGGS
	GLOIRE	GLOIRES
	GLOM	GLOMS
	GLOMERATE	GLOMERATED · GLOMERATES
	GLOMERULE	GLOMERULES
	GLONOIN	GLONOINS
	GLOOM	GLOOMS · GLOOMY
	GLOOMING	GLOOMINGS
	GLOOP	GLOOPS · GLOOPY
	GLOP	GLOPS
	GLORIA	GLORIAS
	GLORIFIER	GLORIFIERS
	GLORIOLE	GLORIOLES
	GLORIOSA	GLORIOSAS
	GLOSS	GLOSSA · GLOSSY
	GLOSSA	GLOSSAE · GLOSSAL · GLOSSAS
AGLOSSAL	**GLOSSAL**	
	GLOSSATOR	GLOSSATORS
	GLOSSEME	GLOSSEMES
	GLOSSER	GLOSSERS
	GLOSSIES	GLOSSIEST
	GLOSSINA	GLOSSINAS
	GLOSSIST	GLOSSISTS
	GLOST	GLOSTS
	GLOUT	GLOUTS
	GLOVE	GLOVED · GLOVER · GLOVES
	GLOVER	GLOVERS
	GLOVING	GLOVINGS
AGLOW	**GLOW**	GLOWS
	GLOWER	GLOWERS
	GLOWLAMP	GLOWLAMPS
	GLOWSTICK	GLOWSTICKS
	GLOWWORM	GLOWWORMS
	GLOXINIA	GLOXINIAS
	GLOZE	GLOZED · GLOZES
	GLOZING	GLOZINGS
	GLUCAGON	GLUCAGONS
	GLUCAN	GLUCANS
	GLUCINA	GLUCINAS
	GLUCINIUM	GLUCINIUMS
	GLUCINUM	GLUCINUMS
	GLUCONATE	GLUCONATES
	GLUCOSE	GLUCOSES
	GLUCOSIDE	GLUCOSIDES

FRONT HOOK	ROOT WORD	END HOOK
	GLUE	GLUED · GLUER · GLUES · GLUEY
	GLUEPOT	GLUEPOTS
	GLUER	GLUERS
	GLUG	GLUGS
	GLUHWEIN	GLUHWEINS
	GLUM	GLUME · GLUMS
	GLUME	GLUMES
	GLUMELLA	GLUMELLAS
	GLUON	GLUONS
	GLURGE	GLURGES
	GLUT	GLUTE · GLUTS
	GLUTAMATE	GLUTAMATES
	GLUTAMINE	GLUTAMINES
	GLUTE	GLUTEI · GLUTEN · GLUTES
	GLUTELIN	GLUTELINS
	GLUTEN	GLUTENS
	GLUTENIN	GLUTENINS
	GLUTTON	GLUTTONS · GLUTTONY
	GLYCAEMIA	GLYCAEMIAS
	GLYCAN	GLYCANS
	GLYCEMIA	GLYCEMIAS
	GLYCERIA	GLYCERIAS
	GLYCERIDE	GLYCERIDES
	GLYCERIN	GLYCERINE · GLYCERINS
	GLYCERINE	GLYCERINES
	GLYCEROL	GLYCEROLS
	GLYCERYL	GLYCERYLS
	GLYCIN	GLYCINE · GLYCINS
	GLYCINE	GLYCINES
	GLYCOCOLL	GLYCOCOLLS
	GLYCOGEN	GLYCOGENS
	GLYCOL	GLYCOLS
	GLYCONIC	GLYCONICS
	GLYCOSE	GLYCOSES
	GLYCOSIDE	GLYCOSIDES
	GLYCOSYL	GLYCOSYLS
	GLYCYL	GLYCYLS
	GLYPH	GLYPHS
	GLYPTAL	GLYPTALS
	GLYPTIC	GLYPTICS
	GMELINITE	GMELINITES
	GNAR	GNARL · GNARR · GNARS
	GNARL	GNARLS · GNARLY
	GNARR	GNARRS
	GNASHER	GNASHERS
	GNAT	GNATS
	GNATHION	GNATHIONS
	GNATHITE	GNATHITES
	GNATLING	GNATLINGS
	GNAW	GNAWN · GNAWS
	GNAWER	GNAWERS
	GNAWING	GNAWINGS
	GNOCCHI	GNOCCHIS
	GNOME	GNOMES
	GNOMIST	GNOMISTS
	GNOMON	GNOMONS
	GNOMONIC	GNOMONICS
AGNOSTIC	GNOSTIC	GNOSTICS
AGNOSTICS	GNOSTICS	
	GNOW	GNOWS
	GNU	GNUS
AGO · EGO · YGO	GO	GOA · GOB · GOD · GOE · GON · GOO · GOR · GOS · GOT · GOV · GOX · GOY
	GOA	GOAD · GOAF · GOAL · GOAS · GOAT
	GOAD	GOADS
	GOADSTER	GOADSTERS
	GOAF	GOAFS
	GOAL	GOALS
	GOALBALL	GOALBALLS

FRONT HOOK	ROOT WORD	END HOOK
	GOALIE	GOALIES
	GOALMOUTH	GOALMOUTHS
	GOALPOST	GOALPOSTS
	GOANNA	GOANNAS
	GOAT	GOATS ▪ GOATY
	GOATEE	GOATEED ▪ GOATEES
	GOATHERD	GOATHERDS
	GOATLING	GOATLINGS
	GOATSKIN	GOATSKINS
	GOATWEED	GOATWEEDS
	GOB	GOBO ▪ GOBS ▪ GOBY
	GOBAN	GOBANG ▪ GOBANS
	GOBANG	GOBANGS
	GOBBELINE	GOBBELINES
	GOBBET	GOBBETS
	GOBBLE	GOBBLED ▪ GOBBLER ▪ GOBBLES
	GOBBLER	GOBBLERS
	GOBIID	GOBIIDS
	GOBIOID	GOBIOIDS
	GOBLET	GOBLETS
	GOBLIN	GOBLINS
	GOBO	GOBOS
	GOBSHITE	GOBSHITES *(offensive)*
	GOBURRA	GOBURRAS
	GOD	GODS
	GODDAM	GODDAMN ▪ GODDAMS
	GODDAMN	GODDAMNS
	GODDEN	GODDENS
	GODET	GODETS
	GODETIA	GODETIAS
	GODFATHER	GODFATHERS
	GODHEAD	GODHEADS
	GODHOOD	GODHOODS
	GODLING	GODLINGS
	GODMOTHER	GODMOTHERS
	GODOWN	GODOWNS
	GODPARENT	GODPARENTS
	GODROON	GODROONS
	GODS	GODSO
	GODSEND	GODSENDS
	GODSHIP	GODSHIPS
	GODSLOT	GODSLOTS
	GODSO	GODSON ▪ GODSOS
	GODSON	GODSONS
	GODSPEED	GODSPEEDS
	GODSQUAD	GODSQUADS *(offensive)*
	GODWARD	GODWARDS
	GODWIT	GODWITS
YGOE	**GOE**	GOEL ▪ GOER ▪ GOES ▪ GOEY
	GOEL	GOELS
	GOER	GOERS
	GOETHITE	GOETHITES
	GOFER	GOFERS
	GOFF	GOFFS
	GOFFER	GOFFERS
	GOFFERING	GOFFERINGS
	GOGGA	GOGGAS
	GOGGLE	GOGGLED ▪ GOGGLER ▪ GOGGLES
	GOGGLER	GOGGLERS
	GOGGLING	GOGGLINGS
	GOGLET	GOGLETS
	GOGO	GOGOS
	GOHONZON	GOHONZONS
AGOING	**GOING**	GOINGS
	GOITER	GOITERS
	GOITRE	GOITRED ▪ GOITRES
	GOITROGEN	GOITROGENS
	GOLCONDA	GOLCONDAS
	GOLD	GOLDS ▪ GOLDY

FRONT HOOK	ROOT WORD	END HOOK
	GOLDARN	GOLDARNS
	GOLDBRICK	GOLDBRICKS
	GOLDBUG	GOLDBUGS
	GOLDCREST	GOLDCRESTS
	GOLDEN	GOLDENS
	GOLDENEYE	GOLDENEYES
	GOLDENROD	GOLDENRODS
	GOLDEYE	GOLDEYES
	GOLDFIELD	GOLDFIELDS
	GOLDMINER	GOLDMINERS
	GOLDSIZE	GOLDSIZES
	GOLDSMITH	GOLDSMITHS
	GOLDSPINK	GOLDSPINKS
	GOLDSTICK	GOLDSTICKS
	GOLDSTONE	GOLDSTONES
	GOLDURN	GOLDURNS
	GOLE	GOLEM · GOLES
	GOLEM	GOLEMS
	GOLF	GOLFS
	GOLFER	GOLFERS
	GOLFIANA	GOLFIANAS
	GOLFING	GOLFINGS
	GOLGOTHA	GOLGOTHAS
	GOLIARD	GOLIARDS · GOLIARDY
	GOLIATH	GOLIATHS
	GOLLAN	GOLLAND · GOLLANS
	GOLLAND	GOLLANDS
	GOLLAR	GOLLARS
	GOLLER	GOLLERS
	GOLLIWOG	GOLLIWOGG · GOLLIWOGS
	GOLLIWOGG	GOLLIWOGGS
	GOLLOP	GOLLOPS
	GOLLOPER	GOLLOPERS
	GOLLYWOG	GOLLYWOGS
	GOLOMYNKA	GOLOMYNKAS
	GOLOSH	GOLOSHE
	GOLOSHE	GOLOSHED · GOLOSHES
	GOLP	GOLPE · GOLPS
	GOLPE	GOLPES
	GOMBEEN	GOMBEENS
	GOMBO	GOMBOS
	GOMBRO	GOMBROS
	GOMBROON	GOMBROONS
	GOMER	GOMERS
	GOMERAL	GOMERALS
	GOMEREL	GOMERELS
	GOMERIL	GOMERILS
	GOMOKU	GOMOKUS
	GOMPA	GOMPAS
	GOMUTI	GOMUTIS
	GOMUTO	GOMUTOS
AGON	GON	GONE · GONG · GONK · GONS
	GONAD	GONADS
	GONDELAY	GONDELAYS
	GONDOLA	GONDOLAS
	GONDOLIER	GONDOLIERS
AGONE	GONE	GONEF · GONER
	GONEF	GONEFS
	GONER	GONERS
	GONFALON	GONFALONS
	GONFANON	GONFANONS
	GONG	GONGS
	GONGSTER	GONGSTERS
	GONGYO	GONGYOS
	GONIATITE	GONIATITES
	GONIDIA	GONIDIAL
	GONIF	GONIFF · GONIFS
	GONIFF	GONIFFS
	GONK	GONKS

FRONT HOOK	ROOT WORD	END HOOK
	GONOCOCCI	GONOCOCCIC
	GONOCYTE	GONOCYTES
	GONODUCT	GONODUCTS
	GONOF	GONOFS
	GONOPH	GONOPHS
	GONOPHORE	GONOPHORES
	GONOPOD	GONOPODS
	GONOPORE	GONOPORES
	GONORRHEA	GONORRHEAL · GONORRHEAS
	GONOSOME	GONOSOMES
AGONS	**GONS**	
	GOO	GOOD · GOOF · GOOG · GOOK · GOOL
		GOON · GOOP · GOOR · GOOS
	GOOBER	GOOBERS
AGOOD	**GOOD**	GOODS · GOODY
	GOODBY	GOODBYE · GOODBYS
	GOODBYE	GOODBYES
	GOODIE	GOODIER · GOODIES
	GOODIES	GOODIEST
	GOODNIGHT	GOODNIGHTS
	GOODSIRE	GOODSIRES
	GOODWILL	GOODWILLS
	GOODYEAR	GOODYEARS
	GOOF	GOOFS · GOOFY
	GOOFBALL	GOOFBALLS
	GOOG	GOOGS
	GOOGLE	GOOGLED · GOOGLES
	GOOGOL	GOOGOLS
	GOOK	GOOKS (offensive) · GOOKY
	GOOL	GOOLD · GOOLS · GOOLY (offensive)
	GOOLD	GOOLDS
	GOOLEY	GOOLEYS (offensive)
	GOOLIE	GOOLIES (offensive)
	GOOMBAH	GOOMBAHS
	GOOMBAY	GOOMBAYS
	GOON	GOONS · GOONY
	GOONDA	GOONDAS
	GOONEY	GOONEYS
	GOONIE	GOONIER · GOONIES
	GOONIES	GOONIEST
	GOOP	GOOPS · GOOPY
	GOOR	GOORS · GOORY
	GOORAL	GOORALS
	GOORIE	GOORIES
	GOOROO	GOOROOS
	GOOS	GOOSE · GOOSY
	GOOSANDER	GOOSANDERS
	GOOSE	GOOSED · GOOSES · GOOSEY
	GOOSEFOOT	GOOSEFOOTS
	GOOSEGOB	GOOSEGOBS
	GOOSEGOG	GOOSEGOGS
	GOOSEHERD	GOOSEHERDS
	GOOSENECK	GOOSENECKS
	GOOSEY	GOOSEYS
	GOOSIES	GOOSIEST
	GOPAK	GOPAKS
	GOPHER	GOPHERS
	GOPURA	GOPURAM · GOPURAS
	GOPURAM	GOPURAMS
	GOR	GORA · GORE · GORI · GORM · GORP · GORY
AGORA	**GORA**	GORAL · GORAS
	GORAL	GORALS
AGORAS	**GORAS**	
	GORCOCK	GORCOCKS
	GORCROW	GORCROWS
	GORDITA	GORDITAS
	GORE	GORED · GORES
	GOREHOUND	GOREHOUNDS
	GORGE	GORGED · GORGER · GORGES · GORGET

FRONT HOOK	ROOT WORD	END HOOK
	GORGER	GORGERS
	GORGERIN	GORGERINS
	GORGET	GORGETS
	GORGIA	GORGIAS
	GORGIO	GORGIOS
	GORGON	GORGONS
	GORGONIAN	GORGONIANS
	GORGONISE	GORGONISED ▪ GORGONISES
	GORGONIZE	GORGONIZED ▪ GORGONIZES
	GORHEN	GORHENS
	GORI	GORIS
	GORILLA	GORILLAS
	GORING	GORINGS
	GORM	GORMS ▪ GORMY
	GORMAND	GORMANDS
	GORP	GORPS
	GORSE	GORSES
	GORSEDD	GORSEDDS
	GORSOON	GORSOONS
EGOS	GOS	GOSH ▪ GOSS
	GOSH	GOSHT
	GOSHAWK	GOSHAWKS
	GOSHT	GOSHTS
	GOSLARITE	GOSLARITES
	GOSLET	GOSLETS
	GOSLING	GOSLINGS
	GOSPEL	GOSPELS
	GOSPELER	GOSPELERS
	GOSPELISE	GOSPELISED ▪ GOSPELISES
	GOSPELIZE	GOSPELIZED ▪ GOSPELIZES
	GOSPELLER	GOSPELLERS
	GOSPODA	GOSPODAR
	GOSPODAR	GOSPODARS
	GOSPORT	GOSPORTS
	GOSS	GOSSE
	GOSSAMER	GOSSAMERS ▪ GOSSAMERY
	GOSSAN	GOSSANS
	GOSSE	GOSSED ▪ GOSSES
	GOSSIB	GOSSIBS
	GOSSIP	GOSSIPS ▪ GOSSIPY
	GOSSIPER	GOSSIPERS
	GOSSIPING	GOSSIPINGS
	GOSSIPPER	GOSSIPPERS
	GOSSOON	GOSSOONS
	GOSSYPOL	GOSSYPOLS
	GOSTER	GOSTERS
	GOT	GOTH
	GOTCHA	GOTCHAS
	GOTH	GOTHS
	GOTHIC	GOTHICS
	GOTHICISE	GOTHICISED ▪ GOTHICISES
	GOTHICISM	GOTHICISMS
	GOTHICIZE	GOTHICIZED ▪ GOTHICIZES
	GOTHITE	GOTHITES
	GOUACHE	GOUACHES
	GOUGE	GOUGED ▪ GOUGER ▪ GOUGES
	GOUGER	GOUGERE ▪ GOUGERS
	GOUGERE	GOUGERES
	GOUJON	GOUJONS
	GOUK	GOUKS
	GOURA	GOURAS
	GOURAMI	GOURAMIS
	GOURD	GOURDE ▪ GOURDS ▪ GOURDY
	GOURDE	GOURDES
	GOURMAND	GOURMANDS
	GOURMET	GOURMETS
	GOUT	GOUTS ▪ GOUTY
	GOUTTE	GOUTTES
	GOUTWEED	GOUTWEEDS

FRONT HOOK	ROOT WORD	END HOOK
	GOUTWORT	GOUTWORTS
AGOUTY	**GOUTY**	
	GOV	GOVS
	GOVERN	GOVERNS
	GOVERNALL	GOVERNALLS
	GOVERNESS	GOVERNESSY
	GOVERNOR	GOVERNORS
	GOWAN	GOWANS · GOWANY
	GOWD	GOWDS
	GOWDSPINK	GOWDSPINKS
	GOWF	GOWFS
	GOWFER	GOWFERS
	GOWK	GOWKS
	GOWL	GOWLS
	GOWLAN	GOWLAND · GOWLANS
	GOWLAND	GOWLANDS
	GOWN	GOWNS
	GOWNBOY	GOWNBOYS
	GOWPEN	GOWPENS
	GOWPENFUL	GOWPENFULS
	GOY	GOYS (offensive)
	GOZZAN	GOZZANS
	GRAAL	GRAALS
	GRAB	GRABS
	GRABBER	GRABBERS
	GRABBLE	GRABBLED · GRABBLER · GRABBLES
	GRABBLER	GRABBLERS
	GRABEN	GRABENS
	GRACE	GRACED · GRACES
	GRACILE	GRACILES
	GRACIOSO	GRACIOSOS
	GRACKLE	GRACKLES
	GRAD	GRADE · GRADS
	GRADABLE	GRADABLES
	GRADATE	GRADATED · GRADATES
	GRADATION	GRADATIONS
	GRADDAN	GRADDANS
	GRADE	GRADED · GRADER · GRADES
	GRADER	GRADERS
	GRADIENT	GRADIENTS
	GRADIN	GRADINE · GRADING · GRADINI · GRADINO · GRADINS
	GRADINE	GRADINES
	GRADUAL	GRADUALS
	GRADUAND	GRADUANDS
	GRADUATE	GRADUATED · GRADUATES
	GRADUATOR	GRADUATORS
	GRAECISE	GRAECISED · GRAECISES
	GRAECIZE	GRAECIZED · GRAECIZES
	GRAFF	GRAFFS
SGRAFFITI	**GRAFFITI**	GRAFFITIS
	GRAFFITIS	GRAFFITIST
SGRAFFITO	**GRAFFITO**	
	GRAFT	GRAFTS
	GRAFTAGE	GRAFTAGES
	GRAFTER	GRAFTERS
	GRAFTING	GRAFTINGS
	GRAHAM	GRAHAMS
	GRAIL	GRAILE · GRAILS
	GRAILE	GRAILES
	GRAIN	GRAINE · GRAINS · GRAINY
	GRAINAGE	GRAINAGES
	GRAINE	GRAINED · GRAINER · GRAINES
	GRAINER	GRAINERS
	GRAINING	GRAININGS
	GRAIP	GRAIPS
	GRAITH	GRAITHS
	GRAKLE	GRAKLES
	GRALLOCH	GRALLOCHS

FRONT HOOK	ROOT WORD	END HOOK
	GRAM	GRAMA = GRAME = GRAMP = GRAMS
	GRAMA	GRAMAS
	GRAMARY	GRAMARYE
	GRAMARYE	GRAMARYES
	GRAMAS	GRAMASH
	GRAME	GRAMES
	GRAMMA	GRAMMAR = GRAMMAS
	GRAMMAGE	GRAMMAGES
	GRAMMAR	GRAMMARS
	GRAMME	GRAMMES
	GRAMOCHE	GRAMOCHES
	GRAMP	GRAMPA = GRAMPS
	GRAMPA	GRAMPAS
	GRAN	GRANA = GRAND = GRANS = GRANT
	GRAND	GRANDE = GRANDS
	GRANDAD	GRANDADS
	GRANDAM	GRANDAME = GRANDAMS
	GRANDAME	GRANDAMES
	GRANDAUNT	GRANDAUNTS
	GRANDDAD	GRANDDADS
	GRANDDAM	GRANDDAMS
	GRANDE	GRANDEE = GRANDER
	GRANDEE	GRANDEES
	GRANDEUR	GRANDEURS
	GRANDKID	GRANDKIDS
	GRANDMA	GRANDMAS
	GRANDMAMA	GRANDMAMAS
	GRANDPA	GRANDPAS
	GRANDPAPA	GRANDPAPAS
	GRANDSIR	GRANDSIRE = GRANDSIRS
	GRANDSIRE	GRANDSIRES
	GRANDSON	GRANDSONS
	GRANFER	GRANFERS
	GRANGE	GRANGER = GRANGES
	GRANGER	GRANGERS
	GRANITA	GRANITAS
	GRANITE	GRANITES
	GRANITISE	GRANITISED = GRANITISES
	GRANITITE	GRANITITES
	GRANITIZE	GRANITIZED = GRANITIZES
	GRANIVORE	GRANIVORES
	GRANNAM	GRANNAMS
	GRANNIE	GRANNIED = GRANNIES
	GRANNOM	GRANNOMS
	GRANOLA	GRANOLAS
	GRANOLITH	GRANOLITHS
	GRANT	GRANTS
	GRANTEE	GRANTEES
	GRANTER	GRANTERS
	GRANTOR	GRANTORS
	GRANULAR	GRANULARY
	GRANULATE	GRANULATED = GRANULATER = GRANULATES
	GRANULE	GRANULES
	GRANULITE	GRANULITES
	GRANULOMA	GRANULOMAS
	GRANULOSE	GRANULOSES
	GRAPE	GRAPED = GRAPES = GRAPEY
	GRAPESEED	GRAPESEEDS
	GRAPESHOT	GRAPESHOTS
	GRAPETREE	GRAPETREES
	GRAPEVINE	GRAPEVINES
	GRAPH	GRAPHS
	GRAPHEME	GRAPHEMES
	GRAPHEMIC	GRAPHEMICS
AGRAPHIC	GRAPHIC	GRAPHICS
	GRAPHITE	GRAPHITES
	GRAPHIUM	GRAPHIUMS
	GRAPLE	GRAPLES
	GRAPLIN	GRAPLINE = GRAPLINS

FRONT HOOK	ROOT WORD	END HOOK
	GRAPLINE	GRAPLINES
	GRAPNEL	GRAPNELS
	GRAPPA	GRAPPAS
	GRAPPLE	GRAPPLED · GRAPPLER · GRAPPLES
	GRAPPLER	GRAPPLERS
	GRAPPLING	GRAPPLINGS
	GRASP	GRASPS
	GRASPER	GRASPERS
	GRASS	GRASSY
	GRASSER	GRASSERS
	GRASSHOOK	GRASSHOOKS
	GRASSING	GRASSINGS
	GRASSLAND	GRASSLANDS
	GRASSPLOT	GRASSPLOTS
	GRASSQUIT	GRASSQUITS
	GRASSROOT	GRASSROOTS
	GRASSUM	GRASSUMS
AGRASTE	**GRASTE**	
	GRAT	GRATE
	GRATE	GRATED · GRATER · GRATES
	GRATER	GRATERS
	GRATICULE	GRATICULES
	GRATIFIER	GRATIFIERS
	GRATIN	GRATINE · GRATING · GRATINS
	GRATINATE	GRATINATED · GRATINATES
	GRATINE	GRATINEE
	GRATINEE	GRATINEED · GRATINEES
	GRATING	GRATINGS
	GRATITUDE	GRATITUDES
	GRATTOIR	GRATTOIRS
	GRATULATE	GRATULATED · GRATULATES
	GRAUNCHER	GRAUNCHERS
	GRAUPEL	GRAUPELS
	GRAV	GRAVE · GRAVS · GRAVY
	GRAVAMEN	GRAVAMENS
	GRAVE	GRAVED · GRAVEL · GRAVEN · GRAVER GRAVES
	GRAVEL	GRAVELS · GRAVELY
	GRAVER	GRAVERS
	GRAVES	GRAVEST
	GRAVESIDE	GRAVESIDES
	GRAVESITE	GRAVESITES
	GRAVEYARD	GRAVEYARDS
	GRAVID	GRAVIDA
	GRAVIDA	GRAVIDAE · GRAVIDAS
	GRAVING	GRAVINGS
	GRAVITATE	GRAVITATED · GRAVITATER · GRAVITATES
	GRAVITINO	GRAVITINOS
	GRAVITON	GRAVITONS
	GRAVURE	GRAVURES
	GRAY	GRAYS
	GRAYBACK	GRAYBACKS
	GRAYBEARD	GRAYBEARDS
	GRAYHOUND	GRAYHOUNDS
	GRAYLAG	GRAYLAGS
	GRAYLE	GRAYLES
	GRAYLING	GRAYLINGS
	GRAYMAIL	GRAYMAILS
	GRAYOUT	GRAYOUTS
	GRAYWACKE	GRAYWACKES
	GRAYWATER	GRAYWATERS
	GRAZE	GRAZED · GRAZER · GRAZES
	GRAZER	GRAZERS
	GRAZIER	GRAZIERS
	GRAZING	GRAZINGS
	GREASE	GREASED · GREASER · GREASES
	GREASER	GREASERS
	GREASIES	GREASIEST
	GREAT	GREATS

FRONT HOOK	ROOT WORD	END HOOK
	GREATCOAT	GREATCOATS
	GREATEN	GREATENS
	GREATEST	GREATESTS
	GREAVE	GREAVED = GREAVES
	GREBE	GREBES
	GRECE	GRECES
	GRECIAN	GRECIANS
	GRECISE	GRECISED = GRECISES
	GRECIZE	GRECIZED = GRECIZES
	GRECQUE	GRECQUES
AGREE	GREE	GREED = GREEK = GREEN = GREES = GREET
	GREECE	GREECES
AGREED	GREED	GREEDS = GREEDY
	GREEGREE	GREEGREES
AGREEING	GREEING	
	GREEKING	GREEKINGS
	GREEN	GREENS = GREENY
	GREENBACK	GREENBACKS
	GREENBELT	GREENBELTS
	GREENBONE	GREENBONES
	GREENBUG	GREENBUGS
	GREENER	GREENERS = GREENERY
	GREENGAGE	GREENGAGES
	GREENHAND	GREENHANDS
	GREENHEAD	GREENHEADS
	GREENHORN	GREENHORNS
	GREENIE	GREENIER = GREENIES
	GREENIES	GREENIEST
	GREENING	GREENINGS
	GREENLET	GREENLETS
	GREENLING	GREENLINGS
	GREENMAIL	GREENMAILS
	GREENROOM	GREENROOMS
	GREENSAND	GREENSANDS
	GREENSOME	GREENSOMES
	GREENTH	GREENTHS
	GREENWAY	GREENWAYS
	GREENWEED	GREENWEEDS
	GREENWING	GREENWINGS
	GREENWOOD	GREENWOODS
AGREES	GREES	GREESE
	GREESE	GREESES
	GREESING	GREESINGS
	GREET	GREETE = GREETS
	GREETE	GREETED = GREETER = GREETES
	GREETER	GREETERS
	GREETING	GREETINGS
	GREFFIER	GREFFIERS
	GREGALE	GREGALES
	GREGARINE	GREGARINES
AGREGE	GREGE	
	GREGO	GREGOS
	GREIGE	GREIGES
	GREIN	GREINS
	GREISEN	GREISENS
	GREMIAL	GREMIALS
	GREMLIN	GREMLINS
	GREMMIE	GREMMIES
	GREMOLATA	GREMOLATAS
	GREN	GRENS = GRENZ
	GRENADE	GRENADES
	GRENADIER	GRENADIERS
	GRENADINE	GRENADINES
	GRESE	GRESES
EGRESSING	GRESSING	GRESSINGS
	GREVE	GREVES
	GREVILLEA	GREVILLEAS
	GREW	GREWS
	GREWHOUND	GREWHOUNDS

FRONT HOOK	ROOT WORD	END HOOK
	GREWSOME	GREWSOMER
	GREY	GREYS
	GREYBACK	GREYBACKS
	GREYBEARD	GREYBEARDS
	GREYHEN	GREYHENS
	GREYHOUND	GREYHOUNDS
	GREYING	GREYINGS
	GREYLAG	GREYLAGS
	GREYLIST	GREYLISTS
	GREYSTONE	GREYSTONES
	GREYWACKE	GREYWACKES
	GRIBBLE	GRIBBLES
	GRICE	GRICED · GRICER · GRICES
	GRICER	GRICERS
	GRICING	GRICINGS
	GRID	GRIDE · GRIDS
	GRIDDER	GRIDDERS
	GRIDDLE	GRIDDLED · GRIDDLES
	GRIDE	GRIDED · GRIDES
	GRIDELIN	GRIDELINS
	GRIDIRON	GRIDIRONS
	GRIDLOCK	GRIDLOCKS
	GRIECE	GRIECED · GRIECES
	GRIEF	GRIEFS
	GRIEFER	GRIEFERS
	GRIEVANCE	GRIEVANCES
	GRIEVANT	GRIEVANTS
	GRIEVE	GRIEVED · GRIEVER · GRIEVES
	GRIEVER	GRIEVERS
	GRIEVING	GRIEVINGS
	GRIFF	GRIFFE · GRIFFS
	GRIFFE	GRIFFES
	GRIFFIN	GRIFFINS
	GRIFFON	GRIFFONS
	GRIFT	GRIFTS
	GRIFTER	GRIFTERS
	GRIG	GRIGS
	GRIGRI	GRIGRIS
	GRIKE	GRIKES
	GRILL	GRILLE · GRILLS
	GRILLADE	GRILLADES
	GRILLAGE	GRILLAGES
	GRILLE	GRILLED · GRILLER · GRILLES
	GRILLER	GRILLERS · GRILLERY
	GRILLING	GRILLINGS
	GRILLION	GRILLIONS
	GRILLROOM	GRILLROOMS
	GRILLWORK	GRILLWORKS
	GRILSE	GRILSES
	GRIM	GRIME · GRIMY
	GRIMACE	GRIMACED · GRIMACER · GRIMACES
	GRIMACER	GRIMACERS
	GRIMALKIN	GRIMALKINS
	GRIME	GRIMED · GRIMES
	GRIMOIRE	GRIMOIRES
AGRIN	GRIN	GRIND · GRINS
	GRIND	GRINDS
	GRINDELIA	GRINDELIAS
	GRINDER	GRINDERS · GRINDERY
	GRINDING	GRINDINGS
	GRINGA	GRINGAS (offensive)
	GRINGO	GRINGOS (offensive)
	GRINNER	GRINNERS
	GRINNING	GRINNINGS
	GRIOT	GRIOTS
	GRIP	GRIPE · GRIPS · GRIPT · GRIPY
	GRIPE	GRIPED · GRIPER · GRIPES · GRIPEY
	GRIPER	GRIPERS
	GRIPPE	GRIPPED · GRIPPER · GRIPPES

FRONT HOOK	ROOT WORD	END HOOK
	GRIPPER	GRIPPERS
	GRIPPLE	GRIPPLES
	GRIPSACK	GRIPSACKS
	GRIPTAPE	GRIPTAPES
	GRIS	GRISE · GRIST · GRISY
	GRISAILLE	GRISAILLES
AGRISE	**GRISE**	GRISED · GRISES
AGRISED	**GRISED**	
AGRISES	**GRISES**	
	GRISETTE	GRISETTES
AGRISING	**GRISING**	
	GRISKIN	GRISKINS
	GRISLIES	GRISLIEST
	GRISON	GRISONS
	GRIST	GRISTS
	GRISTER	GRISTERS
	GRISTLE	GRISTLES
	GRISTMILL	GRISTMILLS
	GRIT	GRITH · GRITS
	GRITH	GRITHS
	GRITSTONE	GRITSTONES
	GRITTER	GRITTERS
	GRIVATION	GRIVATIONS
	GRIVET	GRIVETS
AGRIZE	**GRIZE**	GRIZES
AGRIZES	**GRIZES**	
	GRIZZLE	GRIZZLED · GRIZZLER · GRIZZLES
	GRIZZLER	GRIZZLERS
	GRIZZLIES	GRIZZLIEST
	GROAN	GROANS
	GROANER	GROANERS
	GROANING	GROANINGS
	GROAT	GROATS
	GROCER	GROCERS · GROCERY
	GROCKLE	GROCKLES
	GROG	GROGS
	GROGRAM	GROGRAMS
	GROGSHOP	GROGSHOPS
	GROIN	GROINS
	GROINING	GROININGS
	GROK	GROKS
	GROMA	GROMAS
	GROMET	GROMETS
	GROMMET	GROMMETS
	GROMWELL	GROMWELLS
	GRONE	GRONED · GRONES
	GROOF	GROOFS
	GROOM	GROOMS
	GROOMER	GROOMERS
	GROOMING	GROOMINGS
	GROOVE	GROOVED · GROOVER · GROOVES
	GROOVER	GROOVERS
	GROPE	GROPED · GROPER · GROPES
	GROPER	GROPERS
	GROSBEAK	GROSBEAKS
	GROSCHEN	GROSCHENS
	GROSER	GROSERS · GROSERT
	GROSERT	GROSERTS
	GROSET	GROSETS
	GROSGRAIN	GROSGRAINS
	GROSSART	GROSSARTS
	GROSSER	GROSSERS ·
	GROSSES	GROSSEST
	GROSSULAR	GROSSULARS
	GROSZ	GROSZE · GROSZY
	GROT	GROTS
	GROTESQUE	GROTESQUER · GROTESQUES
	GROTTO	GROTTOS
	GROUCH	GROUCHY

FRONT HOOK	ROOT WORD	END HOOK
	GROUF	GROUFS
	GROUGH	GROUGHS
AGROUND	**GROUND**	GROUNDS
	GROUNDAGE	GROUNDAGES
	GROUNDER	GROUNDERS
	GROUNDHOG	GROUNDHOGS
	GROUNDING	GROUNDINGS
	GROUNDNUT	GROUNDNUTS
	GROUNDOUT	GROUNDOUTS
	GROUNDSEL	GROUNDSELL · GROUNDSELS
	GROUP	GROUPS · GROUPY
	GROUPAGE	GROUPAGES
	GROUPER	GROUPERS
	GROUPIE	GROUPIES
	GROUPING	GROUPINGS
	GROUPIST	GROUPISTS
	GROUPLET	GROUPLETS
	GROUPOID	GROUPOIDS
	GROUPWARE	GROUPWARES
	GROUSE	GROUSED · GROUSER · GROUSES
	GROUSER	GROUSERS
	GROUSES	GROUSEST
	GROUT	GROUTS · GROUTY
	GROUTER	GROUTERS
	GROUTING	GROUTINGS
	GROVE	GROVED · GROVEL · GROVES · GROVET
	GROVEL	GROVELS
	GROVELER	GROVELERS
	GROVELLER	GROVELLERS
	GROVET	GROVETS
	GROW	GROWL · GROWN · GROWS
	GROWER	GROWERS
	GROWING	GROWINGS
	GROWL	GROWLS · GROWLY
	GROWLER	GROWLERS · GROWLERY
	GROWLING	GROWLINGS
	GROWNUP	GROWNUPS
	GROWTH	GROWTHS · GROWTHY
	GROWTHIST	GROWTHISTS
	GROYNE	GROYNES
	GRUB	GRUBS
	GRUBBER	GRUBBERS
	GRUBBLE	GRUBBLED · GRUBBLES
	GRUBSTAKE	GRUBSTAKED · GRUBSTAKER · GRUBSTAKES
	GRUBWORM	GRUBWORMS
	GRUDGE	GRUDGED · GRUDGER · GRUDGES
	GRUDGER	GRUDGERS
	GRUDGING	GRUDGINGS
	GRUE	GRUED · GRUEL · GRUES
	GRUEL	GRUELS
	GRUELER	GRUELERS
	GRUELING	GRUELINGS
	GRUELLER	GRUELLERS
	GRUELLING	GRUELLINGS
	GRUESOME	GRUESOMER
	GRUFE	GRUFES
	GRUFF	GRUFFS · GRUFFY
	GRUGRU	GRUGRUS
	GRUM	GRUME · GRUMP
	GRUMBLE	GRUMBLED · GRUMBLER · GRUMBLES
	GRUMBLER	GRUMBLERS
	GRUMBLING	GRUMBLINGS
	GRUME	GRUMES
	GRUMMET	GRUMMETS
	GRUMP	GRUMPH · GRUMPS · GRUMPY
	GRUMPH	GRUMPHS · GRUMPHY
	GRUMPHIE	GRUMPHIES
	GRUNGE	GRUNGER · GRUNGES
	GRUNGER	GRUNGERS

FRONT HOOK	ROOT WORD	END HOOK
	GRUNION	GRUNIONS
	GRUNT	GRUNTS
	GRUNTER	GRUNTERS
	GRUNTING	GRUNTINGS
	GRUNTLE	GRUNTLED · GRUNTLES
	GRUYERE	GRUYERES
	GRYCE	GRYCES
	GRYDE	GRYDED · GRYDES
	GRYFON	GRYFONS
	GRYKE	GRYKES
	GRYPE	GRYPES
	GRYPHON	GRYPHONS
	GRYSBOK	GRYSBOKS
	GU	GUB · GUE · GUL · GUM · GUN · GUP · GUR · GUS · GUT · GUV · GUY
	GUACAMOLE	GUACAMOLES
	GUACHARO	GUACHAROS
	GUACO	GUACOS
	GUAIAC	GUAIACS
	GUAIACOL	GUAIACOLS
	GUAIACUM	GUAIACUMS
	GUAIOCUM	GUAIOCUMS
	GUAN	GUANA · GUANO · GUANS
IGUANA	**GUANA**	GUANAS · GUANAY
	GUANABANA	GUANABANAS
	GUANACO	GUANACOS
IGUANAS	**GUANAS**	GUANASE
	GUANASE	GUANASES
	GUANAY	GUANAYS
	GUANAZOLO	GUANAZOLOS
	GUANGO	GUANGOS
	GUANIDIN	GUANIDINE · GUANIDINS
	GUANIDINE	GUANIDINES
	GUANIN	GUANINE · GUANINS
	GUANINE	GUANINES
	GUANO	GUANOS
	GUANOSINE	GUANOSINES
	GUANXI	GUANXIS
	GUAR	GUARD · GUARS
	GUARANA	GUARANAS
	GUARANI	GUARANIS
	GUARANTEE	GUARANTEED · GUARANTEES
	GUARANTOR	GUARANTORS
	GUARD	GUARDS
	GUARDAGE	GUARDAGES
	GUARDANT	GUARDANTS
	GUARDDOG	GUARDDOGS
	GUARDEE	GUARDEES
	GUARDER	GUARDERS
	GUARDIAN	GUARDIANS
	GUARDRAIL	GUARDRAILS
	GUARDROOM	GUARDROOMS
	GUARDSHIP	GUARDSHIPS
	GUAVA	GUAVAS
	GUAYABERA	GUAYABERAS
	GUAYULE	GUAYULES
	GUB	GUBS
	GUBBAH	GUBBAHS
	GUBERNIYA	GUBERNIYAS
	GUCK	GUCKS · GUCKY
	GUDDLE	GUDDLED · GUDDLES
	GUDE	GUDES
	GUDESIRE	GUDESIRES
	GUDGEON	GUDGEONS
AGUE	**GUE**	GUES
	GUENON	GUENONS
	GUERDON	GUERDONS
	GUERDONER	GUERDONERS
	GUEREZA	GUEREZAS

FRONT HOOK	ROOT WORD	END HOOK
	GUERIDON	GUERIDONS
	GUERILLA	GUERILLAS
	GUERITE	GUERITES
	GUERNSEY	GUERNSEYS
	GUERRILLA	GUERRILLAS
AGUES	**GUES**	GUESS - GUEST
	GUESSER	GUESSERS
	GUESSING	GUESSINGS
	GUESSWORK	GUESSWORKS
	GUEST	GUESTS
	GUESTEN	GUESTENS
	GUFF	GUFFS
	GUFFAW	GUFFAWS
	GUFFIE	GUFFIES
	GUGA	GUGAS
	GUGGLE	GUGGLED - GUGGLES
	GUGLET	GUGLETS
	GUICHET	GUICHETS
	GUID	GUIDE - GUIDS
	GUIDAGE	GUIDAGES
	GUIDANCE	GUIDANCES
	GUIDE	GUIDED - GUIDER - GUIDES
	GUIDEBOOK	GUIDEBOOKS
	GUIDELINE	GUIDELINES
	GUIDEPOST	GUIDEPOSTS
	GUIDER	GUIDERS
	GUIDESHIP	GUIDESHIPS
	GUIDEWAY	GUIDEWAYS
	GUIDEWORD	GUIDEWORDS
	GUIDING	GUIDINGS
	GUIDON	GUIDONS
	GUILD	GUILDS
	GUILDER	GUILDERS
	GUILDHALL	GUILDHALLS
	GUILDSHIP	GUILDSHIPS
	GUILE	GUILED - GUILER - GUILES
	GUILER	GUILERS
	GUILLEMET	GUILLEMETS
	GUILLEMOT	GUILLEMOTS
	GUILLOCHE	GUILLOCHED - GUILLOCHES
	GUILT	GUILTS - GUILTY
	GUIMBARD	GUIMBARDS
	GUIMP	GUIMPE - GUIMPS
	GUIMPE	GUIMPED - GUIMPES
	GUINEA	GUINEAS
	GUIPURE	GUIPURES
	GUIRO	GUIROS
	GUISARD	GUISARDS
AGUISE	**GUISE**	GUISED - GUISER - GUISES
AGUISED	**GUISED**	
	GUISER	GUISERS
AGUISES	**GUISES**	
AGUISING	**GUISING**	GUISINGS
	GUITAR	GUITARS
	GUITARIST	GUITARISTS
	GUITGUIT	GUITGUITS
	GUIZER	GUIZERS
	GUL	GULA - GULE - GULF - GULL - GULP GULS - GULY
	GULA	GULAG - GULAR - GULAS
	GULAG	GULAGS
	GULDEN	GULDENS
	GULE	GULES
	GULF	GULFS - GULFY
	GULFWEED	GULFWEEDS
	GULL	GULLS - GULLY
	GULLER	GULLERS - GULLERY
	GULLET	GULLETS
	GULLEY	GULLEYS

FRONT HOOK	ROOT WORD	END HOOK
	GULP	GULPH · GULPS · GULPY
	GULPER	GULPERS
	GULPH	GULPHS
	GUM	GUMP · GUMS
	GUMBALL	GUMBALLS
	GUMBO	GUMBOS
	GUMBOIL	GUMBOILS
	GUMBOOT	GUMBOOTS
	GUMBOTIL	GUMBOTILS
	GUMDROP	GUMDROPS
	GUMLINE	GUMLINES
	GUMMA	GUMMAS
	GUMMER	GUMMERS
	GUMMIES	GUMMIEST
	GUMMING	GUMMINGS
	GUMMITE	GUMMITES
	GUMMOSE	GUMMOSES
	GUMNUT	GUMNUTS
	GUMP	GUMPS
	GUMPHION	GUMPHIONS
	GUMPTION	GUMPTIONS
	GUMSHIELD	GUMSHIELDS
	GUMSHOE	GUMSHOED · GUMSHOES
	GUMSUCKER	GUMSUCKERS
	GUMTREE	GUMTREES
	GUMWEED	GUMWEEDS
	GUMWOOD	GUMWOODS
	GUN	GUNG · GUNK · GUNS
	GUNBOAT	GUNBOATS
	GUNCOTTON	GUNCOTTONS
	GUNDOG	GUNDOGS
	GUNFIGHT	GUNFIGHTS
	GUNFIRE	GUNFIRES
	GUNFLINT	GUNFLINTS
	GUNG	GUNGE · GUNGY
	GUNGE	GUNGED · GUNGES
	GUNHOUSE	GUNHOUSES
	GUNITE	GUNITES
	GUNK	GUNKS · GUNKY
	GUNKHOLE	GUNKHOLED · GUNKHOLES
	GUNLAYER	GUNLAYERS
	GUNLOCK	GUNLOCKS
	GUNMAKER	GUNMAKERS
	GUNMETAL	GUNMETALS
	GUNNAGE	GUNNAGES
	GUNNEL	GUNNELS
	GUNNER	GUNNERA · GUNNERS · GUNNERY
	GUNNERA	GUNNERAS
	GUNNING	GUNNINGS
	GUNNYBAG	GUNNYBAGS
	GUNNYSACK	GUNNYSACKS
	GUNPAPER	GUNPAPERS
	GUNPLAY	GUNPLAYS
	GUNPOINT	GUNPOINTS
	GUNPORT	GUNPORTS
	GUNPOWDER	GUNPOWDERS · GUNPOWDERY
	GUNROOM	GUNROOMS
	GUNRUNNER	GUNRUNNERS
	GUNSEL	GUNSELS
	GUNSHIP	GUNSHIPS
	GUNSHOT	GUNSHOTS
	GUNSMITH	GUNSMITHS
	GUNSTICK	GUNSTICKS
	GUNSTOCK	GUNSTOCKS
	GUNSTONE	GUNSTONES
	GUNTER	GUNTERS
	GUNWALE	GUNWALES
	GUNYAH	GUNYAHS
	GUP	GUPS

FRONT HOOK	ROOT WORD	END HOOK
	GUR	GURL · GURN · GURS · GURU
	GURAMI	GURAMIS
	GURDWARA	GURDWARAS
	GURGE	GURGED · GURGES
	GURGLE	GURGLED · GURGLES · GURGLET
	GURGLET	GURGLETS
	GURGOYLE	GURGOYLES
	GURJUN	GURJUNS
	GURL	GURLS · GURLY
	GURLET	GURLETS
	GURN	GURNS
	GURNARD	GURNARDS
	GURNET	GURNETS
	GURNEY	GURNEYS
	GURRAH	GURRAHS
	GURRIER	GURRIERS
	GURS	GURSH
	GURU	GURUS
	GURUDOM	GURUDOMS
	GURUISM	GURUISMS
	GURUSHIP	GURUSHIPS
	GUS	GUSH · GUST
	GUSH	GUSHY
	GUSHER	GUSHERS
	GUSLA	GUSLAR · GUSLAS
	GUSLAR	GUSLARS
	GUSLE	GUSLES
	GUSLI	GUSLIS
	GUSSET	GUSSETS
	GUSSIE	GUSSIED · GUSSIES
	GUST	GUSTO · GUSTS · GUSTY
	GUSTABLE	GUSTABLES
	GUSTATION	GUSTATIONS
	GUSTIE	GUSTIER
	GUSTO	GUSTOS
	GUT	GUTS
	GUTBUCKET	GUTBUCKETS
	GUTCHER	GUTCHERS
	GUTFUL	GUTFULS
	GUTROT	GUTROTS
	GUTS	GUTSY
	GUTSER	GUTSERS
	GUTSFUL	GUTSFULS
	GUTTA	GUTTAE · GUTTAS
	GUTTATE	GUTTATED · GUTTATES
	GUTTATION	GUTTATIONS
	GUTTER	GUTTERS · GUTTERY
	GUTTERING	GUTTERINGS
	GUTTIES	GUTTIEST
	GUTTLE	GUTTLED · GUTTLER · GUTTLES
	GUTTLER	GUTTLERS
	GUTTURAL	GUTTURALS
	GUTZER	GUTZERS
	GUV	GUVS
	GUY	GUYS
	GUYLE	GUYLED · GUYLER · GUYLES
	GUYLER	GUYLERS
	GUYLINE	GUYLINES
	GUYOT	GUYOTS
	GUYS	GUYSE
	GUYSE	GUYSES
	GUZZLE	GUZZLED · GUZZLER · GUZZLES
	GUZZLER	GUZZLERS
	GWEDUC	GWEDUCK · GWEDUCS
	GWEDUCK	GWEDUCKS
	GWINIAD	GWINIADS
	GWYNIAD	GWYNIADS
	GYAL	GYALS
	GYBE	GYBED · GYBES

FRONT HOOK	ROOT WORD	END HOOK
	GYELD	GYELDS
	GYM	GYMP (offensive) ▪ GYMS
	GYMBAL	GYMBALS
	GYMKHANA	GYMKHANAS
	GYMMAL	GYMMALS
	GYMNASIA	GYMNASIAL
	GYMNASIUM	GYMNASIUMS
	GYMNAST	GYMNASTS
	GYMNASTIC	GYMNASTICS
	GYMNOSOPH	GYMNOSOPHS ▪ GYMNOSOPHY
	GYMP	GYMPS (offensive)
	GYMPIE	GYMPIES
	GYMSLIP	GYMSLIPS
	GYNAE	GYNAES
	GYNAECEUM	GYNAECEUMS
	GYNIE	GYNIES
	GYNNEY	GYNNEYS
	GYNOPHOBE	GYNOPHOBES
	GYNOPHORE	GYNOPHORES
	GYOZA	GYOZAS
	GYP	GYPS
	GYPLURE	GYPLURES
	GYPPER	GYPPERS
	GYPPIE	GYPPIES
	GYPPO	GYPPOS (offensive)
	GYPS	GYPSY
	GYPSTER	GYPSTERS
	GYPSUM	GYPSUMS
	GYPSYDOM	GYPSYDOMS
	GYPSYHOOD	GYPSYHOODS
	GYPSYISM	GYPSYISMS
	GYPSYWORT	GYPSYWORTS
	GYRASE	GYRASES
	GYRATE	GYRATED ▪ GYRATES
	GYRATION	GYRATIONS
	GYRATOR	GYRATORS ▪ GYRATORY
	GYRE	GYRED ▪ GYRES
	GYRENE	GYRENES
	GYRFALCON	GYRFALCONS
	GYRO	GYRON ▪ GYROS
	GYROCAR	GYROCARS
	GYRODYNE	GYRODYNES
	GYROLITE	GYROLITES
	GYRON	GYRONS
	GYROPILOT	GYROPILOTS
	GYROPLANE	GYROPLANES
	GYROS	GYROSE
	GYROSCOPE	GYROSCOPES
	GYROSTAT	GYROSTATS
	GYROVAGUE	GYROVAGUES
	GYTE	GYTES
	GYTTJA	GYTTJAS
	GYVE	GYVED ▪ GYVES

H

FRONT HOOK	ROOT WORD	END HOOK
AHA · CHA · SHA · WHA	HA	HAD · HAE · HAG · HAH · HAJ · HAM · HAN
		HAO · HAP · HAS · HAT · HAW · HAY
	HAAF	HAAFS
	HAANEPOOT	HAANEPOOTS
	HAAR	HAARS
	HABANERA	HABANERAS
	HABANERO	HABANEROS
	HABDALAH	HABDALAHS
	HABERDINE	HABERDINES
	HABERGEON	HABERGEONS
	HABIT	HABITS
	HABITAN	HABITANS · HABITANT
	HABITANT	HABITANTS
	HABITAT	HABITATS
	HABITUAL	HABITUALS
	HABITUATE	HABITUATED · HABITUATES
	HABITUDE	HABITUDES
	HABITUE	HABITUES
	HABOOB	HABOOBS
	HABU	HABUS
	HACEK	HACEKS
	HACENDADO	HACENDADOS
RHACHIS	HACHIS	
	HACHURE	HACHURED · HACHURES
	HACIENDA	HACIENDAS
CHACK · SHACK · THACK · WHACK	HACK	HACKS
	HACKAMORE	HACKAMORES
	HACKBOLT	HACKBOLTS
	HACKBUT	HACKBUTS
CHACKED · SHACKED · THACKED · WHACKED	HACKED	
	HACKEE	HACKEES
WHACKER	HACKER	HACKERS · HACKERY
WHACKERS	HACKERS	
	HACKETTE	HACKETTES
	HACKIE	HACKIES
CHACKING · SHACKING · THACKING · WHACKING	HACKING	HACKINGS
WHACKINGS	HACKINGS	
SHACKLE	HACKLE	HACKLED · HACKLER · HACKLES · HACKLET
SHACKLED	HACKLED	
SHACKLER	HACKLER	HACKLERS
SHACKLERS	HACKLERS	
SHACKLES	HACKLES	
	HACKLET	HACKLETS
SHACKLING	HACKLING	
	HACKNEY	HACKNEYS
CHACKS · SHACKS · THACKS · WHACKS	HACKS	
	HACKSAW	HACKSAWN · HACKSAWS
	HACKWORK	HACKWORKS
	HACQUETON	HACQUETONS
CHAD · SHAD	HAD	HADE · HADJ · HADS
CHADARIM	HADARIM	
	HADDIE	HADDIES
SHADDOCK	HADDOCK	HADDOCKS
SHADDOCKS	HADDOCKS	
SHADE	HADE	HADED · HADES
SHADED	HADED	
	HADEDAH	HADEDAHS
SHADES	HADES	
SHADING	HADING	
	HADITH	HADITHS
	HADJ	HADJI
	HADJEE	HADJEES
	HADJI	HADJIS
	HADROME	HADROMES
	HADRON	HADRONS

FRONT HOOK	ROOT WORD	END HOOK
	HADROSAUR	HADROSAURS
CHADS ▪ SHADS	**HADS**	HADST
THAE ▪ WHAE	**HAE**	HAED ▪ HAEM ▪ HAEN ▪ HAES ▪ HAET
	HAEM	HAEMS
	HAEMATEIN	HAEMATEINS
	HAEMATIC	HAEMATICS
	HAEMATIN	HAEMATINS
	HAEMATITE	HAEMATITES
	HAEMATOMA	HAEMATOMAS
	HAEMIN	HAEMINS
	HAEMOCOEL	HAEMOCOELS
	HAEMOCYTE	HAEMOCYTES
	HAEMOSTAT	HAEMOSTATS
	HAET	HAETS
CHAFF	**HAFF**	HAFFS
	HAFFET	HAFFETS
	HAFFIT	HAFFITS
	HAFFLIN	HAFFLINS
CHAFFS	**HAFFS**	
	HAFNIUM	HAFNIUMS
CHAFT ▪ SHAFT	**HAFT**	HAFTS
	HAFTARA	HAFTARAH ▪ HAFTARAS
	HAFTARAH	HAFTARAHS
	HAFTAROT	HAFTAROTH
SHAFTED	**HAFTED**	
SHAFTER	**HAFTER**	HAFTERS
SHAFTERS	**HAFTERS**	
SHAFTING	**HAFTING**	
	HAFTORAH	HAFTORAHS
	HAFTOROT	HAFTOROTH
CHAFTS ▪ SHAFTS	**HAFTS**	
SHAG	**HAG**	HAGG ▪ HAGS
	HAGADIST	HAGADISTS
	HAGBOLT	HAGBOLTS
	HAGBUT	HAGBUTS
	HAGBUTEER	HAGBUTEERS
	HAGBUTTER	HAGBUTTERS
	HAGDEN	HAGDENS
	HAGDON	HAGDONS
	HAGDOWN	HAGDOWNS
	HAGG	HAGGS
	HAGGADA	HAGGADAH ▪ HAGGADAS
	HAGGADAH	HAGGADAHS
	HAGGADIST	HAGGADISTS
	HAGGADOT	HAGGADOTH
	HAGGARD	HAGGARDS
SHAGGED (offensive)	**HAGGED**	
SHAGGING (offensive)	**HAGGING**	
	HAGGIS	HAGGISH
	HAGGLE	HAGGLED ▪ HAGGLER ▪ HAGGLES
	HAGGLER	HAGGLERS
	HAGLET	HAGLETS
	HAGRIDE	HAGRIDER ▪ HAGRIDES
	HAGRIDER	HAGRIDERS
SHAGS (offensive)	**HAGS**	
SHAH	**HAH**	HAHA ▪ HAHS
	HAHA	HAHAS
	HAHNIUM	HAHNIUMS
SHAHS	**HAHS**	
	HAICK	HAICKS
	HAIDUK	HAIDUKS
	HAIK	HAIKA ▪ HAIKS ▪ HAIKU
	HAIKA	HAIKAI
	HAIKU	HAIKUS
	HAIL	HAILS ▪ HAILY
	HAILER	HAILERS
	HAILSHOT	HAILSHOTS
	HAILSTONE	HAILSTONES
	HAILSTORM	HAILSTORMS

FRONT HOOK	ROOT WORD	END HOOK
CHAIN	**HAIN**	HAINS · HAINT
CHAINED	**HAINED**	
CHAINING	**HAINING**	HAININGS
CHAINS	**HAINS**	
	HAINT	HAINTS
	HAIQUE	HAIQUES
CHAIR	**HAIR**	HAIRS · HAIRY
	HAIRBALL	HAIRBALLS
	HAIRBAND	HAIRBANDS
	HAIRBELL	HAIRBELLS
	HAIRCAP	HAIRCAPS
	HAIRCLOTH	HAIRCLOTHS
	HAIRCUT	HAIRCUTS
	HAIRDO	HAIRDOS
	HAIRDRIER	HAIRDRIERS
	HAIRDRYER	HAIRDRYERS
CHAIRED	**HAIRED**	
	HAIRGRIP	HAIRGRIPS
	HAIRIF	HAIRIFS
CHAIRING	**HAIRING**	
	HAIRLINE	HAIRLINES
	HAIRLOCK	HAIRLOCKS
	HAIRNET	HAIRNETS
	HAIRPIECE	HAIRPIECES
	HAIRPIN	HAIRPINS
CHAIRS	**HAIRS**	HAIRST
	HAIRSPRAY	HAIRSPRAYS
	HAIRST	HAIRSTS
	HAIRSTYLE	HAIRSTYLES
	HAIRTAIL	HAIRTAILS
	HAIRWORK	HAIRWORKS
	HAIRWORM	HAIRWORMS
	HAIRYBACK	HAIRYBACKS *(offensive)*
	HAJ	HAJI · HAJJ
BHAJI	**HAJI**	HAJIS
BHAJIS	**HAJIS**	
	HAJJ	HAJJI
	HAJJAH	HAJJAHS
	HAJJI	HAJJIS
	HAKA	HAKAM · HAKAS
	HAKAM	HAKAMS
SHAKE	**HAKE**	HAKEA · HAKES
	HAKEA	HAKEAS
	HAKEEM	HAKEEMS
SHAKES	**HAKES**	
	HAKIM	HAKIMS
	HAKU	HAKUS
	HALACHA	HALACHAS
	HALACHIST	HALACHISTS
	HALACHOT	HALACHOTH
	HALAKAH	HALAKAHS
	HALAKHA	HALAKHAH · HALAKHAS
	HALAKHAH	HALAKHAHS
	HALAKHIST	HALAKHISTS
	HALAKHOT	HALAKHOTH
	HALAKIST	HALAKISTS
	HALAL	HALALA · HALALS
	HALALA	HALALAH · HALALAS
	HALALAH	HALALAHS
	HALATION	HALATIONS
	HALAVAH	HALAVAHS
	HALAZONE	HALAZONES
	HALBERD	HALBERDS
	HALBERT	HALBERTS
	HALCYON	HALCYONS
SHALE · WHALE	**HALE**	HALED · HALER · HALES
SHALED · WHALED	**HALED**	
THALER · WHALER	**HALER**	HALERS · HALERU
THALERS · WHALERS	**HALERS**	

FRONT HOOK	ROOT WORD	END HOOK
SHALES ▪ WHALES	**HALES**	HALEST
	HALF	HALFA ▪ HALFS
	HALFA	HALFAS
	HALFBACK	HALFBACKS
	HALFBEAK	HALFBEAKS
	HALFLIN	HALFLING ▪ HALFLINS
	HALFLING	HALFLINGS
	HALFPACE	HALFPACES
	HALFPIPE	HALFPIPES
	HALFTIME	HALFTIMES
	HALFTONE	HALFTONES
	HALFTRACK	HALFTRACKS
	HALFWIT	HALFWITS
	HALIBUT	HALIBUTS
	HALICORE	HALICORES
	HALID	HALIDE ▪ HALIDS
	HALIDE	HALIDES
	HALIDOM	HALIDOME ▪ HALIDOMS
	HALIDOME	HALIDOMES
	HALIEUTIC	HALIEUTICS
	HALIMOT	HALIMOTE ▪ HALIMOTS
	HALIMOTE	HALIMOTES
SHALING ▪ WHALING	**HALING**	
	HALITE	HALITES
SHALL	**HALL**	HALLO ▪ HALLS
CHALLAH	**HALLAH**	HALLAHS
CHALLAHS	**HALLAHS**	
	HALLAL	HALLALI ▪ HALLALS
	HALLALI	HALLALIS
	HALLALOO	HALLALOOS
CHALLAN	**HALLAN**	HALLANS
CHALLANS	**HALLANS**	
	HALLEL	HALLELS
	HALLIAN	HALLIANS
	HALLIARD	HALLIARDS
	HALLING	HALLINGS
	HALLION	HALLIONS
	HALLMARK	HALLMARKS
	HALLO	HALLOA ▪ HALLOO ▪ HALLOS ▪ HALLOT HALLOW
	HALLOA	HALLOAS
	HALLOO	HALLOOS
CHALLOT ▪ SHALLOT	**HALLOT**	HALLOTH
CHALLOTH	**HALLOTH**	
	HALLOUMI	HALLOUMIS
SHALLOW	**HALLOW**	HALLOWS
SHALLOWED	**HALLOWED**	
SHALLOWER	**HALLOWER**	HALLOWERS
SHALLOWING	**HALLOWING**	
SHALLOWS	**HALLOWS**	
	HALLSTAND	HALLSTANDS
	HALLWAY	HALLWAYS
	HALLYON	HALLYONS
SHALM	**HALM**	HALMA ▪ HALMS
	HALMA	HALMAS
SHALMS	**HALMS**	
	HALO	HALON ▪ HALOS
	HALOBIONT	HALOBIONTS
	HALOCLINE	HALOCLINES
	HALOGEN	HALOGENS
	HALOGETON	HALOGETONS
	HALOID	HALOIDS
	HALON	HALONS
	HALOPHILE	HALOPHILES
	HALOPHOBE	HALOPHOBES
	HALOPHYTE	HALOPHYTES
	HALOSERE	HALOSERES
	HALOTHANE	HALOTHANES
	HALOUMI	HALOUMIS

FRONT HOOK	ROOT WORD	END HOOK
	HALSE	HALSED ▪ HALSER ▪ HALSES
	HALSER	HALSERS
SHALT	**HALT**	HALTS
	HALTER	HALTERE ▪ HALTERS
	HALTERE	HALTERED ▪ HALTERES
	HALTING	HALTINGS
CHALUTZ	**HALUTZ**	
CHALUTZIM	**HALUTZIM**	
	HALVA	HALVAH ▪ HALVAS
	HALVAH	HALVAHS
	HALVE	HALVED ▪ HALVER ▪ HALVES
	HALVER	HALVERS
	HALYARD	HALYARDS
CHAM ▪ SHAM ▪ WHAM	**HAM**	HAME ▪ HAMS
	HAMADA	HAMADAS
	HAMADRYAD	HAMADRYADS
	HAMAL	HAMALS
	HAMARTIA	HAMARTIAS
	HAMATE	HAMATES
	HAMAUL	HAMAULS
SHAMBA	**HAMBA**	
SHAMBLE	**HAMBLE**	HAMBLED ▪ HAMBLES
SHAMBLED	**HAMBLED**	
SHAMBLES	**HAMBLES**	
SHAMBLING	**HAMBLING**	
	HAMBONE	HAMBONED ▪ HAMBONES
	HAMBURG	HAMBURGS
	HAMBURGER	HAMBURGERS
SHAME	**HAME**	HAMED ▪ HAMES
SHAMED	**HAMED**	
SHAMES	**HAMES**	
	HAMFATTER	HAMFATTERS
SHAMING	**HAMING**	
CHAMLET	**HAMLET**	HAMLETS
CHAMLETS	**HAMLETS**	
	HAMMADA	HAMMADAS
	HAMMAL	HAMMALS
	HAMMAM	HAMMAMS
SHAMMED ▪ WHAMMED	**HAMMED**	
SHAMMER	**HAMMER**	HAMMERS
	HAMMERER	HAMMERERS
	HAMMERING	HAMMERINGS
	HAMMERKOP	HAMMERKOPS
SHAMMERS	**HAMMERS**	
	HAMMERTOE	HAMMERTOES
SHAMMING ▪ WHAMMING	**HAMMING**	
	HAMMOCK	HAMMOCKS
CHAMMY ▪ SHAMMY ▪ WHAMMY	**HAMMY**	
CHAMPER	**HAMPER**	HAMPERS
	HAMPERER	HAMPERERS
CHAMPERS	**HAMPERS**	
	HAMPSTER	HAMPSTERS
CHAMS ▪ SHAMS ▪ WHAMS	**HAMS**	
	HAMSTER	HAMSTERS
	HAMSTRING	HAMSTRINGS
	HAMZA	HAMZAH ▪ HAMZAS
	HAMZAH	HAMZAHS
KHAN ▪ SHAN ▪ THAN	**HAN**	HAND ▪ HANG ▪ HANK ▪ HANT
	HANAP	HANAPS
	HANAPER	HANAPERS
CHANCE	**HANCE**	HANCES
CHANCES	**HANCES**	
SHAND	**HAND**	HANDS ▪ HANDY
	HANDBAG	HANDBAGS
	HANDBALL	HANDBALLS
	HANDBELL	HANDBELLS
	HANDBILL	HANDBILLS
	HANDBOOK	HANDBOOKS
	HANDBRAKE	HANDBRAKES

FRONT HOOK	ROOT WORD	END HOOK
	HANDCAR	HANDCARS · HANDCART
	HANDCART	HANDCARTS
	HANDCLAP	HANDCLAPS
	HANDCLASP	HANDCLASPS
	HANDCRAFT	HANDCRAFTS
	HANDCUFF	HANDCUFFS
	HANDER	HANDERS
	HANDFAST	HANDFASTS
	HANDFEED	HANDFEEDS
	HANDFUL	HANDFULS
	HANDGRIP	HANDGRIPS
	HANDGUN	HANDGUNS
	HANDHELD	HANDHELDS
	HANDHOLD	HANDHOLDS
	HANDICAP	HANDICAPS
	HANDISM	HANDISMS
	HANDIWORK	HANDIWORKS
	HANDJAR	HANDJARS
	HANDLE	HANDLED · HANDLER · HANDLES
	HANDLEBAR	HANDLEBARS
CHANDLER	HANDLER	HANDLERS
CHANDLERS	HANDLERS	
	HANDLES	HANDLESS
	HANDLING	HANDLINGS
	HANDLIST	HANDLISTS
	HANDLOOM	HANDLOOMS
	HANDMAID	HANDMAIDS
	HANDOFF	HANDOFFS
	HANDOUT	HANDOUTS
	HANDOVER	HANDOVERS
	HANDPHONE	HANDPHONES
	HANDPICK	HANDPICKS
	HANDPLAY	HANDPLAYS
	HANDPRINT	HANDPRINTS
	HANDRAIL	HANDRAILS
	HANDROLL	HANDROLLS
SHANDS	HANDS	
	HANDSAW	HANDSAWS
	HANDSEL	HANDSELS
	HANDSET	HANDSETS
	HANDSHAKE	HANDSHAKES
	HANDSOME	HANDSOMER · HANDSOMES
	HANDSOMES	HANDSOMEST
	HANDSPIKE	HANDSPIKES
	HANDSTAFF	HANDSTAFFS
	HANDSTAMP	HANDSTAMPS
	HANDSTAND	HANDSTANDS
	HANDSTURN	HANDSTURNS
	HANDTOWEL	HANDTOWELS
	HANDWHEEL	HANDWHEELS
	HANDWORK	HANDWORKS
	HANDWRIT	HANDWRITE
	HANDWRITE	HANDWRITES
SHANDY	HANDY	
	HANDYWORK	HANDYWORKS
	HANEPOOT	HANEPOOTS
BHANG · CHANG · PHANG · WHANG	HANG	HANGI · HANGS
	HANGAR	HANGARS
	HANGBIRD	HANGBIRDS
	HANGDOG	HANGDOGS
CHANGED · PHANGED · WHANGED	HANGED	
CHANGER	HANGER	HANGERS
CHANGERS	HANGERS	
	HANGFIRE	HANGFIRES
	HANGI	HANGIS
CHANGING · PHANGING · WHANGING	HANGING	HANGINGS
	HANGNAIL	HANGNAILS
	HANGNEST	HANGNESTS
	HANGOUT	HANGOUTS

FRONT HOOK	ROOT WORD	END HOOK
	HANGOVER	HANGOVERS
BHANGS · CHANGS · PHANGS · WHANGS	**HANGS**	
	HANGTAG	HANGTAGS
	HANGUP	HANGUPS
KHANJAR	**HANJAR**	HANJARS
KHANJARS	**HANJARS**	
CHANK · SHANK · THANK	**HANK**	HANKS · HANKY
SHANKED · THANKED	**HANKED**	
THANKER	**HANKER**	HANKERS
	HANKERER	HANKERERS
	HANKERING	HANKERINGS
THANKERS	**HANKERS**	
	HANKIE	HANKIES
SHANKING · THANKING	**HANKING**	
CHANKS · SHANKS · THANKS	**HANKS**	
	HANSA	HANSAS
	HANSE	HANSEL · HANSES
	HANSEL	HANSELS
	HANSOM	HANSOMS
CHANT	**HANT**	HANTS
CHANTED	**HANTED**	
CHANTING	**HANTING**	
	HANTLE	HANTLES
CHANTS	**HANTS**	
CHANUKIAH	**HANUKIAH**	HANUKIAHS
CHANUKIAHS	**HANUKIAHS**	
	HANUMAN	HANUMANS
CHAO	**HAO**	
	HAOLE	HAOLES (offensive)
	HAOMA	HAOMAS
CHAP · WHAP	**HAP**	HAPS · HAPU
	HAPHAZARD	HAPHAZARDS
	HAPHTARA	HAPHTARAH · HAPHTARAS
	HAPHTARAH	HAPHTARAHS
	HAPHTAROT	HAPHTAROTH
	HAPKIDO	HAPKIDOS
CHAPLESS	**HAPLESS**	
	HAPLITE	HAPLITES
	HAPLOID	HAPLOIDS · HAPLOIDY
	HAPLONT	HAPLONTS
	HAPLOPIA	HAPLOPIAS
	HAPLOTYPE	HAPLOTYPES
CHAPPED · WHAPPED	**HAPPED**	
	HAPPEN	HAPPENS
	HAPPENING	HAPPENINGS
CHAPPIER	**HAPPIER**	
CHAPPIES	**HAPPIES**	HAPPIEST
CHAPPIEST	**HAPPIEST**	
CHAPPING · WHAPPING	**HAPPING**	
CHAPPY	**HAPPY**	
CHAPS · SHAPS · WHAPS	**HAPS**	
	HAPTEN	HAPTENE · HAPTENS
	HAPTENE	HAPTENES
	HAPTERON	HAPTERONS
	HAPTIC	HAPTICS
	HAPU	HAPUS
	HAPUKA	HAPUKAS
	HAPUKU	HAPUKUS
	HAQUETON	HAQUETONS
	HARAKEKE	HARAKEKES
	HARAM	HARAMS
	HARAMBEE	HARAMBEES
	HARAMDA	HARAMDAS (offensive)
	HARAMDI	HARAMDIS (offensive)
	HARAMZADA	HARAMZADAS
	HARAMZADI	HARAMZADIS
	HARANGUE	HARANGUED · HARANGUER · HARANGUES
	HARANGUER	HARANGUERS
	HARASSER	HARASSERS

FRONT HOOK	ROOT WORD	END HOOK
	HARASSING	HARASSINGS
	HARBINGER	HARBINGERS
	HARBOR	HARBORS
	HARBORAGE	HARBORAGES
	HARBORER	HARBORERS
	HARBORFUL	HARBORFULS
	HARBOUR	HARBOURS
	HARBOURER	HARBOURERS
CHARD ▪ SHARD	HARD	HARDS ▪ HARDY
	HARDBACK	HARDBACKS
	HARDBAG	HARDBAGS
	HARDBAKE	HARDBAKES
	HARDBALL	HARDBALLS
	HARDBEAM	HARDBEAMS
	HARDBOARD	HARDBOARDS
	HARDBOOT	HARDBOOTS
	HARDBOUND	HARDBOUNDS
	HARDCORE	HARDCORES
	HARDCOVER	HARDCOVERS
	HARDEDGE	HARDEDGES
	HARDEN	HARDENS
	HARDENER	HARDENERS
	HARDENING	HARDENINGS
	HARDFACE	HARDFACES
	HARDHACK	HARDHACKS
	HARDHAT	HARDHATS
	HARDHEAD	HARDHEADS
	HARDIES	HARDIEST
	HARDIHEAD	HARDIHEADS
	HARDIHOOD	HARDIHOODS
	HARDIMENT	HARDIMENTS
	HARDLINE	HARDLINER
	HARDLINER	HARDLINERS
	HARDNOSE	HARDNOSED ▪ HARDNOSES
	HARDOKE	HARDOKES
	HARDPACK	HARDPACKS
	HARDPAN	HARDPANS
	HARDROCK	HARDROCKS
CHARDS ▪ SHARDS	HARDS	
	HARDSHIP	HARDSHIPS
	HARDSTAND	HARDSTANDS
	HARDTACK	HARDTACKS
	HARDTOP	HARDTOPS
	HARDWARE	HARDWARES
	HARDWIRE	HARDWIRED ▪ HARDWIRES
	HARDWOOD	HARDWOODS
CHARE ▪ PHARE ▪ SHARE ▪ WHARE	HARE	HARED ▪ HAREM ▪ HARES
	HAREBELL	HAREBELLS
CHARED ▪ SHARED	HARED	
	HAREEM	HAREEMS
	HARELD	HARELDS
	HARELIP	HARELIPS
	HAREM	HAREMS
CHARES ▪ PHARES ▪ SHARES ▪ WHARES	HARES	
	HARESTAIL	HARESTAILS
	HAREWOOD	HAREWOODS
	HARIANA	HARIANAS
	HARICOT	HARICOTS
	HARIJAN	HARIJANS
	HARIM	HARIMS
CHARING ▪ SHARING	HARING	
	HARIOLATE	HARIOLATED ▪ HARIOLATES
	HARIRA	HARIRAS
	HARISSA	HARISSAS
CHARK ▪ SHARK	HARK	HARKS
CHARKED ▪ SHARKED	HARKED	
	HARKEN	HARKENS
	HARKENER	HARKENERS
CHARKING ▪ SHARKING	HARKING	

FRONT HOOK	ROOT WORD	END HOOK
CHARKS ▪ SHARKS	**HARKS**	
	HARL	HARLS
	HARLEQUIN	HARLEQUINS
	HARLING	HARLINGS
	HARLOT	HARLOTS
CHARM ▪ THARM	**HARM**	HARMS
	HARMALA	HARMALAS
	HARMALIN	HARMALINE ▪ HARMALINS
	HARMALINE	HARMALINES
	HARMAN	HARMANS
	HARMATTAN	HARMATTANS
	HARMDOING	HARMDOINGS
CHARMED	**HARMED**	
	HARMEL	HARMELS
CHARMER	**HARMER**	HARMERS
CHARMERS	**HARMERS**	
CHARMFUL	**HARMFUL**	
	HARMIN	HARMINE ▪ HARMING ▪ HARMINS
	HARMINE	HARMINES
CHARMING ▪ PHARMING	**HARMING**	
CHARMLESS	**HARMLESS**	
	HARMONIC	HARMONICA ▪ HARMONICS
	HARMONICA	HARMONICAL ▪ HARMONICAS
	HARMONISE	HARMONISED ▪ HARMONISER ▪ HARMONISES
	HARMONIST	HARMONISTS
CHARMONIUM	**HARMONIUM**	HARMONIUMS
	HARMONIZE	HARMONIZED ▪ HARMONIZER ▪ HARMONIZES
	HARMOST	HARMOSTS ▪ HARMOSTY
	HARMOTOME	HARMOTOMES
CHARMS ▪ THARMS	**HARMS**	
SHARN	**HARN**	HARNS
	HARNESSER	HARNESSERS
SHARNS	**HARNS**	
	HARO	HAROS
PHAROS	**HAROS**	
CHAROSET	**HAROSET**	HAROSETH ▪ HAROSETS
CHAROSETH	**HAROSETH**	HAROSETHS
CHAROSETHS	**HAROSETHS**	
CHAROSETS	**HAROSETS**	
SHARP	**HARP**	HARPS ▪ HARPY
SHARPED	**HARPED**	
SHARPER	**HARPER**	HARPERS
SHARPERS	**HARPERS**	
CHARPIES ▪ SHARPIES	**HARPIES**	
	HARPIN	HARPING ▪ HARPINS
SHARPING	**HARPING**	HARPINGS
SHARPINGS	**HARPINGS**	
	HARPIST	HARPISTS
	HARPOON	HARPOONS
	HARPOONER	HARPOONERS
SHARPS	**HARPS**	
SHARPY	**HARPY**	
	HARQUEBUS	HARQUEBUSE ▪ HARQUEBUSS
	HARRIDAN	HARRIDANS
CHARRIER	**HARRIER**	HARRIERS
GHARRIES	**HARRIES**	
	HARROW	HARROWS
	HARROWER	HARROWERS
	HARROWING	HARROWINGS
	HARRUMPH	HARRUMPHS
CHARRY ▪ GHARRY	**HARRY**	
	HARSHEN	HARSHENS
	HARSLET	HARSLETS
CHART	**HART**	HARTS
	HARTAL	HARTALS
	HARTBEES	HARTBEEST
	HARTBEEST	HARTBEESTS
	HARTEN	HARTENS
CHARTS	**HARTS**	

FRONT HOOK	ROOT WORD	END HOOK
	HARTSHORN	HARTSHORNS
	HARUMPH	HARUMPHS
	HARVEST	HARVESTS
	HARVESTER	HARVESTERS
CHAS	**HAS**	HASH ▪ HASK ▪ HASP ▪ HAST
	HASBIAN	HASBIANS
SHASH	**HASH**	HASHY
SHASHED	**HASHED**	
SHASHES	**HASHES**	
	HASHHEAD	HASHHEADS
SHASHING	**HASHING**	
	HASHMARK	HASHMARKS
	HASK	HASKS
	HASLET	HASLETS
	HASP	HASPS
	HASSAR	HASSARS
	HASSEL	HASSELS
	HASSIUM	HASSIUMS
	HASSLE	HASSLED ▪ HASSLES
	HASSOCK	HASSOCKS ▪ HASSOCKY
GHAST	**HAST**	HASTA ▪ HASTE ▪ HASTY
	HASTATE	HASTATED
CHASTE	**HASTE**	HASTED ▪ HASTEN ▪ HASTES
GHASTED	**HASTED**	
CHASTEN	**HASTEN**	HASTENS
CHASTENED	**HASTENED**	
CHASTENER	**HASTENER**	HASTENERS
CHASTENERS	**HASTENERS**	
CHASTENING	**HASTENING**	
CHASTENS	**HASTENS**	
GHASTING	**HASTING**	HASTINGS
BHAT ▪ CHAT ▪ GHAT ▪ KHAT ▪ PHAT	**HAT**	HATE ▪ HATH ▪ HATS
SHAT (offensive) ▪ THAT ▪ WHAT		
	HATBAND	HATBANDS
THATCH	**HATCH**	
	HATCHBACK	HATCHBACKS
	HATCHECK	HATCHECKS
THATCHED	**HATCHED**	
	HATCHEL	HATCHELS
THATCHER	**HATCHER**	HATCHERS ▪ HATCHERY
THATCHERS	**HATCHERS**	
THATCHES	**HATCHES**	
	HATCHET	HATCHETS ▪ HATCHETY
THATCHING	**HATCHING**	HATCHINGS
THATCHINGS	**HATCHINGS**	
	HATCHLING	HATCHLINGS
	HATCHMENT	HATCHMENTS
	HATCHWAY	HATCHWAYS
	HATE	HATED ▪ HATER ▪ HATES
	HATER	HATERS
	HATERENT	HATERENTS
	HATFUL	HATFULS
	HATGUARD	HATGUARDS
	HATH	HATHA
	HATMAKER	HATMAKERS
	HATPEG	HATPEGS
	HATPIN	HATPINS
	HATRACK	HATRACKS
	HATRED	HATREDS
CHATS ▪ GHATS ▪ KHATS ▪ WHATS	**HATS**	
	HATSTAND	HATSTANDS
CHATTED	**HATTED**	
CHATTER ▪ PHATTER ▪ SHATTER	**HATTER**	HATTERS
CHATTERED ▪ SHATTERED	**HATTERED**	
	HATTERIA	HATTERIAS
CHATTERING ▪ SHATTERING	**HATTERING**	
CHATTERS ▪ SHATTERS	**HATTERS**	
CHATTING	**HATTING**	HATTINGS
	HATTOCK	HATTOCKS

FRONT HOOK	ROOT WORD	END HOOK
	HAUBERK	HAUBERKS
	HAUD	HAUDS
	HAUF	HAUFS
SHAUGH	**HAUGH**	HAUGHS · HAUGHT
SHAUGHS	**HAUGHS**	
	HAUGHT	HAUGHTY
SHAUL	**HAUL**	HAULD · HAULM · HAULS · HAULT
	HAULAGE	HAULAGES
	HAULD	HAULDS
SHAULED	**HAULED**	
	HAULER	HAULERS
	HAULIER	HAULIERS
SHAULING	**HAULING**	
	HAULM	HAULMS · HAULMY
SHAULS	**HAULS**	HAULST
	HAULYARD	HAULYARDS
CHAUNT	**HAUNT**	HAUNTS
CHAUNTED	**HAUNTED**	
CHAUNTER	**HAUNTER**	HAUNTERS
CHAUNTERS	**HAUNTERS**	
CHAUNTING	**HAUNTING**	HAUNTINGS
CHAUNTS	**HAUNTS**	
	HAUSE	HAUSED · HAUSEN · HAUSES
	HAUSEN	HAUSENS
	HAUSFRAU	HAUSFRAUS
	HAUSTORIA	HAUSTORIAL
GHAUT	**HAUT**	HAUTE
	HAUTBOY	HAUTBOYS
	HAUTEUR	HAUTEURS
	HAUYNE	HAUYNES
	HAVARTI	HAVARTIS
	HAVDALAH	HAVDALAHS
	HAVDOLOH	HAVDOLOHS
CHAVE · SHAVE	**HAVE**	HAVEN · HAVER · HAVES
	HAVELOCK	HAVELOCKS
SHAVEN	**HAVEN**	HAVENS
	HAVEOUR	HAVEOURS
SHAVER	**HAVER**	HAVERS
	HAVEREL	HAVERELS
	HAVERING	HAVERINGS
SHAVERS	**HAVERS**	
	HAVERSACK	HAVERSACKS
	HAVERSINE	HAVERSINES
SHAVES	**HAVES**	
	HAVILDAR	HAVILDARS
SHAVING	**HAVING**	HAVINGS
SHAVINGS	**HAVINGS**	
	HAVIOR	HAVIORS
	HAVIOUR	HAVIOURS
	HAVOC	HAVOCS
	HAVOCKER	HAVOCKERS
CHAW · SHAW · THAW	**HAW**	HAWK · HAWM · HAWS
	HAWALA	HAWALAS
	HAWBUCK	HAWBUCKS
CHAWED · SHAWED · THAWED	**HAWED**	
CHAWING · SHAWING · THAWING	**HAWING**	
CHAWK	**HAWK**	HAWKS
	HAWKBELL	HAWKBELLS
	HAWKBILL	HAWKBILLS
	HAWKBIT	HAWKBITS
	HAWKER	HAWKERS
	HAWKEY	HAWKEYS
	HAWKIE	HAWKIES
	HAWKING	HAWKINGS
	HAWKMOTH	HAWKMOTHS
	HAWKNOSE	HAWKNOSES
CHAWKS	**HAWKS**	
	HAWKSBILL	HAWKSBILLS
	HAWKSHAW	HAWKSHAWS

FRONT HOOK	ROOT WORD	END HOOK
	HAWKWEED	HAWKWEEDS
SHAWM	**HAWM**	HAWMS
SHAWMS	**HAWMS**	
CHAWS ▪ SHAWS ▪ THAWS	**HAWS**	HAWSE
	HAWSE	HAWSED ▪ HAWSER ▪ HAWSES
	HAWSEHOLE	HAWSEHOLES
	HAWSEPIPE	HAWSEPIPES
	HAWSER	HAWSERS
	HAWTHORN	HAWTHORNS ▪ HAWTHORNY
CHAY ▪ SHAY	**HAY**	HAYS
	HAYBAND	HAYBANDS
	HAYCOCK	HAYCOCKS
	HAYER	HAYERS
	HAYFIELD	HAYFIELDS
	HAYFORK	HAYFORKS
	HAYING	HAYINGS
	HAYLAGE	HAYLAGES
	HAYLE	HAYLES
	HAYLOFT	HAYLOFTS
	HAYMAKER	HAYMAKERS
	HAYMAKING	HAYMAKINGS
	HAYMOW	HAYMOWS
	HAYRACK	HAYRACKS
	HAYRICK	HAYRICKS
	HAYRIDE	HAYRIDES
CHAYS ▪ SHAYS	**HAYS**	
	HAYSEED	HAYSEEDS
	HAYSEL	HAYSELS
	HAYSTACK	HAYSTACKS
	HAYWARD	HAYWARDS
	HAYWIRE	HAYWIRES
CHAZAN	**HAZAN**	HAZANS
CHAZANIM	**HAZANIM**	
CHAZANS	**HAZANS**	
	HAZARD	HAZARDS
	HAZARDER	HAZARDERS
	HAZARDIZE	HAZARDIZES
	HAZE	HAZED ▪ HAZEL ▪ HAZER ▪ HAZES
GHAZEL	**HAZEL**	HAZELS
	HAZELHEN	HAZELHENS
	HAZELNUT	HAZELNUTS
GHAZELS	**HAZELS**	
	HAZER	HAZERS
	HAZING	HAZINGS
	HAZMAT	HAZMATS
CHAZZAN	**HAZZAN**	HAZZANS
CHAZZANIM	**HAZZANIM**	
CHAZZANS	**HAZZANS**	
CHE ▪ SHE ▪ THE	**HE**	HEH ▪ HEM ▪ HEN ▪ HEP ▪ HER ▪ HES ▪ HET HEW ▪ HEX ▪ HEY
AHEAD	**HEAD**	HEADS ▪ HEADY
	HEADACHE	HEADACHES ▪ HEADACHEY
	HEADAGE	HEADAGES
	HEADBAND	HEADBANDS
	HEADBANG	HEADBANGS
	HEADBOARD	HEADBOARDS
	HEADCASE	HEADCASES
	HEADCHAIR	HEADCHAIRS
	HEADCLOTH	HEADCLOTHS
	HEADCOUNT	HEADCOUNTS
	HEADEND	HEADENDS
	HEADER	HEADERS
	HEADFAST	HEADFASTS
	HEADFRAME	HEADFRAMES
	HEADFUCK	HEADFUCKS (offensive)
	HEADFUL	HEADFULS
	HEADGATE	HEADGATES
	HEADGEAR	HEADGEARS
	HEADGUARD	HEADGUARDS

H

FRONT HOOK	ROOT WORD	END HOOK
	HEADHUNT	HEADHUNTS
SHEADING	**HEADING**	HEADINGS
SHEADINGS	**HEADINGS**	
	HEADLAMP	HEADLAMPS
	HEADLAND	HEADLANDS
	HEADLEASE	HEADLEASES
	HEADLIGHT	HEADLIGHTS
	HEADLINE	HEADLINED ▪ HEADLINER ▪ HEADLINES
	HEADLINER	HEADLINERS
	HEADLOCK	HEADLOCKS
	HEADMARK	HEADMARKS
	HEADNOTE	HEADNOTES
	HEADPEACE	HEADPEACES
	HEADPHONE	HEADPHONES
	HEADPIECE	HEADPIECES
	HEADPIN	HEADPINS
	HEADRACE	HEADRACES
	HEADRAIL	HEADRAILS
	HEADREST	HEADRESTS
	HEADRIG	HEADRIGS
	HEADRING	HEADRINGS
	HEADROOM	HEADROOMS
	HEADROPE	HEADROPES
	HEADSAIL	HEADSAILS
	HEADSET	HEADSETS
	HEADSHAKE	HEADSHAKES
	HEADSHIP	HEADSHIPS
	HEADSHOT	HEADSHOTS
	HEADSPACE	HEADSPACES
	HEADSTALL	HEADSTALLS
	HEADSTAND	HEADSTANDS
	HEADSTAY	HEADSTAYS
	HEADSTICK	HEADSTICKS
	HEADSTOCK	HEADSTOCKS
	HEADSTONE	HEADSTONES
	HEADWARD	HEADWARDS
	HEADWATER	HEADWATERS
	HEADWAY	HEADWAYS
	HEADWIND	HEADWINDS
	HEADWORD	HEADWORDS
	HEADWORK	HEADWORKS
SHEAL ▪ WHEAL	**HEAL**	HEALD ▪ HEALS
	HEALD	HEALDS
SHEALED	**HEALED**	
	HEALEE	HEALEES
	HEALER	HEALERS
SHEALING	**HEALING**	HEALINGS
SHEALINGS	**HEALINGS**	
SHEALS ▪ WHEALS	**HEALS**	
	HEALTH	HEALTHS ▪ HEALTHY
	HEALTHISM	HEALTHISMS
AHEAP ▪ CHEAP	**HEAP**	HEAPS ▪ HEAPY
CHEAPED	**HEAPED**	
CHEAPER	**HEAPER**	HEAPERS
CHEAPING	**HEAPING**	
CHEAPS	**HEAPS**	
	HEAPSTEAD	HEAPSTEADS
CHEAPY	**HEAPY**	
SHEAR ▪ WHEAR	**HEAR**	HEARD ▪ HEARE ▪ HEARS ▪ HEART
	HEARD	HEARDS
WHEARE	**HEARE**	HEARER ▪ HEARES
SHEARER	**HEARER**	HEARERS
SHEARERS	**HEARERS**	
SHEARING	**HEARING**	HEARINGS
SHEARINGS	**HEARINGS**	
	HEARKEN	HEARKENS
	HEARKENER	HEARKENERS
SHEARS	**HEARS**	HEARSE ▪ HEARSY
	HEARSAY	HEARSAYS

FRONT HOOK	ROOT WORD	END HOOK
	HEARSE	HEARSED · HEARSES
	HEART	HEARTH · HEARTS · HEARTY
	HEARTACHE	HEARTACHES
	HEARTBEAT	HEARTBEATS
	HEARTBURN	HEARTBURNS
	HEARTEN	HEARTENS
	HEARTENER	HEARTENERS
	HEARTH	HEARTHS
	HEARTHRUG	HEARTHRUGS
	HEARTIES	HEARTIEST
	HEARTIKIN	HEARTIKINS
	HEARTLAND	HEARTLANDS
	HEARTLET	HEARTLETS
	HEARTLING	HEARTLINGS
	HEARTPEA	HEARTPEAS
	HEARTSEED	HEARTSEEDS
	HEARTWOOD	HEARTWOODS
	HEARTWORM	HEARTWORMS
	HEAST	HEASTE · HEASTS
	HEASTE	HEASTES
CHEAT · WHEAT	**HEAT**	HEATH · HEATS
CHEATABLE	**HEATABLE**	
CHEATED	**HEATED**	
CHEATER · THEATER	**HEATER**	HEATERS
CHEATERS · THEATERS	**HEATERS**	
SHEATH	**HEATH**	HEATHS · HEATHY
	HEATHBIRD	HEATHBIRDS
	HEATHCOCK	HEATHCOCKS
	HEATHEN	HEATHENS
SHEATHER	**HEATHER**	HEATHERS · HEATHERY
SHEATHERS	**HEATHERS**	
	HEATHFOWL	HEATHFOWLS
SHEATHIER	**HEATHIER**	
SHEATHIEST	**HEATHIEST**	
	HEATHLAND	HEATHLANDS
SHEATHLESS	**HEATHLESS**	
SHEATHS	**HEATHS**	
SHEATHY	**HEATHY**	
CHEATING	**HEATING**	HEATINGS
CHEATINGS	**HEATINGS**	
WHEATLESS	**HEATLESS**	
CHEATS · WHEATS	**HEATS**	
	HEATSPOT	HEATSPOTS
	HEAUME	HEAUMES
SHEAVE · THEAVE	**HEAVE**	HEAVED · HEAVEN · HEAVER · HEAVES
SHEAVED	**HEAVED**	
	HEAVEN	HEAVENS
	HEAVER	HEAVERS
SHEAVES · THEAVES	**HEAVES**	
	HEAVIES	HEAVIEST
SHEAVING	**HEAVING**	HEAVINGS
	HEBDOMAD	HEBDOMADS
THEBE	**HEBE**	HEBEN · HEBES
	HEBEN	HEBENS
	HEBENON	HEBENONS
THEBES	**HEBES**	
	HEBETATE	HEBETATED · HEBETATES
	HEBETUDE	HEBETUDES
	HEBONA	HEBONAS
	HEBRAISE	HEBRAISED · HEBRAISES
	HEBRAIZE	HEBRAIZED · HEBRAIZES
	HECATOMB	HECATOMBS
	HECH	HECHT
	HECHT	HECHTS
CHECK	**HECK**	HECKS
	HECKLE	HECKLED · HECKLER · HECKLES
	HECKLER	HECKLERS
	HECKLING	HECKLINGS
CHECKS	**HECKS**	

FRONT HOOK	ROOT WORD	END HOOK
	HECOGENIN	HECOGENINS
	HECTARE	HECTARES
	HECTIC	HECTICS
	HECTOGRAM	HECTOGRAMS
	HECTOR	HECTORS
	HECTORER	HECTORERS
	HECTORING	HECTORINGS
	HECTORISM	HECTORISMS
	HEDDLE	HEDDLED = HEDDLES
CHEDER	**HEDER**	HEDERA = HEDERS
	HEDERA	HEDERAL = HEDERAS
CHEDERS	**HEDERS**	
	HEDGE	HEDGED = HEDGER = HEDGES
	HEDGEBILL	HEDGEBILLS
	HEDGEHOG	HEDGEHOGS
	HEDGEHOP	HEDGEHOPS
	HEDGEPIG	HEDGEPIGS
	HEDGER	HEDGERS
	HEDGEROW	HEDGEROWS
	HEDGING	HEDGINGS
	HEDONIC	HEDONICS
	HEDONISM	HEDONISMS
	HEDONIST	HEDONISTS
	HEDYPHANE	HEDYPHANES
THEED	**HEED**	HEEDS = HEEDY
	HEEDER	HEEDERS
	HEEHAW	HEEHAWS
SHEEL = WHEEL	**HEEL**	HEELS
	HEELBALL	HEELBALLS
SHEELED = WHEELED	**HEELED**	
WHEELER	**HEELER**	HEELERS
WHEELERS	**HEELERS**	
SHEELING = WHEELING	**HEELING**	HEELINGS
WHEELINGS	**HEELINGS**	
WHEELLESS	**HEELLESS**	
	HEELPIECE	HEELPIECES
	HEELPLATE	HEELPLATES
	HEELPOST	HEELPOSTS
SHEELS = WHEELS	**HEELS**	
	HEELTAP	HEELTAPS
PHEEZE = WHEEZE	**HEEZE**	HEEZED = HEEZES
PHEEZED = WHEEZED	**HEEZED**	
PHEEZES = WHEEZES	**HEEZES**	
	HEEZIE	HEEZIES
PHEEZING = WHEEZING	**HEEZING**	
THEFT = WHEFT	**HEFT**	HEFTE = HEFTS = HEFTY
	HEFTE	HEFTED = HEFTER
	HEFTER	HEFTERS
THEFTS = WHEFTS	**HEFTS**	
	HEGARI	HEGARIS
	HEGEMON	HEGEMONS = HEGEMONY
	HEGIRA	HEGIRAS
	HEGUMEN	HEGUMENE = HEGUMENS = HEGUMENY
	HEGUMENE	HEGUMENES
	HEH	HEHS
	HEID	HEIDS
	HEIFER	HEIFERS
	HEIGH	HEIGHT
AHEIGHT	**HEIGHT**	HEIGHTH = HEIGHTS
	HEIGHTEN	HEIGHTENS
	HEIGHTH	HEIGHTHS
	HEIGHTISM	HEIGHTISMS
	HEIL	HEILS
SHEILING	**HEILING**	
	HEINIE	HEINIES
THEIR	**HEIR**	HEIRS
	HEIRDOM	HEIRDOMS
	HEIRLOOM	HEIRLOOMS
THEIRS	**HEIRS**	

FRONT HOOK	ROOT WORD	END HOOK
	HEIRSHIP	HEIRSHIPS
THEIST	**HEIST**	HEISTS
	HEISTER	HEISTERS
THEISTS	**HEISTS**	
	HEITIKI	HEITIKIS
	HEJAB	HEJABS
	HEJIRA	HEJIRAS
	HEJRA	HEJRAS
	HEKETARA	HEKETARAS
	HEKTARE	HEKTARES
	HEKTOGRAM	HEKTOGRAMS
	HELE	HELED ▪ HELES
	HELENIUM	HELENIUMS
	HELIAST	HELIASTS
	HELICLINE	HELICLINES
	HELICOID	HELICOIDS
	HELICON	HELICONS
	HELICONIA	HELICONIAS
	HELICOPT	HELICOPTS
	HELICTITE	HELICTITES
	HELIDECK	HELIDECKS
	HELIDROME	HELIDROMES
	HELILIFT	HELILIFTS
	HELIO	HELIOS
	HELIODOR	HELIODORS
	HELIOGRAM	HELIOGRAMS
	HELIOSTAT	HELIOSTATS
	HELIOTYPE	HELIOTYPED ▪ HELIOTYPES
	HELIOZOAN	HELIOZOANS
	HELIPAD	HELIPADS
	HELIPILOT	HELIPILOTS
	HELIPORT	HELIPORTS
	HELISTOP	HELISTOPS
	HELIUM	HELIUMS
SHELL	**HELL**	HELLO ▪ HELLS
	HELLBROTH	HELLBROTHS
	HELLCAT	HELLCATS
	HELLDIVER	HELLDIVERS
	HELLEBORE	HELLEBORES
SHELLED	**HELLED**	
	HELLENISE	HELLENISED ▪ HELLENISES
	HELLENIZE	HELLENIZED ▪ HELLENIZES
SHELLER	**HELLER**	HELLERI ▪ HELLERS ▪ HELLERY
	HELLERI	HELLERIS
SHELLERS	**HELLERS**	
SHELLFIRE	**HELLFIRE**	HELLFIRES
SHELLFIRES	**HELLFIRES**	
	HELLHOLE	HELLHOLES
	HELLHOUND	HELLHOUNDS
	HELLICAT	HELLICATS
SHELLIER	**HELLIER**	HELLIERS
SHELLING	**HELLING**	
	HELLION	HELLIONS
	HELLKITE	HELLKITES
	HELLO	HELLOS
SHELLS	**HELLS**	
	HELLWARD	HELLWARDS
WHELM	**HELM**	HELMS
WHELMED	**HELMED**	
	HELMER	HELMERS
	HELMET	HELMETS
WHELMING	**HELMING**	
	HELMINTH	HELMINTHS
WHELMS	**HELMS**	
	HELO	HELOS ▪ HELOT
	HELOPHYTE	HELOPHYTES
	HELOT	HELOTS
	HELOTAGE	HELOTAGES
	HELOTISM	HELOTISMS

H

H

FRONT HOOK	ROOT WORD	END HOOK
CHELP ▪ WHELP	**HELP**	HELPS
	HELPDESK	HELPDESKS
CHELPED ▪ WHELPED	**HELPED**	
	HELPER	HELPERS
CHELPING ▪ WHELPING	**HELPING**	HELPINGS
WHELPLESS	**HELPLESS**	
	HELPLINE	HELPLINES
	HELPMATE	HELPMATES
	HELPMEET	HELPMEETS
CHELPS ▪ WHELPS	**HELPS**	
SHELVE	**HELVE**	HELVED ▪ HELVES
SHELVED	**HELVED**	
SHELVES ▪ THELVES	**HELVES**	
	HELVETIUM	HELVETIUMS
SHELVING	**HELVING**	
AHEM ▪ THEM	**HEM**	HEME ▪ HEMP ▪ HEMS
	HEMAGOG	HEMAGOGS
	HEMAGOGUE	HEMAGOGUES
	HEMATEIN	HEMATEINS
RHEMATIC ▪ THEMATIC	**HEMATIC**	HEMATICS
THEMATICS	**HEMATICS**	
	HEMATIN	HEMATINE ▪ HEMATINS
	HEMATINE	HEMATINES
	HEMATINIC	HEMATINICS
	HEMATITE	HEMATITES
	HEMATOMA	HEMATOMAS
	HEMATURIA	HEMATURIAS
RHEME ▪ THEME	**HEME**	HEMES
	HEMELYTRA	HEMELYTRAL
RHEMES ▪ THEMES	**HEMES**	
	HEMIALGIA	HEMIALGIAS
CHEMIC	**HEMIC**	
	HEMICYCLE	HEMICYCLES
	HEMIN	HEMINA ▪ HEMINS
	HEMINA	HEMINAS
	HEMIOLA	HEMIOLAS
	HEMIOLIA	HEMIOLIAS
	HEMIONE	HEMIONES
	HEMIOPIA	HEMIOPIAS
	HEMIOPSIA	HEMIOPSIAS
	HEMIPOD	HEMIPODE ▪ HEMIPODS
	HEMIPODE	HEMIPODES
	HEMIPTER	HEMIPTERS
	HEMISPACE	HEMISPACES
	HEMISTICH	HEMISTICHS
	HEMITROPE	HEMITROPES
	HEMLINE	HEMLINES
	HEMLOCK	HEMLOCKS
	HEMMER	HEMMERS
	HEMOCOEL	HEMOCOELS
	HEMOCYTE	HEMOCYTES
	HEMOLYMPH	HEMOLYMPHS
	HEMOLYSE	HEMOLYSED ▪ HEMOLYSES
	HEMOLYSIN	HEMOLYSING ▪ HEMOLYSINS
	HEMOLYZE	HEMOLYZED ▪ HEMOLYZES
	HEMOPHILE	HEMOPHILES
CHEMOSTAT	**HEMOSTAT**	HEMOSTATS
CHEMOSTATS	**HEMOSTATS**	
	HEMOTOXIN	HEMOTOXINS
	HEMP	HEMPS ▪ HEMPY
	HEMPIE	HEMPIER ▪ HEMPIES
	HEMPIES	HEMPIEST
	HEMPSEED	HEMPSEEDS
	HEMPWEED	HEMPWEEDS
THEN ▪ WHEN	**HEN**	HEND ▪ HENS ▪ HENT
	HENBANE	HENBANES
	HENBIT	HENBITS
THENCE ▪ WHENCE	**HENCE**	
	HENCOOP	HENCOOPS

FRONT HOOK	ROOT WORD	END HOOK
SHEND	**HEND**	HENDS
SHENDING	**HENDING**	
SHENDS	**HENDS**	
	HENEQUEN	HENEQUENS
	HENEQUIN	HENEQUINS
	HENGE	HENGES
	HENHOUSE	HENHOUSES
	HENIQUEN	HENIQUENS
	HENIQUIN	HENIQUINS
	HENLEY	HENLEYS
	HENNA	HENNAS
	HENNER	HENNERS ▪ HENNERY
	HENNIES	HENNIEST
	HENNIN	HENNING ▪ HENNINS
	HENPECK	HENPECKS
	HENRY	HENRYS
THENS ▪ WHENS	**HENS**	
AHENT ▪ SHENT	**HENT**	HENTS
	HEP	HEPS ▪ HEPT
	HEPAR	HEPARS
	HEPARIN	HEPARINS
	HEPATIC	HEPATICA ▪ HEPATICS
	HEPATICA	HEPATICAE ▪ HEPATICAL ▪ HEPATICAS
	HEPATISE	HEPATISED ▪ HEPATISES
	HEPATITE	HEPATITES
	HEPATIZE	HEPATIZED ▪ HEPATIZES
	HEPATOMA	HEPATOMAS
	HEPCAT	HEPCATS
	HEPSTER	HEPSTERS
	HEPTAD	HEPTADS
	HEPTAGLOT	HEPTAGLOTS
	HEPTAGON	HEPTAGONS
	HEPTANE	HEPTANES
	HEPTARCH	HEPTARCHS ▪ HEPTARCHY
	HEPTOSE	HEPTOSES
CHER	**HER**	HERB ▪ HERD ▪ HERE ▪ HERL ▪ HERM
		HERN ▪ HERO ▪ HERS ▪ HERY
	HERALD	HERALDS
	HERALDIST	HERALDISTS
	HERB	HERBS ▪ HERBY
	HERBAGE	HERBAGED ▪ HERBAGES
	HERBAL	HERBALS
	HERBALISM	HERBALISMS
	HERBALIST	HERBALISTS
	HERBAR	HERBARS ▪ HERBARY
	HERBARIA	HERBARIAL ▪ HERBARIAN
	HERBARIAN	HERBARIANS
	HERBARIUM	HERBARIUMS
	HERBELET	HERBELETS
	HERBICIDE	HERBICIDES
	HERBIST	HERBISTS
	HERBIVORE	HERBIVORES
	HERBLET	HERBLETS
	HERBORISE	HERBORISED ▪ HERBORISES
	HERBORIST	HERBORISTS
	HERBORIZE	HERBORIZED ▪ HERBORIZES
	HERCYNITE	HERCYNITES
SHERD	**HERD**	HERDS
	HERDBOY	HERDBOYS
	HERDEN	HERDENS
	HERDER	HERDERS
	HERDIC	HERDICS
SHERDS	**HERDS**	
	HERDWICK	HERDWICKS
CHERE ▪ SHERE ▪ THERE ▪ WHERE	**HERE**	HERES
THEREABOUT ▪ WHEREABOUT	**HEREABOUT**	HEREABOUTS
THEREAFTER ▪ WHEREAFTER	**HEREAFTER**	HEREAFTERS
THEREAT ▪ WHEREAT	**HEREAT**	
THEREAWAY	**HEREAWAY**	HEREAWAYS

369

FRONT HOOK	ROOT WORD	END HOOK
THEREBY · WHEREBY	**HEREBY**	
THEREFROM · WHEREFROM	**HEREFROM**	
THEREIN · WHEREIN	**HEREIN**	
THEREINTO · WHEREINTO	**HEREINTO**	
THERENESS · WHERENESS	**HERENESS**	
THEREOF · WHEREOF	**HEREOF**	
THEREON · WHEREON	**HEREON**	
THERES · WHERES	**HERES**	HERESY
	HERETIC	HERETICS
THERETO · WHERETO	**HERETO**	
THEREUNDER · WHEREUNDER	**HEREUNDER**	
THEREUNTO · WHEREUNTO	**HEREUNTO**	
THEREUPON · WHEREUPON	**HEREUPON**	
THEREWITH · WHEREWITH	**HEREWITH**	
	HERIOT	HERIOTS
	HERISSON	HERISSONS
	HERITAGE	HERITAGES
	HERITOR	HERITORS
	HERL	HERLS
	HERLING	HERLINGS
THERM	**HERM**	HERMA · HERMS
	HERMA	HERMAE · HERMAI
THERMAE	**HERMAE**	
	HERMANDAD	HERMANDADS
	HERMETIC	HERMETICS
	HERMETISM	HERMETISMS
	HERMETIST	HERMETISTS
THERMIT	**HERMIT**	HERMITS
	HERMITAGE	HERMITAGES
	HERMITISM	HERMITISMS
THERMITS	**HERMITS**	
THERMS	**HERMS**	
	HERN	HERNS
	HERNIA	HERNIAE · HERNIAL · HERNIAS
	HERNIATE	HERNIATED · HERNIATES
	HERNSHAW	HERNSHAWS
	HERO	HEROE · HERON · HEROS
	HEROE	HEROES
	HEROIC	HEROICS
	HEROICISE	HEROICISED · HEROICISES
	HEROICIZE	HEROICIZED · HEROICIZES
	HEROIN	HEROINE · HEROINS
	HEROINE	HEROINES
	HEROINISM	HEROINISMS
	HEROISE	HEROISED · HEROISES
	HEROISM	HEROISMS
	HEROIZE	HEROIZED · HEROIZES
	HERON	HERONS
	HERONSEW	HERONSEWS
	HERONSHAW	HERONSHAWS
	HEROON	HEROONS
	HEROSHIP	HEROSHIPS
	HERPETIC	HERPETICS
CHERRIED · WHERRIED	**HERRIED**	
CHERRIES · SHERRIES · WHERRIES	**HERRIES**	
	HERRIMENT	HERRIMENTS
	HERRING	HERRINGS
	HERRINGER	HERRINGERS
CHERRY · SHERRY · WHERRY	**HERRY**	
CHERRYING · WHERRYING	**HERRYING**	
	HERRYMENT	HERRYMENTS
	HERS	HERSE
	HERSALL	HERSALLS
	HERSE	HERSED · HERSES
	HERSHIP	HERSHIPS
	HERY	HERYE
	HERYE	HERYED · HERYES
SHES	**HES**	HESP · HEST
	HESITANCE	HESITANCES

FRONT HOOK	ROOT WORD	END HOOK
	HESITATE	HESITATED ▪ HESITATER ▪ HESITATES
	HESITATER	HESITATERS
	HESITATOR	HESITATORS ▪ HESITATORY
THESP	**HESP**	HESPS
	HESPERID	HESPERIDS
THESPS	**HESPS**	
	HESSIAN	HESSIANS
	HESSITE	HESSITES
	HESSONITE	HESSONITES
CHEST ▪ GHEST	**HEST**	HESTS
CHESTS	**HESTS**	
KHET ▪ SHET ▪ WHET	**HET**	HETE ▪ HETH ▪ HETS
	HETAERA	HETAERAE ▪ HETAERAS
	HETAERISM	HETAERISMS
	HETAERIST	HETAERISTS
	HETAIRA	HETAIRAI ▪ HETAIRAS
	HETAIRIA	HETAIRIAS
	HETAIRISM	HETAIRISMS
	HETAIRIST	HETAIRISTS
THETE	**HETE**	HETES
	HETERO	HETEROS
	HETERODOX	HETERODOXY
	HETERONYM	HETERONYMS
	HETEROPOD	HETEROPODS
THETES	**HETES**	
CHETH ▪ KHETH	**HETH**	HETHS
THETHER ▪ WHETHER	**HETHER**	
CHETHS ▪ KHETHS	**HETHS**	
	HETMAN	HETMANS
	HETMANATE	HETMANATES
KHETS ▪ SHETS ▪ WHETS	**HETS**	
SHEUCH	**HEUCH**	HEUCHS
	HEUCHERA	HEUCHERAS
SHEUCHS	**HEUCHS**	
SHEUGH ▪ WHEUGH	**HEUGH**	HEUGHS
SHEUGHS ▪ WHEUGHS	**HEUGHS**	
	HEUREKA	HEUREKAS
	HEURETIC	HEURETICS
	HEURISM	HEURISMS
	HEURISTIC	HEURISTICS
	HEVEA	HEVEAS
CHEW ▪ PHEW ▪ SHEW ▪ THEW ▪ WHEW	**HEW**	HEWN ▪ HEWS
	HEWABLE	
CHEWED ▪ SHEWED ▪ THEWED ▪ WHEWED	**HEWED**	
CHEWER ▪ SHEWER	**HEWER**	HEWERS
CHEWERS ▪ SHEWERS	**HEWERS**	
CHEWING ▪ SHEWING ▪ WHEWING	**HEWING**	HEWINGS
SHEWN	**HEWN**	
CHEWS ▪ SHEWS ▪ THEWS ▪ WHEWS	**HEWS**	
	HEXACHORD	HEXACHORDS
	HEXACT	HEXACTS
	HEXAD	HEXADE ▪ HEXADS
	HEXADE	HEXADES
	HEXAFOIL	HEXAFOILS
	HEXAGON	HEXAGONS
	HEXAGRAM	HEXAGRAMS
	HEXAHEDRA	HEXAHEDRAL
	HEXAMETER	HEXAMETERS
	HEXAMINE	HEXAMINES
	HEXANE	HEXANES
	HEXAPLA	HEXAPLAR ▪ HEXAPLAS
	HEXAPLOID	HEXAPLOIDS ▪ HEXAPLOIDY
	HEXAPOD	HEXAPODS ▪ HEXAPODY
	HEXARCH	HEXARCHY
	HEXASTICH	HEXASTICHS
	HEXASTYLE	HEXASTYLES
	HEXENE	HEXENES
	HEXER	HEXERS
	HEXEREI	HEXEREIS

H

FRONT HOOK	ROOT WORD	END HOOK
RHEXES	**HEXES**	
	HEXING	HEXINGS
	HEXONE	HEXONES
	HEXOSAN	HEXOSANS
	HEXOSE	HEXOSES
	HEXYL	HEXYLS
	HEXYLENE	HEXYLENES
THEY ▪ WHEY	**HEY**	HEYS
	HEYDAY	HEYDAYS
	HEYDEY	HEYDEYS
	HEYDUCK	HEYDUCKS
WHEYS	**HEYS**	
AHI ▪ CHI ▪ GHI ▪ KHI ▪ PHI	**HI**	HIC ▪ HID ▪ HIE ▪ HIM ▪ HIN ▪ HIP ▪ HIS ▪ HIT
	HIBACHI	HIBACHIS
	HIBAKUSHA	HIBAKUSHAS
	HIBERNATE	HIBERNATED ▪ HIBERNATES
	HIBERNISE	HIBERNISED ▪ HIBERNISES
	HIBERNIZE	HIBERNIZED ▪ HIBERNIZES
CHIC	**HIC**	HICK
	HICATEE	HICATEES
	HICCATEE	HICCATEES
	HICCOUGH	HICCOUGHS
	HICCUP	HICCUPS ▪ HICCUPY
CHICK ▪ THICK	**HICK**	HICKS
	HICKEY	HICKEYS
THICKIE (offensive)	**HICKIE**	HICKIES
THICKIES (offensive)	**HICKIES**	
THICKISH	**HICKISH**	
CHICKORIES	**HICKORIES**	
CHICKORY	**HICKORY**	
CHICKS ▪ THICKS	**HICKS**	
	HICKWALL	HICKWALLS
	HICKYMAL	HICKYMALS
CHID ▪ WHID	**HID**	HIDE
	HIDAGE	HIDAGES
	HIDALGA	HIDALGAS
	HIDALGO	HIDALGOS
CHIDDEN	**HIDDEN**	
	HIDDENITE	HIDDENITES
SHIDDER ▪ WHIDDER	**HIDDER**	HIDDERS
SHIDDERS ▪ WHIDDERS	**HIDDERS**	
CHIDE	**HIDE**	HIDED ▪ HIDER ▪ HIDES
	HIDEAWAY	HIDEAWAYS
CHIDED	**HIDED**	
	HIDEOUT	HIDEOUTS
CHIDER	**HIDER**	HIDERS
CHIDERS	**HIDERS**	
CHIDES	**HIDES**	
CHIDING	**HIDING**	HIDINGS
CHIDINGS	**HIDINGS**	
	HIDLING	HIDLINGS
CHIDLINGS	**HIDLINGS**	
	HIDROTIC	HIDROTICS
	HIE	HIED ▪ HIES
SHIED	**HIED**	
	HIELAMAN	HIELAMANS
	HIERACIUM	HIERACIUMS
	HIERARCH	HIERARCHS ▪ HIERARCHY
	HIERATIC	HIERATICA
	HIERATICA	HIERATICAL ▪ HIERATICAS
	HIEROCRAT	HIEROCRATS
	HIERODULE	HIERODULES
	HIEROGRAM	HIEROGRAMS
RHIES ▪ SHIES	**HIES**	
	HIGGLE	HIGGLED ▪ HIGGLER ▪ HIGGLES
	HIGGLER	HIGGLERS
	HIGGLING	HIGGLINGS
AHIGH ▪ THIGH	**HIGH**	HIGHS ▪ HIGHT

FRONT HOOK	ROOT WORD	END HOOK
	HIGHBALL	HIGHBALLS
	HIGHBOY	HIGHBOYS
	HIGHBROW	HIGHBROWS
	HIGHCHAIR	HIGHCHAIRS
THIGHED	HIGHED	
	HIGHER	HIGHERS
	HIGHFLIER	HIGHFLIERS
	HIGHFLYER	HIGHFLYERS
	HIGHJACK	HIGHJACKS
	HIGHLAND	HIGHLANDS
	HIGHLIFE	HIGHLIFES
	HIGHLIGHT	HIGHLIGHTS
	HIGHRISE	HIGHRISES
	HIGHROAD	HIGHROADS
THIGHS	HIGHS	
	HIGHSPOT	HIGHSPOTS
	HIGHT	HIGHTH ▪ HIGHTS
	HIGHTAIL	HIGHTAILS
	HIGHTH	HIGHTHS
	HIGHTOP	HIGHTOPS
	HIGHVELD	HIGHVELDS
	HIGHWAY	HIGHWAYS
	HIJAB	HIJABS
	HIJACK	HIJACKS
	HIJACKER	HIJACKERS
	HIJRA	HIJRAH ▪ HIJRAS
	HIJRAH	HIJRAHS
	HIKE	HIKED ▪ HIKER ▪ HIKES
	HIKER	HIKERS
	HIKOI	HIKOIS
	HILA	HILAR
CHILD	HILD	
CHILDING	HILDING	HILDINGS
CHILI	HILI	
CHILL ▪ SHILL ▪ THILL	HILL	HILLO ▪ HILLS ▪ HILLY
	HILLCREST	HILLCRESTS
CHILLED ▪ SHILLED	HILLED	
CHILLER ▪ THILLER	HILLER	HILLERS
CHILLERS ▪ THILLERS	HILLERS	
	HILLFORT	HILLFORTS
CHILLIER	HILLIER	
CHILLIEST	HILLIEST	
CHILLINESS	HILLINESS	
CHILLING ▪ SHILLING	HILLING	
	HILLO	HILLOA ▪ HILLOS
	HILLOA	HILLOAS
	HILLOCK	HILLOCKS ▪ HILLOCKY
CHILLS ▪ SHILLS ▪ THILLS	HILLS	
	HILLSIDE	HILLSIDES
	HILLSLOPE	HILLSLOPES
	HILLTOP	HILLTOPS
CHILLY ▪ WHILLY	HILLY	
	HILT	HILTS
SHIM ▪ WHIM	HIM	HIMS
	HIMATION	HIMATIONS
	HIMBO	HIMBOS (offensive)
SHIMS ▪ WHIMS	HIMS	
CHIN ▪ SHIN ▪ THIN ▪ WHIN	HIN	HIND ▪ HING ▪ HINS ▪ HINT
AHIND	HIND	HINDS
	HINDBRAIN	HINDBRAINS
	HINDER	HINDERS
	HINDERER	HINDERERS
	HINDERING	HINDERINGS
	HINDGUT	HINDGUTS
	HINDHEAD	HINDHEADS
	HINDLEG	HINDLEGS
	HINDRANCE	HINDRANCES
	HINDSHANK	HINDSHANKS
	HINDSIGHT	HINDSIGHTS

H

FRONT HOOK	ROOT WORD	END HOOK
	HINDWING	HINDWINGS
AHING ▪ EHING ▪ OHING ▪ THING	**HING**	HINGE ▪ HINGS
WHINGE	**HINGE**	HINGED ▪ HINGER ▪ HINGES
WHINGED	**HINGED**	
WHINGER	**HINGER**	HINGERS
WHINGERS	**HINGERS**	
WHINGES	**HINGES**	
WHINGING	**HINGING**	
THINGS	**HINGS**	
CHINKIER	**HINKIER**	
CHINKIEST	**HINKIEST**	
CHINKY	**HINKY**	
SHINNIED ▪ WHINNIED	**HINNIED**	
SHINNIES ▪ WHINNIES	**HINNIES**	
SHINNY ▪ WHINNY	**HINNY**	
SHINNYING ▪ WHINNYING	**HINNYING**	
CHINS ▪ SHINS ▪ THINS ▪ WHINS	**HINS**	
AHINT	**HINT**	HINTS
	HINTER	HINTERS
	HINTING	HINTINGS
CHINTS	**HINTS**	
	HIOI	HIOIS
CHIP ▪ SHIP ▪ WHIP	**HIP**	HIPS ▪ HIPT
	HIPBONE	HIPBONES
SHIPLESS	**HIPLESS**	
WHIPLIKE	**HIPLIKE**	
	HIPLINE	HIPLINES
	HIPPARCH	HIPPARCHS
CHIPPED ▪ SHIPPED ▪ WHIPPED	**HIPPED**	
SHIPPEN	**HIPPEN**	HIPPENS
SHIPPENS	**HIPPENS**	
CHIPPER ▪ SHIPPER ▪ WHIPPER	**HIPPER**	
CHIPPIE ▪ SHIPPIE	**HIPPIE**	HIPPIER ▪ HIPPIES
	HIPPIEDOM	HIPPIEDOMS
CHIPPIER ▪ WHIPPIER	**HIPPIER**	
CHIPPIES ▪ SHIPPIES	**HIPPIES**	HIPPIEST
CHIPPIEST ▪ WHIPPIEST	**HIPPIEST**	
	HIPPIN	HIPPING ▪ HIPPINS
CHIPPINESS ▪ WHIPPINESS	**HIPPINESS**	
CHIPPING ▪ SHIPPING ▪ WHIPPING	**HIPPING**	HIPPINGS
CHIPPINGS ▪ SHIPPINGS ▪ WHIPPINGS	**HIPPINGS**	
SHIPPO	**HIPPO**	HIPPOS
	HIPPODAME	HIPPODAMES
SHIPPOS	**HIPPOS**	
	HIPPURITE	HIPPURITES
CHIPPY ▪ WHIPPY	**HIPPY**	
	HIPPYDOM	HIPPYDOMS
CHIPS ▪ SHIPS ▪ WHIPS	**HIPS**	
WHIPSTER	**HIPSTER**	HIPSTERS
WHIPSTERS	**HIPSTERS**	
WHIPT	**HIPT**	
	HIRAGANA	HIRAGANAS
	HIRAGE	HIRAGES
SHIRE	**HIRE**	HIRED ▪ HIREE ▪ HIRER ▪ HIRES
	HIREAGE	HIREAGES
SHIRED	**HIRED**	
	HIREE	HIREES
	HIRELING	HIRELINGS *(offensive)*
	HIRER	HIRERS
SHIRES	**HIRES**	
SHIRING	**HIRING**	HIRINGS
CHIRLING ▪ THIRLING ▪ WHIRLING	**HIRLING**	HIRLINGS
WHIRLINGS	**HIRLINGS**	
	HIRPLE	HIRPLED ▪ HIRPLES
	HIRRIENT	HIRRIENTS
	HIRSEL	HIRSELS
	HIRSLE	HIRSLED ▪ HIRSLES
	HIRSUTISM	HIRSUTISMS
	HIRUDIN	HIRUDINS

H

FRONT HOOK	ROOT WORD	END HOOK
AHIS ▪ CHIS ▪ GHIS ▪ KHIS ▪ PHIS ▪ THIS	**HIS**	HISH ▪ HISN ▪ HISS ▪ HIST
SHISH ▪ WHISH	**HISH**	
WHISHED	**HISHED**	
WHISHES	**HISHES**	
PHISHING ▪ WHISHING	**HISHING**	
	HISPANISM	HISPANISMS
WHISS	**HISS**	HISSY
WHISSED	**HISSED**	
	HISSER	HISSERS
WHISSES	**HISSES**	
	HISSIES	HISSIEST
WHISSING	**HISSING**	HISSINGS
SHIST ▪ WHIST	**HIST**	HISTS
	HISTAMIN	HISTAMINE ▪ HISTAMINS
	HISTAMINE	HISTAMINES
WHISTED	**HISTED**	
	HISTIDIN	HISTIDINE ▪ HISTIDINS
	HISTIDINE	HISTIDINES
BHISTIE	**HISTIE**	
WHISTING	**HISTING**	
	HISTOGEN	HISTOGENS ▪ HISTOGENY
	HISTOGRAM	HISTOGRAMS
	HISTONE	HISTONES
	HISTORIAN	HISTORIANS
AHISTORIC	**HISTORIC**	
	HISTORISM	HISTORISMS
	HISTRIO	HISTRION ▪ HISTRIOS
	HISTRION	HISTRIONS
SHISTS ▪ WHISTS	**HISTS**	
CHIT ▪ SHIT (offensive) ▪ WHIT	**HIT**	HITS
	HITCH	HITCHY
	HITCHER	HITCHERS
	HITCHHIKE	HITCHHIKED ▪ HITCHHIKER ▪ HITCHHIKES
	HITHE	HITHER ▪ HITHES
THITHER ▪ WHITHER	**HITHER**	HITHERS
WHITHERED	**HITHERED**	
WHITHERING	**HITHERING**	
WHITHERS	**HITHERS**	
THITHERTO	**HITHERTO**	
SHITLESS	**HITLESS**	
CHITS ▪ SHITS (offensive) ▪ WHITS	**HITS**	
CHITTER ▪ WHITTER	**HITTER**	HITTERS
CHITTERS ▪ WHITTERS	**HITTERS**	
CHITTING ▪ SHITTING (offensive)	**HITTING**	
CHIVE ▪ SHIVE	**HIVE**	HIVED ▪ HIVER ▪ HIVES
CHIVED	**HIVED**	
SHIVER	**HIVER**	HIVERS
SHIVERS	**HIVERS**	
CHIVES ▪ SHIVES	**HIVES**	
	HIVEWARD	HIVEWARDS
CHIVING	**HIVING**	
	HIZEN	HIZENS
CHIZZ ▪ WHIZZ	**HIZZ**	
CHIZZED ▪ WHIZZED	**HIZZED**	
CHIZZES ▪ PHIZZES ▪ WHIZZES	**HIZZES**	
CHIZZING ▪ WHIZZING	**HIZZING**	
	HIZZONER	HIZZONERS
OHM	**HM**	HMM
MHO ▪ OHO ▪ PHO ▪ RHO ▪ THO ▪ WHO ▪ ZHO	**HO**	HOA ▪ HOB ▪ HOC ▪ HOD ▪ HOE ▪ HOG ▪ HOH HOI ▪ HOM ▪ HON ▪ HOO ▪ HOP HOS (offensive) ▪ HOT ▪ HOW ▪ HOX ▪ HOY
WHOA	**HOA**	HOAR ▪ HOAS ▪ HOAX
	HOACTZIN	HOACTZINS
	HOAGIE	HOAGIES
	HOAR	HOARD ▪ HOARS ▪ HOARY
	HOARD	HOARDS
	HOARDER	HOARDERS
	HOARDING	HOARDINGS
	HOARFROST	HOARFROSTS

FRONT HOOK	ROOT WORD	END HOOK
	HOARHEAD	HOARHEADS
	HOARHOUND	HOARHOUNDS
	HOARS	HOARSE
	HOARSE	HOARSEN · HOARSER
	HOARSEN	HOARSENS
	HOAS	HOAST
	HOAST	HOASTS
	HOATZIN	HOATZINS
	HOAXER	HOAXERS
	HOB	HOBO · HOBS
	HOBBER	HOBBERS
	HOBBIT	HOBBITS
	HOBBLE	HOBBLED · HOBBLER · HOBBLES
	HOBBLER	HOBBLERS
	HOBBLING	HOBBLINGS
	HOBBYISM	HOBBYISMS
	HOBBYIST	HOBBYISTS
	HOBDAY	HOBDAYS
	HOBGOBLIN	HOBGOBLINS
	HOBJOB	HOBJOBS
	HOBJOBBER	HOBJOBBERS
	HOBNAIL	HOBNAILS
	HOBNOB	HOBNOBS
	HOBNOBBER	HOBNOBBERS
	HOBO	HOBOS
	HOBODOM	HOBODOMS
	HOBOISM	HOBOISMS
CHOC	**HOC**	HOCK
CHOCK · SHOCK	**HOCK**	HOCKS
CHOCKED · SHOCKED	**HOCKED**	
CHOCKER · SHOCKER	**HOCKER**	HOCKERS
SHOCKERS	**HOCKERS**	
	HOCKEY	HOCKEYS
CHOCKING · SHOCKING	**HOCKING**	
	HOCKLE	HOCKLED · HOCKLES
CHOCKS · SHOCKS	**HOCKS**	
	HOCKSHOP	HOCKSHOPS
SHOD	**HOD**	HODS
	HODAD	HODADS
SHODDEN	**HODDEN**	HODDENS
	HODDIN	HODDING · HODDINS
	HODDLE	HODDLED · HODDLES
KHODJA	**HODJA**	HODJAS
KHODJAS	**HODJAS**	
	HODMANDOD	HODMANDODS
	HODOGRAPH	HODOGRAPHS
	HODOMETER	HODOMETERS
	HODOSCOPE	HODOSCOPES
SHOE	**HOE**	HOED · HOER · HOES
	HOECAKE	HOECAKES
SHOED	**HOED**	
	HOEDOWN	HOEDOWNS
SHOEING	**HOEING**	
SHOER	**HOER**	HOERS
SHOERS	**HOERS**	
SHOES	**HOES**	
CHOG · SHOG	**HOG**	HOGG · HOGH · HOGS
	HOGAN	HOGANS
	HOGBACK	HOGBACKS
	HOGEN	HOGENS
	HOGG	HOGGS
SHOGGED	**HOGGED**	
	HOGGER	HOGGERS · HOGGERY
	HOGGEREL	HOGGERELS
	HOGGET	HOGGETS
	HOGGIN	HOGGING · HOGGINS
SHOGGING	**HOGGING**	HOGGINGS
	HOGH	HOGHS
	HOGHOOD	HOGHOODS

FRONT HOOK	ROOT WORD	END HOOK
	HOGMANAY	HOGMANAYS
	HOGMANE	HOGMANES
	HOGMENAY	HOGMENAYS
	HOGNOSE	HOGNOSED ▪ HOGNOSES
	HOGNUT	HOGNUTS
CHOGS ▪ SHOGS	**HOGS**	
	HOGSHEAD	HOGSHEADS
	HOGTIE	HOGTIED ▪ HOGTIES
	HOGWARD	HOGWARDS
	HOGWEED	HOGWEEDS
PHOH	**HOH**	HOHA ▪ HOHS
PHOHS	**HOHS**	
	HOI	HOIK
	HOICK	HOICKS
	HOIDEN	HOIDENS
	HOIK	HOIKS
	HOISE	HOISED ▪ HOISES
	HOISIN	HOISING ▪ HOISINS
	HOIST	HOISTS
	HOISTER	HOISTERS
	HOISTING	HOISTINGS
	HOISTWAY	HOISTWAYS
CHOKE	**HOKE**	HOKED ▪ HOKES ▪ HOKEY
CHOKED	**HOKED**	
CHOKES	**HOKES**	
CHOKEY	**HOKEY**	
	HOKI	HOKIS
CHOKIER	**HOKIER**	
CHOKIEST	**HOKIEST**	
CHOKING	**HOKING**	
	HOKONUI	HOKONUIS
	HOKUM	HOKUMS
	HOLARD	HOLARDS
AHOLD	**HOLD**	HOLDS
	HOLDALL	HOLDALLS
	HOLDBACK	HOLDBACKS
	HOLDDOWN	HOLDDOWNS
	HOLDER	HOLDERS
	HOLDERBAT	HOLDERBATS
	HOLDFAST	HOLDFASTS
	HOLDING	HOLDINGS
	HOLDOUT	HOLDOUTS
	HOLDOVER	HOLDOVERS
AHOLDS	**HOLDS**	
	HOLDUP	HOLDUPS
DHOLE ▪ THOLE ▪ WHOLE	**HOLE**	HOLED ▪ HOLES ▪ HOLEY
THOLED	**HOLED**	
DHOLES ▪ THOLES ▪ WHOLES	**HOLES**	
	HOLESOM	HOLESOME
WHOLESOME	**HOLESOME**	
	HOLIBUT	HOLIBUTS
	HOLIDAY	HOLIDAYS
	HOLIDAYER	HOLIDAYERS
	HOLIES	HOLIEST
THOLING	**HOLING**	HOLINGS
WHOLISM	**HOLISM**	HOLISMS
WHOLISMS	**HOLISMS**	
WHOLIST	**HOLIST**	HOLISTS
WHOLISTIC	**HOLISTIC**	
WHOLISTS	**HOLISTS**	
	HOLK	HOLKS
CHOLLA	**HOLLA**	HOLLAS
	HOLLAND	HOLLANDS
CHOLLAS	**HOLLAS**	
	HOLLER	HOLLERS
CHOLLERS	**HOLLERS**	
	HOLLIDAM	HOLLIDAMS
	HOLLO	HOLLOA ▪ HOLLOO ▪ HOLLOS ▪ HOLLOW
	HOLLOA	HOLLOAS

FRONT HOOK	ROOT WORD	END HOOK
	HOLLOO	HOLLOOS
	HOLLOW	HOLLOWS
	HOLLOWARE	HOLLOWARES
WHOLLY	**HOLLY**	
	HOLLYHOCK	HOLLYHOCKS
	HOLM	HOLMS
	HOLMIA	HOLMIAS
	HOLMIUM	HOLMIUMS
	HOLOCAUST	HOLOCAUSTS
	HOLOGRAM	HOLOGRAMS
	HOLOGRAPH	HOLOGRAPHS ▪ HOLOGRAPHY
	HOLOHEDRA	HOLOHEDRAL
	HOLON	HOLONS
	HOLOPHOTE	HOLOPHOTES
	HOLOPHYTE	HOLOPHYTES
	HOLOTYPE	HOLOTYPES
DHOLS	**HOLS**	
	HOLSTEIN	HOLSTEINS
	HOLSTER	HOLSTERS
	HOLT	HOLTS
	HOLYDAM	HOLYDAME ▪ HOLYDAMS
	HOLYDAME	HOLYDAMES
	HOLYDAY	HOLYDAYS
	HOLYSTONE	HOLYSTONED ▪ HOLYSTONES
	HOLYTIDE	HOLYTIDES
WHOM	**HOM**	HOMA ▪ HOME ▪ HOMO ▪ HOMS ▪ HOMY
	HOMA	HOMAS
	HOMAGE	HOMAGED ▪ HOMAGER ▪ HOMAGES
	HOMAGER	HOMAGERS
	HOMALOID	HOMALOIDS
	HOMBRE	HOMBRES
	HOMBURG	HOMBURGS
	HOME	HOMED ▪ HOMER ▪ HOMES ▪ HOMEY
	HOMEBIRTH	HOMEBIRTHS
	HOMEBOY	HOMEBOYS
	HOMEBRED	HOMEBREDS
	HOMEBREW	HOMEBREWS
	HOMEBUYER	HOMEBUYERS
	HOMECOMER	HOMECOMERS
	HOMECRAFT	HOMECRAFTS
	HOMEGIRL	HOMEGIRLS
	HOMELAND	HOMELANDS
	HOMELY	HOMELYN
	HOMELYN	HOMELYNS
	HOMEMAKER	HOMEMAKERS
	HOMEOPATH	HOMEOPATHS ▪ HOMEOPATHY
	HOMEOWNER	HOMEOWNERS
	HOMEPAGE	HOMEPAGES
	HOMEPLACE	HOMEPLACES
	HOMEPORT	HOMEPORTS
	HOMER	HOMERS
	HOMEROOM	HOMEROOMS
	HOMESITE	HOMESITES
	HOMESPUN	HOMESPUNS
	HOMESTALL	HOMESTALLS
	HOMESTAND	HOMESTANDS
	HOMESTAY	HOMESTAYS
	HOMESTEAD	HOMESTEADS
	HOMETOWN	HOMETOWNS
	HOMEWARD	HOMEWARDS
	HOMEWARE	HOMEWARES
	HOMEWORK	HOMEWORKS
	HOMEY	HOMEYS
	HOMICIDE	HOMICIDES
	HOMIE	HOMIER ▪ HOMIES
	HOMIES	HOMIEST
	HOMILETIC	HOMILETICS
	HOMILIST	HOMILISTS
	HOMINES	HOMINESS

H

FRONT HOOK	ROOT WORD	END HOOK
	HOMING	HOMINGS
	HOMINIAN	HOMINIANS
	HOMINID	HOMINIDS
	HOMINISE	HOMINISED ▪ HOMINISES
	HOMINIZE	HOMINIZED ▪ HOMINIZES
	HOMINOID	HOMINOIDS
	HOMME	HOMMES
	HOMMOCK	HOMMOCKS
ZHOMO	**HOMO**	HOMOS
	HOMOGRAFT	HOMOGRAFTS
	HOMOGRAPH	HOMOGRAPHS
	HOMOLOG	HOMOLOGS ▪ HOMOLOGY
	HOMOLOGUE	HOMOLOGUES
	HOMOMORPH	HOMOMORPHS ▪ HOMOMORPHY
	HOMONYM	HOMONYMS ▪ HOMONYMY
	HOMOPHILE	HOMOPHILES
	HOMOPHOBE	HOMOPHOBES
	HOMOPHONE	HOMOPHONES
ZHOMOS	**HOMOS**	
	HOMOTYPE	HOMOTYPES
	HOMOUSIAN	HOMOUSIANS
	HOMUNCLE	HOMUNCLES
	HOMUNCULE	HOMUNCULES
CHON ▪ PHON ▪ THON	**HON**	HOND ▪ HONE ▪ HONG ▪ HONK ▪ HONS
	HONAN	HONANS
	HONCHO	HONCHOS
	HOND	HONDA ▪ HONDS
	HONDA	HONDAS
	HONDLE	HONDLED ▪ HONDLES
OHONE ▪ PHONE ▪ RHONE ▪ SHONE	**HONE**	HONED ▪ HONER ▪ HONES ▪ HONEY
PHONED	**HONED**	
PHONER	**HONER**	HONERS
PHONERS	**HONERS**	
PHONES ▪ RHONES	**HONES**	HONEST
	HONEST	HONESTY
	HONEWORT	HONEWORTS
PHONEY	**HONEY**	HONEYS
	HONEYBEE	HONEYBEES
	HONEYBUN	HONEYBUNS
	HONEYCOMB	HONEYCOMBS
	HONEYDEW	HONEYDEWS
PHONEYED	**HONEYED**	
PHONEYING	**HONEYING**	
	HONEYMOON	HONEYMOONS
	HONEYPOT	HONEYPOTS
PHONEYS	**HONEYS**	
	HONEYTRAP	HONEYTRAPS
THONG	**HONG**	HONGI ▪ HONGS
	HONGI	HONGIS
THONGS	**HONGS**	
PHONIED	**HONIED**	
PHONING	**HONING**	
	HONK	HONKS ▪ HONKY
	HONKER	HONKERS
	HONKEY	HONKEYS (*offensive*)
	HONKIE	HONKIES (*offensive*)
SHONKY	**HONKY**	
	HONOR	HONORS
	HONORAND	HONORANDS
	HONOREE	HONOREES
	HONORER	HONORERS
	HONORIFIC	HONORIFICS
	HONOUR	HONOURS
	HONOURER	HONOURERS
CHONS ▪ PHONS	**HONS**	
SHOO	**HOO**	HOOD ▪ HOOF ▪ HOOK ▪ HOON ▪ HOOP ▪ HOOT
	HOOCHIE	HOOCHIES
	HOOD	HOODS ▪ HOODY
	HOODIA	HOODIAS

FRONT HOOK	ROOT WORD	END HOOK
	HOODIE	HOODIER ▪ HOODIES
	HOODIES	HOODIEST
	HOODLUM	HOODLUMS
	HOODMOLD	HOODMOLDS
	HOODOO	HOODOOS
	HOODOOISM	HOODOOISMS
	HOODWINK	HOODWINKS
PHOOEY	**HOOEY**	HOOEYS
CHOOF ▪ WHOOF	**HOOF**	HOOFS
	HOOFBEAT	HOOFBEATS
CHOOFED ▪ WHOOFED	**HOOFED**	
	HOOFER	HOOFERS
CHOOFING ▪ WHOOFING	**HOOFING**	
	HOOFPRINT	HOOFPRINTS
	HOOFROT	HOOFROTS
CHOOFS ▪ WHOOFS	**HOOFS**	
CHOOK ▪ SHOOK	**HOOK**	HOOKA ▪ HOOKS ▪ HOOKY
	HOOKA	HOOKAH ▪ HOOKAS
	HOOKAH	HOOKAHS
	HOOKCHECK	HOOKCHECKS
CHOOKED	**HOOKED**	
	HOOKER	HOOKERS
	HOOKEY	HOOKEYS
CHOOKIES	**HOOKIES**	HOOKIEST
CHOOKING	**HOOKING**	
	HOOKLET	HOOKLETS
	HOOKNOSE	HOOKNOSED ▪ HOOKNOSES
CHOOKS ▪ SHOOKS	**HOOKS**	
	HOOKUP	HOOKUPS
	HOOKWORM	HOOKWORMS
	HOOLACHAN	HOOLACHANS
	HOOLEY	HOOLEYS
	HOOLICAN	HOOLICANS
	HOOLIE	HOOLIER ▪ HOOLIES
DHOOLIES	**HOOLIES**	HOOLIEST
	HOOLIGAN	HOOLIGANS
	HOOLOCK	HOOLOCKS
DHOOLY	**HOOLY**	
SHOON	**HOON**	HOONS
WHOOP	**HOOP**	HOOPS
WHOOPED	**HOOPED**	
WHOOPER	**HOOPER**	
WHOOPERS	**HOOPERS**	HOOPERS
WHOOPING	**HOOPING**	
WHOOPLA	**HOOPLA**	HOOPLAS
WHOOPLAS	**HOOPLAS**	
	HOOPOE	HOOPOES
	HOOPOO	HOOPOOS
WHOOPS	**HOOPS**	
	HOOPSKIRT	HOOPSKIRTS
	HOOPSTER	HOOPSTERS
	HOORAH	HOORAHS
	HOORAY	HOORAYS
	HOORD	HOORDS
	HOOSEGOW	HOOSEGOWS
	HOOSGOW	HOOSGOWS
WHOOSH	**HOOSH**	
WHOOSHED	**HOOSHED**	
WHOOSHES	**HOOSHES**	
WHOOSHING	**HOOSHING**	
BHOOT ▪ SHOOT ▪ WHOOT	**HOOT**	HOOTS ▪ HOOTY
WHOOTED	**HOOTED**	
SHOOTER	**HOOTER**	HOOTERS
SHOOTERS	**HOOTERS**	
SHOOTING ▪ WHOOTING	**HOOTING**	
BHOOTS ▪ SHOOTS ▪ WHOOTS	**HOOTS**	
	HOOVE	HOOVED ▪ HOOVEN ▪ HOOVER ▪ HOOVES
	HOOVER	HOOVERS
CHOP ▪ SHOP ▪ WHOP	**HOP**	HOPE ▪ HOPS

FRONT HOOK	ROOT WORD	END HOOK
	HOPBIND	HOPBINDS
	HOPBINE	HOPBINES
	HOPDOG	HOPDOGS
SHOPE	HOPE	HOPED · HOPER · HOPES
	HOPEFUL	HOPEFULS
	HOPER	HOPERS
	HOPHEAD	HOPHEADS
	HOPLITE	HOPLITES
CHOPPED · SHOPPED · WHOPPED	HOPPED	
CHOPPER · SHOPPER · WHOPPER	HOPPER	HOPPERS
	HOPPERCAR	HOPPERCARS
CHOPPERS · SHOPPERS · WHOPPERS	HOPPERS	
CHOPPIER · SHOPPIER	HOPPIER	
CHOPPIEST · SHOPPIEST	HOPPIEST	
CHOPPING · SHOPPING · WHOPPING	HOPPING	HOPPINGS
CHOPPINGS · SHOPPINGS · WHOPPINGS	HOPPINGS	
	HOPPLE	HOPPLED · HOPPLER · HOPPLES
	HOPPLER	HOPPLERS
CHOPPY · SHOPPY	HOPPY	
CHOPS · SHOPS · WHOPS	HOPS	
	HOPSACK	HOPSACKS
	HOPTOAD	HOPTOADS
	HORA	HORAH · HORAL · HORAS
	HORAH	HORAHS
CHORAL	HORAL	
	HORDE	HORDED · HORDES
CHORDED	HORDED	
	HORDEIN	HORDEINS
CHORDING	HORDING	
	HORDOCK	HORDOCKS
CHORE · SHORE · WHORE	HORE	
	HOREHOUND	HOREHOUNDS
	HORI	HORIS (offensive)
	HORIATIKI	HORIATIKIS
	HORIZON	HORIZONS
	HORKEY	HORKEYS
	HORME	HORMES
	HORMONE	HORMONES
SHORN · THORN	HORN	HORNS · HORNY
	HORNBAG	HORNBAGS (offensive)
	HORNBEAK	HORNBEAKS
	HORNBEAM	HORNBEAMS
THORNBILL	HORNBILL	HORNBILLS
THORNBILLS	HORNBILLS	
	HORNBOOK	HORNBOOKS
	HORNBUG	HORNBUGS
THORNED	HORNED	
	HORNER	HORNERS
	HORNET	HORNETS
	HORNFUL	HORNFULS
	HORNGELD	HORNGELDS
THORNIER	HORNIER	
THORNIEST	HORNIEST	
THORNILY	HORNILY	
THORNINESS	HORNINESS	
THORNING	HORNING	HORNINGS
	HORNIST	HORNISTS
	HORNITO	HORNITOS
THORNLESS	HORNLESS	
	HORNLET	HORNLETS
THORNLIKE	HORNLIKE	
	HORNPIPE	HORNPIPES
	HORNPOUT	HORNPOUTS
THORNS	HORNS	
	HORNSTONE	HORNSTONES
	HORNTAIL	HORNTAILS
	HORNWORK	HORNWORKS
	HORNWORM	HORNWORMS
	HORNWORT	HORNWORTS

FRONT HOOK	ROOT WORD	END HOOK
	HORNWRACK	HORNWRACKS
THORNY	**HORNY**	
	HORNYHEAD	HORNYHEADS
	HORNYWINK	HORNYWINKS
	HOROLOGE	HOROLOGER ▪ HOROLOGES
	HOROLOGER	HOROLOGERS
CHOROLOGY	**HOROLOGY**	
	HOROPITO	HOROPITOS
	HOROPTER	HOROPTERS
	HOROSCOPE	HOROSCOPES
	HORRIBLE	HORRIBLES
	HORROR	HORRORS
KHORS	**HORS**	HORSE ▪ HORST ▪ HORSY
AHORSE	**HORSE**	HORSED ▪ HORSES ▪ HORSEY
AHORSEBACK	**HORSEBACK**	HORSEBACKS
	HORSEBEAN	HORSEBEANS
	HORSECAR	HORSECARS
	HORSEHAIR	HORSEHAIRS
	HORSEHIDE	HORSEHIDES
	HORSEMEAT	HORSEMEATS
	HORSEMINT	HORSEMINTS
	HORSEPLAY	HORSEPLAYS
	HORSEPOND	HORSEPONDS
	HORSERACE	HORSERACES
	HORSESHIT	HORSESHITS
	HORSESHOE	HORSESHOED ▪ HORSESHOER ▪ HORSESHOES
	HORSETAIL	HORSETAILS
	HORSEWAY	HORSEWAYS
	HORSEWEED	HORSEWEEDS
	HORSEWHIP	HORSEWHIPS
	HORSING	HORSINGS
	HORSON	HORSONS
	HORST	HORSTE ▪ HORSTS
	HORSTE	HORSTES
	HORTATION	HORTATIONS
MHOS ▪ OHOS ▪ PHOS ▪ RHOS ▪ ZHOS	**HOS**	HOSE ▪ HOSS ▪ HOST
	HOSANNA	HOSANNAH ▪ HOSANNAS
	HOSANNAH	HOSANNAHS
CHOSE ▪ THOSE ▪ WHOSE	**HOSE**	HOSED ▪ HOSEL ▪ HOSEN ▪ HOSER ▪ HOSES ▪ HOSEY
	HOSEL	HOSELS
CHOSEN	**HOSEN**	
	HOSEPIPE	HOSEPIPES
	HOSER	HOSERS
CHOSES	**HOSES**	
	HOSEY	HOSEYS
	HOSIER	HOSIERS ▪ HOSIERY
	HOSPICE	HOSPICES
	HOSPITAGE	HOSPITAGES
	HOSPITAL	HOSPITALE ▪ HOSPITALS
	HOSPITALE	HOSPITALER ▪ HOSPITALES
	HOSPODAR	HOSPODARS
GHOST	**HOST**	HOSTA ▪ HOSTS
	HOSTA	HOSTAS
	HOSTAGE	HOSTAGES
GHOSTED	**HOSTED**	
	HOSTEL	HOSTELS
	HOSTELER	HOSTELERS
	HOSTELLER	HOSTELLERS
	HOSTIE	HOSTIES
	HOSTILE	HOSTILES
GHOSTING	**HOSTING**	HOSTINGS
GHOSTINGS	**HOSTINGS**	
	HOSTLER	HOSTLERS
GHOSTLY	**HOSTLY**	
GHOSTS	**HOSTS**	
PHOT ▪ SHOT ▪ WHOT	**HOT**	HOTE ▪ HOTS
	HOTBED	HOTBEDS
	HOTBLOOD	HOTBLOODS

FRONT HOOK	ROOT WORD	END HOOK
	HOTCAKE	HOTCAKES
	HOTCHPOT	HOTCHPOTS
	HOTDOG	HOTDOGS
	HOTDOGGER	HOTDOGGERS
SHOTE	HOTE	HOTEL · HOTEN
	HOTEL	HOTELS
	HOTELDOM	HOTELDOMS
	HOTELIER	HOTELIERS
	HOTFOOT	HOTFOOTS
	HOTHEAD	HOTHEADS
	HOTHOUSE	HOTHOUSED · HOTHOUSES
	HOTLINE	HOTLINES
	HOTLINK	HOTLINKS
	HOTPLATE	HOTPLATES
	HOTPOT	HOTPOTS
	HOTROD	HOTRODS
PHOTS · SHOTS	HOTS	
	HOTSHOT	HOTSHOTS
	HOTSPOT	HOTSPOTS
	HOTSPUR	HOTSPURS
SHOTTED	HOTTED	
	HOTTENTOT	HOTTENTOTS
	HOTTER	HOTTERS
	HOTTIE	HOTTIES
SHOTTING	HOTTING	HOTTINGS
	HOUDAH	HOUDAHS
	HOUDAN	HOUDANS
	HOUF	HOUFF · HOUFS
	HOUFF	HOUFFS
CHOUGH · SHOUGH · THOUGH	HOUGH	HOUGHS
CHOUGHS · SHOUGHS	HOUGHS	
	HOUND	HOUNDS
	HOUNDER	HOUNDERS
	HOUNGAN	HOUNGANS
	HOUR	HOURI · HOURS
	HOURI	HOURIS
	HOURPLATE	HOURPLATES
CHOUSE · SHOUSE	HOUSE	HOUSED · HOUSEL · HOUSER · HOUSES HOUSEY
	HOUSEBOAT	HOUSEBOATS
	HOUSEBOY	HOUSEBOYS
	HOUSECARL	HOUSECARLS
	HOUSECOAT	HOUSECOATS
CHOUSED	HOUSED	
	HOUSEFUL	HOUSEFULS
	HOUSEHOLD	HOUSEHOLDS
	HOUSEKEEP	HOUSEKEEPS
	HOUSEL	HOUSELS
	HOUSELEEK	HOUSELEEKS
	HOUSELINE	HOUSELINES
	HOUSEMAID	HOUSEMAIDS
	HOUSEMATE	HOUSEMATES
CHOUSER	HOUSER	HOUSERS
	HOUSEROOM	HOUSEROOMS
CHOUSERS	HOUSERS	
CHOUSES · SHOUSES	HOUSES	
	HOUSESIT	HOUSESITS
	HOUSETOP	HOUSETOPS
	HOUSEWIFE	HOUSEWIFEY
	HOUSEWORK	HOUSEWORKS
CHOUSING	HOUSING	HOUSINGS
	HOUSTONIA	HOUSTONIAS
CHOUT · SHOUT	HOUT	HOUTS
SHOUTED	HOUTED	
SHOUTING	HOUTING	HOUTINGS
SHOUTINGS	HOUTINGS	
CHOUTS · SHOUTS	HOUTS	
SHOVE	HOVE	HOVEA · HOVED · HOVEL · HOVEN · HOVER HOVES

383

FRONT HOOK	ROOT WORD	END HOOK
	HOVEA	HOVEAS
SHOVED	**HOVED**	
SHOVEL	**HOVEL**	HOVELS
SHOVELED	**HOVELED**	
SHOVELING	**HOVELING**	
SHOVELLED	**HOVELLED**	
SHOVELLER	**HOVELLER**	HOVELLERS
SHOVELLERS	**HOVELLERS**	
SHOVELLING	**HOVELLING**	
SHOVELS	**HOVELS**	
SHOVER	**HOVER**	HOVERS
	HOVERER	HOVERERS
	HOVERPORT	HOVERPORTS
SHOVERS	**HOVERS**	
SHOVES	**HOVES**	
SHOVING	**HOVING**	
CHOW ▪ DHOW ▪ SHOW ▪ WHOW	**HOW**	HOWE ▪ HOWF ▪ HOWK ▪ HOWL ▪ HOWS
	HOWDAH	HOWDAHS
	HOWDIE	HOWDIED ▪ HOWDIES
	HOWE	HOWES
	HOWF	HOWFF ▪ HOWFS
	HOWFF	HOWFFS
	HOWITZER	HOWITZERS
CHOWK	**HOWK**	HOWKS
	HOWKER	HOWKERS
CHOWKS	**HOWKS**	
THOWL	**HOWL**	HOWLS
	HOWLBACK	HOWLBACKS
	HOWLER	HOWLERS
	HOWLET	HOWLETS
	HOWLING	HOWLINGS
	HOWLROUND	HOWLROUNDS
THOWLS	**HOWLS**	
	HOWRE	HOWRES
CHOWS ▪ DHOWS ▪ SHOWS	**HOWS**	HOWSO
	HOWTOWDIE	HOWTOWDIES
AHOY	**HOY**	HOYA ▪ HOYS
	HOYA	HOYAS
	HOYDEN	HOYDENS
	HOYDENISM	HOYDENISMS
	HOYLE	HOYLES
	HRYVNA	HRYVNAS
	HRYVNIA	HRYVNIAS
	HRYVNYA	HRYVNYAS
	HUANACO	HUANACOS
	HUAQUERO	HUAQUEROS
	HUARACHE	HUARACHES
	HUARACHO	HUARACHOS
CHUB	**HUB**	HUBS
	HUBBUB	HUBBUBS
	HUBBUBOO	HUBBUBOOS
CHUBBY	**HUBBY**	
	HUBCAP	HUBCAPS
CHUBS	**HUBS**	
CHUCK ▪ SHUCK	**HUCK**	HUCKS
	HUCKABACK	HUCKABACKS
CHUCKLE	**HUCKLE**	HUCKLES
CHUCKLES	**HUCKLES**	
CHUCKS ▪ SHUCKS	**HUCKS**	
	HUCKSTER	HUCKSTERS ▪ HUCKSTERY
	HUDDLE	HUDDLED ▪ HUDDLER ▪ HUDDLES
	HUDDLER	HUDDLERS
	HUDNA	HUDNAS
	HUDUD	HUDUDS
	HUE	HUED ▪ HUER ▪ HUES
	HUER	HUERS
CHUFF	**HUFF**	HUFFS ▪ HUFFY
CHUFFED	**HUFFED**	
CHUFFER	**HUFFER**	HUFFERS

FRONT HOOK	ROOT WORD	END HOOK
CHUFFIER	**HUFFIER**	
CHUFFIEST	**HUFFIEST**	
CHUFFINESS	**HUFFINESS**	
CHUFFING	**HUFFING**	HUFFINGS
	HUFFKIN	HUFFKINS
CHUFFS	**HUFFS**	
CHUFFY	**HUFFY**	
CHUG ▪ THUG	**HUG**	HUGE ▪ HUGS ▪ HUGY
	HUGE	HUGER
CHUGGED	**HUGGED**	
CHUGGER	**HUGGER**	HUGGERS
CHUGGERS	**HUGGERS**	
CHUGGING	**HUGGING**	
SHUGGY	**HUGGY**	
CHUGS ▪ THUGS	**HUGS**	
	HUH	HUHU
	HUHU	HUHUS
	HUI	HUIA ▪ HUIC ▪ HUIS
	HUIA	HUIAS
	HUIPIL	HUIPILS
	HUISACHE	HUISACHES
	HUISSIER	HUISSIERS
	HUITAIN	HUITAINS
	HULA	HULAS
SHULE	**HULE**	HULES
SHULES	**HULES**	
	HULK	HULKS ▪ HULKY
AHULL	**HULL**	HULLO ▪ HULLS ▪ HULLY
	HULLER	HULLERS
	HULLO	HULLOA ▪ HULLOO ▪ HULLOS
	HULLOA	HULLOAS
	HULLOO	HULLOOS
CHUM	**HUM**	HUMA ▪ HUMF ▪ HUMP ▪ HUMS
	HUMA	HUMAN ▪ HUMAS
	HUMAN	HUMANE ▪ HUMANS
	HUMANE	HUMANER
	HUMANHOOD	HUMANHOODS
	HUMANISE	HUMANISED ▪ HUMANISER ▪ HUMANISES
	HUMANISER	HUMANISERS
	HUMANISM	HUMANISMS
	HUMANIST	HUMANISTS
	HUMANIZE	HUMANIZED ▪ HUMANIZER ▪ HUMANIZES
	HUMANIZER	HUMANIZERS
	HUMANKIND	HUMANKINDS
	HUMANOID	HUMANOIDS
	HUMATE	HUMATES
	HUMBLE	HUMBLED ▪ HUMBLER ▪ HUMBLES
	HUMBLEBEE	HUMBLEBEES
	HUMBLER	HUMBLERS
	HUMBLES	HUMBLEST
	HUMBLESSE	HUMBLESSES
THUMBLING	**HUMBLING**	HUMBLINGS
THUMBLINGS	**HUMBLINGS**	
	HUMBUCKER	HUMBUCKERS
	HUMBUG	HUMBUGS
	HUMBUGGER	HUMBUGGERS ▪ HUMBUGGERY
	HUMDINGER	HUMDINGERS
	HUMDRUM	HUMDRUMS
	HUMECT	HUMECTS
	HUMECTANT	HUMECTANTS
	HUMECTATE	HUMECTATED ▪ HUMECTATES
	HUMECTIVE	HUMECTIVES
	HUMERAL	HUMERALS
	HUMF	HUMFS
	HUMHUM	HUMHUMS
	HUMICOLE	HUMICOLES
	HUMIDOR	HUMIDORS
	HUMILIATE	HUMILIATED ▪ HUMILIATES
	HUMINT	HUMINTS

FRONT HOOK	ROOT WORD	END HOOK
	HUMITE	HUMITES
	HUMITURE	HUMITURES
	HUMLIE	HUMLIES
	HUMMAUM	HUMMAUMS
CHUMMED	**HUMMED**	
	HUMMEL	HUMMELS
	HUMMELLER	HUMMELLERS
	HUMMER	HUMMERS
CHUMMING	**HUMMING**	HUMMINGS
	HUMMOCK	HUMMOCKS · HUMMOCKY
	HUMMUM	HUMMUMS
	HUMOGEN	HUMOGENS
	HUMOR	HUMORS
	HUMORESK	HUMORESKS
	HUMORIST	HUMORISTS
	HUMOUR	HUMOURS
CHUMP · THUMP · WHUMP	**HUMP**	HUMPH · HUMPS · HUMPY
	HUMPBACK	HUMPBACKS
CHUMPED · THUMPED · WHUMPED	**HUMPED**	
	HUMPEN	HUMPENS
THUMPER	**HUMPER**	HUMPERS
THUMPERS	**HUMPERS**	
	HUMPH	HUMPHS
	HUMPIES	HUMPIEST
CHUMPING · THUMPING · WHUMPING	**HUMPING**	
CHUMPS · THUMPS · WHUMPS	**HUMPS**	
CHUMS	**HUMS**	
	HUMSTRUM	HUMSTRUMS
	HUMUS	HUMUSY
	HUMVEE	HUMVEES
SHUN	**HUN**	HUNG · HUNH · HUNK · HUNS · HUNT
	HUNCHBACK	HUNCHBACKS
	HUNDRED	HUNDREDS
	HUNDREDER	HUNDREDERS
	HUNDREDOR	HUNDREDORS
	HUNDREDTH	HUNDREDTHS
	HUNGAN	HUNGANS
	HUNGER	HUNGERS
AHUNGERED	**HUNGERED**	
AHUNGRY	**HUNGRY**	
CHUNK · THUNK	**HUNK**	HUNKS · HUNKY
	HUNKER	HUNKERS
	HUNKEY	HUNKEYS
	HUNKIE	HUNKIER · HUNKIES (offensive)
CHUNKIER	**HUNKIER**	
	HUNKIES	HUNKIEST
CHUNKIEST	**HUNKIEST**	
CHUNKS · THUNKS	**HUNKS**	
CHUNKY	**HUNKY**	
SHUNS	**HUNS**	
SHUNT	**HUNT**	HUNTS
	HUNTAWAY	HUNTAWAYS
SHUNTED	**HUNTED**	
CHUNTER · SHUNTER	**HUNTER**	HUNTERS
CHUNTERS · SHUNTERS	**HUNTERS**	
SHUNTING	**HUNTING**	HUNTINGS
SHUNTINGS	**HUNTINGS**	
SHUNTS	**HUNTS**	
WHUP	**HUP**	HUPS
CHUPPAH	**HUPPAH**	HUPPAHS
CHUPPAHS	**HUPPAHS**	
WHUPPED	**HUPPED**	
WHUPPING	**HUPPING**	
WHUPS	**HUPS**	
	HURCHEON	HURCHEONS
	HURDEN	HURDENS
	HURDLE	HURDLED · HURDLER · HURDLES
	HURDLER	HURDLERS
	HURDLING	HURDLINGS

FRONT HOOK	ROOT WORD	END HOOK
CHURL · THURL	**HURL**	HURLS · HURLY
	HURLBAT	HURLBATS
	HURLER	HURLERS
	HURLEY	HURLEYS
	HURLING	HURLINGS
CHURLS · THURLS	**HURLS**	
DHURRA	**HURRA**	HURRAH · HURRAS · HURRAY
	HURRAH	HURRAHS
DHURRAS	**HURRAS**	
	HURRAY	HURRAYS
	HURRICANE	HURRICANES
	HURRIER	HURRIERS
DHURRIES	**HURRIES**	
	HURRYING	HURRYINGS
	HURST	HURSTS
	HURT	HURTS
	HURTER	HURTERS
	HURTLE	HURTLED · HURTLES
	HURTLES	HURTLESS
	HUSBAND	HUSBANDS
	HUSBANDER	HUSBANDERS
SHUSH	**HUSH**	HUSHY
SHUSHED	**HUSHED**	
SHUSHER	**HUSHER**	HUSHERS
SHUSHERS	**HUSHERS**	
SHUSHES	**HUSHES**	
SHUSHING	**HUSHING**	
	HUSK	HUSKS · HUSKY
	HUSKER	HUSKERS
	HUSKIES	HUSKIEST
	HUSKING	HUSKINGS
	HUSO	HUSOS
	HUSS	HUSSY
	HUSSAR	HUSSARS
	HUSSIF	HUSSIFS
	HUSTLE	HUSTLED · HUSTLER · HUSTLES
	HUSTLER	HUSTLERS
	HUSTLING	HUSTLINGS
	HUSWIFE	HUSWIFES
BHUT · CHUT · PHUT · SHUT	**HUT**	HUTS
	HUTCHIE	HUTCHIES
	HUTIA	HUTIAS
	HUTMENT	HUTMENTS
BHUTS · PHUTS · SHUTS	**HUTS**	
PHUTTED	**HUTTED**	
PHUTTING · SHUTTING	**HUTTING**	HUTTINGS
CHUTZPA	**HUTZPA**	HUTZPAH · HUTZPAS
CHUTZPAH	**HUTZPAH**	HUTZPAHS
CHUTZPAHS	**HUTZPAHS**	
CHUTZPAS	**HUTZPAS**	
	HUZOOR	HUZOORS
	HUZZA	HUZZAH · HUZZAS
	HUZZAH	HUZZAHS
	HWYL	HWYLS
	HYACINE	HYACINES
	HYACINTH	HYACINTHS
	HYAENA	HYAENAS
	HYALIN	HYALINE · HYALINS
	HYALINE	HYALINES
	HYALINISE	HYALINISED · HYALINISES
	HYALINIZE	HYALINIZED · HYALINIZES
	HYALITE	HYALITES
	HYALOGEN	HYALOGENS
	HYALOID	HYALOIDS
	HYALONEMA	HYALONEMAS
	HYBRID	HYBRIDS
	HYBRIDISE	HYBRIDISED · HYBRIDISER · HYBRIDISES
	HYBRIDISM	HYBRIDISMS
	HYBRIDIST	HYBRIDISTS

FRONT HOOK	ROOT WORD	END HOOK
	HYBRIDIZE	HYBRIDIZED ▪ HYBRIDIZER ▪ HYBRIDIZES
	HYBRIDOMA	HYBRIDOMAS
	HYDANTOIN	HYDANTOINS
	HYDATHODE	HYDATHODES
	HYDATID	HYDATIDS
	HYDRA	HYDRAE ▪ HYDRAS
	HYDRACID	HYDRACIDS
	HYDRAEMIA	HYDRAEMIAS
	HYDRAGOG	HYDRAGOGS
	HYDRANGEA	HYDRANGEAS
	HYDRANT	HYDRANTH ▪ HYDRANTS
	HYDRANTH	HYDRANTHS
	HYDRAS	HYDRASE
	HYDRASE	HYDRASES
	HYDRATE	HYDRATED ▪ HYDRATES
	HYDRATION	HYDRATIONS
	HYDRATOR	HYDRATORS
	HYDRAULIC	HYDRAULICS
	HYDRAZIDE	HYDRAZIDES
	HYDRAZINE	HYDRAZINES
	HYDREMIA	HYDREMIAS
	HYDRIA	HYDRIAE
	HYDRID	HYDRIDE ▪ HYDRIDS
	HYDRIDE	HYDRIDES
	HYDRILLA	HYDRILLAS
	HYDRO	HYDROS
	HYDROCAST	HYDROCASTS
	HYDROCELE	HYDROCELES
	HYDROFOIL	HYDROFOILS
	HYDROGEL	HYDROGELS
	HYDROGEN	HYDROGENS
	HYDROID	HYDROIDS
	HYDROLASE	HYDROLASES
	HYDROLYSE	HYDROLYSED ▪ HYDROLYSER ▪ HYDROLYSES
	HYDROLYTE	HYDROLYTES
	HYDROLYZE	HYDROLYZED ▪ HYDROLYZER ▪ HYDROLYZES
	HYDROMA	HYDROMAS
	HYDROMEL	HYDROMELS
	HYDRONAUT	HYDRONAUTS
	HYDRONIUM	HYDRONIUMS
	HYDROPATH	HYDROPATHS ▪ HYDROPATHY
	HYDROPS	HYDROPSY
	HYDROPULT	HYDROPULTS
	HYDROSERE	HYDROSERES
	HYDROSKI	HYDROSKIS
	HYDROSOL	HYDROSOLS
	HYDROSOMA	HYDROSOMAL
	HYDROSOME	HYDROSOMES
	HYDROSTAT	HYDROSTATS
	HYDROVANE	HYDROVANES
	HYDROXIDE	HYDROXIDES
	HYDROXY	HYDROXYL
	HYDROXYL	HYDROXYLS
	HYDROZOA	HYDROZOAN
	HYDROZOAN	HYDROZOANS
	HYDYNE	HYDYNES
	HYE	HYED ▪ HYEN ▪ HYES
	HYEN	HYENA ▪ HYENS
	HYENA	HYENAS
	HYGEIST	HYGEISTS
	HYGIEIST	HYGIEISTS
	HYGIENE	HYGIENES
	HYGIENIC	HYGIENICS
	HYGIENIST	HYGIENISTS
	HYGRISTOR	HYGRISTORS
	HYGRODEIK	HYGRODEIKS
	HYGROMA	HYGROMAS
	HYGROPHIL	HYGROPHILE
	HYGROSTAT	HYGROSTATS

FRONT HOOK	ROOT WORD	END HOOK
SHYING	**HYING**	
	HYKE	HYKES
PHYLA	**HYLA**	HYLAS
	HYLDING	HYLDINGS
CHYLE · PHYLE	**HYLE**	HYLEG · HYLES
	HYLEG	HYLEGS
CHYLES	**HYLES**	
PHYLIC	**HYLIC**	
	HYLICISM	HYLICISMS
	HYLICIST	HYLICISTS
	HYLISM	HYLISMS
	HYLIST	HYLISTS
	HYLOBATE	HYLOBATES
	HYLOIST	HYLOISTS
	HYLOPHYTE	HYLOPHYTES
	HYLOZOISM	HYLOZOISMS
	HYLOZOIST	HYLOZOISTS
	HYMEN	HYMENS
	HYMENEAL	HYMENEALS
	HYMENIA	HYMENIAL
	HYMENIUM	HYMENIUMS
	HYMN	HYMNS
	HYMNAL	HYMNALS
	HYMNBOOK	HYMNBOOKS
	HYMNIST	HYMNISTS
	HYMNODIST	HYMNODISTS
	HYNDE	HYNDES
	HYOID	HYOIDS
	HYOSCINE	HYOSCINES
	HYP	HYPE · HYPO · HYPS
	HYPALGIA	HYPALGIAS
	HYPALLAGE	HYPALLAGES
	HYPANTHIA	HYPANTHIAL
	HYPATE	HYPATES
	HYPE	HYPED · HYPER · HYPES
	HYPER	HYPERS
	HYPERBOLA	HYPERBOLAE · HYPERBOLAS
	HYPERBOLE	HYPERBOLES
	HYPERCUBE	HYPERCUBES
	HYPEREMIA	HYPEREMIAS
	HYPERGOL	HYPERGOLS
	HYPERICUM	HYPERICUMS
	HYPERLINK	HYPERLINKS
	HYPERMART	HYPERMARTS
	HYPERNOVA	HYPERNOVAE · HYPERNOVAS
	HYPERNYM	HYPERNYMS · HYPERNYMY
	HYPERON	HYPERONS
	HYPEROPE	HYPEROPES
	HYPEROPIA	HYPEROPIAS
	HYPERPNEA	HYPERPNEAS
	HYPERREAL	HYPERREALS
	HYPERTEXT	HYPERTEXTS
	HYPESTER	HYPESTERS
	HYPHA	HYPHAE · HYPHAL
	HYPHEMIA	HYPHEMIAS
	HYPHEN	HYPHENS
	HYPHENATE	HYPHENATED · HYPHENATES
	HYPHENISE	HYPHENISED · HYPHENISES
	HYPHENISM	HYPHENISMS
	HYPHENIZE	HYPHENIZED · HYPHENIZES
	HYPING	HYPINGS
	HYPNIC	HYPNICS
	HYPNONE	HYPNONES
	HYPNOTEE	HYPNOTEES
	HYPNOTIC	HYPNOTICS
	HYPNOTISE	HYPNOTISED · HYPNOTISER · HYPNOTISES
	HYPNOTISM	HYPNOTISMS
	HYPNOTIST	HYPNOTISTS
	HYPNOTIZE	HYPNOTIZED · HYPNOTIZER · HYPNOTIZES

	FRONT HOOK	ROOT WORD	END HOOK
		HYPNUM	HYPNUMS
		HYPO	HYPOS
		HYPOBLAST	HYPOBLASTS
		HYPOBOLE	HYPOBOLES
		HYPOCAUST	HYPOCAUSTS
		HYPOCIST	HYPOCISTS
		HYPOCOTYL	HYPOCOTYLS
		HYPOCRITE	HYPOCRITES
		HYPODERM	HYPODERMA ▪ HYPODERMS
		HYPODERMA	HYPODERMAL ▪ HYPODERMAS
		HYPOGAEA	HYPOGAEAL ▪ HYPOGAEAN
		HYPOGEA	HYPOGEAL ▪ HYPOGEAN
		HYPOMANIA	HYPOMANIAS
		HYPOMANIC	HYPOMANICS
		HYPOMORPH	HYPOMORPHS
		HYPONEA	HYPONEAS
		HYPONOIA	HYPONOIAS
		HYPONYM	HYPONYMS ▪ HYPONYMY
		HYPOPHYGE	HYPOPHYGES
		HYPOPLOID	HYPOPLOIDS ▪ HYPOPLOIDY
		HYPOPNEA	HYPOPNEAS
		HYPOPNOEA	HYPOPNOEAS
		HYPOPYON	HYPOPYONS
		HYPOSTOME	HYPOSTOMES
		HYPOSTYLE	HYPOSTYLES
		HYPOTHEC	HYPOTHECA ▪ HYPOTHECS
		HYPOTHECA	HYPOTHECAE
		HYPOTONIA	HYPOTONIAS
		HYPOXEMIA	HYPOXEMIAS
		HYPOXIA	HYPOXIAS
		HYRACOID	HYRACOIDS
		HYSON	HYSONS
		HYSSOP	HYSSOPS
		HYSTERIA	HYSTERIAS
		HYSTERIC	HYSTERICS
		HYTHE	HYTHES

FRONT HOOK	ROOT WORD	END HOOK
	IAMB	IAMBI ▪ IAMBS
	IAMBI	IAMBIC
	IAMBIC	IAMBICS
	IAMBIST	IAMBISTS
FIBERISES	**IBERISES**	
VIBEX	**IBEX**	
VIBICES	**IBICES**	
	IBOGAINE	IBOGAINES
	IBUPROFEN	IBUPROFENS
BICE ▪ DICE ▪ FICE ▪ LICE ▪ MICE ▪ NICE PICE ▪ RICE ▪ SICE ▪ TICE ▪ VICE ▪ WICE	**ICE**	ICED ▪ ICER ▪ ICES
	ICEBALL	ICEBALLS
	ICEBERG	ICEBERGS
	ICEBLINK	ICEBLINKS
	ICEBOAT	ICEBOATS
	ICEBOATER	ICEBOATERS
	ICECAP	ICECAPS
DICED ▪ RICED ▪ TICED ▪ VICED	**ICED**	
	ICEFALL	ICEFALLS
	ICEFIELD	ICEFIELDS
	ICEHOUSE	ICEHOUSES
	ICEKHANA	ICEKHANAS
VICELESS	**ICELESS**	
VICELIKE	**ICELIKE**	
	ICEMAKER	ICEMAKERS
	ICEPACK	ICEPACKS
DICER ▪ NICER ▪ RICER	**ICER**	ICERS
DICERS ▪ RICERS	**ICERS**	
BICES ▪ DICES ▪ FICES ▪ RICES ▪ SICES TICES ▪ VICES	**ICES**	
	ICESTONE	ICESTONES
	ICEWINE	ICEWINES
DICH ▪ LICH ▪ MICH ▪ RICH ▪ SICH ▪ TICH WICH	**ICH**	ICHS
MICHED ▪ NICHED ▪ RICHED	**ICHED**	
FICHES ▪ LICHES ▪ MICHES ▪ NICHES RICHES ▪ TICHES ▪ WICHES	**ICHES**	
MICHING ▪ NICHING ▪ RICHING	**ICHING**	
	ICHNEUMON	ICHNEUMONS
	ICHNITE	ICHNITES
	ICHNOLITE	ICHNOLITES
	ICHOR	ICHORS
	ICHTHYOID	ICHTHYOIDS
	ICICLE	ICICLED ▪ ICICLES
DICIER ▪ RICIER	**ICIER**	
DICIEST ▪ RICIEST	**ICIEST**	
DICING ▪ RICING ▪ TICING ▪ VICING	**ICING**	ICINGS
DICINGS	**ICINGS**	
DICK ▪ HICK ▪ KICK ▪ LICK ▪ MICK ▪ NICK PICK ▪ RICK ▪ SICK ▪ TICK ▪ WICK	**ICK**	ICKY
BICKER ▪ DICKER ▪ KICKER ▪ LICKER NICKER ▪ PICKER ▪ RICKER ▪ SICKER TICKER ▪ WICKER ▪ YICKER	**ICKER**	ICKERS
BICKERS ▪ DICKERS ▪ KICKERS ▪ LICKERS NICKERS ▪ PICKERS ▪ RICKERS ▪ TICKERS WICKERS ▪ YICKERS	**ICKERS**	
DICKIER ▪ KICKIER ▪ PICKIER	**ICKIER**	
DICKIEST ▪ KICKIEST ▪ PICKIEST	**ICKIEST**	
PICKILY	**ICKILY**	
PICKINESS	**ICKINESS**	
FICKLE ▪ MICKLE ▪ NICKLE ▪ PICKLE RICKLE ▪ SICKLE ▪ TICKLE	**ICKLE**	ICKLER
FICKLER ▪ MICKLER ▪ PICKLER ▪ TICKLER	**ICKLER**	
FICKLEST ▪ MICKLEST	**ICKLEST**	
DICKY ▪ KICKY ▪ MICKY ▪ NICKY ▪ PICKY TICKY ▪ WICKY	**ICKY**	

FRONT HOOK	ROOT WORD	END HOOK
	ICON	ICONS
	ICONISE	ICONISED ▪ ICONISES
	ICONIZE	ICONIZED ▪ ICONIZES
RICTAL	**ICTAL**	
	ICTERIC	ICTERICS
	ICTERICAL	
	ICTERID	ICTERIDS
RICTUS	**ICTUS**	
RICTUSES	**ICTUSES**	
RICY	**ICY**	
AID ▪ BID ▪ CID ▪ DID ▪ FID ▪ GID ▪ HID ▪ KID ▪ LID ▪ MID ▪ NID ▪ RID ▪ TID ▪ VID ▪ YID *(offensive)*	**ID**	IDE ▪ IDS
AIDANT	**IDANT**	IDANTS
AIDE ▪ BIDE ▪ CIDE ▪ EIDE ▪ HIDE ▪ NIDE ▪ RIDE ▪ SIDE ▪ TIDE ▪ VIDE ▪ WIDE	**IDE**	IDEA ▪ IDEE ▪ IDEM ▪ IDES
	IDEA	IDEAL ▪ IDEAS
	IDEAL	IDEALS
	IDEALISE	IDEALISED ▪ IDEALISER ▪ IDEALISES
	IDEALISER	IDEALISERS
	IDEALISM	IDEALISMS
	IDEALIST	IDEALISTS
	IDEALIZE	IDEALIZED ▪ IDEALIZER ▪ IDEALIZES
	IDEALIZER	IDEALIZERS
	IDEALOGUE	IDEALOGUES
	IDEATE	IDEATED ▪ IDEATES
	IDEATION	IDEATIONS
	IDEE	IDEES
BIDENT ▪ EIDENT ▪ RIDENT	**IDENT**	IDENTS
	IDENTIKIT	IDENTIKITS
BIDENTS	**IDENTS**	
VIDEOGRAM	**IDEOGRAM**	IDEOGRAMS
VIDEOGRAMS	**IDEOGRAMS**	
	IDEOGRAPH	IDEOGRAPHS ▪ IDEOGRAPHY
	IDEOLOGUE	IDEOLOGUES
VIDEOPHONE	**IDEOPHONE**	IDEOPHONES
AIDES ▪ BIDES ▪ CIDES ▪ HIDES ▪ NIDES ▪ RIDES ▪ SIDES ▪ TIDES ▪ WIDES	**IDES**	
	IDIOBLAST	IDIOBLASTS
	IDIOGRAM	IDIOGRAMS
	IDIOGRAPH	IDIOGRAPHS
	IDIOLECT	IDIOLECTS
	IDIOM	IDIOMS
	IDIOPHONE	IDIOPHONES
	IDIOPLASM	IDIOPLASMS
	IDIOT	IDIOTS
	IDIOTICON	IDIOTICONS
	IDIOTISM	IDIOTISMS
	IDIOTYPE	IDIOTYPES
SIDLE	**IDLE**	IDLED ▪ IDLER ▪ IDLES
SIDLED	**IDLED**	
	IDLEHOOD	IDLEHOODS
SIDLER	**IDLER**	IDLERS
SIDLERS	**IDLERS**	
SIDLES	**IDLES**	IDLEST
	IDLESSE	IDLESSES
HIDLING ▪ KIDLING ▪ SIDLING	**IDLING**	
	IDOCRASE	IDOCRASES
	IDOL	IDOLA ▪ IDOLS
EIDOLA	**IDOLA**	
	IDOLATER	IDOLATERS
	IDOLATOR	IDOLATORS
	IDOLISE	IDOLISED ▪ IDOLISER ▪ IDOLISES
	IDOLISER	IDOLISERS
	IDOLISM	IDOLISMS
	IDOLIST	IDOLISTS
	IDOLIZE	IDOLIZED ▪ IDOLIZER ▪ IDOLIZES
	IDOLIZER	IDOLIZERS

FRONT HOOK	ROOT WORD	END HOOK
AIDS ∘ BIDS ∘ CIDS ∘ FIDS ∘ GIDS ∘ KIDS LIDS ∘ MIDS ∘ NIDS ∘ RIDS ∘ TIDS ∘ VIDS YIDS (offensive)	**IDS**	
	IDYL	IDYLL ∘ IDYLS
	IDYLIST	IDYLISTS
	IDYLL	IDYLLS
	IDYLLIST	IDYLLISTS
DIF ∘ GIF ∘ KIF ∘ RIF ∘ SIF	**IF**	IFF ∘ IFS
BIFF ∘ DIFF ∘ JIFF ∘ KIFF ∘ MIFF ∘ NIFF RIFF ∘ TIFF ∘ ZIFF	**IFF**	IFFY
MIFFIER ∘ NIFFIER	**IFFIER**	
MIFFIEST ∘ NIFFIEST	**IFFIEST**	
MIFFINESS	**IFFINESS**	
BIFFY ∘ JIFFY ∘ MIFFY ∘ NIFFY	**IFFY**	
DIFS ∘ KIFS ∘ RIFS	**IFS**	
	IFTAR	IFTARS
	IGAPO	IGAPOS
	IGARAPE	IGARAPES
BIGG ∘ MIGG ∘ RIGG	**IGG**	IGGS
BIGGED ∘ DIGGED ∘ FIGGED ∘ GIGGED JIGGED ∘ LIGGED ∘ PIGGED ∘ RIGGED TIGGED ∘ WIGGED ∘ ZIGGED	**IGGED**	
BIGGING ∘ DIGGING ∘ FIGGING ∘ GIGGING JIGGING ∘ LIGGING ∘ PIGGING ∘ RIGGING TIGGING ∘ WIGGING ∘ ZIGGING	**IGGING**	
BIGGS ∘ MIGGS ∘ RIGGS	**IGGS**	
	IGLOO	IGLOOS
	IGLU	IGLUS
	IGNARO	IGNAROS
	IGNATIA	IGNATIAS
LIGNEOUS	**IGNEOUS**	
	IGNESCENT	IGNESCENTS
DIGNIFIED ∘ LIGNIFIED ∘ SIGNIFIED	**IGNIFIED**	
DIGNIFIES ∘ LIGNIFIES ∘ SIGNIFIES	**IGNIFIES**	
DIGNIFY ∘ LIGNIFY ∘ SIGNIFY	**IGNIFY**	
DIGNIFYING ∘ LIGNIFYING ∘ SIGNIFYING	**IGNIFYING**	
LIGNITE	**IGNITE**	IGNITED ∘ IGNITER ∘ IGNITES
	IGNITER	IGNITERS
LIGNITES	**IGNITES**	
	IGNITION	IGNITIONS
	IGNITOR	IGNITORS
	IGNITRON	IGNITRONS
	IGNOBLE	IGNOBLER
	IGNORANCE	IGNORANCES
	IGNORANT	IGNORANTS
SIGNORE	**IGNORE**	IGNORED ∘ IGNORER ∘ IGNORES
	IGNORER	IGNORERS
SIGNORES	**IGNORES**	
	IGUANA	IGUANAS
	IGUANIAN	IGUANIANS
	IGUANID	IGUANIDS
	IGUANODON	IGUANODONS
	IHRAM	IHRAMS
	IJTIHAD	IJTIHADS
	IKAN	IKANS
	IKAT	IKATS
	IKEBANA	IKEBANAS
EIKON	**IKON**	IKONS
EIKONS	**IKONS**	
PILEA	**ILEA**	ILEAC ∘ ILEAL
PILEUM	**ILEUM**	
PILEUS	**ILEUS**	
SILEX	**ILEX**	
SILEXES	**ILEXES**	
CILIA ∘ MILIA	**ILIA**	ILIAC ∘ ILIAD ∘ ILIAL
	ILIAD	ILIADS
FILIAL	**ILIAL**	
CILICES	**ILICES**	
CILIUM ∘ MILIUM	**ILIUM**	

FRONT HOOK	ROOT WORD	END HOOK
BILK ▪ MILK ▪ SILK	**ILK**	ILKA ▪ ILKS
	ILKADAY	ILKADAYS
BILKS ▪ MILKS ▪ SILKS	**ILKS**	
BILL ▪ CILL ▪ DILL ▪ FILL ▪ GILL ▪ HILL	**ILL**	ILLS ▪ ILLY
JILL ▪ KILL ▪ LILL ▪ MILL ▪ NILL ▪ PILL		
RILL ▪ SILL ▪ TILL ▪ VILL ▪ WILL ▪ YILL		
ZILL		
	ILLAPSE	ILLAPSED ▪ ILLAPSES
	ILLATION	ILLATIONS
	ILLATIVE	ILLATIVES
	ILLEGAL	ILLEGALS
BILLER ▪ FILLER ▪ GILLER ▪ HILLER	**ILLER**	
KILLER ▪ MILLER ▪ SILLER ▪ TILLER		
WILLER		
WILLEST	**ILLEST**	
	ILLIAD	ILLIADS
	ILLINIUM	ILLINIUMS
	ILLIPE	ILLIPES
	ILLISION	ILLISIONS
TILLITE	**ILLITE**	ILLITES
TILLITES	**ILLITES**	
	ILLOGIC	ILLOGICS
BILLS ▪ CILLS ▪ DILLS ▪ FILLS ▪ GILLS	**ILLS**	
HILLS ▪ JILLS ▪ KILLS ▪ LILLS ▪ MILLS		
NILLS ▪ PILLS ▪ RILLS ▪ SILLS ▪ TILLS		
VILLS ▪ WILLS ▪ YILLS ▪ ZILLS		
	ILLTH	ILLTHS
	ILLUDE	ILLUDED ▪ ILLUDES
	ILLUME	ILLUMED ▪ ILLUMES
	ILLUMINE	ILLUMINED ▪ ILLUMINER ▪ ILLUMINES
	ILLUMINER	ILLUMINERS
	ILLUPI	ILLUPIS
	ILLUSION	ILLUSIONS
	ILLUVIA	ILLUVIAL
	ILLUVIATE	ILLUVIATED ▪ ILLUVIATES
	ILLUVIUM	ILLUVIUMS
BILLY ▪ DILLY ▪ FILLY ▪ GILLY ▪ HILLY	**ILLY**	
SILLY ▪ TILLY ▪ WILLY		
	ILMENITE	ILMENITES
	IMAGE	IMAGED ▪ IMAGER ▪ IMAGES
	IMAGER	IMAGERS ▪ IMAGERY
	IMAGINE	IMAGINED ▪ IMAGINER ▪ IMAGINES
	IMAGINER	IMAGINERS
	IMAGING	IMAGINGS
	IMAGINING	IMAGININGS
	IMAGINIST	IMAGINISTS
	IMAGISM	IMAGISMS
	IMAGIST	IMAGISTS
	IMAGO	IMAGOS
	IMAM	IMAMS
	IMAMATE	IMAMATES
	IMARET	IMARETS
	IMARI	IMARIS
	IMAUM	IMAUMS
	IMBALANCE	IMBALANCED ▪ IMBALANCES
	IMBALM	IMBALMS
	IMBALMER	IMBALMERS
MIMBAR	**IMBAR**	IMBARK ▪ IMBARS
	IMBARK	IMBARKS
MIMBARS	**IMBARS**	
	IMBASE	IMBASED ▪ IMBASES
	IMBATHE	IMBATHED ▪ IMBATHES
	IMBECILE	IMBECILES
LIMBED ▪ NIMBED	**IMBED**	IMBEDS
	IMBIBE	IMBIBED ▪ IMBIBER ▪ IMBIBES
	IMBIBER	IMBIBERS
	IMBITTER	IMBITTERS
	IMBIZO	IMBIZOS
	IMBLAZE	IMBLAZED ▪ IMBLAZES

FRONT HOOK	ROOT WORD	END HOOK
	IMBOLDEN	IMBOLDENS
	IMBORDER	IMBORDERS
	IMBOSK	IMBOSKS
	IMBOSOM	IMBOSOMS
	IMBOWER	IMBOWERS
	IMBRANGLE	IMBRANGLED ▪ IMBRANGLES
	IMBRICATE	IMBRICATED ▪ IMBRICATES
	IMBROGLIO	IMBROGLIOS
	IMBROWN	IMBROWNS
	IMBRUE	IMBRUED ▪ IMBRUES
	IMBRUTE	IMBRUTED ▪ IMBRUTES
	IMBUE	IMBUED ▪ IMBUES
	IMBUEMENT	IMBUEMENTS
	IMBURSE	IMBURSED ▪ IMBURSES
TIMID	**IMID**	IMIDE ▪ IMIDO ▪ IMIDS
	IMIDAZOLE	IMIDAZOLES
	IMIDE	IMIDES
	IMINAZOLE	IMINAZOLES
	IMINE	IMINES
	IMINOUREA	IMINOUREAS
LIMITABLE	**IMITABLE**	
	IMITANT	IMITANTS
	IMITATE	IMITATED ▪ IMITATES
LIMITATION	**IMITATION**	IMITATIONS
LIMITATIVE	**IMITATIVE**	
	IMITATOR	IMITATORS
	IMMANACLE	IMMANACLED ▪ IMMANACLES
	IMMANENCE	IMMANENCES
	IMMANTLE	IMMANTLED ▪ IMMANTLES
	IMMASK	IMMASKS
	IMMATURE	IMMATURES
	IMMENSE	IMMENSER
	IMMERGE	IMMERGED ▪ IMMERGES
	IMMERSE	IMMERSED ▪ IMMERSER ▪ IMMERSES
	IMMERSER	IMMERSERS
	IMMERSION	IMMERSIONS
	IMMEW	IMMEWS
GIMMIES ▪ JIMMIES	**IMMIES**	
	IMMIGRANT	IMMIGRANTS
	IMMIGRATE	IMMIGRATED ▪ IMMIGRATES
	IMMINENCE	IMMINENCES
	IMMINGLE	IMMINGLED ▪ IMMINGLES
	IMMISSION	IMMISSIONS
	IMMIT	IMMITS
	IMMIXTURE	IMMIXTURES
	IMMODEST	IMMODESTY
	IMMOLATE	IMMOLATED ▪ IMMOLATES
	IMMOLATOR	IMMOLATORS
	IMMORTAL	IMMORTALS
	IMMOVABLE	IMMOVABLES
	IMMUNE	IMMUNES
	IMMUNISE	IMMUNISED ▪ IMMUNISER ▪ IMMUNISES
	IMMUNISER	IMMUNISERS
	IMMUNIZE	IMMUNIZED ▪ IMMUNIZER ▪ IMMUNIZES
	IMMUNIZER	IMMUNIZERS
	IMMUNOGEN	IMMUNOGENS
	IMMURE	IMMURED ▪ IMMURES
JIMMY	**IMMY**	
DIMP ▪ GIMP ▪ JIMP ▪ LIMP ▪ PIMP ▪ SIMP ▪ WIMP	**IMP**	IMPI ▪ IMPS
	IMPACT	IMPACTS
	IMPACTER	IMPACTERS
	IMPACTION	IMPACTIONS
	IMPACTITE	IMPACTITES
	IMPACTOR	IMPACTORS
	IMPAINT	IMPAINTS
	IMPAIR	IMPAIRS
	IMPAIRER	IMPAIRERS
	IMPAIRING	IMPAIRINGS

FRONT HOOK	ROOT WORD	END HOOK
	IMPALA	IMPALAS
	IMPALE	IMPALED ▪ IMPALER ▪ IMPALES
	IMPALER	IMPALERS
	IMPANEL	IMPANELS
	IMPANNEL	IMPANNELS
	IMPARK	IMPARKS
	IMPARL	IMPARLS
	IMPART	IMPARTS
	IMPARTER	IMPARTERS
	IMPASSE	IMPASSES
	IMPASSION	IMPASSIONS
	IMPASTE	IMPASTED ▪ IMPASTES
	IMPASTO	IMPASTOS
	IMPAVE	IMPAVED ▪ IMPAVES
	IMPAWN	IMPAWNS
	IMPEACHER	IMPEACHERS
	IMPEARL	IMPEARLS
GIMPED (*offensive*) ▪ LIMPED ▪ PIMPED WIMPED	**IMPED**	IMPEDE
	IMPEDANCE	IMPEDANCES
	IMPEDE	IMPEDED ▪ IMPEDER ▪ IMPEDES
	IMPEDER	IMPEDERS
	IMPEDOR	IMPEDORS
	IMPEL	IMPELS
	IMPELLENT	IMPELLENTS
	IMPELLER	IMPELLERS
	IMPELLOR	IMPELLORS
	IMPEND	IMPENDS
	IMPERATOR	IMPERATORS
	IMPERFECT	IMPERFECTS
	IMPERIA	IMPERIAL
	IMPERIAL	IMPERIALS
	IMPERIL	IMPERILS
	IMPERIUM	IMPERIUMS
	IMPETIGO	IMPETIGOS
	IMPETRATE	IMPETRATED ▪ IMPETRATES
	IMPHEE	IMPHEES
	IMPI	IMPIS
GIMPING (*offensive*) ▪ LIMPING ▪ PIMPING WIMPING	**IMPING**	IMPINGE ▪ IMPINGS
	IMPINGE	IMPINGED ▪ IMPINGER ▪ IMPINGES
	IMPINGER	IMPINGERS
LIMPINGS	**IMPINGS**	
	IMPIS	IMPISH
WIMPISH WIMPISHLY	**IMPISH**	
	IMPISHLY	
	IMPLANT	IMPLANTS
	IMPLANTER	IMPLANTERS
	IMPLATE	IMPLATED ▪ IMPLATES
	IMPLEAD	IMPLEADS
	IMPLEADER	IMPLEADERS
DIMPLED ▪ PIMPLED ▪ RIMPLED ▪ SIMPLED WIMPLED	**IMPLED**	
	IMPLEDGE	IMPLEDGED ▪ IMPLEDGES
DIMPLEMENT	**IMPLEMENT**	IMPLEMENTS
	IMPLETE	IMPLETED ▪ IMPLETES
	IMPLETION	IMPLETIONS
SIMPLEX	**IMPLEX**	
SIMPLEXES	**IMPLEXES**	
	IMPLEXION	IMPLEXIONS
	IMPLICATE	IMPLICATED ▪ IMPLICATES
	IMPLICIT	IMPLICITY
SIMPLICITY	**IMPLICITY**	
	IMPLODE	IMPLODED ▪ IMPLODES
	IMPLODENT	IMPLODENTS
	IMPLORE	IMPLORED ▪ IMPLORER ▪ IMPLORES
	IMPLORER	IMPLORERS
	IMPLOSION	IMPLOSIONS
	IMPLOSIVE	IMPLOSIVES

	FRONT HOOK	ROOT WORD	END HOOK
		IMPLUNGE	IMPLUNGED · IMPLUNGES
	DIMPLY · JIMPLY · LIMPLY · PIMPLY SIMPLY	**IMPLY**	
		IMPOCKET	IMPOCKETS
		IMPOLDER	IMPOLDERS
		IMPOLITE	IMPOLITER
		IMPONE	IMPONED · IMPONES
		IMPONENT	IMPONENTS
		IMPORT	IMPORTS
		IMPORTER	IMPORTERS
		IMPORTING	IMPORTINGS
		IMPORTUNE	IMPORTUNED · IMPORTUNER · IMPORTUNES
		IMPOSE	IMPOSED · IMPOSER · IMPOSES
		IMPOSER	IMPOSERS
		IMPOST	IMPOSTS
		IMPOSTER	IMPOSTERS
		IMPOSTOR	IMPOSTORS
		IMPOSTUME	IMPOSTUMED · IMPOSTUMES
		IMPOSTURE	IMPOSTURES
		IMPOT	IMPOTS
		IMPOTENCE	IMPOTENCES
		IMPOTENT	IMPOTENTS
		IMPOUND	IMPOUNDS
		IMPOUNDER	IMPOUNDERS
		IMPOWER	IMPOWERS
		IMPRECATE	IMPRECATED · IMPRECATES
		IMPREGN	IMPREGNS
		IMPRESA	IMPRESAS
		IMPRESARI	IMPRESARIO
		IMPRESE	IMPRESES
		IMPRESS	IMPRESSE
		IMPRESSE	IMPRESSED · IMPRESSER · IMPRESSES
		IMPRESSER	IMPRESSERS
		IMPREST	IMPRESTS
		IMPRINT	IMPRINTS
		IMPRINTER	IMPRINTERS
		IMPRISON	IMPRISONS
		IMPROMPTU	IMPROMPTUS
		IMPROV	IMPROVE · IMPROVS
		IMPROVE	IMPROVED · IMPROVER · IMPROVES
		IMPROVER	IMPROVERS
		IMPROVISE	IMPROVISED · IMPROVISER · IMPROVISES
	DIMPS · GIMPS *(offensive)* · LIMPS · NIMPS PIMPS · SIMPS · TIMPS · WIMPS	**IMPS**	
		IMPSONITE	IMPSONITES
		IMPUDENCE	IMPUDENCES
		IMPUGN	IMPUGNS
		IMPUGNER	IMPUGNERS
		IMPULSE	IMPULSED · IMPULSES
		IMPULSION	IMPULSIONS
		IMPUNDULU	IMPUNDULUS
		IMPURE	IMPURER
		IMPURPLE	IMPURPLED · IMPURPLES
		IMPUTE	IMPUTED · IMPUTER · IMPUTES
		IMPUTER	IMPUTERS
	AIN · BIN · DIN · FIN · GIN · HIN · JIN KIN · LIN · PIN · RIN · SIN · TIN · VIN WIN · YIN · ZIN	**IN**	INK · INN · INS
		INACTION	INACTIONS
		INAMORATA	INAMORATAS
		INAMORATO	INAMORATOS
		INANE	INANER · INANES
		INANES	INANEST
		INANGA	INANGAS
		INANITION	INANITIONS
		INARM	INARMS
		INAUGURAL	INAUGURALS
		INBEING	INBEINGS
		INBOARD	INBOARDS

FRONT HOOK	ROOT WORD	END HOOK
	INBOUND	INBOUNDS
	INBREAK	INBREAKS
	INBREATHE	INBREATHED · INBREATHES
	INBRED	INBREDS
	INBREED	INBREEDS
	INBREEDER	INBREEDERS
	INBRING	INBRINGS
	INBURST	INBURSTS
	INBY	INBYE
	INCAGE	INCAGED · INCAGES
	INCANT	INCANTS
	INCAPABLE	INCAPABLES
	INCARNATE	INCARNATED · INCARNATES
PINCASE	**INCASE**	INCASED · INCASES
PINCASES	**INCASES**	
	INCAUTION	INCAUTIONS
	INCAVE	INCAVED · INCAVES
	INCEDE	INCEDED · INCEDES
	INCENSE	INCENSED · INCENSER · INCENSES
	INCENSER	INCENSERS
	INCENSOR	INCENSORS · INCENSORY
	INCENT	INCENTS
	INCENTER	INCENTERS
	INCENTIVE	INCENTIVES
	INCENTRE	INCENTRES
	INCEPT	INCEPTS
	INCEPTION	INCEPTIONS
	INCEPTIVE	INCEPTIVES
	INCEPTOR	INCEPTORS
	INCEST	INCESTS
CINCH · FINCH · LINCH · PINCH · WINCH	**INCH**	
	INCHASE	INCHASED · INCHASES
CINCHED · FINCHED · PINCHED · WINCHED	**INCHED**	
PINCHER · WINCHER	**INCHER**	INCHERS
PINCHERS · WINCHERS	**INCHERS**	
CINCHES · FINCHES · LINCHES · PINCHES		
WINCHES	**INCHES**	
CINCHING · PINCHING · WINCHING	**INCHING**	
	INCHOATE	INCHOATED · INCHOATES
LINCHPIN	**INCHPIN**	INCHPINS
LINCHPINS	**INCHPINS**	
	INCHWORM	INCHWORMS
	INCIDENCE	INCIDENCES
	INCIDENT	INCIDENTS
	INCIPIT	INCIPITS
	INCISE	INCISED · INCISES
	INCISION	INCISIONS
	INCISOR	INCISORS · INCISORY
	INCISURE	INCISURES
	INCITANT	INCITANTS
ZINCITE	**INCITE**	INCITED · INCITER · INCITES
	INCITER	INCITERS
ZINCITES	**INCITES**	
	INCIVISM	INCIVISMS
	INCLASP	INCLASPS
	INCLE	INCLES
	INCLINE	INCLINED · INCLINER · INCLINES
	INCLINER	INCLINERS
	INCLINING	INCLININGS
	INCLIP	INCLIPS
	INCLOSE	INCLOSED · INCLOSER · INCLOSES
	INCLOSER	INCLOSERS
	INCLOSURE	INCLOSURES
	INCLUDE	INCLUDED · INCLUDES
	INCLUSION	INCLUSIONS
	INCOG	INCOGS
	INCOGNITA	INCOGNITAS
	INCOGNITO	INCOGNITOS
	INCOME	INCOMER · INCOMES

FRONT HOOK	ROOT WORD	END HOOK
	INCOMER	INCOMERS
	INCOMING	INCOMINGS
	INCOMMODE	INCOMMODED · INCOMMODES
	INCONNU	INCONNUE · INCONNUS
	INCONNUE	INCONNUES
	INCORPSE	INCORPSED · INCORPSES
	INCREASE	INCREASED · INCREASER · INCREASES
	INCREASER	INCREASERS
	INCREMATE	INCREMATED · INCREMATES
	INCREMENT	INCREMENTS
	INCRETION	INCRETIONS
	INCRUST	INCRUSTS
	INCUBATE	INCUBATED · INCUBATES
	INCUBATOR	INCUBATORS · INCUBATORY
	INCULCATE	INCULCATED · INCULCATES
	INCULPATE	INCULPATED · INCULPATES
	INCUMBENT	INCUMBENTS
	INCUMBER	INCUMBERS
	INCUNABLE	INCUNABLES
	INCUR	INCURS
	INCURABLE	INCURABLES
	INCURSION	INCURSIONS
	INCURVATE	INCURVATED · INCURVATES
	INCURVE	INCURVED · INCURVES
	INCUS	INCUSE
	INCUSE	INCUSED · INCUSES
	INDABA	INDABAS
	INDAGATE	INDAGATED · INDAGATES
	INDAGATOR	INDAGATORS · INDAGATORY
	INDAMIN	INDAMINE · INDAMINS
	INDAMINE	INDAMINES
	INDART	INDARTS
	INDECORUM	INDECORUMS
	INDENE	INDENES
	INDENT	INDENTS
	INDENTER	INDENTERS
	INDENTION	INDENTIONS
	INDENTOR	INDENTORS
	INDENTURE	INDENTURED · INDENTURES
	INDEW	INDEWS
	INDEXER	INDEXERS
	INDEXICAL	INDEXICALS
	INDEXING	INDEXINGS
	INDICAN	INDICANS · INDICANT
	INDICANT	INDICANTS
VINDICATE	INDICATE	INDICATED · INDICATES
VINDICATED	INDICATED	
VINDICATES	INDICATES	
VINDICATOR	INDICATOR	INDICATORS · INDICATORY
	INDICIA	INDICIAL · INDICIAS
	INDICIUM	INDICIUMS
	INDICT	INDICTS
	INDICTEE	INDICTEES
	INDICTER	INDICTERS
	INDICTION	INDICTIONS
	INDICTOR	INDICTORS
KINDIE	INDIE	INDIES
KINDIES · LINDIES	INDIES	
	INDIGEN	INDIGENE · INDIGENS · INDIGENT
	INDIGENCE	INDIGENCES
	INDIGENE	INDIGENES
	INDIGENT	INDIGENTS
	INDIGEST	INDIGESTS
WINDIGO	INDIGO	INDIGOS
	INDIGOID	INDIGOIDS
WINDIGOS	INDIGOS	
	INDIGOTIN	INDIGOTINS
	INDINAVIR	INDINAVIRS
	INDIRUBIN	INDIRUBINS

FRONT HOOK	ROOT WORD	END HOOK
	INDISPOSE	INDISPOSED ▪ INDISPOSES
	INDITE	INDITED ▪ INDITER ▪ INDITES
	INDITER	INDITERS
	INDIUM	INDIUMS
	INDIVIDUA	INDIVIDUAL
	INDOL	INDOLE ▪ INDOLS
	INDOLE	INDOLES
	INDOLENCE	INDOLENCES
	INDOOR	INDOORS
	INDORSE	INDORSED ▪ INDORSEE ▪ INDORSER INDORSES
	INDORSEE	INDORSEES
	INDORSER	INDORSERS
	INDORSOR	INDORSORS
WINDOW	**INDOW**	INDOWS
WINDOWED	**INDOWED**	
WINDOWING	**INDOWING**	
WINDOWS	**INDOWS**	
	INDOXYL	INDOXYLS
	INDRAFT	INDRAFTS
	INDRAUGHT	INDRAUGHTS
	INDRI	INDRIS
	INDUCE	INDUCED ▪ INDUCER ▪ INDUCES
	INDUCER	INDUCERS
	INDUCT	INDUCTS
	INDUCTEE	INDUCTEES
	INDUCTION	INDUCTIONS
	INDUCTOR	INDUCTORS
	INDUE	INDUED ▪ INDUES
	INDULGE	INDULGED ▪ INDULGER ▪ INDULGES
	INDULGER	INDULGERS
	INDULIN	INDULINE ▪ INDULINS
	INDULINE	INDULINES
	INDULT	INDULTS
	INDUNA	INDUNAS
	INDURATE	INDURATED ▪ INDURATES
	INDUSIA	INDUSIAL
	INDWELL	INDWELLS
	INDWELLER	INDWELLERS
	INEARTH	INEARTHS
	INEBRIANT	INEBRIANTS
	INEBRIATE	INEBRIATED ▪ INEBRIATES
	INERT	INERTS
	INERTIA	INERTIAE ▪ INERTIAL ▪ INERTIAS
	INESSIVE	INESSIVES
	INEXPERT	INEXPERTS
PINFALL	**INFALL**	INFALLS
PINFALLS	**INFALLS**	
	INFAME	INFAMED ▪ INFAMES
	INFAMISE	INFAMISED ▪ INFAMISES
	INFAMIZE	INFAMIZED ▪ INFAMIZES
	INFANT	INFANTA ▪ INFANTE ▪ INFANTS
	INFANTA	INFANTAS
	INFANTE	INFANTES
	INFARCT	INFARCTS
	INFARE	INFARES
	INFATUATE	INFATUATED ▪ INFATUATES
	INFAUNA	INFAUNAE ▪ INFAUNAL ▪ INFAUNAS
	INFECT	INFECTS
	INFECTER	INFECTERS
	INFECTION	INFECTIONS
	INFECTOR	INFECTORS
	INFEFT	INFEFTS
	INFEOFF	INFEOFFS
	INFER	INFERE ▪ INFERS
	INFERENCE	INFERENCES
	INFERIOR	INFERIORS
	INFERNO	INFERNOS
	INFERRER	INFERRERS

FRONT HOOK	ROOT WORD	END HOOK
	INFEST	INFESTS
	INFESTANT	INFESTANTS
	INFESTER	INFESTERS
	INFIDEL	INFIDELS
	INFIELD	INFIELDS
	INFIELDER	INFIELDERS
	INFIGHT	INFIGHTS
	INFIGHTER	INFIGHTERS
	INFILL	INFILLS
	INFILLING	INFILLINGS
	INFIMUM	INFIMUMS
	INFINITE	INFINITES
	INFIRM	INFIRMS
	INFIXION	INFIXIONS
	INFLAME	INFLAMED ▪ INFLAMER ▪ INFLAMES
	INFLAMER	INFLAMERS
	INFLATE	INFLATED ▪ INFLATER ▪ INFLATES
	INFLATER	INFLATERS
	INFLATION	INFLATIONS
	INFLATOR	INFLATORS
	INFLECT	INFLECTS
	INFLECTOR	INFLECTORS
	INFLEXION	INFLEXIONS
	INFLEXURE	INFLEXURES
	INFLICT	INFLICTS
	INFLICTER	INFLICTERS
	INFLICTOR	INFLICTORS
	INFLOW	INFLOWS
	INFLOWING	INFLOWINGS
	INFLUENCE	INFLUENCED ▪ INFLUENCER
		INFLUENCES
	INFLUENT	INFLUENTS
	INFLUENZA	INFLUENZAL ▪ INFLUENZAS
	INFLUXION	INFLUXIONS
	INFO	INFOS
	INFOBAHN	INFOBAHNS
PINFOLD	**INFOLD**	INFOLDS
PINFOLDED	**INFOLDED**	
	INFOLDER	INFOLDERS
PINFOLDING	**INFOLDING**	
PINFOLDS	**INFOLDS**	
	INFOMANIA	INFOMANIAS
	INFORCE	INFORCED ▪ INFORCES
	INFORM	INFORMS
	INFORMANT	INFORMANTS
	INFORMER	INFORMERS
	INFORTUNE	INFORTUNES
	INFRACT	INFRACTS
	INFRACTOR	INFRACTORS
	INFRARED	INFRAREDS
	INFRINGE	INFRINGED ▪ INFRINGER ▪ INFRINGES
	INFRINGER	INFRINGERS
	INFULA	INFULAE
	INFURIATE	INFURIATED ▪ INFURIATES
	INFUSCATE	INFUSCATED
	INFUSE	INFUSED ▪ INFUSER ▪ INFUSES
	INFUSER	INFUSERS
	INFUSION	INFUSIONS
	INFUSORIA	INFUSORIAL ▪ INFUSORIAN
FINGAN	**INGAN**	INGANS
FINGANS	**INGANS**	
	INGATE	INGATES
	INGATHER	INGATHERS
	INGENER	INGENERS
	INGENIUM	INGENIUMS
	INGENU	INGENUE ▪ INGENUS
	INGENUE	INGENUES
	INGEST	INGESTA ▪ INGESTS
	INGESTION	INGESTIONS

FRONT HOOK	ROOT WORD	END HOOK
BINGLE · DINGLE · GINGLE · JINGLE KINGLE · LINGLE · MINGLE · PINGLE SINGLE · TINGLE	**INGINE** **INGLE**	INGINES INGLES
BINGLES · DINGLES · GINGLES · JINGLES KINGLES · LINGLES · MINGLES · PINGLES SINGLES · TINGLES	**INGLENEUK** **INGLENOOK** **INGLES**	INGLENEUKS INGLENOOKS
BINGO · DINGO · JINGO · LINGO · PINGO BINGOES · DINGOES · JINGOES · LINGOES PINGOES	**INGLOBE** **INGO** **INGOES**	INGLOBED · INGLOBES INGOT
DINGOING LINGOT LINGOTS	**INGOING** **INGOT** **INGOTS**	INGOINGS INGOTS
	INGRAFT	INGRAFTS
	INGRAIN	INGRAINS
	INGRATE	INGRATES
	INGROOVE	INGROOVED · INGROOVES
	INGROUP	INGROUPS
	INGROWTH	INGROWTHS
	INGULF	INGULFS
	INGULPH	INGULPHS
	INHABIT	INHABITS
	INHABITER	INHABITERS
	INHABITOR	INHABITORS
	INHALANT	INHALANTS
	INHALATOR	INHALATORS
	INHALE	INHALED · INHALER · INHALES
	INHALER	INHALERS
	INHAUL	INHAULS
	INHAULER	INHAULERS
	INHAUST	INHAUSTS
	INHEARSE	INHEARSED · INHEARSES
	INHERCE	INHERCED · INHERCES
	INHERE	INHERED · INHERES
	INHERENCE	INHERENCES
	INHERIT	INHERITS
	INHERITOR	INHERITORS
	INHESION	INHESIONS
	INHIBIN	INHIBINS
	INHIBIT	INHIBITS
	INHIBITER	INHIBITERS
	INHIBITOR	INHIBITORS · INHIBITORY
	INHOLDER	INHOLDERS
	INHOLDING	INHOLDINGS
	INHOOP	INHOOPS
	INHUMAN	INHUMANE
	INHUMATE	INHUMATED · INHUMATES
	INHUME	INHUMED · INHUMER · INHUMES
	INHUMER	INHUMERS
MINION · PINION MINIONS · PINIONS	**INION** **INIONS**	INIONS
	INISLE	INISLED · INISLES
	INITIAL	INITIALS
	INITIALER	INITIALERS
	INITIATE	INITIATED · INITIATES
	INITIATOR	INITIATORS · INITIATORY
	INJECT	INJECTS
	INJECTANT	INJECTANTS
	INJECTION	INJECTIONS
	INJECTOR	INJECTORS
	INJERA	INJERAS
	INJOINT	INJOINTS
	INJUNCT	INJUNCTS
	INJURE	INJURED · INJURER · INJURES
	INJURER	INJURERS
	INJUSTICE	INJUSTICES

FRONT HOOK	ROOT WORD	END HOOK
BINK · DINK · FINK · GINK · JINK · KINK LINK · MINK · OINK · PINK · RINK · SINK TINK · WINK	**INK**	INKS · INKY
	INKBLOT	INKBLOTS
DINKED · FINKED · JINKED · KINKED LINKED · OINKED · PINKED · RINKED TINKED · WINKED · ZINKED	**INKED**	
DINKER · JINKER · LINKER · PINKER SINKER · TINKER · WINKER	**INKER**	INKERS
JINKERS · LINKERS · PINKERS · SINKERS TINKERS · WINKERS	**INKERS**	
	INKHOLDER	INKHOLDERS
	INKHORN	INKHORNS
DINKIER · HINKIER · KINKIER · PINKIER SINKIER · ZINKIER	**INKIER**	
DINKIEST · HINKIEST · KINKIEST PINKIEST · SINKIEST · ZINKIEST	**INKIEST**	
KINKINESS · PINKINESS	**INKINESS**	
DINKING · FINKING · JINKING KINKING · LINKING · OINKING · PINKING RINKING · SINKING · TINKING · WINKING ZINKING	**INKING**	
KINKLE · TINKLE · WINKLE	**INKLE**	INKLED · INKLES
TINKLED · WINKLED	**INKLED**	
KINKLES · TINKLES · WINKLES	**INKLES**	INKLESS
TINKLING · WINKLING	**INKLING**	INKLINGS
TINKLINGS	**INKLINGS**	
	INKPOT	INKPOTS
BINKS · DINKS · FINKS · GINKS · JINKS KINKS · LINKS · MINKS · OINKS · PINKS RINKS · SINKS · TINKS · WINKS	**INKS**	
	INKSPOT	INKSPOTS
	INKSTAND	INKSTANDS
	INKSTONE	INKSTONES
	INKWELL	INKWELLS
	INKWOOD	INKWOODS
DINKY · HINKY · KINKY · LINKY · PINKY SINKY · ZINKY	**INKY**	
	INLACE	INLACED · INLACES
	INLAND	INLANDS
	INLANDER	INLANDERS
	INLAY	INLAYS
	INLAYER	INLAYERS
	INLAYING	INLAYINGS
	INLET	INLETS
	INLIER	INLIERS
	INLOCK	INLOCKS
	INMATE	INMATES
	INMIGRANT	INMIGRANTS
GINN · JINN · LINN · WINN	**INN**	INNS
	INNAGE	INNAGES
WINNARDS	**INNARDS**	
PINNATE	**INNATE**	
PINNATELY	**INNATELY**	
BINNED · DINNED · FINNED · GINNED LINNED · PINNED · SINNED · TINNED WINNED	**INNED**	
DINNER · FINNER · GINNER · PINNER SINNER · TINNER · WINNER	**INNER**	INNERS
	INNERMOST	INNERMOSTS
DINNERS · FINNERS · GINNERS · PINNERS SINNERS · TINNERS · WINNERS	**INNERS**	
	INNERSOLE	INNERSOLES
	INNERVATE	INNERVATED · INNERVATES
	INNERVE	INNERVED · INNERVES
	INNERWEAR	INNERWEARS
BINNING · DINNING · FINNING · GINNING LINNING · PINNING · RINNING · SINNING TINNING · WINNING	**INNING**	INNINGS

FRONT HOOK	ROOT WORD	END HOOK
GINNINGS ▪ PINNINGS ▪ TINNINGS WINNINGS	**INNINGS**	
	INNKEEPER	INNKEEPERS
	INNOCENCE	INNOCENCES
	INNOCENT	INNOCENTS
	INNOVATE	INNOVATED ▪ INNOVATES
	INNOVATOR	INNOVATORS ▪ INNOVATORY
JINNS ▪ LINNS ▪ WINNS	**INNS**	
	INNUENDO	INNUENDOS
	INNYARD	INNYARDS
	INOCULANT	INOCULANTS
	INOCULATE	INOCULATED ▪ INOCULATES
	INOCULUM	INOCULUMS
	INORB	INORBS
	INOSINE	INOSINES
	INOSITE	INOSITES
	INOSITOL	INOSITOLS
	INPATIENT	INPATIENTS
	INPAYMENT	INPAYMENTS
	INPOUR	INPOURS
	INPOURING	INPOURINGS
	INPUT	INPUTS
	INPUTTER	INPUTTERS
	INQILAB	INQILABS
	INQUERE	INQUERED ▪ INQUERES
	INQUEST	INQUESTS
	INQUIET	INQUIETS
	INQUILINE	INQUILINES
	INQUINATE	INQUINATED ▪ INQUINATES
	INQUIRE	INQUIRED ▪ INQUIRER ▪ INQUIRES
	INQUIRER	INQUIRERS
	INROAD	INROADS
	INRUN	INRUNS
	INRUSHING	INRUSHINGS
AINS ▪ BINS ▪ DINS ▪ FINS ▪ GINS ▪ HINS JINS ▪ KINS ▪ LINS ▪ PINS ▪ RINS ▪ SINS TINS ▪ VINS ▪ WINS ▪ YINS ▪ ZINS	**INS**	
	INSANE	INSANER
	INSANIE	INSANIES
	INSCAPE	INSCAPES
	INSCIENCE	INSCIENCES
	INSCONCE	INSCONCED ▪ INSCONCES
	INSCRIBE	INSCRIBED ▪ INSCRIBER ▪ INSCRIBES
	INSCRIBER	INSCRIBERS
	INSCROLL	INSCROLLS
	INSCULP	INSCULPS ▪ INSCULPT
	INSEAM	INSEAMS
	INSECT	INSECTS
	INSECTION	INSECTIONS
	INSEEM	INSEEMS
	INSELBERG	INSELBERGE ▪ INSELBERGS
	INSERT	INSERTS
	INSERTER	INSERTERS
	INSERTION	INSERTIONS
	INSET	INSETS
PINSETTER PINSETTERS	**INSETTER**	INSETTERS
	INSETTERS	
	INSHEATH	INSHEATHE ▪ INSHEATHS
	INSHEATHE	INSHEATHED ▪ INSHEATHES
	INSHELL	INSHELLS
	INSHELTER	INSHELTERS
KINSHIP KINSHIPS	**INSHIP**	INSHIPS
	INSHIPS	
	INSHRINE	INSHRINED ▪ INSHRINES
	INSIDE	INSIDER ▪ INSIDES
	INSIDER	INSIDERS
	INSIGHT	INSIGHTS
	INSIGNIA	INSIGNIAS
	INSINEW	INSINEWS

FRONT HOOK	ROOT WORD	END HOOK
	INSINUATE	INSINUATED ▪ INSINUATES
	INSIST	INSISTS
	INSISTER	INSISTERS
	INSNARE	INSNARED ▪ INSNARER ▪ INSNARES
	INSNARER	INSNARERS
	INSOLATE	INSOLATED ▪ INSOLATES
	INSOLE	INSOLES
	INSOLENCE	INSOLENCES
	INSOLENT	INSOLENTS
	INSOLUBLE	INSOLUBLES
	INSOLVENT	INSOLVENTS
	INSOMNIA	INSOMNIAC ▪ INSOMNIAS
	INSOMNIAC	INSOMNIACS
	INSOUL	INSOULS
	INSPAN	INSPANS
	INSPECT	INSPECTS
	INSPECTOR	INSPECTORS
	INSPHERE	INSPHERED ▪ INSPHERES
	INSPIRE	INSPIRED ▪ INSPIRER ▪ INSPIRES
	INSPIRER	INSPIRERS
	INSPIRIT	INSPIRITS
	INSTAL	INSTALL ▪ INSTALS
	INSTALL	INSTALLS
	INSTALLER	INSTALLERS
	INSTANCE	INSTANCED ▪ INSTANCES
	INSTANT	INSTANTS
	INSTAR	INSTARS
	INSTATE	INSTATED ▪ INSTATES
	INSTEP	INSTEPS
	INSTIGATE	INSTIGATED ▪ INSTIGATES
	INSTIL	INSTILL ▪ INSTILS
	INSTILL	INSTILLS
	INSTILLER	INSTILLERS
	INSTINCT	INSTINCTS
	INSTITUTE	INSTITUTED ▪ INSTITUTER ▪ INSTITUTES
	INSTROKE	INSTROKES
	INSTRUCT	INSTRUCTS
	INSULA	INSULAE ▪ INSULAR ▪ INSULAS
	INSULANT	INSULANTS
	INSULAR	INSULARS
	INSULATE	INSULATED ▪ INSULATES
	INSULATOR	INSULATORS
	INSULIN	INSULINS
	INSULT	INSULTS
	INSULTER	INSULTERS
	INSURANCE	INSURANCER ▪ INSURANCES
	INSURANT	INSURANTS
	INSURE	INSURED ▪ INSURER ▪ INSURES
	INSURED	INSUREDS
	INSURER	INSURERS
	INSURGENT	INSURGENTS
	INSWATHE	INSWATHED ▪ INSWATHES
	INSWING	INSWINGS
	INSWINGER	INSWINGERS
	INTAGLI	INTAGLIO
	INTAGLIO	INTAGLIOS
	INTAKE	INTAKES
	INTARSIA	INTARSIAS
	INTEGER	INTEGERS
	INTEGRAL	INTEGRALS
	INTEGRAND	INTEGRANDS
	INTEGRANT	INTEGRANTS
	INTEGRATE	INTEGRATED ▪ INTEGRATES
LINTEL	**INTEL**	INTELS
	INTELLECT	INTELLECTS
LINTELS	**INTELS**	
	INTEND	INTENDS
	INTENDANT	INTENDANTS
	INTENDED	INTENDEDS

I

	FRONT HOOK	ROOT WORD	END HOOK
		INTENDER	INTENDERS
		INTENSATE	INTENSATED · INTENSATES
		INTENSE	INTENSER
		INTENSION	INTENSIONS
		INTENSIVE	INTENSIVES
		INTENT	INTENTS
		INTENTION	INTENTIONS
	HINTER · LINTER · MINTER · SINTER TINTER · WINTER	**INTER**	INTERN · INTERS
		INTERACT	INTERACTS
		INTERBED	INTERBEDS
		INTERCEDE	INTERCEDED · INTERCEDER · INTERCEDES
		INTERCEPT	INTERCEPTS
		INTERCOM	INTERCOMS
		INTERCROP	INTERCROPS
		INTERCUT	INTERCUTS
		INTERDEAL	INTERDEALS · INTERDEALT
		INTERDICT	INTERDICTS
		INTERDINE	INTERDINED · INTERDINES
		INTERESS	INTERESSE
		INTERESSE	INTERESSED · INTERESSES
		INTEREST	INTERESTS
		INTERFACE	INTERFACED · INTERFACES
		INTERFERE	INTERFERED · INTERFERER · INTERFERES
		INTERFILE	INTERFILED · INTERFILES
		INTERFLOW	INTERFLOWS
		INTERFOLD	INTERFOLDS
		INTERFUSE	INTERFUSED · INTERFUSES
		INTERGROW	INTERGROWN · INTERGROWS
		INTERIM	INTERIMS
		INTERIOR	INTERIORS
		INTERJECT	INTERJECTS
		INTERJOIN	INTERJOINS
		INTERKNIT	INTERKNITS
		INTERKNOT	INTERKNOTS
		INTERLACE	INTERLACED · INTERLACES
		INTERLAP	INTERLAPS
		INTERLARD	INTERLARDS
		INTERLAY	INTERLAYS
		INTERLEND	INTERLENDS
		INTERLINE	INTERLINED · INTERLINER · INTERLINES
		INTERLINK	INTERLINKS
		INTERLOAN	INTERLOANS
		INTERLOCK	INTERLOCKS
		INTERLOOP	INTERLOOPS
		INTERLOPE	INTERLOPED · INTERLOPER · INTERLOPES
		INTERLUDE	INTERLUDED · INTERLUDES
		INTERMAT	INTERMATS
		INTERMENT	INTERMENTS
		INTERMIT	INTERMITS
		INTERMURE	INTERMURED · INTERMURES
		INTERN	INTERNE · INTERNS
		INTERNAL	INTERNALS
		INTERNE	INTERNED · INTERNEE · INTERNES INTERNET
		INTERNEE	INTERNEES
		INTERNET	INTERNETS
		INTERNIST	INTERNISTS
		INTERNODE	INTERNODES
		INTERPAGE	INTERPAGED · INTERPAGES
		INTERPLAY	INTERPLAYS
		INTERPONE	INTERPONED · INTERPONES
		INTERPOSE	INTERPOSED · INTERPOSER · INTERPOSES
		INTERPRET	INTERPRETS
		INTERRAIL	INTERRAILS
		INTERRUPT	INTERRUPTS
	HINTERS · LINTERS · MINTERS · SINTERS TINTERS · WINTERS	**INTERS**	
		INTERSECT	INTERSECTS

I

FRONT HOOK	ROOT WORD	END HOOK
	INTERSERT	INTERSERTS
	INTERTEXT	INTERTEXTS
	INTERTIE	INTERTIES
	INTERTILL	INTERTILLS
	INTERVAL	INTERVALE · INTERVALS
	INTERVALE	INTERVALES
	INTERVEIN	INTERVEINS
	INTERVENE	INTERVENED · INTERVENER
		INTERVENES
	INTERVIEW	INTERVIEWS
	INTERWIND	INTERWINDS
	INTERWORK	INTERWORKS
	INTERWOVE	INTERWOVEN
	INTERZONE	INTERZONES
	INTESTATE	INTESTATES
	INTESTINE	INTESTINES
	INTHRAL	INTHRALL · INTHRALS
	INTHRALL	INTHRALLS
	INTHRONE	INTHRONED · INTHRONES
	INTI	INTIL · INTIS
	INTIFADA	INTIFADAH · INTIFADAS
	INTIFADAH	INTIFADAHS
	INTIFADEH	INTIFADEHS
	INTIMA	INTIMAE · INTIMAL · INTIMAS
	INTIMATE	INTIMATED · INTIMATER · INTIMATES
	INTIMATER	INTIMATERS
	INTIMISM	INTIMISMS
	INTIMIST	INTIMISTE · INTIMISTS
	INTIMISTE	INTIMISTES
	INTINE	INTINES
	INTITLE	INTITLED · INTITLES
	INTITULE	INTITULED · INTITULES
PINTO	**INTO**	
	INTOMB	INTOMBS
	INTONACO	INTONACOS
	INTONATE	INTONATED · INTONATES
	INTONATOR	INTONATORS
	INTONE	INTONED · INTONER · INTONES
	INTONER	INTONERS
	INTONING	INTONINGS
	INTORSION	INTORSIONS
	INTORT	INTORTS
	INTORTION	INTORTIONS
	INTRADA	INTRADAS · INTRADAY
	INTRANET	INTRANETS
	INTRANT	INTRANTS
	INTREAT	INTREATS
	INTRIGANT	INTRIGANTE · INTRIGANTS
	INTRIGUE	INTRIGUED · INTRIGUER · INTRIGUES
	INTRIGUER	INTRIGUERS
	INTRO	INTRON · INTROS
	INTRODUCE	INTRODUCED · INTRODUCER · INTRODUCES
	INTROIT	INTROITS
	INTROJECT	INTROJECTS
	INTROMIT	INTROMITS
	INTRON	INTRONS
	INTROVERT	INTROVERTS
	INTRUDE	INTRUDED · INTRUDER · INTRUDES
	INTRUDER	INTRUDERS
	INTRUSION	INTRUSIONS
	INTRUSIVE	INTRUSIVES
	INTRUST	INTRUSTS
	INTUBATE	INTUBATED · INTUBATES
	INTUIT	INTUITS
	INTUITION	INTUITIONS
	INTUMESCE	INTUMESCED · INTUMESCES
	INTURN	INTURNS
	INTUSE	INTUSES
	INTWINE	INTWINED · INTWINES

FRONT HOOK	ROOT WORD	END HOOK
	INTWIST	INTWISTS
	INUKSHUK	INUKSHUKS
	INULA	INULAS
	INULAS	INULASE
	INULASE	INULASES
	INULIN	INULINS
	INUMBRATE	INUMBRATED ▪ INUMBRATES
	INUNCTION	INUNCTIONS
	INUNDATE	INUNDATED ▪ INUNDATES
	INUNDATOR	INUNDATORS ▪ INUNDATORY
	INURE	INURED ▪ INURES
	INUREMENT	INUREMENTS
	INURN	INURNS
	INURNMENT	INURNMENTS
	INUSTION	INUSTIONS
	INVADE	INVADED ▪ INVADER ▪ INVADES
	INVADER	INVADERS
	INVALID	INVALIDS
	INVAR	INVARS
	INVARIANT	INVARIANTS
	INVASION	INVASIONS
	INVEAGLE	INVEAGLED ▪ INVEAGLES
	INVECTIVE	INVECTIVES
	INVEIGH	INVEIGHS
	INVEIGHER	INVEIGHERS
	INVEIGLE	INVEIGLED ▪ INVEIGLER ▪ INVEIGLES
	INVEIGLER	INVEIGLERS
	INVENT	INVENTS
	INVENTER	INVENTERS
	INVENTION	INVENTIONS
	INVENTOR	INVENTORS ▪ INVENTORY
	INVERSE	INVERSED ▪ INVERSES
	INVERSION	INVERSIONS
	INVERT	INVERTS
	INVERTASE	INVERTASES
	INVERTER	INVERTERS
	INVERTIN	INVERTING ▪ INVERTINS
	INVERTOR	INVERTORS
	INVEST	INVESTS
	INVESTOR	INVESTORS
	INVIOLATE	INVIOLATED
	INVISIBLE	INVISIBLES
	INVITE	INVITED ▪ INVITEE ▪ INVITER ▪ INVITES
	INVITEE	INVITEES
	INVITER	INVITERS
	INVITING	INVITINGS
	INVOCATE	INVOCATED ▪ INVOCATES
	INVOCATOR	INVOCATORS ▪ INVOCATORY
	INVOICE	INVOICED ▪ INVOICES
	INVOKE	INVOKED ▪ INVOKER ▪ INVOKES
	INVOKER	INVOKERS
	INVOLUCEL	INVOLUCELS
	INVOLUCRA	INVOLUCRAL
	INVOLUCRE	INVOLUCRES
	INVOLUTE	INVOLUTED ▪ INVOLUTES
	INVOLVE	INVOLVED ▪ INVOLVER ▪ INVOLVES
	INVOLVER	INVOLVERS
	INWALL	INWALLS
	INWARD	INWARDS
	INWEAVE	INWEAVED ▪ INWEAVES
	INWICK	INWICKS
	INWIND	INWINDS
	INWIT	INWITH ▪ INWITS
PINWORK ▪ TINWORK	**INWORK**	INWORKS
	INWORKING	INWORKINGS
PINWORKS ▪ TINWORKS	**INWORKS**	
	INWOVE	INWOVEN
	INWRAP	INWRAPS
	INWREATHE	INWREATHED ▪ INWREATHES

FRONT HOOK	ROOT WORD	END HOOK
	INYALA	INYALAS
BIO · GIO	**IO**	ION · IOS
	IODATE	IODATED · IODATES
	IODATION	IODATIONS
	IODID	IODIDE · IODIDS
	IODIDE	IODIDES
	IODIN	IODINE · IODINS
	IODINATE	IODINATED · IODINATES
	IODINE	IODINES
	IODISE	IODISED · IODISER · IODISES
	IODISER	IODISERS
	IODISM	IODISMS
	IODIZE	IODIZED · IODIZER · IODIZES
	IODIZER	IODIZERS
	IODOFORM	IODOFORMS
	IODOPHOR	IODOPHORS
	IODOPSIN	IODOPSINS
	IODURET	IODURETS
	IODYRITE	IODYRITES
	IOLITE	IOLITES
CION · LION · PION	**ION**	IONS
BIONIC · PIONIC	**IONIC**	IONICS
BIONICS	**IONICS**	
LIONISE	**IONISE**	IONISED · IONISER · IONISES
LIONISED	**IONISED**	
LIONISER	**IONISER**	IONISERS
LIONISERS	**IONISERS**	
LIONISES	**IONISES**	
LIONISING	**IONISING**	
	IONIUM	IONIUMS
LIONIZE	**IONIZE**	IONIZED · IONIZER · IONIZES
LIONIZED	**IONIZED**	
LIONIZER	**IONIZER**	IONIZERS
LIONIZERS	**IONIZERS**	
LIONIZES	**IONIZES**	
LIONIZING	**IONIZING**	
	IONOGEN	IONOGENS
	IONOMER	IONOMERS
	IONONE	IONONES
	IONOPAUSE	IONOPAUSES
	IONOPHORE	IONOPHORES
	IONOSONDE	IONOSONDES
CIONS · LIONS · PIONS	**IONS**	
BIOS · GIOS	**IOS**	
BIOTA · DIOTA	**IOTA**	IOTAS
	IOTACISM	IOTACISMS
BIOTAS · DIOTAS	**IOTAS**	
	IPECAC	IPECACS
	IPOMOEA	IPOMOEAS
	IPPON	IPPONS
	IPRINDOLE	IPRINDOLES
TIRADE	**IRADE**	IRADES
TIRADES	**IRADES**	
PIRATE	**IRATE**	IRATER
CIRE · DIRE · FIRE · HIRE · LIRE · MIRE · SIRE · TIRE · VIRE · WIRE	**IRE**	IRED · IRES
AIRED · FIRED · HIRED · MIRED · SIRED · TIRED · VIRED · WIRED	**IRED**	
DIREFUL	**IREFUL**	
DIREFULLY	**IREFULLY**	
FIRELESS · TIRELESS · WIRELESS	**IRELESS**	
EIRENIC · SIRENIC	**IRENIC**	IRENICS
EIRENICAL	**IRENICAL**	
	IRENICISM	IRENICISMS
EIRENICON	**IRENICON**	IRENICONS
EIRENICONS	**IRENICONS**	
CIRES · FIRES · HIRES · MIRES · SIRES · TIRES · VIRES · WIRES	**IRES**	
VIRID	**IRID**	IRIDS

FRONT HOOK	ROOT WORD	END HOOK
VIRIDIAN	**IRIDIAN**	
	IRIDISE	IRIDISED · IRIDISES
	IRIDIUM	IRIDIUMS
	IRIDIZE	IRIDIZED · IRIDIZES
	IRIDOCYTE	IRIDOCYTES
AIRING · FIRING · HIRING · MIRING	**IRING**	
SIRING · TIRING · VIRING · WIRING		
SIRIS	**IRIS**	
	IRISATE	IRISATED · IRISATES
	IRISATION	IRISATIONS
	IRISCOPE	IRISCOPES
	IRITIS	
MIRITIS · TIRITIS	**IRK**	IRKS
BIRK · DIRK · FIRK · KIRK · LIRK · MIRK		
YIRK		
DIRKED · FIRKED · KIRKED · LIRKED	**IRKED**	
YIRKED		
DIRKING · FIRKING · KIRKING · LIRKING	**IRKING**	
YIRKING		
BIRKS · DIRKS · FIRKS · KIRKS · LIRKS	**IRKS**	
MIRKS · YIRKS		
	IROKO	IROKOS
GIRON	**IRON**	IRONE · IRONS · IRONY
	IRONBARK	IRONBARKS
	IRONCLAD	IRONCLADS
	IRONE	IRONED · IRONER · IRONES
	IRONER	IRONERS
GIRONIC · TIRONIC	**IRONIC**	
	IRONIES	IRONIEST
	IRONING	IRONINGS
SIRONISE	**IRONISE**	IRONISED · IRONISES
SIRONISED	**IRONISED**	
SIRONISES	**IRONISES**	
SIRONISING	**IRONISING**	
SIRONIST	**IRONIST**	IRONISTS
SIRONIZE	**IRONIZE**	IRONIZED · IRONIZES
SIRONIZED	**IRONIZED**	
SIRONIZES	**IRONIZES**	
SIRONIZING	**IRONIZING**	
GIRONS	**IRONS**	
	IRONSIDE	IRONSIDES
	IRONSMITH	IRONSMITHS
	IRONSTONE	IRONSTONES
	IRONWARE	IRONWARES
	IRONWEED	IRONWEEDS
	IRONWOOD	IRONWOODS
	IRONWORK	IRONWORKS
	IRRADIATE	IRRADIATED · IRRADIATES
	IRREDENTA	IRREDENTAS
	IRREGULAR	IRREGULARS
	IRRIDENTA	IRRIDENTAS
	IRRIGATE	IRRIGATED · IRRIGATES
	IRRIGATOR	IRRIGATORS
	IRRISION	IRRISIONS
	IRRITANT	IRRITANTS
	IRRITATE	IRRITATED · IRRITATES
	IRRITATOR	IRRITATORS
	IRRUPT	IRRUPTS
	IRRUPTION	IRRUPTIONS
AIS · BIS · CIS · DIS · GIS · HIS · KIS	**IS**	ISH · ISM · ISO
LIS · MIS · NIS · PIS · QIS · SIS · TIS		
VIS · WIS · XIS		
	ISABEL	ISABELS
	ISABELLA	ISABELLAS
	ISAGOGE	ISAGOGES
	ISAGOGIC	ISAGOGICS
	ISALLOBAR	ISALLOBARS
	ISARITHM	ISARITHMS
	ISATIN	ISATINE · ISATINS
	ISATINE	ISATINES

FRONT HOOK	ROOT WORD	END HOOK
	ISBA	ISBAS
	ISCHAEMIA	ISCHAEMIAS
	ISCHEMIA	ISCHEMIAS
	ISCHIA	ISCHIAL
	ISCHURIA	ISCHURIAS
	ISEIKONIA	ISEIKONIAS
BISH ▪ DISH ▪ EISH ▪ FISH ▪ HISH ▪ KISH NISH ▪ PISH ▪ WISH	**ISH**	
BISHES ▪ DISHES ▪ FISHES ▪ HISHES KISHES ▪ NISHES ▪ PISHES ▪ WISHES	**ISHES**	
VISIT	**ISIT**	
	ISLAND	ISLANDS
	ISLANDER	ISLANDERS
AISLE ▪ LISLE	**ISLE**	ISLED ▪ ISLES ▪ ISLET
AISLED ▪ MISLED	**ISLED**	
AISLELESS	**ISLELESS**	
AISLES ▪ LISLES	**ISLES**	
	ISLET	ISLETS
AISLING	**ISLING**	
	ISLOMANIA	ISLOMANIAS
GISM ▪ JISM (offensive)	**ISM**	ISMS
GISMS ▪ JISMS (offensive)	**ISMS**	
	ISNA	ISNAE
MISO ▪ PISO	**ISO**	ISOS
	ISOAMYL	ISOAMYLS
	ISOBAR	ISOBARE ▪ ISOBARS
	ISOBARE	ISOBARES
	ISOBARISM	ISOBARISMS
	ISOBASE	ISOBASES
	ISOBATH	ISOBATHS
	ISOBRONT	ISOBRONTS
	ISOBUTANE	ISOBUTANES
	ISOBUTENE	ISOBUTENES
	ISOBUTYL	ISOBUTYLS
	ISOCHASM	ISOCHASMS
	ISOCHEIM	ISOCHEIMS
	ISOCHIMAL	ISOCHIMALS
	ISOCHIME	ISOCHIMES
	ISOCHOR	ISOCHORE ▪ ISOCHORS
	ISOCHORE	ISOCHORES
	ISOCHRON	ISOCHRONE ▪ ISOCHRONS
	ISOCHRONE	ISOCHRONES
	ISOCLINAL	ISOCLINALS
	ISOCLINE	ISOCLINES
	ISOCLINIC	ISOCLINICS
	ISOCRYMAL	ISOCRYMALS
	ISOCRYME	ISOCRYMES
	ISODOMON	ISODOMONS
	ISODONT	ISODONTS
	ISODONTAL	ISODONTALS
	ISODOSE	ISODOSES
	ISOENZYME	ISOENZYMES
	ISOFORM	ISOFORMS
	ISOGAMETE	ISOGAMETES
MISOGAMIC	**ISOGAMIC**	
MISOGAMIES	**ISOGAMIES**	
MISOGAMY	**ISOGAMY**	
	ISOGON	ISOGONE ▪ ISOGONS ▪ ISOGONY
	ISOGONAL	ISOGONALS
	ISOGONE	ISOGONES
	ISOGONIC	ISOGONICS
	ISOGRAFT	ISOGRAFTS
	ISOGRAM	ISOGRAMS
	ISOGRAPH	ISOGRAPHS
	ISOGRIV	ISOGRIVS
	ISOHEL	ISOHELS
	ISOHYET	ISOHYETS
	ISOHYETAL	ISOHYETALS
	ISOKONT	ISOKONTS

FRONT HOOK	ROOT WORD	END HOOK
	ISOKONTAN	ISOKONTANS
	ISOLATE	ISOLATED · ISOLATES
	ISOLATION	ISOLATIONS
	ISOLATOR	ISOLATORS
	ISOLEAD	ISOLEADS
	ISOLINE	ISOLINES
	ISOLOG	ISOLOGS
	ISOLOGUE	ISOLOGUES
	ISOMER	ISOMERE · ISOMERS
	ISOMERASE	ISOMERASES
	ISOMERE	ISOMERES
	ISOMERISE	ISOMERISED · ISOMERISES
	ISOMERISM	ISOMERISMS
	ISOMERIZE	ISOMERIZED · ISOMERIZES
	ISOMETRIC	ISOMETRICS
	ISOMORPH	ISOMORPHS
	ISONIAZID	ISONIAZIDE · ISONIAZIDS
	ISONOME	ISONOMES
	ISOOCTANE	ISOOCTANES
	ISOPACH	ISOPACHS
	ISOPHONE	ISOPHONES
	ISOPHOTE	ISOPHOTES
	ISOPLETH	ISOPLETHS
	ISOPOD	ISOPODS
	ISOPODAN	ISOPODANS
	ISOPRENE	ISOPRENES
	ISOPROPYL	ISOPROPYLS
	ISOPYCNAL	ISOPYCNALS
	ISOPYCNIC	ISOPYCNICS
MISOS · PISOS	**ISOS**	
	ISOSPIN	ISOSPINS
	ISOTACH	ISOTACHS
	ISOTHERAL	ISOTHERALS
	ISOTHERE	ISOTHERES
	ISOTHERM	ISOTHERMS
	ISOTONE	ISOTONES
	ISOTOPE	ISOTOPES
	ISOTRON	ISOTRONS
	ISOTYPE	ISOTYPES
	ISOZYME	ISOZYMES
	ISPAGHULA	ISPAGHULAS
	ISSEI	ISSEIS
	ISSUANCE	ISSUANCES
TISSUE	**ISSUE**	ISSUED · ISSUER · ISSUES
TISSUED	**ISSUED**	
	ISSUER	ISSUERS
TISSUES	**ISSUES**	
TISSUING	**ISSUING**	
	ISTANA	ISTANAS
	ISTHMI	ISTHMIC
	ISTHMIAN	ISTHMIANS
MISTLE	**ISTLE**	ISTLES
MISTLES	**ISTLES**	
AIT · BIT · CIT · DIT · FIT · GIT · HIT KIT · LIT · NIT · PIT · RIT · SIT · TIT WIT · ZIT	**IT**	ITA · ITS
DITA · PITA · VITA	**ITA**	ITAS
	ITACISM	ITACISMS
	ITALIC	ITALICS
	ITALICISE	ITALICISED · ITALICISES
	ITALICIZE	ITALICIZED · ITALICIZES
DITAS · LITAS · PITAS · VITAS	**ITAS**	
AITCH · BITCH · DITCH · FITCH · HITCH MITCH · PITCH · TITCH · WITCH	**ITCH**	ITCHY
BITCHED · DITCHED · HITCHED · MITCHED PITCHED · WITCHED	**ITCHED**	
AITCHES · BITCHES · DITCHES · FITCHES HITCHES · MITCHES · PITCHES · TITCHES WITCHES	**ITCHES**	

FRONT HOOK	ROOT WORD	END HOOK
BITCHIER · HITCHIER · PITCHIER TITCHIER · WITCHIER	**ITCHIER**	
BITCHIEST · HITCHIEST · PITCHIEST TITCHIEST · WITCHIEST	**ITCHIEST**	
BITCHILY · HITCHILY · PITCHILY	**ITCHILY**	
BITCHINESS · PITCHINESS	**ITCHINESS**	
BITCHING · DITCHING · HITCHING MITCHING · PITCHING · WITCHING	**ITCHING**	ITCHINGS
PITCHINGS · WITCHINGS	**ITCHINGS**	
WITCHWEED	**ITCHWEED**	ITCHWEEDS
WITCHWEEDS	**ITCHWEEDS**	
BITCHY · FITCHY · HITCHY · PITCHY TITCHY · WITCHY	**ITCHY**	
	ITEM	ITEMS
	ITEMISE	ITEMISED · ITEMISER · ITEMISES
	ITEMISER	ITEMISERS
	ITEMIZE	ITEMIZED · ITEMIZER · ITEMIZES
	ITEMIZER	ITEMIZERS
	ITERANCE	ITERANCES
LITERATE	**ITERATE**	ITERATED · ITERATES
LITERATES	**ITERATES**	
LITERATION	**ITERATION**	ITERATIONS
CITHER · DITHER · EITHER · HITHER LITHER · MITHER · NITHER · TITHER WITHER · ZITHER	**ITHER**	
	ITINERANT	ITINERANTS
	ITINERATE	ITINERATED · ITINERATES
AITS · BITS · CITS · DITS · FITS · GITS HITS · KITS · LITS · NITS · PITS · RITS SITS · TITS · WITS · ZITS	**ITS**	
CIVIES	**IVIES**	
	IVORIST	IVORISTS
	IVORYBILL	IVORYBILLS
	IVORYWOOD	IVORYWOODS
	IVRESSE	IVRESSES
JIVY · TIVY	**IVY**	
KIWI	**IWI**	IWIS
KIWIS	**IWIS**	
	IXIA	IXIAS
	IXODID	IXODIDS
	IXORA	IXORAS
	IXTLE	IXTLES
SIZAR	**IZAR**	IZARD · IZARS
LIZARD · RIZARD · VIZARD · WIZARD	**IZARD**	IZARDS
LIZARDS · RIZARDS · VIZARDS · WIZARDS	**IZARDS**	
SIZARS	**IZARS**	
	IZVESTIA	IZVESTIAS
	IZVESTIYA	IZVESTIYAS
DIZZARD · GIZZARD	**IZZARD**	IZZARDS
DIZZARDS · GIZZARDS	**IZZARDS**	
	IZZAT	IZZATS

I

J

FRONT HOOK	ROOT WORD	END HOOK
	JA	JAB = JAG = JAI = JAK = JAM = JAP = JAR JAW = JAY
	JAAP	JAAPS (offensive)
	JAB	JABS
	JABBER	JABBERS
	JABBERER	JABBERERS
	JABBERING	JABBERINGS
	JABBLE	JABBLED = JABBLES
	JABIRU	JABIRUS
	JABORANDI	JABORANDIS
	JABOT	JABOTS
	JACAL	JACALS
	JACAMAR	JACAMARS
	JACANA	JACANAS
	JACARANDA	JACARANDAS
	JACARE	JACARES
	JACINTH	JACINTHE = JACINTHS
	JACINTHE	JACINTHES
	JACK	JACKS = JACKY
	JACKAL	JACKALS
	JACKAROO	JACKAROOS
	JACKBOOT	JACKBOOTS
	JACKDAW	JACKDAWS
	JACKEEN	JACKEENS
	JACKER	JACKERS
	JACKEROO	JACKEROOS
	JACKET	JACKETS
	JACKFRUIT	JACKFRUITS
	JACKING	JACKINGS
	JACKKNIFE	JACKKNIFED = JACKKNIFES
	JACKLEG	JACKLEGS
	JACKLIGHT	JACKLIGHTS
	JACKPLANE	JACKPLANES
	JACKPOT	JACKPOTS
	JACKROLL	JACKROLLS
	JACKS	JACKSY (offensive)
	JACKSCREW	JACKSCREWS
	JACKSHAFT	JACKSHAFTS
	JACKSIE	JACKSIES (offensive)
	JACKSMELT	JACKSMELTS
	JACKSMITH	JACKSMITHS
	JACKSNIPE	JACKSNIPES
	JACKSTAY	JACKSTAYS
	JACKSTONE	JACKSTONES
	JACKSTRAW	JACKSTRAWS
	JACOBIN	JACOBINS
	JACONET	JACONETS
	JACQUARD	JACQUARDS
	JACQUERIE	JACQUERIES
	JACTATION	JACTATIONS
EJACULATE	**JACULATE**	JACULATED = JACULATES
EJACULATED	**JACULATED**	
EJACULATES	**JACULATES**	
EJACULATOR	**JACULATOR**	JACULATORS = JACULATORY
	JACUZZI	JACUZZIS
	JADE	JADED = JADES
	JADEITE	JADEITES
	JAEGER	JAEGERS
	JAFA	JAFAS (offensive)
	JAG	JAGA = JAGG = JAGS
	JAGA	JAGAS
	JAGER	JAGERS
	JAGG	JAGGS = JAGGY
	JAGGER	JAGGERS = JAGGERY
	JAGGIES	JAGGIEST
	JAGHIR	JAGHIRE = JAGHIRS

FRONT HOOK	ROOT WORD	END HOOK
	JAGHIRDAR	JAGHIRDARS
	JAGHIRE	JAGHIRES
	JAGIR	JAGIRS
	JAGRA	JAGRAS
	JAGUAR	JAGUARS
	JAI	JAIL
	JAIL	JAILS
	JAILBIRD	JAILBIRDS
	JAILBREAK	JAILBREAKS
	JAILER	JAILERS
	JAILHOUSE	JAILHOUSES
	JAILOR	JAILORS
	JAK	JAKE ▪ JAKS
	JAKE	JAKES ▪ JAKEY
	JAKEY	JAKEYS (offensive)
	JAKFRUIT	JAKFRUITS
	JALAP	JALAPS
	JALAPENO	JALAPENOS
	JALAPIN	JALAPINS
	JALOP	JALOPS ▪ JALOPY
	JALOUSE	JALOUSED ▪ JALOUSES
	JALOUSIE	JALOUSIED ▪ JALOUSIES
	JAM	JAMB ▪ JAMS
	JAMADAR	JAMADARS
	JAMB	JAMBE ▪ JAMBO ▪ JAMBS ▪ JAMBU
	JAMBALAYA	JAMBALAYAS
	JAMBART	JAMBARTS
	JAMBE	JAMBED ▪ JAMBEE ▪ JAMBER ▪ JAMBES
	JAMBEAU	JAMBEAUX
	JAMBEE	JAMBEES
	JAMBER	JAMBERS
	JAMBIER	JAMBIERS
	JAMBIYA	JAMBIYAH ▪ JAMBIYAS
	JAMBIYAH	JAMBIYAHS
	JAMBO	JAMBOK ▪ JAMBOS
SJAMBOK	**JAMBOK**	JAMBOKS
SJAMBOKKED	**JAMBOKKED**	
SJAMBOKS	**JAMBOKS**	
	JAMBOLAN	JAMBOLANA ▪ JAMBOLANS
	JAMBOLANA	JAMBOLANAS
	JAMBONE	JAMBONES
	JAMBOOL	JAMBOOLS
	JAMBOREE	JAMBOREES
	JAMBU	JAMBUL ▪ JAMBUS
	JAMBUL	JAMBULS
	JAMDANI	JAMDANIS
	JAMJAR	JAMJARS
	JAMMER	JAMMERS
	JAMMIES	JAMMIEST
	JAMMING	JAMMINGS
	JAMPAN	JAMPANI ▪ JAMPANS
	JAMPANEE	JAMPANEES
	JAMPANI	JAMPANIS
	JAMPOT	JAMPOTS
	JANDAL	JANDALS
	JANE	JANES
	JANGLE	JANGLED ▪ JANGLER ▪ JANGLES
	JANGLER	JANGLERS
	JANGLING	JANGLINGS
	JANITOR	JANITORS
	JANIZAR	JANIZARS ▪ JANIZARY
	JANKER	JANKERS
	JANN	JANNS ▪ JANNY
	JANNOCK	JANNOCKS
	JANSKY	JANSKYS
	JANTIES	JANTIEST
	JAP	JAPE ▪ JAPS
	JAPAN	JAPANS
	JAPANISE	JAPANISED ▪ JAPANISES

J

415

J

FRONT HOOK	ROOT WORD	END HOOK
	JAPANIZE	JAPANIZED · JAPANIZES
	JAPANNER	JAPANNERS
	JAPE	JAPED · JAPER · JAPES
	JAPER	JAPERS · JAPERY
	JAPING	JAPINGS
	JAPONICA	JAPONICAS
AJAR	JAR	JARK · JARL · JARP · JARS
	JARARACA	JARARACAS
	JARARAKA	JARARAKAS
	JARFUL	JARFULS
	JARGON	JARGONS · JARGONY
	JARGONEER	JARGONEERS
	JARGONEL	JARGONELS
	JARGONISE	JARGONISED · JARGONISES
	JARGONIST	JARGONISTS
	JARGONIZE	JARGONIZED · JARGONIZES
	JARGOON	JARGOONS
	JARHEAD	JARHEADS
	JARINA	JARINAS
	JARK	JARKS
	JARL	JARLS
	JARLDOM	JARLDOMS
	JARLSBERG	JARLSBERGS
	JAROOL	JAROOLS
	JAROSITE	JAROSITES
	JAROVISE	JAROVISED · JAROVISES
	JAROVIZE	JAROVIZED · JAROVIZES
	JARP	JARPS
	JARRAH	JARRAHS
	JARRING	JARRINGS
	JARTA	JARTAS
	JARUL	JARULS
	JARVEY	JARVEYS
	JARVIE	JARVIES
	JASEY	JASEYS
	JASMIN	JASMINE · JASMINS
	JASMINE	JASMINES
	JASP	JASPE · JASPS
	JASPE	JASPER · JASPES
	JASPER	JASPERS · JASPERY
	JASPERISE	JASPERISED · JASPERISES
	JASPERIZE	JASPERIZED · JASPERIZES
	JASPILITE	JASPILITES
	JASSID	JASSIDS
	JATAKA	JATAKAS
	JATO	JATOS
	JAUK	JAUKS
	JAUNCE	JAUNCED · JAUNCES
	JAUNDICE	JAUNDICED · JAUNDICES
	JAUNSE	JAUNSED · JAUNSES
	JAUNT	JAUNTS · JAUNTY
	JAUNTIE	JAUNTIER · JAUNTIES
	JAUNTIES	JAUNTIEST
	JAUP	JAUPS
	JAVA	JAVAS
	JAVEL	JAVELS
	JAVELIN	JAVELINA · JAVELINS
	JAVELINA	JAVELINAS
	JAW	JAWS
	JAWAN	JAWANS
	JAWARI	JAWARIS
	JAWBATION	JAWBATIONS
	JAWBONE	JAWBONED · JAWBONER · JAWBONES
	JAWBONER	JAWBONERS
	JAWBONING	JAWBONINGS
	JAWFALL	JAWFALLS
	JAWHOLE	JAWHOLES
	JAWING	JAWINGS
	JAWLINE	JAWLINES

FRONT HOOK	ROOT WORD	END HOOK
	JAXIE	JAXIES (offensive)
	JAY	JAYS
	JAYBIRD	JAYBIRDS
	JAYGEE	JAYGEES
	JAYHAWKER	JAYHAWKERS
	JAYVEE	JAYVEES
	JAYWALK	JAYWALKS
	JAYWALKER	JAYWALKERS
	JAZERANT	JAZERANTS
	JAZZ	JAZZY
	JAZZBO	JAZZBOS
	JAZZER	JAZZERS
	JEALOUS	JEALOUSE · JEALOUSY
	JEALOUSE	JEALOUSED · JEALOUSES
	JEAN	JEANS
	JEANETTE	JEANETTES
	JEAT	JEATS
DJEBEL	JEBEL	JEBELS
DJEBELS	JEBELS	
	JEDI	JEDIS
AJEE	JEE	JEED · JEEL · JEEP · JEER · JEES · JEEZ
	JEEL	JEELS · JEELY
	JEELIE	JEELIED · JEELIES
	JEEP	JEEPS
	JEEPNEY	JEEPNEYS
	JEER	JEERS
	JEERER	JEERERS
	JEERING	JEERINGS
	JEFE	JEFES
	JEFF	JEFFS
	JEHAD	JEHADI · JEHADS
	JEHADI	JEHADIS
	JEHADIS	JEHADISM · JEHADIST
	JEHADISM	JEHADISMS
	JEHADIST	JEHADISTS
	JEHU	JEHUS
	JEJUNA	JEJUNAL
	JELAB	JELABS
	JELL	JELLO · JELLS · JELLY
DJELLABA	JELLABA	JELLABAH · JELLABAS
DJELLABAH	JELLABAH	JELLABAHS
DJELLABAHS	JELLABAHS	
DJELLABAS	JELLABAS	
	JELLO	JELLOS
	JELLYBEAN	JELLYBEANS
	JELLYROLL	JELLYROLLS
	JELUTONG	JELUTONGS
	JEMADAR	JEMADARS
DJEMBE	JEMBE	JEMBES
DJEMBES	JEMBES	
	JEMIDAR	JEMIDARS
	JEMIMA	JEMIMAS
	JEMMIES	JEMMIEST
	JENNET	JENNETS
	JENNETING	JENNETINGS
	JEOFAIL	JEOFAILS
	JEOPARD	JEOPARDS · JEOPARDY
	JEOPARDER	JEOPARDERS
	JERBIL	JERBILS
	JERBOA	JERBOAS
	JEREED	JEREEDS
	JEREMIAD	JEREMIADS
	JEREPIGO	JEREPIGOS
	JERFALCON	JERFALCONS
	JERID	JERIDS
	JERK	JERKS · JERKY
	JERKER	JERKERS
	JERKIES	JERKIEST
	JERKIN	JERKING · JERKINS

FRONT HOOK	ROOT WORD	END HOOK
	JERKING	JERKINGS
	JERKWATER	JERKWATERS
	JEROBOAM	JEROBOAMS
	JERQUE	JERQUED · JERQUER · JERQUES
	JERQUER	JERQUERS
	JERQUING	JERQUINGS
	JERREED	JERREEDS
	JERRICAN	JERRICANS
	JERRID	JERRIDS
	JERRYCAN	JERRYCANS
	JERSEY	JERSEYS
	JESS	JESSE
	JESSAMINE	JESSAMINES
	JESSE	JESSED · JESSES
	JESSERANT	JESSERANTS
	JESSIE	JESSIES
	JEST	JESTS
	JESTBOOK	JESTBOOKS
	JESTEE	JESTEES
	JESTER	JESTERS
	JESTING	JESTINGS
	JESUIT	JESUITS (offensive)
	JESUITISM	JESUITISMS (offensive)
	JET	JETE · JETS
	JETBEAD	JETBEADS
	JETE	JETES
	JETFOIL	JETFOILS
	JETLAG	JETLAGS
	JETLINER	JETLINERS
	JETON	JETONS
	JETPLANE	JETPLANES
	JETPORT	JETPORTS
	JETSAM	JETSAMS
	JETSOM	JETSOMS
	JETSON	JETSONS
	JETSTREAM	JETSTREAMS
	JETTATURA	JETTATURAS
	JETTIES	JETTIEST
	JETTISON	JETTISONS
	JETTON	JETTONS
	JETWAY	JETWAYS
	JEU	JEUX
	JEW	JEWS (offensive)
	JEWEL	JEWELS
	JEWELER	JEWELERS
	JEWELLER	JEWELLERS · JEWELLERY
	JEWELWEED	JEWELWEEDS
	JEWIE	JEWIES
	JEZAIL	JEZAILS
	JEZEBEL	JEZEBELS
	JHALA	JHALAS
	JHATKA	JHATKAS
	JIAO	JIAOS
	JIB	JIBB · JIBE · JIBS
	JIBB	JIBBS
DJIBBAH	**JIBBAH**	JIBBAHS
DJIBBAHS	**JIBBAHS**	
	JIBBER	JIBBERS
	JIBBING	JIBBINGS
	JIBBOOM	JIBBOOMS
	JIBE	JIBED · JIBER · JIBES
	JIBER	JIBERS
	JICAMA	JICAMAS
	JICKAJOG	JICKAJOGS
	JIFF	JIFFS · JIFFY
	JIG	JIGS
	JIGABOO	JIGABOOS (offensive)
	JIGAJIG	JIGAJIGS
	JIGAJOG	JIGAJOGS

J

FRONT HOOK	ROOT WORD	END HOOK
	JIGAMAREE	JIGAMAREES
	JIGGER	JIGGERS
	JIGGING	JIGGINGS
	JIGGLE	JIGGLED · JIGGLES
	JIGGUMBOB	JIGGUMBOBS
	JIGJIG	JIGJIGS
	JIGOT	JIGOTS
	JIGSAW	JIGSAWN · JIGSAWS
	JIHAD	JIHADI · JIHADS
	JIHADI	JIHADIS
	JIHADIS	JIHADISM · JIHADIST
	JIHADISM	JIHADISMS
	JIHADIST	JIHADISTS
	JILBAB	JILBABS
	JILGIE	JILGIES
	JILL	JILLS
	JILLAROO	JILLAROOS
	JILLET	JILLETS
	JILLFLIRT	JILLFLIRTS
	JILLION	JILLIONS
	JILT	JILTS
	JILTER	JILTERS
	JIMCRACK	JIMCRACKS
	JIMJAM	JIMJAMS
	JIMMIE	JIMMIED · JIMMIES
	JIMP	JIMPY
DJIN	JIN	JINK · JINN · JINS · JINX
	JINGAL	JINGALL · JINGALS
	JINGALL	JINGALLS
	JINGBANG	JINGBANGS
	JINGLE	JINGLED · JINGLER · JINGLES · JINGLET
	JINGLER	JINGLERS
	JINGLET	JINGLETS
	JINGOISM	JINGOISMS
	JINGOIST	JINGOISTS
	JINJILI	JINJILIS
	JINK	JINKS
	JINKER	JINKERS
DJINN	JINN	JINNE · JINNI · JINNS
	JINNE	JINNEE
DJINNI	JINNI	JINNIS
DJINNS	JINNS	
	JINRIKSHA	JINRIKSHAS
DJINS	JINS	
	JIPIJAPA	JIPIJAPAS
	JIPYAPA	JIPYAPAS
	JIRBLE	JIRBLED · JIRBLES
	JIRD	JIRDS
	JIRGA	JIRGAS
	JIRKINET	JIRKINETS
	JISM	JISMS (offensive)
	JISSOM	JISSOMS (offensive)
	JITNEY	JITNEYS
	JITTER	JITTERS · JITTERY
	JITTERBUG	JITTERBUGS
	JIUJITSU	JIUJITSUS
	JIUJUTSU	JIUJUTSUS
	JIVE	JIVED · JIVER · JIVES · JIVEY
	JIVER	JIVERS
	JIZ	JIZZ
	JNANA	JNANAS
	JO	JOB · JOE · JOG · JOL · JOR · JOT · JOW JOY
	JOANNA	JOANNAS
	JOB	JOBE · JOBS
	JOBATION	JOBATIONS
	JOBBER	JOBBERS · JOBBERY
	JOBBIE	JOBBIES
	JOBBING	JOBBINGS

J

FRONT HOOK	ROOT WORD	END HOOK
	JOBCENTRE	JOBCENTRES
	JOBE	JOBED · JOBES
	JOBERNOWL	JOBERNOWLS
	JOBHOLDER	JOBHOLDERS
	JOBNAME	JOBNAMES
	JOBSEEKER	JOBSEEKERS
	JOBSHARE	JOBSHARES
	JOBSWORTH	JOBSWORTHS
	JOCK	JOCKO · JOCKS
	JOCKETTE	JOCKETTES
	JOCKEY	JOCKEYS
	JOCKEYISM	JOCKEYISMS
	JOCKNEY	JOCKNEYS
	JOCKO	JOCKOS
	JOCKSTRAP	JOCKSTRAPS
	JOCKTELEG	JOCKTELEGS
	JOCULATOR	JOCULATORS
	JODEL	JODELS
	JODHPUR	JODHPURS
SJOE	**JOE**	JOES · JOEY
	JOEY	JOEYS
	JOG	JOGS
	JOGGER	JOGGERS
	JOGGING	JOGGINGS
	JOGGLE	JOGGLED · JOGGLER · JOGGLES
	JOGGLER	JOGGLERS
	JOGTROT	JOGTROTS
	JOHN	JOHNS
	JOHNBOAT	JOHNBOATS
	JOHNNIE	JOHNNIES
	JOHNSON	JOHNSONS (offensive)
	JOIN	JOINS · JOINT
	JOINDER	JOINDERS
	JOINER	JOINERS · JOINERY
	JOINING	JOININGS
	JOINT	JOINTS
	JOINTER	JOINTERS
	JOINTURE	JOINTURED · JOINTURES
	JOINTURES	JOINTURESS
	JOINTWEED	JOINTWEEDS
	JOINTWORM	JOINTWORMS
	JOIST	JOISTS
	JOJOBA	JOJOBAS
	JOKE	JOKED · JOKER · JOKES · JOKEY
	JOKER	JOKERS
	JOKESMITH	JOKESMITHS
	JOKESTER	JOKESTERS
	JOL	JOLE · JOLL · JOLS · JOLT
	JOLE	JOLED · JOLES
	JOLL	JOLLS · JOLLY
	JOLLEY	JOLLEYS
	JOLLEYER	JOLLEYERS
	JOLLEYING	JOLLEYINGS
	JOLLIER	JOLLIERS
	JOLLIES	JOLLIEST
	JOLLIMENT	JOLLIMENTS
	JOLLOP	JOLLOPS
	JOLLYBOAT	JOLLYBOATS
	JOLLYER	JOLLYERS
	JOLLYHEAD	JOLLYHEADS
	JOLLYING	JOLLYINGS
	JOLT	JOLTS · JOLTY
	JOLTER	JOLTERS
	JOLTHEAD	JOLTHEADS
	JOMO	JOMON · JOMOS
	JONCANOE	JONCANOES
	JONG	JONGS
	JONGLEUR	JONGLEURS
	JONNYCAKE	JONNYCAKES

J

FRONT HOOK	ROOT WORD	END HOOK
	JONQUIL	JONQUILS
	JOOK	JOOKS
	JOR	JORS
	JORAM	JORAMS
	JORDAN	JORDANS
	JORDELOO	JORDELOOS
	JORUM	JORUMS
	JOSEPH	JOSEPHS
	JOSHER	JOSHERS
	JOSKIN	JOSKINS
	JOSSER	JOSSERS
	JOSTLE	JOSTLED ▪ JOSTLER ▪ JOSTLES
	JOSTLER	JOSTLERS
	JOSTLING	JOSTLINGS
	JOT	JOTA ▪ JOTS
	JOTA	JOTAS
	JOTTER	JOTTERS
	JOTTING	JOTTINGS
	JOTUN	JOTUNN ▪ JOTUNS
	JOTUNN	JOTUNNS
	JOUAL	JOUALS
	JOUISANCE	JOUISANCES
	JOUK	JOUKS
	JOULE	JOULED ▪ JOULES
	JOUNCE	JOUNCED ▪ JOUNCES
	JOUR	JOURS
	JOURNAL	JOURNALS
	JOURNEY	JOURNEYS
	JOURNEYER	JOURNEYERS
	JOURNO	JOURNOS
	JOUST	JOUSTS
	JOUSTER	JOUSTERS
	JOW	JOWL ▪ JOWS
	JOWAR	JOWARI ▪ JOWARS
	JOWARI	JOWARIS
	JOWL	JOWLS ▪ JOWLY
	JOWLER	JOWLERS
	JOY	JOYS
	JOYANCE	JOYANCES
	JOYPOP	JOYPOPS
	JOYPOPPER	JOYPOPPERS
	JOYRIDE	JOYRIDER ▪ JOYRIDES
	JOYRIDER	JOYRIDERS
	JOYRIDING	JOYRIDINGS
	JOYSTICK	JOYSTICKS
	JUBA	JUBAS
	JUBBAH	JUBBAHS
	JUBE	JUBES
	JUBHAH	JUBHAHS
	JUBILANCE	JUBILANCES
	JUBILATE	JUBILATED ▪ JUBILATES
	JUBILE	JUBILEE ▪ JUBILES
	JUBILEE	JUBILEES
	JUCO	JUCOS
	JUD	JUDO ▪ JUDS ▪ JUDY
	JUDDER	JUDDERS
	JUDGE	JUDGED ▪ JUDGER ▪ JUDGES
	JUDGEMENT	JUDGEMENTS
	JUDGER	JUDGERS
	JUDGESHIP	JUDGESHIPS
	JUDGMENT	JUDGMENTS
	JUDICATOR	JUDICATORS ▪ JUDICATORY
	JUDO	JUDOS
	JUDOGI	JUDOGIS
	JUDOIST	JUDOISTS
	JUDOKA	JUDOKAS
	JUG	JUGA ▪ JUGS
AJUGA	**JUGA**	JUGAL
	JUGAL	JUGALS

J

FRONT HOOK	ROOT WORD	END HOOK
	JUGFUL	JUGFULS
	JUGGING	JUGGINGS
	JUGGLE	JUGGLED · JUGGLER · JUGGLES
	JUGGLER	JUGGLERS · JUGGLERY
	JUGGLING	JUGGLINGS
	JUGHEAD	JUGHEADS
	JUGLET	JUGLETS
	JUGULA	JUGULAR
	JUGULAR	JUGULARS
	JUGULATE	JUGULATED · JUGULATES
	JUGUM	JUGUMS
	JUICE	JUICED · JUICER · JUICES
	JUICEHEAD	JUICEHEADS
	JUICER	JUICERS
	JUJITSU	JUJITSUS
	JUJU	JUJUS
	JUJUBE	JUJUBES
	JUJUISM	JUJUISMS
	JUJUIST	JUJUISTS
	JUJUTSU	JUJUTSUS
	JUKE	JUKED · JUKES
	JUKSKEI	JUKSKEIS
	JUKU	JUKUS
	JULEP	JULEPS
	JULIENNE	JULIENNED · JULIENNES
	JUMAR	JUMARS · JUMART
	JUMART	JUMARTS
	JUMBAL	JUMBALS
	JUMBIE	JUMBIES
	JUMBLE	JUMBLED · JUMBLER · JUMBLES
	JUMBLER	JUMBLERS
	JUMBO	JUMBOS
	JUMBOISE	JUMBOISED · JUMBOISES
	JUMBOIZE	JUMBOIZED · JUMBOIZES
	JUMBUCK	JUMBUCKS
	JUMELLE	JUMELLES
	JUMP	JUMPS · JUMPY
	JUMPER	JUMPERS
	JUMPING	JUMPINGS
	JUMPOFF	JUMPOFFS
	JUMPSUIT	JUMPSUITS
	JUN	JUNK
	JUNCATE	JUNCATES
	JUNCO	JUNCOS
	JUNCTION	JUNCTIONS
	JUNCTURE	JUNCTURES
	JUNEATING	JUNEATINGS
	JUNGLE	JUNGLED · JUNGLES
	JUNGLEGYM	JUNGLEGYMS
	JUNGLI	JUNGLIS
	JUNGLIS	JUNGLIST
	JUNGLIST	JUNGLISTS
	JUNIOR	JUNIORS
	JUNIORATE	JUNIORATES
	JUNIPER	JUNIPERS
	JUNK	JUNKS · JUNKY
	JUNKANOO	JUNKANOOS
	JUNKER	JUNKERS
	JUNKET	JUNKETS
	JUNKETEER	JUNKETEERS
	JUNKETER	JUNKETERS
	JUNKETING	JUNKETINGS
	JUNKETTER	JUNKETTERS
	JUNKIE	JUNKIER · JUNKIES
	JUNKIES	JUNKIEST
	JUNKYARD	JUNKYARDS
	JUNTA	JUNTAS
	JUNTO	JUNTOS
	JUPATI	JUPATIS

FRONT HOOK	ROOT WORD	END HOOK
	JUPE	JUPES
	JUPON	JUPONS
	JURA	JURAL ▪ JURAT
	JURANT	JURANTS
	JURAT	JURATS
	JURE	JUREL
	JUREL	JURELS
	JURIST	JURISTS
	JUROR	JURORS
	JURYMAST	JURYMASTS
GJUS	JUS	JUST
	JUSSIVE	JUSSIVES
	JUST	JUSTS
	JUSTER	JUSTERS
	JUSTICE	JUSTICER ▪ JUSTICES
	JUSTICER	JUSTICERS
	JUSTICIAR	JUSTICIARS ▪ JUSTICIARY
	JUSTIFIER	JUSTIFIERS
	JUSTLE	JUSTLED ▪ JUSTLES
	JUT	JUTE ▪ JUTS
	JUTE	JUTES
	JUVE	JUVES
	JUVENAL	JUVENALS
	JUVENILE	JUVENILES
	JUXTAPOSE	JUXTAPOSED ▪ JUXTAPOSES

J

K

FRONT HOOK	ROOT WORD	END HOOK
AKA • OKA • SKA	**KA**	KAB • KAE • KAF • KAI • KAK • KAM KAS • KAT • KAW • KAY
	KAAMA	KAAMAS
	KAB	KABS
	KABAB	KABABS
	KABADDI	KABADDIS
	KABAKA	KABAKAS
	KABALA	KABALAS
	KABALISM	KABALISMS
	KABALIST	KABALISTS
	KABAR	KABARS
	KABAYA	KABAYAS
	KABBALA	KABBALAH • KABBALAS
	KABBALAH	KABBALAHS
	KABBALISM	KABBALISMS
	KABBALIST	KABBALISTS
	KABELE	KABELES
	KABELJOU	KABELJOUS • KABELJOUW
	KABELJOUW	KABELJOUWS
	KABIKI	KABIKIS
	KABOB	KABOBS
	KABUKI	KABUKIS
	KACCHA	KACCHAS
	KACHAHRI	KACHAHRIS
	KACHERI	KACHERIS
	KACHINA	KACHINAS
	KADAITCHA	KADAITCHAS
	KADE	KADES
	KADI	KADIS
	KAE	KAED • KAES
	KAF	KAFS
	KAFFIR	KAFFIRS
	KAFFIYAH	KAFFIYAHS
	KAFFIYEH	KAFFIYEHS
	KAFILA	KAFILAS
	KAFIR	KAFIRS
	KAFTAN	KAFTANS
	KAGO	KAGOS
	KAGOOL	KAGOOLS
	KAGOUL	KAGOULE • KAGOULS
	KAGOULE	KAGOULES
	KAGU	KAGUS
	KAHAL	KAHALS
	KAHAWAI	KAHAWAIS
	KAHIKATEA	KAHIKATEAS
	KAHUNA	KAHUNAS
	KAI	KAID • KAIE • KAIF • KAIK • KAIL KAIM • KAIN • KAIS
	KAIAK	KAIAKS
	KAID	KAIDS
	KAIE	KAIES
	KAIF	KAIFS
	KAIK	KAIKA • KAIKS
	KAIKA	KAIKAI • KAIKAS
	KAIKAI	KAIKAIS
SKAIL SKAILS	**KAIL**	KAILS
	KAILS	
	KAILYAIRD	KAILYAIRDS
	KAILYARD	KAILYARDS
	KAIM	KAIMS
	KAIMAKAM	KAIMAKAMS
	KAIN	KAING • KAINS
	KAING	KAINGA
	KAINGA	KAINGAS
	KAINIT	KAINITE • KAINITS
	KAINITE	KAINITES

FRONT HOOK	ROOT WORD	END HOOK
	KAIROMONE	KAIROMONES
	KAISER	KAISERS
	KAISERDOM	KAISERDOMS
	KAISERIN	KAISERINS
	KAISERISM	KAISERISMS
	KAIZEN	KAIZENS
	KAJAWAH	KAJAWAHS
	KAJEPUT	KAJEPUTS
	KAK	KAKA ▪ KAKI ▪ KAKS (offensive)
	KAKA	KAKAS
	KAKAPO	KAKAPOS
	KAKEMONO	KAKEMONOS
	KAKI	KAKIS
	KAKIEMON	KAKIEMONS
	KAKODYL	KAKODYLS
	KALAM	KALAMS
	KALAMATA	KALAMATAS
	KALAMDAN	KALAMDANS
	KALAMKARI	KALAMKARIS
	KALANCHOE	KALANCHOES
	KALE	KALES
	KALENDAR	KALENDARS
	KALEYARD	KALEYARDS
	KALI	KALIF ▪ KALIS
	KALIAN	KALIANS
	KALIF	KALIFS
	KALIFATE	KALIFATES
	KALIMBA	KALIMBAS
	KALINITE	KALINITES
	KALIPH	KALIPHS
	KALIPHATE	KALIPHATES
	KALIUM	KALIUMS
	KALLIDIN	KALLIDINS
	KALLITYPE	KALLITYPES
	KALMIA	KALMIAS
	KALONG	KALONGS
	KALOTYPE	KALOTYPES
	KALPA	KALPAC ▪ KALPAK ▪ KALPAS
	KALPAC	KALPACS
	KALPAK	KALPAKS
	KALSOMINE	KALSOMINED ▪ KALSOMINES
	KALUMPIT	KALUMPITS
	KALYPTRA	KALYPTRAS
	KAM	KAMA ▪ KAME ▪ KAMI
	KAMA	KAMAS
	KAMAAINA	KAMAAINAS
	KAMACITE	KAMACITES
	KAMALA	KAMALAS
	KAME	KAMES
	KAMELA	KAMELAS
	KAMERAD	KAMERADS
	KAMI	KAMIK ▪ KAMIS
	KAMICHI	KAMICHIS
	KAMIK	KAMIKS
	KAMIKAZE	KAMIKAZES
	KAMILA	KAMILAS
	KAMPONG	KAMPONGS
	KAMSEEN	KAMSEENS
	KAMSIN	KAMSINS
	KANA	KANAE ▪ KANAS
	KANAKA	KANAKAS
	KANAMYCIN	KANAMYCINS
	KANBAN	KANBANS
	KANE	KANEH ▪ KANES
	KANEH	KANEHS
	KANG	KANGA ▪ KANGS
	KANGA	KANGAS
	KANGAROO	KANGAROOS
	KANGHA	KANGHAS

H

FRONT HOOK	ROOT WORD	END HOOK
	KANJI	KANJIS
IKANS	**KANS**	
	KANT	KANTS
	KANTAR	KANTARS
	KANTELA	KANTELAS
	KANTELE	KANTELES
	KANTEN	KANTENS
	KANTHA	KANTHAS
	KANTIKOY	KANTIKOYS
	KANZU	KANZUS
	KAOLIANG	KAOLIANGS
	KAOLIN	KAOLINE ▪ KAOLINS
	KAOLINE	KAOLINES
	KAOLINISE	KAOLINISED ▪ KAOLINISES
	KAOLINITE	KAOLINITES
	KAOLINIZE	KAOLINIZED ▪ KAOLINIZES
	KAON	KAONS
	KAPA	KAPAS
	KAPH	KAPHS
	KAPOK	KAPOKS
	KAPPA	KAPPAS
	KAPUT	KAPUTT
	KARA	KARAS ▪ KARAT
	KARABINER	KARABINERS
	KARAISM	KARAISMS
	KARAIT	KARAITS
	KARAKA	KARAKAS
	KARAKIA	KARAKIAS
	KARAKUL	KARAKULS
	KARAMU	KARAMUS
	KARANGA	KARANGAS
	KARAOKE	KARAOKES
	KARAT	KARATE ▪ KARATS
	KARATE	KARATES
	KARATEIST	KARATEISTS
	KARATEKA	KARATEKAS
	KARENGO	KARENGOS
	KARITE	KARITES
	KARK	KARKS
	KARMA	KARMAS
	KARN	KARNS
	KARO	KAROO
	KAROO	KAROOS
	KARORO	KAROROS
	KAROSHI	KAROSHIS
	KARRI	KARRIS
	KARROO	KARROOS
	KARSEY	KARSEYS
	KARST	KARSTS
SKART	**KART**	KARTS
	KARTER	KARTERS
	KARTING	KARTINGS
SKARTS	**KARTS**	
	KARYOGRAM	KARYOGRAMS
	KARYON	KARYONS
	KARYOSOME	KARYOSOMES
	KARYOTIN	KARYOTINS
	KARYOTYPE	KARYOTYPED ▪ KARYOTYPES
OKAS ▪ SKAS	**KAS**	
	KASBAH	KASBAHS
	KASHA	KASHAS
	KASHER	KASHERS
	KASHMIR	KASHMIRS
	KASHRUT	KASHRUTH ▪ KASHRUTS
	KASHRUTH	KASHRUTHS
IKAT ▪ SKAT	**KAT**	KATA ▪ KATI ▪ KATS
	KATA	KATAS
	KATAKANA	KATAKANAS
	KATANA	KATANAS

FRONT HOOK	ROOT WORD	END HOOK
	KATCHINA	KATCHINAS
	KATCINA	KATCINAS
	KATHAK	KATHAKS
	KATHAKALI	KATHAKALIS
	KATHODE	KATHODES
	KATI	KATIS
	KATION	KATIONS
	KATIPO	KATIPOS
	KATORGA	KATORGAS
IKATS ▪ SKATS	KATS	
	KATSURA	KATSURAS
	KATTI	KATTIS
	KATYDID	KATYDIDS
	KAUGH	KAUGHS
	KAUMATUA	KAUMATUAS
	KAUPAPA	KAUPAPAS
	KAURI	KAURIS
	KAVA	KAVAS
	KAVAKAVA	KAVAKAVAS
	KAVAS	KAVASS
SKAW	KAW	KAWA ▪ KAWS
	KAWA	KAWAS ▪ KAWAU
	KAWAKAWA	KAWAKAWAS
SKAWS	KAWS	
OKAY	KAY	KAYO ▪ KAYS
	KAYAK	KAYAKS
	KAYAKER	KAYAKERS
	KAYAKING	KAYAKINGS
	KAYLE	KAYLES
	KAYO	KAYOS
	KAYOING	KAYOINGS
OKAYS	KAYS	
	KAZATZKA	KAZATZKAS
	KAZI	KAZIS
	KAZILLION	KAZILLIONS
	KAZOO	KAZOOS
	KBAR	KBARS
	KEA	KEAS
	KEASAR	KEASARS
	KEAVIE	KEAVIES
	KEB	KEBS
	KEBAB	KEBABS
	KEBAR	KEBARS
	KEBBIE	KEBBIES
	KEBBOCK	KEBBOCKS
	KEBBUCK	KEBBUCKS
	KEBELE	KEBELES
	KEBLAH	KEBLAHS
	KEBOB	KEBOBS
	KECK	KECKS
	KECKLE	KECKLED ▪ KECKLES
	KECKLING	KECKLINGS
	KECKS	KECKSY
AKED ▪ EKED	KED	KEDS
	KEDDAH	KEDDAHS
	KEDGE	KEDGED ▪ KEDGER ▪ KEDGES
	KEDGER	KEDGERS
	KEDGEREE	KEDGEREES
SKEEF	KEEF	KEEFS
	KEEK	KEEKS
	KEEKER	KEEKERS
	KEEL	KEELS
	KEELAGE	KEELAGES
	KEELBOAT	KEELBOATS
	KEELER	KEELERS
	KEELHALE	KEELHALED ▪ KEELHALES
	KEELHAUL	KEELHAULS
	KEELIE	KEELIES
	KEELING	KEELINGS

FRONT HOOK	ROOT WORD	END HOOK
	KEELIVINE	KEELIVINES
	KEELSON	KEELSONS
	KEELYVINE	KEELYVINES
SKEEN	**KEEN**	KEENO ▪ KEENS
	KEENER	KEENERS
	KEENING	KEENINGS
	KEENO	KEENOS
SKEENS	**KEENS**	
	KEEP	KEEPS
	KEEPER	KEEPERS
	KEEPING	KEEPINGS
	KEEPNET	KEEPNETS
	KEEPSAKE	KEEPSAKES
	KEESHOND	KEESHONDS
	KEESTER	KEESTERS
SKEET	**KEET**	KEETS
SKEETS	**KEETS**	
	KEEVE	KEEVES
	KEF	KEFS
	KEFFEL	KEFFELS
	KEFFIYAH	KEFFIYAHS
	KEFFIYEH	KEFFIYEHS
	KEFIR	KEFIRS
	KEFUFFLE	KEFUFFLED ▪ KEFUFFLES
SKEG	**KEG**	KEGS
	KEGELER	KEGELERS
SKEGGER	**KEGGER**	KEGGERS
SKEGGERS	**KEGGERS**	
	KEGLER	KEGLERS
	KEGLING	KEGLINGS
SKEGS	**KEGS**	
	KEHUA	KEHUAS
	KEIR	KEIRS
	KEIRETSU	KEIRETSUS
	KEISTER	KEISTERS
	KEITLOA	KEITLOAS
	KEKSYE	KEKSYES
	KELEP	KELEPS
	KELIM	KELIMS
SKELL	**KELL**	KELLS ▪ KELLY
	KELLAUT	KELLAUTS
SKELLIES	**KELLIES**	
SKELLS	**KELLS**	
SKELLY	**KELLY**	
	KELOID	KELOIDS
SKELP	**KELP**	KELPS ▪ KELPY
SKELPED	**KELPED**	
	KELPER	KELPERS
	KELPIE	KELPIES
SKELPING	**KELPING**	
SKELPS	**KELPS**	
	KELSON	KELSONS
	KELT	KELTS ▪ KELTY
SKELTER	**KELTER**	KELTERS
SKELTERS	**KELTERS**	
	KELTIE	KELTIES
	KELVIN	KELVINS
	KEMB	KEMBO ▪ KEMBS
	KEMBLA	KEMBLAS
	KEMBO	KEMBOS
	KEMP	KEMPS ▪ KEMPT ▪ KEMPY
	KEMPER	KEMPERS
	KEMPING	KEMPINGS
	KEMPLE	KEMPLES
SKEN	**KEN**	KENO ▪ KENS ▪ KENT
	KENAF	KENAFS
	KENDO	KENDOS
SKENNED	**KENNED**	
	KENNEL	KENNELS

FRONT HOOK	ROOT WORD	END HOOK
	KENNER	KENNERS
	KENNET	KENNETS = KENNETT
	KENNETT	KENNETTS
SKENNING	KENNING	KENNINGS
	KENO	KENOS
	KENOTIC	KENOTICS
	KENOTRON	KENOTRONS
SKENS	KENS	
	KENT	KENTE = KENTS
	KENTE	KENTED = KENTES
	KENTIA	KENTIAS
	KENTLEDGE	KENTLEDGES
SKEP	KEP	KEPI = KEPS = KEPT
	KEPHALIC	KEPHALICS
	KEPHALIN	KEPHALINS
	KEPHIR	KEPHIRS
	KEPI	KEPIS
SKEPPED	KEPPED	
SKEPPING	KEPPING	
SKEPS	KEPS	
	KERAMIC	KERAMICS
	KERATIN	KERATINS
	KERATOMA	KERATOMAS
	KERATOSE	KERATOSES
	KERB	KERBS
	KERBAYA	KERBAYAS
	KERBING	KERBINGS
	KERBSIDE	KERBSIDES
	KERBSTONE	KERBSTONES
	KERCHIEF	KERCHIEFS
	KEREL	KERELS
	KERF	KERFS
	KERFUFFLE	KERFUFFLED = KERFUFFLES
	KERMA	KERMAS
	KERMES	KERMESS
	KERMESITE	KERMESITES
	KERMESS	KERMESSE
	KERMESSE	KERMESSES
	KERN	KERNE = KERNS
	KERNE	KERNED = KERNEL = KERNES
	KERNEL	KERNELS
	KERNING	KERNINGS
	KERNITE	KERNITES
	KERO	KEROS
	KEROGEN	KEROGENS
	KEROSENE	KEROSENES
	KEROSINE	KEROSINES
	KERPLUNK	KERPLUNKS
	KERRIA	KERRIAS
SKERRIES	KERRIES	
SKERRY	KERRY	
	KERSEY	KERSEYS
	KERVE	KERVED = KERVES
	KERYGMA	KERYGMAS
	KESAR	KESARS
	KEST	KESTS
	KESTREL	KESTRELS
SKET	KET	KETA = KETE = KETO = KETS
	KETA	KETAS
	KETAMINE	KETAMINES
SKETCH	KETCH	
SKETCHES	KETCHES	
SKETCHING	KETCHING	
	KETCHUP	KETCHUPS
	KETENE	KETENES
	KETMIA	KETMIAS
	KETO	KETOL
	KETOL	KETOLS
	KETONE	KETONES

FRONT HOOK	ROOT WORD	END HOOK
	KETONEMIA	KETONEMIAS
	KETONURIA	KETONURIAS
	KETOSE	KETOSES
	KETOXIME	KETOXIMES
SKETS	**KETS**	
	KETTLE	KETTLES
	KETTLEFUL	KETTLEFULS
	KETUBAH	KETUBAHS
	KETUBOT	KETUBOTH
	KEVEL	KEVELS
	KEVIL	KEVILS
	KEWPIE	KEWPIES
	KEY	KEYS
	KEYBOARD	KEYBOARDS
	KEYBUGLE	KEYBUGLES
	KEYBUTTON	KEYBUTTONS
	KEYCARD	KEYCARDS
	KEYHOLE	KEYHOLES
	KEYING	KEYINGS
	KEYLINE	KEYLINES
	KEYLOGGER	KEYLOGGERS
	KEYNOTE	KEYNOTED · KEYNOTER · KEYNOTES
	KEYNOTER	KEYNOTERS
	KEYPAD	KEYPADS
	KEYPAL	KEYPALS
	KEYSET	KEYSETS
	KEYSTER	KEYSTERS
	KEYSTONE	KEYSTONED · KEYSTONES
	KEYSTROKE	KEYSTROKED · KEYSTROKES
	KEYWAY	KEYWAYS
	KEYWORD	KEYWORDS
	KGOTLA	KGOTLAS
	KHADDAR	KHADDARS
	KHADI	KHADIS
	KHAF	KHAFS
	KHAKI	KHAKIS
	KHALAT	KHALATS
	KHALIF	KHALIFA · KHALIFS
	KHALIFA	KHALIFAH · KHALIFAS · KHALIFAT
	KHALIFAH	KHALIFAHS
	KHALIFAT	KHALIFATE · KHALIFATS
	KHALIFATE	KHALIFATES
	KHAMSEEN	KHAMSEENS
	KHAMSIN	KHAMSINS
	KHAN	KHANS
	KHANATE	KHANATES
	KHANDA	KHANDAS
	KHANGA	KHANGAS
	KHANJAR	KHANJARS
	KHANSAMA	KHANSAMAH · KHANSAMAS
	KHANSAMAH	KHANSAMAHS
	KHANUM	KHANUMS
	KHAPH	KHAPHS
	KHARIF	KHARIFS
	KHAT	KHATS
	KHAYA	KHAYAL · KHAYAS
	KHAYAL	KHAYALS
	KHAZEN	KHAZENS
	KHAZI	KHAZIS
	KHEDA	KHEDAH · KHEDAS
	KHEDAH	KHEDAHS
	KHEDIVA	KHEDIVAL · KHEDIVAS
	KHEDIVATE	KHEDIVATES
	KHEDIVE	KHEDIVES
	KHET	KHETH · KHETS
	KHETH	KHETHS
	KHI	KHIS
	KHILAFAT	KHILAFATS
	KHILAT	KHILATS

FRONT HOOK	ROOT WORD	END HOOK
	KHILIM	KHILIMS
	KHIRKAH	KHIRKAHS
	KHODJA	KHODJAS
	KHOJA	KHOJAS
	KHOR	KHORS
	KHOTBAH	KHOTBAHS
	KHOTBEH	KHOTBEHS
	KHOUM	KHOUMS
	KHUD	KHUDS
	KHURTA	KHURTAS
	KHUTBAH	KHUTBAHS
SKI	KI	KID · KIF · KIN · KIP · KIR · KIS · KIT
	KIAAT	KIAATS
	KIANG	KIANGS
	KIAUGH	KIAUGHS
	KIBBE	KIBBEH · KIBBES
	KIBBEH	KIBBEHS
	KIBBI	KIBBIS
	KIBBITZER	KIBBITZERS
	KIBBLE	KIBBLED · KIBBLES
	KIBE	KIBEI · KIBES
	KIBEI	KIBEIS
	KIBITKA	KIBITKAS
	KIBITZER	KIBITZERS
	KIBLA	KIBLAH · KIBLAS
	KIBLAH	KIBLAHS
	KICK	KICKS · KICKY
	KICKABOUT	KICKABOUTS
	KICKBACK	KICKBACKS
	KICKBALL	KICKBALLS
	KICKBOARD	KICKBOARDS
	KICKBOXER	KICKBOXERS
	KICKDOWN	KICKDOWNS
	KICKER	KICKERS
	KICKOFF	KICKOFFS
	KICKSHAW	KICKSHAWS
	KICKSTAND	KICKSTANDS
	KICKSTART	KICKSTARTS
	KICKUP	KICKUPS
SKID	KID	KIDS
SKIDDED	KIDDED	
SKIDDER	KIDDER	KIDDERS
SKIDDERS	KIDDERS	
	KIDDIE	KIDDIED · KIDDIER · KIDDIES
SKIDDIER	KIDDIER	KIDDIERS
SKIDDING	KIDDING	
	KIDDLE	KIDDLES
	KIDDO	KIDDOS
SKIDDY	KIDDY	
	KIDDYWINK	KIDDYWINKS
	KIDEL	KIDELS
	KIDGIE	KIDGIER
	KIDLET	KIDLETS
	KIDLING	KIDLINGS
	KIDNAP	KIDNAPS
	KIDNAPEE	KIDNAPEES
	KIDNAPER	KIDNAPERS
	KIDNAPING	KIDNAPINGS
	KIDNAPPEE	KIDNAPPEES
	KIDNAPPER	KIDNAPPERS
	KIDNEY	KIDNEYS
SKIDS	KIDS	
	KIDSKIN	KIDSKINS
	KIDULT	KIDULTS
	KIDVID	KIDVIDS
	KIEF	KIEFS
	KIEKIE	KIEKIES
	KIELBASA	KIELBASAS

FRONT HOOK	ROOT WORD	END HOOK
SKIER	**KIER**	KIERS
	KIERIE	KIERIES
SKIERS	**KIERS**	
	KIESELGUR	KIESELGURS
	KIESERITE	KIESERITES
	KIESTER	KIESTERS
	KIEVE	KIEVES
	KIF	KIFF ▪ KIFS
SKIFF	**KIFF**	
	KIGHT	KIGHTS
	KIKE	KIKES (offensive)
	KIKOI	KIKOIS
	KIKUMON	KIKUMONS
	KIKUYU	KIKUYUS
	KILDERKIN	KILDERKINS
	KILERG	KILERGS
	KILEY	KILEYS
	KILIM	KILIMS
SKILL	**KILL**	KILLS
	KILLADAR	KILLADARS
	KILLCOW	KILLCOWS
	KILLCROP	KILLCROPS
	KILLDEE	KILLDEER ▪ KILLDEES
	KILLDEER	KILLDEERS
SKILLED	**KILLED**	
	KILLER	KILLERS
	KILLICK	KILLICKS
	KILLIE	KILLIES
SKILLIES	**KILLIES**	
SKILLING	**KILLING**	KILLINGS
SKILLINGS	**KILLINGS**	
	KILLJOY	KILLJOYS
	KILLOCK	KILLOCKS
	KILLOGIE	KILLOGIES
SKILLS	**KILLS**	
	KILLUT	KILLUTS
	KILN	KILNS
	KILO	KILOS
	KILOBAR	KILOBARS
	KILOBASE	KILOBASES
	KILOBAUD	KILOBAUDS
	KILOBIT	KILOBITS
	KILOBYTE	KILOBYTES
	KILOCURIE	KILOCURIES
	KILOCYCLE	KILOCYCLES
	KILOGRAM	KILOGRAMS
	KILOGRAY	KILOGRAYS
	KILOJOULE	KILOJOULES
	KILOLITER	KILOLITERS
	KILOLITRE	KILOLITRES
	KILOMETER	KILOMETERS
	KILOMETRE	KILOMETRES
	KILOMOLE	KILOMOLES
	KILORAD	KILORADS
	KILOTON	KILOTONS
	KILOVOLT	KILOVOLTS
	KILOWATT	KILOWATTS
	KILP	KILPS
	KILT	KILTS ▪ KILTY
	KILTER	KILTERS
	KILTIE	KILTIES
	KILTING	KILTINGS
AKIMBO	**KIMBO**	KIMBOS
	KIMCHEE	KIMCHEES
	KIMCHI	KIMCHIS
SKIMMER	**KIMMER**	KIMMERS
SKIMMERS	**KIMMERS**	
OKIMONO	**KIMONO**	KIMONOS
OKIMONOS	**KIMONOS**	

FRONT HOOK	ROOT WORD	END HOOK
AKIN ▪ SKIN	**KIN**	KINA ▪ KIND ▪ KINE ▪ KING ▪ KINK KINO ▪ KINS
	KINA	KINAS
	KINAKINA	KINAKINAS
	KINARA	KINARAS
	KINAS	KINASE
	KINASE	KINASES
	KINCHIN	KINCHINS
	KINCOB	KINCOBS
	KIND	KINDA ▪ KINDS ▪ KINDY
	KINDER	KINDERS
	KINDIE	KINDIES
	KINDLE	KINDLED ▪ KINDLER ▪ KINDLES
	KINDLER	KINDLERS
	KINDLES	KINDLESS
	KINDLING	KINDLINGS
	KINDRED	KINDREDS
	KINE	KINES
	KINEMA	KINEMAS
	KINEMATIC	KINEMATICS
	KINESCOPE	KINESCOPED ▪ KINESCOPES
AKINESES	**KINESES**	
	KINESIC	KINESICS
AKINESIS	**KINESIS**	
AKINETIC	**KINETIC**	KINETICS
	KINETIN	KINETINS
	KINFOLK	KINFOLKS
AKING ▪ EKING	**KING**	KINGS
	KINGBIRD	KINGBIRDS
	KINGBOLT	KINGBOLTS
	KINGCRAFT	KINGCRAFTS
	KINGCUP	KINGCUPS
	KINGDOM	KINGDOMS
	KINGHOOD	KINGHOODS
	KINGKLIP	KINGKLIPS
	KINGLE	KINGLES ▪ KINGLET
	KINGLES	KINGLESS
	KINGLET	KINGLETS
	KINGLING	KINGLINGS
	KINGMAKER	KINGMAKERS
	KINGPIN	KINGPINS
	KINGPOST	KINGPOSTS
	KINGSHIP	KINGSHIPS
	KINGSIDE	KINGSIDES
	KINGSNAKE	KINGSNAKES
	KINGWOOD	KINGWOODS
	KININ	KININS
SKINK	**KINK**	KINKS ▪ KINKY
	KINKAJOU	KINKAJOUS
SKINKED	**KINKED**	
SKINKING	**KINKING**	
	KINKLE	KINKLES
SKINKS	**KINKS**	
SKINLESS	**KINLESS**	
	KINO	KINOS
	KINONE	KINONES
	KINRED	KINREDS
SKINS	**KINS**	
	KINSFOLK	KINSFOLKS
	KINSHIP	KINSHIPS
	KIOSK	KIOSKS
SKIP	**KIP**	KIPE ▪ KIPP ▪ KIPS
	KIPE	KIPES
	KIPP	KIPPA ▪ KIPPS
	KIPPA	KIPPAS
	KIPPAGE	KIPPAGES
SKIPPED	**KIPPED**	
SKIPPER	**KIPPER**	KIPPERS
SKIPPERED	**KIPPERED**	

433

FRONT HOOK	ROOT WORD	END HOOK
	KIPPERER	KIPPERERS
SKIPPERING	**KIPPERING**	
SKIPPERS	**KIPPERS**	
SKIPPING	**KIPPING**	
SKIPS	**KIPS**	
	KIPSKIN	KIPSKINS
	KIR	KIRK · KIRN · KIRS
	KIRBEH	KIRBEHS
	KIRBIGRIP	KIRBIGRIPS
	KIRIGAMI	KIRIGAMIS
	KIRIMON	KIRIMONS
	KIRK	KIRKS
	KIRKING	KIRKINGS
	KIRKTON	KIRKTONS
	KIRKYAIRD	KIRKYAIRDS
	KIRKYARD	KIRKYARDS
	KIRN	KIRNS
	KIRPAN	KIRPANS
	KIRRI	KIRRIS
	KIRTAN	KIRTANS
	KIRTLE	KIRTLED · KIRTLES
SKIS	**KIS**	KISH · KISS · KIST
	KISAN	KISANS
	KISHKA	KISHKAS
	KISHKE	KISHKES
	KISMAT	KISMATS
	KISMET	KISMETS
	KISS	KISSY
	KISSAGRAM	KISSAGRAMS
	KISSEL	KISSELS
	KISSER	KISSERS
	KISSOGRAM	KISSOGRAMS
	KIST	KISTS
	KISTFUL	KISTFULS
	KISTVAEN	KISTVAENS
SKIT	**KIT**	KITE · KITH · KITS
	KITBAG	KITBAGS
	KITCHEN	KITCHENS
	KITCHENER	KITCHENERS
	KITCHENET	KITCHENETS
SKITE	**KITE**	KITED · KITER · KITES
SKITED	**KITED**	
	KITENGE	KITENGES
	KITER	KITERS
SKITES	**KITES**	
	KITH	KITHE · KITHS
	KITHARA	KITHARAS
	KITHE	KITHED · KITHES
SKITING	**KITING**	KITINGS
	KITLING	KITLINGS
SKITS	**KITS**	
	KITSCH	KITSCHY
	KITSET	KITSETS
	KITTEL	KITTELS
	KITTEN	KITTENS · KITTENY
	KITTIWAKE	KITTIWAKES
SKITTLE	**KITTLE**	KITTLED · KITTLER · KITTLES
SKITTLED	**KITTLED**	
SKITTLES	**KITTLES**	KITTLEST
SKITTLING	**KITTLING**	
	KITTUL	KITTULS
	KIVA	KIVAS
	KIWI	KIWIS
	KIWIFRUIT	KIWIFRUITS
	KLANG	KLANGS
	KLAP	KLAPS
	KLAVERN	KLAVERNS
	KLAVIER	KLAVIERS
	KLAXON	KLAXONS

FRONT HOOK	ROOT WORD	END HOOK
	KLEAGLE	KLEAGLES
	KLEPHT	KLEPHTS
	KLEPHTISM	KLEPHTISMS
	KLEPTO	KLEPTOS
	KLETT	KLETTS
	KLEZMER	KLEZMERS
	KLICK	KLICKS
	KLIK	KLIKS
	KLINKER	KLINKERS
	KLINOSTAT	KLINOSTATS
	KLISTER	KLISTERS
	KLONDIKE	KLONDIKED · KLONDIKER · KLONDIKES
	KLONDIKER	KLONDIKERS
	KLONDYKE	KLONDYKED · KLONDYKER · KLONDYKES
	KLONDYKER	KLONDYKERS
	KLONG	KLONGS
	KLOOCHMAN	KLOOCHMANS
	KLOOF	KLOOFS
	KLUDGE	KLUDGED · KLUDGES · KLUDGEY
	KLUGE	KLUGED · KLUGES
	KLUTZ	KLUTZY
	KLYSTRON	KLYSTRONS
	KNACK	KNACKS · KNACKY
	KNACKER	KNACKERS · KNACKERY
	KNAG	KNAGS
	KNAP	KNAPS
	KNAPPER	KNAPPERS
	KNAPPLE	KNAPPLED · KNAPPLES
	KNAPSACK	KNAPSACKS
	KNAPWEED	KNAPWEEDS
	KNAR	KNARL · KNARS
	KNARL	KNARLS · KNARLY
	KNAUR	KNAURS
	KNAVE	KNAVES
	KNAVESHIP	KNAVESHIPS
	KNAWE	KNAWEL · KNAWES
	KNAWEL	KNAWELS
	KNEAD	KNEADS
	KNEADER	KNEADERS
	KNEE	KNEED · KNEEL · KNEES
	KNEECAP	KNEECAPS
	KNEEHOLE	KNEEHOLES
	KNEEL	KNEELS
	KNEELER	KNEELERS
	KNEEPAD	KNEEPADS
	KNEEPAN	KNEEPANS
	KNEEPIECE	KNEEPIECES
	KNEESOCK	KNEESOCKS
	KNELL	KNELLS
	KNESSET	KNESSETS
	KNEVELL	KNEVELLS
	KNICKER	KNICKERS
	KNIFE	KNIFED · KNIFER · KNIFES
	KNIFER	KNIFERS
	KNIFEREST	KNIFERESTS
	KNIFING	KNIFINGS
	KNIGHT	KNIGHTS
	KNIGHTAGE	KNIGHTAGES
	KNIPHOFIA	KNIPHOFIAS
	KNIT	KNITS
	KNITTER	KNITTERS
	KNITTING	KNITTINGS
	KNITTLE	KNITTLES
	KNITWEAR	KNITWEARS
	KNIVE	KNIVED · KNIVES
	KNOB	KNOBS
	KNOBBER	KNOBBERS
	KNOBBLE	KNOBBLED · KNOBBLES
	KNOBHEAD	KNOBHEADS (offensive)

FRONT HOOK	ROOT WORD	END HOOK
	KNOBSTICK	KNOBSTICKS
	KNOCK	KNOCKS
	KNOCKDOWN	KNOCKDOWNS
	KNOCKER	KNOCKERS
	KNOCKING	KNOCKINGS
	KNOCKOFF	KNOCKOFFS
	KNOCKOUT	KNOCKOUTS
	KNOLL	KNOLLS = KNOLLY
	KNOLLER	KNOLLERS
	KNOP	KNOPS
	KNOSP	KNOSPS
	KNOT	KNOTS
	KNOTHOLE	KNOTHOLES
	KNOTTER	KNOTTERS
	KNOTTING	KNOTTINGS
	KNOTWEED	KNOTWEEDS
	KNOTWORK	KNOTWORKS
	KNOUT	KNOUTS
	KNOW	KNOWE = KNOWN = KNOWS
	KNOWE	KNOWER = KNOWES
	KNOWER	KNOWERS
	KNOWHOW	KNOWHOWS
	KNOWING	KNOWINGS
	KNOWLEDGE	KNOWLEDGED = KNOWLEDGES
	KNOWN	KNOWNS
	KNUB	KNUBS
	KNUBBLE	KNUBBLED = KNUBBLES
	KNUCKLE	KNUCKLED = KNUCKLER = KNUCKLES
	KNUCKLER	KNUCKLERS
	KNUR	KNURL = KNURR = KNURS
	KNURL	KNURLS = KNURLY
	KNURLING	KNURLINGS
	KNURR	KNURRS
	KNUT	KNUTS
	KO	KOA = KOB = KOI = KON = KOP = KOR = KOS KOW
	KOA	KOAN = KOAP = KOAS
	KOALA	KOALAS
	KOAN	KOANS
	KOAP	KOAPS (offensive)
	KOB	KOBO = KOBS
	KOBAN	KOBANG = KOBANS
	KOBANG	KOBANGS
	KOBO	KOBOS
	KOBOLD	KOBOLDS
	KOCHIA	KOCHIAS
	KOEL	KOELS
SKOFF	**KOFF**	KOFFS
SKOFFS	**KOFFS**	
	KOFTA	KOFTAS
	KOFTGAR	KOFTGARI = KOFTGARS
	KOFTGARI	KOFTGARIS
	KOFTWORK	KOFTWORKS
	KOHA	KOHAS
	KOHL	KOHLS
	KOHLRABI	KOHLRABIS
	KOI	KOIS
	KOINE	KOINES
	KOJI	KOJIS
	KOKAKO	KOKAKOS
	KOKANEE	KOKANEES
	KOKER	KOKERS
	KOKOWAI	KOKOWAIS
	KOKRA	KOKRAS
	KOKUM	KOKUMS
	KOLA	KOLAS
	KOLBASI	KOLBASIS
	KOLBASSI	KOLBASSIS
	KOLHOZ	KOLHOZY

FRONT HOOK	ROOT WORD	END HOOK
	KOLKHOS	KOLKHOSY
	KOLKHOZ	KOLKHOZY
	KOLKOZ	KOLKOZY
	KOLO	KOLOS
	KOMATIK	KOMATIKS
	KOMBU	KOMBUS
	KOMISSAR	KOMISSARS
	KOMITAJI	KOMITAJIS
	KOMONDOR	KOMONDORS
IKON	KON	KOND ▪ KONK ▪ KONS
	KONBU	KONBUS
	KOND	KONDO
	KONDO	KONDOS
	KONFYT	KONFYTS
	KONIMETER	KONIMETERS
	KONISCOPE	KONISCOPES
	KONK	KONKS
IKONS	KONS	
	KOODOO	KOODOOS
	KOOK	KOOKS ▪ KOOKY
	KOOKIE	KOOKIER
	KOOLAH	KOOLAHS
	KOORI	KOORIS
	KOP	KOPH ▪ KOPS
	KOPECK	KOPECKS
	KOPEK	KOPEKS
	KOPH	KOPHS
	KOPIYKA	KOPIYKAS
	KOPJE	KOPJES
	KOPPA	KOPPAS
	KOPPIE	KOPPIES
	KOR	KORA ▪ KORE ▪ KORO ▪ KORS ▪ KORU
	KORA	KORAI ▪ KORAS ▪ KORAT
	KORAT	KORATS
	KORE	KORES
	KORERO	KOREROS
	KORFBALL	KORFBALLS
	KORKIR	KORKIRS
	KORMA	KORMAS
	KORORA	KORORAS
	KORU	KORUN ▪ KORUS
	KORUN	KORUNA ▪ KORUNY
	KORUNA	KORUNAS
	KOS	KOSS
	KOSHER	KOSHERS
	KOTO	KOTOS ▪ KOTOW
	KOTOW	KOTOWS
	KOTOWER	KOTOWERS
	KOTWAL	KOTWALS
	KOULAN	KOULANS
	KOUMIS	KOUMISS
	KOUMYS	KOUMYSS
	KOUPREY	KOUPREYS
	KOUSSO	KOUSSOS
	KOW	KOWS
	KOWHAI	KOWHAIS
	KOWTOW	KOWTOWS
	KOWTOWER	KOWTOWERS
	KRAAL	KRAALS
	KRAB	KRABS
	KRAFT	KRAFTS
	KRAIT	KRAITS
	KRAKEN	KRAKENS
	KRAKOWIAK	KRAKOWIAKS
	KRAMERIA	KRAMERIAS
	KRANG	KRANGS
SKRANS	KRANS	
	KRATER	KRATERS
	KRAUT	KRAUTS

FRONT HOOK	ROOT WORD	END HOOK
	KREASOTE	KREASOTED · KREASOTES
	KREATINE	KREATINES
	KREEP	KREEPS
	KREESE	KREESED · KREESES
	KREMLIN	KREMLINS
	KRENG	KRENGS
	KREOSOTE	KREOSOTED · KREOSOTES
	KREUTZER	KREUTZERS
	KREUZER	KREUZERS
	KREWE	KREWES
	KRILL	KRILLS
	KRIMMER	KRIMMERS
	KRONE	KRONEN · KRONER
	KROON	KROONI · KROONS
	KRUBI	KRUBIS
	KRUBUT	KRUBUTS
	KRULLER	KRULLERS
	KRUMHORN	KRUMHORNS
	KRUMKAKE	KRUMKAKES
	KRUMMHORN	KRUMMHORNS
	KRYOLITE	KRYOLITES
	KRYOLITH	KRYOLITHS
	KRYOMETER	KRYOMETERS
	KRYPTON	KRYPTONS
	KRYTRON	KRYTRONS
	KSAR	KSARS
	KUCHEN	KUCHENS
	KUDLIK	KUDLIKS
	KUDO	KUDOS
	KUDU	KUDUS
	KUDZU	KUDZUS
	KUE	KUEH · KUES
	KUFI	KUFIS
	KUFIYAH	KUFIYAHS
	KUGEL	KUGELS
	KUIA	KUIAS
	KUKRI	KUKRIS
	KUKU	KUKUS
	KULA	KULAK · KULAN · KULAS
	KULAK	KULAKI · KULAKS
	KULAN	KULANS
	KULFI	KULFIS
	KULTUR	KULTURS
	KUMARA	KUMARAS
	KUMARAHOU	KUMARAHOUS
	KUMARI	KUMARIS
	KUMERA	KUMERAS
	KUMITE	KUMITES
	KUMMEL	KUMMELS
	KUMQUAT	KUMQUATS
	KUNDALINI	KUNDALINIS
	KUNKAR	KUNKARS
	KUNKUR	KUNKURS
	KUNZITE	KUNZITES
	KURFUFFLE	KURFUFFLED · KURFUFFLES
	KURGAN	KURGANS
	KURI	KURIS
	KURRAJONG	KURRAJONGS
	KURRE	KURRES
	KURSAAL	KURSAALS
	KURTA	KURTAS
	KURU	KURUS
	KURVEY	KURVEYS
	KURVEYOR	KURVEYORS
	KUSSO	KUSSOS
	KUTA	KUTAS
	KUTCH	KUTCHA
	KUTI	KUTIS
	KUTU	KUTUS

FRONT HOOK	ROOT WORD	END HOOK
	KUZU	KUZUS
	KVAS	KVASS
	KVELL	KVELLS
	KVETCH	KVETCHY
	KVETCHER	KVETCHERS
	KWACHA	KWACHAS
	KWAITO	KWAITOS
	KWANZA	KWANZAS
	KWELA	KWELAS
SKY	**KY**	KYE = KYU
	KYACK	KYACKS
	KYAK	KYAKS
	KYANG	KYANGS
	KYANISE	KYANISED = KYANISES
	KYANITE	KYANITES
	KYANIZE	KYANIZED = KYANIZES
	KYAR	KYARS
	KYAT	KYATS
	KYBO	KYBOS
	KYBOS	KYBOSH
	KYE	KYES
	KYLE	KYLES
	KYLIE	KYLIES
	KYLIN	KYLINS
	KYLOE	KYLOES
	KYMOGRAM	KYMOGRAMS
	KYMOGRAPH	KYMOGRAPHS = KYMOGRAPHY
	KYND	KYNDE = KYNDS
	KYNDE	KYNDED = KYNDES
	KYOGEN	KYOGENS
	KYPE	KYPES
	KYRIE	KYRIES
	KYRIELLE	KYRIELLES
SKYTE	**KYTE**	KYTES
SKYTES	**KYTES**	
	KYTHE	KYTHED = KYTHES
	KYU	KYUS

L

FRONT HOOK	ROOT WORD	END HOOK
ALA	**LA**	LAB · LAC · LAD · LAG · LAH · LAM · LAP LAR · LAS · LAT · LAV · LAW · LAX · LAY
	LAAGER	LAAGERS
	LAARI	LAARIS
BLAB · FLAB · SLAB	**LAB**	LABS
	LABARUM	LABARUMS
	LABDA	LABDAS
	LABDACISM	LABDACISMS
	LABDANUM	LABDANUMS
	LABEL	LABELS
	LABELER	LABELERS
FLABELLA · GLABELLA	**LABELLA**	
FLABELLATE	**LABELLATE**	
	LABELLER	LABELLERS
	LABELLIST	LABELLISTS
FLABELLUM	**LABELLUM**	
	LABIA	LABIAL
	LABIAL	LABIALS
	LABIALISE	LABIALISED · LABIALISES
	LABIALISM	LABIALISMS
	LABIALIZE	LABIALIZED · LABIALIZES
	LABIATE	LABIATED · LABIATES
	LABLAB	LABLABS
	LABOR	LABORS
	LABORER	LABORERS
	LABORISM	LABORISMS
	LABORIST	LABORISTS
	LABORITE	LABORITES
	LABOUR	LABOURS
	LABOURER	LABOURERS
	LABOURISM	LABOURISMS
	LABOURIST	LABOURISTS
	LABRADOR	LABRADORS
	LABRET	LABRETS
	LABRID	LABRIDS
	LABROID	LABROIDS
	LABRUM	LABRUMS
BLABS · FLABS · SLABS	**LABS**	
	LABURNUM	LABURNUMS
	LABYRINTH	LABYRINTHS
	LAC	LACE · LACK · LACS · LACY
	LACCOLITE	LACCOLITES
	LACCOLITH	LACCOLITHS
GLACE · PLACE	**LACE**	LACED · LACER · LACES · LACET · LACEY
	LACEBARK	LACEBARKS
PLACED	**LACED**	
PLACELESS	**LACELESS**	
PLACER	**LACER**	LACERS
	LACERATE	LACERATED · LACERATES
PLACERS	**LACERS**	
	LACERTIAN	LACERTIANS
	LACERTID	LACERTIDS
GLACES · PLACES	**LACES**	
PLACET	**LACET**	LACETS
PLACETS	**LACETS**	
	LACEWING	LACEWINGS
	LACEWOOD	LACEWOODS
	LACEWORK	LACEWORKS
	LACHRYMAL	LACHRYMALS
GLACIER	**LACIER**	
PLACING	**LACING**	LACINGS
PLACINGS	**LACINGS**	
	LACINIA	LACINIAE
	LACINIATE	LACINIATED
ALACK · BLACK · CLACK · FLACK · PLACK SLACK	**LACK**	LACKS

FRONT HOOK	ROOT WORD	END HOOK
ALACKADAY	LACKADAY	
BLACKED · CLACKED · FLACKED · SLACKED	LACKED	
BLACKER · CLACKER · FLACKER · SLACKER	LACKER	LACKERS
FLACKERED	LACKERED	
FLACKERING	LACKERING	
CLACKERS · FLACKERS · SLACKERS	LACKERS	
	LACKEY	LACKEYS
BLACKING · CLACKING · FLACKING	LACKING	
SLACKING		
BLACKLAND	LACKLAND	LACKLANDS
BLACKLANDS	LACKLANDS	
BLACKS · CLACKS · FLACKS · PLACKS	LACKS	
SLACKS		
	LACONISM	LACONISMS
	LACQUER	LACQUERS
	LACQUERER	LACQUERERS
	LACQUEY	LACQUEYS
	LACRIMAL	LACRIMALS
	LACROSSE	LACROSSES
	LACRYMAL	LACRYMALS
	LACTAM	LACTAMS
	LACTARIAN	LACTARIANS
	LACTASE	LACTASES
	LACTATE	LACTATED · LACTATES
	LACTATION	LACTATIONS
	LACTEAL	LACTEALS
	LACTONE	LACTONES
	LACTOSE	LACTOSES
	LACUNA	LACUNAE · LACUNAL · LACUNAR · LACUNAS
	LACUNAR	LACUNARS · LACUNARY
	LACUNE	LACUNES
BLAD · CLAD · GLAD	LAD	LADE · LADS · LADY
	LADANUM	LADANUMS
BLADDER · CLADDER · GLADDER	LADDER	LADDERS · LADDERY
BLADDERED	LADDERED	
BLADDERS · CLADDERS	LADDERS	
BLADDERY	LADDERY	
CLADDIE · GLADDIE	LADDIE	LADDIES
CLADDIES · GLADDIES	LADDIES	
BLADE · CLADE · GLADE · SLADE	LADE	LADED · LADEN · LADER · LADES
BLADED	LADED	
	LADEN	LADENS
BLADER	LADER	LADERS
BLADERS	LADERS	
BLADES · CLADES · GLADES · SLADES	LADES	
	LADETTE	LADETTES
	LADHOOD	LADHOODS
BLADING	LADING	LADINGS
BLADINGS	LADINGS	
	LADINO	LADINOS
	LADLE	LADLED · LADLER · LADLES
	LADLEFUL	LADLEFULS
	LADLER	LADLERS
	LADRON	LADRONE · LADRONS
	LADRONE	LADRONES
BLADS · CLADS · GLADS	LADS	
BLADY · GLADY	LADY	
	LADYBIRD	LADYBIRDS
	LADYBOY	LADYBOYS
	LADYBUG	LADYBUGS
	LADYCOW	LADYCOWS
	LADYHOOD	LADYHOODS
	LADYISM	LADYISMS
	LADYKIN	LADYKINS
	LADYLOVE	LADYLOVES
	LADYPALM	LADYPALMS
	LADYSHIP	LADYSHIPS
BLAER	LAER	LAERS
	LAETARE	LAETARES

FRONT HOOK	ROOT WORD	END HOOK
	LAETRILE	LAETRILES
	LAEVIGATE	LAEVIGATED · LAEVIGATES
	LAEVULIN	LAEVULINS
	LAEVULOSE	LAEVULOSES
BLAG · CLAG · FLAG · SLAG	**LAG**	LAGS
	LAGAN	LAGANS
	LAGENA	LAGENAS
	LAGEND	LAGENDS
	LAGER	LAGERS
	LAGGARD	LAGGARDS
BLAGGED · CLAGGED · FLAGGED · SLAGGED	**LAGGED**	
	LAGGEN	LAGGENS
BLAGGER · FLAGGER	**LAGGER**	LAGGERS
BLAGGERS · FLAGGERS	**LAGGERS**	
	LAGGIN	LAGGING · LAGGINS
BLAGGING · CLAGGING · FLAGGING · SLAGGING	**LAGGING**	LAGGINGS
FLAGGINGLY	**LAGGINGLY**	
BLAGGINGS · FLAGGINGS · SLAGGINGS	**LAGGINGS**	
	LAGNAPPE	LAGNAPPES
	LAGNIAPPE	LAGNIAPPES
	LAGOMORPH	LAGOMORPHS
	LAGOON	LAGOONS
BLAGS · CLAGS · FLAGS · SLAGS	**LAGS**	
	LAGUNA	LAGUNAS
	LAGUNE	LAGUNES
BLAH	**LAH**	LAHS
	LAHAR	LAHARS
BLAHS	**LAHS**	
	LAIC	LAICH · LAICS
	LAICH	LAICHS
	LAICISE	LAICISED · LAICISES
	LAICISM	LAICISMS
	LAICIZE	LAICIZED · LAICIZES
PLAID · SLAID	**LAID**	LAIDS
PLAIDED	**LAIDED**	
PLAIDING	**LAIDING**	
PLAIDS	**LAIDS**	
	LAIGH	LAIGHS
GLAIK	**LAIK**	LAIKA · LAIKS
	LAIKA	LAIKAS
	LAIKER	LAIKERS
GLAIKS	**LAIKS**	
BLAIN · ELAIN · PLAIN · SLAIN	**LAIN**	
	LAIPSE	LAIPSED · LAIPSES
FLAIR · GLAIR	**LAIR**	LAIRD · LAIRS · LAIRY
	LAIRAGE	LAIRAGES
	LAIRD	LAIRDS
	LAIRDSHIP	LAIRDSHIPS
GLAIRED	**LAIRED**	
GLAIRIER	**LAIRIER**	
GLAIRIEST	**LAIRIEST**	
GLAIRING	**LAIRING**	
	LAIRISE	LAIRISED · LAIRISES
	LAIRIZE	LAIRIZED · LAIRIZES
FLAIRS · GLAIRS	**LAIRS**	
GLAIRY	**LAIRY**	
	LAISSE	LAISSES
	LAITANCE	LAITANCES
FLAKE · SLAKE	**LAKE**	LAKED · LAKER · LAKES
	LAKEBED	LAKEBEDS
FLAKED · SLAKED	**LAKED**	
	LAKEFRONT	LAKEFRONTS
	LAKELAND	LAKELANDS
	LAKELET	LAKELETS
	LAKEPORT	LAKEPORTS
FLAKER · SLAKER	**LAKER**	LAKERS
FLAKERS · SLAKERS	**LAKERS**	
FLAKES · SLAKES	**LAKES**	

FRONT HOOK	ROOT WORD	END HOOK
	LAKESHORE	LAKESHORES
	LAKESIDE	LAKESIDES
	LAKH	LAKHS
FLAKIER	LAKIER	
FLAKIEST	LAKIEST	
	LAKIN	LAKING · LAKINS
FLAKING · SLAKING	LAKING	LAKINGS
	LAKSA	LAKSAS
FLAKY	LAKY	
	LALANG	LALANGS
	LALDIE	LALDIES
	LALIQUE	LALIQUES
	LALL	LALLS
	LALLAN	LALLAND · LALLANS
	LALLAND	LALLANDS
	LALLATION	LALLATIONS
	LALLING	LALLINGS
	LALLYGAG	LALLYGAGS
BLAM · CLAM · FLAM · GLAM · SLAM	LAM	LAMA · LAMB · LAME · LAMP · LAMS
LLAMA · ULAMA	LAMA	LAMAS
	LAMANTIN	LAMANTINS
LLAMAS · ULAMAS	LAMAS	
	LAMASERAI	LAMASERAIS
	LAMB	LAMBS · LAMBY
	LAMBADA	LAMBADAS
	LAMBAST	LAMBASTE · LAMBASTS
	LAMBASTE	LAMBASTED · LAMBASTES
	LAMBDA	LAMBDAS
CLAMBER	LAMBER	LAMBERS · LAMBERT
CLAMBERS	LAMBERS	
	LAMBERT	LAMBERTS
	LAMBIE	LAMBIER · LAMBIES
	LAMBIES	LAMBIEST
	LAMBING	LAMBINGS
	LAMBITIVE	LAMBITIVES
	LAMBKILL	LAMBKILLS
	LAMBKIN	LAMBKINS
	LAMBLING	LAMBLINGS
	LAMBRUSCO	LAMBRUSCOS
	LAMBSKIN	LAMBSKINS
BLAME · CLAME · FLAME	LAME	LAMED · LAMER · LAMES
	LAMEBRAIN	LAMEBRAINS
BLAMED · FLAMED	LAMED	LAMEDH · LAMEDS
	LAMEDH	LAMEDHS
	LAMELLA	LAMELLAE · LAMELLAR · LAMELLAS
	LAMELLATE	LAMELLATED
	LAMENT	LAMENTS
	LAMENTER	LAMENTERS
	LAMENTING	LAMENTINGS
BLAMER · FLAMER	LAMER	
BLAMES · CLAMES · FLAMES	LAMES	LAMEST
	LAMETER	LAMETERS
	LAMIA	LAMIAE · LAMIAS
	LAMIGER	LAMIGERS
	LAMINA	LAMINAE · LAMINAL · LAMINAR · LAMINAS
	LAMINAL	LAMINALS
	LAMINAR	LAMINARY
	LAMINARIA	LAMINARIAN · LAMINARIAS
	LAMINARIN	LAMINARINS
	LAMINATE	LAMINATED · LAMINATES
	LAMINATOR	LAMINATORS
BLAMING · FLAMING	LAMING	
	LAMINGTON	LAMINGTONS
	LAMININ	LAMININS
	LAMISTER	LAMISTERS
	LAMITER	LAMITERS
CLAMMED · FLAMMED · SLAMMED	LAMMED	
CLAMMER · SLAMMER	LAMMER	LAMMERS
CLAMMERS · SLAMMERS	LAMMERS	

FRONT HOOK	ROOT WORD	END HOOK
	LAMMIE	LAMMIES
	LAMMIGER	LAMMIGERS
CLAMMING ▪ FLAMMING ▪ SLAMMING	**LAMMING**	LAMMINGS
SLAMMINGS	**LAMMINGS**	
CLAMMY	**LAMMY**	
CLAMP	**LAMP**	LAMPS
	LAMPAD	LAMPADS
	LAMPADIST	LAMPADISTS
	LAMPASSE	LAMPASSES
	LAMPBLACK	LAMPBLACKS
CLAMPED	**LAMPED**	
CLAMPER	**LAMPER**	LAMPERN ▪ LAMPERS
	LAMPERN	LAMPERNS
CLAMPERS	**LAMPERS**	
	LAMPHOLE	LAMPHOLES
CLAMPING	**LAMPING**	LAMPINGS
	LAMPION	LAMPIONS
	LAMPLIGHT	LAMPLIGHTS
	LAMPOON	LAMPOONS
	LAMPOONER	LAMPOONERS ▪ LAMPOONERY
	LAMPPOST	LAMPPOSTS
	LAMPREY	LAMPREYS
CLAMPS	**LAMPS**	
	LAMPSHADE	LAMPSHADES
	LAMPSHELL	LAMPSHELLS
	LAMPUKA	LAMPUKAS
	LAMPUKI	LAMPUKIS
	LAMPYRID	LAMPYRIDS
BLAMS ▪ CLAMS ▪ FLAMS ▪ GLAMS ▪ SLAMS	**LAMS**	
	LAMSTER	LAMSTERS
	LANA	LANAI ▪ LANAS
	LANAI	LANAIS
PLANATE	**LANATE**	LANATED
ELANCE ▪ GLANCE	**LANCE**	LANCED ▪ LANCER ▪ LANCES ▪ LANCET
ELANCED ▪ GLANCED	**LANCED**	
	LANCEGAY	LANCEGAYS
	LANCEJACK	LANCEJACKS
	LANCELET	LANCELETS
GLANCER	**LANCER**	LANCERS
GLANCERS	**LANCERS**	
ELANCES ▪ GLANCES	**LANCES**	
	LANCET	LANCETS
	LANCEWOOD	LANCEWOODS
BLANCH ▪ FLANCH ▪ PLANCH	**LANCH**	
BLANCHED ▪ FLANCHED ▪ PLANCHED	**LANCHED**	
BLANCHES ▪ FLANCHES ▪ PLANCHES	**LANCHES**	
BLANCHING ▪ FLANCHING ▪ PLANCHING	**LANCHING**	
	LANCINATE	LANCINATED ▪ LANCINATES
ELANCING ▪ GLANCING	**LANCING**	
ALAND ▪ BLAND ▪ ELAND ▪ GLAND	**LAND**	LANDE ▪ LANDS
	LANDAMMAN	LANDAMMANN ▪ LANDAMMANS
	LANDAU	LANDAUS
	LANDAULET	LANDAULETS
	LANDBOARD	LANDBOARDS
	LANDDAMNE	LANDDAMNED ▪ LANDDAMNES
	LANDDROS	LANDDROST
	LANDDROST	LANDDROSTS
	LANDE	LANDED ▪ LANDER ▪ LANDES
BLANDER ▪ SLANDER	**LANDER**	LANDERS
GLANDERS ▪ SLANDERS	**LANDERS**	
GLANDES	**LANDES**	
	LANDFALL	LANDFALLS
	LANDFILL	LANDFILLS
	LANDFORCE	LANDFORCES
	LANDFORM	LANDFORMS
	LANDGRAB	LANDGRABS
	LANDGRAVE	LANDGRAVES
	LANDING	LANDINGS
	LANDLER	LANDLERS

FRONT HOOK	ROOT WORD	END HOOK
GLANDLESS	**LANDLESS**	
	LANDLINE	LANDLINES
	LANDLOPER	LANDLOPERS
	LANDLORD	LANDLORDS
	LANDMARK	LANDMARKS
	LANDOWNER	LANDOWNERS
	LANDRACE	LANDRACES
	LANDRAIL	LANDRAILS
ALANDS ▪ BLANDS ▪ ELANDS ▪ GLANDS	**LANDS**	
	LANDSCAPE	LANDSCAPED ▪ LANDSCAPER ▪ LANDSCAPES
	LANDSHARK	LANDSHARKS
	LANDSIDE	LANDSIDES
	LANDSKIP	LANDSKIPS
	LANDSLID	LANDSLIDE
	LANDSLIDE	LANDSLIDES
	LANDSLIP	LANDSLIPS
	LANDWARD	LANDWARDS
	LANDWIND	LANDWINDS
ALANE ▪ PLANE ▪ SLANE	**LANE**	LANES
FLANES ▪ PLANES ▪ SLANES	**LANES**	
	LANEWAY	LANEWAYS
ALANG ▪ CLANG ▪ KLANG ▪ SLANG′	**LANG**	
	LANGAHA	LANGAHAS
	LANGAR	LANGARS
CLANGER ▪ FLANGER ▪ SLANGER	**LANGER**	LANGERS (offensive)
CLANGERS ▪ FLANGERS ▪ SLANGERS	**LANGERS**	
	LANGLAUF	LANGLAUFS
	LANGLEY	LANGLEYS
	LANGOUSTE	LANGOUSTES
	LANGRAGE	LANGRAGES
	LANGREL	LANGRELS
	LANGRIDGE	LANGRIDGES
	LANGSHAN	LANGSHANS
	LANGSPEL	LANGSPELS
	LANGSPIEL	LANGSPIELS
	LANGSYNE	LANGSYNES
SLANGUAGE	**LANGUAGE**	LANGUAGED ▪ LANGUAGES
SLANGUAGES	**LANGUAGES**	
	LANGUE	LANGUED ▪ LANGUES ▪ LANGUET
	LANGUET	LANGUETS
	LANGUETTE	LANGUETTES
	LANGUOR	LANGUORS
	LANGUR	LANGURS
	LANIARD	LANIARDS
	LANITAL	LANITALS
BLANK ▪ CLANK ▪ FLANK ▪ PLANK ▪ SLANK	**LANK**	LANKS ▪ LANKY
BLANKED ▪ CLANKED ▪ FLANKED ▪ PLANKED	**LANKED**	
BLANKER ▪ FLANKER	**LANKER**	
BLANKEST	**LANKEST**	
CLANKIER	**LANKIER**	
CLANKIEST	**LANKIEST**	
BLANKING ▪ CLANKING ▪ FLANKING PLANKING	**LANKING**	
BLANKLY	**LANKLY**	
BLANKNESS	**LANKNESS**	
BLANKS ▪ CLANKS ▪ FLANKS ▪ PLANKS	**LANKS**	
BLANKY ▪ CLANKY	**LANKY**	
PLANNER	**LANNER**	LANNERS
	LANNERET	LANNERETS
PLANNERS	**LANNERS**	
	LANOLIN	LANOLINE ▪ LANOLINS
	LANOLINE	LANOLINES
ALANT ▪ PLANT ▪ SLANT	**LANT**	LANTS
	LANTANA	LANTANAS
	LANTERLOO	LANTERLOOS
	LANTERN	LANTERNS
	LANTHANON	LANTHANONS
	LANTHANUM	LANTHANUMS
	LANTHORN	LANTHORNS

FRONT HOOK	ROOT WORD	END HOOK
ALANTS · PLANTS · SLANTS	**LANTS**	
	LANTSKIP	LANTSKIPS
	LANUGO	LANUGOS
	LANYARD	LANYARDS
	LAODICEAN	LAODICEANS
	LAOGAI	LAOGAIS
ALAP · CLAP · FLAP · KLAP · PLAP · SLAP	**LAP**	LAPS
CLAPBOARD	**LAPBOARD**	LAPBOARDS
CLAPBOARDS	**LAPBOARDS**	
	LAPDOG	LAPDOGS
	LAPEL	LAPELS
	LAPFUL	LAPFULS
	LAPIDATE	LAPIDATED · LAPIDATES
	LAPIDIST	LAPIDISTS
	LAPIN	LAPINS
	LAPJE	LAPJES
CLAPPED · FLAPPED · KLAPPED · PLAPPED · SLAPPED	**LAPPED**	
	LAPPEL	LAPPELS
CLAPPER · FLAPPER · SLAPPER	**LAPPER**	LAPPERS
CLAPPERED	**LAPPERED**	
CLAPPERING	**LAPPERING**	
CLAPPERS · FLAPPERS · SLAPPERS	**LAPPERS**	
	LAPPET	LAPPETS
	LAPPIE	LAPPIES
CLAPPING · FLAPPING · KLAPPING · PLAPPING · SLAPPING	**LAPPING**	LAPPINGS
CLAPPINGS · FLAPPINGS	**LAPPINGS**	
ALAPS · CLAPS · FLAPS · KLAPS · PLAPS · SLAPS	**LAPS**	LAPSE
	LAPSANG	LAPSANGS
ELAPSE	**LAPSE**	LAPSED · LAPSER · LAPSES
ELAPSED	**LAPSED**	
	LAPSER	LAPSERS
ELAPSES	**LAPSES**	
ELAPSING	**LAPSING**	
	LAPSTONE	LAPSTONES
	LAPSTRAKE	LAPSTRAKES
	LAPSTREAK	LAPSTREAKS
	LAPTOP	LAPTOPS
	LAPTRAY	LAPTRAYS
	LAPWING	LAPWINGS
	LAPWORK	LAPWORKS
ALAR	**LAR**	LARD · LARE · LARI · LARK · LARN · LARS
	LARBOARD	LARBOARDS
	LARCENER	LARCENERS
	LARCENIST	LARCENISTS
	LARD	LARDS · LARDY
	LARDALITE	LARDALITES
	LARDER	LARDERS
	LARDERER	LARDERERS
	LARDON	LARDONS
	LARDOON	LARDOONS
BLARE · FLARE · GLARE	**LARE**	LAREE · LARES
	LAREE	LAREES
BLARES · FLARES · GLARES	**LARES**	
	LARGE	LARGEN · LARGER · LARGES
	LARGEN	LARGENS
	LARGES	LARGESS · LARGEST
	LARGESS	LARGESSE
	LARGESSE	LARGESSES
	LARGHETTO	LARGHETTOS
	LARGITION	LARGITIONS
	LARGO	LARGOS
	LARI	LARIS
	LARIAT	LARIATS
	LARK	LARKS · LARKY
	LARKER	LARKERS
	LARKSPUR	LARKSPURS

FRONT HOOK	ROOT WORD	END HOOK
	LARMIER	LARMIERS
	LARN	LARNS
BLARNEY	LARNEY	LARNEYS
BLARNEYS	LARNEYS	
	LARRIGAN	LARRIGANS
	LARRIKIN	LARRIKINS
	LARRUP	LARRUPS
	LARRUPER	LARRUPERS
ALARUM	LARUM	LARUMS
ALARUMS	LARUMS	
	LARVA	LARVAE ▪ LARVAL ▪ LARVAS
	LARVATE	LARVATED
	LARVICIDE	LARVICIDES
	LARVIKITE	LARVIKITES
	LARYNGAL	LARYNGALS
	LARYNGEAL	LARYNGEALS
ALAS	LAS	LASE ▪ LASH ▪ LASS ▪ LAST
	LASAGNA	LASAGNAS
	LASAGNE	LASAGNES
	LASCAR	LASCARS
BLASE	LASE	LASED ▪ LASER ▪ LASES
FLASER	LASER	LASERS
	LASERDISC	LASERDISCS
	LASERDISK	LASERDISKS
FLASERS	LASERS	
	LASERWORT	LASERWORTS
BLASH ▪ CLASH ▪ FLASH ▪ PLASH ▪ SLASH	LASH	
CLASHED ▪ FLASHED ▪ PLASHED ▪ SLASHED	LASHED	
CLASHER ▪ FLASHER ▪ PLASHER ▪ SLASHER	LASHER	LASHERS
CLASHERS ▪ FLASHERS ▪ PLASHERS SLASHERS	LASHERS	
BLASHES ▪ CLASHES ▪ FLASHES ▪ PLASHES SLASHES	LASHES	
CLASHING ▪ FLASHING ▪ PLASHING SLASHING	LASHING	LASHINGS
CLASHINGLY ▪ SLASHINGLY	LASHINGLY	
CLASHINGS ▪ FLASHINGS ▪ PLASHINGS SLASHINGS	LASHINGS	
	LASHKAR	LASHKARS
	LASING	LASINGS
FLASKET	LASKET	LASKETS
FLASKETS	LASKETS	
	LASQUE	LASQUES
CLASS ▪ GLASS	LASS	LASSI ▪ LASSO ▪ LASSU
CLASSES ▪ GLASSES	LASSES	
	LASSI	LASSIE ▪ LASSIS
GLASSIE	LASSIE	LASSIES
GLASSIES	LASSIES	
CLASSIS	LASSIS	
	LASSITUDE	LASSITUDES
	LASSO	LASSOS
	LASSOCK	LASSOCKS
	LASSOER	LASSOERS
	LASSU	LASSUS
BLAST ▪ CLAST ▪ PLAST	LAST	LASTS
	LASTAGE	LASTAGES
	LASTBORN	LASTBORNS
BLASTED	LASTED	
BLASTER ▪ PLASTER	LASTER	LASTERS
BLASTERS ▪ PLASTERS	LASTERS	
BLASTING	LASTING	LASTINGS
BLASTINGS	LASTINGS	
BLASTS ▪ CLASTS	LASTS	
BLAT ▪ CLAT ▪ FLAT ▪ PLAT ▪ SLAT	LAT	LATE ▪ LATH ▪ LATI ▪ LATS ▪ LATU
	LATAH	LATAHS
	LATAKIA	LATAKIAS
CLATCH ▪ KLATCH ▪ SLATCH	LATCH	
CLATCHED	LATCHED	
CLATCHES ▪ KLATCHES ▪ SLATCHES	LATCHES	

447

FRONT HOOK	ROOT WORD	END HOOK
	LATCHET	LATCHETS
CLATCHING	**LATCHING**	
	LATCHKEY	LATCHKEYS
ALATE · BLATE · ELATE · PLATE · SLATE	**LATE**	LATED · LATEN · LATER · LATEX
	LATECOMER	LATECOMERS
ALATED · ELATED · PLATED · SLATED	**LATED**	
	LATEEN	LATEENS
	LATEENER	LATEENERS
PLATEN	**LATEN**	LATENS · LATENT
	LATENCE	LATENCES
PLATENS	**LATENS**	
	LATENT	LATENTS
BLATER · ELATER · PLATER · SLATER	**LATER**	
	LATERAL	LATERALS
	LATERBORN	LATERBORNS
	LATERISE	LATERISED · LATERISES
ELATERITE	**LATERITE**	LATERITES
ELATERITES	**LATERITES**	
	LATERIZE	LATERIZED · LATERIZES
BLATEST	**LATEST**	LATESTS
	LATEWAKE	LATEWAKES
	LATEWOOD	LATEWOODS
	LATH	LATHE · LATHI · LATHS · LATHY
	LATHE	LATHED · LATHEE · LATHEN · LATHER · LATHES
	LATHEE	LATHEES
BLATHER · SLATHER	**LATHER**	LATHERS · LATHERY
BLATHERED · SLATHERED	**LATHERED**	
BLATHERER	**LATHERER**	LATHERERS
BLATHERERS	**LATHERERS**	
BLATHERING · SLATHERING	**LATHERING**	
BLATHERS · SLATHERS	**LATHERS**	
	LATHI	LATHIS
	LATHING	LATHINGS
	LATHWORK	LATHWORKS
	LATHYRISM	LATHYRISMS
	LATICIFER	LATICIFERS
	LATICLAVE	LATICLAVES
	LATIGO	LATIGOS
	LATILLA	LATILLAS
	LATIMERIA	LATIMERIAS
PLATINA	**LATINA**	LATINAS
PLATINAS	**LATINAS**	
PLATINISE	**LATINISE**	LATINISED · LATINISES
PLATINISED	**LATINISED**	
PLATINISES	**LATINISES**	
PLATINIZE	**LATINIZE**	LATINIZED · LATINIZES
PLATINIZED	**LATINIZED**	
PLATINIZES	**LATINIZES**	
	LATINO	LATINOS
	LATITAT	LATITATS
PLATITUDE	**LATITUDE**	LATITUDES
PLATITUDES	**LATITUDES**	
	LATKE	LATKES
	LATOSOL	LATOSOLS
	LATRATION	LATRATIONS
	LATRIA	LATRIAS
	LATRINE	LATRINES
	LATRON	LATRONS
BLATS · CLATS · FLATS · PLATS · SLATS	**LATS**	
	LATTE	LATTEN · LATTER · LATTES
FLATTEN	**LATTEN**	LATTENS
FLATTENS	**LATTENS**	
BLATTER · CLATTER · FLATTER · PLATTER · SLATTER	**LATTER**	
	LATTICE	LATTICED · LATTICES
	LATTICING	LATTICINGS
	LATTICINI	LATTICINIO
	LATTIN	LATTINS
	LAUAN	LAUANS

FRONT HOOK	ROOT WORD	END HOOK
	LAUCH	LAUCHS
BLAUD	LAUD	LAUDS
	LAUDANUM	LAUDANUMS
	LAUDATION	LAUDATIONS
	LAUDATIVE	LAUDATIVES
	LAUDATOR	LAUDATORS ▪ LAUDATORY
BLAUDED	LAUDED	
	LAUDER	LAUDERS
BLAUDING	LAUDING	
BLAUDS	LAUDS	
	LAUF	LAUFS
	LAUGH	LAUGHS ▪ LAUGHY
	LAUGHER	LAUGHERS
	LAUGHING	LAUGHINGS
	LAUGHLINE	LAUGHLINES
FLAUGHTER ▪ SLAUGHTER	LAUGHTER	LAUGHTERS
FLAUGHTERS ▪ SLAUGHTERS	LAUGHTERS	
	LAUNCE	LAUNCED ▪ LAUNCES
FLAUNCH	LAUNCH	
FLAUNCHED	LAUNCHED	
	LAUNCHER	LAUNCHERS
FLAUNCHES	LAUNCHES	
FLAUNCHING	LAUNCHING	
	LAUNCHPAD	LAUNCHPADS
	LAUND	LAUNDS
	LAUNDER	LAUNDERS
	LAUNDERER	LAUNDERERS
	LAURA	LAURAE ▪ LAURAS
	LAUREATE	LAUREATED ▪ LAUREATES
	LAUREL	LAURELS
	LAURYL	LAURYLS
	LAUWINE	LAUWINES
	LAV	LAVA ▪ LAVE ▪ LAVS
	LAVA	LAVAS
	LAVABO	LAVABOS
	LAVAGE	LAVAGES
	LAVALAVA	LAVALAVAS
	LAVALIER	LAVALIERE ▪ LAVALIERS
	LAVALIERE	LAVALIERES
	LAVAS	LAVASH
	LAVATERA	LAVATERAS
CLAVATION	LAVATION	LAVATIONS
CLAVATIONS	LAVATIONS	
CLAVE ▪ SLAVE	LAVE	LAVED ▪ LAVER ▪ LAVES
SLAVED	LAVED	
	LAVEER	LAVEERS
	LAVEMENT	LAVEMENTS
	LAVENDER	LAVENDERS
CLAVER ▪ SLAVER	LAVER	LAVERS
	LAVEROCK	LAVEROCKS
CLAVERS ▪ SLAVERS	LAVERS	
CLAVES ▪ SLAVES	LAVES	
SLAVING	LAVING	
SLAVISH	LAVISH	
	LAVISHER	LAVISHERS
	LAVISHES	LAVISHEST
SLAVISHLY	LAVISHLY	
	LAVOLT	LAVOLTA ▪ LAVOLTS
	LAVOLTA	LAVOLTAS
	LAVRA	LAVRAS
	LAVROCK	LAVROCKS
BLAW ▪ CLAW ▪ FLAW ▪ SLAW	LAW	LAWK ▪ LAWN ▪ LAWS
	LAWBOOK	LAWBOOKS
BLAWED ▪ CLAWED ▪ FLAWED	LAWED	
CLAWER	LAWER	
	LAWGIVER	LAWGIVERS
	LAWGIVING	LAWGIVINGS
	LAWIN	LAWINE ▪ LAWING ▪ LAWINS
	LAWINE	LAWINES

FRONT HOOK	ROOT WORD	END HOOK
BLAWING · CLAWING · FLAWING	**LAWING**	LAWINGS
	LAWK	LAWKS
	LAWLAND	LAWLANDS
CLAWLESS · FLAWLESS	**LAWLESS**	
FLAWLESSLY	**LAWLESSLY**	
CLAWLIKE	**LAWLIKE**	
	LAWMAKER	LAWMAKERS
	LAWMAKING	LAWMAKINGS
	LAWMONGER	LAWMONGERS
BLAWN · FLAWN	**LAWN**	LAWNS · LAWNY
	LAWNMOWER	LAWNMOWERS
FLAWNS	**LAWNS**	
BLAWS · CLAWS · FLAWS · SLAWS	**LAWS**	
	LAWSUIT	LAWSUITS
	LAWYER	LAWYERS
	LAWYERING	LAWYERINGS
FLAX	**LAX**	
	LAXATION	LAXATIONS
	LAXATIVE	LAXATIVES
	LAXATOR	LAXATORS
FLAXES	**LAXES**	LAXEST
	LAXISM	LAXISMS
	LAXIST	LAXISTS
ALAY · BLAY · CLAY · FLAY · PLAY · SLAY	**LAY**	LAYS
	LAYABOUT	LAYABOUTS
	LAYAWAY	LAYAWAYS
PLAYBACK	**LAYBACK**	LAYBACKS
PLAYBACKS	**LAYBACKS**	
ALAYED · CLAYED · FLAYED · PLAYED SLAYED	**LAYED**	
FLAYER · PLAYER · SLAYER	**LAYER**	LAYERS
	LAYERAGE	LAYERAGES
	LAYERING	LAYERINGS
FLAYERS · PLAYERS · SLAYERS	**LAYERS**	
	LAYETTE	LAYETTES
	LAYIN	LAYING · LAYINS
ALAYING · CLAYING · FLAYING · PLAYING SLAYING	**LAYING**	LAYINGS
	LAYLOCK	LAYLOCKS
PLAYOFF	**LAYOFF**	LAYOFFS
PLAYOFFS	**LAYOFFS**	
	LAYOUT	LAYOUTS
	LAYOVER	LAYOVERS
	LAYPERSON	LAYPERSONS
ALAYS · BLAYS · CLAYS · FLAYS · PLAYS SLAYS	**LAYS**	
	LAYSHAFT	LAYSHAFTS
	LAYSTALL	LAYSTALLS
PLAYTIME	**LAYTIME**	LAYTIMES
PLAYTIMES	**LAYTIMES**	
	LAYUP	LAYUPS
	LAZAR	LAZARS
	LAZARET	LAZARETS
	LAZARETTE	LAZARETTES
	LAZARETTO	LAZARETTOS
BLAZE · GLAZE	**LAZE**	LAZED · LAZES
BLAZED · GLAZED	**LAZED**	
BLAZES · GLAZES	**LAZES**	
GLAZIER	**LAZIER**	
	LAZIES	LAZIEST
GLAZIEST	**LAZIEST**	
GLAZILY	**LAZILY**	
GLAZINESS	**LAZINESS**	
BLAZING · GLAZING	**LAZING**	
	LAZO	LAZOS
	LAZULI	LAZULIS
	LAZULITE	LAZULITES
	LAZURITE	LAZURITES
GLAZY	**LAZY**	

FRONT HOOK	ROOT WORD	END HOOK
FLEA · ILEA · OLEA · PLEA	LEA	LEAD · LEAF · LEAK · LEAL · LEAM LEAN · LEAP · LEAR · LEAS · LEAT
BLEACH · PLEACH	LEACH	LEACHY
BLEACHABLE	LEACHABLE	
	LEACHATE	LEACHATES
BLEACHED · PLEACHED	LEACHED	
BLEACHER	LEACHER	LEACHERS
BLEACHERS	LEACHERS	
BLEACHES · PLEACHES	LEACHES	
BLEACHING · PLEACHING	LEACHING	LEACHINGS
BLEACHINGS	LEACHINGS	
	LEACHOUR	LEACHOURS
PLEAD	LEAD	LEADS · LEADY
PLEADED	LEADED	
	LEADEN	LEADENS
PLEADER	LEADER	LEADERS
	LEADERENE	LEADERENES
PLEADERS	LEADERS	
PLEADING	LEADING	LEADINGS
PLEADINGLY	LEADINGLY	
PLEADINGS	LEADINGS	
	LEADOFF	LEADOFFS
	LEADPLANT	LEADPLANTS
PLEADS	LEADS	
	LEADSCREW	LEADSCREWS
	LEADWORK	LEADWORKS
	LEADWORT	LEADWORTS
	LEAF	LEAFS · LEAFY
	LEAFAGE	LEAFAGES
	LEAFBUD	LEAFBUDS
	LEAFLET	LEAFLETS
	LEAFLETER	LEAFLETERS
	LEAFSTALK	LEAFSTALKS
	LEAFWORM	LEAFWORMS
	LEAGUE	LEAGUED · LEAGUER · LEAGUES
	LEAGUER	LEAGUERS
BLEAK	LEAK	LEAKS · LEAKY
	LEAKAGE	LEAKAGES
BLEAKER	LEAKER	LEAKERS
BLEAKS	LEAKS	
BLEAKY	LEAKY	
ILEAL	LEAL	
FLEAM · GLEAM	LEAM	LEAMS
GLEAMED	LEAMED	
GLEAMING	LEAMING	
FLEAMS · GLEAMS	LEAMS	
CLEAN · GLEAN	LEAN	LEANS · LEANT · LEANY
CLEANED · GLEANED	LEANED	
CLEANER · GLEANER	LEANER	LEANERS
CLEANERS · GLEANERS	LEANERS	
CLEANEST	LEANEST	
CLEANING · GLEANING	LEANING	LEANINGS
CLEANINGS · GLEANINGS	LEANINGS	
CLEANLY	LEANLY	
CLEANNESS	LEANNESS	
CLEANS · GLEANS	LEANS	
	LEAP	LEAPS · LEAPT
	LEAPER	LEAPERS
	LEAPFROG	LEAPFROGS
BLEAR · CLEAR	LEAR	LEARE · LEARN · LEARS · LEARY
	LEARE	LEARED · LEARES
BLEARED · CLEARED	LEARED	
BLEARIER	LEARIER	
BLEARIEST	LEARIEST	
BLEARINESS	LEARINESS	
BLEARING · CLEARING	LEARING	
	LEARN	LEARNS · LEARNT
	LEARNER	LEARNERS
	LEARNING	LEARNINGS

FRONT HOOK	ROOT WORD	END HOOK
BLEARS · CLEARS	**LEARS**	
BLEARY	**LEARY**	
FLEAS · PLEAS	**LEAS**	LEASE · LEASH · LEAST
PLEASABLE	**LEASABLE**	
PLEASE	**LEASE**	LEASED · LEASER · LEASES
	LEASEBACK	LEASEBACKS
PLEASED	**LEASED**	
	LEASEHOLD	LEASEHOLDS
PLEASER	**LEASER**	LEASERS
PLEASERS	**LEASERS**	
PLEASES	**LEASES**	
PLEASING	**LEASING**	LEASINGS
PLEASINGS	**LEASINGS**	
	LEASOW	LEASOWE · LEASOWS
	LEASOWE	LEASOWED · LEASOWES
	LEAST	LEASTS
PLEASURE	**LEASURE**	LEASURES
PLEASURES	**LEASURES**	
BLEAT · CLEAT · PLEAT	**LEAT**	LEATS
PLEATHER	**LEATHER**	LEATHERN · LEATHERS · LEATHERY
PLEATHERS	**LEATHERS**	
BLEATS · CLEATS · PLEATS	**LEATS**	
CLEAVE · GLEAVE · SLEAVE	**LEAVE**	LEAVED · LEAVEN · LEAVER · LEAVES
CLEAVED · SLEAVED	**LEAVED**	
	LEAVEN	LEAVENS
	LEAVENING	LEAVENINGS
CLEAVER	**LEAVER**	LEAVERS
CLEAVERS	**LEAVERS**	
CLEAVES · GLEAVES · SLEAVES	**LEAVES**	
CLEAVING · SLEAVING	**LEAVING**	LEAVINGS
CLEAVINGS	**LEAVINGS**	
SLEAZE	**LEAZE**	LEAZES
SLEAZES	**LEAZES**	
	LEBBEK	LEBBEKS
	LEBEN	LEBENS
	LECANORA	LECANORAS
	LECHAIM	LECHAIMS
	LECHAYIM	LECHAYIMS
	LECHER	LECHERS · LECHERY
FLECHES	**LECHES**	
	LECHWE	LECHWES
	LECITHIN	LECITHINS
	LECTERN	LECTERNS
	LECTIN	LECTINS
ELECTION · FLECTION	**LECTION**	LECTIONS
ELECTIONS · FLECTIONS	**LECTIONS**	
ELECTOR	**LECTOR**	LECTORS
ELECTORATE	**LECTORATE**	LECTORATES
ELECTORS	**LECTORS**	
	LECTOTYPE	LECTOTYPES
ELECTRESS	**LECTRESS**	
	LECTURE	LECTURED · LECTURER · LECTURES
	LECTURER	LECTURERS
	LECTURN	LECTURNS
	LECYTHI	LECYTHIS
BLED · FLED · GLED · PLED · SLED	**LED**	
	LEDDEN	LEDDENS
FLEDGE · GLEDGE · PLEDGE · SLEDGE	**LEDGE**	LEDGED · LEDGER · LEDGES
FLEDGED · GLEDGED · PLEDGED · SLEDGED	**LEDGED**	
PLEDGER · SLEDGER	**LEDGER**	LEDGERS
PLEDGERS · SLEDGERS	**LEDGERS**	
FLEDGES · GLEDGES · PLEDGES · SLEDGES	**LEDGES**	
FLEDGIER	**LEDGIER**	
FLEDGIEST	**LEDGIEST**	
FLEDGY	**LEDGY**	
	LEDUM	LEDUMS
ALEE · BLEE · FLEE · GLEE · SLEE	**LEE**	LEED · LEEK · LEEP · LEER · LEES · LEET
	LEEAR	LEEARS
	LEEBOARD	LEEBOARDS

FRONT HOOK	ROOT WORD	END HOOK
FLEECH ▪ SLEECH	**LEECH**	
	LEECHDOM	LEECHDOMS
FLEECHED	**LEECHED**	
	LEECHEE	LEECHEES
FLEECHES ▪ SLEECHES	**LEECHES**	
FLEECHING	**LEECHING**	
BLEED ▪ GLEED	**LEED**	
FLEEING ▪ GLEEING	**LEEING**	
CLEEK ▪ GLEEK ▪ SLEEK	**LEEK**	LEEKS
CLEEKS ▪ GLEEKS ▪ SLEEKS	**LEEKS**	
BLEEP ▪ CLEEP ▪ SLEEP	**LEEP**	LEEPS
BLEEPED ▪ CLEEPED	**LEEPED**	
BLEEPING ▪ CLEEPING ▪ SLEEPING	**LEEPING**	
BLEEPS ▪ CLEEPS ▪ SLEEPS	**LEEPS**	
FLEER ▪ SLEER	**LEER**	LEERS ▪ LEERY
FLEERED	**LEERED**	
FLEERING	**LEERING**	LEERINGS
FLEERINGLY	**LEERINGLY**	
FLEERINGS	**LEERINGS**	
FLEERS	**LEERS**	
BLEES ▪ FLEES ▪ GLEES	**LEES**	LEESE
	LEESE	LEESES
FLEET ▪ GLEET ▪ SLEET	**LEET**	LEETS
FLEETS ▪ GLEETS ▪ SLEETS	**LEETS**	
	LEEWARD	LEEWARDS
	LEEWAY	LEEWAYS
ALEFT ▪ CLEFT	**LEFT**	LEFTE ▪ LEFTS ▪ LEFTY
	LEFTE	LEFTER
	LEFTIE	LEFTIES
	LEFTISM	LEFTISMS
	LEFTIST	LEFTISTS
	LEFTMOST	LEFTMOSTS
	LEFTOVER	LEFTOVERS
CLEFTS	**LEFTS**	
	LEFTWARD	LEFTWARDS
CLEG ▪ FLEG ▪ GLEG	**LEG**	LEGS
	LEGAL	LEGALS
	LEGALESE	LEGALESES
	LEGALISE	LEGALISED ▪ LEGALISER ▪ LEGALISES
	LEGALISER	LEGALISERS
	LEGALISM	LEGALISMS
	LEGALIST	LEGALISTS
	LEGALIZE	LEGALIZED ▪ LEGALIZER ▪ LEGALIZES
	LEGALIZER	LEGALIZERS
	LEGATE	LEGATED ▪ LEGATEE ▪ LEGATES
	LEGATEE	LEGATEES
	LEGATION	LEGATIONS
	LEGATO	LEGATOR ▪ LEGATOS
	LEGATOR	LEGATORS
	LEGEND	LEGENDS
	LEGENDISE	LEGENDISED ▪ LEGENDISES
	LEGENDIST	LEGENDISTS
	LEGENDIZE	LEGENDIZED ▪ LEGENDIZES
	LEGER	LEGERS
	LEGERING	LEGERINGS
ALEGGE	**LEGGE**	LEGGED ▪ LEGGER ▪ LEGGES
ALEGGED ▪ FLEGGED	**LEGGED**	
GLEGGER	**LEGGER**	LEGGERS
ALEGGES	**LEGGES**	
	LEGGIER	LEGGIERO
	LEGGIN	LEGGING ▪ LEGGINS
ALEGGING ▪ FLEGGING	**LEGGING**	LEGGINGS
	LEGGISM	LEGGISMS
	LEGHORN	LEGHORNS
	LEGION	LEGIONS
	LEGISLATE	LEGISLATED ▪ LEGISLATES
ELEGIST	**LEGIST**	LEGISTS
ELEGISTS	**LEGISTS**	
ELEGIT	**LEGIT**	LEGITS

FRONT HOOK	ROOT WORD	END HOOK
	LEGITIM	LEGITIMS
ELEGITS	**LEGITS**	
	LEGLAN	LEGLANS
	LEGLEN	LEGLENS
	LEGLET	LEGLETS
	LEGLIN	LEGLINS
	LEGONG	LEGONGS
	LEGROOM	LEGROOMS
CLEGS · FLEGS	**LEGS**	
	LEGUAAN	LEGUAANS
	LEGUME	LEGUMES
	LEGUMIN	LEGUMINS
	LEGWARMER	LEGWARMERS
	LEGWEAR	LEGWEARS
	LEGWORK	LEGWORKS
	LEHAIM	LEHAIMS
	LEHAYIM	LEHAYIMS
	LEHR	LEHRS
	LEHUA	LEHUAS
GLEI · VLEI	**LEI**	LEIR · LEIS
	LEIDGER	LEIDGERS
	LEIGER	LEIGERS
	LEIOMYOMA	LEIOMYOMAS
	LEIPOA	LEIPOAS
	LEIR	LEIRS
GLEIS · VLEIS	**LEIS**	LEISH
	LEISLER	LEISLERS
	LEISTER	LEISTERS
	LEISURE	LEISURED · LEISURES
	LEITMOTIF	LEITMOTIFS
	LEITMOTIV	LEITMOTIVS
	LEK	LEKE · LEKS · LEKU
	LEKGOTLA	LEKGOTLAS
	LEKKING	LEKKINGS
	LEKVAR	LEKVARS
	LEMAN	LEMANS
FLEME	**LEME**	LEMED · LEMEL · LEMES
	LEMEL	LEMELS
FLEMES	**LEMES**	
FLEMING	**LEMING**	
	LEMMA	LEMMAS
	LEMMATISE	LEMMATISED · LEMMATISES
	LEMMATIZE	LEMMATIZED · LEMMATIZES
CLEMMING	**LEMMING**	LEMMINGS
	LEMON	LEMONS · LEMONY
	LEMONADE	LEMONADES
	LEMONWOOD	LEMONWOODS
	LEMPIRA	LEMPIRAS
	LEMUR	LEMURS
	LEMURIAN	LEMURIANS
	LEMURINE	LEMURINES
	LEMUROID	LEMUROIDS
BLEND	**LEND**	LENDS
BLENDER · SLENDER	**LENDER**	LENDERS
BLENDERS	**LENDERS**	
BLENDING	**LENDING**	LENDINGS
BLENDINGS	**LENDINGS**	
BLENDS	**LENDS**	
	LENG	LENGS
ALENGTH	**LENGTH**	LENGTHS · LENGTHY
	LENGTHEN	LENGTHENS
	LENIENCE	LENIENCES
	LENIENT	LENIENTS
	LENITE	LENITED · LENITES
	LENITION	LENITIONS
	LENITIVE	LENITIVES
	LENO	LENOS
GLENS	**LENS**	LENSE
FLENSE	**LENSE**	LENSED · LENSES

FRONT HOOK	ROOT WORD	END HOOK
FLENSED	LENSED	
FLENSES	LENSES	
FLENSING	LENSING	
BLENT · GLENT · OLENT	LENT	LENTI · LENTO
	LENTI	LENTIC · LENTIL
	LENTICEL	LENTICELS
	LENTICLE	LENTICLES
	LENTICULE	LENTICULES
	LENTIL	LENTILS
	LENTISK	LENTISKS
	LENTO	LENTOR · LENTOS
	LENTOID	LENTOIDS
	LENTOR	LENTORS
	LENVOY	LENVOYS
	LEONE	LEONES
	LEOPARD	LEOPARDS
	LEOTARD	LEOTARDS
	LEP	LEPS · LEPT
	LEPER	LEPERS
	LEPIDOTE	LEPIDOTES
	LEPORID	LEPORIDS
	LEPRA	LEPRAS
CLEPT · SLEPT	LEPT	LEPTA
	LEPTIN	LEPTINS
	LEPTOME	LEPTOMES
	LEPTON	LEPTONS
	LEPTOSOME	LEPTOSOMES
	LEPTOTENE	LEPTOTENES
	LEQUEAR	LEQUEARS
	LERE	LERED · LERES
	LERP	LERPS
ALES · OLES · ULES	LES	LESS · LEST
	LESBIAN	LESBIANS
	LESBO	LESBOS (offensive)
	LESION	LESIONS
	LESPEDEZA	LESPEDEZAS
BLESS	LESS	
	LESSEE	LESSEES
	LESSEN	LESSENS
BLESSER	LESSER	
BLESSES	LESSES	
	LESSON	LESSONS
	LESSONING	LESSONINGS
PLESSOR	LESSOR	LESSORS
PLESSORS	LESSORS	
BLEST	LEST	LESTS
BLET	LET	LETS
FLETCH	LETCH	
FLETCHED	LETCHED	
FLETCHES	LETCHES	
FLETCHING	LETCHING	LETCHINGS
FLETCHINGS	LETCHINGS	
	LETDOWN	LETDOWNS
	LETHAL	LETHALS
	LETHE	LETHEE · LETHES
	LETHEE	LETHEES
BLETS	LETS	
BLETTED	LETTED	
	LETTER	LETTERN · LETTERS
	LETTERER	LETTERERS
	LETTERING	LETTERINGS
	LETTERN	LETTERNS
	LETTERSET	LETTERSETS
BLETTING	LETTING	LETTINGS
	LETTRE	LETTRES
	LETTUCE	LETTUCES
	LETUP	LETUPS
	LEU	LEUD
	LEUCAEMIA	LEUCAEMIAS

FRONT HOOK	ROOT WORD	END HOOK
	LEUCEMIA	LEUCEMIAS
CLEUCH · PLEUCH	**LEUCH**	
	LEUCIN	LEUCINE · LEUCINS
	LEUCINE	LEUCINES
	LEUCITE	LEUCITES
	LEUCOCYTE	LEUCOCYTES
	LEUCOMA	LEUCOMAS
	LEUCOSIN	LEUCOSINS
	LEUCOTOME	LEUCOTOMES
	LEUD	LEUDS
CLEUGH · PLEUGH	**LEUGH**	
	LEUKAEMIA	LEUKAEMIAS
	LEUKEMIA	LEUKEMIAS
	LEUKEMIC	LEUKEMICS
	LEUKOCYTE	LEUKOCYTES
	LEUKOMA	LEUKOMAS
	LEUKON	LEUKONS
	LEV	LEVA · LEVE · LEVO · LEVY
	LEVANT	LEVANTS
	LEVANTER	LEVANTERS
	LEVANTINE	LEVANTINES
ELEVATOR	**LEVATOR**	LEVATORS
ELEVATORS	**LEVATORS**	
CLEVE	**LEVE**	LEVEE · LEVEL · LEVER
	LEVEE	LEVEED · LEVEES
	LEVEL	LEVELS
	LEVELER	LEVELERS
	LEVELLER	LEVELLERS
	LEVELLING	LEVELLINGS
CLEVER	**LEVER**	LEVERS
	LEVERAGE	LEVERAGED · LEVERAGES
	LEVERET	LEVERETS
	LEVIATHAN	LEVIATHANS
	LEVIER	LEVIERS
	LEVIGATE	LEVIGATED · LEVIGATES
	LEVIGATOR	LEVIGATORS
ALEVIN	**LEVIN**	LEVINS
ALEVINS	**LEVINS**	
	LEVIRATE	LEVIRATES
CLEVIS	**LEVIS**	
	LEVITATE	LEVITATED · LEVITATES
	LEVITATOR	LEVITATORS
	LEVITE	LEVITES
	LEVODOPA	LEVODOPAS
	LEVULIN	LEVULINS
	LEVULOSE	LEVULOSES
ALEW · BLEW · CLEW · FLEW · PLEW · SLEW	**LEW**	LEWD
	LEWDSTER	LEWDSTERS
	LEWISIA	LEWISIAS
	LEWISITE	LEWISITES
	LEWISSON	LEWISSONS
FLEX · ILEX · PLEX · ULEX	**LEX**	
	LEXEME	LEXEMES
FLEXES · ILEXES · PLEXES · ULEXES	**LEXES**	
	LEXICA	LEXICAL
	LEXICON	LEXICONS
	LEXIGRAM	LEXIGRAMS
BLEY · FLEY · GLEY · SLEY	**LEY**	LEYS
	LEYLANDI	LEYLANDII · LEYLANDIS
	LEYLANDII	LEYLANDIIS
BLEYS · FLEYS · GLEYS · SLEYS	**LEYS**	
	LEZ	LEZZ *(offensive)*
	LEZZ	LEZZA *(offensive)* · LEZZY *(offensive)*
	LEZZA	LEZZAS *(offensive)*
	LEZZIE	LEZZIES *(offensive)*
	LI	LIB · LID · LIE · LIG · LIN · LIP · LIS · LIT
PLIABILITY	**LIABILITY**	
PLIABLE	**LIABLE**	
	LIAISE	LIAISED · LIAISES

FRONT HOOK	ROOT WORD	END HOOK
	LIAISON	LIAISONS
	LIANA	LIANAS
	LIANE	LIANES
	LIANG	LIANGS
	LIAR	LIARD = LIARS = LIART
	LIARD	LIARDS
ALIAS = GLIAS	**LIAS**	
ALIASES	**LIASES**	
GLIB	**LIB**	LIBS
	LIBATE	LIBATED = LIBATES
	LIBATION	LIBATIONS
	LIBBARD	LIBBARDS
GLIBBED	**LIBBED**	
GLIBBER	**LIBBER**	LIBBERS (offensive)
GLIBBING	**LIBBING**	
	LIBECCHIO	LIBECCHIOS
	LIBECCIO	LIBECCIOS
	LIBEL	LIBELS
	LIBELANT	LIBELANTS
	LIBELEE	LIBELEES
	LIBELER	LIBELERS
	LIBELING	LIBELINGS
	LIBELIST	LIBELISTS
	LIBELLANT	LIBELLANTS
	LIBELLEE	LIBELLEES
	LIBELLER	LIBELLERS
	LIBELLING	LIBELLINGS
	LIBER	LIBERO = LIBERS
	LIBERAL	LIBERALS
	LIBERATE	LIBERATED = LIBERATES
	LIBERATOR	LIBERATORS = LIBERATORY
	LIBERO	LIBEROS
	LIBERTINE	LIBERTINES
	LIBIDO	LIBIDOS
	LIBKEN	LIBKENS
	LIBLAB	LIBLABS
	LIBRA	LIBRAE = LIBRAS
	LIBRAIRE	LIBRAIRES
	LIBRAIRIE	LIBRAIRIES
	LIBRARIAN	LIBRARIANS
	LIBRATE	LIBRATED = LIBRATES
	LIBRATION	LIBRATIONS
	LIBRETTO	LIBRETTOS
GLIBS	**LIBS**	
SLICE	**LICE**	
	LICENCE	LICENCED = LICENCEE = LICENCER LICENCES
	LICENCEE	LICENCEES
	LICENCER	LICENCERS
	LICENSE	LICENSED = LICENSEE = LICENSER LICENSES
	LICENSEE	LICENSEES
	LICENSER	LICENSERS
	LICENSOR	LICENSORS
	LICENSURE	LICENSURES
	LICH	LICHI = LICHT
	LICHEE	LICHEES
	LICHEN	LICHENS
	LICHENIN	LICHENING = LICHENINS
	LICHENISM	LICHENISMS
	LICHENIST	LICHENISTS
CLICHES = ELICHES	**LICHES**	
	LICHGATE	LICHGATES
	LICHI	LICHIS
	LICHT	LICHTS
FLICHTER	**LICHTER**	
	LICHWAKE	LICHWAKES
	LICHWAY	LICHWAYS
ELICIT	**LICIT**	

FRONT HOOK	ROOT WORD	END HOOK
CLICK · FLICK · KLICK · SLICK	**LICK**	LICKS
CLICKED · FLICKED · SLICKED	**LICKED**	
CLICKER · FLICKER · SLICKER	**LICKER**	LICKERS
CLICKERS · FLICKERS · SLICKERS	**LICKERS**	
CLICKING · FLICKING · SLICKING	**LICKING**	LICKINGS
CLICKINGS · SLICKINGS	**LICKINGS**	
CLICKS · FLICKS · KLICKS · SLICKS	**LICKS**	
	LICKSPIT	LICKSPITS
	LICORICE	LICORICES
	LICTOR	LICTORS
GLID · OLID · SLID	**LID**	LIDO · LIDS
	LIDAR	LIDARS
	LIDGER	LIDGERS
	LIDO	LIDOS
	LIDOCAINE	LIDOCAINES
PLIE	**LIE**	LIED · LIEF · LIEN · LIER · LIES · LIEU
CLIED · FLIED · PLIED	**LIED**	
	LIEF	LIEFS
	LIEGE	LIEGER · LIEGES
	LIEGEDOM	LIEGEDOMS
	LIEGER	LIEGERS
ALIEN	**LIEN**	LIENS
ALIENABLE	**LIENABLE**	
ALIENS	**LIENS**	
FLIER · PLIER · SLIER	**LIER**	LIERS
	LIERNE	LIERNES
FLIERS · PLIERS	**LIERS**	
CLIES · FLIES · PLIES · VLIES	**LIES**	
	LIEU	LIEUS
SLIEVE	**LIEVE**	LIEVER
	LIFE	LIFER · LIFES
	LIFEBELT	LIFEBELTS
	LIFEBLOOD	LIFEBLOODS
	LIFEBOAT	LIFEBOATS
	LIFEBUOY	LIFEBUOYS
	LIFECARE	LIFECARES
	LIFEGUARD	LIFEGUARDS
	LIFELINE	LIFELINES
	LIFER	LIFERS
	LIFESAVER	LIFESAVERS
	LIFESPAN	LIFESPANS
	LIFESTYLE	LIFESTYLER · LIFESTYLES
	LIFETIME	LIFETIMES
	LIFEWAY	LIFEWAYS
	LIFEWORK	LIFEWORKS
	LIFEWORLD	LIFEWORLDS
CLIFT · GLIFT	**LIFT**	LIFTS
	LIFTBACK	LIFTBACKS
	LIFTBOY	LIFTBOYS
CLIFTED	**LIFTED**	
	LIFTER	LIFTERS
	LIFTGATE	LIFTGATES
	LIFTOFF	LIFTOFFS
CLIFTS · GLIFTS	**LIFTS**	
	LIG	LIGS
	LIGAMENT	LIGAMENTS
	LIGAN	LIGAND · LIGANS
	LIGAND	LIGANDS
	LIGASE	LIGASES
	LIGATE	LIGATED · LIGATES
	LIGATION	LIGATIONS
	LIGATURE	LIGATURED · LIGATURES
	LIGER	LIGERS
	LIGGE	LIGGED · LIGGEN · LIGGER · LIGGES
	LIGGER	LIGGERS
	LIGGING	LIGGINGS
ALIGHT · BLIGHT · FLIGHT · PLIGHT · SLIGHT	**LIGHT**	LIGHTS
	LIGHTBULB	LIGHTBULBS

FRONT HOOK	ROOT WORD	END HOOK
ALIGHTED ▪ BLIGHTED ▪ FLIGHTED PLIGHTED ▪ SLIGHTED	**LIGHTED**	
	LIGHTEN	LIGHTENS
	LIGHTENER	LIGHTENERS
BLIGHTER ▪ PLIGHTER ▪ SLIGHTER	**LIGHTER**	LIGHTERS
BLIGHTERS ▪ PLIGHTERS ▪ SLIGHTERS SLIGHTEST	**LIGHTERS**	
SLIGHTEST	**LIGHTEST**	
	LIGHTFACE	LIGHTFACED ▪ LIGHTFACES
PLIGHTFUL	**LIGHTFUL**	
ALIGHTING ▪ BLIGHTING ▪ FLIGHTING PLIGHTING ▪ SLIGHTING	**LIGHTING**	LIGHTINGS
BLIGHTINGS	**LIGHTINGS**	
SLIGHTISH	**LIGHTISH**	
FLIGHTLESS	**LIGHTLESS**	
SLIGHTLY	**LIGHTLY**	
SLIGHTNESS	**LIGHTNESS**	
	LIGHTNING	LIGHTNINGS
ALIGHTS ▪ BLIGHTS ▪ FLIGHTS ▪ PLIGHTS SLIGHTS	**LIGHTS**	
	LIGHTSHIP	LIGHTSHIPS
	LIGHTWOOD	LIGHTWOODS
	LIGNAGE	LIGNAGES
	LIGNAN	LIGNANS
	LIGNE	LIGNES
	LIGNIN	LIGNINS
	LIGNITE	LIGNITES
	LIGNOSE	LIGNOSES
	LIGNUM	LIGNUMS
	LIGROIN	LIGROINE ▪ LIGROINS
	LIGROINE	LIGROINES
	LIGULA	LIGULAE ▪ LIGULAR ▪ LIGULAS
	LIGULATE	LIGULATED
	LIGULE	LIGULES
	LIGURE	LIGURES
ALIKE ▪ GLIKE ▪ YLIKE	**LIKE**	LIKED ▪ LIKEN ▪ LIKER ▪ LIKES
	LIKEN	LIKENS
ALIKENESS	**LIKENESS**	
	LIKER	LIKERS
GLIKES	**LIKES**	LIKEST
	LIKEWAKE	LIKEWAKES
	LIKEWALK	LIKEWALKS
	LIKIN	LIKING ▪ LIKINS
	LIKING	LIKINGS
	LILAC	LILACS
	LILL	LILLS
	LILLIPUT	LILLIPUTS
	LILO	LILOS
	LILT	LILTS
SLILY	**LILY**	
	LIMA	LIMAN ▪ LIMAS ▪ LIMAX
	LIMACEL	LIMACELS
	LIMACON	LIMACONS
	LIMAIL	LIMAILS
	LIMAN	LIMANS
	LIMATION	LIMATIONS
CLIMAX	**LIMAX**	
CLIMB	**LIMB**	LIMBA ▪ LIMBI ▪ LIMBO ▪ LIMBS ▪ LIMBY
	LIMBA	LIMBAS
	LIMBEC	LIMBECK ▪ LIMBECS
	LIMBECK	LIMBECKS
CLIMBED	**LIMBED**	
CLIMBER	**LIMBER**	LIMBERS
CLIMBERS	**LIMBERS**	
	LIMBI	LIMBIC
BLIMBING ▪ CLIMBING	**LIMBING**	
	LIMBO	LIMBOS
CLIMBS	**LIMBS**	
CLIME ▪ GLIME ▪ SLIME	**LIME**	LIMED ▪ LIMEN ▪ LIMES ▪ LIMEY
	LIMEADE	LIMEADES

FRONT HOOK	ROOT WORD	END HOOK
GLIMED · SLIMED	**LIMED**	
	LIMEKILN	LIMEKILNS
	LIMELIGHT	LIMELIGHTS
	LIMEN	LIMENS
	LIMEPIT	LIMEPITS
	LIMERICK	LIMERICKS
CLIMES · GLIMES · SLIMES	**LIMES**	
	LIMESCALE	LIMESCALES
	LIMESTONE	LIMESTONES
	LIMEWATER	LIMEWATERS
BLIMEY	**LIMEY**	LIMEYS
SLIMIER	**LIMIER**	
SLIMIEST	**LIMIEST**	
	LIMINA	LIMINAL
SLIMINESS	**LIMINESS**	
GLIMING · SLIMING	**LIMING**	LIMINGS
	LIMIT	LIMITS
	LIMITED	LIMITEDS
	LIMITER	LIMITERS
	LIMITING	LIMITINGS
	LIMMA	LIMMAS
GLIMMER · SLIMMER	**LIMMER**	LIMMERS
GLIMMERS · SLIMMERS	**LIMMERS**	
	LIMN	LIMNS
	LIMNAEID	LIMNAEIDS
	LIMNER	LIMNERS
	LIMO	LIMOS
	LIMONENE	LIMONENES
	LIMONITE	LIMONITES
	LIMOUSINE	LIMOUSINES
BLIMP · FLIMP	**LIMP**	LIMPA · LIMPS
	LIMPA	LIMPAS
FLIMPED	**LIMPED**	
	LIMPER	LIMPERS
	LIMPET	LIMPETS
FLIMPING	**LIMPING**	LIMPINGS
	LIMPKIN	LIMPKINS
BLIMPS · FLIMPS	**LIMPS**	LIMPSY
SLIMPSIER	**LIMPSIER**	
SLIMPSIEST	**LIMPSIEST**	
SLIMPSY	**LIMPSY**	
	LIMULOID	LIMULOIDS
BLIMY · SLIMY	**LIMY**	
BLIN	**LIN**	LIND · LINE · LING · LINK · LINN
		LINO · LINS · LINT · LINY
	LINAC	LINACS
	LINAGE	LINAGES
	LINALOL	LINALOLS
	LINALOOL	LINALOOLS
CLINCH · FLINCH	**LINCH**	
CLINCHES · FLINCHES	**LINCHES**	
	LINCHET	LINCHETS
	LINCHPIN	LINCHPINS
	LINCRUSTA	LINCRUSTAS
	LINCTURE	LINCTURES
BLIND	**LIND**	LINDS · LINDY
	LINDANE	LINDANES
	LINDEN	LINDENS
BLINDS	**LINDS**	
BLINDWORM	**LINDWORM**	LINDWORMS
BLINDWORMS	**LINDWORMS**	
ALINE · CLINE	**LINE**	LINED · LINEN · LINER · LINES · LINEY
	LINEAGE	LINEAGES
	LINEAMENT	LINEAMENTS
	LINEARISE	LINEARISED · LINEARISES
	LINEARIZE	LINEARIZED · LINEARIZES
	LINEATE	LINEATED
ALINEATION	**LINEATION**	LINEATIONS
	LINECUT	LINECUTS

FRONT HOOK	ROOT WORD	END HOOK
ALINED	**LINED**	
	LINEN	LINENS · LINENY
	LINEOLATE	LINEOLATED
ALINER	**LINER**	LINERS
ALINERS	**LINERS**	
ALINES · CLINES	**LINES**	
	LINEUP	LINEUPS
BLING · CLING · FLING · PLING · SLING	**LING**	LINGA · LINGO · LINGS · LINGY
	LINGA	LINGAM · LINGAS
	LINGAM	LINGAMS
	LINGCOD	LINGCODS
	LINGEL	LINGELS
BLINGER · CLINGER · FLINGER · SLINGER	**LINGER**	LINGERS
	LINGERER	LINGERERS
	LINGERIE	LINGERIES
	LINGERING	LINGERINGS
CLINGERS · FLINGERS · SLINGERS	**LINGERS**	
CLINGIER	**LINGIER**	
CLINGIEST	**LINGIEST**	
	LINGLE	LINGLES
OLINGO	**LINGO**	LINGOT
	LINGOT	LINGOTS
BLINGS · CLINGS · FLINGS · PLINGS · SLINGS	**LINGS**	
	LINGSTER	LINGSTERS
	LINGUA	LINGUAE · LINGUAL · LINGUAS
	LINGUAL	LINGUALS
	LINGUICA	LINGUICAS
	LINGUINE	LINGUINES
	LINGUINI	LINGUINIS
	LINGUISA	LINGUISAS
	LINGUIST	LINGUISTS
	LINGULA	LINGULAE · LINGULAR · LINGULAS
	LINGULATE	LINGULATED
CLINGY	**LINGY**	
	LINHAY	LINHAYS
	LINIMENT	LINIMENTS
	LININ	LINING · LININS
ALINING	**LINING**	LININGS
	LINISHER	LINISHERS
	LINISHING	LINISHINGS
BLINK · CLINK · PLINK · SLINK	**LINK**	LINKS · LINKY
	LINKAGE	LINKAGES
	LINKBOY	LINKBOYS
BLINKED · CLINKED · PLINKED · SLINKED	**LINKED**	
BLINKER · CLINKER · KLINKER · PLINKER · SLINKER	**LINKER**	LINKERS
BLINKERS · CLINKERS · KLINKERS · PLINKERS · SLINKERS	**LINKERS**	
BLINKING · CLINKING · PLINKING · SLINKING	**LINKING**	
BLINKS · CLINKS · PLINKS · SLINKS	**LINKS**	
	LINKSLAND	LINKSLANDS
	LINKSTER	LINKSTERS
	LINKUP	LINKUPS
	LINKWORK	LINKWORKS
SLINKY	**LINKY**	
	LINN	LINNS · LINNY
BLINNED	**LINNED**	
	LINNET	LINNETS
	LINNEY	LINNEYS
BLINNING	**LINNING**	
	LINO	LINOS
	LINOCUT	LINOCUTS
	LINOLEATE	LINOLEATES
	LINOLEUM	LINOLEUMS
	LINOTYPE	LINOTYPED · LINOTYPER · LINOTYPES
	LINOTYPER	LINOTYPERS
BLINS	**LINS**	

L

FRONT HOOK	ROOT WORD	END HOOK
	LINSANG	LINSANGS
	LINSEED	LINSEEDS
	LINSEY	LINSEYS
	LINSTOCK	LINSTOCKS
CLINT · ELINT · FLINT · GLINT	**LINT**	LINTS · LINTY
FLINTED · GLINTED	**LINTED**	
	LINTEL	LINTELS
SLINTER	**LINTER**	LINTERS
SLINTERS	**LINTERS**	
	LINTIE	LINTIER · LINTIES
FLINTIER · GLINTIER	**LINTIER**	
	LINTIES	LINTIEST
FLINTIEST · GLINTIEST	**LINTIEST**	
FLINTING · GLINTING	**LINTING**	
	LINTOL	LINTOLS
CLINTS · ELINTS · FLINTS · GLINTS	**LINTS**	
	LINTSEED	LINTSEEDS
	LINTSTOCK	LINTSTOCKS
	LINTWHITE	LINTWHITES
FLINTY · GLINTY	**LINTY**	
	LINUM	LINUMS
	LINURON	LINURONS
BLINY	**LINY**	
	LION	LIONS
	LIONCEL	LIONCELS
	LIONCELLE	LIONCELLES
	LIONEL	LIONELS
	LIONET	LIONETS
	LIONISE	LIONISED · LIONISER · LIONISES
	LIONISER	LIONISERS
	LIONISM	LIONISMS
	LIONIZE	LIONIZED · LIONIZER · LIONIZES
	LIONIZER	LIONIZERS
BLIP · CLIP · FLIP · SLIP	**LIP**	LIPA · LIPE · LIPO · LIPS
	LIPAEMIA	LIPAEMIAS
	LIPARITE	LIPARITES
	LIPASE	LIPASES
CLIPE · SLIPE	**LIPE**	
	LIPEMIA	LIPEMIAS
	LIPID	LIPIDE · LIPIDS
	LIPIDE	LIPIDES
	LIPIN	LIPINS
SLIPLESS	**LIPLESS**	
	LIPO	LIPOS
	LIPOCYTE	LIPOCYTES
	LIPOGRAM	LIPOGRAMS
	LIPOID	LIPOIDS
	LIPOMA	LIPOMAS
	LIPOPLAST	LIPOPLASTS
	LIPOSOME	LIPOSOMES
	LIPOSUCK	LIPOSUCKS
BLIPPED · CLIPPED · FLIPPED · SLIPPED	**LIPPED**	
	LIPPEN	LIPPENS
CLIPPER · FLIPPER · SLIPPER	**LIPPER**	LIPPERS
SLIPPERED	**LIPPERED**	
SLIPPERING	**LIPPERING**	
CLIPPERS · FLIPPERS · SLIPPERS	**LIPPERS**	
CLIPPIE	**LIPPIE**	LIPPIER · LIPPIES
SLIPPIER	**LIPPIER**	
CLIPPIES	**LIPPIES**	LIPPIEST
SLIPPIEST	**LIPPIEST**	
SLIPPINESS	**LIPPINESS**	
BLIPPING · CLIPPING · FLIPPING	**LIPPING**	LIPPINGS
SLIPPING		
CLIPPINGS	**LIPPINGS**	
	LIPPITUDE	LIPPITUDES
FLIPPY · SLIPPY	**LIPPY**	
	LIPREAD	LIPREADS
	LIPREADER	LIPREADERS

L

FRONT HOOK	ROOT WORD	END HOOK
BLIPS · CLIPS · FLIPS · SLIPS	**LIPS**	
	LIPSTICK	LIPSTICKS
	LIPURIA	LIPURIAS
	LIQUATE	LIQUATED · LIQUATES
	LIQUATION	LIQUATIONS
	LIQUEFIER	LIQUEFIERS
	LIQUESCE	LIQUESCED · LIQUESCES
	LIQUEUR	LIQUEURS
	LIQUID	LIQUIDS
	LIQUIDATE	LIQUIDATED · LIQUIDATES
	LIQUIDISE	LIQUIDISED · LIQUIDISER · LIQUIDISES
	LIQUIDIZE	LIQUIDIZED · LIQUIDIZER · LIQUIDIZES
	LIQUOR	LIQUORS
	LIQUORICE	LIQUORICES
	LIRA	LIRAS
	LIRIOPE	LIRIOPES
	LIRIPIPE	LIRIPIPES
	LIRIPOOP	LIRIPOOPS
	LIRK	LIRKS
	LIROT	LIROTH
	LIS	LISK · LISP · LIST
FLISK · GLISK	**LISK**	LISKS
FLISKS · GLISKS	**LISKS**	
	LISLE	LISLES
	LISP	LISPS
	LISPER	LISPERS
	LISPING	LISPINGS
	LISPOUND	LISPOUNDS
	LISPUND	LISPUNDS
BLISSES · PLISSES	**LISSES**	
	LISSOM	LISSOME
ALIST · BLIST	**LIST**	LISTS
	LISTEE	LISTEES
	LISTEL	LISTELS
GLISTEN	**LISTEN**	LISTENS
GLISTENED	**LISTENED**	
	LISTENER	LISTENERS
GLISTENING	**LISTENING**	
GLISTENS	**LISTENS**	
BLISTER · GLISTER · KLISTER	**LISTER**	LISTERS
	LISTERIA	LISTERIAL · LISTERIAS
BLISTERS · GLISTERS · KLISTERS	**LISTERS**	
	LISTING	LISTINGS
	LISTSERV	LISTSERVS
ALIT · FLIT · GLIT · SLIT	**LIT**	LITE · LITH · LITS · LITU
	LITCHI	LITCHIS
BLITE · ELITE · FLITE	**LITE**	LITED · LITER · LITES
FLITED	**LITED**	
	LITER	LITERS
ALITERACY	**LITERACY**	
	LITERAL	LITERALS
ALITERATE	**LITERATE**	LITERATES
ALITERATES	**LITERATES**	
	LITERATI	LITERATIM
	LITERATO	LITERATOR
	LITERATOR	LITERATORS
BLITES · ELITES · FLITES	**LITES**	
	LITH	LITHE · LITHO · LITHS
	LITHARGE	LITHARGES
	LITHATE	LITHATES
BLITHE	**LITHE**	LITHED · LITHER · LITHES
BLITHELY	**LITHELY**	
	LITHEMIA	LITHEMIAS
BLITHENESS	**LITHENESS**	
BLITHER · SLITHER	**LITHER**	
	LITHES	LITHEST
BLITHESOME	**LITHESOME**	
BLITHEST	**LITHEST**	
	LITHIA	LITHIAS

FRONT HOOK	ROOT WORD	END HOOK
	LITHISTID	LITHISTIDS
	LITHITE	LITHITES
	LITHIUM	LITHIUMS
	LITHO	LITHOS
	LITHOCYST	LITHOCYSTS
	LITHOPONE	LITHOPONES
	LITHOSOL	LITHOSOLS
	LITHOTOME	LITHOTOMES
	LITIGANT	LITIGANTS
	LITIGATE	LITIGATED · LITIGATES
	LITIGATOR	LITIGATORS
FLITING	**LITING**	
CLITORAL	**LITORAL**	
	LITRE	LITRES
FLITS · GLITS · SLITS	**LITS**	
CLITTER · FLITTER · GLITTER · SLITTER	**LITTER**	LITTERS · LITTERY
	LITTERBAG	LITTERBAGS
	LITTERBUG	LITTERBUGS
CLITTERED · FLITTERED · GLITTERED	**LITTERED**	
	LITTERER	LITTERERS
CLITTERING · FLITTERING · GLITTERING	**LITTERING**	
CLITTERS · FLITTERS · GLITTERS SLITTERS	**LITTERS**	
GLITTERY	**LITTERY**	
	LITTLE	LITTLER · LITTLES
	LITTLES	LITTLEST
	LITTLIE	LITTLIES
	LITTLIN	LITTLING · LITTLINS
	LITTLING	LITTLINGS
	LITTORAL	LITTORALS
	LITURGIC	LITURGICS
	LITURGISM	LITURGISMS
	LITURGIST	LITURGISTS
ALIVE · BLIVE · OLIVE · SLIVE	**LIVE**	LIVED · LIVEN · LIVER · LIVES
SLIVED	**LIVED**	LIVEDO
	LIVEDO	LIVEDOS
	LIVELOD	LIVELODS
	LIVELONG	LIVELONGS
	LIVELOOD	LIVELOODS
SLIVEN	**LIVEN**	LIVENS
	LIVENER	LIVENERS
ALIVENESS	**LIVENESS**	
OLIVER · SLIVER	**LIVER**	LIVERS · LIVERY
SLIVERED	**LIVERED**	
SLIVERING	**LIVERING**	
CLIVERS · OLIVERS · SLIVERS	**LIVERS**	
	LIVERWORT	LIVERWORTS
OLIVES · SLIVES	**LIVES**	LIVEST
	LIVESTOCK	LIVESTOCKS
	LIVETRAP	LIVETRAPS
	LIVEWARE	LIVEWARES
	LIVEYER	LIVEYERE · LIVEYERS
	LIVEYERE	LIVEYERES
	LIVIER	LIVIERS
SLIVING	**LIVING**	LIVINGS
	LIVOR	LIVORS
	LIVRAISON	LIVRAISONS
	LIVRE	LIVRES
	LIVYER	LIVYERS
	LIXIVIA	LIXIVIAL
	LIXIVIATE	LIXIVIATED · LIXIVIATES
	LIXIVIUM	LIXIVIUMS
	LIZARD	LIZARDS
	LIZZIE	LIZZIES
	LLAMA	LLAMAS
	LLANERO	LLANEROS
	LLANO	LLANOS
	LO	LOB · LOD · LOG · LOO · LOP · LOR · LOS LOT · LOU · LOW · LOX · LOY

L

FRONT HOOK	ROOT WORD	END HOOK
	LOAD	LOADS
	LOADEN	LOADENS
	LOADER	LOADERS
	LOADING	LOADINGS
	LOADSPACE	LOADSPACES
	LOADSTAR	LOADSTARS
	LOADSTONE	LOADSTONES
	LOAF	LOAFS
	LOAFER	LOAFERS
	LOAFING	LOAFINGS
CLOAM · GLOAM	**LOAM**	LOAMS · LOAMY
GLOAMING	**LOAMING**	
CLOAMS · GLOAMS	**LOAMS**	
SLOAN	**LOAN**	LOANS
	LOANBACK	LOANBACKS
	LOANER	LOANERS
	LOANING	LOANINGS
SLOANS	**LOANS**	
	LOANSHIFT	LOANSHIFTS
	LOANWORD	LOANWORDS
	LOATH	LOATHE · LOATHY
	LOATHE	LOATHED · LOATHER · LOATHES
	LOATHER	LOATHERS
	LOATHES	LOATHEST
	LOATHING	LOATHINGS
	LOAVE	LOAVED · LOAVES
BLOB · GLOB · SLOB	**LOB**	LOBE · LOBI · LOBO · LOBS
GLOBATE	**LOBATE**	LOBATED
GLOBATED	**LOBATED**	
	LOBATION	LOBATIONS
BLOBBED	**LOBBED**	
CLOBBER · SLOBBER	**LOBBER**	LOBBERS
CLOBBERS · SLOBBERS	**LOBBERS**	
BLOBBING	**LOBBING**	
BLOBBY · GLOBBY · SLOBBY	**LOBBY**	
	LOBBYER	LOBBYERS
	LOBBYGOW	LOBBYGOWS
	LOBBYING	LOBBYINGS
	LOBBYISM	LOBBYISMS
	LOBBYIST	LOBBYISTS
GLOBE	**LOBE**	LOBED · LOBES
GLOBED	**LOBED**	
	LOBEFIN	LOBEFINS
	LOBELET	LOBELETS
	LOBELIA	LOBELIAS
	LOBELINE	LOBELINES
GLOBES	**LOBES**	
GLOBI	**LOBI**	
GLOBING	**LOBING**	LOBINGS
	LOBO	LOBOS
	LOBOLA	LOBOLAS
	LOBOLO	LOBOLOS
	LOBOS	LOBOSE
GLOBOSE	**LOBOSE**	
BLOBS · GLOBS · SLOBS	**LOBS**	
	LOBSCOUSE	LOBSCOUSES
	LOBSTER	LOBSTERS
	LOBSTERER	LOBSTERERS
	LOBSTICK	LOBSTICKS
GLOBULAR	**LOBULAR**	
GLOBULARLY	**LOBULARLY**	
	LOBULATE	LOBULATED
GLOBULE	**LOBULE**	LOBULES
GLOBULES	**LOBULES**	
GLOBUS	**LOBUS**	
	LOBWORM	LOBWORMS
	LOCA	LOCAL
	LOCAL	LOCALE · LOCALS
	LOCALE	LOCALES

L

FRONT HOOK	ROOT WORD	END HOOK
	LOCALISE	LOCALISED · LOCALISER · LOCALISES
	LOCALISER	LOCALISERS
	LOCALISM	LOCALISMS
	LOCALIST	LOCALISTS
	LOCALITE	LOCALITES
	LOCALIZE	LOCALIZED · LOCALIZER · LOCALIZES
	LOCALIZER	LOCALIZERS
	LOCATE	LOCATED · LOCATER · LOCATES
	LOCATER	LOCATERS
	LOCATION	LOCATIONS
	LOCATIVE	LOCATIVES
	LOCATOR	LOCATORS
	LOCH	LOCHS
	LOCHAN	LOCHANS
	LOCHIA	LOCHIAL
BLOCK · CLOCK · FLOCK	**LOCK**	LOCKS
BLOCKABLE	**LOCKABLE**	
BLOCKAGE	**LOCKAGE**	LOCKAGES
BLOCKAGES	**LOCKAGES**	
	LOCKAWAY	LOCKAWAYS
	LOCKDOWN	LOCKDOWNS
BLOCKED · CLOCKED · FLOCKED	**LOCKED**	
BLOCKER · CLOCKER	**LOCKER**	LOCKERS
BLOCKERS · CLOCKERS	**LOCKERS**	
	LOCKET	LOCKETS
	LOCKFUL	LOCKFULS
BLOCKHOUSE	**LOCKHOUSE**	LOCKHOUSES
BLOCKING · CLOCKING · FLOCKING	**LOCKING**	LOCKINGS
BLOCKINGS · CLOCKINGS · FLOCKINGS	**LOCKINGS**	
CLOCKMAKER	**LOCKMAKER**	LOCKMAKERS
	LOCKNUT	LOCKNUTS
	LOCKOUT	LOCKOUTS
	LOCKPICK	LOCKPICKS
	LOCKRAM	LOCKRAMS
BLOCKS · CLOCKS · FLOCKS	**LOCKS**	
	LOCKSET	LOCKSETS
	LOCKSMITH	LOCKSMITHS
	LOCKSTEP	LOCKSTEPS
	LOCKUP	LOCKUPS
	LOCO	LOCOS
	LOCOFOCO	LOCOFOCOS
	LOCOISM	LOCOISMS
	LOCOMOTE	LOCOMOTED · LOCOMOTES
	LOCOMOTOR	LOCOMOTORS · LOCOMOTORY
	LOCOPLANT	LOCOPLANTS
	LOCOWEED	LOCOWEEDS
	LOCULATE	LOCULATED
	LOCULE	LOCULED · LOCULES
	LOCUM	LOCUMS
	LOCUS	LOCUST
	LOCUST	LOCUSTA · LOCUSTS
	LOCUSTA	LOCUSTAE · LOCUSTAL
ELOCUTION	**LOCUTION**	LOCUTIONS
ELOCUTIONS	**LOCUTIONS**	
ELOCUTORY	**LOCUTORY**	
ALOD · CLOD · PLOD	**LOD**	LODE · LODS
GLODE	**LODE**	LODEN · LODES
	LODEN	LODENS
	LODESTAR	LODESTARS
	LODESTONE	LODESTONES
PLODGE	**LODGE**	LODGED · LODGER · LODGES
PLODGED	**LODGED**	
	LODGEMENT	LODGEMENTS
	LODGEPOLE	LODGEPOLES
	LODGER	LODGERS
PLODGES	**LODGES**	
PLODGING	**LODGING**	LODGINGS
	LODGMENT	LODGMENTS

L

FRONT HOOK	ROOT WORD	END HOOK
	LODICULA	LODICULAE
	LODICULE	LODICULES
ALODS ▪ CLODS ▪ PLODS	**LODS**	
	LOERIE	LOERIES
ALOFT	**LOFT**	LOFTS ▪ LOFTY
	LOFTER	LOFTERS
BLOG ▪ CLOG ▪ FLOG ▪ SLOG	**LOG**	LOGE ▪ LOGO ▪ LOGS ▪ LOGY
SLOGAN	**LOGAN**	LOGANS
	LOGANIA	LOGANIAS
SLOGANS	**LOGANS**	
	LOGAOEDIC	LOGAOEDICS
	LOGARITHM	LOGARITHMS
	LOGBOARD	LOGBOARDS
	LOGBOOK	LOGBOOKS
ELOGE	**LOGE**	LOGES
ELOGES	**LOGES**	
	LOGGAT	LOGGATS
CLOGGED ▪ FLOGGED ▪ SLOGGED	**LOGGED**	
BLOGGER ▪ CLOGGER ▪ FLOGGER ▪ SLOGGER	**LOGGER**	LOGGERS
BLOGGERS ▪ CLOGGERS ▪ FLOGGERS	**LOGGERS**	
SLOGGERS		
	LOGGIA	LOGGIAS
	LOGGIE	LOGGIER
CLOGGIER	**LOGGIER**	
CLOGGIEST	**LOGGIEST**	
BLOGGING ▪ CLOGGING ▪ FLOGGING	**LOGGING**	LOGGINGS
SLOGGING		
BLOGGINGS ▪ CLOGGINGS ▪ FLOGGINGS	**LOGGINGS**	
CLOGGY	**LOGGY**	
ALOGIA	**LOGIA**	
	LOGIC	LOGICS
ALOGICAL	**LOGICAL**	
ALOGICALLY	**LOGICALLY**	
	LOGICIAN	LOGICIANS
	LOGICISE	LOGICISED ▪ LOGICISES
	LOGICISM	LOGICISMS
	LOGICIST	LOGICISTS
	LOGICIZE	LOGICIZED ▪ LOGICIZES
	LOGIE	LOGIER ▪ LOGIES
ELOGIES ▪ OLOGIES	**LOGIES**	LOGIEST
	LOGIN	LOGINS
	LOGION	LOGIONS
	LOGISTIC	LOGISTICS
	LOGJAM	LOGJAMS
	LOGJUICE	LOGJUICES
	LOGLINE	LOGLINES
	LOGLOG	LOGLOGS
	LOGO	LOGOI ▪ LOGON ▪ LOGOS
	LOGOFF	LOGOFFS
	LOGOGRAM	LOGOGRAMS
	LOGOGRAPH	LOGOGRAPHS ▪ LOGOGRAPHY
	LOGOGRIPH	LOGOGRIPHS
	LOGOMACH	LOGOMACHS ▪ LOGOMACHY
	LOGON	LOGONS
	LOGOPEDIC	LOGOPEDICS
	LOGOPHILE	LOGOPHILES
	LOGORRHEA	LOGORRHEAS
	LOGOTHETE	LOGOTHETES
	LOGOTYPE	LOGOTYPES
	LOGOUT	LOGOUTS
	LOGROLL	LOGROLLS
	LOGROLLER	LOGROLLERS
BLOGS ▪ CLOGS ▪ FLOGS ▪ SLOGS	**LOGS**	
	LOGWAY	LOGWAYS
	LOGWOOD	LOGWOODS
ELOGY ▪ OLOGY	**LOGY**	
	LOHAN	LOHANS
SLOID	**LOID**	LOIDS
SLOIDS	**LOIDS**	

L

467

FRONT HOOK	ROOT WORD	END HOOK
ALOIN ▪ ELOIN	**LOIN**	LOINS
	LOINCLOTH	LOINCLOTHS
ALOINS ▪ ELOINS	**LOINS**	
	LOIPE	LOIPEN
	LOIR	LOIRS
	LOITER	LOITERS
	LOITERER	LOITERERS
	LOITERING	LOITERINGS
BLOKE ▪ CLOKE	**LOKE**	LOKES
BLOKES ▪ CLOKES	**LOKES**	
	LOLIGO	LOLIGOS
	LOLIUM	LOLIUMS
	LOLL	LOLLS ▪ LOLLY
	LOLLER	LOLLERS
	LOLLIPOP	LOLLIPOPS
	LOLLOP	LOLLOPS ▪ LOLLOPY
	LOLLYGAG	LOLLYGAGS
	LOLLYPOP	LOLLYPOPS
	LOLOG	LOLOGS
	LOMA	LOMAS
	LOME	LOMED ▪ LOMES
	LOMEIN	LOMEINS
	LOMENT	LOMENTA ▪ LOMENTS
	LOMENTUM	LOMENTUMS
ALONE ▪ CLONE	**LONE**	LONER
ALONELY	**LONELY**	
ALONENESS	**LONENESS**	
CLONER	**LONER**	LONERS
CLONERS	**LONERS**	
	LONESOME	LONESOMES
ALONG ▪ FLONG ▪ KLONG ▪ PLONG	**LONG**	LONGA ▪ LONGE ▪ LONGS
	LONGA	LONGAN ▪ LONGAS
	LONGAN	LONGANS
	LONGBOARD	LONGBOARDS
	LONGBOAT	LONGBOATS
	LONGBOW	LONGBOWS
	LONGCLOTH	LONGCLOTHS
PLONGE	**LONGE**	LONGED ▪ LONGER ▪ LONGES
PLONGED	**LONGED**	
	LONGER	LONGERS
	LONGERON	LONGERONS
PLONGES	**LONGES**	LONGEST
	LONGHAIR	LONGHAIRS
	LONGHAND	LONGHANDS
	LONGHEAD	LONGHEADS
	LONGHORN	LONGHORNS
	LONGHOUSE	LONGHOUSES
	LONGICORN	LONGICORNS
PLONGING	**LONGING**	LONGINGS
	LONGITUDE	LONGITUDES
	LONGJUMP	LONGJUMPS
	LONGLINE	LONGLINES
	LONGNECK	LONGNECKS
FLONGS ▪ KLONGS ▪ PLONGS	**LONGS**	
	LONGSHIP	LONGSHIPS
ALONGSHORE	**LONGSHORE**	
	LONGSPUR	LONGSPURS
	LONGUEUR	LONGUEURS
	LONGWALL	LONGWALLS
	LONICERA	LONICERAS
	LOO	LOOF ▪ LOOK ▪ LOOM ▪ LOON ▪ LOOP
		LOOR ▪ LOOS ▪ LOOT
	LOOBIES	LOOBIEST
BLOOEY ▪ FLOOEY	**LOOEY**	LOOEYS
ALOOF ▪ KLOOF	**LOOF**	LOOFA ▪ LOOFS
	LOOFA	LOOFAH ▪ LOOFAS
	LOOFAH	LOOFAHS
	LOOFFUL	LOOFFULS
KLOOFS	**LOOFS**	

FRONT HOOK	ROOT WORD	END HOOK
BLOOIE ▪ FLOOIE	**LOOIE**	LOOIES
PLOOK	**LOOK**	LOOKS
	LOOKALIKE	LOOKALIKES
	LOOKDOWN	LOOKDOWNS
	LOOKER	LOOKERS
	LOOKISM	LOOKISMS
	LOOKIST	LOOKISTS
	LOOKOUT	LOOKOUTS
	LOOKOVER	LOOKOVERS
PLOOKS	**LOOKS**	
	LOOKSISM	LOOKSISMS
	LOOKUP	LOOKUPS
BLOOM ▪ GLOOM ▪ SLOOM	**LOOM**	LOOMS
BLOOMED ▪ GLOOMED ▪ SLOOMED	**LOOMED**	
BLOOMING ▪ GLOOMING ▪ SLOOMING	**LOOMING**	
BLOOMS ▪ GLOOMS ▪ SLOOMS	**LOOMS**	
	LOON	LOONS ▪ LOONY
	LOONEY	LOONEYS
	LOONIE	LOONIER ▪ LOONIES
	LOONIES	LOONIEST
	LOONING	LOONINGS
BLOOP ▪ CLOOP ▪ GLOOP ▪ SLOOP	**LOOP**	LOOPS ▪ LOOPY
BLOOPED ▪ GLOOPED	**LOOPED**	
BLOOPER	**LOOPER**	LOOPERS
BLOOPERS	**LOOPERS**	
	LOOPHOLE	LOOPHOLED ▪ LOOPHOLES
GLOOPIER	**LOOPIER**	
GLOOPIEST	**LOOPIEST**	
BLOOPING ▪ GLOOPING	**LOOPING**	LOOPINGS
BLOOPS ▪ CLOOPS ▪ GLOOPS ▪ SLOOPS	**LOOPS**	
GLOOPY	**LOOPY**	
FLOOR	**LOOR**	LOORD
	LOORD	LOORDS
	LOOS	LOOSE
	LOOSE	LOOSED ▪ LOOSEN ▪ LOOSER ▪ LOOSES
	LOOSEN	LOOSENS
	LOOSENER	LOOSENERS
	LOOSES	LOOSEST
FLOOSIE	**LOOSIE**	LOOSIES
FLOOSIES	**LOOSIES**	
	LOOSING	LOOSINGS
CLOOT ▪ SLOOT	**LOOT**	LOOTS
	LOOTER	LOOTERS
	LOOTING	LOOTINGS
CLOOTS ▪ SLOOTS	**LOOTS**	
CLOP ▪ FLOP ▪ GLOP ▪ PLOP ▪ SLOP	**LOP**	LOPE ▪ LOPS
ELOPE ▪ SLOPE	**LOPE**	LOPED ▪ LOPER ▪ LOPES
ELOPED ▪ SLOPED	**LOPED**	
ELOPER ▪ SLOPER	**LOPER**	LOPERS
ELOPERS ▪ SLOPERS	**LOPERS**	
ELOPES ▪ SLOPES	**LOPES**	
ELOPING ▪ SLOPING	**LOPING**	
	LOPOLITH	LOPOLITHS
CLOPPED ▪ FLOPPED ▪ GLOPPED ▪ PLOPPED SLOPPED	**LOPPED**	
FLOPPER	**LOPPER**	LOPPERS
FLOPPERS	**LOPPERS**	
FLOPPIER ▪ GLOPPIER ▪ SLOPPIER	**LOPPIER**	
FLOPPIES	**LOPPIES**	LOPPIEST
FLOPPIEST ▪ GLOPPIEST ▪ SLOPPIEST	**LOPPIEST**	
CLOPPING ▪ FLOPPING ▪ GLOPPING PLOPPING ▪ SLOPPING	**LOPPING**	LOPPINGS
FLOPPY ▪ GLOPPY ▪ SLOPPY	**LOPPY**	
CLOPS ▪ ELOPS ▪ FLOPS ▪ GLOPS ▪ PLOPS SLOPS	**LOPS**	
	LOPSTICK	LOPSTICKS
	LOQUAT	LOQUATS
FLOR	**LOR**	LORD ▪ LORE ▪ LORN ▪ LORY
FLORAL	**LORAL**	

FRONT HOOK	ROOT WORD	END HOOK
	LORAN	LORANS
	LORAZEPAM	LORAZEPAMS
	LORCHA	LORCHAS
	LORD	LORDS · LORDY
	LORDING	LORDINGS
	LORDKIN	LORDKINS
	LORDLING	LORDLINGS
	LORDOMA	LORDOMAS
	LORDSHIP	LORDSHIPS
BLORE	**LORE**	LOREL · LORES
	LOREL	LORELS
BLORES	**LORES**	
	LORETTE	LORETTES
	LORGNETTE	LORGNETTES
	LORGNON	LORGNONS
	LORIC	LORICA · LORICS
	LORICA	LORICAE
	LORICATE	LORICATED · LORICATES
GLORIES	**LORIES**	
	LORIKEET	LORIKEETS
	LORIMER	LORIMERS
	LORINER	LORINERS
	LORING	LORINGS
	LORIOT	LORIOTS
	LORRELL	LORRELLS
FLORY · GLORY	**LORY**	
	LOS	LOSE · LOSH · LOSS · LOST
CLOSABLE	**LOSABLE**	
CLOSE	**LOSE**	LOSED · LOSEL · LOSEN · LOSER · LOSES
CLOSED	**LOSED**	
	LOSEL	LOSELS
CLOSER	**LOSER**	LOSERS
CLOSERS	**LOSERS**	
CLOSES · ULOSES	**LOSES**	
FLOSH · SLOSH	**LOSH**	
CLOSING	**LOSING**	LOSINGS
CLOSINGS	**LOSINGS**	
	LOSLYF	LOSLYFS *(offensive)*
FLOSS · GLOSS	**LOSS**	LOSSY
FLOSSES · GLOSSES	**LOSSES**	
FLOSSIER · GLOSSIER	**LOSSIER**	
FLOSSIEST · GLOSSIEST	**LOSSIEST**	
GLOSSLESS	**LOSSLESS**	
	LOSSMAKER	LOSSMAKERS
FLOSSY · GLOSSY	**LOSSY**	
GLOST	**LOST**	
BLOT · CLOT · PLOT · SLOT	**LOT**	LOTA · LOTE · LOTH · LOTI · LOTO ·
LOTS		
FLOTA	**LOTA**	LOTAH · LOTAS
	LOTAH	LOTAHS
FLOTAS	**LOTAS**	
CLOTE · FLOTE · ZLOTE	**LOTE**	LOTES
CLOTES · FLOTES	**LOTES**	
CLOTH · SLOTH	**LOTH**	
	LOTHARIO	LOTHARIOS
	LOTI	LOTIC
	LOTION	LOTIONS
	LOTO	LOTOS
BLOTS · CLOTS · PLOTS · SLOTS	**LOTS**	
	LOTTE	LOTTED · LOTTER · LOTTES
BLOTTED · CLOTTED · PLOTTED · SLOTTED	**LOTTED**	
BLOTTER · CLOTTER · PLOTTER · SLOTTER	**LOTTER**	LOTTERS · LOTTERY
BLOTTERS · CLOTTERS · PLOTTERS · SLOTTERS	**LOTTERS**	
BLOTTING · CLOTTING · PLOTTING · SLOTTING	**LOTTING**	
BLOTTO	**LOTTO**	LOTTOS
	LOTUSLAND	LOTUSLANDS
CLOU	**LOU**	LOUD · LOUN · LOUP · LOUR · LOUS · LOUT

L

FRONT HOOK	ROOT WORD	END HOOK
ALOUD = CLOUD	**LOUD**	
	LOUDEN	LOUDENS
	LOUDMOUTH	LOUDMOUTHS
CLOUGH = PLOUGH = SLOUGH	**LOUGH**	LOUGHS
CLOUGHS = PLOUGHS = SLOUGHS	**LOUGHS**	
	LOUIE	LOUIES
	LOUMA	LOUMAS
	LOUN	LOUND = LOUNS
	LOUND	LOUNDS
FLOUNDER	**LOUNDER**	LOUNDERS
FLOUNDERED	**LOUNDERED**	
FLOUNDERS	**LOUNDERS**	
	LOUNGE	LOUNGED = LOUNGER = LOUNGES
	LOUNGER	LOUNGERS
	LOUNGING	LOUNGINGS
	LOUP	LOUPE = LOUPS
	LOUPE	LOUPED = LOUPEN = LOUPES
CLOUR = FLOUR	**LOUR**	LOURE = LOURS = LOURY
	LOURE	LOURED = LOURES
CLOURED = FLOURED	**LOURED**	
	LOURIE	LOURIER = LOURIES
FLOURIER	**LOURIER**	
	LOURIES	LOURIEST
FLOURIEST	**LOURIEST**	
CLOURING = FLOURING	**LOURING**	LOURINGS
CLOURS = FLOURS	**LOURS**	
FLOURY	**LOURY**	
CLOUS	**LOUS**	LOUSE = LOUSY
BLOUSE = FLOUSE	**LOUSE**	LOUSED = LOUSER = LOUSES
BLOUSED = FLOUSED	**LOUSED**	
	LOUSER	LOUSERS
BLOUSES = FLOUSES	**LOUSES**	
	LOUSEWORT	LOUSEWORTS
BLOUSIER	**LOUSIER**	
BLOUSIEST	**LOUSIEST**	
BLOUSILY	**LOUSILY**	
BLOUSING = FLOUSING	**LOUSING**	
BLOUSY	**LOUSY**	
CLOUT = FLOUT = GLOUT	**LOUT**	LOUTS
CLOUTED = FLOUTED = GLOUTED	**LOUTED**	
CLOUTING = FLOUTING = GLOUTING	**LOUTING**	
CLOUTS = FLOUTS = GLOUTS	**LOUTS**	
	LOUVAR	LOUVARS
	LOUVER	LOUVERS
	LOUVRE	LOUVRED = LOUVRES
	LOVAGE	LOVAGES
	LOVAT	LOVATS
CLOVE = GLOVE = SLOVE	**LOVE**	LOVED = LOVER = LOVES = LOVEY
	LOVEBIRD	LOVEBIRDS
	LOVEBITE	LOVEBITES
	LOVEBUG	LOVEBUGS
GLOVED	**LOVED**	
	LOVEFEST	LOVEFESTS
GLOVELESS	**LOVELESS**	
	LOVELIES	LOVELIEST
	LOVELIGHT	LOVELIGHTS
	LOVELOCK	LOVELOCKS
	LOVEMAKER	LOVEMAKERS
CLOVER = GLOVER = PLOVER	**LOVER**	LOVERS
CLOVERED	**LOVERED**	
CLOVERS = GLOVERS = PLOVERS	**LOVERS**	
CLOVES = GLOVES	**LOVES**	
	LOVESEAT	LOVESEATS
	LOVEVINE	LOVEVINES
	LOVEY	LOVEYS
GLOVING	**LOVING**	LOVINGS
GLOVINGS	**LOVINGS**	
ALOW = BLOW = CLOW = FLOW = GLOW = PLOW SLOW	**LOW**	LOWE = LOWN = LOWP = LOWS = LOWT

FRONT HOOK	ROOT WORD	END HOOK
	LOWAN	LOWANS
BLOWBALL	**LOWBALL**	LOWBALLS
BLOWBALLS	**LOWBALLS**	
PLOWBOY	**LOWBOY**	LOWBOYS
PLOWBOYS	**LOWBOYS**	
	LOWBROW	LOWBROWS
BLOWDOWN · SLOWDOWN	**LOWDOWN**	LOWDOWNS
BLOWDOWNS · SLOWDOWNS	**LOWDOWNS**	
ALOWE	**LOWE**	LOWED · LOWER · LOWES
BLOWED · FLOWED · GLOWED · PLOWED · SLOWED	**LOWED**	
BLOWER · FLOWER · GLOWER · PLOWER · SLOWER	**LOWER**	LOWERS · LOWERY
	LOWERCASE	LOWERCASED · LOWERCASES
FLOWERED · GLOWERED	**LOWERED**	
FLOWERIER	**LOWERIER**	
FLOWERIEST	**LOWERIEST**	
FLOWERING · GLOWERING	**LOWERING**	LOWERINGS
FLOWERINGS	**LOWERINGS**	
BLOWERS · FLOWERS · GLOWERS · PLOWERS	**LOWERS**	
FLOWERY	**LOWERY**	
	LOWES	LOWEST
SLOWEST	**LOWEST**	
BLOWING · FLOWING · GLOWING · PLOWING · SLOWING	**LOWING**	LOWINGS
SLOWINGS	**LOWINGS**	
SLOWISH	**LOWISH**	
PLOWLAND	**LOWLAND**	LOWLANDS
	LOWLANDER	LOWLANDERS
PLOWLANDS	**LOWLANDS**	
	LOWLIFE	LOWLIFER · LOWLIFES
	LOWLIFER	LOWLIFERS
	LOWLIGHT	LOWLIGHTS
	LOWLIHEAD	LOWLIHEADS
SLOWLY	**LOWLY**	
BLOWN · CLOWN · FLOWN	**LOWN**	LOWND · LOWNE · LOWNS
	LOWND	LOWNDS
	LOWNE	LOWNED · LOWNES
CLOWNED	**LOWNED**	
	LOWNES	LOWNESS
SLOWNESS	**LOWNESS**	
SLOWNESSES	**LOWNESSES**	
CLOWNING	**LOWNING**	
CLOWNS	**LOWNS**	
	LOWP	LOWPS
	LOWRIDER	LOWRIDERS
	LOWRIE	LOWRIES
BLOWS · CLOWS · FLOWS · GLOWS · PLOWS · SLOWS	**LOWS**	LOWSE
BLOWSE	**LOWSE**	LOWSED · LOWSER · LOWSES
BLOWSED	**LOWSED**	
	LOWSENING	LOWSENINGS
BLOWSES	**LOWSES**	LOWSEST
	LOWT	LOWTS
	LOWVELD	LOWVELDS
	LOXODROME	LOXODROMES
	LOXYGEN	LOXYGENS
CLOY · PLOY	**LOY**	LOYS
	LOYALISM	LOYALISMS
	LOYALIST	LOYALISTS
CLOYS · PLOYS	**LOYS**	
	LOZELL	LOZELLS
	LOZEN	LOZENS
	LOZENGE	LOZENGED · LOZENGES
	LUAU	LUAUS
	LUBBARD	LUBBARDS
BLUBBER · CLUBBER · FLUBBER · SLUBBER	**LUBBER**	LUBBERS
BLUBBERS · CLUBBERS · FLUBBERS · SLUBBERS	**LUBBERS**	

FRONT HOOK	ROOT WORD	END HOOK
	LUBE	LUBED · LUBES
	LUBRA	LUBRAS
	LUBRICANT	LUBRICANTS
	LUBRICATE	LUBRICATED · LUBRICATES
	LUCARNE	LUCARNES
	LUCE	LUCES
	LUCENCE	LUCENCES
	LUCERN	LUCERNE · LUCERNS
	LUCERNE	LUCERNES
	LUCHOT	LUCHOTH
	LUCIFER	LUCIFERS
	LUCIFERIN	LUCIFERINS
	LUCIGEN	LUCIGENS
	LUCITE	LUCITES
CLUCK · PLUCK	**LUCK**	LUCKS · LUCKY
CLUCKED · PLUCKED	**LUCKED**	
	LUCKIE	LUCKIER · LUCKIES
CLUCKIER · PLUCKIER	**LUCKIER**	
	LUCKIES	LUCKIEST
CLUCKIEST · PLUCKIEST	**LUCKIEST**	
PLUCKILY	**LUCKILY**	
PLUCKINESS	**LUCKINESS**	
CLUCKING · PLUCKING	**LUCKING**	
CLUCKS · PLUCKS	**LUCKS**	
CLUCKY · PLUCKY	**LUCKY**	
	LUCRE	LUCRES
	LUCTATION	LUCTATIONS
ELUCUBRATE	**LUCUBRATE**	LUCUBRATED · LUCUBRATES
	LUCUMA	LUCUMAS
	LUCUMO	LUCUMOS
	LUD	LUDE · LUDO · LUDS
BLUDE · ELUDE	**LUDE**	LUDES
	LUDERICK	LUDERICKS
BLUDES · ELUDES	**LUDES**	
	LUDO	LUDOS
	LUDSHIP	LUDSHIPS
BLUES · CLUES · FLUES · GLUES · PLUES · SLUES	**LUES**	
	LUETIC	LUETICS
BLUFF · FLUFF · PLUFF · SLUFF	**LUFF**	LUFFA · LUFFS
	LUFFA	LUFFAS
BLUFFED · FLUFFED · PLUFFED · SLUFFED	**LUFFED**	
BLUFFING · FLUFFING · PLUFFING · SLUFFING	**LUFFING**	
BLUFFS · FLUFFS · PLUFFS · SLUFFS	**LUFFS**	
GLUG · PLUG · SLUG	**LUG**	LUGE · LUGS
KLUGE	**LUGE**	LUGED · LUGER · LUGES
KLUGED	**LUGED**	
	LUGEING	LUGEINGS
	LUGER	LUGERS
KLUGES	**LUGES**	
GLUGGABLE	**LUGGABLE**	LUGGABLES
	LUGGAGE	LUGGAGES
GLUGGED · PLUGGED · SLUGGED	**LUGGED**	
PLUGGER · SLUGGER	**LUGGER**	LUGGERS
PLUGGERS · SLUGGERS	**LUGGERS**	
	LUGGIE	LUGGIES
GLUGGING · PLUGGING · SLUGGING	**LUGGING**	
PLUGHOLE	**LUGHOLE**	LUGHOLES
PLUGHOLES	**LUGHOLES**	
KLUGING	**LUGING**	LUGINGS
GLUGS · PLUGS · SLUGS	**LUGS**	
	LUGSAIL	LUGSAILS
	LUGWORM	LUGWORMS
SLUIT	**LUIT**	
FLUKE	**LUKE**	
	LULIBUB	LULIBUBS
	LULL	LULLS
	LULLER	LULLERS

FRONT HOOK	ROOT WORD	END HOOK
	LULU	LULUS
ALUM · GLUM · PLUM · SLUM	**LUM**	LUMA · LUMP · LUMS
	LUMA	LUMAS
PLUMBAGO	**LUMBAGO**	LUMBAGOS
PLUMBAGOS	**LUMBAGOS**	
	LUMBANG	LUMBANGS
	LUMBAR	LUMBARS
CLUMBER · PLUMBER · SLUMBER	**LUMBER**	LUMBERS
SLUMBERED	**LUMBERED**	
SLUMBERER	**LUMBERER**	LUMBERERS
SLUMBERERS	**LUMBERERS**	
SLUMBERING	**LUMBERING**	LUMBERINGS
CLUMBERS · PLUMBERS · SLUMBERS	**LUMBERS**	
	LUMBRICAL	LUMBRICALS
	LUMEN	LUMENS
ALUMINA	**LUMINA**	LUMINAL
	LUMINAIRE	LUMINAIRES
	LUMINANCE	LUMINANCES
	LUMINANT	LUMINANTS
	LUMINARIA	LUMINARIAS
ALUMINE	**LUMINE**	LUMINED · LUMINES
ALUMINES	**LUMINES**	
	LUMINESCE	LUMINESCED · LUMINESCES
	LUMINISM	LUMINISMS
	LUMINIST	LUMINISTS
ALUMINOUS	**LUMINOUS**	
PLUMMIER · SLUMMIER	**LUMMIER**	
PLUMMIEST · SLUMMIEST	**LUMMIEST**	
FLUMMOX	**LUMMOX**	
FLUMMOXES	**LUMMOXES**	
PLUMMY · SLUMMY	**LUMMY**	
CLUMP · FLUMP · PLUMP · SLUMP	**LUMP**	LUMPS · LUMPY
CLUMPED · FLUMPED · PLUMPED · SLUMPED	**LUMPED**	
PLUMPEN	**LUMPEN**	LUMPENS
PLUMPENS	**LUMPENS**	
CLUMPER · PLUMPER	**LUMPER**	LUMPERS
CLUMPERS · PLUMPERS	**LUMPERS**	
CLUMPIER · GLUMPIER · PLUMPIER	**LUMPIER**	
SLUMPIER		
CLUMPIEST · GLUMPIEST · PLUMPIEST	**LUMPIEST**	
SLUMPIEST		
GLUMPILY	**LUMPILY**	
CLUMPINESS	**LUMPINESS**	
CLUMPING · FLUMPING · PLUMPING	**LUMPING**	
SLUMPING		
CLUMPISH · GLUMPISH · PLUMPISH	**LUMPISH**	
	LUMPKIN	LUMPKINS
CLUMPS · FLUMPS · GLUMPS · PLUMPS	**LUMPS**	
SLUMPS		
CLUMPY · GLUMPY · PLUMPY · SLUMPY	**LUMPY**	
ALUMS · GLUMS · PLUMS · SLUMS	**LUMS**	
	LUNA	LUNAR · LUNAS
	LUNANAUT	LUNANAUTS
	LUNAR	LUNARS · LUNARY
	LUNARIAN	LUNARIANS
	LUNARIST	LUNARISTS
	LUNARNAUT	LUNARNAUTS
	LUNATE	LUNATED · LUNATES
	LUNATIC	LUNATICS
	LUNATION	LUNATIONS
CLUNCH · GLUNCH	**LUNCH**	
GLUNCHED	**LUNCHED**	
	LUNCHEON	LUNCHEONS
	LUNCHER	LUNCHERS
CLUNCHES · GLUNCHES	**LUNCHES**	
GLUNCHING	**LUNCHING**	
	LUNCHMEAT	LUNCHMEATS
	LUNCHROOM	LUNCHROOMS
	LUNCHTIME	LUNCHTIMES

FRONT HOOK	ROOT WORD	END HOOK
	LUNE	LUNES · LUNET
	LUNET	LUNETS
	LUNETTE	LUNETTES
CLUNG · FLUNG · SLUNG	LUNG	LUNGE · LUNGI · LUNGS
	LUNGAN	LUNGANS
BLUNGE · PLUNGE	LUNGE	LUNGED · LUNGEE · LUNGER · LUNGES
BLUNGED · PLUNGED	LUNGED	
	LUNGEE	LUNGEES
BLUNGER · PLUNGER	LUNGER	LUNGERS
BLUNGERS · PLUNGERS	LUNGERS	
BLUNGES · PLUNGES	LUNGES	
	LUNGFUL	LUNGFULS
	LUNGI	LUNGIE · LUNGIS
	LUNGIE	LUNGIES
BLUNGING · PLUNGING	LUNGING	
	LUNGWORM	LUNGWORMS
	LUNGWORT	LUNGWORTS
	LUNGYI	LUNGYIS
	LUNIES	LUNIEST
BLUNK · CLUNK · FLUNK · PLUNK · SLUNK	LUNK	LUNKS
BLUNKER · CLUNKER · FLUNKER · PLUNKER	LUNKER	LUNKERS
BLUNKERS · CLUNKERS · FLUNKERS PLUNKERS	LUNKERS	
	LUNKHEAD	LUNKHEADS
BLUNKS · CLUNKS · FLUNKS · PLUNKS	LUNKS	
BLUNT	LUNT	LUNTS
BLUNTED	LUNTED	
BLUNTING	LUNTING	
BLUNTS	LUNTS	
	LUNULA	LUNULAE · LUNULAR
	LUNULATE	LUNULATED
	LUNULE	LUNULES
	LUNYIE	LUNYIES
	LUPANAR	LUPANARS
	LUPIN	LUPINE · LUPINS
	LUPINE	LUPINES
	LUPULIN	LUPULINE · LUPULINS
BLUR · SLUR	LUR	LURE · LURK · LURS
	LURCHER	LURCHERS
	LURDAN	LURDANE · LURDANS
	LURDANE	LURDANES
	LURDEN	LURDENS
ALURE	LURE	LURED · LURER · LURES · LUREX
	LURER	LURERS
ALURES	LURES	
	LURGI	LURGIS
	LURK	LURKS
	LURKER	LURKERS
	LURKING	LURKINGS
FLURRIES · SLURRIES	LURRIES	
BLURRY · FLURRY · PLURRY · SLURRY	LURRY	
BLURS · SLURS	LURS	
	LURVE	LURVES
	LUSER	LUSERS
BLUSH · FLUSH · PLUSH · SLUSH	LUSH	LUSHY
BLUSHED · FLUSHED · SLUSHED	LUSHED	
BLUSHER · FLUSHER · PLUSHER	LUSHER	LUSHERS
BLUSHERS · FLUSHERS	LUSHERS	
BLUSHES · FLUSHES · PLUSHES · SLUSHES	LUSHES	LUSHEST
FLUSHEST · PLUSHEST	LUSHEST	
FLUSHIER · PLUSHIER · SLUSHIER	LUSHIER	
FLUSHIEST · PLUSHIEST · SLUSHIEST	LUSHIEST	
BLUSHING · FLUSHING · SLUSHING	LUSHING	
PLUSHLY	LUSHLY	
FLUSHNESS · PLUSHNESS	LUSHNESS	
FLUSHY · PLUSHY · SLUSHY	LUSHY	
	LUSK	LUSKS
	LUST	LUSTS · LUSTY
BLUSTER · CLUSTER · FLUSTER	LUSTER	LUSTERS

FRONT HOOK	ROOT WORD	END HOOK
BLUSTERED · CLUSTERED · FLUSTERED	**LUSTERED**	
BLUSTERING · CLUSTERING · FLUSTERING	**LUSTERING**	
BLUSTERS · CLUSTERS · FLUSTERS	**LUSTERS**	
	LUSTIHEAD	LUSTIHEADS
	LUSTIHOOD	LUSTIHOODS
	LUSTRA	LUSTRAL
FLUSTRATE	**LUSTRATE**	LUSTRATED · LUSTRATES
FLUSTRATED	**LUSTRATED**	
FLUSTRATES	**LUSTRATES**	
	LUSTRE	LUSTRED · LUSTRES
	LUSTRINE	LUSTRINES
	LUSTRING	LUSTRINGS
BLUSTROUS	**LUSTROUS**	
	LUSTRUM	LUSTRUMS
	LUTANIST	LUTANISTS
ELUTE · FLUTE · GLUTE	**LUTE**	LUTEA · LUTED · LUTER · LUTES
	LUTEA	LUTEAL
GLUTEAL · PLUTEAL	**LUTEAL**	
	LUTECIUM	LUTECIUMS
ELUTED · FLUTED	**LUTED**	
	LUTEFISK	LUTEFISKS
	LUTEIN	LUTEINS
	LUTEINISE	LUTEINISED · LUTEINISES
	LUTEINIZE	LUTEINIZED · LUTEINIZES
	LUTENIST	LUTENISTS
	LUTEOLIN	LUTEOLINS
FLUTER	**LUTER**	LUTERS
FLUTERS	**LUTERS**	
ELUTES · FLUTES · GLUTES	**LUTES**	
	LUTETIUM	LUTETIUMS
	LUTFISK	LUTFISKS
	LUTHERN	LUTHERNS
	LUTHIER	LUTHIERS
ELUTING · FLUTING	**LUTING**	LUTINGS
FLUTINGS	**LUTINGS**	
FLUTIST	**LUTIST**	LUTISTS
FLUTISTS	**LUTISTS**	
	LUTITE	LUTITES
KLUTZ	**LUTZ**	
KLUTZES	**LUTZES**	
	LUV	LUVS
	LUVVIE	LUVVIES
FLUX	**LUX**	LUXE ·
	LUXATE	LUXATED · LUXATES
	LUXATION	LUXATIONS
	LUXE	LUXES
FLUXES	**LUXES**	
FLUXMETER	**LUXMETER**	LUXMETERS
FLUXMETERS	**LUXMETERS**	
	LUXURIATE	LUXURIATED · LUXURIATES
	LUXURIST	LUXURISTS
	LUZERN	LUZERNS
	LWEI	LWEIS
	LYAM	LYAMS
	LYASE	LYASES
	LYCEE	LYCEES
	LYCEUM	LYCEUMS
	LYCHEE	LYCHEES
	LYCHGATE	LYCHGATES
	LYCOPENE	LYCOPENES
	LYCOPOD	LYCOPODS
	LYCRA	LYCRAS
	LYDDITE	LYDDITES
	LYE	LYES
CLYING · FLYING · PLYING	**LYING**	LYINGS
PLYINGLY	**LYINGLY**	
FLYINGS	**LYINGS**	
	LYKEWAKE	LYKEWAKES
	LYKEWALK	LYKEWALKS

FRONT HOOK	ROOT WORD	END HOOK
	LYM	LYME · LYMS
	LYME	LYMES
	LYMITER	LYMITERS
	LYMPH	LYMPHS
	LYMPHAD	LYMPHADS
	LYMPHATIC	LYMPHATICS
	LYMPHOMA	LYMPHOMAS
	LYNAGE	LYNAGES
	LYNCHER	LYNCHERS
	LYNCHET	LYNCHETS
	LYNCHING	LYNCHINGS
	LYNCHPIN	LYNCHPINS
	LYNE	LYNES
	LYOPHIL	LYOPHILE
	LYOPHILE	LYOPHILED
	LYRATE	LYRATED
	LYRE	LYRES
	LYREBIRD	LYREBIRDS
	LYRIC	LYRICS
	LYRICISE	LYRICISED · LYRICISES
	LYRICISM	LYRICISMS
	LYRICIST	LYRICISTS
	LYRICIZE	LYRICIZED · LYRICIZES
	LYRICON	LYRICONS
	LYRISM	LYRISMS
	LYRIST	LYRISTS
	LYSATE	LYSATES
	LYSE	LYSED · LYSES
	LYSERGIDE	LYSERGIDES
	LYSIMETER	LYSIMETERS
	LYSIN	LYSINE · LYSING · LYSINS
	LYSINE	LYSINES
	LYSOGEN	LYSOGENS · LYSOGENY
	LYSOL	LYSOLS
	LYSOSOME	LYSOSOMES
	LYSOZYME	LYSOZYMES
	LYSSA	LYSSAS
FLYTE	LYTE	LYTED · LYTES
FLYTED	LYTED	
FLYTES	LYTES	
	LYTHE	LYTHES
FLYTING	LYTING	
	LYTTA	LYTTAE · LYTTAS

477

M

FRONT HOOK	ROOT WORD	END HOOK
AMA · SMA	MA	MAA · MAC · MAD · MAE · MAG · MAK · MAL MAM · MAN · MAP · MAR · MAS · MAT · MAW MAX · MAY
	MAA	MAAR · MAAS
	MAAR	MAARE · MAARS
	MABE	MABES
	MABELA	MABELAS
	MAC	MACE · MACH · MACK · MACS
	MACACO	MACACOS
	MACADAM	MACADAMS
	MACADAMIA	MACADAMIAS
	MACAHUBA	MACAHUBAS
	MACALLUM	MACALLUMS
	MACAQUE	MACAQUES
	MACARISE	MACARISED · MACARISES
	MACARISM	MACARISMS
	MACARIZE	MACARIZED · MACARIZES
	MACARONI	MACARONIC · MACARONIS
	MACARONIC	MACARONICS
	MACAROON	MACAROONS
	MACASSAR	MACASSARS
	MACAW	MACAWS
	MACCABAW	MACCABAWS
	MACCABOY	MACCABOYS
	MACCARONI	MACCARONIS
	MACCHIATO	MACCHIATOS
	MACCOBOY	MACCOBOYS
	MACE	MACED · MACER · MACES
	MACEDOINE	MACEDOINES
	MACER	MACERS
	MACERAL	MACERALS
	MACERATE	MACERATED · MACERATER · MACERATES
	MACERATER	MACERATERS
	MACERATOR	MACERATORS
	MACH	MACHE · MACHI · MACHO · MACHS
	MACHAIR	MACHAIRS
	MACHAN	MACHANS
	MACHE	MACHER · MACHES
	MACHER	MACHERS
	MACHETE	MACHETES
	MACHINATE	MACHINATED · MACHINATES
	MACHINE	MACHINED · MACHINES
	MACHINING	MACHININGS
	MACHINIST	MACHINISTS
	MACHISMO	MACHISMOS
	MACHMETER	MACHMETERS
	MACHO	MACHOS
	MACHOISM	MACHOISMS
	MACHREE	MACHREES
	MACHZOR	MACHZORS
SMACK	MACK	MACKS
	MACKEREL	MACKERELS
	MACKINAW	MACKINAWS
	MACKLE	MACKLED · MACKLES
SMACKS	MACKS	
	MACLE	MACLED · MACLES
	MACON	MACONS
	MACOYA	MACOYAS
	MACRAME	MACRAMES
	MACRAMI	MACRAMIS
	MACRO	MACRON · MACROS
	MACROCODE	MACROCODES
	MACROCOSM	MACROCOSMS
	MACROCYST	MACROCYSTS
	MACROCYTE	MACROCYTES
	MACRODOME	MACRODOMES

FRONT HOOK	ROOT WORD	END HOOK
	MACROGLIA	MACROGLIAS
	MACROMERE	MACROMERES
	MACROMOLE	MACROMOLES
	MACRON	MACRONS
	MACROPOD	MACROPODS
	MACROPSIA	MACROPSIAS
	MACRURAN	MACRURANS
EMACS	MACS	
	MACTATION	MACTATIONS
	MACULA	MACULAE · MACULAR · MACULAS
	MACULATE	MACULATED · MACULATES
	MACULE	MACULED · MACULES
	MACUMBA	MACUMBAS
	MAD	MADE · MADS
	MADAFU	MADAFUS
	MADAM	MADAME · MADAMS
	MADAME	MADAMED · MADAMES
	MADCAP	MADCAPS
	MADDEN	MADDENS
	MADDER	MADDERS
	MADDOCK	MADDOCKS
	MADEIRA	MADEIRAS
	MADELEINE	MADELEINES
	MADERISE	MADERISED · MADERISES
	MADERIZE	MADERIZED · MADERIZES
	MADGE	MADGES
	MADHOUSE	MADHOUSES
	MADISON	MADISONS
	MADLING	MADLINGS
	MADONNA	MADONNAS
	MADOQUA	MADOQUAS
	MADRAS	MADRASA
	MADRASA	MADRASAH · MADRASAS
	MADRASAH	MADRASAHS
	MADRASSA	MADRASSAH · MADRASSAS
	MADRASSAH	MADRASSAHS
	MADRE	MADRES
	MADREPORE	MADREPORES
	MADRIGAL	MADRIGALS
	MADRILENE	MADRILENES
	MADRONA	MADRONAS
	MADRONE	MADRONES
	MADRONO	MADRONOS
	MADTOM	MADTOMS
	MADURO	MADUROS
	MADWORT	MADWORTS
	MADZOON	MADZOONS
	MAE	MAES
	MAELID	MAELIDS
	MAELSTROM	MAELSTROMS
	MAENAD	MAENADS
	MAENADISM	MAENADISMS
	MAESTOSO	MAESTOSOS
	MAESTRO	MAESTROS
	MAFFIA	MAFFIAS
	MAFFICK	MAFFICKS
	MAFFICKER	MAFFICKERS
	MAFFLIN	MAFFLING · MAFFLINS
	MAFFLING	MAFFLINGS
	MAFIA	MAFIAS
	MAFIC	MAFICS
	MAFIOSO	MAFIOSOS
	MAFTIR	MAFTIRS
	MAG	MAGE · MAGG · MAGI · MAGS
	MAGAININ	MAGAININS
	MAGALOG	MAGALOGS
	MAGALOGUE	MAGALOGUES
	MAGAZINE	MAGAZINES
	MAGDALEN	MAGDALENE · MAGDALENS

FRONT HOOK	ROOT WORD	END HOOK
	MAGDALENE	MAGDALENES
IMAGE	**MAGE**	MAGES
	MAGENTA	MAGENTAS
IMAGES	**MAGES**	
	MAGESHIP	MAGESHIPS
	MAGG	MAGGS
	MAGGIE	MAGGIES
	MAGGOT	MAGGOTS ▪ MAGGOTY
	MAGI	MAGIC
	MAGIAN	MAGIANS
	MAGIANISM	MAGIANISMS
	MAGIC	MAGICS
	MAGICIAN	MAGICIANS
	MAGILP	MAGILPS
IMAGISM	**MAGISM**	MAGISMS
IMAGISMS	**MAGISMS**	
	MAGISTER	MAGISTERS ▪ MAGISTERY
	MAGISTRAL	MAGISTRALS
	MAGLEV	MAGLEVS
	MAGMA	MAGMAS
	MAGMATISM	MAGMATISMS
	MAGNALIUM	MAGNALIUMS
	MAGNATE	MAGNATES
	MAGNESIA	MAGNESIAL ▪ MAGNESIAN ▪ MAGNESIAS
	MAGNESITE	MAGNESITES
	MAGNESIUM	MAGNESIUMS
	MAGNET	MAGNETO ▪ MAGNETS
	MAGNETAR	MAGNETARS
	MAGNETIC	MAGNETICS
	MAGNETISE	MAGNETISED ▪ MAGNETISER ▪ MAGNETISES
	MAGNETISM	MAGNETISMS
	MAGNETIST	MAGNETISTS
	MAGNETITE	MAGNETITES
	MAGNETIZE	MAGNETIZED ▪ MAGNETIZER ▪ MAGNETIZES
	MAGNETO	MAGNETON ▪ MAGNETOS
	MAGNETON	MAGNETONS
	MAGNETRON	MAGNETRONS
	MAGNIFIC	MAGNIFICO
	MAGNIFICO	MAGNIFICOS
	MAGNIFIER	MAGNIFIERS
	MAGNITUDE	MAGNITUDES
	MAGNOLIA	MAGNOLIAS
	MAGNON	MAGNONS
	MAGNUM	MAGNUMS
	MAGOT	MAGOTS
	MAGPIE	MAGPIES
	MAGUEY	MAGUEYS
	MAHARAJA	MAHARAJAH ▪ MAHARAJAS
	MAHARAJAH	MAHARAJAHS
	MAHARANEE	MAHARANEES
	MAHARANI	MAHARANIS
	MAHARISHI	MAHARISHIS
	MAHATMA	MAHATMAS
	MAHEWU	MAHEWUS
	MAHIMAHI	MAHIMAHIS
	MAHJONG	MAHJONGG ▪ MAHJONGS
	MAHJONGG	MAHJONGGS
	MAHLSTICK	MAHLSTICKS
	MAHMAL	MAHMALS
	MAHOE	MAHOES
	MAHONIA	MAHONIAS
	MAHOUT	MAHOUTS
	MAHSEER	MAHSEERS
	MAHSIR	MAHSIRS
	MAHUA	MAHUAS
	MAHUANG	MAHUANGS
	MAHWA	MAHWAS
	MAHZOR	MAHZORS
	MAIASAUR	MAIASAURA ▪ MAIASAURS

FRONT HOOK	ROOT WORD	END HOOK
	MAIASAURA	MAIASAURAS
	MAID	MAIDS
	MAIDAN	MAIDANS
	MAIDEN	MAIDENS
	MAIDHOOD	MAIDHOODS
	MAIDISM	MAIDISMS
	MAIEUTIC	MAIEUTICS
	MAIGRE	MAIGRES
	MAIHEM	MAIHEMS
SMAIK	MAIK	MAIKO · MAIKS
	MAIKO	MAIKOS
SMAIKS	MAIKS	
EMAIL	MAIL	MAILE · MAILL · MAILS
	MAILBAG	MAILBAGS
	MAILCAR	MAILCARS
	MAILE	MAILED · MAILER · MAILES
EMAILED	MAILED	
	MAILER	MAILERS
	MAILGRAM	MAILGRAMS
EMAILING	MAILING	MAILINGS
	MAILL	MAILLS
	MAILLOT	MAILLOTS
	MAILMERGE	MAILMERGED · MAILMERGES
	MAILROOM	MAILROOMS
EMAILS	MAILS	
	MAILSACK	MAILSACKS
	MAILSHOT	MAILSHOTS
	MAILVAN	MAILVANS
	MAIM	MAIMS
	MAIMER	MAIMERS
	MAIMING	MAIMINGS
AMAIN	MAIN	MAINS
	MAINBOOM	MAINBOOMS
	MAINBRACE	MAINBRACES
	MAINDOOR	MAINDOORS
	MAINFRAME	MAINFRAMES
	MAINLAND	MAINLANDS
	MAINLINE	MAINLINED · MAINLINER · MAINLINES
	MAINLINER	MAINLINERS
	MAINMAST	MAINMASTS
	MAINOR	MAINORS
	MAINOUR	MAINOURS
	MAINPRISE	MAINPRISES
	MAINSAIL	MAINSAILS
	MAINSHEET	MAINSHEETS
	MAINSTAY	MAINSTAYS
	MAINTAIN	MAINTAINS
	MAINTOP	MAINTOPS
	MAINYARD	MAINYARDS
	MAIOLICA	MAIOLICAS
	MAIR	MAIRE · MAIRS
	MAIRE	MAIRES
	MAIREHAU	MAIREHAUS
	MAISE	MAISES
	MAIST	MAISTS
	MAISTER	MAISTERS
	MAISTRING	MAISTRINGS
	MAIZE	MAIZES
	MAJAGUA	MAJAGUAS
	MAJOLICA	MAJOLICAS
	MAJOR	MAJORS
	MAJORAT	MAJORATS
	MAJORDOMO	MAJORDOMOS
	MAJORETTE	MAJORETTES
	MAJORSHIP	MAJORSHIPS
	MAJUSCULE	MAJUSCULES
	MAK	MAKE · MAKI · MAKO · MAKS
	MAKAR	MAKARS
	MAKE	MAKER · MAKES

M

M

FRONT HOOK	ROOT WORD	END HOOK
	MAKEBATE	MAKEBATES
	MAKEFAST	MAKEFASTS
	MAKEOVER	MAKEOVERS
	MAKER	MAKERS
	MAKESHIFT	MAKESHIFTS
	MAKEUP	MAKEUPS
	MAKI	MAKIS
	MAKIMONO	MAKIMONOS
	MAKING	MAKINGS
	MAKO	MAKOS
	MAKUTU	MAKUTUS
	MAL	MALA ▪ MALE ▪ MALI ▪ MALL ▪ MALM MALS ▪ MALT
	MALA	MALAM ▪ MALAR ▪ MALAS ▪ MALAX
	MALACCA	MALACCAS
	MALACHITE	MALACHITES
	MALACIA	MALACIAS
	MALADROIT	MALADROITS
	MALAGUENA	MALAGUENAS
	MALAISE	MALAISES
	MALAM	MALAMS
	MALAMUTE	MALAMUTES
	MALANDER	MALANDERS
	MALANGA	MALANGAS
	MALAPERT	MALAPERTS
	MALAPROP	MALAPROPS
	MALAR	MALARS
	MALARIA	MALARIAL ▪ MALARIAN ▪ MALARIAS
	MALARKEY	MALARKEYS
	MALAROMA	MALAROMAS
	MALATE	MALATES
	MALATHION	MALATHIONS
	MALAXAGE	MALAXAGES
	MALAXATE	MALAXATED ▪ MALAXATES
	MALAXATOR	MALAXATORS
	MALE	MALES
	MALEATE	MALEATES
	MALEDICT	MALEDICTS
	MALEFFECT	MALEFFECTS
	MALEFIC	MALEFICE
	MALEFICE	MALEFICES
	MALEMIUT	MALEMIUTS
	MALEMUTE	MALEMUTES
	MALENGINE	MALENGINES
	MALGRE	MALGRED ▪ MALGRES
	MALI	MALIC ▪ MALIK ▪ MALIS
	MALIC	MALICE
	MALICE	MALICED ▪ MALICES
	MALICHO	MALICHOS
	MALIGN	MALIGNS
	MALIGNANT	MALIGNANTS
	MALIGNER	MALIGNERS
	MALIHINI	MALIHINIS
	MALIK	MALIKS
	MALINE	MALINES
	MALINGER	MALINGERS ▪ MALINGERY
	MALIS	MALISM ▪ MALIST
	MALISM	MALISMS
	MALISON	MALISONS
	MALKIN	MALKINS
SMALL	MALL	MALLS
	MALLAM	MALLAMS
	MALLANDER	MALLANDERS
	MALLARD	MALLARDS
	MALLEATE	MALLEATED ▪ MALLEATES
	MALLECHO	MALLECHOS
SMALLED	MALLED	
	MALLEE	MALLEES
	MALLEMUCK	MALLEMUCKS

FRONT HOOK	ROOT WORD	END HOOK
	MALLENDER	MALLENDERS
	MALLET	MALLETS
SMALLING	MALLING	MALLINGS
	MALLOW	MALLOWS
SMALLS	MALLS	
SMALM	MALM	MALMS · MALMY
	MALMAG	MALMAGS
SMALMS	MALMS	
	MALMSEY	MALMSEYS
	MALMSTONE	MALMSTONES
SMALMY	MALMY	
	MALODOR	MALODORS
	MALODOUR	MALODOURS
	MALONATE	MALONATES
	MALSTICK	MALSTICKS
SMALT	MALT	MALTS · MALTY
	MALTALENT	MALTALENTS
	MALTASE	MALTASES
	MALTED	MALTEDS
	MALTHA	MALTHAS
	MALTING	MALTINGS
	MALTOL	MALTOLS
	MALTOSE	MALTOSES
	MALTREAT	MALTREATS
SMALTS	MALTS	
	MALTSTER	MALTSTERS
	MALTWORM	MALTWORMS
	MALVA	MALVAS
	MALVASIA	MALVASIAN · MALVASIAS
	MALVESIE	MALVESIES
	MALVOISIE	MALVOISIES
	MALWA	MALWAS
	MALWARE	MALWARES
IMAM	MAM	MAMA · MAMS
	MAMA	MAMAS
	MAMAGUY	MAMAGUYS
	MAMALIGA	MAMALIGAS
	MAMBA	MAMBAS
	MAMBO	MAMBOS
	MAMEE	MAMEES
	MAMELON	MAMELONS
	MAMELUCO	MAMELUCOS
	MAMELUKE	MAMELUKES
	MAMEY	MAMEYS
	MAMIE	MAMIES
	MAMILLA	MAMILLAE · MAMILLAR
	MAMILLAR	MAMILLARY
	MAMILLATE	MAMILLATED
	MAMLUK	MAMLUKS
	MAMMA	MAMMAE · MAMMAL · MAMMAS
	MAMMAL	MAMMALS
	MAMMALIAN	MAMMALIANS
	MAMMEE	MAMMEES
	MAMMER	MAMMERS
	MAMMET	MAMMETS
	MAMMEY	MAMMEYS
	MAMMIE	MAMMIES
	MAMMIFER	MAMMIFERS
	MAMMILLA	MAMMILLAE
	MAMMOCK	MAMMOCKS
	MAMMOGRAM	MAMMOGRAMS
	MAMMON	MAMMONS
	MAMMONISM	MAMMONISMS
	MAMMONIST	MAMMONISTS
	MAMMONITE	MAMMONITES
	MAMMOTH	MAMMOTHS
	MAMPARA	MAMPARAS
	MAMPOER	MAMPOERS
IMAMS	MAMS	

M

FRONT HOOK	ROOT WORD	END HOOK
	MAMSELLE	MAMSELLES
	MAMZER	MAMZERS
	MAN	MANA ▪ MAND ▪ MANE ▪ MANG ▪ MANI MANO ▪ MANS ▪ MANY
	MANA	MANAS ▪ MANAT
	MANACLE	MANACLED ▪ MANACLES
	MANAGE	MANAGED ▪ MANAGER ▪ MANAGES
	MANAGER	MANAGERS
	MANAKIN	MANAKINS
	MANANA	MANANAS
	MANAT	MANATI ▪ MANATS ▪ MANATU
	MANATEE	MANATEES
	MANATI	MANATIS
	MANAWA	MANAWAS
	MANCALA	MANCALAS
	MANCHE	MANCHES ▪ MANCHET
	MANCHET	MANCHETS
EMANCIPATE	**MANCIPATE**	MANCIPATED ▪ MANCIPATES
	MANCIPLE	MANCIPLES
	MAND	MANDI
	MANDALA	MANDALAS
	MANDARIN	MANDARINE ▪ MANDARINS
	MANDARINE	MANDARINES
	MANDATE	MANDATED ▪ MANDATES
	MANDATOR	MANDATORS ▪ MANDATORY
	MANDI	MANDIR ▪ MANDIS
	MANDIBLE	MANDIBLES
	MANDILION	MANDILIONS
	MANDIOC	MANDIOCA ▪ MANDIOCS
	MANDIOCA	MANDIOCAS
	MANDIOCCA	MANDIOCCAS
	MANDIR	MANDIRA ▪ MANDIRS
	MANDIRA	MANDIRAS
	MANDOLA	MANDOLAS
	MANDOLIN	MANDOLINE ▪ MANDOLINS
	MANDOLINE	MANDOLINES
	MANDOM	MANDOMS
	MANDORA	MANDORAS
	MANDORLA	MANDORLAS
	MANDRAKE	MANDRAKES
	MANDREL	MANDRELS
	MANDRIL	MANDRILL ▪ MANDRILS
	MANDRILL	MANDRILLS
	MANDUCATE	MANDUCATED ▪ MANDUCATES
	MANDYLION	MANDYLIONS
	MANE	MANED ▪ MANEH ▪ MANES ▪ MANET
	MANEGE	MANEGED ▪ MANEGES
	MANEH	MANEHS
	MANEUVER	MANEUVERS
	MANG	MANGA ▪ MANGE ▪ MANGO ▪ MANGS ▪ MANGY
	MANGA	MANGAL ▪ MANGAS
	MANGABEY	MANGABEYS
	MANGAL	MANGALS
	MANGANATE	MANGANATES
	MANGANESE	MANGANESES
	MANGANIN	MANGANINS
	MANGANITE	MANGANITES
	MANGE	MANGED ▪ MANGEL ▪ MANGER ▪ MANGES MANGEY
	MANGEL	MANGELS
	MANGER	MANGERS
	MANGETOUT	MANGETOUTS
	MANGLE	MANGLED ▪ MANGLER ▪ MANGLES
	MANGLER	MANGLERS
	MANGO	MANGOS
	MANGOLD	MANGOLDS
	MANGONEL	MANGONELS
	MANGOSTAN	MANGOSTANS
	MANGOUSTE	MANGOUSTES

FRONT HOOK	ROOT WORD	END HOOK
	MANGROVE	MANGROVES
	MANGULATE	MANGULATED · MANGULATES
	MANHANDLE	MANHANDLED · MANHANDLES
	MANHATTAN	MANHATTANS
	MANHOLE	MANHOLES
	MANHOOD	MANHOODS
	MANHUNT	MANHUNTS
	MANHUNTER	MANHUNTERS
	MANI	MANIA · MANIC · MANIS
	MANIA	MANIAC · MANIAS
	MANIAC	MANIACS
	MANIC	MANICS
	MANICOTTI	MANICOTTIS
	MANICURE	MANICURED · MANICURES
	MANIFEST	MANIFESTO · MANIFESTS
	MANIFESTO	MANIFESTOS
	MANIFOLD	MANIFOLDS
	MANIHOC	MANIHOCS
	MANIHOT	MANIHOTS
	MANIKIN	MANIKINS
	MANILA	MANILAS
	MANILLA	MANILLAS
	MANILLE	MANILLES
	MANIOC	MANIOCA · MANIOCS
	MANIOCA	MANIOCAS
	MANIPLE	MANIPLES
	MANIPULAR	MANIPULARS
	MANITO	MANITOS · MANITOU
	MANITOU	MANITOUS
	MANITU	MANITUS
	MANJACK	MANJACKS
	MANKIND	MANKINDS
	MANNA	MANNAN · MANNAS
	MANNAN	MANNANS
	MANNEQUIN	MANNEQUINS
	MANNER	MANNERS
	MANNERISM	MANNERISMS
	MANNERIST	MANNERISTS
	MANNIKIN	MANNIKINS
	MANNITE	MANNITES
	MANNITOL	MANNITOLS
	MANNOSE	MANNOSES
	MANO	MANOR · MANOS
	MANOAO	MANOAOS
	MANOEUVRE	MANOEUVRED · MANOEUVRER · MANOEUVRES
	MANOMETER	MANOMETERS
	MANOR	MANORS
	MANPACK	MANPACKS
	MANPOWER	MANPOWERS
	MANRED	MANREDS
	MANRENT	MANRENTS
	MANRIDER	MANRIDERS
	MANROPE	MANROPES
	MANS	MANSE
	MANSARD	MANSARDS
	MANSE	MANSES
	MANSHIFT	MANSHIFTS
	MANSION	MANSIONS
	MANSLAYER	MANSLAYERS
	MANTA	MANTAS
	MANTEAU	MANTEAUS · MANTEAUX
	MANTEEL	MANTEELS
	MANTEL	MANTELS
	MANTELET	MANTELETS
	MANTICORA	MANTICORAS
	MANTICORE	MANTICORES
	MANTID	MANTIDS
	MANTILLA	MANTILLAS
	MANTISSA	MANTISSAS

M

FRONT HOOK	ROOT WORD	END HOOK
	MANTLE	MANTLED · MANTLES · MANTLET
	MANTLET	MANTLETS
	MANTLING	MANTLINGS
	MANTO	MANTOS
	MANTRA	MANTRAM · MANTRAP · MANTRAS
	MANTRAM	MANTRAMS
	MANTRAP	MANTRAPS
	MANTUA	MANTUAS
	MANUAL	MANUALS
	MANUBRIA	MANUBRIAL
	MANUBRIUM	MANUBRIUMS
	MANUHIRI	MANUHIRIS
	MANUKA	MANUKAS
	MANUL	MANULS
	MANUMEA	MANUMEAS
	MANUMIT	MANUMITS
	MANURANCE	MANURANCES
	MANURE	MANURED · MANURER · MANURES
	MANURER	MANURERS
	MANURING	MANURINGS
	MANWARD	MANWARDS
	MANYATA	MANYATAS
	MANYATTA	MANYATTAS
	MANZANITA	MANZANITAS
	MANZELLO	MANZELLOS
	MAORMOR	MAORMORS
	MAP	MAPS
	MAPLE	MAPLES
	MAPLES	MAPLESS
	MAPMAKER	MAPMAKERS
	MAPMAKING	MAPMAKINGS
	MAPPEMOND	MAPPEMONDS
	MAPPER	MAPPERS · MAPPERY
	MAPPING	MAPPINGS
	MAPPIST	MAPPISTS
	MAPSTICK	MAPSTICKS
	MAQUETTE	MAQUETTES
	MAQUI	MAQUIS
	MAQUILA	MAQUILAS
	MAQUISARD	MAQUISARDS
	MAR	MARA · MARC · MARD · MARE · MARG MARK · MARL · MARM · MARS · MART · MARY
	MARA	MARAE · MARAH · MARAS
	MARABI	MARABIS
	MARABOU	MARABOUS · MARABOUT
	MARABOUT	MARABOUTS
	MARABUNTA	MARABUNTAS
	MARACA	MARACAS
	MARAE	MARAES
	MARAGING	MARAGINGS
	MARAH	MARAHS
	MARANATHA	MARANATHAS
	MARANTA	MARANTAS
	MARARI	MARARIS
	MARASCA	MARASCAS
	MARATHON	MARATHONS
	MARAUD	MARAUDS
	MARAUDER	MARAUDERS
	MARAVEDI	MARAVEDIS
	MARBELISE	MARBELISED · MARBELISES
	MARBELIZE	MARBELIZED · MARBELIZES
	MARBLE	MARBLED · MARBLER · MARBLES
	MARBLEISE	MARBLEISED · MARBLEISES
	MARBLEIZE	MARBLEIZED · MARBLEIZES
	MARBLER	MARBLERS
	MARBLING	MARBLINGS
	MARC	MARCH · MARCS
	MARCASITE	MARCASITES
	MARCATO	MARCATOS

FRONT HOOK	ROOT WORD	END HOOK
	MARCEL	MARCELS
	MARCELLA	MARCELLAS
	MARCELLER	MARCELLERS
	MARCHER	MARCHERS
	MARCHES	MARCHESA ▪ MARCHESE ▪ MARCHESI
	MARCHESA	MARCHESAS
	MARCHESE	MARCHESES
	MARCHLAND	MARCHLANDS
	MARCHPANE	MARCHPANES
	MARCONI	MARCONIS
	MARD	MARDY
	MARDIES	MARDIEST
	MARE	MARES
	MAREMMA	MAREMMAS
	MARESCHAL	MARESCHALS
	MARG	MARGE ▪ MARGS
	MARGARIN	MARGARINE ▪ MARGARINS
	MARGARINE	MARGARINES
	MARGARITA	MARGARITAS
	MARGARITE	MARGARITES
	MARGAY	MARGAYS
	MARGE	MARGES
	MARGENT	MARGENTS
	MARGIN	MARGINS
	MARGINAL	MARGINALS
EMARGINATE	MARGINATE	MARGINATED ▪ MARGINATES
	MARGOSA	MARGOSAS
	MARGRAVE	MARGRAVES
	MARIACHI	MARIACHIS
	MARIALITE	MARIALITES
	MARID	MARIDS
	MARIGOLD	MARIGOLDS
	MARIGRAM	MARIGRAMS
	MARIGRAPH	MARIGRAPHS
	MARIHUANA	MARIHUANAS
	MARIJUANA	MARIJUANAS
	MARIMBA	MARIMBAS
	MARIMBIST	MARIMBISTS
	MARINA	MARINAS
	MARINADE	MARINADED ▪ MARINADES
	MARINARA	MARINARAS
	MARINATE	MARINATED ▪ MARINATES
	MARINE	MARINER ▪ MARINES
	MARINER	MARINERA ▪ MARINERS
	MARINERA	MARINERAS
	MARIPOSA	MARIPOSAS
	MARISCHAL	MARISCHALS
	MARITAGE	MARITAGES
	MARJORAM	MARJORAMS
	MARK	MARKA ▪ MARKS
	MARKA	MARKAS
	MARKDOWN	MARKDOWNS
	MARKER	MARKERS
	MARKET	MARKETS
	MARKETEER	MARKETEERS
	MARKETER	MARKETERS
	MARKETING	MARKETINGS
	MARKHOOR	MARKHOORS
	MARKHOR	MARKHORS
	MARKING	MARKINGS
	MARKKA	MARKKAA ▪ MARKKAS
	MARKUP	MARKUPS
	MARL	MARLE ▪ MARLS ▪ MARLY
	MARLE	MARLED ▪ MARLES
	MARLIN	MARLINE ▪ MARLING ▪ MARLINS
	MARLINE	MARLINES
	MARLING	MARLINGS
	MARLITE	MARLITES
	MARLSTONE	MARLSTONES

FRONT HOOK	ROOT WORD	END HOOK
SMARM	**MARM**	MARMS
	MARMALADE	MARMALADES
	MARMALISE	MARMALISED · MARMALISES
	MARMALIZE	MARMALIZED · MARMALIZES
	MARMARISE	MARMARISED · MARMARISES
	MARMARIZE	MARMARIZED · MARMARIZES
	MARMELISE	MARMELISED · MARMELISES
	MARMELIZE	MARMELIZED · MARMELIZES
	MARMITE	MARMITES
	MARMOSE	MARMOSES · MARMOSET
	MARMOSET	MARMOSETS
	MARMOT	MARMOTS
SMARMS	**MARMS**	
	MAROCAIN	MAROCAINS
	MARON	MARONS
	MAROON	MAROONS
	MAROONER	MAROONERS
	MAROONING	MAROONINGS
	MAROQUIN	MAROQUINS
	MAROR	MARORS
	MARPLOT	MARPLOTS
	MARQUE	MARQUEE · MARQUES
	MARQUEE	MARQUEES
	MARQUES	MARQUESS
	MARQUIS	MARQUISE
	MARQUISE	MARQUISES
	MARRAM	MARRAMS
	MARRANO	MARRANOS
	MARRER	MARRERS
	MARRI	MARRIS
	MARRIAGE	MARRIAGES
	MARRIED	MARRIEDS
	MARRIER	MARRIERS
	MARRON	MARRONS
	MARROW	MARROWS · MARROWY
	MARROWFAT	MARROWFATS
	MARRUM	MARRUMS
	MARRYING	MARRYINGS
	MARS	MARSE · MARSH
	MARSALA	MARSALAS
	MARSE	MARSES
	MARSEILLE	MARSEILLES
	MARSH	MARSHY
	MARSHAL	MARSHALL · MARSHALS
	MARSHALER	MARSHALERS
	MARSHALL	MARSHALLS
	MARSHBUCK	MARSHBUCKS
	MARSHLAND	MARSHLANDS
	MARSHWORT	MARSHWORTS
	MARSPORT	MARSPORTS
	MARSQUAKE	MARSQUAKES
	MARSUPIA	MARSUPIAL · MARSUPIAN
	MARSUPIAL	MARSUPIALS
	MARSUPIAN	MARSUPIANS
	MARSUPIUM	MARSUPIUMS
SMART	**MART**	MARTS
	MARTAGON	MARTAGONS
SMARTED	**MARTED**	
	MARTEL	MARTELS
	MARTELLO	MARTELLOS
SMARTEN	**MARTEN**	MARTENS
SMARTENS	**MARTENS**	
	MARTEXT	MARTEXTS
	MARTIAL	MARTIALS
	MARTIAN	MARTIANS
	MARTIN	MARTING · MARTINI · MARTINS
	MARTINET	MARTINETS
SMARTING	**MARTING**	
	MARTINGAL	MARTINGALE · MARTINGALS

FRONT HOOK	ROOT WORD	END HOOK
	MARTINI	MARTINIS
	MARTLET	MARTLETS
SMARTS	MARTS	
	MARTYR	MARTYRS ▪ MARTYRY
	MARTYRDOM	MARTYRDOMS
	MARTYRISE	MARTYRISED ▪ MARTYRISES
	MARTYRIZE	MARTYRIZED ▪ MARTYRIZES
	MARVEL	MARVELS
	MARVER	MARVERS
	MARYBUD	MARYBUDS
	MARYJANE	MARYJANES
	MARZIPAN	MARZIPANS
AMAS	MAS	MASA ▪ MASE ▪ MASH ▪ MASK ▪ MASS MAST ▪ MASU
OMASA	MASA	MASAS
	MASALA	MASALAS
	MASCARA	MASCARAS
	MASCARON	MASCARONS
	MASCLE	MASCLED ▪ MASCLES
	MASCON	MASCONS
	MASCOT	MASCOTS
	MASCULINE	MASCULINES
	MASCULIST	MASCULISTS
	MASE	MASED ▪ MASER ▪ MASES
	MASER	MASERS
SMASH	MASH	MASHY
SMASHED	MASHED	
SMASHER	MASHER	MASHERS
SMASHERS	MASHERS	
SMASHES	MASHES	
	MASHIACH	MASHIACHS
	MASHIE	MASHIER ▪ MASHIES
	MASHIES	MASHIEST
SMASHING	MASHING	MASHINGS
SMASHINGS	MASHINGS	
	MASHLAM	MASHLAMS
	MASHLIM	MASHLIMS
	MASHLIN	MASHLINS
	MASHLOCH	MASHLOCHS
	MASHLUM	MASHLUMS
	MASHUA	MASHUAS
SMASHUP	MASHUP	MASHUPS
SMASHUPS	MASHUPS	
	MASJID	MASJIDS
	MASK	MASKS
	MASKEG	MASKEGS
	MASKER	MASKERS
	MASKING	MASKINGS
	MASLIN	MASLINS
	MASOCHISM	MASOCHISMS
	MASOCHIST	MASOCHISTS
	MASON	MASONS
	MASONITE	MASONITES
	MASOOLAH	MASOOLAHS
	MASQUE	MASQUER ▪ MASQUES
	MASQUER	MASQUERS
AMASS	MASS	MASSA ▪ MASSE ▪ MASSY
	MASSA	MASSAS
	MASSACRE	MASSACRED ▪ MASSACRER ▪ MASSACRES
	MASSACRER	MASSACRERS
	MASSAGE	MASSAGED ▪ MASSAGER ▪ MASSAGES
	MASSAGER	MASSAGERS
	MASSAGIST	MASSAGISTS
	MASSCULT	MASSCULTS
	MASSE	MASSED ▪ MASSES
AMASSED	MASSED	
AMASSES	MASSES	
	MASSETER	MASSETERS
	MASSEUR	MASSEURS

FRONT HOOK	ROOT WORD	END HOOK
	MASSEUSE	MASSEUSES
	MASSICOT	MASSICOTS
	MASSIF	MASSIFS
AMASSING	MASSING	
	MASSIVE	MASSIVES
	MASSOOLA	MASSOOLAS
	MASSYMORE	MASSYMORES
	MAST	MASTS · MASTY
	MASTABA	MASTABAH · MASTABAS
	MASTABAH	MASTABAHS
	MASTER	MASTERS · MASTERY
	MASTERATE	MASTERATES
	MASTERDOM	MASTERDOMS
	MASTERING	MASTERINGS
	MASTHEAD	MASTHEADS
	MASTHOUSE	MASTHOUSES
	MASTIC	MASTICH · MASTICS
	MASTICATE	MASTICATED · MASTICATES
	MASTICH	MASTICHE · MASTICHS
	MASTICHE	MASTICHES
	MASTICOT	MASTICOTS
	MASTIFF	MASTIFFS
	MASTODON	MASTODONS · MASTODONT
	MASTODONT	MASTODONTS
	MASTOID	MASTOIDS
	MASU	MASUS
	MASULA	MASULAS
	MASURIUM	MASURIUMS
	MAT	MATE · MATH · MATS · MATT · MATY
	MATACHIN	MATACHINA · MATACHINI
	MATACHINA	MATACHINAS
	MATADOR	MATADORA · MATADORE · MATADORS
	MATADORA	MATADORAS
	MATADORE	MATADORES
	MATAGOURI	MATAGOURIS
	MATAI	MATAIS
	MATAMATA	MATAMATAS
SMATCH	MATCH	
	MATCHBOOK	MATCHBOOKS
SMATCHED	MATCHED	
	MATCHER	MATCHERS
SMATCHES	MATCHES	
	MATCHET	MATCHETS
SMATCHING	MATCHING	
	MATCHLOCK	MATCHLOCKS
	MATCHMAKE	MATCHMAKER · MATCHMAKES
	MATCHMARK	MATCHMARKS
	MATCHUP	MATCHUPS
	MATCHWOOD	MATCHWOODS
AMATE	MATE	MATED · MATER · MATES · MATEY
AMATED	MATED	
	MATELASSE	MATELASSES
	MATELOT	MATELOTE · MATELOTS
	MATELOTE	MATELOTES
	MATELOTTE	MATELOTTES
	MATER	MATERS
	MATERIAL	MATERIALS
	MATERIEL	MATERIELS
AMATES	MATES	
	MATESHIP	MATESHIPS
	MATEY	MATEYS
	MATFELON	MATFELONS
	MATH	MATHS
	MATICO	MATICOS
	MATIES	MATIEST
	MATILDA	MATILDAS
	MATIN	MATING · MATINS
	MATINEE	MATINEES
AMATING	MATING	MATINGS

FRONT HOOK	ROOT WORD	END HOOK
	MATIPO	MATIPOS
	MATLO	MATLOS ▪ MATLOW
	MATLOW	MATLOWS
	MATOKE	MATOKES
	MATOOKE	MATOOKES
	MATRIARCH	MATRIARCHS ▪ MATRIARCHY
	MATRIC	MATRICE ▪ MATRICS
	MATRICE	MATRICES
	MATRICIDE	MATRICIDES
	MATRICULA	MATRICULAR ▪ MATRICULAS
	MATRON	MATRONS
	MATRONAGE	MATRONAGES
	MATRONISE	MATRONISED ▪ MATRONISES
	MATRONIZE	MATRONIZED ▪ MATRONIZES
	MATSAH	MATSAHS
	MATSURI	MATSURIS
	MATSUTAKE	MATSUTAKES
	MATT	MATTE ▪ MATTS
	MATTAMORE	MATTAMORES
	MATTE	MATTED ▪ MATTER ▪ MATTES
SMATTER	MATTER	MATTERS ▪ MATTERY
SMATTERED	MATTERED	
SMATTERING	MATTERING	
SMATTERS	MATTERS	
	MATTIE	MATTIES
	MATTIN	MATTING ▪ MATTINS
	MATTING	MATTINGS
	MATTOCK	MATTOCKS
	MATTOID	MATTOIDS
	MATURATE	MATURATED ▪ MATURATES
	MATURE	MATURED ▪ MATURER ▪ MATURES
	MATURER	MATURERS
	MATURES	MATUREST
	MATWEED	MATWEEDS
	MATZA	MATZAH ▪ MATZAS
	MATZAH	MATZAHS
	MATZO	MATZOH ▪ MATZOS ▪ MATZOT
	MATZOH	MATZOHS
	MATZOON	MATZOONS
	MATZOT	MATZOTH
	MAUD	MAUDS
	MAUGRE	MAUGRED ▪ MAUGRES
	MAUL	MAULS
	MAULER	MAULERS
	MAULGRE	MAULGRED ▪ MAULGRES
	MAULSTICK	MAULSTICKS
	MAULVI	MAULVIS
	MAUMET	MAUMETS
	MAUN	MAUND
	MAUND	MAUNDS ▪ MAUNDY
	MAUNDER	MAUNDERS
	MAUNDERER	MAUNDERERS
	MAURI	MAURIS
	MAUSOLEA	MAUSOLEAN
	MAUSOLEUM	MAUSOLEUMS
AMAUT	MAUT	MAUTS
	MAUTHER	MAUTHERS
AMAUTS	MAUTS	
	MAUVAIS	MAUVAISE
	MAUVE	MAUVER ▪ MAUVES
	MAUVEIN	MAUVEINE ▪ MAUVEINS
	MAUVEINE	MAUVEINES
	MAUVES	MAUVEST
	MAUVIN	MAUVINE ▪ MAUVINS
	MAUVINE	MAUVINES
	MAVEN	MAVENS
	MAVERICK	MAVERICKS
	MAVIE	MAVIES
	MAVIN	MAVINS

FRONT HOOK	ROOT WORD	END HOOK
	MAVOURNIN	MAVOURNINS
	MAW	MAWK ▪ MAWN ▪ MAWR ▪ MAWS
	MAWK	MAWKS ▪ MAWKY
	MAWKIN	MAWKINS
	MAWMET	MAWMETS
	MAWR	MAWRS
	MAWSEED	MAWSEEDS
	MAWTHER	MAWTHERS
	MAX	MAXI
	MAXI	MAXIM ▪ MAXIS
	MAXICOAT	MAXICOATS
	MAXILLA	MAXILLAE ▪ MAXILLAR ▪ MAXILLAS
	MAXILLAR	MAXILLARY
	MAXILLULA	MAXILLULAE
	MAXIM	MAXIMA ▪ MAXIMS
	MAXIMA	MAXIMAL
	MAXIMAL	MAXIMALS
	MAXIMIN	MAXIMINS
	MAXIMISE	MAXIMISED ▪ MAXIMISER ▪ MAXIMISES
	MAXIMISER	MAXIMISERS
	MAXIMIST	MAXIMISTS
	MAXIMITE	MAXIMITES
	MAXIMIZE	MAXIMIZED ▪ MAXIMIZER ▪ MAXIMIZES
	MAXIMIZER	MAXIMIZERS
	MAXIMUM	MAXIMUMS
	MAXIXE	MAXIXES
	MAXWELL	MAXWELLS
	MAY	MAYA ▪ MAYO ▪ MAYS
	MAYA	MAYAN ▪ MAYAS
	MAYAPPLE	MAYAPPLES
	MAYBE	MAYBES
	MAYBIRD	MAYBIRDS
	MAYDAY	MAYDAYS
	MAYFLOWER	MAYFLOWERS
	MAYHEM	MAYHEMS
	MAYING	MAYINGS
	MAYO	MAYOR ▪ MAYOS
	MAYOR	MAYORS
	MAYORSHIP	MAYORSHIPS
	MAYPOLE	MAYPOLES
	MAYPOP	MAYPOPS
	MAYS	MAYST
	MAYSTER	MAYSTERS
	MAYVIN	MAYVINS
	MAYWEED	MAYWEEDS
	MAZARD	MAZARDS
	MAZARINE	MAZARINES
AMAZE ▪ SMAZE	**MAZE**	MAZED ▪ MAZER ▪ MAZES ▪ MAZEY
AMAZED	**MAZED**	
AMAZEDLY	**MAZEDLY**	
AMAZEDNESS	**MAZEDNESS**	
AMAZEMENT	**MAZEMENT**	MAZEMENTS
AMAZEMENTS	**MAZEMENTS**	
	MAZER	MAZERS
AMAZES ▪ SMAZES	**MAZES**	
	MAZHBI	MAZHBIS
AMAZING	**MAZING**	
	MAZOURKA	MAZOURKAS
	MAZOUT	MAZOUTS
	MAZUMA	MAZUMAS
	MAZURKA	MAZURKAS
	MAZUT	MAZUTS
	MAZZARD	MAZZARDS
	MBAQANGA	MBAQANGAS
	MBIRA	MBIRAS
EME	**ME**	MED ▪ MEE ▪ MEG ▪ MEL ▪ MEM ▪ MEN ▪ MES
		MET ▪ MEU ▪ MEW
	MEACOCK	MEACOCKS
	MEAD	MEADS

FRONT HOOK	ROOT WORD	END HOOK
	MEADOW	MEADOWS ▪ MEADOWY
	MEAGRE	MEAGRER ▪ MEAGRES
	MEAGRES	MEAGREST
	MEAL	MEALS ▪ MEALY
	MEALER	MEALERS
	MEALIE	MEALIER ▪ MEALIES
	MEALIES	MEALIEST
	MEALTIME	MEALTIMES
	MEALWORM	MEALWORMS
	MEALYBUG	MEALYBUGS
	MEAN	MEANE ▪ MEANS ▪ MEANT ▪ MEANY
	MEANDER	MEANDERS
	MEANDERER	MEANDERERS
	MEANE	MEANED ▪ MEANER ▪ MEANES
	MEANER	MEANERS
	MEANES	MEANEST
	MEANIE	MEANIES
	MEANING	MEANINGS
	MEANTIME	MEANTIMES
	MEANWHILE	MEANWHILES
	MEARE	MEARES
SMEARING	**MEARING**	
	MEASE	MEASED ▪ MEASES
	MEASLE	MEASLED ▪ MEASLES
	MEASURE	MEASURED ▪ MEASURER ▪ MEASURES
	MEASURER	MEASURERS
	MEASURING	MEASURINGS
	MEAT	MEATH ▪ MEATS ▪ MEATY
	MEATAXE	MEATAXES
	MEATBALL	MEATBALLS
SMEATH	**MEATH**	MEATHE ▪ MEATHS
	MEATHE	MEATHES
	MEATHEAD	MEATHEADS
SMEATHS	**MEATHS**	
	MEATSPACE	MEATSPACES
	MEAZEL	MEAZELS
	MECCA	MECCAS
	MECHANIC	MECHANICS
	MECHANISE	MECHANISED ▪ MECHANISER ▪ MECHANISES
	MECHANISM	MECHANISMS
	MECHANIST	MECHANISTS
	MECHANIZE	MECHANIZED ▪ MECHANIZER ▪ MECHANIZES
	MECHITZA	MECHITZAS
	MECK	MECKS
	MECLIZINE	MECLIZINES
	MECONATE	MECONATES
	MECONIN	MECONINS
	MECONIUM	MECONIUMS
	MED	MEDS
	MEDACCA	MEDACCAS
	MEDAILLON	MEDAILLONS
	MEDAKA	MEDAKAS
	MEDAL	MEDALS
	MEDALET	MEDALETS
	MEDALIST	MEDALISTS
	MEDALLION	MEDALLIONS
	MEDALLIST	MEDALLISTS
	MEDDLE	MEDDLED ▪ MEDDLER ▪ MEDDLES
	MEDDLER	MEDDLERS
	MEDDLING	MEDDLINGS
	MEDEVAC	MEDEVACS
	MEDIA	MEDIAD ▪ MEDIAE ▪ MEDIAL ▪ MEDIAN
		MEDIAS
	MEDIAEVAL	MEDIAEVALS
	MEDIAL	MEDIALS
	MEDIAN	MEDIANS ▪ MEDIANT
	MEDIANT	MEDIANTS
	MEDIATE	MEDIATED ▪ MEDIATES
	MEDIATION	MEDIATIONS

FRONT HOOK	ROOT WORD	END HOOK
	MEDIATISE	MEDIATISED · MEDIATISES
	MEDIATIZE	MEDIATIZED · MEDIATIZES
	MEDIATOR	MEDIATORS · MEDIATORY
	MEDIC	MEDICK · MEDICO · MEDICS
	MEDICAID	MEDICAIDS
	MEDICAL	MEDICALS
	MEDICANT	MEDICANTS
	MEDICARE	MEDICARES
	MEDICATE	MEDICATED · MEDICATES
	MEDICIDE	MEDICIDES
	MEDICINAL	MEDICINALS
	MEDICINE	MEDICINED · MEDICINER · MEDICINES
	MEDICINER	MEDICINERS
	MEDICK	MEDICKS
	MEDICO	MEDICOS
	MEDIEVAL	MEDIEVALS
	MEDIGAP	MEDIGAPS
	MEDINA	MEDINAS
	MEDITATE	MEDITATED · MEDITATES
	MEDITATOR	MEDITATORS
	MEDIUM	MEDIUMS
	MEDIVAC	MEDIVACS
	MEDLAR	MEDLARS
	MEDLE	MEDLED · MEDLES · MEDLEY
	MEDLEY	MEDLEYS
	MEDRESE	MEDRESES
	MEDRESSEH	MEDRESSEHS
	MEDULLA	MEDULLAE · MEDULLAR · MEDULLAS
	MEDULLAR	MEDULLARY
	MEDULLATE	MEDULLATED
	MEDUSA	MEDUSAE · MEDUSAL · MEDUSAN · MEDUSAS
	MEDUSAN	MEDUSANS
	MEDUSOID	MEDUSOIDS
SMEE	MEE	MEED · MEEK · MEER · MEES · MEET
	MEED	MEEDS
SMEEK	MEEK	
	MEEKEN	MEEKENS
	MEEMIE	MEEMIES
AMEER · EMEER	MEER	MEERS
	MEERCAT	MEERCATS
	MEERKAT	MEERKATS
AMEERS · EMEERS	MEERS	
SMEES	MEES	
	MEET	MEETS
	MEETER	MEETERS
	MEETING	MEETINGS
	MEFF	MEFFS
	MEG	MEGA · MEGS
OMEGA	MEGA	
	MEGABAR	MEGABARS
	MEGABIT	MEGABITS
	MEGABUCK	MEGABUCKS
	MEGABYTE	MEGABYTES
	MEGACURIE	MEGACURIES
	MEGACYCLE	MEGACYCLES
	MEGADEAL	MEGADEALS
	MEGADEATH	MEGADEATHS
	MEGADOSE	MEGADOSES
	MEGADYNE	MEGADYNES
	MEGAFARAD	MEGAFARADS
	MEGAFAUNA	MEGAFAUNAE · MEGAFAUNAL · MEGAFAUNAS
	MEGAFLOP	MEGAFLOPS
	MEGAFLORA	MEGAFLORAE · MEGAFLORAS
	MEGAFOG	MEGAFOGS
	MEGAHIT	MEGAHITS
	MEGAJOULE	MEGAJOULES
	MEGALITH	MEGALITHS
	MEGALITRE	MEGALITRES
	MEGAPHONE	MEGAPHONED · MEGAPHONES

FRONT HOOK	ROOT WORD	END HOOK
	MEGAPHYLL	MEGAPHYLLS
	MEGAPIXEL	MEGAPIXELS
	MEGAPOD	MEGAPODE · MEGAPODS
	MEGAPODE	MEGAPODES
	MEGARA	MEGARAD
	MEGARAD	MEGARADS
	MEGARON	MEGARONS
	MEGASCOPE	MEGASCOPES
	MEGASPORE	MEGASPORES
	MEGASS	MEGASSE
	MEGASSE	MEGASSES
	MEGASTAR	MEGASTARS
	MEGASTORE	MEGASTORES
	MEGATHERE	MEGATHERES
	MEGATON	MEGATONS
	MEGAVOLT	MEGAVOLTS
	MEGAWATT	MEGAWATTS
	MEGILLA	MEGILLAH · MEGILLAS
	MEGILLAH	MEGILLAHS
	MEGILP	MEGILPH · MEGILPS
	MEGILPH	MEGILPHS
	MEGOHM	MEGOHMS
	MEGRIM	MEGRIMS
	MEHNDI	MEHNDIS
	MEIN	MEINS · MEINT · MEINY
	MEINEY	MEINEYS
	MEINIE	MEINIES
	MEIOCYTE	MEIOCYTES
	MEIOFAUNA	MEIOFAUNAL
	MEIONITE	MEIONITES
AMEIOSES	MEIOSES	
AMEIOSIS	MEIOSIS	
	MEIOSPORE	MEIOSPORES
	MEISHI	MEISHIS
	MEISTER	MEISTERS
	MEITH	MEITHS
	MEKKA	MEKKAS
	MEKOMETER	MEKOMETERS
	MEL	MELA · MELD · MELL · MELS · MELT
	MELA	MELAS
	MELALEUCA	MELALEUCAS
	MELAMINE	MELAMINES
	MELAMPODE	MELAMPODES
	MELANGE	MELANGES
	MELANIC	MELANICS
	MELANIN	MELANINS
	MELANISE	MELANISED · MELANISES
	MELANISM	MELANISMS
	MELANIST	MELANISTS
	MELANITE	MELANITES
	MELANIZE	MELANIZED · MELANIZES
	MELANO	MELANOS
	MELANOID	MELANOIDS
	MELANOMA	MELANOMAS
	MELANURIA	MELANURIAS
	MELAPHYRE	MELAPHYRES
	MELATONIN	MELATONINS
	MELD	MELDS
	MELDER	MELDERS
	MELEE	MELEES
	MELENA	MELENAS
	MELIC	MELICK · MELICS
	MELICK	MELICKS
	MELIK	MELIKS
	MELILITE	MELILITES
	MELILOT	MELILOTS
GMELINITE	MELINITE	MELINITES
GMELINITES	MELINITES	
AMELIORATE	MELIORATE	MELIORATED · MELIORATES

495

FRONT HOOK	ROOT WORD	END HOOK
	MELIORISM	MELIORISMS
	MELIORIST	MELIORISTS
	MELISMA	MELISMAS
SMELL	**MELL**	MELLS
	MELLAY	MELLAYS
SMELLED	**MELLED**	
SMELLING	**MELLING**	
	MELLITE	MELLITES
	MELLOTRON	MELLOTRONS
	MELLOW	MELLOWS ▪ MELLOWY
SMELLS	**MELLS**	
	MELOCOTON	MELOCOTONS
	MELODEON	MELODEONS
	MELODIA	MELODIAS
	MELODIC	MELODICA ▪ MELODICS
	MELODICA	MELODICAS
	MELODION	MELODIONS
	MELODISE	MELODISED ▪ MELODISER ▪ MELODISES
	MELODISER	MELODISERS
	MELODIST	MELODISTS
	MELODIZE	MELODIZED ▪ MELODIZER ▪ MELODIZES
	MELODIZER	MELODIZERS
	MELODRAMA	MELODRAMAS
	MELODRAME	MELODRAMES
	MELOID	MELOIDS
	MELOMANIA	MELOMANIAC ▪ MELOMANIAS
	MELON	MELONS
	MELONGENE	MELONGENES
	MELPHALAN	MELPHALANS
SMELT	**MELT**	MELTS ▪ MELTY
	MELTAGE	MELTAGES
	MELTDOWN	MELTDOWNS
SMELTED	**MELTED**	
	MELTEMI	MELTEMIS
SMELTER	**MELTER**	MELTERS
SMELTERS	**MELTERS**	
SMELTING	**MELTING**	MELTINGS
SMELTINGS	**MELTINGS**	
	MELTITH	MELTITHS
	MELTON	MELTONS
SMELTS	**MELTS**	
	MELTWATER	MELTWATERS
	MELUNGEON	MELUNGEONS
	MEM	MEME ▪ MEMO ▪ MEMS
	MEMBER	MEMBERS
	MEMBRANE	MEMBRANED ▪ MEMBRANES
	MEME	MEMES
	MEMENTO	MEMENTOS
	MEMO	MEMOS
	MEMOIR	MEMOIRS
	MEMOIRISM	MEMOIRISMS
	MEMOIRIST	MEMOIRISTS
	MEMORIAL	MEMORIALS
	MEMORISE	MEMORISED ▪ MEMORISER ▪ MEMORISES
	MEMORISER	MEMORISERS
	MEMORIZE	MEMORIZED ▪ MEMORIZER ▪ MEMORIZES
	MEMORIZER	MEMORIZERS
	MEMSAHIB	MEMSAHIBS
AMEN ▪ OMEN	**MEN**	MEND ▪ MENE ▪ MENG ▪ MENO ▪ MENT ▪ MENU
	MENACE	MENACED ▪ MENACER ▪ MENACES
	MENACER	MENACERS
	MENAD	MENADS
	MENADIONE	MENADIONES
AMENAGE	**MENAGE**	MENAGED ▪ MENAGES
AMENAGED	**MENAGED**	
	MENAGERIE	MENAGERIES
AMENAGES	**MENAGES**	
AMENAGING	**MENAGING**	
	MENARCHE	MENARCHES

FRONT HOOK	ROOT WORD	END HOOK
	MENAZON	MENAZONS
AMEND · EMEND	**MEND**	MENDS
AMENDABLE · EMENDABLE	**MENDABLE**	
AMENDED · EMENDED	**MENDED**	
AMENDER · EMENDER	**MENDER**	MENDERS
AMENDERS · EMENDERS	**MENDERS**	
	MENDICANT	MENDICANTS
	MENDIGO	MENDIGOS
AMENDING · EMENDING	**MENDING**	MENDINGS
AMENDS · EMENDS	**MENDS**	
AMENE	**MENE**	MENED · MENES
AMENED · OMENED	**MENED**	
	MENEER	MENEERS
	MENFOLK	MENFOLKS
	MENG	MENGE · MENGS
	MENGE	MENGED · MENGES
	MENHADEN	MENHADENS
	MENHIR	MENHIRS
	MENIAL	MENIALS
	MENILITE	MENILITES
AMENING · OMENING	**MENING**	
	MENOMINEE	MENOMINEES
	MENOMINI	MENOMINIS
	MENOPAUSE	MENOPAUSES
	MENOPOME	MENOPOMES
	MENORAH	MENORAHS
AMENORRHEA	**MENORRHEA**	MENORRHEAS
	MENSA	MENSAE · MENSAL · MENSAS
	MENSCH	MENSCHY
	MENSE	MENSED · MENSES
	MENSTRUA	MENSTRUAL
	MENSTRUUM	MENSTRUUMS
	MENSWEAR	MENSWEARS
AMENT	**MENT**	MENTA · MENTO
AMENTA · OMENTA	**MENTA**	MENTAL
AMENTAL · OMENTAL	**MENTAL**	
	MENTALESE	MENTALESES
	MENTALISM	MENTALISMS
	MENTALIST	MENTALISTS
	MENTATION	MENTATIONS
	MENTEE	MENTEES
	MENTHENE	MENTHENES
	MENTHOL	MENTHOLS
	MENTICIDE	MENTICIDES
	MENTION	MENTIONS
	MENTIONER	MENTIONERS
	MENTO	MENTOR · MENTOS
	MENTOR	MENTORS
	MENTORING	MENTORINGS
AMENTUM · OMENTUM	**MENTUM**	
	MENU	MENUS
	MENUDO	MENUDOS
	MENUISIER	MENUISIERS
	MENYIE	MENYIES
	MEOU	MEOUS
	MEOW	MEOWS
	MEPACRINE	MEPACRINES
	MEPHITIS	MEPHITISM
	MEPHITISM	MEPHITISMS
	MERANTI	MERANTIS
	MERBROMIN	MERBROMINS
	MERC	MERCH · MERCS · MERCY
	MERCAPTAN	MERCAPTANS
	MERCAT	MERCATS
AMERCER	**MERCER**	MERCERS · MERCERY
	MERCERISE	MERCERISED · MERCERISER · MERCERISES
	MERCERIZE	MERCERIZED · MERCERIZER · MERCERIZES
AMERCERS	**MERCERS**	
AMERCES	**MERCES**	

FRONT HOOK	ROOT WORD	END HOOK
	MERCHANT	MERCHANTS
	MERCHET	MERCHETS
AMERCIABLE	**MERCIABLE**	
	MERCURATE	MERCURATED ▪ MERCURATES
	MERCURIAL	MERCURIALS
	MERCURISE	MERCURISED ▪ MERCURISES
	MERCURIZE	MERCURIZED ▪ MERCURIZES
	MERDE	MERDES
	MERE	MERED ▪ MEREL ▪ MERER ▪ MERES
	MEREL	MERELL ▪ MERELS ▪ MERELY
	MERELL	MERELLS
	MERENGUE	MERENGUES
	MERES	MEREST
	MERESTONE	MERESTONES
	MERFOLK	MERFOLKS
	MERGANSER	MERGANSERS
EMERGE	**MERGE**	MERGED ▪ MERGEE ▪ MERGER ▪ MERGES
EMERGED	**MERGED**	
	MERGEE	MERGEES
EMERGENCE	**MERGENCE**	MERGENCES
EMERGENCES	**MERGENCES**	
	MERGER	MERGERS
EMERGES	**MERGES**	
EMERGING	**MERGING**	MERGINGS
	MERI	MERIL ▪ MERIS ▪ MERIT
	MERICARP	MERICARPS
	MERIDIAN	MERIDIANS
	MERIL	MERILS
	MERIMAKE	MERIMAKES
	MERING	MERINGS
	MERINGUE	MERINGUES
	MERINO	MERINOS
	MERIS	MERISM
	MERISM	MERISMS
	MERISTEM	MERISTEMS
	MERIT	MERITS
SMERK	**MERK**	MERKS
	MERKIN	MERKINS
SMERKS	**MERKS**	
	MERL	MERLE ▪ MERLS
	MERLE	MERLES
	MERLIN	MERLING ▪ MERLINS
	MERLING	MERLINGS
	MERLON	MERLONS
	MERLOT	MERLOTS
	MERMAID	MERMAIDS
	MERMAIDEN	MERMAIDENS
	MEROME	MEROMES
	MERONYM	MERONYMS ▪ MERONYMY
	MEROPIA	MEROPIAS
	MEROPIDAN	MEROPIDANS
	MEROSOME	MEROSOMES
	MEROZOITE	MEROZOITES
	MERPEOPLE	MERPEOPLES
	MERRIES	MERRIEST
	MERRIMENT	MERRIMENTS
	MERSALYL	MERSALYLS
	MERSE	MERSES
EMERSION	**MERSION**	MERSIONS
EMERSIONS	**MERSIONS**	
	MERYCISM	MERYCISMS
EMES	**MES**	MESA ▪ MESE ▪ MESH ▪ MESS
	MESA	MESAL ▪ MESAS
	MESAIL	MESAILS
	MESCAL	MESCALS
	MESCALIN	MESCALINE ▪ MESCALINS
	MESCALINE	MESCALINES
	MESCALISM	MESCALISMS
	MESCLUM	MESCLUMS

FRONT HOOK	ROOT WORD	END HOOK
	MESCLUN	MESCLUNS
	MESE	MESEL = MESES
	MESEL	MESELS
EMESES = TMESES	**MESES**	
	MESETA	MESETAS
	MESH	MESHY
	MESHING	MESHINGS
	MESHUGA	MESHUGAH = MESHUGAS
	MESHUGGA	MESHUGGAH
	MESHWORK	MESHWORKS
	MESMERISE	MESMERISED = MESMERISER = MESMERISES
	MESMERISM	MESMERISMS
	MESMERIST	MESMERISTS
	MESMERIZE	MESMERIZED = MESMERIZER = MESMERIZES
	MESNE	MESNES
	MESOBLAST	MESOBLASTS
	MESOCARP	MESOCARPS
	MESODERM	MESODERMS
	MESOGLEA	MESOGLEAL = MESOGLEAS
	MESOGLOEA	MESOGLOEAS
	MESOLITE	MESOLITES
	MESOMERE	MESOMERES
	MESOMORPH	MESOMORPHS = MESOMORPHY
	MESON	MESONS
	MESOPAUSE	MESOPAUSES
	MESOPHILE	MESOPHILES
	MESOPHYL	MESOPHYLL = MESOPHYLS
	MESOPHYLL	MESOPHYLLS
	MESOPHYTE	MESOPHYTES
	MESOSOME	MESOSOMES
	MESOTRON	MESOTRONS
	MESOZOAN	MESOZOANS
	MESPRISE	MESPRISES
	MESPRIZE	MESPRIZES
	MESQUIN	MESQUINE
	MESQUIT	MESQUITE = MESQUITS
	MESQUITE	MESQUITES
	MESS	MESSY
	MESSAGE	MESSAGED = MESSAGES
	MESSAGING	MESSAGINGS
	MESSALINE	MESSALINES
	MESSAN	MESSANS
	MESSENGER	MESSENGERS
	MESSIAH	MESSIAHS
	MESSMATE	MESSMATES
	MESSUAGE	MESSUAGES
	MESTEE	MESTEES
	MESTER	MESTERS
	MESTESO	MESTESOS
	MESTINO	MESTINOS
	MESTIZA	MESTIZAS
	MESTIZO	MESTIZOS
	MESTO	MESTOM
	MESTOM	MESTOME = MESTOMS
	MESTOME	MESTOMES
	MESTRANOL	MESTRANOLS
	MET	META = METE = METH = METS
	META	METAL
AMETABOLIC	**METABOLIC**	
	METAGE	METAGES
	METAIRIE	METAIRIES
	METAL	METALS
	METALHEAD	METALHEADS
	METALISE	METALISED = METALISES
	METALIST	METALISTS
	METALIZE	METALIZED = METALIZES
	METALLIC	METALLICS
	METALLING	METALLINGS
	METALLISE	METALLISED = METALLISES

M

FRONT HOOK	ROOT WORD	END HOOK
	METALLIST	METALLISTS
	METALLIZE	METALLIZED = METALLIZES
	METALLOID	METALLOIDS
	METALMARK	METALMARKS
	METALWARE	METALWARES
	METALWORK	METALWORKS
	METAMALE	METAMALES
	METAMER	METAMERE = METAMERS
	METAMERE	METAMERES
	METANOIA	METANOIAS
	METAPHASE	METAPHASES
	METAPHOR	METAPHORS
	METAPLASM	METAPLASMS
	METARCHON	METARCHONS
	METASOMA	METASOMAS
	METATAG	METATAGS
	METATE	METATES
	METAXYLEM	METAXYLEMS
	METAYAGE	METAYAGES
	METAYER	METAYERS
	METAZOA	METAZOAL = METAZOAN
	METAZOAN	METAZOANS
	METCAST	METCASTS
	METE	METED = METER = METES
	METEOR	METEORS
	METEORISM	METEORISMS
	METEORIST	METEORISTS
	METEORITE	METEORITES
	METEOROID	METEOROIDS
	METEPA	METEPAS
	METER	METERS
	METERAGE	METERAGES
	METESTICK	METESTICKS
	METEWAND	METEWANDS
	METEYARD	METEYARDS
	METFORMIN	METFORMINS
	METH	METHO = METHS
	METHADON	METHADONE = METHADONS
	METHADONE	METHADONES
	METHANAL	METHANALS
	METHANE	METHANES
	METHANOL	METHANOLS
	METHEGLIN	METHEGLINS
	METHINK	METHINKS
	METHO	METHOD = METHOS
	METHOD	METHODS
	METHODISE	METHODISED = METHODISER = METHODISES
	METHODISM	METHODISMS
	METHODIST	METHODISTS
	METHODIZE	METHODIZED = METHODIZER = METHODIZES
	METHOXIDE	METHOXIDES
	METHOXY	METHOXYL
	METHYL	METHYLS
	METHYLAL	METHYLALS
	METHYLASE	METHYLASES
	METHYLATE	METHYLATED = METHYLATES
	METHYLENE	METHYLENES
EMETIC	METIC	METICS
EMETICAL	METICAL	METICALS
EMETICS	METICS	
	METIER	METIERS
	METIF	METIFS
	METISSE	METISSES
	METOL	METOLS
	METONYM	METONYMS = METONYMY
	METOPE	METOPES
	METOPISM	METOPISMS
	METOPON	METOPONS
	METOPRYL	METOPRYLS

FRONT HOOK	ROOT WORD	END HOOK
	METRALGIA	METRALGIAS
	METRAZOL	METRAZOLS
	METRE	METRED = METRES
	METRIC	METRICS
	METRICATE	METRICATED = METRICATES
	METRICIAN	METRICIANS
	METRICISE	METRICISED = METRICISES
	METRICISM	METRICISMS
	METRICIST	METRICISTS
	METRICIZE	METRICIZED = METRICIZES
	METRIFIER	METRIFIERS
	METRIST	METRISTS
	METRO	METROS
	METRONOME	METRONOMES
	METTLE	METTLED = METTLES
	METUMP	METUMPS
EMEU	**MEU**	MEUS
EMEUS	**MEUS**	MEUSE
SMEUSE	**MEUSE**	MEUSED = MEUSES
SMEUSES	**MEUSES**	
	MEVE	MEVED = MEVES
	MEVROU	MEVROUS
SMEW	**MEW**	MEWL = MEWS
	MEWL	MEWLS
	MEWLER	MEWLERS
SMEWS	**MEWS**	
	MEZAIL	MEZAILS
	MEZCAL	MEZCALS
	MEZCALINE	MEZCALINES
	MEZE	MEZES
	MEZEREON	MEZEREONS
	MEZEREUM	MEZEREUMS
	MEZQUIT	MEZQUITE = MEZQUITS
	MEZQUITE	MEZQUITES
	MEZUZA	MEZUZAH = MEZUZAS
	MEZUZAH	MEZUZAHS
	MEZUZOT	MEZUZOTH
	MEZZ	MEZZE = MEZZO
	MEZZALUNA	MEZZALUNAS
	MEZZANINE	MEZZANINES
	MEZZE	MEZZES
	MEZZO	MEZZOS
	MEZZOTINT	MEZZOTINTO = MEZZOTINTS
	MGANGA	MGANGAS
	MHO	MHOS
	MHORR	MHORRS
AMI	**MI**	MIB = MIC = MID = MIG = MIL = MIM = MIR MIS = MIX = MIZ
	MIAOU	MIAOUS
	MIAOW	MIAOWS
	MIASM	MIASMA = MIASMS
	MIASMA	MIASMAL = MIASMAS
	MIAUL	MIAULS
	MIB	MIBS
EMIC	**MIC**	MICA = MICE = MICH = MICK = MICO = MICS
	MICA	MICAS
EMICATE	**MICATE**	MICATED = MICATES
EMICATED	**MICATED**	
EMICATES	**MICATES**	
EMICATING	**MICATING**	
	MICAWBER	MICAWBERS
AMICE	**MICE**	
	MICELL	MICELLA = MICELLE = MICELLS
	MICELLA	MICELLAE = MICELLAR = MICELLAS
	MICELLE	MICELLES
	MICH	MICHE = MICHT
	MICHE	MICHED = MICHER = MICHES
	MICHER	MICHERS
	MICHIGAN	MICHIGANS

FRONT HOOK	ROOT WORD	END HOOK
	MICHING	MICHINGS
	MICHT	MICHTS
	MICK	MICKS (offensive) ▪ MICKY
	MICKEY	MICKEYS
	MICKLE	MICKLER ▪ MICKLES
	MICKLES	MICKLEST
	MICO	MICOS
	MICRO	MICRON ▪ MICROS
	MICROBAR	MICROBARS
	MICROBE	MICROBES
	MICROBEAM	MICROBEAMS
	MICROBREW	MICROBREWS
	MICROCAR	MICROCARD ▪ MICROCARS
	MICROCARD	MICROCARDS
	MICROCHIP	MICROCHIPS
	MICROCODE	MICROCODES
	MICROCOSM	MICROCOSMS
	MICROCYTE	MICROCYTES
	MICRODOT	MICRODOTS
	MICROFILM	MICROFILMS
	MICROFORM	MICROFORMS
	MICROGLIA	MICROGLIAS
	MICROGRAM	MICROGRAMS
	MICROHM	MICROHMS
	MICROJET	MICROJETS
	MICROLITE	MICROLITER ▪ MICROLITES
	MICROLITH	MICROLITHS
	MICROLOAN	MICROLOANS
	MICROMERE	MICROMERES
	MICROMHO	MICROMHOS
	MICROMINI	MICROMINIS
	MICROMOLE	MICROMOLES
OMICRON	MICRON	MICRONS
	MICRONISE	MICRONISED ▪ MICRONISES
	MICRONIZE	MICRONIZED ▪ MICRONIZES
OMICRONS	MICRONS	
	MICROPORE	MICROPORES
	MICROPSIA	MICROPSIAS
	MICROPUMP	MICROPUMPS
	MICROPYLE	MICROPYLES
	MICROSITE	MICROSITES
	MICROSOME	MICROSOMES
	MICROTOME	MICROTOMES
	MICROTONE	MICROTONES
	MICROVOLT	MICROVOLTS
	MICROWATT	MICROWATTS
	MICROWAVE	MICROWAVED ▪ MICROWAVES
	MICROWIRE	MICROWIRES
EMICTION	MICTION	MICTIONS
EMICTIONS	MICTIONS	
	MICTURATE	MICTURATED ▪ MICTURATES
AMID ▪ IMID	MID	MIDI ▪ MIDS
	MIDAIR	MIDAIRS
	MIDBRAIN	MIDBRAINS
	MIDCULT	MIDCULTS
	MIDDAY	MIDDAYS
	MIDDEN	MIDDENS
	MIDDIE	MIDDIES
SMIDDIES	MIDDIES	
	MIDDLE	MIDDLED ▪ MIDDLER ▪ MIDDLES
	MIDDLER	MIDDLERS
	MIDDLING	MIDDLINGS
SMIDDY	MIDDY	
	MIDFIELD	MIDFIELDS
SMIDGE	MIDGE	MIDGES ▪ MIDGET
SMIDGES	MIDGES	
	MIDGET	MIDGETS
	MIDGIE	MIDGIER ▪ MIDGIES
	MIDGIES	MIDGIEST

FRONT HOOK	ROOT WORD	END HOOK
	MIDGUT	MIDGUTS
	MIDI	MIDIS
	MIDINETTE	MIDINETTES
	MIDIRON	MIDIRONS
	MIDISKIRT	MIDISKIRTS
	MIDLAND	MIDLANDS
	MIDLEG	MIDLEGS
	MIDLIFE	MIDLIFER
	MIDLIFER	MIDLIFERS
	MIDLINE	MIDLINES
	MIDLIST	MIDLISTS
	MIDMONTH	MIDMONTHS
AMIDMOST	**MIDMOST**	MIDMOSTS
	MIDNIGHT	MIDNIGHTS
	MIDNOON	MIDNOONS
	MIDPOINT	MIDPOINTS
	MIDRANGE	MIDRANGES
	MIDRASHOT	MIDRASHOTH
	MIDRIB	MIDRIBS
	MIDRIFF	MIDRIFFS
AMIDS - IMIDS	**MIDS**	MIDST
AMIDSHIP	**MIDSHIP**	MIDSHIPS
AMIDSHIPS	**MIDSHIPS**	
	MIDSIZE	MIDSIZED
	MIDSOLE	MIDSOLES
	MIDSPACE	MIDSPACES
AMIDST	**MIDST**	MIDSTS
	MIDSTREAM	MIDSTREAMS
	MIDSUMMER	MIDSUMMERS
	MIDTERM	MIDTERMS
	MIDTOWN	MIDTOWNS
	MIDWAY	MIDWAYS
	MIDWEEK	MIDWEEKS
	MIDWIFE	MIDWIFED - MIDWIFES
	MIDWINTER	MIDWINTERS
	MIDWIVE	MIDWIVED - MIDWIVES
	MIDYEAR	MIDYEARS
	MIELIE	MIELIES
	MIEN	MIENS
	MIEVE	MIEVED - MIEVES
	MIFF	MIFFS - MIFFY
	MIG	MIGG - MIGS
	MIGG	MIGGS
	MIGGLE	MIGGLES
SMIGHT	**MIGHT**	MIGHTS - MIGHTY
SMIGHTS	**MIGHTS**	MIGHTST
	MIGMATITE	MIGMATITES
	MIGNON	MIGNONS
	MIGNONNE	MIGNONNES
	MIGRAINE	MIGRAINES
EMIGRANT	**MIGRANT**	MIGRANTS
EMIGRANTS	**MIGRANTS**	
EMIGRATE	**MIGRATE**	MIGRATED - MIGRATES
EMIGRATED	**MIGRATED**	
EMIGRATES	**MIGRATES**	
EMIGRATING	**MIGRATING**	
EMIGRATION	**MIGRATION**	MIGRATIONS
	MIGRATOR	MIGRATORS - MIGRATORY
EMIGRATORY	**MIGRATORY**	
	MIHI	MIHIS
	MIHRAB	MIHRABS
	MIJNHEER	MIJNHEERS
	MIKADO	MIKADOS
	MIKE	MIKED - MIKES
OMIKRON	**MIKRON**	MIKRONS
OMIKRONS	**MIKRONS**	
	MIKVAH	MIKVAHS
	MIKVEH	MIKVEHS
	MIKVOT	MIKVOTH

FRONT HOOK	ROOT WORD	END HOOK
	MIL	MILD = MILE = MILK = MILL = MILO MILS = MILT
	MILADI	MILADIS
	MILAGE	MILAGES
	MILD	MILDS
	MILDEN	MILDENS
	MILDEW	MILDEWS = MILDEWY
SMILE	**MILE**	MILER = MILES
	MILEAGE	MILEAGES
	MILEPOST	MILEPOSTS
SMILER	**MILER**	MILERS
SMILERS	**MILERS**	
SMILES	**MILES**	
	MILESIMO	MILESIMOS
	MILESTONE	MILESTONES
	MILFOIL	MILFOILS
	MILIARIA	MILIARIAL = MILIARIAS
	MILIEU	MILIEUS = MILIEUX
	MILITANCE	MILITANCES
	MILITANT	MILITANTS
	MILITAR	MILITARY
	MILITATE	MILITATED = MILITATES
	MILITIA	MILITIAS
	MILK	MILKO = MILKS = MILKY
	MILKER	MILKERS
	MILKING	MILKINGS
	MILKMAID	MILKMAIDS
	MILKO	MILKOS
	MILKSHAKE	MILKSHAKES
	MILKSHED	MILKSHEDS
	MILKSOP	MILKSOPS
	MILKTOAST	MILKTOASTS
	MILKWEED	MILKWEEDS
	MILKWOOD	MILKWOODS
	MILKWORT	MILKWORTS
	MILL	MILLE = MILLS
	MILLAGE	MILLAGES
	MILLBOARD	MILLBOARDS
	MILLCAKE	MILLCAKES
	MILLDAM	MILLDAMS
	MILLE	MILLED = MILLER = MILLES = MILLET
	MILLENNIA	MILLENNIAL
	MILLEPED	MILLEPEDE = MILLEPEDS
	MILLEPEDE	MILLEPEDES
	MILLEPORE	MILLEPORES
	MILLER	MILLERS
	MILLERITE	MILLERITES
	MILLET	MILLETS
	MILLHOUSE	MILLHOUSES
	MILLIARD	MILLIARDS
	MILLIARE	MILLIARES
	MILLIBAR	MILLIBARS
	MILLIE	MILLIER = MILLIES *(offensive)*
	MILLIEME	MILLIEMES
	MILLIER	MILLIERS
	MILLIGAL	MILLIGALS
	MILLIGRAM	MILLIGRAMS
	MILLIME	MILLIMES
	MILLIMHO	MILLIMHOS
	MILLIMOLE	MILLIMOLES
	MILLINE	MILLINER = MILLINES
	MILLINER	MILLINERS = MILLINERY
	MILLING	MILLINGS
	MILLIOHM	MILLIOHMS
	MILLION	MILLIONS
	MILLIONTH	MILLIONTHS
	MILLIPED	MILLIPEDE = MILLIPEDS
	MILLIPEDE	MILLIPEDES
	MILLIREM	MILLIREMS

FRONT HOOK	ROOT WORD	END HOOK
	MILLIVOLT	MILLIVOLTS
	MILLIWATT	MILLIWATTS
	MILLOCRAT	MILLOCRATS
	MILLPOND	MILLPONDS
	MILLRACE	MILLRACES
	MILLRIND	MILLRINDS
	MILLRUN	MILLRUNS
	MILLSCALE	MILLSCALES
	MILLSTONE	MILLSTONES
	MILLTAIL	MILLTAILS
	MILLWHEEL	MILLWHEELS
	MILLWORK	MILLWORKS
	MILNEB	MILNEBS
	MILO	MILOR ▪ MILOS
	MILOMETER	MILOMETERS
	MILOR	MILORD ▪ MILORS
	MILORD	MILORDS
	MILPA	MILPAS
	MILSEY	MILSEYS
	MILT	MILTS ▪ MILTY ▪ MILTZ
	MILTER	MILTERS
	MILTONIA	MILTONIAS
	MIM	MIME
	MIMBAR	MIMBARS
	MIME	MIMED ▪ MIMEO ▪ MIMER ▪ MIMES
	MIMEO	MIMEOS
	MIMER	MIMERS
	MIMESTER	MIMESTERS
	MIMETITE	MIMETITES
	MIMIC	MIMICS
	MIMICKER	MIMICKERS
	MIMMICK	MIMMICKS
	MIMOSA	MIMOSAS
	MINA	MINAE ▪ MINAR ▪ MINAS
	MINAR	MINARS
	MINARET	MINARETS
	MINBAR	MINBARS
	MINCE	MINCED ▪ MINCER ▪ MINCES
	MINCEMEAT	MINCEMEATS
	MINCER	MINCERS
	MINCING	MINCINGS
	MIND	MINDS
	MINDER	MINDERS
	MINDFUCK	MINDFUCKS (offensive)
	MINDING	MINDINGS
	MINDSET	MINDSETS
	MINDSHARE	MINDSHARES
AMINE ▪ IMINE	MINE	MINED ▪ MINER ▪ MINES
	MINEFIELD	MINEFIELDS
	MINELAYER	MINELAYERS
	MINEOLA	MINEOLAS
	MINER	MINERS
	MINERAL	MINERALS
AMINES ▪ IMINES	MINES	
	MINESHAFT	MINESHAFTS
	MINESTONE	MINESTONES
	MINETTE	MINETTES
	MINEVER	MINEVERS
	MING	MINGE ▪ MINGS ▪ MINGY
	MINGE	MINGED ▪ MINGER ▪ MINGES (offensive)
	MINGER	MINGERS (offensive)
	MINGIN	MINGING
	MINGLE	MINGLED ▪ MINGLER ▪ MINGLES
	MINGLER	MINGLERS
	MINGLING	MINGLINGS
	MINI	MINIM ▪ MINIS
	MINIATE	MINIATED ▪ MINIATES
	MINIATION	MINIATIONS
	MINIATURE	MINIATURED ▪ MINIATURES

FRONT HOOK	ROOT WORD	END HOOK
	MINIBAR	MINIBARS
	MINIBIKE	MINIBIKER · MINIBIKES
	MINIBIKER	MINIBIKERS
	MINIBREAK	MINIBREAKS
	MINICAB	MINICABS
	MINICAM	MINICAMP · MINICAMS
	MINICAMP	MINICAMPS
	MINICAR	MINICARS
	MINICOM	MINICOMS
	MINIDISC	MINIDISCS
	MINIDISK	MINIDISKS
	MINIKIN	MINIKINS
	MINILAB	MINILABS
	MINIM	MINIMA · MINIMS
	MINIMA	MINIMAL · MINIMAX
	MINIMAL	MINIMALS
	MINIMENT	MINIMENTS
	MINIMILL	MINIMILLS
	MINIMISE	MINIMISED · MINIMISER · MINIMISES
	MINIMISER	MINIMISERS
	MINIMISM	MINIMISMS
	MINIMIST	MINIMISTS
	MINIMIZE	MINIMIZED · MINIMIZER · MINIMIZES
	MINIMIZER	MINIMIZERS
	MINIMOTO	MINIMOTOS
	MINIMUM	MINIMUMS
	MINING	MININGS
	MINION	MINIONS
	MINIPARK	MINIPARKS
	MINIPILL	MINIPILLS
	MINIS	MINISH
	MINISCULE	MINISCULES
	MINISKI	MINISKIS
	MINISKIRT	MINISKIRTS
	MINISTATE	MINISTATES
	MINISTER	MINISTERS
	MINITOWER	MINITOWERS
	MINITRACK	MINITRACKS
	MINIUM	MINIUMS
	MINIVAN	MINIVANS
	MINIVER	MINIVERS
	MINIVET	MINIVETS
	MINK	MINKE · MINKS
	MINKE	MINKES
	MINNEOLA	MINNEOLAS
	MINNICK	MINNICKS
	MINNIE	MINNIES
	MINNOCK	MINNOCKS
	MINNOW	MINNOWS
AMINO · IMINO	MINO	MINOR · MINOS
	MINOR	MINORS
	MINORCA	MINORCAS
	MINORSHIP	MINORSHIPS
	MINOXIDIL	MINOXIDILS
	MINSHUKU	MINSHUKUS
	MINSTER	MINSTERS
	MINSTREL	MINSTRELS
	MINSTRELS	MINSTRELSY
	MINT	MINTS · MINTY
	MINTAGE	MINTAGES
	MINTER	MINTERS
	MINUEND	MINUENDS
	MINUET	MINUETS
	MINUSCULE	MINUSCULES
	MINUTE	MINUTED · MINUTER · MINUTES
	MINUTES	MINUTEST
	MINUTIA	MINUTIAE · MINUTIAL
	MINYAN	MINYANS
	MIOMBO	MIOMBOS

FRONT HOOK	ROOT WORD	END HOOK
	MIOTIC	MIOTICS
	MIQUELET	MIQUELETS
AMIR ▪ EMIR ▪ SMIR	**MIR**	MIRE ▪ MIRI ▪ MIRK ▪ MIRO ▪ MIRS
		MIRV ▪ MIRY
	MIRABELLE	MIRABELLES
	MIRACIDIA	MIRACIDIAL
	MIRACLE	MIRACLES
	MIRADOR	MIRADORS
	MIRAGE	MIRAGES
	MIRANDISE	MIRANDISED ▪ MIRANDISES
	MIRANDIZE	MIRANDIZED ▪ MIRANDIZES
	MIRBANE	MIRBANES
	MIRE	MIRED ▪ MIRES ▪ MIREX
	MIRI	MIRIN
	MIRIN	MIRING ▪ MIRINS
	MIRITI	MIRITIS
SMIRK	**MIRK**	MIRKS ▪ MIRKY
SMIRKER	**MIRKER**	
SMIRKIER	**MIRKIER**	
SMIRKIEST	**MIRKIEST**	
SMIRKILY	**MIRKILY**	
SMIRKS	**MIRKS**	
SMIRKY	**MIRKY**	
	MIRLITON	MIRLITONS
	MIRROR	MIRRORS
AMIRS ▪ EMIRS ▪ SMIRS	**MIRS**	
	MIRTH	MIRTHS
	MIRV	MIRVS
	MIRZA	MIRZAS
AMIS	**MIS**	MISE ▪ MISO ▪ MISS ▪ MIST
	MISACT	MISACTS
	MISADAPT	MISADAPTS
	MISADD	MISADDS
	MISADJUST	MISADJUSTS
	MISADVICE	MISADVICES
	MISADVISE	MISADVISED ▪ MISADVISES
	MISAGENT	MISAGENTS
	MISAIM	MISAIMS
	MISALIGN	MISALIGNS
	MISALLEGE	MISALLEGED ▪ MISALLEGES
	MISALLOT	MISALLOTS
	MISALTER	MISALTERS
	MISARRAY	MISARRAYS
	MISASSAY	MISASSAYS
	MISASSIGN	MISASSIGNS
	MISATONE	MISATONED ▪ MISATONES
	MISAUNTER	MISAUNTERS
	MISAVER	MISAVERS
	MISAWARD	MISAWARDS
	MISBECOME	MISBECOMES
	MISBEGIN	MISBEGINS
	MISBEHAVE	MISBEHAVED ▪ MISBEHAVER ▪ MISBEHAVES
	MISBELIEF	MISBELIEFS
	MISBESEEM	MISBESEEMS
	MISBESTOW	MISBESTOWS
	MISBILL	MISBILLS
	MISBIND	MISBINDS
	MISBIRTH	MISBIRTHS
	MISBRAND	MISBRANDS
	MISBUILD	MISBUILDS
	MISBUTTON	MISBUTTONS
	MISCALL	MISCALLS
	MISCALLER	MISCALLERS
	MISCAST	MISCASTS
	MISCEGEN	MISCEGENE ▪ MISCEGENS
	MISCEGENE	MISCEGENES
	MISCEGINE	MISCEGINES
	MISCHANCE	MISCHANCED ▪ MISCHANCES
	MISCHARGE	MISCHARGED ▪ MISCHARGES

FRONT HOOK	ROOT WORD	END HOOK
	MISCHIEF	MISCHIEFS
	MISCHOICE	MISCHOICES
	MISCHOOSE	MISCHOOSES
	MISCHOSE	MISCHOSEN
	MISCITE	MISCITED · MISCITES
	MISCLAIM	MISCLAIMS
	MISCODE	MISCODED · MISCODES
	MISCOIN	MISCOINS
	MISCOLOR	MISCOLORS
	MISCOLOUR	MISCOLOURS
	MISCOOK	MISCOOKS
	MISCOUNT	MISCOUNTS
	MISCREANT	MISCREANTS
	MISCREATE	MISCREATED · MISCREATES
	MISCREDIT	MISCREDITS
	MISCREED	MISCREEDS
	MISCUE	MISCUED · MISCUES
	MISCUT	MISCUTS
	MISDATE	MISDATED · MISDATES
	MISDEAL	MISDEALS · MISDEALT
	MISDEALER	MISDEALERS
	MISDEED	MISDEEDS
	MISDEEM	MISDEEMS
	MISDEFINE	MISDEFINED · MISDEFINES
	MISDEMEAN	MISDEMEANS
	MISDESERT	MISDESERTS
	MISDIAL	MISDIALS
	MISDIET	MISDIETS
	MISDIRECT	MISDIRECTS
	MISDIVIDE	MISDIVIDED · MISDIVIDES
	MISDOER	MISDOERS
	MISDOING	MISDOINGS
	MISDOUBT	MISDOUBTS
	MISDRAW	MISDRAWN · MISDRAWS
	MISDREAD	MISDREADS
	MISDRIVE	MISDRIVEN · MISDRIVES
	MISE	MISER · MISES
	MISEASE	MISEASES
	MISEAT	MISEATS
	MISEDIT	MISEDITS
	MISEMPLOY	MISEMPLOYS
	MISENROL	MISENROLL · MISENROLS
	MISENROLL	MISENROLLS
	MISENTER	MISENTERS
	MISER	MISERE · MISERS · MISERY
	MISERABLE	MISERABLES
	MISERE	MISERES
	MISERERE	MISERERES
AMISES	**MISES**	
	MISESTEEM	MISESTEEMS
	MISEVENT	MISEVENTS
	MISFAITH	MISFAITHS
	MISFALL	MISFALLS
	MISFARE	MISFARED · MISFARES
	MISFARING	MISFARINGS
	MISFEASOR	MISFEASORS
	MISFEED	MISFEEDS
	MISFEIGN	MISFEIGNS
	MISFIELD	MISFIELDS
	MISFILE	MISFILED · MISFILES
	MISFIRE	MISFIRED · MISFIRES
	MISFIT	MISFITS
	MISFORM	MISFORMS
	MISFRAME	MISFRAMED · MISFRAMES
	MISGAUGE	MISGAUGED · MISGAUGES
	MISGIVE	MISGIVEN · MISGIVES
	MISGIVING	MISGIVINGS
	MISGOVERN	MISGOVERNS
	MISGRADE	MISGRADED · MISGRADES

FRONT HOOK	ROOT WORD	END HOOK
	MISGRAFT	MISGRAFTS
	MISGROW	MISGROWN - MISGROWS
	MISGROWTH	MISGROWTHS
	MISGUGGLE	MISGUGGLED - MISGUGGLES
	MISGUIDE	MISGUIDED - MISGUIDER - MISGUIDES
	MISGUIDER	MISGUIDERS
	MISHANDLE	MISHANDLED - MISHANDLES
	MISHANTER	MISHANTERS
	MISHAP	MISHAPS - MISHAPT
	MISHAPPEN	MISHAPPENS
	MISHEAR	MISHEARD - MISHEARS
	MISHIT	MISHITS
	MISHMEE	MISHMEES
	MISHMI	MISHMIS
	MISINFER	MISINFERS
	MISINFORM	MISINFORMS
	MISINTEND	MISINTENDS
	MISINTER	MISINTERS
	MISJOIN	MISJOINS
	MISJUDGE	MISJUDGED - MISJUDGER - MISJUDGES
	MISJUDGER	MISJUDGERS
	MISKAL	MISKALS
	MISKEEP	MISKEEPS
	MISKEN	MISKENS - MISKENT
	MISKEY	MISKEYS
	MISKICK	MISKICKS
	MISKNOW	MISKNOWN - MISKNOWS
	MISLABEL	MISLABELS
	MISLABOR	MISLABORS
	MISLAY	MISLAYS
	MISLAYER	MISLAYERS
	MISLEAD	MISLEADS
	MISLEADER	MISLEADERS
	MISLEARN	MISLEARNS - MISLEARNT
	MISLEEKE	MISLEEKED - MISLEEKES
	MISLETOE	MISLETOES
	MISLIE	MISLIES
	MISLIGHT	MISLIGHTS
	MISLIKE	MISLIKED - MISLIKER - MISLIKES
	MISLIKER	MISLIKERS
	MISLIKING	MISLIKINGS
	MISLIPPEN	MISLIPPENS
	MISLIVE	MISLIVED - MISLIVES
	MISLOCATE	MISLOCATED - MISLOCATES
	MISLODGE	MISLODGED - MISLODGES
	MISLUCK	MISLUCKS
	MISMAKE	MISMAKES
	MISMANAGE	MISMANAGED - MISMANAGER - MISMANAGES
	MISMARK	MISMARKS
	MISMATE	MISMATED - MISMATES
	MISMEET	MISMEETS
	MISMETRE	MISMETRED - MISMETRES
	MISMOVE	MISMOVED - MISMOVES
	MISNAME	MISNAMED - MISNAMES
	MISNOMER	MISNOMERS
	MISNUMBER	MISNUMBERS
	MISO	MISOS
	MISONEISM	MISONEISMS
	MISONEIST	MISONEISTS
	MISORDER	MISORDERS
	MISORIENT	MISORIENTS
	MISPAGE	MISPAGED - MISPAGES
	MISPAINT	MISPAINTS
	MISPARSE	MISPARSED - MISPARSES
	MISPART	MISPARTS
	MISPEN	MISPENS
	MISPHRASE	MISPHRASED - MISPHRASES
	MISPICKEL	MISPICKELS
	MISPLACE	MISPLACED - MISPLACES

FRONT HOOK	ROOT WORD	END HOOK
	MISPLAN	MISPLANS · MISPLANT
	MISPLANT	MISPLANTS
	MISPLAY	MISPLAYS
	MISPLEAD	MISPLEADS
	MISPLEASE	MISPLEASED · MISPLEASES
	MISPOINT	MISPOINTS
	MISPOISE	MISPOISED · MISPOISES
	MISPRAISE	MISPRAISED · MISPRAISES
	MISPRICE	MISPRICED · MISPRICES
	MISPRINT	MISPRINTS
	MISPRISE	MISPRISED · MISPRISES
	MISPRIZE	MISPRIZED · MISPRIZER · MISPRIZES
	MISPRIZER	MISPRIZERS
	MISQUOTE	MISQUOTED · MISQUOTER · MISQUOTES
	MISQUOTER	MISQUOTERS
	MISRAISE	MISRAISED · MISRAISES
	MISRATE	MISRATED · MISRATES
	MISREAD	MISREADS
	MISRECKON	MISRECKONS
	MISRECORD	MISRECORDS
	MISREFER	MISREFERS
	MISREGARD	MISREGARDS
	MISRELATE	MISRELATED · MISRELATES
	MISRENDER	MISRENDERS
	MISREPORT	MISREPORTS
	MISROUTE	MISROUTED · MISROUTES
	MISRULE	MISRULED · MISRULES
AMISS	**MISS**	MISSA · MISSY
	MISSA	MISSAE · MISSAL · MISSAW · MISSAY
	MISSAL	MISSALS
	MISSAY	MISSAYS
	MISSAYING	MISSAYINGS
	MISSEAT	MISSEATS
	MISSEE	MISSEEM · MISSEEN · MISSEES
	MISSEEM	MISSEEMS
	MISSEL	MISSELS
	MISSEND	MISSENDS
	MISSENSE	MISSENSES
AMISSES	**MISSES**	
	MISSET	MISSETS
	MISSHAPE	MISSHAPED · MISSHAPEN · MISSHAPER MISSHAPES
	MISSHAPER	MISSHAPERS
	MISSHOOD	MISSHOODS
	MISSIES	MISSIEST
EMISSILE	**MISSILE**	MISSILES
	MISSILEER	MISSILEERS
AMISSING	**MISSING**	
EMISSION · OMISSION	**MISSION**	MISSIONS
	MISSIONER	MISSIONERS
EMISSIONS · OMISSIONS	**MISSIONS**	
	MISSIS	MISSISH
EMISSIVE · OMISSIVE	**MISSIVE**	MISSIVES
	MISSORT	MISSORTS
	MISSOUND	MISSOUNDS
	MISSOUT	MISSOUTS
	MISSPACE	MISSPACED · MISSPACES
	MISSPEAK	MISSPEAKS
	MISSPELL	MISSPELLS
	MISSPEND	MISSPENDS
	MISSPOKE	MISSPOKEN
	MISSTAMP	MISSTAMPS
	MISSTART	MISSTARTS
	MISSTATE	MISSTATED · MISSTATES
	MISSTEER	MISSTEERS
	MISSTEP	MISSTEPS
	MISSTOP	MISSTOPS
	MISSTRIKE	MISSTRIKES
	MISSTYLE	MISSTYLED · MISSTYLES

FRONT HOOK	ROOT WORD	END HOOK
	MISSUIT	MISSUITS
	MIST	MISTS • MISTY
	MISTAKE	MISTAKEN • MISTAKER • MISTAKES
	MISTAKER	MISTAKERS
	MISTAKING	MISTAKINGS
	MISTAL	MISTALS
	MISTBOW	MISTBOWS
	MISTELL	MISTELLS
	MISTEMPER	MISTEMPERS
	MISTEND	MISTENDS
	MISTER	MISTERM • MISTERS • MISTERY
	MISTERM	MISTERMS
	MISTHINK	MISTHINKS
	MISTHROW	MISTHROWN • MISTHROWS
	MISTICO	MISTICOS
	MISTIME	MISTIMED • MISTIMES
	MISTING	MISTINGS
	MISTITLE	MISTITLED • MISTITLES
	MISTLE	MISTLED • MISTLES
	MISTLETOE	MISTLETOES
	MISTRACE	MISTRACED • MISTRACES
	MISTRAIN	MISTRAINS
	MISTRAL	MISTRALS
	MISTREAT	MISTREATS
	MISTRIAL	MISTRIALS
	MISTRUST	MISTRUSTS
	MISTRUTH	MISTRUTHS
	MISTRYST	MISTRYSTS
	MISTUNE	MISTUNED • MISTUNES
	MISTUTOR	MISTUTORS
	MISTYPE	MISTYPED • MISTYPES
	MISUNION	MISUNIONS
	MISUSAGE	MISUSAGES
	MISUSE	MISUSED • MISUSER • MISUSES
	MISUSER	MISUSERS
	MISVALUE	MISVALUED • MISVALUES
	MISWEEN	MISWEENS
	MISWEND	MISWENDS
	MISWORD	MISWORDS
	MISWRIT	MISWRITE
	MISWRITE	MISWRITES
	MISYOKE	MISYOKED • MISYOKES
SMITE	**MITE**	MITER • MITES
SMITER	**MITER**	MITERS
	MITERER	MITERERS
SMITERS	**MITERS**	
	MITERWORT	MITERWORTS
SMITES	**MITES**	
	MITHER	MITHERS
SMITHERS	**MITHERS**	
	MITICIDE	MITICIDES
	MITIGATE	MITIGATED • MITIGATES
	MITIGATOR	MITIGATORS • MITIGATORY
	MITOGEN	MITOGENS
	MITOMYCIN	MITOMYCINS
AMITOSES	**MITOSES**	
AMITOSIS	**MITOSIS**	
AMITOTIC	**MITOTIC**	
	MITRAILLE	MITRAILLES
	MITRE	MITRED • MITRES
	MITREWORT	MITREWORTS
	MITSVAH	MITSVAHS
	MITT	MITTS
SMITTEN	**MITTEN**	MITTENS
	MITUMBA	MITUMBAS
AMITY	**MITY**	
	MITZVAH	MITZVAHS
	MIX	MIXT • MIXY
	MIXDOWN	MIXDOWNS

511

FRONT HOOK	ROOT WORD	END HOOK
	MIXEN	MIXENS
	MIXER	MIXERS
	MIXMASTER	MIXMASTERS
	MIXT	MIXTE
	MIXTION	MIXTIONS
	MIXTURE	MIXTURES
	MIXUP	MIXUPS
	MIZ	MIZZ
	MIZEN	MIZENS
	MIZENMAST	MIZENMASTS
	MIZMAZE	MIZMAZES
	MIZUNA	MIZUNAS
	MIZZ	MIZZY
	MIZZEN	MIZZENS
	MIZZLE	MIZZLED · MIZZLES
	MIZZLING	MIZZLINGS
	MIZZONITE	MIZZONITES
HMM · UMM	**MM**	
	MNA	MNAS
	MNEME	MNEMES
	MNEMON	MNEMONS
	MNEMONIC	MNEMONICS
	MNEMONIST	MNEMONISTS
EMO	**MO**	MOA · MOB · MOC · MOD · MOE · MOG · MOI
		MOL · MOM · MON · MOO · MOP · MOR · MOS
		MOT · MOU · MOW · MOY · MOZ
	MOA	MOAI · MOAN · MOAS · MOAT
	MOAN	MOANS
	MOANER	MOANERS
	MOANING	MOANINGS
	MOAT	MOATS
	MOB	MOBE · MOBS · MOBY
	MOBBER	MOBBERS
	MOBBIE	MOBBIES
	MOBBING	MOBBINGS
	MOBBISM	MOBBISMS
	MOBBLE	MOBBLED · MOBBLES
	MOBCAP	MOBCAPS
	MOBE	MOBES
	MOBIE	MOBIES
	MOBILE	MOBILES
	MOBILISE	MOBILISED · MOBILISER · MOBILISES
	MOBILISER	MOBILISERS
	MOBILIZE	MOBILIZED · MOBILIZER · MOBILIZES
	MOBILIZER	MOBILIZERS
	MOBLE	MOBLED · MOBLES
	MOBLOG	MOBLOGS
	MOBLOGGER	MOBLOGGERS
	MOBOCRAT	MOBOCRATS
	MOBSTER	MOBSTERS
	MOC	MOCH · MOCK · MOCS
	MOCASSIN	MOCASSINS
	MOCCASIN	MOCCASINS
	MOCH	MOCHA · MOCHS · MOCHY
	MOCHA	MOCHAS
	MOCHELL	MOCHELLS
	MOCHIE	MOCHIER
	MOCHILA	MOCHILAS
SMOCK	**MOCK**	MOCKS
	MOCKAGE	MOCKAGES
SMOCKED	**MOCKED**	
	MOCKER	MOCKERS · MOCKERY
	MOCKERNUT	MOCKERNUTS
SMOCKING	**MOCKING**	MOCKINGS
SMOCKINGS	**MOCKINGS**	
	MOCKNEY	MOCKNEYS
SMOCKS	**MOCKS**	
	MOCKTAIL	MOCKTAILS
	MOCKUP	MOCKUPS

FRONT HOOK	ROOT WORD	END HOOK
	MOCOCK	MOCOCKS
	MOCUCK	MOCUCKS
	MOCUDDUM	MOCUDDUMS
	MOD	MODE ▪ MODI ▪ MODS
	MODAL	MODALS
	MODALISM	MODALISMS
	MODALIST	MODALISTS
	MODE	MODEL ▪ MODEM ▪ MODER ▪ MODES
	MODEL	MODELS
	MODELER	MODELERS
	MODELING	MODELINGS
	MODELIST	MODELISTS
	MODELLER	MODELLERS
	MODELLING	MODELLINGS
	MODELLO	MODELLOS
	MODEM	MODEMS
	MODENA	MODENAS
	MODER	MODERN ▪ MODERS
	MODERATE	MODERATED ▪ MODERATES
	MODERATO	MODERATOR ▪ MODERATOS
	MODERATOR	MODERATORS
	MODERN	MODERNE ▪ MODERNS
	MODERNE	MODERNER ▪ MODERNES
	MODERNES	MODERNEST
	MODERNISE	MODERNISED ▪ MODERNISER ▪ MODERNISES
	MODERNISM	MODERNISMS
	MODERNIST	MODERNISTS
	MODERNIZE	MODERNIZED ▪ MODERNIZER ▪ MODERNIZES
	MODES	MODEST
	MODEST	MODESTY
	MODGE	MODGED ▪ MODGES
	MODI	MODII
	MODICUM	MODICUMS
	MODIFIER	MODIFIERS
	MODILLION	MODILLIONS
	MODIST	MODISTE ▪ MODISTS
	MODISTE	MODISTES
	MODIWORT	MODIWORTS
	MODULAR	MODULARS
	MODULATE	MODULATED ▪ MODULATES
	MODULATOR	MODULATORS ▪ MODULATORY
	MODULE	MODULES
	MOE	MOER ▪ MOES
	MOELLON	MOELLONS
	MOER	MOERS
	MOFETTE	MOFETTES
	MOFFETTE	MOFFETTES
	MOFFIE	MOFFIES
	MOFO	MOFOS (offensive)
	MOFUSSIL	MOFUSSILS
SMOG	MOG	MOGS
	MOGGAN	MOGGANS
	MOGGIE	MOGGIES
SMOGGY	MOGGY	
	MOGHUL	MOGHULS
SMOGS	MOGS	
	MOGUL	MOGULS
	MOHAIR	MOHAIRS
	MOHAWK	MOHAWKS
	MOHEL	MOHELS
	MOHICAN	MOHICANS
	MOHR	MOHRS
	MOHUR	MOHURS
	MOI	MOIL ▪ MOIT
	MOIDER	MOIDERS
	MOIDORE	MOIDORES
	MOIL	MOILS
SMOILED	MOILED	
	MOILER	MOILERS

FRONT HOOK	ROOT WORD	END HOOK
SMOILING	**MOILING**	
	MOINEAU	MOINEAUS
	MOIRA	MOIRAI
	MOIRE	MOIRES
	MOISER	MOISERS
	MOIST	MOISTS
	MOISTEN	MOISTENS
	MOISTENER	MOISTENERS
	MOISTURE	MOISTURES
	MOIT	MOITS
	MOITHER	MOITHERS
	MOJARRA	MOJARRAS
	MOJO	MOJOS
	MOKADDAM	MOKADDAMS
SMOKE	**MOKE**	MOKES
SMOKES	**MOKES**	
	MOKI	MOKIS
SMOKO	**MOKO**	MOKOS
	MOKOPUNA	MOKOPUNAS
	MOKORO	MOKOROS
SMOKOS	**MOKOS**	
	MOKSHA	MOKSHAS
	MOL	MOLA ▪ MOLD ▪ MOLE ▪ MOLL ▪ MOLS MOLT ▪ MOLY
	MOLA	MOLAL ▪ MOLAR ▪ MOLAS
	MOLAR	MOLARS
	MOLASSE	MOLASSES
	MOLD	MOLDS ▪ MOLDY
	MOLDAVITE	MOLDAVITES
	MOLDBOARD	MOLDBOARDS
SMOLDER	**MOLDER**	MOLDERS
SMOLDERED	**MOLDERED**	
SMOLDERING	**MOLDERING**	
SMOLDERS	**MOLDERS**	
	MOLDING	MOLDINGS
	MOLDWARP	MOLDWARPS
AMOLE	**MOLE**	MOLES
	MOLECAST	MOLECASTS
	MOLECULE	MOLECULES
	MOLEHILL	MOLEHILLS
	MOLEHUNT	MOLEHUNTS
	MOLERAT	MOLERATS
AMOLES	**MOLES**	MOLEST
	MOLESKIN	MOLESKINS
	MOLEST	MOLESTS
	MOLESTER	MOLESTERS
	MOLIMEN	MOLIMENS
	MOLINE	MOLINES ▪ MOLINET
	MOLINET	MOLINETS
	MOLL	MOLLA ▪ MOLLS ▪ MOLLY
	MOLLA	MOLLAH ▪ MOLLAS
	MOLLAH	MOLLAHS
	MOLLIE	MOLLIES
	MOLLIFIER	MOLLIFIERS
	MOLLUSC	MOLLUSCA ▪ MOLLUSCS
	MOLLUSCA	MOLLUSCAN
	MOLLUSCAN	MOLLUSCANS
	MOLLUSK	MOLLUSKS
	MOLLUSKAN	MOLLUSKANS
	MOLLYHAWK	MOLLYHAWKS
	MOLLYMAWK	MOLLYMAWKS
	MOLOCH	MOLOCHS
	MOLOCHISE	MOLOCHISED ▪ MOLOCHISES
	MOLOCHIZE	MOLOCHIZED ▪ MOLOCHIZES
SMOLT ▪ YMOLT	**MOLT**	MOLTO ▪ MOLTS
YMOLTEN	**MOLTEN**	
	MOLTER	MOLTERS
SMOLTS	**MOLTS**	
	MOLYBDATE	MOLYBDATES

FRONT HOOK	ROOT WORD	END HOOK
	MOM	MOME · MOMI · MOMS
	MOME	MOMES
	MOMENT	MOMENTA · MOMENTO · MOMENTS
	MOMENTO	MOMENTOS
	MOMENTUM	MOMENTUMS
	MOMISM	MOMISMS
	MOMMA	MOMMAS
	MOMMET	MOMMETS
	MOMSER	MOMSERS
	MOMZER	MOMZERS
	MON	MONA · MONG · MONK · MONO · MONS · MONY
	MONA	MONAD · MONAL · MONAS
	MONACHISM	MONACHISMS
	MONACHIST	MONACHISTS
	MONACID	MONACIDS
	MONAD	MONADS
	MONADISM	MONADISMS
	MONADNOCK	MONADNOCKS
	MONAL	MONALS
	MONARCH	MONARCHS · MONARCHY
	MONARDA	MONARDAS
	MONASTIC	MONASTICS
	MONAUL	MONAULS
	MONAXON	MONAXONS
	MONAZITE	MONAZITES
	MONDAIN	MONDAINE · MONDAINS
	MONDAINE	MONDAINES
	MONDE	MONDES
	MONDO	MONDOS
	MONELLIN	MONELLINS
	MONEME	MONEMES
	MONER	MONERA
	MONERA	MONERAN
	MONERAN	MONERANS
	MONERGISM	MONERGISMS
	MONETH	MONETHS
	MONETISE	MONETISED · MONETISES
	MONETIZE	MONETIZED · MONETIZES
	MONEY	MONEYS
	MONEYBAG	MONEYBAGS
	MONEYER	MONEYERS
	MONEYWORT	MONEYWORTS
AMONG · EMONG	**MONG**	MONGO · MONGS (offensive)
	MONGCORN	MONGCORNS
	MONGER	MONGERS · MONGERY
	MONGERING	MONGERINGS
	MONGO	MONGOE · MONGOL · MONGOS
	MONGOE	MONGOES
	MONGOL	MONGOLS (offensive)
	MONGOLISM	MONGOLISMS
	MONGOLOID	MONGOLOIDS (offensive)
	MONGOOSE	MONGOOSES
	MONGREL	MONGRELS
	MONGS	MONGST
AMONGST · EMONGST	**MONGST**	
	MONIAL	MONIALS
	MONICKER	MONICKERS
	MONIE	MONIED · MONIES
	MONIKER	MONIKERS
	MONILIA	MONILIAL · MONILIAS
	MONIMENT	MONIMENTS
	MONISM	MONISMS
	MONIST	MONISTS
	MONITION	MONITIONS
	MONITOR	MONITORS · MONITORY
	MONK	MONKS
	MONKEY	MONKEYS
	MONKEYISM	MONKEYISMS
	MONKEYPOD	MONKEYPODS

FRONT HOOK	ROOT WORD	END HOOK
	MONKEYPOT	MONKEYPOTS
	MONKHOOD	MONKHOODS
	MONKSHOOD	MONKSHOODS
	MONO	MONOS
	MONOACID	MONOACIDS
	MONOAMINE	MONOAMINES
	MONOBROW	MONOBROWS
	MONOCARP	MONOCARPS
	MONOCHORD	MONOCHORDS
	MONOCLE	MONOCLED ▪ MONOCLES
	MONOCLINE	MONOCLINES
	MONOCOQUE	MONOCOQUES
	MONOCOT	MONOCOTS
	MONOCOTYL	MONOCOTYLS
	MONOCRAT	MONOCRATS
	MONOCULAR	MONOCULARS
	MONOCYCLE	MONOCYCLES
	MONOCYTE	MONOCYTES
	MONODIST	MONODISTS
	MONODRAMA	MONODRAMAS
	MONOECISM	MONOECISMS
	MONOESTER	MONOESTERS
	MONOFIL	MONOFILS
	MONOFUEL	MONOFUELS
	MONOGLOT	MONOGLOTS
	MONOGRAM	MONOGRAMS
	MONOGRAPH	MONOGRAPHS ▪ MONOGRAPHY
	MONOHULL	MONOHULLS
	MONOKINE	MONOKINES
	MONOKINI	MONOKINIS
	MONOLATER	MONOLATERS
	MONOLAYER	MONOLAYERS
	MONOLITH	MONOLITHS
	MONOLOG	MONOLOGS ▪ MONOLOGY
	MONOLOGUE	MONOLOGUED ▪ MONOLOGUES
	MONOMANIA	MONOMANIAC ▪ MONOMANIAS
	MONOMARK	MONOMARKS
	MONOMER	MONOMERS
	MONOMETER	MONOMETERS
	MONOMIAL	MONOMIALS
	MONONYM	MONONYMS
	MONOPLANE	MONOPLANES
	MONOPLOID	MONOPLOIDS
	MONOPOD	MONOPODE ▪ MONOPODS ▪ MONOPODY
	MONOPODE	MONOPODES
	MONOPODIA	MONOPODIAL
	MONOPOLE	MONOPOLES
	MONOPTERA	MONOPTERAL
	MONOPTOTE	MONOPTOTES
	MONOPULSE	MONOPULSES
	MONORAIL	MONORAILS
	MONORCHID	MONORCHIDS
	MONORHYME	MONORHYMED ▪ MONORHYMES
	MONOS	MONOSY
	MONOSKI	MONOSKIS
	MONOSKIER	MONOSKIERS
	MONOSOME	MONOSOMES
	MONOSOMIC	MONOSOMICS
	MONOSTELE	MONOSTELES
	MONOSTICH	MONOSTICHS
	MONOTINT	MONOTINTS
	MONOTONE	MONOTONED ▪ MONOTONES
	MONOTREME	MONOTREMES
	MONOTROCH	MONOTROCHS
	MONOTYPE	MONOTYPES
	MONOXIDE	MONOXIDES
	MONOXYLON	MONOXYLONS
	MONSIGNOR	MONSIGNORI ▪ MONSIGNORS
	MONSOON	MONSOONS

FRONT HOOK	ROOT WORD	END HOOK
	MONSTER	MONSTERA ▪ MONSTERS
	MONSTERA	MONSTERAS
	MONTADALE	MONTADALES
	MONTAGE	MONTAGED ▪ MONTAGES
	MONTAN	MONTANE ▪ MONTANT
	MONTANE	MONTANES
	MONTANT	MONTANTO ▪ MONTANTS
	MONTANTO	MONTANTOS
	MONTARIA	MONTARIAS
	MONTE	MONTEM ▪ MONTES
	MONTEITH	MONTEITHS
	MONTEM	MONTEMS
	MONTERO	MONTEROS
	MONTH	MONTHS
	MONTHLING	MONTHLINGS
	MONTICLE	MONTICLES
	MONTICULE	MONTICULES
	MONTRE	MONTRES
	MONTURE	MONTURES
	MONUMENT	MONUMENTS
	MONURON	MONURONS
	MONZONITE	MONZONITES
	MOO	MOOD ▪ MOOI ▪ MOOK ▪ MOOL ▪ MOON MOOP ▪ MOOR ▪ MOOS ▪ MOOT
SMOOCH	**MOOCH**	
SMOOCHED	**MOOCHED**	
SMOOCHER	**MOOCHER**	MOOCHERS
SMOOCHERS	**MOOCHERS**	
SMOOCHES	**MOOCHES**	
SMOOCHING	**MOOCHING**	
	MOOD	MOODS ▪ MOODY
	MOODIES	MOODIEST
	MOOK	MOOKS (offensive)
	MOOKTAR	MOOKTARS
	MOOL	MOOLA ▪ MOOLI ▪ MOOLS ▪ MOOLY
	MOOLA	MOOLAH ▪ MOOLAS
	MOOLAH	MOOLAHS
	MOOLEY	MOOLEYS
	MOOLI	MOOLIS
	MOOLOO	MOOLOOS
	MOOLVI	MOOLVIE ▪ MOOLVIS
	MOOLVIE	MOOLVIES
	MOON	MOONS ▪ MOONY
	MOONBEAM	MOONBEAMS
	MOONBOW	MOONBOWS
	MOONDUST	MOONDUSTS
	MOONER	MOONERS
	MOONEYE	MOONEYES
	MOONFACE	MOONFACED ▪ MOONFACES
	MOONIES	MOONIEST
	MOONLET	MOONLETS
	MOONLIGHT	MOONLIGHTS
	MOONPHASE	MOONPHASES
	MOONPORT	MOONPORTS
	MOONQUAKE	MOONQUAKES
	MOONRAKER	MOONRAKERS
	MOONRISE	MOONRISES
	MOONROCK	MOONROCKS
	MOONROOF	MOONROOFS
	MOONSAIL	MOONSAILS
	MOONSCAPE	MOONSCAPES
	MOONSEED	MOONSEEDS
	MOONSET	MOONSETS
	MOONSHEE	MOONSHEES
	MOONSHINE	MOONSHINED ▪ MOONSHINER ▪ MOONSHINES
	MOONSHOT	MOONSHOTS
	MOONSTONE	MOONSTONES
	MOONWALK	MOONWALKS
	MOONWARD	MOONWARDS

FRONT HOOK	ROOT WORD	END HOOK
	MOONWORT	MOONWORTS
	MOOP	MOOPS
SMOOR	**MOOR**	MOORS = MOORY
	MOORAGE	MOORAGES
	MOORBURN	MOORBURNS
	MOORCOCK	MOORCOCKS
SMOORED	**MOORED**	
	MOORFOWL	MOORFOWLS
	MOORHEN	MOORHENS
	MOORILL	MOORILLS
SMOORING	**MOORING**	MOORINGS
	MOORLAND	MOORLANDS
	MOORLOG	MOORLOGS
SMOORS	**MOORS**	
	MOORVA	MOORVAS
	MOORWORT	MOORWORTS
	MOOS	MOOSE
	MOOSEBIRD	MOOSEBIRDS
	MOOSEWOOD	MOOSEWOODS
	MOOSEYARD	MOOSEYARDS
SMOOT	**MOOT**	MOOTS
SMOOTED	**MOOTED**	
	MOOTER	MOOTERS
SMOOTING	**MOOTING**	MOOTINGS
SMOOTS	**MOOTS**	
AMOOVE	**MOOVE**	MOOVED = MOOVES
AMOOVED	**MOOVED**	
AMOOVES	**MOOVES**	
AMOOVING	**MOOVING**	
	MOP	MOPE = MOPS = MOPY
	MOPANE	MOPANES
	MOPANI	MOPANIS
	MOPBOARD	MOPBOARDS
	MOPE	MOPED = MOPER = MOPES = MOPEY
	MOPED	MOPEDS
	MOPEHAWK	MOPEHAWKS
	MOPER	MOPERS = MOPERY
	MOPHEAD	MOPHEADS
	MOPOKE	MOPOKES
	MOPPER	MOPPERS
	MOPPET	MOPPETS
	MOPS	MOPSY
	MOPSTICK	MOPSTICKS
	MOQUETTE	MOQUETTES
	MOR	MORA = MORE = MORN = MORS = MORT
	MORA	MORAE = MORAL = MORAS = MORAT = MORAY
	MORAINE	MORAINES
AMORAL	**MORAL**	MORALE = MORALL = MORALS
	MORALE	MORALES
	MORALISE	MORALISED = MORALISER = MORALISES
	MORALISER	MORALISERS
AMORALISM	**MORALISM**	MORALISMS
AMORALISMS	**MORALISMS**	
AMORALIST	**MORALIST**	MORALISTS
AMORALISTS	**MORALISTS**	
AMORALITY	**MORALITY**	
	MORALIZE	MORALIZED = MORALIZER = MORALIZES
	MORALIZER	MORALIZERS
	MORALL	MORALLS = MORALLY
	MORALLER	MORALLERS
AMORALLY	**MORALLY**	
	MORAS	MORASS
	MORASS	MORASSY
	MORAT	MORATS
	MORAY	MORAYS
	MORCEAU	MORCEAUX
	MORCHA	MORCHAS
	MORDANT	MORDANTS
	MORDENT	MORDENTS

FRONT HOOK	ROOT WORD	END HOOK
SMORE	**MORE**	MOREL · MORES
	MOREEN	MOREENS
	MOREL	MORELS
	MORELLE	MORELLES
	MORELLO	MORELLOS
	MOREPORK	MOREPORKS
SMORES	**MORES**	
	MORESQUE	MORESQUES
	MORGAN	MORGANS
	MORGANITE	MORGANITES
	MORGAY	MORGAYS
	MORGEN	MORGENS
	MORGUE	MORGUES
	MORIA	MORIAS
	MORICHE	MORICHES
	MORION	MORIONS
	MORISCO	MORISCOS
	MORKIN	MORKINS
	MORLING	MORLINGS
	MORMAOR	MORMAORS
	MORN	MORNE · MORNS
	MORNAY	MORNAYS
	MORNE	MORNED · MORNES
	MORNING	MORNINGS
AMORNINGS	**MORNINGS**	
	MOROCCO	MOROCCOS
	MORON	MORONS
	MORONISM	MORONISMS
	MOROSE	MOROSER
AMOROSITY	**MOROSITY**	
	MORPH	MORPHO · MORPHS
	MORPHEME	MORPHEMES
	MORPHEMIC	MORPHEMICS
	MORPHEW	MORPHEWS
	MORPHIA	MORPHIAS
	MORPHIN	MORPHINE · MORPHING · MORPHINS
	MORPHINE	MORPHINES
	MORPHING	MORPHINGS
	MORPHO	MORPHOS
	MORPHOGEN	MORPHOGENS · MORPHOGENY
	MORRA	MORRAS
	MORRELL	MORRELLS
	MORRHUA	MORRHUAS
	MORRICE	MORRICES
	MORRION	MORRIONS
	MORRO	MORROS · MORROW
	MORROW	MORROWS
	MORS	MORSE
	MORSE	MORSEL · MORSES
	MORSEL	MORSELS
	MORSURE	MORSURES
AMORT	**MORT**	MORTS
	MORTAL	MORTALS
	MORTALISE	MORTALISED · MORTALISES
	MORTALIZE	MORTALIZED · MORTALIZES
	MORTAR	MORTARS · MORTARY
	MORTBELL	MORTBELLS
	MORTCLOTH	MORTCLOTHS
	MORTGAGE	MORTGAGED · MORTGAGEE · MORTGAGER
		MORTGAGES
	MORTGAGEE	MORTGAGEES
	MORTGAGER	MORTGAGERS
	MORTGAGOR	MORTGAGORS
	MORTICE	MORTICED · MORTICER · MORTICES
	MORTICER	MORTICERS
	MORTICIAN	MORTICIANS
	MORTIFIER	MORTIFIERS
AMORTISE	**MORTISE**	MORTISED · MORTISER · MORTISES
AMORTISED	**MORTISED**	

519

FRONT HOOK	ROOT WORD	END HOOK
	MORTISER	MORTISERS
AMORTISES	**MORTISES**	
AMORTISING	**MORTISING**	
	MORTLING	MORTLINGS
	MORTMAIN	MORTMAINS
	MORTSAFE	MORTSAFES
	MORULA	MORULAE · MORULAR · MORULAS
	MORWONG	MORWONGS
EMOS	**MOS**	MOSE · MOSH · MOSK · MOSS · MOST
	MOSAIC	MOSAICS
	MOSAICISM	MOSAICISMS
	MOSAICIST	MOSAICISTS
	MOSASAUR	MOSASAURI · MOSASAURS
	MOSCHATE	MOSCHATEL
	MOSCHATEL	MOSCHATELS
	MOSE	MOSED · MOSES · MOSEY
	MOSELLE	MOSELLES
	MOSEY	MOSEYS
	MOSHER	MOSHERS
	MOSHING	MOSHINGS
	MOSK	MOSKS
	MOSKONFYT	MOSKONFYTS
	MOSQUE	MOSQUES
	MOSQUITO	MOSQUITOS
	MOSS	MOSSO · MOSSY
	MOSSBACK	MOSSBACKS
	MOSSER	MOSSERS
	MOSSIE	MOSSIER · MOSSIES
	MOSSIES	MOSSIEST
	MOSSLAND	MOSSLANDS
	MOSSPLANT	MOSSPLANTS
	MOST	MOSTE · MOSTS
	MOSTEST	MOSTESTS
	MOT	MOTE · MOTH · MOTI · MOTS · MOTT · MOTU
EMOTE · SMOTE	**MOTE**	MOTED · MOTEL · MOTEN · MOTES · MOTET · MOTEY
EMOTED	**MOTED**	
	MOTEL	MOTELS
	MOTELIER	MOTELIERS
EMOTES	**MOTES**	
	MOTET	MOTETS · MOTETT
	MOTETT	MOTETTS
	MOTETTIST	MOTETTISTS
	MOTH	MOTHS · MOTHY
	MOTHBALL	MOTHBALLS
SMOTHER	**MOTHER**	MOTHERS · MOTHERY
SMOTHERED	**MOTHERED**	
	MOTHERESE	MOTHERESES
SMOTHERING	**MOTHERING**	MOTHERINGS
SMOTHERS	**MOTHERS**	
SMOTHERY	**MOTHERY**	
	MOTHPROOF	MOTHPROOFS
	MOTI	MOTIF · MOTIS (offensive)
	MOTIF	MOTIFS
	MOTILE	MOTILES
AMOTION · EMOTION	**MOTION**	MOTIONS
EMOTIONAL	**MOTIONAL**	
	MOTIONER	MOTIONERS
	MOTIONIST	MOTIONISTS
AMOTIONS · EMOTIONS	**MOTIONS**	
	MOTIVATE	MOTIVATED · MOTIVATES
	MOTIVATOR	MOTIVATORS
EMOTIVE	**MOTIVE**	MOTIVED · MOTIVES
EMOTIVITY	**MOTIVITY**	
	MOTLEY	MOTLEYS
	MOTMOT	MOTMOTS
	MOTOR	MOTORS · MOTORY
	MOTORAIL	MOTORAILS
	MOTORBIKE	MOTORBIKED · MOTORBIKES

FRONT HOOK	ROOT WORD	END HOOK
	MOTORBOAT	MOTORBOATS
	MOTORCADE	MOTORCADED ▪ MOTORCADES
	MOTORCAR	MOTORCARS
	MOTORDOM	MOTORDOMS
	MOTORHOME	MOTORHOMES
	MOTORING	MOTORINGS
	MOTORISE	MOTORISED ▪ MOTORISES
	MOTORIST	MOTORISTS
	MOTORIUM	MOTORIUMS
	MOTORIZE	MOTORIZED ▪ MOTORIZES
	MOTORSHIP	MOTORSHIPS
	MOTORWAY	MOTORWAYS
	MOTSER	MOTSERS
	MOTT	MOTTE ▪ MOTTO ▪ MOTTS ▪ MOTTY
	MOTTE	MOTTES
	MOTTIES	MOTTIEST
	MOTTLE	MOTTLED ▪ MOTTLER ▪ MOTTLES
	MOTTLER	MOTTLERS
	MOTTLING	MOTTLINGS
	MOTTO	MOTTOS
	MOTU	MOTUS (offensive)
	MOTUCA	MOTUCAS
	MOTZA	MOTZAS
	MOU	MOUE ▪ MOUP ▪ MOUS
SMOUCH	**MOUCH**	
	MOUCHARD	MOUCHARDS
SMOUCHED	**MOUCHED**	
	MOUCHER	MOUCHERS
SMOUCHES	**MOUCHES**	
SMOUCHING	**MOUCHING**	
	MOUCHOIR	MOUCHOIRS
	MOUDIWART	MOUDIWARTS
	MOUDIWORT	MOUDIWORTS
	MOUE	MOUES
	MOUFFLON	MOUFFLONS
	MOUFLON	MOUFLONS
	MOUJIK	MOUJIKS
	MOULAGE	MOULAGES
	MOULD	MOULDS ▪ MOULDY
SMOULDER	**MOULDER**	MOULDERS
SMOULDERED	**MOULDERED**	
SMOULDERS	**MOULDERS**	
	MOULDING	MOULDINGS
	MOULDWARP	MOULDWARPS
	MOULIN	MOULINS
	MOULINET	MOULINETS
	MOULT	MOULTS
	MOULTER	MOULTERS
	MOULTING	MOULTINGS
	MOUND	MOUNDS
	MOUNDBIRD	MOUNDBIRDS
	MOUNSEER	MOUNSEERS
AMOUNT	**MOUNT**	MOUNTS
	MOUNTAIN	MOUNTAINS ▪ MOUNTAINY
	MOUNTANT	MOUNTANTS
AMOUNTED	**MOUNTED**	
	MOUNTER	MOUNTERS
AMOUNTING	**MOUNTING**	MOUNTINGS
AMOUNTS	**MOUNTS**	
	MOUP	MOUPS
	MOURN	MOURNS
	MOURNER	MOURNERS
	MOURNING	MOURNINGS
	MOURNIVAL	MOURNIVALS
	MOUS	MOUSE ▪ MOUST ▪ MOUSY
	MOUSAKA	MOUSAKAS
SMOUSE	**MOUSE**	MOUSED ▪ MOUSER ▪ MOUSES ▪ MOUSEY
	MOUSEBIRD	MOUSEBIRDS
SMOUSED	**MOUSED**	

FRONT HOOK	ROOT WORD	END HOOK
	MOUSEKIN	MOUSEKINS
	MOUSEMAT	MOUSEMATS
	MOUSEOVER	MOUSEOVERS
	MOUSEPAD	MOUSEPADS
SMOUSER	**MOUSER**	MOUSERS ▪ MOUSERY
SMOUSERS	**MOUSERS**	
SMOUSES	**MOUSES**	
	MOUSETAIL	MOUSETAILS
	MOUSETRAP	MOUSETRAPS
	MOUSIE	MOUSIER ▪ MOUSIES
	MOUSIES	MOUSIEST
SMOUSING	**MOUSING**	MOUSINGS
	MOUSLE	MOUSLED ▪ MOUSLES
	MOUSME	MOUSMEE ▪ MOUSMES
	MOUSMEE	MOUSMEES
	MOUSSAKA	MOUSSAKAS
	MOUSSE	MOUSSED ▪ MOUSSES
	MOUST	MOUSTS
	MOUSTACHE	MOUSTACHED ▪ MOUSTACHES
	MOUTAN	MOUTANS
	MOUTER	MOUTERS
	MOUTERER	MOUTERERS
	MOUTH	MOUTHS ▪ MOUTHY
	MOUTHER	MOUTHERS
	MOUTHFEEL	MOUTHFEELS
	MOUTHFUL	MOUTHFULS
	MOUTHPART	MOUTHPARTS
	MOUTON	MOUTONS
	MOVABLE	MOVABLES
AMOVE ▪ EMOVE	**MOVE**	MOVED ▪ MOVER ▪ MOVES
	MOVEABLE	MOVEABLES
AMOVED ▪ EMOVED	**MOVED**	
	MOVEMENT	MOVEMENTS
	MOVER	MOVERS
AMOVES ▪ EMOVES	**MOVES**	
	MOVIE	MOVIES
	MOVIEDOM	MOVIEDOMS
	MOVIEGOER	MOVIEGOERS
	MOVIELAND	MOVIELANDS
	MOVIEOKE	MOVIEOKES
	MOVIEOLA	MOVIEOLAS
AMOVING ▪ EMOVING	**MOVING**	
	MOVIOLA	MOVIOLAS
	MOW	MOWA ▪ MOWN ▪ MOWS
	MOWA	MOWAS
	MOWBURN	MOWBURNS ▪ MOWBURNT
	MOWDIE	MOWDIES
	MOWER	MOWERS
	MOWING	MOWINGS
	MOWRA	MOWRAS
	MOXA	MOXAS
	MOXIE	MOXIES
	MOY	MOYA ▪ MOYL ▪ MOYS
	MOYA	MOYAS
	MOYGASHEL	MOYGASHELS
	MOYL	MOYLE ▪ MOYLS
SMOYLE	**MOYLE**	MOYLED ▪ MOYLES
SMOYLED	**MOYLED**	
SMOYLES	**MOYLES**	
SMOYLING	**MOYLING**	
	MOZ	MOZE ▪ MOZO ▪ MOZZ
	MOZE	MOZED ▪ MOZES
	MOZETTA	MOZETTAS
	MOZO	MOZOS
	MOZZETTA	MOZZETTAS
	MOZZIE	MOZZIES
	MOZZLE	MOZZLES
	MPRET	MPRETS
	MRIDAMGAM	MRIDAMGAMS

FRONT HOOK	ROOT WORD	END HOOK
	MRIDANG	MRIDANGA = MRIDANGS
	MRIDANGA	MRIDANGAM = MRIDANGAS
	MRIDANGAM	MRIDANGAMS
AMU = EMU = UMU	**MU**	MUD = MUG = MUM = MUN = MUS = MUT = MUX
	MUCATE	MUCATES
	MUCH	MUCHO
	MUCHACHO	MUCHACHOS
	MUCHEL	MUCHELL = MUCHELS
	MUCHELL	MUCHELLS
	MUCIGEN	MUCIGENS
	MUCILAGE	MUCILAGES
	MUCIN	MUCINS
	MUCINOGEN	MUCINOGENS
AMUCK	**MUCK**	MUCKS = MUCKY
	MUCKAMUCK	MUCKAMUCKS
	MUCKENDER	MUCKENDERS
	MUCKER	MUCKERS
	MUCKHEAP	MUCKHEAPS
	MUCKLE	MUCKLES
	MUCKLUCK	MUCKLUCKS
	MUCKRAKE	MUCKRAKED = MUCKRAKER = MUCKRAKES
	MUCKRAKER	MUCKRAKERS
AMUCKS	**MUCKS**	
	MUCKSWEAT	MUCKSWEATS
	MUCKWORM	MUCKWORMS
	MUCLUC	MUCLUCS
	MUCOID	MUCOIDS
	MUCOR	MUCORS
	MUCOSA	MUCOSAE = MUCOSAL = MUCOSAS
	MUCRO	MUCROS
	MUCRONATE	MUCRONATED
	MUD	MUDS
	MUDBATH	MUDBATHS
	MUDBUG	MUDBUGS
	MUDCAP	MUDCAPS
	MUDCAT	MUDCATS
	MUDDER	MUDDERS
	MUDDIES	MUDDIEST
	MUDDLE	MUDDLED = MUDDLER = MUDDLES
	MUDDLER	MUDDLERS
	MUDDLING	MUDDLINGS
	MUDEYE	MUDEYES
	MUDFLAP	MUDFLAPS
	MUDFLAT	MUDFLATS
	MUDFLOW	MUDFLOWS
SMUDGE	**MUDGE**	MUDGED = MUDGER = MUDGES
SMUDGED	**MUDGED**	
SMUDGER	**MUDGER**	MUDGERS
SMUDGERS	**MUDGERS**	
SMUDGES	**MUDGES**	
SMUDGING	**MUDGING**	
	MUDGUARD	MUDGUARDS
	MUDHEN	MUDHENS
	MUDHOLE	MUDHOLES
	MUDHOOK	MUDHOOKS
	MUDIR	MUDIRS
	MUDIRIA	MUDIRIAS
	MUDIRIEH	MUDIRIEHS
	MUDLARK	MUDLARKS
	MUDLOGGER	MUDLOGGERS
	MUDPACK	MUDPACKS
	MUDRA	MUDRAS
	MUDROCK	MUDROCKS
	MUDROOM	MUDROOMS
	MUDSCOW	MUDSCOWS
	MUDSILL	MUDSILLS
	MUDSLIDE	MUDSLIDES
	MUDSTONE	MUDSTONES
	MUDWORT	MUDWORTS

FRONT HOOK	ROOT WORD	END HOOK
	MUEDDIN	MUEDDINS
	MUENSTER	MUENSTERS
	MUESLI	MUESLIS
	MUEZZIN	MUEZZINS
	MUFF	MUFFS
	MUFFIN	MUFFING · MUFFINS
	MUFFINEER	MUFFINEERS
	MUFFLE	MUFFLED · MUFFLER · MUFFLES
	MUFFLER	MUFFLERS
	MUFLON	MUFLONS
	MUFTI	MUFTIS
SMUG	**MUG**	MUGG · MUGS
	MUGEARITE	MUGEARITES
	MUGFUL	MUGFULS
	MUGG	MUGGA · MUGGS · MUGGY
	MUGGA	MUGGAR · MUGGAS
	MUGGAR	MUGGARS
SMUGGED	**MUGGED**	
	MUGGEE	MUGGEES
SMUGGER	**MUGGER**	MUGGERS
SMUGGING	**MUGGING**	MUGGINGS
	MUGGUR	MUGGURS
	MUGHAL	MUGHALS
SMUGS	**MUGS**	
	MUGSHOT	MUGSHOTS
	MUGWORT	MUGWORTS
	MUGWUMP	MUGWUMPS
	MUID	MUIDS
	MUIL	MUILS
	MUIR	MUIRS
	MUIRBURN	MUIRBURNS
	MUIST	MUISTS
	MUJIK	MUJIKS
	MUKHTAR	MUKHTARS
	MUKLUK	MUKLUKS
	MUKTUK	MUKTUKS
	MULATTA	MULATTAS
	MULATTO	MULATTOS
	MULCT	MULCTS
EMULE	**MULE**	MULED · MULES · MULEY
EMULED	**MULED**	
EMULES	**MULES**	
	MULETA	MULETAS
	MULETEER	MULETEERS
	MULEY	MULEYS
	MULGA	MULGAS
EMULING	**MULING**	
	MULL	MULLA · MULLS
	MULLA	MULLAH · MULLAS
	MULLAH	MULLAHS
	MULLAHISM	MULLAHISMS
	MULLEIN	MULLEINS
	MULLEN	MULLENS
	MULLER	MULLERS
	MULLET	MULLETS
	MULLEY	MULLEYS
	MULLIGAN	MULLIGANS
	MULLION	MULLIONS
	MULLITE	MULLITES
	MULLOCK	MULLOCKS · MULLOCKY
	MULLOWAY	MULLOWAYS
	MULMUL	MULMULL · MULMULS
	MULMULL	MULMULLS
	MULSE	MULSES
	MULTICAST	MULTICASTS
	MULTICIDE	MULTICIDES
	MULTIFIL	MULTIFILS
	MULTIFOIL	MULTIFOILS
	MULTIFORM	MULTIFORMS

FRONT HOOK	ROOT WORD	END HOOK
	MULTIGYM	MULTIGYMS
	MULTIHULL	MULTIHULLS
	MULTILANE	MULTILANES
	MULTILOBE	MULTILOBED ▪ MULTILOBES
	MULTIPACK	MULTIPACKS
	MULTIPARA	MULTIPARAE ▪ MULTIPARAS
	MULTIPART	MULTIPARTY
	MULTIPED	MULTIPEDE ▪ MULTIPEDS
	MULTIPEDE	MULTIPEDES
	MULTIPLE	MULTIPLES ▪ MULTIPLET ▪ MULTIPLEX
	MULTIPLET	MULTIPLETS
	MULTIPOLE	MULTIPOLES
	MULTITASK	MULTITASKS
	MULTITON	MULTITONE
	MULTITONE	MULTITONES
	MULTITUDE	MULTITUDES
	MULTIUSE	MULTIUSER
	MULTUM	MULTUMS
	MULTURE	MULTURED ▪ MULTURER ▪ MULTURES
	MULTURER	MULTURERS
	MUM	MUMM ▪ MUMP ▪ MUMS ▪ MUMU
	MUMBLE	MUMBLED ▪ MUMBLER ▪ MUMBLES
	MUMBLER	MUMBLERS
	MUMBLING	MUMBLINGS
	MUMCHANCE	MUMCHANCES
	MUMM	MUMMS ▪ MUMMY
	MUMMER	MUMMERS ▪ MUMMERY
	MUMMIA	MUMMIAS
	MUMMICHOG	MUMMICHOGS
	MUMMING	MUMMINGS
	MUMMOCK	MUMMOCKS
	MUMP	MUMPS
	MUMPER	MUMPERS
	MUMS	MUMSY
	MUMU	MUMUS
	MUN	MUNG ▪ MUNI ▪ MUNS ▪ MUNT
	MUNCHABLE	MUNCHABLES
	MUNCHER	MUNCHERS
	MUNCHKIN	MUNCHKINS
	MUNDANE	MUNDANER
	MUNDIC	MUNDICS
	MUNDUNGO	MUNDUNGOS
	MUNG	MUNGA ▪ MUNGO ▪ MUNGS
	MUNGA	MUNGAS
	MUNGCORN	MUNGCORNS
EMUNGED	**MUNGED**	
EMUNGING	**MUNGING**	
	MUNGO	MUNGOS
	MUNGOOSE	MUNGOOSES
	MUNI	MUNIS
	MUNICIPAL	MUNICIPALS
	MUNIMENT	MUNIMENTS
	MUNITE	MUNITED ▪ MUNITES
	MUNITION	MUNITIONS
	MUNNION	MUNNIONS
	MUNSHI	MUNSHIS
	MUNSTER	MUNSTERS
	MUNT	MUNTS *(offensive)* ▪ MUNTU *(offensive)*
	MUNTER	MUNTERS *(offensive)*
	MUNTIN	MUNTING ▪ MUNTINS
	MUNTING	MUNTINGS
	MUNTJAC	MUNTJACS
	MUNTJAK	MUNTJAKS
	MUNTRIE	MUNTRIES
	MUNTU	MUNTUS *(offensive)*
	MUON	MUONS
	MUONIUM	MUONIUMS
	MUPPET	MUPPETS
	MUQADDAM	MUQADDAMS

FRONT HOOK	ROOT WORD	END HOOK
	MURA	MURAL · MURAS
	MURAENA	MURAENAS
	MURAENID	MURAENIDS
	MURAGE	MURAGES
	MURAL	MURALS
	MURALIST	MURALISTS
	MURDER	MURDERS
	MURDEREE	MURDEREES
	MURDERER	MURDERERS
EMURE	**MURE**	MURED · MURES · MUREX
EMURED	**MURED**	
	MUREIN	MUREINS
	MURENA	MURENAS
EMURES	**MURES**	
	MURGEON	MURGEONS
	MURIATE	MURIATED · MURIATES
	MURICATE	MURICATED
	MURID	MURIDS
	MURINE	MURINES
EMURING	**MURING**	
	MURK	MURKS · MURKY
	MURL	MURLS · MURLY
	MURLAIN	MURLAINS
	MURLAN	MURLANS
	MURLIN	MURLING · MURLINS
	MURMUR	MURMURS
	MURMURER	MURMURERS
	MURMURING	MURMURINGS
	MURR	MURRA · MURRE · MURRI · MURRS · MURRY
	MURRA	MURRAM · MURRAS · MURRAY
	MURRAGH	MURRAGHS
	MURRAIN	MURRAINS
	MURRAM	MURRAMS
	MURRAY	MURRAYS
	MURRE	MURREE · MURREN · MURRES · MURREY
	MURREE	MURREES
	MURRELET	MURRELETS
	MURREN	MURRENS
	MURREY	MURREYS
	MURRHA	MURRHAS
	MURRI	MURRIN · MURRIS
	MURRIN	MURRINE · MURRINS
	MURRION	MURRIONS
SMURRY	**MURRY**	
	MURTHER	MURTHERS
	MURTHERER	MURTHERERS
	MURTI	MURTIS
	MURVA	MURVAS
AMUS · EMUS	**MUS**	MUSE · MUSH · MUSK · MUSO · MUSS · MUST
	MUSANG	MUSANGS
	MUSAR	MUSARS
	MUSCA	MUSCAE · MUSCAT
	MUSCADEL	MUSCADELS
	MUSCADET	MUSCADETS
	MUSCADIN	MUSCADINE · MUSCADINS
	MUSCADINE	MUSCADINES
	MUSCARINE	MUSCARINES
	MUSCAT	MUSCATS
	MUSCATEL	MUSCATELS
	MUSCAVADO	MUSCAVADOS
	MUSCID	MUSCIDS
	MUSCLE	MUSCLED · MUSCLES
	MUSCLING	MUSCLINGS
	MUSCONE	MUSCONES
	MUSCOVADO	MUSCOVADOS
	MUSCOVITE	MUSCOVITES
AMUSE	**MUSE**	MUSED · MUSER · MUSES · MUSET
AMUSED	**MUSED**	
AMUSER	**MUSER**	MUSERS

FRONT HOOK	ROOT WORD	END HOOK
AMUSERS	**MUSERS**	
AMUSES	**MUSES**	
	MUSET	MUSETS
	MUSETTE	MUSETTES
AMUSETTE	**MUSETTE**	MUSETTES
AMUSETTES	**MUSETTES**	
	MUSEUM	MUSEUMS
SMUSH	**MUSH**	MUSHA ▪ MUSHY
SMUSHED	**MUSHED**	
	MUSHER	MUSHERS
SMUSHES	**MUSHES**	
SMUSHING	**MUSHING**	
	MUSHMOUTH	MUSHMOUTHS
	MUSHROOM	MUSHROOMS
	MUSIC	MUSICK ▪ MUSICS
	MUSICAL	MUSICALE ▪ MUSICALS
	MUSICALE	MUSICALES
	MUSICIAN	MUSICIANS
	MUSICK	MUSICKS
	MUSICKER	MUSICKERS
	MUSIMON	MUSIMONS
AMUSING	**MUSING**	MUSINGS
AMUSINGLY	**MUSINGLY**	
	MUSIT	MUSITS
AMUSIVE	**MUSIVE**	
	MUSJID	MUSJIDS
	MUSK	MUSKS ▪ MUSKY
	MUSKEG	MUSKEGS
	MUSKET	MUSKETS
	MUSKETEER	MUSKETEERS
	MUSKETOON	MUSKETOONS
	MUSKIE	MUSKIER ▪ MUSKIES
	MUSKIES	MUSKIEST
	MUSKIT	MUSKITS
	MUSKLE	MUSKLES
	MUSKMELON	MUSKMELONS
	MUSKONE	MUSKONES
	MUSKRAT	MUSKRATS
	MUSKROOT	MUSKROOTS
	MUSLIN	MUSLINS
	MUSLINET	MUSLINETS
	MUSMON	MUSMONS
	MUSO	MUSOS
	MUSPIKE	MUSPIKES
	MUSROL	MUSROLS
	MUSS	MUSSE ▪ MUSSY
	MUSSE	MUSSED ▪ MUSSEL ▪ MUSSES
	MUSSEL	MUSSELS
	MUSSITATE	MUSSITATED ▪ MUSSITATES
	MUST	MUSTH ▪ MUSTS ▪ MUSTY
	MUSTACHE	MUSTACHED ▪ MUSTACHES
	MUSTACHIO	MUSTACHIOS
	MUSTANG	MUSTANGS
	MUSTARD	MUSTARDS ▪ MUSTARDY
	MUSTEE	MUSTEES
	MUSTELID	MUSTELIDS
	MUSTELINE	MUSTELINES
	MUSTER	MUSTERS
	MUSTERER	MUSTERERS
	MUSTH	MUSTHS
SMUT	**MUT**	MUTE ▪ MUTI ▪ MUTS ▪ MUTT
	MUTAGEN	MUTAGENS
	MUTANT	MUTANTS
	MUTASE	MUTASES
	MUTATE	MUTATED ▪ MUTATES
	MUTATION	MUTATIONS
SMUTCH	**MUTCH**	
SMUTCHED	**MUTCHED**	
SMUTCHES	**MUTCHES**	
SMUTCHING	**MUTCHING**	

M

FRONT HOOK	ROOT WORD	END HOOK
	MUTCHKIN	MUTCHKINS
	MUTE	MUTED · MUTER · MUTES
	MUTES	MUTEST
	MUTHA	MUTHAS (offensive)
	MUTI	MUTIS
	MUTILATE	MUTILATED · MUTILATES
	MUTILATOR	MUTILATORS
	MUTINE	MUTINED · MUTINES
	MUTINEER	MUTINEERS
	MUTIS	MUTISM
	MUTISM	MUTISMS
	MUTON	MUTONS
	MUTOSCOPE	MUTOSCOPES
SMUTS	**MUTS**	
	MUTT	MUTTS
	MUTTER	MUTTERS
	MUTTERER	MUTTERERS
	MUTTERING	MUTTERINGS
	MUTTON	MUTTONS · MUTTONY
	MUTUAL	MUTUALS
	MUTUALISE	MUTUALISED · MUTUALISES
	MUTUALISM	MUTUALISMS
	MUTUALIST	MUTUALISTS
	MUTUALIZE	MUTUALIZED · MUTUALIZES
	MUTUCA	MUTUCAS
	MUTUEL	MUTUELS
	MUTULE	MUTULES
	MUTUUM	MUTUUMS
	MUUMUU	MUUMUUS
	MUZHIK	MUZHIKS
	MUZJIK	MUZJIKS
	MUZZ	MUZZY
	MUZZLE	MUZZLED · MUZZLER · MUZZLES
	MUZZLER	MUZZLERS
	MVULE	MVULES
	MWALIMU	MWALIMUS
	MY	MYC
	MYAL	MYALL
	MYALGIA	MYALGIAS
	MYALISM	MYALISMS
	MYALIST	MYALISTS
	MYALL	MYALLS
	MYC	MYCS
	MYCELE	MYCELES
	MYCELIA	MYCELIAL · MYCELIAN
	MYCELLA	MYCELLAS
	MYCETOMA	MYCETOMAS
	MYCOBIONT	MYCOBIONTS
	MYCOFLORA	MYCOFLORAE · MYCOFLORAS
	MYCOPHILE	MYCOPHILES
	MYCORHIZA	MYCORHIZAE · MYCORHIZAL · MYCORHIZAS
	MYCOTOXIN	MYCOTOXINS
	MYDRIATIC	MYDRIATICS
	MYELIN	MYELINE · MYELINS
	MYELINE	MYELINES
	MYELOCYTE	MYELOCYTES
	MYELOGRAM	MYELOGRAMS
	MYELOMA	MYELOMAS
	MYELON	MYELONS
	MYGALE	MYGALES
	MYLAR	MYLARS
	MYLODON	MYLODONS · MYLODONT
	MYLODONT	MYLODONTS
	MYLOHYOID	MYLOHYOIDS
	MYLONITE	MYLONITES
	MYNA	MYNAH · MYNAS
	MYNAH	MYNAHS
	MYNHEER	MYNHEERS
	MYOBLAST	MYOBLASTS

M

FRONT HOOK	ROOT WORD	END HOOK
	MYOCARDIA	MYOCARDIAL
	MYOFIBRIL	MYOFIBRILS
	MYOGEN	MYOGENS
	MYOGLOBIN	MYOGLOBINS
	MYOGRAM	MYOGRAMS
	MYOGRAPH	MYOGRAPHS ▪ MYOGRAPHY
	MYOLOGIST	MYOLOGISTS
	MYOMA	MYOMAS
	MYOPE	MYOPES
	MYOPIA	MYOPIAS
	MYOPIC	MYOPICS
	MYOSCOPE	MYOSCOPES
	MYOSIN	MYOSINS
	MYOSOTE	MYOSOTES
	MYOTIC	MYOTICS
	MYOTOME	MYOTOMES
AMYOTONIA	**MYOTONIA**	MYOTONIAS
AMYOTONIAS	**MYOTONIAS**	
	MYOTUBE	MYOTUBES
	MYRBANE	MYRBANES
	MYRIAD	MYRIADS
	MYRIADTH	MYRIADTHS
	MYRIAPOD	MYRIAPODS
	MYRICA	MYRICAS
	MYRINGA	MYRINGAS
	MYRIOPOD	MYRIOPODS
	MYRIORAMA	MYRIORAMAS
	MYRMIDON	MYRMIDONS
	MYROBALAN	MYROBALANS
	MYRRH	MYRRHS
	MYRRHOL	MYRRHOLS
	MYRTLE	MYRTLES
	MYSID	MYSIDS
	MYSOST	MYSOSTS
	MYSTAGOG	MYSTAGOGS ▪ MYSTAGOGY
	MYSTIC	MYSTICS
	MYSTICETE	MYSTICETES
	MYSTICISM	MYSTICISMS
	MYSTIFIER	MYSTIFIERS
	MYSTIQUE	MYSTIQUES
	MYTH	MYTHI ▪ MYTHS ▪ MYTHY
	MYTHI	MYTHIC
	MYTHICISE	MYTHICISED ▪ MYTHICISER ▪ MYTHICISES
	MYTHICISM	MYTHICISMS
	MYTHICIST	MYTHICISTS
	MYTHICIZE	MYTHICIZED ▪ MYTHICIZER ▪ MYTHICIZES
	MYTHISE	MYTHISED ▪ MYTHISES
	MYTHISM	MYTHISMS
	MYTHIST	MYTHISTS
	MYTHIZE	MYTHIZED ▪ MYTHIZES
	MYTHMAKER	MYTHMAKERS
	MYTHOMANE	MYTHOMANES
	MYTHOPOET	MYTHOPOETS
	MYXAMEBA	MYXAMEBAE ▪ MYXAMEBAS
	MYXAMOEBA	MYXAMOEBAE ▪ MYXAMOEBAS
	MYXEDEMA	MYXEDEMAS
	MYXO	MYXOS
	MYXOCYTE	MYXOCYTES
	MYXOEDEMA	MYXOEDEMAS
	MYXOMA	MYXOMAS
	MZEE	MZEES
	MZUNGU	MZUNGUS

M

N

FRONT HOOK	ROOT WORD	END HOOK
ANA • MNA	NA	NAB • NAE • NAG • NAH • NAM • NAN • NAP NAS • NAT • NAW • NAY
	NAAM	NAAMS
	NAAN	NAANS
	NAARTJE	NAARTJES
	NAARTJIE	NAARTJIES
SNAB	NAB	NABE • NABK • NABS
	NABBER	NABBERS
	NABE	NABES
	NABK	NABKS
	NABLA	NABLAS
	NABOB	NABOBS
	NABOBISM	NABOBISMS
SNABS	NABS	
	NACARAT	NACARATS
	NACELLE	NACELLES
	NACH	NACHE • NACHO
	NACHE	NACHES
	NACHO	NACHOS
	NACHTMAAL	NACHTMAALS
	NACKET	NACKETS
	NACRE	NACRED • NACRES
	NACRITE	NACRITES
	NADA	NADAS
	NADIR	NADIRS
	NAETHING	NAETHINGS
	NAEVE	NAEVES
	NAFF	NAFFS
KNAG • SNAG	NAG	NAGA • NAGS
	NAGA	NAGAS
	NAGANA	NAGANAS
	NAGAPIE	NAGAPIES
	NAGARI	NAGARIS
SNAGGED	NAGGED	
	NAGGER	NAGGERS
KNAGGIER • SNAGGIER	NAGGIER	
KNAGGIEST • SNAGGIEST	NAGGIEST	
SNAGGING	NAGGING	
KNAGGY • SNAGGY	NAGGY	
	NAGMAAL	NAGMAALS
	NAGOR	NAGORS
KNAGS • SNAGS	NAGS	
	NAHAL	NAHALS
	NAIAD	NAIADS
	NAIF	NAIFS
	NAIK	NAIKS
SNAIL	NAIL	NAILS
	NAILBITER	NAILBITERS
SNAILED	NAILED	
	NAILER	NAILERS • NAILERY
SNAILERIES	NAILERIES	
SNAILERY	NAILERY	
	NAILFILE	NAILFILES
	NAILFOLD	NAILFOLDS
	NAILHEAD	NAILHEADS
SNAILING	NAILING	NAILINGS
SNAILS	NAILS	
	NAILSET	NAILSETS
	NAINSELL	NAINSELLS
	NAINSOOK	NAINSOOKS
	NAIRA	NAIRAS
	NAIRU	NAIRUS
	NAISSANCE	NAISSANCES
	NAIVE	NAIVER • NAIVES
	NAIVES	NAIVEST
	NAIVETE	NAIVETES

FRONT HOOK	ROOT WORD	END HOOK
SNAKED	**NAKED**	
	NAKER	NAKERS
	NAKFA	NAKFAS
	NALA	NALAS
	NALED	NALEDS
	NALLA	NALLAH ▪ NALLAS
	NALLAH	NALLAHS
	NALOXONE	NALOXONES
	NAM	NAME ▪ NAMS ▪ NAMU
	NAMASKAR	NAMASKARS
	NAMASTE	NAMASTES
	NAME	NAMED ▪ NAMER ▪ NAMES
	NAMECHECK	NAMECHECKS
	NAMEPLATE	NAMEPLATES
	NAMER	NAMERS
	NAMESAKE	NAMESAKES
	NAMETAG	NAMETAGS
	NAMETAPE	NAMETAPES
	NAMING	NAMINGS
GNAMMA	**NAMMA**	
ANAN	**NAN**	NANA ▪ NANE ▪ NANS
ANANA ▪ JNANA	**NANA**	NANAS
ANANAS ▪ JNANAS	**NANAS**	
	NANCE	NANCES (offensive)
	NANDIN	NANDINA ▪ NANDINE ▪ NANDINS
	NANDINA	NANDINAS
	NANDINE	NANDINES
	NANDOO	NANDOOS
	NANDU	NANDUS
INANE	**NANE**	
ONANISM	**NANISM**	NANISMS
ONANISMS	**NANISMS**	
	NANKEEN	NANKEENS
	NANKIN	NANKINS
	NANNA	NANNAS
	NANNIE	NANNIED ▪ NANNIES
	NANNYGAI	NANNYGAIS
	NANOBE	NANOBES
	NANODOT	NANODOTS
	NANOGRAM	NANOGRAMS
	NANOMETER	NANOMETERS
	NANOMETRE	NANOMETRES
	NANOOK	NANOOKS
	NANOTECH	NANOTECHS
	NANOTESLA	NANOTESLAS
	NANOTUBE	NANOTUBES
	NANOWATT	NANOWATTS
	NANOWORLD	NANOWORLDS
KNAP ▪ SNAP	**NAP**	NAPA ▪ NAPE ▪ NAPS
	NAPA	NAPAS
	NAPALM	NAPALMS
	NAPE	NAPED ▪ NAPES
	NAPHTHA	NAPHTHAS
	NAPHTHENE	NAPHTHENES
	NAPHTHOL	NAPHTHOLS
	NAPHTHYL	NAPHTHYLS
	NAPHTOL	NAPHTOLS
	NAPKIN	NAPKINS
SNAPLESS	**NAPLESS**	
	NAPOLEON	NAPOLEONS
	NAPOO	NAPOOS
	NAPPA	NAPPAS
	NAPPE	NAPPED ▪ NAPPER ▪ NAPPES
KNAPPED ▪ SNAPPED	**NAPPED**	
KNAPPER ▪ SNAPPER	**NAPPER**	NAPPERS
KNAPPERS ▪ SNAPPERS	**NAPPERS**	
	NAPPIE	NAPPIER ▪ NAPPIES
SNAPPIER	**NAPPIER**	
	NAPPIES	NAPPIEST

531

FRONT HOOK	ROOT WORD	END HOOK
SNAPPIEST	**NAPPIEST**	
SNAPPINESS	**NAPPINESS**	
KNAPPING · SNAPPING	**NAPPING**	
SNAPPY	**NAPPY**	
	NAPRON	NAPRONS
	NAPROXEN	NAPROXENS
KNAPS · SNAPS	**NAPS**	
	NARC	NARCO · NARCS
	NARCEEN	NARCEENS
	NARCEIN	NARCEINE · NARCEINS
	NARCEINE	NARCEINES
	NARCISM	NARCISMS
	NARCIST	NARCISTS
	NARCO	NARCOS
	NARCOMA	NARCOMAS
	NARCOS	NARCOSE
	NARCOSE	NARCOSES
	NARCOTIC	NARCOTICS
	NARCOTINE	NARCOTINES
	NARCOTISE	NARCOTISED · NARCOTISES
	NARCOTISM	NARCOTISMS
	NARCOTIST	NARCOTISTS
	NARCOTIZE	NARCOTIZED · NARCOTIZES
	NARD	NARDS
	NARDOO	NARDOOS
SNARE	**NARE**	NARES
SNARES	**NARES**	
	NARGHILE	NARGHILES
	NARGILE	NARGILEH · NARGILES
	NARGILEH	NARGILEHS
	NARICORN	NARICORNS
SNARK	**NARK**	NARKS · NARKY
SNARKIER	**NARKIER**	
SNARKIEST	**NARKIEST**	
SNARKS	**NARKS**	
SNARKY	**NARKY**	
	NARRATE	NARRATED · NARRATER · NARRATES
	NARRATER	NARRATERS
ENARRATION	**NARRATION**	NARRATIONS
	NARRATIVE	NARRATIVES
	NARRATOR	NARRATORS · NARRATORY
	NARROW	NARROWS
	NARROWING	NARROWINGS
	NARTJIE	NARTJIES
	NARWAL	NARWALS
	NARWHAL	NARWHALE · NARWHALS
	NARWHALE	NARWHALES
SNARY · UNARY	**NARY**	
ANAS · MNAS	**NAS**	
	NASAL	NASALS
	NASALISE	NASALISED · NASALISES
	NASALISM	NASALISMS
	NASALIZE	NASALIZED · NASALIZES
	NASARD	NASARDS
	NASCENCE	NASCENCES
	NASHGAB	NASHGABS
	NASHI	NASHIS
	NASION	NASIONS
	NASTALIK	NASTALIKS
	NASTIES	NASTIEST
	NASUTE	NASUTES
GNAT	**NAT**	NATS
	NATATION	NATATIONS
	NATATORIA	NATATORIAL
SNATCH	**NATCH**	
SNATCHES	**NATCHES**	
ENATES	**NATES**	
	NATHELESS	NATHELESSE
ENATION	**NATION**	NATIONS

FRONT HOOK	ROOT WORD	END HOOK
	NATIONAL	NATIONALS
ENATIONS	**NATIONS**	
	NATIVE	NATIVES
	NATIVISM	NATIVISMS
	NATIVIST	NATIVISTS
	NATRIUM	NATRIUMS
	NATROLITE	NATROLITES
	NATRON	NATRONS
GNATS	**NATS**	
	NATTER	NATTERS ▪ NATTERY
	NATTERER	NATTERERS
GNATTIER	**NATTIER**	
GNATTIEST	**NATTIEST**	
GNATTY	**NATTY**	
	NATURA	NATURAE ▪ NATURAL
	NATURAL	NATURALS
	NATURE	NATURED ▪ NATURES
	NATURISM	NATURISMS
	NATURIST	NATURISTS
	NAUGAHYDE	NAUGAHYDES
	NAUGHT	NAUGHTS ▪ NAUGHTY
	NAUGHTIES	NAUGHTIEST
	NAUMACHIA	NAUMACHIAE ▪ NAUMACHIAS
	NAUNT	NAUNTS
	NAUSEA	NAUSEAS
	NAUSEANT	NAUSEANTS
	NAUSEATE	NAUSEATED ▪ NAUSEATES
	NAUTIC	NAUTICS
	NAUTILOID	NAUTILOIDS
	NAVAID	NAVAIDS
	NAVALISM	NAVALISMS
	NAVAR	NAVARS
	NAVARCH	NAVARCHS ▪ NAVARCHY
	NAVARHO	NAVARHOS
	NAVARIN	NAVARINS
KNAVE	**NAVE**	NAVEL ▪ NAVES ▪ NAVEW
	NAVEL	NAVELS
	NAVELWORT	NAVELWORTS
KNAVES	**NAVES**	
	NAVETTE	NAVETTES
	NAVEW	NAVEWS
	NAVICERT	NAVICERTS
	NAVICULA	NAVICULAR ▪ NAVICULAS
	NAVICULAR	NAVICULARE ▪ NAVICULARS
	NAVIGATE	NAVIGATED ▪ NAVIGATES
	NAVIGATOR	NAVIGATORS
GNAW ▪ SNAW	**NAW**	
	NAWAB	NAWABS
	NAY	NAYS
	NAYSAY	NAYSAYS
	NAYSAYER	NAYSAYERS
	NAYSAYING	NAYSAYINGS
	NAYWARD	NAYWARDS
	NAYWORD	NAYWORDS
	NAZE	NAZES
	NAZI	NAZIR ▪ NAZIS
	NAZIR	NAZIRS
ANE ▪ ENE ▪ ONE	**NE**	NEB ▪ NED ▪ NEE ▪ NEF ▪ NEG ▪ NEK ▪ NEP ▪ NET ▪ NEW
	NEAFE	NEAFES
	NEAFFE	NEAFFES
	NEAL	NEALS
SNEAP	**NEAP**	NEAPS
SNEAPED	**NEAPED**	
SNEAPING	**NEAPING**	
SNEAPS	**NEAPS**	
ANEAR	**NEAR**	NEARS
ANEARED ▪ UNEARED	**NEARED**	
ANEARING	**NEARING**	
ANEARS	**NEARS**	

N

FRONT HOOK	ROOT WORD	END HOOK
	NEARSIDE	NEARSIDES
	NEAT	NEATH · NEATS
UNEATEN	**NEATEN**	NEATENS
ANEATH · SNEATH · UNEATH	**NEATH**	
	NEATHERD	NEATHERDS
	NEATNIK	NEATNIKS
SNEB	**NEB**	NEBS
SNEBBED	**NEBBED**	
	NEBBICH	NEBBICHS
SNEBBING	**NEBBING**	
	NEBBISH	NEBBISHE · NEBBISHY
	NEBBISHE	NEBBISHER · NEBBISHES
	NEBBISHER	NEBBISHERS
	NEBBUK	NEBBUKS
	NEBECK	NEBECKS
	NEBEK	NEBEKS
	NEBEL	NEBELS
	NEBENKERN	NEBENKERNS
SNEBS	**NEBS**	
	NEBULA	NEBULAE · NEBULAR · NEBULAS
	NEBULE	NEBULES
	NEBULISE	NEBULISED · NEBULISER · NEBULISES
	NEBULISER	NEBULISERS
	NEBULIUM	NEBULIUMS
	NEBULIZE	NEBULIZED · NEBULIZER · NEBULIZES
	NEBULIZER	NEBULIZERS
SNECK	**NECK**	NECKS
	NECKATEE	NECKATEES
	NECKBAND	NECKBANDS
	NECKBEEF	NECKBEEFS
	NECKCLOTH	NECKCLOTHS
SNECKED	**NECKED**	
	NECKER	NECKERS
	NECKGEAR	NECKGEARS
SNECKING	**NECKING**	NECKINGS
	NECKLACE	NECKLACED · NECKLACES
	NECKLET	NECKLETS
	NECKLINE	NECKLINES
	NECKPIECE	NECKPIECES
SNECKS	**NECKS**	
	NECKTIE	NECKTIES
	NECKVERSE	NECKVERSES
	NECKWEAR	NECKWEARS
	NECKWEED	NECKWEEDS
	NECROPHIL	NECROPHILE · NECROPHILS · NECROPHILY
	NECROPOLI	NECROPOLIS
	NECROSE	NECROSED · NECROSES
	NECROTISE	NECROTISED · NECROTISES
	NECROTIZE	NECROTIZED · NECROTIZES
	NECTAR	NECTARS · NECTARY
	NECTARINE	NECTARINES
SNED	**NED**	NEDS (offensive)
	NEDDIES	NEDDIEST
	NEDETTE	NEDETTES (offensive)
SNEDS	**NEDS**	
KNEE · SNEE	**NEE**	NEED · NEEM · NEEP
KNEED · SNEED	**NEED**	NEEDS · NEEDY
	NEEDER	NEEDERS
	NEEDFIRE	NEEDFIRES
	NEEDFUL	NEEDFULS
	NEEDLE	NEEDLED · NEEDLER · NEEDLES
	NEEDLEFUL	NEEDLEFULS
	NEEDLER	NEEDLERS
	NEEDLES	NEEDLESS
	NEEDLING	NEEDLINGS
	NEEDMENT	NEEDMENTS
	NEELD	NEELDS
	NEELE	NEELES
	NEEM	NEEMB · NEEMS

N

FRONT HOOK	ROOT WORD	END HOOK
	NEEMB	NEEMBS
	NEEP	NEEPS
	NEESE	NEESED ▪ NEESES
SNEEZE	**NEEZE**	NEEZED ▪ NEEZES
SNEEZED	**NEEZED**	
SNEEZES	**NEEZES**	
SNEEZING	**NEEZING**	
	NEF	NEFS
	NEG	NEGS
	NEGATE	NEGATED ▪ NEGATER ▪ NEGATES
	NEGATER	NEGATERS
	NEGATION	NEGATIONS
	NEGATIVE	NEGATIVED ▪ NEGATIVES
	NEGATON	NEGATONS
	NEGATOR	NEGATORS ▪ NEGATORY
	NEGATRON	NEGATRONS
	NEGLECT	NEGLECTS
	NEGLECTER	NEGLECTERS
	NEGLECTOR	NEGLECTORS
	NEGLIGE	NEGLIGEE ▪ NEGLIGES
	NEGLIGEE	NEGLIGEES
	NEGOCIANT	NEGOCIANTS
	NEGOTIANT	NEGOTIANTS
	NEGOTIATE	NEGOTIATED ▪ NEGOTIATES
	NEGRITUDE	NEGRITUDES
	NEGROHEAD	NEGROHEADS (offensive)
	NEGROID	NEGROIDS (offensive)
	NEGROISM	NEGROISMS (offensive)
	NEGRONI	NEGRONIS
	NEGROPHIL	NEGROPHILE ▪ NEGROPHILS
	NEIF	NEIFS
	NEIGH	NEIGHS
	NEIGHBOR	NEIGHBORS
	NEIGHBOUR	NEIGHBOURS
	NEINEI	NEINEIS
	NEIVE	NEIVES
	NEK	NEKS
	NEKTON	NEKTONS
	NELLIE	NELLIES
SNELLY	**NELLY**	
	NELSON	NELSONS
	NELUMBIUM	NELUMBIUMS
	NELUMBO	NELUMBOS
ENEMA	**NEMA**	NEMAS
ENEMAS	**NEMAS**	
	NEMATODE	NEMATODES
	NEMERTEAN	NEMERTEANS
	NEMERTIAN	NEMERTIANS
	NEMERTINE	NEMERTINES
	NEMESIA	NEMESIAS
	NEMN	NEMNS
	NEMOPHILA	NEMOPHILAS
	NENE	NENES
	NENNIGAI	NENNIGAIS
	NENUPHAR	NENUPHARS
	NEOBLAST	NEOBLASTS
	NEOCON	NEOCONS
	NEODYMIUM	NEODYMIUMS
	NEOGOTHIC	NEOGOTHICS
	NEOLITH	NEOLITHS
	NEOLOGIAN	NEOLOGIANS
	NEOLOGISE	NEOLOGISED ▪ NEOLOGISES
	NEOLOGISM	NEOLOGISMS
	NEOLOGIST	NEOLOGISTS
	NEOLOGIZE	NEOLOGIZED ▪ NEOLOGIZES
	NEOMORPH	NEOMORPHS
	NEOMYCIN	NEOMYCINS
	NEON	NEONS
	NEONATE	NEONATES

FRONT HOOK	ROOT WORD	END HOOK
	NEONOMIAN	NEONOMIANS
	NEOPAGAN	NEOPAGANS
	NEOPHILE	NEOPHILES
	NEOPHILIA	NEOPHILIAC · NEOPHILIAS
	NEOPHOBE	NEOPHOBES
	NEOPHOBIA	NEOPHOBIAS
	NEOPHYTE	NEOPHYTES
	NEOPILINA	NEOPILINAS
	NEOPLASIA	NEOPLASIAS
	NEOPLASM	NEOPLASMS
	NEOPRENE	NEOPRENES
	NEOTEINIA	NEOTEINIAS
	NEOTERIC	NEOTERICS
	NEOTERISE	NEOTERISED · NEOTERISES
	NEOTERISM	NEOTERISMS
	NEOTERIST	NEOTERISTS
	NEOTERIZE	NEOTERIZED · NEOTERIZES
	NEOTOXIN	NEOTOXINS
	NEOTROPIC	NEOTROPICS
	NEOTYPE	NEOTYPES
	NEP	NEPS
	NEPENTHE	NEPENTHES
	NEPER	NEPERS
	NEPETA	NEPETAS
	NEPHALISM	NEPHALISMS
	NEPHALIST	NEPHALISTS
	NEPHELINE	NEPHELINES
	NEPHELITE	NEPHELITES
	NEPHEW	NEPHEWS
	NEPHOGRAM	NEPHOGRAMS
	NEPHRIDIA	NEPHRIDIAL
	NEPHRISM	NEPHRISMS
	NEPHRITE	NEPHRITES
	NEPHRITIC	NEPHRITICS
	NEPHRON	NEPHRONS
	NEPHROTIC	NEPHROTICS
	NEPIT	NEPITS
	NEPOTISM	NEPOTISMS
	NEPOTIST	NEPOTISTS
	NEPTUNIUM	NEPTUNIUMS
	NERAL	NERALS
	NERD	NERDS · NERDY
	NEREID	NEREIDS
	NERINE	NERINES
	NERITE	NERITES
	NERK	NERKA · NERKS
	NERKA	NERKAS
	NEROL	NEROLI · NEROLS
	NEROLI	NEROLIS
INERTS	**NERTS**	
ENERVATE	**NERVATE**	
ENERVATION	**NERVATION**	NERVATIONS
	NERVATURE	NERVATURES
ENERVE	**NERVE**	NERVED · NERVER · NERVES
ENERVED	**NERVED**	
	NERVELET	NERVELETS
	NERVER	NERVERS
ENERVES	**NERVES**	
	NERVINE	NERVINES
	NERVINES	NERVINESS
ENERVING	**NERVING**	NERVINGS
	NERVULE	NERVULES
	NERVURE	NERVURES
	NESCIENCE	NESCIENCES
	NESCIENT	NESCIENTS
	NEST	NESTS
	NESTER	NESTERS
	NESTFUL	NESTFULS
	NESTING	NESTINGS

FRONT HOOK	ROOT WORD	END HOOK
	NESTLE	NESTLED · NESTLER · NESTLES
	NESTLER	NESTLERS
	NESTLING	NESTLINGS
	NESTOR	NESTORS
	NET	NETE · NETS · NETT
	NETBALL	NETBALLS
	NETBALLER	NETBALLERS
	NETE	NETES
	NETFUL	NETFULS
	NETHEAD	NETHEADS
	NETIZEN	NETIZENS
	NETMINDER	NETMINDERS
	NETOP	NETOPS
	NETSPEAK	NETSPEAKS
	NETSUKE	NETSUKES
	NETT	NETTS · NETTY
	NETTER	NETTERS
	NETTIE	NETTIER · NETTIES
	NETTIES	NETTIEST
	NETTING	NETTINGS
	NETTLE	NETTLED · NETTLER · NETTLES
	NETTLER	NETTLERS
	NETWORK	NETWORKS
	NETWORKER	NETWORKERS
	NEUK	NEUKS
	NEUM	NEUME · NEUMS
PNEUMATIC	**NEUMATIC**	
	NEUME	NEUMES
	NEURALGIA	NEURALGIAS
	NEURATION	NEURATIONS
	NEURAXON	NEURAXONS
	NEURINE	NEURINES
ANEURISM	**NEURISM**	NEURISMS
ANEURISMS	**NEURISMS**	
	NEURITE	NEURITES
	NEURITIC	NEURITICS
	NEUROCHIP	NEUROCHIPS
	NEUROCOEL	NEUROCOELE · NEUROCOELS
	NEUROGLIA	NEUROGLIAL · NEUROGLIAS
	NEUROGRAM	NEUROGRAMS
	NEUROMA	NEUROMAS
	NEUROMAS	NEUROMAST
	NEUROMAST	NEUROMASTS
	NEURON	NEURONE · NEURONS
	NEURONE	NEURONES
	NEUROPATH	NEUROPATHS · NEUROPATHY
	NEUROPIL	NEUROPILS
	NEUROTIC	NEUROTICS
	NEURULA	NEURULAE · NEURULAR · NEURULAS
	NEUSTON	NEUSTONS
	NEUTER	NEUTERS
	NEUTRAL	NEUTRALS
	NEUTRETTO	NEUTRETTOS
	NEUTRINO	NEUTRINOS
	NEUTRON	NEUTRONS
	NEVE	NEVEL · NEVER · NEVES
	NEVEL	NEVELS
KNEVELLED	**NEVELLED**	
KNEVELLING	**NEVELLING**	
	NEVERMIND	NEVERMINDS
ANEW · ENEW · KNEW	**NEW**	NEWS · NEWT
	NEWBIE	NEWBIES
	NEWBORN	NEWBORNS
	NEWCOME	NEWCOMER
	NEWCOMER	NEWCOMERS
ENEWED	**NEWED**	
	NEWEL	NEWELL · NEWELS
	NEWELL	NEWELLS
	NEWFANGLE	NEWFANGLED

537

FRONT HOOK	ROOT WORD	END HOOK
	NEWIE	NEWIES
ENEWING	**NEWING**	
	NEWLYWED	NEWLYWEDS
	NEWMARKET	NEWMARKETS
ENEWS	**NEWS**	NEWSY
	NEWSAGENT	NEWSAGENTS
	NEWSBEAT	NEWSBEATS
	NEWSBOY	NEWSBOYS
	NEWSBREAK	NEWSBREAKS
	NEWSCAST	NEWSCASTS
	NEWSDESK	NEWSDESKS
	NEWSGIRL	NEWSGIRLS
	NEWSGROUP	NEWSGROUPS
	NEWSHAWK	NEWSHAWKS
	NEWSHOUND	NEWSHOUNDS
	NEWSIE	NEWSIER ▪ NEWSIES
	NEWSIES	NEWSIEST
	NEWSMAKER	NEWSMAKERS
	NEWSPAPER	NEWSPAPERS
	NEWSPEAK	NEWSPEAKS
	NEWSPRINT	NEWSPRINTS
	NEWSREEL	NEWSREELS
	NEWSROOM	NEWSROOMS
	NEWSSTAND	NEWSSTANDS
	NEWSTRADE	NEWSTRADES
	NEWSWIRE	NEWSWIRES
	NEWT	NEWTS
	NEWTON	NEWTONS
	NEWWAVER	NEWWAVERS
	NEXT	NEXTS
	NGAIO	NGAIOS
	NGANA	NGANAS
	NGATI	NGATIS
	NGOMA	NGOMAS
	NGULTRUM	NGULTRUMS
	NHANDU	NHANDUS
	NIACIN	NIACINS
	NIAISERIE	NIAISERIES
	NIALAMIDE	NIALAMIDES
SNIB	**NIB**	NIBS
SNIBBED	**NIBBED**	
SNIBBING	**NIBBING**	
	NIBBLE	NIBBLED ▪ NIBBLER ▪ NIBBLES
	NIBBLER	NIBBLERS
	NIBBLING	NIBBLINGS
	NIBLICK	NIBLICKS
SNIBS	**NIBS**	
	NICAD	NICADS
	NICCOLITE	NICCOLITES
	NICE	NICER
	NICHE	NICHED ▪ NICHER ▪ NICHES
	NICHER	NICHERS
	NICHT	NICHTS
SNICK	**NICK**	NICKS ▪ NICKY
	NICKAR	NICKARS
SNICKED	**NICKED**	
	NICKEL	NICKELS
	NICKELINE	NICKELINES
	NICKELISE	NICKELISED ▪ NICKELISES
	NICKELIZE	NICKELIZED ▪ NICKELIZES
KNICKER ▪ SNICKER	**NICKER**	NICKERS
KNICKERED ▪ SNICKERED	**NICKERED**	
SNICKERING	**NICKERING**	
KNICKERS ▪ SNICKERS	**NICKERS**	
SNICKING	**NICKING**	
	NICKLE	NICKLED ▪ NICKLES
	NICKNACK	NICKNACKS
	NICKNAME	NICKNAMED ▪ NICKNAMER ▪ NICKNAMES
	NICKNAMER	NICKNAMERS

FRONT HOOK	ROOT WORD	END HOOK
KNICKPOINT	**NICKPOINT**	NICKPOINTS
KNICKS ▪ SNICKS	**NICKS**	
	NICKSTICK	NICKSTICKS
	NICKUM	NICKUMS
	NICOL	NICOLS
	NICOMPOOP	NICOMPOOPS
	NICOTIAN	NICOTIANA ▪ NICOTIANS
	NICOTIANA	NICOTIANAS
	NICOTIN	NICOTINE ▪ NICOTINS
	NICOTINE	NICOTINED ▪ NICOTINES
	NICTATE	NICTATED ▪ NICTATES
	NICTATION	NICTATIONS
	NICTITATE	NICTITATED ▪ NICTITATES
	NID	NIDE ▪ NIDI ▪ NIDS
	NIDAMENTA	NIDAMENTAL
	NIDATE	NIDATED ▪ NIDATES
	NIDATION	NIDATIONS
	NIDDERING	NIDDERINGS
	NIDDICK	NIDDICKS
SNIDE	**NIDE**	NIDED ▪ NIDES
SNIDED	**NIDED**	
	NIDERING	NIDERINGS
	NIDERLING	NIDERLINGS
SNIDES	**NIDES**	
	NIDGET	NIDGETS
SNIDING	**NIDING**	NIDINGS
	NIDOR	NIDORS
ONIE	**NIE**	NIED ▪ NIEF ▪ NIES
	NIECE	NIECES
	NIEF	NIEFS
	NIELLIST	NIELLISTS
	NIELLO	NIELLOS
SNIES	**NIES**	
	NIEVE	NIEVES
	NIEVEFUL	NIEVEFULS
KNIFE	**NIFE**	NIFES
KNIFES	**NIFES**	
SNIFF	**NIFF**	NIFFS ▪ NIFFY
SNIFFED	**NIFFED**	
SNIFFER	**NIFFER**	NIFFERS
SNIFFERS	**NIFFERS**	
SNIFFIER	**NIFFIER**	
SNIFFIEST	**NIFFIEST**	
SNIFFING	**NIFFING**	
	NIFFNAFF	NIFFNAFFS
SNIFFS	**NIFFS**	
SNIFFY	**NIFFY**	
SNIFTIER	**NIFTIER**	
	NIFTIES	NIFTIEST
SNIFTIEST	**NIFTIEST**	
SNIFTY	**NIFTY**	
	NIGELLA	NIGELLAS
	NIGER	NIGERS (offensive)
	NIGGARD	NIGGARDS
SNIGGER	**NIGGER**	NIGGERS (offensive) ▪ NIGGERY (offensive)
	NIGGERDOM	NIGGERDOMS (offensive)
SNIGGERED	**NIGGERED**	
SNIGGERING	**NIGGERING**	
	NIGGERISM	NIGGERISMS (offensive)
SNIGGERS	**NIGGERS**	
SNIGGLE	**NIGGLE**	NIGGLED ▪ NIGGLER ▪ NIGGLES
SNIGGLED	**NIGGLED**	
SNIGGLER	**NIGGLER**	NIGGLERS
SNIGGLERS	**NIGGLERS**	
SNIGGLES	**NIGGLES**	
SNIGGLING	**NIGGLING**	NIGGLINGS
SNIGGLINGS	**NIGGLINGS**	
ANIGH	**NIGH**	NIGHS ▪ NIGHT
ANIGHT ▪ KNIGHT	**NIGHT**	NIGHTS ▪ NIGHTY

FRONT HOOK	ROOT WORD	END HOOK
	NIGHTBIRD	NIGHTBIRDS
	NIGHTCAP	NIGHTCAPS
	NIGHTCLUB	NIGHTCLUBS
KNIGHTED	**NIGHTED**	
	NIGHTFALL	NIGHTFALLS
	NIGHTFIRE	NIGHTFIRES
	NIGHTGEAR	NIGHTGEARS
	NIGHTGLOW	NIGHTGLOWS
	NIGHTGOWN	NIGHTGOWNS
	NIGHTHAWK	NIGHTHAWKS
	NIGHTIE	NIGHTIES
	NIGHTJAR	NIGHTJARS
KNIGHTLESS	**NIGHTLESS**	
	NIGHTLIFE	NIGHTLIFES
KNIGHTLY	**NIGHTLY**	
	NIGHTMARE	NIGHTMARES
KNIGHTS	**NIGHTS**	
	NIGHTSIDE	NIGHTSIDES
	NIGHTSPOT	NIGHTSPOTS
	NIGHTTIDE	NIGHTTIDES
	NIGHTTIME	NIGHTTIMES
	NIGHTWEAR	NIGHTWEARS
	NIGIRI	NIGIRIS
	NIGRITUDE	NIGRITUDES
	NIGROSIN	NIGROSINE ▪ NIGROSINS
	NIGROSINE	NIGROSINES
	NIHIL	NIHILS
	NIHILISM	NIHILISMS
	NIHILIST	NIHILISTS
	NIHONGA	NIHONGAS
	NIKAU	NIKAUS
ANIL	**NIL**	NILL ▪ NILS
	NILGAI	NILGAIS
	NILGAU	NILGAUS
	NILGHAI	NILGHAIS
	NILGHAU	NILGHAUS
	NILL	NILLS
	NILPOTENT	NILPOTENTS
ANILS	**NILS**	
	NIM	NIMB ▪ NIMS
	NIMB	NIMBI ▪ NIMBS
	NIMBLE	NIMBLER
	NIMBLESSE	NIMBLESSES
	NIMBLEWIT	NIMBLEWITS
	NIMBYISM	NIMBYISMS
	NIMMER	NIMMERS
	NIMROD	NIMRODS
	NINCOM	NINCOMS
	NINCUM	NINCUMS
	NINE	NINES
	NINEBARK	NINEBARKS
	NINEPENCE	NINEPENCES
	NINEPIN	NINEPINS
	NINESCORE	NINESCORES
	NINETEEN	NINETEENS
	NINETIETH	NINETIETHS
	NINHYDRIN	NINHYDRINS
	NINJA	NINJAS
	NINJITSU	NINJITSUS
	NINJUTSU	NINJUTSUS
	NINON	NINONS
	NINTH	NINTHS
	NIOBATE	NIOBATES
	NIOBITE	NIOBITES
	NIOBIUM	NIOBIUMS
SNIP	**NIP**	NIPA ▪ NIPS
	NIPA	NIPAS
	NIPCHEESE	NIPCHEESES
SNIPPED	**NIPPED**	

FRONT HOOK	ROOT WORD	END HOOK
SNIPPER	**NIPPER**	NIPPERS
	NIPPERKIN	NIPPERKINS
SNIPPERS	**NIPPERS**	
SNIPPIER	**NIPPIER**	
SNIPPIEST	**NIPPIEST**	
SNIPPILY	**NIPPILY**	
SNIPPINESS	**NIPPINESS**	
SNIPPING	**NIPPING**	
	NIPPLE	NIPPLED ▪ NIPPLES
SNIPPY	**NIPPY**	
SNIPS	**NIPS**	
	NIPTER	NIPTERS
	NIQAB	NIQABS
	NIRAMIAI	NIRAMIAIS
	NIRL	NIRLS ▪ NIRLY
	NIRLIE	NIRLIER
	NIRVANA	NIRVANAS
ANIS ▪ UNIS	**NIS**	NISH ▪ NISI
	NISEI	NISEIS
	NISGUL	NISGULS
KNISH	**NISH**	
KNISHES	**NISHES**	
	NISSE	NISSES
KNIT ▪ SNIT ▪ UNIT	**NIT**	NITE ▪ NITS
	NITCHIE	NITCHIES (offensive)
UNITE	**NITE**	NITER ▪ NITES
UNITER	**NITER**	NITERS ▪ NITERY
	NITERIE	NITERIES
UNITERS	**NITERS**	
UNITES	**NITES**	
	NITHER	NITHERS
	NITHING	NITHINGS
	NITINOL	NITINOLS
	NITON	NITONS
	NITPICK	NITPICKS ▪ NITPICKY
	NITPICKER	NITPICKERS
	NITRAMINE	NITRAMINES
	NITRATE	NITRATED ▪ NITRATES
	NITRATINE	NITRATINES
	NITRATION	NITRATIONS
	NITRATOR	NITRATORS
	NITRE	NITRES
	NITRID	NITRIDE ▪ NITRIDS
	NITRIDE	NITRIDED ▪ NITRIDES
	NITRIDING	NITRIDINGS
	NITRIFIER	NITRIFIERS
	NITRIL	NITRILE ▪ NITRILS
	NITRILE	NITRILES
	NITRITE	NITRITES
	NITRO	NITROS
	NITROGEN	NITROGENS
	NITROS	NITROSO
	NITROSYL	NITROSYLS
	NITROXYL	NITROXYLS
	NITRY	NITRYL
	NITRYL	NITRYLS
KNITS ▪ SNITS ▪ UNITS	**NITS**	
	NITWIT	NITWITS
	NIVATION	NIVATIONS
	NIX	NIXE ▪ NIXY
	NIXE	NIXED ▪ NIXER ▪ NIXES
	NIXER	NIXERS
	NIXIE	NIXIES
	NIZAM	NIZAMS
	NIZAMATE	NIZAMATES
	NKOSI	NKOSIS
ONO	**NO**	NOB ▪ NOD ▪ NOG ▪ NOH ▪ NOM ▪ NON ▪ NOO NOR ▪ NOS ▪ NOT ▪ NOW ▪ NOX ▪ NOY
	NOAH	NOAHS

FRONT HOOK	ROOT WORD	END HOOK
KNOB · SNOB	**NOB**	NOBS
KNOBBIER · SNOBBIER	**NOBBIER**	
KNOBBIEST · SNOBBIEST	**NOBBIEST**	
SNOBBILY	**NOBBILY**	
KNOBBINESS	**NOBBINESS**	
KNOBBLE	**NOBBLE**	NOBBLED · NOBBLER · NOBBLES
KNOBBLED	**NOBBLED**	
	NOBBLER	NOBBLERS
KNOBBLES	**NOBBLES**	
KNOBBLING	**NOBBLING**	
KNOBBY · SNOBBY	**NOBBY**	
	NOBELIUM	NOBELIUMS
	NOBILESSE	NOBILESSES
	NOBLE	NOBLER · NOBLES
	NOBLES	NOBLEST
	NOBLESSE	NOBLESSES
KNOBS · SNOBS	**NOBS**	
	NOCAKE	NOCAKES
	NOCENT	NOCENTS
	NOCHEL	NOCHELS
KNOCK	**NOCK**	NOCKS
KNOCKED	**NOCKED**	
	NOCKET	NOCKETS
KNOCKING	**NOCKING**	
KNOCKS	**NOCKS**	
	NOCTILIO	NOCTILIOS
	NOCTILUCA	NOCTILUCAE · NOCTILUCAS
	NOCTUA	NOCTUAS
	NOCTUID	NOCTUIDS
	NOCTULE	NOCTULES
	NOCTURIA	NOCTURIAS
	NOCTURN	NOCTURNE · NOCTURNS
	NOCTURNAL	NOCTURNALS
	NOCTURNE	NOCTURNES
SNOD	**NOD**	NODE · NODI · NODS
ANODAL · ENODAL	**NODAL**	
	NODALISE	NODALISED · NODALISES
	NODALIZE	NODALIZED · NODALIZES
ANODALLY	**NODALLY**	
	NODATION	NODATIONS
SNODDED	**NODDED**	
SNODDER	**NODDER**	NODDERS
	NODDIES	NODDIEST
SNODDING	**NODDING**	NODDINGS
	NODDLE	NODDLED · NODDLES
ANODE	**NODE**	NODES
ANODES	**NODES**	
SNODS	**NODS**	
	NODULE	NODULED · NODULES
	NOEL	NOELS
ANOESES	**NOESES**	
ANOESIS	**NOESIS**	
ANOETIC	**NOETIC**	
SNOG	**NOG**	NOGG · NOGS
	NOGG	NOGGS
SNOGGED	**NOGGED**	
	NOGGIN	NOGGING · NOGGINS
SNOGGING	**NOGGING**	NOGGINGS
SNOGS	**NOGS**	
	NOIL	NOILS · NOILY
ANOINT	**NOINT**	NOINTS
ANOINTED	**NOINTED**	
ANOINTER	**NOINTER**	NOINTERS
ANOINTERS	**NOINTERS**	
ANOINTING	**NOINTING**	
ANOINTS	**NOINTS**	
	NOIR	NOIRS
	NOISE	NOISED · NOISES
	NOISENIK	NOISENIKS

FRONT HOOK	ROOT WORD	END HOOK
	NOISETTE	NOISETTES
ANOLE	NOLE	NOLES
ANOLES	NOLES	
	NOLITION	NOLITIONS
KNOLL	NOLL	NOLLS
KNOLLS	NOLLS	
	NOLO	NOLOS
	NOM	NOMA ▪ NOME ▪ NOMS
	NOMA	NOMAD ▪ NOMAS
	NOMAD	NOMADE ▪ NOMADS ▪ NOMADY
	NOMADE	NOMADES
	NOMADISE	NOMADISED ▪ NOMADISES
	NOMADISM	NOMADISMS
	NOMADIZE	NOMADIZED ▪ NOMADIZES
	NOMARCH	NOMARCHS ▪ NOMARCHY
	NOMBRIL	NOMBRILS
GNOME	NOME	NOMEN ▪ NOMES
GNOMES	NOMES	
ANOMIC ▪ GNOMIC	NOMIC	
	NOMINA	NOMINAL
	NOMINAL	NOMINALS
	NOMINATE	NOMINATED ▪ NOMINATES
	NOMINATOR	NOMINATORS
	NOMINEE	NOMINEES
	NOMISM	NOMISMS
	NOMOGRAM	NOMOGRAMS
	NOMOGRAPH	NOMOGRAPHS ▪ NOMOGRAPHY
	NOMOTHETE	NOMOTHETES
ANON	NON	NONA ▪ NONE ▪ NONG ▪ NONI
	NONA	NONAS
	NONACID	NONACIDS
	NONACTION	NONACTIONS
	NONACTOR	NONACTORS
	NONADDICT	NONADDICTS
	NONADULT	NONADULTS
	NONAGE	NONAGED ▪ NONAGES
	NONAGON	NONAGONS
	NONANE	NONANES
	NONANSWER	NONANSWERS
	NONART	NONARTS
	NONARTIST	NONARTISTS
	NONAUTHOR	NONAUTHORS
	NONBANK	NONBANKS
	NONBEING	NONBEINGS
	NONBELIEF	NONBELIEFS
	NONBLACK	NONBLACKS
	NONBOOK	NONBOOKS
	NONCE	NONCES
	NONCOLA	NONCOLAS
	NONCOLOR	NONCOLORS
	NONCOM	NONCOMS
	NONCONCUR	NONCONCURS
	NONCRIME	NONCRIMES
	NONDANCE	NONDANCER ▪ NONDANCES
	NONDANCER	NONDANCERS
	NONDEMAND	NONDEMANDS
	NONDOCTOR	NONDOCTORS
	NONDRIVER	NONDRIVERS
	NONE	NONES ▪ NONET
	NONEDIBLE	NONEDIBLES
	NONEGO	NONEGOS
	NONEQUAL	NONEQUALS
	NONET	NONETS
	NONETHNIC	NONETHNICS
	NONETTE	NONETTES
	NONETTO	NONETTOS
	NONEVENT	NONEVENTS
	NONEXEMPT	NONEXEMPTS
	NONEXPERT	NONEXPERTS

FRONT HOOK	ROOT WORD	END HOOK
	NONFACT	NONFACTS
	NONFACTOR	NONFACTORS
	NONFAN	NONFANS
	NONFARMER	NONFARMERS
	NONFLUID	NONFLUIDS
	NONG	NONGS
	NONGAY	NONGAYS
	NONGLARE	NONGLARES
	NONGOLFER	NONGOLFERS
	NONGUEST	NONGUESTS
	NONGUILT	NONGUILTS
	NONHUMAN	NONHUMANS
	NONHUNTER	NONHUNTERS
	NONI	NONIS
	NONILLION	NONILLIONS
	NONIMAGE	NONIMAGES
	NONINSECT	NONINSECTS
	NONISSUE	NONISSUES
	NONJOINER	NONJOINERS
	NONJUROR	NONJURORS
	NONKOSHER	NONKOSHERS
	NONLAWYER	NONLAWYERS
	NONLEGUME	NONLEGUMES
	NONLIQUID	NONLIQUIDS
	NONLIVING	NONLIVINGS
	NONLOCAL	NONLOCALS
	NONMAJOR	NONMAJORS
	NONMARKET	NONMARKETS
	NONMEMBER	NONMEMBERS
	NONMETAL	NONMETALS
	NONMODERN	NONMODERNS
	NONMORTAL	NONMORTALS
	NONMUSIC	NONMUSICS
	NONMUTANT	NONMUTANTS
	NONNATIVE	NONNATIVES
	NONNOVEL	NONNOVELS
	NONOWNER	NONOWNERS
	NONPAGAN	NONPAGANS
	NONPAPIST	NONPAPISTS
	NONPAREIL	NONPAREILS
	NONPARENT	NONPARENTS
	NONPAST	NONPASTS
	NONPERSON	NONPERSONS
	NONPLAY	NONPLAYS
	NONPLAYER	NONPLAYERS
	NONPROFIT	NONPROFITS
	NONREADER	NONREADERS
	NONRIOTER	NONRIOTERS
	NONRIVAL	NONRIVALS
	NONSECRET	NONSECRETS
	NONSENSE	NONSENSES
	NONSERIAL	NONSERIALS
	NONSIGNER	NONSIGNERS
	NONSKATER	NONSKATERS
	NONSKED	NONSKEDS
	NONSKIER	NONSKIERS
	NONSMOKER	NONSMOKERS
	NONSOLID	NONSOLIDS
	NONSTAPLE	NONSTAPLES
	NONSTICK	NONSTICKY
	NONSTOP	NONSTOPS
	NONSTYLE	NONSTYLES
	NONSUGAR	NONSUGARS
	NONSUIT	NONSUITS
	NONSYSTEM	NONSYSTEMS
	NONTALKER	NONTALKERS
	NONTHEIST	NONTHEISTS
	NONTRUTH	NONTRUTHS
	NONUNION	NONUNIONS

FRONT HOOK	ROOT WORD	END HOOK
	NONUPLE	NONUPLES · NONUPLET
	NONUPLET	NONUPLETS
	NONUSE	NONUSER · NONUSES
	NONUSER	NONUSERS
	NONVECTOR	NONVECTORS
	NONVIEWER	NONVIEWERS
	NONVIRGIN	NONVIRGINS
	NONVOCAL	NONVOCALS
	NONVOTER	NONVOTERS
	NONWAR	NONWARS
	NONWHITE	NONWHITES
	NONWORD	NONWORDS
	NONWORKER	NONWORKERS
	NONWOVEN	NONWOVENS
	NONWRITER	NONWRITERS
	NONYL	NONYLS
	NOO	NOOK · NOON · NOOP
	NOODGE	NOODGED · NOODGES
	NOODLE	NOODLED · NOODLES
	NOODLEDOM	NOODLEDOMS
	NOODLING	NOODLINGS
	NOOGIE	NOOGIES
SNOOK	NOOK	NOOKS · NOOKY
	NOOKIE	NOOKIER · NOOKIES (offensive)
	NOOKIES	NOOKIEST
SNOOKS	NOOKS	
	NOON	NOONS
	NOONDAY	NOONDAYS
	NOONER	NOONERS
	NOONING	NOONINGS
	NOONTIDE	NOONTIDES
	NOONTIME	NOONTIMES
SNOOP	NOOP	NOOPS
SNOOPS	NOOPS	
	NOOSE	NOOSED · NOOSER · NOOSES
	NOOSER	NOOSERS
	NOOSPHERE	NOOSPHERES
	NOOTROPIC	NOOTROPICS
	NOPAL	NOPALS
	NOPALITO	NOPALITOS
	NOR	NORI · NORK · NORM
	NORI	NORIA · NORIS
	NORIA	NORIAS
	NORIMON	NORIMONS
	NORITE	NORITES
	NORK	NORKS
	NORLAND	NORLANDS
ENORM	NORM	NORMA · NORMS
	NORMA	NORMAL · NORMAN · NORMAS
	NORMAL	NORMALS
	NORMALISE	NORMALISED · NORMALISER · NORMALISES
	NORMALIZE	NORMALIZED · NORMALIZER · NORMALIZES
	NORMAN	NORMANS
	NORSEL	NORSELS
	NORSELLER	NORSELLERS
	NORTENA	NORTENAS
	NORTENO	NORTENOS
	NORTH	NORTHS
	NORTHEAST	NORTHEASTS
	NORTHER	NORTHERN · NORTHERS
	NORTHERN	NORTHERNS
	NORTHING	NORTHINGS
	NORTHLAND	NORTHLANDS
	NORTHWARD	NORTHWARDS
	NORTHWEST	NORTHWESTS
	NORWARD	NORWARDS
ONOS	NOS	NOSE · NOSH · NOSY
	NOSE	NOSED · NOSER · NOSES · NOSEY
	NOSEAN	NOSEANS

FRONT HOOK	ROOT WORD	END HOOK
	NOSEBAG	NOSEBAGS
	NOSEBAND	NOSEBANDS
	NOSEBLEED	NOSEBLEEDS
	NOSEDIVE	NOSEDIVED ▪ NOSEDIVES
	NOSEGAY	NOSEGAYS
	NOSEGUARD	NOSEGUARDS
	NOSELITE	NOSELITES
	NOSEPIECE	NOSEPIECES
	NOSER	NOSERS
ENOSES ▪ GNOSES	**NOSES**	
	NOSEWHEEL	NOSEWHEELS
	NOSEY	NOSEYS
	NOSHER	NOSHERS ▪ NOSHERY
	NOSHERIE	NOSHERIES
	NOSIES	NOSIEST
	NOSING	NOSINGS
	NOSODE	NOSODES
	NOSTALGIA	NOSTALGIAS
	NOSTALGIC	NOSTALGICS
	NOSTOC	NOSTOCS
	NOSTRIL	NOSTRILS
	NOSTRUM	NOSTRUMS
KNOT ▪ SNOT	**NOT**	NOTA ▪ NOTE ▪ NOTT
	NOTA	NOTAL
	NOTABLE	NOTABLES
	NOTAEUM	NOTAEUMS
	NOTARISE	NOTARISED ▪ NOTARISES
	NOTARIZE	NOTARIZED ▪ NOTARIZES
	NOTATE	NOTATED ▪ NOTATES
	NOTATION	NOTATIONS
	NOTCH	NOTCHY
	NOTCHBACK	NOTCHBACKS
	NOTCHEL	NOTCHELS
	NOTCHER	NOTCHERS
	NOTCHING	NOTCHINGS
	NOTE	NOTED ▪ NOTER ▪ NOTES
	NOTEBOOK	NOTEBOOKS
	NOTECARD	NOTECARDS
	NOTECASE	NOTECASES
	NOTELET	NOTELETS
	NOTEPAD	NOTEPADS
	NOTEPAPER	NOTEPAPERS
	NOTER	NOTERS
ANOTHER	**NOTHER**	
	NOTHING	NOTHINGS
	NOTICE	NOTICED ▪ NOTICER ▪ NOTICES
	NOTICER	NOTICERS
	NOTIFIER	NOTIFIERS
	NOTION	NOTIONS
	NOTIONIST	NOTIONISTS
	NOTITIA	NOTITIAE ▪ NOTITIAS
	NOTOCHORD	NOTOCHORDS
	NOUGAT	NOUGATS
	NOUGHT	NOUGHTS
	NOUL	NOULD ▪ NOULE ▪ NOULS
	NOULD	NOULDE
	NOULE	NOULES
	NOUMENA	NOUMENAL
	NOUN	NOUNS ▪ NOUNY
	NOUP	NOUPS
	NOURICE	NOURICES
	NOURISHER	NOURISHERS
	NOURITURE	NOURITURES
	NOURSLE	NOURSLED ▪ NOURSLES
	NOUSELL	NOUSELLS
	NOUSLE	NOUSLED ▪ NOUSLES
KNOUT ▪ SNOUT	**NOUT**	
	NOUVEAU	NOUVEAUX
	NOUVELLE	NOUVELLES

FRONT HOOK	ROOT WORD	END HOOK
	NOVA	NOVAE • NOVAS
	NOVATION	NOVATIONS
	NOVEL	NOVELS
	NOVELDOM	NOVELDOMS
	NOVELESE	NOVELESES
	NOVELETTE	NOVELETTES
	NOVELISE	NOVELISED • NOVELISER • NOVELISES
	NOVELISER	NOVELISERS
	NOVELISM	NOVELISMS
	NOVELIST	NOVELISTS
	NOVELIZE	NOVELIZED • NOVELIZER • NOVELIZES
	NOVELIZER	NOVELIZERS
	NOVELLA	NOVELLAE • NOVELLAS
	NOVENA	NOVENAE • NOVENAS
	NOVERINT	NOVERINTS
	NOVICE	NOVICES
	NOVICIATE	NOVICIATES
	NOVITIATE	NOVITIATES
	NOVOCAINE	NOVOCAINES
	NOVUM	NOVUMS
ANOW • ENOW • GNOW • KNOW • SNOW	**NOW**	NOWL • NOWN • NOWS • NOWT • NOWY
	NOWAY	NOWAYS
SNOWED • UNOWED	**NOWED**	
	NOWHERE	NOWHERES
	NOWL	NOWLS
KNOWN	**NOWN**	
ENOWS • GNOWS • KNOWS • SNOWS	**NOWS**	
	NOWT	NOWTS • NOWTY
SNOWY	**NOWY**	
	NOY	NOYS
	NOYADE	NOYADES
	NOYANCE	NOYANCES
	NOYAU	NOYAUS
	NOZZER	NOZZERS
	NOZZLE	NOZZLES
GNU	**NU**	NUB • NUN • NUR • NUS • NUT
	NUANCE	NUANCED • NUANCES
KNUB • SNUB	**NUB**	NUBS
SNUBBED	**NUBBED**	
KNUBBIER • SNUBBIER	**NUBBIER**	
KNUBBIEST • SNUBBIEST	**NUBBIEST**	
	NUBBIN	NUBBING • NUBBINS
SNUBBINESS	**NUBBINESS**	
SNUBBING	**NUBBING**	
KNUBBLE	**NUBBLE**	NUBBLED • NUBBLES
KNUBBLED	**NUBBLED**	
KNUBBLES	**NUBBLES**	
KNUBBLIER	**NUBBLIER**	
KNUBBLIEST	**NUBBLIEST**	
KNUBBLING	**NUBBLING**	
KNUBBLY	**NUBBLY**	
KNUBBY • SNUBBY	**NUBBY**	
	NUBECULA	NUBECULAE
	NUBIA	NUBIAS
KNUBS • SNUBS	**NUBS**	
	NUBUCK	NUBUCKS
	NUCHA	NUCHAE • NUCHAL
	NUCHAL	NUCHALS
	NUCLEASE	NUCLEASES
ANUCLEATE • ENUCLEATE	**NUCLEATE**	NUCLEATED • NUCLEATES
ANUCLEATED • ENUCLEATED	**NUCLEATED**	
ENUCLEATES	**NUCLEATES**	
	NUCLEATOR	NUCLEATORS
	NUCLEI	NUCLEIC • NUCLEIN
	NUCLEIDE	NUCLEIDES
	NUCLEIN	NUCLEINS
	NUCLEOID	NUCLEOIDS
	NUCLEOLE	NUCLEOLES
	NUCLEON	NUCLEONS

FRONT HOOK	ROOT WORD	END HOOK
	NUCLEONIC	NUCLEONICS
	NUCLIDE	NUCLIDES
	NUCULE	NUCULES
	NUDATION	NUDATIONS
	NUDE	NUDER · NUDES
	NUDES	NUDEST
SNUDGE	**NUDGE**	NUDGED · NUDGER · NUDGES
SNUDGED	**NUDGED**	
	NUDGER	NUDGERS
SNUDGES	**NUDGES**	
SNUDGING	**NUDGING**	
	NUDIE	NUDIES
	NUDISM	NUDISMS
	NUDIST	NUDISTS
	NUDNICK	NUDNICKS
	NUDNIK	NUDNIKS
SNUFF	**NUFF**	NUFFS
	NUFFIN	NUFFINS
SNUFFS	**NUFFS**	
	NUGGAR	NUGGARS
	NUGGET	NUGGETS · NUGGETY
	NUISANCE	NUISANCER · NUISANCES
	NUISANCER	NUISANCERS
	NUKE	NUKED · NUKES
	NULL	NULLA · NULLS
	NULLA	NULLAH · NULLAS
	NULLAH	NULLAHS
	NULLIFIER	NULLIFIERS
	NULLING	NULLINGS
	NULLIPARA	NULLIPARAE · NULLIPARAS
	NULLIPORE	NULLIPORES
	NUMB	NUMBS
	NUMBAT	NUMBATS
	NUMBER	NUMBERS
	NUMBERER	NUMBERERS
	NUMBERING	NUMBERINGS
	NUMBSKULL	NUMBSKULLS
	NUMCHUCK	NUMCHUCKS
	NUMDAH	NUMDAHS
ENUMERABLE	**NUMERABLE**	
	NUMERAIRE	NUMERAIRES
	NUMERAL	NUMERALS
ENUMERATE	**NUMERATE**	NUMERATED · NUMERATES
ENUMERATED	**NUMERATED**	
ENUMERATES	**NUMERATES**	
ENUMERATOR	**NUMERATOR**	NUMERATORS
	NUMERIC	NUMERICS
	NUMMULAR	NUMMULARY
	NUMMULITE	NUMMULITES
	NUMNAH	NUMNAHS
	NUMSKULL	NUMSKULLS
	NUN	NUNS
	NUNATAK	NUNATAKS
	NUNCHAKU	NUNCHAKUS
	NUNCHEON	NUNCHEONS
	NUNCIO	NUNCIOS
	NUNCLE	NUNCLES
	NUNCUPATE	NUNCUPATED · NUNCUPATES
	NUNDINE	NUNDINES
	NUNHOOD	NUNHOODS
	NUNNATION	NUNNATIONS
	NUNSHIP	NUNSHIPS
	NUPTIAL	NUPTIALS
KNUR	**NUR**	NURD · NURL · NURR · NURS
	NURAGHI	NURAGHIC
	NURD	NURDS · NURDY
	NURDLE	NURDLED · NURDLES
	NURHAG	NURHAGS
KNURL	**NURL**	NURLS

FRONT HOOK	ROOT WORD	END HOOK
KNURLED	**NURLED**	
KNURLING	**NURLING**	
KNURLS	**NURLS**	
KNURR	**NURR**	NURRS
KNURRS	**NURRS**	
KNURS	**NURS**	NURSE
	NURSE	NURSED · NURSER · NURSES
	NURSELING	NURSELINGS
	NURSEMAID	NURSEMAIDS
	NURSER	NURSERS · NURSERY
	NURSING	NURSINGS
	NURSLE	NURSLED · NURSLES
	NURSLING	NURSLINGS
	NURTURE	NURTURED · NURTURER · NURTURES
	NURTURER	NURTURERS
ANUS · GNUS · ONUS	**NUS**	
KNUT	**NUT**	NUTS
	NUTARIAN	NUTARIANS
	NUTATE	NUTATED · NUTATES
	NUTATION	NUTATIONS
	NUTBUTTER	NUTBUTTERS
	NUTCASE	NUTCASES (offensive)
	NUTGALL	NUTGALLS
	NUTHOUSE	NUTHOUSES (offensive)
	NUTJOBBER	NUTJOBBERS
	NUTLET	NUTLETS
	NUTMEAL	NUTMEALS
	NUTMEAT	NUTMEATS
	NUTMEG	NUTMEGS
	NUTPECKER	NUTPECKERS
	NUTPICK	NUTPICKS
	NUTRIA	NUTRIAS
	NUTRIENT	NUTRIENTS
	NUTRIMENT	NUTRIMENTS
	NUTRITION	NUTRITIONS
	NUTRITIVE	NUTRITIVES
KNUTS	**NUTS**	NUTSO · NUTSY
	NUTSEDGE	NUTSEDGES
	NUTSHELL	NUTSHELLS
	NUTTER	NUTTERS (offensive) · NUTTERY
	NUTTING	NUTTINGS
	NUTWOOD	NUTWOODS
	NUZZER	NUZZERS
SNUZZLE	**NUZZLE**	NUZZLED · NUZZLER · NUZZLES
SNUZZLED	**NUZZLED**	
	NUZZLER	NUZZLERS
SNUZZLES	**NUZZLES**	
SNUZZLING	**NUZZLING**	
ANY · ONY · SNY	**NY**	NYE · NYS
	NYAFF	NYAFFS
INYALA	**NYALA**	NYALAS
INYALAS	**NYALAS**	
	NYANZA	NYANZAS
	NYBBLE	NYBBLES
SNYE	**NYE**	NYED · NYES
SNYES	**NYES**	
	NYLGHAI	NYLGHAIS
	NYLGHAU	NYLGHAUS
	NYLON	NYLONS
	NYMPH	NYMPHA · NYMPHO · NYMPHS
	NYMPHA	NYMPHAE · NYMPHAL
	NYMPHAE	NYMPHAEA
	NYMPHAEUM	NYMPHAEUMS
	NYMPHALID	NYMPHALIDS
	NYMPHET	NYMPHETS
	NYMPHETTE	NYMPHETTES
	NYMPHO	NYMPHOS
	NYSSA	NYSSAS
	NYSTATIN	NYSTATINS

O

FRONT HOOK	ROOT WORD	END HOOK
GOAF · LOAF	OAF	OAFS
GOAFS · LOAFS	OAFS	
BOAK · SOAK	OAK	OAKS · OAKY
BOAKED · SOAKED	OAKED	
SOAKEN	OAKEN	
	OAKENSHAW	OAKENSHAWS
SOAKER	OAKER	OAKERS
SOAKERS	OAKERS	
	OAKIES	OAKIEST
	OAKLING	OAKLINGS
BOAKS · SOAKS	OAKS	
	OAKUM	OAKUMS
	OANSHAGH	OANSHAGHS
BOAR · HOAR · ROAR · SOAR · VOAR	OAR	OARS · OARY
	OARAGE	OARAGES
HOARED · ROARED · SOARED	OARED	
BOARFISH	OARFISH	
BOARFISHES	OARFISHES	
HOARIER · ROARIER	OARIER	
HOARIEST · ROARIEST	OARIEST	
HOARING · ROARING · SOARING	OARING	
	OARLOCK	OARLOCKS
BOARS · HOARS · ROARS · SOARS · VOARS	OARS	
	OARWEED	OARWEEDS
GOARY · HOARY · ROARY	OARY	
BOAST · COAST · HOAST · LOAST · ROAST	OAST	OASTS
TOAST		
	OASTHOUSE	OASTHOUSES
BOASTS · COASTS · HOASTS · ROASTS	OASTS	
TOASTS		
BOAT · COAT · DOAT · GOAT · MOAT	OAT	OATH · OATS
	OATCAKE	OATCAKES
BOATER · COATER · DOATER	OATER	OATERS
BOATERS · COATERS · DOATERS	OATERS	
LOATH	OATH	OATHS
BOATLIKE · GOATLIKE · MOATLIKE	OATLIKE	
	OATMEAL	OATMEALS
BOATS · COATS · DOATS · GOATS · MOATS	OATS	
LOAVES · SOAVES	OAVES	
BOB · COB · DOB · FOB · GOB · HOB · JOB	OB	OBA · OBE · OBI · OBO · OBS
KOB · LOB · MOB · NOB · ROB · SOB · YOB		
BOBA · SOBA	OBA	OBAS
GOBANG · KOBANG	OBANG	OBANGS
GOBANGS · KOBANGS	OBANGS	
BOBAS · SOBAS	OBAS	
	OBBLIGATO	OBBLIGATOS
	OBDURATE	OBDURATED · OBDURATES
	OBDURE	OBDURED · OBDURES
JOBE · LOBE · MOBE · ROBE	OBE	OBES · OBEY
	OBEAH	OBEAHS
	OBEAHISM	OBEAHISMS
BOBECHE	OBECHE	OBECHES
BOBECHES	OBECHES	
	OBEDIENCE	OBEDIENCES
	OBEISANCE	OBEISANCES
	OBEISM	OBEISMS
	OBELI	OBELIA
LOBELIA	OBELIA	OBELIAS
LOBELIAS	OBELIAS	
	OBELISE	OBELISED · OBELISES
	OBELISK	OBELISKS
	OBELISM	OBELISMS
	OBELIZE	OBELIZED · OBELIZES
	OBENTO	OBENTOS
JOBES · LOBES · MOBES · ROBES	OBES	OBESE
	OBESE	OBESER

FRONT HOOK	ROOT WORD	END HOOK
	OBEY	OBEYS
	OBEYER	OBEYERS
	OBFUSCATE	OBFUSCATED · OBFUSCATES
LOBI	**OBI**	OBIA · OBIS · OBIT
COBIA	**OBIA**	OBIAS
COBIAS	**OBIAS**	
	OBIISM	OBIISMS
OOBIT	**OBIT**	OBITS
OOBITS	**OBITS**	
	OBJECT	OBJECTS
	OBJECTION	OBJECTIONS
	OBJECTIVE	OBJECTIVES
	OBJECTOR	OBJECTORS
	OBJET	OBJETS
	OBJURE	OBJURED · OBJURES
	OBJURGATE	OBJURGATED · OBJURGATES
	OBLAST	OBLASTI · OBLASTS
	OBLATE	OBLATES
	OBLATION	OBLATIONS
	OBLIGANT	OBLIGANTS
	OBLIGATE	OBLIGATED · OBLIGATES
	OBLIGATO	OBLIGATOR · OBLIGATOS
	OBLIGATOR	OBLIGATORS · OBLIGATORY
	OBLIGE	OBLIGED · OBLIGEE · OBLIGER · OBLIGES
	OBLIGEE	OBLIGEES
	OBLIGER	OBLIGERS
	OBLIGOR	OBLIGORS
	OBLIQUE	OBLIQUED · OBLIQUER · OBLIQUES
	OBLIQUES	OBLIQUEST
	OBLIVION	OBLIVIONS
	OBLONG	OBLONGS
GOBO · HOBO · KOBO · LOBO · ZOBO	**OBO**	OBOE · OBOL · OBOS
	OBOE	OBOES
GOBOES · HOBOES	**OBOES**	
	OBOIST	OBOISTS
BOBOL	**OBOL**	OBOLE · OBOLI · OBOLS
SOBOLE	**OBOLE**	OBOLES
SOBOLES	**OBOLES**	
BOBOLS	**OBOLS**	
GOBOS · HOBOS · KOBOS · LOBOS · ZOBOS	**OBOS**	
	OBREPTION	OBREPTIONS
BOBS · COBS · DOBS · FOBS · GOBS · HOBS JOBS · KOBS · LOBS · MOBS · NOBS · ROBS SOBS · YOBS	**OBS**	
	OBSCENE	OBSCENER
	OBSCURANT	OBSCURANTS
	OBSCURE	OBSCURED · OBSCURER · OBSCURES
	OBSCURER	OBSCURERS
	OBSCURES	OBSCUREST
	OBSECRATE	OBSECRATED · OBSECRATES
	OBSEQUIE	OBSEQUIES
	OBSERVANT	OBSERVANTS
	OBSERVE	OBSERVED · OBSERVER · OBSERVES
	OBSERVER	OBSERVERS
	OBSESSION	OBSESSIONS
	OBSESSIVE	OBSESSIVES
	OBSESSOR	OBSESSORS
	OBSIDIAN	OBSIDIANS
	OBSIGN	OBSIGNS
	OBSIGNATE	OBSIGNATED · OBSIGNATES
	OBSOLESCE	OBSOLESCED · OBSOLESCES
	OBSOLETE	OBSOLETED · OBSOLETES
	OBSTACLE	OBSTACLES
	OBSTETRIC	OBSTETRICS
	OBSTRUCT	OBSTRUCTS
	OBSTRUENT	OBSTRUENTS
	OBTAIN	OBTAINS
	OBTAINER	OBTAINERS
	OBTEMPER	OBTEMPERS

FRONT HOOK	ROOT WORD	END HOOK
	OBTEND	OBTENDS
	OBTENTION	OBTENTIONS
	OBTEST	OBTESTS
	OBTRUDE	OBTRUDED ▪ OBTRUDER ▪ OBTRUDES
	OBTRUDER	OBTRUDERS
	OBTRUDING	OBTRUDINGS
	OBTRUSION	OBTRUSIONS
	OBTUND	OBTUNDS
	OBTUNDENT	OBTUNDENTS
	OBTURATE	OBTURATED ▪ OBTURATES
	OBTURATOR	OBTURATORS
	OBTUSE	OBTUSER
	OBUMBRATE	OBUMBRATED ▪ OBUMBRATES
	OBVENTION	OBVENTIONS
	OBVERSE	OBVERSES
	OBVERSION	OBVERSIONS
	OBVERT	OBVERTS
	OBVIATE	OBVIATED ▪ OBVIATES
	OBVIATION	OBVIATIONS
	OBVIATOR	OBVIATORS
	OBVOLUTE	OBVOLUTED
COCA ▪ LOCA ▪ SOCA	**OCA**	OCAS
	OCARINA	OCARINAS
COCAS ▪ SOCAS	**OCAS**	
	OCCAM	OCCAMS ▪ OCCAMY
	OCCASION	OCCASIONS
	OCCIDENT	OCCIDENTS
BOCCIES ▪ MOCCIES	**OCCIES**	
	OCCIPITA	OCCIPITAL
	OCCIPITAL	OCCIPITALS
	OCCIPUT	OCCIPUTS
	OCCLUDE	OCCLUDED ▪ OCCLUDER ▪ OCCLUDES
	OCCLUDENT	OCCLUDENTS
	OCCLUDER	OCCLUDERS
	OCCLUSION	OCCLUSIONS
	OCCLUSIVE	OCCLUSIVES
	OCCLUSOR	OCCLUSORS
	OCCULT	OCCULTS
	OCCULTER	OCCULTERS
	OCCULTISM	OCCULTISMS
	OCCULTIST	OCCULTISTS
	OCCUPANCE	OCCUPANCES
	OCCUPANT	OCCUPANTS
	OCCUPATE	OCCUPATED ▪ OCCUPATES
	OCCUPIER	OCCUPIERS
	OCCUR	OCCURS
	OCCURRENT	OCCURRENTS
	OCEAN	OCEANS
	OCEANAUT	OCEANAUTS
	OCEANID	OCEANIDS
LOCELLATE	**OCELLATE**	OCELLATED
	OCELOT	OCELOTS
COCH ▪ LOCH ▪ MOCH ▪ ROCH	**OCH**	OCHE
BOCHE	**OCHE**	OCHER ▪ OCHES
TOCHER	**OCHER**	OCHERS ▪ OCHERY
TOCHERED	**OCHERED**	
TOCHERING	**OCHERING**	
TOCHERS	**OCHERS**	
BOCHES (offensive) ▪ COCHES ▪ ROCHES	**OCHES**	
	OCHIDORE	OCHIDORES
	OCHLOCRAT	OCHLOCRATS
	OCHRE	OCHREA ▪ OCHRED ▪ OCHRES ▪ OCHREY
	OCHREA	OCHREAE
	OCICAT	OCICATS
COCKER ▪ DOCKER ▪ HOCKER ▪ LOCKER MOCKER ▪ ROCKER	**OCKER**	OCKERS
	OCKERISM	OCKERISMS
COCKERS ▪ DOCKERS ▪ HOCKERS ▪ LOCKERS MOCKERS ▪ ROCKERS	**OCKERS**	

FRONT HOOK	ROOT WORD	END HOOK
	OCOTILLO	OCOTILLOS
	OCREA	OCREAE
COCREATE	**OCREATE**	
	OCTA	OCTAD ▪ OCTAL ▪ OCTAN ▪ OCTAS
	OCTACHORD	OCTACHORDS
	OCTAD	OCTADS
	OCTAGON	OCTAGONS
	OCTAHEDRA	OCTAHEDRAL
	OCTAL	OCTALS
	OCTAMETER	OCTAMETERS
	OCTAN	OCTANE ▪ OCTANS ▪ OCTANT
	OCTANE	OCTANES
	OCTANGLE	OCTANGLES
	OCTANOL	OCTANOLS
	OCTANT	OCTANTS
	OCTAPLA	OCTAPLAS
	OCTAPLOID	OCTAPLOIDS ▪ OCTAPLOIDY
	OCTAROON	OCTAROONS
	OCTASTICH	OCTASTICHS
	OCTASTYLE	OCTASTYLES
	OCTAVE	OCTAVES
	OCTAVO	OCTAVOS
	OCTET	OCTETS ▪ OCTETT
	OCTETT	OCTETTE ▪ OCTETTS
	OCTETTE	OCTETTES
	OCTILLION	OCTILLIONS
	OCTOPLOID	OCTOPLOIDS
	OCTOPOD	OCTOPODS
	OCTOPODAN	OCTOPODANS
	OCTOPUS	OCTOPUSH
	OCTOROON	OCTOROONS
	OCTOSTYLE	OCTOSTYLES
	OCTOTHORP	OCTOTHORPS
	OCTROI	OCTROIS
	OCTUOR	OCTUORS
	OCTUPLE	OCTUPLED ▪ OCTUPLES ▪ OCTUPLET OCTUPLEX
	OCTUPLET	OCTUPLETS
	OCTYL	OCTYLS
JOCULAR ▪ LOCULAR ▪ VOCULAR	**OCULAR**	OCULARS
	OCULARIST	OCULARISTS
JOCULARLY	**OCULARLY**	
LOCULATE	**OCULATE**	OCULATED
LOCULATED	**OCULATED**	
LOCULI	**OCULI**	
	OCULIST	OCULISTS
LOCULUS	**OCULUS**	
BOD ▪ COD ▪ DOD ▪ GOD ▪ HOD ▪ LOD ▪ MOD NOD ▪ POD ▪ ROD ▪ SOD ▪ TOD ▪ YOD	**OD**	ODA ▪ ODD ▪ ODE ▪ ODS
CODA ▪ SODA	**ODA**	ODAH ▪ ODAL ▪ ODAS
	ODAH	ODAHS
MODAL ▪ NODAL ▪ PODAL	**ODAL**	ODALS
	ODALIQUE	ODALIQUES
	ODALISK	ODALISKS
	ODALISQUE	ODALISQUES
	ODALLER	ODALLERS
MODALS	**ODALS**	
CODAS ▪ SODAS	**ODAS**	
	ODD	ODDS
	ODDBALL	ODDBALLS
CODDER ▪ DODDER ▪ FODDER ▪ NODDER	**ODDER**	
	ODDMENT	ODDMENTS
	ODDSMAKER	ODDSMAKERS
BODE ▪ CODE ▪ LODE ▪ MODE ▪ NODE ▪ RODE YODE	**ODE**	ODEA ▪ ODES
	ODEON	ODEONS
BODES ▪ CODES ▪ LODES ▪ MODES ▪ NODES RODES	**ODES**	
	ODEUM	ODEUMS

FRONT HOOK	ROOT WORD	END HOOK
IODIC · SODIC	**ODIC**	
IODISM	**ODISM**	ODISMS
IODISMS	**ODISMS**	
CODIST · MODIST	**ODIST**	ODISTS
CODISTS · MODISTS	**ODISTS**	
PODIUM · SODIUM	**ODIUM**	ODIUMS
PODIUMS · SODIUMS	**ODIUMS**	
HODOGRAPH	**ODOGRAPH**	ODOGRAPHS
HODOGRAPHS	**ODOGRAPHS**	
HODOMETER	**ODOMETER**	ODOMETERS
HODOMETERS	**ODOMETERS**	
HODOMETRY · IODOMETRY	**ODOMETRY**	
	ODONATE	ODONATES
	ODONATIST	ODONATISTS
	ODONTIST	ODONTISTS
	ODONTOID	ODONTOIDS
	ODONTOMA	ODONTOMAS
	ODOR	ODORS
	ODORANT	ODORANTS
	ODORISE	ODORISED · ODORISES
	ODORIZE	ODORIZED · ODORIZES
	ODOUR	ODOURS
BODS · CODS · DODS · GODS · HODS · LODS MODS · NODS · PODS · RODS · SODS · TODS YODS	**ODS**	ODSO
GODSO	**ODSO**	ODSOS
GODSOS	**ODSOS**	
	ODYL	ODYLE · ODYLS
	ODYLE	ODYLES
	ODYLISM	ODYLISMS
	ODYSSEY	ODYSSEYS
DOE · FOE · GOE · HOE · JOE · MOE · ROE TOE · VOE · WOE	**OE**	OES
	OECIST	OECISTS
	OEDEMA	OEDEMAS
	OEDOMETER	OEDOMETERS
	OEILLADE	OEILLADES
POENOLOGY	**OENOLOGY**	
	OENOMANIA	OENOMANIAS
	OENOMEL	OENOMELS
	OENOMETER	OENOMETERS
	OENOPHIL	OENOPHILE · OENOPHILS · OENOPHILY
	OENOPHILE	OENOPHILES
	OENOTHERA	OENOTHERAS
	OERLIKON	OERLIKONS
	OERSTED	OERSTEDS
DOES · FOES · GOES · HOES · JOES · MOES NOES · ROES · TOES · VOES · WOES	**OES**	
	OESTRIN	OESTRINS
	OESTRIOL	OESTRIOLS
	OESTROGEN	OESTROGENS
	OESTRONE	OESTRONES
	OESTRUM	OESTRUMS
	OEUVRE	OEUVRES
DOF · OOF · WOF	**OF**	OFF · OFT
	OFAY	OFAYS *(offensive)*
BOFF · COFF · DOFF · GOFF · KOFF · TOFF	**OFF**	OFFS
	OFFAL	OFFALS
	OFFBEAT	OFFBEATS
	OFFCAST	OFFCASTS
	OFFCUT	OFFCUTS
BOFFED · COFFED · DOFFED · GOFFED	**OFFED**	
	OFFENCE	OFFENCES
	OFFEND	OFFENDS
	OFFENDER	OFFENDERS
	OFFENSE	OFFENSES
	OFFENSIVE	OFFENSIVES
COFFER · DOFFER · GOFFER	**OFFER**	OFFERS
COFFERED · GOFFERED	**OFFERED**	

FRONT HOOK	ROOT WORD	END HOOK
	OFFEREE	OFFEREES
	OFFERER	OFFERERS
COFFERING ▪ GOFFERING	**OFFERING**	OFFERINGS
GOFFERINGS	**OFFERINGS**	
	OFFEROR	OFFERORS
COFFERS ▪ DOFFERS ▪ GOFFERS	**OFFERS**	
	OFFICE	OFFICER ▪ OFFICES
	OFFICER	OFFICERS
	OFFICIAL	OFFICIALS
	OFFICIANT	OFFICIANTS
	OFFICIATE	OFFICIATED ▪ OFFICIATES
	OFFICINAL	OFFICINALS
BOFFING ▪ COFFING ▪ DOFFING ▪ GOFFING	**OFFING**	OFFINGS
TOFFISH	**OFFISH**	
	OFFLOAD	OFFLOADS
	OFFPRINT	OFFPRINTS
	OFFPUT	OFFPUTS
	OFFRAMP	OFFRAMPS
BOFFS ▪ COFFS ▪ DOFFS ▪ GOFFS ▪ KOFFS	**OFFS**	
TOFFS		
	OFFSADDLE	OFFSADDLED ▪ OFFSADDLES
	OFFSCUM	OFFSCUMS
	OFFSEASON	OFFSEASONS
	OFFSET	OFFSETS
	OFFSHOOT	OFFSHOOTS
	OFFSHORE	OFFSHORES
	OFFSIDE	OFFSIDER ▪ OFFSIDES
	OFFSIDER	OFFSIDERS
	OFFSPRING	OFFSPRINGS
	OFFSTAGE	OFFSTAGES
	OFFTAKE	OFFTAKES
	OFLAG	OFLAGS
COFT ▪ LOFT ▪ SOFT ▪ TOFT	**OFT**	
SOFTEN	**OFTEN**	
SOFTENER	**OFTENER**	
LOFTER ▪ SOFTER	**OFTER**	
SOFTEST	**OFTEST**	
	OGAM	OGAMS
	OGDOAD	OGDOADS
YOGEE	**OGEE**	OGEES
YOGEES	**OGEES**	
HOGGIN ▪ NOGGIN	**OGGIN**	OGGINS
HOGGINS ▪ NOGGINS	**OGGINS**	
	OGHAM	OGHAMS
	OGHAMIST	OGHAMISTS
	OGIVE	OGIVES
BOGLE ▪ FOGLE	**OGLE**	OGLED ▪ OGLER ▪ OGLES
	OGLER	OGLERS
BOGLES ▪ FOGLES	**OGLES**	
	OGLING	OGLINGS
	OGRE	OGRES
	OGREISM	OGREISMS
	OGRES	OGRESS
	OGRISM	OGRISMS
BOH ▪ DOH ▪ FOH ▪ HOH ▪ NOH ▪ OOH ▪ POH	**OH**	OHM ▪ OHO ▪ OHS
SOH		
HOHED ▪ OOHED	**OHED**	
	OHIA	OHIAS
HOHING ▪ OOHING	**OHING**	
	OHM	OHMS
	OHMAGE	OHMAGES
	OHMMETER	OHMMETERS
BOHO ▪ COHO ▪ SOHO ▪ TOHO	**OHO**	OHOS
BOHOS ▪ COHOS ▪ TOHOS	**OHOS**	
BOHS ▪ DOHS ▪ FOHS ▪ HOHS ▪ OOHS ▪ SOHS	**OHS**	
BOI ▪ HOI ▪ KOI ▪ MOI ▪ POI	**OI**	OIK ▪ OIL
HOIK	**OIK**	OIKS (offensive)
	OIKIST	OIKISTS
HOIKS	**OIKS**	

FRONT HOOK	ROOT WORD	END HOOK
BOIL · COIL · FOIL · MOIL · NOIL · ROIL SOIL · TOIL	OIL	OILS · OILY
	OILBIRD	OILBIRDS
	OILCAMP	OILCAMPS
	OILCAN	OILCANS
	OILCLOTH	OILCLOTHS
	OILCUP	OILCUPS
BOILED · COILED · DOILED · FOILED MOILED · ROILED · SOILED · TOILED	OILED	
BOILER · COILER · MOILER · TOILER	OILER	OILERS · OILERY
BOILERIES	OILERIES	
BOILERS · COILERS · MOILERS · TOILERS	OILERS	
BOILERY	OILERY	
	OILFIELD	OILFIELDS
	OILHOLE	OILHOLES
ROILIER · SOILIER	OILIER	
ROILIEST · SOILIEST	OILIEST	
SOILINESS	OILINESS	
BOILING · COILING · FOILING · MOILING ROILING · SOILING · TOILING	OILING	
	OILLET	OILLETS
	OILNUT	OILNUTS
	OILPAPER	OILPAPERS
BOILS · COILS · FOILS · MOILS · NOILS ROILS · SOILS · TOILS	OILS	
	OILSEED	OILSEEDS
	OILSKIN	OILSKINS
	OILSTONE	OILSTONES
	OILWAY	OILWAYS
DOILY · NOILY · ROILY · SOILY	OILY	
BOINK	OINK	OINKS
BOINKED	OINKED	
BOINKING	OINKING	
BOINKS	OINKS	
	OINOMEL	OINOMELS
JOINT · NOINT · POINT	OINT	OINTS
JOINTED · NOINTED · POINTED	OINTED	
JOINTING · NOINTING · POINTING	OINTING	
	OINTMENT	OINTMENTS
JOINTS · NOINTS · POINTS	OINTS	
	OITICICA	OITICICAS
	OJIME	OJIMES
HOKA	OKA	OKAS · OKAY
	OKAPI	OKAPIS
TOKAY	OKAY	OKAYS
TOKAYS	OKAYS	
BOKE · COKE · HOKE · JOKE · LOKE · MOKE POKE · ROKE · SOKE · TOKE · WOKE · YOKE	OKE	OKEH · OKES
	OKEH	OKEHS
BOKES · COKES · HOKES · JOKES · LOKES MOKES · POKES · ROKES · SOKES · TOKES YOKES	OKES	
	OKEYDOKE	OKEYDOKEY
	OKIMONO	OKIMONOS
KOKRA	OKRA	OKRAS
KOKRAS	OKRAS	
	OKTA	OKTAS
BOLD · COLD · FOLD · GOLD · HOLD · MOLD SOLD · TOLD · WOLD · YOLD	OLD	OLDS · OLDY
BOLDEN · GOLDEN · HOLDEN	OLDEN	OLDENS
BOLDENED · GOLDENED	OLDENED	
BOLDENING · GOLDENING	OLDENING	
BOLDENS · GOLDENS	OLDENS	
BOLDER · COLDER · FOLDER · GOLDER HOLDER · MOLDER · POLDER · SOLDER	OLDER	
BOLDEST · COLDEST · GOLDEST	OLDEST	
COLDIE	OLDIE	OLDIES
COLDIES	OLDIES	
COLDISH · GOLDISH	OLDISH	

FRONT HOOK	ROOT WORD	END HOOK
BOLDNESS · COLDNESS	**OLDNESS**	
BOLDNESSES · COLDNESSES	**OLDNESSES**	
BOLDS · COLDS · FOLDS · GOLDS · HOLDS	**OLDS**	
MOLDS · SOLDS · WOLDS		
	OLDSQUAW	OLDSQUAWS
	OLDSTER	OLDSTERS
	OLDSTYLE	OLDSTYLES
GOLDY · MOLDY	**OLDY**	
BOLE · COLE · DOLE · GOLE · HOLE · JOLE	**OLE**	OLEA · OLEO · OLES
MOLE · NOLE · POLE · ROLE · SOLE · VOLE		
	OLEANDER	OLEANDERS
	OLEARIA	OLEARIAS
	OLEASTER	OLEASTERS
	OLEATE	OLEATES
	OLECRANON	OLECRANONS
	OLEFIN	OLEFINE · OLEFINS
	OLEFINE	OLEFINES
SOLEIN	**OLEIN**	OLEINE · OLEINS
	OLEINE	OLEINES
DOLENT	**OLENT**	
	OLEO	OLEOS
	OLEOGRAPH	OLEOGRAPHS · OLEOGRAPHY
	OLEORESIN	OLEORESINS
BOLES · COLES · DOLES · GOLES · HOLES	**OLES**	
JOLES · MOLES · NOLES · POLES · ROLES		
SOLES · TOLES · VOLES		
	OLESTRA	OLESTRAS
	OLEUM	OLEUMS
	OLFACT	OLFACTS
	OLFACTION	OLFACTIONS
	OLIBANUM	OLIBANUMS
	OLICOOK	OLICOOKS
SOLID	**OLID**	
	OLIGAEMIA	OLIGAEMIAS
	OLIGARCH	OLIGARCHS · OLIGARCHY
	OLIGEMIA	OLIGEMIAS
	OLIGIST	OLIGISTS
	OLIGOGENE	OLIGOGENES
	OLIGOMER	OLIGOMERS
	OLIGURIA	OLIGURIAS
	OLINGO	OLINGOS
FOLIO · POLIO	**OLIO**	OLIOS
FOLIOS · POLIOS	**OLIOS**	
	OLIPHANT	OLIPHANTS
SOLIVE	**OLIVE**	OLIVER · OLIVES · OLIVET
	OLIVENITE	OLIVENITES
	OLIVER	OLIVERS
SOLIVES	**OLIVES**	
	OLIVET	OLIVETS
	OLIVINE	OLIVINES
HOLLA · MOLLA	**OLLA**	OLLAS · OLLAV
	OLLAMH	OLLAMHS
HOLLAS · MOLLAS	**OLLAS**	
	OLLAV	OLLAVS
GOLLER · HOLLER · LOLLER · POLLER	**OLLER**	OLLERS
ROLLER · SOLLER · TOLLER		
GOLLERS · HOLLERS · LOLLERS · POLLERS	**OLLERS**	
ROLLERS · SOLLERS · TOLLERS		
COLLIE · MOLLIE · TOLLIE	**OLLIE**	OLLIES
COLLIES · DOLLIES · FOLLIES · GOLLIES	**OLLIES**	
HOLLIES · JOLLIES · LOLLIES · MOLLIES		
POLLIES · TOLLIES · WOLLIES		
HOLM	**OLM**	OLMS
HOLMS	**OLMS**	
OOLOGIES	**OLOGIES**	
OOLOGIST	**OLOGIST**	OLOGISTS
OOLOGISTS	**OLOGISTS**	
	OLOGOAN	OLOGOANS
OOLOGY	**OLOGY**	

FRONT HOOK	ROOT WORD	END HOOK
	OLOLIUQUI	OLOLIUQUIS
DOLOROSO	**OLOROSO**	OLOROSOS
GOLPE	**OLPE**	OLPES
GOLPES	**OLPES**	
	OLYCOOK	OLYCOOKS
	OLYKOEK	OLYKOEKS
	OLYMPIAD	OLYMPIADS
DOM · HOM · MOM · NOM · OOM · POM · ROM SOM · TOM · YOM	**OM**	OMS
	OMADHAUN	OMADHAUNS
	OMASA	OMASAL
BOMBER · COMBER · SOMBER	**OMBER**	OMBERS
BOMBERS · COMBERS · SOMBERS	**OMBERS**	
HOMBRE · SOMBRE	**OMBRE**	OMBRES
	OMBRELLA	OMBRELLAS
HOMBRES · SOMBRES	**OMBRES**	
	OMBROPHIL	OMBROPHILE · OMBROPHILS
KOMBU	**OMBU**	OMBUS
KOMBUS	**OMBUS**	
	OMEGA	OMEGAS
	OMELET	OMELETS
	OMELETTE	OMELETTES
NOMEN · WOMEN	**OMEN**	OMENS
LOMENTA · MOMENTA · TOMENTA	**OMENTA**	OMENTAL
LOMENTUM · MOMENTUM · TOMENTUM	**OMENTUM**	OMENTUMS
LOMENTUMS · MOMENTUMS	**OMENTUMS**	
COMER · GOMER · HOMER · VOMER	**OMER**	OMERS
COMERS · GOMERS · HOMERS · VOMERS	**OMERS**	
	OMERTA	OMERTAS
	OMICRON	OMICRONS
	OMIKRON	OMIKRONS
	OMISSION	OMISSIONS
VOMIT	**OMIT**	OMITS
VOMITS	**OMITS**	
	OMITTANCE	OMITTANCES
	OMITTER	OMITTERS
	OMLAH	OMLAHS
	OMMATIDIA	OMMATIDIAL
	OMNIARCH	OMNIARCHS
SOMNIFIC	**OMNIFIC**	
	OMNIRANGE	OMNIRANGES
	OMNIUM	OMNIUMS
	OMNIVORE	OMNIVORES
	OMOHYOID	OMOHYOIDS
	OMOPHAGIA	OMOPHAGIAS
	OMOPLATE	OMOPLATES
	OMOV	OMOVS
	OMPHACITE	OMPHACITES
	OMPHALI	OMPHALIC
	OMRAH	OMRAHS
COMS · DOMS · HOMS · MOMS · NOMS · OOMS POMS · ROMS · SOMS · TOMS	**OMS**	
BON · CON · DON · EON · FON · GON · HON ION · KON · MON · NON · OON · SON · TON WON · YON	**ON**	ONE · ONO · ONS · ONY
	ONAGER	ONAGERS
	ONANISM	ONANISMS
	ONANIST	ONANISTS
	ONBEAT	ONBEATS
BONCE · NONCE · PONCE · SONCE	**ONCE**	ONCER · ONCES · ONCET
	ONCER	ONCERS
BONCES · NONCES · PONCES (offensive) SONCES	**ONCES**	
	ONCIDIUM	ONCIDIUMS
	ONCOGEN	ONCOGENE · ONCOGENS
	ONCOGENE	ONCOGENES
	ONCOLYTIC	ONCOLYTICS
	ONCOME	ONCOMES
	ONCOMETER	ONCOMETERS

FRONT HOOK	ROOT WORD	END HOOK
	ONCOMING	ONCOMINGS
	ONCOST	ONCOSTS
	ONDATRA	ONDATRAS
	ONDINE	ONDINES
BONDING = FONDING = PONDING	**ONDING**	ONDINGS
BONDINGS	**ONDINGS**	
	ONDOGRAM	ONDOGRAMS
	ONDOGRAPH	ONDOGRAPHS
BONE = CONE = DONE = FONE = GONE = HONE = LONE = NONE = PONE = RONE = SONE = TONE = ZONE	**ONE**	ONER = ONES
LONELY	**ONELY**	
DONENESS = GONENESS = LONENESS	**ONENESS**	
DONENESSES = GONENESSES = LONENESSES	**ONENESSES**	
BONER = DONER = GONER = HONER = LONER = MONER = TONER = ZONER	**ONER**	ONERS = ONERY
BONERS = GONERS = HONERS = LONERS = TONERS = ZONERS	**ONERS**	
BONES = CONES = HONES = JONES = NONES = PONES = RONES = SONES = TONES = ZONES	**ONES**	
ZONETIME	**ONETIME**	
BONEYER = MONEYER	**ONEYER**	ONEYERS
MONEYERS	**ONEYERS**	
	ONEYRE	ONEYRES
	ONFALL	ONFALLS
	ONFLOW	ONFLOWS
	ONGAONGA	ONGAONGAS
	ONGOING	ONGOINGS
BONIE = MONIE	**ONIE**	
GONION = RONION	**ONION**	ONIONS = ONIONY
RONIONS	**ONIONS**	
	ONIONSKIN	ONIONSKINS
CONIUM = GONIUM = IONIUM	**ONIUM**	ONIUMS
CONIUMS = IONIUMS	**ONIUMS**	
	ONLAY	ONLAYS
	ONLINE	ONLINER
	ONLINER	ONLINERS
	ONLOAD	ONLOADS
	ONLOOKER	ONLOOKERS
FONLY = SONLY	**ONLY**	
CONNED = DONNED = FONNED = WONNED	**ONNED**	
CONNING = DONNING = FONNING = KONNING = RONNING = WONNING	**ONNING**	
MONO	**ONO**	ONOS
	ONOMASTIC	ONOMASTICS
MONOS	**ONOS**	
CONS = DONS = EONS = FONS = GONS = HONS = IONS = KONS = MONS = OONS = PONS = SONS = TONS = WONS	**ONS**	ONST
	ONSET	ONSETS
	ONSETTER	ONSETTERS
	ONSETTING	ONSETTINGS
	ONSHORING	ONSHORINGS
	ONSIDE	ONSIDES
	ONSLAUGHT	ONSLAUGHTS
	ONSTEAD	ONSTEADS
PONTIC	**ONTIC**	
CONTO	**ONTO**	
BONUS = CONUS = TONUS	**ONUS**	
BONUSES = NONUSES = TONUSES	**ONUSES**	
	ONWARD	ONWARDS
BONY = CONY = MONY = PONY = TONY	**ONY**	ONYX
	ONYCHA	ONYCHAS
	ONYCHIA	ONYCHIAS
	ONYCHITE	ONYCHITES
	ONYCHIUM	ONYCHIUMS
BOO = COO = DOO = GOO = HOO = LOO = MOO = NOO = POO = ROO = TOO = WOO = ZOO	**OO**	OOF = OOH = OOM = OON = OOP = OOR = OOS = OOT
	OOBIT	OOBITS

FRONT HOOK	ROOT WORD	END HOOK
	OOCYST	OOCYSTS
	OOCYTE	OOCYTES
BOODLES · DOODLES · NOODLES · POODLES	**OODLES**	
COOF · GOOF · HOOF · LOOF · POOF · ROOF WOOF · YOOF	**OOF**	OOFS · OOFY
BOOFIER · GOOFIER · POOFIER (offensive) ROOFIER · WOOFIER	**OOFIER**	
BOOFIEST · GOOFIEST · POOFIEST (offensive) ROOFIEST · WOOFIEST	**OOFIEST**	
COOFS · GOOFS · HOOFS · LOOFS POOFS (offensive) · ROOFS · WOOFS · YOOFS	**OOFS**	
BOOFY · GOOFY · POOFY (offensive) · ROOFY WOOFY	**OOFY**	
ZOOGAMETE	**OOGAMETE**	OOGAMETES
ZOOGAMETES	**OOGAMETES**	
ZOOGAMIES	**OOGAMIES**	
ZOOGAMOUS	**OOGAMOUS**	
ZOOGAMY	**OOGAMY**	
NOOGENESES	**OOGENESES**	
NOOGENESIS	**OOGENESIS**	
ZOOGENIES	**OOGENIES**	
ZOOGENY	**OOGENY**	
	OOGONIA	OOGONIAL
	OOGONIUM	OOGONIUMS
BOOH · POOH	**OOH**	OOHS
BOOHED · POOHED	**OOHED**	
BOOHING · POOHING	**OOHING**	
BOOHS · POOHS	**OOHS**	
ZOOIDAL	**OOIDAL**	
HOOLACHAN	**OOLACHAN**	OOLACHANS
HOOLACHANS	**OOLACHANS**	
	OOLAKAN	OOLAKANS
ZOOLITE	**OOLITE**	OOLITES
ZOOLITES	**OOLITES**	
ZOOLITH	**OOLITH**	OOLITHS
ZOOLITHS	**OOLITHS**	
ZOOLITIC	**OOLITIC**	
ZOOLOGIC	**OOLOGIC**	
ZOOLOGICAL	**OOLOGICAL**	
NOOLOGIES · ZOOLOGIES	**OOLOGIES**	
ZOOLOGIST	**OOLOGIST**	OOLOGISTS
ZOOLOGISTS	**OOLOGISTS**	
NOOLOGY · ZOOLOGY	**OOLOGY**	
	OOLONG	OOLONGS
BOOM · COOM · DOOM · LOOM · ROOM · SOOM TOOM · ZOOM	**OOM**	OOMS
	OOMIAC	OOMIACK · OOMIACS
	OOMIACK	OOMIACKS
	OOMIAK	OOMIAKS
	OOMPAH	OOMPAHS
	OOMPH	OOMPHS
BOOMS · COOMS · DOOMS · LOOMS · ROOMS SOOMS · TOOMS · ZOOMS	**OOMS**	
	OOMYCETE	OOMYCETES
BOON · COON · DOON · GOON · HOON · LOON MOON · NOON · POON · ROON · SOON · TOON WOON · ZOON	**OON**	OONS · OONT
BOONS · COONS · GOONS · HOONS · LOONS MOONS · NOONS · POONS · ROONS · TOONS WOONS · ZOONS	**OONS**	
	OONT	OONTS
COOP · GOOP · HOOP · LOOP · MOOP · NOOP POOP · ROOP · SOOP · YOOP	**OOP**	OOPS
COOPED · HOOPED · LOOPED · MOOPED POOPED · ROOPED · SOOPED	**OOPED**	
	OOPHORON	OOPHORONS
ZOOPHYTE	**OOPHYTE**	OOPHYTES
ZOOPHYTES	**OOPHYTES**	
ZOOPHYTIC	**OOPHYTIC**	

FRONT HOOK	ROOT WORD	END HOOK
COOPING · HOOPING · LOOPING · MOOPING POOPING · ROOPING · SOOPING	**OOPING**	
COOPS · GOOPS · HOOPS · LOOPS · MOOPS NOOPS · POOPS · ROOPS · SOOPS · WOOPS YOOPS	**OOPS**	
BOOR · DOOR · GOOR · LOOR · MOOR · POOR	**OOR**	
WOORALI	**OORALI**	OORALIS
WOORALIS	**OORALIS**	
	OORIAL	OORIALS
COORIE · GOORIE · TOORIE	**OORIE**	OORIER
MOORIER	**OORIER**	
MOORIEST	**OORIEST**	
BOOS · COOS · DOOS · GOOS · LOOS · MOOS POOS · ROOS · WOOS · ZOOS	**OOS**	OOSE · OOSY
BOOSE · GOOSE · LOOSE · MOOSE · NOOSE ROOSE · WOOSE	**OOSE**	OOSES
BOOSES · GOOSES · LOOSES · NOOSES ROOSES · WOOSES	**OOSES**	
GOOSIER	**OOSIER**	
GOOSIEST	**OOSIEST**	
ZOOSPERM	**OOSPERM**	OOSPERMS
ZOOSPERMS	**OOSPERMS**	
NOOSPHERE	**OOSPHERE**	OOSPHERES
NOOSPHERES	**OOSPHERES**	
ZOOSPORE	**OOSPORE**	OOSPORES
ZOOSPORES	**OOSPORES**	
ZOOSPORIC	**OOSPORIC**	
ZOOSPOROUS	**OOSPOROUS**	
GOOSY	**OOSY**	
BOOT · COOT · FOOT · HOOT · LOOT · MOOT POOT · ROOT · SOOT · TOOT · WOOT · ZOOT	**OOT**	OOTS
	OOTHECA	OOTHECAE · OOTHECAL
	OOTID	OOTIDS
BOOTS · COOTS · FOOTS · HOOTS · LOOTS MOOTS · POOTS · ROOTS · SOOTS · TOOTS	**OOTS**	
BOOZE · COOZE	**OOZE**	OOZED · OOZES
BOOZED	**OOZED**	
BOOZES · COOZES (offensive)	**OOZES**	
BOOZIER · WOOZIER	**OOZIER**	
BOOZIEST · WOOZIEST	**OOZIEST**	
BOOZILY · WOOZILY	**OOZILY**	
BOOZINESS · WOOZINESS	**OOZINESS**	
BOOZING	**OOZING**	
BOOZY · DOOZY · WOOZY	**OOZY**	
BOP · COP · DOP · FOP · HOP · KOP · LOP MOP · OOP · POP · SOP · TOP · WOP (offensive)	**OP**	OPE · OPS · OPT
	OPACIFIER	OPACIFIERS
	OPAH	OPAHS
COPAL · NOPAL	**OPAL**	OPALS
	OPALESCE	OPALESCED · OPALESCES
	OPALINE	OPALINES
COPALS · NOPALS	**OPALS**	
	OPAQUE	OPAQUED · OPAQUER · OPAQUES
	OPAQUES	OPAQUEST
	OPCODE	OPCODES
COPE · DOPE · HOPE · LOPE · MOPE · NOPE POPE · ROPE · TOPE	**OPE**	OPED · OPEN · OPES
COPED · DOPED · HOPED · LOPED · MOPED OOPED · ROPED · TOPED	**OPED**	
COPEN	**OPEN**	OPENS
	OPENER	OPENERS
	OPENING	OPENINGS
COPENS	**OPENS**	
	OPENSIDE	OPENSIDES
	OPENWORK	OPENWORKS
	OPEPE	OPEPES
POPERA	**OPERA**	OPERAS
	OPERAGOER	OPERAGOERS
	OPERAND	OPERANDS

FRONT HOOK	ROOT WORD	END HOOK
	OPERANT	OPERANTS
POPERAS	**OPERAS**	
	OPERATE	OPERATED ▪ OPERATES
	OPERATIC	OPERATICS
	OPERATION	OPERATIONS
	OPERATISE	OPERATISED ▪ OPERATISES
	OPERATIVE	OPERATIVES
	OPERATIZE	OPERATIZED ▪ OPERATIZES
	OPERATOR	OPERATORS
	OPERCELE	OPERCELES
	OPERCULA	OPERCULAR
	OPERCULAR	OPERCULARS
	OPERCULE	OPERCULES
	OPERCULUM	OPERCULUMS
	OPERETTA	OPERETTAS
	OPERON	OPERONS
COPES ▪ DOPES ▪ HOPES ▪ LOPES ▪ MOPES POPES ▪ ROPES ▪ TOPES	**OPES**	
	OPHIDIAN	OPHIDIANS
	OPHIOLITE	OPHIOLITES
	OPHITE	OPHITES
	OPHIURA	OPHIURAN ▪ OPHIURAS
	OPHIURAN	OPHIURANS
	OPHIURID	OPHIURIDS
	OPHIUROID	OPHIUROIDS
	OPIATE	OPIATED ▪ OPIATES
	OPIFICER	OPIFICERS
	OPINE	OPINED ▪ OPINES
COPING ▪ DOPING ▪ HOPING ▪ LOPING MOPING ▪ OOPING ▪ ROPING ▪ TOPING	**OPING**	
	OPINION	OPINIONS
	OPIOID	OPIOIDS
	OPIUM	OPIUMS
	OPIUMISM	OPIUMISMS
	OPOBALSAM	OPOBALSAMS
	OPODELDOC	OPODELDOCS
	OPORICE	OPORICES
	OPOSSUM	OPOSSUMS
	OPPIDAN	OPPIDANS
	OPPILATE	OPPILATED ▪ OPPILATES
ZOPPO	**OPPO**	OPPOS
	OPPONENT	OPPONENTS
	OPPOS	OPPOSE
	OPPOSE	OPPOSED ▪ OPPOSER ▪ OPPOSES
	OPPOSER	OPPOSERS
	OPPOSITE	OPPOSITES
	OPPRESSOR	OPPRESSORS
	OPPUGN	OPPUGNS
	OPPUGNANT	OPPUGNANTS
	OPPUGNER	OPPUGNERS
BOPS ▪ COPS ▪ DOPS ▪ FOPS ▪ HOPS ▪ KOPS LOPS ▪ MOPS ▪ OOPS ▪ POPS ▪ SOPS ▪ TOPS WOPS (offensive)	**OPS**	
	OPSIMATH	OPSIMATHS ▪ OPSIMATHY
	OPSIN	OPSINS
	OPSOMANIA	OPSOMANIAC ▪ OPSOMANIAS
	OPSONIN	OPSONINS
	OPSONISE	OPSONISED ▪ OPSONISES
	OPSONIUM	OPSONIUMS
	OPSONIZE	OPSONIZED ▪ OPSONIZES
	OPT	OPTS
	OPTANT	OPTANTS
	OPTATIVE	OPTATIVES
COPTER	**OPTER**	OPTERS
COPTERS	**OPTERS**	
	OPTIC	OPTICS
	OPTICIAN	OPTICIANS
	OPTICIST	OPTICISTS
	OPTIMA	OPTIMAL

FRONT HOOK	ROOT WORD	END HOOK
	OPTIMATE	OPTIMATES
	OPTIME	OPTIMES
	OPTIMISE	OPTIMISED ▪ OPTIMISER ▪ OPTIMISES
	OPTIMISER	OPTIMISERS
	OPTIMISM	OPTIMISMS
	OPTIMIST	OPTIMISTS
	OPTIMIZE	OPTIMIZED ▪ OPTIMIZER ▪ OPTIMIZES
	OPTIMIZER	OPTIMIZERS
	OPTIMUM	OPTIMUMS
	OPTION	OPTIONS
	OPTIONAL	OPTIONALS
	OPTIONEE	OPTIONEES
	OPTOMETER	OPTOMETERS
	OPTOPHONE	OPTOPHONES
	OPULENCE	OPULENCES
	OPUNTIA	OPUNTIAS
MOPUS	**OPUS**	
	OPUSCLE	OPUSCLES
	OPUSCULA	OPUSCULAR
	OPUSCULE	OPUSCULES
MOPUSES	**OPUSES**	
	OQUASSA	OQUASSAS
BOR ▪ COR ▪ DOR ▪ FOR ▪ GOR ▪ JOR ▪ KOR LOR ▪ MOR ▪ NOR ▪ OOR ▪ TOR ▪ VOR	**OR**	ORA ▪ ORB ▪ ORC ▪ ORD ▪ ORE ▪ ORF ▪ ORS ORT
BORA ▪ FORA ▪ GORA ▪ HORA ▪ KORA ▪ MORA SORA ▪ TORA	**ORA**	ORAD ▪ ORAL
	ORACH	ORACHE
	ORACHE	ORACHES
CORACLE	**ORACLE**	ORACLED ▪ ORACLES
CORACLES	**ORACLES**	
DORAD	**ORAD**	
BORAL ▪ CORAL ▪ GORAL ▪ HORAL ▪ LORAL MORAL ▪ PORAL ▪ RORAL ▪ SORAL	**ORAL**	ORALS
MORALISM	**ORALISM**	ORALISMS
MORALISMS	**ORALISMS**	
MORALIST	**ORALIST**	ORALISTS
MORALISTS	**ORALISTS**	
MORALITIES	**ORALITIES**	
MORALITY	**ORALITY**	
MORALLY	**ORALLY**	
BORALS ▪ CORALS ▪ GORALS ▪ MORALS	**ORALS**	
	ORANG	ORANGE ▪ ORANGS ▪ ORANGY
	ORANGE	ORANGER ▪ ORANGES ▪ ORANGEY
	ORANGEADE	ORANGEADES
	ORANGER	ORANGERY
	ORANGERIE	ORANGERIES
	ORANGES	ORANGEST
	ORANGUTAN	ORANGUTANS
VORANT	**ORANT**	ORANTS
	ORARIA	ORARIAN
	ORARIAN	ORARIANS
	ORARION	ORARIONS
	ORARIUM	ORARIUMS
BORATE ▪ LORATE	**ORATE**	ORATED ▪ ORATES
BORATED	**ORATED**	
BORATES	**ORATES**	
BORATING	**ORATING**	
	ORATION	ORATIONS
	ORATOR	ORATORS ▪ ORATORY
	ORATORIAN	ORATORIANS
	ORATORIO	ORATORIOS
MORATORY	**ORATORY**	
DORB ▪ FORB ▪ SORB	**ORB**	ORBS ▪ ORBY
SORBED	**ORBED**	
SORBING ▪ ZORBING	**ORBING**	
	ORBIT	ORBITA ▪ ORBITS ▪ ORBITY
	ORBITA	ORBITAL ▪ ORBITAS
	ORBITAL	ORBITALS
	ORBITER	ORBITERS

FRONT HOOK	ROOT WORD	END HOOK
DORBS · FORBS · SORBS	**ORBS**	
CORBY · FORBY	**ORBY**	
TORC	**ORC**	ORCA · ORCS
	ORCA	ORCAS
	ORCEIN	ORCEINS
	ORCHARD	ORCHARDS
	ORCHAT	ORCHATS
	ORCHEL	ORCHELS
	ORCHELLA	ORCHELLAS
	ORCHESTIC	ORCHESTICS
	ORCHESTRA	ORCHESTRAL · ORCHESTRAS
	ORCHID	ORCHIDS
	ORCHIDIST	ORCHIDISTS
	ORCHIL	ORCHILS
	ORCHILLA	ORCHILLAS
	ORCIN	ORCINE · ORCINS
PORCINE	**ORCINE**	ORCINES
	ORCINOL	ORCINOLS
TORCS	**ORCS**	
BORD · CORD · FORD · LORD · SORD · WORD	**ORD**	ORDO · ORDS
	ORDAIN	ORDAINS
	ORDAINER	ORDAINERS
	ORDALIUM	ORDALIUMS
	ORDEAL	ORDEALS
BORDER · CORDER	**ORDER**	ORDERS
BORDERED	**ORDERED**	
BORDERER	**ORDERER**	ORDERERS
BORDERERS	**ORDERERS**	
BORDERING	**ORDERING**	ORDERINGS
BORDERLESS	**ORDERLESS**	
BORDERS · CORDERS	**ORDERS**	
	ORDINAIRE	ORDINAIRES
	ORDINAL	ORDINALS
	ORDINANCE	ORDINANCES
	ORDINAND	ORDINANDS
	ORDINANT	ORDINANTS
	ORDINAR	ORDINARS · ORDINARY
	ORDINATE	ORDINATED · ORDINATES
	ORDINEE	ORDINEES
SORDINES	**ORDINES**	
	ORDNANCE	ORDNANCES
FORDO · SORDO	**ORDO**	ORDOS
BORDS · CORDS · FORDS · LORDS · SORDS · WORDS	**ORDS**	
BORDURE	**ORDURE**	ORDURES
BORDURES	**ORDURES**	
BORE · CORE · DORE · FORE · GORE · HORE KORE · LORE · MORE · PORE · RORE · SORE TORE · WORE · YORE	**ORE**	ORES
	OREAD	OREADS
	OREGANO	OREGANOS
	OREIDE	OREIDES
	OREODONT	OREODONTS
BORES · CORES · FORES · GORES · KORES LORES · MORES · PORES · RORES · SORES TORES · YORES	**ORES**	
	OREWEED	OREWEEDS
CORF	**ORF**	ORFE · ORFS
	ORFE	ORFES
	ORFRAY	ORFRAYS
MORGAN	**ORGAN**	ORGANA · ORGANS
	ORGANDIE	ORGANDIES
	ORGANELLE	ORGANELLES
	ORGANIC	ORGANICS
	ORGANISE	ORGANISED · ORGANISER · ORGANISES
	ORGANISER	ORGANISERS
	ORGANISM	ORGANISMS
	ORGANIST	ORGANISTS
	ORGANIZE	ORGANIZED · ORGANIZER · ORGANIZES
	ORGANIZER	ORGANIZERS

FRONT HOOK	ROOT WORD	END HOOK
	ORGANON	ORGANONS
	ORGANOSOL	ORGANOSOLS
MORGANS	**ORGANS**	
	ORGANUM	ORGANUMS
	ORGANZA	ORGANZAS
	ORGANZINE	ORGANZINES
	ORGASM	ORGASMS
	ORGEAT	ORGEATS
GORGIA	**ORGIA**	ORGIAC ▪ ORGIAS
GORGIAS	**ORGIAS**	ORGIAST
	ORGIAST	ORGIASTS
PORGIES	**ORGIES**	
FORGONE	**ORGONE**	ORGONES
MORGUE	**ORGUE**	ORGUES
MORGUES	**ORGUES**	
PORGY	**ORGY**	
	ORIBATID	ORIBATIDS
	ORIBI	ORIBIS
	ORICALCHE	ORICALCHES
	ORICHALC	ORICHALCS
	ORIEL	ORIELS
	ORIENT	ORIENTS
	ORIENTAL	ORIENTALS
	ORIENTATE	ORIENTATED ▪ ORIENTATES
	ORIENTEER	ORIENTEERS
	ORIENTER	ORIENTERS
	ORIFICE	ORIFICES
	ORIFLAMME	ORIFLAMMES
	ORIGAMI	ORIGAMIS
	ORIGAN	ORIGANE ▪ ORIGANS
	ORIGANE	ORIGANES
	ORIGANUM	ORIGANUMS
	ORIGIN	ORIGINS
	ORIGINAL	ORIGINALS
	ORIGINATE	ORIGINATED ▪ ORIGINATES
	ORILLION	ORILLIONS
	ORINASAL	ORINASALS
	ORIOLE	ORIOLES
	ORISHA	ORISHAS
	ORISON	ORISONS
	ORIXA	ORIXAS
	ORLE	ORLES
	ORLON	ORLONS
	ORLOP	ORLOPS
DORMER ▪ FORMER ▪ WORMER	**ORMER**	ORMERS
DORMERS ▪ FORMERS ▪ WORMERS	**ORMERS**	
	ORMOLU	ORMOLUS
	ORNAMENT	ORNAMENTS
	ORNATE	ORNATER
	ORNITHINE	ORNITHINES
	OROGEN	OROGENS ▪ OROGENY
HOROGRAPHY	**OROGRAPHY**	
	OROIDE	OROIDES
HOROLOGIES	**OROLOGIES**	
HOROLOGIST	**OROLOGIST**	OROLOGISTS
HOROLOGY	**OROLOGY**	
	OROMETER	OROMETERS
	OROPESA	OROPESAS
	ORPHAN	ORPHANS
	ORPHANAGE	ORPHANAGES
	ORPHANISM	ORPHANISMS
	ORPHARION	ORPHARIONS
MORPHIC	**ORPHIC**	
	ORPHISM	ORPHISMS
	ORPHREY	ORPHREYS
	ORPIMENT	ORPIMENTS
	ORPIN	ORPINE ▪ ORPINS
FORPINE	**ORPINE**	ORPINES
FORPINES	**ORPINES**	

FRONT HOOK	ROOT WORD	END HOOK
MORRA ▪ SORRA	**ORRA**	
MORRICE	**ORRICE**	ORRICES
MORRICES	**ORRICES**	
MORRIS	**ORRIS**	
MORRISES	**ORRISES**	
	ORRISROOT	ORRISROOTS
BORS ▪ CORS ▪ DORS ▪ HORS ▪ JORS ▪ KORS MORS ▪ TORS ▪ VORS	**ORS**	
	ORSEILLE	ORSEILLES
BORT ▪ DORT ▪ FORT ▪ MORT ▪ PORT ▪ RORT SORT ▪ TORT ▪ WORT	**ORT**	ORTS
	ORTANIQUE	ORTANIQUES
	ORTHICON	ORTHICONS
	ORTHO	ORTHOS
	ORTHODOX	ORTHODOXY
	ORTHOPOD	ORTHOPODS
	ORTHOPTER	ORTHOPTERA ▪ ORTHOPTERS
	ORTHOPTIC	ORTHOPTICS
PORTHOS	**ORTHOS**	
PORTHOSES	**ORTHOSES**	
	ORTHOTIC	ORTHOTICS
	ORTHOTIST	ORTHOTISTS
	ORTHOTONE	ORTHOTONES
PORTOLAN	**ORTOLAN**	ORTOLANS
PORTOLANS	**ORTOLANS**	
BORTS ▪ DORTS ▪ FORTS ▪ MORTS ▪ PORTS RORTS ▪ SORTS ▪ TORTS ▪ WORTS	**ORTS**	
	ORVAL	ORVALS
	ORZO	ORZOS
BOS ▪ COS ▪ DOS ▪ GOS ▪ HOS (offensive) ▪ IOS KOS ▪ LOS ▪ MOS ▪ NOS ▪ OOS ▪ POS ▪ SOS WOS ▪ YOS ▪ ZOS	**OS**	OSE
	OSCAR	OSCARS
	OSCILLATE	OSCILLATED ▪ OSCILLATES
	OSCINE	OSCINES
	OSCITANCE	OSCITANCES
	OSCITATE	OSCITATED ▪ OSCITATES
	OSCULA	OSCULAR
	OSCULATE	OSCULATED ▪ OSCULATES
	OSCULE	OSCULES
COSE ▪ DOSE ▪ HOSE ▪ LOSE ▪ MOSE ▪ NOSE OOSE ▪ POSE ▪ ROSE ▪ TOSE	**OSE**	OSES
COSES ▪ DOSES ▪ HOSES ▪ KOSES ▪ LOSES MOSES ▪ NOSES ▪ OOSES ▪ POSES ▪ ROSES TOSES	**OSES**	
	OSETRA	OSETRAS
	OSHAC	OSHACS
COSIER ▪ HOSIER ▪ NOSIER ▪ OOSIER POSIER ▪ ROSIER	**OSIER**	OSIERS ▪ OSIERY
HOSIERIES	**OSIERIES**	
COSIERS ▪ HOSIERS ▪ ROSIERS	**OSIERS**	
HOSIERY	**OSIERY**	
	OSMATE	OSMATES
	OSMIATE	OSMIATES
COSMIC	**OSMIC**	OSMICS
COSMICALLY	**OSMICALLY**	
	OSMIUM	OSMIUMS
	OSMOL	OSMOLE ▪ OSMOLS
	OSMOLE	OSMOLES
	OSMOMETER	OSMOMETERS
	OSMOSE	OSMOSED ▪ OSMOSES
COSMOSES ▪ KOSMOSES	**OSMOSES**	
	OSMUND	OSMUNDA ▪ OSMUNDS
	OSMUNDA	OSMUNDAS
	OSMUNDINE	OSMUNDINES
	OSNABURG	OSNABURGS
	OSPREY	OSPREYS
FOSSA	**OSSA**	
	OSSARIUM	OSSARIUMS

FRONT HOOK	ROOT WORD	END HOOK
	OSSATURE	OSSATURES
	OSSEIN	OSSEINS
	OSSELET	OSSELETS
	OSSETER	OSSETERS
	OSSETRA	OSSETRAS
	OSSICLE	OSSICLES
	OSSIFIER	OSSIFIERS
	OSSIFRAGA	OSSIFRAGAS
	OSSIFRAGE	OSSIFRAGES
	OSTENT	OSTENTS
	OSTEOCYTE	OSTEOCYTES
	OSTEODERM	OSTEODERMS
	OSTEOGEN	OSTEOGENS · OSTEOGENY
	OSTEOID	OSTEOIDS
	OSTEOMA	OSTEOMAS
	OSTEOPATH	OSTEOPATHS · OSTEOPATHY
	OSTEOTOME	OSTEOTOMES
	OSTIA	OSTIAL
	OSTINATO	OSTINATOS
	OSTIOLE	OSTIOLES
HOSTLER · JOSTLER	**OSTLER**	OSTLERS
HOSTLERS · JOSTLERS	**OSTLERS**	
POSTMARK	**OSTMARK**	OSTMARKS
POSTMARKS	**OSTMARKS**	
	OSTOMATE	OSTOMATES
	OSTRACISE	OSTRACISED · OSTRACISER · OSTRACISES
	OSTRACISM	OSTRACISMS
	OSTRACIZE	OSTRACIZED · OSTRACIZER · OSTRACIZES
	OSTRACOD	OSTRACODE · OSTRACODS
	OSTRACODE	OSTRACODES
	OSTREGER	OSTREGERS
	OTALGIA	OTALGIAS
NOTARIES · ROTARIES · VOTARIES	**OTARIES**	
NOTARY · ROTARY · VOTARY	**OTARY**	
BOTHER · FOTHER · LOTHER · MOTHER	**OTHER**	OTHERS
NOTHER · POTHER · ROTHER · TOTHER		
BOTHERS · FOTHERS · MOTHERS · POTHERS	**OTHERS**	
ROTHERS		
LOTIC	**OTIC**	
	OTOCYST	OTOCYSTS
	OTOLITH	OTOLITHS
	OTOLOGIST	OTOLOGISTS
	OTORRHOEA	OTORRHOEAS
	OTOSCOPE	OTOSCOPES
COTTAR	**OTTAR**	OTTARS
COTTARS	**OTTARS**	
	OTTAVA	OTTAVAS
	OTTAVINO	OTTAVINOS
COTTER · DOTTER · HOTTER · JOTTER	**OTTER**	OTTERS
LOTTER · POTTER · ROTTER · TOTTER		
COTTERED · HOTTERED · POTTERED	**OTTERED**	
TOTTERED		
COTTERING · HOTTERING · POTTERING	**OTTERING**	
TOTTERING		
COTTERS · DOTTERS · HOTTERS · JOTTERS	**OTTERS**	
LOTTERS · POTTERS · ROTTERS · TOTTERS		
LOTTO · MOTTO · POTTO	**OTTO**	OTTOS
	OTTOMAN	OTTOMANS
LOTTOS · MOTTOS · POTTOS	**OTTOS**	
	OTTRELITE	OTTRELITES
FOU · LOU · MOU · SOU · YOU	**OU**	OUD · OUK · OUP · OUR · OUS · OUT
	OUABAIN	OUABAINS
	OUAKARI	OUAKARIS
WOUBIT	**OUBIT**	OUBITS
WOUBITS	**OUBITS**	
	OUBLIETTE	OUBLIETTES
COUCH · MOUCH · POUCH · TOUCH · VOUCH	**OUCH**	OUCHT
COUCHED · DOUCHED · MOUCHED · POUCHED	**OUCHED**	
TOUCHED · VOUCHED		

567

FRONT HOOK	ROOT WORD	END HOOK
BOUCHES = COUCHES = DOUCHES = MOUCHES POUCHES = ROUCHES = TOUCHES VOUCHES	OUCHES	
COUCHING = DOUCHING = MOUCHING POUCHING = TOUCHING = VOUCHING	OUCHING	
	OUCHT	OUCHTS
FOUD = LOUD	OUD	OUDS
FOUDS	OUDS	
ROUGHLY = TOUGHLY	OUGHLY	
BOUGHT = DOUGHT = FOUGHT = MOUGHT NOUGHT = ROUGHT = SOUGHT	OUGHT	OUGHTS
BOUGHTS = NOUGHTS	OUGHTS	
	OUGLIE	OUGLIED = OUGLIES
	OUGUIYA	OUGUIYAS
	OUIJA	OUIJAS
	OUISTITI	OUISTITIS
BOUK = DOUK = GOUK = JOUK = POUK = SOUK TOUK = YOUK = ZOUK	OUK	OUKS
BOUKS = DOUKS = GOUKS = JOUKS = POUKS SOUKS = TOUKS = YOUKS = ZOUKS	OUKS	
	OULACHON	OULACHONS
	OULAKAN	OULAKANS
COULD = MOULD = NOULD = WOULD	OULD	
BOULDER = FOULDER = MOULDER = POULDER	OULDER	
COULDEST = WOULDEST	OULDEST	
	OULK	OULKS
	OULONG	OULONGS
DOUMA = LOUMA	OUMA	OUMAS
DOUMAS = LOUMAS	OUMAS	
BOUNCE = JOUNCE = POUNCE = ROUNCE	OUNCE	OUNCES
BOUNCES = JOUNCES = POUNCES = ROUNCES	OUNCES	
WOUNDY	OUNDY	
COUP = DOUP = LOUP = MOUP = NOUP = ROUP = SOUP	OUP	OUPA = OUPH = OUPS
	OUPA	OUPAS
COUPED = LOUPED = MOUPED = POUPED ROUPED = SOUPED	OUPED	
	OUPH	OUPHE = OUPHS
	OUPHE	OUPHES
COUPING = LOUPING = MOUPING = POUPING ROUPING = SOUPING	OUPING	
COUPS = DOUPS = LOUPS = MOUPS = NOUPS ROUPS = SOUPS	OUPS	
COUR = DOUR = FOUR = HOUR = JOUR = LOUR POUR = SOUR = TOUR = YOUR	OUR	OURN = OURS
WOURALI	OURALI	OURALIS
WOURALIS	OURALIS	
	OURANG	OURANGS
	OURARI	OURARIS
	OUREBI	OUREBIS
COURIE = LOURIE = POURIE = TOURIE	OURIE	OURIER
COURIER = LOURIER	OURIER	
LOURIEST	OURIEST	
BOURN = MOURN = YOURN	OURN	
COURS = FOURS = HOURS = JOURS = LOURS POURS = SOURS = TOURS = YOURS	OURS	
YOURSELF	OURSELF	
YOURSELVES	OURSELVES	
FOUS = LOUS = MOUS = NOUS = SOUS = YOUS	OUS	OUST
HOUSEL	OUSEL	OUSELS
HOUSELS	OUSELS	
JOUST = MOUST = ROUST	OUST	OUSTS
JOUSTED = MOUSTED = ROUSTED	OUSTED	
JOUSTER = ROUSTER	OUSTER	OUSTERS
JOUSTERS = ROUSTERS	OUSTERS	
JOUSTING = MOUSTING = ROUSTING	OUSTING	
	OUSTITI	OUSTITIS
JOUSTS = MOUSTS = ROUSTS	OUSTS	
BOUT = DOUT = GOUT = HOUT = LOUT = NOUT POUT = ROUT = SOUT = TOUT	OUT	OUTS

FRONT HOOK	ROOT WORD	END HOOK
	OUTACT	OUTACTS
	OUTADD	OUTADDS
	OUTAGE	OUTAGES
	OUTARGUE	OUTARGUED · OUTARGUES
	OUTASK	OUTASKS
	OUTBACK	OUTBACKS
	OUTBACKER	OUTBACKERS
	OUTBAKE	OUTBAKED · OUTBAKES
	OUTBAR	OUTBARK · OUTBARS
	OUTBARK	OUTBARKS
	OUTBAWL	OUTBAWLS
	OUTBEAM	OUTBEAMS
	OUTBEG	OUTBEGS
	OUTBID	OUTBIDS
	OUTBIDDER	OUTBIDDERS
	OUTBLAZE	OUTBLAZED · OUTBLAZES
	OUTBLEAT	OUTBLEATS
	OUTBLOOM	OUTBLOOMS
	OUTBLUFF	OUTBLUFFS
	OUTBOARD	OUTBOARDS
	OUTBOAST	OUTBOASTS
	OUTBOUND	OUTBOUNDS
	OUTBRAG	OUTBRAGS
	OUTBRAVE	OUTBRAVED · OUTBRAVES
	OUTBRAWL	OUTBRAWLS
	OUTBRAZEN	OUTBRAZENS
	OUTBREAK	OUTBREAKS
	OUTBREED	OUTBREEDS
	OUTBRIBE	OUTBRIBED · OUTBRIBES
	OUTBROKE	OUTBROKEN
	OUTBUILD	OUTBUILDS
	OUTBULGE	OUTBULGED · OUTBULGES
	OUTBULK	OUTBULKS
	OUTBURN	OUTBURNS · OUTBURNT
	OUTBURST	OUTBURSTS
	OUTBUY	OUTBUYS
	OUTBY	OUTBYE
	OUTCALL	OUTCALLS
	OUTCAPER	OUTCAPERS
	OUTCAST	OUTCASTE · OUTCASTS
	OUTCASTE	OUTCASTED · OUTCASTES
	OUTCAVIL	OUTCAVILS
	OUTCHARGE	OUTCHARGED · OUTCHARGES
	OUTCHARM	OUTCHARMS
	OUTCHEAT	OUTCHEATS
	OUTCHID	OUTCHIDE
	OUTCHIDE	OUTCHIDED · OUTCHIDES
	OUTCLIMB	OUTCLIMBS
	OUTCOME	OUTCOMES
	OUTCOOK	OUTCOOKS
	OUTCOUNT	OUTCOUNTS
	OUTCRAWL	OUTCRAWLS
	OUTCROP	OUTCROPS
	OUTCROW	OUTCROWD · OUTCROWS
	OUTCROWD	OUTCROWDS
	OUTCURSE	OUTCURSED · OUTCURSES
	OUTCURVE	OUTCURVES
	OUTDANCE	OUTDANCED · OUTDANCES
	OUTDARE	OUTDARED · OUTDARES
	OUTDATE	OUTDATED · OUTDATES
	OUTDAZZLE	OUTDAZZLED · OUTDAZZLES
	OUTDEBATE	OUTDEBATED · OUTDEBATES
	OUTDESIGN	OUTDESIGNS
	OUTDODGE	OUTDODGED · OUTDODGES
	OUTDOER	OUTDOERS
	OUTDOOR	OUTDOORS
	OUTDOORS	OUTDOORSY
	OUTDRAG	OUTDRAGS
	OUTDRAW	OUTDRAWN · OUTDRAWS

C

FRONT HOOK	ROOT WORD	END HOOK
	OUTDREAM	OUTDREAMS · OUTDREAMT
	OUTDRINK	OUTDRINKS
	OUTDRIVE	OUTDRIVEN · OUTDRIVES
	OUTDROP	OUTDROPS
	OUTDUEL	OUTDUELS
	OUTDURE	OUTDURED · OUTDURES
	OUTDWELL	OUTDWELLS
	OUTEARN	OUTEARNS
	OUTEAT	OUTEATS
DOUTED · HOUTED · LOUTED · POUTED ROUTED · TOUTED	**OUTED**	
	OUTEDGE	OUTEDGES
COUTER · DOUTER · FOUTER · MOUTER POUTER · ROUTER · SOUTER · TOUTER	**OUTER**	OUTERS
	OUTERCOAT	OUTERCOATS
COUTERS · DOUTERS · FOUTERS · MOUTERS POUTERS · ROUTERS · SOUTERS · TOUTERS	**OUTERS**	
	OUTERWEAR	OUTERWEARS
	OUTFABLE	OUTFABLED · OUTFABLES
	OUTFACE	OUTFACED · OUTFACES
	OUTFALL	OUTFALLS
	OUTFAST	OUTFASTS
	OUTFAWN	OUTFAWNS
	OUTFEAST	OUTFEASTS
	OUTFEEL	OUTFEELS
	OUTFENCE	OUTFENCED · OUTFENCES
	OUTFIELD	OUTFIELDS
	OUTFIGHT	OUTFIGHTS
	OUTFIGURE	OUTFIGURED · OUTFIGURES
	OUTFIND	OUTFINDS
	OUTFIRE	OUTFIRED · OUTFIRES
	OUTFIT	OUTFITS
	OUTFITTER	OUTFITTERS
	OUTFLANK	OUTFLANKS
GOUTFLIES	**OUTFLIES**	
	OUTFLING	OUTFLINGS
	OUTFLOAT	OUTFLOATS
	OUTFLOW	OUTFLOWN · OUTFLOWS
GOUTFLY	**OUTFLY**	
	OUTFOOL	OUTFOOLS
	OUTFOOT	OUTFOOTS
	OUTFROWN	OUTFROWNS
	OUTFUMBLE	OUTFUMBLED · OUTFUMBLES
	OUTGAIN	OUTGAINS
	OUTGALLOP	OUTGALLOPS
	OUTGAMBLE	OUTGAMBLED · OUTGAMBLES
	OUTGATE	OUTGATES
	OUTGAZE	OUTGAZED · OUTGAZES
	OUTGIVE	OUTGIVEN · OUTGIVES
	OUTGIVING	OUTGIVINGS
	OUTGLARE	OUTGLARED · OUTGLARES
	OUTGLEAM	OUTGLEAMS
	OUTGLOW	OUTGLOWS
	OUTGNAW	OUTGNAWN · OUTGNAWS
	OUTGOER	OUTGOERS
	OUTGOING	OUTGOINGS
	OUTGRIN	OUTGRINS
	OUTGROUP	OUTGROUPS
	OUTGROW	OUTGROWN · OUTGROWS
	OUTGROWTH	OUTGROWTHS
	OUTGUARD	OUTGUARDS
	OUTGUIDE	OUTGUIDED · OUTGUIDES
	OUTGUN	OUTGUNS
	OUTHANDLE	OUTHANDLED · OUTHANDLES
	OUTHAUL	OUTHAULS
	OUTHAULER	OUTHAULERS
	OUTHEAR	OUTHEARD · OUTHEARS
COUTHER · MOUTHER · POUTHER · SOUTHER	**OUTHER**	
	OUTHIRE	OUTHIRED · OUTHIRES

FRONT HOOK	ROOT WORD	END HOOK
	OUTHIT	OUTHITS
	OUTHOMER	OUTHOMERS
	OUTHOUSE	OUTHOUSES
	OUTHOWL	OUTHOWLS
	OUTHUMOR	OUTHUMORS
	OUTHUNT	OUTHUNTS
	OUTHUSTLE	OUTHUSTLED ▪ OUTHUSTLES
	OUTHYRE	OUTHYRED ▪ OUTHYRES
DOUTING ▪ HOUTING ▪ LOUTING ▪ POUTING ROUTING ▪ TOUTING	**OUTING**	OUTINGS
HOUTINGS ▪ POUTINGS ▪ ROUTINGS	**OUTINGS**	
	OUTJEST	OUTJESTS
	OUTJET	OUTJETS
	OUTJOCKEY	OUTJOCKEYS
	OUTJUGGLE	OUTJUGGLED ▪ OUTJUGGLES
	OUTJUMP	OUTJUMPS
	OUTJUT	OUTJUTS
	OUTKEEP	OUTKEEPS
	OUTKICK	OUTKICKS
	OUTKILL	OUTKILLS
	OUTLAND	OUTLANDS
	OUTLANDER	OUTLANDERS
	OUTLAST	OUTLASTS
	OUTLAUGH	OUTLAUGHS
	OUTLAUNCE	OUTLAUNCED ▪ OUTLAUNCES
	OUTLAW	OUTLAWS
	OUTLAY	OUTLAYS
	OUTLEAD	OUTLEADS
	OUTLEAP	OUTLEAPS ▪ OUTLEAPT
	OUTLEARN	OUTLEARNS ▪ OUTLEARNT
	OUTLER	OUTLERS
	OUTLET	OUTLETS
	OUTLIE	OUTLIED ▪ OUTLIER ▪ OUTLIES
	OUTLIER	OUTLIERS
	OUTLINE	OUTLINED ▪ OUTLINER ▪ OUTLINES
	OUTLINER	OUTLINERS
	OUTLIVE	OUTLIVED ▪ OUTLIVER ▪ OUTLIVES
	OUTLIVER	OUTLIVERS
	OUTLOOK	OUTLOOKS
	OUTLOVE	OUTLOVED ▪ OUTLOVES
	OUTLUSTRE	OUTLUSTRED ▪ OUTLUSTRES
	OUTMAN	OUTMANS
	OUTMANTLE	OUTMANTLED ▪ OUTMANTLES
	OUTMASTER	OUTMASTERS
	OUTMODE	OUTMODED ▪ OUTMODES
	OUTMOVE	OUTMOVED ▪ OUTMOVES
	OUTMUSCLE	OUTMUSCLED ▪ OUTMUSCLES
	OUTNAME	OUTNAMED ▪ OUTNAMES
	OUTNIGHT	OUTNIGHTS
	OUTNUMBER	OUTNUMBERS
	OUTOFFICE	OUTOFFICES
	OUTPACE	OUTPACED ▪ OUTPACES
	OUTPAINT	OUTPAINTS
	OUTPART	OUTPARTS
	OUTPEEP	OUTPEEPS
	OUTPEER	OUTPEERS
	OUTPEOPLE	OUTPEOPLED ▪ OUTPEOPLES
	OUTPLACE	OUTPLACED ▪ OUTPLACER ▪ OUTPLACES
	OUTPLACER	OUTPLACERS
	OUTPLAN	OUTPLANS
	OUTPLAY	OUTPLAYS
	OUTPLOD	OUTPLODS
	OUTPLOT	OUTPLOTS
	OUTPOINT	OUTPOINTS
	OUTPOLL	OUTPOLLS
	OUTPORT	OUTPORTS
	OUTPORTER	OUTPORTERS
	OUTPOST	OUTPOSTS
	OUTPOUR	OUTPOURS

FRONT HOOK	ROOT WORD	END HOOK
	OUTPOURER	OUTPOURERS
	OUTPOWER	OUTPOWERS
	OUTPRAY	OUTPRAYS
	OUTPREEN	OUTPREENS
	OUTPRICE	OUTPRICED · OUTPRICES
	OUTPRIZE	OUTPRIZED · OUTPRIZES
	OUTPULL	OUTPULLS
	OUTPUPIL	OUTPUPILS
	OUTPURSUE	OUTPURSUED · OUTPURSUES
	OUTPUT	OUTPUTS
	OUTQUOTE	OUTQUOTED · OUTQUOTES
	OUTRACE	OUTRACED · OUTRACES
	OUTRAGE	OUTRAGED · OUTRAGES
	OUTRAISE	OUTRAISED · OUTRAISES
	OUTRAN	OUTRANG · OUTRANK
	OUTRANCE	OUTRANCES
	OUTRANG	OUTRANGE
	OUTRANGE	OUTRANGED · OUTRANGES
	OUTRANK	OUTRANKS
	OUTRATE	OUTRATED · OUTRATES
	OUTRAVE	OUTRAVED · OUTRAVES
FOUTRE	**OUTRE**	OUTRED
	OUTREAD	OUTREADS
	OUTREASON	OUTREASONS
	OUTRECKON	OUTRECKONS
FOUTRED	**OUTRED**	OUTREDS
	OUTREDDEN	OUTREDDENS
	OUTREIGN	OUTREIGNS
	OUTRELIEF	OUTRELIEFS
	OUTREMER	OUTREMERS
	OUTRIDE	OUTRIDER · OUTRIDES
	OUTRIDER	OUTRIDERS
	OUTRIG	OUTRIGS
	OUTRIGGER	OUTRIGGERS
FOUTRING	**OUTRING**	OUTRINGS
	OUTRIVAL	OUTRIVALS
	OUTRO	OUTROS · OUTROW
	OUTROAR	OUTROARS
	OUTROCK	OUTROCKS
	OUTROLL	OUTROLLS
	OUTROOP	OUTROOPS
	OUTROOPER	OUTROOPERS
	OUTROOT	OUTROOTS
	OUTROPE	OUTROPER · OUTROPES
	OUTROPER	OUTROPERS
	OUTROW	OUTROWS
	OUTRUN	OUTRUNG · OUTRUNS
	OUTRUNNER	OUTRUNNERS
BOUTS · DOUTS · GOUTS · HOUTS · LOUTS POUTS · ROUTS · SOUTS · TOUTS	**OUTS**	
	OUTSAIL	OUTSAILS
	OUTSAVOR	OUTSAVORS
	OUTSAY	OUTSAYS
	OUTSCHEME	OUTSCHEMED · OUTSCHEMES
	OUTSCOLD	OUTSCOLDS
	OUTSCOOP	OUTSCOOPS
	OUTSCORE	OUTSCORED · OUTSCORES
	OUTSCORN	OUTSCORNS
	OUTSCREAM	OUTSCREAMS
	OUTSEE	OUTSEEN · OUTSEES
	OUTSELL	OUTSELLS
	OUTSERT	OUTSERTS
	OUTSERVE	OUTSERVED · OUTSERVES
	OUTSET	OUTSETS
	OUTSHAME	OUTSHAMED · OUTSHAMES
	OUTSHINE	OUTSHINED · OUTSHINES
	OUTSHOOT	OUTSHOOTS
	OUTSHOT	OUTSHOTS
	OUTSHOUT	OUTSHOUTS

FRONT HOOK	ROOT WORD	END HOOK
	OUTSIDE	OUTSIDER ▪ OUTSIDES
	OUTSIDER	OUTSIDERS
	OUTSIGHT	OUTSIGHTS
	OUTSIN	OUTSING ▪ OUTSINS
	OUTSING	OUTSINGS
	OUTSIT	OUTSITS
	OUTSIZE	OUTSIZED ▪ OUTSIZES
	OUTSKATE	OUTSKATED ▪ OUTSKATES
	OUTSKIRT	OUTSKIRTS
	OUTSLEEP	OUTSLEEPS
	OUTSLICK	OUTSLICKS
	OUTSMART	OUTSMARTS
	OUTSMELL	OUTSMELLS
	OUTSMILE	OUTSMILED ▪ OUTSMILES
	OUTSMOKE	OUTSMOKED ▪ OUTSMOKES
	OUTSNORE	OUTSNORED ▪ OUTSNORES
	OUTSOAR	OUTSOARS
	OUTSOLE	OUTSOLES
	OUTSOURCE	OUTSOURCED ▪ OUTSOURCES
	OUTSPAN	OUTSPANS
	OUTSPEAK	OUTSPEAKS
	OUTSPEED	OUTSPEEDS
	OUTSPELL	OUTSPELLS
	OUTSPEND	OUTSPENDS
	OUTSPOKE	OUTSPOKEN
	OUTSPORT	OUTSPORTS
	OUTSPREAD	OUTSPREADS
	OUTSPRING	OUTSPRINGS
	OUTSPRINT	OUTSPRINTS
	OUTSTAND	OUTSTANDS
	OUTSTARE	OUTSTARED ▪ OUTSTARES
	OUTSTART	OUTSTARTS
	OUTSTATE	OUTSTATED ▪ OUTSTATES
	OUTSTAY	OUTSTAYS
	OUTSTEER	OUTSTEERS
	OUTSTEP	OUTSTEPS
	OUTSTRAIN	OUTSTRAINS
	OUTSTRIDE	OUTSTRIDES
	OUTSTRIKE	OUTSTRIKES
	OUTSTRIP	OUTSTRIPS
	OUTSTRIVE	OUTSTRIVEN ▪ OUTSTRIVES
	OUTSTROKE	OUTSTROKES
	OUTSTUNT	OUTSTUNTS
	OUTSULK	OUTSULKS
	OUTSUM	OUTSUMS
	OUTSWEAR	OUTSWEARS
	OUTSWEEP	OUTSWEEPS
	OUTSWELL	OUTSWELLS
	OUTSWIM	OUTSWIMS
	OUTSWING	OUTSWINGS
	OUTTAKE	OUTTAKEN ▪ OUTTAKES
	OUTTALK	OUTTALKS
	OUTTASK	OUTTASKS
	OUTTELL	OUTTELLS
	OUTTHANK	OUTTHANKS
	OUTTHIEVE	OUTTHIEVED ▪ OUTTHIEVES
	OUTTHINK	OUTTHINKS
	OUTTHROB	OUTTHROBS
	OUTTHROW	OUTTHROWN ▪ OUTTHROWS
	OUTTHRUST	OUTTHRUSTS
	OUTTONGUE	OUTTONGUED ▪ OUTTONGUES
	OUTTOP	OUTTOPS
	OUTTOWER	OUTTOWERS
	OUTTRADE	OUTTRADED ▪ OUTTRADES
	OUTTRAVEL	OUTTRAVELS
	OUTTRICK	OUTTRICKS
	OUTTROT	OUTTROTS
	OUTTRUMP	OUTTRUMPS
	OUTTURN	OUTTURNS

FRONT HOOK	ROOT WORD	END HOOK
	OUTVALUE	OUTVALUED · OUTVALUES
	OUTVAUNT	OUTVAUNTS
	OUTVENOM	OUTVENOMS
	OUTVIE	OUTVIED · OUTVIES
	OUTVOICE	OUTVOICED · OUTVOICES
	OUTVOTE	OUTVOTED · OUTVOTER · OUTVOTES
	OUTVOTER	OUTVOTERS
	OUTWAIT	OUTWAITS
	OUTWALK	OUTWALKS
	OUTWAR	OUTWARD · OUTWARS
	OUTWARD	OUTWARDS
	OUTWASTE	OUTWASTED · OUTWASTES
	OUTWEAR	OUTWEARS · OUTWEARY
GOUTWEED	**OUTWEED**	OUTWEEDS
GOUTWEEDS	**OUTWEEDS**	
	OUTWEEP	OUTWEEPS
	OUTWEIGH	OUTWEIGHS
	OUTWELL	OUTWELLS
	OUTWHIRL	OUTWHIRLS
	OUTWICK	OUTWICKS
	OUTWILE	OUTWILED · OUTWILES
	OUTWILL	OUTWILLS
	OUTWIN	OUTWIND · OUTWING · OUTWINS
	OUTWIND	OUTWINDS
	OUTWING	OUTWINGS
	OUTWIT	OUTWITH · OUTWITS
	OUTWORK	OUTWORKS
	OUTWORKER	OUTWORKERS
	OUTWORTH	OUTWORTHS
	OUTWREST	OUTWRESTS
	OUTWRIT	OUTWRITE
	OUTWRITE	OUTWRITES
	OUTYELL	OUTYELLS
	OUTYELP	OUTYELPS
	OUTYIELD	OUTYIELDS
COUVERT	**OUVERT**	OUVERTE
	OUVRAGE	OUVRAGES
	OUVRIER	OUVRIERE · OUVRIERS
	OUVRIERE	OUVRIERES
	OUZEL	OUZELS
	OUZO	OUZOS
NOVA	**OVA**	OVAL
	OVAL	OVALS
	OVALBUMIN	OVALBUMINS
COVARIES	**OVARIES**	
	OVARIOLE	OVARIOLES
COVARY	**OVARY**	
BOVATE	**OVATE**	OVATED · OVATES
NOVATED	**OVATED**	
BOVATES	**OVATES**	
NOVATION	**OVATION**	OVATIONS
NOVATIONS	**OVATIONS**	
	OVATOR	OVATORS
HOVEL · NOVEL	**OVEL**	OVELS
HOVELS · NOVELS	**OVELS**	
COVEN · DOVEN · HOVEN · ROVEN · WOVEN	**OVEN**	OVENS
	OVENBIRD	OVENBIRDS
DOVENED	**OVENED**	
DOVENING	**OVENING**	
COVENS · DOVENS · WOVENS	**OVENS**	
	OVENWARE	OVENWARES
	OVENWOOD	OVENWOODS
COVER · DOVER · HOVER · LOVER · MOVER · ROVER	**OVER**	OVERS · OVERT
COVERABLE	**OVERABLE**	
	OVERACT	OVERACTS
COVERAGE	**OVERAGE**	OVERAGED · OVERAGES
COVERAGES	**OVERAGES**	
COVERALL	**OVERALL**	OVERALLS

FRONT HOOK	ROOT WORD	END HOOK
COVERALLED	OVERALLED	
COVERALLS	OVERALLS	
	OVERARM	OVERARMS
	OVERAWE	OVERAWED · OVERAWES
	OVERBAKE	OVERBAKED · OVERBAKES
	OVERBEAR	OVERBEARS
	OVERBEAT	OVERBEATS
	OVERBET	OVERBETS
	OVERBID	OVERBIDS
	OVERBILL	OVERBILLS
	OVERBITE	OVERBITES
	OVERBLOW	OVERBLOWN · OVERBLOWS
	OVERBOIL	OVERBOILS
	OVERBOOK	OVERBOOKS
	OVERBOOT	OVERBOOTS
	OVERBORN	OVERBORNE
	OVERBOUND	OVERBOUNDS
	OVERBRAKE	OVERBRAKED · OVERBRAKES
	OVERBREED	OVERBREEDS
	OVERBRIEF	OVERBRIEFS
	OVERBRIM	OVERBRIMS
	OVERBROW	OVERBROWS
	OVERBROWS	OVERBROWSE
	OVERBUILD	OVERBUILDS
	OVERBULK	OVERBULKS
	OVERBURN	OVERBURNS · OVERBURNT
	OVERBUY	OVERBUYS
	OVERCALL	OVERCALLS
	OVERCAST	OVERCASTS
	OVERCHECK	OVERCHECKS
	OVERCHILL	OVERCHILLS
	OVERCLAIM	OVERCLAIMS
	OVERCLEAN	OVERCLEANS
	OVERCLEAR	OVERCLEARS
	OVERCLOUD	OVERCLOUDS
	OVERCLOY	OVERCLOYS
	OVERCOAT	OVERCOATS
	OVERCOLOR	OVERCOLORS
	OVERCOME	OVERCOMER · OVERCOMES
	OVERCOMER	OVERCOMERS
	OVERCOOK	OVERCOOKS
	OVERCOOL	OVERCOOLS
	OVERCOUNT	OVERCOUNTS
	OVERCOVER	OVERCOVERS
	OVERCRAM	OVERCRAMS
	OVERCRAW	OVERCRAWS
	OVERCROP	OVERCROPS
	OVERCROW	OVERCROWD · OVERCROWS
	OVERCROWD	OVERCROWDS
	OVERCURE	OVERCURED · OVERCURES
	OVERCUT	OVERCUTS
	OVERDARE	OVERDARED · OVERDARES
	OVERDECK	OVERDECKS
	OVERDO	OVERDOG
	OVERDOER	OVERDOERS
	OVERDOG	OVERDOGS
	OVERDOSE	OVERDOSED · OVERDOSES
	OVERDRAFT	OVERDRAFTS
	OVERDRAW	OVERDRAWN · OVERDRAWS
	OVERDRINK	OVERDRINKS
	OVERDRIVE	OVERDRIVEN · OVERDRIVES
	OVERDUB	OVERDUBS
	OVERDUST	OVERDUSTS
	OVERDYE	OVERDYED · OVERDYER · OVERDYES
	OVERDYER	OVERDYERS
	OVEREAT	OVEREATS
	OVEREATER	OVEREATERS
COVERED · DOVERED · HOVERED · LOVERED	OVERED	
	OVEREDIT	OVEREDITS

C

575

FRONT HOOK	ROOT WORD	END HOOK
	OVEREGG	OVEREGGS
	OVEREMOTE	OVEREMOTED · OVEREMOTES
	OVEREXERT	OVEREXERTS
	OVEREYE	OVEREYED · OVEREYES
	OVERFALL	OVERFALLS
	OVERFAVOR	OVERFAVORS
	OVERFEAR	OVERFEARS
	OVERFEED	OVERFEEDS
	OVERFILL	OVERFILLS
HOVERFLIES	OVERFLIES	
	OVERFLOOD	OVERFLOODS
	OVERFLOW	OVERFLOWN · OVERFLOWS
HOVERFLY	OVERFLY	
	OVERFOLD	OVERFOLDS
	OVERFUND	OVERFUNDS
	OVERGALL	OVERGALLS
	OVERGANG	OVERGANGS
	OVERGEAR	OVERGEARS
	OVERGET	OVERGETS
	OVERGILD	OVERGILDS
	OVERGIRD	OVERGIRDS
	OVERGIVE	OVERGIVEN · OVERGIVES
	OVERGLAZE	OVERGLAZED · OVERGLAZES
	OVERGLOOM	OVERGLOOMS
	OVERGO	OVERGOT
	OVERGOAD	OVERGOADS
	OVERGOING	OVERGOINGS
	OVERGORGE	OVERGORGED · OVERGORGES
	OVERGRADE	OVERGRADED · OVERGRADES
	OVERGRAIN	OVERGRAINS
	OVERGRAZE	OVERGRAZED · OVERGRAZES
	OVERGREEN	OVERGREENS
	OVERGROW	OVERGROWN · OVERGROWS
	OVERHAILE	OVERHAILED · OVERHAILES
	OVERHAIR	OVERHAIRS
	OVERHALE	OVERHALED · OVERHALES
	OVERHAND	OVERHANDS
	OVERHANG	OVERHANGS
	OVERHASTE	OVERHASTES
	OVERHATE	OVERHATED · OVERHATES
	OVERHAUL	OVERHAULS
	OVERHEAD	OVERHEADS
	OVERHEAP	OVERHEAPS
	OVERHEAR	OVERHEARD · OVERHEARS
	OVERHEAT	OVERHEATS
	OVERHENT	OVERHENTS
	OVERHIT	OVERHITS
	OVERHOLD	OVERHOLDS
	OVERHONOR	OVERHONORS
	OVERHOPE	OVERHOPED · OVERHOPES
	OVERHUNT	OVERHUNTS
	OVERHYPE	OVERHYPED · OVERHYPES
COVERING · DOVERING · HOVERING	OVERING	
	OVERISSUE	OVERISSUED · OVERISSUES
	OVERJOY	OVERJOYS
	OVERJUMP	OVERJUMPS
	OVERKEEP	OVERKEEPS
	OVERKILL	OVERKILLS
	OVERKING	OVERKINGS
	OVERLABOR	OVERLABORS
	OVERLADE	OVERLADED · OVERLADEN · OVERLADES
	OVERLAND	OVERLANDS
	OVERLAP	OVERLAPS
	OVERLARD	OVERLARDS
	OVERLAY	OVERLAYS
	OVERLEAP	OVERLEAPS · OVERLEAPT
	OVERLEARN	OVERLEARNS · OVERLEARNT
	OVERLEND	OVERLENDS
COVERLET	OVERLET	OVERLETS

FRONT HOOK	ROOT WORD	END HOOK
COVERLETS	**OVERLETS**	
	OVERLIE	OVERLIER ▪ OVERLIES
	OVERLIER	OVERLIERS
	OVERLIGHT	OVERLIGHTS
	OVERLIVE	OVERLIVED ▪ OVERLIVES
	OVERLOAD	OVERLOADS
	OVERLOCK	OVERLOCKS
	OVERLOOK	OVERLOOKS
	OVERLORD	OVERLORDS
	OVERLOVE	OVERLOVED ▪ OVERLOVES
LOVERLY	**OVERLY**	
	OVERMAN	OVERMANS ▪ OVERMANY
	OVERMAST	OVERMASTS
	OVERMELT	OVERMELTS
	OVERMILK	OVERMILKS
	OVERMINE	OVERMINED ▪ OVERMINES
COVERMOUNT	**OVERMOUNT**	OVERMOUNTS
	OVERNAME	OVERNAMED ▪ OVERNAMES
	OVERNET	OVERNETS
	OVERNIGHT	OVERNIGHTS
	OVERPACK	OVERPACKS
	OVERPAINT	OVERPAINTS
	OVERPART	OVERPARTS
	OVERPAY	OVERPAYS
	OVERPEDAL	OVERPEDALS
	OVERPEER	OVERPEERS
	OVERPLAID	OVERPLAIDS
	OVERPLAN	OVERPLANS ▪ OVERPLANT
	OVERPLANT	OVERPLANTS
	OVERPLAY	OVERPLAYS
	OVERPLOT	OVERPLOTS
	OVERPOISE	OVERPOISED ▪ OVERPOISES
	OVERPOST	OVERPOSTS
	OVERPOWER	OVERPOWERS
	OVERPRICE	OVERPRICED ▪ OVERPRICES
	OVERPRINT	OVERPRINTS
	OVERPRIZE	OVERPRIZED ▪ OVERPRIZES
	OVERPUMP	OVERPUMPS
	OVERRACK	OVERRACKS
	OVERRAKE	OVERRAKED ▪ OVERRAKES
	OVERRAN	OVERRANK
	OVERRATE	OVERRATED ▪ OVERRATES
	OVERREACT	OVERREACTS
	OVERREAD	OVERREADS
	OVERRED	OVERREDS
	OVERREN	OVERRENS
	OVERRIDE	OVERRIDER ▪ OVERRIDES
	OVERRIDER	OVERRIDERS
	OVERRIPE	OVERRIPEN
	OVERRIPEN	OVERRIPENS
	OVERROAST	OVERROASTS
	OVERRUFF	OVERRUFFS
	OVERRULE	OVERRULED ▪ OVERRULER ▪ OVERRULES
	OVERRULER	OVERRULERS
	OVERRUN	OVERRUNS
COVERS ▪ DOVERS ▪ HOVERS ▪ LOVERS MOVERS ▪ ROVERS	**OVERS**	
	OVERSAIL	OVERSAILS
	OVERSALE	OVERSALES
	OVERSALT	OVERSALTS
	OVERSAUCE	OVERSAUCED ▪ OVERSAUCES
	OVERSAVE	OVERSAVED ▪ OVERSAVES
	OVERSCALE	OVERSCALED
	OVERSCORE	OVERSCORED ▪ OVERSCORES
	OVERSEA	OVERSEAS
	OVERSEE	OVERSEED ▪ OVERSEEN ▪ OVERSEER OVERSEES
	OVERSEED	OVERSEEDS
	OVERSEER	OVERSEERS

FRONT HOOK	ROOT WORD	END HOOK
	OVERSELL	OVERSELLS
	OVERSET	OVERSETS
	OVERSEW	OVERSEWN · OVERSEWS
	OVERSHADE	OVERSHADED · OVERSHADES
	OVERSHINE	OVERSHINES
	OVERSHIRT	OVERSHIRTS
	OVERSHOE	OVERSHOES
	OVERSHOOT	OVERSHOOTS
	OVERSHOT	OVERSHOTS
	OVERSIDE	OVERSIDES
	OVERSIGHT	OVERSIGHTS
	OVERSIZE	OVERSIZED · OVERSIZES
	OVERSKIP	OVERSKIPS
	OVERSKIRT	OVERSKIRTS
	OVERSLEEP	OVERSLEEPS
COVERSLIP	OVERSLIP	OVERSLIPS · OVERSLIPT
COVERSLIPS	OVERSLIPS	
	OVERSMOKE	OVERSMOKED · OVERSMOKES
	OVERSOAK	OVERSOAKS
	OVERSOUL	OVERSOULS
	OVERSOW	OVERSOWN · OVERSOWS
	OVERSPEND	OVERSPENDS
	OVERSPICE	OVERSPICED · OVERSPICES
	OVERSPILL	OVERSPILLS
	OVERSPIN	OVERSPINS
	OVERSTAFF	OVERSTAFFS
	OVERSTAIN	OVERSTAINS
	OVERSTAND	OVERSTANDS
	OVERSTARE	OVERSTARED · OVERSTARES
	OVERSTATE	OVERSTATED · OVERSTATES
	OVERSTAY	OVERSTAYS
	OVERSTEER	OVERSTEERS
	OVERSTEP	OVERSTEPS
	OVERSTINK	OVERSTINKS
	OVERSTIR	OVERSTIRS
	OVERSTOCK	OVERSTOCKS
	OVERSTREW	OVERSTREWN · OVERSTREWS
	OVERSTUFF	OVERSTUFFS
	OVERSUP	OVERSUPS
	OVERSWAY	OVERSWAYS
	OVERSWEAR	OVERSWEARS
	OVERSWELL	OVERSWELLS
	OVERSWIM	OVERSWIMS
	OVERSWING	OVERSWINGS
COVERT	OVERT	
	OVERTAKE	OVERTAKEN · OVERTAKES
	OVERTALK	OVERTALKS
	OVERTASK	OVERTASKS
	OVERTEEM	OVERTEEMS
	OVERTHIN	OVERTHINK
	OVERTHINK	OVERTHINKS
	OVERTHROW	OVERTHROWN · OVERTHROWS
	OVERTIME	OVERTIMED · OVERTIMER · OVERTIMES
	OVERTIMER	OVERTIMERS
	OVERTIP	OVERTIPS
	OVERTIRE	OVERTIRED · OVERTIRES
COVERTLY	OVERTLY	
COVERTNESS	OVERTNESS	
	OVERTOIL	OVERTOILS
	OVERTONE	OVERTONES
	OVERTOP	OVERTOPS
	OVERTOWER	OVERTOWERS
	OVERTRADE	OVERTRADED · OVERTRADES
HOVERTRAIN	OVERTRAIN	OVERTRAINS
	OVERTREAT	OVERTREATS
	OVERTRICK	OVERTRICKS
	OVERTRIM	OVERTRIMS
	OVERTRIP	OVERTRIPS
	OVERTRUMP	OVERTRUMPS

FRONT HOOK	ROOT WORD	END HOOK
	OVERTRUST	OVERTRUSTS
COVERTURE	OVERTURE	OVERTURED ▪ OVERTURES
COVERTURES	OVERTURES	
	OVERTURN	OVERTURNS
	OVERTYPE	OVERTYPED ▪ OVERTYPES
	OVERURGE	OVERURGED ▪ OVERURGES
	OVERUSE	OVERUSED ▪ OVERUSES
	OVERVALUE	OVERVALUED ▪ OVERVALUES
	OVERVEIL	OVERVEILS
	OVERVIEW	OVERVIEWS
	OVERVOTE	OVERVOTED ▪ OVERVOTES
	OVERWARM	OVERWARMS
	OVERWATER	OVERWATERS
	OVERWEAR	OVERWEARS ▪ OVERWEARY
	OVERWEEN	OVERWEENS
	OVERWEIGH	OVERWEIGHS ▪ OVERWEIGHT
	OVERWET	OVERWETS
	OVERWHELM	OVERWHELMS
	OVERWIND	OVERWINDS
	OVERWING	OVERWINGS
	OVERWORD	OVERWORDS
	OVERWORK	OVERWORKS
	OVERWREST	OVERWRESTS
	OVERWRITE	OVERWRITES
	OVERYEAR	OVERYEARS
	OVERZEAL	OVERZEALS
	OVICIDE	OVICIDES
	OVIDUCT	OVIDUCTS
BOVINE	OVINE	OVINES
BOVINES	OVINES	
	OVIPOSIT	OVIPOSITS
	OVIRAPTOR	OVIRAPTORS
	OVISAC	OVISACS
	OVIST	OVISTS
	OVOID	OVOIDS
	OVOIDAL	OVOIDALS
	OVOLO	OVOLOS
	OVONIC	OVONICS
	OVULAR	OVULARY
	OVULATE	OVULATED ▪ OVULATES
	OVULATION	OVULATIONS
	OVULE	OVULES
	OVUM	
	NOVUM	
BOW ▪ COW ▪ DOW ▪ HOW ▪ JOW ▪ KOW ▪ LOW MOW ▪ NOW ▪ POW ▪ ROW ▪ SOW ▪ TOW ▪ VOW WOW ▪ YOW	OW	OWE ▪ OWL ▪ OWN ▪ OWT
	OWCHE	OWCHES
HOWE ▪ LOWE ▪ YOWE	OWE	OWED ▪ OWER ▪ OWES
BOWED ▪ COWED ▪ DOWED ▪ JOWED ▪ LOWED MOWED ▪ NOWED ▪ ROWED ▪ SOWED ▪ TOWED VOWED ▪ WOWED ▪ YOWED	OWED	
BOWER ▪ COWER ▪ DOWER ▪ LOWER ▪ MOWER POWER ▪ ROWER ▪ SOWER ▪ TOWER ▪ VOWER	OWER	
	OWERLOUP	OWERLOUPS
BOWES ▪ HOWES ▪ LOWES ▪ YOWES	OWES	
BOWING ▪ COWING ▪ DOWING ▪ JOWING LOWING ▪ MOWING ▪ ROWING ▪ SOWING TOWING ▪ VOWING ▪ WOWING ▪ YOWING	OWING	
BOWL ▪ COWL ▪ DOWL ▪ FOWL ▪ GOWL ▪ HOWL JOWL ▪ NOWL ▪ SOWL ▪ YOWL	OWL	OWLS ▪ OWLY
BOWLED ▪ COWLED ▪ FOWLED ▪ GOWLED HOWLED ▪ JOWLED ▪ SOWLED ▪ YOWLED	OWLED	
BOWLER ▪ FOWLER ▪ HOWLER ▪ JOWLER YOWLER	OWLER	OWLERS ▪ OWLERY
BOWLERS ▪ FOWLERS ▪ HOWLERS ▪ JOWLERS YOWLERS	OWLERS	
HOWLET	OWLET	OWLETS
HOWLETS	OWLETS	
DOWLIER ▪ JOWLIER ▪ LOWLIER	OWLIER	

FRONT HOOK	ROOT WORD	END HOOK
DOWLIEST · JOWLIEST · LOWLIEST	OWLIEST	
BOWLING · COWLING · FOWLING · GOWLING HOWLING · JOWLING · SOWLING · YOWLING	OWLING	
BOWLLIKE	OWLLIKE	
BOWLS · COWLS · DOWLS · FOWLS · GOWLS HOWLS · JOWLS · SOWLS · YOWLS	OWLS	
DOWLY · JOWLY · LOWLY	OWLY	
DOWN · GOWN · LOWN · MOWN · NOWN · POWN SOWN · TOWN	OWN	OWNS
BOWNED · DOWNED · GOWNED · LOWNED	OWNED	
DOWNER	OWNER	OWNERS
DOWNERS	OWNERS	
	OWNERSHIP	OWNERSHIPS
BOWNING · DOWNING · GOWNING · LOWNING	OWNING	
DOWNS · GOWNS · LOWNS · POWNS · TOWNS	OWNS	
HOWRE · POWRE	OWRE	OWRES
	OWRECOME	OWRECOMES
	OWRELAY	OWRELAYS
HOWRES · POWRES	OWRES	
	OWREWORD	OWREWORDS
COWRIE · LOWRIE	OWRIE	OWRIER
BOWSE · DOWSE · LOWSE · SOWSE · TOWSE	OWSE	OWSEN
DOWT · LOWT · NOWT · ROWT · TOWT	OWT	OWTS
DOWTS · LOWTS · NOWTS · ROWTS · TOWTS	OWTS	
BOX · COX · FOX · GOX · HOX · LOX · NOX POX · SOX · VOX · WOX	OX	OXO · OXY
	OXACILLIN	OXACILLINS
	OXALATE	OXALATED · OXALATES
	OXAZEPAM	OXAZEPAMS
	OXAZINE	OXAZINES
	OXBLOOD	OXBLOODS
	OXBOW	OXBOWS
	OXCART	OXCARTS
BOXEN · WOXEN	OXEN	
BOXER	OXER	OXERS
BOXERS	OXERS	
BOXES · COXES · FOXES · GOXES · HOXES LOXES · NOXES · POXES	OXES	
	OXEYE	OXEYES
	OXFORD	OXFORDS
	OXGANG	OXGANGS
	OXGATE	OXGATES
	OXHEAD	OXHEADS
	OXHEART	OXHEARTS
	OXHIDE	OXHIDES
	OXID	OXIDE · OXIDS
	OXIDANT	OXIDANTS
	OXIDASE	OXIDASES
	OXIDATE	OXIDATED · OXIDATES
	OXIDATION	OXIDATIONS
	OXIDE	OXIDES
	OXIDISE	OXIDISED · OXIDISER · OXIDISES
	OXIDISER	OXIDISERS
	OXIDIZE	OXIDIZED · OXIDIZER · OXIDIZES
	OXIDIZER	OXIDIZERS
	OXIM	OXIME · OXIMS
	OXIME	OXIMES
	OXIMETER	OXIMETERS
	OXLAND	OXLANDS
BOXLIKE · FOXLIKE	OXLIKE	
	OXLIP	OXLIPS
	OXONIUM	OXONIUMS
	OXPECKER	OXPECKERS
	OXSLIP	OXSLIPS
FOXTAIL	OXTAIL	OXTAILS
FOXTAILS	OXTAILS	
	OXTER	OXTERS
	OXTONGUE	OXTONGUES
BOXY · COXY · DOXY · FOXY · POXY	OXY	

FRONT HOOK	ROOT WORD	END HOOK
	OXYACID	OXYACIDS
	OXYCODONE	OXYCODONES
LOXYGEN	**OXYGEN**	OXYGENS
	OXYGENASE	OXYGENASES
	OXYGENATE	OXYGENATED · OXYGENATES
	OXYGENISE	OXYGENISED · OXYGENISER · OXYGENISES
	OXYGENIZE	OXYGENIZED · OXYGENIZER · OXYGENIZES
LOXYGENS	**OXYGENS**	
	OXYMEL	OXYMELS
	OXYMORON	OXYMORONS
	OXYPHIL	OXYPHILE · OXYPHILS
	OXYPHILE	OXYPHILES
	OXYSALT	OXYSALTS
	OXYSOME	OXYSOMES
	OXYTOCIC	OXYTOCICS
	OXYTOCIN	OXYTOCINS
	OXYTONE	OXYTONES
BOY · COY · DOY · FOY · GOY · HOY · JOY LOY · MOY · NOY · SOY · TOY	**OY**	OYE · OYS
	OYE	OYER · OYES · OYEZ
COYER · FOYER · TOYER	**OYER**	OYERS
FOYERS · TOYERS	**OYERS**	
NOYES	**OYES**	
NOYESES	**OYESES**	
BOYS · COYS · DOYS · FOYS · GOYS (offensive) HOYS · JOYS · LOYS · MOYS · NOYS · SOYS TOYS	**OYS**	
ROYSTER	**OYSTER**	OYSTERS
ROYSTERED	**OYSTERED**	
ROYSTERER	**OYSTERER**	OYSTERERS
ROYSTERERS	**OYSTERERS**	
ROYSTERING	**OYSTERING**	OYSTERINGS
ROYSTERS	**OYSTERS**	
	OYSTRIGE	OYSTRIGES
	OZAENA	OZAENAS
	OZALID	OZALIDS
	OZEKI	OZEKIS
	OZOCERITE	OZOCERITES
	OZOKERITE	OZOKERITES
	OZONATE	OZONATED · OZONATES
	OZONATION	OZONATIONS
	OZONE	OZONES
	OZONIDE	OZONIDES
	OZONISE	OZONISED · OZONISER · OZONISES
	OZONISER	OZONISERS
	OZONIZE	OZONIZED · OZONIZER · OZONIZES
	OZONIZER	OZONIZERS
MOZZIE	**OZZIE**	OZZIES
MOZZIES · POZZIES	**OZZIES**	

O

P

FRONT HOOK	ROOT WORD	END HOOK
SPA	**PA**	PAC · PAD · PAH · PAL · PAM · PAN · PAP PAR · PAS · PAT · PAV · PAW · PAX · PAY
	PAAL	PAALS
	PABLUM	PABLUMS
	PABOUCHE	PABOUCHES
	PABULUM	PABULUMS
	PAC	PACA · PACE · PACK · PACO · PACS PACT · PACY
	PACA	PACAS
	PACATION	PACATIONS
APACE · SPACE	**PACE**	PACED · PACER · PACES · PACEY
SPACED	**PACED**	
	PACEMAKER	PACEMAKERS
SPACER	**PACER**	PACERS
SPACERS	**PACERS**	
SPACES	**PACES**	
	PACEWAY	PACEWAYS
SPACEY	**PACEY**	
	PACHA	PACHAK · PACHAS
	PACHADOM	PACHADOMS
	PACHAK	PACHAKS
	PACHALIC	PACHALICS
	PACHINKO	PACHINKOS
	PACHISI	PACHISIS
	PACHOULI	PACHOULIS
	PACHUCO	PACHUCOS
	PACHYDERM	PACHYDERMS
	PACHYTENE	PACHYTENES
SPACIER	**PACIER**	
SPACIEST	**PACIEST**	
OPACIFIED	**PACIFIED**	
OPACIFIER	**PACIFIER**	PACIFIERS
OPACIFIERS	**PACIFIERS**	
OPACIFIES	**PACIFIES**	
	PACIFISM	PACIFISMS
	PACIFIST	PACIFISTS
OPACIFY	**PACIFY**	
OPACIFYING	**PACIFYING**	
SPACING	**PACING**	
	PACK	PACKS
	PACKAGE	PACKAGED · PACKAGER · PACKAGES
	PACKAGER	PACKAGERS
	PACKAGING	PACKAGINGS
	PACKBOARD	PACKBOARDS
	PACKER	PACKERS
	PACKET	PACKETS
	PACKFONG	PACKFONGS
	PACKFRAME	PACKFRAMES
	PACKHORSE	PACKHORSES
	PACKING	PACKINGS
	PACKSACK	PACKSACKS
	PACKSHEET	PACKSHEETS
	PACKSTAFF	PACKSTAFFS
	PACKWAY	PACKWAYS
	PACO	PACOS
EPACT	**PACT**	PACTA · PACTS
	PACTION	PACTIONS
EPACTS	**PACTS**	
SPACY	**PACY**	
	PAD	PADI · PADS
	PADANG	PADANGS
	PADAUK	PADAUKS
	PADDER	PADDERS
	PADDING	PADDINGS
	PADDLE	PADDLED · PADDLER · PADDLES
	PADDLER	PADDLERS

FRONT HOOK	ROOT WORD	END HOOK
	PADDLING	PADDLINGS
	PADDOCK	PADDOCKS
	PADDYWACK	PADDYWACKS
	PADELLA	PADELLAS
	PADEMELON	PADEMELONS
	PADERERO	PADEREROS
	PADI	PADIS
	PADISHAH	PADISHAHS
	PADLE	PADLES
	PADLOCK	PADLOCKS
	PADMA	PADMAS
	PADNAG	PADNAGS
	PADOUK	PADOUKS
	PADRE	PADRES
	PADRONE	PADRONES
	PADRONISM	PADRONISMS
	PADSAW	PADSAWS
	PADSHAH	PADSHAHS
	PADUASOY	PADUASOYS
	PADYMELON	PADYMELONS
	PAEAN	PAEANS
	PAEANISM	PAEANISMS
	PAEDERAST	PAEDERASTS ▪ PAEDERASTY
	PAEDEUTIC	PAEDEUTICS
	PAELLA	PAELLAS
	PAENULA	PAENULAE ▪ PAENULAS
	PAEON	PAEONS ▪ PAEONY
	PAEONIC	PAEONICS
	PAESAN	PAESANI ▪ PAESANO ▪ PAESANS
	PAESANO	PAESANOS
	PAGAN	PAGANS
	PAGANDOM	PAGANDOMS
	PAGANISE	PAGANISED ▪ PAGANISER ▪ PAGANISES
	PAGANISER	PAGANISERS
	PAGANISM	PAGANISMS
	PAGANIST	PAGANISTS
	PAGANIZE	PAGANIZED ▪ PAGANIZER ▪ PAGANIZES
	PAGANIZER	PAGANIZERS
APAGE	PAGE	PAGED ▪ PAGER ▪ PAGES
	PAGEANT	PAGEANTS
	PAGEBOY	PAGEBOYS
	PAGEFUL	PAGEFULS
	PAGEHOOD	PAGEHOODS
	PAGER	PAGERS
	PAGEVIEW	PAGEVIEWS
	PAGINATE	PAGINATED ▪ PAGINATES
	PAGING	PAGINGS
	PAGLE	PAGLES
	PAGOD	PAGODA ▪ PAGODS
	PAGODA	PAGODAS
	PAGRI	PAGRIS
	PAGURIAN	PAGURIANS
	PAGURID	PAGURIDS
OPAH	PAH	PAHS
	PAHLAVI	PAHLAVIS
	PAHOEHOE	PAHOEHOES
OPAHS	PAHS	
APAID	PAID	
	PAIDEUTIC	PAIDEUTICS
	PAIDLE	PAIDLES
	PAIGLE	PAIGLES
	PAIK	PAIKS
SPAIL	PAIL	PAILS
	PAILFUL	PAILFULS
	PAILLARD	PAILLARDS
	PAILLASSE	PAILLASSES
	PAILLETTE	PAILLETTES
	PAILLON	PAILLONS
SPAILS	PAILS	

FRONT HOOK	ROOT WORD	END HOOK
SPAIN	PAIN	PAINS · PAINT
SPAINED	PAINED	
	PAINIM	PAINIMS
SPAINING	PAINING	
SPAINS	PAINS	
	PAINT	PAINTS · PAINTY
	PAINTBALL	PAINTBALLS
	PAINTER	PAINTERS
	PAINTING	PAINTINGS
	PAINTURE	PAINTURES
	PAINTWORK	PAINTWORKS
	PAIOCK	PAIOCKE · PAIOCKS
	PAIOCKE	PAIOCKES
	PAIR	PAIRE · PAIRS
	PAIRE	PAIRED · PAIRER · PAIRES
	PAIRES	PAIREST
	PAIRIAL	PAIRIALS
	PAIRING	PAIRINGS
	PAIS	PAISA · PAISE
	PAISA	PAISAN · PAISAS
	PAISAN	PAISANA · PAISANO · PAISANS
	PAISANA	PAISANAS
	PAISANO	PAISANOS
	PAISLEY	PAISLEYS
	PAITRICK	PAITRICKS
	PAJAMA	PAJAMAS
	PAJOCK	PAJOCKE · PAJOCKS
	PAJOCKE	PAJOCKES
	PAKAHI	PAKAHIS
	PAKAPOO	PAKAPOOS
	PAKEHA	PAKEHAS
	PAKFONG	PAKFONGS
	PAKIHI	PAKIHIS
	PAKOKO	PAKOKOS
	PAKORA	PAKORAS
	PAKTHONG	PAKTHONGS
	PAKTONG	PAKTONGS
OPAL	PAL	PALE · PALL · PALM · PALP · PALS · PALY
	PALABRA	PALABRAS
	PALACE	PALACED · PALACES
	PALADIN	PALADINS
	PALAESTRA	PALAESTRAE · PALAESTRAL · PALAESTRAS
	PALAFITTE	PALAFITTES
	PALAGI	PALAGIS
	PALAMA	PALAMAE
	PALAMINO	PALAMINOS
	PALAMPORE	PALAMPORES
	PALANKEEN	PALANKEENS
	PALANQUIN	PALANQUINS
	PALAPA	PALAPAS
	PALATAL	PALATALS
	PALATE	PALATED · PALATES
	PALATINE	PALATINES
	PALAVER	PALAVERS
	PALAVERER	PALAVERERS
	PALAY	PALAYS
	PALAZZO	PALAZZOS
SPALE	PALE	PALEA · PALED · PALER · PALES · PALET
	PALEA	PALEAE · PALEAL
	PALEBUCK	PALEBUCKS
OPALED	PALED	
	PALEFACE	PALEFACES (offensive)
	PALEMPORE	PALEMPORES
	PALEOLITH	PALEOLITHS
	PALEOSOL	PALEOSOLS
SPALES	PALES	PALEST
	PALESTRA	PALESTRAE · PALESTRAL · PALESTRAS
	PALET	PALETS
	PALETOT	PALETOTS

FRONT HOOK	ROOT WORD	END HOOK
	PALETTE	PALETTES
	PALFREY	PALFREYS
	PALIKAR	PALIKARS
	PALILALIA	PALILALIAS
	PALING	PALINGS
	PALINKA	PALINKAS
	PALINODE	PALINODES
	PALINOPIA	PALINOPIAS
	PALISADE	PALISADED ▪ PALISADES
	PALKEE	PALKEES
	PALKI	PALKIS
SPALL	PALL	PALLA ▪ PALLS ▪ PALLY
	PALLA	PALLAE ▪ PALLAH
	PALLADIUM	PALLADIUMS
	PALLAH	PALLAHS
SPALLED	PALLED	
	PALLET	PALLETS
	PALLETISE	PALLETISED ▪ PALLETISER ▪ PALLETISES
	PALLETIZE	PALLETIZED ▪ PALLETIZER ▪ PALLETIZES
	PALLETTE	PALLETTES
	PALLIA	PALLIAL
	PALLIARD	PALLIARDS
	PALLIASSE	PALLIASSES
	PALLIATE	PALLIATED ▪ PALLIATES
	PALLIATOR	PALLIATORS ▪ PALLIATORY
SPALLING	PALLING	
	PALLIUM	PALLIUMS
	PALLONE	PALLONES
	PALLOR	PALLORS
SPALLS	PALLS	
	PALM	PALMS ▪ PALMY
	PALMAR	PALMARY
	PALMATE	PALMATED
	PALMATION	PALMATIONS
	PALMER	PALMERS
	PALMETTE	PALMETTES
	PALMETTO	PALMETTOS
	PALMFUL	PALMFULS
	PALMHOUSE	PALMHOUSES
	PALMIE	PALMIER ▪ PALMIES ▪ PALMIET
	PALMIES	PALMIEST
	PALMIET	PALMIETS
	PALMIPED	PALMIPEDE ▪ PALMIPEDS
	PALMIPEDE	PALMIPEDES
	PALMIST	PALMISTS
	PALMISTER	PALMISTERS
	PALMITATE	PALMITATES
	PALMITIN	PALMITINS
	PALMTOP	PALMTOPS
	PALMYRA	PALMYRAS
	PALOLO	PALOLOS
	PALOMINO	PALOMINOS
	PALOOKA	PALOOKAS
	PALOVERDE	PALOVERDES
	PALP	PALPI ▪ PALPS
	PALPATE	PALPATED ▪ PALPATES
	PALPATION	PALPATIONS
	PALPATOR	PALPATORS ▪ PALPATORY
	PALPEBRA	PALPEBRAE ▪ PALPEBRAL ▪ PALPEBRAS
	PALPITATE	PALPITATED ▪ PALPITATES
OPALS	PALS	PALSY
	PALSGRAVE	PALSGRAVES
	PALSHIP	PALSHIPS
	PALSIES	PALSIEST
	PALSTAFF	PALSTAFFS
	PALSTAVE	PALSTAVES
	PALTER	PALTERS
	PALTERER	PALTERERS
	PALUDISM	PALUDISMS

P

FRONT HOOK	ROOT WORD	END HOOK
SPAM	PAM	PAMS
	PAMPA	PAMPAS
	PAMPEAN	PAMPEANS
	PAMPER	PAMPERO · PAMPERS
	PAMPERER	PAMPERERS
	PAMPERO	PAMPEROS
	PAMPHLET	PAMPHLETS
	PAMPHREY	PAMPHREYS
	PAMPOEN	PAMPOENS
	PAMPOOTIE	PAMPOOTIES
SPAMS	PAMS	
SPAN	PAN	PAND · PANE · PANG · PANS · PANT
	PANACEA	PANACEAN · PANACEAS
	PANACHAEA	PANACHAEAS
	PANACHE	PANACHES
	PANADA	PANADAS
	PANAMA	PANAMAS
	PANATELA	PANATELAS
	PANATELLA	PANATELLAS
	PANBROIL	PANBROILS
	PANCAKE	PANCAKED · PANCAKES
	PANCE	PANCES
	PANCETTA	PANCETTAS
	PANCHAYAT	PANCHAYATS
	PANCHEON	PANCHEONS
	PANCHION	PANCHIONS
	PANCRATIA	PANCRATIAN
	PAND	PANDA · PANDS · PANDY
	PANDA	PANDAR · PANDAS
	PANDAR	PANDARS
	PANDATION	PANDATIONS
	PANDECT	PANDECTS
	PANDEMIA	PANDEMIAN · PANDEMIAS
	PANDEMIC	PANDEMICS
	PANDER	PANDERS
	PANDERER	PANDERERS
	PANDERISM	PANDERISMS
	PANDIT	PANDITS
	PANDOOR	PANDOORS
	PANDORA	PANDORAS
	PANDORE	PANDORES
	PANDOUR	PANDOURS
	PANDURA	PANDURAS
	PANDURATE	PANDURATED
SPANE	PANE	PANED · PANEL · PANES
SPANED	PANED	
	PANEER	PANEERS
	PANEGOISM	PANEGOISMS
	PANEGYRIC	PANEGYRICA · PANEGYRICS
	PANEL	PANELS
	PANELING	PANELINGS
	PANELIST	PANELISTS
	PANELLING	PANELLINGS
	PANELLIST	PANELLISTS
SPANES	PANES	
	PANETELA	PANETELAS
	PANETELLA	PANETELLAS
	PANETTONE	PANETTONES
	PANFUL	PANFULS
SPANG	PANG	PANGA · PANGS
	PANGA	PANGAS
SPANGED	PANGED	
	PANGEN	PANGENE · PANGENS
	PANGENE	PANGENES
SPANGING	PANGING	
	PANGOLIN	PANGOLINS
	PANGRAM	PANGRAMS
SPANGS	PANGS	
	PANHANDLE	PANHANDLED · PANHANDLER · PANHANDLES

FRONT HOOK	ROOT WORD	END HOOK
	PANIC	PANICK ▪ PANICS
	PANICK	PANICKS ▪ PANICKY
	PANICLE	PANICLED ▪ PANICLES
	PANICUM	PANICUMS
	PANIER	PANIERS
	PANIM	PANIMS
SPANING	**PANING**	
	PANISC	PANISCS
	PANISK	PANISKS
	PANISLAM	PANISLAMS
	PANLOGISM	PANLOGISMS
	PANMIXIA	PANMIXIAS
	PANNAGE	PANNAGES
	PANNE	PANNED ▪ PANNER ▪ PANNES
SPANNED	**PANNED**	
SPANNER	**PANNER**	PANNERS
SPANNERS	**PANNERS**	
	PANNICK	PANNICKS
	PANNICLE	PANNICLES
	PANNIER	PANNIERS
	PANNIKEL	PANNIKELL ▪ PANNIKELS
	PANNIKELL	PANNIKELLS
	PANNIKIN	PANNIKINS
SPANNING	**PANNING**	PANNINGS
	PANOCHA	PANOCHAS
	PANOCHE	PANOCHES
	PANORAMA	PANORAMAS
	PANPIPE	PANPIPES
SPANS	**PANS**	PANSY
	PANSEXUAL	PANSEXUALS
	PANT	PANTO ▪ PANTS ▪ PANTY
	PANTABLE	PANTABLES
	PANTALEON	PANTALEONS
	PANTALET	PANTALETS
	PANTALON	PANTALONE ▪ PANTALONS
	PANTALONE	PANTALONES
	PANTALOON	PANTALOONS
	PANTER	PANTERS
	PANTHEISM	PANTHEISMS
	PANTHEIST	PANTHEISTS
	PANTHENOL	PANTHENOLS
	PANTHEON	PANTHEONS
	PANTHER	PANTHERS
	PANTIE	PANTIES
	PANTILE	PANTILED ▪ PANTILES
	PANTILING	PANTILINGS
	PANTINE	PANTINES
	PANTING	PANTINGS
	PANTLER	PANTLERS
	PANTO	PANTON ▪ PANTOS
	PANTOFFLE	PANTOFFLES
	PANTOFLE	PANTOFLES
	PANTOMIME	PANTOMIMED ▪ PANTOMIMES
	PANTON	PANTONS
	PANTOUFLE	PANTOUFLES
	PANTOUM	PANTOUMS
	PANTSUIT	PANTSUITS
	PANTUN	PANTUNS
	PANZER	PANZERS
	PANZOOTIC	PANZOOTICS
	PAP	PAPA ▪ PAPE ▪ PAPS
	PAPA	PAPAL ▪ PAPAS ▪ PAPAW
	PAPADAM	PAPADAMS
	PAPADOM	PAPADOMS
	PAPADUM	PAPADUMS
	PAPAIN	PAPAINS
	PAPALISE	PAPALISED ▪ PAPALISES
	PAPALISM	PAPALISMS
	PAPALIST	PAPALISTS

FRONT HOOK	ROOT WORD	END HOOK
	PAPALIZE	PAPALIZED · PAPALIZES
	PAPAW	PAPAWS
	PAPAYA	PAPAYAN · PAPAYAS
	PAPE	PAPER · PAPES
	PAPER	PAPERS · PAPERY
	PAPERBACK	PAPERBACKS
	PAPERBARK	PAPERBARKS
	PAPERBOY	PAPERBOYS
	PAPERCLIP	PAPERCLIPS
	PAPERER	PAPERERS
	PAPERGIRL	PAPERGIRLS
	PAPERING	PAPERINGS
	PAPERWARE	PAPERWARES
	PAPERWORK	PAPERWORKS
	PAPETERIE	PAPETERIES
	PAPHIAN	PAPHIANS
	PAPILIO	PAPILIOS
	PAPILLA	PAPILLAE · PAPILLAR
	PAPILLAR	PAPILLARY
	PAPILLATE	PAPILLATED
	PAPILLOMA	PAPILLOMAS
	PAPILLON	PAPILLONS
	PAPILLOTE	PAPILLOTES
	PAPILLULE	PAPILLULES
	PAPISHER	PAPISHERS (offensive)
	PAPISM	PAPISMS (offensive)
	PAPIST	PAPISTS (offensive)
	PAPOOSE	PAPOOSES
	PAPPADAM	PAPPADAMS
	PAPPADOM	PAPPADOMS
	PAPPIES	PAPPIEST
	PAPPOOSE	PAPPOOSES
	PAPRICA	PAPRICAS
	PAPRIKA	PAPRIKAS
	PAPULA	PAPULAE · PAPULAR
	PAPULE	PAPULES
SPAR	**PAR**	PARA · PARD · PARE · PARK · PARP
		PARR · PARS · PART
	PARA	PARAE · PARAS
	PARABLAST	PARABLASTS
SPARABLE	**PARABLE**	PARABLED · PARABLES
SPARABLES	**PARABLES**	
	PARABOLA	PARABOLAS
	PARABOLE	PARABOLES
	PARABRAKE	PARABRAKES
	PARACHOR	PARACHORS
	PARACHUTE	PARACHUTED · PARACHUTES
	PARACLETE	PARACLETES
	PARACME	PARACMES
	PARADE	PARADED · PARADER · PARADES
	PARADER	PARADERS
	PARADIGM	PARADIGMS
	PARADISE	PARADISES
	PARADOR	PARADORS
	PARADOX	PARADOXY
	PARADOXER	PARADOXERS
	PARADROP	PARADROPS
	PARAFFIN	PARAFFINE · PARAFFINS · PARAFFINY
	PARAFFINE	PARAFFINED · PARAFFINES
	PARAFFLE	PARAFFLES
	PARAFLE	PARAFLES
	PARAFOIL	PARAFOILS
	PARAFORM	PARAFORMS
	PARAGE	PARAGES
	PARAGLIDE	PARAGLIDED · PARAGLIDER · PARAGLIDES
	PARAGOGE	PARAGOGES
	PARAGOGUE	PARAGOGUES
	PARAGON	PARAGONS
	PARAGRAM	PARAGRAMS

FRONT HOOK	ROOT WORD	END HOOK
	PARAGRAPH	PARAGRAPHS
	PARAKEET	PARAKEETS
	PARAKELIA	PARAKELIAS
	PARAKITE	PARAKITES
	PARALALIA	PARALALIAS
	PARALEGAL	PARALEGALS
	PARALEXIA	PARALEXIAS
	PARALLEL	PARALLELS
	PARALOGIA	PARALOGIAS
	PARALYSE	PARALYSED ▪ PARALYSER ▪ PARALYSES
	PARALYSER	PARALYSERS
	PARALYTIC	PARALYTICS
	PARALYZE	PARALYZED ▪ PARALYZER ▪ PARALYZES
	PARALYZER	PARALYZERS
	PARAMATTA	PARAMATTAS
	PARAMEDIC	PARAMEDICO ▪ PARAMEDICS
	PARAMENT	PARAMENTA ▪ PARAMENTS
	PARAMESE	PARAMESES
	PARAMETER	PARAMETERS
	PARAMO	PARAMOS
	PARAMORPH	PARAMORPHS
	PARAMOUNT	PARAMOUNTS
	PARAMOUR	PARAMOURS
	PARAMYLUM	PARAMYLUMS
	PARANETE	PARANETES
	PARANG	PARANGS
	PARANOEA	PARANOEAS
	PARANOEIC	PARANOEICS
	PARANOIA	PARANOIAC ▪ PARANOIAS
	PARANOIAC	PARANOIACS
	PARANOIC	PARANOICS
	PARANOID	PARANOIDS
	PARANYM	PARANYMS
	PARANYMPH	PARANYMPHS
	PARAPENTE	PARAPENTES
	PARAPET	PARAPETS
	PARAPH	PARAPHS
	PARAPODIA	PARAPODIAL
	PARAQUAT	PARAQUATS
	PARAQUET	PARAQUETS
	PARAQUITO	PARAQUITOS
	PARARHYME	PARARHYMES
	PARASAIL	PARASAILS
	PARASANG	PARASANGS
	PARASCEVE	PARASCEVES
	PARASHAH	PARASHAHS
	PARASHOT	PARASHOTH
	PARASITE	PARASITES
	PARASOL	PARASOLS
	PARATHA	PARATHAS
	PARATHION	PARATHIONS
	PARATROOP	PARATROOPS
	PARAVANE	PARAVANES
	PARAWING	PARAWINGS
	PARAZOA	PARAZOAN
	PARAZOAN	PARAZOANS
	PARBAKE	PARBAKED ▪ PARBAKES
	PARBOIL	PARBOILS
	PARBREAK	PARBREAKS
	PARBUCKLE	PARBUCKLED ▪ PARBUCKLES
	PARCEL	PARCELS
	PARCENER	PARCENERS
EPARCH	PARCH	
	PARCHEESI	PARCHEESIS
	PARCHES	PARCHESI
	PARCHESI	PARCHESIS
	PARCHISI	PARCHISIS
	PARCHMENT	PARCHMENTS ▪ PARCHMENTY
	PARCLOSE	PARCLOSES

FRONT HOOK	ROOT WORD	END HOOK
SPARD	**PARD**	PARDI · PARDS · PARDY
	PARDAH	PARDAHS
	PARDAL	PARDALE · PARDALS
	PARDALE	PARDALES
	PARDALOTE	PARDALOTES
	PARDI	PARDIE
	PARDNER	PARDNERS
	PARDON	PARDONS
	PARDONER	PARDONERS
	PARDONING	PARDONINGS
SPARE	**PARE**	PARED · PAREO · PARER · PARES · PAREU PAREV
	PARECISM	PARECISMS
SPARED	**PARED**	
	PAREGORIC	PAREGORICS
	PAREIRA	PAREIRAS
	PARELLA	PARELLAS
	PARELLE	PARELLES
	PARENT	PARENTS
	PARENTAGE	PARENTAGES
	PARENTING	PARENTINGS
	PAREO	PAREOS
SPARER	**PARER**	PARERA · PARERS
SPARERS	**PARERS**	
SPARES	**PARES**	
	PARETIC	PARETICS
	PAREU	PAREUS
	PAREV	PAREVE
	PARFAIT	PARFAITS
	PARFLECHE	PARFLECHES
	PARGANA	PARGANAS
	PARGASITE	PARGASITES
SPARGE	**PARGE**	PARGED · PARGES · PARGET
SPARGED	**PARGED**	
SPARGES	**PARGES**	
	PARGET	PARGETS
	PARGETER	PARGETERS
	PARGETING	PARGETINGS
SPARGING	**PARGING**	PARGINGS
	PARGO	PARGOS
	PARGYLINE	PARGYLINES
	PARHYPATE	PARHYPATES
	PARIAH	PARIAHS
	PARIAL	PARIALS
	PARIAN	PARIANS
	PARIETAL	PARIETALS
SPARING	**PARING**	PARINGS
	PARIS	PARISH
	PARISCHAN	PARISCHANE · PARISCHANS
	PARISHAD	PARISHADS
	PARISHEN	PARISHENS
	PARISON	PARISONS
	PARITOR	PARITORS
SPARK	**PARK**	PARKA · PARKI · PARKS · PARKY
	PARKA	PARKAS
	PARKADE	PARKADES
SPARKED	**PARKED**	
	PARKEE	PARKEES
SPARKER	**PARKER**	PARKERS
SPARKERS	**PARKERS**	
	PARKETTE	PARKETTES
	PARKI	PARKIE · PARKIN · PARKIS
SPARKIE	**PARKIE**	PARKIER · PARKIES
SPARKIER	**PARKIER**	
SPARKIES	**PARKIES**	PARKIEST
SPARKIEST	**PARKIEST**	
	PARKIN	PARKING · PARKINS
SPARKING	**PARKING**	PARKINGS
	PARKIS	PARKISH

FRONT HOOK	ROOT WORD	END HOOK
SPARKISH	PARKISH	
	PARKLAND	PARKLANDS
SPARKLY	PARKLY	
	PARKOUR	PARKOURS
SPARKS	PARKS	
	PARKWARD	PARKWARDS
	PARKWAY	PARKWAYS
SPARKY	PARKY	
	PARLANCE	PARLANCES
	PARLAY	PARLAYS
	PARLE	PARLED ▪ PARLES ▪ PARLEY
	PARLEMENT	PARLEMENTS
	PARLEY	PARLEYS
	PARLEYER	PARLEYERS
	PARLEYVOO	PARLEYVOOS
SPARLING	PARLING	
	PARLOR	PARLORS
	PARLOUR	PARLOURS
	PARMESAN	PARMESANS
	PAROCHIN	PAROCHINE ▪ PAROCHINS
	PAROCHINE	PAROCHINES
	PARODIST	PARODISTS
	PAROEMIA	PAROEMIAC ▪ PAROEMIAL ▪ PAROEMIAS
	PAROEMIAC	PAROEMIACS
	PAROL	PAROLE ▪ PAROLS
	PAROLE	PAROLED ▪ PAROLEE ▪ PAROLES
	PAROLEE	PAROLEES
	PARONYM	PARONYMS ▪ PARONYMY
	PAROQUET	PAROQUETS
	PAROSMIA	PAROSMIAS
	PAROTID	PAROTIDS
	PAROTOID	PAROTOIDS
	PAROUSIA	PAROUSIAS
	PAROXYSM	PAROXYSMS
	PARP	PARPS
	PARPANE	PARPANES
	PARPEN	PARPEND ▪ PARPENS ▪ PARPENT
	PARPEND	PARPENDS
	PARPENT	PARPENTS
	PARPOINT	PARPOINTS
	PARQUET	PARQUETS
	PARR	PARRA ▪ PARRS ▪ PARRY
	PARRA	PARRAL ▪ PARRAS
	PARRAKEET	PARRAKEETS
	PARRAL	PARRALS
SPARRED	PARRED	
	PARREL	PARRELS
	PARRHESIA	PARRHESIAS
	PARRICIDE	PARRICIDES
	PARRIDGE	PARRIDGES
SPARRIER	PARRIER	PARRIERS
SPARRING	PARRING	
	PARROCK	PARROCKS
	PARROKET	PARROKETS
	PARROQUET	PARROQUETS
	PARROT	PARROTS ▪ PARROTY
	PARROTER	PARROTERS
SPARRY	PARRY	
SPARS	PARS	PARSE
SPARSE	PARSE	PARSEC ▪ PARSED ▪ PARSER ▪ PARSES
	PARSEC	PARSECS
SPARSER	PARSER	PARSERS
	PARSING	PARSINGS
	PARSLEY	PARSLEYS
	PARSNEP	PARSNEPS
	PARSNIP	PARSNIPS
	PARSON	PARSONS
	PARSONAGE	PARSONAGES
APART ▪ SPART	PART	PARTI ▪ PARTS ▪ PARTY

FRONT HOOK	ROOT WORD	END HOOK
	PARTAKE	PARTAKEN · PARTAKER · PARTAKES
	PARTAKER	PARTAKERS
	PARTAKING	PARTAKINGS
SPARTAN	PARTAN	PARTANS
SPARTANS	PARTANS	
	PARTER	PARTERS
	PARTERRE	PARTERRES
	PARTI	PARTIM · PARTIS
	PARTIAL	PARTIALS
	PARTICLE	PARTICLES
	PARTIER	PARTIERS
	PARTING	PARTINGS
	PARTISAN	PARTISANS
	PARTITA	PARTITAS
	PARTITION	PARTITIONS
	PARTITIVE	PARTITIVES
	PARTITURA	PARTITURAS
	PARTIZAN	PARTIZANS
	PARTLET	PARTLETS
	PARTNER	PARTNERS
	PARTON	PARTONS
	PARTRIDGE	PARTRIDGES
SPARTS	PARTS	
	PARTURE	PARTURES
	PARTWORK	PARTWORKS
	PARTYER	PARTYERS
	PARTYGOER	PARTYGOERS
	PARTYISM	PARTYISMS
	PARURA	PARURAS
	PARURE	PARURES
	PARVENU	PARVENUE · PARVENUS
	PARVENUE	PARVENUES
	PARVIS	PARVISE
	PARVISE	PARVISES
	PARVO	PARVOS
	PARVOLIN	PARVOLINE · PARVOLINS
	PARVOLINE	PARVOLINES
SPAS · UPAS	PAS	PASE · PASH · PASS · PAST
	PASCAL	PASCALS
	PASCHAL	PASCHALS
	PASE	PASEO · PASES
	PASEAR	PASEARS
	PASELA	PASELAS
	PASEO	PASEOS
UPASES	PASES	
	PASH	PASHA · PASHM
	PASHA	PASHAS
	PASHADOM	PASHADOMS
	PASHALIC	PASHALICS
	PASHALIK	PASHALIKS
	PASHIM	PASHIMS
	PASHKA	PASHKAS
	PASHM	PASHMS
	PASHMINA	PASHMINAS
	PASODOBLE	PASODOBLES
	PASPALUM	PASPALUMS
	PASQUIL	PASQUILS
	PASQUILER	PASQUILERS
	PASS	PASSE
	PASSADE	PASSADES
	PASSADO	PASSADOS
	PASSAGE	PASSAGED · PASSAGER · PASSAGES
	PASSALONG	PASSALONGS
	PASSAMENT	PASSAMENTS
	PASSATA	PASSATAS
	PASSBAND	PASSBANDS
	PASSBOOK	PASSBOOKS
	PASSE	PASSED · PASSEE · PASSEL · PASSER · PASSES

FRONT HOOK	ROOT WORD	END HOOK
	PASSEL	PASSELS
	PASSEMENT	PASSEMENTS
	PASSENGER	PASSENGERS
	PASSEPIED	PASSEPIEDS
	PASSER	PASSERS
	PASSERINE	PASSERINES
	PASSING	PASSINGS
	PASSION	PASSIONS
	PASSIONAL	PASSIONALS
	PASSIVATE	PASSIVATED · PASSIVATES
	PASSIVE	PASSIVES
	PASSIVISM	PASSIVISMS
	PASSIVIST	PASSIVISTS
	PASSKEY	PASSKEYS
	PASSMEN	PASSMENT
	PASSMENT	PASSMENTS
	PASSOUT	PASSOUTS
	PASSOVER	PASSOVERS
	PASSPORT	PASSPORTS
	PASSWORD	PASSWORDS
	PAST	PASTA · PASTE · PASTS · PASTY
	PASTA	PASTAS
	PASTANCE	PASTANCES
	PASTE	PASTED · PASTEL · PASTER · PASTES
	PASTEDOWN	PASTEDOWNS
	PASTEL	PASTELS
	PASTELIST	PASTELISTS
	PASTER	PASTERN · PASTERS
	PASTERN	PASTERNS
	PASTEUP	PASTEUPS
	PASTICCI	PASTICCIO
	PASTICCIO	PASTICCIOS
	PASTICHE	PASTICHES
	PASTIE	PASTIER · PASTIES
	PASTIES	PASTIEST
	PASTIL	PASTILS · PASTILY
	PASTILLE	PASTILLES
	PASTIME	PASTIMES
	PASTINA	PASTINAS
	PASTING	PASTINGS
	PASTITSIO	PASTITSIOS
	PASTITSO	PASTITSOS
	PASTOR	PASTORS
	PASTORAL	PASTORALE · PASTORALI · PASTORALS
	PASTORALE	PASTORALES
	PASTORATE	PASTORATES
	PASTORIUM	PASTORIUMS
	PASTRAMI	PASTRAMIS
	PASTROMI	PASTROMIS
	PASTURAGE	PASTURAGES
	PASTURE	PASTURED · PASTURER · PASTURES
	PASTURER	PASTURERS
SPAT	PAT	PATE · PATH · PATS · PATU · PATY
	PATACA	PATACAS
	PATAGIA	PATAGIAL
	PATAMAR	PATAMARS
	PATBALL	PATBALLS
	PATCH	PATCHY
	PATCHER	PATCHERS · PATCHERY
	PATCHING	PATCHINGS
	PATCHOCKE	PATCHOCKES
	PATCHOULI	PATCHOULIS
	PATCHWORK	PATCHWORKS
SPATE	PATE	PATED · PATEN · PATER · PATES
	PATELLA	PATELLAE · PATELLAR · PATELLAS
	PATEN	PATENS · PATENT
	PATENT	PATENTS
	PATENTEE	PATENTEES
	PATENTOR	PATENTORS

FRONT HOOK	ROOT WORD	END HOOK
	PATER	PATERA · PATERS
	PATERA	PATERAE
	PATERCOVE	PATERCOVES
	PATERERO	PATEREROS
SPATES	**PATES**	
	PATH	PATHS
SPATHED	**PATHED**	
APATHETIC	**PATHETIC**	PATHETICS
SPATHIC	**PATHIC**	PATHICS
	PATHNAME	PATHNAMES
	PATHOGEN	PATHOGENE · PATHOGENS · PATHOGENY
	PATHOGENE	PATHOGENES
	PATHWAY	PATHWAYS
	PATIENCE	PATIENCES
	PATIENT	PATIENTS
	PATIN	PATINA · PATINE · PATINS
	PATINA	PATINAE · PATINAS
	PATINAE	PATINAED
	PATINATE	PATINATED · PATINATES
	PATINE	PATINED · PATINES
	PATINISE	PATINISED · PATINISES
	PATINIZE	PATINIZED · PATINIZES
	PATIO	PATIOS
	PATISSIER	PATISSIERS
	PATOOTIE	PATOOTIES
	PATRIAL	PATRIALS
	PATRIARCH	PATRIARCHS · PATRIARCHY
	PATRIATE	PATRIATED · PATRIATES
	PATRICIAN	PATRICIANS
	PATRICIDE	PATRICIDES
	PATRICK	PATRICKS
	PATRIOT	PATRIOTS
	PATRISTIC	PATRISTICS
	PATROL	PATROLS
	PATROLLER	PATROLLERS
	PATRON	PATRONS
	PATRONAGE	PATRONAGED · PATRONAGES
	PATRONISE	PATRONISED · PATRONISER · PATRONISES
	PATRONIZE	PATRONIZED · PATRONIZER · PATRONIZES
	PATRONNE	PATRONNES
	PATROON	PATROONS
SPATS	**PATS**	PATSY
	PATTAMAR	PATTAMARS
	PATTE	PATTED · PATTEE · PATTEN · PATTER · PATTES
SPATTED	**PATTED**	
SPATTEE	**PATTEE**	
	PATTEN	PATTENS
SPATTER	**PATTER**	PATTERN · PATTERS
SPATTERED	**PATTERED**	
	PATTERER	PATTERERS
SPATTERING	**PATTERING**	
	PATTERN	PATTERNS
SPATTERS	**PATTERS**	
	PATTIE	PATTIES
SPATTING	**PATTING**	
	PATTLE	PATTLES
	PATTYPAN	PATTYPANS
	PATU	PATUS
	PATULIN	PATULINS
	PATUTUKI	PATUTUKIS
	PATZER	PATZERS
	PAUA	PAUAS
	PAUCAL	PAUCALS
SPAUL	**PAUL**	PAULS
	PAULDRON	PAULDRONS
	PAULIN	PAULINS
	PAULOWNIA	PAULOWNIAS
SPAULS	**PAULS**	

FRONT HOOK	ROOT WORD	END HOOK
	PAUNCE	PAUNCES
	PAUNCH	PAUNCHY
	PAUPER	PAUPERS
	PAUPERISE	PAUPERISED ▪ PAUPERISES
	PAUPERISM	PAUPERISMS
	PAUPERIZE	PAUPERIZED ▪ PAUPERIZES
	PAUPIETTE	PAUPIETTES
	PAUROPOD	PAUROPODS
	PAUSE	PAUSED ▪ PAUSER ▪ PAUSES
	PAUSER	PAUSERS
	PAUSING	PAUSINGS
	PAV	PAVE ▪ PAVS
	PAVAGE	PAVAGES
	PAVAN	PAVANE ▪ PAVANS
	PAVANE	PAVANES
	PAVE	PAVED ▪ PAVEN ▪ PAVER ▪ PAVES
	PAVEMENT	PAVEMENTS
	PAVEN	PAVENS
	PAVER	PAVERS
	PAVILION	PAVILIONS
	PAVILLON	PAVILLONS
SPAVIN	**PAVIN**	PAVING ▪ PAVINS
	PAVING	PAVINGS
SPAVINS	**PAVINS**	
	PAVIOR	PAVIORS
	PAVIOUR	PAVIOURS
	PAVIS	PAVISE
	PAVISE	PAVISER ▪ PAVISES
	PAVISER	PAVISERS
	PAVISSE	PAVISSES
	PAVLOVA	PAVLOVAS
	PAVONAZZO	PAVONAZZOS
	PAVONE	PAVONES
SPAW	**PAW**	PAWA ▪ PAWK ▪ PAWL ▪ PAWN ▪ PAWS
	PAWA	PAWAS ▪ PAWAW
	PAWAW	PAWAWS
	PAWER	PAWERS
	PAWK	PAWKS ▪ PAWKY
SPAWL	**PAWL**	PAWLS
SPAWLS	**PAWLS**	
SPAWN	**PAWN**	PAWNS
	PAWNAGE	PAWNAGES
	PAWNCE	PAWNCES
SPAWNED	**PAWNED**	
	PAWNEE	PAWNEES
SPAWNER	**PAWNER**	PAWNERS
SPAWNERS	**PAWNERS**	
SPAWNING	**PAWNING**	
	PAWNOR	PAWNORS
SPAWNS	**PAWNS**	
	PAWNSHOP	PAWNSHOPS
	PAWPAW	PAWPAWS
SPAWS	**PAWS**	
	PAXIUBA	PAXIUBAS
APAY ▪ SPAY	**PAY**	PAYS
	PAYABLE	PAYABLES
	PAYBACK	PAYBACKS
	PAYCHECK	PAYCHECKS
	PAYDAY	PAYDAYS
SPAYED	**PAYED**	
	PAYEE	PAYEES
	PAYER	PAYERS
	PAYFONE	PAYFONES
	PAYGRADE	PAYGRADES
APAYING ▪ SPAYING	**PAYING**	PAYINGS
	PAYLOAD	PAYLOADS
	PAYMASTER	PAYMASTERS
	PAYMENT	PAYMENTS
	PAYNIM	PAYNIMS

FRONT HOOK	ROOT WORD	END HOOK
	PAYOFF	PAYOFFS
	PAYOLA	PAYOLAS
	PAYOR	PAYORS
	PAYOUT	PAYOUTS
	PAYPHONE	PAYPHONES
	PAYROLL	PAYROLLS
APAYS · SPAYS	PAYS	PAYSD
	PAYSAGE	PAYSAGES
	PAYSAGIST	PAYSAGISTS
	PAYSLIP	PAYSLIPS
APE · OPE	PE	PEA · PEC · PED · PEE · PEG · PEH · PEN PEP · PER · PES · PET · PEW
	PEA	PEAG · PEAK · PEAL · PEAN · PEAR PEAS · PEAT
	PEACE	PEACED · PEACES
	PEACENIK	PEACENIKS
	PEACETIME	PEACETIMES
	PEACH	PEACHY
	PEACHBLOW	PEACHBLOWS
	PEACHER	PEACHERS
	PEACOAT	PEACOATS
	PEACOCK	PEACOCKS · PEACOCKY
	PEACOD	PEACODS
	PEAFOWL	PEAFOWLS
	PEAG	PEAGE · PEAGS
	PEAGE	PEAGES
	PEAHEN	PEAHENS
APEAK · SPEAK	PEAK	PEAKS · PEAKY
SPEAKING	PEAKING	
SPEAKS	PEAKS	
SPEAL	PEAL	PEALS
SPEALS	PEALS	
SPEAN	PEAN	PEANS
SPEANED	PEANED	
SPEANING	PEANING	
SPEANS	PEANS	
	PEANUT	PEANUTS
	PEAPOD	PEAPODS
SPEAR	PEAR	PEARE · PEARL · PEARS · PEART
	PEARCE	PEARCED · PEARCES
	PEARE	PEARES
	PEARL	PEARLS · PEARLY
	PEARLER	PEARLERS
	PEARLIES	PEARLIEST
	PEARLIN	PEARLING · PEARLINS
	PEARLING	PEARLINGS
	PEARLITE	PEARLITES
	PEARLWORT	PEARLWORTS
	PEARMAIN	PEARMAINS
SPEARS	PEARS	PEARST
	PEARWOOD	PEARWOODS
	PEAS	PEASE
	PEASANT	PEASANTS · PEASANTY
	PEASCOD	PEASCODS
	PEASE	PEASED · PEASEN · PEASES
	PEASECOD	PEASECODS
	PEASOUPER	PEASOUPERS
SPEAT	PEAT	PEATS · PEATY
	PEATLAND	PEATLANDS
SPEATS	PEATS	
	PEATSHIP	PEATSHIPS
	PEAVEY	PEAVEYS
	PEAZE	PEAZED · PEAZES
	PEBA	PEBAS
	PEBBLE	PEBBLED · PEBBLES
	PEBBLING	PEBBLINGS
	PEBRINE	PEBRINES
SPEC	PEC	PECH · PECK · PECS
	PECAN	PECANS

FRONT HOOK	ROOT WORD	END HOOK
	PECCAVI	PECCAVIS
	PECH	PECHS
	PECHAN	PECHANS
SPECK	**PECK**	PECKE = PECKS = PECKY
	PECKE	PECKED = PECKER = PECKES
SPECKED	**PECKED**	
	PECKER	PECKERS *(offensive)*
SPECKIER	**PECKIER**	
SPECKIEST	**PECKIEST**	
SPECKING	**PECKING**	PECKINGS
SPECKS	**PECKS**	
SPECKY	**PECKY**	
	PECORINO	PECORINOS
SPECS	**PECS**	
	PECTASE	PECTASES
SPECTATE	**PECTATE**	PECTATES
SPECTATES	**PECTATES**	
	PECTEN	PECTENS
	PECTIN	PECTINS
	PECTINATE	PECTINATED
	PECTISE	PECTISED = PECTISES
	PECTIZE	PECTIZED = PECTIZES
	PECTOLITE	PECTOLITES
	PECTORAL	PECTORALS
	PECTOSE	PECTOSES
SPECULATE	**PECULATE**	PECULATED = PECULATES
SPECULATED	**PECULATED**	
SPECULATES	**PECULATES**	
SPECULATOR	**PECULATOR**	PECULATORS
	PECULIA	PECULIAR
	PECULIAR	PECULIARS
APED = OPED = SPED	**PED**	PEDS
	PEDAGOG	PEDAGOGS = PEDAGOGY
	PEDAGOGIC	PEDAGOGICS
	PEDAGOGUE	PEDAGOGUED = PEDAGOGUES
	PEDAL	PEDALO = PEDALS
	PEDALER	PEDALERS
	PEDALFER	PEDALFERS
	PEDALIER	PEDALIERS
	PEDALLER	PEDALLERS
	PEDALLING	PEDALLINGS
	PEDALO	PEDALOS
	PEDANT	PEDANTS
	PEDANTISE	PEDANTISED = PEDANTISES
	PEDANTISM	PEDANTISMS
	PEDANTIZE	PEDANTIZED = PEDANTIZES
	PEDDER	PEDDERS
	PEDDLE	PEDDLED = PEDDLER = PEDDLES
	PEDDLER	PEDDLERS = PEDDLERY
	PEDDLING	PEDDLINGS
	PEDERAST	PEDERASTS = PEDERASTY
	PEDERERO	PEDEREROS
	PEDESTAL	PEDESTALS
	PEDIATRIC	PEDIATRICS
	PEDICAB	PEDICABS
	PEDICEL	PEDICELS
	PEDICLE	PEDICLED = PEDICLES
	PEDICURE	PEDICURED = PEDICURES
	PEDIGREE	PEDIGREED = PEDIGREES
	PEDIMENT	PEDIMENTS
	PEDIPALP	PEDIPALPI = PEDIPALPS
	PEDLAR	PEDLARS = PEDLARY
	PEDLER	PEDLERS = PEDLERY
	PEDOCAL	PEDOCALS
	PEDOMETER	PEDOMETERS
	PEDOPHILE	PEDOPHILES
	PEDRAIL	PEDRAILS
	PEDRERO	PEDREROS
	PEDRO	PEDROS

FRONT HOOK	ROOT WORD	END HOOK
	PEDUNCLE	PEDUNCLED ▪ PEDUNCLES
EPEE	**PEE**	PEED (offensive) ▪ PEEK ▪ PEEL ▪ PEEN PEEP ▪ PEER ▪ PEES
	PEEBEEN	PEEBEENS
	PEECE	PEECES
SPEED	**PEED**	
APEEK	**PEEK**	PEEKS
	PEEKABO	PEEKABOO ▪ PEEKABOS
	PEEKABOO	PEEKABOOS
	PEEKAPOO	PEEKAPOOS
SPEEL	**PEEL**	PEELS
SPEELED	**PEELED**	
SPEELER	**PEELER**	PEELERS
SPEELERS	**PEELERS**	
SPEELING	**PEELING**	PEELINGS
SPEELS	**PEELS**	
	PEEN	PEENS
	PEENGE	PEENGED ▪ PEENGES
	PEEOY	PEEOYS
	PEEP	PEEPE ▪ PEEPS
	PEEPE	PEEPED ▪ PEEPER ▪ PEEPES
	PEEPER	PEEPERS
	PEEPHOLE	PEEPHOLES
	PEEPSHOW	PEEPSHOWS
	PEEPUL	PEEPULS
SPEER	**PEER**	PEERS ▪ PEERY
	PEERAGE	PEERAGES
SPEERED	**PEERED**	
	PEERIE	PEERIER ▪ PEERIES
	PEERIES	PEERIEST
SPEERING	**PEERING**	
SPEERS	**PEERS**	
EPEES	**PEES**	
	PEESWEEP	PEESWEEPS
	PEETWEET	PEETWEETS
	PEEVE	PEEVED ▪ PEEVER ▪ PEEVES
	PEEVER	PEEVERS
	PEEWEE	PEEWEES
	PEEWIT	PEEWITS
	PEG	PEGH ▪ PEGS
	PEGBOARD	PEGBOARDS
	PEGGING	PEGGINGS
	PEGH	PEGHS
	PEGMATITE	PEGMATITES
	PEH	PEHS
	PEIGNOIR	PEIGNOIRS
	PEIN	PEINS
	PEINCT	PEINCTS
SPEISE	**PEISE**	PEISED ▪ PEISES
SPEISES	**PEISES**	
	PEISHWA	PEISHWAH ▪ PEISHWAS
	PEISHWAH	PEISHWAHS
	PEIZE	PEIZED ▪ PEIZES
	PEJORATE	PEJORATED ▪ PEJORATES
	PEKAN	PEKANS
	PEKE	PEKES
	PEKEPOO	PEKEPOOS
	PEKIN	PEKINS
	PEKOE	PEKOES
	PELA	PELAS
	PELAGE	PELAGES
	PELAGIAN	PELAGIANS
	PELAGIC	PELAGICS
	PELE	PELES
	PELECYPOD	PELECYPODS
	PELERINE	PELERINES
	PELF	PELFS
	PELHAM	PELHAMS
	PELICAN	PELICANS

FRONT HOOK	ROOT WORD	END HOOK
	PELISSE	PELISSES
	PELITE	PELITES
SPELL	PELL	PELLS
	PELLACH	PELLACHS
	PELLACK	PELLACKS
	PELLAGRA	PELLAGRAS
	PELLAGRIN	PELLAGRINS
	PELLET	PELLETS
	PELLETISE	PELLETISED · PELLETISER · PELLETISES
	PELLETIZE	PELLETIZED · PELLETIZER · PELLETIZES
	PELLICLE	PELLICLES
	PELLMELL	PELLMELLS
	PELLOCK	PELLOCKS
SPELLS	PELLS	
	PELLUM	PELLUMS
	PELMA	PELMAS
	PELMANISM	PELMANISMS
	PELMET	PELMETS
	PELOID	PELOIDS
	PELORIA	PELORIAN · PELORIAS
	PELORISM	PELORISMS
	PELOTA	PELOTAS
	PELOTON	PELOTONS
SPELT	PELT	PELTA · PELTS
	PELTA	PELTAE · PELTAS
	PELTAS	PELTAST
	PELTAST	PELTASTS
	PELTATION	PELTATIONS
SPELTER	PELTER	PELTERS
SPELTERS	PELTERS	
	PELTING	PELTINGS
SPELTS	PELTS	
	PELVIC	PELVICS
	PEMBINA	PEMBINAS
	PEMBROKE	PEMBROKES
	PEMICAN	PEMICANS
	PEMMICAN	PEMMICANS
	PEMOLINE	PEMOLINES
OPEN	PEN	PEND · PENE · PENI · PENK · PENS · PENT
	PENALISE	PENALISED · PENALISES
	PENALIZE	PENALIZED · PENALIZES
	PENANCE	PENANCED · PENANCES
	PENANG	PENANGS
SPENCE	PENCE	PENCEL · PENCES
	PENCEL	PENCELS
SPENCES	PENCES	
	PENCHANT	PENCHANTS
	PENCIL	PENCILS
	PENCILER	PENCILERS
	PENCILING	PENCILINGS
	PENCILLER	PENCILLERS
	PENCRAFT	PENCRAFTS
SPEND · UPEND	PEND	PENDS · PENDU
	PENDANT	PENDANTS
UPENDED	PENDED	
	PENDENT	PENDENTS
	PENDICLE	PENDICLER · PENDICLES
	PENDICLER	PENDICLERS
SPENDING · UPENDING	PENDING	
	PENDRAGON	PENDRAGONS
SPENDS · UPENDS	PENDS	
	PENDULATE	PENDULATED · PENDULATES
	PENDULE	PENDULES
	PENDULUM	PENDULUMS
	PENE	PENED · PENES
OPENED	PENED	
	PENEPLAIN	PENEPLAINS
	PENEPLANE	PENEPLANES
	PENETRANT	PENETRANTS

FRONT HOOK	ROOT WORD	END HOOK
	PENETRATE	PENETRATED · PENETRATES
	PENFOLD	PENFOLDS
	PENFUL	PENFULS
	PENGO	PENGOS
	PENGUIN	PENGUINS
	PENHOLDER	PENHOLDERS
	PENI	PENIE · PENIS
	PENICIL	PENICILS
	PENIE	PENIES
OPENING	PENING	
	PENINSULA	PENINSULAR · PENINSULAS
	PENISTONE	PENISTONES
	PENITENCE	PENITENCES
	PENITENT	PENITENTS
	PENK	PENKS
	PENLIGHT	PENLIGHTS
	PENLITE	PENLITES
	PENNA	PENNAE · PENNAL
	PENNAL	PENNALS
	PENNALISM	PENNALISMS
	PENNAME	PENNAMES
	PENNANT	PENNANTS
	PENNATE	PENNATED
	PENNATULA	PENNATULAE · PENNATULAS
	PENNE	PENNED · PENNER · PENNES
	PENNEECH	PENNEECHS
	PENNEECK	PENNEECKS
	PENNER	PENNERS
	PENNI	PENNIA · PENNIS
	PENNINE	PENNINES
	PENNINITE	PENNINITES
	PENNON	PENNONS
	PENNONCEL	PENNONCELS
	PENNYBOY	PENNYBOYS
	PENNYFEE	PENNYFEES
	PENNYLAND	PENNYLANDS
	PENNYWORT	PENNYWORTH · PENNYWORTS
	PENOCHE	PENOCHES
	PENONCEL	PENONCELS
	PENPOINT	PENPOINTS
	PENPUSHER	PENPUSHERS
OPENS	PENS	
	PENSEE	PENSEES
	PENSEL	PENSELS
	PENSIL	PENSILE · PENSILS
	PENSION	PENSIONE · PENSIONS
	PENSIONE	PENSIONED · PENSIONER · PENSIONES
	PENSIONER	PENSIONERS
	PENSTEMON	PENSTEMONS
	PENSTER	PENSTERS
	PENSTOCK	PENSTOCKS
	PENSUM	PENSUMS
SPENT	PENT	PENTS
	PENTACLE	PENTACLES
	PENTACT	PENTACTS
	PENTAD	PENTADS
	PENTAGON	PENTAGONS
	PENTAGRAM	PENTAGRAMS
	PENTALPHA	PENTALPHAS
	PENTANE	PENTANES
	PENTANGLE	PENTANGLES
	PENTANOL	PENTANOLS
	PENTARCH	PENTARCHS · PENTARCHY
	PENTEL	PENTELS
	PENTENE	PENTENES
	PENTHIA	PENTHIAS
	PENTHOUSE	PENTHOUSED · PENTHOUSES
	PENTICE	PENTICED · PENTICES
	PENTISE	PENTISED · PENTISES

FRONT HOOK	ROOT WORD	END HOOK
	PENTODE	PENTODES
	PENTOSAN	PENTOSANE · PENTOSANS
	PENTOSANE	PENTOSANES
	PENTOSE	PENTOSES
	PENTOSIDE	PENTOSIDES
	PENTOXIDE	PENTOXIDES
	PENTROOF	PENTROOFS
	PENTYL	PENTYLS
	PENTYLENE	PENTYLENES
	PENUCHE	PENUCHES
	PENUCHI	PENUCHIS
	PENUCHLE	PENUCHLES
	PENUCKLE	PENUCKLES
	PENULT	PENULTS
	PENULTIMA	PENULTIMAS
	PENUMBRA	PENUMBRAE · PENUMBRAL · PENUMBRAS
	PEON	PEONS · PEONY
	PEONAGE	PEONAGES
	PEONISM	PEONISMS
	PEOPLE	PEOPLED · PEOPLER · PEOPLES
	PEOPLER	PEOPLERS
	PEP	PEPO · PEPS
	PEPERINO	PEPERINOS
	PEPEROMIA	PEPEROMIAS
	PEPERONI	PEPERONIS
	PEPINO	PEPINOS
	PEPLUM	PEPLUMS
	PEPO	PEPOS
	PEPONIDA	PEPONIDAS
	PEPONIUM	PEPONIUMS
	PEPPER	PEPPERS · PEPPERY
	PEPPERER	PEPPERERS
	PEPPERING	PEPPERINGS
	PEPPERONI	PEPPERONIS
	PEPSIN	PEPSINE · PEPSINS
	PEPSINATE	PEPSINATED · PEPSINATES
	PEPSINE	PEPSINES
	PEPTALK	PEPTALKS
	PEPTIC	PEPTICS
	PEPTID	PEPTIDE · PEPTIDS
	PEPTIDASE	PEPTIDASES
	PEPTIDE	PEPTIDES
	PEPTISE	PEPTISED · PEPTISER · PEPTISES
	PEPTISER	PEPTISERS
	PEPTIZE	PEPTIZED · PEPTIZER · PEPTIZES
	PEPTIZER	PEPTIZERS
	PEPTONE	PEPTONES
	PEPTONISE	PEPTONISED · PEPTONISER · PEPTONISES
	PEPTONIZE	PEPTONIZED · PEPTONIZER · PEPTONIZES
	PEQUISTE	PEQUISTES
APER	PER	PERE · PERI · PERK · PERM · PERN · PERP · PERT · PERV
	PERACID	PERACIDS
	PERAEON	PERAEONS
	PERAEOPOD	PERAEOPODS
	PERAI	PERAIS
	PERBORATE	PERBORATES
	PERCALE	PERCALES
	PERCALINE	PERCALINES
	PERCE	PERCED · PERCEN · PERCES
	PERCEIVE	PERCEIVED · PERCEIVER · PERCEIVES
	PERCEIVER	PERCEIVERS
	PERCEN	PERCENT
	PERCENT	PERCENTS
	PERCEPT	PERCEPTS
	PERCHER	PERCHERS · PERCHERY
	PERCHERON	PERCHERONS
	PERCHING	PERCHINGS
	PERCOID	PERCOIDS

FRONT HOOK	ROOT WORD	END HOOK
	PERCOLATE	PERCOLATED · PERCOLATES
	PERCOLIN	PERCOLINS
	PERCUSSOR	PERCUSSORS
	PERDITION	PERDITIONS
EPERDU	**PERDU**	PERDUE · PERDUS
EPERDUE	**PERDUE**	PERDUES
	PERDURE	PERDURED · PERDURES
	PERE	PEREA · PERES
	PEREGAL	PEREGALS
	PEREGRIN	PEREGRINE · PEREGRINS
	PEREGRINE	PEREGRINES
	PEREION	PEREIONS
	PEREIOPOD	PEREIOPODS
	PEREIRA	PEREIRAS
	PERENNATE	PERENNATED · PERENNATES
	PERENNIAL	PERENNIALS
	PERENTIE	PERENTIES
	PEREON	PEREONS
	PEREOPOD	PEREOPODS
	PERFECT	PERFECTA · PERFECTI · PERFECTO PERFECTS
	PERFECTA	PERFECTAS
	PERFECTER	PERFECTERS
	PERFECTO	PERFECTOR · PERFECTOS
	PERFECTOR	PERFECTORS
	PERFERVOR	PERFERVORS
	PERFIN	PERFING · PERFINS
	PERFING	PERFINGS
	PERFORATE	PERFORATED · PERFORATES
	PERFORM	PERFORMS
	PERFORMER	PERFORMERS
	PERFUME	PERFUMED · PERFUMER · PERFUMES
	PERFUMER	PERFUMERS · PERFUMERY
	PERFUMIER	PERFUMIERS
	PERFUSATE	PERFUSATES
	PERFUSE	PERFUSED · PERFUSES
	PERFUSION	PERFUSIONS
	PERGOLA	PERGOLAS
	PERGUNNAH	PERGUNNAHS
	PERI	PERIL · PERIS
	PERIAGUA	PERIAGUAS
	PERIANTH	PERIANTHS
	PERIAPT	PERIAPTS
	PERIBLAST	PERIBLASTS
	PERIBLEM	PERIBLEMS
	PERICARP	PERICARPS
	PERICLASE	PERICLASES
	PERICLINE	PERICLINES
	PERICOPE	PERICOPES
	PERICYCLE	PERICYCLES
	PERIDERM	PERIDERMS
	PERIDIA	PERIDIAL
	PERIDINIA	PERIDINIAN
	PERIDIUM	PERIDIUMS
	PERIDOT	PERIDOTE · PERIDOTS
	PERIDOTE	PERIDOTES
	PERIDROME	PERIDROMES
	PERIGEE	PERIGEES
	PERIGON	PERIGONE · PERIGONS
	PERIGONE	PERIGONES
	PERIGONIA	PERIGONIAL
	PERIHELIA	PERIHELIAL
	PERIKARYA	PERIKARYAL
	PERIL	PERILS
	PERILLA	PERILLAS
	PERILUNE	PERILUNES
	PERILYMPH	PERILYMPHS
	PERIMETER	PERIMETERS
	PERIMORPH	PERIMORPHS

FRONT HOOK	ROOT WORD	END HOOK
	PERINAEUM	PERINAEUMS
	PERINEA	PERINEAL
	PERINEUM	PERINEUMS
	PERIOD	PERIODS
	PERIODATE	PERIODATES
APERIODIC	PERIODIC	
	PERIODID	PERIODIDE ▪ PERIODIDS
	PERIODIDE	PERIODIDES
	PERIOST	PERIOSTS
	PERIOSTEA	PERIOSTEAL
	PERIOTIC	PERIOTICS
	PERIPETIA	PERIPETIAN ▪ PERIPETIAS
	PERIPLASM	PERIPLASMS
	PERIPLAST	PERIPLASTS
	PERIPROCT	PERIPROCTS
	PERIPTER	PERIPTERS ▪ PERIPTERY
	PERIQUE	PERIQUES
	PERIS	PERISH
	PERISARC	PERISARCS
	PERISCIAN	PERISCIANS
	PERISCOPE	PERISCOPES
	PERISHER	PERISHERS
	PERISPERM	PERISPERMS
	PERISTOME	PERISTOMES
	PERISTYLE	PERISTYLES
	PERITONEA	PERITONEAL
	PERITRACK	PERITRACKS
	PERITRICH	PERITRICHA ▪ PERITRICHS
	PERIWIG	PERIWIGS
	PERJURE	PERJURED ▪ PERJURER ▪ PERJURES
	PERJURER	PERJURERS
	PERK	PERKS ▪ PERKY
	PERKIN	PERKING ▪ PERKINS
	PERLEMOEN	PERLEMOENS
	PERLITE	PERLITES
SPERM	PERM	PERMS
	PERMALLOY	PERMALLOYS
	PERMANENT	PERMANENTS
	PERMEANCE	PERMEANCES
	PERMEANT	PERMEANTS
	PERMEASE	PERMEASES
	PERMEATE	PERMEATED ▪ PERMEATES
	PERMEATOR	PERMEATORS
	PERMIE	PERMIES
	PERMIT	PERMITS
	PERMITTEE	PERMITTEES
	PERMITTER	PERMITTERS
SPERMS	PERMS	
	PERMUTATE	PERMUTATED ▪ PERMUTATES
	PERMUTE	PERMUTED ▪ PERMUTES
	PERN	PERNS
	PERNOD	PERNODS
	PERONE	PERONES
	PERORATE	PERORATED ▪ PERORATES
	PERORATOR	PERORATORS
	PEROVSKIA	PEROVSKIAS
	PEROXID	PEROXIDE ▪ PEROXIDS
	PEROXIDE	PEROXIDED ▪ PEROXIDES
	PERP	PERPS
	PERPEND	PERPENDS
	PERPENT	PERPENTS
	PERPETUAL	PERPETUALS
	PERPLEXER	PERPLEXERS
	PERRIER	PERRIERS
	PERRON	PERRONS
	PERRUQUE	PERRUQUES
	PERSALT	PERSALTS
SPERSE	PERSE	PERSES
	PERSECUTE	PERSECUTED ▪ PERSECUTEE ▪ PERSECUTES

FRONT HOOK	ROOT WORD	END HOOK
	PERSELINE	PERSELINES
SPERSES	**PERSES**	
	PERSEVERE	PERSEVERED · PERSEVERES
	PERSICO	PERSICOS · PERSICOT
	PERSICOT	PERSICOTS
	PERSIENNE	PERSIENNES
	PERSIMMON	PERSIMMONS
SPERSING	**PERSING**	
	PERSIST	PERSISTS
	PERSISTER	PERSISTERS
	PERSON	PERSONA · PERSONS
	PERSONA	PERSONAE · PERSONAL · PERSONAS
	PERSONAGE	PERSONAGES
	PERSONAL	PERSONALS
	PERSONATE	PERSONATED · PERSONATES
	PERSONISE	PERSONISED · PERSONISES
	PERSONIZE	PERSONIZED · PERSONIZES
	PERSONNEL	PERSONNELS
	PERSPIRE	PERSPIRED · PERSPIRES
SPERST	**PERST**	
	PERSUADE	PERSUADED · PERSUADER · PERSUADES
	PERSUADER	PERSUADERS
.	**PERSUE**	PERSUED · PERSUES
	PERSWADE	PERSWADED · PERSWADES
APERT	**PERT**	PERTS
	PERTAIN	PERTAINS
	PERTAKE	PERTAKEN · PERTAKES
	PERTHITE	PERTHITES
	PERTINENT	PERTINENTS
APERTNESS	**PERTNESS**	
	PERTURB	PERTURBS
	PERTURBER	PERTURBERS
	PERTUSE	PERTUSED
	PERTUSION	PERTUSIONS
	PERUKE	PERUKED · PERUKES
	PERUSAL	PERUSALS
	PERUSE	PERUSED · PERUSER · PERUSES
	PERUSER	PERUSERS
	PERV	PERVE · PERVS
	PERVADE	PERVADED · PERVADER · PERVADES
	PERVADER	PERVADERS
	PERVASION	PERVASIONS
	PERVE	PERVED · PERVES
	PERVERSE	PERVERSER
	PERVERT	PERVERTS
	PERVERTER	PERVERTERS
	PERVIATE	PERVIATED · PERVIATES
APES · OPES	**PES**	PESO · PEST
	PESADE	PESADES
	PESANT	PESANTE · PESANTS
	PESAUNT	PESAUNTS
	PESETA	PESETAS
	PESEWA	PESEWAS
	PESHWA	PESHWAS
	PESO	PESOS
	PESSIMA	PESSIMAL
	PESSIMISM	PESSIMISMS
	PESSIMIST	PESSIMISTS
	PEST	PESTO · PESTS · PESTY
	PESTER	PESTERS
	PESTERER	PESTERERS
	PESTHOLE	PESTHOLES
	PESTHOUSE	PESTHOUSES
	PESTICIDE	PESTICIDES
	PESTLE	PESTLED · PESTLES
	PESTO	PESTOS
SPET	**PET**	PETS
	PETABYTE	PETABYTES
	PETAL	PETALS

FRONT HOOK	ROOT WORD	END HOOK
	PETALISM	PETALISMS
APETALOUS	**PETALOUS**	
	PETANQUE	PETANQUES
	PETAR	PETARA · PETARD · PETARS · PETARY
	PETARA	PETARAS
	PETARD	PETARDS
	PETAURIST	PETAURISTS
	PETCOCK	PETCOCKS
	PETECHIA	PETECHIAE · PETECHIAL
	PETER	PETERS
	PETERSHAM	PETERSHAMS
	PETHER	PETHERS
	PETHIDINE	PETHIDINES
	PETIOLATE	PETIOLATED
	PETIOLE	PETIOLED · PETIOLES
	PETIOLULE	PETIOLULES
	PETIT	PETITE
	PETITE	PETITES
	PETITION	PETITIONS
	PETNAP	PETNAPS
	PETNAPER	PETNAPERS
	PETNAPING	PETNAPINGS
	PETNAPPER	PETNAPPERS
	PETRALE	PETRALES
	PETRE	PETREL · PETRES
	PETREL	PETRELS
	PETRIFIER	PETRIFIERS
	PETROGRAM	PETROGRAMS
	PETROL	PETROLS
	PETROLAGE	PETROLAGES
	PETROLEUM	PETROLEUMS
	PETROLEUR	PETROLEURS
	PETRONEL	PETRONELS
	PETROSAL	PETROSALS
SPETS	**PETS**	
	PETSAI	PETSAIS
	PETTER	PETTERS
	PETTICOAT	PETTICOATS
	PETTIES	PETTIEST
	PETTIFOG	PETTIFOGS
SPETTING	**PETTING**	PETTINGS
	PETTLE	PETTLED · PETTLES
	PETULANCE	PETULANCES
	PETUNIA	PETUNIAS
	PETUNTSE	PETUNTSES
	PETUNTZE	PETUNTZES
SPEW	**PEW**	PEWS
	PEWEE	PEWEES
	PEWHOLDER	PEWHOLDERS
	PEWIT	PEWITS
SPEWS	**PEWS**	
	PEWTER	PEWTERS
	PEWTERER	PEWTERERS
	PEYOTE	PEYOTES
	PEYOTISM	PEYOTISMS
	PEYOTIST	PEYOTISTS
	PEYOTL	PEYOTLS
	PEYSE	PEYSED · PEYSES
	PEYTRAL	PEYTRALS
	PEYTREL	PEYTRELS
	PEZANT	PEZANTS
	PFENNIG	PFENNIGE · PFENNIGS
	PFENNING	PFENNINGS
	PHACELIA	PHACELIAS
	PHACOLITE	PHACOLITES
	PHACOLITH	PHACOLITHS
	PHAEISM	PHAEISMS
	PHAENOGAM	PHAENOGAMS
	PHAETON	PHAETONS

FRONT HOOK	ROOT WORD	END HOOK
	PHAGE	PHAGES
	PHAGEDENA	PHAGEDENAS
	PHAGOCYTE	PHAGOCYTES
	PHAGOSOME	PHAGOSOMES
	PHALANGE	PHALANGER ▪ PHALANGES
	PHALANGER	PHALANGERS
	PHALANGID	PHALANGIDS
	PHALAROPE	PHALAROPES
	PHALLI	PHALLIC ▪ PHALLIN
	PHALLIN	PHALLINS
	PHALLISM	PHALLISMS
	PHALLIST	PHALLISTS
UPHANG	PHANG	PHANGS
UPHANGING	PHANGING	
UPHANGS	PHANGS	
	PHANSIGAR	PHANSIGARS
	PHANTASIM	PHANTASIME ▪ PHANTASIMS
	PHANTASM	PHANTASMA ▪ PHANTASMS
	PHANTASMA	PHANTASMAL
	PHANTAST	PHANTASTS
	PHANTOM	PHANTOMS ▪ PHANTOMY
	PHANTOSME	PHANTOSMES
	PHARAOH	PHARAOHS
	PHARE	PHARES
	PHARISEE	PHARISEES
	PHARMA	PHARMAS
	PHARMING	PHARMINGS
	PHARYNGAL	PHARYNGALS
	PHASE	PHASED ▪ PHASES
	PHASEDOWN	PHASEDOWNS
	PHASEOLIN	PHASEOLINS
	PHASEOUT	PHASEOUTS
APHASIC	PHASIC	
	PHASING	PHASINGS
	PHASMID	PHASMIDS
	PHASOR	PHASORS
	PHEASANT	PHEASANTS
	PHEAZAR	PHEAZARS
	PHEER	PHEERE ▪ PHEERS
	PHEERE	PHEERES
	PHEESE	PHEESED ▪ PHEESES
	PHEEZE	PHEEZED ▪ PHEEZES
	PHELLEM	PHELLEMS
	PHELLOGEN	PHELLOGENS
	PHELONION	PHELONIONS
	PHENACITE	PHENACITES
	PHENAKISM	PHENAKISMS
	PHENAKITE	PHENAKITES
	PHENATE	PHENATES
	PHENAZIN	PHENAZINE ▪ PHENAZINS
	PHENAZINE	PHENAZINES
SPHENE	PHENE	PHENES
SPHENES	PHENES	
	PHENETIC	PHENETICS
	PHENETOL	PHENETOLE ▪ PHENETOLS
	PHENETOLE	PHENETOLES
	PHENGITE	PHENGITES
SPHENIC	PHENIC	
	PHENOGAM	PHENOGAMS
	PHENOL	PHENOLS
	PHENOLATE	PHENOLATED ▪ PHENOLATES
	PHENOLIC	PHENOLICS
	PHENOM	PHENOMS
	PHENOMENA	PHENOMENAL ▪ PHENOMENAS
	PHENOTYPE	PHENOTYPED ▪ PHENOTYPES
	PHENOXIDE	PHENOXIDES
	PHENYL	PHENYLS
	PHENYLENE	PHENYLENES
	PHENYTOIN	PHENYTOINS

FRONT HOOK	ROOT WORD	END HOOK
	PHEON	PHEONS
APHERESES	PHERESES	
APHERESIS	PHERESIS	
	PHEROMONE	PHEROMONES
	PHESE	PHESED ▪ PHESES
APHESES	PHESES	
	PHI	PHIS ▪ PHIZ
	PHIAL	PHIALS
	PHILABEG	PHILABEGS
	PHILAMOT	PHILAMOTS
	PHILANDER	PHILANDERS
	PHILHORSE	PHILHORSES
	PHILIBEG	PHILIBEGS
	PHILIPPIC	PHILIPPICS
	PHILISTIA	PHILISTIAS
	PHILLABEG	PHILLABEGS
	PHILLIBEG	PHILLIBEGS
	PHILOMATH	PHILOMATHS ▪ PHILOMATHY
	PHILOMEL	PHILOMELA ▪ PHILOMELS
	PHILOMELA	PHILOMELAS
	PHILOMOT	PHILOMOTS
	PHILOPENA	PHILOPENAS
	PHILTER	PHILTERS
	PHILTRE	PHILTRED ▪ PHILTRES
	PHINNOCK	PHINNOCKS
APHIS	PHIS	
	PHISHING	PHISHINGS
	PHIZOG	PHIZOGS
	PHLEGM	PHLEGMS ▪ PHLEGMY
	PHLEGMON	PHLEGMONS
	PHLOEM	PHLOEMS
	PHLORIZIN	PHLORIZINS
	PHLYCTENA	PHLYCTENAE
	PHO	PHOH ▪ PHON ▪ PHOS ▪ PHOT
	PHOBIA	PHOBIAS
	PHOBIC	PHOBICS
	PHOBISM	PHOBISMS
	PHOBIST	PHOBISTS
	PHOCA	PHOCAE ▪ PHOCAS
	PHOEBE	PHOEBES
	PHOH	PHOHS
	PHON	PHONE ▪ PHONO ▪ PHONS ▪ PHONY
	PHONATE	PHONATED ▪ PHONATES
	PHONATHON	PHONATHONS
	PHONATION	PHONATIONS
	PHONE	PHONED ▪ PHONER ▪ PHONES ▪ PHONEY
	PHONECAM	PHONECAMS
	PHONECARD	PHONECARDS
	PHONEME	PHONEMES
	PHONEMIC	PHONEMICS
	PHONER	PHONERS
	PHONETIC	PHONETICS
	PHONETISE	PHONETISED ▪ PHONETISES
	PHONETISM	PHONETISMS
	PHONETIST	PHONETISTS
	PHONETIZE	PHONETIZED ▪ PHONETIZES
	PHONEY	PHONEYS
APHONIC	PHONIC	PHONICS
APHONICS	PHONICS	
APHONIES	PHONIES	PHONIEST
	PHONMETER	PHONMETERS
	PHONO	PHONON ▪ PHONOS
	PHONOGRAM	PHONOGRAMS
	PHONOLITE	PHONOLITES
	PHONON	PHONONS
	PHONOPORE	PHONOPORES
	PHONOTYPE	PHONOTYPED ▪ PHONOTYPER ▪ PHONOTYPES
APHONY	PHONY	
EPHORATE	PHORATE	PHORATES

FRONT HOOK	ROOT WORD	END HOOK
EPHORATES	**PHORATES**	
	PHORMIUM	PHORMIUMS
	PHORONID	PHORONIDS
	PHOSGENE	PHOSGENES
	PHOSPHATE	PHOSPHATED · PHOSPHATES
	PHOSPHENE	PHOSPHENES
	PHOSPHID	PHOSPHIDE · PHOSPHIDS
	PHOSPHIDE	PHOSPHIDES
	PHOSPHIN	PHOSPHINE · PHOSPHINS
	PHOSPHINE	PHOSPHINES
	PHOSPHITE	PHOSPHITES
	PHOSPHOR	PHOSPHORE · PHOSPHORI · PHOSPHORS
	PHOSPHORE	PHOSPHORES · PHOSPHORET
	PHOSPHORI	PHOSPHORIC
	PHOT	PHOTO · PHOTS
APHOTIC	**PHOTIC**	PHOTICS
	PHOTINIA	PHOTINIAS
	PHOTISM	PHOTISMS
	PHOTO	PHOTOG · PHOTON · PHOTOS
	PHOTOCELL	PHOTOCELLS
	PHOTOFIT	PHOTOFITS
	PHOTOG	PHOTOGS
	PHOTOGEN	PHOTOGENE · PHOTOGENS · PHOTOGENY
	PHOTOGENE	PHOTOGENES
	PHOTOGRAM	PHOTOGRAMS
	PHOTOLYSE	PHOTOLYSED · PHOTOLYSES
	PHOTOLYZE	PHOTOLYZED · PHOTOLYZES
	PHOTOMAP	PHOTOMAPS
	PHOTOMASK	PHOTOMASKS
	PHOTON	PHOTONS
	PHOTONIC	PHOTONICS
	PHOTOPHIL	PHOTOPHILS · PHOTOPHILY
	PHOTOPIA	PHOTOPIAS
	PHOTOPLAY	PHOTOPLAYS
	PHOTOPSIA	PHOTOPSIAS
	PHOTOSCAN	PHOTOSCANS
	PHOTOSET	PHOTOSETS
	PHOTOSTAT	PHOTOSTATS
	PHOTOTUBE	PHOTOTUBES
	PHOTOTYPE	PHOTOTYPED · PHOTOTYPES
	PHRASE	PHRASED · PHRASER · PHRASES
	PHRASER	PHRASERS
	PHRASING	PHRASINGS
	PHREAK	PHREAKS
	PHREAKER	PHREAKERS
	PHREAKING	PHREAKINGS
	PHRENETIC	PHRENETICS
	PHRENISM	PHRENISMS
	PHRYGANA	PHRYGANAS
	PHTHALATE	PHTHALATES
	PHTHALEIN	PHTHALEINS
	PHTHALIN	PHTHALINS
	PHTHISIC	PHTHISICS
	PHUT	PHUTS
	PHYCOCYAN	PHYCOCYANS
	PHYLA	PHYLAE · PHYLAR
	PHYLARCH	PHYLARCHS · PHYLARCHY
	PHYLETIC	PHYLETICS
	PHYLLID	PHYLLIDS
	PHYLLITE	PHYLLITES
	PHYLLO	PHYLLOS
	PHYLLODE	PHYLLODES
	PHYLLODIA	PHYLLODIAL
	PHYLLOID	PHYLLOIDS
	PHYLLOME	PHYLLOMES
	PHYLLOPOD	PHYLLOPODS
	PHYSALIA	PHYSALIAS
	PHYSED	PHYSEDS
	PHYSETER	PHYSETERS

FRONT HOOK	ROOT WORD	END HOOK
	PHYSIC	PHYSICS
	PHYSICAL	PHYSICALS
	PHYSICIAN	PHYSICIANS
	PHYSICISM	PHYSICISMS
	PHYSICIST	PHYSICISTS
	PHYSIO	PHYSIOS
	PHYSIQUE	PHYSIQUED ▪ PHYSIQUES
	PHYTANE	PHYTANES
	PHYTIN	PHYTINS
	PHYTOL	PHYTOLS
	PHYTOLITH	PHYTOLITHS
	PHYTON	PHYTONS
	PHYTOTRON	PHYTOTRONS
	PI	PIA ▪ PIC ▪ PIE ▪ PIG ▪ PIN ▪ PIP ▪ PIR PIS ▪ PIT ▪ PIU ▪ PIX
	PIA	PIAL ▪ PIAN ▪ PIAS
	PIAFFE	PIAFFED ▪ PIAFFER ▪ PIAFFES
	PIAFFER	PIAFFERS
SPIAL	PIAL	
APIAN	PIAN	PIANO ▪ PIANS
	PIANETTE	PIANETTES
	PIANINO	PIANINOS
	PIANISM	PIANISMS
	PIANIST	PIANISTE ▪ PIANISTS
	PIANISTE	PIANISTES
	PIANO	PIANOS
	PIANOLIST	PIANOLISTS
APIARIST	PIARIST	PIARISTS
APIARISTS	PIARISTS	
	PIASABA	PIASABAS
	PIASAVA	PIASAVAS
	PIASSABA	PIASSABAS
	PIASSAVA	PIASSAVAS
	PIASTER	PIASTERS
	PIASTRE	PIASTRES
	PIAZZA	PIAZZAS
	PIBAL	PIBALS
	PIBROCH	PIBROCHS
EPIC ▪ SPIC	PIC	PICA ▪ PICE ▪ PICK ▪ PICS
SPICA	PICA	PICAL ▪ PICAS
	PICACHO	PICACHOS
	PICADILLO	PICADILLOS
	PICADOR	PICADORS
APICAL ▪ EPICAL	PICAL	
	PICAMAR	PICAMARS
	PICARA	PICARAS
	PICARIAN	PICARIANS
	PICARO	PICAROS
	PICAROON	PICAROONS
SPICAS	PICAS	
	PICAYUNE	PICAYUNES
	PICCADILL	PICCADILLO ▪ PICCADILLS ▪ PICCADILLY
	PICCANIN	PICCANINS (offensive)
	PICCOLO	PICCOLOS
SPICE	PICE	
EPICENE	PICENE	PICENES
EPICENES	PICENES	
	PICHOLINE	PICHOLINES
	PICHURIM	PICHURIMS
SPICK	PICK	PICKS ▪ PICKY
	PICKABACK	PICKABACKS
	PICKADIL	PICKADILL ▪ PICKADILS
	PICKADILL	PICKADILLO ▪ PICKADILLS ▪ PICKADILLY
	PICKAPACK	PICKAPACKS
	PICKAROON	PICKAROONS
	PICKAX	PICKAXE
	PICKAXE	PICKAXED ▪ PICKAXES
	PICKBACK	PICKBACKS
	PICKEER	PICKEERS

FRONT HOOK	ROOT WORD	END HOOK
	PICKEERER	PICKEERERS
SPICKER (offensive)	**PICKER**	PICKERS ▪ PICKERY
	PICKEREL	PICKERELS
	PICKET	PICKETS
	PICKETER	PICKETERS
	PICKETING	PICKETINGS
	PICKIN	PICKING ▪ PICKINS
	PICKING	PICKINGS
	PICKLE	PICKLED ▪ PICKLER ▪ PICKLES
	PICKLER	PICKLERS
	PICKLOCK	PICKLOCKS
	PICKMAW	PICKMAWS
	PICKOFF	PICKOFFS
SPICKS (offensive)	**PICKS**	
	PICKTHANK	PICKTHANKS
	PICKUP	PICKUPS
	PICKWICK	PICKWICKS
	PICLORAM	PICLORAMS
	PICNIC	PICNICS
	PICNICKER	PICNICKERS
	PICOCURIE	PICOCURIES
	PICOFARAD	PICOFARADS
	PICOGRAM	PICOGRAMS
	PICOLIN	PICOLINE ▪ PICOLINS
	PICOLINE	PICOLINES
	PICOMETER	PICOMETERS
	PICOMETRE	PICOMETRES
	PICOMOLE	PICOMOLES
	PICONG	PICONGS
	PICOT	PICOTE ▪ PICOTS
	PICOTE	PICOTED ▪ PICOTEE
	PICOTEE	PICOTEES
	PICOTITE	PICOTITES
	PICOWAVE	PICOWAVED ▪ PICOWAVES
	PICQUET	PICQUETS
	PICRA	PICRAS
	PICRATE	PICRATED ▪ PICRATES
	PICRITE	PICRITES
EPICRITIC	**PICRITIC**	
EPICS ▪ SPICS (offensive)	**PICS**	
	PICTARNIE	PICTARNIES
	PICTOGRAM	PICTOGRAMS
	PICTORIAL	PICTORIALS
	PICTURAL	PICTURALS
	PICTURE	PICTURED ▪ PICTURES
	PICTURISE	PICTURISED ▪ PICTURISES
	PICTURIZE	PICTURIZED ▪ PICTURIZES
	PICUL	PICULS
	PIDDLE	PIDDLED ▪ PIDDLER ▪ PIDDLES
	PIDDLER	PIDDLERS
	PIDDOCK	PIDDOCKS
	PIDGEON	PIDGEONS
	PIDGIN	PIDGINS
	PIDGINISE	PIDGINISED ▪ PIDGINISES
	PIDGINIZE	PIDGINIZED ▪ PIDGINIZES
SPIE	**PIE**	PIED ▪ PIER ▪ PIES ▪ PIET
	PIEBALD	PIEBALDS
APIECE	**PIECE**	PIECED ▪ PIECEN ▪ PIECER ▪ PIECES
	PIECEMEAL	PIECEMEALS
	PIECEN	PIECENS
	PIECENER	PIECENERS
	PIECER	PIECERS
	PIECEWORK	PIECEWORKS
	PIECING	PIECINGS
	PIECRUST	PIECRUSTS
SPIED	**PIED**	
	PIEDFORT	PIEDFORTS
	PIEDMONT	PIEDMONTS
	PIEFORT	PIEFORTS

FRONT HOOK	ROOT WORD	END HOOK
	PIEHOLE	PIEHOLES
	PIEND	PIENDS
	PIEPLANT	PIEPLANTS
	PIEPOWDER	PIEPOWDERS
SPIER	**PIER**	PIERS ▪ PIERT
	PIERAGE	PIERAGES
	PIERCE	PIERCED ▪ PIERCER ▪ PIERCES
	PIERCER	PIERCERS
	PIERCING	PIERCINGS
	PIERID	PIERIDS
	PIERRETTE	PIERRETTES
	PIERROT	PIERROTS
SPIERS	**PIERS**	PIERST
	PIERT	PIERTS
SPIES	**PIES**	
	PIET	PIETA ▪ PIETS ▪ PIETY
	PIETA	PIETAS
	PIETISM	PIETISMS
	PIETIST	PIETISTS
	PIFFERO	PIFFEROS
	PIFFLE	PIFFLED ▪ PIFFLER ▪ PIFFLES
	PIFFLER	PIFFLERS
	PIG	PIGS
	PIGBOAT	PIGBOATS
	PIGEON	PIGEONS
	PIGEONITE	PIGEONITES
	PIGFACE	PIGFACES
	PIGFEED	PIGFEEDS
	PIGGIE	PIGGIER ▪ PIGGIES
	PIGGIES	PIGGIEST
	PIGGIN	PIGGING ▪ PIGGINS
	PIGGING	PIGGINGS
	PIGGYBACK	PIGGYBACKS
SPIGHT ▪ YPIGHT	**PIGHT**	PIGHTS
SPIGHTED	**PIGHTED**	
SPIGHTING	**PIGHTING**	
	PIGHTLE	PIGHTLES
SPIGHTS	**PIGHTS**	
	PIGLET	PIGLETS
	PIGLING	PIGLINGS
	PIGMEAT	PIGMEATS
	PIGMENT	PIGMENTS
	PIGNERATE	PIGNERATED ▪ PIGNERATES
	PIGNOLI	PIGNOLIA ▪ PIGNOLIS
	PIGNOLIA	PIGNOLIAS
	PIGNORATE	PIGNORATED ▪ PIGNORATES
	PIGNUT	PIGNUTS
	PIGOUT	PIGOUTS
	PIGPEN	PIGPENS
	PIGSCONCE	PIGSCONCES
	PIGSKIN	PIGSKINS
	PIGSNEY	PIGSNEYS
	PIGSNIE	PIGSNIES
	PIGSTICK	PIGSTICKS
	PIGSWILL	PIGSWILLS
	PIGTAIL	PIGTAILS
	PIGWEED	PIGWEEDS
	PIKA	PIKAS ▪ PIKAU
	PIKAKE	PIKAKES
	PIKAU	PIKAUS
SPIKE	**PIKE**	PIKED ▪ PIKER ▪ PIKES ▪ PIKEY
SPIKED	**PIKED**	
SPIKELET	**PIKELET**	PIKELETS
SPIKELETS	**PIKELETS**	
SPIKER	**PIKER**	PIKERS
SPIKERS	**PIKERS**	
SPIKES	**PIKES**	
	PIKESTAFF	PIKESTAFFS
SPIKEY	**PIKEY**	PIKEYS *(offensive)*

FRONT HOOK	ROOT WORD	END HOOK
	PIKI	PIKIS
SPIKING	**PIKING**	PIKINGS
	PIKUL	PIKULS
	PILA	PILAF ▪ PILAO ▪ PILAR ▪ PILAU ▪ PILAW
	PILAF	PILAFF ▪ PILAFS
	PILAFF	PILAFFS
	PILAO	PILAOS
	PILASTER	PILASTERS
	PILAU	PILAUS
	PILAW	PILAWS
	PILCHARD	PILCHARDS
	PILCHER	PILCHERS
	PILCORN	PILCORNS
	PILCROW	PILCROWS
SPILE	**PILE**	PILEA ▪ PILED ▪ PILEI ▪ PILER ▪ PILES
	PILEA	PILEAS
	PILEATE	PILEATED
SPILED	**PILED**	
	PILER	PILERS
SPILES	**PILES**	
	PILEUP	PILEUPS
	PILEWORK	PILEWORKS
	PILEWORT	PILEWORTS
	PILFER	PILFERS ▪ PILFERY
	PILFERAGE	PILFERAGES
	PILFERER	PILFERERS
	PILFERING	PILFERINGS
	PILGARLIC	PILGARLICK ▪ PILGARLICS
	PILGRIM	PILGRIMS
	PILGRIMER	PILGRIMERS
	PILI	PILIS
SPILING	**PILING**	PILINGS
SPILINGS	**PILINGS**	
SPILL	**PILL**	PILLS
SPILLAGE	**PILLAGE**	PILLAGED ▪ PILLAGER ▪ PILLAGES
	PILLAGER	PILLAGERS
SPILLAGES	**PILLAGES**	
	PILLAR	PILLARS
	PILLARIST	PILLARISTS
	PILLAU	PILLAUS
SPILLED	**PILLED**	
	PILLHEAD	PILLHEADS
	PILLICOCK	PILLICOCKS
	PILLIE	PILLIES
SPILLING	**PILLING**	PILLINGS
SPILLINGS	**PILLINGS**	
	PILLION	PILLIONS
	PILLOCK	PILLOCKS
	PILLORISE	PILLORISED ▪ PILLORISES
	PILLORIZE	PILLORIZED ▪ PILLORIZES
	PILLOW	PILLOWS ▪ PILLOWY
SPILLS	**PILLS**	
	PILLWORM	PILLWORMS
	PILLWORT	PILLWORTS
	PILOT	PILOTS
	PILOTAGE	PILOTAGES
	PILOTING	PILOTINGS
	PILOW	PILOWS
	PILSENER	PILSENERS
	PILSNER	PILSNERS
	PILULA	PILULAE ▪ PILULAR ▪ PILULAS
	PILULE	PILULES
	PIMA	PIMAS
	PIMENT	PIMENTO ▪ PIMENTS
	PIMENTO	PIMENTON ▪ PIMENTOS
	PIMENTON	PIMENTONS
	PIMIENTO	PIMIENTOS
	PIMP	PIMPS
	PIMPERNEL	PIMPERNELS

FRONT HOOK	ROOT WORD	END HOOK
	PIMPLE	PIMPLED ▪ PIMPLES
SPIN	**PIN**	PINA ▪ PINE ▪ PING ▪ PINK ▪ PINS PINT ▪ PINY
SPINA	**PINA**	PINAS
SPINACEOUS	**PINACEOUS**	
	PINACOID	PINACOIDS
	PINAFORE	PINAFORED ▪ PINAFORES
	PINAKOID	PINAKOIDS
	PINANG	PINANGS
SPINAS	**PINAS**	
	PINASTER	PINASTERS
	PINATA	PINATAS
	PINBALL	PINBALLS
	PINBONE	PINBONES
	PINCASE	PINCASES
	PINCER	PINCERS
	PINCHBECK	PINCHBECKS
	PINCHBUG	PINCHBUGS
	PINCHCOCK	PINCHCOCKS
	PINCHECK	PINCHECKS
	PINCHER	PINCHERS
	PINCHFIST	PINCHFISTS
	PINCHGUT	PINCHGUTS
	PINCHING	PINCHINGS
	PINDAN	PINDANS
	PINDAREE	PINDAREES
	PINDARI	PINDARIS
	PINDER	PINDERS
SPINDLING	**PINDLING**	
	PINDOWN	PINDOWNS
OPINE ▪ SPINE	**PINE**	PINED ▪ PINES ▪ PINEY
	PINEAL	PINEALS
	PINEAPPLE	PINEAPPLES
	PINECONE	PINECONES
OPINED ▪ SPINED	**PINED**	
	PINELAND	PINELANDS
SPINELIKE	**PINELIKE**	
	PINENE	PINENES
OPINES ▪ SPINES	**PINES**	
	PINESAP	PINESAPS
	PINEWOOD	PINEWOODS
	PINFALL	PINFALLS
	PINFOLD	PINFOLDS
APING ▪ OPING	**PING**	PINGO ▪ PINGS
	PINGER	PINGERS
	PINGLE	PINGLED ▪ PINGLER ▪ PINGLES
	PINGLER	PINGLERS
	PINGO	PINGOS
	PINGPONG	PINGPONGS
	PINGUIN	PINGUINS
	PINHEAD	PINHEADS
	PINHOLE	PINHOLES
	PINHOOKER	PINHOOKERS
SPINIER	**PINIER**	
	PINIES	PINIEST
SPINIEST	**PINIEST**	
OPINING	**PINING**	
OPINION	**PINION**	PINIONS
OPINIONED	**PINIONED**	
OPINIONS	**PINIONS**	
	PINITE	PINITES
	PINITOL	PINITOLS
SPINK	**PINK**	PINKO ▪ PINKS ▪ PINKY
	PINKEN	PINKENS
	PINKER	PINKERS
	PINKERTON	PINKERTONS
	PINKEY	PINKEYE ▪ PINKEYS
	PINKEYE	PINKEYES
	PINKIE	PINKIER ▪ PINKIES

FRONT HOOK	ROOT WORD	END HOOK
	PINKIES	PINKIEST
	PINKING	PINKINGS
	PINKO	PINKOS
	PINKROOT	PINKROOTS
SPINKS	**PINKS**	
	PINNA	PINNAE ▪ PINNAL ▪ PINNAS
	PINNACE	PINNACES
	PINNACLE	PINNACLED ▪ PINNACLES
	PINNATE	PINNATED
	PINNATION	PINNATIONS
SPINNER	**PINNER**	PINNERS
SPINNERS	**PINNERS**	
SPINNET	**PINNET**	PINNETS
SPINNETS	**PINNETS**	
	PINNIE	PINNIES
SPINNIES	**PINNIES**	
SPINNING	**PINNING**	PINNINGS
SPINNINGS	**PINNINGS**	
	PINNIPED	PINNIPEDE ▪ PINNIPEDS
	PINNIPEDE	PINNIPEDES
	PINNOCK	PINNOCKS
	PINNULA	PINNULAE ▪ PINNULAR ▪ PINNULAS
	PINNULATE	PINNULATED
	PINNULE	PINNULES
SPINNY	**PINNY**	
	PINOCHLE	PINOCHLES
	PINOCLE	PINOCLES
	PINOLE	PINOLES
	PINON	PINONS
	PINOT	PINOTS
	PINPOINT	PINPOINTS
	PINPRICK	PINPRICKS
SPINS	**PINS**	
	PINSCHER	PINSCHERS
	PINSETTER	PINSETTERS
	PINSTRIPE	PINSTRIPES
	PINSWELL	PINSWELLS
	PINT	PINTA ▪ PINTO ▪ PINTS
	PINTA	PINTAS
	PINTABLE	PINTABLES
	PINTADA	PINTADAS
	PINTADERA	PINTADERAS
	PINTADO	PINTADOS
	PINTAIL	PINTAILS
	PINTANO	PINTANOS
	PINTLE	PINTLES
SPINTO	**PINTO**	PINTOS
SPINTOS	**PINTOS**	
	PINTSIZE	PINTSIZED
	PINUP	PINUPS
	PINWALE	PINWALES
	PINWEED	PINWEEDS
	PINWHEEL	PINWHEELS
	PINWORK	PINWORKS
	PINWORM	PINWORMS
SPINY	**PINY**	
	PINYON	PINYONS
	PIOLET	PIOLETS
	PION	PIONS ▪ PIONY
	PIONEER	PIONEERS
	PIONER	PIONERS
	PIONEY	PIONEYS
	PIONING	PIONINGS
	PIOY	PIOYE ▪ PIOYS
	PIOYE	PIOYES
	PIP	PIPA ▪ PIPE ▪ PIPI ▪ PIPS ▪ PIPY
	PIPA	PIPAL ▪ PIPAS
	PIPAGE	PIPAGES
	PIPAL	PIPALS

FRONT HOOK	ROOT WORD	END HOOK
	PIPE	PIPED ▪ PIPER ▪ PIPES ▪ PIPET
	PIPEAGE	PIPEAGES
	PIPECLAY	PIPECLAYS
	PIPEFUL	PIPEFULS
	PIPELINE	PIPELINED ▪ PIPELINES
	PIPER	PIPERS
	PIPERINE	PIPERINES
	PIPERONAL	PIPERONALS
	PIPESTEM	PIPESTEMS
	PIPESTONE	PIPESTONES
	PIPET	PIPETS
	PIPETTE	PIPETTED ▪ PIPETTES
	PIPEWORK	PIPEWORKS
	PIPEWORT	PIPEWORTS
	PIPI	PIPIS ▪ PIPIT
	PIPING	PIPINGS
	PIPISTREL	PIPISTRELS
	PIPIT	PIPITS
	PIPKIN	PIPKINS
	PIPPIN	PIPPING ▪ PIPPINS
	PIPSQUEAK	PIPSQUEAKS
	PIPUL	PIPULS
	PIQUANCE	PIQUANCES
	PIQUE	PIQUED ▪ PIQUES ▪ PIQUET
	PIQUET	PIQUETS
	PIQUILLO	PIQUILLOS
	PIR	PIRL ▪ PIRN ▪ PIRS
	PIRACETAM	PIRACETAMS
	PIRAGUA	PIRAGUAS
	PIRAI	PIRAIS
	PIRANA	PIRANAS
	PIRANHA	PIRANHAS
	PIRARUCU	PIRARUCUS
	PIRATE	PIRATED ▪ PIRATES
SPIRATED	**PIRATED**	
	PIRAYA	PIRAYAS
	PIRL	PIRLS
	PIRLICUE	PIRLICUED ▪ PIRLICUES
	PIRN	PIRNS
	PIRNIE	PIRNIES
	PIROG	PIROGI
	PIROGUE	PIROGUES
	PIROPLASM	PIROPLASMA ▪ PIROPLASMS
	PIROQUE	PIROQUES
	PIROUETTE	PIROUETTED ▪ PIROUETTER ▪ PIROUETTES
	PIS	PISE ▪ PISH ▪ PISO ▪ PISS
	PISCATOR	PISCATORS ▪ PISCATORY
	PISCINA	PISCINAE ▪ PISCINAL ▪ PISCINAS
	PISCINE	PISCINES
	PISCIVORE	PISCIVORES
	PISCO	PISCOS
	PISE	PISES
APISH	**PISH**	
	PISHER	PISHERS
	PISHOGE	PISHOGES
	PISHOGUE	PISHOGUES
	PISIFORM	PISIFORMS
	PISMIRE	PISMIRES
	PISO	PISOS
	PISOLITE	PISOLITES
	PISOLITH	PISOLITHS
	PISSANT	PISSANTS *(offensive)*
	PISSER	PISSERS *(offensive)*
	PISSHEAD	PISSHEADS *(offensive)*
	PISSOIR	PISSOIRS *(offensive)*
	PISTACHE	PISTACHES
	PISTACHIO	PISTACHIOS
	PISTAREEN	PISTAREENS
	PISTE	PISTES

FRONT HOOK	ROOT WORD	END HOOK
	PISTIL	PISTILS
	PISTOL	PISTOLE ▪ PISTOLS
	PISTOLE	PISTOLED ▪ PISTOLES ▪ PISTOLET
	PISTOLEER	PISTOLEERS
	PISTOLERO	PISTOLEROS
EPISTOLET	**PISTOLET**	PISTOLETS
EPISTOLETS	**PISTOLETS**	
	PISTOLIER	PISTOLIERS
	PISTON	PISTONS
	PISTOU	PISTOUS
SPIT	**PIT**	PITA ▪ PITH ▪ PITS ▪ PITY
	PITA	PITAS
	PITAHAYA	PITAHAYAS
	PITAPAT	PITAPATS
	PITARA	PITARAH ▪ PITARAS
	PITARAH	PITARAHS
	PITAYA	PITAYAS
	PITCH	PITCHY
	PITCHBEND	PITCHBENDS
SPITCHER	**PITCHER**	PITCHERS
	PITCHFORK	PITCHFORKS
	PITCHING	PITCHINGS
	PITCHOUT	PITCHOUTS
	PITCHPINE	PITCHPINES
	PITCHPIPE	PITCHPIPES
	PITCHPOLE	PITCHPOLED ▪ PITCHPOLES
	PITFALL	PITFALLS
	PITH	PITHS ▪ PITHY
	PITHBALL	PITHBALLS
	PITHEAD	PITHEADS
	PITIER	PITIERS
	PITMAN	PITMANS
	PITON	PITONS
	PITPROP	PITPROPS
SPITS	**PITS**	
	PITSAW	PITSAWS
	PITTA	PITTAS
	PITTANCE	PITTANCES
SPITTED	**PITTED**	
SPITTEN	**PITTEN**	
SPITTER	**PITTER**	PITTERS
SPITTERS	**PITTERS**	
SPITTING	**PITTING**	PITTINGS
SPITTINGS	**PITTINGS**	
	PITTITE	PITTITES
	PITUITA	PITUITAS
	PITUITE	PITUITES
	PITUITRIN	PITUITRINS
	PITURI	PITURIS
	PIU	PIUM
OPIUM	**PIUM**	PIUMS
OPIUMS	**PIUMS**	
	PIUPIU	PIUPIUS
	PIVOT	PIVOTS
	PIVOTER	PIVOTERS
	PIVOTING	PIVOTINGS
	PIX	PIXY
	PIXEL	PIXELS
	PIXIE	PIXIES
	PIZAZZ	PIZAZZY
	PIZE	PIZED ▪ PIZES
	PIZZA	PIZZAS ▪ PIZZAZ
	PIZZAZ	PIZZAZZ
	PIZZAZZ	PIZZAZZY
	PIZZELLE	PIZZELLES
	PIZZERIA	PIZZERIAS
	PIZZICATO	PIZZICATOS
	PIZZLE	PIZZLES
	PLACARD	PLACARDS

FRONT HOOK	ROOT WORD	END HOOK
	PLACATE	PLACATED ▪ PLACATER ▪ PLACATES
	PLACATER	PLACATERS
	PLACATION	PLACATIONS
	PLACCAT	PLACCATE ▪ PLACCATS
	PLACCATE	PLACCATES
	PLACE	PLACED ▪ PLACER ▪ PLACES ▪ PLACET
	PLACEBO	PLACEBOS
	PLACEKICK	PLACEKICKS
	PLACEMEN	PLACEMENT
	PLACEMENT	PLACEMENTS
	PLACENTA	PLACENTAE ▪ PLACENTAL ▪ PLACENTAS
APLACENTAL	PLACENTAL	PLACENTALS
	PLACER	PLACERS
	PLACET	PLACETS
	PLACING	PLACINGS
	PLACIT	PLACITA ▪ PLACITS
	PLACK	PLACKS
	PLACKET	PLACKETS
	PLACODERM	PLACODERMS
	PLACOID	PLACOIDS
	PLAFOND	PLAFONDS
	PLAGE	PLAGES
	PLAGIUM	PLAGIUMS
	PLAGUE	PLAGUED ▪ PLAGUER ▪ PLAGUES ▪ PLAGUEY
	PLAGUER	PLAGUERS
	PLAICE	PLAICES
UPLAID	PLAID	PLAIDS
	PLAIDING	PLAIDINGS
	PLAIN	PLAINS ▪ PLAINT
	PLAINANT	PLAINANTS
	PLAINING	PLAININGS
	PLAINSONG	PLAINSONGS
	PLAINT	PLAINTS
	PLAINTEXT	PLAINTEXTS
	PLAINTIFF	PLAINTIFFS
	PLAINWORK	PLAINWORKS
	PLAISTER	PLAISTERS
	PLAIT	PLAITS
	PLAITER	PLAITERS
	PLAITING	PLAITINGS
	PLAN	PLANE ▪ PLANK ▪ PLANS ▪ PLANT
	PLANARIA	PLANARIAN ▪ PLANARIAS
	PLANARIAN	PLANARIANS
	PLANATION	PLANATIONS
	PLANCH	PLANCHE
	PLANCHE	PLANCHED ▪ PLANCHES ▪ PLANCHET
	PLANCHET	PLANCHETS
	PLANE	PLANED ▪ PLANER ▪ PLANES ▪ PLANET
	PLANELOAD	PLANELOADS
	PLANER	PLANERS
	PLANESIDE	PLANESIDES
	PLANET	PLANETS
APLANETIC	PLANETIC	
	PLANETOID	PLANETOIDS
	PLANFORM	PLANFORMS
	PLANISHER	PLANISHERS
	PLANK	PLANKS
	PLANKING	PLANKINGS
	PLANKTER	PLANKTERS
	PLANKTON	PLANKTONS
	PLANNER	PLANNERS
	PLANNING	PLANNINGS
	PLANOSOL	PLANOSOLS
	PLANT	PLANTA ▪ PLANTS
	PLANTA	PLANTAE ▪ PLANTAR ▪ PLANTAS
	PLANTAGE	PLANTAGES
	PLANTAIN	PLANTAINS
	PLANTER	PLANTERS
	PLANTING	PLANTINGS

FRONT HOOK	ROOT WORD	END HOOK
	PLANTLET	PLANTLETS
	PLANTLING	PLANTLINGS
	PLANTULE	PLANTULES
	PLANULA	PLANULAE · PLANULAR
	PLANURIA	PLANURIAS
	PLAP	PLAPS
	PLAQUE	PLAQUES
	PLAQUETTE	PLAQUETTES
SPLASH	**PLASH**	PLASHY
SPLASHED	**PLASHED**	
SPLASHER	**PLASHER**	PLASHERS
SPLASHERS	**PLASHERS**	
SPLASHES	**PLASHES**	
	PLASHET	PLASHETS
SPLASHIER	**PLASHIER**	
SPLASHIEST	**PLASHIEST**	
SPLASHING	**PLASHING**	PLASHINGS
SPLASHINGS	**PLASHINGS**	
SPLASHY	**PLASHY**	
	PLASM	PLASMA · PLASMS
	PLASMA	PLASMAS
	PLASMAGEL	PLASMAGELS
	PLASMASOL	PLASMASOLS
	PLASMID	PLASMIDS
	PLASMIN	PLASMINS
	PLASMODIA	PLASMODIAL
	PLASMOID	PLASMOIDS
	PLASMON	PLASMONS
YPLAST	**PLAST**	PLASTE
	PLASTE	PLASTER
	PLASTER	PLASTERS · PLASTERY
	PLASTERER	PLASTERERS
APLASTIC	**PLASTIC**	PLASTICS
	PLASTID	PLASTIDS
	PLASTIQUE	PLASTIQUES
	PLASTISOL	PLASTISOLS
	PLASTRON	PLASTRONS
	PLASTRUM	PLASTRUMS
SPLAT	**PLAT**	PLATE · PLATS · PLATY
	PLATAN	PLATANE · PLATANS
	PLATANE	PLATANES
	PLATANNA	PLATANNAS
	PLATBAND	PLATBANDS
	PLATE	PLATED · PLATEN · PLATER · PLATES
	PLATEASM	PLATEASMS
	PLATEAU	PLATEAUS · PLATEAUX
	PLATEFUL	PLATEFULS
	PLATELET	PLATELETS
	PLATEMARK	PLATEMARKS
	PLATEN	PLATENS
	PLATER	PLATERS
	PLATFORM	PLATFORMS
	PLATIES	PLATIEST
	PLATINA	PLATINAS
	PLATING	PLATINGS
	PLATINISE	PLATINISED · PLATINISES
	PLATINIZE	PLATINIZED · PLATINIZES
	PLATINOID	PLATINOIDS
	PLATINUM	PLATINUMS
	PLATITUDE	PLATITUDES
	PLATONIC	PLATONICS
	PLATONISM	PLATONISMS
	PLATOON	PLATOONS
SPLATS	**PLATS**	
SPLATTED	**PLATTED**	
SPLATTER	**PLATTER**	PLATTERS
SPLATTERS	**PLATTERS**	
SPLATTING	**PLATTING**	PLATTINGS
SPLATTINGS	**PLATTINGS**	

FRONT HOOK	ROOT WORD	END HOOK
	PLATY	PLATYS
	PLATYSMA	PLATYSMAS
	PLAUDIT	PLAUDITE · PLAUDITS
SPLAY · UPLAY	**PLAY**	PLAYA · PLAYS
	PLAYA	PLAYAS
	PLAYACT	PLAYACTS
	PLAYACTOR	PLAYACTORS
	PLAYBACK	PLAYBACKS
	PLAYBILL	PLAYBILLS
	PLAYBOOK	PLAYBOOKS
	PLAYBOY	PLAYBOYS
	PLAYDATE	PLAYDATES
	PLAYDAY	PLAYDAYS
	PLAYDOWN	PLAYDOWNS
SPLAYED	**PLAYED**	
	PLAYER	PLAYERS
	PLAYFIELD	PLAYFIELDS
	PLAYGIRL	PLAYGIRLS
	PLAYGOER	PLAYGOERS
	PLAYGOING	PLAYGOINGS
	PLAYGROUP	PLAYGROUPS
	PLAYHOUSE	PLAYHOUSES
SPLAYING · UPLAYING	**PLAYING**	
	PLAYLAND	PLAYLANDS
	PLAYLET	PLAYLETS
	PLAYLIST	PLAYLISTS
	PLAYMAKER	PLAYMAKERS
	PLAYMATE	PLAYMATES
	PLAYOFF	PLAYOFFS
	PLAYPEN	PLAYPENS
	PLAYROOM	PLAYROOMS
SPLAYS · UPLAYS	**PLAYS**	
	PLAYSUIT	PLAYSUITS
	PLAYTHING	PLAYTHINGS
	PLAYTIME	PLAYTIMES
	PLAZA	PLAZAS
	PLEA	PLEAD · PLEAS · PLEAT
UPLEAD	**PLEAD**	PLEADS
	PLEADER	PLEADERS
UPLEADING	**PLEADING**	PLEADINGS
UPLEADS	**PLEADS**	
	PLEAS	PLEASE
	PLEASANCE	PLEASANCES
	PLEASE	PLEASED · PLEASER · PLEASES
	PLEASER	PLEASERS
	PLEASING	PLEASINGS
	PLEASURE	PLEASURED · PLEASURER · PLEASURES
	PLEASURER	PLEASURERS
	PLEAT	PLEATS
	PLEATER	PLEATERS
	PLEATHER	PLEATHERS
	PLEB	PLEBE · PLEBS
	PLEBE	PLEBES
	PLEBEIAN	PLEBEIANS
	PLECTRE	PLECTRES
	PLECTRON	PLECTRONS
	PLECTRUM	PLECTRUMS
UPLED	**PLED**	
	PLEDGE	PLEDGED · PLEDGEE · PLEDGER · PLEDGES · PLEDGET
	PLEDGEE	PLEDGEES
	PLEDGEOR	PLEDGEORS
	PLEDGER	PLEDGERS
	PLEDGET	PLEDGETS
	PLEDGOR	PLEDGORS
	PLEIAD	PLEIADS
	PLENILUNE	PLENILUNES
	PLENIPO	PLENIPOS
	PLENISHER	PLENISHERS

FRONT HOOK	ROOT WORD	END HOOK
	PLENISM	PLENISMS
	PLENIST	PLENISTS
	PLENITUDE	PLENITUDES
APLENTY	**PLENTY**	
	PLENUM	PLENUMS
	PLEON	PLEONS
	PLEONASM	PLEONASMS
	PLEONAST	PLEONASTE ▪ PLEONASTS
	PLEONASTE	PLEONASTES
	PLEONEXIA	PLEONEXIAS
	PLEOPOD	PLEOPODS
	PLERION	PLERIONS
	PLEROMA	PLEROMAS
	PLEROME	PLEROMES
	PLESSOR	PLESSORS
	PLETHORA	PLETHORAS
	PLEUCH	PLEUCHS
	PLEUGH	PLEUGHS
	PLEURA	PLEURAE ▪ PLEURAL ▪ PLEURAS
	PLEURITIC	PLEURITICS
	PLEUSTON	PLEUSTONS
	PLEW	PLEWS
	PLEXOR	PLEXORS
	PLEXURE	PLEXURES
	PLICA	PLICAE ▪ PLICAL
	PLICATE	PLICATED ▪ PLICATES
	PLICATION	PLICATIONS
	PLICATURE	PLICATURES
	PLIE	PLIED ▪ PLIER ▪ PLIES
	PLIER	PLIERS
UPLIGHT ▪ YPLIGHT	**PLIGHT**	PLIGHTS
UPLIGHTED	**PLIGHTED**	
UPLIGHTER	**PLIGHTER**	PLIGHTERS
UPLIGHTERS	**PLIGHTERS**	
UPLIGHTING	**PLIGHTING**	
UPLIGHTS	**PLIGHTS**	
	PLIM	PLIMS
	PLIMSOL	PLIMSOLE ▪ PLIMSOLL ▪ PLIMSOLS
	PLIMSOLE	PLIMSOLES
	PLIMSOLL	PLIMSOLLS
	PLING	PLINGS
UPLINK	**PLINK**	PLINKS
UPLINKED	**PLINKED**	
	PLINKER	PLINKERS
UPLINKING	**PLINKING**	PLINKINGS
UPLINKINGS	**PLINKINGS**	
UPLINKS	**PLINKS**	
	PLINTH	PLINTHS
	PLIOFILM	PLIOFILMS
	PLIOSAUR	PLIOSAURS
	PLIOTRON	PLIOTRONS
	PLISKIE	PLISKIES
	PLISSE	PLISSES
	PLOAT	PLOATS
	PLOD	PLODS
	PLODDER	PLODDERS
	PLODDING	PLODDINGS
SPLODGE	**PLODGE**	PLODGED ▪ PLODGES
SPLODGED	**PLODGED**	
SPLODGES	**PLODGES**	
SPLODGING	**PLODGING**	
	PLONG	PLONGD ▪ PLONGE ▪ PLONGS
	PLONGE	PLONGED ▪ PLONGES
	PLONK	PLONKO ▪ PLONKS ▪ PLONKY
	PLONKER	PLONKERS
	PLONKING	PLONKINGS
	PLONKO	PLONKOS
UPLOOK	**PLOOK**	PLOOKS ▪ PLOOKY
	PLOOKIE	PLOOKIER

FRONT HOOK	ROOT WORD	END HOOK
UPLOOKS	**PLOOKS**	
	PLOP	PLOPS
	PLOSION	PLOSIONS
	PLOSIVE	PLOSIVES
	PLOT	PLOTS ▪ PLOTZ
	PLOTLINE	PLOTLINES
	PLOTTAGE	PLOTTAGES
	PLOTTER	PLOTTERS
	PLOTTIE	PLOTTIER ▪ PLOTTIES
	PLOTTIES	PLOTTIEST
	PLOTTING	PLOTTINGS
	PLOUGH	PLOUGHS
	PLOUGHBOY	PLOUGHBOYS
	PLOUGHER	PLOUGHERS
	PLOUGHING	PLOUGHINGS
	PLOUK	PLOUKS ▪ PLOUKY
	PLOUKIE	PLOUKIER
	PLOUTER	PLOUTERS
	PLOVER	PLOVERS ▪ PLOVERY
	PLOW	PLOWS
	PLOWBACK	PLOWBACKS
	PLOWBOY	PLOWBOYS
	PLOWER	PLOWERS
	PLOWHEAD	PLOWHEADS
	PLOWLAND	PLOWLANDS
	PLOWSHARE	PLOWSHARES
	PLOWSTAFF	PLOWSTAFFS
	PLOWTER	PLOWTERS
	PLOY	PLOYS
	PLU	PLUE ▪ PLUG ▪ PLUM ▪ PLUS
	PLUCK	PLUCKS ▪ PLUCKY
	PLUCKER	PLUCKERS
	PLUE	PLUES
	PLUFF	PLUFFS ▪ PLUFFY
	PLUG	PLUGS
	PLUGBOARD	PLUGBOARDS
	PLUGGER	PLUGGERS
	PLUGGING	PLUGGINGS
	PLUGHOLE	PLUGHOLES
	PLUGOLA	PLUGOLAS
	PLUM	PLUMB ▪ PLUME ▪ PLUMP ▪ PLUMS ▪ PLUMY
	PLUMAGE	PLUMAGED ▪ PLUMAGES
	PLUMB	PLUMBS
	PLUMBAGO	PLUMBAGOS
	PLUMBATE	PLUMBATES
	PLUMBER	PLUMBERS ▪ PLUMBERY
	PLUMBING	PLUMBINGS
	PLUMBISM	PLUMBISMS
	PLUMBITE	PLUMBITES
	PLUMBUM	PLUMBUMS
	PLUMCOT	PLUMCOTS
	PLUME	PLUMED ▪ PLUMES
	PLUMELET	PLUMELETS
	PLUMERIA	PLUMERIAS
	PLUMIPED	PLUMIPEDS
	PLUMIST	PLUMISTS
	PLUMMET	PLUMMETS
	PLUMP	PLUMPS ▪ PLUMPY
	PLUMPEN	PLUMPENS
	PLUMPER	PLUMPERS
	PLUMPIE	PLUMPIER
	PLUMULA	PLUMULAE ▪ PLUMULAR
	PLUMULE	PLUMULES
	PLUNDER	PLUNDERS
	PLUNDERER	PLUNDERERS
	PLUNGE	PLUNGED ▪ PLUNGER ▪ PLUNGES
	PLUNGER	PLUNGERS
	PLUNGING	PLUNGINGS
	PLUNK	PLUNKS ▪ PLUNKY

FRONT HOOK	ROOT WORD	END HOOK
	PLUNKER	PLUNKERS
	PLURAL	PLURALS
	PLURALISE	PLURALISED · PLURALISER · PLURALISES
	PLURALISM	PLURALISMS
	PLURALIST	PLURALISTS
	PLURALIZE	PLURALIZED · PLURALIZER · PLURALIZES
	PLURIPARA	PLURIPARAE · PLURIPARAS
	PLURISIE	PLURISIES
	PLUS	PLUSH
	PLUSAGE	PLUSAGES
	PLUSH	PLUSHY
	PLUSHES	PLUSHEST
	PLUSSAGE	PLUSSAGES
	PLUTOCRAT	PLUTOCRATS
	PLUTON	PLUTONS
	PLUTONISM	PLUTONISMS
	PLUTONIUM	PLUTONIUMS
	PLUVIAL	PLUVIALS
	PLYER	PLYERS
UPLYING	**PLYING**	
	PLYWOOD	PLYWOODS
	PNEUMA	PNEUMAS
	PNEUMATIC	PNEUMATICS
	PNEUMONIA	PNEUMONIAS
	PNEUMONIC	PNEUMONICS
APO · UPO	**PO**	POA · POD · POH · POI · POL · POM · POO POP · POS · POT · POW · POX · POZ
	POA	POAS
	POACH	POACHY
	POACHER	POACHERS
	POACHING	POACHINGS
	POAKA	POAKAS
	POAKE	POAKES
	POBLANO	POBLANOS
	POBOY	POBOYS
	POCHARD	POCHARDS
	POCHAY	POCHAYS
	POCHETTE	POCHETTES
	POCHOIR	POCHOIRS
	POCK	POCKS · POCKY
	POCKARD	POCKARDS
	POCKET	POCKETS
	POCKETER	POCKETERS
	POCKETFUL	POCKETFULS
	POCKIES	POCKIEST
	POCKMARK	POCKMARKS
	POCKPIT	POCKPITS
	POCOSEN	POCOSENS
	POCOSIN	POCOSINS
	POCOSON	POCOSONS
APOD · SPOD	**POD**	PODS
	PODAGRA	PODAGRAL · PODAGRAS
APODAL	**PODAL**	
	PODCAST	PODCASTS
	PODCASTER	PODCASTERS
	PODDIE	PODDIER · PODDIES
SPODDIER	**PODDIER**	
	PODDIES	PODDIEST
SPODDIEST	**PODDIEST**	
	PODDLE	PODDLED · PODDLES
SPODDY	**PODDY**	
	PODESTA	PODESTAS
	PODGE	PODGES
	PODIA	PODIAL
	PODITE	PODITES
SPODIUM	**PODIUM**	PODIUMS
SPODIUMS	**PODIUMS**	
	PODLEY	PODLEYS
	PODOCARP	PODOCARPS

FRONT HOOK	ROOT WORD	END HOOK
	PODOMERE	PODOMERES
APODS · SPODS	PODS	
	PODSOL	PODSOLS
	PODSOLISE	PODSOLISED · PODSOLISES
	PODSOLIZE	PODSOLIZED · PODSOLIZES
	PODZOL	PODZOLS
	PODZOLISE	PODZOLISED · PODZOLISES
	PODZOLIZE	PODZOLIZED · PODZOLIZES
	POECHORE	POECHORES
	POEM	POEMS
	POEP	POEPS
	POEPOL	POEPOLS (offensive)
	POET	POETS
	POETASTER	POETASTERS · POETASTERY
	POETIC	POETICS
	POETICAL	POETICALS
	POETICISE	POETICISED · POETICISES
	POETICISM	POETICISMS
	POETICIZE	POETICIZED · POETICIZES
	POETICULE	POETICULES
	POETISE	POETISED · POETISER · POETISES
	POETISER	POETISERS
	POETIZE	POETIZED · POETIZER · POETIZES
	POETIZER	POETIZERS
	POETRESSE	POETRESSES
	POETSHIP	POETSHIPS
	POFFLE	POFFLES
	POGEY	POGEYS
	POGGE	POGGES
	POGO	POGOS
	POGOER	POGOERS
	POGONIA	POGONIAS
	POGONIP	POGONIPS
	POGROM	POGROMS
	POGROMIST	POGROMISTS
	POHIRI	POHIRIS
	POI	POIS
	POIGNANCE	POIGNANCES
	POILU	POILUS
	POINCIANA	POINCIANAS
	POIND	POINDS
	POINDER	POINDERS
	POINDING	POINDINGS
	POINT	POINTE · POINTS · POINTY
	POINTE	POINTED · POINTEL · POINTER · POINTES
	POINTEL	POINTELS
	POINTELLE	POINTELLES
	POINTER	POINTERS
	POINTING	POINTINGS
	POIS	POISE
	POISE	POISED · POISER · POISES
	POISER	POISERS
	POISON	POISONS
	POISONER	POISONERS
	POISSON	POISSONS
	POITIN	POITINS
	POITREL	POITRELS
	POITRINE	POITRINES
	POKAL	POKALS
SPOKE	POKE	POKED · POKER · POKES · POKEY
SPOKED	POKED	
	POKEFUL	POKEFULS
	POKELOGAN	POKELOGANS
	POKER	POKERS
	POKEROOT	POKEROOTS
	POKERWORK	POKERWORKS
SPOKES	POKES	
	POKEWEED	POKEWEEDS
	POKEY	POKEYS

FRONT HOOK	ROOT WORD	END HOOK
	POKIE	POKIER ▪ POKIES
	POKIES	POKIEST
SPOKING	**POKING**	
	POL	POLE ▪ POLK ▪ POLL ▪ POLO ▪ POLS ▪ POLT ▪ POLY
	POLACCA	POLACCAS
	POLACRE	POLACRES
	POLAR	POLARS
	POLARISE	POLARISED ▪ POLARISER ▪ POLARISES
	POLARISER	POLARISERS
	POLARIZE	POLARIZED ▪ POLARIZER ▪ POLARIZES
	POLARIZER	POLARIZERS
	POLARON	POLARONS
	POLDER	POLDERS
	POLE	POLED ▪ POLER ▪ POLES ▪ POLEY
	POLEAX	POLEAXE
	POLEAXE	POLEAXED ▪ POLEAXES
	POLECAT	POLECATS
	POLEMARCH	POLEMARCHS
	POLEMIC	POLEMICS
	POLEMISE	POLEMISED ▪ POLEMISES
	POLEMIST	POLEMISTS
	POLEMIZE	POLEMIZED ▪ POLEMIZES
	POLENTA	POLENTAS
	POLER	POLERS
	POLESTAR	POLESTARS
	POLEY	POLEYN ▪ POLEYS
	POLEYN	POLEYNS
	POLIANITE	POLIANITES
	POLICE	POLICED ▪ POLICER ▪ POLICES
	POLICER	POLICERS
	POLICING	POLICINGS
	POLING	POLINGS
	POLIO	POLIOS
	POLIS	POLISH
	POLISHER	POLISHERS
	POLISHING	POLISHINGS
	POLITBURO	POLITBUROS
	POLITE	POLITER
	POLITESSE	POLITESSES
	POLITIC	POLITICK ▪ POLITICO ▪ POLITICS
APOLITICAL	**POLITICAL**	
	POLITICK	POLITICKS
	POLITICO	POLITICOS
	POLITIQUE	POLITIQUES
	POLJE	POLJES
	POLK	POLKA ▪ POLKS
	POLKA	POLKAS
	POLL	POLLS ▪ POLLY
	POLLACK	POLLACKS
	POLLAN	POLLANS
	POLLARD	POLLARDS
	POLLEE	POLLEES
	POLLEN	POLLENS ▪ POLLENT
	POLLENATE	POLLENATED ▪ POLLENATES
	POLLER	POLLERS
	POLLICIE	POLLICIES
	POLLINATE	POLLINATED ▪ POLLINATES
	POLLING	POLLINGS
	POLLINISE	POLLINISED ▪ POLLINISER ▪ POLLINISES
	POLLINIZE	POLLINIZED ▪ POLLINIZER ▪ POLLINIZES
	POLLIST	POLLISTS
	POLLIWIG	POLLIWIGS
	POLLIWOG	POLLIWOGS
	POLLOCK	POLLOCKS
	POLLSTER	POLLSTERS
	POLLTAKER	POLLTAKERS
	POLLUCITE	POLLUCITES
	POLLUSION	POLLUSIONS
	POLLUTANT	POLLUTANTS

P

FRONT HOOK	ROOT WORD	END HOOK
	POLLUTE	POLLUTED · POLLUTER · POLLUTES
	POLLUTER	POLLUTERS
	POLLUTION	POLLUTIONS
	POLLYANNA	POLLYANNAS
	POLLYWIG	POLLYWIGS
	POLLYWOG	POLLYWOGS
	POLO	POLOS
	POLOIST	POLOISTS
	POLONAISE	POLONAISES
	POLONIE	POLONIES
	POLONISE	POLONISED · POLONISES
	POLONISM	POLONISMS
	POLONIUM	POLONIUMS
	POLONIZE	POLONIZED · POLONIZES
	POLT	POLTS
	POLTROON	POLTROONS
	POLVERINE	POLVERINES
	POLY	POLYP · POLYS
	POLYAMIDE	POLYAMIDES
	POLYAMINE	POLYAMINES
	POLYANTHA	POLYANTHAS
	POLYARCH	POLYARCHY
	POLYAXIAL	POLYAXIALS
	POLYAXON	POLYAXONS
	POLYBRID	POLYBRIDS
	POLYCHETE	POLYCHETES
	POLYCOT	POLYCOTS
	POLYENE	POLYENES
	POLYESTER	POLYESTERS
	POLYGALA	POLYGALAS
	POLYGAM	POLYGAMS · POLYGAMY
	POLYGENE	POLYGENES
	POLYGLOT	POLYGLOTS · POLYGLOTT
	POLYGLOTT	POLYGLOTTS
	POLYGON	POLYGONS · POLYGONY
	POLYGONUM	POLYGONUMS
	POLYGRAPH	POLYGRAPHS · POLYGRAPHY
	POLYHEDRA	POLYHEDRAL
	POLYIMIDE	POLYIMIDES
	POLYLEMMA	POLYLEMMAS
	POLYMATH	POLYMATHS · POLYMATHY
	POLYMER	POLYMERS · POLYMERY
	POLYMORPH	POLYMORPHS
	POLYMYXIN	POLYMYXINS
	POLYNIA	POLYNIAS
	POLYNYA	POLYNYAS
	POLYOL	POLYOLS
	POLYOMA	POLYOMAS
	POLYOMINO	POLYOMINOS
	POLYONYM	POLYONYMS · POLYONYMY
	POLYP	POLYPE · POLYPI · POLYPS
	POLYPE	POLYPED · POLYPES
	POLYPED	POLYPEDS
	POLYPHON	POLYPHONE · POLYPHONS · POLYPHONY
	POLYPHONE	POLYPHONES
	POLYPIDE	POLYPIDES
	POLYPIDOM	POLYPIDOMS
	POLYPILL	POLYPILLS
	POLYPITE	POLYPITES
	POLYPLOID	POLYPLOIDS · POLYPLOIDY
	POLYPNEA	POLYPNEAS
	POLYPOD	POLYPODS · POLYPODY
	POLYPORE	POLYPORES
	POLYPTYCH	POLYPTYCHS
	POLYSEME	POLYSEMES
	POLYSOME	POLYSOMES
	POLYSOMIC	POLYSOMICS
	POLYTHENE	POLYTHENES
	POLYTYPE	POLYTYPES

P

FRONT HOOK	ROOT WORD	END HOOK
	POLYURIA	POLYURIAS
	POLYVINYL	POLYVINYLS
	POLYWATER	POLYWATERS
	POLYZOA	POLYZOAN
	POLYZOAN	POLYZOANS
	POM	POME ▪ POMO ▪ POMP ▪ POMS
	POMACE	POMACES
	POMADE	POMADED ▪ POMADES
	POMANDER	POMANDERS
	POMATUM	POMATUMS
	POMBE	POMBES
	POME	POMES
	POMELO	POMELOS
	POMEROY	POMEROYS
	POMFRET	POMFRETS
	POMMEL	POMMELE ▪ POMMELS
	POMMELE	POMMELED
	POMMIE	POMMIES (offensive)
	POMO	POMOS
	POMOERIUM	POMOERIUMS
	POMP	POMPS
	POMPADOUR	POMPADOURS
	POMPANO	POMPANOS
	POMPELO	POMPELOS
	POMPEY	POMPEYS
	POMPILID	POMPILIDS
	POMPION	POMPIONS
	POMPOM	POMPOMS
	POMPON	POMPONS
	POMPOON	POMPOONS
	POMROY	POMROYS
	POMWATER	POMWATERS
	PONCE	PONCED (offensive) ▪ PONCES (offensive) PONCEY
	PONCEAU	PONCEAUS ▪ PONCEAUX
	PONCHO	PONCHOS
	POND	PONDS
	PONDAGE	PONDAGES
	PONDER	PONDERS
	PONDERATE	PONDERATED ▪ PONDERATES
	PONDERER	PONDERERS
	PONDEROSA	PONDEROSAS
	PONDOK	PONDOKS
	PONDOKKIE	PONDOKKIES
	PONDWEED	PONDWEEDS
	PONE	PONES ▪ PONEY
	PONEY	PONEYS
	PONG	PONGA ▪ PONGO ▪ PONGS ▪ PONGY
	PONGA	PONGAS
SPONGED	**PONGED**	
	PONGEE	PONGEES
	PONGID	PONGIDS
SPONGIER	**PONGIER**	
SPONGIEST	**PONGIEST**	
SPONGING	**PONGING**	
	PONGO	PONGOS
SPONGY	**PONGY**	
	PONIARD	PONIARDS
	PONK	PONKS
	PONT	PONTS ▪ PONTY
	PONTAGE	PONTAGES
	PONTIANAC	PONTIANACS
	PONTIANAK	PONTIANAKS
	PONTIE	PONTIES
	PONTIFF	PONTIFFS
	PONTIFIC	PONTIFICE
	PONTIFICE	PONTIFICES
	PONTIL	PONTILE ▪ PONTILS
	PONTILE	PONTILES

P

FRONT HOOK	ROOT WORD	END HOOK
	PONTON	PONTONS
	PONTONEER	PONTONEERS
	PONTONIER	PONTONIERS
SPONTOON	**PONTOON**	PONTOONS
	PONTOONER	PONTOONERS
SPONTOONS	**PONTOONS**	
	PONYSKIN	PONYSKINS
	PONYTAIL	PONYTAILS
	PONZU	PONZUS
	POO	POOD ▪ POOF ▪ POOH ▪ POOK ▪ POOL POON ▪ POOP ▪ POOR ▪ POOS ▪ POOT
	POOD	POODS
	POODLE	POODLES
SPOOF	**POOF**	POOFS (offensive) ▪ POOFY (offensive)
SPOOFS	**POOFS**	
	POOFTAH	POOFTAHS (offensive)
	POOFTER	POOFTERS (offensive)
SPOOFY	**POOFY**	
	POOGYE	POOGYES
	POOH	POOHS
	POOJA	POOJAH ▪ POOJAS
	POOJAH	POOJAHS
SPOOK	**POOK**	POOKA ▪ POOKS
	POOKA	POOKAS
SPOOKING	**POOKING**	
SPOOKS	**POOKS**	
SPOOL	**POOL**	POOLS
SPOOLED	**POOLED**	
SPOOLER	**POOLER**	POOLERS
SPOOLERS	**POOLERS**	
	POOLHALL	POOLHALLS
SPOOLING	**POOLING**	
	POOLROOM	POOLROOMS
SPOOLS	**POOLS**	
	POOLSIDE	POOLSIDES
SPOON	**POON**	POONS
	POONAC	POONACS
	POONCE	POONCED (offensive) ▪ POONCES (offensive)
SPOONS	**POONS**	
	POONTANG	POONTANGS (offensive)
APOOP	**POOP**	POOPS
	POOPER	POOPERS
SPOOR	**POOR**	POORI ▪ POORT
SPOORER	**POORER**	
	POORHOUSE	POORHOUSES
	POORI	POORIS
	POORIS	POORISH
	POORMOUTH	POORMOUTHS
	POORT	POORTS
	POORTITH	POORTITHS
	POORWILL	POORWILLS
SPOOT	**POOT**	POOTS
	POOTER	POOTERS
	POOTLE	POOTLED ▪ POOTLES
SPOOTS	**POOTS**	
	POOVE	POOVES (offensive)
	POP	POPE ▪ POPS
	POPADUM	POPADUMS
	POPCORN	POPCORNS
	POPE	POPES
	POPEDOM	POPEDOMS
	POPEHOOD	POPEHOODS
	POPELING	POPELINGS (offensive)
	POPERA	POPERAS
	POPERIN	POPERINS
	POPESHIP	POPESHIPS
	POPETTE	POPETTES
	POPGUN	POPGUNS
	POPINJAY	POPINJAYS

FRONT HOOK	ROOT WORD	END HOOK
	POPJOY	POPJOYS
	POPLAR	POPLARS
	POPLIN	POPLINS
	POPOVER	POPOVERS
	POPPA	POPPAS
	POPPADOM	POPPADOMS
	POPPADUM	POPPADUMS
	POPPER	POPPERS
	POPPERING	POPPERINGS
	POPPET	POPPETS
	POPPIES	POPPIEST
	POPPIT	POPPITS
	POPPLE	POPPLED · POPPLES
	POPPYCOCK	POPPYCOCKS
	POPPYHEAD	POPPYHEADS
	POPRIN	POPRINS
	POPS	POPSY
	POPSICLE	POPSICLES
	POPSIE	POPSIES
	POPSTER	POPSTERS
	POPULACE	POPULACES
	POPULAR	POPULARS
	POPULATE	POPULATED · POPULATES
	POPULISM	POPULISMS
	POPULIST	POPULISTS
SPORAL	**PORAL**	
	PORBEAGLE	PORBEAGLES
	PORCELAIN	PORCELAINS
	PORCINI	PORCINIS
	PORCUPINE	PORCUPINES
SPORE	**PORE**	PORED · PORER · PORES
SPORED	**PORED**	
	PORER	PORERS
SPORES	**PORES**	
	PORGE	PORGED · PORGES
	PORGIE	PORGIES
	PORIFER	PORIFERS
	PORIFERAN	PORIFERANS
	PORINA	PORINAS
SPORING	**PORING**	
	PORISM	PORISMS
	PORK	PORKS · PORKY
	PORKER	PORKERS
	PORKIES	PORKIEST
	PORKLING	PORKLINGS
	PORKPIE	PORKPIES
	PORKWOOD	PORKWOODS
	PORN	PORNO · PORNS · PORNY
	PORNO	PORNOS
	PORNOMAG	PORNOMAGS
	POROMERIC	POROMERICS
	POROSCOPE	POROSCOPES
	POROSE	POROSES
	PORPESS	PORPESSE
	PORPESSE	PORPESSES
	PORPHYRIA	PORPHYRIAS
	PORPHYRIN	PORPHYRINS
	PORPHYRIO	PORPHYRIOS
	PORPOISE	PORPOISED · PORPOISES
	PORRECT	PORRECTS
	PORRENGER	PORRENGERS
	PORRIDGE	PORRIDGES
	PORRIGO	PORRIGOS
	PORRINGER	PORRINGERS
APORT · SPORT	**PORT**	PORTA · PORTS · PORTY
	PORTA	PORTAL · PORTAS
SPORTABLE	**PORTABLE**	PORTABLES
	PORTAGE	PORTAGED · PORTAGES
	PORTAGUE	PORTAGUES

P

FRONT HOOK	ROOT WORD	END HOOK
	PORTAL	PORTALS
SPORTANCE	**PORTANCE**	PORTANCES
SPORTANCES	**PORTANCES**	
	PORTAPACK	PORTAPACKS
	PORTAPAK	PORTAPAKS
	PORTATIVE	PORTATIVES
SPORTED	**PORTED**	
	PORTEND	PORTENDS
	PORTENT	PORTENTS
SPORTER	**PORTER**	PORTERS
	PORTERAGE	PORTERAGES
SPORTERS	**PORTERS**	
	PORTESS	PORTESSE
	PORTESSE	PORTESSES
	PORTFIRE	PORTFIRES
	PORTFOLIO	PORTFOLIOS
	PORTHOLE	PORTHOLES
	PORTHOUSE	PORTHOUSES
	PORTICO	PORTICOS
SPORTIER	**PORTIER**	PORTIERE
	PORTIERE	PORTIERED ▪ PORTIERES
SPORTIEST	**PORTIEST**	
	PORTIGUE	PORTIGUES
SPORTING	**PORTING**	
	PORTION	PORTIONS
	PORTIONER	PORTIONERS
	PORTLAND	PORTLANDS
	PORTLAST	PORTLASTS
SPORTLESS	**PORTLESS**	
	PORTOISE	PORTOISES
	PORTOLAN	PORTOLANI ▪ PORTOLANO ▪ PORTOLANS
	PORTOLANO	PORTOLANOS
	PORTRAIT	PORTRAITS
	PORTRAY	PORTRAYS
	PORTRAYAL	PORTRAYALS
	PORTRAYER	PORTRAYERS
	PORTREEVE	PORTREEVES
SPORTS	**PORTS**	
	PORTULACA	PORTULACAS
	PORTULAN	PORTULANS
SPORTY	**PORTY**	
	PORWIGGLE	PORWIGGLES
APOS ▪ EPOS	**POS**	POSE ▪ POSH ▪ POSS ▪ POST ▪ POSY
	POSADA	POSADAS
	POSAUNE	POSAUNES
	POSE	POSED ▪ POSER ▪ POSES ▪ POSEY
	POSER	POSERS
EPOSES	**POSES**	
	POSEUR	POSEURS
	POSEUSE	POSEUSES
SPOSH	**POSH**	POSHO
SPOSHES	**POSHES**	POSHEST
	POSHO	POSHOS
	POSHTEEN	POSHTEENS
	POSIES	POSIEST
	POSING	POSINGS
	POSIT	POSITS
	POSITIF	POSITIFS
	POSITION	POSITIONS
	POSITIVE	POSITIVER ▪ POSITIVES
	POSITIVES	POSITIVEST
	POSITON	POSITONS
	POSITRON	POSITRONS
	POSNET	POSNETS
	POSOLE	POSOLES
	POSS	POSSE
	POSSE	POSSED ▪ POSSER ▪ POSSES ▪ POSSET
	POSSER	POSSERS
	POSSES	POSSESS

P

FRONT HOOK	ROOT WORD	END HOOK
	POSSESSOR	POSSESSORS · POSSESSORY
	POSSET	POSSETS
	POSSIBLE	POSSIBLER · POSSIBLES
	POSSIBLES	POSSIBLEST
	POSSIE	POSSIES
OPOSSUM	**POSSUM**	POSSUMS
OPOSSUMS	**POSSUMS**	
	POST	POSTS
	POSTAGE	POSTAGES
	POSTAL	POSTALS
	POSTBAG	POSTBAGS
	POSTBOY	POSTBOYS
	POSTCARD	POSTCARDS
	POSTCAVA	POSTCAVAE · POSTCAVAL · POSTCAVAS
	POSTCODE	POSTCODED · POSTCODES
	POSTDATE	POSTDATED · POSTDATES
	POSTDOC	POSTDOCS
	POSTEEN	POSTEENS
	POSTER	POSTERN · POSTERS
	POSTERIOR	POSTERIORS
	POSTERN	POSTERNS
	POSTFACE	POSTFACES
	POSTFORM	POSTFORMS
	POSTGRAD	POSTGRADS
	POSTHASTE	POSTHASTES
	POSTHEAT	POSTHEATS
	POSTHOLE	POSTHOLES
	POSTHORSE	POSTHORSES
	POSTHOUSE	POSTHOUSES
	POSTICHE	POSTICHES
	POSTIE	POSTIES
APOSTIL	**POSTIL**	POSTILS
	POSTILION	POSTILIONS
	POSTILLER	POSTILLERS
APOSTILS	**POSTILS**	
	POSTIN	POSTING · POSTINS
	POSTING	POSTINGS
	POSTIQUE	POSTIQUES
	POSTLUDE	POSTLUDES
	POSTMARK	POSTMARKS
	POSTOP	POSTOPS
	POSTPONE	POSTPONED · POSTPONER · POSTPONES
	POSTPONER	POSTPONERS
	POSTPOSE	POSTPOSED · POSTPOSES
	POSTRIDER	POSTRIDERS
	POSTSYNC	POSTSYNCS
	POSTTEEN	POSTTEENS
	POSTTEST	POSTTESTS
	POSTULANT	POSTULANTS
	POSTULATE	POSTULATED · POSTULATES
	POSTURE	POSTURED · POSTURER · POSTURES
	POSTURER	POSTURERS
	POSTURISE	POSTURISED · POSTURISES
	POSTURIST	POSTURISTS
	POSTURIZE	POSTURIZED · POSTURIZES
SPOT	**POT**	POTE · POTS · POTT
	POTABLE	POTABLES
	POTAE	POTAES
	POTAGE	POTAGER · POTAGES
	POTAGER	POTAGERS
	POTASS	POTASSA
	POTASSA	POTASSAS
	POTASSIUM	POTASSIUMS
	POTATION	POTATIONS
	POTATOBUG	POTATOBUGS
	POTBOIL	POTBOILS
	POTBOILER	POTBOILERS
	POTBOY	POTBOYS
	POTCH	POTCHE

P

FRONT HOOK	ROOT WORD	END HOOK
	POTCHE	POTCHED ▪ POTCHER ▪ POTCHES
	POTCHER	POTCHERS
	POTE	POTED ▪ POTES
	POTEEN	POTEENS
	POTENCE	POTENCES
	POTENT	POTENTS
	POTENTATE	POTENTATES
	POTENTIAL	POTENTIALS
	POTENTISE	POTENTISED ▪ POTENTISES
	POTENTIZE	POTENTIZED ▪ POTENTIZES
	POTFUL	POTFULS
	POTGUN	POTGUNS
	POTHEAD	POTHEADS
APOTHECARY	POTHECARY	
	POTHEEN	POTHEENS
	POTHER	POTHERB ▪ POTHERS ▪ POTHERY
	POTHERB	POTHERBS
	POTHOLDER	POTHOLDERS
	POTHOLE	POTHOLED ▪ POTHOLER ▪ POTHOLES
	POTHOLER	POTHOLERS
	POTHOLING	POTHOLINGS
	POTHOOK	POTHOOKS
	POTHOUSE	POTHOUSES
	POTHUNTER	POTHUNTERS
	POTICHE	POTICHES
	POTIN	POTING ▪ POTINS
	POTION	POTIONS
	POTLACH	POTLACHE
	POTLACHE	POTLACHES
	POTLINE	POTLINES
	POTLUCK	POTLUCKS
	POTOMETER	POTOMETERS
	POTOO	POTOOS
	POTOROO	POTOROOS
	POTPIE	POTPIES
	POTPOURRI	POTPOURRIS
SPOTS	POTS	POTSY
	POTSHARD	POTSHARDS
	POTSHARE	POTSHARES
	POTSHERD	POTSHERDS
	POTSHOP	POTSHOPS
	POTSHOT	POTSHOTS
	POTSIE	POTSIES
	POTSTONE	POTSTONES
	POTT	POTTO ▪ POTTS ▪ POTTY
	POTTAGE	POTTAGES
SPOTTED	POTTED	
	POTTEEN	POTTEENS
SPOTTER	POTTER	POTTERS ▪ POTTERY
	POTTERER	POTTERERS
	POTTERING	POTTERINGS
SPOTTERS	POTTERS	
SPOTTIER	POTTIER	
SPOTTIES	POTTIES	POTTIEST
SPOTTIEST	POTTIEST	
SPOTTINESS	POTTINESS	
SPOTTING	POTTING	
	POTTINGAR	POTTINGARS
	POTTINGER	POTTINGERS
	POTTLE	POTTLES
	POTTO	POTTOS
SPOTTY	POTTY	
	POTWALLER	POTWALLERS
	POTZER	POTZERS
	POUCH	POUCHY
	POUCHFUL	POUCHFULS
	POUDER	POUDERS
	POUDRE	POUDRES
	POUF	POUFF ▪ POUFS

FRONT HOOK	ROOT WORD	END HOOK
	POUFF	POUFFE · POUFFS · POUFFY (offensive)
	POUFFE	POUFFED · POUFFES
	POUFTAH	POUFTAHS (offensive)
	POUFTER	POUFTERS (offensive)
	POUK	POUKE · POUKS
	POUKE	POUKES
	POULAINE	POULAINES
	POULARD	POULARDE · POULARDS
	POULARDE	POULARDES
	POULDER	POULDERS
	POULDRE	POULDRES
	POULDRON	POULDRONS
	POULE	POULES
	POULP	POULPE · POULPS
	POULPE	POULPES
	POULT	POULTS
	POULTER	POULTERS
	POULTERER	POULTERERS
	POULTICE	POULTICED · POULTICES
	POUNCE	POUNCED · POUNCER · POUNCES · POUNCET
	POUNCER	POUNCERS
	POUNCET	POUNCETS
	POUND	POUNDS
	POUNDAGE	POUNDAGES
	POUNDAL	POUNDALS
	POUNDCAKE	POUNDCAKES
	POUNDER	POUNDERS
	POUPE	POUPED · POUPES
	POUR	POURS
	POURBOIRE	POURBOIRES
	POURER	POURERS
	POURIE	POURIES
	POURING	POURINGS
	POURPOINT	POURPOINTS
	POURSEW	POURSEWS
	POURSUE	POURSUED · POURSUES
	POURSUIT	POURSUITS
	POURTRAY	POURTRAYD · POURTRAYS
	POUSOWDIE	POUSOWDIES
	POUSSE	POUSSES
	POUSSETTE	POUSSETTED · POUSSETTES
	POUSSIE	POUSSIES
	POUSSIN	POUSSINS
SPOUT	**POUT**	POUTS · POUTY
SPOUTED	**POUTED**	
SPOUTER	**POUTER**	POUTERS
SPOUTERS	**POUTERS**	
	POUTHER	POUTHERS
SPOUTIER	**POUTIER**	
SPOUTIEST	**POUTIEST**	
	POUTINE	POUTINES
SPOUTING	**POUTING**	POUTINGS
SPOUTINGS	**POUTINGS**	
SPOUTS	**POUTS**	
SPOUTY	**POUTY**	
	POW	POWN · POWS
	POWAN	POWANS
	POWDER	POWDERS · POWDERY
	POWDERER	POWDERERS
	POWELLISE	POWELLISED · POWELLISES
	POWELLITE	POWELLITES
	POWELLIZE	POWELLIZED · POWELLIZES
	POWER	POWERS
	POWERBOAT	POWERBOATS
	POWERPLAY	POWERPLAYS
	POWHIRI	POWHIRIS
	POWIN	POWINS
	POWN	POWND · POWNS · POWNY
	POWND	POWNDS

FRONT HOOK	ROOT WORD	END HOOK
	POWNEY	POWNEYS
	POWNIE	POWNIES
	POWRE	POWRED ▪ POWRES
	POWTER	POWTERS
	POWWOW	POWWOWS
	POX	POXY
EPOXY	POXY	
	POYNT	POYNTS
	POYOU	POYOUS
	POYSE	POYSED ▪ POYSES
	POYSON	POYSONS
	POZ	POZZ
	POZOLE	POZOLES
	POZZ	POZZY
	POZZOLAN	POZZOLANA ▪ POZZOLANS
	POZZOLANA	POZZOLANAS
	PRAAM	PRAAMS
	PRABBLE	PRABBLES
	PRACHARAK	PRACHARAKS
APRACTIC	PRACTIC	PRACTICE ▪ PRACTICK ▪ PRACTICS
	PRACTICAL	PRACTICALS
	PRACTICE	PRACTICED ▪ PRACTICER ▪ PRACTICES
	PRACTICER	PRACTICERS
	PRACTICK	PRACTICKS
	PRACTICUM	PRACTICUMS
	PRACTIQUE	PRACTIQUES
	PRACTISE	PRACTISED ▪ PRACTISER ▪ PRACTISES
	PRACTISER	PRACTISERS
	PRACTOLOL	PRACTOLOLS
SPRAD	PRAD	PRADS
	PRAEAMBLE	PRAEAMBLES
	PRAECIPE	PRAECIPES
	PRAEDIAL	PRAEDIALS
	PRAEFECT	PRAEFECTS
	PRAELECT	PRAELECTS
	PRAENOMEN	PRAENOMENS
	PRAETOR	PRAETORS
	PRAGMATIC	PRAGMATICS
	PRAHU	PRAHUS
	PRAIRIE	PRAIRIED ▪ PRAIRIES
UPRAISE	PRAISE	PRAISED ▪ PRAISER ▪ PRAISES
	PRAISEACH	PRAISEACHS
UPRAISED	PRAISED	
UPRAISER	PRAISER	PRAISERS
UPRAISERS	PRAISERS	
UPRAISES	PRAISES	
UPRAISING	PRAISING	PRAISINGS
	PRAJNA	PRAJNAS
	PRALINE	PRALINES
	PRAM	PRAMS
	PRANA	PRANAS
	PRANAYAMA	PRANAYAMAS
	PRANCE	PRANCED ▪ PRANCER ▪ PRANCES
	PRANCER	PRANCERS
	PRANCING	PRANCINGS
	PRANCK	PRANCKE ▪ PRANCKS
	PRANCKE	PRANCKED ▪ PRANCKES
SPRANG	PRANG	PRANGS
SPRANGS	PRANGS	
	PRANK	PRANKS ▪ PRANKY
	PRANKING	PRANKINGS
	PRANKLE	PRANKLED ▪ PRANKLES
	PRANKSTER	PRANKSTERS
	PRAO	PRAOS
	PRASE	PRASES
SPRAT	PRAT	PRATE ▪ PRATS ▪ PRATT ▪ PRATY
UPRATE	PRATE	PRATED ▪ PRATER ▪ PRATES
UPRATED	PRATED	
	PRATER	PRATERS

FRONT HOOK	ROOT WORD	END HOOK
UPRATES	**PRATES**	
	PRATFALL	PRATFALLS
	PRATIE	PRATIES
UPRATING	**PRATING**	PRATINGS
	PRATIQUE	PRATIQUES
SPRATS	**PRATS**	
	PRATT	PRATTS
SPRATTLE	**PRATTLE**	PRATTLED ▪ PRATTLER ▪ PRATTLES
SPRATTLED	**PRATTLED**	
	PRATTLER	PRATTLERS
SPRATTLES	**PRATTLES**	
SPRATTLING	**PRATTLING**	
	PRAU	PRAUS
	PRAUNCE	PRAUNCED ▪ PRAUNCES
	PRAWLE	PRAWLES
	PRAWLIN	PRAWLINS
	PRAWN	PRAWNS
	PRAWNER	PRAWNERS
SPRAY	**PRAY**	PRAYS
SPRAYED	**PRAYED**	
SPRAYER	**PRAYER**	PRAYERS
SPRAYERS	**PRAYERS**	
SPRAYING	**PRAYING**	PRAYINGS
SPRAYINGS	**PRAYINGS**	
SPRAYS	**PRAYS**	
	PRE	PREE ▪ PREM ▪ PREP ▪ PREX ▪ PREY ▪ PREZ
	PREABSORB	PREABSORBS
	PREACCUSE	PREACCUSED ▪ PREACCUSES
	PREACE	PREACED ▪ PREACES
UPREACH	**PREACH**	PREACHY
UPREACHED	**PREACHED**	
	PREACHER	PREACHERS
UPREACHES	**PREACHES**	
UPREACHING	**PREACHING**	PREACHINGS
	PREACT	PREACTS
	PREADAPT	PREADAPTS
	PREADJUST	PREADJUSTS
	PREADMIT	PREADMITS
	PREADOPT	PREADOPTS
	PREADULT	PREADULTS
	PREALLOT	PREALLOTS
	PREALTER	PREALTERS
	PREAMBLE	PREAMBLED ▪ PREAMBLES
	PREAMP	PREAMPS
	PREARM	PREARMS
	PREASE	PREASED ▪ PREASES
	PREASSE	PREASSED ▪ PREASSES
	PREASSIGN	PREASSIGNS
	PREASSURE	PREASSURED ▪ PREASSURES
	PREATTUNE	PREATTUNED ▪ PREATTUNES
	PREAUDIT	PREAUDITS
	PREAVER	PREAVERS
	PREBAKE	PREBAKED ▪ PREBAKES
	PREBEND	PREBENDS
	PREBID	PREBIDS
	PREBILL	PREBILLS
	PREBIND	PREBINDS
	PREBIRTH	PREBIRTHS
	PREBOARD	PREBOARDS
	PREBOIL	PREBOILS
	PREBOOK	PREBOOKS
	PREBUDGET	PREBUDGETS
	PREBUILD	PREBUILDS
	PREBUTTAL	PREBUTTALS
	PREBUY	PREBUYS
	PRECANCEL	PRECANCELS
	PRECANCER	PRECANCERS
	PRECAST	PRECASTS
	PRECAVA	PRECAVAE ▪ PRECAVAL

P

FRONT HOOK	ROOT WORD	END HOOK
	PRECEDE	PRECEDED · PRECEDES
	PRECEDENT	PRECEDENTS
	PRECENSOR	PRECENSORS
	PRECENT	PRECENTS
	PRECENTOR	PRECENTORS
	PRECEPIT	PRECEPITS
	PRECEPT	PRECEPTS
	PRECEPTOR	PRECEPTORS · PRECEPTORY
	PRECHARGE	PRECHARGED · PRECHARGES
	PRECHECK	PRECHECKS
	PRECHILL	PRECHILLS
	PRECHOOSE	PRECHOOSES
	PRECHOSE	PRECHOSEN
	PRECIEUSE	PRECIEUSES
	PRECINCT	PRECINCTS
	PRECIPE	PRECIPES
	PRECIPICE	PRECIPICED · PRECIPICES
	PRECIS	PRECISE
	PRECISE	PRECISED · PRECISER · PRECISES
	PRECISES	PRECISEST
	PRECISIAN	PRECISIANS
	PRECISION	PRECISIONS
	PRECLEAN	PRECLEANS
	PRECLEAR	PRECLEARS
	PRECLUDE	PRECLUDED · PRECLUDES
	PRECOCIAL	PRECOCIALS
	PRECODE	PRECODED · PRECODES
	PRECONISE	PRECONISED · PRECONISES
	PRECONIZE	PRECONIZED · PRECONIZES
	PRECOOK	PRECOOKS
	PRECOOKER	PRECOOKERS
	PRECOOL	PRECOOLS
	PRECREASE	PRECREASED · PRECREASES
	PRECURE	PRECURED · PRECURES
	PRECURRER	PRECURRERS
	PRECURSE	PRECURSES
	PRECURSOR	PRECURSORS · PRECURSORY
	PRECUT	PRECUTS
	PREDATE	PREDATED · PREDATES
	PREDATION	PREDATIONS
	PREDATISM	PREDATISMS
	PREDATOR	PREDATORS · PREDATORY
	PREDAWN	PREDAWNS
	PREDEATH	PREDEATHS
	PREDEDUCT	PREDEDUCTS
	PREDEFINE	PREDEFINED · PREDEFINES
	PREDELLA	PREDELLAS
	PREDESIGN	PREDESIGNS
	PREDIAL	PREDIALS
	PREDICANT	PREDICANTS
	PREDICATE	PREDICATED · PREDICATES
	PREDICT	PREDICTS
	PREDICTER	PREDICTERS
	PREDICTOR	PREDICTORS
	PREDIGEST	PREDIGESTS
	PREDIKANT	PREDIKANTS
	PREDINNER	PREDINNERS
	PREDOOM	PREDOOMS
	PREDRILL	PREDRILLS
	PREDUSK	PREDUSKS
SPREE	**PREE**	PREED · PREEN · PREES
SPREED	**PREED**	
	PREEDIT	PREEDITS
SPREEING	**PREEING**	
	PREELECT	PREELECTS
	PREEMIE	PREEMIES
	PREEMPT	PREEMPTS
	PREEMPTOR	PREEMPTORS
	PREEN	PREENS

FRONT HOOK	ROOT WORD	END HOOK
	PREENACT	PREENACTS
	PREENER	PREENERS
	PREERECT	PREERECTS
SPREES	**PREES**	
	PREEVE	PREEVED ▪ PREEVES
	PREEXCITE	PREEXCITED ▪ PREEXCITES
	PREEXEMPT	PREEXEMPTS
	PREEXIST	PREEXISTS
	PREEXPOSE	PREEXPOSED ▪ PREEXPOSES
	PREFAB	PREFABS
	PREFACE	PREFACED ▪ PREFACER ▪ PREFACES
	PREFACER	PREFACERS
	PREFADE	PREFADED ▪ PREFADES
	PREFECT	PREFECTS
	PREFER	PREFERS
	PREFERRER	PREFERRERS
	PREFIGURE	PREFIGURED ▪ PREFIGURES
	PREFILE	PREFILED ▪ PREFILES
	PREFIRE	PREFIRED ▪ PREFIRES
	PREFIXION	PREFIXIONS
	PREFLIGHT	PREFLIGHTS
	PREFORM	PREFORMS
	PREFORMAT	PREFORMATS
	PREFRANK	PREFRANKS
	PREFREEZE	PREFREEZES
	PREFROZE	PREFROZEN
	PREFUND	PREFUNDS
	PREGAME	PREGAMES
	PREGNANCE	PREGNANCES
	PREGROWTH	PREGROWTHS
	PREGUIDE	PREGUIDED ▪ PREGUIDES
	PREHANDLE	PREHANDLED ▪ PREHANDLES
	PREHARDEN	PREHARDENS
	PREHEAT	PREHEATS
	PREHEATER	PREHEATERS
	PREHEND	PREHENDS
	PREHENSOR	PREHENSORS ▪ PREHENSORY
	PREHNITE	PREHNITES
	PREHUMAN	PREHUMANS
	PREIF	PREIFE ▪ PREIFS
	PREIFE	PREIFES
	PREIMPOSE	PREIMPOSED ▪ PREIMPOSES
	PREINFORM	PREINFORMS
	PREINSERT	PREINSERTS
	PREINVITE	PREINVITED ▪ PREINVITES
	PREJUDGE	PREJUDGED ▪ PREJUDGER ▪ PREJUDGES
	PREJUDGER	PREJUDGERS
	PREJUDICE	PREJUDICED ▪ PREJUDICES
	PREJUDIZE	PREJUDIZES
	PRELATE	PRELATES
	PRELATES	PRELATESS
	PRELATION	PRELATIONS
	PRELATISE	PRELATISED ▪ PRELATISES
	PRELATISM	PRELATISMS
	PRELATIST	PRELATISTS
	PRELATIZE	PRELATIZED ▪ PRELATIZES
	PRELATURE	PRELATURES
	PRELECT	PRELECTS
	PRELECTOR	PRELECTORS
	PRELIM	PRELIMS
	PRELIMIT	PRELIMITS
	PRELOAD	PRELOADS
	PRELOCATE	PRELOCATED ▪ PRELOCATES
	PRELUDE	PRELUDED ▪ PRELUDER ▪ PRELUDES
	PRELUDER	PRELUDERS
	PRELUDI	PRELUDIO
	PRELUSION	PRELUSIONS
	PREM	PREMS ▪ PREMY
	PREMARKET	PREMARKETS

FRONT HOOK	ROOT WORD	END HOOK
	PREMATURE	PREMATURES
	PREMED	PREMEDS
	PREMEDIC	PREMEDICS
	PREMIE	PREMIER ▪ PREMIES
	PREMIER	PREMIERE ▪ PREMIERS
	PREMIERE	PREMIERED ▪ PREMIERES
	PREMISE	PREMISED ▪ PREMISES
	PREMIUM	PREMIUMS
	PREMIX	PREMIXT
	PREMOLAR	PREMOLARS
	PREMOLD	PREMOLDS
	PREMOTION	PREMOTIONS
	PREMOVE	PREMOVED ▪ PREMOVES
	PRENAME	PRENAMES
	PRENASAL	PRENASALS
	PRENATAL	PRENATALS
	PRENOMEN	PRENOMENS
	PRENOMINA	PRENOMINAL
	PRENOTION	PRENOTIONS
SPRENT	PRENT	PRENTS
	PRENTICE	PRENTICED ▪ PRENTICES
	PRENUMBER	PRENUMBERS
	PRENUP	PRENUPS
	PREOBTAIN	PREOBTAINS
	PREOP	PREOPS
	PREOPTION	PREOPTIONS
	PREORDAIN	PREORDAINS
	PREORDER	PREORDERS
	PREP	PREPS
	PREPACK	PREPACKS
	PREPARE	PREPARED ▪ PREPARER ▪ PREPARES
	PREPARER	PREPARERS
	PREPASTE	PREPASTED ▪ PREPASTES
	PREPAVE	PREPAVED ▪ PREPAVES
	PREPAY	PREPAYS
	PREPENSE	PREPENSED ▪ PREPENSES
	PREPLACE	PREPLACED ▪ PREPLACES
	PREPLAN	PREPLANS ▪ PREPLANT
	PREPONE	PREPONED ▪ PREPONES
	PREPOSE	PREPOSED ▪ PREPOSES
	PREPOSTOR	PREPOSTORS
	PREPPIE	PREPPIER ▪ PREPPIES
	PREPPIES	PREPPIEST
	PREPREG	PREPREGS
	PREPRICE	PREPRICED ▪ PREPRICES
	PREPRINT	PREPRINTS
	PREPUCE	PREPUCES
	PREPUPA	PREPUPAE ▪ PREPUPAL ▪ PREPUPAS
	PREQUEL	PREQUELS
	PRERECORD	PRERECORDS
	PRERINSE	PRERINSED ▪ PRERINSES
	PRESAGE	PRESAGED ▪ PRESAGER ▪ PRESAGES
	PRESAGER	PRESAGERS
	PRESALE	PRESALES
	PRESBYOPE	PRESBYOPES
	PRESBYTE	PRESBYTER ▪ PRESBYTES
	PRESBYTER	PRESBYTERS ▪ PRESBYTERY
	PRESCHOOL	PRESCHOOLS
	PRESCIND	PRESCINDS
	PRESCORE	PRESCORED ▪ PRESCORES
	PRESCREEN	PRESCREENS
	PRESCRIBE	PRESCRIBED ▪ PRESCRIBER ▪ PRESCRIBES
	PRESCRIPT	PRESCRIPTS
	PRESE	PRESES ▪ PRESET
	PRESEASON	PRESEASONS
	PRESELECT	PRESELECTS
	PRESELL	PRESELLS
	PRESENCE	PRESENCES
	PRESENT	PRESENTS

FRONT HOOK	ROOT WORD	END HOOK
	PRESENTEE	PRESENTEES
	PRESENTER	PRESENTERS
	PRESERVE	PRESERVED ▪ PRESERVER ▪ PRESERVES
	PRESERVER	PRESERVERS
	PRESET	PRESETS
	PRESETTLE	PRESETTLED ▪ PRESETTLES
	PRESHAPE	PRESHAPED ▪ PRESHAPES
	PRESHIP	PRESHIPS
	PRESHOW	PRESHOWN ▪ PRESHOWS
	PRESHRINK	PRESHRINKS
	PRESIDE	PRESIDED ▪ PRESIDER ▪ PRESIDES
	PRESIDENT	PRESIDENTS
	PRESIDER	PRESIDERS
	PRESIDIA	PRESIDIAL
	PRESIDIO	PRESIDIOS
	PRESIDIUM	PRESIDIUMS
	PRESIFT	PRESIFTS
	PRESIGNAL	PRESIGNALS
	PRESLICE	PRESLICED ▪ PRESLICES
	PRESOAK	PRESOAKS
	PRESOLVE	PRESOLVED ▪ PRESOLVES
	PRESORT	PRESORTS
	PRESSER	PRESSERS
	PRESSFAT	PRESSFATS
	PRESSFUL	PRESSFULS
	PRESSGANG	PRESSGANGS
	PRESSIE	PRESSIES
	PRESSING	PRESSINGS
	PRESSION	PRESSIONS
	PRESSMARK	PRESSMARKS
	PRESSOR	PRESSORS
	PRESSROOM	PRESSROOMS
	PRESSRUN	PRESSRUNS
	PRESSURE	PRESSURED ▪ PRESSURES
	PRESSWORK	PRESSWORKS
UPREST	**PREST**	PRESTO ▪ PRESTS
	PRESTAMP	PRESTAMPS
	PRESTER	PRESTERS
	PRESTIGE	PRESTIGES
	PRESTO	PRESTOS
	PRESTORE	PRESTORED ▪ PRESTORES
UPRESTS	**PRESTS**	
	PRESUME	PRESUMED ▪ PRESUMER ▪ PRESUMES
	PRESUMER	PRESUMERS
	PRESUMMIT	PRESUMMITS
	PRESURVEY	PRESURVEYS
	PRETAPE	PRETAPED ▪ PRETAPES
	PRETASTE	PRETASTED ▪ PRETASTES
	PRETEEN	PRETEENS
	PRETELL	PRETELLS
	PRETENCE	PRETENCES
	PRETEND	PRETENDS
	PRETENDER	PRETENDERS
	PRETENSE	PRETENSES
	PRETERIST	PRETERISTS
	PRETERIT	PRETERITE ▪ PRETERITS
	PRETERITE	PRETERITES
	PRETERM	PRETERMS
	PRETERMIT	PRETERMITS
	PRETEST	PRETESTS
	PRETEXT	PRETEXTS
	PRETOR	PRETORS
	PRETORIAN	PRETORIANS
	PRETRAIN	PRETRAINS
	PRETREAT	PRETREATS
	PRETRIAL	PRETRIALS
	PRETRIM	PRETRIMS
	PRETTIES	PRETTIEST
	PRETTYISM	PRETTYISMS

FRONT HOOK	ROOT WORD	END HOOK
	PRETYPE	PRETYPED · PRETYPES
	PRETZEL	PRETZELS
	PREUNION	PREUNIONS
	PREUNITE	PREUNITED · PREUNITES
	PREVAIL	PREVAILS
	PREVAILER	PREVAILERS
	PREVALENT	PREVALENTS
	PREVALUE	PREVALUED · PREVALUES
	PREVE	PREVED · PREVES
	PREVENE	PREVENED · PREVENES
	PREVENT	PREVENTS
	PREVENTER	PREVENTERS
	PREVERB	PREVERBS
	PREVIEW	PREVIEWS
	PREVIEWER	PREVIEWERS
	PREVISE	PREVISED · PREVISES
	PREVISION	PREVISIONS
	PREVISIT	PREVISITS
	PREVISOR	PREVISORS
	PREVUE	PREVUED · PREVUES
	PREWAR	PREWARM · PREWARN
	PREWARM	PREWARMS
	PREWARN	PREWARNS
	PREWEIGH	PREWEIGHS
	PREWIRE	PREWIRED · PREWIRES
	PREWORK	PREWORKS
	PREWRAP	PREWRAPS
	PREWYN	PREWYNS
	PREX	PREXY
	PREY	PREYS
	PREYER	PREYERS
	PREZZIE	PREZZIES
	PRIAL	PRIALS
	PRIAPI	PRIAPIC
	PRIAPISM	PRIAPISMS
	PRIBBLE	PRIBBLES
	PRICE	PRICED · PRICER · PRICES · PRICEY
	PRICER	PRICERS
	PRICING	PRICINGS
	PRICK	PRICKS · PRICKY
	PRICKER	PRICKERS
	PRICKET	PRICKETS
	PRICKING	PRICKINGS
	PRICKLE	PRICKLED · PRICKLES
	PRICKLING	PRICKLINGS
	PRICKWOOD	PRICKWOODS
	PRIDE	PRIDED · PRIDES
	PRIEDIEU	PRIEDIEUS · PRIEDIEUX
	PRIEF	PRIEFE · PRIEFS
	PRIEFE	PRIEFES
SPRIER	PRIER	PRIERS
	PRIES	PRIEST
SPRIEST	PRIEST	PRIESTS
	PRIEVE	PRIEVED · PRIEVES
SPRIG	PRIG	PRIGS
SPRIGGED	PRIGGED	
SPRIGGER	PRIGGER	PRIGGERS · PRIGGERY
SPRIGGERS	PRIGGERS	
SPRIGGING	PRIGGING	PRIGGINGS
	PRIGGISM	PRIGGISMS
SPRIGS	PRIGS	
	PRILL	PRILLS
	PRIM	PRIMA · PRIME · PRIMI · PRIMO · PRIMP PRIMS · PRIMY
	PRIMA	PRIMAL · PRIMAS
	PRIMAGE	PRIMAGES
	PRIMATAL	PRIMATALS
	PRIMATE	PRIMATES
	PRIMATIAL	PRIMATIALS

FRONT HOOK	ROOT WORD	END HOOK
	PRIMAVERA	PRIMAVERAS
	PRIME	PRIMED ▪ PRIMER ▪ PRIMES
	PRIMER	PRIMERO ▪ PRIMERS
	PRIMERO	PRIMEROS
	PRIMEUR	PRIMEURS
	PRIMINE	PRIMINES
	PRIMING	PRIMINGS
	PRIMIPARA	PRIMIPARAE ▪ PRIMIPARAS
	PRIMITIVE	PRIMITIVES
	PRIMMER	PRIMMERS
	PRIMO	PRIMOS
	PRIMORDIA	PRIMORDIAL
	PRIMP	PRIMPS
	PRIMROSE	PRIMROSED ▪ PRIMROSES
	PRIMSIE	PRIMSIER
	PRIMULA	PRIMULAS
	PRIMULINE	PRIMULINES
	PRINCE	PRINCED ▪ PRINCES
	PRINCEDOM	PRINCEDOMS
	PRINCEKIN	PRINCEKINS
	PRINCELET	PRINCELETS
	PRINCES	PRINCESS
	PRINCESS	PRINCESSE
	PRINCESSE	PRINCESSES
	PRINCIPAL	PRINCIPALS
	PRINCIPI	PRINCIPIA
	PRINCIPIA	PRINCIPIAL
	PRINCIPLE	PRINCIPLED ▪ PRINCIPLES
	PRINCOCK	PRINCOCKS
	PRINK	PRINKS
	PRINKER	PRINKERS
SPRINT	**PRINT**	PRINTS
SPRINTED	**PRINTED**	
SPRINTER	**PRINTER**	PRINTERS ▪ PRINTERY
SPRINTERS	**PRINTERS**	
	PRINTHEAD	PRINTHEADS
SPRINTING	**PRINTING**	PRINTINGS
SPRINTINGS	**PRINTINGS**	
	PRINTOUT	PRINTOUTS
SPRINTS	**PRINTS**	
	PRION	PRIONS
	PRIOR	PRIORS ▪ PRIORY
	PRIORATE	PRIORATES
APRIORITY	**PRIORITY**	
	PRIORSHIP	PRIORSHIPS
	PRISAGE	PRISAGES
EPRISE ▪ UPRISE	**PRISE**	PRISED ▪ PRISER ▪ PRISES
UPRISER	**PRISER**	PRISERE ▪ PRISERS
	PRISERE	PRISERES
UPRISERS	**PRISERS**	
UPRISES	**PRISES**	
UPRISING	**PRISING**	
	PRISM	PRISMS ▪ PRISMY
	PRISMOID	PRISMOIDS
	PRISON	PRISONS
	PRISONER	PRISONERS
	PRISS	PRISSY
	PRISSIES	PRISSIEST
	PRISTANE	PRISTANES
	PRIVADO	PRIVADOS
	PRIVATE	PRIVATER ▪ PRIVATES
	PRIVATEER	PRIVATEERS
	PRIVATES	PRIVATEST
	PRIVATION	PRIVATIONS
	PRIVATISE	PRIVATISED ▪ PRIVATISER ▪ PRIVATISES
	PRIVATISM	PRIVATISMS
	PRIVATIST	PRIVATISTS
	PRIVATIVE	PRIVATIVES
	PRIVATIZE	PRIVATIZED ▪ PRIVATIZER ▪ PRIVATIZES

FRONT HOOK	ROOT WORD	END HOOK
	PRIVET	PRIVETS
	PRIVIES	PRIVIEST
	PRIVILEGE	PRIVILEGED ▪ PRIVILEGES
	PRIZE	PRIZED ▪ PRIZER ▪ PRIZES
	PRIZER	PRIZERS
	PRO	PROA ▪ PROB ▪ PROD ▪ PROF ▪ PROG
		PROM ▪ PROO ▪ PROP ▪ PROS ▪ PROW
	PROA	PROAS
	PROACTION	PROACTIONS
	PROB	PROBE ▪ PROBS
	PROBABLE	PROBABLES
	PROBAND	PROBANDS
	PROBANG	PROBANGS
	PROBATE	PROBATED ▪ PROBATES
	PROBATION	PROBATIONS
	PROBE	PROBED ▪ PROBER ▪ PROBES
	PROBER	PROBERS
	PROBIOTIC	PROBIOTICS
	PROBIT	PROBITS ▪ PROBITY
	PROBLEM	PROBLEMS
	PROCAINE	PROCAINES
	PROCAMBIA	PROCAMBIAL
	PROCARP	PROCARPS
	PROCARYON	PROCARYONS
	PROCEDURE	PROCEDURES
	PROCEED	PROCEEDS
	PROCEEDER	PROCEEDERS
	PROCESSER	PROCESSERS
	PROCESSOR	PROCESSORS
	PROCINCT	PROCINCTS
	PROCLAIM	PROCLAIMS
	PROCLITIC	PROCLITICS
	PROCONSUL	PROCONSULS
	PROCREANT	PROCREANTS
	PROCREATE	PROCREATED ▪ PROCREATES
	PROCTOR	PROCTORS
	PROCURAL	PROCURALS
	PROCURE	PROCURED ▪ PROCURER ▪ PROCURES
	PROCURER	PROCURERS
	PROCURES	PROCURESS
	PROCUREUR	PROCUREURS
SPROD	PROD	PRODS
	PRODDER	PRODDERS
	PRODIGAL	PRODIGALS
	PRODITOR	PRODITORS ▪ PRODITORY
	PRODNOSE	PRODNOSED ▪ PRODNOSES
	PRODROME	PRODROMES
	PRODROMI	PRODROMIC
	PRODRUG	PRODRUGS
SPRODS	PRODS	
	PRODUCE	PRODUCED ▪ PRODUCER ▪ PRODUCES
	PRODUCER	PRODUCERS
	PRODUCT	PRODUCTS
	PROEM	PROEMS
	PROEMBRYO	PROEMBRYOS
	PROENZYME	PROENZYMES
	PROETTE	PROETTES
	PROF	PROFS
	PROFANE	PROFANED ▪ PROFANER ▪ PROFANES
	PROFANER	PROFANERS
	PROFESSOR	PROFESSORS
	PROFFER	PROFFERS
	PROFFERER	PROFFERERS
	PROFILE	PROFILED ▪ PROFILER ▪ PROFILES
	PROFILER	PROFILERS
	PROFILING	PROFILINGS
	PROFILIST	PROFILISTS
	PROFIT	PROFITS
	PROFITEER	PROFITEERS

FRONT HOOK	ROOT WORD	END HOOK
	PROFITER	PROFITERS
	PROFITING	PROFITINGS
	PROFORMA	PROFORMAS
	PROFOUND	PROFOUNDS
	PROFUSE	PROFUSER
	PROFUSER	PROFUSERS
	PROFUSION	PROFUSIONS
SPROG	**PROG**	PROGS
	PROGERIA	PROGERIAS
	PROGESTIN	PROGESTINS
	PROGGER	PROGGERS
	PROGNOSE	PROGNOSED · PROGNOSES
	PROGRADE	PROGRADED · PROGRADES
	PROGRAM	PROGRAMS
	PROGRAMER	PROGRAMERS
	PROGRAMME	PROGRAMMED · PROGRAMMER · PROGRAMMES
SPROGS	**PROGS**	
	PROHIBIT	PROHIBITS
	PROIGN	PROIGNS
	PROIN	PROINE · PROINS
	PROINE	PROINED · PROINES
	PROJECT	PROJECTS
	PROJECTOR	PROJECTORS
	PROJET	PROJETS
	PROKARYON	PROKARYONS
	PROKARYOT	PROKARYOTE · PROKARYOTS
	PROKE	PROKED · PROKER · PROKES
	PROKER	PROKERS
	PROLACTIN	PROLACTINS
	PROLAMIN	PROLAMINE · PROLAMINS
	PROLAMINE	PROLAMINES
	PROLAN	PROLANS
	PROLAPSE	PROLAPSED · PROLAPSES
	PROLATE	PROLATED · PROLATES
	PROLATION	PROLATIONS
	PROLE	PROLED · PROLEG · PROLER · PROLES
	PROLEG	PROLEGS
	PROLER	PROLERS
	PROLICIDE	PROLICIDES
	PROLINE	PROLINES
UPROLL	**PROLL**	PROLLS
UPROLLED	**PROLLED**	
	PROLLER	PROLLERS
UPROLLING	**PROLLING**	
UPROLLS	**PROLLS**	
	PROLOG	PROLOGS
	PROLOGISE	PROLOGISED · PROLOGISES
	PROLOGIST	PROLOGISTS
	PROLOGIZE	PROLOGIZED · PROLOGIZES
	PROLOGUE	PROLOGUED · PROLOGUES
	PROLONG	PROLONGE · PROLONGS
	PROLONGE	PROLONGED · PROLONGER · PROLONGES
	PROLONGER	PROLONGERS
	PROLUSION	PROLUSIONS
EPROM	**PROM**	PROMO · PROMS
	PROMENADE	PROMENADED · PROMENADER · PROMENADES
	PROMETAL	PROMETALS
	PROMINE	PROMINES
	PROMISE	PROMISED · PROMISEE · PROMISER PROMISES
	PROMISEE	PROMISEES
	PROMISER	PROMISERS
	PROMISOR	PROMISORS
	PROMISSOR	PROMISSORS · PROMISSORY
	PROMMER	PROMMERS
	PROMO	PROMOS
	PROMOTE	PROMOTED · PROMOTER · PROMOTES
	PROMOTER	PROMOTERS
	PROMOTION	PROMOTIONS

FRONT HOOK	ROOT WORD	END HOOK
	PROMOTOR	PROMOTORS
	PROMPT	PROMPTS
	PROMPTER	PROMPTERS
	PROMPTING	PROMPTINGS
	PROMPTURE	PROMPTURES
EPROMS	**PROMS**	
	PROMULGE	PROMULGED · PROMULGES
	PRONATE	PRONATED · PRONATES
	PRONATION	PRONATIONS
	PRONATOR	PRONATORS
	PRONE	PRONER · PRONES
	PRONES	PRONEST
	PRONEUR	PRONEURS
SPRONG	**PRONG**	PRONGS
	PRONGBUCK	PRONGBUCKS
	PRONGHORN	PRONGHORNS
	PRONK	PRONKS
	PRONOTA	PRONOTAL
	PRONOUN	PRONOUNS
	PRONOUNCE	PRONOUNCED · PRONOUNCER · PRONOUNCES
	PRONUNCIO	PRONUNCIOS
	PROO	PROOF
	PROOEMION	PROOEMIONS
	PROOEMIUM	PROOEMIUMS
	PROOF	PROOFS
	PROOFER	PROOFERS
	PROOFING	PROOFINGS
	PROOFREAD	PROOFREADS
	PROOFROOM	PROOFROOMS
	PROOTIC	PROOTICS
	PROP	PROPS
	PROPAGATE	PROPAGATED · PROPAGATES
	PROPAGE	PROPAGED · PROPAGES
	PROPAGULE	PROPAGULES
	PROPALE	PROPALED · PROPALES
	PROPANE	PROPANES
	PROPANOL	PROPANOLS
	PROPANONE	PROPANONES
	PROPEL	PROPELS
	PROPELLER	PROPELLERS
	PROPELLOR	PROPELLORS
	PROPEND	PROPENDS
	PROPENE	PROPENES
	PROPENOL	PROPENOLS
	PROPER	PROPERS
	PROPERDIN	PROPERDINS
	PROPHAGE	PROPHAGES
	PROPHASE	PROPHASES
	PROPHET	PROPHETS
	PROPHYLL	PROPHYLLS
	PROPINE	PROPINED · PROPINES
	PROPJET	PROPJETS
	PROPODEON	PROPODEONS
	PROPODEUM	PROPODEUMS
	PROPONE	PROPONED · PROPONES
	PROPONENT	PROPONENTS
	PROPOSAL	PROPOSALS
	PROPOSE	PROPOSED · PROPOSER · PROPOSES
	PROPOSER	PROPOSERS
	PROPOSITA	PROPOSITAE
	PROPOUND	PROPOUNDS
	PROPPANT	PROPPANTS
	PROPRETOR	PROPRETORS
	PROPULSOR	PROPULSORS · PROPULSORY
	PROPYL	PROPYLA · PROPYLS
	PROPYLENE	PROPYLENES
	PROPYLITE	PROPYLITES
	PROPYLON	PROPYLONS
	PRORATE	PRORATED · PRORATES

P

FRONT HOOK	ROOT WORD	END HOOK
	PRORATION	PRORATIONS
	PRORE	PRORES
	PRORECTOR	PRORECTORS
	PROROGATE	PROROGATED · PROROGATES
	PROROGUE	PROROGUED · PROROGUES
	PROS	PROSE · PROSO · PROSS · PROST · PROSY
	PROSAISM	PROSAISMS
	PROSAIST	PROSAISTS
	PROSATEUR	PROSATEURS
	PROSCRIBE	PROSCRIBED · PROSCRIBER · PROSCRIBES
	PROSCRIPT	PROSCRIPTS
UPROSE	**PROSE**	PROSED · PROSER · PROSES
	PROSECT	PROSECTS
	PROSECTOR	PROSECTORS
	PROSECUTE	PROSECUTED · PROSECUTES
	PROSELYTE	PROSELYTED · PROSELYTES
	PROSER	PROSERS
	PROSEUCHA	PROSEUCHAE
	PROSIMIAN	PROSIMIANS
	PROSING	PROSINGS
	PROSO	PROSOS
	PROSODIAN	PROSODIANS
	PROSODIST	PROSODISTS
	PROSOMA	PROSOMAL · PROSOMAS
	PROSOPON	PROSOPONS
	PROSPECT	PROSPECTS
	PROSPER	PROSPERS
	PROSSIE	PROSSIES
	PROSTATE	PROSTATES
	PROSTIE	PROSTIES
	PROSTOMIA	PROSTOMIAL
	PROSTRATE	PROSTRATED · PROSTRATES
	PROSTYLE	PROSTYLES
	PROSUMER	PROSUMERS
	PROTAMIN	PROTAMINE · PROTAMINS
	PROTAMINE	PROTAMINES
	PROTANOPE	PROTANOPES
	PROTEA	PROTEAN · PROTEAS
	PROTEAN	PROTEANS
	PROTEAS	PROTEASE
	PROTEASE	PROTEASES
	PROTECT	PROTECTS
	PROTECTER	PROTECTERS
	PROTECTOR	PROTECTORS · PROTECTORY
	PROTEGE	PROTEGEE · PROTEGES
	PROTEGEE	PROTEGEES
	PROTEI	PROTEID · PROTEIN
	PROTEID	PROTEIDE · PROTEIDS
	PROTEIDE	PROTEIDES
	PROTEIN	PROTEINS
	PROTEND	PROTENDS
	PROTENSE	PROTENSES
	PROTEOME	PROTEOMES
	PROTEOMIC	PROTEOMICS
	PROTEOSE	PROTEOSES
	PROTEST	PROTESTS
	PROTESTER	PROTESTERS
	PROTESTOR	PROTESTORS
	PROTHALLI	PROTHALLIA · PROTHALLIC
	PROTHYL	PROTHYLS
	PROTIST	PROTISTS
	PROTISTAN	PROTISTANS
	PROTIUM	PROTIUMS
	PROTOCOL	PROTOCOLS
	PROTODERM	PROTODERMS
	PROTOGINE	PROTOGINES
	PROTON	PROTONS
	PROTONATE	PROTONATED · PROTONATES
	PROTONEMA	PROTONEMAL

P

FRONT HOOK	ROOT WORD	END HOOK
	PROTOPOD	PROTOPODS
	PROTORE	PROTORES
	PROTOSTAR	PROTOSTARS
	PROTOTYPE	PROTOTYPED · PROTOTYPES
	PROTOXID	PROTOXIDE · PROTOXIDS
	PROTOXIDE	PROTOXIDES
	PROTOZOA	PROTOZOAL · PROTOZOAN
	PROTOZOAN	PROTOZOANS
	PROTOZOON	PROTOZOONS
	PROTRACT	PROTRACTS
	PROTRUDE	PROTRUDED · PROTRUDES
	PROTYL	PROTYLE · PROTYLS
	PROTYLE	PROTYLES
	PROUL	PROULS
	PROULER	PROULERS
	PROUSTITE	PROUSTITES
	PROVAND	PROVANDS
	PROVE	PROVED · PROVEN · PROVER · PROVES
	PROVEDOR	PROVEDORE · PROVEDORS
	PROVEDORE	PROVEDORES
	PROVEN	PROVEND
	PROVEND	PROVENDS
	PROVENDER	PROVENDERS
	PROVER	PROVERB · PROVERS
	PROVERB	PROVERBS
	PROVIANT	PROVIANTS
	PROVIDE	PROVIDED · PROVIDER · PROVIDES
	PROVIDER	PROVIDERS
	PROVIDOR	PROVIDORS
	PROVINCE	PROVINCES
	PROVINE	PROVINED · PROVINES
	PROVING	PROVINGS
	PROVISION	PROVISIONS
	PROVISO	PROVISOR · PROVISOS
	PROVISOR	PROVISORS · PROVISORY
	PROVOCANT	PROVOCANTS
	PROVOKE	PROVOKED · PROVOKER · PROVOKES
	PROVOKER	PROVOKERS
	PROVOLONE	PROVOLONES
	PROVOST	PROVOSTS
	PROW	PROWL · PROWS
	PROWL	PROWLS
	PROWLER	PROWLERS
	PROWLING	PROWLINGS
	PROXEMIC	PROXEMICS
	PROYN	PROYNE · PROYNS
	PROYNE	PROYNED · PROYNES
	PROZYMITE	PROZYMITES
	PRUDE	PRUDES
	PRUDENCE	PRUDENCES
	PRUINA	PRUINAS
	PRUINE	PRUINES
	PRUNE	PRUNED · PRUNER · PRUNES
	PRUNELLA	PRUNELLAS
	PRUNELLE	PRUNELLES
	PRUNELLO	PRUNELLOS
	PRUNER	PRUNERS
	PRUNING	PRUNINGS
	PRUNT	PRUNTS
	PRURIENCE	PRURIENCES
	PRURIGO	PRURIGOS
	PRUSIK	PRUSIKS
	PRUSSIATE	PRUSSIATES
	PRUTA	PRUTAH
	PRUTOT	PRUTOTH
SPRY	**PRY**	PRYS
SPRYER	**PRYER**	PRYERS
	PRYING	PRYINGS
	PRYS	PRYSE

FRONT HOOK	ROOT WORD	END HOOK
	PRYSE	PRYSED · PRYSES
	PSALM	PSALMS
	PSALMBOOK	PSALMBOOKS
	PSALMIST	PSALMISTS
	PSALTER	PSALTERS · PSALTERY
	PSALTERIA	PSALTERIAN
	PSAMMITE	PSAMMITES
	PSAMMON	PSAMMONS
	PSCHENT	PSCHENTS
	PSELLISM	PSELLISMS
	PSEPHISM	PSEPHISMS
	PSEPHITE	PSEPHITES
	PSEUD	PSEUDO · PSEUDS
	PSEUDO	PSEUDOS
	PSEUDONYM	PSEUDONYMS
	PSEUDOPOD	PSEUDOPODS
	PSHAW	PSHAWS
	PSI	PSIS
	PSILOCIN	PSILOCINS
	PSION	PSIONS
	PSIONIC	PSIONICS
APSIS	**PSIS**	
	PSOCID	PSOCIDS
	PSORA	PSORAS
	PSORALEA	PSORALEAS
	PSORALEN	PSORALENS
	PSORIATIC	PSORIATICS
	PSYCH	PSYCHE · PSYCHO · PSYCHS
	PSYCHE	PSYCHED · PSYCHES
	PSYCHIC	PSYCHICS
	PSYCHISM	PSYCHISMS
	PSYCHIST	PSYCHISTS
	PSYCHO	PSYCHOS (offensive)
	PSYCHOID	PSYCHOIDS
	PSYCHOTIC	PSYCHOTICS
	PSYLLA	PSYLLAS
	PSYLLID	PSYLLIDS
	PSYLLIUM	PSYLLIUMS
	PSYOP	PSYOPS
	PSYWAR	PSYWARS
	PTARMIC	PTARMICS
	PTARMIGAN	PTARMIGANS
APTERIA	**PTERIA**	
	PTERIDINE	PTERIDINES
	PTERIN	PTERINS
	PTEROPOD	PTEROPODS
	PTEROSAUR	PTEROSAURS
	PTERYGIA	PTERYGIAL
APTERYGIAL	**PTERYGIAL**	PTERYGIALS
	PTERYGIUM	PTERYGIUMS
	PTERYGOID	PTERYGOIDS
	PTERYLA	PTERYLAE
	PTISAN	PTISANS
	PTOMAIN	PTOMAINE · PTOMAINS
	PTOMAINE	PTOMAINES
APTOTIC	**PTOTIC**	
	PTYALIN	PTYALINS
	PTYALISE	PTYALISED · PTYALISES
	PTYALISM	PTYALISMS
	PTYALIZE	PTYALIZED · PTYALIZES
	PUB	PUBE · PUBS
	PUBE	PUBES
	PUBLIC	PUBLICS
	PUBLICAN	PUBLICANS
	PUBLICISE	PUBLICISED · PUBLICISES
	PUBLICIST	PUBLICISTS
	PUBLICIZE	PUBLICIZED · PUBLICIZES
	PUBLISHER	PUBLISHERS
	PUCAN	PUCANS

P

FRONT HOOK	ROOT WORD	END HOOK
	PUCCOON	PUCCOONS
	PUCE	PUCER · PUCES
	PUCELAGE	PUCELAGES
	PUCELLE	PUCELLES
	PUCES	PUCEST
	PUCK	PUCKA · PUCKS
	PUCKER	PUCKERS · PUCKERY
	PUCKERER	PUCKERERS
	PUCKFIST	PUCKFISTS
	PUCKLE	PUCKLES
SPUD	PUD	PUDS · PUDU
	PUDDEN	PUDDENS
	PUDDENING	PUDDENINGS
SPUDDER	PUDDER	PUDDERS
SPUDDERS	PUDDERS	
SPUDDING	PUDDING	PUDDINGS · PUDDINGY
SPUDDINGS	PUDDINGS	
SPUDDLE	PUDDLE	PUDDLED · PUDDLER · PUDDLES
	PUDDLER	PUDDLERS
SPUDDLES	PUDDLES	
	PUDDLING	PUDDLINGS
	PUDDOCK	PUDDOCKS
SPUDDY	PUDDY	
	PUDENDA	PUDENDAL
	PUDGE	PUDGES
	PUDOR	PUDORS
SPUDS	PUDS	PUDSY
	PUDU	PUDUS
	PUEBLO	PUEBLOS
SPUER	PUER	PUERS
	PUERILISM	PUERILISMS
	PUERPERA	PUERPERAE · PUERPERAL
SPUERS	PUERS	
	PUFF	PUFFS · PUFFY
	PUFFBALL	PUFFBALLS
	PUFFBIRD	PUFFBIRDS
	PUFFER	PUFFERS · PUFFERY
	PUFFIN	PUFFING · PUFFINS
	PUFFING	PUFFINGS
	PUFTALOON	PUFTALOONS
SPUG	PUG	PUGH · PUGS
	PUGAREE	PUGAREES
	PUGGAREE	PUGGAREES
	PUGGIE	PUGGIER · PUGGIES
SPUGGIES	PUGGIES	PUGGIEST
	PUGGING	PUGGINGS
	PUGGLE	PUGGLED · PUGGLES
	PUGGREE	PUGGREES
SPUGGY	PUGGY	
	PUGIL	PUGILS
	PUGILISM	PUGILISMS
	PUGILIST	PUGILISTS
	PUGMARK	PUGMARKS
	PUGREE	PUGREES
SPUGS	PUGS	
	PUH	PUHA
	PUHA	PUHAS
	PUIRTITH	PUIRTITHS
	PUISNE	PUISNES
	PUISSANCE	PUISSANCES
	PUJA	PUJAH · PUJAS
	PUJAH	PUJAHS
	PUKATEA	PUKATEAS
	PUKE	PUKED · PUKER · PUKES
	PUKEKO	PUKEKOS
	PUKER	PUKERS
	PUKU	PUKUS
	PUL	PULA · PULE · PULI · PULK · PULL PULP · PULS · PULU · PULY

P

FRONT HOOK	ROOT WORD	END HOOK
	PULA	PULAO · PULAS
	PULAO	PULAOS
	PULDRON	PULDRONS
SPULE	**PULE**	PULED · PULER · PULES
	PULER	PULERS
SPULES	**PULES**	
	PULI	PULIK · PULIS
	PULICIDE	PULICIDES
	PULING	PULINGS
EPULIS	**PULIS**	
	PULK	PULKA · PULKS
	PULKA	PULKAS
	PULKHA	PULKHAS
	PULL	PULLI · PULLS
	PULLBACK	PULLBACKS
	PULLER	PULLERS
	PULLET	PULLETS
	PULLEY	PULLEYS
	PULLMAN	PULLMANS
	PULLOUT	PULLOUTS
	PULLOVER	PULLOVERS
	PULLULATE	PULLULATED · PULLULATES
	PULLUP	PULLUPS
	PULMONATE	PULMONATES
	PULMONIC	PULMONICS
	PULMOTOR	PULMOTORS
	PULP	PULPS · PULPY
	PULPBOARD	PULPBOARDS
	PULPER	PULPERS
	PULPIT	PULPITS
	PULPITEER	PULPITEERS
	PULPITER	PULPITERS
	PULPITUM	PULPITUMS
	PULPMILL	PULPMILLS
	PULPSTONE	PULPSTONES
	PULPWOOD	PULPWOODS
	PULQUE	PULQUES
	PULS	PULSE
	PULSAR	PULSARS
	PULSATE	PULSATED · PULSATES
	PULSATION	PULSATIONS
	PULSATOR	PULSATORS · PULSATORY
	PULSE	PULSED · PULSER · PULSES
	PULSEJET	PULSEJETS
	PULSER	PULSERS
	PULSIDGE	PULSIDGES
	PULSION	PULSIONS
	PULSOJET	PULSOJETS
	PULTAN	PULTANS
	PULTON	PULTONS
	PULTOON	PULTOONS
	PULTUN	PULTUNS
	PULTURE	PULTURES
	PULU	PULUS
OPULUS	**PULUS**	
	PULVER	PULVERS
	PULVERINE	PULVERINES
	PULVERISE	PULVERISED · PULVERISER · PULVERISES
	PULVERIZE	PULVERIZED · PULVERIZER · PULVERIZES
	PULVIL	PULVILS
	PULVILIO	PULVILIOS
	PULVILLE	PULVILLED · PULVILLES
	PULVILLI	PULVILLIO
	PULVILLIO	PULVILLIOS
	PULVINAR	PULVINARS
	PULVINATE	PULVINATED
	PULVINULE	PULVINULES
	PULWAR	PULWARS
	PUMA	PUMAS

FRONT HOOK	ROOT WORD	END HOOK
	PUMELO	PUMELOS
	PUMICATE	PUMICATED · PUMICATES
	PUMICE	PUMICED · PUMICER · PUMICES
	PUMICER	PUMICERS
	PUMICITE	PUMICITES
	PUMIE	PUMIES
	PUMMEL	PUMMELO · PUMMELS
	PUMMELO	PUMMELOS
	PUMP	PUMPS
	PUMPER	PUMPERS
	PUMPHOOD	PUMPHOODS
	PUMPION	PUMPIONS
	PUMPKIN	PUMPKING · PUMPKINS
	PUMPKING	PUMPKINGS
SPUMY	**PUMY**	
SPUN	**PUN**	PUNA · PUNG · PUNK · PUNS · PUNT · PUNY
	PUNA	PUNAS
	PUNALUA	PUNALUAN · PUNALUAS
	PUNCE	PUNCED · PUNCES
	PUNCH	PUNCHY
	PUNCHBAG	PUNCHBAGS
	PUNCHBALL	PUNCHBALLS
	PUNCHBOWL	PUNCHBOWLS
	PUNCHEON	PUNCHEONS
	PUNCHER	PUNCHERS
	PUNCTATE	PUNCTATED
	PUNCTATOR	PUNCTATORS
	PUNCTILIO	PUNCTILIOS
	PUNCTO	PUNCTOS
	PUNCTUATE	PUNCTUATED · PUNCTUATES
	PUNCTULE	PUNCTULES
	PUNCTURE	PUNCTURED · PUNCTURER · PUNCTURES
	PUNCTURER	PUNCTURERS
	PUNDIT	PUNDITS
	PUNG	PUNGA · PUNGS
	PUNGA	PUNGAS
	PUNGENCE	PUNGENCES
	PUNGLE	PUNGLED · PUNGLES
	PUNISHER	PUNISHERS
	PUNITION	PUNITIONS
	PUNJI	PUNJIS
SPUNK	**PUNK**	PUNKA · PUNKS · PUNKY
	PUNKA	PUNKAH · PUNKAS
	PUNKAH	PUNKAHS
	PUNKER	PUNKERS
	PUNKEY	PUNKEYS
SPUNKIE	**PUNKIE**	PUNKIER · PUNKIES
SPUNKIER	**PUNKIER**	
SPUNKIES	**PUNKIES**	PUNKIEST
SPUNKIEST	**PUNKIEST**	
	PUNKIN	PUNKINS
SPUNKINESS	**PUNKINESS**	
SPUNKS	**PUNKS**	
SPUNKY	**PUNKY**	
	PUNNER	PUNNERS
	PUNNET	PUNNETS
	PUNNING	PUNNINGS
	PUNSTER	PUNSTERS
	PUNT	PUNTO · PUNTS · PUNTY
	PUNTEE	PUNTEES
	PUNTER	PUNTERS
	PUNTO	PUNTOS
	PUP	PUPA · PUPS · PUPU
	PUPA	PUPAE · PUPAL · PUPAS
	PUPARIA	PUPARIAL
	PUPATE	PUPATED · PUPATES
	PUPATION	PUPATIONS
	PUPIL	PUPILS
	PUPILAGE	PUPILAGES

P

FRONT HOOK	ROOT WORD	END HOOK
	PUPILAR	PUPILARY
	PUPILLAGE	PUPILLAGES
	PUPILLAR	PUPILLARY
	PUPILSHIP	PUPILSHIPS
	PUPPET	PUPPETS
	PUPPETEER	PUPPETEERS
	PUPPODUM	PUPPODUMS
	PUPPYDOM	PUPPYDOMS
	PUPPYHOOD	PUPPYHOODS
	PUPPYISM	PUPPYISMS
	PUPU	PUPUS
	PUPUNHA	PUPUNHAS
SPUR	**PUR**	PURE · PURI · PURL · PURR · PURS
	PURANA	PURANAS
	PURCHASE	PURCHASED · PURCHASER · PURCHASES
	PURCHASER	PURCHASERS
	PURDA	PURDAH · PURDAS
	PURDAH	PURDAHS
	PURDONIUM	PURDONIUMS
	PURE	PURED · PUREE · PURER · PURES
	PUREBLOOD	PUREBLOODS
	PUREBRED	PUREBREDS
	PUREE	PUREED · PUREES
	PURES	PUREST
	PURFLE	PURFLED · PURFLER · PURFLES
	PURFLER	PURFLERS
	PURFLING	PURFLINGS
	PURGATION	PURGATIONS
	PURGATIVE	PURGATIVES
SPURGE	**PURGE**	PURGED · PURGER · PURGES
	PURGER	PURGERS
SPURGES	**PURGES**	
	PURGING	PURGINGS
	PURI	PURIM · PURIN · PURIS
	PURIFIER	PURIFIERS
	PURIM	PURIMS
	PURIN	PURINE · PURING · PURINS
	PURINE	PURINES
	PURIRI	PURIRIS
	PURIS	PURISM · PURIST
	PURISM	PURISMS
	PURIST	PURISTS
	PURITAN	PURITANS
	PURL	PURLS
	PURLER	PURLERS
	PURLICUE	PURLICUED · PURLICUES
	PURLIEU	PURLIEUS
	PURLIN	PURLINE · PURLING · PURLINS
	PURLINE	PURLINES
SPURLING	**PURLING**	PURLINGS
SPURLINGS	**PURLINGS**	
	PURLOIN	PURLOINS
	PURLOINER	PURLOINERS
	PUROMYCIN	PUROMYCINS
	PURPIE	PURPIES
	PURPLE	PURPLED · PURPLER · PURPLES
	PURPLES	PURPLEST
	PURPORT	PURPORTS
	PURPOSE	PURPOSED · PURPOSES
	PURPURA	PURPURAS
	PURPURE	PURPURES
	PURPURIN	PURPURINS
	PURR	PURRS
SPURRED	**PURRED**	
SPURRING	**PURRING**	PURRINGS
SPURRINGS	**PURRINGS**	
SPURS	**PURS**	PURSE · PURSY
	PURSE	PURSED · PURSER · PURSES · PURSEW
	PURSEFUL	PURSEFULS

P

FRONT HOOK	ROOT WORD	END HOOK
	PURSER	PURSERS
	PURSEW	PURSEWS
	PURSLAIN	PURSLAINS
	PURSLANE	PURSLANES
	PURSUAL	PURSUALS
	PURSUANCE	PURSUANCES
	PURSUE	PURSUED · PURSUER · PURSUES
	PURSUER	PURSUERS
	PURSUING	PURSUINGS
	PURSUIT	PURSUITS
	PURULENCE	PURULENCES
	PURVEY	PURVEYS
	PURVEYOR	PURVEYORS
	PURVIEW	PURVIEWS
OPUS	**PUS**	PUSH · PUSS
OPUSES	**PUSES**	
	PUSH	PUSHY
	PUSHBALL	PUSHBALLS
	PUSHCART	PUSHCARTS
	PUSHCHAIR	PUSHCHAIRS
	PUSHDOWN	PUSHDOWNS
	PUSHER	PUSHERS
	PUSHOVER	PUSHOVERS
	PUSHPIN	PUSHPINS
	PUSHROD	PUSHRODS
	PUSHUP	PUSHUPS
	PUSLE	PUSLED · PUSLES · PUSLEY
	PUSLEY	PUSLEYS
	PUSS	PUSSY
	PUSSEL	PUSSELS
	PUSSER	PUSSERS
	PUSSIES	PUSSIEST
	PUSSLEY	PUSSLEYS
	PUSSYCAT	PUSSYCATS
	PUSSYFOOT	PUSSYFOOTS
	PUSTULANT	PUSTULANTS
	PUSTULATE	PUSTULATED · PUSTULATES
	PUSTULE	PUSTULED · PUSTULES
	PUT	PUTS · PUTT · PUTZ
	PUTCHEON	PUTCHEONS
	PUTCHER	PUTCHERS
	PUTCHOCK	PUTCHOCKS
	PUTCHUK	PUTCHUKS
	PUTDOWN	PUTDOWNS
	PUTEAL	PUTEALS
	PUTELI	PUTELIS
	PUTLOCK	PUTLOCKS
	PUTLOG	PUTLOGS
	PUTOFF	PUTOFFS
	PUTON	PUTONS
	PUTONGHUA	PUTONGHUAS
	PUTOUT	PUTOUTS
	PUTREFIER	PUTREFIERS
	PUTSCHIST	PUTSCHISTS
	PUTT	PUTTI · PUTTO · PUTTS · PUTTY
	PUTTEE	PUTTEES
SPUTTER	**PUTTER**	PUTTERS
SPUTTERED	**PUTTERED**	
SPUTTERER	**PUTTERER**	PUTTERERS
SPUTTERERS	**PUTTERERS**	
SPUTTERING	**PUTTERING**	
SPUTTERS	**PUTTERS**	
	PUTTI	PUTTIE
	PUTTIE	PUTTIED · PUTTIER · PUTTIES
	PUTTIER	PUTTIERS
	PUTTING	PUTTINGS
	PUTTOCK	PUTTOCKS
	PUTTYROOT	PUTTYROOTS
	PUTURE	PUTURES

FRONT HOOK	ROOT WORD	END HOOK
	PUY	PUYS
	PUZEL	PUZELS
	PUZZEL	PUZZELS
	PUZZLE	PUZZLED · PUZZLER · PUZZLES
	PUZZLEDOM	PUZZLEDOMS
	PUZZLER	PUZZLERS
	PUZZOLANA	PUZZOLANAS
	PYA	PYAS · PYAT
	PYAEMIA	PYAEMIAS
	PYAT	PYATS
	PYCNIDIA	PYCNIDIAL
	PYCNITE	PYCNITES
	PYCNON	PYCNONS
	PYE	PYES · PYET
	PYEBALD	PYEBALDS
	PYELOGRAM	PYELOGRAMS
	PYEMIA	PYEMIAS
	PYENGADU	PYENGADUS
	PYET	PYETS
	PYGAL	PYGALS
	PYGARG	PYGARGS
	PYGIDIA	PYGIDIAL
	PYGIDIUM	PYGIDIUMS
	PYGMYISM	PYGMYISMS
	PYGOSTYLE	PYGOSTYLES
	PYIN	PYINS
	PYINKADO	PYINKADOS
	PYJAMA	PYJAMAS
	PYKNIC	PYKNICS
	PYKNOSOME	PYKNOSOMES
	PYLON	PYLONS
	PYLORI	PYLORIC
	PYNE	PYNED · PYNES
	PYODERMA	PYODERMAS
	PYONER	PYONERS
	PYORRHEA	PYORRHEAL · PYORRHEAS
	PYORRHOEA	PYORRHOEAL · PYORRHOEAS
	PYOT	PYOTS
	PYRACANTH	PYRACANTHA · PYRACANTHS
	PYRALID	PYRALIDS
	PYRALIDID	PYRALIDIDS
	PYRAMID	PYRAMIDS
	PYRAMIDON	PYRAMIDONS
	PYRAN	PYRANS
	PYRANOSE	PYRANOSES
	PYRAZOLE	PYRAZOLES
SPYRE	**PYRE**	PYRES · PYREX
	PYRENE	PYRENES
	PYRENEITE	PYRENEITES
	PYRENOID	PYRENOIDS
SPYRES	**PYRES**	
	PYRETHRIN	PYRETHRINS
	PYRETHRUM	PYRETHRUMS
APYRETIC	**PYRETIC**	
APYREXIA	**PYREXIA**	PYREXIAL · PYREXIAS
APYREXIAS	**PYREXIAS**	
	PYRIDINE	PYRIDINES
	PYRIDOXAL	PYRIDOXALS
	PYRIDOXIN	PYRIDOXINE · PYRIDOXINS
	PYRITE	PYRITES
	PYRITISE	PYRITISED · PYRITISES
	PYRITIZE	PYRITIZED · PYRITIZES
	PYRO	PYROS
	PYROCERAM	PYROCERAMS
	PYROCLAST	PYROCLASTS
	PYROGEN	PYROGENS
	PYROLA	PYROLAS
	PYROLATER	PYROLATERS
	PYROLISE	PYROLISED · PYROLISES

FRONT HOOK	ROOT WORD	END HOOK
	PYROLIZE	PYROLIZED ▪ PYROLIZES
	PYROLYSE	PYROLYSED ▪ PYROLYSER ▪ PYROLYSES
	PYROLYSER	PYROLYSERS
	PYROLYZE	PYROLYZED ▪ PYROLYZER ▪ PYROLYZES
	PYROLYZER	PYROLYZERS
	PYROMANIA	PYROMANIAC ▪ PYROMANIAS
	PYROMETER	PYROMETERS
	PYRONE	PYRONES
	PYRONINE	PYRONINES
	PYROPE	PYROPES
	PYROPHONE	PYROPHONES
	PYROSCOPE	PYROSCOPES
	PYROSOME	PYROSOMES
	PYROSTAT	PYROSTATS
	PYROXENE	PYROXENES
	PYROXYLE	PYROXYLES
	PYROXYLIN	PYROXYLINE ▪ PYROXYLINS
	PYRRHIC	PYRRHICS
	PYRROL	PYRROLE ▪ PYRROLS
	PYRROLE	PYRROLES
	PYRUVATE	PYRUVATES
	PYTHIUM	PYTHIUMS
	PYTHON	PYTHONS
	PYURIA	PYURIAS
	PYXIE	PYXIES

P

Q

FRONT HOOK	ROOT WORD	END HOOK
	QABALA	QABALAH · QABALAS
	QABALAH	QABALAHS
	QABALISM	QABALISMS
	QABALIST	QABALISTS
	QADI	QADIS
	QAID	QAIDS
	QAIMAQAM	QAIMAQAMS
	QALAMDAN	QALAMDANS
	QANAT	QANATS
	QASIDA	QASIDAS
	QAT	QATS
	QAWWAL	QAWWALI · QAWWALS
	QAWWALI	QAWWALIS
	QI	QIS
	QIBLA	QIBLAS
	QIGONG	QIGONGS
	QINDAR	QINDARS
	QINGHAOSU	QINGHAOSUS
	QINTAR	QINTARS
	QIVIUT	QIVIUTS
	QOPH	QOPHS
	QORMA	QORMAS
AQUA	**QUA**	QUAD · QUAG · QUAI · QUAT · QUAY
	QUAALUDE	QUAALUDES
	QUACK	QUACKS · QUACKY
	QUACKER	QUACKERS · QUACKERY
	QUACKISM	QUACKISMS
	QUACKLE	QUACKLED · QUACKLES
SQUAD	**QUAD**	QUADS
SQUADDED	**QUADDED**	
SQUADDING	**QUADDING**	
	QUADRANT	QUADRANTS
	QUADRAT	QUADRATE · QUADRATS
	QUADRATE	QUADRATED · QUADRATES
	QUADRATIC	QUADRATICS
	QUADRELLA	QUADRELLAS
	QUADRIC	QUADRICS
	QUADRICEP	QUADRICEPS
	QUADRIGA	QUADRIGAE · QUADRIGAS
	QUADRILLE	QUADRILLED · QUADRILLER · QUADRILLES
	QUADRIVIA	QUADRIVIAL
	QUADROON	QUADROONS (offensive)
	QUADRUMAN	QUADRUMANE · QUADRUMANS
	QUADRUPED	QUADRUPEDS
	QUADRUPLE	QUADRUPLED · QUADRUPLES · QUADRUPLET QUADRUPLEX
SQUADS	**QUADS**	
	QUAERE	QUAERED · QUAERES
	QUAESITUM	QUAESITUMS
	QUAESTOR	QUAESTORS
	QUAFF	QUAFFS
	QUAFFER	QUAFFERS
	QUAG	QUAGS
	QUAGGA	QUAGGAS
	QUAGMIRE	QUAGMIRED · QUAGMIRES
	QUAHAUG	QUAHAUGS
	QUAHOG	QUAHOGS
	QUAI	QUAIL · QUAIR · QUAIS
	QUAICH	QUAICHS
	QUAIGH	QUAIGHS
SQUAIL	**QUAIL**	QUAILS
SQUAILED	**QUAILED**	
SQUAILING	**QUAILING**	QUAILINGS
SQUAILINGS	**QUAILINGS**	
SQUAILS	**QUAILS**	
	QUAIR	QUAIRS

FRONT HOOK	ROOT WORD	END HOOK
	QUAKE	QUAKED · QUAKER · QUAKES
	QUAKER	QUAKERS
	QUAKING	QUAKINGS
	QUALIFIER	QUALIFIERS
EQUALITIES	QUALITIES	
EQUALITY	QUALITY	
	QUALM	QUALMS · QUALMY
	QUANDANG	QUANDANGS
	QUANDONG	QUANDONGS
	QUANGO	QUANGOS
	QUANNET	QUANNETS
EQUANT	QUANT	QUANTA · QUANTS
	QUANTA	QUANTAL
	QUANTIC	QUANTICS
	QUANTILE	QUANTILES
	QUANTISE	QUANTISED · QUANTISER · QUANTISES
	QUANTISER	QUANTISERS
	QUANTIZE	QUANTIZED · QUANTIZER · QUANTIZES
	QUANTIZER	QUANTIZERS
	QUANTONG	QUANTONGS
EQUANTS	QUANTS	
SQUARE	QUARE	QUARER
	QUARENDEN	QUARENDENS
	QUARENDER	QUARENDERS
SQUARER	QUARER	
SQUAREST	QUAREST	
SQUARK	QUARK	QUARKS
SQUARKS	QUARKS	
	QUARREL	QUARRELS
	QUARRELER	QUARRELERS
	QUARRIAN	QUARRIANS
	QUARRIER	QUARRIERS
	QUARRION	QUARRIONS
	QUARRYING	QUARRYINGS
	QUART	QUARTE · QUARTO · QUARTS · QUARTZ
	QUARTAN	QUARTANS
	QUARTE	QUARTER · QUARTES · QUARTET
	QUARTER	QUARTERN · QUARTERS
	QUARTERER	QUARTERERS
	QUARTERN	QUARTERNS
	QUARTET	QUARTETS · QUARTETT
	QUARTETT	QUARTETTE · QUARTETTI · QUARTETTO · QUARTETTS
	QUARTETTE	QUARTETTES
	QUARTIC	QUARTICS
	QUARTIER	QUARTIERS
	QUARTILE	QUARTILES
	QUARTO	QUARTOS
	QUARTZ	QUARTZY
	QUARTZITE	QUARTZITES
	QUASAR	QUASARS
SQUASH	QUASH	
SQUASHED	QUASHED	
	QUASHEE	QUASHEES
SQUASHER	QUASHER	QUASHERS
SQUASHERS	QUASHERS	
SQUASHES	QUASHES	
	QUASHIE	QUASHIES
SQUASHING	QUASHING	
	QUASSIA	QUASSIAS
	QUASSIN	QUASSINS
SQUAT	QUAT	QUATE · QUATS
EQUATE	QUATE	
	QUATORZE	QUATORZES
	QUATRAIN	QUATRAINS
	QUATRE	QUATRES
SQUATS	QUATS	
	QUAVER	QUAVERS · QUAVERY
	QUAVERER	QUAVERERS

FRONT HOOK	ROOT WORD	END HOOK
	QUAVERING	QUAVERINGS
	QUAY	QUAYD · QUAYS
	QUAYAGE	QUAYAGES
	QUAYSIDE	QUAYSIDES
	QUBIT	QUBITS
	QUBYTE	QUBYTES
	QUEACH	QUEACHY
	QUEAN	QUEANS
	QUEBRACHO	QUEBRACHOS
	QUEEN	QUEENS · QUEENY
	QUEENCAKE	QUEENCAKES
	QUEENDOM	QUEENDOMS
	QUEENHOOD	QUEENHOODS
	QUEENIE	QUEENIER · QUEENIES
	QUEENIES	QUEENIEST
	QUEENING	QUEENINGS
	QUEENITE	QUEENITES
	QUEENLET	QUEENLETS
	QUEENSHIP	QUEENSHIPS
	QUEENSIDE	QUEENSIDES
	QUEER	QUEERS
	QUEERCORE	QUEERCORES
	QUEERDOM	QUEERDOMS
	QUEEST	QUEESTS
SQUELCH	**QUELCH**	
SQUELCHED	**QUELCHED**	
SQUELCHES	**QUELCHES**	
SQUELCHING	**QUELCHING**	
	QUELEA	QUELEAS
	QUELL	QUELLS
	QUELLER	QUELLERS
	QUEME	QUEMED · QUEMES
	QUENA	QUENAS
	QUENCHER	QUENCHERS
	QUENCHING	QUENCHINGS
	QUENELLE	QUENELLES
	QUERCETIN	QUERCETINS
	QUERCETUM	QUERCETUMS
	QUERCITIN	QUERCITINS
	QUERIDA	QUERIDAS
	QUERIER	QUERIERS
	QUERIST	QUERISTS
	QUERN	QUERNS
	QUERYING	QUERYINGS
	QUEST	QUESTS
	QUESTANT	QUESTANTS
	QUESTER	QUESTERS
	QUESTING	QUESTINGS
	QUESTION	QUESTIONS
	QUESTOR	QUESTORS
	QUESTRIST	QUESTRISTS
	QUETHE	QUETHES
	QUETZAL	QUETZALS
	QUEUE	QUEUED · QUEUER · QUEUES
	QUEUEING	QUEUEINGS
	QUEUER	QUEUERS
	QUEUING	QUEUINGS
	QUEY	QUEYN · QUEYS
	QUEYN	QUEYNS
	QUEYNIE	QUEYNIES
	QUEZAL	QUEZALS
	QUIBBLE	QUIBBLED · QUIBBLER · QUIBBLES
	QUIBBLER	QUIBBLERS
	QUIBBLING	QUIBBLINGS
	QUIBLIN	QUIBLINS
	QUICH	QUICHE
	QUICHE	QUICHED · QUICHES
	QUICK	QUICKS
	QUICKBEAM	QUICKBEAMS

FRONT HOOK	ROOT WORD	END HOOK
	QUICKEN	QUICKENS
	QUICKENER	QUICKENERS
	QUICKIE	QUICKIES
	QUICKLIME	QUICKLIMES
	QUICKSAND	QUICKSANDS
	QUICKSET	QUICKSETS
	QUICKSTEP	QUICKSTEPS
EQUID ▪ SQUID	**QUID**	QUIDS
	QUIDAM	QUIDAMS
	QUIDDIT	QUIDDITS ▪ QUIDDITY
	QUIDDLE	QUIDDLED ▪ QUIDDLER ▪ QUIDDLES
	QUIDDLER	QUIDDLERS
	QUIDNUNC	QUIDNUNCS
EQUIDS ▪ SQUIDS	**QUIDS**	
	QUIESCE	QUIESCED ▪ QUIESCES
	QUIET	QUIETS
	QUIETEN	QUIETENS
	QUIETENER	QUIETENERS
	QUIETER	QUIETERS
	QUIETING	QUIETINGS
	QUIETISM	QUIETISMS
	QUIETIST	QUIETISTS
	QUIETIVE	QUIETIVES
	QUIETUDE	QUIETUDES
SQUIFF	**QUIFF**	QUIFFS
	QUIGHT	QUIGHTS
SQUILL	**QUILL**	QUILLS
	QUILLAI	QUILLAIA ▪ QUILLAIS
	QUILLAIA	QUILLAIAS
	QUILLAJA	QUILLAJAS
	QUILLBACK	QUILLBACKS
	QUILLET	QUILLETS
	QUILLING	QUILLINGS
	QUILLON	QUILLONS
SQUILLS	**QUILLS**	
	QUILLWORK	QUILLWORKS
	QUILLWORT	QUILLWORTS
	QUILT	QUILTS
	QUILTER	QUILTERS
	QUILTING	QUILTINGS
	QUIM	QUIMS *(offensive)*
	QUIN	QUINA ▪ QUINE ▪ QUINO ▪ QUINS ▪ QUINT
	QUINA	QUINAS
	QUINCE	QUINCES
	QUINCHE	QUINCHED ▪ QUINCHES
SQUINCHED	**QUINCHED**	
SQUINCHES	**QUINCHES**	
SQUINCHING	**QUINCHING**	
EQUINE	**QUINE**	QUINES
	QUINELA	QUINELAS
	QUINELLA	QUINELLAS
EQUINES	**QUINES**	
	QUINIDINE	QUINIDINES
	QUINIE	QUINIES
	QUINIELA	QUINIELAS
SQUINIES	**QUINIES**	
	QUININ	QUININA ▪ QUININE ▪ QUININS
	QUININA	QUININAS
	QUININE	QUININES
	QUINNAT	QUINNATS
	QUINO	QUINOA ▪ QUINOL ▪ QUINOS
	QUINOA	QUINOAS
	QUINOID	QUINOIDS
	QUINOL	QUINOLS
	QUINOLIN	QUINOLINE ▪ QUINOLINS
	QUINOLINE	QUINOLINES
	QUINOLONE	QUINOLONES
	QUINONE	QUINONES
	QUINQUINA	QUINQUINAS

FRONT HOOK	ROOT WORD	END HOOK
	QUINS	QUINSY
SQUINT	**QUINT**	QUINTA · QUINTE · QUINTS
	QUINTA	QUINTAL · QUINTAN · QUINTAR · QUINTAS
	QUINTAIN	QUINTAINS
	QUINTAL	QUINTALS
	QUINTAN	QUINTANS
	QUINTAR	QUINTARS
	QUINTE	QUINTES · QUINTET
	QUINTET	QUINTETS · QUINTETT
	QUINTETT	QUINTETTE · QUINTETTI · QUINTETTO
		QUINTETTS
	QUINTETTE	QUINTETTES
	QUINTIC	QUINTICS
	QUINTILE	QUINTILES
	QUINTIN	QUINTINS
	QUINTROON	QUINTROONS
SQUINTS	**QUINTS**	
	QUINTUPLE	QUINTUPLED · QUINTUPLES · QUINTUPLET
	QUINZE	QUINZES
EQUIP	**QUIP**	QUIPO · QUIPS · QUIPU
	QUIPO	QUIPOS
EQUIPPED	**QUIPPED**	
EQUIPPER	**QUIPPER**	QUIPPERS
EQUIPPERS	**QUIPPERS**	
EQUIPPING	**QUIPPING**	
	QUIPPU	QUIPPUS
EQUIPS	**QUIPS**	
	QUIPSTER	QUIPSTERS
	QUIPU	QUIPUS
SQUIRE	**QUIRE**	QUIRED · QUIRES
SQUIRED	**QUIRED**	
SQUIRES	**QUIRES**	
SQUIRING	**QUIRING**	
	QUIRISTER	QUIRISTERS
	QUIRK	QUIRKS · QUIRKY
SQUIRT	**QUIRT**	QUIRTS
SQUIRTED	**QUIRTED**	
SQUIRTING	**QUIRTING**	
SQUIRTS	**QUIRTS**	
	QUISLING	QUISLINGS
	QUIST	QUISTS
SQUIT	**QUIT**	QUITE · QUITS
SQUITCH	**QUITCH**	
SQUITCHES	**QUITCHES**	
	QUITCLAIM	QUITCLAIMS
	QUITE	QUITED · QUITES
EQUITES	**QUITES**	
	QUITRENT	QUITRENTS
SQUITS	**QUITS**	
	QUITTAL	QUITTALS
	QUITTANCE	QUITTANCED · QUITTANCES
	QUITTER	QUITTERS
	QUITTOR	QUITTORS
AQUIVER	**QUIVER**	QUIVERS · QUIVERY
	QUIVERER	QUIVERERS
	QUIVERFUL	QUIVERFULS
	QUIVERING	QUIVERINGS
	QUIXOTE	QUIXOTES
	QUIXOTISM	QUIXOTISMS
SQUIZ	**QUIZ**	
	QUIZZER	QUIZZERS · QUIZZERY
SQUIZZES	**QUIZZES**	
	QUIZZING	QUIZZINGS
	QUOD	QUODS
	QUODLIBET	QUODLIBETS
	QUODLIN	QUODLINS
	QUOHOG	QUOHOGS
	QUOIF	QUOIFS
	QUOIN	QUOINS

FRONT HOOK	ROOT WORD	END HOOK
	QUOIST	QUOISTS
	QUOIT	QUOITS
	QUOITER	QUOITERS
	QUOKKA	QUOKKAS
	QUOLL	QUOLLS
	QUOMODO	QUOMODOS
	QUONK	QUONKS
	QUOP	QUOPS
	QUORUM	QUORUMS
	QUOTA	QUOTAS
	QUOTATION	QUOTATIONS
	QUOTATIVE	QUOTATIVES
	QUOTE	QUOTED · QUOTER · QUOTES
	QUOTER	QUOTERS
	QUOTH	QUOTHA
	QUOTIDIAN	QUOTIDIANS
	QUOTIENT	QUOTIENTS
	QUOTITION	QUOTITIONS
	QUOTUM	QUOTUMS
	QUYTE	QUYTED · QUYTES
	QWERTY	QWERTYS

R

FRONT HOOK	ROOT WORD	END HOOK
	RABANNA	RABANNAS
	RABAT	RABATO = RABATS
	RABATINE	RABATINES
	RABATMENT	RABATMENTS
	RABATO	RABATOS
	RABATTE	RABATTED = RABATTES
	RABATTING	RABATTINGS
DRABBET	**RABBET**	RABBETS
DRABBETS	**RABBETS**	
	RABBI	RABBIN = RABBIS = RABBIT
	RABBIN	RABBINS
	RABBINATE	RABBINATES
	RABBINIC	RABBINICS
	RABBINISM	RABBINISMS
	RABBINIST	RABBINISTS
	RABBINITE	RABBINITES
FRABBIT	**RABBIT**	RABBITO = RABBITS = RABBITY
	RABBITER	RABBITERS
	RABBITO	RABBITOH = RABBITOS
	RABBITOH	RABBITOHS
BRABBLE = DRABBLE = GRABBLE = PRABBLE	**RABBLE**	RABBLED = RABBLER = RABBLES
BRABBLED = DRABBLED = GRABBLED	**RABBLED**	
BRABBLER = DRABBLER = GRABBLER	**RABBLER**	RABBLERS
BRABBLERS = DRABBLERS = GRABBLERS	**RABBLERS**	
BRABBLES = DRABBLES = GRABBLES = PRABBLES	**RABBLES**	
BRABBLING = DRABBLING = GRABBLING	**RABBLING**	RABBLINGS
DRABBLINGS	**RABBLINGS**	
	RABBONI	RABBONIS
	RABI	RABIC = RABID = RABIS
ARABIC	**RABIC**	
ARABIS	**RABIS**	
	RACAHOUT	RACAHOUTS
	RACCAHOUT	RACCAHOUTS
	RACCOON	RACCOONS
BRACE = GRACE = TRACE	**RACE**	RACED = RACER = RACES
	RACECARD	RACECARDS
BRACED = GRACED = TRACED	**RACED**	
	RACEGOER	RACEGOERS
	RACEGOING	RACEGOINGS
	RACEHORSE	RACEHORSES
	RACEMATE	RACEMATES
	RACEME	RACEMED = RACEMES
	RACEMISE	RACEMISED = RACEMISES
	RACEMISM	RACEMISMS
	RACEMIZE	RACEMIZED = RACEMIZES
	RACEPATH	RACEPATHS
BRACER = TRACER	**RACER**	RACERS
BRACERS = TRACERS	**RACERS**	
BRACES = GRACES = TRACES	**RACES**	
	RACETRACK	RACETRACKS
	RACEWALK	RACEWALKS
	RACEWAY	RACEWAYS
BRACH = ORACH	**RACH**	RACHE
ORACHE	**RACHE**	RACHES = RACHET
BRACHES = ORACHES	**RACHES**	
BRACHET	**RACHET**	RACHETS
BRACHETS	**RACHETS**	
BRACHIAL	**RACHIAL**	
	RACHILLA	RACHILLAE = RACHILLAS
ARACHIS	**RACHIS**	
ARACHISES	**RACHISES**	
TRACHITIS	**RACHITIS**	
	RACIALISE	RACIALISED = RACIALISES
	RACIALISM	RACIALISMS
	RACIALIST	RACIALISTS

FRONT HOOK	ROOT WORD	END HOOK
	RACIALIZE	RACIALIZED ▪ RACIALIZES
	RACIATION	RACIATIONS
BRACING ▪ GRACING ▪ TRACING	**RACING**	RACINGS
BRACINGS ▪ TRACINGS	**RACINGS**	
	RACISM	RACISMS
	RACIST	RACISTS
BRACK ▪ CRACK ▪ DRACK ▪ FRACK ▪ TRACK WRACK	**RACK**	RACKS
CRACKED ▪ TRACKED ▪ WRACKED	**RACKED**	
CRACKER ▪ TRACKER	**RACKER**	RACKERS
CRACKERS ▪ TRACKERS	**RACKERS**	
BRACKET ▪ CRACKET	**RACKET**	RACKETS ▪ RACKETT ▪ RACKETY
BRACKETED	**RACKETED**	
	RACKETEER	RACKETEERS
	RACKETER	RACKETERS
BRACKETING	**RACKETING**	
BRACKETS ▪ CRACKETS	**RACKETS**	
	RACKETT	RACKETTS
WRACKFUL	**RACKFUL**	RACKFULS
CRACKING ▪ FRACKING ▪ TRACKING WRACKING	**RACKING**	RACKINGS
CRACKINGS ▪ FRACKINGS ▪ TRACKINGS	**RACKINGS**	
CRACKLE ▪ GRACKLE	**RACKLE**	
BRACKS ▪ CRACKS ▪ TRACKS ▪ WRACKS	**RACKS**	
	RACKWORK	RACKWORKS
	RACLETTE	RACLETTES
	RACLOIR	RACLOIRS
	RACON	RACONS
	RACONTEUR	RACONTEURS
	RACOON	RACOONS
	RACQUET	RACQUETS
ORACY	**RACY**	
BRAD ▪ DRAD ▪ GRAD ▪ ORAD ▪ PRAD ▪ TRAD	**RAD**	RADE ▪ RADS
	RADAR	RADARS
BRADDED	**RADDED**	
BRADDING	**RADDING**	
	RADDLE	RADDLED ▪ RADDLES
	RADDOCKE	RADDOCKES
GRADE ▪ IRADE ▪ TRADE	**RADE**	
	RADGE	RADGER ▪ RADGES
	RADGES	RADGEST
	RADIAL	RADIALE ▪ RADIALS
	RADIALISE	RADIALISED ▪ RADIALISES
	RADIALIZE	RADIALIZED ▪ RADIALIZES
	RADIAN	RADIANS ▪ RADIANT
	RADIANCE	RADIANCES
	RADIANT	RADIANTS
	RADIATA	RADIATAS
ERADIATE	**RADIATE**	RADIATED ▪ RADIATES
ERADIATED	**RADIATED**	
ERADIATES	**RADIATES**	
ERADIATING	**RADIATING**	
ERADIATION	**RADIATION**	RADIATIONS
	RADIATOR	RADIATORS ▪ RADIATORY
	RADICAL	RADICALS
	RADICAND	RADICANDS
ERADICANT	**RADICANT**	
ERADICATE	**RADICATE**	RADICATED ▪ RADICATES
ERADICATED	**RADICATED**	
ERADICATES	**RADICATES**	
	RADICCHIO	RADICCHIOS
	RADICEL	RADICELS
	RADICLE	RADICLES
	RADICULE	RADICULES
	RADIO	RADIOS
	RADIOGOLD	RADIOGOLDS
	RADIOGRAM	RADIOGRAMS
	RADIOTHON	RADIOTHONS
	RADIUM	RADIUMS

FRONT HOOK	ROOT WORD	END HOOK
	RADOME	RADOMES
	RADON	RADONS
BRADS · GRADS · PRADS · TRADS	**RADS**	
	RADULA	RADULAE · RADULAR · RADULAS
	RADWASTE	RADWASTES
	RAFALE	RAFALES
DRAFF · GRAFF	**RAFF**	RAFFS
	RAFFIA	RAFFIAS
	RAFFINATE	RAFFINATES
	RAFFINOSE	RAFFINOSES
DRAFFISH	**RAFFISH**	
	RAFFLE	RAFFLED · RAFFLER · RAFFLES
	RAFFLER	RAFFLERS
	RAFFLESIA	RAFFLESIAS
DRAFFS · GRAFFS	**RAFFS**	
CRAFT · DRAFT · GRAFT · KRAFT	**RAFT**	RAFTS
CRAFTED · DRAFTED · GRAFTED	**RAFTED**	
CRAFTER · DRAFTER · GRAFTER	**RAFTER**	RAFTERS
	RAFTERING	RAFTERINGS
CRAFTERS · DRAFTERS · GRAFTERS	**RAFTERS**	
CRAFTING · DRAFTING · GRAFTING	**RAFTING**	RAFTINGS
DRAFTINGS · GRAFTINGS	**RAFTINGS**	
CRAFTS · DRAFTS · GRAFTS · KRAFTS	**RAFTS**	
CRAFTSMAN · DRAFTSMAN	**RAFTSMAN**	
CRAFTSMEN · DRAFTSMEN	**RAFTSMEN**	
BRAG · CRAG · DRAG · FRAG	**RAG**	RAGA · RAGE · RAGG · RAGI · RAGS
	RAGA	RAGAS
	RAGBAG	RAGBAGS
	RAGBOLT	RAGBOLTS
	RAGE	RAGED · RAGEE · RAGER · RAGES
DRAGEE	**RAGEE**	RAGEES
DRAGEES	**RAGEES**	
	RAGER	RAGERS
	RAGG	RAGGA · RAGGS · RAGGY
	RAGGA	RAGGAS
BRAGGED · CRAGGED · DRAGGED · FRAGGED	**RAGGED**	RAGGEDY
	RAGGEE	RAGGEES
BRAGGIER · CRAGGIER · DRAGGIER	**RAGGIER**	
	RAGGIES	RAGGIEST
BRAGGIEST · CRAGGIEST · DRAGGIEST	**RAGGIEST**	
BRAGGING · DRAGGING · FRAGGING	**RAGGING**	RAGGINGS
BRAGGINGS · FRAGGINGS	**RAGGINGS**	
DRAGGLE	**RAGGLE**	RAGGLED · RAGGLES
DRAGGLED	**RAGGLED**	
DRAGGLES	**RAGGLES**	
DRAGGLING	**RAGGLING**	
BRAGGY · CRAGGY · DRAGGY	**RAGGY**	
	RAGHEAD	RAGHEADS *(offensive)*
TRAGI	**RAGI**	RAGIS
	RAGING	RAGINGS
	RAGINI	RAGINIS
	RAGLAN	RAGLANS
	RAGMAN	RAGMANS
	RAGMEN	RAGMENT
FRAGMENT	**RAGMENT**	RAGMENTS
FRAGMENTS	**RAGMENTS**	
	RAGOUT	RAGOUTS
	RAGPICKER	RAGPICKERS
BRAGS · CRAGS · DRAGS · FRAGS	**RAGS**	
	RAGSTONE	RAGSTONES
	RAGTAG	RAGTAGS
	RAGTIME	RAGTIMER · RAGTIMES
	RAGTIMER	RAGTIMERS
	RAGTOP	RAGTOPS
	RAGWEED	RAGWEEDS
	RAGWHEEL	RAGWHEELS
	RAGWORK	RAGWORKS
	RAGWORM	RAGWORMS
	RAGWORT	RAGWORTS

FRONT HOOK	ROOT WORD	END HOOK
	RAH	RAHS
	RAHUI	RAHUIS
	RAI	RAIA · RAID · RAIK · RAIL · RAIN RAIS · RAIT
	RAIA	RAIAS
BRAID	**RAID**	RAIDS
BRAIDED	**RAIDED**	
BRAIDER	**RAIDER**	RAIDERS
BRAIDERS	**RAIDERS**	
BRAIDING	**RAIDING**	RAIDINGS
BRAIDINGS	**RAIDINGS**	
BRAIDS	**RAIDS**	
TRAIK	**RAIK**	RAIKS
TRAIKED	**RAIKED**	
TRAIKING	**RAIKING**	
TRAIKS	**RAIKS**	
BRAIL · DRAIL · FRAIL · GRAIL · TRAIL	**RAIL**	RAILE · RAILS
	RAILBED	RAILBEDS
	RAILBIRD	RAILBIRDS
	RAILCAR	RAILCARD · RAILCARS
	RAILCARD	RAILCARDS
GRAILE	**RAILE**	RAILED · RAILER · RAILES
BRAILED · DRAILED · TRAILED	**RAILED**	
FRAILER · TRAILER	**RAILER**	RAILERS
TRAILERS	**RAILERS**	
GRAILES	**RAILES**	
TRAILHEAD	**RAILHEAD**	RAILHEADS
TRAILHEADS	**RAILHEADS**	
BRAILING · DRAILING · TRAILING	**RAILING**	RAILINGS
TRAILINGLY	**RAILINGLY**	
TRAILLESS	**RAILLESS**	
FRAILLY	**RAILLY**	
	RAILROAD	RAILROADS
BRAILS · DRAILS · FRAILS · GRAILS TRAILS	**RAILS**	
	RAILWAY	RAILWAYS
	RAIMENT	RAIMENTS
BRAIN · DRAIN · GRAIN · TRAIN	**RAIN**	RAINE · RAINS · RAINY
TRAINBAND	**RAINBAND**	RAINBANDS
TRAINBANDS	**RAINBANDS**	
	RAINBIRD	RAINBIRDS
	RAINBOW	RAINBOWS · RAINBOWY
	RAINCHECK	RAINCHECKS
	RAINCOAT	RAINCOATS
	RAINDATE	RAINDATES
	RAINDROP	RAINDROPS
GRAINE	**RAINE**	RAINED · RAINES
BRAINED · DRAINED · GRAINED · TRAINED	**RAINED**	
GRAINES	**RAINES**	
	RAINFALL	RAINFALLS
BRAINIER · GRAINIER	**RAINIER**	
BRAINIEST · GRAINIEST	**RAINIEST**	
BRAINILY	**RAINILY**	
BRAININESS · GRAININESS	**RAININESS**	
BRAINING · DRAINING · GRAINING TRAINING	**RAINING**	
BRAINLESS · GRAINLESS · TRAINLESS	**RAINLESS**	
	RAINMAKER	RAINMAKERS
	RAINOUT	RAINOUTS
	RAINPROOF	RAINPROOFS
BRAINS · DRAINS · GRAINS · TRAINS	**RAINS**	
	RAINSPOUT	RAINSPOUTS
BRAINSTORM	**RAINSTORM**	RAINSTORMS
BRAINWASH	**RAINWASH**	
	RAINWATER	RAINWATERS
	RAINWEAR	RAINWEARS
BRAINY · GRAINY	**RAINY**	
BRAIRD	**RAIRD**	RAIRDS
BRAIRDS	**RAIRDS**	

FRONT HOOK	ROOT WORD	END HOOK
	RAIS	RAISE
ARAISE · BRAISE · FRAISE · PRAISE	**RAISE**	RAISED · RAISER · RAISES
ARAISED · BRAISED · FRAISED · PRAISED	**RAISED**	
PRAISER	**RAISER**	RAISERS
PRAISERS	**RAISERS**	
ARAISES · BRAISES · FRAISES · PRAISES	**RAISES**	
	RAISIN	RAISING · RAISINS · RAISINY
ARAISING · BRAISING · FRAISING · PRAISING	**RAISING**	RAISINGS
PRAISINGS	**RAISINGS**	
KRAIT · TRAIT	**RAIT**	RAITA · RAITS
	RAITA	RAITAS
KRAITS · TRAITS	**RAITS**	
	RAIYAT	RAIYATS
	RAJ	RAJA
	RAJA	RAJAH · RAJAS
	RAJAH	RAJAHS
	RAJAHSHIP	RAJAHSHIPS
	RAJASHIP	RAJASHIPS
BRAKE · CRAKE · DRAKE	**RAKE**	RAKED · RAKEE · RAKER · RAKES
BRAKED · CRAKED	**RAKED**	
	RAKEE	RAKEES
	RAKEHELL	RAKEHELLS · RAKEHELLY
	RAKEOFF	RAKEOFFS
	RAKER	RAKERS · RAKERY
BRAKES · CRAKES · DRAKES	**RAKES**	
	RAKESHAME	RAKESHAMES
	RAKI	RAKIS
BRAKING · CRAKING	**RAKING**	RAKINGS
	RAKIS	RAKISH
	RAKSHAS	RAKSHASA
	RAKSHASA	RAKSHASAS
	RAKU	RAKUS
	RALE	RALES
	RALLIER	RALLIERS
ORALLY	**RALLY**	RALLYE
	RALLYE	RALLYES
	RALLYING	RALLYINGS
	RALLYIST	RALLYISTS
	RALPH	RALPHS *(offensive)*
CRAM · DRAM · GRAM · PRAM · TRAM	**RAM**	RAMI · RAMP · RAMS
	RAMADA	RAMADAS
	RAMAKIN	RAMAKINS
	RAMBLA	RAMBLAS
BRAMBLE	**RAMBLE**	RAMBLED · RAMBLER · RAMBLES
BRAMBLED	**RAMBLED**	
	RAMBLER	RAMBLERS
BRAMBLES	**RAMBLES**	
BRAMBLING	**RAMBLING**	RAMBLINGS
BRAMBLINGS	**RAMBLINGS**	
	RAMBUTAN	RAMBUTANS
	RAMCAT	RAMCATS
	RAMEE	RAMEES
	RAMEKIN	RAMEKINS
	RAMEN	RAMENS
	RAMEQUIN	RAMEQUINS
	RAMET	RAMETS
	RAMI	RAMIE · RAMIN · RAMIS
	RAMIE	RAMIES
	RAMILIE	RAMILIES
	RAMILLIE	RAMILLIES
	RAMIN	RAMINS
	RAMJET	RAMJETS
CRAMMED · DRAMMED · TRAMMED	**RAMMED**	
TRAMMEL	**RAMMEL**	RAMMELS
TRAMMELS	**RAMMELS**	
CRAMMER	**RAMMER**	RAMMERS
CRAMMERS	**RAMMERS**	
TRAMMIES	**RAMMIES**	RAMMIEST
CRAMMING · DRAMMING · TRAMMING	**RAMMING**	

R

FRONT HOOK	ROOT WORD	END HOOK
	RAMMLE	RAMMLES
	RAMONA	RAMONAS
CRAMP ▪ GRAMP ▪ TRAMP	**RAMP**	RAMPS
	RAMPAGE	RAMPAGED ▪ RAMPAGER ▪ RAMPAGES
	RAMPAGER	RAMPAGERS
	RAMPAGING	RAMPAGINGS
	RAMPART	RAMPARTS
	RAMPAUGE	RAMPAUGED ▪ RAMPAUGES
CRAMPED ▪ TRAMPED	**RAMPED**	
CRAMPER ▪ TRAMPER	**RAMPER**	RAMPERS
CRAMPERS ▪ TRAMPERS	**RAMPERS**	
	RAMPICK	RAMPICKS
	RAMPIKE	RAMPIKES
CRAMPING ▪ TRAMPING	**RAMPING**	RAMPINGS
TRAMPINGS	**RAMPINGS**	
	RAMPION	RAMPIONS
	RAMPIRE	RAMPIRED ▪ RAMPIRES
	RAMPOLE	RAMPOLES
CRAMPS ▪ GRAMPS ▪ TRAMPS	**RAMPS**	
	RAMROD	RAMRODS
CRAMS ▪ DRAMS ▪ GRAMS ▪ PRAMS ▪ TRAMS	**RAMS**	
	RAMSHORN	RAMSHORNS
	RAMSON	RAMSONS
	RAMTIL	RAMTILS
	RAMTILLA	RAMTILLAS
BRAN ▪ CRAN ▪ GRAN	**RAN**	RANA ▪ RAND ▪ RANG ▪ RANI ▪ RANK ▪ RANT
GRANA ▪ PRANA	**RANA**	RANAS
	RANARIUM	RANARIUMS
PRANAS	**RANAS**	
PRANCE ▪ TRANCE	**RANCE**	RANCED ▪ RANCEL ▪ RANCES
PRANCED ▪ TRANCED	**RANCED**	
	RANCEL	RANCELS
PRANCES ▪ TRANCES	**RANCES**	
BRANCH ▪ CRANCH	**RANCH**	RANCHO
BRANCHED ▪ CRANCHED	**RANCHED**	
BRANCHER	**RANCHER**	RANCHERO ▪ RANCHERS
	RANCHERIA	RANCHERIAS
	RANCHERIE	RANCHERIES
	RANCHERO	RANCHEROS
BRANCHERS	**RANCHERS**	
BRANCHES ▪ CRANCHES ▪ TRANCHES	**RANCHES**	
BRANCHING ▪ CRANCHING	**RANCHING**	RANCHINGS
BRANCHINGS	**RANCHINGS**	
BRANCHLESS	**RANCHLESS**	
BRANCHLIKE	**RANCHLIKE**	
	RANCHO	RANCHOS
PRANCING ▪ TRANCING	**RANCING**	
	RANCOR	RANCORS
	RANCOUR	RANCOURS
BRAND ▪ GRAND	**RAND**	RANDS ▪ RANDY
	RANDAN	RANDANS
BRANDED	**RANDED**	
	RANDEM	RANDEMS
	RANDIE	RANDIER ▪ RANDIES
BRANDIES	**RANDIES**	RANDIEST
BRANDING	**RANDING**	
	RANDLORD	RANDLORDS
	RANDOM	RANDOMS
	RANDOMISE	RANDOMISED ▪ RANDOMISER ▪ RANDOMISES
	RANDOMIZE	RANDOMIZED ▪ RANDOMIZER ▪ RANDOMIZES
	RANDON	RANDONS
BRANDS ▪ GRANDS	**RANDS**	
BRANDY	**RANDY**	
	RANEE	RANEES
KRANG ▪ ORANG ▪ PRANG ▪ WRANG	**RANG**	RANGE ▪ RANGI ▪ RANGY
	RANGATIRA	RANGATIRAS
GRANGE ▪ ORANGE	**RANGE**	RANGED ▪ RANGER ▪ RANGES
PRANGED ▪ WRANGED	**RANGED**	
	RANGELAND	RANGELANDS

FRONT HOOK	ROOT WORD	END HOOK
FRANGER · GRANGER · ORANGER	**RANGER**	RANGERS
FRANGERS · GRANGERS	**RANGERS**	
GRANGES · ORANGES	**RANGES**	
	RANGI	RANGIS
ORANGIER	**RANGIER**	
ORANGIEST	**RANGIEST**	
PRANGING · WRANGING	**RANGING**	RANGINGS
	RANGIORA	RANGIORAS
	RANGOLI	RANGOLIS
ORANGY	**RANGY**	
	RANI	RANID · RANIS
	RANID	RANIDS
BRANK · CRANK · DRANK · FRANK · PRANK · TRANK	**RANK**	RANKE · RANKS
	RANKE	RANKED · RANKER · RANKES
BRANKED · CRANKED · FRANKED · PRANKED	**RANKED**	
CRANKER · FRANKER	**RANKER**	RANKERS
FRANKERS	**RANKERS**	
	RANKES	RANKEST
CRANKEST · FRANKEST	**RANKEST**	
BRANKING · CRANKING · FRANKING · PRANKING	**RANKING**	RANKINGS
PRANKINGS	**RANKINGS**	
CRANKISH · PRANKISH	**RANKISH**	
	RANKISM	RANKISMS
CRANKLE · PRANKLE	**RANKLE**	RANKLED · RANKLES
CRANKLED · PRANKLED	**RANKLED**	
CRANKLES · PRANKLES	**RANKLES**	RANKLESS
CRANKLING · PRANKLING	**RANKLING**	
CRANKLY · FRANKLY	**RANKLY**	
CRANKNESS · FRANKNESS	**RANKNESS**	
BRANKS · CRANKS · FRANKS · PRANKS · TRANKS	**RANKS**	
	RANKSHIFT	RANKSHIFTS
	RANPIKE	RANPIKES
	RANSACK	RANSACKS
	RANSACKER	RANSACKERS
	RANSEL	RANSELS
	RANSHAKLE	RANSHAKLED · RANSHAKLES
TRANSOM	**RANSOM**	RANSOMS
TRANSOMED	**RANSOMED**	
	RANSOMER	RANSOMERS
TRANSOMS	**RANSOMS**	
BRANT · DRANT · GRANT · ORANT · TRANT	**RANT**	RANTS
DRANTED · GRANTED · TRANTED	**RANTED**	
GRANTER · TRANTER	**RANTER**	RANTERS
	RANTERISM	RANTERISMS
GRANTERS · TRANTERS	**RANTERS**	
DRANTING · GRANTING · TRANTING	**RANTING**	RANTINGS
	RANTIPOLE	RANTIPOLED · RANTIPOLES
BRANTS · CRANTS · DRANTS · GRANTS · ORANTS · TRANTS	**RANTS**	
	RANULA	RANULAR · RANULAS
GRANULAR	**RANULAR**	
	RANZEL	RANZELS
	RAOULIA	RAOULIAS
CRAP · DRAP · FRAP · TRAP · WRAP	**RAP**	RAPE · RAPS · RAPT
CRAPE · DRAPE · FRAPE · GRAPE · TRAPE	**RAPE**	RAPED · RAPER · RAPES
CRAPED · DRAPED · GRAPED · TRAPED	**RAPED**	
DRAPER	**RAPER**	RAPERS
DRAPERS	**RAPERS**	
CRAPES · DRAPES · GRAPES · TRAPES	**RAPES**	
GRAPESEED	**RAPESEED**	RAPESEEDS
GRAPESEEDS	**RAPESEEDS**	
	RAPHANIA	RAPHANIAS
	RAPHE	RAPHES
	RAPHIA	RAPHIAS
	RAPHIDE	RAPHIDES
	RAPID	RAPIDS

R

FRONT HOOK	ROOT WORD	END HOOK
CRAPIER ▪ DRAPIER ▪ GRAPIER DRAPIERS	**RAPIER**	RAPIERS
	RAPIERS	
	RAPINE	RAPINES
CRAPING ▪ DRAPING ▪ GRAPING ▪ TRAPING	**RAPING**	
	RAPIST	RAPISTS
	RAPLOCH	RAPLOCHS
	RAPPAREE	RAPPAREES
FRAPPE	**RAPPE**	RAPPED ▪ RAPPEE ▪ RAPPEL ▪ RAPPEN RAPPER ▪ RAPPES
CRAPPED ▪ DRAPPED ▪ FRAPPED ▪ TRAPPED WRAPPED	**RAPPED**	
FRAPPEE	**RAPPEE**	RAPPEES
	RAPPEL	RAPPELS
CRAPPER ▪ TRAPPER ▪ WRAPPER	**RAPPER**	RAPPERS
CRAPPERS (offensive) ▪ TRAPPERS ▪ WRAPPERS FRAPPES	**RAPPERS**	
	RAPPES	
CRAPPING ▪ DRAPPING ▪ FRAPPING TRAPPING ▪ WRAPPING	**RAPPING**	RAPPINGS
TRAPPINGS ▪ WRAPPINGS	**RAPPINGS**	
	RAPPORT	RAPPORTS
CRAPS ▪ DRAPS ▪ FRAPS ▪ TRAPS ▪ WRAPS TRAPT ▪ WRAPT ▪ YRAPT	**RAPS**	
	RAPT	
	RAPTOR	RAPTORS
	RAPTURE	RAPTURED ▪ RAPTURES
	RAPTURISE	RAPTURISED ▪ RAPTURISES
	RAPTURIST	RAPTURISTS
	RAPTURIZE	RAPTURIZED ▪ RAPTURIZES
CRARE ▪ URARE	**RARE**	RARED ▪ RAREE ▪ RARER ▪ RARES
	RAREBIT	RAREBITS
	RAREFIER	RAREFIERS
	RARERIPE	RARERIPES
CRARES ▪ URARES	**RARES**	RAREST
	RARK	RARKS
BRAS ▪ ERAS ▪ FRAS	**RAS**	RASE ▪ RASH ▪ RASP ▪ RAST
	RASBORA	RASBORAS
	RASCAILLE	RASCAILLES
	RASCAL	RASCALS
	RASCALDOM	RASCALDOMS
	RASCALISM	RASCALISMS
	RASCASSE	RASCASSES
	RASCHEL	RASCHELS
ERASE ▪ PRASE ▪ URASE	**RASE**	RASED ▪ RASER ▪ RASES
ERASED	**RASED**	
ERASER	**RASER**	RASERS
ERASERS	**RASERS**	
BRASES ▪ CRASES ▪ ERASES ▪ PRASES URASES	**RASES**	
BRASH ▪ CRASH ▪ TRASH	**RASH**	
BRASHED ▪ CRASHED ▪ TRASHED	**RASHED**	
BRASHER ▪ CRASHER ▪ TRASHER	**RASHER**	RASHERS
CRASHERS ▪ TRASHERS	**RASHERS**	
BRASHES ▪ CRASHES ▪ TRASHES	**RASHES**	RASHEST
BRASHEST	**RASHEST**	
	RASHIE	RASHIES
BRASHING ▪ CRASHING ▪ TRASHING	**RASHING**	
BRASHLY	**RASHLY**	
BRASHNESS	**RASHNESS**	
ERASING	**RASING**	
	RASMALAI	RASMALAIS
GRASP	**RASP**	RASPS ▪ RASPY
GRASPED	**RASPED**	
GRASPER	**RASPER**	RASPERS
GRASPERS	**RASPERS**	
GRASPING	**RASPING**	RASPINGS
GRASPINGLY	**RASPINGLY**	
GRASPS	**RASPS**	
WRASSE	**RASSE**	RASSES
BRASSES ▪ FRASSES ▪ GRASSES ▪ TRASSES WRASSES	**RASSES**	

FRONT HOOK	ROOT WORD	END HOOK
WRASSLE	**RASSLE**	RASSLED · RASSLES
WRASSLED	**RASSLED**	
WRASSLES	**RASSLES**	
WRASSLING	**RASSLING**	
BRAST · WRAST	**RAST**	RASTA
	RASTER	RASTERS
	RASTERISE	RASTERISED · RASTERISES
	RASTERIZE	RASTERIZED · RASTERIZES
	RASTRUM	RASTRUMS
ERASURE	**RASURE**	RASURES
ERASURES	**RASURES**	
BRAT · DRAT · FRAT · GRAT · PRAT · TRAT	**RAT**	RATA · RATE · RATH · RATO · RATS · RATU
	RATA	RATAL · RATAN · RATAS
	RATABLE	RATABLES
	RATAFEE	RATAFEES
	RATAFIA	RATAFIAS
	RATAL	RATALS
	RATAN	RATANS · RATANY
	RATAPLAN	RATAPLANS
	RATATAT	RATATATS
	RATBAG	RATBAGS (offensive)
CRATCH · FRATCH	**RATCH**	
CRATCHES · FRATCHES	**RATCHES**	
BRATCHET	**RATCHET**	RATCHETS
BRATCHETS	**RATCHETS**	
FRATCHING	**RATCHING**	
CRATE · FRATE · GRATE · IRATE · ORATE	**RATE**	RATED · RATEL · RATER · RATES
PRATE · URATE · WRATE		
CRATED · GRATED · ORATED · PRATED	**RATED**	
	RATEEN	RATEENS
	RATEL	RATELS
	RATEMETER	RATEMETERS
	RATEPAYER	RATEPAYERS
CRATER · FRATER · GRATER · IRATER	**RATER**	RATERS
KRATER · PRATER		
CRATERS · FRATERS · GRATERS · KRATERS	**RATERS**	
PRATERS		
CRATES · GRATES · ORATES · PRATES	**RATES**	
URATES		
	RATFINK	RATFINKS
WRATH	**RATH**	RATHA · RATHE · RATHS
	RATHA	RATHAS
	RATHE	RATHER
	RATHERIPE	RATHERIPES
	RATHOLE	RATHOLES
	RATHOUSE	RATHOUSES
	RATHRIPE	RATHRIPES
WRATHS	**RATHS**	
	RATICIDE	RATICIDES
GRATIFIED	**RATIFIED**	
GRATIFIER	**RATIFIER**	RATIFIERS
GRATIFIERS	**RATIFIERS**	
GRATIFIES	**RATIFIES**	
GRATIFY	**RATIFY**	
GRATIFYING	**RATIFYING**	
GRATINE	**RATINE**	RATINES
CRATING · GRATING · ORATING · PRATING	**RATING**	RATINGS
GRATINGS · PRATINGS	**RATINGS**	
	RATIO	RATION · RATIOS
ORATION	**RATION**	RATIONS
	RATIONAL	RATIONALE · RATIONALS
	RATIONALE	RATIONALES
ORATIONS	**RATIONS**	
	RATITE	RATITES
	RATLIN	RATLINE · RATLING · RATLINS
	RATLINE	RATLINES
BRATLING	**RATLING**	RATLINGS
BRATLINGS	**RATLINGS**	
	RATO	RATOO · RATOS

FRONT HOOK	ROOT WORD	END HOOK
	RATOO	RATOON · RATOOS
	RATOON	RATOONS
	RATOONER	RATOONERS
BRATPACK	RATPACK	RATPACKS
BRATPACKS	RATPACKS	
BRATS · DRATS · FRATS · PRATS · TRATS	RATS	
	RATSBANE	RATSBANES
	RATTAIL	RATTAILS
	RATTAN	RATTANS
DRATTED · PRATTED	RATTED	
	RATTEEN	RATTEENS
	RATTEN	RATTENS
	RATTENER	RATTENERS
	RATTENING	RATTENINGS
	RATTER	RATTERS · RATTERY
BRATTIER	RATTIER	
BRATTIEST	RATTIEST	
BRATTINESS	RATTINESS	
DRATTING · PRATTING	RATTING	RATTINGS
BRATTISH	RATTISH	
BRATTLE · PRATTLE	RATTLE	RATTLED · RATTLER · RATTLES
	RATTLEBAG	RATTLEBAGS
PRATTLEBOX	RATTLEBOX	
BRATTLED · PRATTLED	RATTLED	
PRATTLER	RATTLER	RATTLERS
PRATTLERS	RATTLERS	
BRATTLES · PRATTLES	RATTLES	
	RATTLIN	RATTLINE · RATTLING · RATTLINS
	RATTLINE	RATTLINES
BRATTLING · PRATTLING	RATTLING	RATTLINGS
BRATTLINGS	RATTLINGS	
	RATTON	RATTONS
	RATTOON	RATTOONS
	RATTRAP	RATTRAPS
BRATTY	RATTY	
	RATU	RATUS
	RAUCLE	RAUCLER
DRAUGHT · FRAUGHT	RAUGHT	
	RAUN	RAUNS
BRAUNCH · CRAUNCH · GRAUNCH	RAUNCH	RAUNCHY
BRAUNCHED · CRAUNCHED · GRAUNCHED	RAUNCHED	
BRAUNCHES · CRAUNCHES · GRAUNCHES	RAUNCHES	
CRAUNCHIER	RAUNCHIER	
BRAUNCHING · CRAUNCHING · GRAUNCHING	RAUNCHING	
CRAUNCHY	RAUNCHY	
	RAUNGE	RAUNGED · RAUNGES
	RAUPATU	RAUPATUS
	RAURIKI	RAURIKIS
	RAUWOLFIA	RAUWOLFIAS
	RAVAGE	RAVAGED · RAVAGER · RAVAGES
	RAVAGER	RAVAGERS
BRAVE · CRAVE · DRAVE · GRAVE · TRAVE	RAVE	RAVED · RAVEL · RAVEN · RAVER · RAVES
BRAVED · CRAVED · GRAVED	RAVED	
GRAVEL · TRAVEL	RAVEL	RAVELS
GRAVELED · TRAVELED	RAVELED	
TRAVELER	RAVELER	RAVELERS
TRAVELERS	RAVELERS	
	RAVELIN	RAVELING · RAVELINS
GRAVELING · TRAVELING	RAVELING	RAVELINGS
TRAVELINGS	RAVELINGS	
GRAVELLED · TRAVELLED	RAVELLED	
TRAVELLER	RAVELLER	RAVELLERS
TRAVELLERS	RAVELLERS	
GRAVELLING · TRAVELLING	RAVELLING	RAVELLINGS
GRAVELLY	RAVELLY	
	RAVELMENT	RAVELMENTS
GRAVELS · TRAVELS	RAVELS	
CRAVEN · GRAVEN	RAVEN	RAVENS
CRAVENED	RAVENED	

FRONT HOOK	ROOT WORD	END HOOK
	RAVENER	RAVENERS
CRAVENING	**RAVENING**	RAVENINGS
CRAVENS	**RAVENS**	
BRAVER · CRAVER · GRAVER	**RAVER**	RAVERS
BRAVERS · CRAVERS · GRAVERS	**RAVERS**	
BRAVES · CRAVES · GRAVES · TRAVES	**RAVES**	
	RAVIGOTE	RAVIGOTES
	RAVIGOTTE	RAVIGOTTES
	RAVIN	RAVINE · RAVING · RAVINS
	RAVINE	RAVINED · RAVINES
BRAVING · CRAVING · GRAVING	**RAVING**	RAVINGS
CRAVINGS · GRAVINGS	**RAVINGS**	
	RAVIOLI	RAVIOLIS
YRAVISHED	**RAVISHED**	
	RAVISHER	RAVISHERS
BRAW · CRAW · DRAW	**RAW**	RAWN · RAWS
	RAWBONE	RAWBONED
BRAWER · DRAWER	**RAWER**	
BRAWEST	**RAWEST**	
	RAWHEAD	RAWHEADS
	RAWHIDE	RAWHIDED · RAWHIDES
	RAWIN	RAWING · RAWINS
DRAWING	**RAWING**	RAWINGS
DRAWINGS	**RAWINGS**	
BRAWLY · CRAWLY · DRAWLY	**RAWLY**	
BRAWN · DRAWN · PRAWN	**RAWN**	RAWNS
BRAWNS · PRAWNS	**RAWNS**	
BRAWS · CRAWS · DRAWS	**RAWS**	
PRAXES	**RAXES**	
BRAY · CRAY · DRAY · FRAY · GRAY · PRAY · TRAY	**RAY**	RAYA · RAYS
	RAYA	RAYAH · RAYAS
	RAYAH	RAYAHS
BRAYED · DRAYED · FRAYED · GRAYED · PRAYED	**RAYED**	
BRAYING · DRAYING · FRAYING · GRAYING · PRAYING	**RAYING**	
GRAYLE	**RAYLE**	RAYLED · RAYLES · RAYLET
GRAYLES	**RAYLES**	RAYLESS
	RAYLET	RAYLETS
GRAYLING	**RAYLING**	
TRAYNE	**RAYNE**	RAYNES
TRAYNES	**RAYNES**	
CRAYON	**RAYON**	RAYONS
CRAYONS	**RAYONS**	
BRAYS · CRAYS · DRAYS · FRAYS · GRAYS · PRAYS · TRAYS	**RAYS**	
BRAZE · CRAZE · GRAZE	**RAZE**	RAZED · RAZEE · RAZER · RAZES
BRAZED · CRAZED · GRAZED	**RAZED**	
	RAZEE	RAZEED · RAZEES
BRAZER · GRAZER	**RAZER**	RAZERS
BRAZERS · GRAZERS	**RAZERS**	
BRAZES · CRAZES · GRAZES	**RAZES**	
BRAZING · CRAZING · GRAZING	**RAZING**	
	RAZOO	RAZOOS
	RAZOR	RAZORS
	RAZORBACK	RAZORBACKS
	RAZORBILL	RAZORBILLS
	RAZURE	RAZURES
	RAZZIA	RAZZIAS
FRAZZLE	**RAZZLE**	RAZZLES
FRAZZLES	**RAZZLES**	
ARE · ERE · IRE · ORE · PRE · URE	**RE**	REB · REC · RED · REE · REF · REG · REH · REI · REM · REN · REO · REP · RES · RET · REV · REW · REX · REZ
PREABSORB	**REABSORB**	REABSORBS
PREABSORBS	**REABSORBS**	
	REACCEDE	REACCEDED · REACCEDES
	REACCENT	REACCENTS

FRONT HOOK	ROOT WORD	END HOOK
	REACCEPT	REACCEPTS
	REACCLAIM	REACCLAIMS
PREACCUSE	**REACCUSE**	REACCUSED · REACCUSES
PREACCUSED	**REACCUSED**	
PREACCUSES	**REACCUSES**	
AREACH · BREACH · CREACH · PREACH	**REACH**	
PREACHABLE	**REACHABLE**	
AREACHED · BREACHED · PREACHED	**REACHED**	
BREACHER · PREACHER · TREACHER	**REACHER**	REACHERS
BREACHERS · PREACHERS · TREACHERS	**REACHERS**	
AREACHES · BREACHES · PREACHES	**REACHES**	
AREACHING · BREACHING · PREACHING	**REACHING**	
	REACQUIRE	REACQUIRED · REACQUIRES
PREACT	**REACT**	REACTS
	REACTANCE	REACTANCES
	REACTANT	REACTANTS
PREACTED	**REACTED**	
PREACTING	**REACTING**	
	REACTION	REACTIONS
	REACTOR	REACTORS
PREACTS	**REACTS**	
	REACTUATE	REACTUATED · REACTUATES
AREAD · BREAD · DREAD · OREAD · TREAD	**READ**	READD · READS · READY
PREADAPT	**READAPT**	READAPTS
PREADAPTED	**READAPTED**	
PREADAPTS	**READAPTS**	
	READD	READDS
	READDICT	READDICTS
DREADER · TREADER	**READER**	READERS
DREADERS · TREADERS	**READERS**	
	READIES	READIEST
AREADING · BREADING · DREADING TREADING	**READING**	READINGS
TREADINGS	**READINGS**	
PREADJUST	**READJUST**	READJUSTS
PREADJUSTS	**READJUSTS**	
PREADMIT	**READMIT**	READMITS
PREADMITS	**READMITS**	
PREADOPT	**READOPT**	READOPTS
PREADOPTED	**READOPTED**	
PREADOPTS	**READOPTS**	
	READORN	READORNS
	READOUT	READOUTS
AREADS · BREADS · DREADS · OREADS TREADS	**READS**	
	READVANCE	READVANCED · READVANCES
	READVISE	READVISED · READVISES
BREADY	**READY**	
	READYMADE	READYMADES
	REAEDIFY	REAEDIFYE
	REAEDIFYE	REAEDIFYED · REAEDIFYES
	REAFFIRM	REAFFIRMS
	REAGENT	REAGENTS
	REAGIN	REAGINS
BREAK · CREAK · FREAK · WREAK	**REAK**	REAKS
CREAKED · FREAKED · WREAKED	**REAKED**	
BREAKING · CREAKING · FREAKING WREAKING	**REAKING**	
	REAKS	
BREAKS · CREAKS · FREAKS · WREAKS	**REAKS**	
AREAL · UREAL	**REAL**	REALM · REALO · REALS
	REALES	REALEST
	REALGAR	REALGARS
	REALIGN	REALIGNS
	REALISE	REALISED · REALISER · REALISES
	REALISER	REALISERS
	REALISM	REALISMS
	REALIST	REALISTS
	REALIZE	REALIZED · REALIZER · REALIZES
	REALIZER	REALIZERS

FRONT HOOK	ROOT WORD	END HOOK
	REALLIE	REALLIED · REALLIES
PREALLOT	**REALLOT**	REALLOTS
PREALLOTS	**REALLOTS**	
AREALLY	**REALLY**	
	REALM	REALMS
	REALO	REALOS
PREALTER	**REALTER**	REALTERS
PREALTERED	**REALTERED**	
PREALTERS	**REALTERS**	
	REALTIE	REALTIES
	REALTOR	REALTORS
BREAM · CREAM · DREAM	**REAM**	REAME · REAMS · REAMY
	REAME	REAMED · REAMER · REAMES
BREAMED · CREAMED · DREAMED	**REAMED**	
	REAMEND	REAMENDS
CREAMER · DREAMER	**REAMER**	REAMERS
CREAMERS · DREAMERS	**REAMERS**	
CREAMIER · DREAMIER	**REAMIER**	
CREAMIEST · DREAMIEST	**REAMIEST**	
BREAMING · CREAMING · DREAMING	**REAMING**	
BREAMS · CREAMS · DREAMS	**REAMS**	
CREAMY · DREAMY	**REAMY**	
	REAN	REANS
	REANALYSE	REANALYSED · REANALYSES
	REANALYZE	REANALYZED · REANALYZES
	REANIMATE	REANIMATED · REANIMATES
	REANOINT	REANOINTS
	REANSWER	REANSWERS
	REAP	REAPS
	REAPER	REAPERS
	REAPHOOK	REAPHOOKS
	REAPPAREL	REAPPARELS
	REAPPEAR	REAPPEARS
PREAPPLIED	**REAPPLIED**	
PREAPPLIES	**REAPPLIES**	
PREAPPLY	**REAPPLY**	
PREAPPOINT	**REAPPOINT**	REAPPOINTS
PREAPPROVE	**REAPPROVE**	REAPPROVED · REAPPROVES
AREAR · DREAR	**REAR**	REARM · REARS
DREARER	**REARER**	REARERS
	REARGUARD	REARGUARDS
	REARGUE	REARGUED · REARGUES
	REARHORSE	REARHORSES
DREARING	**REARING**	
	REARISE	REARISEN · REARISES
PREARM	**REARM**	REARMS
PREARMED	**REARMED**	
PREARMING	**REARMING**	
PREARMS	**REARMS**	
	REAROUSAL	REAROUSALS
	REAROUSE	REAROUSED · REAROUSES
PREARRANGE	**REARRANGE**	REARRANGED · REARRANGER · REARRANGES
	REARREST	REARRESTS
DREARS	**REARS**	
	REARWARD	REARWARDS
	REASCEND	REASCENDS
	REASCENT	REASCENTS
TREASON	**REASON**	REASONS
	REASONER	REASONERS
	REASONING	REASONINGS
TREASONS	**REASONS**	
	REASSAIL	REASSAILS
	REASSERT	REASSERTS
PREASSIGN	**REASSIGN**	REASSIGNS
PREASSIGNS	**REASSIGNS**	
	REASSORT	REASSORTS
	REASSUME	REASSUMED · REASSUMES
PREASSURE	**REASSURE**	REASSURED · REASSURER · REASSURES
PREASSURED	**REASSURED**	

FRONT HOOK	ROOT WORD	END HOOK
	REASSURER	REASSURERS
PREASSURES	**REASSURES**	
BREAST	**REAST**	REASTS ▪ REASTY
BREASTED	**REASTED**	
BREASTING	**REASTING**	
BREASTS	**REASTS**	
	REATA	REATAS
CREATE	**REATE**	REATES
CREATES	**REATES**	
	REATTACK	REATTACKS
	REATTAIN	REATTAINS
	REATTEMPT	REATTEMPTS
	REAVAIL	REAVAILS
GREAVE	**REAVE**	REAVED ▪ REAVER ▪ REAVES
GREAVED	**REAVED**	
PREAVER	**REAVER**	REAVERS
PREAVERS	**REAVERS**	
GREAVES	**REAVES**	
GREAVING	**REAVING**	
	REAVOW	REAVOWS
	REAWAKE	REAWAKED ▪ REAWAKEN ▪ REAWAKES
	REAWAKEN	REAWAKENS
	REAWOKE	REAWOKEN
	REB	REBS
	REBACK	REBACKS
	REBADGE	REBADGED ▪ REBADGES
	REBAIT	REBAITS
	REBALANCE	REBALANCED ▪ REBALANCES
	REBAPTISE	REBAPTISED ▪ REBAPTISES
	REBAPTISM	REBAPTISMS
	REBAPTIZE	REBAPTIZED ▪ REBAPTIZES
	REBAR	REBARS
	REBATE	REBATED ▪ REBATER ▪ REBATES
	REBATER	REBATERS
	REBATO	REBATOS
	REBBE	REBBES
	REBBETZIN	REBBETZINS
	REBEC	REBECK ▪ REBECS
	REBECK	REBECKS
	REBEGIN	REBEGINS
	REBEL	REBELS
	REBELDOM	REBELDOMS
	REBELLER	REBELLERS
	REBELLION	REBELLIONS
	REBELLOW	REBELLOWS
PREBID	**REBID**	REBIDS
PREBIDDEN	**REBIDDEN**	
PREBIDDING	**REBIDDING**	
PREBIDS	**REBIDS**	
PREBILL	**REBILL**	REBILLS
PREBILLED	**REBILLED**	
PREBILLING	**REBILLING**	
PREBILLS	**REBILLS**	
PREBIND	**REBIND**	REBINDS
PREBINDING	**REBINDING**	
PREBINDS	**REBINDS**	
PREBIRTH	**REBIRTH**	REBIRTHS
PREBIRTHS	**REBIRTHS**	
	REBIT	REBITE
	REBITE	REBITES
	REBLEND	REBLENDS
	REBLOOM	REBLOOMS
	REBLOSSOM	REBLOSSOMS
PREBOARD	**REBOARD**	REBOARDS
PREBOARDED	**REBOARDED**	
PREBOARDS	**REBOARDS**	
	REBOATION	REBOATIONS
PREBOIL	**REBOIL**	REBOILS
PREBOILED	**REBOILED**	

673

FRONT HOOK	ROOT WORD	END HOOK
PREBOILING	**REBOILING**	
PREBOILS	**REBOILS**	
PREBOOK	**REBOOK**	REBOOKS
PREBOOKED	**REBOOKED**	
PREBOOKING	**REBOOKING**	
PREBOOKS	**REBOOKS**	
	REBOOT	REBOOTS
	REBOP	REBOPS
	REBORE	REBORED = REBORES
PREBORN	**REBORN**	
	REBORROW	REBORROWS
	REBOTTLE	REBOTTLED = REBOTTLES
PREBOUGHT	**REBOUGHT**	
PREBOUND	**REBOUND**	REBOUNDS
	REBOUNDER	REBOUNDERS
	REBOZO	REBOZOS
	REBRACE	REBRACED = REBRACES
	REBRAND	REBRANDS
	REBREED	REBREEDS
	REBUFF	REBUFFS
PREBUILD	**REBUILD**	REBUILDS
PREBUILDS	**REBUILDS**	
PREBUILT	**REBUILT**	
	REBUKE	REBUKED = REBUKER = REBUKES
	REBUKER	REBUKERS
	REBURIAL	REBURIALS
	REBUT	REBUTS
	REBUTMENT	REBUTMENTS
PREBUTTAL	**REBUTTAL**	REBUTTALS
PREBUTTALS	**REBUTTALS**	
	REBUTTER	REBUTTERS
	REBUTTON	REBUTTONS
PREBUY	**REBUY**	REBUYS
PREBUYING	**REBUYING**	
PREBUYS	**REBUYS**	
	REC	RECK = RECS
	RECAL	RECALL = RECALS
	RECALESCE	RECALESCED = RECALESCES
	RECALL	RECALLS
	RECALLER	RECALLERS
	RECALMENT	RECALMENTS
	RECAMIER	RECAMIERS
	RECANE	RECANED = RECANES
	RECANT	RECANTS
	RECANTER	RECANTERS
	RECAP	RECAPS
	RECAPTION	RECAPTIONS
	RECAPTOR	RECAPTORS
	RECAPTURE	RECAPTURED = RECAPTURER = RECAPTURES
	RECARPET	RECARPETS
PRECAST	**RECAST**	RECASTS
PRECASTING	**RECASTING**	
PRECASTS	**RECASTS**	
	RECATALOG	RECATALOGS
PRECAUTION	**RECAUTION**	RECAUTIONS
	RECCE	RECCED = RECCES
	RECCO	RECCOS
PRECEDE	**RECEDE**	RECEDED = RECEDES
PRECEDED	**RECEDED**	
PRECEDES	**RECEDES**	
PRECEDING	**RECEDING**	
	RECEIPT	RECEIPTS
	RECEIPTOR	RECEIPTORS
	RECEIVAL	RECEIVALS
	RECEIVE	RECEIVED = RECEIVER = RECEIVES
	RECEIVER	RECEIVERS
	RECEIVING	RECEIVINGS
	RECEMENT	RECEMENTS
	RECENSE	RECENSED = RECENSES

R

FRONT HOOK	ROOT WORD	END HOOK
	RECENSION	RECENSIONS
PRECENSOR	**RECENSOR**	RECENSORS
PRECENSORS	**RECENSORS**	
PRECENT	**RECENT**	
	RECENTRE	RECENTRED · RECENTRES
PRECEPT	**RECEPT**	RECEPTS
	RECEPTION	RECEPTIONS
PRECEPTIVE	**RECEPTIVE**	
PRECEPTOR	**RECEPTOR**	RECEPTORS
PRECEPTORS	**RECEPTORS**	
PRECEPTS	**RECEPTS**	
PRECESS	**RECESS**	
PRECESSED	**RECESSED**	
PRECESSES	**RECESSES**	
PRECESSING	**RECESSING**	
PRECESSION	**RECESSION**	RECESSIONS
	RECESSIVE	RECESSIVES
	RECHANGE	RECHANGED · RECHANGES
	RECHANNEL	RECHANNELS
PRECHARGE	**RECHARGE**	RECHARGED · RECHARGER · RECHARGES
PRECHARGED	**RECHARGED**	
	RECHARGER	RECHARGERS
PRECHARGES	**RECHARGES**	
	RECHART	RECHARTS
	RECHARTER	RECHARTERS
	RECHATE	RECHATES
	RECHAUFFE	RECHAUFFES
	RECHEAT	RECHEATS
PRECHECK	**RECHECK**	RECHECKS
PRECHECKED	**RECHECKED**	
PRECHECKS	**RECHECKS**	
	RECHEW	RECHEWS
PRECHOOSE	**RECHOOSE**	RECHOOSES
PRECHOOSES	**RECHOOSES**	
PRECHOSE	**RECHOSE**	RECHOSEN
PRECHOSEN	**RECHOSEN**	
PRECIPE	**RECIPE**	RECIPES
PRECIPES	**RECIPES**	
	RECIPIENT	RECIPIENTS
	RECIRCLE	RECIRCLED · RECIRCLES
PRECISION	**RECISION**	RECISIONS
PRECISIONS	**RECISIONS**	
	RECIT	RECITE · RECITS
	RECITAL	RECITALS
	RECITE	RECITED · RECITER · RECITES
PRECITED	**RECITED**	
	RECITER	RECITERS
DRECK · TRECK · WRECK	**RECK**	RECKS
TRECKED · WRECKED	**RECKED**	
TRECKING · WRECKING	**RECKING**	
FRECKLING	**RECKLING**	RECKLINGS
FRECKLINGS	**RECKLINGS**	
	RECKON	RECKONS
	RECKONER	RECKONERS
	RECKONING	RECKONINGS
DRECKS · TRECKS · WRECKS	**RECKS**	
	RECLAD	RECLADS
	RECLAIM	RECLAIMS
	RECLAIMER	RECLAIMERS
	RECLAME	RECLAMES
	RECLASP	RECLASPS
PRECLEAN	**RECLEAN**	RECLEANS
PRECLEANED	**RECLEANED**	
PRECLEANS	**RECLEANS**	
	RECLIMB	RECLIMBS
	RECLINE	RECLINED · RECLINER · RECLINES
	RECLINER	RECLINERS
	RECLOSE	RECLOSED · RECLOSES
	RECLOTHE	RECLOTHED · RECLOTHES

FRONT HOOK	ROOT WORD	END HOOK
	RECLUSE	RECLUSES
PRECLUSION	**RECLUSION**	RECLUSIONS
PRECLUSIVE	**RECLUSIVE**	
	RECOAL	RECOALS
	RECOAT	RECOATS
	RECOCK	RECOCKS
PRECODE	**RECODE**	RECODED ▪ RECODES
PRECODED	**RECODED**	
PRECODES	**RECODES**	
PRECODING	**RECODING**	
PRECOGNISE	**RECOGNISE**	RECOGNISED ▪ RECOGNISEE ▪ RECOGNISER
		RECOGNISES
PRECOGNIZE	**RECOGNIZE**	RECOGNIZED ▪ RECOGNIZEE ▪ RECOGNIZER
		RECOGNIZES
	RECOIL	RECOILS
	RECOILER	RECOILERS
	RECOIN	RECOINS
	RECOINAGE	RECOINAGES
	RECOLLECT	RECOLLECTS
	RECOLLET	RECOLLETS
	RECOLOR	RECOLORS
	RECOMB	RECOMBS
	RECOMBINE	RECOMBINED ▪ RECOMBINES
	RECOMFORT	RECOMFORTS
	RECOMMEND	RECOMMENDS
	RECOMMIT	RECOMMITS
	RECOMPACT	RECOMPACTS
	RECOMPILE	RECOMPILED ▪ RECOMPILES
PRECOMPOSE	**RECOMPOSE**	RECOMPOSED ▪ RECOMPOSES
PRECOMPUTE	**RECOMPUTE**	RECOMPUTED ▪ RECOMPUTES
	RECON	RECONS
	RECONCILE	RECONCILED ▪ RECONCILER ▪ RECONCILES
	RECONDUCT	RECONDUCTS
	RECONFER	RECONFERS
	RECONFINE	RECONFINED ▪ RECONFINES
	RECONFIRM	RECONFIRMS
	RECONNECT	RECONNECTS
	RECONQUER	RECONQUERS
	RECONSIGN	RECONSIGNS
	RECONSOLE	RECONSOLED ▪ RECONSOLES
	RECONSULT	RECONSULTS
PRECONTACT	**RECONTACT**	RECONTACTS
	RECONTOUR	RECONTOURS
	RECONVENE	RECONVENED ▪ RECONVENES
	RECONVERT	RECONVERTS
	RECONVEY	RECONVEYS
	RECONVICT	RECONVICTS
PRECOOK	**RECOOK**	RECOOKS
PRECOOKED	**RECOOKED**	
PRECOOKING	**RECOOKING**	
PRECOOKS	**RECOOKS**	
	RECORD	RECORDS
	RECORDER	RECORDERS
	RECORDING	RECORDINGS
	RECORDIST	RECORDISTS
	RECORK	RECORKS
	RECOUNT	RECOUNTS
	RECOUNTAL	RECOUNTALS
	RECOUNTER	RECOUNTERS
PRECOUP	**RECOUP**	RECOUPE ▪ RECOUPS
	RECOUPE	RECOUPED
	RECOUPLE	RECOUPLED ▪ RECOUPLES
	RECOURE	RECOURED ▪ RECOURES
	RECOURSE	RECOURSED ▪ RECOURSES
	RECOVER	RECOVERS ▪ RECOVERY
	RECOVEREE	RECOVEREES
	RECOVERER	RECOVERERS
	RECOVEROR	RECOVERORS
	RECOWER	RECOWERS

FRONT HOOK	ROOT WORD	END HOOK
	RECOYLE	RECOYLED ▪ RECOYLES
	RECRATE	RECRATED ▪ RECRATES
	RECREANCE	RECREANCES
	RECREANT	RECREANTS
	RECREATE	RECREATED ▪ RECREATES
	RECREATOR	RECREATORS
	RECREMENT	RECREMENTS
	RECROWN	RECROWNS
	RECRUIT	RECRUITS
	RECRUITAL	RECRUITALS
	RECRUITER	RECRUITERS
	RECTA	RECTAL
	RECTANGLE	RECTANGLED ▪ RECTANGLES
	RECTIFIER	RECTIFIERS
ERECTION	**RECTION**	RECTIONS
ERECTIONS	**RECTIONS**	
	RECTITUDE	RECTITUDES
	RECTO	RECTOR ▪ RECTOS
	RECTOCELE	RECTOCELES
ERECTOR	**RECTOR**	RECTORS ▪ RECTORY
	RECTORATE	RECTORATES
	RECTORIAL	RECTORIALS
ERECTORS	**RECTORS**	
	RECTUM	RECTUMS
	RECUILE	RECUILED ▪ RECUILES
	RECULE	RECULED ▪ RECULES
	RECUR	RECURE ▪ RECURS
PRECURE	**RECURE**	RECURED ▪ RECURES
PRECURED	**RECURED**	
PRECURES	**RECURES**	
PRECURING	**RECURING**	
	RECURSION	RECURSIONS
PRECURSIVE	**RECURSIVE**	
	RECURVE	RECURVED ▪ RECURVES
	RECUSAL	RECUSALS
	RECUSANCE	RECUSANCES
	RECUSANT	RECUSANTS
	RECUSE	RECUSED ▪ RECUSES
PRECUT	**RECUT**	RECUTS
PRECUTS	**RECUTS**	
PRECUTTING	**RECUTTING**	
	RECYCLATE	RECYCLATES
	RECYCLE	RECYCLED ▪ RECYCLER ▪ RECYCLES
	RECYCLER	RECYCLERS
	RECYCLIST	RECYCLISTS
ARED ▪ BRED ▪ CRED ▪ ERED ▪ IRED	**RED**	REDD ▪ REDE ▪ REDO ▪ REDS
	REDACT	REDACTS
	REDACTION	REDACTIONS
	REDACTOR	REDACTORS
	REDAMAGE	REDAMAGED ▪ REDAMAGES
	REDAN	REDANS
	REDARGUE	REDARGUED ▪ REDARGUES
PREDATE	**REDATE**	REDATED ▪ REDATES
PREDATED	**REDATED**	
PREDATES	**REDATES**	
PREDATING	**REDATING**	
	REDBACK	REDBACKS
	REDBAIT	REDBAITS
	REDBAITER	REDBAITERS
	REDBAY	REDBAYS
	REDBIRD	REDBIRDS
	REDBONE	REDBONES
	REDBREAST	REDBREASTS
	REDBRICK	REDBRICKS
	REDBUD	REDBUDS
	REDBUG	REDBUGS
	REDCAP	REDCAPS
	REDCOAT	REDCOATS
AREDD	**REDD**	REDDS ▪ REDDY

R

FRONT HOOK	ROOT WORD	END HOOK
	REDDEN	REDDENS
	REDDENDO	REDDENDOS
	REDDER	REDDERS
	REDDING	REDDINGS
TREDDLE	**REDDLE**	REDDLED · REDDLES
TREDDLED	**REDDLED**	
TREDDLES	**REDDLES**	
TREDDLING	**REDDLING**	
AREDE · BREDE	**REDE**	REDED · REDES
	REDEAL	REDEALS · REDEALT
	REDEAR	REDEARS
	REDECIDE	REDECIDED · REDECIDES
	REDECRAFT	REDECRAFTS
BREDED	**REDED**	
	REDEEM	REDEEMS
	REDEEMER	REDEEMERS
	REDEFEAT	REDEFEATS
	REDEFECT	REDEFECTS
PREDEFINE	**REDEFINE**	REDEFINED · REDEFINES
PREDEFINED	**REDEFINED**	
PREDEFINES	**REDEFINES**	
	REDELIVER	REDELIVERS · REDELIVERY
	REDEMAND	REDEMANDS
	REDEPLOY	REDEPLOYS
PREDEPOSIT	**REDEPOSIT**	REDEPOSITS
AREDES · BREDES	**REDES**	
	REDESCEND	REDESCENDS
PREDESIGN	**REDESIGN**	REDESIGNS
PREDESIGNS	**REDESIGNS**	
PREDEVELOP	**REDEVELOP**	REDEVELOPS
	REDEYE	REDEYES
	REDFIN	REDFINS
	REDFOOT	REDFOOTS
	REDHEAD	REDHEADS
	REDHORSE	REDHORSES
UREDIA	**REDIA**	REDIAE · REDIAL · REDIAS
PREDIAL · UREDIAL	**REDIAL**	REDIALS
PREDIALS	**REDIALS**	
	REDICTATE	REDICTATED · REDICTATES
PREDIGEST	**REDIGEST**	REDIGESTS
PREDIGESTS	**REDIGESTS**	
AREDING · BREDING	**REDING**	
	REDINGOTE	REDINGOTES
	REDIP	REDIPS · REDIPT
	REDIRECT	REDIRECTS
	REDISPLAY	REDISPLAYS
PREDISPOSE	**REDISPOSE**	REDISPOSED · REDISPOSES
	REDISTIL	REDISTILL · REDISTILS
	REDISTILL	REDISTILLS
	REDIVIDE	REDIVIDED · REDIVIDES
	REDIVORCE	REDIVORCED · REDIVORCES
	REDLEG	REDLEGS (offensive)
	REDLINE	REDLINED · REDLINER · REDLINES
	REDLINER	REDLINERS
	REDLINING	REDLININGS
	REDNECK	REDNECKS (offensive)
CREDO · UREDO	**REDO**	REDON · REDOS · REDOX
	REDOCK	REDOCKS
	REDOLENCE	REDOLENCES
	REDON	REDONE · REDONS
CREDOS · UREDOS	**REDOS**	
	REDOUBLE	REDOUBLED · REDOUBLER · REDOUBLES
	REDOUBLER	REDOUBLERS
	REDOUBT	REDOUBTS
	REDOUND	REDOUNDS
	REDOUT	REDOUTS
	REDOWA	REDOWAS
	REDPOLL	REDPOLLS
PREDRAFT	**REDRAFT**	REDRAFTS

FRONT HOOK	ROOT WORD	END HOOK
	REDRAW	REDRAWN ▪ REDRAWS
	REDRAWER	REDRAWERS
	REDREAM	REDREAMS ▪ REDREAMT
	REDRESSER	REDRESSERS
	REDRESSOR	REDRESSORS
PREDRIED	**REDRIED**	
PREDRIES	**REDRIES**	
PREDRILL	**REDRILL**	REDRILLS
PREDRILLED	**REDRILLED**	
PREDRILLS	**REDRILLS**	
	REDRIVE	REDRIVEN ▪ REDRIVES
	REDROOT	REDROOTS
PREDRY	**REDRY**	
PREDRYING	**REDRYING**	
BREDS ▪ CREDS	**REDS**	
	REDSHANK	REDSHANKS
	REDSHIFT	REDSHIFTS
	REDSHIRT	REDSHIRTS
	REDSKIN	REDSKINS (offensive)
	REDSTART	REDSTARTS
	REDSTREAK	REDSTREAKS
	REDTAIL	REDTAILS
	REDTOP	REDTOPS
	REDUB	REDUBS
	REDUCE	REDUCED ▪ REDUCER ▪ REDUCES
	REDUCER	REDUCERS
	REDUCTANT	REDUCTANTS
	REDUCTASE	REDUCTASES
	REDUCTION	REDUCTIONS
	REDUCTOR	REDUCTORS
	REDUIT	REDUITS
	REDUVIID	REDUVIIDS
	REDWARE	REDWARES
	REDWATER	REDWATERS
	REDWING	REDWINGS
	REDWOOD	REDWOODS
	REDYE	REDYED ▪ REDYES
BREE ▪ CREE ▪ DREE ▪ FREE ▪ GREE ▪ PREE ▪ TREE	**REE**	REED ▪ REEF ▪ REEK ▪ REEL ▪ REEN
	REES	
	REEARN	REEARNS
	REEBOK	REEBOKS
BREECH	**REECH**	REECHO ▪ REECHY
BREECHED	**REECHED**	
BREECHES	**REECHES**	
	REECHIE	REECHIER
BREECHING	**REECHING**	
BREED ▪ CREED ▪ DREED ▪ FREED ▪ GREED ▪ PREED ▪ TREED	**REED**	REEDE ▪ REEDS ▪ REEDY
	REEDBED	REEDBEDS
	REEDBIRD	REEDBIRDS
	REEDBUCK	REEDBUCKS
	REEDE	REEDED ▪ REEDEN ▪ REEDER ▪ REEDES
BREEDER	**REEDER**	REEDERS
BREEDERS	**REEDERS**	
GREEDIER	**REEDIER**	
GREEDIEST	**REEDIEST**	
GREEDILY	**REEDILY**	
GREEDINESS	**REEDINESS**	
BREEDING	**REEDING**	REEDINGS
BREEDINGS	**REEDINGS**	
PREEDIT	**REEDIT**	REEDITS
PREEDITED	**REEDITED**	
PREEDITING	**REEDITING**	
	REEDITION	REEDITIONS
PREEDITS	**REEDITS**	
	REEDLING	REEDLINGS
	REEDMACE	REEDMACES
FREEDMAN	**REEDMAN**	
FREEDMEN	**REEDMEN**	

FRONT HOOK	ROOT WORD	END HOOK
BREEDS · CREEDS · GREEDS	**REEDS**	
	REEDSTOP	REEDSTOPS
	REEDUCATE	REEDUCATED · REEDUCATES
GREEDY	**REEDY**	
	REEF	REEFS · REEFY
	REEFER	REEFERS
	REEFING	REEFINGS
	REEJECT	REEJECTS
CREEK · GREEK	**REEK**	REEKS · REEKY
GREEKED	**REEKED**	
	REEKER	REEKERS
	REEKIE	REEKIER
CREEKIER	**REEKIER**	
CREEKIEST	**REEKIEST**	
GREEKING	**REEKING**	
BREEKS · CREEKS	**REEKS**	
CREEKY	**REEKY**	
CREEL	**REEL**	REELS
PREELECT	**REELECT**	REELECTS
PREELECTED	**REELECTED**	
PREELECTS	**REELECTS**	
CREELED	**REELED**	
	REELER	REELERS
	REELEVATE	REELEVATED · REELEVATES
CREELING	**REELING**	REELINGS
CREELS	**REELS**	
	REEMBARK	REEMBARKS
	REEMBRACE	REEMBRACED · REEMBRACES
	REEMERGE	REEMERGED · REEMERGES
	REEMIT	REEMITS
	REEMPLOY	REEMPLOYS
GREEN · PREEN · TREEN	**REEN**	REENS
PREENACT	**REENACT**	REENACTS
PREENACTED	**REENACTED**	
	REENACTOR	REENACTORS
PREENACTS	**REENACTS**	
	REENDOW	REENDOWS
	REENFORCE	REENFORCED · REENFORCES
GREENGAGE	**REENGAGE**	REENGAGED · REENGAGES
GREENGAGES	**REENGAGES**	
	REENGRAVE	REENGRAVED · REENGRAVES
	REENJOY	REENJOYS
	REENLARGE	REENLARGED · REENLARGES
	REENLIST	REENLISTS
	REENROLL	REENROLLS
GREENS · PREENS · TREENS	**REENS**	
	REENSLAVE	REENSLAVED · REENSLAVES
	REENTER	REENTERS
	REENTRANT	REENTRANTS
	REEQUIP	REEQUIPS
PREERECT	**REERECT**	REERECTS
PREERECTED	**REERECTED**	
PREERECTS	**REERECTS**	
BREES · CREES · DREES · FREES · GREES	**REES**	REEST
PREES · TREES		
BREEST · FREEST	**REEST**	REESTS · REESTY
BREESTS	**REESTS**	
PREEVE	**REEVE**	REEVED · REEVES
PREEVED	**REEVED**	
PREEVES	**REEVES**	
PREEVING	**REEVING**	
	REEVOKE	REEVOKED · REEVOKES
	REEXAMINE	REEXAMINED · REEXAMINES
	REEXECUTE	REEXECUTED · REEXECUTES
	REEXHIBIT	REEXHIBITS
	REEXPEL	REEXPELS
	REEXPLAIN	REEXPLAINS
	REEXPLORE	REEXPLORED · REEXPLORES
	REEXPORT	REEXPORTS

FRONT HOOK	ROOT WORD	END HOOK
PREEXPOSE	**REEXPOSE**	REEXPOSED · REEXPOSES
PREEXPOSED	**REEXPOSED**	
PREEXPOSES	**REEXPOSES**	
TREF	**REF**	REFS · REFT
PREFACE	**REFACE**	REFACED · REFACES
PREFACED	**REFACED**	
PREFACES	**REFACES**	
PREFACING	**REFACING**	
	REFALL	REFALLS
	REFASHION	REFASHIONS
	REFASTEN	REFASTENS
PREFECT	**REFECT**	REFECTS
	REFECTION	REFECTIONS
PREFECTS	**REFECTS**	
	REFEED	REFEEDS
	REFEEL	REFEELS
	REFEL	REFELL · REFELS · REFELT
	REFENCE	REFENCED · REFENCES
PREFER	**REFER**	REFERS
PREFERABLE	**REFERABLE**	
	REFEREE	REFEREED · REFEREES
PREFERENCE	**REFERENCE**	REFERENCED · REFERENCER · REFERENCES
	REFERENT	REFERENTS
	REFERRAL	REFERRALS
PREFERRED	**REFERRED**	
PREFERRER	**REFERRER**	REFERRERS
PREFERRERS	**REFERRERS**	
PREFERRING	**REFERRING**	
PREFERS	**REFERS**	
	REFFO	REFFOS (offensive)
PREFIGHT	**REFIGHT**	REFIGHTS
PREFIGURE	**REFIGURE**	REFIGURED · REFIGURES
PREFIGURED	**REFIGURED**	
PREFIGURES	**REFIGURES**	
PREFILE	**REFILE**	REFILED · REFILES
PREFILED	**REFILED**	
PREFILES	**REFILES**	
PREFILING	**REFILING**	
	REFILL	REFILLS
PREFILLED	**REFILLED**	
	REFILM	REFILMS
	REFILTER	REFILTERS
PREFINANCE	**REFINANCE**	REFINANCED · REFINANCES
	REFIND	REFINDS
	REFINE	REFINED · REFINER · REFINES
	REFINER	REFINERS · REFINERY
	REFINING	REFININGS
PREFIRE	**REFIRE**	REFIRED · REFIRES
PREFIRED	**REFIRED**	
PREFIRES	**REFIRES**	
PREFIRING	**REFIRING**	
	REFIT	REFITS
	REFITMENT	REFITMENTS
	REFITTING	REFITTINGS
PREFIX	**REFIX**	
PREFIXED	**REFIXED**	
PREFIXES	**REFIXES**	
PREFIXING	**REFIXING**	
	REFLAG	REFLAGS
	REFLATE	REFLATED · REFLATES
	REFLATION	REFLATIONS
	REFLECT	REFLECTS
	REFLECTER	REFLECTERS
	REFLECTOR	REFLECTORS
	REFLET	REFLETS
	REFLEXION	REFLEXIONS
	REFLEXIVE	REFLEXIVES
	REFLOAT	REFLOATS
	REFLOOD	REFLOODS

F

FRONT HOOK	ROOT WORD	END HOOK
	REFLOW	REFLOWN ▪ REFLOWS
	REFLOWER	REFLOWERS
	REFLOWING	REFLOWINGS
	REFLUENCE	REFLUENCES
PREFOCUS	**REFOCUS**	
PREFOCUSED	**REFOCUSED**	
PREFOCUSES	**REFOCUSES**	
	REFOLD	REFOLDS
	REFOOT	REFOOTS
	REFOREST	REFORESTS
	REFORGE	REFORGED ▪ REFORGES
PREFORM	**REFORM**	REFORMS
	REFORMADE	REFORMADES
	REFORMADO	REFORMADOS
PREFORMAT	**REFORMAT**	REFORMATE ▪ REFORMATS
	REFORMATE	REFORMATES
PREFORMATS	**REFORMATS**	
PREFORMED	**REFORMED**	
	REFORMER	REFORMERS
PREFORMING	**REFORMING**	REFORMINGS
	REFORMISM	REFORMISMS
	REFORMIST	REFORMISTS
PREFORMS	**REFORMS**	
	REFOUND	REFOUNDS
	REFOUNDER	REFOUNDERS
	REFRACT	REFRACTS
	REFRACTOR	REFRACTORS ▪ REFRACTORY
	REFRAIN	REFRAINS
	REFRAINER	REFRAINERS
	REFRAME	REFRAMED ▪ REFRAMES
PREFREEZE	**REFREEZE**	REFREEZES
PREFREEZES	**REFREEZES**	
	REFRESHEN	REFRESHENS
	REFRESHER	REFRESHERS
	REFRINGE	REFRINGED ▪ REFRINGES
	REFRONT	REFRONTS
PREFROZE	**REFROZE**	REFROZEN
PREFROZEN	**REFROZEN**	
	REFUEL	REFUELS
	REFUGE	REFUGED ▪ REFUGEE ▪ REFUGES
	REFUGEE	REFUGEES
PREFULGENT	**REFULGENT**	
PREFUND	**REFUND**	REFUNDS
PREFUNDED	**REFUNDED**	
	REFUNDER	REFUNDERS
PREFUNDING	**REFUNDING**	
PREFUNDS	**REFUNDS**	
	REFUSAL	REFUSALS
	REFUSE	REFUSED ▪ REFUSER ▪ REFUSES
	REFUSENIK	REFUSENIKS
	REFUSER	REFUSERS
	REFUSION	REFUSIONS
	REFUSNIK	REFUSNIKS
	REFUTAL	REFUTALS
	REFUTE	REFUTED ▪ REFUTER ▪ REFUTES
	REFUTER	REFUTERS
AREG ▪ DREG	**REG**	REGO ▪ REGS
	REGAIN	REGAINS
	REGAINER	REGAINERS
	REGAL	REGALE ▪ REGALS
GREGALE	**REGALE**	REGALED ▪ REGALER ▪ REGALES
	REGALER	REGALERS
GREGALES	**REGALES**	
	REGALIA	REGALIAN ▪ REGALIAS
	REGALISM	REGALISMS
	REGALIST	REGALISTS
	REGAR	REGARD ▪ REGARS
	REGARD	REGARDS
	REGARDER	REGARDERS

R

FRONT HOOK	ROOT WORD	END HOOK
	REGATHER	REGATHERS
	REGATTA	REGATTAS
	REGAUGE	REGAUGED = REGAUGES
	REGEAR	REGEARS
	REGELATE	REGELATED = REGELATES
	REGENCE	REGENCES
	REGENT	REGENTS
	REGES	REGEST
	REGEST	REGESTS
	REGGAE	REGGAES
	REGGO	REGGOS
	REGICIDE	REGICIDES
	REGIE	REGIES
	REGILD	REGILDS
	REGIME	REGIMEN = REGIMES
	REGIMEN	REGIMENS = REGIMENT
	REGIMENT	REGIMENTS
	REGINA	REGINAE = REGINAL = REGINAS
	REGION	REGIONS
	REGIONAL	REGIONALS
	REGISSEUR	REGISSEURS
	REGISTER	REGISTERS
	REGISTRAR	REGISTRARS = REGISTRARY
	REGIVE	REGIVEN = REGIVES
	REGLAZE	REGLAZED = REGLAZES
	REGLET	REGLETS
	REGLOW	REGLOWS
	REGLUE	REGLUED = REGLUES
BREGMA	REGMA	
	REGMAKER	REGMAKERS
BREGMATA	REGMATA	
	REGNA	REGNAL
PREGNANCY	REGNANCY	
PREGNANT	REGNANT	
GREGO	REGO	REGOS
	REGOLITH	REGOLITHS
	REGORGE	REGORGED = REGORGES
GREGOS	REGOS	
	REGOSOL	REGOSOLS
	REGRADE	REGRADED = REGRADES
	REGRAFT	REGRAFTS
	REGRANT	REGRANTS
	REGRATE	REGRATED = REGRATER = REGRATES
	REGRATER	REGRATERS
	REGRATING	REGRATINGS
	REGRATOR	REGRATORS
	REGREDE	REGREDED = REGREDES
	REGREEN	REGREENS
	REGREET	REGREETS
	REGRESSOR	REGRESSORS
	REGRET	REGRETS
	REGRETTER	REGRETTERS
	REGRIND	REGRINDS
	REGROOM	REGROOMS
	REGROOVE	REGROOVED = REGROOVES
	REGROUP	REGROUPS
	REGROW	REGROWN = REGROWS
PREGROWTH	REGROWTH	REGROWTHS
PREGROWTHS	REGROWTHS	
DREGS	REGS	
	REGUERDON	REGUERDONS
	REGULA	REGULAE = REGULAR
	REGULAR	REGULARS
	REGULATE	REGULATED = REGULATES
	REGULATOR	REGULATORS = REGULATORY
	REGULISE	REGULISED = REGULISES
	REGULIZE	REGULIZED = REGULIZES
	REGULO	REGULOS
	REGUR	REGURS

FRONT HOOK	ROOT WORD	END HOOK
	REH	REHS
	REHAB	REHABS
	REHABBER	REHABBERS
	REHAMMER	REHAMMERS
PREHANDLE	**REHANDLE**	REHANDLED ▪ REHANDLES
PREHANDLED	**REHANDLED**	
PREHANDLES	**REHANDLES**	
	REHANG	REHANGS
PREHARDEN	**REHARDEN**	REHARDENS
PREHARDENS	**REHARDENS**	
	REHEAR	REHEARD ▪ REHEARS
	REHEARING	REHEARINGS
	REHEARS	REHEARSE
	REHEARSAL	REHEARSALS
	REHEARSE	REHEARSED ▪ REHEARSER ▪ REHEARSES
	REHEARSER	REHEARSERS
PREHEAT	**REHEAT**	REHEATS
PREHEATED	**REHEATED**	
PREHEATER	**REHEATER**	REHEATERS
PREHEATERS	**REHEATERS**	
PREHEATING	**REHEATING**	REHEATINGS
PREHEATS	**REHEATS**	
	REHEEL	REHEELS
	REHEM	REHEMS
	REHINGE	REHINGED ▪ REHINGES
	REHIRE	REHIRED ▪ REHIRES
PREHIRING	**REHIRING**	
	REHOBOAM	REHOBOAMS
	REHOUSE	REHOUSED ▪ REHOUSES
	REHOUSING	REHOUSINGS
	REHYDRATE	REHYDRATED ▪ REHYDRATES
BREI	**REI**	REIF ▪ REIK ▪ REIN ▪ REIS
PREIF ▪ TREIF	**REIF**	REIFS ▪ REIFY
	REIFIER	REIFIERS
PREIFS	**REIFS**	
	REIGN	REIGNS
	REIGNITE	REIGNITED ▪ REIGNITES
	REIK	REIKI ▪ REIKS
	REIKI	REIKIS
	REILLUME	REILLUMED ▪ REILLUMES
	REIMAGE	REIMAGED ▪ REIMAGES
	REIMAGINE	REIMAGINED ▪ REIMAGINES
	REIMBURSE	REIMBURSED ▪ REIMBURSER ▪ REIMBURSES
	REIMMERSE	REIMMERSED ▪ REIMMERSES
	REIMPLANT	REIMPLANTS
	REIMPORT	REIMPORTS
PREIMPOSE	**REIMPOSE**	REIMPOSED ▪ REIMPOSES
PREIMPOSED	**REIMPOSED**	
PREIMPOSES	**REIMPOSES**	
GREIN	**REIN**	REINK ▪ REINS
	REINCITE	REINCITED ▪ REINCITES
	REINCUR	REINCURS
	REINDEER	REINDEERS
	REINDICT	REINDICTS
	REINDUCE	REINDUCED ▪ REINDUCES
	REINDUCT	REINDUCTS
GREINED	**REINED**	
	REINETTE	REINETTES
	REINFECT	REINFECTS
	REINFLAME	REINFLAMED ▪ REINFLAMES
	REINFLATE	REINFLATED ▪ REINFLATES
	REINFORCE	REINFORCED ▪ REINFORCER ▪ REINFORCES
PREINFORM	**REINFORM**	REINFORMS
PREINFORMS	**REINFORMS**	
	REINFUND	REINFUNDS
	REINFUSE	REINFUSED ▪ REINFUSES
	REINHABIT	REINHABITS
GREINING	**REINING**	
	REINJECT	REINJECTS

FRONT HOOK	ROOT WORD	END HOOK
	REINJURE	REINJURED ▪ REINJURES
	REINK	REINKS
GREINS	REINS	
PREINSERT	REINSERT	REINSERTS
PREINSERTS	REINSERTS	
	REINSPECT	REINSPECTS
	REINSPIRE	REINSPIRED ▪ REINSPIRES
	REINSTAL	REINSTALL ▪ REINSTALS
	REINSTALL	REINSTALLS
	REINSTATE	REINSTATED ▪ REINSTATES
	REINSURE	REINSURED ▪ REINSURER ▪ REINSURES
	REINSURER	REINSURERS
	REINTER	REINTERS
	REINVADE	REINVADED ▪ REINVADES
	REINVENT	REINVENTS
	REINVEST	REINVESTS
PREINVITE	REINVITE	REINVITED ▪ REINVITES
PREINVITED	REINVITED	
PREINVITES	REINVITES	
	REINVOKE	REINVOKED ▪ REINVOKES
	REINVOLVE	REINVOLVED ▪ REINVOLVES
	REIRD	REIRDS
BREIS	REIS	REIST
	REISSUE	REISSUED ▪ REISSUER ▪ REISSUES
	REISSUER	REISSUERS
BREIST	REIST	REISTS
	REISTAFEL	REISTAFELS
BREISTS	REISTS	
	REITBOK	REITBOKS
	REITER	REITERS
	REITERATE	REITERATED ▪ REITERATES
	REIVE	REIVED ▪ REIVER ▪ REIVES
	REIVER	REIVERS
	REJACKET	REJACKETS
	REJECT	REJECTS
	REJECTEE	REJECTEES
	REJECTER	REJECTERS
	REJECTION	REJECTIONS
	REJECTOR	REJECTORS
	REJIG	REJIGS
	REJIGGER	REJIGGERS
	REJOICE	REJOICED ▪ REJOICER ▪ REJOICES
	REJOICER	REJOICERS
	REJOICING	REJOICINGS
	REJOIN	REJOINS
	REJOINDER	REJOINDERS
	REJONEO	REJONEOS
	REJOURN	REJOURNS
PREJUDGE	REJUDGE	REJUDGED ▪ REJUDGES
PREJUDGED	REJUDGED	
PREJUDGES	REJUDGES	
PREJUDGING	REJUDGING	
	REJUGGLE	REJUGGLED ▪ REJUGGLES
	REKE	REKED ▪ REKES ▪ REKEY
	REKEY	REKEYS
	REKINDLE	REKINDLED ▪ REKINDLES
	REKNIT	REKNITS
	REKNOT	REKNOTS
	RELABEL	RELABELS
	RELACE	RELACED ▪ RELACES
	RELACHE	RELACHES
	RELACQUER	RELACQUERS
	RELAND	RELANDS
	RELAPSE	RELAPSED ▪ RELAPSER ▪ RELAPSES
	RELAPSER	RELAPSERS
PRELATE	RELATE	RELATED ▪ RELATER ▪ RELATES
	RELATER	RELATERS
PRELATES	RELATES	
PRELATION	RELATION	RELATIONS

685

FRONT HOOK	ROOT WORD	END HOOK
PRELATIONS	**RELATIONS**	
	RELATIVE	RELATIVES
	RELATOR	RELATORS
PRELAUNCH	**RELAUNCH**	
	RELAUNDER	RELAUNDERS
	RELAXANT	RELAXANTS
	RELAXER	RELAXERS
	RELAXIN	RELAXING - RELAXINS
	RELAY	RELAYS
	RELEARN	RELEARNS - RELEARNT
	RELEASE	RELEASED - RELEASEE - RELEASER RELEASES
	RELEASEE	RELEASEES
	RELEASER	RELEASERS
	RELEASOR	RELEASORS
	RELEGATE	RELEGATED - RELEGATES
	RELEND	RELENDS
	RELENT	RELENTS
	RELENTING	RELENTINGS
	RELET	RELETS
	RELETTER	RELETTERS
	RELEVANCE	RELEVANCES
	RELEVE	RELEVES
	RELIABLE	RELIABLES
	RELIANCE	RELIANCES
	RELIC	RELICS - RELICT
	RELICENSE	RELICENSED - RELICENSES
	RELICT	RELICTS
	RELICTION	RELICTIONS
	RELIE	RELIED - RELIEF - RELIER - RELIES
	RELIEF	RELIEFS
	RELIER	RELIERS
	RELIEVE	RELIEVED - RELIEVER - RELIEVES
	RELIEVER	RELIEVERS
	RELIEVO	RELIEVOS
	RELIGHT	RELIGHTS
	RELIGION	RELIGIONS
	RELINE	RELINED - RELINES
	RELINK	RELINKS
	RELIQUE	RELIQUES
	RELIST	RELISTS
	RELIVE	RELIVED - RELIVER - RELIVES
	RELIVER	RELIVERS
PRELIVES	**RELIVES**	
	RELLENO	RELLENOS
PRELOAD	**RELOAD**	RELOADS
PRELOADED	**RELOADED**	
	RELOADER	RELOADERS
PRELOADING	**RELOADING**	
PRELOADS	**RELOADS**	
	RELOAN	RELOANS
PRELOCATE	**RELOCATE**	RELOCATED - RELOCATEE - RELOCATES
PRELOCATED	**RELOCATED**	
	RELOCATEE	RELOCATEES
PRELOCATES	**RELOCATES**	
	RELOCATOR	RELOCATORS
	RELOCK	RELOCKS
	RELOOK	RELOOKS
	RELUCT	RELUCTS
	RELUCTATE	RELUCTATED - RELUCTATES
	RELUME	RELUMED - RELUMES
	RELUMINE	RELUMINED - RELUMINES
CREM - PREM	**REM**	REMS
PREMADE	**REMADE**	REMADES
	REMAIL	REMAILS
	REMAIN	REMAINS
	REMAINDER	REMAINDERS
CREMAINS	**REMAINS**	
	REMAKE	REMAKER - REMAKES

686

FRONT HOOK	ROOT WORD	END HOOK
	REMAKER	REMAKERS
PREMAN	**REMAN**	REMAND = REMANS
	REMAND	REMANDS
	REMANENCE	REMANENCES
	REMANENT	REMANENTS
	REMANET	REMANETS
	REMANIE	REMANIES
	REMAP	REMAPS
	REMARK	REMARKS
	REMARKER	REMARKERS
PREMARKET	**REMARKET**	REMARKETS
PREMARKETS	**REMARKETS**	
	REMARQUE	REMARQUED = REMARQUES
CREMASTER	**REMASTER**	REMASTERS
CREMASTERS	**REMASTERS**	
CREMATE	**REMATE**	REMATED = REMATES
CREMATED	**REMATED**	
CREMATES	**REMATES**	
CREMATING	**REMATING**	
	REMBLAI	REMBLAIS
TREMBLE	**REMBLE**	REMBLED = REMBLES
TREMBLED	**REMBLED**	
TREMBLES	**REMBLES**	
TREMBLING	**REMBLING**	
	REMEAD	REMEADS
PREMEASURE	**REMEASURE**	REMEASURED = REMEASURES
	REMEDE	REMEDED = REMEDES
	REMEDIAT	REMEDIATE
	REMEDIATE	REMEDIATED = REMEDIATES
PREMEET	**REMEET**	REMEETS
	REMEID	REMEIDS
	REMELT	REMELTS
	REMEMBER	REMEMBERS
PREMEN	**REMEN**	REMEND = REMENS
	REMEND	REMENDS
	REMERGE	REMERGED = REMERGES
	REMIGATE	REMIGATED = REMIGATES
	REMIGRATE	REMIGRATED = REMIGRATES
	REMIND	REMINDS
	REMINDER	REMINDERS
	REMINISCE	REMINISCED = REMINISCER = REMINISCES
	REMINT	REMINTS
PREMISE	**REMISE**	REMISED = REMISES
PREMISED	**REMISED**	
PREMISES	**REMISES**	
PREMISING	**REMISING**	
PREMISS	**REMISS**	
	REMISSION	REMISSIONS
FREMIT	**REMIT**	REMITS
	REMITMENT	REMITMENTS
FREMITS	**REMITS**	
	REMITTAL	REMITTALS
	REMITTEE	REMITTEES
	REMITTER	REMITTERS
	REMITTOR	REMITTORS
PREMIX	**REMIX**	REMIXT
PREMIXED	**REMIXED**	
PREMIXES	**REMIXES**	
PREMIXING	**REMIXING**	
PREMIXT	**REMIXT**	
	REMIXTURE	REMIXTURES
	REMNANT	REMNANTS
	REMODEL	REMODELS
	REMODELER	REMODELERS
PREMODIFY	**REMODIFY**	
PREMOISTEN	**REMOISTEN**	REMOISTENS
	REMOLADE	REMOLADES
PREMOLD	**REMOLD**	REMOLDS
PREMOLDED	**REMOLDED**	

FRONT HOOK	ROOT WORD	END HOOK
PREMOLDING	**REMOLDING**	
PREMOLDS	**REMOLDS**	
	REMONTANT	REMONTANTS
	REMONTOIR	REMONTOIRE · REMONTOIRS
	REMORA	REMORAS
PREMORSE	**REMORSE**	REMORSES
	REMOTE	REMOTER · REMOTES
	REMOTES	REMOTEST
PREMOTION	**REMOTION**	REMOTIONS
PREMOTIONS	**REMOTIONS**	
	REMOULADE	REMOULADES
	REMOULD	REMOULDS
	REMOUNT	REMOUNTS
	REMOVAL	REMOVALS
PREMOVE	**REMOVE**	REMOVED · REMOVER · REMOVES
PREMOVED	**REMOVED**	
	REMOVER	REMOVERS
PREMOVES	**REMOVES**	
PREMOVING	**REMOVING**	
CREMS · PREMS	**REMS**	
	REMUAGE	REMUAGES
	REMUDA	REMUDAS
	REMUEUR	REMUEURS
	REMURMUR	REMURMURS
BREN · GREN · WREN	**REN**	REND · RENK · RENS · RENT · RENY
	RENAGUE	RENAGUED · RENAGUES
TRENAIL	**RENAIL**	RENAILS
TRENAILS	**RENAILS**	
PRENAME	**RENAME**	RENAMED · RENAMES
PRENAMES	**RENAMES**	
CRENATURE	**RENATURE**	RENATURED · RENATURES
CRENATURES	**RENATURES**	
	RENAY	RENAYS
	RENCONTRE	RENCONTRES
TREND	**REND**	RENDS
TRENDED	**RENDED**	
	RENDER	RENDERS
	RENDERER	RENDERERS
	RENDERING	RENDERINGS
TRENDING	**RENDING**	
	RENDITION	RENDITIONS
TRENDS	**RENDS**	
	RENDZINA	RENDZINAS
	RENEGADE	RENEGADED · RENEGADES
	RENEGADO	RENEGADOS
	RENEGATE	RENEGATES
	RENEGE	RENEGED · RENEGER · RENEGES
	RENEGER	RENEGERS
	RENEGUE	RENEGUED · RENEGUER · RENEGUES
	RENEGUER	RENEGUERS
	RENEST	RENESTS
	RENEW	RENEWS
	RENEWABLE	RENEWABLES
	RENEWAL	RENEWALS
	RENEWER	RENEWERS
	RENEWING	RENEWINGS
	RENEY	RENEYS
	RENFORCE	RENFORCED · RENFORCES
	RENGA	RENGAS
	RENIG	RENIGS
	RENIN	RENINS
	RENITENCE	RENITENCES
	RENMINBI	RENMINBIS
	RENNASE	RENNASES
BRENNE · FRENNE	**RENNE**	RENNED · RENNES · RENNET
GRENNED	**RENNED**	
BRENNES	**RENNES**	
	RENNET	RENNETS
	RENNIN	RENNING · RENNINS

FRONT HOOK	ROOT WORD	END HOOK
BRENNING · GRENNING	**RENNING**	RENNINGS
	RENOGRAM	RENOGRAMS
PRENOTIFY	**RENOTIFY**	
	RENOUNCE	RENOUNCED · RENOUNCER · RENOUNCES
	RENOUNCER	RENOUNCERS
	RENOVATE	RENOVATED · RENOVATES
	RENOVATOR	RENOVATORS
	RENOWN	RENOWNS
	RENOWNER	RENOWNERS
BRENS · GRENS · WRENS	**RENS**	
BRENT · DRENT · PRENT · URENT · YRENT	**RENT**	RENTE · RENTS
TRENTAL	**RENTAL**	RENTALS
	RENTALLER	RENTALLERS
TRENTALS	**RENTALS**	
	RENTE	RENTED · RENTER · RENTES
PRENTED	**RENTED**	
BRENTER	**RENTER**	RENTERS
	RENTIER	RENTIERS
PRENTING	**RENTING**	RENTINGS
BRENTS · PRENTS	**RENTS**	
PRENUMBER	**RENUMBER**	RENUMBERS
PRENUMBERS	**RENUMBERS**	
	RENVERSE	RENVERSED · RENVERSES
	RENVOI	RENVOIS
	RENVOY	RENVOYS
	REO	REOS
	REOBJECT	REOBJECTS
	REOBSERVE	REOBSERVED · REOBSERVES
PREOBTAIN	**REOBTAIN**	REOBTAINS
PREOBTAINS	**REOBTAINS**	
PREOCCUPY	**REOCCUPY**	
	REOCCUR	REOCCURS
	REOFFEND	REOFFENDS
	REOFFER	REOFFERS
	REOIL	REOILS
	REOPEN	REOPENS
	REOPENER	REOPENERS
PREOPENING	**REOPENING**	
	REOPERATE	REOPERATED · REOPERATES
	REOPPOSE	REOPPOSED · REOPPOSES
PREORDAIN	**REORDAIN**	REORDAINS
PREORDAINS	**REORDAINS**	
PREORDER	**REORDER**	REORDERS
PREORDERED	**REORDERED**	
PREORDERS	**REORDERS**	
	REORIENT	REORIENTS
	REOUTFIT	REOUTFITS
	REOXIDISE	REOXIDISED · REOXIDISES
	REOXIDIZE	REOXIDIZED · REOXIDIZES
PREP	**REP**	REPO · REPP · REPS
PREPACK	**REPACK**	REPACKS
PREPACKAGE	**REPACKAGE**	REPACKAGED · REPACKAGER · REPACKAGES
PREPACKED	**REPACKED**	
PREPACKING	**REPACKING**	
PREPACKS	**REPACKS**	
PREPAID	**REPAID**	
	REPAINT	REPAINTS
	REPAIR	REPAIRS
	REPAIRER	REPAIRERS
	REPANEL	REPANELS
	REPAPER	REPAPERS
	REPARK	REPARKS
	REPARTEE	REPARTEED · REPARTEES
	REPASSAGE	REPASSAGES
	REPAST	REPASTS
PREPASTED	**REPASTED**	
PREPASTING	**REPASTING**	
	REPASTURE	REPASTURES
	REPATTERN	REPATTERNS

FRONT HOOK	ROOT WORD	END HOOK
PREPAVE	**REPAVE**	REPAVED · REPAVES
PREPAVED	**REPAVED**	
PREPAVES	**REPAVES**	
PREPAVING	**REPAVING**	
PREPAY	**REPAY**	REPAYS
PREPAYABLE	**REPAYABLE**	
PREPAYING	**REPAYING**	
PREPAYMENT	**REPAYMENT**	REPAYMENTS
PREPAYS	**REPAYS**	
	REPEAL	REPEALS
	REPEALER	REPEALERS
	REPEAT	REPEATS
	REPEATER	REPEATERS
	REPEATING	REPEATINGS
	REPECHAGE	REPECHAGES
	REPEG	REPEGS
	REPEL	REPELS
	REPELLANT	REPELLANTS
	REPELLENT	REPELLENTS
	REPELLER	REPELLERS
	REPENT	REPENTS
	REPENTANT	REPENTANTS
	REPENTER	REPENTERS
	REPEOPLE	REPEOPLED · REPEOPLES
	REPERK	REPERKS
	REPERUSAL	REPERUSALS
	REPERUSE	REPERUSED · REPERUSES
	REPETEND	REPETENDS
	REPHRASE	REPHRASED · REPHRASES
	REPIGMENT	REPIGMENTS
	REPIN	REPINE · REPINS
	REPINE	REPINED · REPINER · REPINES
	REPINER	REPINERS
	REPINING	REPININGS
	REPIQUE	REPIQUED · REPIQUES
	REPLA	REPLAN · REPLAY
PREPLACE	**REPLACE**	REPLACED · REPLACER · REPLACES
PREPLACED	**REPLACED**	
	REPLACER	REPLACERS
PREPLACES	**REPLACES**	
PREPLACING	**REPLACING**	
PREPLAN	**REPLAN**	REPLANS · REPLANT
PREPLANNED	**REPLANNED**	
PREPLANS	**REPLANS**	
PREPLANT	**REPLANT**	REPLANTS
	REPLASTER	REPLASTERS
	REPLATE	REPLATED · REPLATES
	REPLAY	REPLAYS
	REPLEAD	REPLEADS
	REPLEADER	REPLEADERS
	REPLEDGE	REPLEDGED · REPLEDGES
	REPLETE	REPLETED · REPLETES
	REPLETION	REPLETIONS
	REPLEVIN	REPLEVINS
	REPLICA	REPLICAS
	REPLICAS	REPLICASE
	REPLICASE	REPLICASES
	REPLICATE	REPLICATED · REPLICATES
	REPLICON	REPLICONS
	REPLIER	REPLIERS
	REPLOT	REPLOTS
	REPLOW	REPLOWS
	REPLUM	REPLUMB
	REPLUMB	REPLUMBS
	REPLUNGE	REPLUNGED · REPLUNGES
	REPO	REPOS · REPOT
	REPOINT	REPOINTS
	REPOLL	REPOLLS
PREPONE	**REPONE**	REPONED · REPONES

FRONT HOOK	ROOT WORD	END HOOK
PREPONED	**REPONED**	
PREPONES	**REPONES**	
PREPONING	**REPONING**	
	REPORT	REPORTS
	REPORTAGE	REPORTAGES
	REPORTER	REPORTERS
	REPORTING	REPORTINGS
	REPOS	REPOSE = REPOST
	REPOSAL	REPOSALL = REPOSALS
	REPOSALL	REPOSALLS
PREPOSE	**REPOSE**	REPOSED = REPOSER = REPOSES
PREPOSED	**REPOSED**	
	REPOSER	REPOSERS
PREPOSES	**REPOSES**	
PREPOSING	**REPOSING**	
	REPOSIT	REPOSITS
PREPOSITOR	**REPOSITOR**	REPOSITORS = REPOSITORY
PREPOSSESS	**REPOSSESS**	
	REPOST	REPOSTS
	REPOSURE	REPOSURES
	REPOT	REPOTS
	REPOTTING	REPOTTINGS
	REPOUR	REPOURS
	REPOUSSE	REPOUSSES
	REPOWER	REPOWERS
	REPP	REPPS
PREPPED	**REPPED**	
PREPPING	**REPPING**	REPPINGS
	REPREEVE	REPREEVED = REPREEVES
	REPREHEND	REPREHENDS
	REPRESENT	REPRESENTS
PREPRESS	**REPRESS**	
	REPRESSER	REPRESSERS
	REPRESSOR	REPRESSORS
PREPRICE	**REPRICE**	REPRICED = REPRICES
PREPRICED	**REPRICED**	
PREPRICES	**REPRICES**	
PREPRICING	**REPRICING**	
	REPRIEFE	REPRIEFES
	REPRIEVAL	REPRIEVALS
	REPRIEVE	REPRIEVED = REPRIEVER = REPRIEVES
	REPRIEVER	REPRIEVERS
	REPRIMAND	REPRIMANDS
	REPRIME	REPRIMED = REPRIMES
PREPRINT	**REPRINT**	REPRINTS
PREPRINTED	**REPRINTED**	
	REPRINTER	REPRINTERS
PREPRINTS	**REPRINTS**	
	REPRISAL	REPRISALS
	REPRISE	REPRISED = REPRISES
	REPRIVE	REPRIVED = REPRIVES
	REPRIZE	REPRIZED = REPRIZES
	REPRO	REPROS
	REPROBATE	REPROBATED = REPROBATER = REPROBATES
	REPROBE	REPROBED = REPROBES
PREPROCESS	**REPROCESS**	
	REPRODUCE	REPRODUCED = REPRODUCER = REPRODUCES
PREPROGRAM	**REPROGRAM**	REPROGRAMS
	REPROOF	REPROOFS
	REPROVAL	REPROVALS
	REPROVE	REPROVED = REPROVER = REPROVES
	REPROVER	REPROVERS
	REPROVING	REPROVINGS
	REPRYVE	REPRYVED = REPRYVES
PREPS	**REPS**	
	REPTATION	REPTATIONS
	REPTILE	REPTILES
	REPTILIA	REPTILIAN
	REPTILIAN	REPTILIANS

R

FRONT HOOK	ROOT WORD	END HOOK
	REPUBLIC	REPUBLICS
	REPUDIATE	REPUDIATED · REPUDIATES
	REPUGN	REPUGNS
	REPULP	REPULPS
	REPULSE	REPULSED · REPULSER · REPULSES
	REPULSER	REPULSERS
	REPULSION	REPULSIONS
	REPUMP	REPUMPS
	REPUNIT	REPUNITS
	REPURE	REPURED · REPURES
	REPURPOSE	REPURPOSED · REPURPOSES
	REPURSUE	REPURSUED · REPURSUES
	REPUTE	REPUTED · REPUTES
	REPUTING	REPUTINGS
PREQUALIFY	**REQUALIFY**	
	REQUERE	REQUERED · REQUERES
	REQUEST	REQUESTS
	REQUESTER	REQUESTERS
	REQUESTOR	REQUESTORS
	REQUICKEN	REQUICKENS
	REQUIEM	REQUIEMS
	REQUIGHT	REQUIGHTS
	REQUIN	REQUINS
	REQUIRE	REQUIRED · REQUIRER · REQUIRES
	REQUIRER	REQUIRERS
	REQUIRING	REQUIRINGS
	REQUISITE	REQUISITES
	REQUIT	REQUITE · REQUITS
	REQUITAL	REQUITALS
	REQUITE	REQUITED · REQUITER · REQUITES
	REQUITER	REQUITERS
	REQUOTE	REQUOTED · REQUOTES
	REQUOYLE	REQUOYLED · REQUOYLES
	RERACK	RERACKS
	RERADIATE	RERADIATED · RERADIATES
	RERAIL	RERAILS
	RERAISE	RERAISED · RERAISES
	REREAD	REREADS
PREREADING	**REREADING**	REREADINGS
	REREBRACE	REREBRACES
PRERECORD	**RERECORD**	RERECORDS
PRERECORDS	**RERECORDS**	
	REREDOSSE	REREDOSSES
PRERELEASE	**RERELEASE**	RERELEASED · RERELEASES
	REREMIND	REREMINDS
	RERENT	RERENTS
	REREPEAT	REREPEATS
PREREVIEW	**REREVIEW**	REREVIEWS
	REREVISE	REREVISED · REREVISES
	REREWARD	REREWARDS
	RERIG	RERIGS
	RERISE	RERISEN · RERISES
	REROLL	REROLLS
	REROLLER	REROLLERS
	REROOF	REROOFS
	REROUTE	REROUTED · REROUTES
	RERUN	RERUNS
ARES · ERES · IRES · ORES · TRES · URES	**RES**	RESH · REST
	RESADDLE	RESADDLED · RESADDLES
	RESAIL	RESAILS
PRESALE	**RESALE**	RESALES
PRESALES	**RESALES**	
	RESALGAR	RESALGARS
	RESALUTE	RESALUTED · RESALUTES
	RESAMPLE	RESAMPLED · RESAMPLES
	RESAW	RESAWN · RESAWS
	RESAY	RESAYS
	RESCALE	RESCALED · RESCALES
PRESCHOOL	**RESCHOOL**	RESCHOOLS

R

FRONT HOOK	ROOT WORD	END HOOK
PRESCHOOLS	**RESCHOOLS**	
PRESCIND	**RESCIND**	RESCINDS
PRESCINDED	**RESCINDED**	
	RESCINDER	RESCINDERS
PRESCINDS	**RESCINDS**	
PRESCORE	**RESCORE**	RESCORED ▪ RESCORES
PRESCORED	**RESCORED**	
PRESCORES	**RESCORES**	
PRESCORING	**RESCORING**	
PRESCREEN	**RESCREEN**	RESCREENS
PRESCREENS	**RESCREENS**	
PRESCRIPT	**RESCRIPT**	RESCRIPTS
PRESCRIPTS	**RESCRIPTS**	
	RESCUE	RESCUED ▪ RESCUER ▪ RESCUES
	RESCUER	RESCUERS
	RESCULPT	RESCULPTS
	RESEAL	RESEALS
PRESEASON	**RESEASON**	RESEASONS
PRESEASONS	**RESEASONS**	
	RESEAT	RESEATS
	RESEAU	RESEAUS ▪ RESEAUX
	RESECT	RESECTS
	RESECTION	RESECTIONS
	RESECURE	RESECURED ▪ RESECURES
	RESEDA	RESEDAS
	RESEE	RESEED ▪ RESEEK ▪ RESEEN ▪ RESEES
	RESEED	RESEEDS
	RESEEK	RESEEKS
	RESEIZE	RESEIZED ▪ RESEIZES
	RESEIZURE	RESEIZURES
PRESELECT	**RESELECT**	RESELECTS
PRESELECTS	**RESELECTS**	
PRESELL	**RESELL**	RESELLS
	RESELLER	RESELLERS
PRESELLING	**RESELLING**	
PRESELLS	**RESELLS**	
	RESEMBLE	RESEMBLED ▪ RESEMBLER ▪ RESEMBLES
	RESEMBLER	RESEMBLERS
	RESEND	RESENDS
PRESENT	**RESENT**	RESENTS
PRESENTED	**RESENTED**	
PRESENTER	**RESENTER**	RESENTERS
PRESENTERS	**RESENTERS**	
PRESENTING	**RESENTING**	
PRESENTIVE	**RESENTIVE**	
PRESENTS	**RESENTS**	
	RESERPINE	RESERPINES
PRESERVE	**RESERVE**	RESERVED ▪ RESERVER ▪ RESERVES
PRESERVED	**RESERVED**	
PRESERVER	**RESERVER**	RESERVERS
PRESERVERS	**RESERVERS**	
PRESERVES	**RESERVES**	
PRESERVICE	**RESERVICE**	RESERVICED ▪ RESERVICES
PRESERVING	**RESERVING**	
	RESERVIST	RESERVISTS
	RESERVOIR	RESERVOIRS
GRESES ▪ PRESES ▪ URESES	**RESES**	
PRESET	**RESET**	RESETS
PRESETS	**RESETS**	
	RESETTER	RESETTERS
PRESETTING	**RESETTING**	
PRESETTLE	**RESETTLE**	RESETTLED ▪ RESETTLES
PRESETTLED	**RESETTLED**	
PRESETTLES	**RESETTLES**	
	RESEW	RESEWN ▪ RESEWS
FRESH	**RESH**	
PRESHAPE	**RESHAPE**	RESHAPED ▪ RESHAPER ▪ RESHAPES
PRESHAPED	**RESHAPED**	
	RESHAPER	RESHAPERS

R

FRONT HOOK	ROOT WORD	END HOOK
PRESHAPES	**RESHAPES**	
PRESHAPING	**RESHAPING**	
	RESHARPEN	RESHARPENS
	RESHAVE	RESHAVED · RESHAVEN · RESHAVES
FRESHES	**RESHES**	
	RESHINE	RESHINED · RESHINES
	RESHINGLE	RESHINGLED · RESHINGLES
PRESHIP	**RESHIP**	RESHIPS
PRESHIPPED	**RESHIPPED**	
	RESHIPPER	RESHIPPERS
PRESHIPS	**RESHIPS**	
	RESHOE	RESHOED · RESHOES
	RESHOOT	RESHOOTS
PRESHOW	**RESHOW**	RESHOWN · RESHOWS
PRESHOWED	**RESHOWED**	
	RESHOWER	RESHOWERS
PRESHOWING	**RESHOWING**	
PRESHOWN	**RESHOWN**	
PRESHOWS	**RESHOWS**	
	RESHUFFLE	RESHUFFLED · RESHUFFLES
	RESIANCE	RESIANCES
	RESIANT	RESIANTS
	RESID	RESIDE · RESIDS
PRESIDE	**RESIDE**	RESIDED · RESIDER · RESIDES
PRESIDED	**RESIDED**	
	RESIDENCE	RESIDENCES
PRESIDENCY	**RESIDENCY**	
PRESIDENT	**RESIDENT**	RESIDENTS
PRESIDENTS	**RESIDENTS**	
PRESIDER	**RESIDER**	RESIDERS
PRESIDERS	**RESIDERS**	
PRESIDES	**RESIDES**	
PRESIDING	**RESIDING**	
	RESIDUA	RESIDUAL
	RESIDUAL	RESIDUALS
	RESIDUE	RESIDUES
	RESIDUUM	RESIDUUMS
PRESIFT	**RESIFT**	RESIFTS
PRESIFTED	**RESIFTED**	
PRESIFTING	**RESIFTING**	
PRESIFTS	**RESIFTS**	
	RESIGHT	RESIGHTS
	RESIGN	RESIGNS
	RESIGNER	RESIGNERS
	RESILE	RESILED · RESILES
	RESILIN	RESILING · RESILINS
	RESILVER	RESILVERS
	RESIN	RESINS · RESINY
	RESINATA	RESINATAS
	RESINATE	RESINATED · RESINATES
	RESINER	RESINERS
	RESINISE	RESINISED · RESINISES
	RESINIZE	RESINIZED · RESINIZES
	RESINOID	RESINOIDS
	RESIST	RESISTS
	RESISTANT	RESISTANTS
	RESISTENT	RESISTENTS
	RESISTER	RESISTERS
	RESISTOR	RESISTORS
	RESIT	RESITE · RESITS
	RESITE	RESITED · RESITES
	RESITTING	RESITTINGS
	RESITUATE	RESITUATED · RESITUATES
	RESIZE	RESIZED · RESIZES
	RESKEW	RESKEWS
	RESKILL	RESKILLS
	RESKUE	RESKUED · RESKUES
	RESLATE	RESLATED · RESLATES
	RESMELT	RESMELTS

R

694

FRONT HOOK	ROOT WORD	END HOOK
	RESMOOTH	RESMOOTHS
	RESNATRON	RESNATRONS
PRESOAK	**RESOAK**	RESOAKS
PRESOAKED	**RESOAKED**	
PRESOAKING	**RESOAKING**	
PRESOAKS	**RESOAKS**	
	RESOD	RESODS
	RESOFTEN	RESOFTENS
	RESOJET	RESOJETS
PRESOLD	**RESOLD**	
	RESOLDER	RESOLDERS
	RESOLE	RESOLED · RESOLES
	RESOLUTE	RESOLUTER · RESOLUTES
	RESOLUTES	RESOLUTEST
PRESOLVE	**RESOLVE**	RESOLVED · RESOLVER · RESOLVES
PRESOLVED	**RESOLVED**	
	RESOLVENT	RESOLVENTS
	RESOLVER	RESOLVERS
PRESOLVES	**RESOLVES**	
PRESOLVING	**RESOLVING**	
	RESONANCE	RESONANCES
	RESONANT	RESONANTS
	RESONATE	RESONATED · RESONATES
	RESONATOR	RESONATORS
	RESORB	RESORBS
	RESORCIN	RESORCINS
PRESORT	**RESORT**	RESORTS
PRESORTED	**RESORTED**	
	RESORTER	RESORTERS
PRESORTING	**RESORTING**	
PRESORTS	**RESORTS**	
	RESOUND	RESOUNDS
	RESOURCE	RESOURCED · RESOURCES
	RESOW	RESOWN · RESOWS
	RESPACE	RESPACED · RESPACES
	RESPADE	RESPADED · RESPADES
	RESPEAK	RESPEAKS
PRESPECIFY	**RESPECIFY**	
	RESPECT	RESPECTS
	RESPECTER	RESPECTERS
	RESPELL	RESPELLS
	RESPIRE	RESPIRED · RESPIRES
	RESPITE	RESPITED · RESPITES
	RESPLEND	RESPLENDS
	RESPLICE	RESPLICED · RESPLICES
PRESPLIT	**RESPLIT**	RESPLITS
	RESPOKE	RESPOKEN
	RESPOND	RESPONDS
	RESPONDER	RESPONDERS
	RESPONSE	RESPONSER · RESPONSES
	RESPONSER	RESPONSERS
	RESPONSOR	RESPONSORS · RESPONSORY
	RESPONSUM	RESPONSUMS
	RESPOOL	RESPOOLS
	RESPOT	RESPOTS
	RESPRAY	RESPRAYS
	RESPREAD	RESPREADS
	RESPRING	RESPRINGS
	RESPROUT	RESPROUTS
	RESSALDAR	RESSALDARS
CREST · DREST · PREST · TREST · WREST	**REST**	RESTO · RESTS · RESTY
	RESTABLE	RESTABLED · RESTABLES
	RESTACK	RESTACKS
	RESTAFF	RESTAFFS
	RESTAGE	RESTAGED · RESTAGES
PRESTAMP	**RESTAMP**	RESTAMPS
PRESTAMPED	**RESTAMPED**	
PRESTAMPS	**RESTAMPS**	
	RESTART	RESTARTS

FRONT HOOK	ROOT WORD	END HOOK
	RESTARTER	RESTARTERS
	RESTATE	RESTATED ▪ RESTATES
PRESTATION	**RESTATION**	RESTATIONS
CRESTED ▪ PRESTED ▪ WRESTED	**RESTED**	
	RESTEM	RESTEMS
PRESTER ▪ WRESTER	**RESTER**	RESTERS
PRESTERS ▪ WRESTERS	**RESTERS**	
CRESTING ▪ PRESTING ▪ WRESTING	**RESTING**	RESTINGS
CRESTINGS	**RESTINGS**	
	RESTITUTE	RESTITUTED ▪ RESTITUTES
CRESTLESS	**RESTLESS**	
PRESTO	**RESTO**	RESTOS
	RESTOCK	RESTOCKS
	RESTOKE	RESTOKED ▪ RESTOKES
	RESTORAL	RESTORALS
PRESTORE	**RESTORE**	RESTORED ▪ RESTORER ▪ RESTORES
PRESTORED	**RESTORED**	
	RESTORER	RESTORERS
PRESTORES	**RESTORES**	
PRESTORING	**RESTORING**	
PRESTOS	**RESTOS**	
	RESTRAIN	RESTRAINS ▪ RESTRAINT
	RESTRAINT	RESTRAINTS
PRESTRESS	**RESTRESS**	
	RESTRICT	RESTRICTS
PRESTRIKE	**RESTRIKE**	RESTRIKES
	RESTRING	RESTRINGE ▪ RESTRINGS
	RESTRINGE	RESTRINGED ▪ RESTRINGES
	RESTRIVE	RESTRIVEN ▪ RESTRIVES
	RESTROOM	RESTROOMS
CRESTS ▪ PRESTS ▪ TRESTS ▪ WRESTS	**RESTS**	
	RESTUFF	RESTUFFS
	RESTUMP	RESTUMPS
	RESTYLE	RESTYLED ▪ RESTYLES
	RESUBJECT	RESUBJECTS
	RESUBMIT	RESUBMITS
	RESULT	RESULTS
	RESULTANT	RESULTANTS
PRESUMABLE	**RESUMABLE**	
PRESUME	**RESUME**	RESUMED ▪ RESUMER ▪ RESUMES
PRESUMED	**RESUMED**	
PRESUMER	**RESUMER**	RESUMERS
PRESUMERS	**RESUMERS**	
PRESUMES	**RESUMES**	
PRESUMING	**RESUMING**	
	RESUMMON	RESUMMONS
	RESURFACE	RESURFACED ▪ RESURFACER ▪ RESURFACES
	RESURGE	RESURGED ▪ RESURGES
	RESURRECT	RESURRECTS
PRESURVEY	**RESURVEY**	RESURVEYS
PRESURVEYS	**RESURVEYS**	
	RESUSPEND	RESUSPENDS
	RESWALLOW	RESWALLOWS
ARET ▪ FRET ▪ TRET	**RET**	RETE ▪ RETS
	RETABLE	RETABLES
	RETACK	RETACKS
	RETACKLE	RETACKLED ▪ RETACKLES
	RETAG	RETAGS
	RETAIL	RETAILS
	RETAILER	RETAILERS
	RETAILING	RETAILINGS
	RETAILOR	RETAILORS
	RETAIN	RETAINS
	RETAINER	RETAINERS
	RETAKE	RETAKEN ▪ RETAKER ▪ RETAKES
	RETAKER	RETAKERS
	RETAKING	RETAKINGS
	RETALIATE	RETALIATED ▪ RETALIATES
	RETAMA	RETAMAS

R

FRONT HOOK	ROOT WORD	END HOOK
PRETAPE	**RETAPE**	RETAPED ▪ RETAPES
PRETAPED	**RETAPED**	
PRETAPES	**RETAPES**	
PRETAPING	**RETAPING**	
	RETARD	RETARDS
	RETARDANT	RETARDANTS
	RETARDATE	RETARDATES
	RETARDER	RETARDERS
	RETARGET	RETARGETS
PRETASTE	**RETASTE**	RETASTED ▪ RETASTES
PRETASTED	**RETASTED**	
PRETASTES	**RETASTES**	
PRETASTING	**RETASTING**	
PRETAX	**RETAX**	
WRETCH	**RETCH**	
WRETCHED	**RETCHED**	
WRETCHES	**RETCHES**	
ARETE	**RETE**	RETEM ▪ RETES
	RETEAM	RETEAMS
	RETEAR	RETEARS
PRETELL	**RETELL**	RETELLS
	RETELLER	RETELLERS
PRETELLING	**RETELLING**	RETELLINGS
PRETELLS	**RETELLS**	
	RETEM	RETEMS
	RETEMPER	RETEMPERS
	RETENE	RETENES
	RETENTION	RETENTIONS
ARETES	**RETES**	RETEST
PRETEST	**RETEST**	RETESTS
PRETESTED	**RETESTED**	
PRETESTING	**RETESTING**	
PRETESTS	**RETESTS**	
	RETEXTURE	RETEXTURED ▪ RETEXTURES
	RETHINK	RETHINKS
	RETHINKER	RETHINKERS
	RETHREAD	RETHREADS
	RETIA	RETIAL
	RETICELLA	RETICELLAS
	RETICENCE	RETICENCES
	RETICLE	RETICLES
	RETICULA	RETICULAR
	RETICULAR	RETICULARY
	RETICULE	RETICULES
	RETICULUM	RETICULUMS
	RETIE	RETIED ▪ RETIES
	RETIGHTEN	RETIGHTENS
	RETILE	RETILED ▪ RETILES
	RETIME	RETIMED ▪ RETIMES
	RETINA	RETINAE ▪ RETINAL ▪ RETINAS
	RETINAL	RETINALS
	RETINE	RETINES
	RETINENE	RETINENES
	RETINITE	RETINITES
CRETINOID	**RETINOID**	RETINOIDS
CRETINOIDS	**RETINOIDS**	
	RETINOL	RETINOLS
	RETINT	RETINTS
	RETINUE	RETINUED ▪ RETINUES
	RETINULA	RETINULAE ▪ RETINULAR ▪ RETINULAS
	RETIRAL	RETIRALS
	RETIRANT	RETIRANTS
	RETIRE	RETIRED ▪ RETIREE ▪ RETIRER ▪ RETIRES
	RETIREE	RETIREES
	RETIRER	RETIRERS
	RETITLE	RETITLED ▪ RETITLES
PRETOLD	**RETOLD**	
	RETOOL	RETOOLS
	RETORSION	RETORSIONS

R

FRONT HOOK	ROOT WORD	END HOOK
	RETORT	RETORTS
	RETORTER	RETORTERS
	RETORTION	RETORTIONS
	RETOTAL	RETOTALS
	RETOUCHER	RETOUCHERS
	RETOUR	RETOURS
	RETRACE	RETRACED · RETRACER · RETRACES
	RETRACER	RETRACERS
	RETRACK	RETRACKS
	RETRACT	RETRACTS
	RETRACTOR	RETRACTORS
	RETRAICT	RETRAICTS
PRETRAIN	**RETRAIN**	RETRAINS
PRETRAINED	**RETRAINED**	
	RETRAINEE	RETRAINEES
PRETRAINS	**RETRAINS**	
	RETRAIT	RETRAITE · RETRAITS · RETRAITT
	RETRAITE	RETRAITES
	RETRAITT	RETRAITTS
	RETRATE	RETRATED · RETRATES
	RETREAD	RETREADS
PRETREAT	**RETREAT**	RETREATS
PRETREATED	**RETREATED**	
	RETREATER	RETREATERS
PRETREATS	**RETREATS**	
	RETREE	RETREES
PRETRIAL	**RETRIAL**	RETRIALS
PRETRIALS	**RETRIALS**	
	RETRIBUTE	RETRIBUTED · RETRIBUTES
	RETRIEVAL	RETRIEVALS
	RETRIEVE	RETRIEVED · RETRIEVER · RETRIEVES
	RETRIEVER	RETRIEVERS
PRETRIM	**RETRIM**	RETRIMS
PRETRIMMED	**RETRIMMED**	
PRETRIMS	**RETRIMS**	
	RETRO	RETROD · RETROS
	RETROACT	RETROACTS
	RETROCEDE	RETROCEDED · RETROCEDES
	RETRODICT	RETRODICTS
	RETROFIRE	RETROFIRED · RETROFIRES
	RETROFIT	RETROFITS
	RETROJECT	RETROJECTS
	RETRONYM	RETRONYMS
	RETROPACK	RETROPACKS
	RETROVERT	RETROVERTS
ARETS · FRETS · TRETS	**RETS**	
	RETSINA	RETSINAS
ARETTED · FRETTED	**RETTED**	
ARETTING · FRETTING	**RETTING**	
	RETUND	RETUNDS
	RETUNE	RETUNED · RETUNES
	RETURF	RETURFS
	RETURN	RETURNS
	RETURNEE	RETURNEES
	RETURNER	RETURNERS
	RETURNIK	RETURNIKS
	RETWIST	RETWISTS
PRETYPE	**RETYPE**	RETYPED · RETYPES
PRETYPED	**RETYPED**	
PRETYPES	**RETYPES**	
PRETYPING	**RETYPING**	
PREUNION	**REUNION**	REUNIONS
PREUNIONS	**REUNIONS**	
PREUNITE	**REUNITE**	REUNITED · REUNITER · REUNITES
PREUNITED	**REUNITED**	
	REUNITER	REUNITERS
PREUNITES	**REUNITES**	
PREUNITING	**REUNITING**	
	REUPTAKE	REUPTAKES

FRONT HOOK	ROOT WORD	END HOOK
	REURGE	REURGED ▪ REURGES
	REUSABLE	REUSABLES
	REUSE	REUSED ▪ REUSES
	REUTILISE	REUTILISED ▪ REUTILISES
	REUTILIZE	REUTILIZED ▪ REUTILIZES
	REUTTER	REUTTERS
EREV	**REV**	REVS
	REVALENTA	REVALENTAS
	REVALUATE	REVALUATED ▪ REVALUATES
PREVALUE	**REVALUE**	REVALUED ▪ REVALUES
PREVALUED	**REVALUED**	
PREVALUES	**REVALUES**	
PREVALUING	**REVALUING**	
	REVAMP	REVAMPS
	REVAMPER	REVAMPERS
	REVAMPING	REVAMPINGS
	REVANCHE	REVANCHES
	REVEAL	REVEALS
	REVEALER	REVEALERS
	REVEALING	REVEALINGS
	REVEILLE	REVEILLES
	REVEL	REVELS
	REVELATOR	REVELATORS ▪ REVELATORY
	REVELER	REVELERS
	REVELLER	REVELLERS
	REVELLING	REVELLINGS
	REVELMENT	REVELMENTS
	REVENANT	REVENANTS
	REVENGE	REVENGED ▪ REVENGER ▪ REVENGES
	REVENGER	REVENGERS
	REVENGING	REVENGINGS
	REVENUE	REVENUED ▪ REVENUER ▪ REVENUES
	REVENUER	REVENUERS
PREVERB	**REVERB**	REVERBS
PREVERBS	**REVERBS**	
	REVERE	REVERED ▪ REVERER ▪ REVERES
	REVERENCE	REVERENCED ▪ REVERENCER ▪ REVERENCES
	REVEREND	REVERENDS
	REVERER	REVERERS
	REVERIE	REVERIES
	REVERIST	REVERISTS
	REVERS	REVERSE ▪ REVERSI ▪ REVERSO
	REVERSAL	REVERSALS
	REVERSE	REVERSED ▪ REVERSER ▪ REVERSES
	REVERSER	REVERSERS
	REVERSI	REVERSIS
	REVERSING	REVERSINGS
	REVERSION	REVERSIONS
	REVERSO	REVERSOS
	REVERT	REVERTS
	REVERTANT	REVERTANTS
	REVERTER	REVERTERS
	REVEST	REVESTS
BREVET ▪ TREVET	**REVET**	REVETS
	REVETMENT	REVETMENTS
BREVETS ▪ TREVETS	**REVETS**	
BREVETTED	**REVETTED**	
BREVETTING	**REVETTING**	
	REVEUR	REVEURS
	REVEUSE	REVEUSES
	REVIBRATE	REVIBRATED ▪ REVIBRATES
	REVICTUAL	REVICTUALS
	REVIE	REVIED ▪ REVIES ▪ REVIEW
PREVIEW	**REVIEW**	REVIEWS
	REVIEWAL	REVIEWALS
PREVIEWED	**REVIEWED**	
PREVIEWER	**REVIEWER**	REVIEWERS
PREVIEWERS	**REVIEWERS**	
PREVIEWING	**REVIEWING**	

FRONT HOOK	ROOT WORD	END HOOK
PREVIEWS	**REVIEWS**	
	REVILE	REVILED · REVILER · REVILES
	REVILER	REVILERS
	REVILING	REVILINGS
	REVIOLATE	REVIOLATED · REVIOLATES
	REVISAL	REVISALS
PREVISE	**REVISE**	REVISED · REVISER · REVISES
PREVISED	**REVISED**	
	REVISER	REVISERS
BREVISES · PREVISES · TREVISES	**REVISES**	
PREVISING	**REVISING**	
PREVISION	**REVISION**	REVISIONS
PREVISIONS	**REVISIONS**	
PREVISIT	**REVISIT**	REVISITS
PREVISITED	**REVISITED**	
PREVISITS	**REVISITS**	
PREVISOR	**REVISOR**	REVISORS · REVISORY
PREVISORS	**REVISORS**	
	REVIVAL	REVIVALS
	REVIVE	REVIVED · REVIVER · REVIVES
	REVIVER	REVIVERS
	REVIVING	REVIVINGS
	REVIVOR	REVIVORS
	REVOICE	REVOICED · REVOICES
	REVOKE	REVOKED · REVOKER · REVOKES
	REVOKER	REVOKERS
	REVOLT	REVOLTS
	REVOLTER	REVOLTERS
	REVOLVE	REVOLVED · REVOLVER · REVOLVES
	REVOLVER	REVOLVERS
	REVOLVING	REVOLVINGS
	REVOTE	REVOTED · REVOTES
EREVS	**REVS**	
PREVUE	**REVUE**	REVUES
PREVUES	**REVUES**	
	REVUIST	REVUISTS
	REVULSION	REVULSIONS
	REVULSIVE	REVULSIVES
AREW · BREW · CREW · DREW · GREW · TREW	**REW**	REWS
	REWAKE	REWAKED · REWAKEN · REWAKES
	REWAKEN	REWAKENS
	REWARD	REWARDS
	REWARDER	REWARDERS
	REWAREWA	REWAREWAS
PREWARM	**REWARM**	REWARMS
PREWARMED	**REWARMED**	
PREWARMING	**REWARMING**	
PREWARMS	**REWARMS**	
PREWASH	**REWASH**	
PREWASHED	**REWASHED**	
PREWASHES	**REWASHES**	
PREWASHING	**REWASHING**	
	REWEAR	REWEARS
	REWEAVE	REWEAVED · REWEAVES
BREWED · CREWED · GREWED	**REWED**	REWEDS
PREWEIGH	**REWEIGH**	REWEIGHS
PREWEIGHED	**REWEIGHED**	
PREWEIGHS	**REWEIGHS**	
	REWELD	REWELDS
	REWET	REWETS
	REWIDEN	REWIDENS
	REWIN	REWIND · REWINS
	REWIND	REWINDS
	REWINDER	REWINDERS
PREWIRE	**REWIRE**	REWIRED · REWIRES
PREWIRED	**REWIRED**	
PREWIRES	**REWIRES**	
PREWIRING	**REWIRING**	
	REWOKE	REWOKEN

R

FRONT HOOK	ROOT WORD	END HOOK
	REWORD	REWORDS
PREWORK	**REWORK**	REWORKS
PREWORKED	**REWORKED**	
PREWORKING	**REWORKING**	
PREWORKS	**REWORKS**	
PREWORN	**REWORN**	
	REWOVE	REWOVEN
PREWRAP	**REWRAP**	REWRAPS · REWRAPT
PREWRAPPED	**REWRAPPED**	
PREWRAPS	**REWRAPS**	
	REWRITE	REWRITER · REWRITES
	REWRITER	REWRITERS
PREWRITING	**REWRITING**	
BREWS · CREWS · GREWS · TREWS	**REWS**	
	REWTH	REWTHS
GREX · PREX	**REX**	
GREXES · PREXES	**REXES**	
	REXINE	REXINES
	REYNARD	REYNARDS
PREZ · TREZ	**REZ**	
	REZERO	REZEROS
	REZONE	REZONED · REZONES
	RHABDOID	RHABDOIDS
	RHABDOM	RHABDOME · RHABDOMS
	RHABDOME	RHABDOMES
	RHACHILLA	RHACHILLAS
	RHAMNOSE	RHAMNOSES
	RHANJA	RHANJAS
	RHAPHE	RHAPHES
	RHAPHIDE	RHAPHIDES
	RHAPONTIC	RHAPONTICS
	RHAPSODE	RHAPSODES
	RHEA	RHEAS
	RHEBOK	RHEBOKS
	RHEME	RHEMES
	RHENIUM	RHENIUMS
	RHEOBASE	RHEOBASES
	RHEOCHORD	RHEOCHORDS
	RHEOCORD	RHEOCORDS
	RHEOMETER	RHEOMETERS
	RHEOPHIL	RHEOPHILE
	RHEOPHILE	RHEOPHILES
	RHEOSTAT	RHEOSTATS
	RHEOTOME	RHEOTOMES
	RHEOTROPE	RHEOTROPES
	RHETOR	RHETORS
	RHETORIC	RHETORICS
	RHETORISE	RHETORISED · RHETORISES
	RHETORIZE	RHETORIZED · RHETORIZES
	RHEUM	RHEUMS · RHEUMY
	RHEUMATIC	RHEUMATICS
	RHEUMATIZ	RHEUMATIZE
	RHIGOLENE	RHIGOLENES
	RHIME	RHIMES
	RHINE	RHINES
	RHINO	RHINOS
	RHINOLITH	RHINOLITHS
	RHIPIDION	RHIPIDIONS
	RHIPIDIUM	RHIPIDIUMS
	RHIZINE	RHIZINES
	RHIZOBIA	RHIZOBIAL
	RHIZOCARP	RHIZOCARPS
	RHIZOCAUL	RHIZOCAULS
	RHIZOID	RHIZOIDS
	RHIZOME	RHIZOMES
	RHIZOPOD	RHIZOPODS
	RHO	RHOS
	RHODAMIN	RHODAMINE · RHODAMINS
	RHODAMINE	RHODAMINES

R

FRONT HOOK	ROOT WORD	END HOOK
	RHODANATE	RHODANATES
	RHODANISE	RHODANISED · RHODANISES
	RHODANIZE	RHODANIZED · RHODANIZES
	RHODIE	RHODIES
	RHODINAL	RHODINALS
	RHODIUM	RHODIUMS
	RHODOLITE	RHODOLITES
	RHODONITE	RHODONITES
	RHODOPSIN	RHODOPSINS
	RHODORA	RHODORAS
	RHOEADINE	RHOEADINES
	RHOMB	RHOMBI · RHOMBS
	RHOMBI	RHOMBIC
	RHOMBOI	RHOMBOID
	RHOMBOID	RHOMBOIDS
	RHONE	RHONES
	RHOPALISM	RHOPALISMS
	RHOTACISE	RHOTACISED · RHOTACISES
	RHOTACISM	RHOTACISMS
	RHOTACIST	RHOTACISTS
	RHOTACIZE	RHOTACIZED · RHOTACIZES
	RHUBARB	RHUBARBS · RHUBARBY
	RHUMB	RHUMBA · RHUMBS
	RHUMBA	RHUMBAS
	RHYME	RHYMED · RHYMER · RHYMES
	RHYMER	RHYMERS
	RHYMESTER	RHYMESTERS
	RHYMIST	RHYMISTS
	RHYNE	RHYNES
	RHYOLITE	RHYOLITES
	RHYTHM	RHYTHMI · RHYTHMS
	RHYTHMI	RHYTHMIC
ARHYTHMIC	**RHYTHMIC**	RHYTHMICS
	RHYTHMISE	RHYTHMISED · RHYTHMISES
	RHYTHMIST	RHYTHMISTS
	RHYTHMIZE	RHYTHMIZED · RHYTHMIZES
	RHYTIDOME	RHYTIDOMES
	RHYTINA	RHYTINAS
	RHYTON	RHYTONS
ARIA	**RIA**	RIAL · RIAS
PRIAL · TRIAL · URIAL	**RIAL**	RIALS
PRIALS · TRIALS · URIALS	**RIALS**	
	RIALTO	RIALTOS
CRIANT	**RIANT**	
ARIAS	**RIAS**	
	RIATA	RIATAS
CRIB · DRIB · FRIB	**RIB**	RIBA · RIBS
	RIBA	RIBAS
	RIBALD	RIBALDS
	RIBAND	RIBANDS
	RIBATTUTA	RIBATTUTAS
	RIBAUD	RIBAUDS
	RIBAVIRIN	RIBAVIRINS
	RIBBAND	RIBBANDS
CRIBBED · DRIBBED	**RIBBED**	
CRIBBER · DRIBBER	**RIBBER**	RIBBERS
CRIBBERS · DRIBBERS	**RIBBERS**	
CRIBBING · DRIBBING	**RIBBING**	RIBBINGS
CRIBBINGS	**RIBBINGS**	
	RIBBON	RIBBONS · RIBBONY
	RIBCAGE	RIBCAGES
BRIBES · TRIBES	**RIBES**	
	RIBIBE	RIBIBES
	RIBIBLE	RIBIBLES
	RIBIER	RIBIERS
DRIBLET · TRIBLET	**RIBLET**	RIBLETS
DRIBLETS · TRIBLETS	**RIBLETS**	
	RIBOSE	RIBOSES
	RIBOSOME	RIBOSOMES

FRONT HOOK	ROOT WORD	END HOOK
	RIBOZYME	RIBOZYMES
CRIBS ▪ DRIBS ▪ FRIBS	**RIBS**	
	RIBSTON	RIBSTONE ▪ RIBSTONS
	RIBSTONE	RIBSTONES
CRIBWORK	**RIBWORK**	RIBWORKS
CRIBWORKS	**RIBWORKS**	
	RIBWORT	RIBWORTS
DRICE ▪ GRICE ▪ PRICE ▪ TRICE	**RICE**	RICED ▪ RICER ▪ RICES ▪ RICEY
	RICEBIRD	RICEBIRDS
GRICED ▪ PRICED ▪ TRICED	**RICED**	
GRICER ▪ PRICER	**RICER**	RICERS
	RICERCAR	RICERCARE ▪ RICERCARI ▪ RICERCARS
	RICERCARE	RICERCARES
	RICERCATA	RICERCATAS
GRICERS ▪ PRICERS	**RICERS**	
DRICES ▪ GRICES ▪ PRICES ▪ TRICES	**RICES**	
PRICEY	**RICEY**	
	RICH	RICHT
	RICHEN	RICHENS
	RICHES	RICHEST
	RICHESSE	RICHESSES
BRICHT ▪ FRICHT	**RICHT**	RICHTS
FRICHTED	**RICHTED**	
BRICHTER	**RICHTER**	
BRICHTEST	**RICHTEST**	
FRICHTING	**RICHTING**	
FRICHTS	**RICHTS**	
	RICHWEED	RICHWEEDS
PRICIER	**RICIER**	
PRICIEST	**RICIEST**	
	RICIN	RICING ▪ RICINS
GRICING ▪ PRICING ▪ TRICING	**RICING**	
BRICK ▪ CRICK ▪ ERICK ▪ PRICK ▪ TRICK WRICK	**RICK**	RICKS
BRICKED ▪ CRICKED ▪ PRICKED ▪ TRICKED WRICKED	**RICKED**	
PRICKER ▪ TRICKER	**RICKER**	RICKERS
PRICKERS ▪ TRICKERS	**RICKERS**	
CRICKETS ▪ PRICKETS	**RICKETS**	
CRICKEY	**RICKEY**	RICKEYS
BRICKING ▪ CRICKING ▪ FRICKING PRICKING ▪ TRICKING ▪ WRICKING	**RICKING**	
BRICKLE ▪ PRICKLE ▪ TRICKLE	**RICKLE**	RICKLES
BRICKLES ▪ PRICKLES ▪ TRICKLES	**RICKLES**	
PRICKLY ▪ TRICKLY	**RICKLY**	
	RICKRACK	RICKRACKS
BRICKS ▪ CRICKS ▪ ERICKS ▪ PRICKS TRICKS ▪ WRICKS	**RICKS**	
	RICKSHA	RICKSHAS ▪ RICKSHAW
	RICKSHAW	RICKSHAWS
	RICKSTAND	RICKSTANDS
	RICKSTICK	RICKSTICKS
BRICKYARD	**RICKYARD**	RICKYARDS
BRICKYARDS	**RICKYARDS**	
	RICOCHET	RICOCHETS
	RICOTTA	RICOTTAS
	RICRAC	RICRACS
PRICY	**RICY**	
ARID ▪ GRID ▪ IRID	**RID**	RIDE ▪ RIDS
	RIDDANCE	RIDDANCES
GRIDDED	**RIDDED**	
GRIDDER	**RIDDER**	RIDDERS
GRIDDERS	**RIDDERS**	
GRIDDLE	**RIDDLE**	RIDDLED ▪ RIDDLER ▪ RIDDLES
GRIDDLED	**RIDDLED**	
	RIDDLER	RIDDLERS
GRIDDLES	**RIDDLES**	
GRIDDLING	**RIDDLING**	RIDDLINGS
BRIDE ▪ GRIDE ▪ PRIDE ▪ TRIDE	**RIDE**	RIDER ▪ RIDES

FRONT HOOK	ROOT WORD	END HOOK
TRIDENT	**RIDENT**	
ARIDER	**RIDER**	RIDERS
	RIDERSHIP	RIDERSHIPS
BRIDES · GRIDES · IRIDES · PRIDES	**RIDES**	
BRIDGE · FRIDGE	**RIDGE**	RIDGED · RIDGEL · RIDGER · RIDGES
	RIDGEBACK	RIDGEBACKS
BRIDGED · FRIDGED	**RIDGED**	
	RIDGEL	RIDGELS
	RIDGELINE	RIDGELINES
	RIDGELING	RIDGELINGS
	RIDGEPOLE	RIDGEPOLES
	RIDGER	RIDGERS
BRIDGES · FRIDGES	**RIDGES**	
	RIDGETOP	RIDGETOPS
	RIDGETREE	RIDGETREES
	RIDGEWAY	RIDGEWAYS
	RIDGIL	RIDGILS
BRIDGING · FRIDGING	**RIDGING**	RIDGINGS
BRIDGINGS	**RIDGINGS**	
	RIDGLING	RIDGLINGS
	RIDICULE	RIDICULED · RIDICULER · RIDICULES
	RIDICULER	RIDICULERS
BRIDING · GRIDING · PRIDING	**RIDING**	RIDINGS
	RIDLEY	RIDLEYS
	RIDOTTO	RIDOTTOS
GRIDS · IRIDS	**RIDS**	
ARIEL · ORIEL	**RIEL**	RIELS
ARIELS · ORIELS	**RIELS**	
	RIEM	RIEMS
	RIEMPIE	RIEMPIES
	RIESLING	RIESLINGS
GRIEVE · PRIEVE	**RIEVE**	RIEVER · RIEVES
GRIEVER	**RIEVER**	RIEVERS
GRIEVERS	**RIEVERS**	
GRIEVES · PRIEVES	**RIEVES**	
GRIEVING · PRIEVING	**RIEVING**	
	RIF	RIFE · RIFF · RIFS · RIFT
	RIFAMPIN	RIFAMPINS
	RIFAMYCIN	RIFAMYCINS
	RIFE	RIFER
GRIFF · TRIFF	**RIFF**	RIFFS
	RIFFAGE	RIFFAGES
	RIFFLE	RIFFLED · RIFFLER · RIFFLES
	RIFFLER	RIFFLERS
	RIFFOLA	RIFFOLAS
	RIFFRAFF	RIFFRAFFS
GRIFFS	**RIFFS**	
TRIFLE	**RIFLE**	RIFLED · RIFLER · RIFLES
	RIFLEBIRD	RIFLEBIRDS
TRIFLED	**RIFLED**	
TRIFLER	**RIFLER**	RIFLERS · RIFLERY
TRIFLERS	**RIFLERS**	
TRIFLES	**RIFLES**	
TRIFLING	**RIFLING**	RIFLINGS
TRIFLINGS	**RIFLINGS**	
	RIFLIP	RIFLIPS
DRIFT · GRIFT	**RIFT**	RIFTE · RIFTS · RIFTY
	RIFTE	RIFTED
DRIFTED · GRIFTED	**RIFTED**	
DRIFTIER	**RIFTIER**	
DRIFTIEST	**RIFTIEST**	
DRIFTING · GRIFTING	**RIFTING**	
DRIFTLESS	**RIFTLESS**	
DRIFTS · GRIFTS	**RIFTS**	
DRIFTY	**RIFTY**	
BRIG · FRIG · GRIG · PRIG · TRIG	**RIG**	RIGG · RIGS
	RIGADOON	RIGADOONS
	RIGATONI	RIGATONIS
	RIGAUDON	RIGAUDONS

FRONT HOOK	ROOT WORD	END HOOK
	RIGG	RIGGS
	RIGGALD	RIGGALDS
FRIGGED (offensive) · GRIGGED · PRIGGED · TRIGGED	**RIGGED**	
FRIGGER (offensive) · PRIGGER · TRIGGER	**RIGGER**	RIGGERS
FRIGGERS (offensive) · PRIGGERS · TRIGGERS	**RIGGERS**	
FRIGGING (offensive) · GRIGGING · TRIGGING	**RIGGING**	RIGGINGS
FRIGGINGS (offensive) · PRIGGINGS	**RIGGINGS**	
PRIGGISH	**RIGGISH**	
ARIGHT · BRIGHT · FRIGHT · WRIGHT	**RIGHT**	RIGHTO · RIGHTS · RIGHTY
FRIGHTED	**RIGHTED**	
BRIGHTEN · FRIGHTEN	**RIGHTEN**	RIGHTENS
BRIGHTENED · FRIGHTENED	**RIGHTENED**	
BRIGHTENS · FRIGHTENS	**RIGHTENS**	
BRIGHTER	**RIGHTER**	RIGHTERS
BRIGHTEST	**RIGHTEST**	
FRIGHTFUL	**RIGHTFUL**	
FRIGHTING	**RIGHTING**	RIGHTINGS
BRIGHTISH	**RIGHTISH**	
	RIGHTISM	RIGHTISMS
	RIGHTIST	RIGHTISTS
BRIGHTLY	**RIGHTLY**	
BRIGHTNESS	**RIGHTNESS**	
	RIGHTO	RIGHTOS
BRIGHTS · FRIGHTS · WRIGHTS	**RIGHTS**	
	RIGHTSIZE	RIGHTSIZED · RIGHTSIZES
	RIGHTWARD	RIGHTWARDS
FRIGID	**RIGID**	RIGIDS
FRIGIDER	**RIGIDER**	
FRIGIDEST	**RIGIDEST**	
	RIGIDISE	RIGIDISED · RIGIDISES
FRIGIDITY	**RIGIDITY**	
	RIGIDIZE	RIGIDIZED · RIGIDIZES
FRIGIDLY	**RIGIDLY**	
FRIGIDNESS	**RIGIDNESS**	
	RIGLIN	RIGLING · RIGLINS
	RIGLING	RIGLINGS
	RIGMAROLE	RIGMAROLES
	RIGOL	RIGOLL · RIGOLS
	RIGOLL	RIGOLLS
	RIGOR	RIGORS
	RIGORISM	RIGORISMS
	RIGORIST	RIGORISTS
	RIGOUR	RIGOURS
	RIGOUT	RIGOUTS
BRIGS · FRIGS (offensive) · GRIGS · PRIGS · TRIGS	**RIGS**	
	RIGSDALER	RIGSDALERS
	RIGWIDDIE	RIGWIDDIES
	RIGWOODIE	RIGWOODIES
	RIJSTAFEL	RIJSTAFELS
	RIKISHA	RIKISHAS
	RIKSHAW	RIKSHAWS
	RILE	RILED · RILES · RILEY
ARILED	**RILED**	
BRILL · DRILL · FRILL · GRILL · KRILL · PRILL · TRILL	**RILL**	RILLE · RILLS
GRILLE	**RILLE**	RILLED · RILLES · RILLET
DRILLED · FRILLED · GRILLED · PRILLED · TRILLED	**RILLED**	
GRILLES	**RILLES**	
	RILLET	RILLETS
DRILLING · FRILLING · GRILLING · PRILLING · TRILLING	**RILLING**	
	RILLMARK	RILLMARKS
BRILLS · DRILLS · FRILLS · GRILLS · KRILLS · PRILLS · TRILLS	**RILLS**	
BRIM · CRIM · GRIM · PRIM · TRIM	**RIM**	RIMA · RIME · RIMS · RIMU · RIMY

FRONT HOOK	ROOT WORD	END HOOK
PRIMA	**RIMA**	RIMAE
	RIMAYE	RIMAYES
CRIME ▪ GRIME ▪ PRIME	**RIME**	RIMED ▪ RIMER ▪ RIMES
CRIMED ▪ GRIMED ▪ PRIMED	**RIMED**	
CRIMELESS	**RIMELESS**	
PRIMER ▪ TRIMER	**RIMER**	RIMERS
PRIMERS ▪ TRIMERS	**RIMERS**	
CRIMES ▪ GRIMES ▪ PRIMES	**RIMES**	
TRIMESTER	**RIMESTER**	RIMESTERS
TRIMESTERS	**RIMESTERS**	
	RIMFIRE	RIMFIRES
GRIMIER	**RIMIER**	
GRIMIEST	**RIMIEST**	
GRIMINESS	**RIMINESS**	
BRIMING ▪ CRIMING ▪ GRIMING ▪ PRIMING	**RIMING**	
	RIMLAND	RIMLANDS
BRIMLESS	**RIMLESS**	
BRIMMED ▪ PRIMMED ▪ TRIMMED	**RIMMED**	
BRIMMER ▪ CRIMMER ▪ GRIMMER ▪ KRIMMER	**RIMMER**	RIMMERS
PRIMMER ▪ TRIMMER		
BRIMMERS ▪ CRIMMERS ▪ KRIMMERS	**RIMMERS**	
PRIMMERS ▪ TRIMMERS		
BRIMMING ▪ PRIMMING ▪ TRIMMING	**RIMMING**	RIMMINGS
TRIMMINGS	**RIMMINGS**	
CRIMPLE	**RIMPLE**	RIMPLED ▪ RIMPLES
CRIMPLED	**RIMPLED**	
CRIMPLES	**RIMPLES**	
CRIMPLING	**RIMPLING**	
	RIMROCK	RIMROCKS
BRIMS ▪ CRIMS ▪ PRIMS ▪ TRIMS	**RIMS**	
	RIMSHOT	RIMSHOTS
	RIMU	RIMUS
PRIMUS	**RIMUS**	
GRIMY ▪ PRIMY	**RIMY**	
BRIN ▪ GRIN ▪ TRIN	**RIN**	RIND ▪ RINE ▪ RING ▪ RINK ▪ RINS
GRIND	**RIND**	RINDS ▪ RINDY
BRINDED ▪ GRINDED	**RINDED**	
GRINDING	**RINDING**	
GRINDS	**RINDS**	
BRINE ▪ CRINE ▪ TRINE ▪ URINE	**RINE**	RINES
BRINES ▪ CRINES ▪ TRINES ▪ URINES	**RINES**	
BRING ▪ ERING ▪ IRING ▪ WRING	**RING**	RINGS
	RINGBARK	RINGBARKS
	RINGBIT	RINGBITS
	RINGBOLT	RINGBOLTS
	RINGBONE	RINGBONES
	RINGDOVE	RINGDOVES
CRINGED ▪ FRINGED ▪ WRINGED	**RINGED**	
BRINGER ▪ CRINGER ▪ WRINGER	**RINGER**	RINGERS
BRINGERS ▪ CRINGERS ▪ WRINGERS	**RINGERS**	
	RINGGIT	RINGGITS
BRINGING ▪ CRINGING ▪ FRINGING	**RINGING**	RINGINGS
WRINGING		
CRINGINGLY	**RINGINGLY**	
BRINGINGS ▪ CRINGINGS ▪ WRINGINGS	**RINGINGS**	
	RINGLET	RINGLETS
	RINGNECK	RINGNECKS
BRINGS ▪ WRINGS	**RINGS**	
	RINGSIDE	RINGSIDER ▪ RINGSIDES
	RINGSIDER	RINGSIDERS
	RINGSTAND	RINGSTANDS
	RINGSTER	RINGSTERS
	RINGTAIL	RINGTAILS
	RINGTAW	RINGTAWS
	RINGTONE	RINGTONES
	RINGWAY	RINGWAYS
	RINGWOMB	RINGWOMBS
	RINGWORK	RINGWORKS
	RINGWORM	RINGWORMS

R

FRONT HOOK	ROOT WORD	END HOOK
BRINK · DRINK · PRINK	**RINK**	RINKS
PRINKED	**RINKED**	
DRINKING · PRINKING	**RINKING**	
BRINKS · DRINKS · PRINKS	**RINKS**	
GRINNING	**RINNING**	
BRINS · GRINS · TRINS	**RINS**	RINSE
	RINSE	RINSED · RINSER · RINSES
	RINSER	RINSERS
	RINSING	RINSINGS
	RIOJA	RIOJAS
ARIOT · GRIOT	**RIOT**	RIOTS
	RIOTER	RIOTERS
	RIOTING	RIOTINGS
	RIOTISE	RIOTISES
	RIOTIZE	RIOTIZES
GRIOTS	**RIOTS**	
DRIP · GRIP · TRIP	**RIP**	RIPE · RIPP · RIPS · RIPT
	RIPARIAN	RIPARIANS
	RIPCORD	RIPCORDS
CRIPE · GRIPE · TRIPE	**RIPE**	RIPED · RIPEN · RIPER · RIPES
	RIPECK	RIPECKS
GRIPED	**RIPED**	
	RIPEN	RIPENS
	RIPENER	RIPENERS
GRIPER	**RIPER**	RIPERS
GRIPERS	**RIPERS**	
CRIPES · GRIPES · TRIPES	**RIPES**	RIPEST
	RIPIENIST	RIPIENISTS
	RIPIENO	RIPIENOS
GRIPING	**RIPING**	
	RIPOFF	RIPOFFS
	RIPOST	RIPOSTE · RIPOSTS
	RIPOSTE	RIPOSTED · RIPOSTES
	RIPP	RIPPS
DRIPPED · GRIPPED · TRIPPED	**RIPPED**	
DRIPPER · FRIPPER · GRIPPER · TRIPPER	**RIPPER**	RIPPERS
DRIPPERS · FRIPPERS · GRIPPERS · TRIPPERS	**RIPPERS**	
DRIPPIER · GRIPPIER · TRIPPIER	**RIPPIER**	RIPPIERS
DRIPPING · GRIPPING · TRIPPING	**RIPPING**	
GRIPPINGLY · TRIPPINGLY	**RIPPINGLY**	
ARIPPLE · CRIPPLE · GRIPPLE · TRIPPLE	**RIPPLE**	RIPPLED · RIPPLER · RIPPLES · RIPPLET
CRIPPLED · TRIPPLED	**RIPPLED**	
CRIPPLER · TRIPPLER	**RIPPLER**	RIPPLERS
CRIPPLERS · TRIPPLERS	**RIPPLERS**	
CRIPPLES · GRIPPLES · TRIPPLES	**RIPPLES**	
	RIPPLET	RIPPLETS
CRIPPLING · TRIPPLING	**RIPPLING**	RIPPLINGS
CRIPPLINGS	**RIPPLINGS**	
	RIPRAP	RIPRAPS
DRIPS · GRIPS · TRIPS	**RIPS**	
	RIPSAW	RIPSAWN · RIPSAWS
	RIPSTOP	RIPSTOPS
DRIPT · GRIPT	**RIPT**	
	RIPTIDE	RIPTIDES
	RIRORIRO	RIRORIROS
	RISALDAR	RISALDARS
ARISE · BRISE · CRISE · FRISE · GRISE · PRISE	**RISE**	RISEN · RISER · RISES
ARISEN	**RISEN**	
PRISER	**RISER**	RISERS
PRISERS	**RISERS**	
ARISES · BRISES · CRISES · FRISES · GRISES · IRISES · KRISES · PRISES	**RISES**	
	RISHI	RISHIS
	RISIBLE	RISIBLES
ARISING · GRISING · IRISING · KRISING · PRISING	**RISING**	RISINGS
BRISK · FRISK	**RISK**	RISKS · RISKY

FRONT HOOK	ROOT WORD	END HOOK
BRISKED = FRISKED	**RISKED**	
BRISKER = FRISKER	**RISKER**	RISKERS
FRISKERS	**RISKERS**	
FRISKFUL	**RISKFUL**	
FRISKIER	**RISKIER**	
FRISKIEST	**RISKIEST**	
FRISKILY	**RISKILY**	
FRISKINESS	**RISKINESS**	
BRISKING = FRISKING	**RISKING**	
BRISKS = FRISKS	**RISKS**	
BRISKY = FRISKY	**RISKY**	
	RISOTTO	RISOTTOS
CRISP	**RISP**	RISPS
CRISPED	**RISPED**	
CRISPING	**RISPING**	RISPINGS
CRISPS	**RISPS**	
	RISQUE	RISQUES
	RISSOLE	RISSOLES
	RISTRA	RISTRAS
BRIT = CRIT = FRIT = GRIT = WRIT	**RIT**	RITE = RITS = RITT = RITZ
	RITARD	RITARDS
TRITE = URITE = WRITE	**RITE**	RITES
	RITENUTO	RITENUTOS
FRITES = TRITES = URITES = WRITES	**RITES**	
	RITONAVIR	RITONAVIRS
	RITORNEL	RITORNELL = RITORNELS
	RITORNELL	RITORNELLE = RITORNELLI = RITORNELLO RITORNELLS
BRITS = CRITS = FRITS = GRITS = WRITS	**RITS**	
BRITT = FRITT	**RITT**	RITTS
FRITTED = GRITTED	**RITTED**	
CRITTER = FRITTER = GRITTER	**RITTER**	RITTERS
CRITTERS = FRITTERS = GRITTERS	**RITTERS**	
FRITTING = GRITTING	**RITTING**	
BRITTS = FRITTS	**RITTS**	
	RITUAL	RITUALS
	RITUALISE	RITUALISED = RITUALISES
	RITUALISM	RITUALISMS
	RITUALIST	RITUALISTS
	RITUALIZE	RITUALIZED = RITUALIZES
FRITZ	**RITZ**	RITZY
FRITZES (offensive)	**RITZES**	
	RIVA	RIVAL = RIVAS
	RIVAGE	RIVAGES
	RIVAL	RIVALS
	RIVALISE	RIVALISED = RIVALISES
	RIVALIZE	RIVALIZED = RIVALIZES
	RIVALSHIP	RIVALSHIPS
DRIVE	**RIVE**	RIVED = RIVEL = RIVEN = RIVER = RIVES RIVET
DRIVEL	**RIVEL**	RIVELS
DRIVELLED	**RIVELLED**	
DRIVELLING	**RIVELLING**	
DRIVELS	**RIVELS**	
DRIVEN	**RIVEN**	
DRIVER	**RIVER**	RIVERS = RIVERY
	RIVERAIN	RIVERAINS
	RIVERBANK	RIVERBANKS
	RIVERBED	RIVERBEDS
	RIVERBOAT	RIVERBOATS
	RIVERET	RIVERETS
	RIVERHEAD	RIVERHEADS
DRIVERLESS	**RIVERLESS**	
DRIVERS	**RIVERS**	
	RIVERSIDE	RIVERSIDES
	RIVERWARD	RIVERWARDS
	RIVERWAY	RIVERWAYS
	RIVERWEED	RIVERWEEDS
DRIVES	**RIVES**	

R

FRONT HOOK	ROOT WORD	END HOOK
GRIVET ▪ PRIVET ▪ TRIVET	**RIVET**	RIVETS
	RIVETER	RIVETERS
	RIVETING	RIVETINGS
GRIVETS ▪ PRIVETS ▪ TRIVETS	**RIVETS**	
	RIVIERA	RIVIERAS
	RIVIERE	RIVIERES
DRIVING	**RIVING**	
	RIVLIN	RIVLINS
	RIVO	RIVOS
	RIVULET	RIVULETS
	RIYAL	RIYALS
FRIZ	**RIZ**	RIZA
	RIZA	RIZAS
	RIZARD	RIZARDS
	RIZZAR	RIZZARS ▪ RIZZART
	RIZZART	RIZZARTS
FRIZZER	**RIZZER**	RIZZERS
FRIZZERS	**RIZZERS**	
	RIZZOR	RIZZORS
BROACH	**ROACH**	
BROACHED	**ROACHED**	
BROACHES	**ROACHES**	
BROACHING	**ROACHING**	
BROAD ▪ TROAD	**ROAD**	ROADS
	ROADBED	ROADBEDS
	ROADBLOCK	ROADBLOCKS
	ROADCRAFT	ROADCRAFTS
	ROADEO	ROADEOS
	ROADHOUSE	ROADHOUSES
	ROADIE	ROADIES
	ROADING	ROADINGS
	ROADKILL	ROADKILLS
BROADS ▪ TROADS	**ROADS**	
	ROADSHOW	ROADSHOWS
BROADSIDE	**ROADSIDE**	ROADSIDES
BROADSIDES	**ROADSIDES**	
	ROADSTEAD	ROADSTEADS
	ROADSTER	ROADSTERS
BROADWAY	**ROADWAY**	ROADWAYS
BROADWAYS	**ROADWAYS**	
	ROADWORK	ROADWORKS
	ROAM	ROAMS
	ROAMER	ROAMERS
	ROAMING	ROAMINGS
GROAN	**ROAN**	ROANS
GROANS	**ROANS**	
	ROAR	ROARS ▪ ROARY
	ROARER	ROARERS
	ROARIE	ROARIER
	ROARING	ROARINGS
	ROAST	ROASTS
	ROASTER	ROASTERS
	ROASTING	ROASTINGS
	ROATE	ROATED ▪ ROATES
TROATED	**ROATED**	
TROATING	**ROATING**	
PROB	**ROB**	ROBE ▪ ROBS
	ROBALO	ROBALOS
PROBAND	**ROBAND**	ROBANDS
PROBANDS	**ROBANDS**	
	ROBBER	ROBBERS ▪ ROBBERY
	ROBBIN	ROBBING ▪ ROBBINS
PROBE	**ROBE**	ROBED ▪ ROBES
PROBED	**ROBED**	
PROBES	**ROBES**	
	ROBIN	ROBING ▪ ROBINS
PROBING	**ROBING**	ROBINGS
	ROBINIA	ROBINIAS
	ROBLE	ROBLES

FRONT HOOK	ROOT WORD	END HOOK
	ROBORANT	ROBORANTS
	ROBOT	ROBOTS
	ROBOTIC	ROBOTICS
	ROBOTISE	ROBOTISED ▪ ROBOTISES
	ROBOTISM	ROBOTISMS
	ROBOTIZE	ROBOTIZED ▪ ROBOTIZES
PROBS	**ROBS**	
	ROBURITE	ROBURITES
	ROBUST	ROBUSTA
	ROBUSTA	ROBUSTAS
CROC	**ROC**	ROCH ▪ ROCK ▪ ROCS
	ROCAILLE	ROCAILLES
	ROCAMBOLE	ROCAMBOLES
BROCH	**ROCH**	
BROCHES ▪ CROCHES ▪ TROCHES	**ROCHES**	
CROCHET	**ROCHET**	ROCHETS
CROCHETS	**ROCHETS**	
BROCK ▪ CROCK ▪ FROCK ▪ TROCK	**ROCK**	ROCKS ▪ ROCKY
	ROCKABY	ROCKABYE
	ROCKABYE	ROCKABYES
	ROCKAWAY	ROCKAWAYS
BROCKED ▪ CROCKED ▪ FROCKED ▪ TROCKED	**ROCKED**	
	ROCKER	ROCKERS ▪ ROCKERY
CROCKERIES	**ROCKERIES**	
CROCKERY	**ROCKERY**	
BROCKET ▪ CROCKET	**ROCKET**	ROCKETS
CROCKETED	**ROCKETED**	
	ROCKETEER	ROCKETEERS
	ROCKETER	ROCKETERS
BROCKETS ▪ CROCKETS	**ROCKETS**	
	ROCKFALL	ROCKFALLS
	ROCKHOUND	ROCKHOUNDS
	ROCKIER	ROCKIERS
CROCKING ▪ FROCKING ▪ TROCKING	**ROCKING**	ROCKINGS
FROCKINGS	**ROCKINGS**	
	ROCKLAY	ROCKLAYS
FROCKLESS	**ROCKLESS**	
	ROCKLING	ROCKLINGS
	ROCKOON	ROCKOONS
	ROCKROSE	ROCKROSES
BROCKS ▪ CROCKS ▪ FROCKS ▪ TROCKS	**ROCKS**	
	ROCKSHAFT	ROCKSHAFTS
	ROCKSLIDE	ROCKSLIDES
	ROCKWATER	ROCKWATERS
	ROCKWEED	ROCKWEEDS
	ROCKWORK	ROCKWORKS
	ROCOCO	ROCOCOS
	ROCQUET	ROCQUETS
CROCS	**ROCS**	
BROD ▪ PROD ▪ TROD	**ROD**	RODE ▪ RODS
BRODDED ▪ PRODDED	**RODDED**	
BRODDING ▪ PRODDING	**RODDING**	RODDINGS
ERODE ▪ TRODE	**RODE**	RODED ▪ RODEO ▪ RODES
ERODED	**RODED**	
ERODENT	**RODENT**	RODENTS
ERODENTS	**RODENTS**	
	RODEO	RODEOS
ERODES ▪ TRODES	**RODES**	
	RODEWAY	RODEWAYS
	RODFISHER	RODFISHERS
	RODGERSIA	RODGERSIAS
ERODING	**RODING**	RODINGS
BRODS ▪ PRODS ▪ TRODS	**RODS**	
	RODSTER	RODSTERS
FROE	**ROE**	ROED ▪ ROES
	ROEBUCK	ROEBUCKS
	ROEMER	ROEMERS
	ROENTGEN	ROENTGENS
FROES	**ROES**	

FRONT HOOK	ROOT WORD	END HOOK
	ROESTONE	ROESTONES
	ROGALLO	ROGALLOS
	ROGATION	ROGATIONS
DROGER	**ROGER**	ROGERS (offensive)
	ROGERING	ROGERINGS (offensive)
DROGERS	**ROGERS**	
	ROGNON	ROGNONS
BROGUE ▪ DROGUE	**ROGUE**	ROGUED ▪ ROGUES
BROGUERIES	**ROGUERIES**	
BROGUERY	**ROGUERY**	
BROGUES ▪ DROGUES	**ROGUES**	
	ROGUESHIP	ROGUESHIPS
BROGUISH	**ROGUISH**	
BROIL ▪ DROIL	**ROIL**	ROILS ▪ ROILY
BROILED ▪ DROILED	**ROILED**	
BROILING ▪ DROILING	**ROILING**	
BROILS ▪ DROILS	**ROILS**	
GROIN ▪ PROIN	**ROIN**	ROINS
GROINED ▪ PROINED	**ROINED**	
GROINING ▪ PROINING	**ROINING**	
GROINS ▪ PROINS	**ROINS**	
	ROIST	ROISTS
	ROISTER	ROISTERS
	ROISTERER	ROISTERERS
	ROJAK	ROJAKS
	ROJI	ROJIS
GROK	**ROK**	ROKE ▪ ROKS ▪ ROKY
BROKE ▪ PROKE ▪ TROKE ▪ WROKE	**ROKE**	ROKED ▪ ROKER ▪ ROKES
BROKED ▪ PROKED ▪ TROKED	**ROKED**	
	ROKELAY	ROKELAYS
BROKER ▪ PROKER	**ROKER**	ROKERS
BROKERS ▪ PROKERS	**ROKERS**	
BROKES ▪ PROKES ▪ TROKES	**ROKES**	
BROKING ▪ PROKING ▪ TROKING	**ROKING**	
GROKS	**ROKS**	
	ROLAG	ROLAGS
	ROLAMITE	ROLAMITES
DROLE ▪ PROLE	**ROLE**	ROLES
DROLES ▪ PROLES	**ROLES**	
	ROLF	ROLFS
	ROLFER	ROLFERS
	ROLFING	ROLFINGS
DROLL ▪ PROLL ▪ TROLL	**ROLL**	ROLLS
	ROLLAWAY	ROLLAWAYS
	ROLLBACK	ROLLBACKS
	ROLLBAR	ROLLBARS
DROLLED ▪ PROLLED ▪ TROLLED	**ROLLED**	
DROLLER ▪ PROLLER ▪ TROLLER	**ROLLER**	ROLLERS
PROLLERS ▪ TROLLERS	**ROLLERS**	
	ROLLICK	ROLLICKS ▪ ROLLICKY
DROLLING ▪ PROLLING ▪ TROLLING	**ROLLING**	ROLLINGS
DROLLINGS ▪ TROLLINGS	**ROLLINGS**	
	ROLLMOP	ROLLMOPS
	ROLLNECK	ROLLNECKS
	ROLLOCK	ROLLOCKS
	ROLLOUT	ROLLOUTS
	ROLLOVER	ROLLOVERS
DROLLS ▪ PROLLS ▪ TROLLS	**ROLLS**	
	ROLLWAY	ROLLWAYS
FROM ▪ PROM	**ROM**	ROMA ▪ ROMP ▪ ROMS
AROMA ▪ GROMA	**ROMA**	ROMAL ▪ ROMAN ▪ ROMAS
FROMAGE	**ROMAGE**	ROMAGES
FROMAGES	**ROMAGES**	
	ROMAIKA	ROMAIKAS
	ROMAINE	ROMAINES
	ROMAJI	ROMAJIS
BROMAL	**ROMAL**	ROMALS
BROMALS	**ROMALS**	
	ROMAN	ROMANO ▪ ROMANS

R

FRONT HOOK	ROOT WORD	END HOOK
	ROMANCE	ROMANCED · ROMANCER · ROMANCES
	ROMANCER	ROMANCERS
	ROMANCING	ROMANCINGS
	ROMANISE	ROMANISED · ROMANISES
	ROMANIZE	ROMANIZED · ROMANIZES
	ROMANO	ROMANOS
	ROMANTIC	ROMANTICS
	ROMANZA	ROMANZAS
AROMAS · GROMAS	**ROMAS**	
	ROMAUNT	ROMAUNTS
	ROMCOM	ROMCOMS
	ROMELDALE	ROMELDALES
	ROMEO	ROMEOS
	ROMNEYA	ROMNEYAS
TROMP	**ROMP**	ROMPS
TROMPED	**ROMPED**	
	ROMPER	ROMPERS
TROMPING	**ROMPING**	
TROMPS	**ROMPS**	
PROMS	**ROMS**	
	RONCADOR	RONCADORS
	RONDACHE	RONDACHES
	RONDAVEL	RONDAVELS
	RONDE	RONDEL · RONDES
	RONDEAU	RONDEAUX
	RONDEL	RONDELS
	RONDELET	RONDELETS
	RONDELLE	RONDELLES
	RONDINO	RONDINOS
	RONDO	RONDOS
	RONDURE	RONDURES
CRONE · DRONE · GRONE · IRONE · KRONE PRONE · TRONE	**RONE**	RONEO · RONES
	RONEO	RONEOS
	RONEPIPE	RONEPIPES
CRONES · DRONES · GRONES · IRONES PRONES · TRONES	**RONES**	
PRONG · WRONG	**RONG**	
	RONGGENG	RONGGENGS
	RONIN	RONINS
	RONION	RONIONS
	RONNE	RONNEL
	RONNEL	RONNELS
	RONNIE	RONNIES
FRONT	**RONT**	RONTE · RONTS
	RONTE	RONTES
FRONTES	**RONTES**	
	RONTGEN	RONTGENS
FRONTS	**RONTS**	
	RONYON	RONYONS (offensive)
BRONZER	**RONZER**	RONZERS
BRONZERS	**RONZERS**	
BROO · PROO	**ROO**	ROOD · ROOF · ROOK · ROOM · ROON ROOP · ROOS · ROOT
BROOD	**ROOD**	ROODS
BROODS	**ROODS**	
GROOF · PROOF	**ROOF**	ROOFS · ROOFY
PROOFED	**ROOFED**	
PROOFER	**ROOFER**	ROOFERS
PROOFERS	**ROOFERS**	
	ROOFIE	ROOFIER · ROOFIES
	ROOFIES	ROOFIEST
PROOFING	**ROOFING**	ROOFINGS
PROOFINGS	**ROOFINGS**	
PROOFLESS	**ROOFLESS**	
	ROOFLINE	ROOFLINES
GROOFS · PROOFS	**ROOFS**	
	ROOFSCAPE	ROOFSCAPES
	ROOFTOP	ROOFTOPS

R

FRONT HOOK	ROOT WORD	END HOOK
	ROOFTREE	ROOFTREES
	ROOIKAT	ROOIKATS
	ROOINEK	ROOINEKS *(offensive)*
BROOK ▪ CROOK ▪ DROOK	**ROOK**	ROOKS ▪ ROOKY
BROOKED ▪ CROOKED ▪ DROOKED	**ROOKED**	
CROOKERIES	**ROOKERIES**	
CROOKERY	**ROOKERY**	
BROOKIE	**ROOKIE**	ROOKIER ▪ ROOKIES
BROOKIES	**ROOKIES**	ROOKIEST
BROOKING ▪ CROOKING ▪ DROOKING	**ROOKING**	
BROOKS ▪ CROOKS ▪ DROOKS	**ROOKS**	
BROOM ▪ GROOM ▪ VROOM	**ROOM**	ROOMS ▪ ROOMY
BROOMED ▪ GROOMED ▪ VROOMED	**ROOMED**	
GROOMER	**ROOMER**	ROOMERS
GROOMERS	**ROOMERS**	
	ROOMETTE	ROOMETTES
	ROOMFUL	ROOMFULS
	ROOMIE	ROOMIER ▪ ROOMIES
BROOMIER	**ROOMIER**	
	ROOMIES	ROOMIEST
BROOMIEST	**ROOMIEST**	
BROOMING ▪ GROOMING ▪ VROOMING	**ROOMING**	
	ROOMMATE	ROOMMATES
BROOMS ▪ GROOMS ▪ VROOMS	**ROOMS**	
BROOMY	**ROOMY**	
CROON ▪ KROON	**ROON**	ROONS
CROONS ▪ KROONS	**ROONS**	
DROOP ▪ TROOP	**ROOP**	ROOPS ▪ ROOPY
DROOPED ▪ TROOPED	**ROOPED**	
DROOPIER	**ROOPIER**	
DROOPIEST	**ROOPIEST**	
DROOPING ▪ TROOPING	**ROOPING**	
DROOPS ▪ TROOPS	**ROOPS**	
DROOPY	**ROOPY**	
	ROORBACH	ROORBACHS
	ROORBACK	ROORBACKS
BROOS	**ROOS**	ROOSA ▪ ROOSE ▪ ROOST
	ROOSA	ROOSAS
BROOSE	**ROOSE**	ROOSED ▪ ROOSER ▪ ROOSES
	ROOSER	ROOSERS
BROOSES	**ROOSES**	
	ROOST	ROOSTS
	ROOSTER	ROOSTERS
WROOT	**ROOT**	ROOTS ▪ ROOTY
	ROOTAGE	ROOTAGES
	ROOTCAP	ROOTCAPS
WROOTED	**ROOTED**	
	ROOTER	ROOTERS
	ROOTHOLD	ROOTHOLDS
	ROOTIES	ROOTIEST
WROOTING	**ROOTING**	ROOTINGS
	ROOTLE	ROOTLED ▪ ROOTLES ▪ ROOTLET
	ROOTLES	ROOTLESS
	ROOTLET	ROOTLETS
WROOTS	**ROOTS**	ROOTSY
	ROOTSTALK	ROOTSTALKS
	ROOTSTOCK	ROOTSTOCKS
	ROOTWORM	ROOTWORMS
GROPE ▪ TROPE	**ROPE**	ROPED ▪ ROPER ▪ ROPES ▪ ROPEY
GROPED ▪ TROPED	**ROPED**	
GROPER ▪ PROPER	**ROPER**	ROPERS ▪ ROPERY
GROPERS ▪ PROPERS	**ROPERS**	
GROPES ▪ TROPES	**ROPES**	
	ROPEWALK	ROPEWALKS
	ROPEWAY	ROPEWAYS
	ROPEWORK	ROPEWORKS
GROPING ▪ TROPING	**ROPING**	ROPINGS
	ROQUE	ROQUES ▪ ROQUET
CROQUET	**ROQUET**	ROQUETS

FRONT HOOK	ROOT WORD	END HOOK
CROQUETED	**ROQUETED**	
CROQUETING	**ROQUETING**	
CROQUETS	**ROQUETS**	
CROQUETTE	**ROQUETTE**	ROQUETTES
CROQUETTES	**ROQUETTES**	
CRORE • FRORE • PRORE	**RORE**	RORES
CRORES • PRORES	**RORES**	
	RORIE	RORIER
	RORQUAL	RORQUALS
	RORT	RORTS • RORTY
	RORTER	RORTERS
FRORY	**RORY**	
	ROSACE	ROSACEA • ROSACES
	ROSACEA	ROSACEAS
	ROSAKER	ROSAKERS
	ROSALIA	ROSALIAS
	ROSANILIN	ROSANILINE • ROSANILINS
	ROSARIA	ROSARIAN
	ROSARIAN	ROSARIANS
	ROSARIUM	ROSARIUMS
	ROSBIF	ROSBIFS
	ROSCOE	ROSCOES
AROSE • BROSE • EROSE • PROSE	**ROSE**	ROSED • ROSES • ROSET
	ROSEBAY	ROSEBAYS
	ROSEBOWL	ROSEBOWLS
	ROSEBUD	ROSEBUDS
PROSED	**ROSED**	
	ROSEHIP	ROSEHIPS
PROSELIKE	**ROSELIKE**	
	ROSELLA	ROSELLAS
	ROSELLE	ROSELLES
	ROSEOLA	ROSEOLAR • ROSEOLAS
	ROSEROOT	ROSEROOTS
BROSES • EROSES • PROSES • UROSES	**ROSES**	
	ROSESLUG	ROSESLUGS
GROSET	**ROSET**	ROSETS • ROSETY
GROSETS	**ROSETS**	
	ROSETTE	ROSETTED • ROSETTES
	ROSEWATER	ROSEWATERS
	ROSEWOOD	ROSEWOODS
	ROSHI	ROSHIS
CROSIER • PROSIER	**ROSIER**	ROSIERE • ROSIERS
	ROSIERE	ROSIERES
CROSIERS	**ROSIERS**	
	ROSIES	ROSIEST
PROSIEST	**ROSIEST**	
PROSILY	**ROSILY**	
	ROSIN	ROSING • ROSINS • ROSINY
	ROSINATE	ROSINATES
	ROSINER	ROSINERS
PROSINESS	**ROSINESS**	
PROSING	**ROSING**	
	ROSINOL	ROSINOLS
	ROSINWEED	ROSINWEEDS
PROSIT	**ROSIT**	ROSITS
	ROSMARINE	ROSMARINES
	ROSOGLIO	ROSOGLIOS
	ROSOLIO	ROSOLIOS
CROSSER • GROSSER	**ROSSER**	ROSSERS
CROSSERS • GROSSERS • TROSSERS	**ROSSERS**	
CROST • FROST • PROST	**ROST**	ROSTI • ROSTS
FROSTED	**ROSTED**	
	ROSTELLA	ROSTELLAR
	ROSTELLUM	ROSTELLUMS
	ROSTER	ROSTERS
	ROSTERING	ROSTERINGS
	ROSTI	ROSTIS
FROSTING	**ROSTING**	
	ROSTRA	ROSTRAL

FRONT HOOK	ROOT WORD	END HOOK
EROSTRATE ▪ PROSTRATE	**ROSTRATE**	ROSTRATED
PROSTRATED	**ROSTRATED**	
	ROSTRUM	ROSTRUMS
FROSTS	**ROSTS**	
	ROSULA	ROSULAS
BROSY ▪ PROSY	**ROSY**	
GROT ▪ TROT ▪ VROT	**ROT**	ROTA ▪ ROTE ▪ ROTI ▪ ROTL ▪ ROTO ▪ ROTS
	ROTA	ROTAL ▪ ROTAN ▪ ROTAS
	ROTACHUTE	ROTACHUTES
CROTAL	**ROTAL**	
	ROTAMETER	ROTAMETERS
	ROTAN	ROTANS
	ROTAPLANE	ROTAPLANES
	ROTATE	ROTATED ▪ ROTATES
	ROTATION	ROTATIONS
	ROTATOR	ROTATORS ▪ ROTATORY
	ROTAVATE	ROTAVATED ▪ ROTAVATES
	ROTAVATOR	ROTAVATORS
CROTCH	**ROTCH**	ROTCHE
	ROTCHE	ROTCHES
CROTCHES	**ROTCHES**	
	ROTCHIE	ROTCHIES
WROTE	**ROTE**	ROTED ▪ ROTES
	ROTENONE	ROTENONES
	ROTGUT	ROTGUTS
BROTHER ▪ FROTHER	**ROTHER**	ROTHERS
BROTHERS ▪ FROTHERS	**ROTHERS**	
	ROTI	ROTIS
	ROTIFER	ROTIFERS
	ROTIFERAN	ROTIFERANS
	ROTL	ROTLS
	ROTO	ROTON ▪ ROTOR ▪ ROTOS
	ROTOGRAPH	ROTOGRAPHS
	ROTOLO	ROTOLOS
CROTON ▪ PROTON	**ROTON**	ROTONS
CROTONS ▪ PROTONS	**ROTONS**	
	ROTOR	ROTORS
	ROTOTILL	ROTOTILLS
	ROTOVATE	ROTOVATED ▪ ROTOVATES
	ROTOVATOR	ROTOVATORS
GROTS ▪ TROTS	**ROTS**	
	ROTTAN	ROTTANS
	ROTTE	ROTTED ▪ ROTTEN ▪ ROTTER ▪ ROTTES
TROTTED	**ROTTED**	
	ROTTEN	ROTTENS
TROTTER	**ROTTER**	ROTTERS
TROTTERS	**ROTTERS**	
TROTTING	**ROTTING**	
	ROTULA	ROTULAE ▪ ROTULAS
OROTUND	**ROTUND**	ROTUNDA ▪ ROTUNDS
	ROTUNDA	ROTUNDAS
OROTUNDITY	**ROTUNDITY**	
	ROTURIER	ROTURIERS
TROUBLE	**ROUBLE**	ROUBLES
TROUBLES	**ROUBLES**	
	ROUCHE	ROUCHES
CROUCHES ▪ GROUCHES ▪ TROUCHES	**ROUCHES**	
	ROUCOU	ROUCOUS
	ROUE	ROUEN ▪ ROUES
	ROUEN	ROUENS
	ROUGE	ROUGED ▪ ROUGES
BROUGH ▪ GROUGH ▪ TROUGH	**ROUGH**	ROUGHS ▪ ROUGHT ▪ ROUGHY
	ROUGHAGE	ROUGHAGES
	ROUGHBACK	ROUGHBACKS
	ROUGHCAST	ROUGHCASTS
TROUGHED	**ROUGHED**	
	ROUGHEN	ROUGHENS
	ROUGHER	ROUGHERS
	ROUGHHEW	ROUGHHEWN ▪ ROUGHHEWS

715

FRONT HOOK	ROOT WORD	END HOOK
	ROUGHIE	ROUGHIES
TROUGHING	**ROUGHING**	
	ROUGHLEG	ROUGHLEGS
	ROUGHNECK	ROUGHNECKS
BROUGHS · GROUGHS · TROUGHS	**ROUGHS**	
BROUGHT · DROUGHT · WROUGHT	**ROUGHT**	
FROUGHY	**ROUGHY**	
	ROUILLE	ROUILLES
PROUL	**ROUL**	ROULE · ROULS
	ROULADE	ROULADES
TROULE	**ROULE**	ROULES
	ROULEAU	ROULEAUS · ROULEAUX
TROULES	**ROULES**	
	ROULETTE	ROULETTED · ROULETTES
PROULS	**ROULS**	
	ROUM	ROUMS
	ROUMING	ROUMINGS
FROUNCE · TROUNCE	**ROUNCE**	ROUNCES
FROUNCES · TROUNCES	**ROUNCES**	
	ROUNCEVAL	ROUNCEVALS
AROUND · GROUND	**ROUND**	ROUNDS
	ROUNDBALL	ROUNDBALLS
GROUNDED	**ROUNDED**	
GROUNDEDLY	**ROUNDEDLY**	
	ROUNDEL	ROUNDELS
	ROUNDELAY	ROUNDELAYS
GROUNDER	**ROUNDER**	ROUNDERS
GROUNDERS	**ROUNDERS**	
	ROUNDHAND	ROUNDHANDS
	ROUNDHEEL	ROUNDHEELS
GROUNDING	**ROUNDING**	ROUNDINGS
GROUNDINGS	**ROUNDINGS**	
	ROUNDLE	ROUNDLES · ROUNDLET
	ROUNDLET	ROUNDLETS
GROUNDS	**ROUNDS**	
GROUNDSMAN	**ROUNDSMAN**	
GROUNDSMEN	**ROUNDSMEN**	
	ROUNDTRIP	ROUNDTRIPS
	ROUNDUP	ROUNDUPS
	ROUNDURE	ROUNDURES
GROUNDWOOD	**ROUNDWOOD**	ROUNDWOODS
	ROUNDWORM	ROUNDWORMS
CROUP · GROUP	**ROUP**	ROUPS · ROUPY
CROUPED · GROUPED · TROUPED	**ROUPED**	
CROUPIER	**ROUPIER**	
CROUPIEST	**ROUPIEST**	
CROUPILY	**ROUPILY**	
CROUPING · GROUPING · TROUPING	**ROUPING**	
CROUPS · GROUPS	**ROUPS**	
CROUPY · GROUPY	**ROUPY**	
AROUSE · CROUSE · GROUSE · TROUSE	**ROUSE**	ROUSED · ROUSER · ROUSES
AROUSED · GROUSED	**ROUSED**	
	ROUSEMENT	ROUSEMENTS
AROUSER · GROUSER · TROUSER	**ROUSER**	ROUSERS
AROUSERS · GROUSERS · TROUSERS	**ROUSERS**	
AROUSES · GROUSES · TROUSES	**ROUSES**	
AROUSING · GROUSING	**ROUSING**	
TROUSSEAU	**ROUSSEAU**	ROUSSEAUS
TROUSSEAUS	**ROUSSEAUS**	
	ROUSSETTE	ROUSSETTES
	ROUST	ROUSTS
	ROUSTER	ROUSTERS
CROUT · GROUT · TROUT	**ROUT**	ROUTE · ROUTH · ROUTS
CROUTE	**ROUTE**	ROUTED · ROUTER · ROUTES
GROUTED	**ROUTED**	
GROUTER · TROUTER	**ROUTER**	ROUTERS
GROUTERS · TROUTERS	**ROUTERS**	
CROUTES	**ROUTES**	
	ROUTEWAY	ROUTEWAYS

R

FRONT HOOK	ROOT WORD	END HOOK
DROUTH	**ROUTH**	ROUTHS
	ROUTHIE	ROUTHIER
DROUTHIER	**ROUTHIER**	
DROUTHIEST	**ROUTHIEST**	
DROUTHS	**ROUTHS**	
	ROUTINE	ROUTINES
	ROUTINEER	ROUTINEERS
GROUTING ▪ TROUTING	**ROUTING**	ROUTINGS
GROUTINGS ▪ TROUTINGS	**ROUTINGS**	
	ROUTINISE	ROUTINISED ▪ ROUTINISES
	ROUTINISM	ROUTINISMS
	ROUTINIST	ROUTINISTS
	ROUTINIZE	ROUTINIZED ▪ ROUTINIZES
CROUTS ▪ GROUTS ▪ TROUTS	**ROUTS**	
DROVE ▪ GROVE ▪ PROVE ▪ TROVE	**ROVE**	ROVED ▪ ROVEN ▪ ROVER ▪ ROVES
DROVED ▪ GROVED ▪ PROVED	**ROVED**	
PROVEN	**ROVEN**	
DROVER ▪ PROVER ▪ TROVER	**ROVER**	ROVERS
DROVERS ▪ PROVERS ▪ TROVERS	**ROVERS**	
DROVES ▪ GROVES ▪ PROVES ▪ TROVES	**ROVES**	
DROVING ▪ PROVING	**ROVING**	ROVINGS
DROVINGS ▪ PROVINGS	**ROVINGS**	
AROW ▪ BROW ▪ CROW ▪ DROW ▪ FROW ▪ GROW	**ROW**	ROWS ▪ ROWT
PROW ▪ TROW ▪ VROW		
GROWABLE	**ROWABLE**	
	ROWAN	ROWANS
	ROWBOAT	ROWBOATS
	ROWDEDOW	ROWDEDOWS
CROWDIES	**ROWDIES**	ROWDIEST
CROWDY	**ROWDY**	
	ROWDYDOW	ROWDYDOWS
	ROWDYISM	ROWDYISMS
BROWED ▪ CROWED ▪ TROWED	**ROWED**	
TROWEL	**ROWEL**	ROWELS
TROWELED	**ROWELED**	
TROWELING	**ROWELING**	
TROWELLED	**ROWELLED**	
TROWELLING	**ROWELLING**	
TROWELS	**ROWELS**	
	ROWEN	ROWENS
CROWER ▪ GROWER ▪ PROWER	**ROWER**	ROWERS
CROWERS ▪ GROWERS	**ROWERS**	
CROWING ▪ GROWING ▪ TROWING	**ROWING**	ROWINGS
GROWINGS	**ROWINGS**	
	ROWLOCK	ROWLOCKS
	ROWME	ROWMES
DROWND	**ROWND**	ROWNDS
DROWNDED	**ROWNDED**	
	ROWNDELL	ROWNDELLS
DROWNDING	**ROWNDING**	
DROWNDS	**ROWNDS**	
	ROWOVER	ROWOVERS
BROWS ▪ CROWS ▪ DROWS ▪ FROWS ▪ GROWS	**ROWS**	
PROWS ▪ TROWS ▪ VROWS		
	ROWT	ROWTH ▪ ROWTS
GROWTH ▪ TROWTH	**ROWTH**	ROWTHS
GROWTHS ▪ TROWTHS	**ROWTHS**	
	ROYAL	ROYALS
	ROYALET	ROYALETS
	ROYALISE	ROYALISED ▪ ROYALISES
	ROYALISM	ROYALISMS
	ROYALIST	ROYALISTS
	ROYALIZE	ROYALIZED ▪ ROYALIZES
	ROYALMAST	ROYALMASTS
GROYNE ▪ PROYNE	**ROYNE**	ROYNED ▪ ROYNES
PROYNED	**ROYNED**	
GROYNES ▪ PROYNES	**ROYNES**	
PROYNING	**ROYNING**	
	ROYST	ROYSTS

R

FRONT HOOK	ROOT WORD	END HOOK
	ROYSTER	ROYSTERS
	ROYSTERER	ROYSTERERS
	ROZELLE	ROZELLES
	ROZET	ROZETS
	ROZIT	ROZITS
	ROZZER	ROZZERS
	RUANA	RUANAS
DRUB · GRUB	**RUB**	RUBE · RUBS · RUBY
	RUBABOO	RUBABOOS
	RUBACE	RUBACES
	RUBASSE	RUBASSES
	RUBATO	RUBATOS
	RUBBABOO	RUBBABOOS
DRUBBED · GRUBBED	**RUBBED**	
DRUBBER · GRUBBER	**RUBBER**	RUBBERS · RUBBERY ·
	RUBBERISE	RUBBERISED · RUBBERISES
	RUBBERIZE	RUBBERIZED · RUBBERIZES
DRUBBERS · GRUBBERS	**RUBBERS**	
DRUBBING · GRUBBING	**RUBBING**	RUBBINGS
DRUBBINGS	**RUBBINGS**	
	RUBBISH	RUBBISHY
	RUBBIT	RUBBITY
GRUBBLE	**RUBBLE**	RUBBLED · RUBBLES
GRUBBLED	**RUBBLED**	
GRUBBLES	**RUBBLES**	
GRUBBLING	**RUBBLING**	
	RUBBOARD	RUBBOARDS
GRUBBY	**RUBBY**	
	RUBDOWN	RUBDOWNS
	RUBE	RUBEL · RUBES (offensive)
	RUBEL	RUBELS
	RUBELLA	RUBELLAN · RUBELLAS
	RUBELLAN	RUBELLANS
	RUBELLITE	RUBELLITES
	RUBEOLA	RUBEOLAR · RUBEOLAS
ERUBESCENT	**RUBESCENT**	
	RUBICELLE	RUBICELLES
	RUBICON	RUBICONS
	RUBIDIUM	RUBIDIUMS
	RUBIES	RUBIEST
	RUBIGO	RUBIGOS
	RUBIN	RUBINE · RUBINS
	RUBINE	RUBINES
	RUBLE	RUBLES
	RUBOFF	RUBOFFS
	RUBOUT	RUBOUTS
	RUBRIC	RUBRICS
	RUBRICATE	RUBRICATED · RUBRICATES
	RUBRICIAN	RUBRICIANS
DRUBS · GRUBS	**RUBS**	
	RUBSTONE	RUBSTONES
URUBUS	**RUBUS**	
	RUC	RUCK · RUCS
	RUCHE	RUCHED · RUCHES
	RUCHING	RUCHINGS
CRUCK · TRUCK	**RUCK**	RUCKS
TRUCKED	**RUCKED**	
TRUCKING	**RUCKING**	
BRUCKLE · TRUCKLE	**RUCKLE**	RUCKLED · RUCKLES
TRUCKLED	**RUCKLED**	
TRUCKLES	**RUCKLES**	
TRUCKLING	**RUCKLING**	
TRUCKMAN	**RUCKMAN**	
TRUCKMEN	**RUCKMEN**	
CRUCKS · TRUCKS	**RUCKS**	
	RUCKSACK	RUCKSACKS
	RUCKSEAT	RUCKSEATS
	RUCOLA	RUCOLAS
ERUCTATION	**RUCTATION**	RUCTATIONS

R

FRONT HOOK	ROOT WORD	END HOOK
	RUCTION	RUCTIONS
CRUD	**RUD**	RUDD = RUDE = RUDS
	RUDBECKIA	RUDBECKIAS
	RUDD	RUDDS = RUDDY
CRUDDED	**RUDDED**	
	RUDDER	RUDDERS
CRUDDIER	**RUDDIER**	
	RUDDIES	RUDDIEST
CRUDDIEST	**RUDDIEST**	
CRUDDING	**RUDDING**	
CRUDDLE	**RUDDLE**	RUDDLED = RUDDLES
CRUDDLED	**RUDDLED**	
CRUDDLES	**RUDDLES**	
CRUDDLING	**RUDDLING**	
	RUDDOCK	RUDDOCKS
CRUDDY	**RUDDY**	
CRUDE = PRUDE	**RUDE**	RUDER = RUDES
CRUDELY	**RUDELY**	
CRUDENESS	**RUDENESS**	
CRUDER	**RUDER**	RUDERY
	RUDERAL	RUDERALS
PRUDERIES	**RUDERIES**	
PRUDERY	**RUDERY**	
CRUDES = PRUDES	**RUDES**	RUDEST
CRUDEST	**RUDEST**	
	RUDIE	RUDIES
	RUDIMENT	RUDIMENTS
PRUDISH	**RUDISH**	
CRUDS	**RUDS**	
CRUE = GRUE = TRUE	**RUE**	RUED = RUER = RUES
GRUED = TRUED	**RUED**	
GRUEING = TRUEING	**RUEING**	RUEINGS
	RUELLE	RUELLES
	RUELLIA	RUELLIAS
TRUER	**RUER**	RUERS
CRUES = GRUES = TRUES	**RUES**	
GRUFF	**RUFF**	RUFFE = RUFFS
TRUFFE	**RUFFE**	RUFFED = RUFFES
GRUFFED	**RUFFED**	
TRUFFES	**RUFFES**	
	RUFFIAN	RUFFIANS
	RUFFIN	RUFFING = RUFFINS
GRUFFING	**RUFFING**	
TRUFFLE	**RUFFLE**	RUFFLED = RUFFLER = RUFFLES
TRUFFLED	**RUFFLED**	
	RUFFLER	RUFFLERS
TRUFFLES	**RUFFLES**	
TRUFFLING	**RUFFLING**	RUFFLINGS
TRUFFLINGS	**RUFFLINGS**	
GRUFFLY	**RUFFLY**	
GRUFFS	**RUFFS**	
	RUFIYAA	RUFIYAAS
DRUG = FRUG = TRUG	**RUG**	RUGA = RUGS
	RUGA	RUGAE = RUGAL
FRUGAL	**RUGAL**	
DRUGGED = FRUGGED	**RUGGED**	
	RUGGEDISE	RUGGEDISED = RUGGEDISES
	RUGGEDIZE	RUGGEDIZED = RUGGEDIZES
DRUGGER	**RUGGER**	RUGGERS
DRUGGERS	**RUGGERS**	
DRUGGIER	**RUGGIER**	
DRUGGIEST	**RUGGIEST**	
DRUGGING = FRUGGING	**RUGGING**	RUGGINGS
DRUGGY	**RUGGY**	
ARUGOLA	**RUGOLA**	RUGOLAS
ARUGOLAS	**RUGOLAS**	
	RUGOSA	RUGOSAS
DRUGS = FRUGS = TRUGS	**RUGS**	
BRUIN	**RUIN**	RUING = RUINS

FRONT HOOK	ROOT WORD	END HOOK
	RUINATE	RUINATED · RUINATES
	RUINATION	RUINATIONS
	RUINER	RUINERS
GRUING · TRUING	**RUING**	RUINGS
	RUINING	RUININGS
BRUINS	**RUINS**	
	RUKH	RUKHS
BRULE	**RULE**	RULED · RULER · RULES
	RULER	RULERS
	RULERSHIP	RULERSHIPS
BRULES	**RULES**	
	RULING	RULINGS
	RULLION	RULLIONS
	RULLOCK	RULLOCKS
TRULY	**RULY**	
ARUM · DRUM · GRUM	**RUM**	RUME · RUMP · RUMS
	RUMAKI	RUMAKIS
BRUMAL	**RUMAL**	RUMALS
	RUMBA	RUMBAS
	RUMBELOW	RUMBELOWS
CRUMBLE · DRUMBLE · GRUMBLE	**RUMBLE**	RUMBLED · RUMBLER · RUMBLES
CRUMBLED · DRUMBLED · GRUMBLED	**RUMBLED**	
GRUMBLER	**RUMBLER**	RUMBLERS
GRUMBLERS	**RUMBLERS**	
CRUMBLES · DRUMBLES · GRUMBLES	**RUMBLES**	
CRUMBLIER · GRUMBLIER	**RUMBLIER**	
CRUMBLIEST · GRUMBLIEST	**RUMBLIEST**	
CRUMBLING · DRUMBLING · GRUMBLING	**RUMBLING**	RUMBLINGS
CRUMBLINGS · GRUMBLINGS	**RUMBLINGS**	
CRUMBLY · GRUMBLY	**RUMBLY**	
	RUMBO	RUMBOS
BRUME · GRUME	**RUME**	RUMEN · RUMES
CRUMEN	**RUMEN**	RUMENS
CRUMENS	**RUMENS**	
BRUMES · GRUMES	**RUMES**	
	RUMINA	RUMINAL
	RUMINANT	RUMINANTS
	RUMINATE	RUMINATED · RUMINATES
	RUMINATOR	RUMINATORS
	RUMKIN	RUMKINS
DRUMLY · GRUMLY	**RUMLY**	
	RUMMAGE	RUMMAGED · RUMMAGER · RUMMAGES
	RUMMAGER	RUMMAGERS
BRUMMER · DRUMMER · GRUMMER	**RUMMER**	RUMMERS
BRUMMERS · DRUMMERS	**RUMMERS**	
GRUMMEST	**RUMMEST**	
CRUMMIER	**RUMMIER**	
CRUMMIES · DRUMMIES	**RUMMIES**	RUMMIEST
CRUMMIEST	**RUMMIEST**	
CRUMMINESS	**RUMMINESS**	
CRUMMY · DRUMMY	**RUMMY**	
GRUMNESS	**RUMNESS**	
GRUMNESSES	**RUMNESSES**	
	RUMOR	RUMORS
	RUMOUR	RUMOURS
	RUMOURER	RUMOURERS
CRUMP · FRUMP · GRUMP · TRUMP	**RUMP**	RUMPO · RUMPS · RUMPY
CRUMPED · FRUMPED · GRUMPED · TRUMPED	**RUMPED**	
CRUMPING · FRUMPING · GRUMPING · TRUMPING	**RUMPING**	
CRUMPLE · FRUMPLE	**RUMPLE**	RUMPLED · RUMPLES
CRUMPLED · FRUMPLED	**RUMPLED**	
CRUMPLES · FRUMPLES	**RUMPLES**	RUMPLESS
TRUMPLESS	**RUMPLESS**	
CRUMPLIER	**RUMPLIER**	
CRUMPLIEST	**RUMPLIEST**	
CRUMPLING · FRUMPLING	**RUMPLING**	
CRUMPLY	**RUMPLY**	
	RUMPO	RUMPOS (offensive)

FRONT HOOK	ROOT WORD	END HOOK
CRUMPS ▪ FRUMPS ▪ GRUMPS ▪ TRUMPS	**RUMPS**	
CRUMPY ▪ FRUMPY ▪ GRUMPY	**RUMPY**	
	RUMRUNNER	RUMRUNNERS
ARUMS ▪ DRUMS	**RUMS**	
	RUN	RUND ▪ RUNE ▪ RUNG ▪ RUNS ▪ RUNT
	RUNABOUT	RUNABOUTS
	RUNAGATE	RUNAGATES
	RUNAROUND	RUNAROUNDS
	RUNAWAY	RUNAWAYS
	RUNBACK	RUNBACKS
BRUNCH ▪ CRUNCH	**RUNCH**	
BRUNCHES ▪ CRUNCHES	**RUNCHES**	
	RUND	RUNDS
	RUNDALE	RUNDALES
TRUNDLE	**RUNDLE**	RUNDLED ▪ RUNDLES ▪ RUNDLET
TRUNDLED	**RUNDLED**	
TRUNDLES	**RUNDLES**	
	RUNDLET	RUNDLETS
	RUNDOWN	RUNDOWNS
PRUNE	**RUNE**	RUNED ▪ RUNES
	RUNECRAFT	RUNECRAFTS
PRUNED	**RUNED**	
PRUNES	**RUNES**	
BRUNG ▪ WRUNG	**RUNG**	RUNGS
CRUNKLE	**RUNKLE**	RUNKLED ▪ RUNKLES
CRUNKLED	**RUNKLED**	
CRUNKLES	**RUNKLES**	
CRUNKLING	**RUNKLING**	
	RUNLET	RUNLETS
TRUNNEL	**RUNNEL**	RUNNELS
TRUNNELS	**RUNNELS**	
	RUNNER	RUNNERS
	RUNNET	RUNNETS
	RUNNING	RUNNINGS
TRUNNION	**RUNNION**	RUNNIONS (offensive)
TRUNNIONS	**RUNNIONS**	
	RUNOFF	RUNOFFS
	RUNOUT	RUNOUTS
	RUNOVER	RUNOVERS
	RUNRIG	RUNRIGS
	RUNROUND	RUNROUNDS
BRUNT ▪ GRUNT ▪ PRUNT	**RUNT**	RUNTS ▪ RUNTY
BRUNTED ▪ GRUNTED ▪ PRUNTED	**RUNTED**	
BRUNTS ▪ GRUNTS ▪ PRUNTS	**RUNTS**	
	RUNWAY	RUNWAYS
	RUPEE	RUPEES
	RUPIA	RUPIAH ▪ RUPIAS
	RUPIAH	RUPIAHS
	RUPTURE	RUPTURED ▪ RUPTURES
CRURAL	**RURAL**	RURALS
	RURALISE	RURALISED ▪ RURALISES
	RURALISM	RURALISMS
	RURALIST	RURALISTS
	RURALITE	RURALITES
	RURALIZE	RURALIZED ▪ RURALIZES
	RURP	RURPS
	RURU	RURUS
	RUSA	RUSAS
	RUSALKA	RUSALKAS
CRUSE ▪ DRUSE	**RUSE**	RUSES
CRUSES ▪ DRUSES ▪ URUSES	**RUSES**	
BRUSH ▪ CRUSH ▪ FRUSH	**RUSH**	RUSHY
BRUSHED ▪ CRUSHED ▪ FRUSHED	**RUSHED**	
	RUSHEE	RUSHEES
BRUSHER ▪ CRUSHER	**RUSHER**	RUSHERS
BRUSHERS ▪ CRUSHERS	**RUSHERS**	
BRUSHES ▪ CRUSHES ▪ FRUSHES	**RUSHES**	
BRUSHIER	**RUSHIER**	
BRUSHIEST	**RUSHIEST**	

R

FRONT HOOK	ROOT WORD	END HOOK
BRUSHING ▪ CRUSHING ▪ FRUSHING	**RUSHING**	RUSHINGS
BRUSHINGS	**RUSHINGS**	
	RUSHLIGHT	RUSHLIGHTS
BRUSHLIKE	**RUSHLIKE**	
BRUSHY	**RUSHY**	
BRUSK	**RUSK**	RUSKS
	RUSMA	RUSMAS
	RUSSE	RUSSEL ▪ RUSSET
	RUSSEL	RUSSELS
	RUSSET	RUSSETS ▪ RUSSETY
	RUSSETING	RUSSETINGS
	RUSSIA	RUSSIAS
	RUSSULA	RUSSULAE ▪ RUSSULAS
BRUST ▪ CRUST ▪ FRUST ▪ TRUST	**RUST**	RUSTS ▪ RUSTY
TRUSTABLE	**RUSTABLE**	
CRUSTED ▪ TRUSTED	**RUSTED**	
	RUSTIC	RUSTICS
	RUSTICAL	RUSTICALS
	RUSTICATE	RUSTICATED ▪ RUSTICATES
	RUSTICISE	RUSTICISED ▪ RUSTICISES
	RUSTICISM	RUSTICISMS
	RUSTICIZE	RUSTICIZED ▪ RUSTICIZES
CRUSTIER ▪ TRUSTIER	**RUSTIER**	
CRUSTIEST ▪ TRUSTIEST	**RUSTIEST**	
CRUSTILY ▪ TRUSTILY	**RUSTILY**	
CRUSTINESS ▪ TRUSTINESS	**RUSTINESS**	
BRUSTING ▪ CRUSTING ▪ TRUSTING	**RUSTING**	RUSTINGS
	RUSTLE	RUSTLED ▪ RUSTLER ▪ RUSTLES
	RUSTLER	RUSTLERS
	RUSTLES	RUSTLESS
CRUSTLESS ▪ TRUSTLESS	**RUSTLESS**	
	RUSTLING	RUSTLINGS
	RUSTPROOF	RUSTPROOFS
	RUSTRE	RUSTRED ▪ RUSTRES
BRUSTS ▪ CRUSTS ▪ FRUSTS ▪ TRUSTS	**RUSTS**	
CRUSTY ▪ TRUSTY	**RUSTY**	
BRUT	**RUT**	RUTH ▪ RUTS
	RUTABAGA	RUTABAGAS
TRUTH	**RUTH**	RUTHS
	RUTHENIUM	RUTHENIUMS
TRUTHFUL	**RUTHFUL**	
TRUTHFULLY	**RUTHFULLY**	
TRUTHLESS	**RUTHLESS**	
TRUTHS	**RUTHS**	
	RUTILE	RUTILES
	RUTIN	RUTINS
BRUTS	**RUTS**	
	RUTTER	RUTTERS
	RUTTING	RUTTINGS
	RYA	RYAL ▪ RYAS
	RYAL	RYALS
	RYBAT	RYBATS
	RYBAUDRYE	RYBAUDRYES
TRYE	**RYE**	RYES
	RYEBREAD	RYEBREADS
	RYEFLOUR	RYEFLOURS
	RYEPECK	RYEPECKS
GRYKE ▪ TRYKE	**RYKE**	RYKED ▪ RYKES
GRYKES ▪ TRYKES	**RYKES**	
	RYMME	RYMMED ▪ RYMMES
	RYND	RYNDS
	RYOKAN	RYOKANS
	RYOT	RYOTS
	RYOTWARI	RYOTWARIS
GRYPE	**RYPE**	RYPER
	RYPECK	RYPECKS

R

S

FRONT HOOK	ROOT WORD	END HOOK
	SAB	SABE ▪ SABS
	SABADILLA	SABADILLAS
	SABAL	SABALS
	SABATON	SABATONS
	SABAYON	SABAYONS
	SABBAT	SABBATH ▪ SABBATS
	SABBATH	SABBATHS
	SABBATIC	SABBATICS
	SABBATISE	SABBATISED ▪ SABBATISES
	SABBATISM	SABBATISMS
	SABBATIZE	SABBATIZED ▪ SABBATIZES
	SABE	SABED ▪ SABER ▪ SABES
ISABELLA	**SABELLA**	SABELLAS
ISABELLAS	**SABELLAS**	
	SABER	SABERS
	SABIN	SABINE ▪ SABINS
	SABINE	SABINES
	SABIR	SABIRS
	SABKHA	SABKHAH ▪ SABKHAS ▪ SABKHAT
	SABKHAH	SABKHAHS
	SABKHAT	SABKHATS
USABLE	**SABLE**	SABLED ▪ SABLES
	SABOT	SABOTS
	SABOTAGE	SABOTAGED ▪ SABOTAGES
	SABOTEUR	SABOTEURS
	SABOTIER	SABOTIERS
	SABRA	SABRAS
	SABRE	SABRED ▪ SABRES
	SABREUR	SABREURS
	SABURRA	SABURRAL ▪ SABURRAS
	SAC	SACK ▪ SACS
	SACATON	SACATONS
	SACBUT	SACBUTS
	SACCADE	SACCADES
	SACCHARIN	SACCHARINE ▪ SACCHARINS
	SACCHARUM	SACCHARUMS
	SACCULATE	SACCULATED
	SACCULE	SACCULES
	SACHEM	SACHEMS
	SACHEMDOM	SACHEMDOMS
	SACHET	SACHETS
	SACK	SACKS
	SACKAGE	SACKAGES
	SACKBUT	SACKBUTS
	SACKCLOTH	SACKCLOTHS
	SACKER	SACKERS
	SACKFUL	SACKFULS
	SACKING	SACKINGS
	SACQUE	SACQUES
	SACRA	SACRAL
	SACRAL	SACRALS
	SACRALGIA	SACRALGIAS
	SACRALISE	SACRALISED ▪ SACRALISES
	SACRALIZE	SACRALIZED ▪ SACRALIZES
	SACRAMENT	SACRAMENTS
	SACRARIA	SACRARIAL
	SACRIFICE	SACRIFICED ▪ SACRIFICER ▪ SACRIFICES
	SACRILEGE	SACRILEGES
	SACRING	SACRINGS
	SACRIST	SACRISTS ▪ SACRISTY
	SACRISTAN	SACRISTANS
	SACRUM	SACRUMS
	SAD	SADE ▪ SADI ▪ SADO ▪ SADS
	SADDEN	SADDENS
	SADDHU	SADDHUS
	SADDLE	SADDLED ▪ SADDLER ▪ SADDLES

FRONT HOOK	ROOT WORD	END HOOK
	SADDLEBAG	SADDLEBAGS
	SADDLEBOW	SADDLEBOWS
	SADDLER	SADDLERS · SADDLERY
	SADDO	SADDOS
TSADE	**SADE**	SADES
TSADES	**SADES**	
	SADHANA	SADHANAS
	SADHE	SADHES
	SADHU	SADHUS
TSADI	**SADI**	SADIS
	SADIRON	SADIRONS
TSADIS	**SADIS**	SADISM · SADIST
	SADISM	SADISMS
	SADIST	SADISTS
	SADO	SADOS
	SADZA	SADZAS
	SAECULUM	SAECULUMS
	SAETER	SAETERS
	SAFARI	SAFARIS
	SAFARIS	SAFARIST
	SAFARIST	SAFARISTS
	SAFE	SAFED · SAFER · SAFES
	SAFEGUARD	SAFEGUARDS
	SAFELIGHT	SAFELIGHTS
	SAFES	SAFEST
	SAFFIAN	SAFFIANS
	SAFFLOWER	SAFFLOWERS
	SAFFRON	SAFFRONS · SAFFRONY
	SAFRANIN	SAFRANINE · SAFRANINS
	SAFRANINE	SAFRANINES
	SAFROL	SAFROLE · SAFROLS
	SAFROLE	SAFROLES
	SAFRONAL	SAFRONALS
	SAG	SAGA · SAGE · SAGO · SAGS · SAGY
	SAGA	SAGAS
	SAGAMORE	SAGAMORES
	SAGAPENUM	SAGAPENUMS
	SAGBUT	SAGBUTS
USAGE	**SAGE**	SAGER · SAGES
	SAGENE	SAGENES
	SAGENES	SAGENESS
	SAGENITE	SAGENITES
USAGER	**SAGER**	
USAGES	**SAGES**	SAGEST
	SAGGAR	SAGGARD · SAGGARS
	SAGGARD	SAGGARDS
	SAGGER	SAGGERS
	SAGGING	SAGGINGS
	SAGINATE	SAGINATED · SAGINATES
	SAGITTA	SAGITTAL · SAGITTAS
	SAGO	SAGOS
	SAGOIN	SAGOINS
	SAGOUIN	SAGOUINS
	SAGUARO	SAGUAROS
	SAGUIN	SAGUINS
	SAHEB	SAHEBS
	SAHIB	SAHIBA · SAHIBS
	SAHIBA	SAHIBAH · SAHIBAS
	SAHIBAH	SAHIBAHS
	SAHIWAL	SAHIWALS
	SAHUARO	SAHUAROS
	SAI	SAIC · SAID · SAIL · SAIM · SAIN
		SAIR · SAIS
	SAIBLING	SAIBLINGS
	SAIC	SAICE · SAICK · SAICS
	SAICE	SAICES
	SAICK	SAICKS
	SAID	SAIDS
	SAIDS	SAIDST

FRONT HOOK	ROOT WORD	END HOOK
	SAIGA	SAIGAS
	SAIKEI	SAIKEIS
	SAIL	SAILS
	SAILBOARD	SAILBOARDS
	SAILBOAT	SAILBOATS
	SAILCLOTH	SAILCLOTHS
	SAILER	SAILERS
	SAILING	SAILINGS
	SAILMAKER	SAILMAKERS
	SAILOR	SAILORS
	SAILORING	SAILORINGS
	SAILPLANE	SAILPLANED ▪ SAILPLANER ▪ SAILPLANES
	SAILROOM	SAILROOMS
	SAIM	SAIMS
	SAIMIN	SAIMINS
	SAIMIRI	SAIMIRIS
	SAIN	SAINE ▪ SAINS ▪ SAINT
	SAINE	SAINED
	SAINFOIN	SAINFOINS
	SAINT	SAINTS
	SAINTDOM	SAINTDOMS
	SAINTFOIN	SAINTFOINS
	SAINTHOOD	SAINTHOODS
	SAINTISM	SAINTISMS
	SAINTLING	SAINTLINGS
	SAINTSHIP	SAINTSHIPS
	SAIQUE	SAIQUES
	SAIR	SAIRS
	SAIS	SAIST
	SAITH	SAITHE ▪ SAITHS
	SAITHE	SAITHES
	SAIYID	SAIYIDS
	SAJOU	SAJOUS
	SAKAI	SAKAIS
	SAKE	SAKER ▪ SAKES
	SAKER	SAKERS
	SAKERET	SAKERETS
	SAKI	SAKIA ▪ SAKIS
	SAKIA	SAKIAS
	SAKIEH	SAKIEHS
	SAKIYEH	SAKIYEHS
	SAKSAUL	SAKSAULS
	SAL	SALE ▪ SALL ▪ SALP ▪ SALS ▪ SALT
	SALAAM	SALAAMS
	SALAD	SALADE ▪ SALADS
	SALADANG	SALADANGS
	SALADE	SALADES
	SALADING	SALADINGS
	SALAL	SALALS
	SALAMI	SALAMIS
	SALAMON	SALAMONS
	SALANGANE	SALANGANES
	SALARIAT	SALARIATS
	SALBAND	SALBANDS
	SALCHOW	SALCHOWS
	SALE	SALEP ▪ SALES ▪ SALET
	SALEP	SALEPS
	SALERING	SALERINGS
	SALEROOM	SALEROOMS
	SALESGIRL	SALESGIRLS
	SALESROOM	SALESROOMS
	SALET	SALETS
	SALEYARD	SALEYARDS
	SALFERN	SALFERNS
	SALIAUNCE	SALIAUNCES
	SALICET	SALICETA ▪ SALICETS
	SALICETUM	SALICETUMS
	SALICIN	SALICINE ▪ SALICINS
	SALICINE	SALICINES

S

FRONT HOOK	ROOT WORD	END HOOK
	SALIENCE	SALIENCES
	SALIENT	SALIENTS
	SALIGOT	SALIGOTS
	SALIMETER	SALIMETERS
	SALINA	SALINAS
	SALINE	SALINES
	SALINISE	SALINISED · SALINISES
	SALINIZE	SALINIZED · SALINIZES
	SALIVA	SALIVAL · SALIVAS
	SALIVATE	SALIVATED · SALIVATES
	SALIVATOR	SALIVATORS
	SALL	SALLE · SALLY
	SALLAD	SALLADS
	SALLAL	SALLALS
	SALLE	SALLEE · SALLES · SALLET
	SALLEE	SALLEES
	SALLET	SALLETS
	SALLIER	SALLIERS
	SALLOW	SALLOWS · SALLOWY
	SALLYPORT	SALLYPORTS
	SALMI	SALMIS
	SALMON	SALMONS
	SALMONET	SALMONETS
	SALMONID	SALMONIDS
	SALMONOID	SALMONOIDS
	SALOL	SALOLS
	SALOMETER	SALOMETERS
	SALON	SALONS
	SALOON	SALOONS
	SALOOP	SALOOPS
	SALOP	SALOPS
	SALP	SALPA · SALPS
	SALPA	SALPAE · SALPAS
	SALPIAN	SALPIANS
	SALPICON	SALPICONS
	SALPID	SALPIDS
	SALS	SALSA · SALSE
	SALSA	SALSAS
	SALSE	SALSES
	SALSILLA	SALSILLAS
	SALT	SALTO · SALTS · SALTY
	SALTANT	SALTANTS
	SALTATE	SALTATED · SALTATES
	SALTATION	SALTATIONS
	SALTCAT	SALTCATS
	SALTCHUCK	SALTCHUCKS
PSALTER	**SALTER**	SALTERN · SALTERS
	SALTERN	SALTERNS
PSALTERS	**SALTERS**	
	SALTIE	SALTIER · SALTIES
	SALTIER	SALTIERS
	SALTIES	SALTIEST
	SALTINE	SALTINES
	SALTINES	SALTINESS
	SALTING	SALTINGS
	SALTIRE	SALTIRES
	SALTO	SALTOS
	SALTPAN	SALTPANS
	SALTPETER	SALTPETERS
	SALTPETRE	SALTPETRES
	SALTWORK	SALTWORKS
	SALTWORT	SALTWORTS
	SALUE	SALUED · SALUES
	SALUKI	SALUKIS
	SALURETIC	SALURETICS
	SALUTE	SALUTED · SALUTER · SALUTES
	SALUTER	SALUTERS
	SALVAGE	SALVAGED · SALVAGEE · SALVAGER SALVAGES

S

FRONT HOOK	ROOT WORD	END HOOK
	SALVAGEE	SALVAGEES
	SALVAGER	SALVAGERS
	SALVARSAN	SALVARSANS
	SALVATION	SALVATIONS
	SALVE	SALVED ▪ SALVER ▪ SALVES
	SALVER	SALVERS
	SALVETE	SALVETES
	SALVIA	SALVIAS
	SALVING	SALVINGS
	SALVO	SALVOR ▪ SALVOS
	SALVOR	SALVORS
	SAM	SAMA ▪ SAME ▪ SAMP ▪ SAMS
	SAMA	SAMAN ▪ SAMAS
	SAMAAN	SAMAANS
	SAMADHI	SAMADHIS
	SAMAN	SAMANS
	SAMARA	SAMARAS
	SAMARITAN	SAMARITANS
	SAMARIUM	SAMARIUMS
TSAMBA	**SAMBA**	SAMBAL ▪ SAMBAR ▪ SAMBAS
	SAMBAL	SAMBALS
	SAMBAR	SAMBARS
TSAMBAS	**SAMBAS**	
	SAMBHAR	SAMBHARS
	SAMBHUR	SAMBHURS
	SAMBO	SAMBOS (offensive)
	SAMBUCA	SAMBUCAS
	SAMBUKE	SAMBUKES
	SAMBUR	SAMBURS
YSAME	**SAME**	SAMEK ▪ SAMEL ▪ SAMEN ▪ SAMES ▪ SAMEY
	SAMECH	SAMECHS
	SAMEK	SAMEKH ▪ SAMEKS
	SAMEKH	SAMEKHS
	SAMEL	SAMELY
	SAMFOO	SAMFOOS
	SAMFU	SAMFUS
	SAMIEL	SAMIELS
	SAMISEN	SAMISENS
	SAMITE	SAMITES
	SAMITHI	SAMITHIS
	SAMITI	SAMITIS
	SAMIZDAT	SAMIZDATS
	SAMLET	SAMLETS
	SAMLOR	SAMLORS
	SAMOSA	SAMOSAS
	SAMOVAR	SAMOVARS
	SAMOYED	SAMOYEDS
	SAMP	SAMPI ▪ SAMPS
	SAMPAN	SAMPANS
	SAMPHIRE	SAMPHIRES
	SAMPI	SAMPIS
	SAMPIRE	SAMPIRES
	SAMPLE	SAMPLED ▪ SAMPLER ▪ SAMPLES
	SAMPLER	SAMPLERS ▪ SAMPLERY
	SAMPLING	SAMPLINGS
	SAMSARA	SAMSARAS
	SAMSHOO	SAMSHOOS
	SAMSHU	SAMSHUS
	SAMURAI	SAMURAIS
	SAN	SAND ▪ SANE ▪ SANG ▪ SANK ▪ SANS ▪ SANT
	SANBENITO	SANBENITOS
	SANCAI	SANCAIS
	SANCHO	SANCHOS
	SANCTION	SANCTIONS
	SANCTUM	SANCTUMS
	SAND	SANDS ▪ SANDY
	SANDAL	SANDALS
	SANDARAC	SANDARACH ▪ SANDARACS
	SANDARACH	SANDARACHS

S

FRONT HOOK	ROOT WORD	END HOOK
	SANDBAG	SANDBAGS
	SANDBANK	SANDBANKS
	SANDBAR	SANDBARS
	SANDBLAST	SANDBLASTS
	SANDBOY	SANDBOYS
	SANDBUR	SANDBURR · SANDBURS
	SANDBURR	SANDBURRS
	SANDCRACK	SANDCRACKS
	SANDDAB	SANDDABS
	SANDEK	SANDEKS
	SANDER	SANDERS
	SANDHEAP	SANDHEAPS
	SANDHI	SANDHIS
	SANDHILL	SANDHILLS
	SANDHOG	SANDHOGS
	SANDING	SANDINGS
	SANDIVER	SANDIVERS
	SANDLING	SANDLINGS
	SANDLOT	SANDLOTS
	SANDPAPER	SANDPAPERS · SANDPAPERY
	SANDPEEP	SANDPEEPS
	SANDPILE	SANDPILES
	SANDPIPER	SANDPIPERS
	SANDPIT	SANDPITS
	SANDPUMP	SANDPUMPS
	SANDSHOE	SANDSHOES
	SANDSOAP	SANDSOAPS
	SANDSPOUT	SANDSPOUTS
	SANDSPUR	SANDSPURS
	SANDSTONE	SANDSTONES
	SANDSTORM	SANDSTORMS
	SANDWORM	SANDWORMS
	SANDWORT	SANDWORTS
	SANE	SANED · SANER · SANES
	SANES	SANEST
	SANG	SANGA · SANGH · SANGO · SANGS
	SANGA	SANGAR · SANGAS
	SANGAR	SANGARS
	SANGAREE	SANGAREES
	SANGER	SANGERS
	SANGFROID	SANGFROIDS
	SANGH	SANGHS
	SANGHAT	SANGHATS
	SANGLIER	SANGLIERS
	SANGO	SANGOS
	SANGOMA	SANGOMAS
	SANGRIA	SANGRIAS
	SANGUINE	SANGUINED · SANGUINES
	SANICLE	SANICLES
	SANIDINE	SANIDINES
	SANITARIA	SANITARIAN
	SANITATE	SANITATED · SANITATES
	SANITISE	SANITISED · SANITISER · SANITISES
	SANITISER	SANITISERS
	SANITIZE	SANITIZED · SANITIZER · SANITIZES
	SANITIZER	SANITIZERS
	SANJAK	SANJAKS
	SANK	SANKO
	SANKO	SANKOS
	SANNIE	SANNIES
	SANNOP	SANNOPS
	SANNUP	SANNUPS
	SANNYASI	SANNYASIN · SANNYASIS
	SANNYASIN	SANNYASINS
	SANPAN	SANPANS
	SANPRO	SANPROS
	SANS	SANSA
	SANSA	SANSAR · SANSAS
	SANSAR	SANSARS

S

FRONT HOOK	ROOT WORD	END HOOK
	SANSEI	SANSEIS
	SANSERIF	SANSERIFS
	SANT	SANTO · SANTS
	SANTAL	SANTALS
	SANTALIN	SANTALINS
	SANTALOL	SANTALOLS
	SANTERA	SANTERAS
	SANTERIA	SANTERIAS
	SANTERO	SANTEROS
	SANTIR	SANTIRS
	SANTO	SANTOL · SANTON · SANTOS
	SANTOL	SANTOLS
	SANTOLINA	SANTOLINAS
	SANTON	SANTONS
	SANTONICA	SANTONICAS
	SANTONIN	SANTONINS
	SANTOOR	SANTOORS
	SANTOUR	SANTOURS
	SANTUR	SANTURS
	SANYASI	SANYASIS
	SAOUARI	SAOUARIS
	SAP	SAPS
	SAPAJOU	SAPAJOUS
	SAPAN	SAPANS
	SAPANWOOD	SAPANWOODS
	SAPELE	SAPELES
	SAPHEAD	SAPHEADS
	SAPHENA	SAPHENAE · SAPHENAS
	SAPIENCE	SAPIENCES
	SAPIENT	SAPIENTS
	SAPLING	SAPLINGS
	SAPODILLA	SAPODILLAS
	SAPOGENIN	SAPOGENINS
	SAPONARIA	SAPONARIAS
	SAPONIN	SAPONINE · SAPONINS
	SAPONINE	SAPONINES
	SAPONITE	SAPONITES
	SAPOR	SAPORS
	SAPOTA	SAPOTAS
	SAPOTE	SAPOTES
	SAPOUR	SAPOURS
	SAPPAN	SAPPANS
	SAPPER	SAPPERS
	SAPPHIC	SAPPHICS
	SAPPHIRE	SAPPHIRED · SAPPHIRES
	SAPPHISM	SAPPHISMS
	SAPPHIST	SAPPHISTS
	SAPPLE	SAPPLED · SAPPLES
	SAPRAEMIA	SAPRAEMIAS
	SAPREMIA	SAPREMIAS
	SAPROBE	SAPROBES
	SAPROLITE	SAPROLITES
	SAPROPEL	SAPROPELS
	SAPSAGO	SAPSAGOS
	SAPSUCKER	SAPSUCKERS
	SAPUCAIA	SAPUCAIAS
	SAPWOOD	SAPWOODS
ASAR · KSAR · OSAR · TSAR	SAR	SARD · SARI · SARK · SARS
	SARABAND	SARABANDE · SARABANDS
	SARABANDE	SARABANDES
	SARAFAN	SARAFANS
	SARAN	SARANS
	SARANGI	SARANGIS
	SARAPE	SARAPES
	SARBACANE	SARBACANES
	SARCASM	SARCASMS
	SARCENET	SARCENETS
	SARCINA	SARCINAE · SARCINAS
	SARCOCARP	SARCOCARPS

FRONT HOOK	ROOT WORD	END HOOK
	SARCODE	SARCODES
	SARCOID	SARCOIDS
	SARCOMA	SARCOMAS
	SARCOMERE	SARCOMERES
	SARCONET	SARCONETS
	SARCOSOME	SARCOSOMES
	SARD	SARDS
	SARDANA	SARDANAS
	SARDAR	SARDARS
	SARDEL	SARDELS
	SARDELLE	SARDELLES
	SARDINE	SARDINED ▪ SARDINES
	SAREE	SAREES
	SARGASSO	SARGASSOS
	SARGASSUM	SARGASSUMS
	SARGE	SARGES
	SARGO	SARGOS
	SARI	SARIN ▪ SARIS
	SARIN	SARING ▪ SARINS
	SARK	SARKS ▪ SARKY
	SARKING	SARKINGS
	SARMENT	SARMENTA ▪ SARMENTS
	SARMIE	SARMIES
	SARNEY	SARNEYS
	SARNIE	SARNIES
	SAROD	SARODE ▪ SARODS
	SARODE	SARODES
	SARODIST	SARODISTS
	SARONG	SARONGS
	SARRASIN	SARRASINS
	SARRAZIN	SARRAZINS
KSARS ▪ TSARS	**SARS**	
	SARSAR	SARSARS
	SARSDEN	SARSDENS
	SARSEN	SARSENS
	SARSENET	SARSENETS
	SARSNET	SARSNETS
	SARTOR	SARTORS
	SASARARA	SASARARAS
	SASER	SASERS
	SASHAY	SASHAYS
	SASHIMI	SASHIMIS
	SASIN	SASINE ▪ SASINS
	SASINE	SASINES
	SASKATOON	SASKATOONS
	SASS	SASSE ▪ SASSY
	SASSARARA	SASSARARAS
	SASSE	SASSED ▪ SASSES
	SASSIES	SASSIEST
	SASSOLIN	SASSOLINS
	SASSOLITE	SASSOLITES
	SASSWOOD	SASSWOODS
	SASSYWOOD	SASSYWOODS
	SASTRA	SASTRAS
	SAT	SATE ▪ SATI
	SATAI	SATAIS
	SATANG	SATANGS
	SATANISM	SATANISMS
	SATANIST	SATANISTS
	SATARA	SATARAS
	SATAY	SATAYS
	SATCHEL	SATCHELS
	SATE	SATED ▪ SATEM ▪ SATES
	SATEEN	SATEENS
	SATELLITE	SATELLITED ▪ SATELLITES
	SATI	SATIN ▪ SATIS
	SATIATE	SATIATED ▪ SATIATES
	SATIATION	SATIATIONS
ISATIN	**SATIN**	SATING ▪ SATINS ▪ SATINY

S

FRONT HOOK	ROOT WORD	END HOOK
	SATINET	SATINETS
	SATINETTA	SATINETTAS
	SATINETTE	SATINETTES
	SATINPOD	SATINPODS
ISATINS	**SATINS**	
	SATINWOOD	SATINWOODS
	SATIRE	SATIRES
	SATIRISE	SATIRISED · SATIRISER · SATIRISES
	SATIRISER	SATIRISERS
	SATIRIST	SATIRISTS
	SATIRIZE	SATIRIZED · SATIRIZER · SATIRIZES
	SATIRIZER	SATIRIZERS
	SATISFICE	SATISFICED · SATISFICER · SATISFICES
	SATISFIER	SATISFIERS
	SATORI	SATORIS
	SATRAP	SATRAPS · SATRAPY
	SATSUMA	SATSUMAS
	SATURANT	SATURANTS
	SATURATE	SATURATED · SATURATER · SATURATES
	SATURATER	SATURATERS
	SATURATOR	SATURATORS
	SATURNIID	SATURNIIDS
	SATURNISM	SATURNISMS
	SATURNIST	SATURNISTS
	SATYR	SATYRA · SATYRS
	SATYRA	SATYRAL · SATYRAS
	SATYRAL	SATYRALS
	SATYRID	SATYRIDS
	SATYRISK	SATYRISKS
	SAU	SAUL · SAUT
	SAUBA	SAUBAS
	SAUCE	SAUCED · SAUCER · SAUCES
	SAUCEBOAT	SAUCEBOATS
	SAUCEPAN	SAUCEPANS
	SAUCEPOT	SAUCEPOTS
	SAUCER	SAUCERS
	SAUCERFUL	SAUCERFULS
	SAUCH	SAUCHS
	SAUCIER	SAUCIERS
	SAUCISSE	SAUCISSES
	SAUCISSON	SAUCISSONS
	SAUFGARD	SAUFGARDS
	SAUGER	SAUGERS
	SAUGH	SAUGHS · SAUGHY
	SAUL	SAULS · SAULT
	SAULGE	SAULGES
	SAULIE	SAULIES
	SAULT	SAULTS
	SAUNA	SAUNAS
	SAUNT	SAUNTS
	SAUNTER	SAUNTERS
	SAUNTERER	SAUNTERERS
	SAUREL	SAURELS
	SAURIAN	SAURIANS
	SAUROPOD	SAUROPODS
	SAUSAGE	SAUSAGES
	SAUT	SAUTE · SAUTS
	SAUTE	SAUTED · SAUTES
	SAUTERNE	SAUTERNES
	SAUTOIR	SAUTOIRE · SAUTOIRS
	SAUTOIRE	SAUTOIRES
	SAV	SAVE · SAVS
	SAVAGE	SAVAGED · SAVAGER · SAVAGES
	SAVAGEDOM	SAVAGEDOMS
	SAVAGER	SAVAGERY
	SAVAGES	SAVAGEST
	SAVAGISM	SAVAGISMS
	SAVANNA	SAVANNAH · SAVANNAS
	SAVANNAH	SAVANNAHS

FRONT HOOK	ROOT WORD	END HOOK
	SAVANT	SAVANTE • SAVANTS
	SAVANTE	SAVANTES
	SAVARIN	SAVARINS
	SAVATE	SAVATES
	SAVE	SAVED • SAVER • SAVES • SAVEY
	SAVEGARD	SAVEGARDS
	SAVELOY	SAVELOYS
	SAVER	SAVERS
	SAVEY	SAVEYS
	SAVIN	SAVINE • SAVING • SAVINS
	SAVINE	SAVINES
	SAVING	SAVINGS
	SAVIOR	SAVIORS
	SAVIOUR	SAVIOURS
	SAVOR	SAVORS • SAVORY
	SAVORER	SAVORERS
	SAVORIES	SAVORIEST
	SAVOUR	SAVOURS • SAVOURY
	SAVOURER	SAVOURERS
	SAVOURIES	SAVOURIEST
	SAVOY	SAVOYS
	SAVOYARD	SAVOYARDS
	SAVVEY	SAVVEYS
	SAVVIES	SAVVIEST
	SAW	SAWN • SAWS
	SAWAH	SAWAHS
	SAWBILL	SAWBILLS
	SAWBLADE	SAWBLADES
	SAWBUCK	SAWBUCKS
	SAWDER	SAWDERS
	SAWDUST	SAWDUSTS • SAWDUSTY
	SAWER	SAWERS
	SAWHORSE	SAWHORSES
	SAWING	SAWINGS
	SAWLOG	SAWLOGS
	SAWMILL	SAWMILLS
	SAWNEY	SAWNEYS (offensive)
	SAWPIT	SAWPITS
	SAWSHARK	SAWSHARKS
	SAWTIMBER	SAWTIMBERS
	SAWYER	SAWYERS
	SAX	SAXE
	SAXAUL	SAXAULS
	SAXE	SAXES
	SAXHORN	SAXHORNS
	SAXIFRAGE	SAXIFRAGES
	SAXITOXIN	SAXITOXINS
	SAXONITE	SAXONITES
	SAXOPHONE	SAXOPHONES
	SAXTUBA	SAXTUBAS
	SAY	SAYS
	SAYED	SAYEDS
	SAYER	SAYERS
	SAYID	SAYIDS
	SAYING	SAYINGS
	SAYON	SAYONS
	SAYONARA	SAYONARAS
	SAYS	SAYST
	SAYYID	SAYYIDS
	SAZERAC	SAZERACS
	SAZHEN	SAZHENS
	SCAB	SCABS
	SCABBARD	SCABBARDS
	SCABBLE	SCABBLED • SCABBLES
	SCABIOSA	SCABIOSAS
	SCABLAND	SCABLANDS
	SCAD	SCADS
	SCAFF	SCAFFS
	SCAFFIE	SCAFFIES

FRONT HOOK	ROOT WORD	END HOOK
	SCAFFOLD	SCAFFOLDS
	SCAG	SCAGS
	SCAGLIA	SCAGLIAS
	SCAGLIOLA	SCAGLIOLAS
	SCAIL	SCAILS
	SCAITH	SCAITHS
	SCALA	SCALAE ▪ SCALAR
ESCALADE	**SCALADE**	SCALADES
ESCALADES	**SCALADES**	
ESCALADO	**SCALADO**	SCALADOS
	SCALAGE	SCALAGES
	SCALAR	SCALARE ▪ SCALARS
	SCALARE	SCALARES
ESCALATION	**SCALATION**	SCALATIONS
	SCALAWAG	SCALAWAGS
	SCALD	SCALDS
	SCALDER	SCALDERS
	SCALDHEAD	SCALDHEADS
	SCALDING	SCALDINGS
	SCALDSHIP	SCALDSHIPS
	SCALE	SCALED ▪ SCALER ▪ SCALES
	SCALEPAN	SCALEPANS
	SCALER	SCALERS
	SCALETAIL	SCALETAILS
	SCALEUP	SCALEUPS
	SCALEWORK	SCALEWORKS
ESCALIER	**SCALIER**	
	SCALING	SCALINGS
	SCALL	SCALLS ▪ SCALLY
	SCALLAWAG	SCALLAWAGS
	SCALLION	SCALLIONS
ESCALLOP	**SCALLOP**	SCALLOPS
ESCALLOPED	**SCALLOPED**	
	SCALLOPER	SCALLOPERS
ESCALLOPS	**SCALLOPS**	
	SCALLYWAG	SCALLYWAGS
	SCALOGRAM	SCALOGRAMS
	SCALP	SCALPS
	SCALPEL	SCALPELS
	SCALPER	SCALPERS
	SCALPING	SCALPINGS
	SCALPRUM	SCALPRUMS
	SCAM	SCAMP ▪ SCAMS
	SCAMBLE	SCAMBLED ▪ SCAMBLER ▪ SCAMBLES
	SCAMBLER	SCAMBLERS
	SCAMBLING	SCAMBLINGS
	SCAMEL	SCAMELS
	SCAMMER	SCAMMERS
	SCAMP	SCAMPI ▪ SCAMPS
	SCAMPER	SCAMPERS
	SCAMPERER	SCAMPERERS
	SCAMPI	SCAMPIS
	SCAMPING	SCAMPINGS
	SCAMPIS	SCAMPISH
	SCAMSTER	SCAMSTERS
	SCAMTO	SCAMTOS
	SCAN	SCAND ▪ SCANS ▪ SCANT
	SCANDAL	SCANDALS
	SCANDIA	SCANDIAS
	SCANDIUM	SCANDIUMS
	SCANNER	SCANNERS
	SCANNING	SCANNINGS
	SCANSION	SCANSIONS
	SCANT	SCANTS ▪ SCANTY
	SCANTIES	SCANTIEST
	SCANTLE	SCANTLED ▪ SCANTLES
	SCANTLING	SCANTLINGS
	SCAPA	SCAPAS
ESCAPE	**SCAPE**	SCAPED ▪ SCAPES

S

FRONT HOOK	ROOT WORD	END HOOK
ESCAPED	**SCAPED**	
	SCAPEGOAT	SCAPEGOATS
ESCAPELESS	**SCAPELESS**	
ESCAPEMENT	**SCAPEMENT**	SCAPEMENTS
ESCAPES	**SCAPES**	
	SCAPHOID	SCAPHOIDS
	SCAPHOPOD	SCAPHOPODS
ESCAPING	**SCAPING**	
	SCAPOLITE	SCAPOLITES
	SCAPPLE	SCAPPLED · SCAPPLES
	SCAPULA	SCAPULAE · SCAPULAR · SCAPULAS
	SCAPULAR	SCAPULARS · SCAPULARY
ESCAR · OSCAR	**SCAR**	SCARE · SCARF · SCARP · SCARS · SCART
		SCARY
	SCARAB	SCARABS
	SCARABAEI	SCARABAEID
	SCARABEE	SCARABEES
	SCARABOID	SCARABOIDS
	SCARCE	SCARCER
	SCARE	SCARED · SCARER · SCARES · SCAREY
	SCARECROW	SCARECROWS
ASCARED	**SCARED**	
	SCAREHEAD	SCAREHEADS
	SCARER	SCARERS
	SCARF	SCARFS
	SCARFER	SCARFERS
	SCARFING	SCARFINGS
	SCARFPIN	SCARFPINS
	SCARFSKIN	SCARFSKINS
	SCARIFIER	SCARIFIERS
	SCARLET	SCARLETS
	SCARMOGE	SCARMOGES
ESCARP	**SCARP**	SCARPA · SCARPH · SCARPS
	SCARPA	SCARPAS
ESCARPED	**SCARPED**	
	SCARPER	SCARPERS
	SCARPH	SCARPHS
ESCARPING	**SCARPING**	SCARPINGS
ESCARPS	**SCARPS**	
	SCARRE	SCARRED · SCARRES
	SCARRING	SCARRINGS
ESCARS · OSCARS	**SCARS**	
	SCART	SCARTH · SCARTS
	SCARTH	SCARTHS
	SCAT	SCATH · SCATS · SCATT
	SCATBACK	SCATBACKS
	SCATH	SCATHE · SCATHS
	SCATHE	SCATHED · SCATHES
	SCATOLE	SCATOLES
	SCATT	SCATTS · SCATTY
	SCATTER	SCATTERS · SCATTERY
	SCATTERER	SCATTERERS
	SCATTING	SCATTINGS
	SCAUD	SCAUDS
	SCAUP	SCAUPS
	SCAUPER	SCAUPERS
	SCAUR	SCAURS · SCAURY
	SCAVAGE	SCAVAGER · SCAVAGES
	SCAVAGER	SCAVAGERS
	SCAVENGE	SCAVENGED · SCAVENGER · SCAVENGES
	SCAVENGER	SCAVENGERS · SCAVENGERY
	SCAW	SCAWS
	SCAWTITE	SCAWTITES
	SCAZON	SCAZONS
	SCAZONTIC	SCAZONTICS
	SCEAT	SCEATT
	SCEDULE	SCEDULED · SCEDULES
	SCELERAT	SCELERATE · SCELERATS
	SCELERATE	SCELERATES

FRONT HOOK	ROOT WORD	END HOOK
	SCENA	SCENAS
	SCENARIO	SCENARIOS
	SCENARISE	SCENARISED ▪ SCENARISES
	SCENARIST	SCENARISTS
	SCENARIZE	SCENARIZED ▪ SCENARIZES
ASCEND	SCEND	SCENDS
ASCENDED	SCENDED	
ASCENDING	SCENDING	
ASCENDS	SCENDS	
	SCENE	SCENED ▪ SCENES
	SCENIC	SCENICS
ASCENT	SCENT	SCENTS
	SCENTING	SCENTINGS
ASCENTS	SCENTS	
	SCEPTER	SCEPTERS
	SCEPTIC	SCEPTICS
	SCEPTRE	SCEPTRED ▪ SCEPTRES
	SCERNE	SCERNED ▪ SCERNES
	SCHANSE	SCHANSES
	SCHANTZE	SCHANTZES
	SCHANZE	SCHANZES
	SCHAPPE	SCHAPPED ▪ SCHAPPES
	SCHAPSKA	SCHAPSKAS
	SCHATCHEN	SCHATCHENS
	SCHAV	SCHAVS
	SCHECHITA	SCHECHITAH ▪ SCHECHITAS
	SCHEDULE	SCHEDULED ▪ SCHEDULER ▪ SCHEDULES
	SCHEDULER	SCHEDULERS
	SCHEELITE	SCHEELITES
	SCHELLUM	SCHELLUMS
	SCHELM	SCHELMS
	SCHEMA	SCHEMAS
	SCHEMATIC	SCHEMATICS
	SCHEME	SCHEMED ▪ SCHEMER ▪ SCHEMES
	SCHEMER	SCHEMERS
	SCHEMIE	SCHEMIES (offensive)
	SCHEMING	SCHEMINGS
	SCHERZO	SCHERZOS
	SCHIAVONE	SCHIAVONES
	SCHIEDAM	SCHIEDAMS
	SCHILLER	SCHILLERS
	SCHILLING	SCHILLINGS
	SCHIMMEL	SCHIMMELS
	SCHISM	SCHISMA ▪ SCHISMS
	SCHISMA	SCHISMAS
	SCHIST	SCHISTS
	SCHIZO	SCHIZOS (offensive)
	SCHIZOID	SCHIZOIDS
	SCHIZONT	SCHIZONTS
	SCHIZOPOD	SCHIZOPODS
	SCHLAGER	SCHLAGERS
	SCHLEMIEL	SCHLEMIELS
	SCHLEMIHL	SCHLEMIHLS
	SCHLEP	SCHLEPP ▪ SCHLEPS
	SCHLEPP	SCHLEPPS ▪ SCHLEPPY
	SCHLEPPER	SCHLEPPERS
	SCHLICH	SCHLICHS
	SCHLIERE	SCHLIEREN
	SCHLOCK	SCHLOCKS ▪ SCHLOCKY
	SCHLOCKER	SCHLOCKERS
	SCHLONG	SCHLONGS (offensive)
	SCHLUB	SCHLUBS
	SCHLUMP	SCHLUMPS ▪ SCHLUMPY
	SCHMALTZ	SCHMALTZY
	SCHMALZ	SCHMALZY
	SCHMATTE	SCHMATTES
	SCHMEAR	SCHMEARS
	SCHMECK	SCHMECKS
	SCHMEER	SCHMEERS

FRONT HOOK	ROOT WORD	END HOOK
	SCHMELZ	SCHMELZE
	SCHMELZE	SCHMELZES
	SCHMO	SCHMOE ▪ SCHMOS
	SCHMOCK	SCHMOCKS
	SCHMOE	SCHMOES
	SCHMOOS	SCHMOOSE
	SCHMOOSE	SCHMOOSED ▪ SCHMOOSES
	SCHMOOZ	SCHMOOZE ▪ SCHMOOZY
	SCHMOOZE	SCHMOOZED ▪ SCHMOOZER ▪ SCHMOOZES
	SCHMOOZER	SCHMOOZERS
	SCHMUCK	SCHMUCKS
	SCHMUTTER	SCHMUTTERS
	SCHNAPPER	SCHNAPPERS
	SCHNAUZER	SCHNAUZERS
	SCHNECKE	SCHNECKEN
	SCHNITZEL	SCHNITZELS
	SCHNOOK	SCHNOOKS
	SCHNORKEL	SCHNORKELS
	SCHNORR	SCHNORRS
	SCHNORRER	SCHNORRERS
	SCHNOZ	SCHNOZZ
	SCHNOZZLE	SCHNOZZLES
	SCHOLAR	SCHOLARS
	SCHOLARCH	SCHOLARCHS
	SCHOLIAST	SCHOLIASTS
	SCHOLIUM	SCHOLIUMS
	SCHOOL	SCHOOLE ▪ SCHOOLS
	SCHOOLBAG	SCHOOLBAGS
	SCHOOLBOY	SCHOOLBOYS
	SCHOOLDAY	SCHOOLDAYS
	SCHOOLE	SCHOOLED ▪ SCHOOLES
	SCHOOLIE	SCHOOLIES
	SCHOOLING	SCHOOLINGS
	SCHOOLKID	SCHOOLKIDS
	SCHOONER	SCHOONERS
	SCHORL	SCHORLS
	SCHOUT	SCHOUTS
	SCHRIK	SCHRIKS
	SCHROD	SCHRODS
	SCHTICK	SCHTICKS
	SCHTIK	SCHTIKS
	SCHTOOK	SCHTOOKS
	SCHTUCK	SCHTUCKS
	SCHUIT	SCHUITS
	SCHUL	SCHULN ▪ SCHULS
	SCHUSSER	SCHUSSERS
	SCHUYT	SCHUYTS
	SCHVARTZE	SCHVARTZES
	SCHWA	SCHWAS
	SCHWARTZE	SCHWARTZES
	SCIAENID	SCIAENIDS
	SCIAENOID	SCIAENOIDS
	SCIARID	SCIARIDS
	SCIATIC	SCIATICA ▪ SCIATICS
	SCIATICA	SCIATICAL ▪ SCIATICAS
	SCIENCE	SCIENCED ▪ SCIENCES
	SCIENTISE	SCIENTISED ▪ SCIENTISES
	SCIENTISM	SCIENTISMS
	SCIENTIST	SCIENTISTS
	SCIENTIZE	SCIENTIZED ▪ SCIENTIZES
	SCILLA	SCILLAS
	SCIMETAR	SCIMETARS
	SCIMITAR	SCIMITARS
	SCIMITER	SCIMITERS
	SCINCOID	SCINCOIDS
	SCINTILLA	SCINTILLAE ▪ SCINTILLAS
	SCIOLISM	SCIOLISMS
	SCIOLIST	SCIOLISTS
	SCION	SCIONS

FRONT HOOK	ROOT WORD	END HOOK
	SCIOPHYTE	SCIOPHYTES
	SCIROC	SCIROCS
	SCIROCCO	SCIROCCOS
	SCISSEL	SCISSELS
	SCISSIL	SCISSILE ▪ SCISSILS
	SCISSION	SCISSIONS
	SCISSOR	SCISSORS
	SCISSORER	SCISSORERS
	SCISSURE	SCISSURES
	SCIURID	SCIURIDS
	SCIURINE	SCIURINES
	SCLAFF	SCLAFFS
	SCLAFFER	SCLAFFERS
	SCLATE	SCLATED ▪ SCLATES
	SCLAUNDER	SCLAUNDERS
	SCLAVE	SCLAVES
	SCLERA	SCLERAE ▪ SCLERAL ▪ SCLERAS
	SCLERE	SCLERES
	SCLEREID	SCLEREIDE ▪ SCLEREIDS
	SCLEREIDE	SCLEREIDES
	SCLEREMA	SCLEREMAS
	SCLERITE	SCLERITES
	SCLEROMA	SCLEROMAS
	SCLEROSE	SCLEROSED ▪ SCLEROSES
	SCLEROTAL	SCLEROTALS
	SCLEROTIA	SCLEROTIAL
	SCLEROTIC	SCLEROTICS
	SCLEROTIN	SCLEROTINS
	SCLIFF	SCLIFFS
	SCLIM	SCLIMS
	SCOFF	SCOFFS
	SCOFFER	SCOFFERS
	SCOFFING	SCOFFINGS
	SCOFFLAW	SCOFFLAWS
	SCOG	SCOGS
	SCOINSON	SCOINSONS
	SCOLD	SCOLDS
	SCOLDER	SCOLDERS
	SCOLDING	SCOLDINGS
	SCOLECID	SCOLECIDS
	SCOLECITE	SCOLECITES
	SCOLIOMA	SCOLIOMAS
	SCOLLOP	SCOLLOPS
	SCOLYTID	SCOLYTIDS
	SCOLYTOID	SCOLYTOIDS
	SCOMBRID	SCOMBRIDS
	SCOMBROID	SCOMBROIDS
ASCONCE	SCONCE	SCONCED ▪ SCONCES
	SCONCHEON	SCONCHEONS
	SCONE	SCONES
	SCONTION	SCONTIONS
	SCOOG	SCOOGS
	SCOOP	SCOOPS
	SCOOPER	SCOOPERS
	SCOOPFUL	SCOOPFULS
	SCOOPING	SCOOPINGS
	SCOOT	SCOOTS
	SCOOTER	SCOOTERS
	SCOP	SCOPA ▪ SCOPE ▪ SCOPS
	SCOPA	SCOPAE ▪ SCOPAS
	SCOPE	SCOPED ▪ SCOPES
	SCOPELID	SCOPELIDS
	SCOPELOID	SCOPELOIDS
	SCOPOLINE	SCOPOLINES
	SCOPULA	SCOPULAE ▪ SCOPULAS
	SCORCHER	SCORCHERS
	SCORCHING	SCORCHINGS
	SCORE	SCORED ▪ SCORER ▪ SCORES
	SCORECARD	SCORECARDS

FRONT HOOK	ROOT WORD	END HOOK
	SCORELINE	SCORELINES
	SCOREPAD	SCOREPADS
	SCORER	SCORERS
	SCORIA	SCORIAC ▪ SCORIAE
	SCORIFIER	SCORIFIERS
	SCORING	SCORINGS
	SCORN	SCORNS
	SCORNER	SCORNERS
	SCORNING	SCORNINGS
	SCORODITE	SCORODITES
	SCORPER	SCORPERS
	SCORPIOID	SCORPIOIDS
	SCORPION	SCORPIONS
	SCORSE	SCORSED ▪ SCORSER ▪ SCORSES
	SCORSER	SCORSERS
ASCOT ▪ ESCOT	**SCOT**	SCOTS
	SCOTER	SCOTERS
	SCOTIA	SCOTIAS
	SCOTOMA	SCOTOMAS
	SCOTOMIA	SCOTOMIAS
	SCOTOPIA	SCOTOPIAS
ASCOTS ▪ ESCOTS	**SCOTS**	
	SCOTTIE	SCOTTIES
	SCOUG	SCOUGS
	SCOUNDREL	SCOUNDRELS
	SCOUP	SCOUPS
	SCOUR	SCOURS
	SCOURER	SCOURERS
	SCOURGE	SCOURGED ▪ SCOURGER ▪ SCOURGES
	SCOURGER	SCOURGERS
	SCOURIE	SCOURIES
	SCOURING	SCOURINGS
	SCOURS	SCOURSE
	SCOURSE	SCOURSED ▪ SCOURSES
	SCOUSE	SCOUSER ▪ SCOUSES
	SCOUSER	SCOUSERS
	SCOUT	SCOUTH ▪ SCOUTS
	SCOUTER	SCOUTERS
	SCOUTH	SCOUTHS
	SCOUTHER	SCOUTHERS ▪ SCOUTHERY
	SCOUTING	SCOUTINGS
	SCOW	SCOWL ▪ SCOWP ▪ SCOWS
	SCOWDER	SCOWDERS
	SCOWL	SCOWLS
	SCOWLER	SCOWLERS
	SCOWP	SCOWPS
	SCOWRER	SCOWRERS
	SCOWRIE	SCOWRIES
	SCOWTH	SCOWTHS
	SCOWTHER	SCOWTHERS
	SCOZZA	SCOZZAS
	SCRAB	SCRABS
	SCRABBLE	SCRABBLED ▪ SCRABBLER ▪ SCRABBLES
	SCRABBLER	SCRABBLERS
	SCRAE	SCRAES
	SCRAG	SCRAGS
	SCRAICH	SCRAICHS
	SCRAIGH	SCRAIGHS
	SCRAM	SCRAMB ▪ SCRAMS
	SCRAMB	SCRAMBS
	SCRAMBLE	SCRAMBLED ▪ SCRAMBLER ▪ SCRAMBLES
	SCRAMBLER	SCRAMBLERS
	SCRAMJET	SCRAMJETS
	SCRAN	SCRANS
	SCRANNEL	SCRANNELS
	SCRAP	SCRAPE ▪ SCRAPS
	SCRAPBOOK	SCRAPBOOKS
	SCRAPE	SCRAPED ▪ SCRAPER ▪ SCRAPES
	SCRAPEGUT	SCRAPEGUTS

FRONT HOOK	ROOT WORD	END HOOK
	SCRAPER	SCRAPERS
	SCRAPHEAP	SCRAPHEAPS
	SCRAPIE	SCRAPIES
	SCRAPING	SCRAPINGS
	SCRAPPAGE	SCRAPPAGES
	SCRAPPER	SCRAPPERS
	SCRAPPLE	SCRAPPLES
	SCRAPYARD	SCRAPYARDS
	SCRAT	SCRATS
	SCRATCH	SCRATCHY
	SCRATCHER	SCRATCHERS
	SCRATCHIE	SCRATCHIER · SCRATCHIES
	SCRATTLE	SCRATTLED · SCRATTLES
	SCRAUCH	SCRAUCHS
	SCRAUGH	SCRAUGHS
	SCRAW	SCRAWL · SCRAWM · SCRAWP · SCRAWS
	SCRAWL	SCRAWLS · SCRAWLY
	SCRAWLER	SCRAWLERS
	SCRAWLING	SCRAWLINGS
	SCRAWM	SCRAWMS
	SCRAWP	SCRAWPS
	SCRAY	SCRAYE · SCRAYS
	SCRAYE	SCRAYES
	SCREAK	SCREAKS · SCREAKY
	SCREAM	SCREAMS
	SCREAMER	SCREAMERS
	SCREE	SCREED · SCREEN · SCREES · SCREET
	SCREECH	SCREECHY
	SCREECHER	SCREECHERS
	SCREED	SCREEDS
	SCREEDER	SCREEDERS
	SCREEDING	SCREEDINGS
	SCREEN	SCREENS
	SCREENER	SCREENERS
	SCREENFUL	SCREENFULS
	SCREENIE	SCREENIES
	SCREENING	SCREENINGS
	SCREET	SCREETS
	SCREEVE	SCREEVED · SCREEVER · SCREEVES
	SCREEVER	SCREEVERS
	SCREEVING	SCREEVINGS
	SCREICH	SCREICHS
	SCREIGH	SCREIGHS
	SCREW	SCREWS · SCREWY
	SCREWBALL	SCREWBALLS
	SCREWBEAN	SCREWBEANS
	SCREWER	SCREWERS
	SCREWING	SCREWINGS
	SCREWTOP	SCREWTOPS
	SCREWUP	SCREWUPS
	SCREWWORM	SCREWWORMS
ASCRIBABLE	**SCRIBABLE**	
	SCRIBBLE	SCRIBBLED · SCRIBBLER · SCRIBBLES
	SCRIBBLER	SCRIBBLERS
ASCRIBE · ESCRIBE	**SCRIBE**	SCRIBED · SCRIBER · SCRIBES
ASCRIBED · ESCRIBED	**SCRIBED**	
	SCRIBER	SCRIBERS
ASCRIBES · ESCRIBES	**SCRIBES**	
ASCRIBING · ESCRIBING	**SCRIBING**	SCRIBINGS
	SCRIBISM	SCRIBISMS
	SCRIECH	SCRIECHS
	SCRIENE	SCRIENES
	SCRIEVE	SCRIEVED · SCRIEVES
	SCRIGGLE	SCRIGGLED · SCRIGGLES
	SCRIKE	SCRIKED · SCRIKES
	SCRIM	SCRIMP · SCRIMS
	SCRIMMAGE	SCRIMMAGED · SCRIMMAGER · SCRIMMAGES
	SCRIMP	SCRIMPS · SCRIMPY
	SCRIMPER	SCRIMPERS

FRONT HOOK	ROOT WORD	END HOOK
	SCRIMSHAW	SCRIMSHAWS
	SCRIMURE	SCRIMURES
	SCRINE	SCRINES
	SCRIP	SCRIPS · SCRIPT
	SCRIPPAGE	SCRIPPAGES
	SCRIPT	SCRIPTS
	SCRIPTER	SCRIPTERS
	SCRIPTURE	SCRIPTURES
	SCRIVE	SCRIVED · SCRIVES
	SCRIVENER	SCRIVENERS
	SCROBE	SCROBES
	SCROD	SCRODS
	SCROFULA	SCROFULAS
	SCROG	SCROGS
	SCROGGIE	SCROGGIER
	SCROGGIN	SCROGGINS
ESCROLL	SCROLL	SCROLLS
ESCROLLS	SCROLLS	
	SCROME	SCROMED · SCROMES
	SCROOGE	SCROOGED · SCROOGES
	SCROOP	SCROOPS
	SCRORP	SCRORPS
	SCROTA	SCROTAL
	SCROTE	SCROTES (offensive)
	SCROTUM	SCROTUMS
	SCROUGE	SCROUGED · SCROUGER · SCROUGES
	SCROUGER	SCROUGERS
	SCROUNGE	SCROUNGED · SCROUNGER · SCROUNGES
	SCROUNGER	SCROUNGERS
ESCROW	SCROW	SCROWL · SCROWS
	SCROWDGE	SCROWDGED · SCROWDGES
	SCROWL	SCROWLE · SCROWLS
	SCROWLE	SCROWLED · SCROWLES
ESCROWS	SCROWS	
	SCROYLE	SCROYLES
	SCRUB	SCRUBS
	SCRUBBER	SCRUBBERS (offensive)
	SCRUBBING	SCRUBBINGS
	SCRUBLAND	SCRUBLANDS
	SCRUFF	SCRUFFS · SCRUFFY
	SCRUM	SCRUMP · SCRUMS
	SCRUMDOWN	SCRUMDOWNS
	SCRUMMAGE	SCRUMMAGED · SCRUMMAGER · SCRUMMAGES
	SCRUMMIE	SCRUMMIER · SCRUMMIES
	SCRUMMIES	SCRUMMIEST
	SCRUMP	SCRUMPS · SCRUMPY
	SCRUMPLE	SCRUMPLED · SCRUMPLES
	SCRUNCH	SCRUNCHY
	SCRUNCHIE	SCRUNCHIER · SCRUNCHIES
	SCRUNT	SCRUNTS · SCRUNTY
	SCRUPLE	SCRUPLED · SCRUPLER · SCRUPLES
	SCRUPLER	SCRUPLERS ·
	SCRUTATOR	SCRUTATORS
	SCRUTO	SCRUTOS
	SCRUTOIRE	SCRUTOIRES
	SCRUZE	SCRUZED · SCRUZES
	SCRYER	SCRYERS
	SCRYING	SCRYINGS
	SCRYNE	SCRYNES
	SCUBA	SCUBAS
	SCUCHIN	SCUCHINS
	SCUD	SCUDI · SCUDO · SCUDS
	SCUDDALER	SCUDDALERS
	SCUDDER	SCUDDERS
	SCUDDLE	SCUDDLED · SCUDDLES
	SCUDLER	SCUDLERS
ESCUDO	SCUDO	
	SCUFF	SCUFFS
	SCUFFER	SCUFFERS

S

FRONT HOOK	ROOT WORD	END HOOK
	SCUFFLE	SCUFFLED ▪ SCUFFLER ▪ SCUFFLES
	SCUFFLER	SCUFFLERS
	SCUFT	SCUFTS
	SCUG	SCUGS
	SCUL	SCULK ▪ SCULL ▪ SCULP ▪ SCULS
	SCULK	SCULKS
	SCULKER	SCULKERS
	SCULL	SCULLE ▪ SCULLS
	SCULLE	SCULLED ▪ SCULLER ▪ SCULLES
	SCULLER	SCULLERS ▪ SCULLERY
	SCULLING	SCULLINGS
	SCULLION	SCULLIONS
	SCULP	SCULPS ▪ SCULPT
	SCULPIN	SCULPING ▪ SCULPINS
	SCULPT	SCULPTS
	SCULPTOR	SCULPTORS
	SCULPTURE	SCULPTURED ▪ SCULPTURES
	SCUM	SCUMS
	SCUMBAG	SCUMBAGS (offensive)
	SCUMBER	SCUMBERS
	SCUMBLE	SCUMBLED ▪ SCUMBLES
	SCUMBLING	SCUMBLINGS
	SCUMMER	SCUMMERS
	SCUMMING	SCUMMINGS
	SCUNCHEON	SCUNCHEONS
	SCUNGE	SCUNGED ▪ SCUNGES
	SCUNGILLI	SCUNGILLIS
	SCUNNER	SCUNNERS
	SCUP	SCUPS
	SCUPPAUG	SCUPPAUGS
	SCUPPER	SCUPPERS
	SCUR	SCURF ▪ SCURS
	SCURF	SCURFS ▪ SCURFY
	SCURRIER	SCURRIERS
	SCURRIL	SCURRILE
	SCURRIOUR	SCURRIOURS
	SCURVIES	SCURVIEST
	SCUSE	SCUSED ▪ SCUSES
	SCUT	SCUTA ▪ SCUTE ▪ SCUTS
	SCUTA	SCUTAL
	SCUTAGE	SCUTAGES
	SCUTATION	SCUTATIONS
ESCUTCHEON	**SCUTCHEON**	SCUTCHEONS
	SCUTCHER	SCUTCHERS
	SCUTCHING	SCUTCHINGS
	SCUTE	SCUTES
	SCUTELLA	SCUTELLAR
	SCUTIGER	SCUTIGERS
	SCUTTER	SCUTTERS
	SCUTTLE	SCUTTLED ▪ SCUTTLER ▪ SCUTTLES
	SCUTTLER	SCUTTLERS
	SCUTWORK	SCUTWORKS
	SCUZZ	SCUZZY
	SCUZZBALL	SCUZZBALLS
	SCYE	SCYES
	SCYTALE	SCYTALES
	SCYTHE	SCYTHED ▪ SCYTHER ▪ SCYTHES
	SCYTHER	SCYTHERS
	SDAINE	SDAINED ▪ SDAINES
	SDAYN	SDAYNS
	SDEIGN	SDEIGNE ▪ SDEIGNS
	SDEIGNE	SDEIGNED ▪ SDEIGNES
	SDEIN	SDEINS
ASEA	**SEA**	SEAL ▪ SEAM ▪ SEAN ▪ SEAR ▪ SEAS ▪ SEAT
	SEABAG	SEABAGS
	SEABANK	SEABANKS
	SEABED	SEABEDS
	SEABIRD	SEABIRDS
	SEABLITE	SEABLITES

S

FRONT HOOK	ROOT WORD	END HOOK
	SEABOARD	SEABOARDS
	SEABOOT	SEABOOTS
	SEABOTTLE	SEABOTTLES
	SEACOAST	SEACOASTS
	SEACOCK	SEACOCKS
	SEACRAFT	SEACRAFTS
	SEADOG	SEADOGS
	SEADROME	SEADROMES
	SEAFARER	SEAFARERS
	SEAFARING	SEAFARINGS
	SEAFLOOR	SEAFLOORS
	SEAFOLK	SEAFOLKS
	SEAFOOD	SEAFOODS
	SEAFOWL	SEAFOWLS
	SEAFRONT	SEAFRONTS
	SEAGULL	SEAGULLS
	SEAHAWK	SEAHAWKS
	SEAHOG	SEAHOGS
	SEAHORSE	SEAHORSES
	SEAHOUND	SEAHOUNDS
	SEAKALE	SEAKALES
	SEAL	SEALS
	SEALANT	SEALANTS
	SEALCH	SEALCHS
	SEALER	SEALERS ▪ SEALERY
	SEALGH	SEALGHS
	SEALIFT	SEALIFTS
	SEALINE	SEALINES
	SEALING	SEALINGS
	SEALPOINT	SEALPOINTS
	SEALSKIN	SEALSKINS
	SEALYHAM	SEALYHAMS
	SEAM	SEAME ▪ SEAMS ▪ SEAMY
	SEAMAID	SEAMAIDS
	SEAMARK	SEAMARKS
	SEAME	SEAMED ▪ SEAMEN ▪ SEAMER ▪ SEAMES
	SEAMER	SEAMERS
	SEAMOUNT	SEAMOUNTS
	SEAMSET	SEAMSETS
	SEAMSTER	SEAMSTERS
	SEAN	SEANS
	SEANCE	SEANCES
	SEAPIECE	SEAPIECES
	SEAPLANE	SEAPLANES
	SEAPORT	SEAPORTS
	SEAQUAKE	SEAQUAKES
	SEAR	SEARE ▪ SEARS
	SEARAT	SEARATS
	SEARCE	SEARCED ▪ SEARCES
	SEARCHER	SEARCHERS
	SEARE	SEARED ▪ SEARER
	SEARING	SEARINGS
	SEAROBIN	SEAROBINS
	SEAS	SEASE
	SEASCAPE	SEASCAPES
	SEASCOUT	SEASCOUTS
	SEASE	SEASED ▪ SEASES
	SEASHELL	SEASHELLS
	SEASHORE	SEASHORES
	SEASIDE	SEASIDES
	SEASON	SEASONS
	SEASONAL	SEASONALS
	SEASONER	SEASONERS
	SEASONING	SEASONINGS
	SEASPEAK	SEASPEAKS
	SEASTRAND	SEASTRANDS
	SEASURE	SEASURES
	SEAT	SEATS
	SEATBACK	SEATBACKS

S

FRONT HOOK	ROOT WORD	END HOOK
	SEATBELT	SEATBELTS
	SEATER	SEATERS
	SEATING	SEATINGS
	SEATMATE	SEATMATES
	SEATRAIN	SEATRAINS
	SEATROUT	SEATROUTS
	SEATWORK	SEATWORKS
	SEAWALL	SEAWALLS
	SEAWAN	SEAWANS · SEAWANT
	SEAWANT	SEAWANTS
	SEAWARD	SEAWARDS
	SEAWARE	SEAWARES
	SEAWATER	SEAWATERS
	SEAWAY	SEAWAYS
	SEAWEED	SEAWEEDS
	SEAWORM	SEAWORMS
	SEAZE	SEAZED · SEAZES
	SEBATE	SEBATES
	SEBESTEN	SEBESTENS
	SEBORRHEA	SEBORRHEAL · SEBORRHEAS
	SEBUM	SEBUMS
	SEC	SECH · SECO · SECS · SECT
	SECALOSE	SECALOSES
	SECANT	SECANTS
	SECATEUR	SECATEURS
	SECCO	SECCOS
	SECEDE	SECEDED · SECEDER · SECEDES
	SECEDER	SECEDERS
	SECERN	SECERNS
	SECERNENT	SECERNENTS
	SECESHER	SECESHERS
	SECESSION	SECESSIONS
	SECH	SECHS
	SECKEL	SECKELS
	SECKLE	SECKLES
	SECLUDE	SECLUDED · SECLUDES
	SECLUSION	SECLUSIONS
	SECODONT	SECODONTS
	SECONAL	SECONALS
	SECOND	SECONDE · SECONDI · SECONDO · SECONDS
	SECONDE	SECONDED · SECONDEE · SECONDER
		SECONDES
	SECONDEE	SECONDEES
	SECONDER	SECONDERS
	SECPAR	SECPARS
	SECRET	SECRETA · SECRETE · SECRETS
	SECRETAGE	SECRETAGES
	SECRETE	SECRETED · SECRETER · SECRETES
	SECRETES	SECRETEST
	SECRETIN	SECRETING · SECRETINS
	SECRETION	SECRETIONS
	SECRETOR	SECRETORS · SECRETORY
	SECT	SECTS
	SECTARIAN	SECTARIANS
	SECTATOR	SECTATORS
	SECTION	SECTIONS
	SECTIONAL	SECTIONALS
	SECTOR	SECTORS
	SECTORIAL	SECTORIALS
	SECTORISE	SECTORISED · SECTORISES
	SECTORIZE	SECTORIZED · SECTORIZES
	SECULAR	SECULARS
	SECULUM	SECULUMS
	SECUNDINE	SECUNDINES
	SECURANCE	SECURANCES
	SECURE	SECURED · SECURER · SECURES
	SECURER	SECURERS
	SECURES	SECUREST
	SECURITAN	SECURITANS

S

FRONT HOOK	ROOT WORD	END HOOK
USED	**SED**	
	SEDAN	SEDANS
	SEDATE	SEDATED · SEDATER · SEDATES
	SEDATES	SEDATEST
	SEDATION	SEDATIONS
	SEDATIVE	SEDATIVES
	SEDER	SEDERS
	SEDERUNT	SEDERUNTS
	SEDGE	SEDGED · SEDGES
	SEDGELAND	SEDGELANDS
	SEDIMENT	SEDIMENTS
	SEDITION	SEDITIONS
	SEDUCE	SEDUCED · SEDUCER · SEDUCES
	SEDUCER	SEDUCERS
	SEDUCING	SEDUCINGS
	SEDUCTION	SEDUCTIONS
	SEDUCTOR	SEDUCTORS
	SEDUM	SEDUMS
	SEE	SEED · SEEK · SEEL · SEEM · SEEN
		SEEP · SEER · SEES
	SEED	SEEDS · SEEDY
	SEEDBED	SEEDBEDS
	SEEDCAKE	SEEDCAKES
	SEEDCASE	SEEDCASES
	SEEDEATER	SEEDEATERS
	SEEDER	SEEDERS
	SEEDING	SEEDINGS
	SEEDLING	SEEDLINGS
	SEEDLIP	SEEDLIPS
	SEEDPOD	SEEDPODS
	SEEDSTOCK	SEEDSTOCKS
	SEEDTIME	SEEDTIMES
	SEEING	SEEINGS
	SEEK	SEEKS
	SEEKER	SEEKERS
	SEEL	SEELD · SEELS · SEELY
	SEELIE	SEELIER
	SEELING	SEELINGS
	SEEM	SEEMS
	SEEMER	SEEMERS
	SEEMING	SEEMINGS
	SEEMLIHED	SEEMLIHEDS
	SEEMLYHED	SEEMLYHEDS
	SEEP	SEEPS · SEEPY
	SEEPAGE	SEEPAGES
	SEER	SEERS
	SEESAW	SEESAWS
	SEETHE	SEETHED · SEETHER · SEETHES
	SEETHER	SEETHERS
	SEETHING	SEETHINGS
	SEG	SEGO · SEGS
	SEGAR	SEGARS
	SEGGAR	SEGGARS
	SEGHOL	SEGHOLS
	SEGHOLATE	SEGHOLATES
	SEGMENT	SEGMENTS
	SEGNO	SEGNOS
	SEGO	SEGOL · SEGOS
	SEGOL	SEGOLS
	SEGOLATE	SEGOLATES
	SEGREGANT	SEGREGANTS
	SEGREGATE	SEGREGATED · SEGREGATES
	SEGUE	SEGUED · SEGUES
	SEI	SEIF · SEIK · SEIL · SEIR · SEIS
	SEICENTO	SEICENTOS
	SEICHE	SEICHES
	SEIDEL	SEIDELS
	SEIF	SEIFS
	SEIGNEUR	SEIGNEURS · SEIGNEURY

FRONT HOOK	ROOT WORD	END HOOK
	SEIGNIOR	SEIGNIORS · SEIGNIORY
	SEIL	SEILS
	SEINE	SEINED · SEINER · SEINES
	SEINER	SEINERS
	SEINING	SEININGS
	SEIR	SEIRS
	SEIS	SEISE · SEISM
	SEISE	SEISED · SEISER · SEISES
	SEISER	SEISERS
	SEISIN	SEISING · SEISINS
	SEISING	SEISINGS
	SEISM	SEISMS
ASEISMIC	**SEISMIC**	
	SEISMISM	SEISMISMS
	SEISOR	SEISORS
	SEISURE	SEISURES
	SEITAN	SEITANS
	SEITEN	SEITENS
ASEITIES	**SEITIES**	
ASEITY	**SEITY**	
	SEIZE	SEIZED · SEIZER · SEIZES
	SEIZER	SEIZERS
	SEIZIN	SEIZING · SEIZINS
	SEIZING	SEIZINGS
	SEIZOR	SEIZORS
	SEIZURE	SEIZURES
	SEKT	SEKTS
	SEL	SELD · SELE · SELF · SELL · SELS
	SELACHIAN	SELACHIANS
	SELADANG	SELADANGS
	SELAH	SELAHS
	SELAMLIK	SELAMLIKS
	SELE	SELES
	SELECT	SELECTA · SELECTS
	SELECTA	SELECTAS
	SELECTEE	SELECTEES
	SELECTION	SELECTIONS
	SELECTOR	SELECTORS
	SELENATE	SELENATES
	SELENIDE	SELENIDES
	SELENITE	SELENITES
	SELENIUM	SELENIUMS
	SELF	SELFS
	SELFDOM	SELFDOMS
	SELFHEAL	SELFHEALS
	SELFHOOD	SELFHOODS
	SELFING	SELFINGS
	SELFISM	SELFISMS
	SELFIST	SELFISTS
	SELFWARD	SELFWARDS
	SELICTAR	SELICTARS
	SELKIE	SELKIES
	SELL	SELLA · SELLE · SELLS
	SELLA	SELLAE · SELLAS
	SELLE	SELLER · SELLES
	SELLER	SELLERS
	SELLOFF	SELLOFFS
	SELLOTAPE	SELLOTAPED · SELLOTAPES
	SELLOUT	SELLOUTS
	SELSYN	SELSYNS
	SELTZER	SELTZERS
	SELVA	SELVAS
	SELVAGE	SELVAGED · SELVAGEE · SELVAGES
	SELVAGEE	SELVAGEES
	SELVEDGE	SELVEDGED · SELVEDGES
	SEMAINIER	SEMAINIERS
	SEMANTEME	SEMANTEMES
	SEMANTIC	SEMANTICS
	SEMANTIDE	SEMANTIDES

FRONT HOOK	ROOT WORD	END HOOK
	SEMAPHORE	SEMAPHORED · SEMAPHORES
	SEMBLABLE	SEMBLABLES
	SEMBLANCE	SEMBLANCES
	SEMBLANT	SEMBLANTS
	SEMBLE	SEMBLED · SEMBLES
	SEME	SEMEE · SEMEN · SEMES
	SEMEE	SEMEED
	SEMEIOTIC	SEMEIOTICS
	SEMEME	SEMEMES
	SEMEN	SEMENS
	SEMESTER	SEMESTERS
	SEMI	SEMIE · SEMIS
	SEMIANGLE	SEMIANGLES
	SEMIBOLD	SEMIBOLDS
	SEMIBREVE	SEMIBREVES
	SEMIBULL	SEMIBULLS
	SEMICOLON	SEMICOLONS · SEMICOLONY
	SEMICOMA	SEMICOMAS
	SEMIDOME	SEMIDOMED · SEMIDOMES
	SEMIDWARF	SEMIDWARFS
	SEMIE	SEMIES
	SEMIFINAL	SEMIFINALS
	SEMIFLUID	SEMIFLUIDS
	SEMIGROUP	SEMIGROUPS
	SEMIHOBO	SEMIHOBOS
	SEMILLON	SEMILLONS
	SEMILUNE	SEMILUNES
	SEMIMAT	SEMIMATT
	SEMIMATT	SEMIMATTE
	SEMIMETAL	SEMIMETALS
	SEMINA	SEMINAL · SEMINAR
	SEMINAR	SEMINARS · SEMINARY
	SEMINATE	SEMINATED · SEMINATES
	SEMINOMA	SEMINOMAD · SEMINOMAS
	SEMINOMAD	SEMINOMADS
	SEMIOTIC	SEMIOTICS
	SEMIPED	SEMIPEDS
	SEMIPLUME	SEMIPLUMES
	SEMIPRO	SEMIPROS
	SEMIROUND	SEMIROUNDS
	SEMISOLID	SEMISOLIDS
	SEMITAR	SEMITARS
	SEMITAUR	SEMITAURS
	SEMITIST	SEMITISTS
	SEMITONE	SEMITONES
	SEMITRUCK	SEMITRUCKS
	SEMIVOWEL	SEMIVOWELS
	SEMMIT	SEMMITS
	SEMOLINA	SEMOLINAS
	SEMPLE	SEMPLER
	SEMPSTER	SEMPSTERS
	SEMSEM	SEMSEMS
	SEMUNCIA	SEMUNCIAE · SEMUNCIAL · SEMUNCIAS
	SEN	SENA · SEND · SENE · SENS · SENT
	SENA	SENAS
	SENATE	SENATES
	SENATOR	SENATORS
	SEND	SENDS
	SENDAL	SENDALS
	SENDER	SENDERS
	SENDING	SENDINGS
	SENDOFF	SENDOFFS
	SENDUP	SENDUPS
	SENECA	SENECAS
	SENECIO	SENECIOS
	SENEGA	SENEGAS
	SENESCHAL	SENESCHALS
	SENGREEN	SENGREENS
	SENHOR	SENHORA · SENHORS

FRONT HOOK	ROOT WORD	END HOOK
	SENHORA	SENHORAS
	SENHORITA	SENHORITAS
	SENILE	SENILES
	SENIOR	SENIORS
	SENNA	SENNAS
	SENNACHIE	SENNACHIES
	SENNET	SENNETS
	SENNIGHT	SENNIGHTS
	SENNIT	SENNITS
	SENOPIA	SENOPIAS
	SENOR	SENORA ▪ SENORS
	SENORA	SENORAS
	SENORITA	SENORITAS
	SENS	SENSA ▪ SENSE ▪ SENSI
	SENSATE	SENSATED ▪ SENSATES
	SENSATION	SENSATIONS
	SENSE	SENSED ▪ SENSEI ▪ SENSES
	SENSEI	SENSEIS
	SENSI	SENSIS
	SENSIBLE	SENSIBLER ▪ SENSIBLES
	SENSIBLES	SENSIBLEST
	SENSILLA	SENSILLAE
	SENSING	SENSINGS
	SENSIS	SENSISM ▪ SENSIST
	SENSISM	SENSISMS
	SENSIST	SENSISTS
	SENSITISE	SENSITISED ▪ SENSITISER ▪ SENSITISES
	SENSITIVE	SENSITIVES
	SENSITIZE	SENSITIZED ▪ SENSITIZER ▪ SENSITIZES
	SENSOR	SENSORS ▪ SENSORY
	SENSORIA	SENSORIAL
	SENSORIUM	SENSORIUMS
	SENT	SENTE ▪ SENTI ▪ SENTS
	SENTE	SENTED
	SENTENCE	SENTENCED ▪ SENTENCER ▪ SENTENCES
	SENTENCER	SENTENCERS
	SENTENTIA	SENTENTIAE ▪ SENTENTIAL
	SENTIENCE	SENTIENCES
	SENTIENT	SENTIENTS
	SENTIMENT	SENTIMENTS
	SENTIMO	SENTIMOS
	SENTINEL	SENTINELS
	SEPAD	SEPADS
	SEPAL	SEPALS
ASEPALOUS	**SEPALOUS**	
	SEPARATE	SEPARATED ▪ SEPARATES
	SEPARATOR	SEPARATORS ▪ SEPARATORY
	SEPARATUM	SEPARATUMS
	SEPHEN	SEPHENS
	SEPIA	SEPIAS
	SEPIMENT	SEPIMENTS
	SEPIOLITE	SEPIOLITES
	SEPIOST	SEPIOSTS
	SEPIUM	SEPIUMS
	SEPOY	SEPOYS
	SEPPUKU	SEPPUKUS
ASEPSES	**SEPSES**	
ASEPSIS	**SEPSIS**	
	SEPT	SEPTA ▪ SEPTS
	SEPTA	SEPTAL
	SEPTAGE	SEPTAGES
	SEPTARIA	SEPTARIAN
ASEPTATE	**SEPTATE**	
	SEPTATION	SEPTATIONS
	SEPTEMVIR	SEPTEMVIRI ▪ SEPTEMVIRS
	SEPTENNIA	SEPTENNIAL
	SEPTET	SEPTETS
	SEPTETTE	SEPTETTES
ASEPTIC	**SEPTIC**	SEPTICS

FRONT HOOK	ROOT WORD	END HOOK
ASEPTICS	**SEPTICS**	
	SEPTIME	SEPTIMES
	SEPTIMOLE	SEPTIMOLES
	SEPTLEVA	SEPTLEVAS
	SEPTUM	SEPTUMS
	SEPTUOR	SEPTUORS
	SEPTUPLE	SEPTUPLED · SEPTUPLES · SEPTUPLET
	SEPTUPLET	SEPTUPLETS
	SEPULCHER	SEPULCHERS
	SEPULCHRE	SEPULCHRED · SEPULCHRES
	SEPULTURE	SEPULTURED · SEPULTURES
	SEQUEL	SEQUELA · SEQUELS
	SEQUELA	SEQUELAE
	SEQUELISE	SEQUELISED · SEQUELISES
	SEQUELIZE	SEQUELIZED · SEQUELIZES
	SEQUENCE	SEQUENCED · SEQUENCER · SEQUENCES
	SEQUENCER	SEQUENCERS
	SEQUENT	SEQUENTS
	SEQUESTER	SEQUESTERS
	SEQUESTRA	SEQUESTRAL
	SEQUIN	SEQUINS
	SEQUITUR	SEQUITURS
	SEQUOIA	SEQUOIAS
USER	**SER**	SERA · SERE · SERF · SERK · SERR · SERS
	SERA	SERAC · SERAI · SERAL
	SERAC	SERACS
	SERAFILE	SERAFILES
	SERAFIN	SERAFINS
	SERAGLIO	SERAGLIOS
	SERAI	SERAIL · SERAIS
	SERAIL	SERAILS
	SERANG	SERANGS
	SERAPE	SERAPES
	SERAPH	SERAPHS
	SERAPHIM	SERAPHIMS
	SERAPHIN	SERAPHINE · SERAPHINS
	SERAPHINE	SERAPHINES
	SERASKIER	SERASKIERS
	SERDAB	SERDABS
	SERE	SERED · SERER · SERES
	SEREIN	SEREINS
	SERENADE	SERENADED · SERENADER · SERENADES
	SERENADER	SERENADERS
	SERENATA	SERENATAS
	SERENATE	SERENATES
	SERENE	SERENED · SERENER · SERENES
	SERENES	SERENEST
	SERES	SEREST
	SERF	SERFS
	SERFAGE	SERFAGES
	SERFDOM	SERFDOMS
	SERFHOOD	SERFHOODS
	SERFSHIP	SERFSHIPS
	SERGE	SERGED · SERGER · SERGES
	SERGEANT	SERGEANTS · SERGEANTY
	SERGER	SERGERS
	SERGING	SERGINGS
	SERIAL	SERIALS
	SERIALISE	SERIALISED · SERIALISES
	SERIALISM	SERIALISMS
	SERIALIST	SERIALISTS
	SERIALIZE	SERIALIZED · SERIALIZES
	SERIATE	SERIATED · SERIATES
	SERIATION	SERIATIONS
	SERICIN	SERICINS
	SERICITE	SERICITES
	SERICON	SERICONS
	SERIEMA	SERIEMAS
	SERIF	SERIFS

FRONT HOOK	ROOT WORD	END HOOK
	SERIGRAPH	SERIGRAPHS · SERIGRAPHY
	SERIN	SERINE · SERING · SERINS
ESERINE	**SERINE**	SERINES
ESERINES	**SERINES**	
	SERINETTE	SERINETTES
	SERING	SERINGA
	SERINGA	SERINGAS
	SERIPH	SERIPHS
	SERJEANT	SERJEANTS · SERJEANTY
	SERK	SERKS
	SERKALI	SERKALIS
	SERMON	SERMONS
	SERMONEER	SERMONEERS
	SERMONER	SERMONERS
	SERMONET	SERMONETS
	SERMONING	SERMONINGS
	SERMONISE	SERMONISED · SERMONISER · SERMONISES
	SERMONIZE	SERMONIZED · SERMONIZER · SERMONIZES
	SERON	SERONS
	SEROON	SEROONS
	SEROSA	SEROSAE · SEROSAL · SEROSAS
	SEROTINE	SEROTINES
	SEROTONIN	SEROTONINS
	SEROTYPE	SEROTYPED · SEROTYPES
	SEROVAR	SEROVARS
	SEROW	SEROWS
	SERPENT	SERPENTS
	SERPIGO	SERPIGOS
	SERPULA	SERPULAE
	SERPULID	SERPULIDS
	SERPULITE	SERPULITES
	SERR	SERRA · SERRE · SERRS · SERRY
	SERRA	SERRAE · SERRAN · SERRAS
	SERRAN	SERRANO · SERRANS
	SERRANID	SERRANIDS
	SERRANO	SERRANOS
	SERRANOID	SERRANOIDS
	SERRATE	SERRATED · SERRATES
	SERRATION	SERRATIONS
	SERRATURE	SERRATURES
	SERRE	SERRED · SERRES
	SERREFILE	SERREFILES
	SERRULATE	SERRULATED
USERS	**SERS**	
	SERUEWE	SERUEWED · SERUEWES
	SERUM	SERUMS
	SERVAL	SERVALS
	SERVANT	SERVANTS
	SERVE	SERVED · SERVER · SERVES
	SERVER	SERVERS · SERVERY
	SERVEWE	SERVEWED · SERVEWES
	SERVICE	SERVICED · SERVICER · SERVICES
	SERVICER	SERVICERS
	SERVIETTE	SERVIETTES
	SERVILE	SERVILES
	SERVILISM	SERVILISMS
	SERVING	SERVINGS
	SERVITOR	SERVITORS
	SERVITUDE	SERVITUDES
	SERVLET	SERVLETS
	SERVO	SERVOS
	SERVQUAL	SERVQUALS
	SESAME	SESAMES
	SESAMOID	SESAMOIDS
	SESE	SESEY
	SESELI	SESELIS
	SESS	SESSA
	SESSION	SESSIONS
	SESSPOOL	SESSPOOLS

FRONT HOOK	ROOT WORD	END HOOK
	SESTERCE	SESTERCES
	SESTET	SESTETS · SESTETT
	SESTETT	SESTETTE · SESTETTO · SESTETTS
	SESTETTE	SESTETTES
	SESTETTO	SESTETTOS
	SESTINA	SESTINAS
	SESTINE	SESTINES
	SESTON	SESTONS
	SET	SETA · SETS · SETT
	SETA	SETAE · SETAL
	SETBACK	SETBACKS
	SETENANT	SETENANTS
	SETLINE	SETLINES
	SETOFF	SETOFFS
	SETON	SETONS
	SETOUT	SETOUTS
	SETSCREW	SETSCREWS
	SETT	SETTS
	SETTEE	SETTEES
	SETTER	SETTERS
	SETTING	SETTINGS
	SETTLE	SETTLED · SETTLER · SETTLES
	SETTLER	SETTLERS
	SETTLING	SETTLINGS
	SETTLOR	SETTLORS
	SETUALE	SETUALES
	SETULE	SETULES
	SETUP	SETUPS
	SETWALL	SETWALLS
	SEVEN	SEVENS
	SEVENTEEN	SEVENTEENS
	SEVENTH	SEVENTHS
	SEVER	SEVERE · SEVERS · SEVERY
	SEVERAL	SEVERALS
	SEVERANCE	SEVERANCES
	SEVERE	SEVERED · SEVERER
	SEVICHE	SEVICHES
	SEVRUGA	SEVRUGAS
	SEW	SEWN · SEWS
	SEWAGE	SEWAGES
	SEWAN	SEWANS
	SEWAR	SEWARS
	SEWEL	SEWELS
	SEWELLEL	SEWELLELS
	SEWEN	SEWENS
	SEWER	SEWERS
	SEWERAGE	SEWERAGES
	SEWERING	SEWERINGS
	SEWIN	SEWING · SEWINS
	SEWING	SEWINGS
	SEX	SEXT · SEXY
	SEXAHOLIC	SEXAHOLICS
	SEXENNIAL	SEXENNIALS
	SEXER	SEXERS
	SEXERCISE	SEXERCISES
	SEXFOIL	SEXFOILS
	SEXISM	SEXISMS
	SEXIST	SEXISTS
	SEXPERT	SEXPERTS
	SEXPOT	SEXPOTS
	SEXT	SEXTO · SEXTS
	SEXTAIN	SEXTAINS
	SEXTAN	SEXTANS · SEXTANT
	SEXTANT	SEXTANTS
	SEXTET	SEXTETS · SEXTETT
	SEXTETT	SEXTETTE · SEXTETTS
	SEXTETTE	SEXTETTES
	SEXTILE	SEXTILES
	SEXTO	SEXTON · SEXTOS

FRONT HOOK	ROOT WORD	END HOOK
	SEXTOLET	SEXTOLETS
	SEXTON	SEXTONS
	SEXTUOR	SEXTUORS
	SEXTUPLE	SEXTUPLED ▪ SEXTUPLES ▪ SEXTUPLET
	SEXTUPLET	SEXTUPLETS
ASEXUAL	**SEXUAL**	
	SEXUALISE	SEXUALISED ▪ SEXUALISES
	SEXUALISM	SEXUALISMS
	SEXUALIST	SEXUALISTS
ASEXUALITY	**SEXUALITY**	
	SEXUALIZE	SEXUALIZED ▪ SEXUALIZES
ASEXUALLY	**SEXUALLY**	
	SEY	SEYS
	SEYEN	SEYENS
	SEYSURE	SEYSURES
	SFORZANDO	SFORZANDOS
	SFORZATO	SFORZATOS
	SFUMATO	SFUMATOS
ASH ▪ ISH	**SH**	SHA ▪ SHE ▪ SHH ▪ SHY
	SHA	SHAD ▪ SHAG ▪ SHAH ▪ SHAM ▪ SHAN
		SHAT (offensive) ▪ SHAW ▪ SHAY
	SHABBLE	SHABBLES
	SHABRACK	SHABRACKS
	SHACK	SHACKO ▪ SHACKS
	SHACKLE	SHACKLED ▪ SHACKLER ▪ SHACKLES
	SHACKLER	SHACKLERS
	SHACKO	SHACKOS
	SHAD	SHADE ▪ SHADS ▪ SHADY
	SHADBLOW	SHADBLOWS
	SHADCHAN	SHADCHANS
	SHADDOCK	SHADDOCKS
	SHADE	SHADED ▪ SHADER ▪ SHADES
	SHADER	SHADERS
	SHADING	SHADINGS
	SHADKHAN	SHADKHANS
	SHADOOF	SHADOOFS
	SHADOW	SHADOWS ▪ SHADOWY
	SHADOWER	SHADOWERS
	SHADOWING	SHADOWINGS
	SHADRACH	SHADRACHS
	SHADUF	SHADUFS
	SHAFT	SHAFTS
	SHAFTER	SHAFTERS
	SHAFTING	SHAFTINGS
	SHAG	SHAGS (offensive)
	SHAGBARK	SHAGBARKS
	SHAGREEN	SHAGREENS
	SHAGROON	SHAGROONS
	SHAH	SHAHS
	SHAHADA	SHAHADAS
	SHAHDOM	SHAHDOMS
	SHAIKH	SHAIKHS
	SHAIRD	SHAIRDS
	SHAIRN	SHAIRNS
	SHAITAN	SHAITANS
ASHAKE	**SHAKE**	SHAKED ▪ SHAKEN ▪ SHAKER ▪ SHAKES
	SHAKEDOWN	SHAKEDOWNS
	SHAKEOUT	SHAKEOUTS
	SHAKER	SHAKERS
	SHAKEUP	SHAKEUPS
	SHAKING	SHAKINGS
	SHAKO	SHAKOS
	SHAKUDO	SHAKUDOS
	SHALE	SHALED ▪ SHALES ▪ SHALEY
	SHALL	SHALLI
	SHALLI	SHALLIS
	SHALLON	SHALLONS
	SHALLOON	SHALLOONS
	SHALLOP	SHALLOPS

FRONT HOOK	ROOT WORD	END HOOK
	SHALLOT	SHALLOTS
	SHALLOW	SHALLOWS
	SHALM	SHALMS
	SHALOM	SHALOMS
	SHALOT	SHALOTS
	SHALWAR	SHALWARS
	SHAM	SHAMA ▪ SHAME ▪ SHAMS
	SHAMA	SHAMAN ▪ SHAMAS
	SHAMAN	SHAMANS
	SHAMANISM	SHAMANISMS
	SHAMANIST	SHAMANISTS
	SHAMATEUR	SHAMATEURS
	SHAMBA	SHAMBAS
	SHAMBLE	SHAMBLED ▪ SHAMBLES
	SHAMBLING	SHAMBLINGS
ASHAME	**SHAME**	SHAMED ▪ SHAMER ▪ SHAMES
ASHAMED	**SHAMED**	
	SHAMER	SHAMERS
ASHAMES	**SHAMES**	
	SHAMIANA	SHAMIANAH ▪ SHAMIANAS
	SHAMIANAH	SHAMIANAHS
	SHAMINA	SHAMINAS
ASHAMING	**SHAMING**	
	SHAMISEN	SHAMISENS
	SHAMMAS	SHAMMASH
	SHAMMER	SHAMMERS
	SHAMOY	SHAMOYS
	SHAMPOO	SHAMPOOS
	SHAMPOOER	SHAMPOOERS
	SHAMROCK	SHAMROCKS
	SHAN	SHAND ▪ SHANK ▪ SHANS
	SHANACHIE	SHANACHIES
	SHAND	SHANDS ▪ SHANDY
	SHANGHAI	SHANGHAIS
	SHANK	SHANKS
	SHANKBONE	SHANKBONES
	SHANTEY	SHANTEYS
	SHANTI	SHANTIH ▪ SHANTIS
	SHANTIH	SHANTIHS
	SHANTUNG	SHANTUNGS
	SHAPE	SHAPED ▪ SHAPEN ▪ SHAPER ▪ SHAPES
	SHAPER	SHAPERS
	SHAPEUP	SHAPEUPS
	SHAPING	SHAPINGS
	SHARD	SHARDS
	SHARE	SHARED ▪ SHARER ▪ SHARES
	SHARECROP	SHARECROPS
	SHARER	SHARERS
	SHAREWARE	SHAREWARES
	SHARIA	SHARIAH ▪ SHARIAS ▪ SHARIAT
	SHARIAH	SHARIAHS
	SHARIAT	SHARIATS
	SHARIF	SHARIFS
	SHARING	SHARINGS
	SHARK	SHARKS
	SHARKER	SHARKERS
	SHARKING	SHARKINGS
	SHARKSKIN	SHARKSKINS
	SHARN	SHARNS ▪ SHARNY
	SHARP	SHARPS ▪ SHARPY
	SHARPEN	SHARPENS
	SHARPENER	SHARPENERS
	SHARPER	SHARPERS
	SHARPIE	SHARPIES
	SHARPING	SHARPINGS
	SHASHLICK	SHASHLICKS
	SHASHLIK	SHASHLIKS
	SHASLIK	SHASLIKS
	SHASTER	SHASTERS

FRONT HOOK	ROOT WORD	END HOOK
	SHASTRA	SHASTRAS
	SHATTER	SHATTERS ▪ SHATTERY
	SHATTERER	SHATTERERS
	SHAUCHLE	SHAUCHLED ▪ SHAUCHLES
	SHAUGH	SHAUGHS
	SHAUL	SHAULS
	SHAVE	SHAVED ▪ SHAVEN ▪ SHAVER ▪ SHAVES
	SHAVELING	SHAVELINGS (offensive)
	SHAVER	SHAVERS
	SHAVETAIL	SHAVETAILS
	SHAVIE	SHAVIES
	SHAVING	SHAVINGS
PSHAW	**SHAW**	SHAWL ▪ SHAWM ▪ SHAWN ▪ SHAWS
PSHAWED	**SHAWED**	
PSHAWING	**SHAWING**	
	SHAWL	SHAWLS
	SHAWLEY	SHAWLEYS (offensive)
	SHAWLIE	SHAWLIES (offensive)
	SHAWLING	SHAWLINGS
	SHAWM	SHAWMS
PSHAWS	**SHAWS**	
	SHAY	SHAYA ▪ SHAYS
	SHAYA	SHAYAS
	SHCHI	SHCHIS
	SHE	SHEA ▪ SHED ▪ SHES ▪ SHET ▪ SHEW
	SHEA	SHEAF ▪ SHEAL ▪ SHEAR ▪ SHEAS
	SHEADING	SHEADINGS
	SHEAF	SHEAFS ▪ SHEAFY
	SHEAL	SHEALS
	SHEALING	SHEALINGS
	SHEAR	SHEARS
	SHEARER	SHEARERS
	SHEARING	SHEARINGS
	SHEARLEG	SHEARLEGS
	SHEARLING	SHEARLINGS
	SHEATH	SHEATHE ▪ SHEATHS ▪ SHEATHY
	SHEATHE	SHEATHED ▪ SHEATHER ▪ SHEATHES
	SHEATHER	SHEATHERS
	SHEATHING	SHEATHINGS
	SHEAVE	SHEAVED ▪ SHEAVES
	SHEBANG	SHEBANGS
	SHEBEAN	SHEBEANS
	SHEBEEN	SHEBEENS
	SHEBEENER	SHEBEENERS
	SHECHITA	SHECHITAH ▪ SHECHITAS
	SHECHITAH	SHECHITAHS
ASHED	**SHED**	SHEDS
	SHEDDER	SHEDDERS
	SHEDDING	SHEDDINGS
	SHEDFUL	SHEDFULS
	SHEDLOAD	SHEDLOADS
	SHEEL	SHEELS
	SHEEN	SHEENS ▪ SHEENY (offensive)
	SHEENEY	SHEENEYS (offensive)
	SHEENIE	SHEENIER ▪ SHEENIES (offensive)
	SHEENIES	SHEENIEST
	SHEEP	SHEEPO ▪ SHEEPY
	SHEEPCOT	SHEEPCOTE ▪ SHEEPCOTS
	SHEEPCOTE	SHEEPCOTES
	SHEEPDOG	SHEEPDOGS
	SHEEPFOLD	SHEEPFOLDS
	SHEEPHEAD	SHEEPHEADS
	SHEEPO	SHEEPOS
	SHEEPSKIN	SHEEPSKINS
	SHEEPWALK	SHEEPWALKS
	SHEER	SHEERS
	SHEERLEG	SHEERLEGS
	SHEET	SHEETS ▪ SHEETY
	SHEETER	SHEETERS

FRONT HOOK	ROOT WORD	END HOOK
	SHEETING	SHEETINGS
	SHEETROCK	SHEETROCKS
	SHEEVE	SHEEVES
	SHEHITA	SHEHITAH ▪ SHEHITAS
	SHEHITAH	SHEHITAHS
	SHEIK	SHEIKH ▪ SHEIKS
	SHEIKDOM	SHEIKDOMS
	SHEIKH	SHEIKHA ▪ SHEIKHS
	SHEIKHA	SHEIKHAS
	SHEIKHDOM	SHEIKHDOMS
	SHEILA	SHEILAS
	SHEILING	SHEILINGS
	SHEITAN	SHEITANS
	SHEKEL	SHEKELS
	SHELDDUCK	SHELDDUCKS
	SHELDRAKE	SHELDRAKES
	SHELDUCK	SHELDUCKS
	SHELF	SHELFS ▪ SHELFY
	SHELFFUL	SHELFFULS
	SHELFROOM	SHELFROOMS
	SHELL	SHELLS ▪ SHELLY
	SHELLAC	SHELLACK ▪ SHELLACS
	SHELLACK	SHELLACKS
	SHELLBACK	SHELLBACKS
	SHELLBARK	SHELLBARKS
	SHELLDUCK	SHELLDUCKS
	SHELLER	SHELLERS
	SHELLFIRE	SHELLFIRES
	SHELLFUL	SHELLFULS
	SHELLING	SHELLINGS
	SHELLWORK	SHELLWORKS
	SHELTA	SHELTAS
	SHELTER	SHELTERS ▪ SHELTERY
	SHELTERER	SHELTERERS
	SHELTIE	SHELTIES
	SHELVE	SHELVED ▪ SHELVER ▪ SHELVES
	SHELVER	SHELVERS
	SHELVING	SHELVINGS
	SHEMOZZLE	SHEMOZZLED ▪ SHEMOZZLES
YSHEND	**SHEND**	SHENDS
YSHENDING	**SHENDING**	
YSHENDS	**SHENDS**	
YSHENT	**SHENT**	
	SHEOL	SHEOLS
	SHEPHERD	SHEPHERDS
	SHEQEL	SHEQELS
	SHERANG	SHERANGS
	SHERBERT	SHERBERTS
	SHERBET	SHERBETS
	SHERD	SHERDS
	SHEREEF	SHEREEFS
	SHERIA	SHERIAS ▪ SHERIAT
	SHERIAT	SHERIATS
	SHERIF	SHERIFF ▪ SHERIFS
	SHERIFF	SHERIFFS
	SHERLOCK	SHERLOCKS
	SHEROOT	SHEROOTS
	SHERPA	SHERPAS
	SHERWANI	SHERWANIS
ASHES ▪ ISHES	**SHES**	
ASHET	**SHET**	SHETS
	SHETLAND	SHETLANDS
ASHETS	**SHETS**	
	SHEUCH	SHEUCHS
	SHEUGH	SHEUGHS
	SHEVA	SHEVAS
	SHEW	SHEWN ▪ SHEWS
	SHEWBREAD	SHEWBREADS
	SHEWEL	SHEWELS

FRONT HOOK	ROOT WORD	END HOOK
	SHEWER	SHEWERS
	SHIAI	SHIAIS
	SHIATSU	SHIATSUS
	SHIATZU	SHIATZUS
	SHIBAH	SHIBAHS
	SHIBUICHI	SHIBUICHIS
	SHICKER	SHICKERS
	SHICKSA	SHICKSAS *(offensive)*
	SHIDDER	SHIDDERS
	SHIEL	SHIELD · SHIELS
	SHIELD	SHIELDS
	SHIELDER	SHIELDERS
	SHIELDING	SHIELDINGS
	SHIELING	SHIELINGS
ASHIER	**SHIER**	SHIERS
	SHIES	SHIEST
ASHIEST	**SHIEST**	
	SHIFT	SHIFTS · SHIFTY
	SHIFTER	SHIFTERS
	SHIFTING	SHIFTINGS
	SHIFTWORK	SHIFTWORKS
	SHIGELLA	SHIGELLAE · SHIGELLAS
	SHIITAKE	SHIITAKES
	SHIKAR	SHIKARI · SHIKARS
	SHIKAREE	SHIKAREES
	SHIKARI	SHIKARIS
	SHIKKER	SHIKKERS
	SHIKSA	SHIKSAS *(offensive)*
	SHIKSE	SHIKSEH *(offensive)* · SHIKSES *(offensive)*
	SHIKSEH	SHIKSEHS *(offensive)*
	SHILL	SHILLS
	SHILLABER	SHILLABERS
	SHILLALA	SHILLALAH · SHILLALAS
	SHILLALAH	SHILLALAHS
	SHILLELAH	SHILLELAHS
	SHILLING	SHILLINGS
	SHIM	SHIMS
	SHIMAAL	SHIMAALS
	SHIMMER	SHIMMERS · SHIMMERY
	SHIMMEY	SHIMMEYS
	SHIMOZZLE	SHIMOZZLES
	SHIN	SHINE · SHINS · SHINY
	SHINBONE	SHINBONES
	SHINDIG	SHINDIGS
	SHINDY	SHINDYS
ASHINE	**SHINE**	SHINED · SHINER · SHINES
	SHINER	SHINERS
	SHINES	SHINESS
ASHINESS	**SHINESS**	
ASHINESSES	**SHINESSES**	
	SHINGLE	SHINGLED · SHINGLER · SHINGLES
	SHINGLER	SHINGLERS
	SHINGLING	SHINGLINGS
	SHINGUARD	SHINGUARDS
	SHINIES	SHINIEST
	SHINJU	SHINJUS
	SHINKIN	SHINKINS
	SHINLEAF	SHINLEAFS
	SHINNE	SHINNED · SHINNES · SHINNEY
	SHINNEY	SHINNEYS
	SHIP	SHIPS
	SHIPBOARD	SHIPBOARDS
	SHIPFUL	SHIPFULS
	SHIPLAP	SHIPLAPS
	SHIPLOAD	SHIPLOADS
	SHIPMATE	SHIPMATES
	SHIPMEN	SHIPMENT
	SHIPMENT	SHIPMENTS
	SHIPOWNER	SHIPOWNERS

	FRONT HOOK	ROOT WORD	END HOOK
		SHIPPEN	SHIPPENS
		SHIPPER	SHIPPERS
		SHIPPIE	SHIPPIES
		SHIPPING	SHIPPINGS
		SHIPPO	SHIPPON ▪ SHIPPOS
		SHIPPON	SHIPPONS
		SHIPPOUND	SHIPPOUNDS
		SHIPSIDE	SHIPSIDES
		SHIPWAY	SHIPWAYS
		SHIPWORM	SHIPWORMS
		SHIPWRECK	SHIPWRECKS
		SHIPYARD	SHIPYARDS
		SHIR	SHIRE ▪ SHIRK ▪ SHIRR ▪ SHIRS ▪ SHIRT
		SHIRALEE	SHIRALEES
		SHIRE	SHIRED ▪ SHIRES
		SHIRK	SHIRKS
		SHIRKER	SHIRKERS
		SHIRR	SHIRRA ▪ SHIRRS
		SHIRRA	SHIRRAS
		SHIRRALEE	SHIRRALEES
		SHIRRING	SHIRRINGS
		SHIRT	SHIRTS ▪ SHIRTY
		SHIRTBAND	SHIRTBANDS
		SHIRTING	SHIRTINGS
		SHIRTTAIL	SHIRTTAILS
		SHISH	SHISHA
		SHISHA	SHISHAS
		SHISO	SHISOS
		SHIST	SHISTS
		SHIT	SHITE (offensive) ▪ SHITS (offensive)
		SHITAKE	SHITAKES
		SHITE	SHITED (offensive) ▪ SHITES (offensive)
		SHITHEAD	SHITHEADS (offensive)
		SHITHOLE	SHITHOLES (offensive)
		SHITLIST	SHITLISTS (offensive)
		SHITLOAD	SHITLOADS (offensive)
		SHITTAH	SHITTAHS
		SHITTIM	SHITTIMS
		SHIV	SHIVA ▪ SHIVE ▪ SHIVS
		SHIVA	SHIVAH ▪ SHIVAS
		SHIVAH	SHIVAHS
		SHIVAREE	SHIVAREED ▪ SHIVAREES
		SHIVE	SHIVER ▪ SHIVES
	ASHIVER	**SHIVER**	SHIVERS ▪ SHIVERY
		SHIVERER	SHIVERERS
		SHIVERING	SHIVERINGS
		SHIVITI	SHIVITIS
		SHIVOO	SHIVOOS
		SHLEMIEHL	SHLEMIEHLS
		SHLEMIEL	SHLEMIELS
		SHLEP	SHLEPP ▪ SHLEPS
		SHLEPP	SHLEPPS
		SHLEPPER	SHLEPPERS
		SHLIMAZEL	SHLIMAZELS
		SHLOCK	SHLOCKS ▪ SHLOCKY
		SHLOSHIM	SHLOSHIMS
		SHLUB	SHLUBS
		SHLUMP	SHLUMPS ▪ SHLUMPY
		SHMALTZ	SHMALTZY
		SHMATTE	SHMATTES
		SHMEAR	SHMEARS
		SHMEK	SHMEKS
		SHMOCK	SHMOCKS
		SHMOOSE	SHMOOSED ▪ SHMOOSES
		SHMOOZE	SHMOOZED ▪ SHMOOZES
		SHMUCK	SHMUCKS
		SHNOOK	SHNOOKS
		SHNORRER	SHNORRERS
		SHOAL	SHOALS ▪ SHOALY

FRONT HOOK	ROOT WORD	END HOOK
	SHOALING	SHOALINGS
	SHOAT	SHOATS
	SHOCHET	SHOCHETS
	SHOCK	SHOCKS
	SHOCKER	SHOCKERS
	SHODDIES	SHODDIEST
	SHODER	SHODERS
	SHOE	SHOED ▪ SHOER ▪ SHOES
	SHOEBILL	SHOEBILLS
	SHOEBLACK	SHOEBLACKS
	SHOEHORN	SHOEHORNS
	SHOEING	SHOEINGS
	SHOELACE	SHOELACES
	SHOEMAKER	SHOEMAKERS
	SHOEPAC	SHOEPACK ▪ SHOEPACS
	SHOEPACK	SHOEPACKS
	SHOER	SHOERS
	SHOESHINE	SHOESHINES
	SHOETREE	SHOETREES
	SHOFAR	SHOFARS
	SHOG	SHOGI ▪ SHOGS
	SHOGGLE	SHOGGLED ▪ SHOGGLES
	SHOGI	SHOGIS
	SHOGUN	SHOGUNS
	SHOGUNATE	SHOGUNATES
	SHOJI	SHOJIS
	SHOLA	SHOLAS
	SHOLOM	SHOLOMS
	SHONEEN	SHONEENS
	SHOO	SHOOK ▪ SHOOL ▪ SHOON ▪ SHOOS ▪ SHOOT
	SHOOGIE	SHOOGIED ▪ SHOOGIES
	SHOOGLE	SHOOGLED ▪ SHOOGLES
	SHOOK	SHOOKS
	SHOOL	SHOOLE ▪ SHOOLS
	SHOOLE	SHOOLED ▪ SHOOLES
	SHOORA	SHOORAS
	SHOOT	SHOOTS
	SHOOTDOWN	SHOOTDOWNS
	SHOOTER	SHOOTERS
	SHOOTING	SHOOTINGS
	SHOOTIST	SHOOTISTS
	SHOOTOUT	SHOOTOUTS
	SHOP	SHOPE ▪ SHOPS
	SHOPBOARD	SHOPBOARDS
	SHOPBOY	SHOPBOYS
	SHOPFRONT	SHOPFRONTS
	SHOPFUL	SHOPFULS
	SHOPGIRL	SHOPGIRLS
	SHOPHAR	SHOPHARS
	SHOPLIFT	SHOPLIFTS
	SHOPPE	SHOPPED ▪ SHOPPER ▪ SHOPPES
	SHOPPER	SHOPPERS
	SHOPPING	SHOPPINGS
	SHOPTALK	SHOPTALKS
	SHORAN	SHORANS
ASHORE	SHORE	SHORED ▪ SHORER ▪ SHORES
	SHOREBIRD	SHOREBIRDS
	SHORELINE	SHORELINES
	SHORER	SHORERS
	SHOREWARD	SHOREWARDS
	SHOREWEED	SHOREWEEDS
	SHORING	SHORINGS
	SHORL	SHORLS
	SHORT	SHORTS ▪ SHORTY
	SHORTAGE	SHORTAGES
	SHORTCAKE	SHORTCAKES
	SHORTCUT	SHORTCUTS
	SHORTEN	SHORTENS
	SHORTENER	SHORTENERS

FRONT HOOK	ROOT WORD	END HOOK
	SHORTFALL	SHORTFALLS
	SHORTGOWN	SHORTGOWNS
	SHORTHAIR	SHORTHAIRS
	SHORTHAND	SHORTHANDS
	SHORTHEAD	SHORTHEADS
	SHORTHORN	SHORTHORNS
	SHORTIA	SHORTIAS
	SHORTIE	SHORTIES
	SHORTLIST	SHORTLISTS
	SHORTSTOP	SHORTSTOPS
	SHORTWAVE	SHORTWAVED ▪ SHORTWAVES
	SHOT	SHOTE ▪ SHOTS ▪ SHOTT
	SHOTE	SHOTES
	SHOTFIRER	SHOTFIRERS
	SHOTGUN	SHOTGUNS
	SHOTHOLE	SHOTHOLES
	SHOTMAKER	SHOTMAKERS
	SHOTPUT	SHOTPUTS
	SHOTT	SHOTTE ▪ SHOTTS
	SHOTTE	SHOTTED ▪ SHOTTEN ▪ SHOTTES
	SHOTTLE	SHOTTLES
	SHOUGH	SHOUGHS
	SHOULDER	SHOULDERS
	SHOUSE	SHOUSES
	SHOUT	SHOUTS ▪ SHOUTY
	SHOUTER	SHOUTERS
	SHOUTHER	SHOUTHERS
	SHOUTING	SHOUTINGS
	SHOUTLINE	SHOUTLINES
	SHOVE	SHOVED ▪ SHOVEL ▪ SHOVER ▪ SHOVES
	SHOVEL	SHOVELS
	SHOVELER	SHOVELERS
	SHOVELFUL	SHOVELFULS
	SHOVELLER	SHOVELLERS
	SHOVER	SHOVERS
	SHOVING	SHOVINGS
	SHOW	SHOWD ▪ SHOWN ▪ SHOWS ▪ SHOWY
	SHOWBOAT	SHOWBOATS
	SHOWBREAD	SHOWBREADS
	SHOWCASE	SHOWCASED ▪ SHOWCASES
	SHOWD	SHOWDS
	SHOWDOWN	SHOWDOWNS
	SHOWER	SHOWERS ▪ SHOWERY
	SHOWERER	SHOWERERS
	SHOWERING	SHOWERINGS
	SHOWGHE	SHOWGHES
	SHOWGIRL	SHOWGIRLS
	SHOWING	SHOWINGS
	SHOWOFF	SHOWOFFS
	SHOWPIECE	SHOWPIECES
	SHOWPLACE	SHOWPLACES
	SHOWRING	SHOWRINGS
	SHOWROOM	SHOWROOMS
	SHOWTIME	SHOWTIMES
	SHOWYARD	SHOWYARDS
	SHOYU	SHOYUS
	SHRADDHA	SHRADDHAS
	SHRAPNEL	SHRAPNELS
	SHRED	SHREDS
	SHREDDER	SHREDDERS
	SHREDDING	SHREDDINGS
	SHREEK	SHREEKS
	SHREIK	SHREIKS
	SHREW	SHREWD ▪ SHREWS
	SHREWDIE	SHREWDIES
	SHRI	SHRIS
	SHRIEK	SHRIEKS ▪ SHRIEKY
	SHRIEKER	SHRIEKERS
	SHRIEKING	SHRIEKINGS

FRONT HOOK	ROOT WORD	END HOOK
	SHRIEVE	SHRIEVED ▪ SHRIEVES
	SHRIFT	SHRIFTS
	SHRIGHT	SHRIGHTS
	SHRIKE	SHRIKED ▪ SHRIKES
	SHRILL	SHRILLS ▪ SHRILLY
	SHRILLING	SHRILLINGS
	SHRIMP	SHRIMPS ▪ SHRIMPY
	SHRIMPER	SHRIMPERS
	SHRIMPING	SHRIMPINGS
	SHRINE	SHRINED ▪ SHRINES
	SHRINK	SHRINKS
	SHRINKAGE	SHRINKAGES
	SHRINKER	SHRINKERS
	SHRIVE	SHRIVED ▪ SHRIVEL ▪ SHRIVEN ▪ SHRIVER SHRIVES
	SHRIVEL	SHRIVELS
	SHRIVER	SHRIVERS
	SHRIVING	SHRIVINGS
	SHROFF	SHROFFS
	SHROFFAGE	SHROFFAGES
	SHROOM	SHROOMS
	SHROOMER	SHROOMERS
	SHROUD	SHROUDS ▪ SHROUDY
	SHROUDING	SHROUDINGS
	SHROVE	SHROVED ▪ SHROVES
	SHROW	SHROWD ▪ SHROWS
	SHRUB	SHRUBS
	SHRUBLAND	SHRUBLANDS
	SHRUG	SHRUGS
	SHTCHI	SHTCHIS
	SHTETEL	SHTETELS
	SHTETL	SHTETLS
	SHTICK	SHTICKS ▪ SHTICKY
	SHTIK	SHTIKS
	SHTOOK	SHTOOKS
	SHTUCK	SHTUCKS
	SHTUM	SHTUMM
	SHTUP	SHTUPS
	SHUBUNKIN	SHUBUNKINS
	SHUCK	SHUCKS
	SHUCKER	SHUCKERS
	SHUCKING	SHUCKINGS
	SHUDDER	SHUDDERS ▪ SHUDDERY
	SHUFFLE	SHUFFLED ▪ SHUFFLER ▪ SHUFFLES
	SHUFFLER	SHUFFLERS
	SHUFFLING	SHUFFLINGS
	SHUFTI	SHUFTIS
	SHUL	SHULE ▪ SHULN ▪ SHULS
	SHULE	SHULED ▪ SHULES
	SHUN	SHUNS ▪ SHUNT
	SHUNNER	SHUNNERS
	SHUNPIKE	SHUNPIKED ▪ SHUNPIKER ▪ SHUNPIKES
	SHUNPIKER	SHUNPIKERS
	SHUNT	SHUNTS
	SHUNTER	SHUNTERS
	SHUNTING	SHUNTINGS
	SHURA	SHURAS
	SHUSHER	SHUSHERS
	SHUT	SHUTE ▪ SHUTS
	SHUTDOWN	SHUTDOWNS
	SHUTE	SHUTED ▪ SHUTES
	SHUTEYE	SHUTEYES
	SHUTOFF	SHUTOFFS
	SHUTOUT	SHUTOUTS
	SHUTTER	SHUTTERS
	SHUTTLE	SHUTTLED ▪ SHUTTLER ▪ SHUTTLES
	SHUTTLER	SHUTTLERS
	SHVARTZE	SHVARTZES
	SHWA	SHWAS

FRONT HOOK	ROOT WORD	END HOOK
	SHWANPAN	SHWANPANS
	SHWESHWE	SHWESHWES
ASHY	**SHY**	
	SHYER	SHYERS
	SHYLOCK	SHYLOCKS
	SHYPOO	SHYPOOS
	SHYSTER	SHYSTERS
PSI	**SI**	SIB • SIC • SIF • SIK • SIM • SIN • SIP SIR • SIS • SIT • SIX
	SIAL	SIALS
	SIALID	SIALIDS
	SIALIDAN	SIALIDANS
	SIALOGRAM	SIALOGRAMS
	SIALOLITH	SIALOLITHS
	SIALON	SIALONS
	SIAMANG	SIAMANGS
	SIAMESE	SIAMESED • SIAMESES
	SIAMEZE	SIAMEZED • SIAMEZES
	SIB	SIBB • SIBS
	SIBB	SIBBS
	SIBILANCE	SIBILANCES
	SIBILANT	SIBILANTS
	SIBILATE	SIBILATED • SIBILATES
	SIBILATOR	SIBILATORS • SIBILATORY
	SIBLING	SIBLINGS
	SIBSHIP	SIBSHIPS
	SIBYL	SIBYLS
	SIC	SICE • SICH • SICK • SICS
	SICCATIVE	SICCATIVES
	SICE	SICES
	SICH	SICHT
	SICHT	SICHTS
	SICILIANO	SICILIANOS
	SICK	SICKO • SICKS
	SICKBAY	SICKBAYS
	SICKBED	SICKBEDS
	SICKEE	SICKEES
	SICKEN	SICKENS
	SICKENER	SICKENERS
	SICKENING	SICKENINGS
	SICKIE	SICKIES
	SICKLE	SICKLED • SICKLES
	SICKLEMIA	SICKLEMIAS
	SICKLIES	SICKLIEST
	SICKNURSE	SICKNURSES
	SICKO	SICKOS
	SICKOUT	SICKOUTS
	SICKROOM	SICKROOMS
	SIDA	SIDAS
	SIDALCEA	SIDALCEAS
	SIDDHA	SIDDHAS
	SIDDHI	SIDDHIS
	SIDDHUISM	SIDDHUISMS
	SIDDUR	SIDDURS
ASIDE	**SIDE**	SIDED • SIDER • SIDES
	SIDEARM	SIDEARMS
	SIDEBAND	SIDEBANDS
	SIDEBAR	SIDEBARS
	SIDEBOARD	SIDEBOARDS
	SIDECAR	SIDECARS
	SIDECHECK	SIDECHECKS
	SIDEHILL	SIDEHILLS
	SIDEKICK	SIDEKICKS
	SIDELIGHT	SIDELIGHTS
	SIDELINE	SIDELINED • SIDELINER • SIDELINES
	SIDELINER	SIDELINERS
	SIDELOCK	SIDELOCKS
	SIDENOTE	SIDENOTES
	SIDEPATH	SIDEPATHS

FRONT HOOK	ROOT WORD	END HOOK
	SIDEPIECE	SIDEPIECES
	SIDER	SIDERS
	SIDERATE	SIDERATED · SIDERATES
	SIDERITE	SIDERITES
	SIDEROAD	SIDEROADS
ASIDES	SIDES	
	SIDESHOOT	SIDESHOOTS
	SIDESHOW	SIDESHOWS
	SIDESLIP	SIDESLIPS
	SIDESPIN	SIDESPINS
	SIDESTEP	SIDESTEPS
	SIDESWIPE	SIDESWIPED · SIDESWIPER · SIDESWIPES
	SIDETRACK	SIDETRACKS
	SIDEWALK	SIDEWALKS
	SIDEWALL	SIDEWALLS
	SIDEWARD	SIDEWARDS
	SIDEWAY	SIDEWAYS
	SIDEWHEEL	SIDEWHEELS
	SIDH	SIDHA · SIDHE
	SIDHA	SIDHAS
	SIDING	SIDINGS
	SIDLE	SIDLED · SIDLER · SIDLES
	SIDLER	SIDLERS
	SIECLE	SIECLES
	SIEGE	SIEGED · SIEGER · SIEGES
	SIEGER	SIEGERS
	SIEN	SIENS · SIENT
	SIENITE	SIENITES
	SIENNA	SIENNAS
	SIENT	SIENTS
	SIEROZEM	SIEROZEMS
	SIERRA	SIERRAN · SIERRAS
	SIESTA	SIESTAS
	SIETH	SIETHS
	SIEUR	SIEURS
	SIEVE	SIEVED · SIEVES
	SIEVERT	SIEVERTS
	SIF	SIFT
	SIFAKA	SIFAKAS
	SIFFLE	SIFFLED · SIFFLES
	SIFFLEUR	SIFFLEURS
	SIFFLEUSE	SIFFLEUSES
	SIFT	SIFTS
	SIFTER	SIFTERS
	SIFTING	SIFTINGS
	SIGANID	SIGANIDS
	SIGH	SIGHS · SIGHT
	SIGHER	SIGHERS
	SIGHT	SIGHTS
	SIGHTER	SIGHTERS
	SIGHTING	SIGHTINGS
	SIGHTLINE	SIGHTLINES
	SIGHTSEE	SIGHTSEEN · SIGHTSEER · SIGHTSEES
	SIGHTSEER	SIGHTSEERS
	SIGIL	SIGILS
	SIGLA	SIGLAS
	SIGMA	SIGMAS
	SIGMATE	SIGMATED · SIGMATES
	SIGMATION	SIGMATIONS
	SIGMATISM	SIGMATISMS
	SIGMATRON	SIGMATRONS
	SIGMOID	SIGMOIDS
	SIGN	SIGNA · SIGNS
	SIGNA	SIGNAL
	SIGNAGE	SIGNAGES
	SIGNAL	SIGNALS
	SIGNALER	SIGNALERS
	SIGNALING	SIGNALINGS
	SIGNALISE	SIGNALISED · SIGNALISES

FRONT HOOK	ROOT WORD	END HOOK
	SIGNALIZE	SIGNALIZED ▪ SIGNALIZES
	SIGNALLER	SIGNALLERS
	SIGNALMEN	SIGNALMENT
	SIGNATURE	SIGNATURES
	SIGNBOARD	SIGNBOARDS
	SIGNEE	SIGNEES
	SIGNER	SIGNERS
	SIGNET	SIGNETS
	SIGNEURIE	SIGNEURIES
	SIGNIEUR	SIGNIEURS
	SIGNIFIED	SIGNIFIEDS
	SIGNIFIER	SIGNIFIERS
	SIGNING	SIGNINGS
	SIGNIOR	SIGNIORI ▪ SIGNIORS ▪ SIGNIORY
	SIGNOR	SIGNORA ▪ SIGNORE ▪ SIGNORI ▪ SIGNORS ▪ SIGNORY
	SIGNORA	SIGNORAS
	SIGNORE	SIGNORES
	SIGNORI	SIGNORIA
	SIGNORIA	SIGNORIAL ▪ SIGNORIAS
	SIGNORINA	SIGNORINAS
	SIGNPOST	SIGNPOSTS
	SIJO	SIJOS
	SIK	SIKA ▪ SIKE
	SIKA	SIKAS
	SIKE	SIKER ▪ SIKES
	SILAGE	SILAGED ▪ SILAGES
	SILANE	SILANES
	SILASTIC	SILASTICS
	SILD	SILDS
ESILE	**SILE**	SILED ▪ SILEN ▪ SILER ▪ SILES ▪ SILEX
	SILEN	SILENE ▪ SILENI ▪ SILENS ▪ SILENT
	SILENCE	SILENCED ▪ SILENCER ▪ SILENCES
	SILENCER	SILENCERS
	SILENE	SILENES
	SILENT	SILENTS
	SILER	SILERS
ESILES	**SILES**	
	SILESIA	SILESIAS
	SILICA	SILICAS
	SILICATE	SILICATED ▪ SILICATES
	SILICIDE	SILICIDES
	SILICIUM	SILICIUMS
	SILICLE	SILICLES
	SILICON	SILICONE ▪ SILICONS
	SILICONE	SILICONES
	SILICOTIC	SILICOTICS
	SILICULA	SILICULAE ▪ SILICULAS
	SILICULE	SILICULES
	SILIQUA	SILIQUAE ▪ SILIQUAS
	SILIQUE	SILIQUES
	SILK	SILKS ▪ SILKY
	SILKALENE	SILKALENES
	SILKALINE	SILKALINES
	SILKEN	SILKENS
	SILKIE	SILKIER ▪ SILKIES
	SILKIES	SILKIEST
	SILKOLINE	SILKOLINES
	SILKTAIL	SILKTAILS
	SILKWEED	SILKWEEDS
	SILKWORM	SILKWORMS
	SILL	SILLS ▪ SILLY
	SILLABUB	SILLABUBS
	SILLADAR	SILLADARS
	SILLER	SILLERS
	SILLIBUB	SILLIBUBS
	SILLIES	SILLIEST
	SILLOCK	SILLOCKS
	SILO	SILOS

FRONT HOOK	ROOT WORD	END HOOK
	SILOXANE	SILOXANES
	SILPHIUM	SILPHIUMS
	SILT	SILTS ▪ SILTY
	SILTATION	SILTATIONS
	SILTSTONE	SILTSTONES
	SILURID	SILURIDS
	SILURIST	SILURISTS
	SILUROID	SILUROIDS
	SILVA	SILVAE ▪ SILVAN ▪ SILVAS
	SILVAN	SILVANS
	SILVER	SILVERN ▪ SILVERS ▪ SILVERY
	SILVERER	SILVERERS
	SILVEREYE	SILVEREYES
	SILVERING	SILVERINGS
	SILVERISE	SILVERISED ▪ SILVERISES
	SILVERIZE	SILVERIZED ▪ SILVERIZES
	SIM	SIMA ▪ SIMI ▪ SIMP ▪ SIMS
	SIMA	SIMAR ▪ SIMAS
	SIMAR	SIMARS
	SIMAROUBA	SIMAROUBAS
	SIMARRE	SIMARRES
	SIMARUBA	SIMARUBAS
	SIMAZINE	SIMAZINES
	SIMBA	SIMBAS
	SIMI	SIMIS
	SIMIAN	SIMIANS
	SIMILE	SIMILES
	SIMILISE	SIMILISED ▪ SIMILISES
	SIMILIZE	SIMILIZED ▪ SIMILIZES
	SIMILOR	SIMILORS
	SIMITAR	SIMITARS
	SIMKIN	SIMKINS
	SIMLIN	SIMLINS
	SIMMER	SIMMERS
	SIMNEL	SIMNELS
	SIMOLEON	SIMOLEONS
	SIMONIAC	SIMONIACS
	SIMONISE	SIMONISED ▪ SIMONISES
	SIMONIST	SIMONISTS
	SIMONIZE	SIMONIZED ▪ SIMONIZES
	SIMOOM	SIMOOMS
	SIMOON	SIMOONS
	SIMORG	SIMORGS
	SIMP	SIMPS
	SIMPAI	SIMPAIS
	SIMPER	SIMPERS
	SIMPERER	SIMPERERS
	SIMPERING	SIMPERINGS
	SIMPKIN	SIMPKINS
	SIMPLE	SIMPLED ▪ SIMPLER ▪ SIMPLES ▪ SIMPLEX
	SIMPLER	SIMPLERS
	SIMPLES	SIMPLEST
	SIMPLESSE	SIMPLESSES
	SIMPLETON	SIMPLETONS
	SIMPLICIA	SIMPLICIAL
	SIMPLING	SIMPLINGS
	SIMPLISM	SIMPLISMS
	SIMPLIST	SIMPLISTE ▪ SIMPLISTS
	SIMUL	SIMULS
	SIMULACRE	SIMULACRES
	SIMULANT	SIMULANTS
	SIMULAR	SIMULARS
	SIMULATE	SIMULATED ▪ SIMULATES
	SIMULATOR	SIMULATORS ▪ SIMULATORY
	SIMULCAST	SIMULCASTS
	SIMULIUM	SIMULIUMS
	SIMURG	SIMURGH ▪ SIMURGS
	SIMURGH	SIMURGHS
	SIN	SIND ▪ SINE ▪ SING ▪ SINH ▪ SINK ▪ SINS

FRONT HOOK	ROOT WORD	END HOOK
	SINAPISM	SINAPISMS
	SINCERE	SINCERER
	SINCIPITA	SINCIPITAL
	SINCIPUT	SINCIPUTS
	SIND	SINDS
	SINDING	SINDINGS
	SINDON	SINDONS
	SINE	SINED · SINES · SINEW
	SINECURE	SINECURES
	SINEW	SINEWS · SINEWY
	SINFONIA	SINFONIAS
USING	SING	SINGE · SINGS
	SINGALONG	SINGALONGS
	SINGE	SINGED · SINGER · SINGES
	SINGER	SINGERS
	SINGING	SINGINGS
	SINGLE	SINGLED · SINGLES · SINGLET
	SINGLEDOM	SINGLEDOMS
	SINGLET	SINGLETS
	SINGLETON	SINGLETONS
	SINGLING	SINGLINGS
	SINGSONG	SINGSONGS · SINGSONGY
	SINGSPIEL	SINGSPIELS
	SINGULAR	SINGULARS · SINGULARY
	SINGULT	SINGULTS
	SINH	SINHS
	SINICISE	SINICISED · SINICISES
	SINICIZE	SINICIZED · SINICIZES
	SINISTRAL	SINISTRALS
	SINK	SINKS · SINKY
	SINKAGE	SINKAGES
	SINKER	SINKERS
	SINKHOLE	SINKHOLES
	SINKING	SINKINGS
	SINNER	SINNERS
	SINNET	SINNETS
	SINNINGIA	SINNINGIAS
	SINOLOGUE	SINOLOGUES
	SINOPIA	SINOPIAS
	SINOPITE	SINOPITES
	SINTER	SINTERS · SINTERY
	SINUATE	SINUATED · SINUATES
	SINUATION	SINUATIONS
	SINUSOID	SINUSOIDS
	SIP	SIPE · SIPS
	SIPE	SIPED · SIPES
	SIPHON	SIPHONS
	SIPHONAGE	SIPHONAGES
	SIPHONET	SIPHONETS
	SIPHUNCLE	SIPHUNCLES
	SIPPER	SIPPERS
	SIPPET	SIPPETS
	SIPPLE	SIPPLED · SIPPLES
	SIR	SIRE · SIRI · SIRS
	SIRCAR	SIRCARS
	SIRDAR	SIRDARS
	SIRE	SIRED · SIREE · SIREN · SIRES
	SIREE	SIREES
	SIREN	SIRENS
	SIRENIAN	SIRENIANS
	SIRENISE	SIRENISED · SIRENISES
	SIRENIZE	SIRENIZED · SIRENIZES
	SIRGANG	SIRGANGS
	SIRI	SIRIH · SIRIS
	SIRIH	SIRIHS
	SIRKAR	SIRKARS
	SIRLOIN	SIRLOINS
	SIRNAME	SIRNAMED · SIRNAMES
	SIROC	SIROCS

FRONT HOOK	ROOT WORD	END HOOK
	SIROCCO	SIROCCOS
	SIRONISE	SIRONISED ▪ SIRONISES
	SIRONIZE	SIRONIZED ▪ SIRONIZES
	SIRRA	SIRRAH ▪ SIRRAS
	SIRRAH	SIRRAHS
	SIRREE	SIRREES
	SIRUP	SIRUPS ▪ SIRUPY
	SIRVENTE	SIRVENTES
PSIS	**SIS**	SISS ▪ SIST
	SISAL	SISALS
	SISKIN	SISKINS
	SISS	SISSY
	SISSIES	SISSIEST
	SISSOO	SISSOOS
	SIST	SISTS
	SISTER	SISTERS
	SISTRUM	SISTRUMS
ISIT	**SIT**	SITE ▪ SITH ▪ SITS ▪ SITZ
	SITAR	SITARS
	SITARIST	SITARISTS
	SITATUNGA	SITATUNGAS
	SITCOM	SITCOMS
	SITE	SITED ▪ SITES
	SITELLA	SITELLAS
	SITFAST	SITFASTS
	SITH	SITHE
	SITHE	SITHED ▪ SITHEE ▪ SITHEN ▪ SITHES
	SITHEN	SITHENS
	SITKAMER	SITKAMERS
	SITREP	SITREPS
	SITTAR	SITTARS
	SITTELLA	SITTELLAS
	SITTER	SITTERS
	SITTING	SITTINGS
	SITUATE	SITUATED ▪ SITUATES
	SITUATION	SITUATIONS
	SITULA	SITULAE
	SITUP	SITUPS
	SITUTUNGA	SITUTUNGAS
	SITZKRIEG	SITZKRIEGS
	SITZMARK	SITZMARKS
	SIVER	SIVERS
	SIXAIN	SIXAINE ▪ SIXAINS
	SIXAINE	SIXAINES
	SIXER	SIXERS
	SIXMO	SIXMOS
	SIXPENCE	SIXPENCES
	SIXSCORE	SIXSCORES
	SIXTE	SIXTES
	SIXTEEN	SIXTEENS
	SIXTEENER	SIXTEENERS
	SIXTEENMO	SIXTEENMOS
	SIXTEENTH	SIXTEENTHS
	SIXTH	SIXTHS
	SIXTIETH	SIXTIETHS
	SIZAR	SIZARS
	SIZARSHIP	SIZARSHIPS
	SIZE	SIZED ▪ SIZEL ▪ SIZER ▪ SIZES
	SIZEISM	SIZEISMS
	SIZEIST	SIZEISTS
	SIZEL	SIZELS
	SIZER	SIZERS
	SIZING	SIZINGS
	SIZISM	SIZISMS
	SIZIST	SIZISTS
	SIZZLE	SIZZLED ▪ SIZZLER ▪ SIZZLES
	SIZZLER	SIZZLERS
	SIZZLING	SIZZLINGS
	SJAMBOK	SJAMBOKS

FRONT HOOK	ROOT WORD	END HOOK
	SKA	SKAG · SKAS · SKAT · SKAW
	SKAG	SKAGS
	SKAIL	SKAILS
	SKAITH	SKAITHS
	SKALD	SKALDS
	SKALDSHIP	SKALDSHIPS
	SKANGER	SKANGERS (offensive)
	SKANK	SKANKS · SKANKY
	SKANKER	SKANKERS
	SKANKING	SKANKINGS
	SKART	SKARTH · SKARTS
	SKARTH	SKARTHS
	SKAT	SKATE · SKATS · SKATT
	SKATE	SKATED · SKATER · SKATES
	SKATEPARK	SKATEPARKS
	SKATER	SKATERS
	SKATING	SKATINGS
	SKATOL	SKATOLE · SKATOLS
	SKATOLE	SKATOLES
	SKATT	SKATTS
	SKAW	SKAWS
	SKEAN	SKEANE · SKEANS
	SKEANE	SKEANES
	SKEAR	SKEARS · SKEARY
	SKEDADDLE	SKEDADDLED · SKEDADDLER · SKEDADDLES
	SKEE	SKEED · SKEEF · SKEEN · SKEER · SKEES · SKEET
	SKEECHAN	SKEECHANS
	SKEEN	SKEENS
	SKEER	SKEERS · SKEERY
	SKEET	SKEETS
	SKEETER	SKEETERS
	SKEG	SKEGG · SKEGS
	SKEGG	SKEGGS
	SKEGGER	SKEGGERS
	SKEIN	SKEINS
	SKELDER	SKELDERS
	SKELETON	SKELETONS
	SKELF	SKELFS
	SKELL	SKELLS · SKELLY
	SKELLIE	SKELLIED · SKELLIER · SKELLIES
	SKELLIES	SKELLIEST
	SKELLOCH	SKELLOCHS
	SKELLUM	SKELLUMS
	SKELM	SKELMS
	SKELP	SKELPS
	SKELPING	SKELPINGS
	SKELTER	SKELTERS
	SKELUM	SKELUMS
	SKEN	SKENE · SKENS
	SKENE	SKENES
	SKEO	SKEOS
	SKEP	SKEPS
	SKEPFUL	SKEPFULS
	SKEPTIC	SKEPTICS
ASKER · ESKER	**SKER**	SKERS
	SKERRICK	SKERRICKS
ASKERS · ESKERS	**SKERS**	
	SKET	SKETS
	SKETCH	SKETCHY
	SKETCHER	SKETCHERS
	SKETCHPAD	SKETCHPADS
ASKEW	**SKEW**	SKEWS
	SKEWBACK	SKEWBACKS
	SKEWBALD	SKEWBALDS
	SKEWER	SKEWERS
ASKEWNESS	**SKEWNESS**	
	SKI	SKID · SKIM · SKIN · SKIO · SKIP · SKIS · SKIT

FRONT HOOK	ROOT WORD	END HOOK
	SKIAGRAM	SKIAGRAMS
	SKIAGRAPH	SKIAGRAPHS
	SKIASCOPE	SKIASCOPES
	SKIATRON	SKIATRONS
	SKIBOB	SKIBOBS
	SKIBOBBER	SKIBOBBERS
	SKID	SKIDS
	SKIDDER	SKIDDERS
	SKIDDOO	SKIDDOOS
	SKIDLID	SKIDLIDS
	SKIDOO	SKIDOOS
	SKIDPAN	SKIDPANS
	SKIDWAY	SKIDWAYS
	SKIER	SKIERS
ESKIES	SKIES	
	SKIFF	SKIFFS
	SKIFFLE	SKIFFLED ▪ SKIFFLES
	SKIFFLES	SKIFFLESS
	SKIING	SKIINGS
	SKIJORER	SKIJORERS
	SKIJORING	SKIJORINGS
	SKILL	SKILLS ▪ SKILLY
	SKILLET	SKILLETS
	SKILLIES	SKILLIEST
	SKILLING	SKILLINGS
	SKILLION	SKILLIONS
	SKIM	SKIMO ▪ SKIMP ▪ SKIMS
	SKIMBOARD	SKIMBOARDS
	SKIMMER	SKIMMERS
	SKIMMIA	SKIMMIAS
	SKIMMING	SKIMMINGS
	SKIMO	SKIMOS (offensive)
	SKIMOBILE	SKIMOBILED ▪ SKIMOBILES
	SKIMP	SKIMPS ▪ SKIMPY
	SKIN	SKINK ▪ SKINS ▪ SKINT
	SKINCARE	SKINCARES
	SKINFLICK	SKINFLICKS
	SKINFLINT	SKINFLINTS ▪ SKINFLINTY
	SKINFOOD	SKINFOODS
	SKINFUL	SKINFULS
	SKINHEAD	SKINHEADS
	SKINK	SKINKS
	SKINKER	SKINKERS
	SKINNER	SKINNERS
	SKIO	SKIOS
	SKIORING	SKIORINGS
	SKIP	SKIPS
	SKIPJACK	SKIPJACKS
	SKIPLANE	SKIPLANES
	SKIPPER	SKIPPERS
	SKIPPET	SKIPPETS
	SKIPPING	SKIPPINGS
	SKIRL	SKIRLS
	SKIRLING	SKIRLINGS
	SKIRR	SKIRRS
	SKIRRET	SKIRRETS
	SKIRT	SKIRTS
	SKIRTER	SKIRTERS
	SKIRTING	SKIRTINGS
	SKIT	SKITE ▪ SKITS
	SKITE	SKITED ▪ SKITES
	SKITTER	SKITTERS ▪ SKITTERY
	SKITTLE	SKITTLED ▪ SKITTLES
	SKIVE	SKIVED ▪ SKIVER ▪ SKIVES
	SKIVER	SKIVERS
	SKIVIE	SKIVIER
	SKIVING	SKIVINGS
	SKLATE	SKLATED ▪ SKLATES
ASKLENT	SKLENT	SKLENTS

FRONT HOOK	ROOT WORD	END HOOK
	SKLIFF	SKLIFFS
	SKLIM	SKLIMS
	SKOAL	SKOALS
	SKOFF	SKOFFS
	SKOKIAAN	SKOKIAANS
	SKOL	SKOLS
	SKOLLIE	SKOLLIES
	SKOOL	SKOOLS
	SKORT	SKORTS
	SKRAN	SKRANS
	SKREEGH	SKREEGHS
	SKREEN	SKREENS
	SKREIGH	SKREIGHS
	SKRIECH	SKRIECHS
	SKRIEGH	SKRIEGHS
	SKRIK	SKRIKE ▪ SKRIKS
	SKRIKE	SKRIKED ▪ SKRIKES
	SKRIMMAGE	SKRIMMAGED ▪ SKRIMMAGES
	SKRIMP	SKRIMPS
	SKRUMP	SKRUMPS
	SKRYER	SKRYERS
	SKUA	SKUAS
	SKUDLER	SKUDLERS
	SKUG	SKUGS
	SKULK	SKULKS
	SKULKER	SKULKERS
	SKULKING	SKULKINGS
	SKULL	SKULLS
	SKULLCAP	SKULLCAPS
	SKULPIN	SKULPINS
	SKUMMER	SKUMMERS
	SKUNK	SKUNKS ▪ SKUNKY
	SKUNKBIRD	SKUNKBIRDS
	SKUNKWEED	SKUNKWEEDS
	SKUTTLE	SKUTTLED ▪ SKUTTLES
ESKY	**SKY**	SKYF ▪ SKYR
	SKYBOARD	SKYBOARDS
	SKYBORN	SKYBORNE
	SKYBRIDGE	SKYBRIDGES
	SKYCAP	SKYCAPS
	SKYDIVE	SKYDIVED ▪ SKYDIVER ▪ SKYDIVES
	SKYDIVER	SKYDIVERS
	SKYDIVING	SKYDIVINGS
	SKYER	SKYERS
	SKYF	SKYFS
	SKYHOME	SKYHOMES
	SKYHOOK	SKYHOOKS
	SKYJACK	SKYJACKS
	SKYJACKER	SKYJACKERS
	SKYLAB	SKYLABS
	SKYLARK	SKYLARKS
	SKYLARKER	SKYLARKERS
	SKYLIGHT	SKYLIGHTS
	SKYLINE	SKYLINES
	SKYR	SKYRE ▪ SKYRS
	SKYRE	SKYRED ▪ SKYRES
	SKYROCKET	SKYROCKETS
	SKYSAIL	SKYSAILS
	SKYSCAPE	SKYSCAPES
	SKYSURF	SKYSURFS
	SKYSURFER	SKYSURFERS
	SKYTE	SKYTED ▪ SKYTES
	SKYWALK	SKYWALKS
	SKYWARD	SKYWARDS
	SKYWAY	SKYWAYS
	SKYWRITE	SKYWRITER ▪ SKYWRITES
	SKYWRITER	SKYWRITERS
	SLAB	SLABS
	SLABBER	SLABBERS ▪ SLABBERY

FRONT HOOK	ROOT WORD	END HOOK
	SLABBERER	SLABBERERS
	SLABSTONE	SLABSTONES
	SLACK	SLACKS
	SLACKEN	SLACKENS
	SLACKENER	SLACKENERS
	SLACKER	SLACKERS
	SLADANG	SLADANGS
	SLADE	SLADES
	SLAE	SLAES
	SLAG	SLAGS
	SLAGGING	SLAGGINGS
	SLAIRG	SLAIRGS
	SLAISTER	SLAISTERS ▪ SLAISTERY
ASLAKE	SLAKE	SLAKED ▪ SLAKER ▪ SLAKES
ASLAKED ▪ YSLAKED	SLAKED	
	SLAKER	SLAKERS
ASLAKES	SLAKES	
ASLAKING	SLAKING	
	SLALOM	SLALOMS
	SLALOMER	SLALOMERS
	SLALOMIST	SLALOMISTS
	SLAM	SLAMS
	SLAMDANCE	SLAMDANCED ▪ SLAMDANCES
	SLAMMAKIN	SLAMMAKINS
	SLAMMER	SLAMMERS
	SLAMMING	SLAMMINGS
ISLANDER	SLANDER	SLANDERS
	SLANDERER	SLANDERERS
ISLANDERS	SLANDERS	
	SLANE	SLANES
	SLANG	SLANGS ▪ SLANGY
	SLANGER	SLANGERS
	SLANGING	SLANGINGS
	SLANGUAGE	SLANGUAGES
ASLANT	SLANT	SLANTS ▪ SLANTY
	SLANTER	SLANTERS
	SLAP	SLAPS
	SLAPHEAD	SLAPHEADS (offensive)
	SLAPJACK	SLAPJACKS
	SLAPPER	SLAPPERS
	SLAPSHOT	SLAPSHOTS
	SLAPSTICK	SLAPSTICKS
	SLART	SLARTS
	SLASHER	SLASHERS
	SLASHFEST	SLASHFESTS
	SLASHING	SLASHINGS
	SLAT	SLATE ▪ SLATS ▪ SLATY
	SLATE	SLATED ▪ SLATER ▪ SLATES ▪ SLATEY
	SLATER	SLATERS
	SLATHER	SLATHERS
	SLATING	SLATINGS
	SLATTER	SLATTERN ▪ SLATTERS ▪ SLATTERY
	SLATTERN	SLATTERNS
	SLATTING	SLATTINGS
	SLAUGHTER	SLAUGHTERS ▪ SLAUGHTERY
	SLAVE	SLAVED ▪ SLAVER ▪ SLAVES ▪ SLAVEY
	SLAVER	SLAVERS ▪ SLAVERY
	SLAVERER	SLAVERERS
	SLAVEY	SLAVEYS
	SLAVOCRAT	SLAVOCRATS
	SLAVOPHIL	SLAVOPHILE ▪ SLAVOPHILS
	SLAW	SLAWS
	SLAY	SLAYS
	SLAYER	SLAYERS
	SLEAVE	SLEAVED ▪ SLEAVES
	SLEAZE	SLEAZES
	SLEAZEBAG	SLEAZEBAGS (offensive)
	SLEAZOID	SLEAZOIDS
ISLED	SLED	SLEDS

FRONT HOOK	ROOT WORD	END HOOK
	SLEDDER	SLEDDERS
	SLEDDING	SLEDDINGS
	SLEDGE	SLEDGED ▪ SLEDGER ▪ SLEDGES
	SLEDGER	SLEDGERS
	SLEDGING	SLEDGINGS
	SLEE	SLEEK ▪ SLEEP ▪ SLEER ▪ SLEET
	SLEECH	SLEECHY
	SLEEK	SLEEKS ▪ SLEEKY
	SLEEKEN	SLEEKENS
	SLEEKER	SLEEKERS
	SLEEKING	SLEEKINGS
ASLEEP	**SLEEP**	SLEEPS ▪ SLEEPY
	SLEEPER	SLEEPERS ▪ SLEEPERY
	SLEEPING	SLEEPINGS
	SLEEPOUT	SLEEPOUTS
	SLEEPOVER	SLEEPOVERS
	SLEEPSUIT	SLEEPSUITS
	SLEEPWALK	SLEEPWALKS
	SLEET	SLEETS ▪ SLEETY
	SLEEVE	SLEEVED ▪ SLEEVER ▪ SLEEVES
	SLEEVEEN	SLEEVEENS
	SLEEVELET	SLEEVELETS
	SLEEVER	SLEEVERS
	SLEEVING	SLEEVINGS
	SLEIGH	SLEIGHS ▪ SLEIGHT
	SLEIGHER	SLEIGHERS
	SLEIGHING	SLEIGHINGS
	SLEIGHT	SLEIGHTS
	SLENTER	SLENTERS
	SLEUTH	SLEUTHS
	SLEW	SLEWS
	SLEY	SLEYS
	SLICE	SLICED ▪ SLICER ▪ SLICES
	SLICER	SLICERS
	SLICING	SLICINGS
	SLICK	SLICKS
	SLICKEN	SLICKENS
	SLICKENER	SLICKENERS
	SLICKER	SLICKERS
	SLICKING	SLICKINGS
	SLICKROCK	SLICKROCKS
	SLICKSTER	SLICKSTERS
	SLID	SLIDE
	SLIDDER	SLIDDERS ▪ SLIDDERY
	SLIDE	SLIDED ▪ SLIDER ▪ SLIDES
	SLIDER	SLIDERS
	SLIDEWAY	SLIDEWAYS
	SLIDING	SLIDINGS
	SLIEVE	SLIEVES
	SLIGHT	SLIGHTS
	SLIGHTER	SLIGHTERS
	SLIM	SLIME ▪ SLIMS ▪ SLIMY
	SLIMDOWN	SLIMDOWNS
	SLIME	SLIMED ▪ SLIMES
	SLIMEBALL	SLIMEBALLS
	SLIMMER	SLIMMERS
	SLIMMING	SLIMMINGS
	SLIMS	SLIMSY
ISLING	**SLING**	SLINGS
	SLINGBACK	SLINGBACKS
	SLINGER	SLINGERS
	SLINGSHOT	SLINGSHOTS
	SLINK	SLINKS ▪ SLINKY
	SLINKER	SLINKERS
	SLINKSKIN	SLINKSKINS
	SLINKWEED	SLINKWEEDS
	SLINTER	SLINTERS
	SLIOTAR	SLIOTARS
	SLIP	SLIPE ▪ SLIPS ▪ SLIPT

S

FRONT HOOK	ROOT WORD	END HOOK
	SLIPCASE	SLIPCASED · SLIPCASES
	SLIPCOVER	SLIPCOVERS
	SLIPE	SLIPED · SLIPES
	SLIPFORM	SLIPFORMS
	SLIPKNOT	SLIPKNOTS
	SLIPNOOSE	SLIPNOOSES
	SLIPOUT	SLIPOUTS
	SLIPOVER	SLIPOVERS
	SLIPPAGE	SLIPPAGES
	SLIPPER	SLIPPERS · SLIPPERY
	SLIPRAIL	SLIPRAILS
	SLIPSHEET	SLIPSHEETS
	SLIPSLOP	SLIPSLOPS
	SLIPSOLE	SLIPSOLES
	SLIPUP	SLIPUPS
	SLIPWARE	SLIPWARES
	SLIPWAY	SLIPWAYS
	SLIT	SLITS
	SLITHER	SLITHERS · SLITHERY
	SLITTER	SLITTERS
	SLIVE	SLIVED · SLIVEN · SLIVER · SLIVES
	SLIVER	SLIVERS
	SLIVERER	SLIVERERS
	SLIVOVIC	SLIVOVICA
	SLIVOVICA	SLIVOVICAS
	SLOAN	SLOANS
	SLOB	SLOBS
	SLOBBER	SLOBBERS · SLOBBERY
	SLOBBERER	SLOBBERERS
	SLOBLAND	SLOBLANDS
	SLOCKEN	SLOCKENS
	SLOE	SLOES
	SLOETHORN	SLOETHORNS
	SLOETREE	SLOETREES
	SLOG	SLOGS
	SLOGAN	SLOGANS
	SLOGANEER	SLOGANEERS
	SLOGANISE	SLOGANISED · SLOGANISES
	SLOGANIZE	SLOGANIZED · SLOGANIZES
	SLOGGER	SLOGGERS
	SLOID	SLOIDS
	SLOJD	SLOJDS
	SLOKEN	SLOKENS
	SLOMMOCK	SLOMMOCKS
	SLOOM	SLOOMS · SLOOMY
	SLOOP	SLOOPS
	SLOOT	SLOOTS
	SLOP	SLOPE · SLOPS · SLOPY
ASLOPE	**SLOPE**	SLOPED · SLOPER · SLOPES
	SLOPER	SLOPERS
	SLOPWORK	SLOPWORKS
	SLORM	SLORMS
ASLOSH	**SLOSH**	SLOSHY
	SLOSHING	SLOSHINGS
	SLOT	SLOTH · SLOTS
	SLOTBACK	SLOTBACKS
	SLOTH	SLOTHS
	SLOTTER	SLOTTERS
	SLOUCH	SLOUCHY
	SLOUCHER	SLOUCHERS
	SLOUGH	SLOUGHS · SLOUGHY
	SLOVE	SLOVEN
	SLOVEN	SLOVENS
	SLOW	SLOWS
	SLOWBACK	SLOWBACKS
	SLOWDOWN	SLOWDOWNS
	SLOWING	SLOWINGS
	SLOWPOKE	SLOWPOKES
	SLOWWORM	SLOWWORMS

FRONT HOOK	ROOT WORD	END HOOK
	SLOYD	SLOYDS
	SLUB	SLUBB · SLUBS
	SLUBB	SLUBBS · SLUBBY
	SLUBBER	SLUBBERS
	SLUBBING	SLUBBINGS
	SLUDGE	SLUDGED · SLUDGES
	SLUE	SLUED · SLUES
	SLUFF	SLUFFS
	SLUG	SLUGS
	SLUGABED	SLUGABEDS
	SLUGFEST	SLUGFESTS
	SLUGGABED	SLUGGABEDS
	SLUGGARD	SLUGGARDS
	SLUGGER	SLUGGERS
	SLUGHORN	SLUGHORNE · SLUGHORNS
	SLUGHORNE	SLUGHORNES
	SLUICE	SLUICED · SLUICES
	SLUICEWAY	SLUICEWAYS
	SLUIT	SLUITS
	SLUM	SLUMP · SLUMS
	SLUMBER	SLUMBERS · SLUMBERY
	SLUMBERER	SLUMBERERS
	SLUMGUM	SLUMGUMS
	SLUMISM	SLUMISMS
	SLUMLORD	SLUMLORDS
	SLUMMER	SLUMMERS
	SLUMMING	SLUMMINGS
	SLUMMOCK	SLUMMOCKS
	SLUMP	SLUMPS · SLUMPY
	SLUNGSHOT	SLUNGSHOTS
	SLUR	SLURB · SLURP · SLURS
	SLURB	SLURBS
	SLURP	SLURPS
	SLURPER	SLURPERS
	SLUSE	SLUSES
	SLUSH	SLUSHY
	SLUSHIES	SLUSHIEST
	SLUT	SLUTS (offensive)
	SLUTCH	SLUTCHY
	SLYPE	SLYPES
	SMAAK	SMAAKS
	SMACK	SMACKS
	SMACKER	SMACKERS
	SMACKHEAD	SMACKHEADS
	SMACKING	SMACKINGS
	SMAIK	SMAIKS
	SMALL	SMALLS
	SMALLAGE	SMALLAGES
	SMALLBOY	SMALLBOYS
	SMALLSAT	SMALLSATS
	SMALM	SMALMS · SMALMY
	SMALT	SMALTI · SMALTO · SMALTS
	SMALTINE	SMALTINES
	SMALTITE	SMALTITES
	SMALTO	SMALTOS
	SMARAGD	SMARAGDE · SMARAGDS
	SMARAGDE	SMARAGDES
	SMARM	SMARMS · SMARMY
	SMART	SMARTS · SMARTY
	SMARTARSE	SMARTARSED (offensive)
		SMARTARSES (offensive)
	SMARTEN	SMARTENS
	SMARTIE	SMARTIES
	SMARTWEED	SMARTWEEDS
	SMASHER	SMASHERS
	SMASHEROO	SMASHEROOS
	SMASHING	SMASHINGS
	SMASHUP	SMASHUPS
	SMATTER	SMATTERS

S

FRONT HOOK	ROOT WORD	END HOOK
	SMATTERER	SMATTERERS
	SMAZE	SMAZES
ASMEAR	SMEAR	SMEARS ▪ SMEARY
	SMEARCASE	SMEARCASES
	SMEARER	SMEARERS
	SMEATH	SMEATHS
	SMECTITE	SMECTITES
	SMEDDUM	SMEDDUMS
	SMEE	SMEE ▪ SMEES
	SMEEK	SMEEKS
	SMEETH	SMEETHS
	SMEGMA	SMEGMAS
	SMELL	SMELLS ▪ SMELLY
	SMELLER	SMELLERS
	SMELLIES	SMELLIEST
	SMELLING	SMELLINGS
	SMELT	SMELTS
	SMELTER	SMELTERS ▪ SMELTERY
	SMELTING	SMELTINGS
	SMERK	SMERKS
	SMEUSE	SMEUSES
	SMEW	SMEWS
	SMICKER	SMICKERS
	SMICKET	SMICKETS
	SMIDGE	SMIDGEN ▪ SMIDGES
	SMIDGEN	SMIDGENS
	SMIDGEON	SMIDGEONS
	SMIDGIN	SMIDGINS
	SMIERCASE	SMIERCASES
	SMIGHT	SMIGHTS
	SMILE	SMILED ▪ SMILER ▪ SMILES ▪ SMILET SMILEY
	SMILER	SMILERS
	SMILET	SMILETS
	SMILEY	SMILEYS
	SMILING	SMILINGS
	SMILODON	SMILODONS
	SMIR	SMIRK ▪ SMIRR ▪ SMIRS
	SMIRCHER	SMIRCHERS
	SMIRK	SMIRKS ▪ SMIRKY
	SMIRKER	SMIRKERS
	SMIRR	SMIRRS ▪ SMIRRY
	SMIRTING	SMIRTINGS
	SMIT	SMITE ▪ SMITH ▪ SMITS
	SMITE	SMITER ▪ SMITES
	SMITER	SMITERS
	SMITH	SMITHS ▪ SMITHY
	SMOCK	SMOCKS
	SMOCKING	SMOCKINGS
	SMOG	SMOGS
	SMOILE	SMOILED ▪ SMOILES
	SMOKE	SMOKED ▪ SMOKER ▪ SMOKES ▪ SMOKEY
	SMOKEHO	SMOKEHOS
	SMOKEHOOD	SMOKEHOODS
	SMOKEJACK	SMOKEJACKS
	SMOKEPOT	SMOKEPOTS
	SMOKER	SMOKERS
	SMOKETREE	SMOKETREES
	SMOKIES	SMOKIEST
	SMOKING	SMOKINGS
	SMOKO	SMOKOS
	SMOLDER	SMOLDERS
	SMOLT	SMOLTS
	SMOOCH	SMOOCHY
	SMOOCHER	SMOOCHERS
	SMOODGE	SMOODGED ▪ SMOODGES
	SMOOGE	SMOOGED ▪ SMOOGES
	SMOOR	SMOORS
	SMOOT	SMOOTH ▪ SMOOTS

S

FRONT HOOK	ROOT WORD	END HOOK
	SMOOTH	SMOOTHS · SMOOTHY
	SMOOTHEN	SMOOTHENS
	SMOOTHER	SMOOTHERS
	SMOOTHES	SMOOTHEST
	SMOOTHIE	SMOOTHIES
	SMOOTHING	SMOOTHINGS
	SMORBROD	SMORBRODS
	SMORE	SMORED · SMORES
	SMOTHER	SMOTHERS · SMOTHERY
	SMOTHERER	SMOTHERERS
ASMOULDER	**SMOULDER**	SMOULDERS
	SMOUSE	SMOUSED · SMOUSER · SMOUSES
	SMOUSER	SMOUSERS
	SMOUT	SMOUTS
	SMOWT	SMOWTS
	SMOYLE	SMOYLED · SMOYLES
	SMRITI	SMRITIS
	SMUDGE	SMUDGED · SMUDGER · SMUDGES
	SMUDGER	SMUDGERS
	SMUDGING	SMUDGINGS
	SMUG	SMUGS
	SMUGGER	SMUGGERY
	SMUGGLE	SMUGGLED · SMUGGLER · SMUGGLES
	SMUGGLER	SMUGGLERS
	SMUGGLING	SMUGGLINGS
	SMUR	SMURS
	SMURFING	SMURFINGS
	SMUT	SMUTS
	SMUTCH	SMUTCHY
	SMYTRIE	SMYTRIES
	SNAB	SNABS
	SNABBLE	SNABBLED · SNABBLES
	SNACK	SNACKS
	SNACKER	SNACKERS
	SNACKETTE	SNACKETTES
	SNAFFLE	SNAFFLED · SNAFFLES
	SNAFU	SNAFUS
	SNAG	SNAGS
	SNAIL	SNAILS · SNAILY
	SNAKE	SNAKED · SNAKES · SNAKEY
	SNAKEBIRD	SNAKEBIRDS
	SNAKEBIT	SNAKEBITE
	SNAKEBITE	SNAKEBITES
	SNAKEHEAD	SNAKEHEADS
	SNAKEPIT	SNAKEPITS
	SNAKEROOT	SNAKEROOTS
	SNAKESKIN	SNAKESKINS
	SNAKEWEED	SNAKEWEEDS
	SNAKEWOOD	SNAKEWOODS
	SNAP	SNAPS
	SNAPBACK	SNAPBACKS
	SNAPHANCE	SNAPHANCES
	SNAPLINK	SNAPLINKS
	SNAPPER	SNAPPERS
	SNAPPING	SNAPPINGS
	SNAPSHOT	SNAPSHOTS
	SNAPTIN	SNAPTINS
	SNAPWEED	SNAPWEEDS
	SNAR	SNARE · SNARF · SNARK · SNARL · SNARS SNARY
	SNARE	SNARED · SNARER · SNARES
	SNARER	SNARERS
	SNARF	SNARFS
	SNARING	SNARINGS
	SNARK	SNARKS · SNARKY
	SNARL	SNARLS · SNARLY
	SNARLER	SNARLERS
	SNARLING	SNARLINGS
	SNASTE	SNASTES

S

FRONT HOOK	ROOT WORD	END HOOK
	SNATCH	SNATCHY
	SNATCHER	SNATCHERS
	SNATCHING	SNATCHINGS
	SNATH	SNATHE = SNATHS
	SNATHE	SNATHES
	SNAW	SNAWS
	SNEAD	SNEADS
	SNEAK	SNEAKS = SNEAKY
	SNEAKER	SNEAKERS
	SNEAKUP	SNEAKUPS
	SNEAP	SNEAPS
	SNEATH	SNEATHS
	SNEB	SNEBS
	SNEBBE	SNEBBED = SNEBBES
	SNECK	SNECKS
	SNED	SNEDS
	SNEE	SNEED = SNEER = SNEES
	SNEER	SNEERS = SNEERY
	SNEERER	SNEERERS
	SNEERING	SNEERINGS
	SNEES	SNEESH
	SNEESHAN	SNEESHANS
	SNEESHIN	SNEESHING = SNEESHINS
	SNEESHING	SNEESHINGS
	SNEEZE	SNEEZED = SNEEZER = SNEEZES
	SNEEZER	SNEEZERS
	SNEEZING	SNEEZINGS
	SNELL	SNELLS = SNELLY
	SNIB	SNIBS
	SNICK	SNICKS
	SNICKER	SNICKERS = SNICKERY
	SNICKERER	SNICKERERS
	SNICKET	SNICKETS
	SNIDE	SNIDED = SNIDER = SNIDES = SNIDEY
	SNIDES	SNIDEST
	SNIFF	SNIFFS = SNIFFY
	SNIFFER	SNIFFERS
	SNIFFING	SNIFFINGS
	SNIFFLE	SNIFFLED = SNIFFLER = SNIFFLES
	SNIFFLER	SNIFFLERS
	SNIFT	SNIFTS = SNIFTY
	SNIFTER	SNIFTERS
	SNIG	SNIGS
	SNIGGER	SNIGGERS
	SNIGGERER	SNIGGERERS
	SNIGGLE	SNIGGLED = SNIGGLER = SNIGGLES
	SNIGGLER	SNIGGLERS
	SNIGGLING	SNIGGLINGS
	SNIGLET	SNIGLETS
	SNIP	SNIPE = SNIPS = SNIPY
	SNIPE	SNIPED = SNIPER = SNIPES
	SNIPER	SNIPERS
	SNIPING	SNIPINGS
	SNIPPER	SNIPPERS
	SNIPPET	SNIPPETS = SNIPPETY
	SNIPPING	SNIPPINGS
	SNIRT	SNIRTS
	SNIRTLE	SNIRTLED = SNIRTLES
	SNIT	SNITS
	SNITCH	SNITCHY
	SNITCHER	SNITCHERS
	SNIVEL	SNIVELS
	SNIVELER	SNIVELERS
	SNIVELLER	SNIVELLERS
	SNOB	SNOBS
	SNOBBISM	SNOBBISMS
	SNOBLING	SNOBLINGS
	SNOD	SNODS
	SNOEK	SNOEKS

S

FRONT HOOK	ROOT WORD	END HOOK
	SNOG	SNOGS
	SNOKE	SNOKED · SNOKES
	SNOOD	SNOODS
	SNOOK	SNOOKS
	SNOOKER	SNOOKERS
	SNOOL	SNOOLS
	SNOOP	SNOOPS · SNOOPY
	SNOOPER	SNOOPERS
	SNOOT	SNOOTS · SNOOTY
	SNOOTFUL	SNOOTFULS
	SNOOZE	SNOOZED · SNOOZER · SNOOZES
	SNOOZER	SNOOZERS
	SNOOZLE	SNOOZLED · SNOOZLES
	SNORE	SNORED · SNORER · SNORES
	SNORER	SNORERS
	SNORING	SNORINGS
	SNORKEL	SNORKELS
	SNORKELER	SNORKELERS
	SNORT	SNORTS · SNORTY
	SNORTER	SNORTERS
	SNORTING	SNORTINGS
	SNOT	SNOTS
	SNOTTER	SNOTTERS · SNOTTERY
	SNOTTIE	SNOTTIER · SNOTTIES
	SNOTTIES	SNOTTIEST
	SNOUT	SNOUTS · SNOUTY
	SNOW	SNOWK · SNOWS · SNOWY
	SNOWBALL	SNOWBALLS
	SNOWBANK	SNOWBANKS
	SNOWBELL	SNOWBELLS
	SNOWBELT	SNOWBELTS
	SNOWBIRD	SNOWBIRDS
	SNOWBLINK	SNOWBLINKS
	SNOWBOARD	SNOWBOARDS
	SNOWBOOT	SNOWBOOTS
	SNOWCAP	SNOWCAPS
	SNOWCAT	SNOWCATS
	SNOWDRIFT	SNOWDRIFTS
	SNOWDROP	SNOWDROPS
	SNOWFALL	SNOWFALLS
	SNOWFIELD	SNOWFIELDS
	SNOWFLAKE	SNOWFLAKES
	SNOWFLECK	SNOWFLECKS
	SNOWFLICK	SNOWFLICKS
	SNOWK	SNOWKS
	SNOWLAND	SNOWLANDS
	SNOWLINE	SNOWLINES
	SNOWMAKER	SNOWMAKERS
	SNOWMELT	SNOWMELTS
	SNOWMOLD	SNOWMOLDS
	SNOWPACK	SNOWPACKS
	SNOWPLOW	SNOWPLOWS
	SNOWSCAPE	SNOWSCAPES
	SNOWSHED	SNOWSHEDS
	SNOWSHOE	SNOWSHOED · SNOWSHOER · SNOWSHOES
	SNOWSHOER	SNOWSHOERS
	SNOWSLIDE	SNOWSLIDES
	SNOWSLIP	SNOWSLIPS
	SNOWSTORM	SNOWSTORMS
	SNOWSUIT	SNOWSUITS
	SNUB	SNUBS
	SNUBBE	SNUBBED · SNUBBER · SNUBBES
	SNUBBER	SNUBBERS
	SNUBBING	SNUBBINGS
	SNUDGE	SNUDGED · SNUDGES
	SNUFF	SNUFFS · SNUFFY
	SNUFFER	SNUFFERS
	SNUFFING	SNUFFINGS
	SNUFFLE	SNUFFLED · SNUFFLER · SNUFFLES

S

FRONT HOOK	ROOT WORD	END HOOK
	SNUFFLER	SNUFFLERS
	SNUFFLING	SNUFFLINGS
	SNUG	SNUGS
	SNUGGER	SNUGGERY
	SNUGGERIE	SNUGGERIES
	SNUGGLE	SNUGGLED · SNUGGLES
	SNUZZLE	SNUZZLED · SNUZZLES
	SNY	SNYE
	SNYE	SNYES
DSO · ISO	SO	SOB · SOC · SOD · SOG · SOH · SOL · SOM SON · SOP · SOS · SOT · SOU · SOV · SOW SOX · SOY
	SOAK	SOAKS
	SOAKAGE	SOAKAGES
	SOAKAWAY	SOAKAWAYS
	SOAKER	SOAKERS
	SOAKING	SOAKINGS
	SOAP	SOAPS · SOAPY
	SOAPBARK	SOAPBARKS
	SOAPER	SOAPERS
	SOAPIE	SOAPIER · SOAPIES
	SOAPIES	SOAPIEST
	SOAPLAND	SOAPLANDS
	SOAPROOT	SOAPROOTS
	SOAPSTONE	SOAPSTONES
	SOAPSUDS	SOAPSUDSY
	SOAPWORT	SOAPWORTS
	SOAR	SOARE · SOARS
	SOARE	SOARED · SOARER · SOARES
	SOARER	SOARERS
	SOARING	SOARINGS
	SOAVE	SOAVES
	SOB	SOBA · SOBS
	SOBA	SOBAS
	SOBBER	SOBBERS
	SOBBING	SOBBINGS
	SOBER	SOBERS
	SOBERISE	SOBERISED · SOBERISES
	SOBERIZE	SOBERIZED · SOBERIZES
	SOBOLE	SOBOLES
	SOBRIQUET	SOBRIQUETS
	SOC	SOCA · SOCK · SOCS
	SOCA	SOCAS
	SOCAGE	SOCAGER · SOCAGES
	SOCAGER	SOCAGERS
	SOCCAGE	SOCCAGES
	SOCCER	SOCCERS
	SOCIABLE	SOCIABLES
ASOCIAL	SOCIAL	SOCIALS
	SOCIALISE	SOCIALISED · SOCIALISER · SOCIALISES
	SOCIALISM	SOCIALISMS
	SOCIALIST	SOCIALISTS
	SOCIALITE	SOCIALITES
	SOCIALIZE	SOCIALIZED · SOCIALIZER · SOCIALIZES
ASOCIALS	SOCIALS	
	SOCIATE	SOCIATES
	SOCIATION	SOCIATIONS
	SOCIOGRAM	SOCIOGRAMS
	SOCIOLECT	SOCIOLECTS
	SOCIOPATH	SOCIOPATHS · SOCIOPATHY
	SOCK	SOCKO · SOCKS
	SOCKET	SOCKETS
	SOCKETTE	SOCKETTES
	SOCKEYE	SOCKEYES
	SOCLE	SOCLES
	SOD	SODA · SODS
	SODA	SODAS
	SODAIN	SODAINE
	SODALIST	SODALISTS

S

FRONT HOOK	ROOT WORD	END HOOK
	SODALITE	SODALITES
	SODAMIDE	SODAMIDES
	SODBUSTER	SODBUSTERS
	SODDEN	SODDENS
	SODDIES	SODDIEST
	SODGER	SODGERS
	SODIUM	SODIUMS
	SODOM	SODOMS ▪ SODOMY
	SODOMISE	SODOMISED (offensive)
		SODOMISES (offensive)
	SODOMIST	SODOMISTS
	SODOMITE	SODOMITES
	SODOMIZE	SODOMIZED (offensive) ▪ SODOMIZES (offensive)
	SOFA	SOFAR ▪ SOFAS
	SOFABED	SOFABEDS
	SOFAR	SOFARS
	SOFFIT	SOFFITS
	SOFT	SOFTA ▪ SOFTS ▪ SOFTY
	SOFTA	SOFTAS
	SOFTBACK	SOFTBACKS
	SOFTBALL	SOFTBALLS
	SOFTBOUND	SOFTBOUNDS
	SOFTCOVER	SOFTCOVERS
	SOFTEN	SOFTENS
	SOFTENER	SOFTENERS
	SOFTENING	SOFTENINGS
	SOFTHEAD	SOFTHEADS
	SOFTIE	SOFTIES
	SOFTLING	SOFTLINGS
	SOFTSHELL	SOFTSHELLS
	SOFTWARE	SOFTWARES
	SOFTWOOD	SOFTWOODS
	SOG	SOGS
	SOGER	SOGERS
	SOGGING	SOGGINGS
	SOH	SOHO ▪ SOHS
	SOIGNE	SOIGNEE
	SOIL	SOILS ▪ SOILY
	SOILAGE	SOILAGES
	SOILING	SOILINGS
	SOILURE	SOILURES
	SOIREE	SOIREES
	SOJA	SOJAS
	SOJOURN	SOJOURNS
	SOJOURNER	SOJOURNERS
	SOKAH	SOKAHS
	SOKE	SOKEN ▪ SOKES
	SOKEN	SOKENS
	SOKOL	SOKOLS
	SOL	SOLA ▪ SOLD ▪ SOLE ▪ SOLI ▪ SOLO ▪ SOLS
	SOLA	SOLAH ▪ SOLAN ▪ SOLAR ▪ SOLAS
	SOLACE	SOLACED ▪ SOLACER ▪ SOLACES
	SOLACER	SOLACERS
	SOLAH	SOLAHS
	SOLAN	SOLAND ▪ SOLANO ▪ SOLANS
	SOLAND	SOLANDS
	SOLANDER	SOLANDERS
	SOLANIN	SOLANINE ▪ SOLANINS
	SOLANINE	SOLANINES
	SOLANO	SOLANOS
	SOLANUM	SOLANUMS
	SOLAR	SOLARS
	SOLARISE	SOLARISED ▪ SOLARISES
	SOLARISM	SOLARISMS
	SOLARIST	SOLARISTS
	SOLARIUM	SOLARIUMS
	SOLARIZE	SOLARIZED ▪ SOLARIZES
ISOLATE	SOLATE	SOLATED ▪ SOLATES
ISOLATED	SOLATED	

S

FRONT HOOK	ROOT WORD	END HOOK
ISOLATES	SOLATES	
ISOLATING	SOLATING	
ISOLATION	SOLATION	SOLATIONS
ISOLATIONS	SOLATIONS	
	SOLD	SOLDE · SOLDI · SOLDO · SOLDS
	SOLDADO	SOLDADOS
	SOLDAN	SOLDANS
	SOLDE	SOLDER · SOLDES
	SOLDER	SOLDERS
	SOLDERER	SOLDERERS
	SOLDERING	SOLDERINGS
	SOLDIER	SOLDIERS · SOLDIERY
	SOLE	SOLED · SOLEI · SOLER · SOLES
	SOLECISE	SOLECISED · SOLECISES
	SOLECISM	SOLECISMS
	SOLECIST	SOLECISTS
	SOLECIZE	SOLECIZED · SOLECIZES
	SOLEI	SOLEIN
	SOLEMNISE	SOLEMNISED · SOLEMNISER · SOLEMNISES
	SOLEMNIZE	SOLEMNIZED · SOLEMNIZER · SOLEMNIZES
	SOLENETTE	SOLENETTES
	SOLENODON	SOLENODONS
	SOLENOID	SOLENOIDS
	SOLEPLATE	SOLEPLATES
	SOLEPRINT	SOLEPRINTS
	SOLER	SOLERA · SOLERS
	SOLERA	SOLERAS
	SOLERET	SOLERETS
	SOLFATARA	SOLFATARAS
	SOLFEGE	SOLFEGES
	SOLFEGGI	SOLFEGGIO
	SOLFEGGIO	SOLFEGGIOS
	SOLFERINO	SOLFERINOS
	SOLI	SOLID
	SOLICIT	SOLICITS · SOLICITY
	SOLICITOR	SOLICITORS
	SOLID	SOLIDI · SOLIDS
	SOLIDAGO	SOLIDAGOS
	SOLIDARE	SOLIDARES
	SOLIDATE	SOLIDATED · SOLIDATES
	SOLIDISM	SOLIDISMS
	SOLIDIST	SOLIDISTS
	SOLIDUM	SOLIDUMS
	SOLION	SOLIONS
	SOLIPED	SOLIPEDS
	SOLIPSISM	SOLIPSISMS
	SOLIPSIST	SOLIPSISTS
	SOLIQUID	SOLIQUIDS
	SOLITAIRE	SOLITAIRES
	SOLITO	SOLITON
	SOLITON	SOLITONS
	SOLITUDE	SOLITUDES
	SOLIVE	SOLIVES
	SOLLAR	SOLLARS
	SOLLER	SOLLERS
	SOLLERET	SOLLERETS
	SOLLICKER	SOLLICKERS
	SOLO	SOLON · SOLOS
	SOLOIST	SOLOISTS
	SOLON	SOLONS
	SOLONCHAK	SOLONCHAKS
	SOLPUGID	SOLPUGIDS
	SOLSTICE	SOLSTICES
	SOLUBLE	SOLUBLES
	SOLUM	SOLUMS
	SOLUTE	SOLUTES
	SOLUTION	SOLUTIONS
	SOLVATE	SOLVATED · SOLVATES
	SOLVATION	SOLVATIONS

S

FRONT HOOK	ROOT WORD	END HOOK
	SOLVE	SOLVED ▪ SOLVER ▪ SOLVES
	SOLVENT	SOLVENTS
	SOLVER	SOLVERS
	SOM	SOMA ▪ SOME ▪ SOMS ▪ SOMY
	SOMA	SOMAN ▪ SOMAS
	SOMAN	SOMANS
	SOMASCOPE	SOMASCOPES
	SOMATISM	SOMATISMS
	SOMATIST	SOMATISTS
	SOMBER	SOMBERS
	SOMBRE	SOMBRED ▪ SOMBRER ▪ SOMBRES
	SOMBRER	SOMBRERO
	SOMBRERO	SOMBREROS
	SOMBRES	SOMBREST
	SOMEONE	SOMEONES
	SOMEPLACE	SOMEPLACES
	SOMERSET	SOMERSETS
	SOMETHING	SOMETHINGS
	SOMETIME	SOMETIMES
	SOMEWAY	SOMEWAYS
	SOMEWHAT	SOMEWHATS
	SOMEWHERE	SOMEWHERES
	SOMEWHILE	SOMEWHILES
	SOMITE	SOMITES
	SOMMELIER	SOMMELIERS
	SOMNIATE	SOMNIATED ▪ SOMNIATES
	SON	SONE ▪ SONG ▪ SONS
	SONANCE	SONANCES
	SONANT	SONANTS
	SONAR	SONARS
	SONATA	SONATAS
	SONATINA	SONATINAS
	SONCE	SONCES
	SONDAGE	SONDAGES
	SONDE	SONDER ▪ SONDES
	SONDELI	SONDELIS
	SONDER	SONDERS
	SONE	SONES
	SONERI	SONERIS
	SONG	SONGS
	SONGBIRD	SONGBIRDS
	SONGBOOK	SONGBOOKS
	SONGCRAFT	SONGCRAFTS
	SONGFEST	SONGFESTS
	SONGKOK	SONGKOKS
	SONGOLOLO	SONGOLOLOS
	SONGSMITH	SONGSMITHS
	SONGSTER	SONGSTERS
	SONHOOD	SONHOODS
	SONIC	SONICS
	SONICATE	SONICATED ▪ SONICATES
	SONICATOR	SONICATORS
	SONNE	SONNES ▪ SONNET
	SONNET	SONNETS
	SONNETEER	SONNETEERS
	SONNETISE	SONNETISED ▪ SONNETISES
	SONNETIZE	SONNETIZED ▪ SONNETIZES
	SONOBUOY	SONOBUOYS
	SONOGRAM	SONOGRAMS
	SONOGRAPH	SONOGRAPHS ▪ SONOGRAPHY
	SONOMETER	SONOMETERS
	SONORANT	SONORANTS
	SONS	SONSE ▪ SONSY
	SONSE	SONSES
	SONSHIP	SONSHIPS
	SONSIE	SONSIER
	SONTAG	SONTAGS
	SOOCHONG	SOOCHONGS
	SOOGEE	SOOGEED ▪ SOOGEES

S

FRONT HOOK	ROOT WORD	END HOOK
	SOOGIE	SOOGIED = SOOGIES
	SOOJEY	SOOJEYS
	SOOK	SOOKS
	SOOL	SOOLE = SOOLS
	SOOLE	SOOLED = SOOLES
	SOOM	SOOMS
	SOONER	SOONERS
	SOOP	SOOPS
	SOOPING	SOOPINGS
	SOOT	SOOTE = SOOTH = SOOTS = SOOTY
	SOOTE	SOOTED = SOOTES
	SOOTERKIN	SOOTERKINS
	SOOTFLAKE	SOOTFLAKES
	SOOTH	SOOTHE = SOOTHS
	SOOTHE	SOOTHED = SOOTHER = SOOTHES
	SOOTHER	SOOTHERS
	SOOTHES	SOOTHEST
	SOOTHING	SOOTHINGS
	SOOTHSAY	SOOTHSAYS
	SOP	SOPH = SOPS
	SOPAPILLA	SOPAPILLAS
	SOPH	SOPHS = SOPHY
	SOPHISM	SOPHISMS
	SOPHIST	SOPHISTS
	SOPHISTER	SOPHISTERS
	SOPHOMORE	SOPHOMORES
	SOPITE	SOPITED = SOPITES
	SOPOR	SOPORS
	SOPORIFIC	SOPORIFICS
	SOPPING	SOPPINGS
	SOPRANINO	SOPRANINOS
	SOPRANIST	SOPRANISTS
	SOPRANO	SOPRANOS
PSORA	SORA	SORAL = SORAS
	SORAGE	SORAGES
PSORAS	SORAS	
	SORB	SORBO = SORBS
	SORBARIA	SORBARIAS
	SORBATE	SORBATES
	SORBENT	SORBENTS
	SORBET	SORBETS
	SORBITE	SORBITES
	SORBITISE	SORBITISED = SORBITISES
	SORBITIZE	SORBITIZED = SORBITIZES
	SORBITOL	SORBITOLS
	SORBOSE	SORBOSES
	SORCERER	SORCERERS
	SORD	SORDA = SORDO = SORDS
	SORDINE	SORDINES
	SORDO	SORDOR
	SORDOR	SORDORS
	SORE	SORED = SOREE = SOREL = SORER = SORES SOREX
	SOREDIA	SOREDIAL
	SOREE	SOREES
	SOREHEAD	SOREHEADS
	SOREHON	SOREHONS
	SOREL	SORELL = SORELS = SORELY
	SORELL	SORELLS
TSORES	SORES	SOREST
	SORGHO	SORGHOS
	SORGHUM	SORGHUMS
	SORGO	SORGOS
	SORING	SORINGS
	SORN	SORNS
	SORNER	SORNERS
	SORNING	SORNINGS
	SOROBAN	SOROBANS
	SOROCHE	SOROCHES

S

FRONT HOOK	ROOT WORD	END HOOK
	SORORATE	SORORATES
	SORORISE	SORORISED · SORORISES
	SORORIZE	SORORIZED · SORORIZES
	SORPTION	SORPTIONS
	SORRA	SORRAS
	SORREL	SORRELS
	SORROW	SORROWS
	SORROWER	SORROWERS
	SORROWING	SORROWINGS
	SORT	SORTA · SORTS
	SORTA	SORTAL
	SORTAL	SORTALS
	SORTANCE	SORTANCES
	SORTATION	SORTATIONS
	SORTER	SORTERS
	SORTIE	SORTIED · SORTIES
	SORTILEGE	SORTILEGER · SORTILEGES
	SORTING	SORTINGS
	SORTITION	SORTITIONS
	SORTMENT	SORTMENTS
DSOS · ISOS	**SOS**	SOSS
	SOSATIE	SOSATIES
	SOSSING	SOSSINGS
	SOSTENUTO	SOSTENUTOS
	SOT	SOTH · SOTS
	SOTH	SOTHS
	SOTOL	SOTOLS
	SOTTING	SOTTINGS
	SOTTISIER	SOTTISIERS
	SOU	SOUK · SOUL · SOUM · SOUP · SOUR · SOUS · SOUT
	SOUARI	SOUARIS
	SOUBISE	SOUBISES
	SOUBRETTE	SOUBRETTES
	SOUCAR	SOUCARS
	SOUCE	SOUCED · SOUCES
	SOUCHONG	SOUCHONGS
	SOUDAN	SOUDANS
	SOUFFLE	SOUFFLED · SOUFFLES
	SOUGH	SOUGHS · SOUGHT
	SOUK	SOUKS
	SOUL	SOULS
	SOULDAN	SOULDANS
	SOULDIER	SOULDIERS
	SOULMATE	SOULMATES
	SOUM	SOUMS
	SOUMING	SOUMINGS
	SOUND	SOUNDS
	SOUNDBITE	SOUNDBITES
	SOUNDCARD	SOUNDCARDS
	SOUNDER	SOUNDERS
	SOUNDING	SOUNDINGS
	SOUNDPOST	SOUNDPOSTS
	SOUP	SOUPS · SOUPY
	SOUPCON	SOUPCONS
	SOUPER	SOUPERS
	SOUPFIN	SOUPFINS
	SOUPLE	SOUPLED · SOUPLES
	SOUPLES	SOUPLESS
	SOUPSPOON	SOUPSPOONS
	SOUR	SOURS
	SOURBALL	SOURBALLS
	SOURCE	SOURCED · SOURCES
	SOURCING	SOURCINGS
	SOURDINE	SOURDINES
	SOURDOUGH	SOURDOUGHS
	SOURING	SOURINGS
	SOUROCK	SOUROCKS
	SOURS	SOURSE

S

FRONT HOOK	ROOT WORD	END HOOK
	SOURSE	SOURSES
	SOURSOP	SOURSOPS
	SOURWOOD	SOURWOODS
	SOUS	SOUSE
	SOUSE	SOUSED ▪ SOUSES
	SOUSING	SOUSINGS
	SOUSLIK	SOUSLIKS
	SOUT	SOUTH ▪ SOUTS
	SOUTACHE	SOUTACHES
	SOUTANE	SOUTANES
	SOUTAR	SOUTARS
	SOUTENEUR	SOUTENEURS
	SOUTER	SOUTERS
	SOUTH	SOUTHS
	SOUTHEAST	SOUTHEASTS
	SOUTHER	SOUTHERN ▪ SOUTHERS
	SOUTHERN	SOUTHERNS
	SOUTHING	SOUTHINGS
	SOUTHLAND	SOUTHLANDS
	SOUTHPAW	SOUTHPAWS
	SOUTHRON	SOUTHRONS
	SOUTHSAY	SOUTHSAYS
	SOUTHWARD	SOUTHWARDS
	SOUTHWEST	SOUTHWESTS
	SOUTIE	SOUTIES (offensive)
	SOUTPIEL	SOUTPIELS (offensive)
	SOUVENIR	SOUVENIRS
	SOUVLAKI	SOUVLAKIA ▪ SOUVLAKIS
	SOUVLAKIA	SOUVLAKIAS
	SOV	SOVS
	SOVENANCE	SOVENANCES
	SOVEREIGN	SOVEREIGNS
	SOVIET	SOVIETS
	SOVIETISE	SOVIETISED ▪ SOVIETISES
	SOVIETISM	SOVIETISMS
	SOVIETIST	SOVIETISTS
	SOVIETIZE	SOVIETIZED ▪ SOVIETIZES
	SOVKHOZ	SOVKHOZY
	SOVRAN	SOVRANS
	SOW	SOWF ▪ SOWL ▪ SOWM ▪ SOWN ▪ SOWP ▪ SOWS
	SOWAR	SOWARS
	SOWARREE	SOWARREES
	SOWBACK	SOWBACKS
	SOWBREAD	SOWBREADS
	SOWCAR	SOWCARS
	SOWCE	SOWCED ▪ SOWCES
	SOWER	SOWERS
	SOWF	SOWFF ▪ SOWFS
	SOWFF	SOWFFS
	SOWING	SOWINGS
	SOWL	SOWLE ▪ SOWLS
	SOWLE	SOWLED ▪ SOWLES
	SOWM	SOWMS
	SOWN	SOWND ▪ SOWNE
	SOWND	SOWNDS
	SOWNE	SOWNES
	SOWP	SOWPS
	SOWS	SOWSE
	SOWSE	SOWSED ▪ SOWSES
	SOWSSE	SOWSSED ▪ SOWSSES
	SOWTER	SOWTERS
	SOWTH	SOWTHS
	SOY	SOYA ▪ SOYS
	SOYA	SOYAS
	SOYBEAN	SOYBEANS
	SOYLE	SOYLES
	SOYMILK	SOYMILKS
	SOZIN	SOZINE ▪ SOZINS
	SOZINE	SOZINES

S

FRONT HOOK	ROOT WORD	END HOOK
	SOZZLE	SOZZLED ▪ SOZZLES
	SPA	SPAE ▪ SPAG ▪ SPAM ▪ SPAN ▪ SPAR SPAS ▪ SPAT ▪ SPAW ▪ SPAY ▪ SPAZ
	SPACE	SPACED ▪ SPACER ▪ SPACES ▪ SPACEY
	SPACEBAND	SPACEBANDS
	SPACELAB	SPACELABS
	SPACEPORT	SPACEPORTS
	SPACER	SPACERS
	SPACESHIP	SPACESHIPS
	SPACESUIT	SPACESUITS
	SPACEWALK	SPACEWALKS
	SPACING	SPACINGS
	SPACKLE	SPACKLED ▪ SPACKLES
	SPADASSIN	SPADASSINS
	SPADE	SPADED ▪ SPADER ▪ SPADES
	SPADEFUL	SPADEFULS
	SPADER	SPADERS
	SPADEWORK	SPADEWORKS
	SPADGER	SPADGERS
	SPADILLE	SPADILLES
	SPADILLIO	SPADILLIOS
	SPADILLO	SPADILLOS
	SPADO	SPADOS
	SPADROON	SPADROONS
	SPAE	SPAED ▪ SPAER ▪ SPAES
	SPAEING	SPAEINGS
	SPAER	SPAERS
	SPAETZLE	SPAETZLES
	SPAG	SPAGS
	SPAGERIC	SPAGERICS
	SPAGERIST	SPAGERISTS
	SPAGHETTI	SPAGHETTIS
	SPAGIRIC	SPAGIRICS
	SPAGIRIST	SPAGIRISTS
	SPAGYRIC	SPAGYRICS
	SPAGYRIST	SPAGYRISTS
	SPAHEE	SPAHEES
	SPAHI	SPAHIS
	SPAIL	SPAILS
	SPAIN	SPAING ▪ SPAINS
	SPAING	SPAINGS
	SPAIRGE	SPAIRGED ▪ SPAIRGES
	SPAIT	SPAITS
	SPALD	SPALDS
	SPALDEEN	SPALDEENS
	SPALE	SPALES
	SPALL	SPALLE ▪ SPALLS
	SPALLE	SPALLED ▪ SPALLER ▪ SPALLES
	SPALLER	SPALLERS
	SPALLING	SPALLINGS
	SPALPEEN	SPALPEENS
	SPALT	SPALTS
	SPAM	SPAMS
	SPAMBOT	SPAMBOTS
	SPAMMER	SPAMMERS
	SPAMMIE	SPAMMIER ▪ SPAMMIES
	SPAMMIES	SPAMMIEST
	SPAMMING	SPAMMINGS
	SPAN	SPANE ▪ SPANG ▪ SPANK ▪ SPANS
	SPANAEMIA	SPANAEMIAS
	SPANCEL	SPANCELS
	SPANDREL	SPANDRELS
	SPANDRIL	SPANDRILS
	SPANE	SPANED ▪ SPANES
	SPANG	SPANGS
	SPANGHEW	SPANGHEWS
	SPANGLE	SPANGLED ▪ SPANGLER ▪ SPANGLES SPANGLET
	SPANGLER	SPANGLERS

S

FRONT HOOK	ROOT WORD	END HOOK
	SPANGLET	SPANGLETS
	SPANGLING	SPANGLINGS
	SPANIEL	SPANIELS
	SPANK	SPANKS
	SPANKER	SPANKERS
	SPANKING	SPANKINGS
	SPANNER	SPANNERS
	SPANSPEK	SPANSPEKS
	SPANSULE	SPANSULES
	SPANWORM	SPANWORMS
	SPAR	SPARD · SPARE · SPARK · SPARS · SPART
	SPARABLE	SPARABLES
	SPARE	SPARED · SPARER · SPARES
	SPARER	SPARERS
	SPARERIB	SPARERIBS
	SPARES	SPAREST
	SPARGE	SPARGED · SPARGER · SPARGES
	SPARGER	SPARGERS
	SPARID	SPARIDS
	SPARK	SPARKE · SPARKS · SPARKY
	SPARKE	SPARKED · SPARKER · SPARKES
	SPARKER	SPARKERS
	SPARKIE	SPARKIER · SPARKIES
	SPARKIES	SPARKIEST
ASPARKLE	SPARKLE	SPARKLED · SPARKLER · SPARKLES SPARKLET
	SPARKLER	SPARKLERS
	SPARKLES	SPARKLESS
	SPARKLET	SPARKLETS
	SPARKLIES	SPARKLIEST
	SPARKLING	SPARKLINGS
	SPARKPLUG	SPARKPLUGS
	SPARLING	SPARLINGS
	SPAROID	SPAROIDS
	SPARRE	SPARRED · SPARRER · SPARRES
	SPARRER	SPARRERS
	SPARRING	SPARRINGS
	SPARROW	SPARROWS
	SPARS	SPARSE
	SPARSE	SPARSER
	SPART	SPARTH · SPARTS
	SPARTAN	SPARTANS
	SPARTEINE	SPARTEINES
	SPARTERIE	SPARTERIES
	SPARTH	SPARTHE · SPARTHS
	SPARTHE	SPARTHES
	SPARTINA	SPARTINAS
	SPAS	SPASM
	SPASM	SPASMS
	SPASTIC	SPASTICS (offensive)
	SPAT	SPATE · SPATS
	SPATE	SPATES
	SPATFALL	SPATFALLS
	SPATHE	SPATHED · SPATHES
	SPATLESE	SPATLESEN · SPATLESES
	SPATTEE	SPATTEES
	SPATTER	SPATTERS
	SPATULA	SPATULAR · SPATULAS
	SPATULE	SPATULES
	SPATZLE	SPATZLES
	SPAUL	SPAULD · SPAULS
	SPAULD	SPAULDS
	SPAVIE	SPAVIES · SPAVIET
	SPAVIN	SPAVINS
	SPAW	SPAWL · SPAWN · SPAWS
	SPAWL	SPAWLS
	SPAWN	SPAWNS · SPAWNY
	SPAWNER	SPAWNERS
	SPAWNING	SPAWNINGS

FRONT HOOK	ROOT WORD	END HOOK
	SPAY	SPAYD ▪ SPAYS
	SPAYAD	SPAYADS
	SPAYD	SPAYDS
	SPAZ	SPAZA ▪ SPAZZ (offensive)
	SPEAK	SPEAKS
	SPEAKER	SPEAKERS
	SPEAKING	SPEAKINGS
	SPEAKOUT	SPEAKOUTS
	SPEAL	SPEALS
	SPEAN	SPEANS
	SPEAR	SPEARS ▪ SPEARY
	SPEARER	SPEARERS
	SPEARGUN	SPEARGUNS
	SPEARHEAD	SPEARHEADS
	SPEARMINT	SPEARMINTS
	SPEARWORT	SPEARWORTS
	SPEAT	SPEATS
	SPEC	SPECK ▪ SPECS
ESPECIAL	**SPECIAL**	SPECIALS
ESPECIALLY	**SPECIALLY**	
	SPECIATE	SPECIATED ▪ SPECIATES
	SPECIE	SPECIES
	SPECIFIC	SPECIFICS
	SPECIFIER	SPECIFIERS
	SPECIMEN	SPECIMENS
	SPECK	SPECKS ▪ SPECKY
	SPECKLE	SPECKLED ▪ SPECKLES
	SPECKLES	SPECKLESS
	SPECTACLE	SPECTACLED ▪ SPECTACLES
	SPECTATE	SPECTATED ▪ SPECTATES
	SPECTATOR	SPECTATORS
	SPECTER	SPECTERS
	SPECTRA	SPECTRAL
	SPECTRE	SPECTRES
	SPECTRIN	SPECTRINS
	SPECTRUM	SPECTRUMS
	SPECULA	SPECULAR
	SPECULATE	SPECULATED ▪ SPECULATES
	SPECULUM	SPECULUMS
	SPEED	SPEEDO ▪ SPEEDS ▪ SPEEDY
	SPEEDBALL	SPEEDBALLS
	SPEEDBOAT	SPEEDBOATS
	SPEEDER	SPEEDERS
	SPEEDING	SPEEDINGS
	SPEEDO	SPEEDOS
	SPEEDREAD	SPEEDREADS
	SPEEDSTER	SPEEDSTERS
	SPEEDUP	SPEEDUPS
	SPEEDWAY	SPEEDWAYS
	SPEEDWELL	SPEEDWELLS
	SPEEL	SPEELS
	SPEELER	SPEELERS
	SPEER	SPEERS
	SPEERING	SPEERINGS
	SPEIL	SPEILS
	SPEIR	SPEIRS
	SPEIRING	SPEIRINGS
	SPEISE	SPEISES
	SPEK	SPEKS
	SPEKBOOM	SPEKBOOMS
	SPELD	SPELDS
	SPELDER	SPELDERS
	SPELDIN	SPELDING ▪ SPELDINS
	SPELDING	SPELDINGS
	SPELDRIN	SPELDRING ▪ SPELDRINS
	SPELDRING	SPELDRINGS
	SPELK	SPELKS
	SPELL	SPELLS
	SPELLBIND	SPELLBINDS

S

FRONT HOOK	ROOT WORD	END HOOK
	SPELLDOWN	SPELLDOWNS
	SPELLER	SPELLERS
	SPELLICAN	SPELLICANS
	SPELLING	SPELLINGS
	SPELT	SPELTS ▪ SPELTZ
	SPELTER	SPELTERS
	SPELUNK	SPELUNKS
	SPELUNKER	SPELUNKERS
	SPENCE	SPENCER ▪ SPENCES
	SPENCER	SPENCERS
	SPEND	SPENDS ▪ SPENDY
	SPENDALL	SPENDALLS
	SPENDER	SPENDERS
	SPENDING	SPENDINGS
	SPENSE	SPENSES
	SPERLING	SPERLINGS
	SPERM	SPERMS
	SPERMATIA	SPERMATIAL
	SPERMATIC	SPERMATICS
	SPERMATID	SPERMATIDS
	SPERMINE	SPERMINES
	SPERRE	SPERRED ▪ SPERRES
ASPERSE	SPERSE	SPERSED ▪ SPERSES
ASPERSED	SPERSED	
ASPERSES	SPERSES	
ASPERSING	SPERSING	
	SPERTHE	SPERTHES
	SPET	SPETS
	SPEUG	SPEUGS
	SPEW	SPEWS ▪ SPEWY
	SPEWER	SPEWERS
	SPHAER	SPHAERE ▪ SPHAERS
	SPHAERE	SPHAERES
	SPHAERITE	SPHAERITES
	SPHAGNUM	SPHAGNUMS
	SPHAIREE	SPHAIREES
	SPHEAR	SPHEARE ▪ SPHEARS
	SPHEARE	SPHEARES
	SPHENDONE	SPHENDONES
	SPHENE	SPHENES
	SPHENODON	SPHENODONS ▪ SPHENODONT
	SPHENOID	SPHENOIDS
	SPHERE	SPHERED ▪ SPHERES
ASPHERIC	SPHERIC	SPHERICS
ASPHERICAL	SPHERICAL	
	SPHEROID	SPHEROIDS
	SPHERULE	SPHERULES
	SPHINCTER	SPHINCTERS
	SPHINGID	SPHINGIDS
ESPIAL	SPIAL	SPIALS
ESPIALS	SPIALS	
ASPIC	SPIC	SPICA ▪ SPICE ▪ SPICK ▪ SPICS (offensive) SPICY
	SPICA	SPICAE ▪ SPICAS
	SPICATE	SPICATED
	SPICCATO	SPICCATOS
	SPICE	SPICED ▪ SPICER ▪ SPICES ▪ SPICEY
	SPICER	SPICERS ▪ SPICERY
	SPICILEGE	SPICILEGES
ASPICK	SPICK	SPICKS (offensive)
	SPICKNEL	SPICKNELS
ASPICKS	SPICKS	
ASPICS	SPICS	
	SPICULA	SPICULAE ▪ SPICULAR
	SPICULE	SPICULES
	SPIDE	SPIDER ▪ SPIDES (offensive)
	SPIDER	SPIDERS ▪ SPIDERY
	SPIDERWEB	SPIDERWEBS
	SPIE	SPIED ▪ SPIEL ▪ SPIER ▪ SPIES

S

FRONT HOOK	ROOT WORD	END HOOK
ESPIED	**SPIED**	
	SPIEGEL	SPIEGELS
	SPIEL	SPIELS
	SPIELER	SPIELERS
ESPIER	**SPIER**	SPIERS
ESPIERS	**SPIERS**	
ESPIES	**SPIES**	
	SPIF	SPIFF ▪ SPIFS
	SPIFF	SPIFFS ▪ SPIFFY
	SPIFFIES	SPIFFIEST
	SPIGHT	SPIGHTS
	SPIGNEL	SPIGNELS
	SPIGOT	SPIGOTS
	SPIK	SPIKE ▪ SPIKS (offensive) ▪ SPIKY
	SPIKE	SPIKED ▪ SPIKER ▪ SPIKES ▪ SPIKEY
	SPIKELET	SPIKELETS
	SPIKENARD	SPIKENARDS
	SPIKER	SPIKERS ▪ SPIKERY
	SPILE	SPILED ▪ SPILES
	SPILIKIN	SPILIKINS
	SPILING	SPILINGS
	SPILITE	SPILITES
	SPILL	SPILLS
	SPILLAGE	SPILLAGES
	SPILLER	SPILLERS
	SPILLIKIN	SPILLIKINS
	SPILLING	SPILLINGS
	SPILLOVER	SPILLOVERS
	SPILLWAY	SPILLWAYS
	SPILOSITE	SPILOSITES
	SPILT	SPILTH
	SPILTH	SPILTHS
	SPIM	SPIMS
	SPIN	SPINA ▪ SPINE ▪ SPINK ▪ SPINS ▪ SPINY
	SPINA	SPINAE ▪ SPINAL ▪ SPINAR ▪ SPINAS
	SPINACENE	SPINACENES
	SPINACH	SPINACHY
	SPINAGE	SPINAGES
	SPINAL	SPINALS
	SPINAR	SPINARS
	SPINDLE	SPINDLED ▪ SPINDLER ▪ SPINDLES
	SPINDLER	SPINDLERS
	SPINDLING	SPINDLINGS
	SPINDRIFT	SPINDRIFTS
ASPINE	**SPINE**	SPINED ▪ SPINEL ▪ SPINES ▪ SPINET
	SPINEL	SPINELS
	SPINELLE	SPINELLES
ASPINES	**SPINES**	
	SPINET	SPINETS
	SPINETTE	SPINETTES
	SPINK	SPINKS
	SPINNAKER	SPINNAKERS
	SPINNER	SPINNERS ▪ SPINNERY
	SPINNERET	SPINNERETS
	SPINNET	SPINNETS
	SPINNEY	SPINNEYS
	SPINNING	SPINNINGS
	SPINODE	SPINODES
	SPINOFF	SPINOFFS
	SPINOR	SPINORS
	SPINOUT	SPINOUTS
	SPINSTER	SPINSTERS
	SPINTEXT	SPINTEXTS
	SPINTO	SPINTOS
	SPINULA	SPINULAE
	SPINULE	SPINULES
	SPIRACLE	SPIRACLES
	SPIRACULA	SPIRACULAR
	SPIRAEA	SPIRAEAS

S

FRONT HOOK	ROOT WORD	END HOOK
	SPIRAL	SPIRALS
	SPIRALISM	SPIRALISMS
	SPIRALIST	SPIRALISTS
ASPIRANT	SPIRANT	
ASPIRANTS	SPIRANTS	
	SPIRASTER	SPIRASTERS
ASPIRATED	SPIRATED	
ASPIRATION	SPIRATION	SPIRATIONS
ASPIRE	SPIRE	SPIREA = SPIRED = SPIREM = SPIRES
	SPIREA	SPIREAS
ASPIRED	SPIRED	
	SPIRELET	SPIRELETS
	SPIREM	SPIREME = SPIREMS
	SPIREME	SPIREMES
ASPIRES	SPIRES	
	SPIRIC	SPIRICS
	SPIRILLA	SPIRILLAR
ASPIRING	SPIRING	
	SPIRIT	SPIRITS = SPIRITY
	SPIRITING	SPIRITINGS
	SPIRITISM	SPIRITISMS
	SPIRITIST	SPIRITISTS
	SPIRITUAL	SPIRITUALS
	SPIRLING	SPIRLINGS
	SPIROGRAM	SPIROGRAMS
	SPIROGYRA	SPIROGYRAS
	SPIRT	SPIRTS
	SPIRTLE	SPIRTLES
	SPIRULA	SPIRULAE = SPIRULAS
	SPIRULINA	SPIRULINAS
	SPIT	SPITE = SPITS = SPITZ
	SPITAL	SPITALS
	SPITBALL	SPITBALLS
	SPITE	SPITED = SPITES
	SPITFIRE	SPITFIRES
	SPITTER	SPITTERS
	SPITTING	SPITTINGS
	SPITTLE	SPITTLES
	SPITTOON	SPITTOONS
	SPIV	SPIVS
	SPLAKE	SPLAKES
	SPLASH	SPLASHY
	SPLASHER	SPLASHERS
	SPLASHING	SPLASHINGS
	SPLAT	SPLATS
	SPLATTER	SPLATTERS
	SPLATTING	SPLATTINGS
	SPLAY	SPLAYS
	SPLEEN	SPLEENS = SPLEENY
	SPLENDOR	SPLENDORS
	SPLENDOUR	SPLENDOURS
	SPLENETIC	SPLENETICS
	SPLENIA	SPLENIAL
ASPLENIUM	SPLENIUM	SPLENIUMS
ASPLENIUMS	SPLENIUMS	
	SPLENT	SPLENTS
	SPLEUCHAN	SPLEUCHANS
	SPLICE	SPLICED = SPLICER = SPLICES
	SPLICER	SPLICERS
	SPLIFF	SPLIFFS
	SPLINE	SPLINED = SPLINES
	SPLINT	SPLINTS
	SPLINTER	SPLINTERS = SPLINTERY
	SPLIT	SPLITS
	SPLITTER	SPLITTERS
	SPLODGE	SPLODGED = SPLODGES
	SPLORE	SPLORES
	SPLOTCH	SPLOTCHY
	SPLURGE	SPLURGED = SPLURGER = SPLURGES

FRONT HOOK	ROOT WORD	END HOOK
	SPLURGER	SPLURGERS
	SPLUTTER	SPLUTTERS · SPLUTTERY
	SPOD	SPODE · SPODS
	SPODE	SPODES
	SPODIUM	SPODIUMS
	SPODOGRAM	SPODOGRAMS
	SPODOSOL	SPODOSOLS
	SPODUMENE	SPODUMENES
	SPOIL	SPOILS · SPOILT
	SPOILAGE	SPOILAGES
	SPOILER	SPOILERS
	SPOILFIVE	SPOILFIVES
	SPOKE	SPOKED · SPOKEN · SPOKES
	SPOLIATE	SPOLIATED · SPOLIATES
	SPOLIATOR	SPOLIATORS · SPOLIATORY
	SPONDAIC	SPONDAICS
	SPONDEE	SPONDEES
	SPONDYL	SPONDYLS
	SPONGE	SPONGED · SPONGER · SPONGES
	SPONGEBAG	SPONGEBAGS
	SPONGER	SPONGERS
	SPONGIN	SPONGING · SPONGINS
	SPONSING	SPONSINGS
	SPONSION	SPONSIONS
	SPONSON	SPONSONS
	SPONSOR	SPONSORS
	SPONTOON	SPONTOONS
	SPOOF	SPOOFS · SPOOFY
	SPOOFER	SPOOFERS · SPOOFERY
	SPOOFING	SPOOFINGS
	SPOOK	SPOOKS · SPOOKY
	SPOOL	SPOOLS
	SPOOLER	SPOOLERS
	SPOOLING	SPOOLINGS
	SPOOM	SPOOMS
	SPOON	SPOONS · SPOONY
	SPOONBAIT	SPOONBAITS
	SPOONBILL	SPOONBILLS
	SPOONEY	SPOONEYS
	SPOONFUL	SPOONFULS
	SPOONIES	SPOONIEST
	SPOOR	SPOORS
	SPOORER	SPOORERS
	SPOOT	SPOOTS
	SPORANGIA	SPORANGIAL
	SPORE	SPORED · SPORES
	SPORICIDE	SPORICIDES
	SPORIDESM	SPORIDESMS
	SPORIDIA	SPORIDIAL
	SPOROCARP	SPOROCARPS
	SPOROCYST	SPOROCYSTS
	SPOROCYTE	SPOROCYTES
	SPOROPHYL	SPOROPHYLL · SPOROPHYLS
	SPOROZOA	SPOROZOAL · SPOROZOAN
	SPOROZOAN	SPOROZOANS
	SPORRAN	SPORRANS
ASPORT	**SPORT**	SPORTS · SPORTY
	SPORTANCE	SPORTANCES
ASPORTED	**SPORTED**	
	SPORTER	SPORTERS
	SPORTIES	SPORTIEST
ASPORTING	**SPORTING**	
ASPORTS	**SPORTS**	
	SPORULATE	SPORULATED · SPORULATES
	SPORULE	SPORULES
	SPOSH	SPOSHY
	SPOT	SPOTS
	SPOTLIGHT	SPOTLIGHTS
	SPOTTER	SPOTTERS

S

FRONT HOOK	ROOT WORD	END HOOK
	SPOTTIE	SPOTTIER · SPOTTIES
	SPOTTIES	SPOTTIEST
	SPOTTING	SPOTTINGS
	SPOUSAGE	SPOUSAGES
ESPOUSAL	**SPOUSAL**	SPOUSALS
ESPOUSALS	**SPOUSALS**	
ESPOUSE	**SPOUSE**	SPOUSED · SPOUSES
ESPOUSED	**SPOUSED**	
ESPOUSES	**SPOUSES**	
ESPOUSING	**SPOUSING**	
ASPOUT	**SPOUT**	SPOUTS · SPOUTY
	SPOUTER	SPOUTERS
	SPOUTING	SPOUTINGS
	SPRACKLE	SPRACKLED · SPRACKLES
	SPRADDLE	SPRADDLED · SPRADDLES
	SPRAG	SPRAGS
	SPRAIN	SPRAINS · SPRAINT
	SPRAINT	SPRAINTS
	SPRANG	SPRANGS
	SPRANGLE	SPRANGLED · SPRANGLES
	SPRAT	SPRATS
	SPRATTLE	SPRATTLED · SPRATTLES
	SPRAUCHLE	SPRAUCHLED · SPRAUCHLES
ASPRAWL	**SPRAWL**	SPRAWLS · SPRAWLY
	SPRAWLER	SPRAWLERS
	SPRAY	SPRAYS
	SPRAYER	SPRAYERS
	SPRAYING	SPRAYINGS
ASPREAD	**SPREAD**	SPREADS
	SPREADER	SPREADERS
	SPREADING	SPREADINGS
	SPREAGH	SPREAGHS
	SPREATHE	SPREATHED · SPREATHES
	SPREAZE	SPREAZED · SPREAZES
	SPRED	SPREDD · SPREDS
	SPREDD	SPREDDE · SPREDDS
	SPREDDE	SPREDDEN · SPREDDES
	SPREE	SPREED · SPREES
	SPREETHE	SPREETHED · SPREETHES
	SPREEZE	SPREEZED · SPREEZES
	SPREKELIA	SPREKELIAS
	SPREW	SPREWS
	SPRIG	SPRIGS
	SPRIGGER	SPRIGGERS
	SPRIGHT	SPRIGHTS
	SPRIGTAIL	SPRIGTAILS
	SPRING	SPRINGE · SPRINGS · SPRINGY
	SPRINGAL	SPRINGALD · SPRINGALS
	SPRINGALD	SPRINGALDS
	SPRINGBOK	SPRINGBOKS
	SPRINGE	SPRINGED · SPRINGER · SPRINGES
	SPRINGER	SPRINGERS
	SPRINGING	SPRINGINGS
	SPRINGLE	SPRINGLES · SPRINGLET
	SPRINGLES	SPRINGLESS
	SPRINGLET	SPRINGLETS
	SPRINKLE	SPRINKLED · SPRINKLER · SPRINKLES
	SPRINKLER	SPRINKLERS
	SPRINT	SPRINTS
	SPRINTER	SPRINTERS
	SPRINTING	SPRINTINGS
ESPRIT	**SPRIT**	SPRITE · SPRITS · SPRITZ
	SPRITE	SPRITES
ESPRITS	**SPRITS**	
	SPRITSAIL	SPRITSAILS
	SPRITZER	SPRITZERS
	SPRITZIG	SPRITZIGS
	SPROCKET	SPROCKETS
	SPROD	SPRODS

S

FRONT HOOK	ROOT WORD	END HOOK
	SPROG	SPROGS
ASPROUT	**SPROUT**	SPROUTS
	SPROUTING	SPROUTINGS
	SPRUCE	SPRUCED ▪ SPRUCER ▪ SPRUCES
	SPRUCES	SPRUCEST
	SPRUE	SPRUES
	SPRUG	SPRUGS
	SPRUIK	SPRUIKS
	SPRUIKER	SPRUIKERS
	SPRUIT	SPRUITS
	SPUD	SPUDS
	SPUDDER	SPUDDERS
	SPUDDING	SPUDDINGS
	SPUDDLE	SPUDDLES
	SPUE	SPUED ▪ SPUER ▪ SPUES
	SPUER	SPUERS
	SPUG	SPUGS
	SPUILZIE	SPUILZIED ▪ SPUILZIES
	SPULE	SPULES
	SPULYE	SPULYED ▪ SPULYES
	SPULYIE	SPULYIED ▪ SPULYIES
	SPULZIE	SPULZIED ▪ SPULZIES
	SPUMANTE	SPUMANTES
	SPUME	SPUMED ▪ SPUMES
	SPUMONE	SPUMONES
	SPUMONI	SPUMONIS
	SPUN	SPUNK
	SPUNGE	SPUNGES
	SPUNK	SPUNKS ▪ SPUNKY
	SPUNKIE	SPUNKIER ▪ SPUNKIES
	SPUNKIES	SPUNKIEST
	SPUNYARN	SPUNYARNS
	SPUR	SPURN ▪ SPURS ▪ SPURT
	SPURGALL	SPURGALLS
	SPURGE	SPURGES
	SPURLING	SPURLINGS
	SPURN	SPURNE ▪ SPURNS
	SPURNE	SPURNED ▪ SPURNER ▪ SPURNES
	SPURNER	SPURNERS
	SPURNING	SPURNINGS
	SPURRER	SPURRERS
	SPURREY	SPURREYS
	SPURRIER	SPURRIERS
	SPURRIES	SPURRIEST
	SPURRING	SPURRINGS
	SPURT	SPURTS
	SPURTER	SPURTERS
	SPURTLE	SPURTLES
	SPURWAY	SPURWAYS
	SPUTNIK	SPUTNIKS
	SPUTTER	SPUTTERS ▪ SPUTTERY
	SPUTTERER	SPUTTERERS
ESPY	**SPY**	
	SPYAL	SPYALS
	SPYHOLE	SPYHOLES
ESPYING	**SPYING**	SPYINGS
	SPYMASTER	SPYMASTERS
	SPYPLANE	SPYPLANES
	SPYRE	SPYRES
	SPYWARE	SPYWARES
	SQUAB	SQUABS
	SQUABBLE	SQUABBLED ▪ SQUABBLER ▪ SQUABBLES
	SQUABBLER	SQUABBLERS
	SQUACCO	SQUACCOS
	SQUAD	SQUADS
	SQUADDIE	SQUADDIES
	SQUADRON	SQUADRONE ▪ SQUADRONS
	SQUADRONE	SQUADRONED ▪ SQUADRONES
	SQUAIL	SQUAILS

S

FRONT HOOK	ROOT WORD	END HOOK
	SQUAILER	SQUAILERS
	SQUAILING	SQUAILINGS
	SQUALENE	SQUALENES
	SQUALL	SQUALLS ▪ SQUALLY
	SQUALLER	SQUALLERS
	SQUALLING	SQUALLINGS
	SQUALOR	SQUALORS
	SQUAMA	SQUAMAE
	SQUAMATE	SQUAMATES
	SQUAME	SQUAMES
	SQUAMELLA	SQUAMELLAS
	SQUAMOSAL	SQUAMOSALS
	SQUAMULA	SQUAMULAS
	SQUAMULE	SQUAMULES
	SQUANDER	SQUANDERS
	SQUARE	SQUARED ▪ SQUARER ▪ SQUARES
	SQUARER	SQUARERS
	SQUARES	SQUAREST
	SQUARIAL	SQUARIALS
	SQUARING	SQUARINGS
	SQUARK	SQUARKS
	SQUARSON	SQUARSONS
	SQUASH	SQUASHY
	SQUASHER	SQUASHERS
ASQUAT	**SQUAT**	SQUATS
	SQUATTER	SQUATTERS
	SQUATTLE	SQUATTLED ▪ SQUATTLES
	SQUAW	SQUAWK ▪ SQUAWS (offensive)
	SQUAWK	SQUAWKS ▪ SQUAWKY
	SQUAWKER	SQUAWKERS
	SQUAWKING	SQUAWKINGS
	SQUAWROOT	SQUAWROOTS
	SQUEAK	SQUEAKS ▪ SQUEAKY
	SQUEAKER	SQUEAKERS ▪ SQUEAKERY
	SQUEAKING	SQUEAKINGS
	SQUEAL	SQUEALS
	SQUEALER	SQUEALERS
	SQUEALING	SQUEALINGS
	SQUEEGEE	SQUEEGEED ▪ SQUEEGEES
	SQUEEZE	SQUEEZED ▪ SQUEEZER ▪ SQUEEZES
	SQUEEZER	SQUEEZERS
	SQUEEZING	SQUEEZINGS
	SQUEG	SQUEGS
	SQUEGGER	SQUEGGERS
	SQUEGGING	SQUEGGINGS
	SQUELCH	SQUELCHY
	SQUELCHER	SQUELCHERS
	SQUIB	SQUIBS
	SQUIBBING	SQUIBBINGS
	SQUID	SQUIDS
	SQUIDGE	SQUIDGED ▪ SQUIDGES
	SQUIER	SQUIERS
	SQUIFF	SQUIFFY
	SQUIFFER	SQUIFFERS
	SQUIGGLE	SQUIGGLED ▪ SQUIGGLER ▪ SQUIGGLES
	SQUIGGLER	SQUIGGLERS
	SQUILGEE	SQUILGEED ▪ SQUILGEES
	SQUILL	SQUILLA ▪ SQUILLS
	SQUILLA	SQUILLAE ▪ SQUILLAS
	SQUILLION	SQUILLIONS
	SQUINNIES	SQUINNIEST
ASQUINT	**SQUINT**	SQUINTS ▪ SQUINTY
	SQUINTER	SQUINTERS
	SQUINTING	SQUINTINGS
	SQUIRAGE	SQUIRAGES
	SQUIRARCH	SQUIRARCHS ▪ SQUIRARCHY
ESQUIRE	**SQUIRE**	SQUIRED ▪ SQUIRES
	SQUIREAGE	SQUIREAGES
ESQUIRED	**SQUIRED**	

S

FRONT HOOK	ROOT WORD	END HOOK
	SQUIREDOM	SQUIREDOMS
	SQUIREEN	SQUIREENS
ESQUIRES	**SQUIRES**	SQUIRESS
ESQUIRESS	**SQUIRESS**	
ESQUIRING	**SQUIRING**	
	SQUIRM	SQUIRMS ▪ SQUIRMY
	SQUIRMER	SQUIRMERS
	SQUIRR	SQUIRRS
	SQUIRREL	SQUIRRELS ▪ SQUIRRELY
	SQUIRT	SQUIRTS
	SQUIRTER	SQUIRTERS
	SQUIRTING	SQUIRTINGS
	SQUISH	SQUISHY
	SQUIT	SQUITS
	SQUOOSH	SQUOOSHY
	SRADDHA	SRADDHAS
	SRADHA	SRADHAS
	SRI	SRIS
EST ▪ PST	**ST**	STY
	STAB	STABS
	STABBER	STABBERS
	STABBING	STABBINGS
	STABILATE	STABILATES
	STABILE	STABILES
	STABILISE	STABILISED ▪ STABILISER ▪ STABILISES
	STABILIZE	STABILIZED ▪ STABILIZER ▪ STABILIZES
ASTABLE	**STABLE**	STABLED ▪ STABLER ▪ STABLES
	STABLEBOY	STABLEBOYS
	STABLER	STABLERS
	STABLES	STABLEST
	STABLING	STABLINGS
ESTABLISH	**STABLISH**	
	STACCATO	STACCATOS
	STACK	STACKS
	STACKER	STACKERS
	STACKET	STACKETS
	STACKING	STACKINGS
	STACKROOM	STACKROOMS
	STACKUP	STACKUPS
	STACKYARD	STACKYARDS
	STACTE	STACTES
	STADDA	STADDAS
	STADDLE	STADDLES
	STADE	STADES
	STADIA	STADIAL ▪ STADIAS
	STADIAL	STADIALS
	STADIUM	STADIUMS
	STAFF	STAFFS
	STAFFAGE	STAFFAGES
	STAFFER	STAFFERS
	STAFFROOM	STAFFROOMS
	STAG	STAGE ▪ STAGS ▪ STAGY
	STAGE	STAGED ▪ STAGER ▪ STAGES ▪ STAGEY
	STAGEFUL	STAGEFULS
	STAGEHAND	STAGEHANDS
	STAGER	STAGERS ▪ STAGERY
	STAGGARD	STAGGARDS
	STAGGART	STAGGARTS
	STAGGER	STAGGERS ▪ STAGGERY
	STAGGERER	STAGGERERS
	STAGGIE	STAGGIER ▪ STAGGIES
	STAGGIES	STAGGIEST
	STAGHOUND	STAGHOUNDS
	STAGING	STAGINGS
	STAGNANCE	STAGNANCES
	STAGNATE	STAGNATED ▪ STAGNATES
	STAIG	STAIGS
	STAIN	STAINS
	STAINER	STAINERS

S

FRONT HOOK	ROOT WORD	END HOOK
	STAINING	STAININGS
	STAIR	STAIRS
	STAIRCASE	STAIRCASED · STAIRCASES
	STAIRFOOT	STAIRFOOTS
	STAIRHEAD	STAIRHEADS
	STAIRLIFT	STAIRLIFTS
	STAIRSTEP	STAIRSTEPS
	STAIRWAY	STAIRWAYS
	STAIRWELL	STAIRWELLS
	STAIRWORK	STAIRWORKS
	STAITH	STAITHE · STAITHS
	STAITHE	STAITHES
	STAKE	STAKED · STAKES
	STAKEOUT	STAKEOUTS
	STALAG	STALAGS
	STALE	STALED · STALER · STALES
	STALEMATE	STALEMATED · STALEMATES
	STALEST	STALEST
	STALK	STALKO · STALKS · STALKY
	STALKER	STALKERS
	STALKING	STALKINGS
	STALL	STALLS
	STALLAGE	STALLAGES
	STALLING	STALLINGS
	STALLION	STALLIONS
	STALWART	STALWARTS
	STALWORTH	STALWORTHS
	STAMEN	STAMENS
	STAMINA	STAMINAL · STAMINAS
	STAMINODE	STAMINODES
	STAMMEL	STAMMELS
	STAMMER	STAMMERS
	STAMMERER	STAMMERERS
	STAMP	STAMPS
	STAMPED	STAMPEDE · STAMPEDO
	STAMPEDE	STAMPEDED · STAMPEDER · STAMPEDES
	STAMPEDER	STAMPEDERS
	STAMPEDO	STAMPEDOS
	STAMPER	STAMPERS
	STAMPING	STAMPINGS
	STANCE	STANCES
	STANCHEL	STANCHELS
	STANCHER	STANCHERS
	STANCHES	STANCHEST
	STANCHING	STANCHINGS
	STANCHION	STANCHIONS
	STAND	STANDS
	STANDARD	STANDARDS
	STANDBY	STANDBYS
	STANDDOWN	STANDDOWNS
	STANDEE	STANDEES
	STANDER	STANDERS
	STANDFAST	STANDFASTS
	STANDGALE	STANDGALES
	STANDING	STANDINGS
	STANDOFF	STANDOFFS
	STANDOUT	STANDOUTS
	STANDOVER	STANDOVERS
	STANDPIPE	STANDPIPES
	STANDUP	STANDUPS
	STANE	STANED · STANES
	STANG	STANGS
	STANHOPE	STANHOPES
	STANIEL	STANIELS
	STANINE	STANINES
	STANK	STANKS
	STANNATE	STANNATES
	STANNATOR	STANNATORS
	STANNEL	STANNELS

FRONT HOOK	ROOT WORD	END HOOK
	STANNITE	STANNITES
	STANNUM	STANNUMS
	STANOL	STANOLS
	STANYEL	STANYELS
	STANZA	STANZAS
	STANZE	STANZES
	STANZO	STANZOS
	STAP	STAPH · STAPS
	STAPELIA	STAPELIAS
	STAPH	STAPHS
	STAPLE	STAPLED · STAPLER · STAPLES
	STAPLER	STAPLERS
	STAPPLE	STAPPLES
	STAR	STARE · STARK · STARN · STARR · STARS · START
	STARAGEN	STARAGENS
ASTARBOARD	**STARBOARD**	STARBOARDS
	STARBURST	STARBURSTS
	STARCH	STARCHY
	STARCHER	STARCHERS
	STARDOM	STARDOMS
	STARDRIFT	STARDRIFTS
	STARDUST	STARDUSTS
ASTARE	**STARE**	STARED · STARER · STARES
	STARER	STARERS
	STARFRUIT	STARFRUITS
	STARGAZE	STARGAZED · STARGAZER · STARGAZES
	STARGAZER	STARGAZERS
	STARING	STARINGS
	STARK	STARKS
	STARKEN	STARKENS
	STARKER	STARKERS
	STARLET	STARLETS
	STARLIGHT	STARLIGHTS
	STARLING	STARLINGS
	STARN	STARNS
	STARNIE	STARNIES
	STARNOSE	STARNOSES
	STAROSTA	STAROSTAS
	STARR	STARRS · STARRY
	STARRING	STARRINGS
	STARSHINE	STARSHINES
	STARSHIP	STARSHIPS
	STARSPOT	STARSPOTS
	STARSTONE	STARSTONES
ASTART	**START**	STARTS
ASTARTED	**STARTED**	
	STARTER	STARTERS
ASTARTING	**STARTING**	STARTINGS
	STARTLE	STARTLED · STARTLER · STARTLES
	STARTLER	STARTLERS
	STARTLING	STARTLINGS
ASTARTS	**STARTS**	STARTSY
	STARTUP	STARTUPS
	STARVE	STARVED · STARVER · STARVES
	STARVER	STARVERS
	STARVING	STARVINGS
	STARWORT	STARWORTS
	STASHIE	STASHIES
	STASIDION	STASIDIONS
	STAT	STATE · STATS
ESTATE	**STATE**	STATED · STATER · STATES
ESTATED	**STATED**	
	STATEHOOD	STATEHOODS
	STATELET	STATELETS
	STATEMENT	STATEMENTS
	STATER	STATERS
	STATEROOM	STATEROOMS
ESTATES	**STATES**	

FRONT HOOK	ROOT WORD	END HOOK
ESTATESMAN	**STATESMAN**	
ESTATESMEN	**STATESMEN**	
ASTATIC	**STATIC**	STATICE · STATICS
	STATICE	STATICES
	STATIN	STATING · STATINS
ESTATING	**STATING**	
	STATION	STATIONS
	STATIONER	STATIONERS · STATIONERY
	STATISM	STATISMS
	STATIST	STATISTS
	STATISTIC	STATISTICS
	STATIVE	STATIVES
	STATOCYST	STATOCYSTS
	STATOLITH	STATOLITHS
	STATOR	STATORS
	STATUA	STATUAS
	STATUE	STATUED · STATUES
	STATUETTE	STATUETTES
	STATURE	STATURED · STATURES
	STATUS	STATUSY
	STATUTE	STATUTES
	STAUMREL	STAUMRELS
	STAUN	STAUNS
	STAUNCHER	STAUNCHERS
	STAUNCHES	STAUNCHEST
	STAVE	STAVED · STAVES
	STAVUDINE	STAVUDINES
	STAW	STAWS
	STAY	STAYS
	STAYAWAY	STAYAWAYS
	STAYER	STAYERS
	STAYMAKER	STAYMAKERS
	STAYNE	STAYNED · STAYNES
	STAYRE	STAYRES
	STAYSAIL	STAYSAILS
	STEAD	STEADS · STEADY
	STEADICAM	STEADICAMS
	STEADIER	STEADIERS
	STEADIES	STEADIEST
	STEADING	STEADINGS
	STEAK	STEAKS
OSTEAL	**STEAL**	STEALE · STEALS · STEALT
	STEALAGE	STEALAGES
	STEALE	STEALED · STEALER · STEALES
	STEALER	STEALERS
	STEALING	STEALINGS
	STEALT	STEALTH
	STEALTH	STEALTHS · STEALTHY
	STEAM	STEAMS · STEAMY
	STEAMBOAT	STEAMBOATS
	STEAMER	STEAMERS
	STEAMIE	STEAMIER · STEAMIES
	STEAMIES	STEAMIEST
	STEAMING	STEAMINGS
	STEAMROLL	STEAMROLLS
	STEAMSHIP	STEAMSHIPS
	STEAN	STEANE · STEANS
	STEANE	STEANED · STEANES
	STEANING	STEANINGS
	STEAPSIN	STEAPSINS
	STEAR	STEARD · STEARE · STEARS
	STEARAGE	STEARAGES
	STEARATE	STEARATES
	STEARE	STEARED · STEARES
	STEARIN	STEARINE · STEARING · STEARINS
	STEARINE	STEARINES
	STEATITE	STEATITES
	STEATOMA	STEATOMAS
	STED	STEDD · STEDE · STEDS

FRONT HOOK	ROOT WORD	END HOOK
	STEDD	STEDDE ▪ STEDDS ▪ STEDDY
	STEDDE	STEDDED ▪ STEDDES
	STEDE	STEDED ▪ STEDES
	STEED	STEEDS ▪ STEEDY
	STEEK	STEEKS
	STEEL	STEELD ▪ STEELS ▪ STEELY
	STEELBOW	STEELBOWS
	STEELHEAD	STEELHEADS
	STEELIE	STEELIER ▪ STEELIES
	STEELIES	STEELIEST
	STEELING	STEELINGS
	STEELWARE	STEELWARES
	STEELWORK	STEELWORKS
	STEELYARD	STEELYARDS
ESTEEM	**STEEM**	STEEMS
ESTEEMED	**STEEMED**	
ESTEEMING	**STEEMING**	
ESTEEMS	**STEEMS**	
	STEEN	STEENS
	STEENBOK	STEENBOKS
	STEENBUCK	STEENBUCKS
	STEENING	STEENINGS
	STEENKIRK	STEENKIRKS
	STEEP	STEEPS ▪ STEEPY
	STEEPEN	STEEPENS
	STEEPER	STEEPERS
	STEEPLE	STEEPLED ▪ STEEPLES
	STEER	STEERS ▪ STEERY
	STEERAGE	STEERAGES
	STEERER	STEERERS
	STEERING	STEERINGS
	STEERLING	STEERLINGS
	STEEVE	STEEVED ▪ STEEVER ▪ STEEVES
	STEEVES	STEEVEST
	STEEVING	STEEVINGS
	STEGODON	STEGODONS ▪ STEGODONT
	STEGODONT	STEGODONTS
	STEGOMYIA	STEGOMYIAS
	STEGOSAUR	STEGOSAURS
	STEIL	STEILS
	STEIN	STEINS
	STEINBOCK	STEINBOCKS
	STEINBOK	STEINBOKS
	STEINING	STEININGS
	STEINKIRK	STEINKIRKS
	STELA	STELAE ▪ STELAI ▪ STELAR
	STELE	STELES
ASTELIC	**STELIC**	
	STELL	STELLA ▪ STELLS
	STELLA	STELLAR ▪ STELLAS
	STELLATE	STELLATED
	STELLERID	STELLERIDS
	STELLION	STELLIONS
	STELLITE	STELLITES
	STEM	STEME ▪ STEMS
	STEMBOK	STEMBOKS
	STEMBUCK	STEMBUCKS
	STEME	STEMED ▪ STEMES
	STEMHEAD	STEMHEADS
	STEMLET	STEMLETS
	STEMMA	STEMMAS
	STEMME	STEMMED ▪ STEMMER ▪ STEMMES
	STEMMER	STEMMERS ▪ STEMMERY
	STEMMING	STEMMINGS
	STEMPEL	STEMPELS
	STEMPLE	STEMPLES
	STEMSON	STEMSONS
	STEMWARE	STEMWARES
	STEN	STEND ▪ STENO ▪ STENS ▪ STENT

FRONT HOOK	ROOT WORD	END HOOK
	STENCH	STENCHY
	STENCIL	STENCILS
	STENCILER	STENCILERS
	STEND	STENDS
	STENGAH	STENGAHS
	STENLOCK	STENLOCKS
	STENO	STENOS
	STENOBATH	STENOBATHS
	STENOTYPE	STENOTYPED ▪ STENOTYPER ▪ STENOTYPES
OSTENT	**STENT**	STENTS
	STENTOR	STENTORS
	STENTOUR	STENTOURS
OSTENTS	**STENTS**	
	STEP	STEPS ▪ STEPT
	STEPBAIRN	STEPBAIRNS
	STEPDAME	STEPDAMES
	STEPHANE	STEPHANES
	STEPNEY	STEPNEYS
	STEPPE	STEPPED ▪ STEPPER ▪ STEPPES
	STEPPER	STEPPERS
	STEPSON	STEPSONS
	STEPSTOOL	STEPSTOOLS
	STERADIAN	STERADIANS
	STERCULIA	STERCULIAS
	STERE	STEREO ▪ STERES
	STEREO	STEREOS
	STEREOME	STEREOMES
	STERIGMA	STERIGMAS
	STERILANT	STERILANTS
	STERILISE	STERILISED ▪ STERILISER ▪ STERILISES
	STERILIZE	STERILIZED ▪ STERILIZER ▪ STERILIZES
	STERLET	STERLETS
	STERLING	STERLINGS
ASTERN	**STERN**	STERNA ▪ STERNS
	STERNA	STERNAL
	STERNAGE	STERNAGES
ASTERNAL	**STERNAL**	
	STERNEBRA	STERNEBRAE
	STERNFAST	STERNFASTS
	STERNITE	STERNITES
	STERNPORT	STERNPORTS
	STERNPOST	STERNPOSTS
	STERNSON	STERNSONS
	STERNUM	STERNUMS
	STERNWARD	STERNWARDS
	STERNWAY	STERNWAYS
ASTEROID	**STEROID**	STEROIDS
ASTEROIDAL	**STEROIDAL**	
ASTEROIDS	**STEROIDS**	
	STEROL	STEROLS
	STERTOR	STERTORS
	STERVE	STERVED ▪ STERVES
	STET	STETS
	STETSON	STETSONS
	STEVEDORE	STEVEDORED ▪ STEVEDORES
	STEVEN	STEVENS
	STEW	STEWS ▪ STEWY
	STEWARD	STEWARDS
	STEWBUM	STEWBUMS
	STEWER	STEWERS
	STEWING	STEWINGS
	STEWPAN	STEWPANS
	STEWPOND	STEWPONDS
	STEWPOT	STEWPOTS
ASTHENIA	**STHENIA**	STHENIAS
ASTHENIAS	**STHENIAS**	
ASTHENIC	**STHENIC**	
	STIBBLE	STIBBLER ▪ STIBBLES
	STIBBLER	STIBBLERS

S

FRONT HOOK	ROOT WORD	END HOOK
	STIBINE	STIBINES
	STIBIUM	STIBIUMS
	STIBNITE	STIBNITES
	STICCADO	STICCADOS
	STICCATO	STICCATOS
	STICH	STICHS
	STICK	STICKS · STICKY
	STICKBALL	STICKBALLS
	STICKER	STICKERS
	STICKFUL	STICKFULS
	STICKIES	STICKIEST
	STICKING	STICKINGS
	STICKJAW	STICKJAWS
	STICKLE	STICKLED · STICKLER · STICKLES
	STICKLER	STICKLERS
	STICKOUT	STICKOUTS
	STICKPIN	STICKPINS
	STICKSEED	STICKSEEDS
	STICKUM	STICKUMS
	STICKUP	STICKUPS
	STICKWEED	STICKWEEDS
	STICKWORK	STICKWORKS
	STICTION	STICTIONS
	STIDDIE	STIDDIED · STIDDIES
	STIE	STIED · STIES
	STIEVE	STIEVER
	STIFF	STIFFS · STIFFY
	STIFFEN	STIFFENS
	STIFFENER	STIFFENERS
	STIFFIE	STIFFIES (offensive)
	STIFFWARE	STIFFWARES
	STIFLE	STIFLED · STIFLER · STIFLES
	STIFLER	STIFLERS
	STIFLING	STIFLINGS
	STIGMA	STIGMAL · STIGMAS
ASTIGMATIC	**STIGMATIC**	STIGMATICS
	STIGME	STIGMES
	STILB	STILBS
	STILBENE	STILBENES
	STILBITE	STILBITES
	STILE	STILED · STILES · STILET
	STILET	STILETS
	STILETTO	STILETTOS
	STILL	STILLS · STILLY
	STILLAGE	STILLAGES
	STILLBORN	STILLBORNS
	STILLER	STILLERS
	STILLING	STILLINGS
	STILLION	STILLIONS
	STILLROOM	STILLROOMS
	STILT	STILTS · STILTY
	STILTBIRD	STILTBIRDS
	STILTER	STILTERS
	STILTING	STILTINGS
	STIM	STIME · STIMS · STIMY
	STIME	STIMED · STIMES
	STIMIE	STIMIED · STIMIES
	STIMULANT	STIMULANTS
	STIMULATE	STIMULATED · STIMULATER · STIMULATES
	STING	STINGO · STINGS · STINGY
	STINGAREE	STINGAREES
	STINGBULL	STINGBULLS
	STINGER	STINGERS
	STINGIES	STINGIEST
	STINGING	STINGINGS
	STINGO	STINGOS
	STINGRAY	STINGRAYS
	STINK	STINKO · STINKS · STINKY
	STINKARD	STINKARDS

S

FRONT HOOK	ROOT WORD	END HOOK
	STINKBUG	STINKBUGS
	STINKER	STINKERS
	STINKEROO	STINKEROOS
	STINKHORN	STINKHORNS
	STINKING	STINKINGS
	STINKPOT	STINKPOTS
	STINKWEED	STINKWEEDS
	STINKWOOD	STINKWOODS
	STINT	STINTS ▪ STINTY
	STINTER	STINTERS
	STINTING	STINTINGS
	STIPA	STIPAS
	STIPE	STIPED ▪ STIPEL ▪ STIPES
	STIPEL	STIPELS
	STIPEND	STIPENDS
	STIPPLE	STIPPLED ▪ STIPPLER ▪ STIPPLES
	STIPPLER	STIPPLERS
	STIPPLING	STIPPLINGS
	STIPULAR	STIPULARY
ESTIPULATE	**STIPULATE**	STIPULATED ▪ STIPULATES
	STIPULE	STIPULED ▪ STIPULES
ASTIR	**STIR**	STIRE ▪ STIRK ▪ STIRP ▪ STIRS
	STIRABOUT	STIRABOUTS
	STIRE	STIRED ▪ STIRES
	STIRK	STIRKS
	STIRP	STIRPS
	STIRRA	STIRRAH ▪ STIRRAS
	STIRRAH	STIRRAHS
	STIRRE	STIRRED ▪ STIRRER ▪ STIRRES
	STIRRER	STIRRERS
	STIRRING	STIRRINGS
	STIRRUP	STIRRUPS
	STISHIE	STISHIES
	STITCHER	STITCHERS ▪ STITCHERY
	STITCHING	STITCHINGS
	STIVE	STIVED ▪ STIVER ▪ STIVES
	STIVER	STIVERS
	STOA	STOAE ▪ STOAI ▪ STOAS ▪ STOAT
	STOAT	STOATS
	STOB	STOBS
	STOCCADO	STOCCADOS
	STOCCATA	STOCCATAS
	STOCK	STOCKS ▪ STOCKY
	STOCKADE	STOCKADED ▪ STOCKADES
	STOCKAGE	STOCKAGES
	STOCKCAR	STOCKCARS
	STOCKER	STOCKERS
	STOCKHORN	STOCKHORNS
	STOCKINET	STOCKINETS
	STOCKING	STOCKINGS
	STOCKIST	STOCKISTS
	STOCKLIST	STOCKLISTS
	STOCKLOCK	STOCKLOCKS
	STOCKPILE	STOCKPILED ▪ STOCKPILER ▪ STOCKPILES
	STOCKPOT	STOCKPOTS
	STOCKROOM	STOCKROOMS
	STOCKTAKE	STOCKTAKEN ▪ STOCKTAKES
	STOCKWORK	STOCKWORKS
	STOCKYARD	STOCKYARDS
	STODGE	STODGED ▪ STODGER ▪ STODGES
	STODGER	STODGERS
	STOEP	STOEPS
	STOGEY	STOGEYS
	STOGIE	STOGIES
	STOIC	STOICS
	STOICISM	STOICISMS
	STOIT	STOITS
	STOITER	STOITERS
	STOKE	STOKED ▪ STOKER ▪ STOKES

S

FRONT HOOK	ROOT WORD	END HOOK
	STOKEHOLD	STOKEHOLDS
	STOKEHOLE	STOKEHOLES
	STOKER	STOKERS
	STOKESIA	STOKESIAS
	STOKVEL	STOKVELS
	STOLE	STOLED ▪ STOLEN ▪ STOLES
	STOLLEN	STOLLENS
	STOLON	STOLONS
	STOLPORT	STOLPORTS
	STOMA	STOMAL ▪ STOMAS
	STOMACH	STOMACHS ▪ STOMACHY
	STOMACHER	STOMACHERS
	STOMACHIC	STOMACHICS
	STOMACK	STOMACKS
	STOMATA	STOMATAL
ASTOMATAL	**STOMATAL**	
OSTOMATE	**STOMATE**	STOMATES
OSTOMATES	**STOMATES**	
ASTOMATOUS	**STOMATOUS**	
	STOMIUM	STOMIUMS
	STOMODAEA	STOMODAEAL
	STOMODEA	STOMODEAL
	STOMODEUM	STOMODEUMS
	STOMP	STOMPS
	STOMPER	STOMPERS
	STOMPIE	STOMPIES
	STOND	STONDS
ASTONE	**STONE**	STONED ▪ STONEN ▪ STONER ▪ STONES STONEY
	STONEBOAT	STONEBOATS
	STONECAST	STONECASTS
	STONECHAT	STONECHATS
	STONECROP	STONECROPS
ASTONED	**STONED**	
	STONEHAND	STONEHANDS
	STONER	STONERN ▪ STONERS
	STONERAG	STONERAGS
	STONERAW	STONERAWS
ASTONES	**STONES**	
	STONESHOT	STONESHOTS
	STONEWALL	STONEWALLS
	STONEWARE	STONEWARES
	STONEWORK	STONEWORKS
	STONEWORT	STONEWORTS
ASTONIED	**STONIED**	
ASTONIES	**STONIES**	STONIEST
ASTONING	**STONING**	STONINGS
ASTONISH	**STONISH**	
ASTONISHED	**STONISHED**	
ASTONISHES	**STONISHES**	
	STONK	STONKS
	STONKER	STONKERS
	STONN	STONNE ▪ STONNS
	STONNE	STONNED ▪ STONNES
ASTONY	**STONY**	
ASTONYING	**STONYING**	
	STOOGE	STOOGED ▪ STOOGES
	STOOK	STOOKS
	STOOKER	STOOKERS
	STOOKIE	STOOKIES
	STOOL	STOOLS
	STOOLBALL	STOOLBALLS
	STOOLIE	STOOLIES
ASTOOP	**STOOP**	STOOPE ▪ STOOPS
	STOOPBALL	STOOPBALLS
	STOOPE	STOOPED ▪ STOOPER ▪ STOOPES
	STOOPER	STOOPERS
	STOOR	STOORS
	STOOSHIE	STOOSHIES

S

FRONT HOOK	ROOT WORD	END HOOK
ESTOP	**STOP**	STOPE ▪ STOPS ▪ STOPT
	STOPBANK	STOPBANKS
	STOPCOCK	STOPCOCKS
	STOPE	STOPED ▪ STOPER ▪ STOPES
	STOPER	STOPERS
	STOPGAP	STOPGAPS
	STOPING	STOPINGS
	STOPLIGHT	STOPLIGHTS
	STOPOFF	STOPOFFS
	STOPOVER	STOPOVERS
ESTOPPAGE	**STOPPAGE**	STOPPAGES
ESTOPPAGES	**STOPPAGES**	
ESTOPPED	**STOPPED**	
	STOPPER	STOPPERS
ESTOPPING	**STOPPING**	STOPPINGS
	STOPPLE	STOPPLED ▪ STOPPLES
ESTOPS	**STOPS**	
	STOPWORD	STOPWORDS
	STORABLE	STORABLES
	STORAGE	STORAGES
	STORE	STORED ▪ STORER ▪ STORES ▪ STOREY
	STORER	STORERS
	STOREROOM	STOREROOMS
	STORESHIP	STORESHIPS
	STOREY	STOREYS
	STORGE	STORGES
	STORIETTE	STORIETTES
	STORK	STORKS
	STORM	STORMS ▪ STORMY
	STORMBIRD	STORMBIRDS
	STORMER	STORMERS
	STORMING	STORMINGS
	STORYBOOK	STORYBOOKS
	STORYETTE	STORYETTES
	STORYING	STORYINGS
	STORYLINE	STORYLINES
	STOT	STOTS ▪ STOTT
	STOTIN	STOTINS
	STOTT	STOTTS
	STOTTER	STOTTERS
	STOTTIE	STOTTIES
	STOUN	STOUND ▪ STOUNS
ASTOUND	**STOUND**	STOUNDS
ASTOUNDED	**STOUNDED**	
ASTOUNDING	**STOUNDING**	
ASTOUNDS	**STOUNDS**	
	STOUP	STOUPS
	STOUR	STOURE ▪ STOURS ▪ STOURY
	STOURE	STOURES
	STOURIE	STOURIER
	STOUSHIE	STOUSHIES
	STOUT	STOUTH ▪ STOUTS
	STOUTEN	STOUTENS
	STOUTH	STOUTHS
	STOVAINE	STOVAINES
	STOVE	STOVED ▪ STOVER ▪ STOVES
	STOVEPIPE	STOVEPIPES
ESTOVER	**STOVER**	STOVERS
ESTOVERS	**STOVERS**	
	STOVETOP	STOVETOPS
	STOVING	STOVINGS
	STOW	STOWN ▪ STOWP ▪ STOWS
	STOWAGE	STOWAGES
	STOWAWAY	STOWAWAYS
	STOWDOWN	STOWDOWNS
	STOWER	STOWERS
	STOWING	STOWINGS
	STOWN	STOWND
	STOWND	STOWNDS

S

FRONT HOOK	ROOT WORD	END HOOK
	STOWP	STOWPS
	STOWRE	STOWRES
	STRABISM	STRABISMS
	STRAD	STRADS
ASTRADDLE	**STRADDLE**	STRADDLED · STRADDLER · STRADDLES
	STRADDLER	STRADDLERS
	STRADIOT	STRADIOTS
	STRAE	STRAES
	STRAFE	STRAFED · STRAFER · STRAFES
	STRAFER	STRAFERS
	STRAFF	STRAFFS
	STRAG	STRAGS
	STRAGGLE	STRAGGLED · STRAGGLER · STRAGGLES
	STRAGGLER	STRAGGLERS
	STRAIGHT	STRAIGHTS
	STRAIK	STRAIKS
	STRAIN	STRAINS · STRAINT
	STRAINER	STRAINERS
	STRAINING	STRAININGS
	STRAINT	STRAINTS
	STRAIT	STRAITS
	STRAITEN	STRAITENS
	STRAKE	STRAKED · STRAKES
	STRAMACON	STRAMACONS
	STRAMAZON	STRAMAZONS
	STRAMMEL	STRAMMELS
	STRAMP	STRAMPS
ASTRAND	**STRAND**	STRANDS
	STRANDER	STRANDERS
	STRANG	STRANGE
ESTRANGE	**STRANGE**	STRANGER · STRANGES
ESTRANGER	**STRANGER**	STRANGERS
ESTRANGERS	**STRANGERS**	
ESTRANGES	**STRANGES**	STRANGEST
	STRANGLE	STRANGLED · STRANGLER · STRANGLES
	STRANGLER	STRANGLERS
	STRAP	STRAPS
	STRAPHANG	STRAPHANGS
	STRAPLINE	STRAPLINES
	STRAPPADO	STRAPPADOS
	STRAPPER	STRAPPERS
	STRAPPING	STRAPPINGS
	STRAPWORT	STRAPWORTS
	STRATA	STRATAL · STRATAS
	STRATAGEM	STRATAGEMS
	STRATEGIC	STRATEGICS
	STRATH	STRATHS
	STRATUM	STRATUMS
	STRAUCHT	STRAUCHTS
	STRAUGHT	STRAUGHTS
	STRAVAGE	STRAVAGED · STRAVAGES
	STRAVAIG	STRAVAIGS
	STRAW	STRAWN · STRAWS · STRAWY
	STRAWWORM	STRAWWORMS
ASTRAY · ESTRAY	**STRAY**	STRAYS
ESTRAYED	**STRAYED**	
	STRAYER	STRAYERS
ESTRAYING	**STRAYING**	STRAYINGS
	STRAYLING	STRAYLINGS
ESTRAYS	**STRAYS**	
	STRAYVE	STRAYVED · STRAYVES
	STREAK	STREAKS · STREAKY
	STREAKER	STREAKERS
	STREAKING	STREAKINGS
	STREAM	STREAMS · STREAMY
	STREAMBED	STREAMBEDS
	STREAMER	STREAMERS
	STREAMING	STREAMINGS
	STREAMLET	STREAMLETS

S

FRONT HOOK	ROOT WORD	END HOOK
	STREEK	STREEKS
	STREEKER	STREEKERS
	STREEL	STREELS
	STREET	STREETS ▪ STREETY
	STREETAGE	STREETAGES
	STREETBOY	STREETBOYS
	STREETCAR	STREETCARS
	STREETFUL	STREETFULS
	STREIGHT	STREIGHTS
	STREIGNE	STREIGNED ▪ STREIGNES
	STRELITZ	STRELITZI
	STRELITZI	STRELITZIA
	STRENE	STRENES
	STRENGTH	STRENGTHS
	STREP	STREPS
	STRESSOR	STRESSORS
	STRETCH	STRETCHY
	STRETCHER	STRETCHERS
	STRETTA	STRETTAS
	STRETTO	STRETTOS
	STREUSEL	STREUSELS
	STREW	STREWN ▪ STREWS
	STREWAGE	STREWAGES
	STREWER	STREWERS
	STREWING	STREWINGS
	STREWMENT	STREWMENTS
	STRIA	STRIAE
	STRIATE	STRIATED ▪ STRIATES
	STRIATION	STRIATIONS
	STRIATUM	STRIATUMS
	STRIATURE	STRIATURES
ESTRICH ▪ OSTRICH	**STRICH**	
ESTRICHES ▪ OSTRICHES	**STRICHES**	
	STRICK	STRICKS
	STRICKLE	STRICKLED ▪ STRICKLES
ASTRICT	**STRICT**	
ASTRICTION	**STRICTION**	STRICTIONS
	STRICTURE	STRICTURED ▪ STRICTURES
	STRIDDLE	STRIDDLED ▪ STRIDDLES
ASTRIDE	**STRIDE**	STRIDER ▪ STRIDES
	STRIDENCE	STRIDENCES
	STRIDER	STRIDERS
	STRIDOR	STRIDORS
	STRIFE	STRIFES
	STRIFT	STRIFTS
	STRIG	STRIGA ▪ STRIGS
	STRIGA	STRIGAE
	STRIGIL	STRIGILS
	STRIKE	STRIKER ▪ STRIKES
	STRIKEOUT	STRIKEOUTS
	STRIKER	STRIKERS
	STRIKING	STRIKINGS
	STRING	STRINGS ▪ STRINGY
ASTRINGED	**STRINGED**	
ASTRINGENT	**STRINGENT**	
ASTRINGER	**STRINGER**	STRINGERS
ASTRINGERS	**STRINGERS**	
ASTRINGING	**STRINGING**	STRINGINGS
	STRINKLE	STRINKLED ▪ STRINKLES
	STRIP	STRIPE ▪ STRIPS ▪ STRIPT ▪ STRIPY
	STRIPE	STRIPED ▪ STRIPER ▪ STRIPES ▪ STRIPEY
	STRIPER	STRIPERS
	STRIPING	STRIPINGS
	STRIPLING	STRIPLINGS
	STRIPPER	STRIPPERS
	STRIPPING	STRIPPINGS
	STRIVE	STRIVED ▪ STRIVEN ▪ STRIVER ▪ STRIVES
	STRIVER	STRIVERS
	STRIVING	STRIVINGS

S

FRONT HOOK	ROOT WORD	END HOOK
	STROAM	STROAMS
	STROBE	STROBED ‧ STROBES
	STROBIL	STROBILA ‧ STROBILE ‧ STROBILI STROBILS
	STROBILA	STROBILAE ‧ STROBILAR
	STROBILE	STROBILES
	STROBING	STROBINGS
	STRODDLE	STRODDLED ‧ STRODDLES
	STRODLE	STRODLED ‧ STRODLES
	STROKE	STROKED ‧ STROKEN ‧ STROKER ‧ STROKES
	STROKER	STROKERS
	STROKING	STROKINGS
	STROLL	STROLLS
	STROLLER	STROLLERS
	STROLLING	STROLLINGS
	STROMA	STROMAL
	STROMB	STROMBS
	STROND	STRONDS
	STRONGARM	STRONGARMS
	STRONGYL	STRONGYLE ‧ STRONGYLS
	STRONGYLE	STRONGYLES
	STRONTIA	STRONTIAN ‧ STRONTIAS
	STRONTIAN	STRONTIANS
	STRONTIUM	STRONTIUMS
	STROOK	STROOKE
	STROOKE	STROOKEN ‧ STROOKES
	STROP	STROPS
	STROPHE	STROPHES
	STROPHOID	STROPHOIDS
	STROPPER	STROPPERS
	STROUD	STROUDS
	STROUDING	STROUDINGS
	STROUP	STROUPS
	STROUPACH	STROUPACHS
	STROUPAN	STROUPANS
	STROUT	STROUTS
	STROW	STROWN ‧ STROWS
	STROWER	STROWERS
	STROWING	STROWINGS
	STROY	STROYS
	STROYER	STROYERS
	STRUCTURE	STRUCTURED ‧ STRUCTURES
	STRUDEL	STRUDELS
	STRUGGLE	STRUGGLED ‧ STRUGGLER ‧ STRUGGLES
	STRUGGLER	STRUGGLERS
ESTRUM	STRUM	STRUMA ‧ STRUMS
	STRUMA	STRUMAE ‧ STRUMAS
	STRUMMEL	STRUMMELS
	STRUMMER	STRUMMERS
	STRUMPET	STRUMPETS
ESTRUMS	STRUMS	
	STRUNT	STRUNTS
ASTRUT	STRUT	STRUTS
	STRUTTER	STRUTTERS
	STRUTTING	STRUTTINGS
	STRYCHNIA	STRYCHNIAS
	STUB	STUBS
	STUBBIE	STUBBIER ‧ STUBBIES
	STUBBIES	STUBBIEST
	STUBBLE	STUBBLED ‧ STUBBLES
	STUBBORN	STUBBORNS
	STUCCO	STUCCOS
	STUCCOER	STUCCOERS
	STUCK	STUCKS
	STUD	STUDS ‧ STUDY
	STUDBOOK	STUDBOOKS
	STUDDIE	STUDDIES
	STUDDING	STUDDINGS
	STUDDLE	STUDDLES

S

FRONT HOOK	ROOT WORD	END HOOK
	STUDENT	STUDENTS · STUDENTY
	STUDFARM	STUDFARMS
	STUDHORSE	STUDHORSES
	STUDIER	STUDIERS
	STUDIO	STUDIOS
	STUDWORK	STUDWORKS
	STUFF	STUFFS · STUFFY
	STUFFER	STUFFERS
	STUFFING	STUFFINGS
	STUIVER	STUIVERS
	STULL	STULLS
	STULM	STULMS
	STUM	STUMM · STUMP · STUMS
	STUMBLE	STUMBLED · STUMBLER · STUMBLES
	STUMBLER	STUMBLERS
	STUMER	STUMERS
	STUMMEL	STUMMELS
	STUMP	STUMPS · STUMPY
	STUMPAGE	STUMPAGES
	STUMPER	STUMPERS
	STUMPIES	STUMPIEST
	STUMPWORK	STUMPWORKS
ASTUN	**STUN**	STUNG · STUNK · STUNS · STUNT
ASTUNNED	**STUNNED**	
	STUNNER	STUNNERS
ASTUNNING	**STUNNING**	STUNNINGS
ASTUNS	**STUNS**	
	STUNSAIL	STUNSAILS
	STUNT	STUNTS
	STUPA	STUPAS
	STUPE	STUPED · STUPES
	STUPEFIER	STUPEFIERS
	STUPID	STUPIDS
	STUPOR	STUPORS
	STUPRATE	STUPRATED · STUPRATES
	STURDIES	STURDIEST
	STURGEON	STURGEONS
	STURMER	STURMERS
	STURT	STURTS
	STUSHIE	STUSHIES
	STUTTER	STUTTERS
	STUTTERER	STUTTERERS
	STY	STYE
	STYE	STYED · STYES
ASTYLAR	**STYLAR**	
	STYLE	STYLED · STYLER · STYLES · STYLET
	STYLEBOOK	STYLEBOOKS
	STYLER	STYLERS
	STYLET	STYLETS
	STYLI	STYLIE
	STYLIE	STYLIER
	STYLING	STYLINGS
	STYLISE	STYLISED · STYLISER · STYLISES
	STYLISER	STYLISERS
	STYLIST	STYLISTS
	STYLISTIC	STYLISTICS
	STYLITE	STYLITES
	STYLITISM	STYLITISMS
	STYLIZE	STYLIZED · STYLIZER · STYLIZES
	STYLIZER	STYLIZERS
	STYLO	STYLOS
	STYLOBATE	STYLOBATES
	STYLOID	STYLOIDS
	STYLOLITE	STYLOLITES
	STYLOPISE	STYLOPISED · STYLOPISES
	STYLOPIZE	STYLOPIZED · STYLOPIZES
	STYME	STYMED · STYMES
	STYMIE	STYMIED · STYMIES
	STYPTIC	STYPTICS

S

807

FRONT HOOK	ROOT WORD	END HOOK
	STYRE	STYRED · STYRES
	STYRENE	STYRENES
	STYROFOAM	STYROFOAMS
	STYTE	STYTED · STYTES
	SUASION	SUASIONS
	SUAVE	SUAVER
	SUB	SUBA · SUBS
TSUBA	**SUBA**	SUBAH · SUBAS
	SUBABBOT	SUBABBOTS
	SUBACT	SUBACTS
	SUBACTION	SUBACTIONS
	SUBADAR	SUBADARS
	SUBADULT	SUBADULTS
	SUBAGENT	SUBAGENTS
	SUBAH	SUBAHS
	SUBAHDAR	SUBAHDARS · SUBAHDARY
	SUBAHSHIP	SUBAHSHIPS
	SUBALTERN	SUBALTERNS
	SUBARCTIC	SUBARCTICS
	SUBAREA	SUBAREAS
TSUBAS	**SUBAS**	
	SUBATOM	SUBATOMS
	SUBATOMIC	SUBATOMICS
	SUBBASE	SUBBASES
	SUBBASIN	SUBBASINS
	SUBBIE	SUBBIES
	SUBBING	SUBBINGS
	SUBBLOCK	SUBBLOCKS
	SUBBREED	SUBBREEDS
	SUBBUREAU	SUBBUREAUS · SUBBUREAUX
	SUBCANTOR	SUBCANTORS
	SUBCASTE	SUBCASTES
	SUBCAUSE	SUBCAUSES
	SUBCELL	SUBCELLS
	SUBCELLAR	SUBCELLARS
	SUBCENTER	SUBCENTERS
	SUBCHASER	SUBCHASERS
	SUBCHIEF	SUBCHIEFS
	SUBCHORD	SUBCHORDS
	SUBCLAIM	SUBCLAIMS
	SUBCLAN	SUBCLANS
	SUBCLAUSE	SUBCLAUSES
	SUBCLERK	SUBCLERKS
	SUBCODE	SUBCODES
	SUBCONSUL	SUBCONSULS
	SUBCOOL	SUBCOOLS
	SUBCOSTA	SUBCOSTAE · SUBCOSTAL
	SUBCOSTAL	SUBCOSTALS
	SUBCRUST	SUBCRUSTS
	SUBCULT	SUBCULTS
	SUBDEACON	SUBDEACONS
	SUBDEALER	SUBDEALERS
	SUBDEAN	SUBDEANS
	SUBDEB	SUBDEBS
	SUBDEPOT	SUBDEPOTS
	SUBDEW	SUBDEWS
	SUBDIVIDE	SUBDIVIDED · SUBDIVIDER · SUBDIVIDES
	SUBDUAL	SUBDUALS
	SUBDUCE	SUBDUCED · SUBDUCES
	SUBDUCT	SUBDUCTS
	SUBDUE	SUBDUED · SUBDUER · SUBDUES
	SUBDUER	SUBDUERS
	SUBDWARF	SUBDWARFS
	SUBEDAR	SUBEDARS
	SUBEDIT	SUBEDITS
	SUBEDITOR	SUBEDITORS
	SUBEPOCH	SUBEPOCHS
	SUBER	SUBERS
	SUBERATE	SUBERATES

S

FRONT HOOK	ROOT WORD	END HOOK
	SUBERIN	SUBERINS
	SUBERISE	SUBERISED · SUBERISES
	SUBERIZE	SUBERIZED · SUBERIZES
	SUBFEU	SUBFEUS
	SUBFIELD	SUBFIELDS
	SUBFILE	SUBFILES
	SUBFLOOR	SUBFLOORS
	SUBFOSSIL	SUBFOSSILS
	SUBFRAME	SUBFRAMES
	SUBFUSC	SUBFUSCS
	SUBFUSK	SUBFUSKS
	SUBGENRE	SUBGENRES
	SUBGOAL	SUBGOALS
	SUBGRADE	SUBGRADES
	SUBGRAPH	SUBGRAPHS
	SUBGROUP	SUBGROUPS
	SUBGUM	SUBGUMS
	SUBHA	SUBHAS
	SUBHEAD	SUBHEADS
	SUBHUMAN	SUBHUMANS
	SUBIDEA	SUBIDEAS
	SUBIMAGO	SUBIMAGOS
	SUBINCISE	SUBINCISED · SUBINCISES
	SUBINFEUD	SUBINFEUDS
	SUBITEM	SUBITEMS
	SUBITISE	SUBITISED · SUBITISES
	SUBITIZE	SUBITIZED · SUBITIZES
	SUBJECT	SUBJECTS
	SUBJOIN	SUBJOINS
	SUBJUGATE	SUBJUGATED · SUBJUGATES
	SUBLATE	SUBLATED · SUBLATES
	SUBLATION	SUBLATIONS
	SUBLEASE	SUBLEASED · SUBLEASES
	SUBLESSEE	SUBLESSEES
	SUBLESSOR	SUBLESSORS
	SUBLET	SUBLETS
	SUBLETTER	SUBLETTERS
	SUBLEVEL	SUBLEVELS
	SUBLIMATE	SUBLIMATED · SUBLIMATES
	SUBLIME	SUBLIMED · SUBLIMER · SUBLIMES
	SUBLIMER	SUBLIMERS
	SUBLIMES	SUBLIMEST
	SUBLIMING	SUBLIMINGS
	SUBLIMISE	SUBLIMISED · SUBLIMISES
	SUBLIMIT	SUBLIMITS · SUBLIMITY
	SUBLIMIZE	SUBLIMIZED · SUBLIMIZES
	SUBLINE	SUBLINES
	SUBLOT	SUBLOTS
	SUBLUNAR	SUBLUNARY
	SUBLUXATE	SUBLUXATED · SUBLUXATES
	SUBMARINE	SUBMARINED · SUBMARINER · SUBMARINES
	SUBMARKET	SUBMARKETS
	SUBMEN	SUBMENU
	SUBMENTA	SUBMENTAL
	SUBMENU	SUBMENUS
	SUBMERGE	SUBMERGED · SUBMERGES
	SUBMERSE	SUBMERSED · SUBMERSES
	SUBMICRON	SUBMICRONS
	SUBMIT	SUBMITS
	SUBMITTAL	SUBMITTALS
	SUBMITTER	SUBMITTERS
	SUBMUCOSA	SUBMUCOSAE · SUBMUCOSAL · SUBMUCOSAS
	SUBNET	SUBNETS
	SUBNICHE	SUBNICHES
	SUBNORMAL	SUBNORMALS
	SUBOCTAVE	SUBOCTAVES
	SUBOFFICE	SUBOFFICER · SUBOFFICES
	SUBORDER	SUBORDERS
	SUBORN	SUBORNS

S

FRONT HOOK	ROOT WORD	END HOOK
	SUBORNER	SUBORNERS
	SUBOSCINE	SUBOSCINES
	SUBOXIDE	SUBOXIDES
	SUBPANEL	SUBPANELS
	SUBPAR	SUBPART
	SUBPART	SUBPARTS
	SUBPENA	SUBPENAS
	SUBPERIOD	SUBPERIODS
	SUBPHASE	SUBPHASES
	SUBPHYLA	SUBPHYLAR
	SUBPLOT	SUBPLOTS
	SUBPOENA	SUBPOENAS
	SUBPRIOR	SUBPRIORS
	SUBRACE	SUBRACES
	SUBREGION	SUBREGIONS
	SUBRENT	SUBRENTS
	SUBRING	SUBRINGS
	SUBROGATE	SUBROGATED ▪ SUBROGATES
	SUBRULE	SUBRULES
	SUBSALE	SUBSALES
	SUBSAMPLE	SUBSAMPLED ▪ SUBSAMPLES
	SUBSCALE	SUBSCALES
	SUBSCRIBE	SUBSCRIBED ▪ SUBSCRIBER ▪ SUBSCRIBES
	SUBSCRIPT	SUBSCRIPTS
	SUBSECT	SUBSECTS
	SUBSECTOR	SUBSECTORS
	SUBSENSE	SUBSENSES
	SUBSERE	SUBSERES
	SUBSERVE	SUBSERVED ▪ SUBSERVES
	SUBSET	SUBSETS
	SUBSHAFT	SUBSHAFTS
	SUBSHELL	SUBSHELLS
	SUBSHRUB	SUBSHRUBS
	SUBSIDE	SUBSIDED ▪ SUBSIDER ▪ SUBSIDES
	SUBSIDER	SUBSIDERS
	SUBSIDISE	SUBSIDISED ▪ SUBSIDISER ▪ SUBSIDISES
	SUBSIDIZE	SUBSIDIZED ▪ SUBSIDIZER ▪ SUBSIDIZES
	SUBSIST	SUBSISTS
	SUBSISTER	SUBSISTERS
	SUBSITE	SUBSITES
	SUBSIZAR	SUBSIZARS
	SUBSKILL	SUBSKILLS
	SUBSOIL	SUBSOILS
	SUBSOILER	SUBSOILERS
	SUBSONG	SUBSONGS
	SUBSPACE	SUBSPACES
	SUBSTAGE	SUBSTAGES
	SUBSTANCE	SUBSTANCES
	SUBSTATE	SUBSTATES
	SUBSTRACT	SUBSTRACTS
	SUBSTRATA	SUBSTRATAL
	SUBSTRATE	SUBSTRATES
	SUBSTRUCT	SUBSTRUCTS
	SUBSTYLE	SUBSTYLES
	SUBSUME	SUBSUMED ▪ SUBSUMES
	SUBSYSTEM	SUBSYSTEMS
	SUBTACK	SUBTACKS
	SUBTASK	SUBTASKS
	SUBTAXON	SUBTAXONS
	SUBTEEN	SUBTEENS
	SUBTENANT	SUBTENANTS
	SUBTEND	SUBTENDS
	SUBTENSE	SUBTENSES
	SUBTENURE	SUBTENURES
	SUBTEST	SUBTESTS
	SUBTEXT	SUBTEXTS
	SUBTHEME	SUBTHEMES
	SUBTIL	SUBTILE
	SUBTILE	SUBTILER

S

FRONT HOOK	ROOT WORD	END HOOK
	SUBTILIN	SUBTILINS
	SUBTILISE	SUBTILISED ▪ SUBTILISER ▪ SUBTILISES
	SUBTILIZE	SUBTILIZED ▪ SUBTILIZER ▪ SUBTILIZES
	SUBTITLE	SUBTITLED ▪ SUBTITLES
	SUBTLE	SUBTLER
	SUBTONE	SUBTONES
	SUBTONIC	SUBTONICS
	SUBTOPIA	SUBTOPIAN ▪ SUBTOPIAS
	SUBTOPIC	SUBTOPICS
	SUBTOTAL	SUBTOTALS
	SUBTRACT	SUBTRACTS
	SUBTREND	SUBTRENDS
	SUBTRIBE	SUBTRIBES
	SUBTROPIC	SUBTROPICS
	SUBTRUDE	SUBTRUDED ▪ SUBTRUDES
	SUBTUNIC	SUBTUNICS
	SUBTYPE	SUBTYPES
	SUBUCULA	SUBUCULAS
	SUBUNIT	SUBUNITS
	SUBURB	SUBURBS
	SUBURBAN	SUBURBANS
	SUBURBIA	SUBURBIAS
	SUBVASSAL	SUBVASSALS
	SUBVENE	SUBVENED ▪ SUBVENES
	SUBVERSAL	SUBVERSALS
	SUBVERSE	SUBVERSED ▪ SUBVERSES
	SUBVERT	SUBVERTS
	SUBVERTER	SUBVERTERS
	SUBVICAR	SUBVICARS
	SUBWARDEN	SUBWARDENS
	SUBWAY	SUBWAYS
	SUBWOOFER	SUBWOOFERS
	SUBWORLD	SUBWORLDS
	SUBWRITER	SUBWRITERS
	SUBZONE	SUBZONES
	SUCCADE	SUCCADES
	SUCCAH	SUCCAHS
	SUCCEED	SUCCEEDS
	SUCCEEDER	SUCCEEDERS
	SUCCENTOR	SUCCENTORS
	SUCCES	SUCCESS
	SUCCESSOR	SUCCESSORS
	SUCCINATE	SUCCINATES
	SUCCINITE	SUCCINITES
	SUCCINYL	SUCCINYLS
	SUCCOR	SUCCORS ▪ SUCCORY
	SUCCORER	SUCCORERS
	SUCCOS	SUCCOSE
	SUCCOT	SUCCOTH
	SUCCOUR	SUCCOURS
	SUCCOURER	SUCCOURERS
	SUCCUBA	SUCCUBAE ▪ SUCCUBAS
	SUCCULENT	SUCCULENTS
	SUCCUMB	SUCCUMBS
	SUCCUMBER	SUCCUMBERS
	SUCCURSAL	SUCCURSALE ▪ SUCCURSALS
	SUCCUS	SUCCUSS
	SUCK	SUCKS ▪ SUCKY
	SUCKEN	SUCKENS
	SUCKENER	SUCKENERS
	SUCKER	SUCKERS
	SUCKET	SUCKETS
	SUCKING	SUCKINGS
	SUCKLE	SUCKLED ▪ SUCKLER ▪ SUCKLES
	SUCKLER	SUCKLERS
	SUCKLES	SUCKLESS
	SUCKLING	SUCKLINGS
	SUCRALOSE	SUCRALOSES
	SUCRASE	SUCRASES

FRONT HOOK	ROOT WORD	END HOOK
	SUCRE	SUCRES
	SUCRIER	SUCRIERS
	SUCROSE	SUCROSES
	SUCTION	SUCTIONS
	SUCTORIAN	SUCTORIANS
	SUCURUJU	SUCURUJUS
	SUD	SUDD = SUDS
	SUDAMINA	SUDAMINAL
	SUDATE	SUDATED = SUDATES
	SUDATION	SUDATIONS
	SUDD	SUDDS
ASUDDEN	**SUDDEN**	SUDDENS
	SUDDER	SUDDERS
	SUDOR	SUDORS
	SUDORIFIC	SUDORIFICS
	SUDS	SUDSY
	SUDSER	SUDSERS
	SUE	SUED = SUER = SUES = SUET
	SUED	SUEDE
	SUEDE	SUEDED = SUEDES
	SUEDETTE	SUEDETTES
	SUER	SUERS
	SUET	SUETS = SUETY
	SUFFARI	SUFFARIS
	SUFFER	SUFFERS
	SUFFERER	SUFFERERS
	SUFFERING	SUFFERINGS
	SUFFETE	SUFFETES
	SUFFICE	SUFFICED = SUFFICER = SUFFICES
	SUFFICER	SUFFICERS
	SUFFIXION	SUFFIXIONS
	SUFFLATE	SUFFLATED = SUFFLATES
	SUFFOCATE	SUFFOCATED = SUFFOCATES
	SUFFRAGAN	SUFFRAGANS
	SUFFRAGE	SUFFRAGES
	SUFFUSE	SUFFUSED = SUFFUSES
	SUFFUSION	SUFFUSIONS
	SUGAN	SUGANS
	SUGAR	SUGARS = SUGARY
	SUGARCANE	SUGARCANES
	SUGARCOAT	SUGARCOATS
	SUGARER	SUGARERS
	SUGARING	SUGARINGS
	SUGARPLUM	SUGARPLUMS
	SUGGEST	SUGGESTS
	SUGGESTER	SUGGESTERS
	SUGGING	SUGGINGS
	SUGH	SUGHS
	SUI	SUID = SUIT
	SUICIDE	SUICIDED = SUICIDES
	SUID	SUIDS
	SUIDIAN	SUIDIANS
	SUING	SUINGS
	SUINT	SUINTS
	SUIPLAP	SUIPLAPS
	SUIT	SUITE = SUITS
	SUITCASE	SUITCASES
	SUITE	SUITED = SUITER = SUITES
	SUITER	SUITERS
	SUITING	SUITINGS
	SUITOR	SUITORS
	SUIVANTE	SUIVANTES
	SUJEE	SUJEES
	SUK	SUKH = SUKS
	SUKH	SUKHS
	SUKIYAKI	SUKIYAKIS
	SUKKAH	SUKKAHS
	SUKKOT	SUKKOTH
	SULCALISE	SULCALISED = SULCALISES

S

FRONT HOOK	ROOT WORD	END HOOK
	SULCALIZE	SULCALIZED · SULCALIZES
	SULCATE	SULCATED
	SULCATION	SULCATIONS
	SULDAN	SULDANS
	SULFA	SULFAS
	SULFATASE	SULFATASES
	SULFATE	SULFATED · SULFATES
	SULFATION	SULFATIONS
	SULFID	SULFIDE · SULFIDS
	SULFIDE	SULFIDES
	SULFINYL	SULFINYLS
	SULFITE	SULFITES
	SULFONATE	SULFONATED · SULFONATES
	SULFONE	SULFONES
	SULFONIUM	SULFONIUMS
	SULFONYL	SULFONYLS
	SULFOXIDE	SULFOXIDES
	SULFUR	SULFURS · SULFURY
	SULFURATE	SULFURATED · SULFURATES
	SULFURET	SULFURETS
	SULFURISE	SULFURISED · SULFURISES
	SULFURIZE	SULFURIZED · SULFURIZES
	SULFURY	SULFURYL
	SULFURYL	SULFURYLS
	SULK	SULKS · SULKY
	SULKER	SULKERS
	SULKIES	SULKIEST
	SULLAGE	SULLAGES
	SULLEN	SULLENS
	SULPHA	SULPHAS
	SULPHATE	SULPHATED · SULPHATES
	SULPHID	SULPHIDE · SULPHIDS
	SULPHIDE	SULPHIDES
	SULPHINYL	SULPHINYLS
	SULPHITE	SULPHITES
	SULPHONE	SULPHONES
	SULPHONYL	SULPHONYLS
	SULPHUR	SULPHURS · SULPHURY
	SULPHURET	SULPHURETS
	SULPHURY	SULPHURYL
	SULPHURYL	SULPHURYLS
	SULTAN	SULTANA · SULTANS
	SULTANA	SULTANAS
	SULTANATE	SULTANATES
	SULU	SULUS
	SUM	SUMO · SUMP · SUMS · SUMY
	SUMAC	SUMACH · SUMACS
	SUMACH	SUMACHS
	SUMATRA	SUMATRAS
	SUMMA	SUMMAE · SUMMAR · SUMMAS · SUMMAT
	SUMMAND	SUMMANDS
	SUMMAR	SUMMARY
	SUMMARISE	SUMMARISED · SUMMARISER · SUMMARISES
	SUMMARIST	SUMMARISTS
	SUMMARIZE	SUMMARIZED · SUMMARIZER · SUMMARIZES
	SUMMAT	SUMMATE · SUMMATS
	SUMMATE	SUMMATED · SUMMATES
	SUMMATION	SUMMATIONS
	SUMMER	SUMMERS · SUMMERY
	SUMMERING	SUMMERINGS
	SUMMERSET	SUMMERSETS
	SUMMING	SUMMINGS
	SUMMIST	SUMMISTS
	SUMMIT	SUMMITS
	SUMMITEER	SUMMITEERS
	SUMMON	SUMMONS
	SUMMONER	SUMMONERS
	SUMO	SUMOS
	SUMOIST	SUMOISTS

S

FRONT HOOK	ROOT WORD	END HOOK
	SUMOTORI	SUMOTORIS
	SUMP	SUMPH = SUMPS
	SUMPH	SUMPHS
	SUMPIT	SUMPITS
	SUMPITAN	SUMPITANS
	SUMPTER	SUMPTERS
	SUMPWEED	SUMPWEEDS
	SUN	SUNG = SUNK = SUNN = SUNS
	SUNBAKE	SUNBAKED = SUNBAKES
	SUNBATH	SUNBATHE = SUNBATHS
	SUNBATHE	SUNBATHED = SUNBATHER = SUNBATHES
	SUNBATHER	SUNBATHERS
	SUNBEAM	SUNBEAMS = SUNBEAMY
	SUNBED	SUNBEDS
	SUNBELT	SUNBELTS
	SUNBIRD	SUNBIRDS
	SUNBLIND	SUNBLINDS
	SUNBLOCK	SUNBLOCKS
	SUNBONNET	SUNBONNETS
	SUNBOW	SUNBOWS
	SUNBURN	SUNBURNS = SUNBURNT
	SUNBURST	SUNBURSTS
	SUNCHOKE	SUNCHOKES
	SUNDAE	SUNDAES
	SUNDARI	SUNDARIS
	SUNDECK	SUNDECKS
ASUNDER	**SUNDER**	SUNDERS
	SUNDERER	SUNDERERS
	SUNDERING	SUNDERINGS
	SUNDEW	SUNDEWS
	SUNDIAL	SUNDIALS
	SUNDOG	SUNDOGS
	SUNDOWN	SUNDOWNS
	SUNDOWNER	SUNDOWNERS
	SUNDRA	SUNDRAS
	SUNDRI	SUNDRIS
	SUNFLOWER	SUNFLOWERS
	SUNGAR	SUNGARS
	SUNGLOW	SUNGLOWS
	SUNGREBE	SUNGREBES
	SUNHAT	SUNHATS
	SUNK	SUNKS
	SUNKET	SUNKETS
	SUNKIE	SUNKIES
	SUNLAMP	SUNLAMPS
	SUNLAND	SUNLANDS
	SUNLIGHT	SUNLIGHTS
	SUNN	SUNNA = SUNNS = SUNNY
	SUNNA	SUNNAH = SUNNAS
	SUNNAH	SUNNAHS
	SUNNIES	SUNNIEST
	SUNRAY	SUNRAYS
	SUNRISE	SUNRISES
	SUNRISING	SUNRISINGS
	SUNROOF	SUNROOFS
	SUNROOM	SUNROOMS
	SUNSCALD	SUNSCALDS
	SUNSCREEN	SUNSCREENS
	SUNSEEKER	SUNSEEKERS
	SUNSET	SUNSETS
	SUNSHADE	SUNSHADES
	SUNSHINE	SUNSHINES
	SUNSPOT	SUNSPOTS
	SUNSTAR	SUNSTARS
	SUNSTONE	SUNSTONES
	SUNSTROKE	SUNSTROKES
	SUNSUIT	SUNSUITS
	SUNTAN	SUNTANS
	SUNTRAP	SUNTRAPS

s

FRONT HOOK	ROOT WORD	END HOOK
	SUNUP	SUNUPS
	SUNWARD	SUNWARDS
	SUP	SUPE · SUPS
	SUPAWN	SUPAWNS
	SUPE	SUPER · SUPES
	SUPER	SUPERB · SUPERS
	SUPERADD	SUPERADDS
	SUPERATE	SUPERATED · SUPERATES
	SUPERATOM	SUPERATOMS
	SUPERBANK	SUPERBANKS
	SUPERBIKE	SUPERBIKES
	SUPERBOMB	SUPERBOMBS
	SUPERBRAT	SUPERBRATS
	SUPERBUG	SUPERBUGS
	SUPERCAR	SUPERCARS
	SUPERCEDE	SUPERCEDED · SUPERCEDES
	SUPERCLUB	SUPERCLUBS
	SUPERCOIL	SUPERCOILS
	SUPERCOOL	SUPERCOOLS
	SUPERCOP	SUPERCOPS
	SUPERCOW	SUPERCOWS
	SUPEREGO	SUPEREGOS
	SUPERETTE	SUPERETTES
	SUPERFAN	SUPERFANS
	SUPERFARM	SUPERFARMS
	SUPERFIRM	SUPERFIRMS
	SUPERFUND	SUPERFUNDS
	SUPERFUSE	SUPERFUSED · SUPERFUSES
	SUPERGENE	SUPERGENES
	SUPERGLUE	SUPERGLUED · SUPERGLUES
	SUPERGUN	SUPERGUNS
	SUPERHEAT	SUPERHEATS
	SUPERHET	SUPERHETS
	SUPERHIT	SUPERHITS
	SUPERHIVE	SUPERHIVES
	SUPERHYPE	SUPERHYPED · SUPERHYPES
	SUPERIOR	SUPERIORS
	SUPERJET	SUPERJETS
	SUPERJOCK	SUPERJOCKS
	SUPERLIE	SUPERLIES
	SUPERLOAD	SUPERLOADS
	SUPERLOO	SUPERLOOS
	SUPERMALE	SUPERMALES
	SUPERMART	SUPERMARTS
	SUPERMIND	SUPERMINDS
	SUPERMINI	SUPERMINIS
	SUPERMOM	SUPERMOMS
	SUPERMOTO	SUPERMOTOS
	SUPERNATE	SUPERNATES
	SUPERNOVA	SUPERNOVAE · SUPERNOVAS
	SUPERPIMP	SUPERPIMPS
	SUPERPORT	SUPERPORTS
	SUPERPOSE	SUPERPOSED · SUPERPOSES
	SUPERPRO	SUPERPROS
	SUPERRACE	SUPERRACES
	SUPERROAD	SUPERROADS
	SUPERSALE	SUPERSALES
	SUPERSALT	SUPERSALTS
	SUPERSAUR	SUPERSAURS
	SUPERSEDE	SUPERSEDED · SUPERSEDER · SUPERSEDES
	SUPERSELL	SUPERSELLS
	SUPERSHOW	SUPERSHOWS
	SUPERSIZE	SUPERSIZED · SUPERSIZES
	SUPERSTAR	SUPERSTARS
	SUPERSTUD	SUPERSTUDS
	SUPERVENE	SUPERVENED · SUPERVENES
	SUPERVISE	SUPERVISED · SUPERVISEE · SUPERVISES
	SUPERWAIF	SUPERWAIFS
	SUPERWAVE	SUPERWAVES

S

FRONT HOOK	ROOT WORD	END HOOK
	SUPERWEED	SUPERWEEDS
	SUPERWIDE	SUPERWIDES
	SUPINATE	SUPINATED · SUPINATES
	SUPINATOR	SUPINATORS
	SUPINE	SUPINES
	SUPPAWN	SUPPAWNS
	SUPPER	SUPPERS
	SUPPLANT	SUPPLANTS
	SUPPLE	SUPPLED · SUPPLER · SUPPLES
	SUPPLES	SUPPLEST
	SUPPLIAL	SUPPLIALS
	SUPPLIANT	SUPPLIANTS
	SUPPLICAT	SUPPLICATE · SUPPLICATS
	SUPPLIER	SUPPLIERS
	SUPPORT	SUPPORTS
	SUPPORTER	SUPPORTERS
	SUPPOSAL	SUPPOSALS
	SUPPOSE	SUPPOSED · SUPPOSER · SUPPOSES
	SUPPOSER	SUPPOSERS
	SUPPOSING	SUPPOSINGS
	SUPPURATE	SUPPURATED · SUPPURATES
	SUPREME	SUPREMER · SUPREMES
	SUPREMES	SUPREMEST
	SUPREMO	SUPREMOS
	SUQ	SUQS
	SUR	SURA · SURD · SURE · SURF
	SURA	SURAH · SURAL · SURAS · SURAT
	SURAH	SURAHS
	SURAMIN	SURAMINS
	SURANCE	SURANCES
	SURAT	SURATS
	SURBAHAR	SURBAHARS
	SURBASE	SURBASED · SURBASES
	SURBATE	SURBATED · SURBATES
	SURBED	SURBEDS
	SURCEASE	SURCEASED · SURCEASES
	SURCHARGE	SURCHARGED · SURCHARGER · SURCHARGES
	SURCINGLE	SURCINGLED · SURCINGLES
	SURCOAT	SURCOATS
	SURD	SURDS
USURE	**SURE**	SURED · SURER · SURES
USURED	**SURED**	
USURER	**SURER**	
USURES	**SURES**	SUREST
	SURF	SURFS · SURFY
	SURFACE	SURFACED · SURFACER · SURFACES
	SURFACER	SURFACERS
	SURFACING	SURFACINGS
	SURFBIRD	SURFBIRDS
	SURFBOARD	SURFBOARDS
	SURFBOAT	SURFBOATS
	SURFEIT	SURFEITS
	SURFEITER	SURFEITERS
	SURFER	SURFERS
	SURFIE	SURFIER · SURFIES
	SURFIES	SURFIEST
	SURFING	SURFINGS
	SURFRIDER	SURFRIDERS
	SURGE	SURGED · SURGER · SURGES
	SURGEON	SURGEONS
	SURGER	SURGERS · SURGERY
	SURGING	SURGINGS
	SURICATE	SURICATES
	SURIMI	SURIMIS
USURING	**SURING**	
	SURLOIN	SURLOINS
	SURMASTER	SURMASTERS
	SURMISAL	SURMISALS
	SURMISE	SURMISED · SURMISER · SURMISES

S

FRONT HOOK	ROOT WORD	END HOOK
	SURMISER	SURMISERS
	SURMISING	SURMISINGS
	SURMOUNT	SURMOUNTS
	SURMULLET	SURMULLETS
	SURNAME	SURNAMED · SURNAMER · SURNAMES
	SURNAMER	SURNAMERS
	SURPASSER	SURPASSERS
	SURPLICE	SURPLICED · SURPLICES
	SURPRINT	SURPRINTS
	SURPRISAL	SURPRISALS
	SURPRISE	SURPRISED · SURPRISER · SURPRISES
	SURPRISER	SURPRISERS
	SURPRIZE	SURPRIZED · SURPRIZES
	SURRA	SURRAS
	SURREBUT	SURREBUTS
	SURREJOIN	SURREJOINS
	SURRENDER	SURRENDERS
	SURREY	SURREYS
	SURROGATE	SURROGATED · SURROGATES
	SURROUND	SURROUNDS
	SURROYAL	SURROYALS
	SURTITLE	SURTITLES
	SURTOUT	SURTOUTS
	SURUCUCU	SURUCUCUS
	SURVEIL	SURVEILS
	SURVEILLE	SURVEILLED · SURVEILLES
	SURVEY	SURVEYS
	SURVEYAL	SURVEYALS
	SURVEYING	SURVEYINGS
	SURVEYOR	SURVEYORS
	SURVIEW	SURVIEWS
	SURVIVAL	SURVIVALS
	SURVIVE	SURVIVED · SURVIVER · SURVIVES
	SURVIVER	SURVIVERS
	SURVIVOR	SURVIVORS
	SUS	SUSS · SUSU
	SUSCEPTOR	SUSCEPTORS
	SUSCITATE	SUSCITATED · SUSCITATES
	SUSHI	SUSHIS
	SUSLIK	SUSLIKS
	SUSPECT	SUSPECTS
	SUSPECTER	SUSPECTERS
	SUSPEND	SUSPENDS
	SUSPENDER	SUSPENDERS
	SUSPENS	SUSPENSE
	SUSPENSE	SUSPENSER · SUSPENSES
	SUSPENSER	SUSPENSERS
	SUSPENSOR	SUSPENSORS · SUSPENSORY
	SUSPICION	SUSPICIONS
	SUSPIRE	SUSPIRED · SUSPIRES
	SUSTAIN	SUSTAINS
	SUSTAINER	SUSTAINERS
	SUSU	SUSUS
	SUSURRATE	SUSURRATED · SUSURRATES
	SUTLER	SUTLERS · SUTLERY
	SUTOR	SUTORS
	SUTRA	SUTRAS
	SUTTA	SUTTAS
	SUTTEE	SUTTEES
	SUTTEEISM	SUTTEEISMS
	SUTTLE	SUTTLED · SUTTLES
	SUTTLETIE	SUTTLETIES
	SUTURE	SUTURED · SUTURES
	SUZERAIN	SUZERAINS
	SVASTIKA	SVASTIKAS
	SVEDBERG	SVEDBERGS
	SVELTE	SVELTER
	SWAB	SWABS
	SWABBER	SWABBERS

FRONT HOOK	ROOT WORD	END HOOK
	SWABBIE	SWABBIES
	SWAD	SWADS
	SWADDIE	SWADDIES
	SWADDLE	SWADDLED · SWADDLER · SWADDLES
	SWADDLER	SWADDLERS
	SWAG	SWAGE · SWAGS
	SWAGE	SWAGED · SWAGER · SWAGES
	SWAGER	SWAGERS
	SWAGGER	SWAGGERS
	SWAGGERER	SWAGGERERS
	SWAGGIE	SWAGGIES
	SWAGSHOP	SWAGSHOPS
	SWAIL	SWAILS
	SWAIN	SWAINS
	SWAINING	SWAININGS
	SWALE	SWALED · SWALES
	SWALING	SWALINGS
	SWALLET	SWALLETS
	SWALLOW	SWALLOWS
	SWALLOWER	SWALLOWERS
	SWAM	SWAMI · SWAMP · SWAMY
	SWAMI	SWAMIS
	SWAMP	SWAMPS · SWAMPY
	SWAMPER	SWAMPERS
	SWAMPLAND	SWAMPLANDS
	SWAN	SWANG · SWANK · SWANS
	SWANHERD	SWANHERDS
	SWANK	SWANKS · SWANKY
	SWANKER	SWANKERS
	SWANKEY	SWANKEYS
	SWANKIE	SWANKIER · SWANKIES
	SWANKIES	SWANKIEST
	SWANKPOT	SWANKPOTS
	SWANNIE	SWANNIER · SWANNIES
	SWANNIES	SWANNIEST
	SWANNING	SWANNINGS
	SWANPAN	SWANPANS
	SWANSDOWN	SWANSDOWNS
	SWANSKIN	SWANSKINS
	SWAP	SWAPS · SWAPT
	SWAPPER	SWAPPERS
	SWAPPING	SWAPPINGS
	SWAPTION	SWAPTIONS
	SWARAJISM	SWARAJISMS
	SWARAJIST	SWARAJISTS
USWARD	SWARD	SWARDS · SWARDY
USWARDS	SWARDS	
	SWARF	SWARFS
ASWARM	SWARM	SWARMS
	SWARMER	SWARMERS
	SWARMING	SWARMINGS
	SWART	SWARTH · SWARTY
	SWARTH	SWARTHS · SWARTHY
	SWARVE	SWARVED · SWARVES
	SWASH	SWASHY
	SWASHER	SWASHERS
	SWASHING	SWASHINGS
	SWASHWORK	SWASHWORKS
	SWASTICA	SWASTICAS
	SWASTIKA	SWASTIKAS
	SWAT	SWATH · SWATS
	SWATH	SWATHE · SWATHS · SWATHY
	SWATHE	SWATHED · SWATHER · SWATHES
	SWATHER	SWATHERS
	SWATTER	SWATTERS
	SWATTING	SWATTINGS
ASWAY	SWAY	SWAYL · SWAYS
	SWAYBACK	SWAYBACKS
	SWAYER	SWAYERS

S

FRONT HOOK	ROOT WORD	END HOOK
	SWAYING	SWAYINGS
	SWAYL	SWAYLS
	SWAYLING	SWAYLINGS
	SWAZZLE	SWAZZLES
	SWEAL	SWEALS
	SWEALING	SWEALINGS
	SWEAR	SWEARD ▪ SWEARS
	SWEARD	SWEARDS
	SWEARER	SWEARERS
	SWEARING	SWEARINGS
	SWEARWORD	SWEARWORDS
	SWEAT	SWEATS ▪ SWEATY
	SWEATBAND	SWEATBANDS
	SWEATER	SWEATERS
	SWEATING	SWEATINGS
	SWEATSHOP	SWEATSHOPS
	SWEATSUIT	SWEATSUITS
	SWEDE	SWEDES
	SWEDGER	SWEDGERS
	SWEE	SWEED ▪ SWEEL ▪ SWEEP ▪ SWEER ▪ SWEES SWEET
	SWEEL	SWEELS
	SWEENEY	SWEENEYS
	SWEEP	SWEEPS ▪ SWEEPY
	SWEEPBACK	SWEEPBACKS
	SWEEPER	SWEEPERS
	SWEEPING	SWEEPINGS
	SWEER	SWEERS ▪ SWEERT
	SWEET	SWEETS ▪ SWEETY
	SWEETCORN	SWEETCORNS
	SWEETEN	SWEETENS
	SWEETENER	SWEETENERS
	SWEETIE	SWEETIES
	SWEETING	SWEETINGS
	SWEETMEAT	SWEETMEATS
	SWEETPEA	SWEETPEAS
	SWEETSHOP	SWEETSHOPS
	SWEETSOP	SWEETSOPS
	SWEETWOOD	SWEETWOODS
	SWEIR	SWEIRS ▪ SWEIRT
	SWELCHIE	SWELCHIES
	SWELL	SWELLS
	SWELLDOM	SWELLDOMS
	SWELLER	SWELLERS
	SWELLHEAD	SWELLHEADS
	SWELLING	SWELLINGS
	SWELT	SWELTS
	SWELTER	SWELTERS
	SWEPTWING	SWEPTWINGS
	SWERF	SWERFS
	SWERVE	SWERVED ▪ SWERVER ▪ SWERVES
	SWERVER	SWERVERS
	SWERVING	SWERVINGS
	SWEVEN	SWEVENS
	SWEY	SWEYS
	SWIDDEN	SWIDDENS
	SWIFT	SWIFTS ▪ SWIFTY
	SWIFTER	SWIFTERS
	SWIFTIE	SWIFTIES
	SWIFTLET	SWIFTLETS
	SWIG	SWIGS
	SWIGGER	SWIGGERS
	SWILER	SWILERS
	SWILL	SWILLS
	SWILLER	SWILLERS
	SWILLING	SWILLINGS
ASWIM	**SWIM**	SWIMS
	SWIMMER	SWIMMERS
	SWIMMERET	SWIMMERETS

S

819

FRONT HOOK	ROOT WORD	END HOOK
	SWIMMING	SWIMMINGS
	SWIMSUIT	SWIMSUITS
	SWIMWEAR	SWIMWEARS
	SWINDGE	SWINDGED · SWINDGES
	SWINDLE	SWINDLED · SWINDLER · SWINDLES
	SWINDLER	SWINDLERS
	SWINDLING	SWINDLINGS
	SWINE	SWINES
	SWINEHERD	SWINEHERDS
	SWINEHOOD	SWINEHOODS
ASWING	**SWING**	SWINGE · SWINGS · SWINGY
	SWINGBEAT	SWINGBEATS
	SWINGBOAT	SWINGBOATS
	SWINGBY	SWINGBYS
	SWINGE	SWINGED · SWINGER · SWINGES
	SWINGER	SWINGERS
	SWINGING	SWINGINGS
	SWINGISM	SWINGISMS
	SWINGLE	SWINGLED · SWINGLES
	SWINGLING	SWINGLINGS
	SWINGTREE	SWINGTREES
	SWINK	SWINKS
	SWINKER	SWINKERS
	SWINNEY	SWINNEYS
	SWIPE	SWIPED · SWIPER · SWIPES · SWIPEY
	SWIPER	SWIPERS
	SWIPLE	SWIPLES
	SWIPPLE	SWIPPLES
	SWIRE	SWIRES
ASWIRL	**SWIRL**	SWIRLS · SWIRLY
	SWISH	SWISHY
	SWISHER	SWISHERS
	SWISHES	SWISHEST
	SWISHING	SWISHINGS
	SWISSING	SWISSINGS
	SWITCH	SWITCHY
	SWITCHEL	SWITCHELS
	SWITCHER	SWITCHERS
	SWITCHING	SWITCHINGS
	SWITH	SWITHE
	SWITHE	SWITHER
	SWITHER	SWITHERS
	SWIVE	SWIVED · SWIVEL · SWIVES · SWIVET
	SWIVEL	SWIVELS
	SWIVET	SWIVETS
	SWIZ	SWIZZ
	SWIZZLE	SWIZZLED · SWIZZLER · SWIZZLES
	SWIZZLER	SWIZZLERS
	SWOB	SWOBS
	SWOBBER	SWOBBERS
	SWOFFER	SWOFFERS
	SWOFFING	SWOFFINGS
	SWONE	SWONES
ASWOON	**SWOON**	SWOONS · SWOONY
	SWOONER	SWOONERS
	SWOONING	SWOONINGS
	SWOOP	SWOOPS · SWOOPY
	SWOOPER	SWOOPERS
	SWOP	SWOPS · SWOPT
	SWOPPER	SWOPPERS
	SWOPPING	SWOPPINGS
	SWORD	SWORDS
	SWORDBILL	SWORDBILLS
	SWORDER	SWORDERS
	SWORDPLAY	SWORDPLAYS
	SWORDTAIL	SWORDTAILS
	SWOT	SWOTS
	SWOTTER	SWOTTERS
	SWOTTING	SWOTTINGS

S

FRONT HOOK	ROOT WORD	END HOOK
	SWOUN	SWOUND · SWOUNE · SWOUNS
	SWOUND	SWOUNDS
	SWOUNE	SWOUNED · SWOUNES
	SWOWND	SWOWNDS
	SWOWNE	SWOWNES
	SWOZZLE	SWOZZLES
	SYBARITE	SYBARITES
	SYBBE	SYBBES
	SYBIL	SYBILS
	SYBO	SYBOE · SYBOW
	SYBOE	SYBOES
	SYBOTISM	SYBOTISMS
	SYBOW	SYBOWS
	SYCAMINE	SYCAMINES
	SYCAMORE	SYCAMORES
	SYCE	SYCEE · SYCES
	SYCEE	SYCEES
	SYCOMORE	SYCOMORES
	SYCOPHANT	SYCOPHANTS
	SYE	SYED · SYEN · SYES
	SYEN	SYENS
	SYENITE	SYENITES
	SYKE	SYKER · SYKES
	SYLI	SYLIS
	SYLLABI	SYLLABIC
ASYLLABIC	**SYLLABIC**	SYLLABICS
	SYLLABISE	SYLLABISED · SYLLABISES
	SYLLABISM	SYLLABISMS
	SYLLABIZE	SYLLABIZED · SYLLABIZES
	SYLLABLE	SYLLABLED · SYLLABLES
	SYLLABUB	SYLLABUBS
	SYLLOGISE	SYLLOGISED · SYLLOGISER · SYLLOGISES
	SYLLOGISM	SYLLOGISMS
	SYLLOGIST	SYLLOGISTS
	SYLLOGIZE	SYLLOGIZED · SYLLOGIZER · SYLLOGIZES
	SYLPH	SYLPHS · SYLPHY
	SYLPHID	SYLPHIDE · SYLPHIDS
	SYLPHIDE	SYLPHIDES
	SYLVA	SYLVAE · SYLVAN · SYLVAS
	SYLVAN	SYLVANS
	SYLVANER	SYLVANERS
	SYLVANITE	SYLVANITES
	SYLVIA	SYLVIAS
	SYLVIN	SYLVINE · SYLVINS
	SYLVINE	SYLVINES
	SYLVINITE	SYLVINITES
	SYLVITE	SYLVITES
	SYMAR	SYMARS
	SYMBION	SYMBIONS · SYMBIONT
	SYMBIONT	SYMBIONTS
	SYMBIOT	SYMBIOTE · SYMBIOTS
	SYMBIOTE	SYMBIOTES
	SYMBOL	SYMBOLE · SYMBOLS
	SYMBOLE	SYMBOLED · SYMBOLES
	SYMBOLIC	SYMBOLICS
	SYMBOLISE	SYMBOLISED · SYMBOLISER · SYMBOLISES
	SYMBOLISM	SYMBOLISMS
	SYMBOLIST	SYMBOLISTS
	SYMBOLIZE	SYMBOLIZED · SYMBOLIZER · SYMBOLIZES
	SYMITAR	SYMITARE · SYMITARS
	SYMITARE	SYMITARES
ASYMMETRIC	**SYMMETRIC**	
ASYMMETRY	**SYMMETRY**	
	SYMPATHIN	SYMPATHINS
	SYMPHILE	SYMPHILES
	SYMPLAST	SYMPLASTS
	SYMPLOCE	SYMPLOCES
	SYMPODIA	SYMPODIAL
	SYMPOSIA	SYMPOSIAC · SYMPOSIAL

S

FRONT HOOK	ROOT WORD	END HOOK
	SYMPOSIAC	SYMPOSIACS
	SYMPOSIUM	SYMPOSIUMS
	SYMPTOM	SYMPTOMS
ASYMPTOTIC	**SYMPTOTIC**	
	SYN	SYNC · SYND · SYNE
	SYNAGOG	SYNAGOGS
	SYNAGOGUE	SYNAGOGUES
	SYNALEPHA	SYNALEPHAS
	SYNANON	SYNANONS
	SYNAPHEA	SYNAPHEAS
	SYNAPHEIA	SYNAPHEIAS
	SYNAPSE	SYNAPSED · SYNAPSES
ASYNAPSES	**SYNAPSES**	
	SYNAPSID	SYNAPSIDS
ASYNAPSIS	**SYNAPSIS**	
	SYNAPTASE	SYNAPTASES
	SYNAPTE	SYNAPTES
	SYNC	SYNCH · SYNCS
	SYNCARP	SYNCARPS · SYNCARPY
	SYNCH	SYNCHS
	SYNCHRO	SYNCHROS
ASYNCHRONY	**SYNCHRONY**	
	SYNCLINAL	SYNCLINALS
	SYNCLINE	SYNCLINES
	SYNCOM	SYNCOMS
	SYNCOPATE	SYNCOPATED · SYNCOPATES
	SYNCOPE	SYNCOPES
	SYNCYTIA	SYNCYTIAL
	SYND	SYNDS
	SYNDACTYL	SYNDACTYLS · SYNDACTYLY
	SYNDET	SYNDETS
ASYNDETIC	**SYNDETIC**	
ASYNDETON	**SYNDETON**	SYNDETONS
ASYNDETONS	**SYNDETONS**	
	SYNDIC	SYNDICS
	SYNDICATE	SYNDICATED · SYNDICATES
	SYNDING	SYNDINGS
	SYNDROME	SYNDROMES
	SYNE	SYNED · SYNES
	SYNECHIA	SYNECHIAS
	SYNECTIC	SYNECTICS
	SYNEDRIA	SYNEDRIAL
ASYNERGIA	**SYNERGIA**	SYNERGIAS
ASYNERGIAS	**SYNERGIAS**	
	SYNERGID	SYNERGIDS
ASYNERGIES	**SYNERGIES**	
	SYNERGISE	SYNERGISED · SYNERGISES
	SYNERGISM	SYNERGISMS
	SYNERGIST	SYNERGISTS
	SYNERGIZE	SYNERGIZED · SYNERGIZES
ASYNERGY	**SYNERGY**	
	SYNFUEL	SYNFUELS
	SYNGRAPH	SYNGRAPHS
	SYNKARYON	SYNKARYONS
	SYNOD	SYNODS
	SYNODAL	SYNODALS
	SYNOECETE	SYNOECETES
	SYNOECISE	SYNOECISED · SYNOECISES
	SYNOECISM	SYNOECISMS
	SYNOECIZE	SYNOECIZED · SYNOECIZES
	SYNOEKETE	SYNOEKETES
	SYNONYM	SYNONYME · SYNONYMS · SYNONYMY
	SYNONYME	SYNONYMES
	SYNOPSIS	SYNOPSISE
	SYNOPSISE	SYNOPSISED · SYNOPSISES
	SYNOPSIZE	SYNOPSIZED · SYNOPSIZES
	SYNOPTIC	SYNOPTICS
	SYNOPTIST	SYNOPTISTS
	SYNOVIA	SYNOVIAL · SYNOVIAS

S

FRONT HOOK	ROOT WORD	END HOOK
	SYNROC	SYNROCS
ASYNTACTIC	**SYNTACTIC**	SYNTACTICS
	SYNTAGM	SYNTAGMA = SYNTAGMS
	SYNTAGMA	SYNTAGMAS
	SYNTAN	SYNTANS
	SYNTH	SYNTHS
	SYNTHESIS	SYNTHESISE = SYNTHESIST
	SYNTHETIC	SYNTHETICS
	SYNTHON	SYNTHONS
	SYNTHPOP	SYNTHPOPS
	SYNTONIN	SYNTONINS
	SYNTONISE	SYNTONISED = SYNTONISES
	SYNTONIZE	SYNTONIZED = SYNTONIZES
	SYNURA	SYNURAE
	SYPE	SYPED = SYPES
	SYPH	SYPHS
	SYPHER	SYPHERS
	SYPHERING	SYPHERINGS
	SYPHILIS	SYPHILISE
	SYPHILISE	SYPHILISED = SYPHILISES
	SYPHILIZE	SYPHILIZED = SYPHILIZES
	SYPHILOMA	SYPHILOMAS
	SYPHON	SYPHONS
	SYRAH	SYRAHS
	SYREN	SYRENS
	SYRETTE	SYRETTES
	SYRINGA	SYRINGAS
	SYRINGE	SYRINGED = SYRINGES
	SYRPHIAN	SYRPHIANS
	SYRPHID	SYRPHIDS
	SYRUP	SYRUPS = SYRUPY
	SYSADMIN	SYSADMINS
	SYSOP	SYSOPS
	SYSSITIA	SYSSITIAS
	SYSTEM	SYSTEMS
	SYSTEMIC	SYSTEMICS
	SYSTEMISE	SYSTEMISED = SYSTEMISER = SYSTEMISES
	SYSTEMIZE	SYSTEMIZED = SYSTEMIZER = SYSTEMIZES
ASYSTOLE	**SYSTOLE**	SYSTOLES
ASYSTOLES	**SYSTOLES**	
ASYSTOLIC	**SYSTOLIC**	
	SYSTYLE	SYSTYLES
	SYTHE	SYTHES
	SYVER	SYVERS

S

T

FRONT HOOK	ROOT WORD	END HOOK
ETA ▪ ITA ▪ UTA	**TA**	TAB ▪ TAD ▪ TAE ▪ TAG ▪ TAI ▪ TAJ ▪ TAK TAM ▪ TAN ▪ TAO ▪ TAP ▪ TAR ▪ TAS ▪ TAT TAU ▪ TAV ▪ TAW ▪ TAX ▪ TAY
	TAAL	TAALS
ATAATA	**TAATA**	TAATAS
ATAATAS	**TAATAS**	
STAB	**TAB**	TABI ▪ TABS ▪ TABU
	TABANID	TABANIDS
	TABARD	TABARDS
	TABARET	TABARETS
	TABASHEER	TABASHEERS
	TABASHIR	TABASHIRS
STABBED	**TABBED**	
	TABBINET	TABBINETS
STABBING	**TABBING**	
	TABBOULEH	TABBOULEHS
	TABBOULI	TABBOULIS
	TABBYHOOD	TABBYHOODS
	TABELLION	TABELLIONS
	TABER	TABERD ▪ TABERS
	TABERD	TABERDS
	TABERDAR	TABERDARS
	TABETIC	TABETICS
	TABI	TABID ▪ TABIS
	TABINET	TABINETS
	TABLA	TABLAS
	TABLATURE	TABLATURES
STABLE	**TABLE**	TABLED ▪ TABLES ▪ TABLET
	TABLEAU	TABLEAUS ▪ TABLEAUX
STABLED	**TABLED**	
	TABLEFUL	TABLEFULS
	TABLELAND	TABLELANDS
STABLEMATE	**TABLEMATE**	TABLEMATES
STABLES	**TABLES**	
	TABLET	TABLETS
	TABLETOP	TABLETOPS
	TABLEWARE	TABLEWARES
	TABLIER	TABLIERS
STABLING	**TABLING**	TABLINGS
STABLINGS	**TABLINGS**	
	TABLOID	TABLOIDS ▪ TABLOIDY
	TABOGGAN	TABOGGANS
	TABOO	TABOOS
	TABOOLEY	TABOOLEYS
	TABOR	TABORS
	TABORER	TABORERS
	TABORET	TABORETS
	TABORIN	TABORINE ▪ TABORING ▪ TABORINS
	TABORINE	TABORINES
	TABOULEH	TABOULEHS
	TABOULI	TABOULIS
	TABOUR	TABOURS
	TABOURER	TABOURERS
	TABOURET	TABOURETS
	TABOURIN	TABOURING ▪ TABOURINS
	TABRERE	TABRERES
	TABRET	TABRETS
STABS	**TABS**	
	TABU	TABUN ▪ TABUS
	TABULA	TABULAE ▪ TABULAR
	TABULATE	TABULATED ▪ TABULATES
	TABULATOR	TABULATORS ▪ TABULATORY
	TABULI	TABULIS
	TABUN	TABUNS
	TACAHOUT	TACAHOUTS
	TACAMAHAC	TACAMAHACS

FRONT HOOK	ROOT WORD	END HOOK
	TACAN	TACANS
	TACE	TACES · TACET
	TACET	TACETS
	TACH	TACHE · TACHO · TACHS
	TACHE	TACHES
	TACHINID	TACHINIDS
	TACHISM	TACHISME · TACHISMS
	TACHISME	TACHISMES
	TACHIST	TACHISTE · TACHISTS
	TACHISTE	TACHISTES
	TACHO	TACHOS
	TACHOGRAM	TACHOGRAMS
	TACHYLITE	TACHYLITES
	TACHYLYTE	TACHYLYTES
	TACHYON	TACHYONS
	TACHYPNEA	TACHYPNEAS
STACK	**TACK**	TACKS · TACKY
	TACKBOARD	TACKBOARDS
STACKED	**TACKED**	
STACKER	**TACKER**	TACKERS
STACKERS	**TACKERS**	
STACKET	**TACKET**	TACKETS · TACKETY
STACKETS	**TACKETS**	
	TACKIES	TACKIEST
	TACKIFIER	TACKIFIERS
STACKING	**TACKING**	TACKINGS
STACKINGS	**TACKINGS**	
	TACKLE	TACKLED · TACKLER · TACKLES
	TACKLER	TACKLERS
	TACKLES	TACKLESS
STACKLESS	**TACKLESS**	
	TACKLING	TACKLINGS
STACKS	**TACKS**	
	TACMAHACK	TACMAHACKS
	TACNODE	TACNODES
	TACO	TACOS
	TACONITE	TACONITES
	TACRINE	TACRINES
	TACT	TACTS
ATACTIC	**TACTIC**	TACTICS
	TACTICIAN	TACTICIANS
	TACTILIST	TACTILISTS
	TACTION	TACTIONS
	TACTISM	TACTISMS
	TAD	TADS
	TADDIE	TADDIES
	TADPOLE	TADPOLES
	TAE	TAED · TAEL · TAES
	TAEDIUM	TAEDIUMS
	TAEKWONDO	TAEKWONDOS
	TAEL	TAELS
	TAENIA	TAENIAE · TAENIAS
	TAFFAREL	TAFFARELS
	TAFFEREL	TAFFERELS
	TAFFETA	TAFFETAS
	TAFFIA	TAFFIAS
	TAFFRAIL	TAFFRAILS
	TAFIA	TAFIAS
STAG	**TAG**	TAGS
	TAGALONG	TAGALONGS
	TAGAREEN	TAGAREENS
	TAGBOARD	TAGBOARDS
	TAGGANT	TAGGANTS
STAGGED	**TAGGED**	
	TAGGEE	TAGGEES
STAGGER	**TAGGER**	TAGGERS
STAGGERS	**TAGGERS**	
STAGGIER	**TAGGIER**	
STAGGIEST	**TAGGIEST**	

825

FRONT HOOK	ROOT WORD	END HOOK
STAGGING	**TAGGING**	TAGGINGS
STAGGY	**TAGGY**	
	TAGHAIRM	TAGHAIRMS
	TAGINE	TAGINES
	TAGLINE	TAGLINES
	TAGLIONI	TAGLIONIS
	TAGMEME	TAGMEMES
	TAGMEMIC	TAGMEMICS
	TAGRAG	TAGRAGS
STAGS	**TAGS**	
	TAGUAN	TAGUANS
	TAHA	TAHAS
	TAHINA	TAHINAS
	TAHINI	TAHINIS
	TAHOU	TAHOUS
	TAHR	TAHRS
	TAHSIL	TAHSILS
	TAHSILDAR	TAHSILDARS
	TAI	TAIG ▪ TAIL ▪ TAIN ▪ TAIS ▪ TAIT
	TAIAHA	TAIAHAS
STAIG	**TAIG**	TAIGA ▪ TAIGS (offensive)
	TAIGA	TAIGAS
	TAIGLE	TAIGLED ▪ TAIGLES
STAIGS	**TAIGS**	
	TAIKONAUT	TAIKONAUTS
	TAIL	TAILS
	TAILARD	TAILARDS
	TAILBACK	TAILBACKS
	TAILBOARD	TAILBOARDS
	TAILBONE	TAILBONES
	TAILCOAT	TAILCOATS
	TAILENDER	TAILENDERS
	TAILER	TAILERS
	TAILERON	TAILERONS
	TAILFAN	TAILFANS
	TAILFIN	TAILFINS
	TAILGATE	TAILGATED ▪ TAILGATER ▪ TAILGATES
	TAILGATER	TAILGATERS
	TAILING	TAILINGS
	TAILLAMP	TAILLAMPS
	TAILLE	TAILLES
	TAILLES	TAILLESS
	TAILLEUR	TAILLEURS
	TAILLIE	TAILLIES
	TAILLIGHT	TAILLIGHTS
	TAILOR	TAILORS
	TAILORING	TAILORINGS
	TAILPIECE	TAILPIECES
	TAILPIPE	TAILPIPED ▪ TAILPIPES
	TAILPLANE	TAILPLANES
	TAILRACE	TAILRACES
	TAILSKID	TAILSKIDS
	TAILSLIDE	TAILSLIDES
	TAILSPIN	TAILSPINS
	TAILSTOCK	TAILSTOCKS
	TAILWATER	TAILWATERS
	TAILWHEEL	TAILWHEELS
	TAILWIND	TAILWINDS
	TAILYE	TAILYES
	TAILZIE	TAILZIES
STAIN	**TAIN**	TAINS ▪ TAINT
STAINS	**TAINS**	
	TAINT	TAINTS
	TAINTURE	TAINTURES
	TAIPAN	TAIPANS
	TAIRA	TAIRAS
	TAIS	TAISH
	TAIT	TAITS
	TAIVER	TAIVERS ▪ TAIVERT

T

FRONT HOOK	ROOT WORD	END HOOK
	TAJINE	TAJINES
	TAK	TAKA ▪ TAKE ▪ TAKI ▪ TAKS ▪ TAKY
	TAKA	TAKAS
	TAKAHE	TAKAHES
	TAKAMAKA	TAKAMAKAS
STAKE	TAKE	TAKEN ▪ TAKER ▪ TAKES
	TAKEAWAY	TAKEAWAYS
	TAKEDOWN	TAKEDOWNS
	TAKEOFF	TAKEOFFS
STAKEOUT	TAKEOUT	TAKEOUTS
STAKEOUTS	TAKEOUTS	
	TAKEOVER	TAKEOVERS
	TAKER	TAKERS
STAKES	TAKES	
	TAKEUP	TAKEUPS
	TAKHI	TAKHIS
	TAKI	TAKIN ▪ TAKIS
	TAKIN	TAKING ▪ TAKINS
STAKING	TAKING	TAKINGS
	TALA	TALAK ▪ TALAQ ▪ TALAR ▪ TALAS
	TALAK	TALAKS
	TALANT	TALANTS
	TALAPOIN	TALAPOINS
	TALAQ	TALAQS
	TALAR	TALARS
	TALAUNT	TALAUNTS
	TALAYOT	TALAYOTS
	TALBOT	TALBOTS
	TALBOTYPE	TALBOTYPES
	TALC	TALCS ▪ TALCY
	TALCUM	TALCUMS
STALE	TALE	TALEA ▪ TALER ▪ TALES
	TALEA	TALEAE
	TALEGALLA	TALEGALLAS
	TALEGGIO	TALEGGIOS
	TALENT	TALENTS
STALER	TALER	TALERS
STALES	TALES	
	TALION	TALIONS
	TALIPAT	TALIPATS
	TALIPED	TALIPEDS
	TALIPOT	TALIPOTS
	TALISMAN	TALISMANS
STALK	TALK	TALKS ▪ TALKY
	TALKATHON	TALKATHONS
	TALKBACK	TALKBACKS
STALKED	TALKED	
STALKER	TALKER	TALKERS
STALKERS	TALKERS	
	TALKFEST	TALKFESTS
	TALKIE	TALKIER ▪ TALKIES
STALKIER	TALKIER	
	TALKIES	TALKIEST
STALKIEST	TALKIEST	
STALKINESS	TALKINESS	
STALKING	TALKING	TALKINGS
STALKINGS	TALKINGS	
STALKS	TALKS	
STALKY	TALKY	
STALL	TALL	TALLS ▪ TALLY
STALLAGE	TALLAGE	TALLAGED ▪ TALLAGES
STALLAGES	TALLAGES	
	TALLAT	TALLATS
	TALLBOY	TALLBOYS
	TALLENT	TALLENTS
	TALLET	TALLETS
	TALLIATE	TALLIATED ▪ TALLIATES
	TALLIER	TALLIERS
	TALLIS	TALLISH

FRONT HOOK	ROOT WORD	END HOOK
	TALLIT	TALLITH ▪ TALLITS
	TALLITH	TALLITHS
	TALLITOT	TALLITOTH
	TALLOL	TALLOLS
	TALLOT	TALLOTS
	TALLOW	TALLOWS ▪ TALLOWY
STALLS	**TALLS**	
	TALLYHO	TALLYHOS
	TALLYSHOP	TALLYSHOPS
	TALMA	TALMAS
	TALMUD	TALMUDS
	TALMUDISM	TALMUDISMS
ETALON	**TALON**	TALONS
ETALONS	**TALONS**	
	TALOOKA	TALOOKAS
	TALPA	TALPAE ▪ TALPAS
	TALUK	TALUKA ▪ TALUKS
	TALUKA	TALUKAS
	TALUKDAR	TALUKDARS
	TALWEG	TALWEGS
	TAM	TAME ▪ TAMP ▪ TAMS
	TAMAL	TAMALE ▪ TAMALS
	TAMALE	TAMALES
	TAMANDU	TAMANDUA ▪ TAMANDUS
	TAMANDUA	TAMANDUAS
	TAMANOIR	TAMANOIRS
	TAMANU	TAMANUS
	TAMARA	TAMARAO ▪ TAMARAS ▪ TAMARAU
	TAMARACK	TAMARACKS
	TAMARAO	TAMARAOS
	TAMARAU	TAMARAUS
	TAMARI	TAMARIN ▪ TAMARIS
	TAMARILLO	TAMARILLOS
	TAMARIN	TAMARIND ▪ TAMARINS
	TAMARIND	TAMARINDS
	TAMARIS	TAMARISK
	TAMARISK	TAMARISKS
	TAMASHA	TAMASHAS
	TAMBAC	TAMBACS
	TAMBAK	TAMBAKS
	TAMBALA	TAMBALAS
	TAMBER	TAMBERS
	TAMBOUR	TAMBOURA ▪ TAMBOURS
	TAMBOURA	TAMBOURAS
	TAMBOURER	TAMBOURERS
	TAMBOURIN	TAMBOURINE ▪ TAMBOURING ▪ TAMBOURINS
	TAMBUR	TAMBURA ▪ TAMBURS
	TAMBURA	TAMBURAS
	TAMBURIN	TAMBURINS
	TAME	TAMED ▪ TAMER ▪ TAMES
	TAMEIN	TAMEINS
	TAMER	TAMERS
	TAMES	TAMEST
ETAMIN	**TAMIN**	TAMINE ▪ TAMING ▪ TAMINS
ETAMINE	**TAMINE**	TAMINES
ETAMINES	**TAMINES**	
	TAMING	TAMINGS
ETAMINS	**TAMINS**	
	TAMIS	TAMISE
	TAMISE	TAMISES
	TAMMAR	TAMMARS
	TAMMIE	TAMMIED ▪ TAMMIES
	TAMOXIFEN	TAMOXIFENS
STAMP	**TAMP**	TAMPS
	TAMPALA	TAMPALAS
	TAMPAN	TAMPANS
STAMPED	**TAMPED**	
STAMPER	**TAMPER**	TAMPERS
	TAMPERER	TAMPERERS

FRONT HOOK	ROOT WORD	END HOOK
	TAMPERING	TAMPERINGS
STAMPERS	**TAMPERS**	
STAMPING	**TAMPING**	TAMPINGS
STAMPINGS	**TAMPINGS**	
	TAMPION	TAMPIONS
	TAMPON	TAMPONS
	TAMPONADE	TAMPONADES
	TAMPONAGE	TAMPONAGES
STAMPS	**TAMPS**	
	TAMWORTH	TAMWORTHS
	TAN	TANA ▪ TANE ▪ TANG ▪ TANH ▪ TANK ▪ TANS
	TANA	TANAS
	TANADAR	TANADARS
	TANAGER	TANAGERS
	TANAGRA	TANAGRAS
	TANAISTE	TANAISTES
	TANBARK	TANBARKS
	TANDEM	TANDEMS
	TANDOOR	TANDOORI ▪ TANDOORS
	TANDOORI	TANDOORIS
STANE	**TANE**	
STANG	**TANG**	TANGA ▪ TANGI ▪ TANGO ▪ TANGS ▪ TANGY
	TANGA	TANGAS
STANGED	**TANGED**	
	TANGELO	TANGELOS
	TANGENCE	TANGENCES
	TANGENT	TANGENTS
	TANGERINE	TANGERINES
	TANGHIN	TANGHINS
	TANGHININ	TANGHININS
	TANGI	TANGIE ▪ TANGIS
	TANGIBLE	TANGIBLES
	TANGIE	TANGIER ▪ TANGIES
	TANGIES	TANGIEST
STANGING	**TANGING**	
	TANGLE	TANGLED ▪ TANGLER ▪ TANGLES
	TANGLER	TANGLERS
	TANGLING	TANGLINGS
	TANGO	TANGOS
	TANGOIST	TANGOISTS
	TANGRAM	TANGRAMS
STANGS	**TANGS**	
	TANGUN	TANGUNS
	TANH	TANHS
	TANIST	TANISTS
	TANIWHA	TANIWHAS
STANK	**TANK**	TANKA ▪ TANKS ▪ TANKY
	TANKA	TANKAS
	TANKAGE	TANKAGES
	TANKARD	TANKARDS
STANKED	**TANKED**	
	TANKER	TANKERS
	TANKFUL	TANKFULS
	TANKIA	TANKIAS
STANKING	**TANKING**	TANKINGS
	TANKINI	TANKINIS
STANKS	**TANKS**	
	TANKSHIP	TANKSHIPS
	TANLING	TANLINGS
	TANNA	TANNAH ▪ TANNAS
	TANNAGE	TANNAGES
	TANNAH	TANNAHS
STANNATE	**TANNATE**	TANNATES
STANNATES	**TANNATES**	
	TANNER	TANNERS ▪ TANNERY
STANNIC	**TANNIC**	
	TANNIE	TANNIES
	TANNIN	TANNING ▪ TANNINS
	TANNING	TANNINGS

829

FRONT HOOK	ROOT WORD	END HOOK
	TANNOY	TANNOYS
	TANREC	TANRECS
	TANS	TANSY
	TANTALATE	TANTALATES
	TANTALISE	TANTALISED · TANTALISER · TANTALISES
	TANTALISM	TANTALISMS
	TANTALITE	TANTALITES
	TANTALIZE	TANTALIZED · TANTALIZER · TANTALIZES
	TANTALUM	TANTALUMS
	TANTARA	TANTARAS
	TANTARARA	TANTARARAS
	TANTRA	TANTRAS
	TANTRISM	TANTRISMS
	TANTRUM	TANTRUMS
	TANUKI	TANUKIS
	TANYARD	TANYARDS
	TANZANITE	TANZANITES
	TAO	TAOS
	TAOISEACH	TAOISEACHS
	TAONGA	TAONGAS
ATAP · STAP	TAP	TAPA · TAPE · TAPS · TAPU
	TAPA	TAPAS
	TAPACOLO	TAPACOLOS
	TAPACULO	TAPACULOS
	TAPADERA	TAPADERAS
	TAPADERO	TAPADEROS
	TAPALO	TAPALOS
ETAPE	TAPE	TAPED · TAPEN · TAPER · TAPES · TAPET
	TAPELINE	TAPELINES
	TAPENADE	TAPENADES
	TAPER	TAPERS
	TAPERER	TAPERERS
	TAPERING	TAPERINGS
ETAPES · STAPES	TAPES	
	TAPET	TAPETA · TAPETI · TAPETS
	TAPETA	TAPETAL
	TAPETI	TAPETIS
	TAPEWORM	TAPEWORMS
	TAPHOLE	TAPHOLES
	TAPHOUSE	TAPHOUSES
	TAPIOCA	TAPIOCAS
	TAPIR	TAPIRS
	TAPIS	TAPIST
	TAPIST	TAPISTS
	TAPPA	TAPPAS
STAPPED	TAPPED	
	TAPPER	TAPPERS
	TAPPET	TAPPETS
	TAPPICE	TAPPICED · TAPPICES
STAPPING	TAPPING	TAPPINGS
	TAPROOM	TAPROOMS
	TAPROOT	TAPROOTS
ATAPS · STAPS	TAPS	
	TAPSTER	TAPSTERS
	TAPU	TAPUS
	TAQUERIA	TAQUERIAS
STAR	TAR	TARA · TARE · TARN · TARO · TARP TARS · TART
	TARA	TARAS
	TARAKIHI	TARAKIHIS
	TARAMA	TARAMAS
	TARAMEA	TARAMEAS
	TARAND	TARANDS
	TARANTARA	TARANTARAS
	TARANTAS	TARANTASS
	TARANTISM	TARANTISMS
	TARANTIST	TARANTISTS
	TARANTULA	TARANTULAE · TARANTULAS
	TARAXACUM	TARAXACUMS

FRONT HOOK	ROOT WORD	END HOOK
	TARBOGGIN	TARBOGGINS
	TARBOUCHE	TARBOUCHES
	TARBOY	TARBOYS
	TARCEL	TARCELS
	TARDIES	TARDIEST
	TARDYON	TARDYONS
STARE	**TARE**	TARED ▪ TARES
STARED	**TARED**	
STARES	**TARES**	
	TARGE	TARGED ▪ TARGES ▪ TARGET
	TARGET	TARGETS
	TARGETEER	TARGETEERS
	TARIFF	TARIFFS
STARING	**TARING**	TARINGS
STARINGS	**TARINGS**	
	TARLATAN	TARLATANS
	TARLETAN	TARLETANS
	TARMAC	TARMACS
STARN	**TARN**	TARNS
	TARNATION	TARNATIONS
	TARNISHER	TARNISHERS
STARNS	**TARNS**	
	TARO	TAROC ▪ TAROK ▪ TAROS ▪ TAROT
	TAROC	TAROCS
	TAROK	TAROKS
	TAROT	TAROTS
	TARP	TARPS
	TARPAN	TARPANS
	TARPAPER	TARPAPERS
	TARPAULIN	TARPAULING ▪ TARPAULINS
	TARPON	TARPONS
	TARRAGON	TARRAGONS
	TARRE	TARRED ▪ TARRES
STARRED	**TARRED**	
	TARRIANCE	TARRIANCES
STARRIER	**TARRIER**	TARRIERS
	TARRIES	TARRIEST
STARRIEST	**TARRIEST**	
STARRINESS	**TARRINESS**	
STARRING	**TARRING**	TARRINGS
STARRINGS	**TARRINGS**	
	TARROCK	TARROCKS
	TARROW	TARROWS
STARRY	**TARRY**	
STARS	**TARS**	TARSI
	TARSAL	TARSALS
	TARSALGIA	TARSALGIAS
	TARSEAL	TARSEALS
	TARSEL	TARSELS
	TARSI	TARSIA
	TARSIA	TARSIAS
	TARSIER	TARSIERS
	TARSIPED	TARSIPEDS
START	**TART**	TARTS ▪ TARTY
	TARTAN	TARTANA ▪ TARTANE ▪ TARTANS
	TARTANA	TARTANAS
	TARTANE	TARTANED ▪ TARTANES
	TARTAR	TARTARE ▪ TARTARS
	TARTARE	TARTARES
	TARTARISE	TARTARISED ▪ TARTARISES
	TARTARIZE	TARTARIZED ▪ TARTARIZES
STARTED	**TARTED**	
STARTER	**TARTER**	
	TARTINE	TARTINES
	TARTINES	TARTINESS
STARTING	**TARTING**	
STARTISH	**TARTISH**	
	TARTLET	TARTLETS
STARTLY	**TARTLY**	

FRONT HOOK	ROOT WORD	END HOOK
	TARTRATE	TARTRATED ▪ TARTRATES
STARTS	**TARTS**	
	TARTUFE	TARTUFES
	TARTUFFE	TARTUFFES
	TARWEED	TARWEEDS
	TARWHINE	TARWHINES
	TARZAN	TARZANS
ETAS ▪ ITAS ▪ UTAS	**TAS**	TASH ▪ TASK ▪ TASS
	TASAR	TASARS
	TASER	TASERS
STASH	**TASH**	
STASHED	**TASHED**	
STASHES	**TASHES**	
STASHING	**TASHING**	
	TASIMETER	TASIMETERS
	TASK	TASKS
	TASKBAR	TASKBARS
	TASKER	TASKERS
	TASKING	TASKINGS
	TASKWORK	TASKWORKS
	TASLET	TASLETS
	TASS	TASSE
	TASSE	TASSEL ▪ TASSES ▪ TASSET
	TASSEL	TASSELL ▪ TASSELS
	TASSELL	TASSELLS ▪ TASSELLY
	TASSET	TASSETS
	TASSIE	TASSIES
	TASTE	TASTED ▪ TASTER ▪ TASTES
	TASTER	TASTERS
	TASTEVIN	TASTEVINS
	TASTING	TASTINGS
ETAT ▪ STAT	**TAT**	TATE ▪ TATH ▪ TATS ▪ TATT ▪ TATU
	TATAMI	TATAMIS
	TATAR	TATARS
STATE	**TATE**	TATER ▪ TATES
STATER	**TATER**	TATERS
STATERS	**TATERS**	
STATES	**TATES**	
	TATH	TATHS
	TATIE	TATIES
	TATLER	TATLERS
	TATOU	TATOUS
	TATOUAY	TATOUAYS
ETATS ▪ STATS	**TATS**	
	TATSOI	TATSOIS
	TATT	TATTS ▪ TATTY
	TATTER	TATTERS ▪ TATTERY
	TATTIE	TATTIER ▪ TATTIES
	TATTIES	TATTIEST
	TATTING	TATTINGS
	TATTLE	TATTLED ▪ TATTLER ▪ TATTLES
	TATTLER	TATTLERS
	TATTLING	TATTLINGS
	TATTOO	TATTOOS
	TATTOOER	TATTOOERS
	TATTOOIST	TATTOOISTS
	TATTOW	TATTOWS
	TATU	TATUS
STATUED	**TATUED**	
STATUS	**TATUS**	
	TAU	TAUS ▪ TAUT
	TAUBE	TAUBES
	TAUHINU	TAUHINUS
	TAUIWI	TAUIWIS
	TAUNT	TAUNTS
	TAUNTER	TAUNTERS
	TAUNTING	TAUNTINGS
	TAUON	TAUONS
	TAUPE	TAUPES

FRONT HOOK	ROOT WORD	END HOOK
	TAUPIE	TAUPIES
	TAURINE	TAURINES
	TAUT	TAUTS
	TAUTAUG	TAUTAUGS
	TAUTEN	TAUTENS
	TAUTOG	TAUTOGS
	TAUTOMER	TAUTOMERS
	TAUTONYM	TAUTONYMS ▪ TAUTONYMY
	TAV	TAVA ▪ TAVS
	TAVA	TAVAH ▪ TAVAS
	TAVAH	TAVAHS
	TAVER	TAVERN ▪ TAVERS ▪ TAVERT
	TAVERN	TAVERNA ▪ TAVERNS
	TAVERNA	TAVERNAS
	TAVERNER	TAVERNERS
STAW	TAW	TAWA ▪ TAWS ▪ TAWT
	TAWA	TAWAI ▪ TAWAS
	TAWAI	TAWAIS
	TAWDRIES	TAWDRIEST
STAWED	TAWED	
	TAWER	TAWERS ▪ TAWERY
	TAWHAI	TAWHAIS
	TAWIE	TAWIER
STAWING	TAWING	TAWINGS
	TAWNEY	TAWNEYS
	TAWNIES	TAWNIEST
	TAWPIE	TAWPIES
STAWS	TAWS	TAWSE
	TAWSE	TAWSED ▪ TAWSES
	TAWT	TAWTS
	TAWTIE	TAWTIER
	TAX	TAXA ▪ TAXI
	TAXABLE	TAXABLES
	TAXAMETER	TAXAMETERS
	TAXATION	TAXATIONS
	TAXEME	TAXEMES
	TAXER	TAXERS
	TAXI	TAXIS
	TAXIARCH	TAXIARCHS
	TAXICAB	TAXICABS
ATAXIES	TAXIES	
	TAXIMETER	TAXIMETERS
	TAXING	TAXINGS
	TAXIPLANE	TAXIPLANES
	TAXITE	TAXITES
	TAXIWAY	TAXIWAYS
	TAXOL	TAXOLS
	TAXON	TAXONS
	TAXONOMER	TAXONOMERS
	TAXOR	TAXORS
	TAXPAYER	TAXPAYERS
	TAXPAYING	TAXPAYINGS
STAY	TAY	TAYS
	TAYASSUID	TAYASSUIDS
	TAYRA	TAYRAS
STAYS	TAYS	
	TAZZA	TAZZAS
	TCHICK	TCHICKS
	TCHOTCHKE	TCHOTCHKES
ATE ▪ UTE	TE	TEA ▪ TEC ▪ TED ▪ TEE ▪ TEF ▪ TEG ▪ TEL ▪ TEN ▪ TES ▪ TET ▪ TEW ▪ TEX
	TEA	TEAD ▪ TEAK ▪ TEAL ▪ TEAM ▪ TEAR ▪ TEAS ▪ TEAT
	TEABOARD	TEABOARDS
	TEABOWL	TEABOWLS
	TEABREAD	TEABREADS
	TEACAKE	TEACAKES
	TEACART	TEACARTS
	TEACHER	TEACHERS

FRONT HOOK	ROOT WORD	END HOOK
	TEACHING	TEACHINGS
	TEACUP	TEACUPS
	TEACUPFUL	TEACUPFULS
STEAD	**TEAD**	TEADE • TEADS
	TEADE	TEADES
STEADS	**TEADS**	
	TEAGLE	TEAGLED • TEAGLES
	TEAHOUSE	TEAHOUSES
STEAK	**TEAK**	TEAKS
	TEAKETTLE	TEAKETTLES
STEAKS	**TEAKS**	
	TEAKWOOD	TEAKWOODS
STEAL	**TEAL**	TEALS
STEALS	**TEALS**	
STEAM	**TEAM**	TEAMS
	TEAMAKER	TEAMAKERS
STEAMED	**TEAMED**	
STEAMER	**TEAMER**	TEAMERS
STEAMERS	**TEAMERS**	
STEAMING	**TEAMING**	TEAMINGS
STEAMINGS	**TEAMINGS**	
	TEAMMATE	TEAMMATES
STEAMS	**TEAMS**	
	TEAMSTER	TEAMSTERS
	TEAMWORK	TEAMWORKS
	TEAPOT	TEAPOTS
	TEAPOY	TEAPOYS
STEAR	**TEAR**	TEARS • TEARY
	TEARAWAY	TEARAWAYS
	TEARDOWN	TEARDOWNS
	TEARDROP	TEARDROPS
STEARED	**TEARED**	
	TEARER	TEARERS
STEARING	**TEARING**	
	TEAROOM	TEAROOMS
STEARS	**TEARS**	
	TEARSHEET	TEARSHEETS
	TEARSTAIN	TEARSTAINS
	TEARSTRIP	TEARSTRIPS
	TEAS	TEASE
	TEASE	TEASED • TEASEL • TEASER • TEASES
	TEASEL	TEASELS
	TEASELER	TEASELERS
	TEASELING	TEASELINGS
	TEASELLER	TEASELLERS
	TEASER	TEASERS
	TEASHOP	TEASHOPS
	TEASING	TEASINGS
	TEASPOON	TEASPOONS
	TEAT	TEATS
	TEATASTER	TEATASTERS
	TEATIME	TEATIMES
	TEAWARE	TEAWARES
	TEAZE	TEAZED • TEAZEL • TEAZES
	TEAZEL	TEAZELS
	TEAZLE	TEAZLED • TEAZLES
	TEBBAD	TEBBADS
	TEC	TECH • TECS
	TECH	TECHS • TECHY
	TECHIE	TECHIER • TECHIES
	TECHIES	TECHIEST
ATECHNIC	**TECHNIC**	TECHNICS
	TECHNICAL	TECHNICALS
	TECHNIKON	TECHNIKONS
	TECHNIQUE	TECHNIQUES
	TECHNO	TECHNOS
	TECHNOPOP	TECHNOPOPS
	TECKEL	TECKELS
	TECTA	TECTAL

FRONT HOOK	ROOT WORD	END HOOK
	TECTITE	TECTITES
	TECTONIC	TECTONICS
	TECTONISM	TECTONISMS
	TECTUM	TECTUMS
STED	**TED**	TEDS · TEDY
STEDDED	**TEDDED**	
	TEDDER	TEDDERS
	TEDDIE	TEDDIES
STEDDIES	**TEDDIES**	
STEDDING	**TEDDING**	
STEDDY	**TEDDY**	
	TEDIUM	TEDIUMS
STEDS	**TEDS**	
	TEE	TEED · TEEK · TEEL · TEEM · TEEN
		TEER · TEES
STEED	**TEED**	
STEEK	**TEEK**	
STEEL	**TEEL**	TEELS
STEELS	**TEELS**	
STEEM	**TEEM**	TEEMS
STEEMED	**TEEMED**	
	TEEMER	TEEMERS
STEEMING	**TEEMING**	
STEEMS	**TEEMS**	
STEEN	**TEEN**	TEEND · TEENE · TEENS · TEENY
	TEENAGE	TEENAGED · TEENAGER
	TEENAGER	TEENAGERS
	TEEND	TEENDS
	TEENE	TEENED · TEENER · TEENES
STEENED	**TEENED**	
	TEENER	TEENERS
STEENING	**TEENING**	
STEENS	**TEENS**	TEENSY
	TEEPEE	TEEPEES
STEER	**TEER**	TEERS
STEERED	**TEERED**	
STEERING	**TEERING**	
STEERS	**TEERS**	
	TEETER	TEETERS
	TEETH	TEETHE
	TEETHE	TEETHED · TEETHER · TEETHES
	TEETHER	TEETHERS
	TEETHING	TEETHINGS
	TEETOTAL	TEETOTALS
	TEETOTUM	TEETOTUMS
	TEF	TEFF · TEFS
	TEFF	TEFFS
	TEFLON	TEFLONS
	TEG	TEGG · TEGS · TEGU
	TEGG	TEGGS
	TEGMENTA	TEGMENTAL
	TEGMINA	TEGMINAL
	TEGU	TEGUA · TEGUS
	TEGUA	TEGUAS
	TEGUEXIN	TEGUEXINS
	TEGULA	TEGULAE · TEGULAR
	TEGUMEN	TEGUMENT
	TEGUMENT	TEGUMENTS
	TEHR	TEHRS
	TEIID	TEIIDS
STEIL	**TEIL**	TEILS
STEILS	**TEILS**	
	TEIND	TEINDS
	TEKKIE	TEKKIES
	TEKTITE	TEKTITES
	TEL	TELA · TELD · TELE · TELL · TELS · TELT
STELA	**TELA**	TELAE
STELAE	**TELAE**	
	TELAMON	TELAMONS

T

FRONT HOOK	ROOT WORD	END HOOK
	TELCO	TELCOS
STELE	**TELE**	TELES ▪ TELEX
	TELECAST	TELECASTS
	TELECHIR	TELECHIRS
	TELECINE	TELECINES
	TELECOM	TELECOMS
	TELEDU	TELEDUS
	TELEFILM	TELEFILMS
	TELEGA	TELEGAS
	TELEGRAM	TELEGRAMS
	TELEGRAPH	TELEGRAPHS ▪ TELEGRAPHY
	TELEMARK	TELEMARKS
	TELEMATIC	TELEMATICS
	TELEMETER	TELEMETERS
	TELEOSAUR	TELEOSAURS
	TELEOST	TELEOSTS
	TELEPATH	TELEPATHS ▪ TELEPATHY
	TELEPHEME	TELEPHEMES
	TELEPHONE	TELEPHONED ▪ TELEPHONER ▪ TELEPHONES
	TELEPHOTO	TELEPHOTOS
	TELEPLAY	TELEPLAYS
	TELEPOINT	TELEPOINTS
	TELEPORT	TELEPORTS
	TELERAN	TELERANS
STELES	**TELES**	TELESM
	TELESALE	TELESALES
	TELESCOPE	TELESCOPED ▪ TELESCOPES
	TELESEME	TELESEMES
	TELESHOP	TELESHOPS
	TELESM	TELESMS
	TELESTIC	TELESTICH ▪ TELESTICS
	TELESTICH	TELESTICHS
	TELETEX	TELETEXT
	TELETEXT	TELETEXTS
	TELETHON	TELETHONS
	TELETRON	TELETRONS
	TELETYPE	TELETYPED ▪ TELETYPES
	TELEVIEW	TELEVIEWS
	TELEVISE	TELEVISED ▪ TELEVISER ▪ TELEVISES
	TELEVISER	TELEVISERS
	TELEVISOR	TELEVISORS
	TELFER	TELFERS
	TELFERAGE	TELFERAGES
	TELFORD	TELFORDS
	TELIA	TELIAL
ATELIC ▪ STELIC	**TELIC**	
STELL	**TELL**	TELLS ▪ TELLY
STELLAR	**TELLAR**	TELLARS
	TELLEN	TELLENS
	TELLER	TELLERS
	TELLIN	TELLING ▪ TELLINS
STELLING	**TELLING**	TELLINGS
STELLS	**TELLS**	
	TELLTALE	TELLTALES
	TELLURATE	TELLURATES
	TELLURIAN	TELLURIANS
	TELLURIDE	TELLURIDES
	TELLURION	TELLURIONS
	TELLURISE	TELLURISED ▪ TELLURISES
	TELLURITE	TELLURITES
	TELLURIUM	TELLURIUMS
	TELLURIZE	TELLURIZED ▪ TELLURIZES
	TELLY	TELLYS
	TELNET	TELNETS
	TELOME	TELOMES
	TELOMERE	TELOMERES
	TELOPHASE	TELOPHASES
	TELPHER	TELPHERS
	TELSON	TELSONS

T

FRONT HOOK	ROOT WORD	END HOOK
	TEMAZEPAM	TEMAZEPAMS
	TEMBLOR	TEMBLORS
STEME	**TEME**	TEMED ▪ TEMES
ITEMED ▪ STEMED	**TEMED**	
STEMES	**TEMES**	
	TEMP	TEMPI ▪ TEMPO ▪ TEMPS ▪ TEMPT
	TEMPEH	TEMPEHS
	TEMPER	TEMPERA ▪ TEMPERS
	TEMPERA	TEMPERAS
	TEMPERATE	TEMPERATED ▪ TEMPERATES
	TEMPERER	TEMPERERS
	TEMPERING	TEMPERINGS
	TEMPEST	TEMPESTS
	TEMPLAR	TEMPLARS
	TEMPLATE	TEMPLATES
STEMPLE	**TEMPLE**	TEMPLED ▪ TEMPLES ▪ TEMPLET
STEMPLES	**TEMPLES**	
	TEMPLET	TEMPLETS
	TEMPO	TEMPOS
ATEMPORAL	**TEMPORAL**	TEMPORALS
	TEMPORISE	TEMPORISED ▪ TEMPORISER ▪ TEMPORISES
	TEMPORIZE	TEMPORIZED ▪ TEMPORIZER ▪ TEMPORIZES
	TEMPT	TEMPTS
	TEMPTER	TEMPTERS
	TEMPTING	TEMPTINGS
	TEMPURA	TEMPURAS
ITEMS ▪ STEMS	**TEMS**	TEMSE
	TEMSE	TEMSED ▪ TEMSES
	TEMULENCE	TEMULENCES
ETEN ▪ STEN	**TEN**	TEND ▪ TENE ▪ TENS ▪ TENT
	TENACE	TENACES
	TENACULUM	TENACULUMS
	TENAIL	TENAILS
	TENAILLE	TENAILLES
	TENAILLON	TENAILLONS
	TENANT	TENANTS
STENCH	**TENCH**	
STENCHES	**TENCHES**	
STEND	**TEND**	TENDS ▪ TENDU
	TENDANCE	TENDANCES
STENDED	**TENDED**	
	TENDENCE	TENDENCES
	TENDER	TENDERS
	TENDERER	TENDERERS
	TENDERING	TENDERINGS
	TENDERISE	TENDERISED ▪ TENDERISER ▪ TENDERISES
	TENDERIZE	TENDERIZED ▪ TENDERIZER ▪ TENDERIZES
STENDING	**TENDING**	
	TENDON	TENDONS
	TENDRE	TENDRES
	TENDRESSE	TENDRESSES
	TENDRIL	TENDRILS
	TENDRON	TENDRONS
STENDS	**TENDS**	
	TENDU	TENDUS
CTENE	**TENE**	TENES ▪ TENET
	TENEBRIO	TENEBRIOS
	TENEBRISM	TENEBRISMS
	TENEBRIST	TENEBRISTS
	TENEMENT	TENEMENTS
	TENENDUM	TENENDUMS
CTENES	**TENES**	
	TENET	TENETS
	TENFOLD	TENFOLDS
	TENGE	TENGES
	TENIA	TENIAE ▪ TENIAS
	TENIACIDE	TENIACIDES
	TENIAFUGE	TENIAFUGES
	TENNE	TENNER ▪ TENNES

FRONT HOOK	ROOT WORD	END HOOK
	TENNER	TENNERS
	TENNIS	TENNIST
	TENNIST	TENNISTS
	TENNO	TENNOS
	TENON	TENONS
	TENONER	TENONERS
	TENOR	TENORS
	TENORIST	TENORISTS
	TENORITE	TENORITES
	TENOROON	TENOROONS
	TENOUR	TENOURS
	TENPENCE	TENPENCES
	TENPIN	TENPINS
	TENREC	TENRECS
ETENS ▪ STENS	**TENS**	TENSE
	TENSE	TENSED ▪ TENSER ▪ TENSES
	TENSES	TENSEST
	TENSION	TENSIONS
	TENSIONER	TENSIONERS
	TENSON	TENSONS
	TENSOR	TENSORS
STENT	**TENT**	TENTH ▪ TENTS ▪ TENTY
	TENTACLE	TENTACLED ▪ TENTACLES
	TENTACULA	TENTACULAR
	TENTAGE	TENTAGES
	TENTATION	TENTATIONS
	TENTATIVE	TENTATIVES
STENTED	**TENTED**	
	TENTER	TENTERS
	TENTFUL	TENTFULS
	TENTH	TENTHS
	TENTIE	TENTIER
	TENTIGO	TENTIGOS
STENTING	**TENTING**	TENTINGS
	TENTMAKER	TENTMAKERS
	TENTORIA	TENTORIAL
	TENTORIUM	TENTORIUMS
STENTS	**TENTS**	
	TENUE	TENUES
	TENURE	TENURED ▪ TENURES
	TENUTO	TENUTOS
	TENZON	TENZONS
	TEOCALLI	TEOCALLIS
	TEOPAN	TEOPANS
	TEOSINTE	TEOSINTES
	TEPA	TEPAL ▪ TEPAS
	TEPAL	TEPALS
	TEPEE	TEPEES
	TEPHIGRAM	TEPHIGRAMS
	TEPHRA	TEPHRAS
	TEPHRITE	TEPHRITES
	TEPHROITE	TEPHROITES
	TEPOY	TEPOYS
	TEQUILA	TEQUILAS
	TEQUILLA	TEQUILLAS
	TERABYTE	TERABYTES
	TERAFLOP	TERAFLOPS
	TERAGLIN	TERAGLINS
	TERAI	TERAIS
	TERAKIHI	TERAKIHIS
	TERAOHM	TERAOHMS
	TERAPHIM	TERAPHIMS
	TERATISM	TERATISMS
	TERATOGEN	TERATOGENS ▪ TERATOGENY
	TERATOMA	TERATOMAS
	TERAWATT	TERAWATTS
	TERBIA	TERBIAS
	TERBIUM	TERBIUMS
	TERCE	TERCEL ▪ TERCES ▪ TERCET

T

FRONT HOOK	ROOT WORD	END HOOK
	TERCEL	TERCELS
	TERCELET	TERCELETS
	TERCET	TERCETS
	TERCIO	TERCIOS
	TEREBENE	TEREBENES
	TEREBINTH	TEREBINTHS
	TEREBRA	TEREBRAE ▪ TEREBRAS
	TEREBRANT	TEREBRANTS
	TEREBRATE	TEREBRATED ▪ TEREBRATES
	TEREDO	TEREDOS
	TEREFA	TEREFAH
	TEREK	TEREKS
STERES	**TERES**	
	TERETE	TERETES
	TERF	TERFE ▪ TERFS
	TERFE	TERFES
	TERGA	TERGAL
	TERGITE	TERGITES
	TERIYAKI	TERIYAKIS
	TERM	TERMS
	TERMAGANT	TERMAGANTS
	TERMER	TERMERS
	TERMINAL	TERMINALS
	TERMINATE	TERMINATED ▪ TERMINATES
	TERMINER	TERMINERS
	TERMINISM	TERMINISMS
	TERMINIST	TERMINISTS
	TERMITE	TERMITES
	TERMOR	TERMORS
	TERMTIME	TERMTIMES
STERN	**TERN**	TERNE ▪ TERNS
ETERNAL ▪ STERNAL	**TERNAL**	
ETERNE	**TERNE**	TERNED ▪ TERNES
STERNED	**TERNED**	
STERNING	**TERNING**	
	TERNION	TERNIONS
STERNS	**TERNS**	
	TERPENE	TERPENES
	TERPENOID	TERPENOIDS
	TERPINEOL	TERPINEOLS
	TERPINOL	TERPINOLS
	TERRA	TERRAE ▪ TERRAS
	TERRACE	TERRACED ▪ TERRACES
	TERRACING	TERRACINGS
	TERRAFORM	TERRAFORMS
	TERRAIN	TERRAINS
	TERRAMARE	TERRAMARES
	TERRANE	TERRANES
	TERRAPIN	TERRAPINS
	TERRARIUM	TERRARIUMS
	TERRAZZO	TERRAZZOS
	TERREEN	TERREENS
	TERRELLA	TERRELLAS
	TERRENE	TERRENES
	TERRET	TERRETS
	TERRIBLE	TERRIBLES
	TERRICOLE	TERRICOLES
	TERRIER	TERRIERS
	TERRIFIER	TERRIFIERS
	TERRINE	TERRINES
	TERRIT	TERRITS
	TERROIR	TERROIRS
	TERROR	TERRORS
	TERRORISE	TERRORISED ▪ TERRORISER ▪ TERRORISES
	TERRORISM	TERRORISMS
	TERRORIST	TERRORISTS
	TERRORIZE	TERRORIZED ▪ TERRORIZER ▪ TERRORIZES
	TERSE	TERSER
	TERSION	TERSIONS

T

FRONT HOOK	ROOT WORD	END HOOK
	TERTIA	TERTIAL ▪ TERTIAN ▪ TERTIAS
	TERTIAL	TERTIALS
	TERTIAN	TERTIANS
	TERYLENE	TERYLENES
	TERZETTA	TERZETTAS
	TERZETTO	TERZETTOS
ATES ▪ UTES	**TES**	TEST
	TESLA	TESLAS
	TESSELATE	TESSELATED ▪ TESSELATES
	TESSELLA	TESSELLAE ▪ TESSELLAR
	TESSERA	TESSERAE ▪ TESSERAL
	TESSERACT	TESSERACTS
	TESSITURA	TESSITURAS
	TEST	TESTA ▪ TESTE ▪ TESTS ▪ TESTY
	TESTA	TESTAE
	TESTACEAN	TESTACEANS
	TESTAMENT	TESTAMENTS
	TESTAMUR	TESTAMURS
	TESTATE	TESTATES
	TESTATION	TESTATIONS
	TESTATOR	TESTATORS
	TESTATUM	TESTATUMS
	TESTE	TESTED ▪ TESTEE ▪ TESTER ▪ TESTES
	TESTEE	TESTEES
	TESTER	TESTERN ▪ TESTERS
	TESTERN	TESTERNS
	TESTICLE	TESTICLES
	TESTIFIER	TESTIFIERS
	TESTING	TESTINGS
	TESTON	TESTONS
	TESTOON	TESTOONS
	TESTRIL	TESTRILL ▪ TESTRILS
	TESTRILL	TESTRILLS
	TESTUDO	TESTUDOS
STET	**TET**	TETE ▪ TETH ▪ TETS
	TETANIC	TETANICS
	TETANISE	TETANISED ▪ TETANISES
	TETANIZE	TETANIZED ▪ TETANIZES
	TETE	TETES
	TETH	TETHS
	TETHER	TETHERS
	TETOTUM	TETOTUMS
	TETRA	TETRAD ▪ TETRAS
	TETRACID	TETRACIDS
	TETRACT	TETRACTS
	TETRAD	TETRADS
	TETRADITE	TETRADITES
	TETRAGON	TETRAGONS
	TETRAGRAM	TETRAGRAMS
	TETRAMER	TETRAMERS
	TETRAPLA	TETRAPLAS
	TETRAPOD	TETRAPODS ▪ TETRAPODY
	TETRARCH	TETRARCHS ▪ TETRARCHY
	TETRAXON	TETRAXONS
	TETRI	TETRIS
	TETRODE	TETRODES
	TETRONAL	TETRONALS
	TETROXID	TETROXIDE ▪ TETROXIDS
	TETROXIDE	TETROXIDES
	TETRYL	TETRYLS
STETS	**TETS**	
	TETTER	TETTERS
	TEUCHAT	TEUCHATS
	TEUCHTER	TEUCHTERS *(offensive)*
	TEUTONISE	TEUTONISED ▪ TEUTONISES
	TEUTONIZE	TEUTONIZED ▪ TEUTONIZES
	TEVATRON	TEVATRONS
STEW	**TEW**	TEWS
	TEWART	TEWARTS

T

FRONT HOOK	ROOT WORD	END HOOK
STEWED	**TEWED**	
	TEWEL	TEWELS
	TEWHIT	TEWHITS
STEWING	**TEWING**	
	TEWIT	TEWITS
STEWS	**TEWS**	
	TEX	TEXT
	TEXT	TEXTS
	TEXTBOOK	TEXTBOOKS
	TEXTER	TEXTERS
	TEXTILE	TEXTILES
	TEXTPHONE	TEXTPHONES
	TEXTURE	TEXTURED ▪ TEXTURES
	TEXTURISE	TEXTURISED ▪ TEXTURISES
	TEXTURIZE	TEXTURIZED ▪ TEXTURIZES
	THACK	THACKS
	THAGI	THAGIS
	THAIRM	THAIRMS
	THALAMI	THALAMIC
	THALER	THALERS
	THALI	THALIS
	THALLI	THALLIC
	THALLIUM	THALLIUMS
	THALWEG	THALWEGS
	THAN	THANA ▪ THANE ▪ THANK ▪ THANS
	THANA	THANAH ▪ THANAS
	THANADAR	THANADARS
	THANAGE	THANAGES
	THANAH	THANAHS
	THANATISM	THANATISMS
	THANATIST	THANATISTS
ETHANE	**THANE**	THANES
	THANEDOM	THANEDOMS
	THANEHOOD	THANEHOODS
ETHANES	**THANES**	
	THANESHIP	THANESHIPS
	THANGKA	THANGKAS
	THANK	THANKS
	THANKER	THANKERS
	THANKING	THANKINGS
	THANKYOU	THANKYOUS
	THANNA	THANNAH ▪ THANNAS
	THANNAH	THANNAHS
	THAR	THARM ▪ THARS
	THARM	THARMS
	THATCH	THATCHT ▪ THATCHY
	THATCHER	THATCHERS
	THATCHING	THATCHINGS
	THAUMATIN	THAUMATINS
	THAW	THAWS ▪ THAWY
	THAWER	THAWERS
	THAWING	THAWINGS
ETHE	**THE**	THEE ▪ THEM ▪ THEN ▪ THEW ▪ THEY
	THEATER	THEATERS
	THEATRE	THEATRES
	THEATRIC	THEATRICS
	THEAVE	THEAVES
	THEBAINE	THEBAINES
	THEBE	THEBES
	THECA	THECAE ▪ THECAL
	THECODONT	THECODONTS
	THEE	THEED ▪ THEEK ▪ THEES
	THEEK	THEEKS
	THEELIN	THEELINS
	THEELOL	THEELOLS
	THEFT	THEFTS
	THEGN	THEGNS
	THEIC	THEICS
	THEIN	THEINE ▪ THEINS

FRONT HOOK	ROOT WORD	END HOOK
	THEINE	THEINES
	THEIR	THEIRS
ATHEISM	THEISM	THEISMS
ATHEISMS	THEISMS	
ATHEIST	THEIST	THEISTS
ATHEISTIC	THEISTIC	
ATHEISTS	THEISTS	
	THELEMENT	THELEMENTS
	THEM	THEMA = THEME
ATHEMATIC	THEMATIC	THEMATICS
	THEME	THEMED = THEMES
	THEN	THENS
	THENABOUT	THENABOUTS
	THENAGE	THENAGES
	THENAR	THENARS
	THEOCRAT	THEOCRATS
	THEOLOG	THEOLOGS = THEOLOGY
	THEOLOGER	THEOLOGERS
	THEOLOGUE	THEOLOGUES
ATHEOLOGY	THEOLOGY	
	THEOMANIA	THEOMANIAC = THEOMANIAS
	THEORBIST	THEORBISTS
	THEORBO	THEORBOS
	THEOREM	THEOREMS
	THEORETIC	THEORETICS
	THEORIC	THEORICS
	THEORIQUE	THEORIQUES
	THEORISE	THEORISED = THEORISER = THEORISES
	THEORISER	THEORISERS
	THEORIST	THEORISTS
	THEORIZE	THEORIZED = THEORIZER = THEORIZES
	THEORIZER	THEORIZERS
	THEOSOPH	THEOSOPHS = THEOSOPHY
	THEOW	THEOWS
	THERALITE	THERALITES
	THERAPIST	THERAPISTS
	THERAPSID	THERAPSIDS
	THERBLIG	THERBLIGS
	THERE	THERES
	THEREFOR	THEREFORE
	THEREMIN	THEREMINS
	THERIAC	THERIACA = THERIACS
	THERIACA	THERIACAL = THERIACAS
	THERIAN	THERIANS
	THERM	THERME = THERMS
	THERMAL	THERMALS
	THERME	THERMEL = THERMES
	THERMEL	THERMELS
	THERMETTE	THERMETTES
	THERMIDOR	THERMIDORS
	THERMION	THERMIONS
	THERMIT	THERMITE = THERMITS
	THERMITE	THERMITES
	THERMOSET	THERMOSETS
	THERMOTIC	THERMOTICS
	THEROPOD	THEROPODS
	THESE	THESES
	THESP	THESPS
	THESPIAN	THESPIANS
	THETA	THETAS
	THETE	THETES
	THEURGIST	THEURGISTS
	THEW	THEWS = THEWY
	THIAMIN	THIAMINE = THIAMINS
	THIAMINE	THIAMINES
	THIAZIDE	THIAZIDES
	THIAZIN	THIAZINE = THIAZINS
	THIAZINE	THIAZINES
	THIAZOL	THIAZOLE = THIAZOLS

T

FRONT HOOK	ROOT WORD	END HOOK
	THIAZOLE	THIAZOLES
	THIBET	THIBETS
	THIBLE	THIBLES
	THICK	THICKO ▪ THICKS ▪ THICKY (offensive)
	THICKEN	THICKENS
	THICKENER	THICKENERS
	THICKET	THICKETS ▪ THICKETY
	THICKHEAD	THICKHEADS
	THICKIE	THICKIES (offensive)
	THICKO	THICKOS (offensive)
	THICKSET	THICKSETS
	THICKSKIN	THICKSKINS
	THIEVE	THIEVED ▪ THIEVES
	THIEVING	THIEVINGS
	THIG	THIGH ▪ THIGS
	THIGGER	THIGGERS
	THIGGING	THIGGINGS
	THIGH	THIGHS
	THIGHBONE	THIGHBONES
	THILL	THILLS
	THILLER	THILLERS
	THIMBLE	THIMBLED ▪ THIMBLES
	THIN	THINE ▪ THING ▪ THINK ▪ THINS
	THINCLAD	THINCLADS
	THINDOWN	THINDOWNS
	THING	THINGS ▪ THINGY
	THINGHOOD	THINGHOODS
	THINGIES	THINGIEST
	THINK	THINKS
	THINKER	THINKERS
	THINKING	THINKINGS
	THINNER	THINNERS
	THINNING	THINNINGS
	THIO	THIOL
	THIOFURAN	THIOFURANS
	THIOL	THIOLS
	THIONATE	THIONATES
	THIONIN	THIONINE ▪ THIONINS
ETHIONINE	**THIONINE**	THIONINES
ETHIONINES	**THIONINES**	
	THIONYL	THIONYLS
	THIOPHEN	THIOPHENE ▪ THIOPHENS
	THIOPHENE	THIOPHENES
	THIOTEPA	THIOTEPAS
	THIOUREA	THIOUREAS
	THIR	THIRD ▪ THIRL
	THIRAM	THIRAMS
	THIRD	THIRDS
	THIRDING	THIRDINGS
	THIRL	THIRLS
	THIRLAGE	THIRLAGES
ATHIRST	**THIRST**	THIRSTS ▪ THIRSTY
	THIRSTER	THIRSTERS
	THIRTEEN	THIRTEENS
	THIRTIETH	THIRTIETHS
	THISTLE	THISTLES
	THIVEL	THIVELS
	THO	THON ▪ THOU
	THOFT	THOFTS
	THOLE	THOLED ▪ THOLES
	THOLEIITE	THOLEIITES
	THOLEPIN	THOLEPINS
	THOLOBATE	THOLOBATES
	THON	THONG
	THONG	THONGS
	THORIA	THORIAS
	THORITE	THORITES
	THORIUM	THORIUMS
	THORN	THORNS ▪ THORNY

843

FRONT HOOK	ROOT WORD	END HOOK
	THORNBACK	THORNBACKS
	THORNBILL	THORNBILLS
	THORNTREE	THORNTREES
	THORO	THORON
	THORON	THORONS
	THOROUGH	THOROUGHS
	THORP	THORPE · THORPS
	THORPE	THORPES
	THOU	THOUS
	THOUGH	THOUGHT
	THOUGHT	THOUGHTS
	THOUSAND	THOUSANDS
	THOWEL	THOWELS
	THOWL	THOWLS
	THRAIPING	THRAIPINGS
	THRALDOM	THRALDOMS
	THRALL	THRALLS
	THRALLDOM	THRALLDOMS
	THRANG	THRANGS
	THRAPPLE	THRAPPLED · THRAPPLES
	THRASHER	THRASHERS
	THRASHING	THRASHINGS
	THRAVE	THRAVES
	THRAW	THRAWN · THRAWS
	THREAD	THREADS · THREADY
	THREADER	THREADERS
	THREADFIN	THREADFINS
	THREAP	THREAPS
	THREAPER	THREAPERS
	THREAT	THREATS
	THREATEN	THREATENS
	THREAVE	THREAVES
	THREE	THREEP · THREES
	THREEP	THREEPS
	THREEPER	THREEPERS
	THREESOME	THREESOMES
	THRENE	THRENES
	THRENODE	THRENODES
	THREONINE	THREONINES
	THRESHEL	THRESHELS
	THRESHER	THRESHERS
	THRESHING	THRESHINGS
	THRESHOLD	THRESHOLDS
	THRID	THRIDS
	THRIDACE	THRIDACES
	THRIFT	THRIFTS · THRIFTY
ATHRILL	THRILL	THRILLS · THRILLY
	THRILLER	THRILLERS
	THRIMSA	THRIMSAS
	THRIP	THRIPS
	THRISSEL	THRISSELS
	THRIST	THRISTS · THRISTY
	THRISTLE	THRISTLES
	THRIVE	THRIVED · THRIVEN · THRIVER · THRIVES
	THRIVER	THRIVERS
	THRIVING	THRIVINGS
	THRO	THROB · THROE · THROW
	THROAT	THROATS · THROATY
ATHROB	THROB	THROBS
	THROBBER	THROBBERS
	THROBBING	THROBBINGS
	THROE	THROED · THROES
	THROMBI	THROMBIN
	THROMBIN	THROMBINS
	THROMBOSE	THROMBOSED · THROMBOSES
	THRONE	THRONED · THRONES
	THRONG	THRONGS
	THRONGING	THRONGINGS
	THRONNER	THRONNERS

FRONT HOOK	ROOT WORD	END HOOK
	THROPPLE	THROPPLED ▪ THROPPLES
	THROSTLE	THROSTLES
	THROTTLE	THROTTLED ▪ THROTTLER ▪ THROTTLES
	THROTTLER	THROTTLERS
	THROW	THROWE ▪ THROWN ▪ THROWS
	THROWAWAY	THROWAWAYS
	THROWBACK	THROWBACKS
	THROWE	THROWER ▪ THROWES
	THROWER	THROWERS
	THROWING	THROWINGS
	THROWSTER	THROWSTERS
	THRU	THRUM
	THRUM	THRUMS
	THRUMMER	THRUMMERS
	THRUMMING	THRUMMINGS
	THRUPUT	THRUPUTS
	THRUST	THRUSTS
	THRUSTER	THRUSTERS
	THRUSTING	THRUSTINGS
	THRUSTOR	THRUSTORS
	THRUWAY	THRUWAYS
	THRYMSA	THRYMSAS
	THUD	THUDS
	THUG	THUGS
	THUGGEE	THUGGEES
	THUGGISM	THUGGISMS
	THUGGO	THUGGOS
	THUJA	THUJAS
	THULIA	THULIAS
	THULITE	THULITES
	THULIUM	THULIUMS
	THUMB	THUMBS ▪ THUMBY
	THUMBHOLE	THUMBHOLES
	THUMBKIN	THUMBKINS
	THUMBLING	THUMBLINGS
	THUMBNAIL	THUMBNAILS
	THUMBNUT	THUMBNUTS
	THUMBPOT	THUMBPOTS
	THUMBTACK	THUMBTACKS
	THUMP	THUMPS
	THUMPER	THUMPERS
	THUNDER	THUNDERS ▪ THUNDERY
YTHUNDERED	**THUNDERED**	
	THUNDERER	THUNDERERS
	THUNK	THUNKS
	THURIBLE	THURIBLES
	THURIFER	THURIFERS
	THURL	THURLS
	THUYA	THUYAS
	THWACK	THWACKS
	THWACKER	THWACKERS
	THWACKING	THWACKINGS
	THWAITE	THWAITES
ATHWART	**THWART**	THWARTS
	THWARTER	THWARTERS
	THWARTING	THWARTINGS
	THYLACINE	THYLACINES
	THYLAKOID	THYLAKOIDS
	THYLOSE	THYLOSES
	THYME	THYMES ▪ THYMEY
	THYMI	THYMIC
	THYMIDINE	THYMIDINES
	THYMINE	THYMINES
	THYMOCYTE	THYMOCYTES
	THYMOL	THYMOLS
	THYMOSIN	THYMOSINS
	THYRATRON	THYRATRONS
	THYREOID	THYREOIDS
	THYRISTOR	THYRISTORS

FRONT HOOK	ROOT WORD	END HOOK
	THYROID	THYROIDS
	THYROXIN	THYROXINE ▪ THYROXINS
	THYROXINE	THYROXINES
	THYRSE	THYRSES
	TI	TIC ▪ TID ▪ TIE ▪ TIG ▪ TIL ▪ TIN ▪ TIP ▪ TIS ▪ TIT ▪ TIX
	TIAR	TIARA ▪ TIARS
	TIARA	TIARAS
	TIBIA	TIBIAE ▪ TIBIAL ▪ TIBIAS
STIBIAL	**TIBIAL**	
ETIC ▪ OTIC	**TIC**	TICE ▪ TICH ▪ TICK ▪ TICS
	TICAL	TICALS
	TICE	TICED ▪ TICES
STICH	**TICH**	TICHY
STICK	**TICK**	TICKS ▪ TICKY
STICKED	**TICKED**	
	TICKEN	TICKENS
STICKER	**TICKER**	TICKERS
STICKERS	**TICKERS**	
	TICKET	TICKETS
	TICKETING	TICKETINGS
	TICKEY	TICKEYS
STICKIES	**TICKIES**	
STICKING	**TICKING**	TICKINGS
STICKINGS	**TICKINGS**	
	TICKLACE	TICKLACES
STICKLE	**TICKLE**	TICKLED ▪ TICKLER ▪ TICKLES
STICKLED	**TICKLED**	
STICKLER	**TICKLER**	TICKLERS
STICKLERS	**TICKLERS**	
STICKLES	**TICKLES**	
STICKLING	**TICKLING**	TICKLINGS
STICKS	**TICKS**	
STICKSEED	**TICKSEED**	TICKSEEDS
STICKSEEDS	**TICKSEEDS**	
	TICKTACK	TICKTACKS
	TICKTOCK	TICKTOCKS
STICKY	**TICKY**	
	TICTAC	TICTACS
	TICTOC	TICTOCS
	TID	TIDE ▪ TIDS ▪ TIDY
	TIDBIT	TIDBITS
STIDDIES	**TIDDIES**	TIDDIEST
	TIDDLE	TIDDLED ▪ TIDDLER ▪ TIDDLES ▪ TIDDLEY
	TIDDLER	TIDDLERS
	TIDDLEY	TIDDLEYS
	TIDDLIES	TIDDLIEST
	TIDE	TIDED ▪ TIDES
	TIDELAND	TIDELANDS
	TIDEMARK	TIDEMARKS
	TIDEMILL	TIDEMILLS
	TIDERIP	TIDERIPS
	TIDEWATER	TIDEWATERS
	TIDEWAVE	TIDEWAVES
	TIDEWAY	TIDEWAYS
	TIDIER	TIDIERS
	TIDIES	TIDIEST
	TIDING	TIDINGS
	TIDIVATE	TIDIVATED ▪ TIDIVATES
STIE	**TIE**	TIED ▪ TIER ▪ TIES
	TIEBACK	TIEBACKS
	TIEBREAK	TIEBREAKS
	TIECLASP	TIECLASPS
STIED	**TIED**	
	TIEPIN	TIEPINS
	TIER	TIERS
	TIERCE	TIERCED ▪ TIERCEL ▪ TIERCES ▪ TIERCET
	TIERCEL	TIERCELS
	TIERCELET	TIERCELETS

T

FRONT HOOK	ROOT WORD	END HOOK
	TIERCERON	TIERCERONS
	TIERCET	TIERCETS
	TIEROD	TIERODS
STIES	**TIES**	
	TIETAC	TIETACK · TIETACS
	TIETACK	TIETACKS
STIFF	**TIFF**	TIFFS
STIFFED	**TIFFED**	
	TIFFIN	TIFFING · TIFFINS
STIFFING	**TIFFING**	TIFFINGS
STIFFS	**TIFFS**	
	TIFT	TIFTS
	TIG	TIGE · TIGS
	TIGE	TIGER · TIGES
	TIGER	TIGERS · TIGERY
	TIGEREYE	TIGEREYES
	TIGERISM	TIGERISMS
	TIGHT	TIGHTS
	TIGHTEN	TIGHTENS
	TIGHTENER	TIGHTENERS
	TIGHTROPE	TIGHTROPES
	TIGHTWAD	TIGHTWADS
	TIGHTWIRE	TIGHTWIRES
	TIGLON	TIGLONS
	TIGON	TIGONS
	TIGRIDIA	TIGRIDIAS
	TIKA	TIKAS
	TIKANGA	TIKANGAS
	TIKE	TIKES (offensive)
	TIKI	TIKIS
	TIKKA	TIKKAS
	TIKOLOSHE	TIKOLOSHES
	TIL	TILE · TILL · TILS · TILT
	TILAK	TILAKS
	TILAPIA	TILAPIAS
	TILDE	TILDES
STILE · UTILE	**TILE**	TILED · TILER · TILES
STILED	**TILED**	
	TILER	TILERS · TILERY
STILES	**TILES**	
STILING	**TILING**	TILINGS
STILL	**TILL**	TILLS · TILLY
STILLAGE	**TILLAGE**	TILLAGES
STILLAGES	**TILLAGES**	
STILLED	**TILLED**	
STILLER	**TILLER**	TILLERS
STILLERS	**TILLERS**	
	TILLICUM	TILLICUMS
STILLIER	**TILLIER**	
STILLIEST	**TILLIEST**	
STILLING	**TILLING**	TILLINGS
STILLINGS	**TILLINGS**	
	TILLITE	TILLITES
STILLS	**TILLS**	
STILLY	**TILLY**	
ATILT · STILT	**TILT**	TILTH · TILTS
STILTED	**TILTED**	
STILTER	**TILTER**	TILTERS
STILTERS	**TILTERS**	
	TILTH	TILTHS
STILTING	**TILTING**	TILTINGS
STILTINGS	**TILTINGS**	
	TILTMETER	TILTMETERS
	TILTROTOR	TILTROTORS
STILTS	**TILTS**	
	TILTYARD	TILTYARDS
	TIMARAU	TIMARAUS
	TIMARIOT	TIMARIOTS
	TIMBAL	TIMBALE · TIMBALS

FRONT HOOK	ROOT WORD	END HOOK
	TIMBALE	TIMBALES
	TIMBER	TIMBERS · TIMBERY
	TIMBERING	TIMBERINGS
	TIMBO	TIMBOS
	TIMBRE	TIMBREL · TIMBRES
	TIMBREL	TIMBRELS
STIME	**TIME**	TIMED · TIMER · TIMES
	TIMEBOMB	TIMEBOMBS
	TIMECARD	TIMECARDS
STIMED	**TIMED**	
	TIMEFRAME	TIMEFRAMES
	TIMELINE	TIMELINES
	TIMELINES	TIMELINESS
	TIMENOGUY	TIMENOGUYS
	TIMEOUT	TIMEOUTS
	TIMEPIECE	TIMEPIECES
	TIMER	TIMERS
STIMES	**TIMES**	
	TIMESAVER	TIMESAVERS
	TIMESCALE	TIMESCALES
	TIMETABLE	TIMETABLED · TIMETABLES
	TIMEWORK	TIMEWORKS
STIMING	**TIMING**	TIMINGS
	TIMIST	TIMISTS
	TIMOLOL	TIMOLOLS
	TIMON	TIMONS
	TIMONEER	TIMONEERS
	TIMPANIST	TIMPANISTS
	TIMPANUM	TIMPANUMS
	TIN	TIND · TINE · TING · TINK · TINS TINT · TINY
	TINAJA	TINAJAS
	TINAMOU	TINAMOUS
	TINCAL	TINCALS
	TINCHEL	TINCHELS
	TINCT	TINCTS
	TINCTURE	TINCTURED · TINCTURES
	TIND	TINDS
	TINDAL	TINDALS
	TINDER	TINDERS · TINDERY
	TINE	TINEA · TINED · TINES
	TINEA	TINEAL · TINEAS
	TINEID	TINEIDS
	TINFOIL	TINFOILS
	TINFUL	TINFULS
STING	**TING**	TINGE · TINGS
	TINGE	TINGED · TINGES
STINGED	**TINGED**	
STINGING	**TINGING**	
ATINGLE	**TINGLE**	TINGLED · TINGLER · TINGLES
	TINGLER	TINGLERS
	TINGLING	TINGLINGS
STINGS	**TINGS**	
	TINGUAITE	TINGUAITES
	TINHORN	TINHORNS
	TINIES	TINIEST
STINK	**TINK**	TINKS
STINKER	**TINKER**	TINKERS
	TINKERER	TINKERERS
	TINKERING	TINKERINGS
STINKERS	**TINKERS**	
	TINKERTOY	TINKERTOYS
STINKING	**TINKING**	
	TINKLE	TINKLED · TINKLER · TINKLES
	TINKLER	TINKLERS
	TINKLING	TINKLINGS
STINKS	**TINKS**	
	TINNER	TINNERS
	TINNIE	TINNIER · TINNIES

FRONT HOOK	ROOT WORD	END HOOK
	TINNIES	TINNIEST
	TINNING	TINNINGS
	TINPLATE	TINPLATED ▪ TINPLATES
	TINPOT	TINPOTS
	TINSEL	TINSELS
	TINSEY	TINSEYS
	TINSMITH	TINSMITHS
	TINSTONE	TINSTONES
STINT	**TINT**	TINTS ▪ TINTY
	TINTACK	TINTACKS
STINTED	**TINTED**	
STINTER	**TINTER**	TINTERS
STINTERS	**TINTERS**	
STINTIER	**TINTIER**	
STINTIEST	**TINTIEST**	
STINTING	**TINTING**	TINTINGS
STINTINGS	**TINTINGS**	
STINTLESS	**TINTLESS**	
	TINTOOKIE	TINTOOKIES
STINTS	**TINTS**	
STINTY	**TINTY**	
	TINTYPE	TINTYPES
	TINWARE	TINWARES
	TINWORK	TINWORKS
	TIP	TIPI ▪ TIPS ▪ TIPT
	TIPCART	TIPCARTS
	TIPCAT	TIPCATS
	TIPI	TIPIS
	TIPOFF	TIPOFFS
	TIPPEE	TIPPEES
	TIPPER	TIPPERS
	TIPPET	TIPPETS
	TIPPING	TIPPINGS
STIPPLE	**TIPPLE**	TIPPLED ▪ TIPPLER ▪ TIPPLES
STIPPLED	**TIPPLED**	
STIPPLER	**TIPPLER**	TIPPLERS
STIPPLERS	**TIPPLERS**	
STIPPLES	**TIPPLES**	
STIPPLING	**TIPPLING**	
	TIPPYTOE	TIPPYTOED ▪ TIPPYTOES
	TIPS	TIPSY
	TIPSHEET	TIPSHEETS
	TIPSTAFF	TIPSTAFFS
	TIPSTER	TIPSTERS
	TIPSTOCK	TIPSTOCKS
	TIPTOE	TIPTOED ▪ TIPTOES
	TIPTOP	TIPTOPS
	TIPTRONIC	TIPTRONICS
	TIPULA	TIPULAS
	TIPUNA	TIPUNAS
	TIRADE	TIRADES
	TIRAGE	TIRAGES
	TIRAMISU	TIRAMISUS
	TIRASSE	TIRASSES
STIRE	**TIRE**	TIRED ▪ TIRES
STIRED	**TIRED**	
	TIRELING	TIRELINGS
STIRES	**TIRES**	
STIRING	**TIRING**	TIRINGS
	TIRITI	TIRITIS
	TIRL	TIRLS
	TIRO	TIROS
	TIRR	TIRRS
STIRRED	**TIRRED**	
STIRRING	**TIRRING**	
	TIRRIT	TIRRITS
	TIRRIVEE	TIRRIVEES
	TIRRIVIE	TIRRIVIES
UTIS	**TIS**	

FRONT HOOK	ROOT WORD	END HOOK
	TISANE	TISANES
	TISICK	TISICKS
	TISSUE	TISSUED = TISSUES = TISSUEY
	TIT	TITE = TITI = TITS
	TITAN	TITANS
	TITANATE	TITANATES
	TITANIA	TITANIAS
	TITANIS	TITANISM
	TITANISM	TITANISMS
	TITANITE	TITANITES
	TITANIUM	TITANIUMS
	TITBIT	TITBITS
STITCH	TITCH	TITCHY
STITCHES	TITCHES	
	TITE	TITER
	TITER	TITERS
	TITFER	TITFERS
	TITHE	TITHED = TITHER = TITHES
	TITHER	TITHERS
	TITHING	TITHINGS
	TITHONIA	TITHONIAS
	TITI	TITIS
	TITIAN	TITIANS
	TITILLATE	TITILLATED = TITILLATES
OTITIS	TITIS	
	TITIVATE	TITIVATED = TITIVATES
	TITIVATOR	TITIVATORS
	TITLARK	TITLARKS
	TITLE	TITLED = TITLER = TITLES
	TITLER	TITLERS
	TITLING	TITLINGS
	TITLIST	TITLISTS
	TITOKI	TITOKIS
	TITRANT	TITRANTS
	TITRATE	TITRATED = TITRATES
	TITRATION	TITRATIONS
	TITRATOR	TITRATORS
	TITRE	TITRES
	TITTER	TITTERS
	TITTERER	TITTERERS
	TITTERING	TITTERINGS
	TITTIE	TITTIES
	TITTIVATE	TITTIVATED = TITTIVATES
	TITTLE	TITTLED = TITTLES
	TITTLEBAT	TITTLEBATS
	TITTUP	TITTUPS = TITTUPY
	TITUBATE	TITUBATED = TITUBATES
	TITULAR	TITULARS = TITULARY
	TITULE	TITULED = TITULES
	TITUP	TITUPS = TITUPY
STIVY	TIVY	
	TIZZ	TIZZY
	TJANTING	TJANTINGS
	TO	TOC = TOD = TOE = TOG = TOM = TON = TOO TOP = TOR = TOT = TOW = TOY
	TOAD	TOADS = TOADY
	TOADEATER	TOADEATERS
	TOADSTONE	TOADSTONES
	TOADSTOOL	TOADSTOOLS
	TOADYISM	TOADYISMS
	TOAST	TOASTS = TOASTY
	TOASTER	TOASTERS
	TOASTIE	TOASTIER = TOASTIES
	TOASTIES	TOASTIEST
	TOASTING	TOASTINGS
	TOAZE	TOAZED = TOAZES
	TOBACCO	TOBACCOS
	TOBOGGAN	TOBOGGANS
	TOBOGGIN	TOBOGGINS

FRONT HOOK	ROOT WORD	END HOOK
ATOC	**TOC**	TOCK ▪ TOCO ▪ TOCS
STOCCATA	**TOCCATA**	TOCCATAS
STOCCATAS	**TOCCATAS**	
	TOCCATINA	TOCCATINAS
	TOCHER	TOCHERS
STOCK	**TOCK**	TOCKS ▪ TOCKY
STOCKED	**TOCKED**	
STOCKIER	**TOCKIER**	
STOCKIEST	**TOCKIEST**	
STOCKING	**TOCKING**	
	TOCKLEY	TOCKLEYS *(offensive)*
STOCKS	**TOCKS**	
STOCKY	**TOCKY**	
	TOCO	TOCOS
ATOCS	**TOCS**	
	TOCSIN	TOCSINS
	TOD	TODS ▪ TODY
	TODAY	TODAYS
	TODDE	TODDED ▪ TODDES
	TODDLE	TODDLED ▪ TODDLER ▪ TODDLES
	TODDLER	TODDLERS
	TOE	TOEA ▪ TOED ▪ TOES ▪ TOEY
	TOEA	TOEAS
	TOEBIE	TOEBIES
	TOECAP	TOECAPS
	TOECLIP	TOECLIPS
	TOEHOLD	TOEHOLDS
	TOENAIL	TOENAILS
	TOEPIECE	TOEPIECES
	TOEPLATE	TOEPLATES
	TOERAG	TOERAGS *(offensive)*
	TOERAGGER	TOERAGGERS
	TOESHOE	TOESHOES
	TOETOE	TOETOES
	TOFF	TOFFS ▪ TOFFY
	TOFFEE	TOFFEES
	TOFFIES	TOFFIEST
	TOFT	TOFTS
	TOFU	TOFUS
	TOFUTTI	TOFUTTIS
	TOG	TOGA ▪ TOGE ▪ TOGS
	TOGA	TOGAE ▪ TOGAS
	TOGAE	TOGAED
	TOGATE	TOGATED
	TOGE	TOGED ▪ TOGES
	TOGGER	TOGGERS ▪ TOGGERY
	TOGGLE	TOGGLED ▪ TOGGLER ▪ TOGGLES
	TOGGLER	TOGGLERS
	TOGUE	TOGUES
	TOHEROA	TOHEROAS
	TOHO	TOHOS
	TOHUNGA	TOHUNGAS
	TOIL	TOILE ▪ TOILS
ETOILE	**TOILE**	TOILED ▪ TOILER ▪ TOILES ▪ TOILET
	TOILER	TOILERS
ETOILES	**TOILES**	
	TOILET	TOILETS
	TOILETTE	TOILETTES
	TOILINET	TOILINETS
	TOILING	TOILINGS
	TOING	TOINGS
	TOISE	TOISES
	TOISEACH	TOISEACHS
	TOISECH	TOISECHS
	TOISON	TOISONS
STOIT	**TOIT**	TOITS
STOITED	**TOITED**	
STOITING	**TOITING**	
	TOITOI	TOITOIS

FRONT HOOK	ROOT WORD	END HOOK
STOITS	**TOITS**	
	TOKAMAK	TOKAMAKS
	TOKAY	TOKAYS
ATOKE ▪ STOKE	**TOKE**	TOKED ▪ TOKEN ▪ TOKER ▪ TOKES
STOKED	**TOKED**	
	TOKEN	TOKENS
	TOKENISM	TOKENISMS
STOKER	**TOKER**	TOKERS
STOKERS	**TOKERS**	
ATOKES ▪ STOKES	**TOKES**	
STOKING	**TOKING**	
	TOKO	TOKOS
	TOKOLOSHE	TOKOLOSHES
	TOKOLOSHI	TOKOLOSHIS
	TOKOMAK	TOKOMAKS
	TOKONOMA	TOKONOMAS
	TOKOTOKO	TOKOTOKOS
	TOKTOKKIE	TOKTOKKIES
	TOLA	TOLAN ▪ TOLAR ▪ TOLAS
	TOLAN	TOLANE ▪ TOLANS
	TOLANE	TOLANES
	TOLAR	TOLARS
	TOLBOOTH	TOLBOOTHS
STOLE	**TOLE**	TOLED ▪ TOLES
STOLED	**TOLED**	TOLEDO
	TOLEDO	TOLEDOS
	TOLERANCE	TOLERANCES
	TOLERATE	TOLERATED ▪ TOLERATES
	TOLERATOR	TOLERATORS
STOLES	**TOLES**	
	TOLEWARE	TOLEWARES
	TOLIDIN	TOLIDINE ▪ TOLIDINS
	TOLIDINE	TOLIDINES
	TOLING	TOLINGS
ATOLL	**TOLL**	TOLLS ▪ TOLLY
	TOLLAGE	TOLLAGES
	TOLLBAR	TOLLBARS
	TOLLBOOTH	TOLLBOOTHS
	TOLLER	TOLLERS
	TOLLGATE	TOLLGATES
	TOLLHOUSE	TOLLHOUSES
	TOLLIE	TOLLIES
	TOLLING	TOLLINGS
ATOLLS	**TOLLS**	
	TOLLWAY	TOLLWAYS
	TOLSEL	TOLSELS
	TOLSEY	TOLSEYS
	TOLT	TOLTS
	TOLTER	TOLTERS
	TOLU	TOLUS
	TOLUATE	TOLUATES
	TOLUENE	TOLUENES
	TOLUID	TOLUIDE ▪ TOLUIDS
	TOLUIDE	TOLUIDES
	TOLUIDIDE	TOLUIDIDES
	TOLUIDIN	TOLUIDINE ▪ TOLUIDINS
	TOLUIDINE	TOLUIDINES
	TOLUOL	TOLUOLE ▪ TOLUOLS
	TOLUOLE	TOLUOLES
	TOLUYL	TOLUYLS
	TOLYL	TOLYLS
	TOLZEY	TOLZEYS
ATOM	**TOM**	TOMB ▪ TOME ▪ TOMO ▪ TOMS
	TOMAHAWK	TOMAHAWKS
	TOMALLEY	TOMALLEYS
	TOMAN	TOMANS
	TOMATILLO	TOMATILLOS
	TOMB	TOMBS
	TOMBAC	TOMBACK ▪ TOMBACS

FRONT HOOK	ROOT WORD	END HOOK
	TOMBACK	TOMBACKS
	TOMBAK	TOMBAKS
	TOMBOC	TOMBOCS
	TOMBOLA	TOMBOLAS
	TOMBOLO	TOMBOLOS
	TOMBOY	TOMBOYS
	TOMBSTONE	TOMBSTONES
	TOMCAT	TOMCATS
	TOMCOD	TOMCODS
	TOME	TOMES
	TOMFOOL	TOMFOOLS
STOMIA	**TOMIA**	TOMIAL
STOMIUM	**TOMIUM**	
	TOMMYROT	TOMMYROTS
	TOMO	TOMOS
	TOMOGRAM	TOMOGRAMS
	TOMOGRAPH	TOMOGRAPHS ▪ TOMOGRAPHY
	TOMORROW	TOMORROWS
	TOMPION	TOMPIONS
	TOMPON	TOMPONS
ATOMS	**TOMS**	
	TOMTIT	TOMTITS
	TON	TONE ▪ TONG ▪ TONK ▪ TONS ▪ TONY
ATONAL	**TONAL**	
	TONALITE	TONALITES
ATONALITY	**TONALITY**	
ATONALLY	**TONALLY**	
	TONDINO	TONDINOS
	TONDO	TONDOS
ATONE ▪ STONE	**TONE**	TONED ▪ TONER ▪ TONES ▪ TONEY
	TONEARM	TONEARMS
ATONED ▪ STONED	**TONED**	
STONELESS	**TONELESS**	
	TONEME	TONEMES
	TONEPAD	TONEPADS
ATONER ▪ STONER	**TONER**	TONERS
ATONERS ▪ STONERS	**TONERS**	
ATONES ▪ STONES	**TONES**	
	TONETIC	TONETICS
	TONETTE	TONETTES
STONEY	**TONEY**	
STONG	**TONG**	TONGA ▪ TONGS
	TONGA	TONGAS
	TONGER	TONGERS
	TONGSTER	TONGSTERS
	TONGUE	TONGUED ▪ TONGUES
	TONGUELET	TONGUELETS
	TONGUING	TONGUINGS
ATONIC	**TONIC**	TONICS
ATONICITY	**TONICITY**	
ATONICS	**TONICS**	
STONIER	**TONIER**	
ATONIES ▪ STONIES	**TONIES**	TONIEST
STONIEST	**TONIEST**	
	TONIGHT	TONIGHTS
ATONING ▪ STONING	**TONING**	TONINGS
STONINGS	**TONINGS**	
STONISH	**TONISH**	
	TONITE	TONITES
STONK	**TONK**	TONKA ▪ TONKS
STONKED	**TONKED**	
STONKER	**TONKER**	TONKERS
STONKERS	**TONKERS**	
STONKING	**TONKING**	
STONKS	**TONKS**	
	TONLET	TONLETS
	TONNAG	TONNAGE ▪ TONNAGS
	TONNAGE	TONNAGES
STONNE	**TONNE**	TONNER ▪ TONNES

FRONT HOOK	ROOT WORD	END HOOK
	TONNEAU	TONNEAUS ▪ TONNEAUX
	TONNELL	TONNELLS
	TONNER	TONNERS
STONNES	**TONNES**	
	TONOMETER	TONOMETERS
	TONOPLAST	TONOPLASTS
	TONSIL	TONSILS
	TONSILLAR	TONSILLARY
	TONSOR	TONSORS
	TONSURE	TONSURED ▪ TONSURES
	TONTINE	TONTINER ▪ TONTINES
	TONTINER	TONTINERS
ATONY ▪ STONY	**TONY**	
	TOO	TOOK ▪ TOOL ▪ TOOM ▪ TOON ▪ TOOT
	TOOART	TOOARTS
STOOK	**TOOK**	
STOOL	**TOOL**	TOOLS
	TOOLBAG	TOOLBAGS
	TOOLBAR	TOOLBARS
STOOLED	**TOOLED**	
	TOOLER	TOOLERS
	TOOLHEAD	TOOLHEADS
	TOOLHOUSE	TOOLHOUSES
STOOLING	**TOOLING**	TOOLINGS
	TOOLKIT	TOOLKITS
	TOOLMAKER	TOOLMAKERS
	TOOLROOM	TOOLROOMS
STOOLS	**TOOLS**	
	TOOLSET	TOOLSETS
	TOOLSHED	TOOLSHEDS
	TOOM	TOOMS
	TOON	TOONS
	TOONIE	TOONIES
	TOORIE	TOORIES
STOOSHIE	**TOOSHIE**	
	TOOT	TOOTH ▪ TOOTS
	TOOTER	TOOTERS
	TOOTH	TOOTHS ▪ TOOTHY
	TOOTHACHE	TOOTHACHES
	TOOTHCOMB	TOOTHCOMBS
	TOOTHFUL	TOOTHFULS
	TOOTHING	TOOTHINGS
	TOOTHPICK	TOOTHPICKS
	TOOTHWORT	TOOTHWORTS
	TOOTLE	TOOTLED ▪ TOOTLER ▪ TOOTLES
	TOOTLER	TOOTLERS
	TOOTS	TOOTSY
	TOOTSIE	TOOTSIES
ATOP ▪ STOP	**TOP**	TOPE ▪ TOPH ▪ TOPI ▪ TOPO ▪ TOPS
	TOPALGIA	TOPALGIAS
	TOPARCH	TOPARCHS ▪ TOPARCHY
	TOPCOAT	TOPCOATS
STOPE	**TOPE**	TOPED ▪ TOPEE ▪ TOPEK ▪ TOPER ▪ TOPES
STOPED	**TOPED**	
	TOPEE	TOPEES
	TOPEK	TOPEKS
STOPER	**TOPER**	TOPERS
STOPERS	**TOPERS**	
STOPES	**TOPES**	
	TOPFUL	TOPFULL
	TOPH	TOPHE ▪ TOPHI ▪ TOPHS
	TOPHE	TOPHES
	TOPI	TOPIC ▪ TOPIS
	TOPIARIST	TOPIARISTS
ATOPIC	**TOPIC**	TOPICS
STOPING	**TOPING**	
	TOPKICK	TOPKICKS
	TOPKNOT	TOPKNOTS
STOPLESS	**TOPLESS**	

FRONT HOOK	ROOT WORD	END HOOK
	TOPLINE	TOPLINED · TOPLINER · TOPLINES
	TOPLINER	TOPLINERS
	TOPMAKER	TOPMAKERS
	TOPMAKING	TOPMAKINGS
	TOPMAST	TOPMASTS
	TOPMINNOW	TOPMINNOWS
	TOPO	TOPOI · TOPOS
	TOPOGRAPH	TOPOGRAPHS · TOPOGRAPHY
	TOPONYM	TOPONYMS · TOPONYMY
	TOPONYMIC	TOPONYMICS
	TOPOTYPE	TOPOTYPES
STOPPED	**TOPPED**	
STOPPER	**TOPPER**	TOPPERS
STOPPERS	**TOPPERS**	
STOPPING	**TOPPING**	TOPPINGS
STOPPINGS	**TOPPINGS**	
STOPPLE	**TOPPLE**	TOPPLED · TOPPLES
STOPPLED	**TOPPLED**	
STOPPLES	**TOPPLES**	
STOPPLING	**TOPPLING**	
STOPS	**TOPS**	
	TOPSAIL	TOPSAILS
	TOPSIDE	TOPSIDER · TOPSIDES
	TOPSIDER	TOPSIDERS
	TOPSOIL	TOPSOILS
	TOPSPIN	TOPSPINS
	TOPSTONE	TOPSTONES
	TOPWORK	TOPWORKS
	TOQUE	TOQUES · TOQUET
	TOQUET	TOQUETS
	TOQUILLA	TOQUILLAS
	TOR	TORA · TORC · TORE · TORI · TORN TORO · TORR · TORS · TORT · TORY
	TORA	TORAH · TORAN · TORAS
	TORAH	TORAHS
	TORAN	TORANA · TORANS
	TORANA	TORANAS
	TORBANITE	TORBANITES
	TORC	TORCH · TORCS
	TORCH	TORCHY
	TORCHER	TORCHERE · TORCHERS
	TORCHERE	TORCHERES
	TORCHIER	TORCHIERE · TORCHIERS
	TORCHIERE	TORCHIERES
	TORCHING	TORCHINGS
	TORCHON	TORCHONS
	TORCHWOOD	TORCHWOODS
	TORCULAR	TORCULARS
	TORDION	TORDIONS
STORE	**TORE**	TORES
	TOREADOR	TOREADORS
	TORERO	TOREROS
STORES	**TORES**	
	TOREUTIC	TOREUTICS
	TORGOCH	TORGOCHS
	TORI	TORIC · TORII
	TORIC	TORICS
STORIES	**TORIES**	
	TORMENT	TORMENTA · TORMENTS
	TORMENTER	TORMENTERS
	TORMENTIL	TORMENTILS
	TORMENTOR	TORMENTORS
	TORMENTUM	TORMENTUMS
	TORMINA	TORMINAL
	TORNADE	TORNADES
	TORNADO	TORNADOS
	TORNILLO	TORNILLOS
	TORO	TOROS · TOROT
	TOROID	TOROIDS

FRONT HOOK	ROOT WORD	END HOOK
	TOROS	TOROSE
	TOROT	TOROTH
	TORPEDO	TORPEDOS
	TORPEDOER	TORPEDOERS
	TORPID	TORPIDS
	TORPITUDE	TORPITUDES
	TORPOR	TORPORS
	TORQUATE	TORQUATED
	TORQUE	TORQUED ▪ TORQUER ▪ TORQUES
	TORQUER	TORQUERS
	TORR	TORRS
	TORRENT	TORRENTS
	TORRET	TORRETS
	TORS	TORSE ▪ TORSI ▪ TORSK ▪ TORSO
	TORSADE	TORSADES
	TORSE	TORSEL ▪ TORSES
	TORSEL	TORSELS
	TORSION	TORSIONS
	TORSK	TORSKS
	TORSO	TORSOS
	TORT	TORTA ▪ TORTE ▪ TORTS
	TORTA	TORTAS
	TORTE	TORTEN ▪ TORTES
	TORTILLA	TORTILLAS
	TORTILLON	TORTILLONS
	TORTOISE	TORTOISES
	TORTONI	TORTONIS
	TORTRICID	TORTRICIDS
	TORTURE	TORTURED ▪ TORTURER ▪ TORTURES
	TORTURER	TORTURERS
	TORTURING	TORTURINGS
	TORULA	TORULAE ▪ TORULAS
	TORULI	TORULIN
	TORULIN	TORULINS
	TORULOSE	TORULOSES
STORY	**TORY**	
	TOSA	TOSAS
	TOSE	TOSED ▪ TOSES
PTOSES	**TOSES**	
	TOSH	TOSHY
	TOSHACH	TOSHACHS
	TOSHER	TOSHERS
STOSS	**TOSS**	TOSSY
	TOSSER	TOSSERS (offensive)
STOSSES	**TOSSES**	
	TOSSING	TOSSINGS
	TOSSPOT	TOSSPOTS (offensive)
	TOSSUP	TOSSUPS
YTOST	**TOST**	
	TOSTADA	TOSTADAS
	TOSTADO	TOSTADOS
STOT	**TOT**	TOTE ▪ TOTS
	TOTAL	TOTALS
	TOTALISE	TOTALISED ▪ TOTALISER ▪ TOTALISES
	TOTALISER	TOTALISERS
	TOTALISM	TOTALISMS
	TOTALIST	TOTALISTS
	TOTALIZE	TOTALIZED ▪ TOTALIZER ▪ TOTALIZES
	TOTALIZER	TOTALIZERS
	TOTAQUINE	TOTAQUINES
	TOTARA	TOTARAS
	TOTE	TOTED ▪ TOTEM ▪ TOTER ▪ TOTES
	TOTEM	TOTEMS
	TOTEMISM	TOTEMISMS
	TOTEMIST	TOTEMISTS
	TOTEMITE	TOTEMITES
	TOTER	TOTERS
	TOTIENT	TOTIENTS
	TOTITIVE	TOTITIVES

T

FRONT HOOK	ROOT WORD	END HOOK
STOTS	**TOTS**	
STOTTED	**TOTTED**	
STOTTER	**TOTTER**	TOTTERS ▪ TOTTERY
STOTTERED	**TOTTERED**	
	TOTTERER	TOTTERERS
STOTTERING	**TOTTERING**	TOTTERINGS
STOTTERS	**TOTTERS**	
STOTTIE	**TOTTIE**	TOTTIER ▪ TOTTIES
STOTTIES	**TOTTIES**	TOTTIEST
STOTTING	**TOTTING**	TOTTINGS
	TOUCAN	TOUCANS
	TOUCANET	TOUCANETS
	TOUCH	TOUCHE ▪ TOUCHY
	TOUCHBACK	TOUCHBACKS
	TOUCHDOWN	TOUCHDOWNS
	TOUCHE	TOUCHED ▪ TOUCHER ▪ TOUCHES
	TOUCHER	TOUCHERS
	TOUCHHOLE	TOUCHHOLES
	TOUCHING	TOUCHINGS
	TOUCHLINE	TOUCHLINES
	TOUCHMARK	TOUCHMARKS
	TOUCHPAD	TOUCHPADS
	TOUCHTONE	TOUCHTONES
	TOUCHUP	TOUCHUPS
	TOUCHWOOD	TOUCHWOODS
	TOUGH	TOUGHS ▪ TOUGHY
	TOUGHEN	TOUGHENS
	TOUGHENER	TOUGHENERS
	TOUGHIE	TOUGHIES
	TOUK	TOUKS
STOUN	**TOUN**	TOUNS
STOUNS	**TOUNS**	
	TOUPEE	TOUPEES
	TOUPET	TOUPETS
STOUR	**TOUR**	TOURS
	TOURACO	TOURACOS
	TOURER	TOURERS
STOURIE	**TOURIE**	TOURIES
	TOURING	TOURINGS
	TOURISM	TOURISMS
	TOURIST	TOURISTA ▪ TOURISTS ▪ TOURISTY
	TOURISTA	TOURISTAS
	TOURNEY	TOURNEYS
	TOURNEYER	TOURNEYERS
	TOURNURE	TOURNURES
STOURS	**TOURS**	
	TOURTIERE	TOURTIERES
	TOUSE	TOUSED ▪ TOUSER ▪ TOUSES
	TOUSER	TOUSERS
	TOUSING	TOUSINGS
	TOUSLE	TOUSLED ▪ TOUSLES
	TOUSTIE	TOUSTIER
STOUT	**TOUT**	TOUTS
STOUTER	**TOUTER**	TOUTERS
	TOUTIE	TOUTIER
STOUTS	**TOUTS**	
	TOUZE	TOUZED ▪ TOUZES
	TOUZLE	TOUZLED ▪ TOUZLES
STOW	**TOW**	TOWN ▪ TOWS ▪ TOWT ▪ TOWY
STOWABLE	**TOWABLE**	
STOWAGE	**TOWAGE**	TOWAGES
STOWAGES	**TOWAGES**	
	TOWARD	TOWARDS
STOWAWAY	**TOWAWAY**	TOWAWAYS
STOWAWAYS	**TOWAWAYS**	
	TOWBAR	TOWBARS
	TOWBOAT	TOWBOATS
STOWED	**TOWED**	
	TOWEL	TOWELS

FRONT HOOK	ROOT WORD	END HOOK
	TOWELETTE	TOWELETTES
	TOWELHEAD	TOWELHEADS
	TOWELING	TOWELINGS
	TOWELLING	TOWELLINGS
STOWER	TOWER	TOWERS = TOWERY
STOWERS	TOWERS	
	TOWHEAD	TOWHEADS
	TOWHEE	TOWHEES
	TOWIE	TOWIER = TOWIES
	TOWIES	TOWIEST
STOWING	TOWING	TOWINGS
STOWINGS	TOWINGS	
	TOWKAY	TOWKAYS
	TOWLINE	TOWLINES
	TOWMON	TOWMOND = TOWMONS = TOWMONT
	TOWMOND	TOWMONDS
	TOWMONT	TOWMONTS
STOWN	TOWN	TOWNS = TOWNY
	TOWNEE	TOWNEES
	TOWNHOME	TOWNHOMES
	TOWNHOUSE	TOWNHOUSES
	TOWNIE	TOWNIER = TOWNIES
	TOWNIES	TOWNIEST
	TOWNLAND	TOWNLANDS
	TOWNLET	TOWNLETS
	TOWNLING	TOWNLINGS
	TOWNSCAPE	TOWNSCAPED = TOWNSCAPES
	TOWNSFOLK	TOWNSFOLKS
	TOWNSHIP	TOWNSHIPS
	TOWNSKIP	TOWNSKIPS
	TOWPATH	TOWPATHS
	TOWPLANE	TOWPLANES
	TOWROPE	TOWROPES
STOWS	TOWS	TOWSE = TOWSY
	TOWSACK	TOWSACKS
	TOWSE	TOWSED = TOWSER = TOWSES
	TOWSER	TOWSERS
	TOWT	TOWTS
	TOWZE	TOWZED = TOWZES
	TOXAEMIA	TOXAEMIAS
	TOXAPHENE	TOXAPHENES
	TOXEMIA	TOXEMIAS
	TOXIC	TOXICS
	TOXICANT	TOXICANTS
	TOXIN	TOXINE = TOXINS
	TOXINE	TOXINES
	TOXOCARA	TOXOCARAS
	TOXOID	TOXOIDS
	TOY	TOYO = TOYS
	TOYER	TOYERS
	TOYING	TOYINGS
	TOYO	TOYON = TOYOS
	TOYON	TOYONS
	TOYSHOP	TOYSHOPS
	TOZE	TOZED = TOZES
	TOZIE	TOZIES
	TRABEATE	TRABEATED
	TRABECULA	TRABECULAE = TRABECULAR = TRABECULAS
	TRACE	TRACED = TRACER = TRACES
	TRACER	TRACERS = TRACERY
	TRACEUR	TRACEURS
	TRACHEA	TRACHEAE = TRACHEAL = TRACHEAS
	TRACHEATE	TRACHEATED = TRACHEATES
	TRACHEID	TRACHEIDE = TRACHEIDS
	TRACHEIDE	TRACHEIDES
	TRACHEOLE	TRACHEOLES
	TRACHLE	TRACHLED = TRACHLES
	TRACHOMA	TRACHOMAS
	TRACHYTE	TRACHYTES

FRONT HOOK	ROOT WORD	END HOOK
	TRACING	TRACINGS
	TRACK	TRACKS
	TRACKAGE	TRACKAGES
	TRACKBALL	TRACKBALLS
	TRACKER	TRACKERS
	TRACKING	TRACKINGS
	TRACKPAD	TRACKPADS
	TRACKROAD	TRACKROADS
	TRACKSIDE	TRACKSIDES
	TRACKSUIT	TRACKSUITS
	TRACKWAY	TRACKWAYS
	TRACT	TRACTS
	TRACTATE	TRACTATES
	TRACTATOR	TRACTATORS
	TRACTION	TRACTIONS
	TRACTOR	TRACTORS
STRAD	TRAD	TRADE ▪ TRADS
	TRADE	TRADED ▪ TRADER ▪ TRADES
	TRADEMARK	TRADEMARKS
	TRADENAME	TRADENAMES
	TRADEOFF	TRADEOFFS
	TRADER	TRADERS
	TRADING	TRADINGS
	TRADITION	TRADITIONS
	TRADITOR	TRADITORS
STRADS	TRADS	
	TRADUCE	TRADUCED ▪ TRADUCER ▪ TRADUCES
	TRADUCER	TRADUCERS
	TRADUCIAN	TRADUCIANS
	TRADUCING	TRADUCINGS
	TRAFFIC	TRAFFICS
	TRAGEDIAN	TRAGEDIANS
	TRAGELAPH	TRAGELAPHS
	TRAGI	TRAGIC
	TRAGIC	TRAGICS
	TRAGOPAN	TRAGOPANS
	TRAGULE	TRAGULES
	TRAHISON	TRAHISONS
STRAIK	TRAIK	TRAIKS
STRAIKED	TRAIKED	
STRAIKING	TRAIKING	
STRAIKS	TRAIKS	
	TRAIL	TRAILS
	TRAILER	TRAILERS
	TRAILHEAD	TRAILHEADS
STRAIN	TRAIN	TRAINS
	TRAINBAND	TRAINBANDS
STRAINED	TRAINED	
	TRAINEE	TRAINEES
STRAINER	TRAINER	TRAINERS
STRAINERS	TRAINERS	
	TRAINFUL	TRAINFULS
STRAINING	TRAINING	TRAININGS
STRAININGS	TRAININGS	
	TRAINLOAD	TRAINLOADS
STRAINS	TRAINS	
	TRAINWAY	TRAINWAYS
	TRAIPSE	TRAIPSED ▪ TRAIPSES
	TRAIPSING	TRAIPSINGS
STRAIT	TRAIT	TRAITS
	TRAITOR	TRAITORS
STRAITS	TRAITS	
	TRAJECT	TRAJECTS
	TRAM	TRAMP ▪ TRAMS
	TRAMCAR	TRAMCARS
	TRAMEL	TRAMELL ▪ TRAMELS
	TRAMELL	TRAMELLS
	TRAMLINE	TRAMLINED ▪ TRAMLINES
STRAMMEL	TRAMMEL	TRAMMELS

FRONT HOOK	ROOT WORD	END HOOK
	TRAMMELER	TRAMMELERS
STRAMMELS	**TRAMMELS**	
	TRAMMIE	TRAMMIES
STRAMP	**TRAMP**	TRAMPS · TRAMPY
STRAMPED	**TRAMPED**	
	TRAMPER	TRAMPERS
	TRAMPET	TRAMPETS
	TRAMPETTE	TRAMPETTES
STRAMPING	**TRAMPING**	TRAMPINGS
	TRAMPLE	TRAMPLED · TRAMPLER · TRAMPLES
	TRAMPLER	TRAMPLERS
	TRAMPLING	TRAMPLINGS
	TRAMPOLIN	TRAMPOLINE · TRAMPOLINS
STRAMPS	**TRAMPS**	
	TRAMROAD	TRAMROADS
	TRAMWAY	TRAMWAYS
	TRANCE	TRANCED · TRANCES
	TRANCHE	TRANCHES · TRANCHET
	TRANCHET	TRANCHETS
	TRANECT	TRANECTS
	TRANGAM	TRANGAMS
STRANGLE	**TRANGLE**	TRANGLES
STRANGLES	**TRANGLES**	
	TRANK	TRANKS
	TRANKUM	TRANKUMS
	TRANNIE	TRANNIES
	TRANQ	TRANQS
	TRANS	TRANSE
	TRANSACT	TRANSACTS
	TRANSAXLE	TRANSAXLES
	TRANSCEND	TRANSCENDS
	TRANSDUCE	TRANSDUCED · TRANSDUCER · TRANSDUCES
	TRANSE	TRANSES
	TRANSECT	TRANSECTS
	TRANSENNA	TRANSENNAS
	TRANSEPT	TRANSEPTS
	TRANSFECT	TRANSFECTS
	TRANSFER	TRANSFERS
	TRANSFIX	TRANSFIXT
	TRANSFORM	TRANSFORMS
	TRANSFUSE	TRANSFUSED · TRANSFUSER · TRANSFUSES
	TRANSGENE	TRANSGENES
	TRANSHIP	TRANSHIPS
	TRANSHUME	TRANSHUMED · TRANSHUMES
	TRANSIENT	TRANSIENTS
	TRANSIRE	TRANSIRES
	TRANSIT	TRANSITS
	TRANSLATE	TRANSLATED · TRANSLATES
	TRANSMEW	TRANSMEWS
	TRANSMIT	TRANSMITS
	TRANSMOVE	TRANSMOVED · TRANSMOVES
	TRANSMUTE	TRANSMUTED · TRANSMUTER · TRANSMUTES
	TRANSOM	TRANSOMS
	TRANSONIC	TRANSONICS
	TRANSPIRE	TRANSPIRED · TRANSPIRES
	TRANSPORT	TRANSPORTS
	TRANSPOSE	TRANSPOSED · TRANSPOSER · TRANSPOSES
	TRANSSHIP	TRANSSHIPS
	TRANSUDE	TRANSUDED · TRANSUDES
	TRANSUME	TRANSUMED · TRANSUMES
	TRANSUMPT	TRANSUMPTS
	TRANSVEST	TRANSVESTS
	TRANT	TRANTS
	TRANTER	TRANTERS
STRAP	**TRAP**	TRAPE · TRAPS · TRAPT
	TRAPAN	TRAPANS
	TRAPANNER	TRAPANNERS
	TRAPBALL	TRAPBALLS
	TRAPDOOR	TRAPDOORS

FRONT HOOK	ROOT WORD	END HOOK
	TRAPE	TRAPED ▪ TRAPES
	TRAPESING	TRAPESINGS
	TRAPEZE	TRAPEZED ▪ TRAPEZES
	TRAPEZIA	TRAPEZIAL
	TRAPEZIST	TRAPEZISTS
	TRAPEZIUM	TRAPEZIUMS
	TRAPEZOID	TRAPEZOIDS
STRAPLINE	**TRAPLINE**	TRAPLINES
STRAPLINES	**TRAPLINES**	
	TRAPNEST	TRAPNESTS
STRAPPED	**TRAPPED**	
STRAPPER	**TRAPPER**	TRAPPERS
STRAPPERS	**TRAPPERS**	
STRAPPIER	**TRAPPIER**	
STRAPPIEST	**TRAPPIEST**	
STRAPPING	**TRAPPING**	TRAPPINGS
STRAPPINGS	**TRAPPINGS**	
STRAPPY	**TRAPPY**	
	TRAPROCK	TRAPROCKS
STRAPS	**TRAPS**	
	TRAPUNTO	TRAPUNTOS
	TRASH	TRASHY
	TRASHCAN	TRASHCANS
	TRASHER	TRASHERS ▪ TRASHERY
	TRASHTRIE	TRASHTRIES
STRASS	**TRASS**	
STRASSES	**TRASSES**	
	TRAT	TRATS ▪ TRATT
	TRATT	TRATTS
	TRATTORIA	TRATTORIAS
	TRAUCHLE	TRAUCHLED ▪ TRAUCHLES
	TRAUMA	TRAUMAS
	TRAVAIL	TRAVAILS
	TRAVE	TRAVEL ▪ TRAVES
	TRAVEL	TRAVELS
	TRAVELER	TRAVELERS
	TRAVELING	TRAVELINGS
	TRAVELLER	TRAVELLERS
	TRAVELOG	TRAVELOGS
	TRAVERSAL	TRAVERSALS
	TRAVERSE	TRAVERSED ▪ TRAVERSER ▪ TRAVERSES
	TRAVERSER	TRAVERSERS
	TRAVERTIN	TRAVERTINE ▪ TRAVERTINS
	TRAVOIS	TRAVOISE
	TRAVOISE	TRAVOISES
	TRAWL	TRAWLS
	TRAWLER	TRAWLERS
	TRAWLEY	TRAWLEYS
	TRAWLING	TRAWLINGS
	TRAWLNET	TRAWLNETS
STRAY	**TRAY**	TRAYS
	TRAYBIT	TRAYBITS
	TRAYFUL	TRAYFULS
	TRAYNE	TRAYNED ▪ TRAYNES
STRAYS	**TRAYS**	
	TRAZODONE	TRAZODONES
	TREACHER	TREACHERS ▪ TREACHERY
	TREACHOUR	TREACHOURS
	TREACLE	TREACLED ▪ TREACLES
	TREAD	TREADS
	TREADER	TREADERS
	TREADING	TREADINGS
	TREADLE	TREADLED ▪ TREADLER ▪ TREADLES
	TREADLER	TREADLERS
	TREADLES	TREADLESS
	TREADLING	TREADLINGS
	TREADMILL	TREADMILLS
	TREAGUE	TREAGUES
	TREASON	TREASONS

FRONT HOOK	ROOT WORD	END HOOK
	TREASURE	TREASURED ▪ TREASURER ▪ TREASURES
	TREASURER	TREASURERS
	TREAT	TREATS ▪ TREATY
	TREATER	TREATERS
	TREATING	TREATINGS
	TREATISE	TREATISES
	TREATMENT	TREATMENTS
	TREBBIANO	TREBBIANOS
	TREBLE	TREBLED ▪ TREBLES
	TREBUCHET	TREBUCHETS
	TREBUCKET	TREBUCKETS
	TRECENTO	TRECENTOS
	TRECK	TRECKS
	TREDDLE	TREDDLED ▪ TREDDLES
	TREDILLE	TREDILLES
	TREDRILLE	TREDRILLES
	TREE	TREED ▪ TREEN ▪ TREES
	TREEHOUSE	TREEHOUSES
	TREELAWN	TREELAWNS
	TREEN	TREENS
	TREENAIL	TREENAILS
	TREENWARE	TREENWARES
	TREESHIP	TREESHIPS
	TREETOP	TREETOPS
	TREEWARE	TREEWARES
	TREF	TREFA
	TREFA	TREFAH
	TREFOIL	TREFOILS
	TREGETOUR	TREGETOURS
	TREHALA	TREHALAS
	TREHALOSE	TREHALOSES
	TREIF	TREIFA
	TREILLAGE	TREILLAGED ▪ TREILLAGES
	TREILLE	TREILLES
	TREK	TREKS
	TREKKER	TREKKERS
	TREMA	TREMAS
	TREMATODE	TREMATODES
	TREMATOID	TREMATOIDS
ATREMBLE	TREMBLE	TREMBLED ▪ TREMBLER ▪ TREMBLES
	TREMBLER	TREMBLERS
	TREMBLING	TREMBLINGS
	TREMIE	TREMIES
	TREMOLANT	TREMOLANTS
	TREMOLITE	TREMOLITES
	TREMOLO	TREMOLOS
	TREMOR	TREMORS
	TREMULANT	TREMULANTS
	TREMULATE	TREMULATED ▪ TREMULATES
	TRENAIL	TRENAILS
	TRENCHARD	TRENCHARDS
	TRENCHER	TRENCHERS
	TREND	TRENDS ▪ TRENDY
	TRENDIES	TRENDIEST
	TRENDOID	TRENDOIDS
	TRENDYISM	TRENDYISMS
	TRENISE	TRENISES
	TRENTAL	TRENTALS
	TREPAN	TREPANG ▪ TREPANS
	TREPANG	TREPANGS
	TREPANNER	TREPANNERS
	TREPHINE	TREPHINED ▪ TREPHINER ▪ TREPHINES
	TREPHINER	TREPHINERS
	TREPONEMA	TREPONEMAL ▪ TREPONEMAS
	TREPONEME	TREPONEMES
	TRES	TRESS ▪ TREST
STRESS	TRESS	TRESSY
STRESSED	TRESSED	
	TRESSEL	TRESSELS

FRONT HOOK	ROOT WORD	END HOOK
STRESSES	TRESSES	
STRESSING	TRESSING	
	TRESSOUR	TRESSOURS
	TRESSURE	TRESSURED · TRESSURES
	TREST	TRESTS
	TRESTLE	TRESTLES
	TRET	TRETS
	TRETINOIN	TRETINOINS
	TREVALLY	TREVALLYS
	TREVET	TREVETS
	TREVIS	TREVISS
STREW	TREW	TREWS
STREWS	TREWS	
	TREY	TREYS
	TREYBIT	TREYBITS
	TRIAC	TRIACS · TRIACT
	TRIACID	TRIACIDS
	TRIAD	TRIADS
	TRIADIC	TRIADICS
	TRIADISM	TRIADISMS
	TRIADIST	TRIADISTS
	TRIAGE	TRIAGED · TRIAGES
ATRIAL	TRIAL	TRIALS
	TRIALISM	TRIALISMS
	TRIALIST	TRIALISTS
	TRIALLING	TRIALLINGS
	TRIALLIST	TRIALLISTS
	TRIALOGUE	TRIALOGUES
	TRIALWARE	TRIALWARES
	TRIANGLE	TRIANGLED · TRIANGLES
	TRIARCH	TRIARCHS · TRIARCHY
	TRIATHLON	TRIATHLONS
	TRIATIC	TRIATICS
	TRIAXIAL	TRIAXIALS
	TRIAXON	TRIAXONS
	TRIAZIN	TRIAZINE · TRIAZINS
	TRIAZINE	TRIAZINES
	TRIAZOLE	TRIAZOLES
	TRIBADE	TRIBADES
	TRIBADISM	TRIBADISMS
	TRIBAL	TRIBALS
	TRIBALISM	TRIBALISMS
	TRIBALIST	TRIBALISTS
	TRIBBLE	TRIBBLES
	TRIBE	TRIBES
	TRIBLET	TRIBLETS
	TRIBRACH	TRIBRACHS
	TRIBULATE	TRIBULATED · TRIBULATES
	TRIBUNAL	TRIBUNALS
	TRIBUNATE	TRIBUNATES
	TRIBUNE	TRIBUNES
	TRIBUTE	TRIBUTER · TRIBUTES
	TRIBUTER	TRIBUTERS
	TRICAR	TRICARS
	TRICE	TRICED · TRICEP · TRICES
	TRICEP	TRICEPS
	TRICERION	TRICERIONS
	TRICHINA	TRICHINAE · TRICHINAL · TRICHINAS
	TRICHITE	TRICHITES
	TRICHOME	TRICHOMES
	TRICHORD	TRICHORDS
STRICK	TRICK	TRICKS · TRICKY
	TRICKER	TRICKERS · TRICKERY
	TRICKIE	TRICKIER
	TRICKING	TRICKINGS
STRICKLE	TRICKLE	TRICKLED · TRICKLES · TRICKLET
STRICKLED	TRICKLED	
STRICKLES	TRICKLES	TRICKLESS
	TRICKLET	TRICKLETS

FRONT HOOK	ROOT WORD	END HOOK
STRICKLING STRICKS	**TRICKLING** **TRICKS** **TRICKSTER** **TRICLAD** **TRICLOSAN** **TRICOLOR** **TRICOLOUR** **TRICORN** **TRICORNE** **TRICOT** **TRICOTINE** **TRICTRAC** **TRICUSPID** **TRICYCLE** **TRICYCLER** **TRICYCLIC** **TRIDACNA** **TRIDARN**	TRICKLINGS TRICKSY TRICKSTERS TRICLADS TRICLOSANS TRICOLORS TRICOLOURS TRICORNE ▪ TRICORNS TRICORNES TRICOTS TRICOTINES TRICTRACS TRICUSPIDS TRICYCLED ▪ TRICYCLER ▪ TRICYCLES TRICYCLERS TRICYCLICS TRIDACNAS TRIDARNS
STRIDE STRIDENT	**TRIDE** **TRIDENT** **TRIDUUM** **TRIDYMITE** **TRIE** **TRIELLA** **TRIENE** **TRIENNIA** **TRIENNIAL** **TRIENNIUM**	 TRIDENTS TRIDUUMS TRIDYMITES TRIED ▪ TRIER ▪ TRIES TRIELLAS TRIENES TRIENNIAL TRIENNIALS TRIENNIUMS
ETRIER	**TRIER** **TRIERARCH**	TRIERS TRIERARCHS ▪ TRIERARCHY
ETRIERS	**TRIERS** **TRIFACIAL** **TRIFECTA** **TRIFFID** **TRIFLE** **TRIFLER** **TRIFLING** **TRIFOCAL** **TRIFOLIUM** **TRIFORIA**	 TRIFACIALS TRIFECTAS TRIFFIDS ▪ TRIFFIDY TRIFLED ▪ TRIFLER ▪ TRIFLES TRIFLERS TRIFLINGS TRIFOCALS TRIFOLIUMS TRIFORIAL
STRIG	**TRIG** **TRIGAMIST**	TRIGO ▪ TRIGS TRIGAMISTS
STRIGGED	**TRIGGED** **TRIGGER**	 TRIGGERS
STRIGGING	**TRIGGING** **TRIGLOT** **TRIGLYPH** **TRIGO** **TRIGON** **TRIGRAM** **TRIGRAPH**	 TRIGLOTS TRIGLYPHS TRIGON ▪ TRIGOS TRIGONS TRIGRAMS TRIGRAPHS
STRIGS	**TRIGS** **TRIHEDRA** **TRIHEDRAL** **TRIHEDRON** **TRIHYBRID** **TRIJET**	 TRIHEDRAL TRIHEDRALS TRIHEDRONS TRIHYBRIDS TRIJETS
STRIKE STRIKES	**TRIKE** **TRIKES** **TRILBY** **TRILEMMA** **TRILITH** **TRILITHON** **TRILL** **TRILLER** **TRILLING** **TRILLION** **TRILLIUM** **TRILOBATE**	TRIKES TRILBYS TRILEMMAS TRILITHS TRILITHONS TRILLO ▪ TRILLS TRILLERS TRILLINGS TRILLIONS TRILLIUMS TRILOBATED

FRONT HOOK	ROOT WORD	END HOOK
	TRILOBE	TRILOBED · TRILOBES
	TRILOBITE	TRILOBITES
	TRIM	TRIMS
	TRIMARAN	TRIMARANS
	TRIMER	TRIMERS
	TRIMERISM	TRIMERISMS
	TRIMESTER	TRIMESTERS
	TRIMETER	TRIMETERS
	TRIMMER	TRIMMERS
	TRIMMING	TRIMMINGS
	TRIMORPH	TRIMORPHS
	TRIMOTOR	TRIMOTORS
	TRIMTAB	TRIMTABS
	TRIN	TRINE · TRINS
	TRINDLE	TRINDLED · TRINDLES
	TRINE	TRINED · TRINES
	TRINGLE	TRINGLES
	TRINITRIN	TRINITRINS
	TRINKET	TRINKETS
	TRINKETER	TRINKETERS
	TRINKUM	TRINKUMS
	TRINOMIAL	TRINOMIALS
	TRIO	TRIOL · TRIOR · TRIOS
	TRIODE	TRIODES
	TRIOL	TRIOLS
	TRIOLEIN	TRIOLEINS
	TRIOLET	TRIOLETS
	TRIONYM	TRIONYMS
	TRIOR	TRIORS
	TRIOS	TRIOSE
	TRIOSE	TRIOSES
	TRIOXID	TRIOXIDE · TRIOXIDS
	TRIOXIDE	TRIOXIDES
	TRIOXYGEN	TRIOXYGENS
ATRIP · STRIP	**TRIP**	TRIPE · TRIPS · TRIPY
	TRIPACK	TRIPACKS
STRIPE	**TRIPE**	TRIPES · TRIPEY
STRIPES	**TRIPES**	
STRIPEY	**TRIPEY**	
	TRIPHONE	TRIPHONES
STRIPIER	**TRIPIER**	
STRIPIEST	**TRIPIEST**	
	TRIPITAKA	TRIPITAKAS
	TRIPLANE	TRIPLANES
	TRIPLE	TRIPLED · TRIPLES · TRIPLET · TRIPLEX
	TRIPLET	TRIPLETS
STRIPLING	**TRIPLING**	TRIPLINGS
STRIPLINGS	**TRIPLINGS**	
	TRIPLITE	TRIPLITES
	TRIPLOID	TRIPLOIDS · TRIPLOIDY
	TRIPOD	TRIPODS · TRIPODY
	TRIPOLI	TRIPOLIS
STRIPPED	**TRIPPED**	
STRIPPER	**TRIPPER**	TRIPPERS · TRIPPERY
STRIPPERS	**TRIPPERS**	
	TRIPPET	TRIPPETS
STRIPPING	**TRIPPING**	TRIPPINGS
STRIPPINGS	**TRIPPINGS**	
	TRIPPLE	TRIPPLED · TRIPPLER · TRIPPLES
	TRIPPLER	TRIPPLERS
STRIPS	**TRIPS**	
	TRIPTAN	TRIPTANE · TRIPTANS
	TRIPTANE	TRIPTANES
	TRIPTOTE	TRIPTOTES
	TRIPTYCA	TRIPTYCAS
	TRIPTYCH	TRIPTYCHS
	TRIPTYQUE	TRIPTYQUES
	TRIPUDIUM	TRIPUDIUMS
	TRIPWIRE	TRIPWIRES

	FRONT HOOK	ROOT WORD	END HOOK
	STRIPY	**TRIPY**	
		TRIQUETRA	TRIQUETRAL ▪ TRIQUETRAS
		TRIREME	TRIREMES
		TRISAGION	TRISAGIONS
		TRISCELE	TRISCELES
		TRISECT	TRISECTS
		TRISECTOR	TRISECTORS
		TRISEME	TRISEMES
		TRISHAW	TRISHAWS
		TRISKELE	TRISKELES
		TRISOME	TRISOMES
		TRISOMIC	TRISOMICS
		TRIST	TRISTE
		TRISTESSE	TRISTESSES
		TRISTEZA	TRISTEZAS
		TRISTICH	TRISTICHS
		TRISUL	TRISULA ▪ TRISULS
		TRISULA	TRISULAS
		TRITE	TRITER ▪ TRITES
		TRITES	TRITEST
		TRITHEISM	TRITHEISMS
		TRITHEIST	TRITHEISTS
		TRITHING	TRITHINGS
		TRITIATE	TRITIATED ▪ TRITIATES
		TRITICAL	TRITICALE
		TRITICALE	TRITICALES
		TRITICISM	TRITICISMS
		TRITICUM	TRITICUMS
		TRITIDE	TRITIDES
		TRITIUM	TRITIUMS
		TRITOMA	TRITOMAS
		TRITON	TRITONE ▪ TRITONS
		TRITONE	TRITONES
		TRITONIA	TRITONIAS
		TRITURATE	TRITURATED ▪ TRITURATES
		TRIUMPH	TRIUMPHS
		TRIUMPHAL	TRIUMPHALS
		TRIUMPHER	TRIUMPHERS ▪ TRIUMPHERY
		TRIUMVIR	TRIUMVIRI ▪ TRIUMVIRS ▪ TRIUMVIRY
		TRIUNE	TRIUNES
		TRIVALVE	TRIVALVED ▪ TRIVALVES
		TRIVET	TRIVETS
		TRIVIA	TRIVIAL
		TRIVIUM	TRIVIUMS
		TRIZONE	TRIZONES
		TROAD	TROADE ▪ TROADS
		TROADE	TROADES
		TROAK	TROAKS
		TROAT	TROATS
		TROCAR	TROCARS
		TROCHAIC	TROCHAICS
		TROCHAR	TROCHARS
		TROCHE	TROCHEE ▪ TROCHES
		TROCHEE	TROCHEES
		TROCHI	TROCHIL
		TROCHIL	TROCHILI ▪ TROCHILS
		TROCHILI	TROCHILIC
		TROCHISK	TROCHISKS
		TROCHITE	TROCHITES
		TROCHLEA	TROCHLEAE ▪ TROCHLEAR ▪ TROCHLEAS
		TROCHLEAR	TROCHLEARS
		TROCHOID	TROCHOIDS
		TROCK	TROCKS
		TROD	TRODE ▪ TRODS
	STRODE	**TRODE**	TRODES
		TROELIE	TROELIES
		TROFFER	TROFFERS
		TROG	TROGS
		TROGON	TROGONS

T

FRONT HOOK	ROOT WORD	END HOOK
	TROIKA	TROIKAS
	TROILISM	TROILISMS
	TROILIST	TROILISTS
	TROILITE	TROILITES
STROKE	**TROKE**	TROKED ▪ TROKES
STROKED	**TROKED**	
STROKES	**TROKES**	
STROKING	**TROKING**	
	TROLAND	TROLANDS
STROLL	**TROLL**	TROLLS ▪ TROLLY
STROLLED	**TROLLED**	
STROLLER	**TROLLER**	TROLLERS
STROLLERS	**TROLLERS**	
	TROLLEY	TROLLEYS
STROLLING	**TROLLING**	TROLLINGS
STROLLINGS	**TROLLINGS**	
	TROLLOP	TROLLOPS (offensive) ▪ TROLLOPY (offensive)
	TROLLOPEE	TROLLOPEES
STROLLS	**TROLLS**	
	TROMBONE	TROMBONES
	TROMINO	TROMINOS
	TROMMEL	TROMMELS
	TROMP	TROMPE ▪ TROMPS
	TROMPE	TROMPED ▪ TROMPES
	TRON	TRONA ▪ TRONC ▪ TRONE ▪ TRONK ▪ TRONS
	TRONA	TRONAS
	TRONC	TRONCS
	TRONE	TRONES
	TRONK	TRONKS
	TROOLIE	TROOLIES
	TROOP	TROOPS
	TROOPER	TROOPERS
	TROOPIAL	TROOPIALS
	TROOPSHIP	TROOPSHIPS
	TROOSTITE	TROOSTITES
STROP	**TROP**	TROPE
	TROPE	TROPED ▪ TROPES
	TROPEOLIN	TROPEOLINS
	TROPHI	TROPHIC
ATROPHIC ▪ STROPHIC	**TROPHIC**	
ATROPHIED	**TROPHIED**	
ATROPHIES	**TROPHIES**	
ATROPHY	**TROPHY**	
ATROPHYING	**TROPHYING**	
	TROPIC	TROPICS
	TROPICAL	TROPICALS
ATROPIN	**TROPIN**	TROPINE ▪ TROPING ▪ TROPINS
ATROPINE	**TROPINE**	TROPINES
ATROPINES	**TROPINES**	
ATROPINS	**TROPINS**	
ATROPISM	**TROPISM**	TROPISMS
ATROPISMS	**TROPISMS**	
	TROPIST	TROPISTS
	TROPONIN	TROPONINS
STROSSERS	**TROSSERS**	
	TROT	TROTH ▪ TROTS
	TROTH	TROTHS
	TROTLINE	TROTLINES
	TROTTER	TROTTERS
	TROTTING	TROTTINGS
	TROTTOIR	TROTTOIRS
	TROTYL	TROTYLS
	TROUBLE	TROUBLED ▪ TROUBLER ▪ TROUBLES
	TROUBLER	TROUBLERS
	TROUBLING	TROUBLINGS
	TROUGH	TROUGHS
	TROULE	TROULED ▪ TROULES
	TROUNCE	TROUNCED ▪ TROUNCER ▪ TROUNCES
	TROUNCER	TROUNCERS

FRONT HOOK	ROOT WORD	END HOOK
	TROUNCING	TROUNCINGS
	TROUPE	TROUPED ▪ TROUPER ▪ TROUPES
	TROUPER	TROUPERS
	TROUPIAL	TROUPIALS
	TROUSE	TROUSER ▪ TROUSES
	TROUSER	TROUSERS
	TROUSSEAU	TROUSSEAUS ▪ TROUSSEAUX
STROUT	**TROUT**	TROUTS ▪ TROUTY
	TROUTER	TROUTERS
STROUTING	**TROUTING**	TROUTINGS
	TROUTLET	TROUTLETS
	TROUTLING	TROUTLINGS
STROUTS	**TROUTS**	
	TROUVERE	TROUVERES
	TROUVEUR	TROUVEURS
STROVE	**TROVE**	TROVER ▪ TROVES
	TROVER	TROVERS
STROW	**TROW**	TROWS
STROWED	**TROWED**	
	TROWEL	TROWELS
	TROWELER	TROWELERS
	TROWELLER	TROWELLERS
STROWING	**TROWING**	
STROWS	**TROWS**	
	TROWTH	TROWTHS
STROY	**TROY**	TROYS
STROYS	**TROYS**	
	TRUANT	TRUANTS
	TRUCAGE	TRUCAGES
	TRUCE	TRUCED ▪ TRUCES
	TRUCHMAN	TRUCHMANS
STRUCK	**TRUCK**	TRUCKS
	TRUCKAGE	TRUCKAGES
	TRUCKER	TRUCKERS
	TRUCKFUL	TRUCKFULS
	TRUCKIE	TRUCKIES
	TRUCKING	TRUCKINGS
	TRUCKLE	TRUCKLED ▪ TRUCKLER ▪ TRUCKLES
	TRUCKLER	TRUCKLERS
	TRUCKLINE	TRUCKLINES
	TRUCKLING	TRUCKLINGS
	TRUCKLOAD	TRUCKLOADS
	TRUCKSTOP	TRUCKSTOPS
	TRUDGE	TRUDGED ▪ TRUDGEN ▪ TRUDGER ▪ TRUDGES
	TRUDGEN	TRUDGENS
	TRUDGEON	TRUDGEONS
	TRUDGER	TRUDGERS
	TRUDGING	TRUDGINGS
	TRUE	TRUED ▪ TRUER ▪ TRUES
	TRUEBLUE	TRUEBLUES
	TRUELOVE	TRUELOVES
	TRUES	TRUEST
	TRUFFE	TRUFFES
	TRUFFLE	TRUFFLED ▪ TRUFFLES
	TRUFFLING	TRUFFLINGS
	TRUG	TRUGO ▪ TRUGS
	TRUGO	TRUGOS
	TRUISM	TRUISMS
	TRULL	TRULLS
	TRUMEAU	TRUMEAUX
	TRUMP	TRUMPS
STRUMPET	**TRUMPET**	TRUMPETS
STRUMPETED	**TRUMPETED**	
	TRUMPETER	TRUMPETERS
STRUMPETS	**TRUMPETS**	
	TRUMPING	TRUMPINGS
	TRUNCATE	TRUNCATED ▪ TRUNCATES
	TRUNCHEON	TRUNCHEONS
	TRUNDLE	TRUNDLED ▪ TRUNDLER ▪ TRUNDLES

T

FRONT HOOK	ROOT WORD	END HOOK
	TRUNDLER	TRUNDLERS
	TRUNK	TRUNKS
	TRUNKFUL	TRUNKFULS
	TRUNKING	TRUNKINGS
	TRUNNEL	TRUNNELS
	TRUNNION	TRUNNIONS
	TRUQUAGE	TRUQUAGES
	TRUQUEUR	TRUQUEURS
	TRUSSER	TRUSSERS
	TRUSSING	TRUSSINGS
	TRUST	TRUSTS ▪ TRUSTY
	TRUSTEE	TRUSTEED ▪ TRUSTEES
	TRUSTER	TRUSTERS
	TRUSTIES	TRUSTIEST
	TRUSTOR	TRUSTORS
	TRUTH	TRUTHS ▪ TRUTHY
	TRY	TRYE ▪ TRYP
	TRYE	TRYER
	TRYER	TRYERS
	TRYING	TRYINGS
	TRYKE	TRYKES
	TRYOUT	TRYOUTS
	TRYP	TRYPS
	TRYPSIN	TRYPSINS
	TRYSAIL	TRYSAILS
	TRYST	TRYSTE ▪ TRYSTS
	TRYSTE	TRYSTED ▪ TRYSTER ▪ TRYSTES
	TRYSTER	TRYSTERS
	TSADDIK	TSADDIKS
	TSADDIQ	TSADDIQS
	TSADE	TSADES
	TSADI	TSADIS
	TSAMBA	TSAMBAS
	TSANTSA	TSANTSAS
	TSAR	TSARS
	TSARDOM	TSARDOMS
	TSAREVNA	TSAREVNAS
	TSARINA	TSARINAS
	TSARISM	TSARISMS
	TSARIST	TSARISTS
	TSARITSA	TSARITSAS
	TSARITZA	TSARITZAS
	TSATSKE	TSATSKES
	TSESSEBE	TSESSEBES
	TSETSE	TSETSES
	TSIGANE	TSIGANES
	TSK	TSKS
	TSKTSK	TSKTSKS
	TSOTSI	TSOTSIS
	TSUBA	TSUBAS
	TSUNAMI	TSUNAMIC ▪ TSUNAMIS
	TSUTSUMU	TSUTSUMUS
	TUAN	TUANS
	TUART	TUARTS
	TUATARA	TUATARAS
	TUATERA	TUATERAS
	TUATH	TUATHS
STUB	**TUB**	TUBA ▪ TUBE ▪ TUBS
	TUBA	TUBAE ▪ TUBAL ▪ TUBAR ▪ TUBAS
	TUBAGE	TUBAGES
	TUBAIST	TUBAISTS
STUBBED	**TUBBED**	
	TUBBER	TUBBERS
STUBBIER	**TUBBIER**	
STUBBIEST	**TUBBIEST**	
STUBBINESS	**TUBBINESS**	
STUBBING	**TUBBING**	TUBBINGS
STUBBY	**TUBBY**	
	TUBE	TUBED ▪ TUBER ▪ TUBES

FRONT HOOK	ROOT WORD	END HOOK
	TUBEFUL	TUBEFULS
	TUBENOSE	TUBENOSES
	TUBER	TUBERS
	TUBERCLE	TUBERCLED · TUBERCLES
	TUBERCULA	TUBERCULAR
	TUBERCULE	TUBERCULES
	TUBEROSE	TUBEROSES
	TUBEWORK	TUBEWORKS
	TUBEWORM	TUBEWORMS
	TUBFAST	TUBFASTS
	TUBFUL	TUBFULS
	TUBICOLE	TUBICOLES
	TUBIFICID	TUBIFICIDS
	TUBING	TUBINGS
	TUBIST	TUBISTS
STUBS	TUBS	
	TUBULATE	TUBULATED · TUBULATES
	TUBULATOR	TUBULATORS
	TUBULE	TUBULES
	TUBULIN	TUBULINS
	TUBULURE	TUBULURES
	TUCHUN	TUCHUNS
STUCK	TUCK	TUCKS
	TUCKAHOE	TUCKAHOES
	TUCKER	TUCKERS
	TUCKERBAG	TUCKERBAGS
	TUCKET	TUCKETS
STUCKS	TUCKS	
	TUCKSHOP	TUCKSHOPS
	TUCOTUCO	TUCOTUCOS
	TUCUTUCO	TUCUTUCOS
	TUCUTUCU	TUCUTUCUS
	TUFA	TUFAS
STUFF	TUFF	TUFFE · TUFFS
	TUFFE	TUFFES · TUFFET
	TUFFET	TUFFETS
STUFFS	TUFFS	
	TUFT	TUFTS · TUFTY
	TUFTER	TUFTERS
	TUFTING	TUFTINGS
	TUG	TUGS
	TUGBOAT	TUGBOATS
	TUGGER	TUGGERS
	TUGGING	TUGGINGS
	TUGHRA	TUGHRAS
	TUGHRIK	TUGHRIKS
	TUGRA	TUGRAS
	TUGRIK	TUGRIKS
ETUI · PTUI	TUI	TUIS
	TUILLE	TUILLES
	TUILLETTE	TUILLETTES
	TUILYIE	TUILYIED · TUILYIES
	TUILZIE	TUILZIED · TUILZIES
	TUINA	TUINAS
ETUIS	TUIS	TUISM
	TUISM	TUISMS
	TUITION	TUITIONS
	TUKTOO	TUKTOOS
	TUKTU	TUKTUS
	TULADI	TULADIS
	TULAREMIA	TULAREMIAS
	TULBAN	TULBANS
	TULCHAN	TULCHANS
	TULE	TULES
	TULIP	TULIPS
	TULIPANT	TULIPANTS
	TULIPWOOD	TULIPWOODS
	TULLE	TULLES
	TULLIBEE	TULLIBEES

T

FRONT HOOK	ROOT WORD	END HOOK
	TULPA	TULPAS
	TULWAR	TULWARS
STUM	**TUM**	TUMP ▪ TUMS
STUMBLE	**TUMBLE**	TUMBLED ▪ TUMBLER ▪ TUMBLES
	TUMBLEBUG	TUMBLEBUGS
STUMBLED	**TUMBLED**	
STUMBLER	**TUMBLER**	TUMBLERS
STUMBLERS	**TUMBLERS**	
STUMBLES	**TUMBLES**	
	TUMBLESET	TUMBLESETS
STUMBLING	**TUMBLING**	TUMBLINGS
	TUMBREL	TUMBRELS
	TUMBRIL	TUMBRILS
	TUMESCE	TUMESCED ▪ TUMESCES
	TUMMLER	TUMMLERS
	TUMOR	TUMORS
	TUMOUR	TUMOURS
STUMP	**TUMP**	TUMPS ▪ TUMPY
STUMPED	**TUMPED**	
STUMPIER	**TUMPIER**	
STUMPIEST	**TUMPIEST**	
STUMPING	**TUMPING**	
	TUMPLINE	TUMPLINES
STUMPS	**TUMPS**	
STUMPY	**TUMPY**	
STUMS	**TUMS**	
	TUMSHIE	TUMSHIES
	TUMULAR	TUMULARY
	TUMULT	TUMULTS
STUN	**TUN**	TUNA ▪ TUND ▪ TUNE ▪ TUNG ▪ TUNS ▪ TUNY
	TUNA	TUNAS
	TUND	TUNDS
	TUNDRA	TUNDRAS
	TUNDUN	TUNDUNS
	TUNE	TUNED ▪ TUNER ▪ TUNES
	TUNER	TUNERS
	TUNESMITH	TUNESMITHS
	TUNEUP	TUNEUPS
STUNG	**TUNG**	TUNGS
	TUNGSTATE	TUNGSTATES
	TUNGSTEN	TUNGSTENS
	TUNGSTITE	TUNGSTITES
	TUNIC	TUNICA ▪ TUNICS
	TUNICA	TUNICAE
	TUNICATE	TUNICATED ▪ TUNICATES
	TUNICIN	TUNICINS
	TUNICLE	TUNICLES
	TUNING	TUNINGS
	TUNNAGE	TUNNAGES
STUNNED	**TUNNED**	
	TUNNEL	TUNNELS
	TUNNELER	TUNNELERS
	TUNNELING	TUNNELINGS
	TUNNELLER	TUNNELLERS
STUNNING	**TUNNING**	TUNNINGS
STUNNINGS	**TUNNINGS**	
STUNS	**TUNS**	
	TUP	TUPS
	TUPEK	TUPEKS
	TUPELO	TUPELOS
	TUPIK	TUPIKS
	TUPLE	TUPLES
	TUPPENCE	TUPPENCES
	TUPUNA	TUPUNAS
	TUQUE	TUQUES
	TURACIN	TURACINS
	TURACO	TURACOS ▪ TURACOU
	TURACOU	TURACOUS
	TURBAN	TURBAND ▪ TURBANS ▪ TURBANT

T

FRONT HOOK	ROOT WORD	END HOOK
	TURBAND	TURBANDS
	TURBANT	TURBANTS
	TURBETH	TURBETHS
	TURBIDITE	TURBIDITES
	TURBINAL	TURBINALS
	TURBINATE	TURBINATED · TURBINATES
	TURBINE	TURBINED · TURBINES
	TURBIT	TURBITH · TURBITS
	TURBITH	TURBITHS
	TURBO	TURBOS · TURBOT
	TURBOCAR	TURBOCARS
	TURBOFAN	TURBOFANS
	TURBOJET	TURBOJETS
	TURBOND	TURBONDS
	TURBOPROP	TURBOPROPS
	TURBOT	TURBOTS
	TURCOPOLE	TURCOPOLES
	TURD	TURDS *(offensive)*
	TURDION	TURDIONS
	TUREEN	TUREENS
	TURF	TURFS · TURFY
	TURFING	TURFINGS
	TURFITE	TURFITES
	TURFSKI	TURFSKIS
	TURGITE	TURGITES
	TURGOR	TURGORS
	TURION	TURIONS
	TURISTA	TURISTAS
	TURK	TURKS *(offensive)*
	TURKEY	TURKEYS
	TURLOUGH	TURLOUGHS
	TURM	TURME · TURMS
	TURME	TURMES
	TURMERIC	TURMERICS
	TURMOIL	TURMOILS
	TURN	TURNS
	TURNABOUT	TURNABOUTS
	TURNAGAIN	TURNAGAINS
	TURNBACK	TURNBACKS
	TURNCOAT	TURNCOATS
	TURNCOCK	TURNCOCKS
	TURNDOWN	TURNDOWNS
	TURNDUN	TURNDUNS
	TURNER	TURNERS · TURNERY
	TURNHALL	TURNHALLS
	TURNING	TURNINGS
	TURNIP	TURNIPS
	TURNKEY	TURNKEYS
	TURNOFF	TURNOFFS
	TURNON	TURNONS
	TURNOUT	TURNOUTS
	TURNOVER	TURNOVERS
	TURNPIKE	TURNPIKES
	TURNROUND	TURNROUNDS
	TURNSKIN	TURNSKINS
	TURNSOLE	TURNSOLES
	TURNSPIT	TURNSPITS
	TURNSTILE	TURNSTILES
	TURNSTONE	TURNSTONES
	TURNTABLE	TURNTABLES
	TURNUP	TURNUPS
	TUROPHILE	TUROPHILES
	TURPETH	TURPETHS
	TURPITUDE	TURPITUDES
	TURQUOIS	TURQUOISE
	TURQUOISE	TURQUOISES
	TURRET	TURRETS
	TURRIBANT	TURRIBANTS
	TURTLE	TURTLED · TURTLER · TURTLES

FRONT HOOK	ROOT WORD	END HOOK
	TURTLER	TURTLERS
	TURTLING	TURTLINGS
	TUSCHE	TUSCHES
	TUSH	TUSHY
STUSHIE	**TUSHIE**	TUSHIES
STUSHIES	**TUSHIES**	
	TUSHKAR	TUSHKARS
	TUSHKER	TUSHKERS
	TUSK	TUSKS · TUSKY
	TUSKAR	TUSKARS
	TUSKER	TUSKERS
	TUSKING	TUSKINGS
	TUSSAH	TUSSAHS
	TUSSAR	TUSSARS
	TUSSEH	TUSSEHS
	TUSSER	TUSSERS
	TUSSLE	TUSSLED · TUSSLES
	TUSSOCK	TUSSOCKS · TUSSOCKY
	TUSSOR	TUSSORE · TUSSORS
	TUSSORE	TUSSORES
	TUSSUCK	TUSSUCKS
	TUSSUR	TUSSURS
	TUT	TUTS · TUTU
	TUTANIA	TUTANIAS
	TUTEE	TUTEES
	TUTELAGE	TUTELAGES
	TUTELAR	TUTELARS · TUTELARY
	TUTENAG	TUTENAGS
	TUTIORISM	TUTIORISMS
	TUTIORIST	TUTIORISTS
	TUTOR	TUTORS
	TUTORAGE	TUTORAGES
	TUTORIAL	TUTORIALS
	TUTORING	TUTORINGS
	TUTORISE	TUTORISED · TUTORISES
	TUTORISM	TUTORISMS
	TUTORIZE	TUTORIZED · TUTORIZES
	TUTORSHIP	TUTORSHIPS
	TUTOYER	TUTOYERS
	TUTSAN	TUTSANS
	TUTTI	TUTTIS
	TUTTING	TUTTINGS
	TUTU	TUTUS
	TUTWORK	TUTWORKS
	TUTWORKER	TUTWORKERS
	TUXEDO	TUXEDOS
	TUYER	TUYERE · TUYERS
	TUYERE	TUYERES
	TWA	TWAE · TWAL · TWAS · TWAT · TWAY
	TWADDLE	TWADDLED · TWADDLER · TWADDLES
	TWADDLER	TWADDLERS
	TWADDLING	TWADDLINGS
	TWAE	TWAES
ATWAIN	**TWAIN**	TWAINS
	TWAITE	TWAITES
	TWAL	TWALS
	TWANG	TWANGS · TWANGY
	TWANGER	TWANGERS
	TWANGING	TWANGINGS
	TWANGLE	TWANGLED · TWANGLER · TWANGLES
	TWANGLER	TWANGLERS
	TWANGLING	TWANGLINGS
	TWANK	TWANKS · TWANKY
	TWANKAY	TWANKAYS
	TWASOME	TWASOMES
	TWAT	TWATS (offensive)
	TWATTLE	TWATTLED · TWATTLER · TWATTLES
	TWATTLER	TWATTLERS
	TWATTLING	TWATTLINGS

FRONT HOOK	ROOT WORD	END HOOK
	TWAY	TWAYS
	TWAYBLADE	TWAYBLADES
	TWEAK	TWEAKS • TWEAKY
	TWEAKER	TWEAKERS
	TWEAKING	TWEAKINGS
ETWEE	TWEE	TWEED • TWEEL • TWEEN • TWEER • TWEET
	TWEED	TWEEDS • TWEEDY
	TWEEDLE	TWEEDLED • TWEEDLER • TWEEDLES
	TWEEDLER	TWEEDLERS
ATWEEL	TWEEL	TWEELS • TWEELY
ATWEEN	TWEEN	TWEENS • TWEENY
	TWEENAGER	TWEENAGERS
	TWEENER	TWEENERS
	TWEENIE	TWEENIES
	TWEER	TWEERS
	TWEET	TWEETS
	TWEETER	TWEETERS
	TWEEZE	TWEEZED • TWEEZER • TWEEZES
	TWEEZER	TWEEZERS
	TWELFTH	TWELFTHS
	TWELVE	TWELVES
	TWELVEMO	TWELVEMOS
	TWENTIETH	TWENTIETHS
	TWERP	TWERPS • TWERPY
	TWIBIL	TWIBILL • TWIBILS
	TWIBILL	TWIBILLS
	TWICE	TWICER
	TWICER	TWICERS
	TWIDDLE	TWIDDLED • TWIDDLER • TWIDDLES
	TWIDDLER	TWIDDLERS
	TWIDDLING	TWIDDLINGS
	TWIER	TWIERS
	TWIG	TWIGS
	TWIGGER	TWIGGERS
	TWIGHT	TWIGHTS
	TWIGLOO	TWIGLOOS
	TWILIGHT	TWILIGHTS
	TWILL	TWILLS • TWILLY
	TWILLING	TWILLINGS
	TWILT	TWILTS
	TWIN	TWINE • TWINK • TWINS • TWINY
	TWINE	TWINED • TWINER • TWINES
	TWINER	TWINERS
	TWINGE	TWINGED • TWINGES
	TWINING	TWININGS
	TWINJET	TWINJETS
	TWINK	TWINKS
	TWINKIE	TWINKIES
	TWINKLE	TWINKLED • TWINKLER • TWINKLES
	TWINKLER	TWINKLERS
	TWINKLING	TWINKLINGS
	TWINLING	TWINLINGS
	TWINNING	TWINNINGS
	TWINSET	TWINSETS
	TWINSHIP	TWINSHIPS
	TWINTER	TWINTERS
	TWIRE	TWIRED • TWIRES
	TWIRL	TWIRLS • TWIRLY
	TWIRLER	TWIRLERS
	TWIRP	TWIRPS • TWIRPY
	TWISCAR	TWISCARS
	TWIST	TWISTS • TWISTY
	TWISTER	TWISTERS
	TWISTING	TWISTINGS
	TWISTOR	TWISTORS
	TWIT	TWITE • TWITS
	TWITCH	TWITCHY
	TWITCHER	TWITCHERS
	TWITCHING	TWITCHINGS

T

FRONT HOOK	ROOT WORD	END HOOK
	TWITE	TWITES
	TWITTEN	TWITTENS
ATWITTER	TWITTER	TWITTERS · TWITTERY
	TWITTERER	TWITTERERS
	TWITTING	TWITTINGS
ATWIXT	TWIXT	
	TWIZZLE	TWIZZLED · TWIZZLES
	TWO	TWOS
	TWOCCER	TWOCCERS
	TWOCCING	TWOCCINGS
	TWOCKER	TWOCKERS
	TWOCKING	TWOCKINGS
	TWOER	TWOERS
	TWOFER	TWOFERS
	TWOFOLD	TWOFOLDS
	TWONIE	TWONIES
	TWOONIE	TWOONIES
	TWOPENCE	TWOPENCES
	TWOSEATER	TWOSEATERS
	TWOSOME	TWOSOMES
	TWYER	TWYERE · TWYERS
	TWYERE	TWYERES
	TYCHISM	TYCHISMS
	TYCOON	TYCOONS
	TYCOONATE	TYCOONATES
STYE	TYE	TYED · TYEE · TYER · TYES
STYED	TYED	
	TYEE	TYEES
	TYER	TYERS
STYES	TYES	
	TYG	TYGS
	TYIN	TYING
STYING	TYING	
	TYKE	TYKES (offensive)
STYLER	TYLER	TYLERS
STYLERS	TYLERS	
	TYLOPOD	TYLOPODS
	TYLOSIN	TYLOSINS
	TYLOTE	TYLOTES
	TYMBAL	TYMBALS
	TYMP	TYMPS
	TYMPAN	TYMPANA · TYMPANI · TYMPANO · TYMPANS
		TYMPANY
	TYMPANA	TYMPANAL
	TYMPANI	TYMPANIC
	TYMPANIC	TYMPANICS
	TYMPANIST	TYMPANISTS
	TYMPANUM	TYMPANUMS
	TYND	TYNDE
	TYNE	TYNED · TYNES
	TYPE	TYPED · TYPES · TYPEY
	TYPEBAR	TYPEBARS
	TYPECASE	TYPECASES
	TYPECAST	TYPECASTS
	TYPEFACE	TYPEFACES
	TYPESET	TYPESETS
	TYPESTYLE	TYPESTYLES
	TYPEWRITE	TYPEWRITER · TYPEWRITES
	TYPHOID	TYPHOIDS
	TYPHOIDIN	TYPHOIDINS
	TYPHON	TYPHONS
	TYPHOON	TYPHOONS
ATYPIC · ETYPIC	TYPIC	
ATYPICAL · ETYPICAL	TYPICAL	
ATYPICALLY	TYPICALLY	
	TYPIFIER	TYPIFIERS
	TYPING	TYPINGS
	TYPIST	TYPISTS
	TYPO	TYPOS

FRONT HOOK	ROOT WORD	END HOOK
	TYPOGRAPH	TYPOGRAPHS ▪ TYPOGRAPHY
	TYPOMANIA	TYPOMANIAS
	TYPP	TYPPS
	TYPTO	TYPTOS
	TYRAMINE	TYRAMINES
	TYRAN	TYRANS ▪ TYRANT
	TYRANNE	TYRANNED ▪ TYRANNES
	TYRANNES	TYRANNESS
	TYRANNIS	TYRANNISE
	TYRANNISE	TYRANNISED ▪ TYRANNISER ▪ TYRANNISES
	TYRANNIZE	TYRANNIZED ▪ TYRANNIZER ▪ TYRANNIZES
	TYRANT	TYRANTS
STYRE	TYRE	TYRED ▪ TYRES
STYRED	TYRED	
STYRES	TYRES	
STYRING	TYRING	
	TYRO	TYROS
	TYROCIDIN	TYROCIDINE ▪ TYROCIDINS
	TYROPITTA	TYROPITTAS
	TYROSINE	TYROSINES
	TYSTIE	TYSTIES
STYTE	TYTE	
	TYTHE	TYTHED ▪ TYTHES
	TZADDIK	TZADDIKS
	TZADDIQ	TZADDIQS
	TZAR	TZARS
	TZARDOM	TZARDOMS
	TZAREVNA	TZAREVNAS
	TZARINA	TZARINAS
	TZARISM	TZARISMS
	TZARIST	TZARISTS
	TZARITZA	TZARITZAS
	TZATZIKI	TZATZIKIS
	TZETSE	TZETSES
	TZETZE	TZETZES
	TZIGANE	TZIGANES
	TZITZIT	TZITZITH

U

FRONT HOOK	ROOT WORD	END HOOK
OUAKARI	**UAKARI**	UAKARIS
OUAKARIS	**UAKARIS**	
SUBEROUS ▪ TUBEROUS	**UBEROUS**	
PUBERTIES	**UBERTIES**	
PUBERTY	**UBERTY**	
DUBIETIES	**UBIETIES**	
DUBIETY	**UBIETY**	
	UBIQUITIN	UBIQUITINS
BUCKERS ▪ DUCKERS ▪ FUCKERS (offensive)	**UCKERS**	
MUCKERS ▪ PUCKERS ▪ SUCKERS ▪ TUCKERS		
YUCKERS		
	UDAL	UDALS
	UDALLER	UDALLERS
BUDDER ▪ DUDDER ▪ JUDDER ▪ MUDDER	**UDDER**	UDDERS
PUDDER ▪ RUDDER ▪ SUDDER		
JUDDERED ▪ PUDDERED	**UDDERED**	
RUDDERLESS	**UDDERLESS**	
BUDDERS ▪ DUDDERS ▪ JUDDERS ▪ MUDDERS	**UDDERS**	
PUDDERS ▪ RUDDERS ▪ SUDDERS		
BUDO ▪ JUDO ▪ KUDO ▪ LUDO	**UDO**	UDON ▪ UDOS
	UDOMETER	UDOMETERS
	UDON	UDONS
BUDOS ▪ JUDOS ▪ KUDOS ▪ LUDOS	**UDOS**	
BUDS ▪ CUDS ▪ DUDS ▪ FUDS ▪ JUDS ▪ LUDS	**UDS**	
MUDS ▪ OUDS ▪ PUDS ▪ RUDS ▪ SUDS ▪ WUDS		
QUEY	**UEY**	UEYS
QUEYS	**UEYS**	
BUFO	**UFO**	UFOS
	UFOLOGIST	UFOLOGISTS
BUFOS	**UFOS**	
BUG ▪ DUG ▪ FUG ▪ HUG ▪ JUG ▪ LUG ▪ MUG	**UG**	UGH ▪ UGS
PUG ▪ RUG ▪ TUG ▪ VUG ▪ YUG		
	UGALI	UGALIS
BUGGED ▪ FUGGED ▪ HUGGED ▪ JUGGED	**UGGED**	
LUGGED ▪ MUGGED ▪ PUGGED ▪ RUGGED		
TUGGED		
BUGGING ▪ FUGGING ▪ HUGGING ▪ JUGGING	**UGGING**	
LUGGING ▪ MUGGING ▪ PUGGING ▪ RUGGING		
SUGGING ▪ TUGGING		
EUGH ▪ PUGH ▪ SUGH ▪ VUGH	**UGH**	UGHS
EUGHS ▪ SUGHS ▪ VUGHS	**UGHS**	
OUGLIED	**UGLIED**	
FUGLIER (offensive)	**UGLIER**	
OUGLIES	**UGLIES**	UGLIEST
FUGLIEST (offensive)	**UGLIEST**	
	UGLIFIER	UGLIFIERS
FUGLY	**UGLY**	
BUGS ▪ DUGS ▪ FUGS ▪ HUGS ▪ JUGS ▪ LUGS	**UGS**	
MUGS ▪ PUGS ▪ RUGS ▪ TUGS ▪ VUGS ▪ YUGS		
DUH ▪ HUH ▪ PUH	**UH**	
	UHLAN	UHLANS
	UHURU	UHURUS
	UINTAHITE	UINTAHITES
	UINTAITE	UINTAITES
	UITLANDER	UITLANDERS
	UJAMAA	UJAMAAS
	UKASE	UKASES
BUKE ▪ CUKE ▪ DUKE ▪ JUKE ▪ LUKE ▪ NUKE	**UKE**	UKES
PUKE ▪ YUKE		
	UKELELE	UKELELES
BUKES ▪ CUKES ▪ DUKES ▪ JUKES ▪ NUKES	**UKES**	
PUKES ▪ YUKES		
	UKULELE	UKULELES
	ULAMA	ULAMAS
KULAN ▪ YULAN	**ULAN**	ULANS
KULANS ▪ YULANS	**ULANS**	

877

FRONT HOOK	ROOT WORD	END HOOK
	ULCER	ULCERS
	ULCERATE	ULCERATED · ULCERATES
DULE · GULE · HULE · MULE · PULE · RULE TULE · YULE	**ULE**	ULES · ULEX
	ULEMA	ULEMAS
DULES · GULES · HULES · MULES · PULES RULES · TULES · YULES	**ULES**	
CULEX	**ULEX**	
CULEXES	**ULEXES**	
	ULEXITE	ULEXITES
	ULICON	ULICONS
FULIGINOUS	**ULIGINOUS**	
	ULIKON	ULIKONS
FULLAGE · SULLAGE	**ULLAGE**	ULLAGED · ULLAGES
FULLAGES · SULLAGES	**ULLAGES**	
BULLING · CULLING · DULLING · FULLING GULLING · HULLING · LULLING · MULLING NULLING · PULLING · WULLING	**ULLING**	ULLINGS
BULLINGS · CULLINGS · NULLINGS	**ULLINGS**	
	ULMIN	ULMINS
	ULNA	ULNAD · ULNAE · ULNAR · ULNAS
	ULNAR	ULNARE
DULOSES	**ULOSES**	
DULOSIS	**ULOSIS**	
	ULSTER	ULSTERS
	ULTIMA	ULTIMAS
	ULTIMATE	ULTIMATED · ULTIMATES
	ULTIMATUM	ULTIMATUMS
	ULTION	ULTIONS
	ULTRA	ULTRAS
	ULTRAHEAT	ULTRAHEATS
	ULTRAISM	ULTRAISMS
	ULTRAIST	ULTRAISTS
	ULTRARED	ULTRAREDS
LULU · PULU · SULU · ZULU	**ULU**	ULUS
	ULULATE	ULULATED · ULULATES
	ULULATION	ULULATIONS
LULUS · PULUS · SULUS · ZULUS	**ULUS**	
VULVA	**ULVA**	ULVAS
VULVAS	**ULVAS**	
	ULYIE	ULYIES
	ULZIE	ULZIES
BUM · CUM · FUM · GUM · HUM · LUM · MUM RUM · SUM · TUM · VUM · YUM	**UM**	UMM · UMP · UMU
	UMAMI	UMAMIS
	UMANGITE	UMANGITES
	UMBEL	UMBELS
	UMBELLATE	UMBELLATED
	UMBELLET	UMBELLETS
	UMBELLULE	UMBELLULES
CUMBER · DUMBER · LUMBER · NUMBER	**UMBER**	UMBERS · UMBERY
CUMBERED · LUMBERED · NUMBERED	**UMBERED**	
CUMBERING · LUMBERING · NUMBERING	**UMBERING**	
CUMBERS · LUMBERS · NUMBERS	**UMBERS**	
	UMBILICAL	UMBILICALS
BUMBLE · FUMBLE · HUMBLE · JUMBLE MUMBLE · RUMBLE · TUMBLE	**UMBLE**	UMBLES
BUMBLES · FUMBLES · HUMBLES · JUMBLES MUMBLES · NUMBLES · RUMBLES · TUMBLES	**UMBLES**	
BUMBO · DUMBO · GUMBO · JUMBO · RUMBO	**UMBO**	UMBOS
BUMBOS · DUMBOS · GUMBOS · JUMBOS RUMBOS	**UMBOS**	
	UMBRA	UMBRAE · UMBRAL · UMBRAS
	UMBRAGE	UMBRAGED · UMBRAGES
	UMBRE	UMBREL · UMBRES
TUMBREL	**UMBREL**	UMBRELS
	UMBRELLA	UMBRELLAS
	UMBRELLO	UMBRELLOS
TUMBRELS	**UMBRELS**	

FRONT HOOK	ROOT WORD	END HOOK
	UMBRERE	UMBRERES
	UMBRETTE	UMBRETTES
	UMBRIERE	UMBRIERES
TUMBRIL	**UMBRIL**	UMBRILS
TUMBRILS	**UMBRILS**	
CUMBROUS	**UMBROUS**	
	UMFAZI	UMFAZIS
	UMIAC	UMIACK · UMIACS
	UMIACK	UMIACKS
	UMIAK	UMIAKS
	UMIAQ	UMIAQS
	UMLAUT	UMLAUTS
	UMLUNGU	UMLUNGUS
MUMM	**UMM**	
BUMP · DUMP · GUMP · HUMP · JUMP · LUMP	**UMP**	UMPH · UMPS · UMPY
MUMP · PUMP · RUMP · SUMP · TUMP · YUMP		
BUMPED · DUMPED · GUMPED · HUMPED	**UMPED**	
JUMPED · LUMPED · MUMPED · PUMPED		
RUMPED · TUMPED · YUMPED		
BUMPH · HUMPH · SUMPH	**UMPH**	
YUMPIE	**UMPIE**	UMPIES
DUMPIES · HUMPIES · RUMPIES · YUMPIES	**UMPIES**	
BUMPING · DUMPING · GUMPING · HUMPING	**UMPING**	
JUMPING · LUMPING · MUMPING · PUMPING		
RUMPING · TUMPING · YUMPING		
	UMPIRAGE	UMPIRAGES
	UMPIRE	UMPIRED · UMPIRES
BUMPS · DUMPS · GUMPS · HUMPS · JUMPS	**UMPS**	
LUMPS · MUMPS · PUMPS · RUMPS · SUMPS		
TUMPS · YUMPS		
	UMPTEENTH	UMPTEENTHS
HUMPTY · NUMPTY	**UMPTY**	
BUMPY · DUMPY · HUMPY · JUMPY · LUMPY	**UMPY**	
RUMPY · TUMPY		
MUMU	**UMU**	
	UMWELT	UMWELTS
BUN · DUN · FUN · GUN · HUN · JUN · MUN	**UN**	UNI · UNS
NUN · PUN · RUN · SUN · TUN		
TUNABLE	**UNABLE**	
	UNAI	UNAIS
	UNAKIN	UNAKING
	UNAKITE	UNAKITES
	UNALIST	UNALISTS
	UNANCHOR	UNANCHORS
	UNAPPAREL	UNAPPARELS
	UNARM	UNARMS
LUNARY	**UNARY**	
	UNAU	UNAUS
	UNAWAKE	UNAWAKED
	UNAWARE	UNAWARES
	UNBAG	UNBAGS
SUNBAKED	**UNBAKED**	
	UNBALANCE	UNBALANCED · UNBALANCES
	UNBALE	UNBALED · UNBALES
	UNBAN	UNBANS
	UNBANDAGE	UNBANDAGED · UNBANDAGES
	UNBAPTISE	UNBAPTISED · UNBAPTISES
	UNBAPTIZE	UNBAPTIZED · UNBAPTIZES
	UNBAR	UNBARE · UNBARK · UNBARS
	UNBARE	UNBARED · UNBARES
	UNBARK	UNBARKS
SUNBATHED	**UNBATHED**	
	UNBE	UNBED
	UNBEAR	UNBEARS
SUNBEATEN	**UNBEATEN**	
SUNBED	**UNBED**	UNBEDS
SUNBEDS	**UNBEDS**	
	UNBEGET	UNBEGETS
	UNBEGUILE	UNBEGUILED · UNBEGUILES

FRONT HOOK	ROOT WORD	END HOOK
	UNBEING	UNBEINGS
	UNBELIEF	UNBELIEFS
	UNBELIEVE	UNBELIEVED · UNBELIEVER · UNBELIEVES
SUNBELT	**UNBELT**	UNBELTS
SUNBELTS	**UNBELTS**	
	UNBEND	UNBENDS
	UNBENDING	UNBENDINGS
	UNBESEEM	UNBESEEMS
	UNBESPEAK	UNBESPEAKS
	UNBESPOKE	UNBESPOKEN
	UNBIND	UNBINDS
	UNBINDING	UNBINDINGS
	UNBISHOP	UNBISHOPS
	UNBITT	UNBITTS
SUNBLIND	**UNBLIND**	UNBLINDS
SUNBLINDS	**UNBLINDS**	
SUNBLOCK	**UNBLOCK**	UNBLOCKS
SUNBLOCKS	**UNBLOCKS**	
	UNBOLT	UNBOLTS
	UNBONE	UNBONED · UNBONES
SUNBONNET	**UNBONNET**	UNBONNETS
SUNBONNETS	**UNBONNETS**	
	UNBOOT	UNBOOTS
	UNBORN	UNBORNE
	UNBOSOM	UNBOSOMS
	UNBOSOMER	UNBOSOMERS
	UNBOTTLE	UNBOTTLED · UNBOTTLES
	UNBRACE	UNBRACED · UNBRACES
	UNBRAID	UNBRAIDS
	UNBRAKE	UNBRAKED · UNBRAKES
	UNBRIDLE	UNBRIDLED · UNBRIDLES
SUNBRIGHT	**UNBRIGHT**	
	UNBROKE	UNBROKEN
	UNBUCKLE	UNBUCKLED · UNBUCKLES
	UNBUILD	UNBUILDS
	UNBUNDLE	UNBUNDLED · UNBUNDLER · UNBUNDLES
	UNBUNDLER	UNBUNDLERS
	UNBURDEN	UNBURDENS
SUNBURNED	**UNBURNED**	
SUNBURNT	**UNBURNT**	
	UNBURROW	UNBURROWS
	UNBURTHEN	UNBURTHENS
	UNBUTTON	UNBUTTONS
	UNCAGE	UNCAGED · UNCAGES
	UNCAKE	UNCAKED · UNCAKES
	UNCANDOUR	UNCANDOURS
	UNCAP	UNCAPE · UNCAPS
	UNCAPE	UNCAPED · UNCAPES
	UNCART	UNCARTS
	UNCASE	UNCASED · UNCASES
JUNCATE	**UNCATE**	
BUNCE · DUNCE · OUNCE · PUNCE	**UNCE**	UNCES
BUNCES · DUNCES · OUNCES · PUNCES	**UNCES**	
	UNCHAIN	UNCHAINS
	UNCHAIR	UNCHAIRS
	UNCHARGE	UNCHARGED · UNCHARGES
	UNCHARM	UNCHARMS
	UNCHARNEL	UNCHARNELS
	UNCHASTE	UNCHASTER
	UNCHECK	UNCHECKS
	UNCHILD	UNCHILDS
SUNCHOKE	**UNCHOKE**	UNCHOKED · UNCHOKES
SUNCHOKES	**UNCHOKES**	
	UNCI	UNCIA
	UNCIA	UNCIAE · UNCIAL
	UNCIAL	UNCIALS
	UNCIFORM	UNCIFORMS
	UNCINARIA	UNCINARIAS
RUNCINATE	**UNCINATE**	UNCINATED

FRONT HOOK	ROOT WORD	END HOOK
	UNCIPHER	UNCIPHERS
	UNCLAMP	UNCLAMPS
	UNCLASP	UNCLASPS
NUNCLE	**UNCLE**	UNCLED = UNCLES = UNCLEW
NUNCLES	**UNCLES**	
	UNCLESHIP	UNCLESHIPS
	UNCLEW	UNCLEWS
	UNCLIP	UNCLIPS = UNCLIPT
	UNCLOAK	UNCLOAKS
	UNCLOG	UNCLOGS
	UNCLOSE	UNCLOSED = UNCLOSES
	UNCLOTHE	UNCLOTHED = UNCLOTHES
	UNCLOUD	UNCLOUDS = UNCLOUDY
	UNCLUTTER	UNCLUTTERS
BUNCO = JUNCO	**UNCO**	UNCOS = UNCOY
	UNCOATING	UNCOATINGS
	UNCOCK	UNCOCKS
JUNCOES	**UNCOES**	UNCOEST
	UNCOFFIN	UNCOFFINS
	UNCOIL	UNCOILS
	UNCOLT	UNCOLTS
	UNCOMBINE	UNCOMBINED = UNCOMBINES
	UNCONCERN	UNCONCERNS
	UNCONFINE	UNCONFINED = UNCONFINES
	UNCONFUSE	UNCONFUSED = UNCONFUSES
	UNCONGEAL	UNCONGEALS
	UNCOPE	UNCOPED = UNCOPES
	UNCORD	UNCORDS
	UNCORK	UNCORKS
BUNCOS = JUNCOS	**UNCOS**	
	UNCOUPLE	UNCOUPLED = UNCOUPLER = UNCOUPLES
	UNCOUPLER	UNCOUPLERS
	UNCOVER	UNCOVERS
	UNCOWL	UNCOWLS
	UNCRATE	UNCRATED = UNCRATES
	UNCREATE	UNCREATED = UNCREATES
	UNCROWN	UNCROWNS
	UNCRUMPLE	UNCRUMPLED = UNCRUMPLES
FUNCTION = JUNCTION	**UNCTION**	UNCTIONS
FUNCTIONS = JUNCTIONS	**UNCTIONS**	
	UNCUFF	UNCUFFS
	UNCURB	UNCURBS
	UNCURL	UNCURLS
	UNCURSE	UNCURSED = UNCURSES
	UNCURTAIN	UNCURTAINS
JUNCUS	**UNCUS**	
	UNCUT	UNCUTE
	UNDAM	UNDAMS
	UNDATE	UNDATED
	UNDAZZLE	UNDAZZLED = UNDAZZLES
BUNDE	**UNDE**	UNDEE = UNDER
	UNDEAF	UNDEAFS
	UNDECAGON	UNDECAGONS
	UNDECEIVE	UNDECEIVED = UNDECEIVER = UNDECEIVES
	UNDECIDED	UNDECIDEDS
SUNDECK	**UNDECK**	UNDECKS
SUNDECKS	**UNDECKS**	
	UNDELIGHT	UNDELIGHTS
DUNDER = FUNDER = SUNDER	**UNDER**	UNDERN
	UNDERACT	UNDERACTS
	UNDERAGE	UNDERAGED = UNDERAGES
	UNDERARM	UNDERARMS
	UNDERBAKE	UNDERBAKED = UNDERBAKES
	UNDERBEAR	UNDERBEARS
	UNDERBID	UNDERBIDS
	UNDERBIT	UNDERBITE
	UNDERBITE	UNDERBITES
	UNDERBRIM	UNDERBRIMS
	UNDERBUD	UNDERBUDS

FRONT HOOK	ROOT WORD	END HOOK
	UNDERBUY	UNDERBUYS
	UNDERCARD	UNDERCARDS
	UNDERCART	UNDERCARTS
	UNDERCAST	UNDERCASTS
	UNDERCLAY	UNDERCLAYS
	UNDERCLUB	UNDERCLUBS
	UNDERCOAT	UNDERCOATS
	UNDERCOOK	UNDERCOOKS
	UNDERCOOL	UNDERCOOLS
	UNDERCUT	UNDERCUTS
	UNDERDECK	UNDERDECKS
	UNDERDO	UNDERDOG
	UNDERDOER	UNDERDOERS
	UNDERDOG	UNDERDOGS
	UNDERDOSE	UNDERDOSED ▪ UNDERDOSES
	UNDERDRAW	UNDERDRAWN ▪ UNDERDRAWS
	UNDEREAT	UNDEREATS
	UNDERFEED	UNDERFEEDS
	UNDERFELT	UNDERFELTS
	UNDERFIRE	UNDERFIRED ▪ UNDERFIRES
	UNDERFLOW	UNDERFLOWS
	UNDERFONG	UNDERFONGS
	UNDERFOOT	UNDERFOOTS
	UNDERFUND	UNDERFUNDS
	UNDERFUR	UNDERFURS
	UNDERGIRD	UNDERGIRDS
	UNDERGO	UNDERGOD
	UNDERGOD	UNDERGODS
	UNDERGOER	UNDERGOERS
	UNDERGOWN	UNDERGOWNS
	UNDERGRAD	UNDERGRADS
	UNDERHAIR	UNDERHAIRS
	UNDERHAND	UNDERHANDS
	UNDERHEAT	UNDERHEATS
	UNDERJAW	UNDERJAWS
	UNDERKEEP	UNDERKEEPS
	UNDERKILL	UNDERKILLS
	UNDERKING	UNDERKINGS
	UNDERLAP	UNDERLAPS
	UNDERLAY	UNDERLAYS
	UNDERLET	UNDERLETS
	UNDERLIE	UNDERLIER ▪ UNDERLIES
	UNDERLIER	UNDERLIERS
	UNDERLINE	UNDERLINED ▪ UNDERLINEN ▪ UNDERLINES
	UNDERLING	UNDERLINGS
	UNDERLIP	UNDERLIPS
	UNDERLOAD	UNDERLOADS
	UNDERMAN	UNDERMANS
	UNDERMINE	UNDERMINED ▪ UNDERMINER ▪ UNDERMINES
	UNDERN	UNDERNS
	UNDERNOTE	UNDERNOTED ▪ UNDERNOTES
	UNDERPART	UNDERPARTS
	UNDERPAY	UNDERPAYS
	UNDERPEEP	UNDERPEEPS
	UNDERPIN	UNDERPINS
	UNDERPLAY	UNDERPLAYS
	UNDERPLOT	UNDERPLOTS
	UNDERPROP	UNDERPROPS
	UNDERRATE	UNDERRATED ▪ UNDERRATES
	UNDERRUN	UNDERRUNS
	UNDERSAY	UNDERSAYS
	UNDERSEA	UNDERSEAL ▪ UNDERSEAS
	UNDERSEAL	UNDERSEALS
	UNDERSELL	UNDERSELLS
	UNDERSET	UNDERSETS
	UNDERSIDE	UNDERSIDES
	UNDERSIGN	UNDERSIGNS
	UNDERSIZE	UNDERSIZED
	UNDERSOIL	UNDERSOILS

FRONT HOOK	ROOT WORD	END HOOK
	UNDERSONG	UNDERSONGS
	UNDERSPIN	UNDERSPINS
	UNDERTAKE	UNDERTAKEN ▪ UNDERTAKER ▪ UNDERTAKES
	UNDERTIME	UNDERTIMED ▪ UNDERTIMES
	UNDERTINT	UNDERTINTS
	UNDERTONE	UNDERTONED ▪ UNDERTONES
	UNDERTOW	UNDERTOWS
	UNDERUSE	UNDERUSED ▪ UNDERUSES
	UNDERVEST	UNDERVESTS
	UNDERVOTE	UNDERVOTES
	UNDERWEAR	UNDERWEARS
	UNDERWING	UNDERWINGS
	UNDERWIRE	UNDERWIRED ▪ UNDERWIRES
	UNDERWIT	UNDERWITS
	UNDERWOOD	UNDERWOODS
	UNDERWOOL	UNDERWOOLS
	UNDERWORK	UNDERWORKS
	UNDESERT	UNDESERTS
	UNDESERVE	UNDESERVED ▪ UNDESERVER ▪ UNDESERVES
BUNDIES ▪ CUNDIES ▪ FUNDIES ▪ GUNDIES	**UNDIES**	
	UNDIGHT	UNDIGHTS
NUNDINE	**UNDINE**	UNDINES
NUNDINES	**UNDINES**	
	UNDINISM	UNDINISMS
	UNDOCK	UNDOCKS
	UNDOER	UNDOERS
	UNDOING	UNDOINGS
	UNDOUBLE	UNDOUBLED ▪ UNDOUBLES
	UNDRAPE	UNDRAPED ▪ UNDRAPES
	UNDRAW	UNDRAWN ▪ UNDRAWS
SUNDRESS	**UNDRESS**	
SUNDRESSES	**UNDRESSES**	
	UNDULANCE	UNDULANCES
	UNDULATE	UNDULATED ▪ UNDULATES
	UNDULATOR	UNDULATORS ▪ UNDULATORY
BUNDY ▪ CUNDY ▪ FUNDY ▪ GUNDY ▪ OUNDY	**UNDY**	
BUNDYING	**UNDYING**	
	UNEARTH	UNEARTHS
	UNEASE	UNEASES
	UNEDGE	UNEDGED ▪ UNEDGES
	UNEQUAL	UNEQUALS
	UNESSENCE	UNESSENCED ▪ UNESSENCES
	UNFACT	UNFACTS
FUNFAIR	**UNFAIR**	UNFAIRS
FUNFAIRS	**UNFAIRS**	
	UNFAITH	UNFAITHS
	UNFASTEN	UNFASTENS
	UNFENCE	UNFENCED ▪ UNFENCES
	UNFETTER	UNFETTERS
	UNFIT	UNFITS
	UNFIX	UNFIXT
	UNFOLD	UNFOLDS
	UNFOLDER	UNFOLDERS
	UNFOLDING	UNFOLDINGS
	UNFOOL	UNFOOLS
	UNFORM	UNFORMS
	UNFORTUNE	UNFORTUNED ▪ UNFORTUNES
GUNFOUGHT	**UNFOUGHT**	
	UNFRAUGHT	UNFRAUGHTS
	UNFREE	UNFREED ▪ UNFREES
	UNFREEDOM	UNFREEDOMS
	UNFREEZE	UNFREEZES
	UNFRIEND	UNFRIENDS
	UNFROCK	UNFROCKS
	UNFROZE	UNFROZEN
	UNFURL	UNFURLS
	UNGAG	UNGAGS
	UNGEAR	UNGEARS
PUNGENTLY	**UNGENTLY**	

FRONT HOOK	ROOT WORD	END HOOK
	UNGET	UNGETS
	UNGILD	UNGILDS
	UNGIRD	UNGIRDS
	UNGIRT	UNGIRTH
	UNGIRTH	UNGIRTHS
	UNGLOVE	UNGLOVED · UNGLOVES
	UNGLUE	UNGLUED · UNGLUES
	UNGOD	UNGODS
	UNGOWN	UNGOWNS
	UNGUARD	UNGUARDS
	UNGUENT	UNGUENTA · UNGUENTS
	UNGULA	UNGULAE · UNGULAR
	UNGULATE	UNGULATES
	UNGUM	UNGUMS
	UNGYVE	UNGYVED · UNGYVES
	UNHAIR	UNHAIRS
	UNHAIRER	UNHAIRERS
	UNHALLOW	UNHALLOWS
	UNHAND	UNHANDS · UNHANDY
	UNHANG	UNHANGS
	UNHAPPIES	UNHAPPIEST
	UNHARBOUR	UNHARBOURS
	UNHASP	UNHASPS
SUNHAT	**UNHAT**	UNHATS
SUNHATS	**UNHATS**	
	UNHATTING	UNHATTINGS
	UNHEAD	UNHEADS
	UNHEAL	UNHEALS
	UNHEALTH	UNHEALTHS · UNHEALTHY
	UNHEARSE	UNHEARSED · UNHEARSES
	UNHEART	UNHEARTS
	UNHELE	UNHELED · UNHELES
	UNHELM	UNHELMS
	UNHINGE	UNHINGED · UNHINGES
	UNHIVE	UNHIVED · UNHIVES
	UNHOARD	UNHOARDS
NUNHOOD	**UNHOOD**	UNHOODS
NUNHOODS	**UNHOODS**	
	UNHOOK	UNHOOKS
	UNHOOP	UNHOOPS
	UNHORSE	UNHORSED · UNHORSES
FUNHOUSE · GUNHOUSE	**UNHOUSE**	UNHOUSED · UNHOUSES
FUNHOUSES · GUNHOUSES	**UNHOUSES**	
	UNHUSK	UNHUSKS
MUNI	**UNI**	UNIS · UNIT
	UNIBROW	UNIBROWS
	UNICORN	UNICORNS
	UNICYCLE	UNICYCLED · UNICYCLES
	UNIFACE	UNIFACES
MUNIFIED	**UNIFIED**	
	UNIFIER	UNIFIERS
MUNIFIES	**UNIFIES**	
CUNIFORM	**UNIFORM**	UNIFORMS
CUNIFORMS	**UNIFORMS**	
MUNIFY	**UNIFY**	
MUNIFYING	**UNIFYING**	UNIFYINGS
	UNINSTALL	UNINSTALLS
	UNINSURED	UNINSUREDS
BUNION	**UNION**	UNIONS
	UNIONISE	UNIONISED · UNIONISER · UNIONISES
	UNIONISER	UNIONISERS
	UNIONISM	UNIONISMS
	UNIONIST	UNIONISTS
	UNIONIZE	UNIONIZED · UNIONIZER · UNIONIZES
	UNIONIZER	UNIONIZERS
BUNIONS	**UNIONS**	
	UNIPED	UNIPEDS
	UNIPOD	UNIPODS
	UNIQUE	UNIQUER · UNIQUES

J

FRONT HOOK	ROOT WORD	END HOOK
	UNIQUES	UNIQUEST
MUNIS	**UNIS**	
	UNISON	UNISONS
	UNIT	UNITE · UNITS · UNITY
	UNITAGE	UNITAGES
	UNITARD	UNITARDS
	UNITARIAN	UNITARIANS
DUNITE · GUNITE · MUNITE	**UNITE**	UNITED · UNITER · UNITES
MUNITED	**UNITED**	
	UNITER	UNITERS
DUNITES · GUNITES · MUNITES	**UNITES**	
MUNITING	**UNITING**	UNITINGS
MUNITION · PUNITION	**UNITION**	UNITIONS
MUNITIONS · PUNITIONS	**UNITIONS**	
	UNITISE	UNITISED · UNITISER · UNITISES
	UNITISER	UNITISERS
PUNITIVE	**UNITIVE**	
PUNITIVELY	**UNITIVELY**	
	UNITIZE	UNITIZED · UNITIZER · UNITIZES
	UNITIZER	UNITIZERS
	UNITRUST	UNITRUSTS
	UNIVALENT	UNIVALENTS
	UNIVALVE	UNIVALVED · UNIVALVES
	UNIVERSAL	UNIVERSALS
	UNIVERSE	UNIVERSES
	UNIVOCAL	UNIVOCALS
	UNJAM	UNJAMS
	UNJOINT	UNJOINTS
BUNKED · DUNKED · FUNKED · JUNKED	**UNKED**	
	UNKENNEL	UNKENNELS
JUNKET · SUNKET	**UNKET**	
BUNKING · DUNKING · FUNKING · JUNKING	**UNKING**	UNKINGS
	UNKINK	UNKINKS
	UNKNIGHT	UNKNIGHTS
	UNKNIT	UNKNITS
	UNKNOT	UNKNOTS
	UNKNOWING	UNKNOWINGS
	UNKNOWN	UNKNOWNS
	UNLACE	UNLACED · UNLACES
	UNLADE	UNLADED · UNLADEN · UNLADES
	UNLADING	UNLADINGS
	UNLAST	UNLASTE
	UNLAW	UNLAWS
	UNLAY	UNLAYS
	UNLEAD	UNLEADS
	UNLEADED	UNLEADEDS
	UNLEARN	UNLEARNS · UNLEARNT
GUNLESS · RUNLESS · SUNLESS	**UNLESS**	
RUNLET	**UNLET**	
	UNLEVEL	UNLEVELS
	UNLID	UNLIDS
NUNLIKE · SUNLIKE	**UNLIKE**	UNLIKED · UNLIKES
	UNLIMBER	UNLIMBERS
	UNLIME	UNLIMED · UNLIMES
	UNLINE	UNLINED · UNLINES
	UNLINK	UNLINKS
SUNLIT	**UNLIT**	
	UNLIVE	UNLIVED · UNLIVES
	UNLOAD	UNLOADS
	UNLOADER	UNLOADERS
	UNLOADING	UNLOADINGS
GUNLOCK	**UNLOCK**	UNLOCKS
GUNLOCKS	**UNLOCKS**	
	UNLOOSE	UNLOOSED · UNLOOSEN · UNLOOSES
	UNLOOSEN	UNLOOSENS
	UNLORD	UNLORDS
	UNLOVE	UNLOVED · UNLOVES
	UNMAKE	UNMAKER · UNMAKES
GUNMAKER	**UNMAKER**	UNMAKERS

FRONT HOOK	ROOT WORD	END HOOK
GUNMAKERS	**UNMAKERS**	
	UNMAKING	UNMAKINGS
GUNMAN	**UNMAN**	UNMANS
	UNMANACLE	UNMANACLED · UNMANACLES
	UNMANTLE	UNMANTLED · UNMANTLES
	UNMARRIED	UNMARRIEDS
	UNMASK	UNMASKS
	UNMASKER	UNMASKERS
	UNMASKING	UNMASKINGS
	UNMEW	UNMEWS
	UNMINGLE	UNMINGLED · UNMINGLES
	UNMITER	UNMITERS
	UNMITRE	UNMITRED · UNMITRES
	UNMIX	UNMIXT
	UNMOLD	UNMOLDS
	UNMOOR	UNMOORS
	UNMORTISE	UNMORTISED · UNMORTISES
	UNMOULD	UNMOULDS
	UNMOUNT	UNMOUNTS
	UNMUFFLE	UNMUFFLED · UNMUFFLES
	UNMUZZLE	UNMUZZLED · UNMUZZLES
	UNNAIL	UNNAILS
	UNNERVE	UNNERVED · UNNERVES
DUNNEST · FUNNEST	**UNNEST**	UNNESTS
	UNNOBLE	UNNOBLED · UNNOBLES
	UNORDER	UNORDERS
	UNPACK	UNPACKS
	UNPACKER	UNPACKERS
	UNPACKING	UNPACKINGS
	UNPAINT	UNPAINTS
	UNPANEL	UNPANELS
	UNPANNEL	UNPANNELS
GUNPAPER	**UNPAPER**	UNPAPERS
GUNPAPERS	**UNPAPERS**	
	UNPAY	UNPAYS
	UNPEG	UNPEGS
	UNPEN	UNPENS · UNPENT
	UNPEOPLE	UNPEOPLED · UNPEOPLES
	UNPERSON	UNPERSONS
	UNPERVERT	UNPERVERTS
	UNPICK	UNPICKS
	UNPILE	UNPILED · UNPILES
	UNPIN	UNPINS
	UNPLACE	UNPLACED · UNPLACES
	UNPLAIT	UNPLAITS
	UNPLUG	UNPLUGS
	UNPLUMB	UNPLUMBS
	UNPLUME	UNPLUMED · UNPLUMES
	UNPOISON	UNPOISONS
	UNPOPE	UNPOPED · UNPOPES
	UNPRAISE	UNPRAISED · UNPRAISES
	UNPRAY	UNPRAYS
	UNPREDICT	UNPREDICTS
	UNPREPARE	UNPREPARED · UNPREPARES
	UNPRIEST	UNPRIESTS
	UNPRISON	UNPRISONS
	UNPROP	UNPROPS
	UNPROVIDE	UNPROVIDED · UNPROVIDES
	UNPROVOKE	UNPROVOKED · UNPROVOKES
	UNPUCKER	UNPUCKERS
	UNPURSE	UNPURSED · UNPURSES
	UNPUZZLE	UNPUZZLED · UNPUZZLES
	UNQUEEN	UNQUEENS
	UNQUIET	UNQUIETS
	UNQUOTE	UNQUOTED · UNQUOTES
	UNRAKE	UNRAKED · UNRAKES
	UNRAVEL	UNRAVELS
	UNREAD	UNREADY
	UNREALISE	UNREALISED · UNREALISES

J

FRONT HOOK	ROOT WORD	END HOOK
	UNREALISM	UNREALISMS
	UNREALIZE	UNREALIZED · UNREALIZES
	UNREASON	UNREASONS
	UNREAVE	UNREAVED · UNREAVES
	UNRED	UNREDY
	UNREEL	UNREELS
	UNREELER	UNREELERS
	UNREEVE	UNREEVED · UNREEVES
	UNREIN	UNREINS
	UNREPAIR	UNREPAIRS
	UNRESERVE	UNRESERVED · UNRESERVES
	UNREST	UNRESTS
	UNRETIRE	UNRETIRED · UNRETIRES
	UNRIDDLE	UNRIDDLED · UNRIDDLER · UNRIDDLES
	UNRIDDLER	UNRIDDLERS
RUNRIG	**UNRIG**	UNRIGS
	UNRIGHT	UNRIGHTS
RUNRIGS	**UNRIGS**	
	UNRIP	UNRIPE · UNRIPS
	UNRIPE	UNRIPER
	UNRIPPING	UNRIPPINGS
	UNRIVET	UNRIVETS
	UNROBE	UNROBED · UNROBES
	UNROLL	UNROLLS
SUNROOF	**UNROOF**	UNROOFS
SUNROOFS	**UNROOFS**	
	UNROOST	UNROOSTS
	UNROOT	UNROOTS
	UNROPE	UNROPED · UNROPES
RUNROUND	**UNROUND**	UNROUNDS
RUNROUNDS	**UNROUNDS**	
	UNROVE	UNROVEN
	UNRUFFLE	UNRUFFLED · UNRUFFLES
	UNRULE	UNRULED · UNRULES
BUNS · DUNS · FUNS · GUNS · HUNS · MUNS NUNS · PUNS · RUNS · SUNS · TUNS	**UNS**	
	UNSADDLE	UNSADDLED · UNSADDLES
	UNSAFE	UNSAFER
	UNSAINT	UNSAINTS
	UNSATIATE	UNSATIATED
	UNSAY	UNSAYS
	UNSAYABLE	UNSAYABLES
	UNSCALE	UNSCALED · UNSCALES
	UNSCREW	UNSCREWS
	UNSEAL	UNSEALS
	UNSEAM	UNSEAMS
	UNSEASON	UNSEASONS
	UNSEAT	UNSEATS
	UNSEEL	UNSEELS
	UNSEEMING	UNSEEMINGS
	UNSEEN	UNSEENS
	UNSELF	UNSELFS
	UNSELL	UNSELLS
	UNSENSE	UNSENSED · UNSENSES
SUNSET	**UNSET**	UNSETS
SUNSETS	**UNSETS**	
SUNSETTING	**UNSETTING**	
	UNSETTLE	UNSETTLED · UNSETTLES
	UNSEW	UNSEWN · UNSEWS
	UNSEX	UNSEXY
	UNSHACKLE	UNSHACKLED · UNSHACKLES
	UNSHADOW	UNSHADOWS
	UNSHALE	UNSHALED · UNSHALES
	UNSHAPE	UNSHAPED · UNSHAPEN · UNSHAPES
	UNSHEATHE	UNSHEATHED · UNSHEATHES
DUNSHED	**UNSHED**	
	UNSHELL	UNSHELLS
	UNSHIFT	UNSHIFTS
GUNSHIP · NUNSHIP	**UNSHIP**	UNSHIPS

887

FRONT HOOK	ROOT WORD	END HOOK
GUNSHIPS = NUNSHIPS	**UNSHIPS**	
	UNSHOE	UNSHOED = UNSHOES
	UNSHOOT	UNSHOOTS
GUNSHOT	**UNSHOT**	
	UNSHOUT	UNSHOUTS
	UNSHROUD	UNSHROUDS
	UNSHUT	UNSHUTS
	UNSHUTTER	UNSHUTTERS
	UNSIGHT	UNSIGHTS
	UNSINEW	UNSINEWS
	UNSLING	UNSLINGS
	UNSLUICE	UNSLUICED = UNSLUICES
	UNSMOOTH	UNSMOOTHS
	UNSNAG	UNSNAGS
	UNSNAP	UNSNAPS
	UNSNARL	UNSNARLS
	UNSNECK	UNSNECKS
	UNSOCKET	UNSOCKETS
	UNSOLDER	UNSOLDERS
	UNSOUL	UNSOULS
	UNSPAR	UNSPARS
	UNSPEAK	UNSPEAKS
	UNSPELL	UNSPELLS
	UNSPHERE	UNSPHERED = UNSPHERES
	UNSPOKE	UNSPOKEN
	UNSPOOL	UNSPOOLS
SUNSPOTTED	**UNSPOTTED**	
	UNSTABLE	UNSTABLER
	UNSTACK	UNSTACKS
	UNSTATE	UNSTATED = UNSTATES
	UNSTEEL	UNSTEELS
	UNSTEP	UNSTEPS
GUNSTICK	**UNSTICK**	UNSTICKS
GUNSTICKS	**UNSTICKS**	
GUNSTOCK	**UNSTOCK**	UNSTOCKS
GUNSTOCKS	**UNSTOCKS**	
	UNSTOP	UNSTOPS
	UNSTOPPER	UNSTOPPERS
	UNSTOW	UNSTOWS
	UNSTRAP	UNSTRAPS
	UNSTRING	UNSTRINGS
	UNSTRIP	UNSTRIPS
SUNSTRUCK	**UNSTRUCK**	
SUNSUIT	**UNSUIT**	UNSUITS
SUNSUITS	**UNSUITS**	
	UNSURE	UNSURED = UNSURER
	UNSWADDLE	UNSWADDLED = UNSWADDLES
	UNSWATHE	UNSWATHED = UNSWATHES
	UNSWEAR	UNSWEARS
	UNTACK	UNTACKS
	UNTACKLE	UNTACKLED = UNTACKLES
	UNTAME	UNTAMED = UNTAMES
	UNTANGLE	UNTANGLED = UNTANGLES
SUNTANNED	**UNTANNED**	
	UNTEAM	UNTEAMS
	UNTEMPER	UNTEMPERS
	UNTENANT	UNTENANTS
	UNTENT	UNTENTS = UNTENTY
	UNTETHER	UNTETHERS
	UNTHAW	UNTHAWS
	UNTHINK	UNTHINKS
	UNTHREAD	UNTHREADS
	UNTHRIFT	UNTHRIFTS = UNTHRIFTY
	UNTHRONE	UNTHRONED = UNTHRONES
	UNTIDIES	UNTIDIEST
AUNTIE	**UNTIE**	UNTIED = UNTIES
AUNTIES = PUNTIES	**UNTIES**	
	UNTIL	UNTILE
	UNTILE	UNTILED = UNTILES

FRONT HOOK	ROOT WORD	END HOOK
MUNTIN	**UNTIN**	UNTINS
MUNTINS	**UNTINS**	
JUNTO · PUNTO	**UNTO**	
	UNTOMB	UNTOMBS
	UNTRACE	UNTRACED · UNTRACES
	UNTRACK	UNTRACKS
	UNTREAD	UNTREADS
	UNTRIM	UNTRIMS
	UNTRUE	UNTRUER
	UNTRUISM	UNTRUISMS
	UNTRUSSER	UNTRUSSERS
	UNTRUST	UNTRUSTS · UNTRUSTY
	UNTRUTH	UNTRUTHS
	UNTUCK	UNTUCKS
	UNTUNE	UNTUNED · UNTUNES
	UNTURF	UNTURFS
	UNTURN	UNTURNS
	UNTWINE	UNTWINED · UNTWINES
	UNTWIST	UNTWISTS
	UNTYING	UNTYINGS
	UNUNBIUM	UNUNBIUMS
	UNUNUNIUM	UNUNUNIUMS
	UNVAIL	UNVAILE · UNVAILS
	UNVAILE	UNVAILED · UNVAILES
	UNVEIL	UNVEILS
	UNVEILER	UNVEILERS
	UNVEILING	UNVEILINGS
	UNVIRTUE	UNVIRTUES
	UNVISOR	UNVISORS
	UNVIZARD	UNVIZARDS
	UNVOICE	UNVOICED · UNVOICES
	UNVOICING	UNVOICINGS
	UNWARE	UNWARES
	UNWARIE	UNWARIER
	UNWASHED	UNWASHEDS
	UNWATER	UNWATERS · UNWATERY
	UNWEAL	UNWEALS
	UNWEAPON	UNWEAPONS
	UNWEAVE	UNWEAVES
	UNWEIGHT	UNWEIGHTS
	UNWELCOME	UNWELCOMED
	UNWILL	UNWILLS
	UNWIND	UNWINDS
	UNWINDER	UNWINDERS
	UNWINDING	UNWINDINGS
	UNWIRE	UNWIRED · UNWIRES
	UNWISDOM	UNWISDOMS
SUNWISE	**UNWISE**	UNWISER
	UNWIT	UNWITS
	UNWIVE	UNWIVED · UNWIVES
	UNWOMAN	UNWOMANS
	UNWON	UNWONT
	UNWORK	UNWORKS
	UNWORTH	UNWORTHS · UNWORTHY
	UNWOVE	UNWOVEN
	UNWRAP	UNWRAPS
	UNWREATHE	UNWREATHED · UNWREATHES
	UNWRINKLE	UNWRINKLED · UNWRINKLES
	UNWRITE	UNWRITES
	UNYOKE	UNYOKED · UNYOKES
	UNZIP	UNZIPS
CUP · DUP · GUP · HUP · OUP · PUP · SUP · TUP · YUP	**UP**	UPO · UPS
HUPAITHRIC	**UPAITHRIC**	
OUPAS · PUPAS · ZUPAS	**UPAS**	
	UPBEAR	UPBEARS
CUPBEARER	**UPBEARER**	UPBEARERS
CUPBEARERS	**UPBEARERS**	
	UPBEAT	UPBEATS

FRONT HOOK	ROOT WORD	END HOOK
	UPBIND	UPBINDS
	UPBLOW	UPBLOWN · UPBLOWS
	UPBOIL	UPBOILS
	UPBOW	UPBOWS
	UPBRAID	UPBRAIDS
	UPBRAIDER	UPBRAIDERS
	UPBRAY	UPBRAYS
	UPBREAK	UPBREAKS
	UPBRING	UPBRINGS
	UPBROKE	UPBROKEN
	UPBUILD	UPBUILDS
	UPBUILDER	UPBUILDERS
	UPBURST	UPBURSTS
	UPBY	UPBYE
	UPCAST	UPCASTS
	UPCHEER	UPCHEERS
	UPCHUCK	UPCHUCKS
	UPCLIMB	UPCLIMBS
	UPCLOSE	UPCLOSED · UPCLOSES
	UPCOIL	UPCOILS
	UPCOME	UPCOMES
	UPCURL	UPCURLS
	UPCURVE	UPCURVED · UPCURVES
	UPDART	UPDARTS
	UPDATE	UPDATED · UPDATER · UPDATES
	UPDATER	UPDATERS
	UPDIVE	UPDIVED · UPDIVES
	UPDO	UPDOS
	UPDRAFT	UPDRAFTS
	UPDRAG	UPDRAGS
	UPDRAUGHT	UPDRAUGHTS
	UPDRAW	UPDRAWN · UPDRAWS
	UPEND	UPENDS
	UPFILL	UPFILLS
	UPFILLING	UPFILLINGS
	UPFLING	UPFLINGS
	UPFLOW	UPFLOWS
	UPFOLD	UPFOLDS
	UPFOLLOW	UPFOLLOWS
	UPFURL	UPFURLS
	UPGANG	UPGANGS
	UPGATHER	UPGATHERS
	UPGAZE	UPGAZED · UPGAZES
	UPGIRD	UPGIRDS
	UPGOING	UPGOINGS
	UPGRADE	UPGRADED · UPGRADER · UPGRADES
	UPGRADER	UPGRADERS
	UPGROW	UPGROWN · UPGROWS
	UPGROWING	UPGROWINGS
	UPGROWTH	UPGROWTHS
	UPHANG	UPHANGS
	UPHAUD	UPHAUDS
	UPHEAP	UPHEAPS
	UPHEAPING	UPHEAPINGS
	UPHEAVAL	UPHEAVALS
	UPHEAVE	UPHEAVED · UPHEAVER · UPHEAVES
	UPHEAVER	UPHEAVERS
	UPHILL	UPHILLS
	UPHOARD	UPHOARDS
	UPHOIST	UPHOISTS
	UPHOLD	UPHOLDS
	UPHOLDER	UPHOLDERS
	UPHOLDING	UPHOLDINGS
	UPHOLSTER	UPHOLSTERS · UPHOLSTERY
	UPHOORD	UPHOORDS
EUPHROE	**UPHROE**	UPHROES
EUPHROES	**UPHROES**	
	UPHURL	UPHURLS
	UPJET	UPJETS

J

FRONT HOOK	ROOT WORD	END HOOK
	UPKEEP	UPKEEPS
	UPKNIT	UPKNITS
	UPLAND	UPLANDS
	UPLANDER	UPLANDERS
	UPLAY	UPLAYS
	UPLEAD	UPLEADS
	UPLEAN	UPLEANS ▪ UPLEANT
	UPLEAP	UPLEAPS ▪ UPLEAPT
	UPLIFT	UPLIFTS
	UPLIFTER	UPLIFTERS
	UPLIFTING	UPLIFTINGS
	UPLIGHT	UPLIGHTS
	UPLIGHTER	UPLIGHTERS
	UPLINK	UPLINKS
	UPLINKING	UPLINKINGS
	UPLOAD	UPLOADS
	UPLOCK	UPLOCKS
	UPLOOK	UPLOOKS
DUPLYING	**UPLYING**	
	UPMAKE	UPMAKER ▪ UPMAKES
	UPMAKER	UPMAKERS
	UPMAKING	UPMAKINGS
	UPMANSHIP	UPMANSHIPS
	UPO	UPON
JUPON ▪ YUPON	**UPON**	
CUPPED ▪ DUPPED ▪ HUPPED ▪ PUPPED SUPPED ▪ TUPPED	**UPPED**	
CUPPER ▪ SUPPER	**UPPER**	UPPERS
	UPPERCASE	UPPERCASED ▪ UPPERCASES
	UPPERCUT	UPPERCUTS
	UPPERPART	UPPERPARTS
CUPPERS ▪ SUPPERS	**UPPERS**	
	UPPILE	UPPILED ▪ UPPILES
CUPPING ▪ DUPPING ▪ HUPPING ▪ PUPPING SUPPING ▪ TUPPING	**UPPING**	UPPINGS
CUPPINGS	**UPPINGS**	
	UPPROP	UPPROPS
	UPRAISE	UPRAISED ▪ UPRAISER ▪ UPRAISES
	UPRAISER	UPRAISERS
	UPRATE	UPRATED ▪ UPRATES
	UPREAR	UPREARS
	UPREST	UPRESTS
	UPRIGHT	UPRIGHTS
	UPRISAL	UPRISALS
	UPRISE	UPRISEN ▪ UPRISER ▪ UPRISES
	UPRISER	UPRISERS
	UPRISING	UPRISINGS
	UPRIST	UPRISTS
	UPRIVER	UPRIVERS
	UPROAR	UPROARS
	UPROLL	UPROLLS
	UPROOT	UPROOTS
	UPROOTAL	UPROOTALS
	UPROOTER	UPROOTERS
	UPROOTING	UPROOTINGS
	UPROUSE	UPROUSED ▪ UPROUSES
	UPRUN	UPRUNS
CUPS ▪ DUPS ▪ GUPS ▪ HUPS ▪ OUPS ▪ PUPS SUPS ▪ TUPS ▪ YUPS	**UPS**	UPSY
	UPSCALE	UPSCALED ▪ UPSCALES
	UPSEE	UPSEES
	UPSEND	UPSENDS
	UPSET	UPSETS
	UPSETTER	UPSETTERS
	UPSETTING	UPSETTINGS
	UPSEY	UPSEYS
	UPSHIFT	UPSHIFTS
	UPSHOOT	UPSHOOTS
	UPSHOT	UPSHOTS

FRONT HOOK	ROOT WORD	END HOOK
	UPSIDE	UPSIDES
	UPSILON	UPSILONS
	UPSITTING	UPSITTINGS
	UPSIZE	UPSIZED = UPSIZES
	UPSKILL	UPSKILLS
	UPSOAR	UPSOARS
	UPSPEAK	UPSPEAKS
	UPSPEAR	UPSPEARS
	UPSPOKE	UPSPOKEN
	UPSPRING	UPSPRINGS
	UPSTAGE	UPSTAGED = UPSTAGER = UPSTAGES
	UPSTAGER	UPSTAGERS
	UPSTAIR	UPSTAIRS
	UPSTAND	UPSTANDS
	UPSTARE	UPSTARED = UPSTARES
	UPSTART	UPSTARTS
	UPSTATE	UPSTATER = UPSTATES
	UPSTATER	UPSTATERS
	UPSTAY	UPSTAYS
	UPSTEP	UPSTEPS
	UPSTIR	UPSTIRS
	UPSTREAM	UPSTREAMS
	UPSTROKE	UPSTROKES
	UPSURGE	UPSURGED = UPSURGES
	UPSWARM	UPSWARMS
	UPSWAY	UPSWAYS
	UPSWEEP	UPSWEEPS
	UPSWELL	UPSWELLS
	UPSWING	UPSWINGS
	UPTA	UPTAK
	UPTAK	UPTAKE = UPTAKS
	UPTAKE	UPTAKEN = UPTAKES
	UPTALK	UPTALKS
	UPTEAR	UPTEARS
	UPTEMPO	UPTEMPOS
	UPTHROW	UPTHROWN = UPTHROWS
	UPTHRUST	UPTHRUSTS
	UPTHUNDER	UPTHUNDERS
	UPTICK	UPTICKS
	UPTIE	UPTIED = UPTIES
	UPTILT	UPTILTS
	UPTIME	UPTIMES
	UPTITLING	UPTITLINGS
	UPTOWN	UPTOWNS
	UPTOWNER	UPTOWNERS
	UPTRAIN	UPTRAINS
	UPTREND	UPTRENDS
	UPTURN	UPTURNS
	UPTURNING	UPTURNINGS
	UPVALUE	UPVALUED = UPVALUES
	UPWAFT	UPWAFTS
	UPWARD	UPWARDS
	UPWELL	UPWELLS
	UPWELLING	UPWELLINGS
	UPWHIRL	UPWHIRLS
	UPWIND	UPWINDS
	UPWRAP	UPWRAPS
BUR = CUR = FUR = GUR = LUR = NUR = OUR = PUR = SUR	**UR**	URB = URD = URE = URN = URP
	URACIL	URACILS
	URAEMIA	URAEMIAS
OURALI	**URALI**	URALIS
OURALIS	**URALIS**	
RURALITE	**URALITE**	URALITES
RURALITES	**URALITES**	
	URALITISE	URALITISED = URALITISES
	URALITIZE	URALITIZED = URALITIZES
	URANIA	URANIAN = URANIAS
PURANIC	**URANIC**	

J

FRONT HOOK	ROOT WORD	END HOOK
	URANIDE	URANIDES
	URANIN	URANINS
	URANINITE	URANINITES
	URANISM	URANISMS
	URANITE	URANITES
	URANIUM	URANIUMS
	URANYL	URANYLS
	URAO	URAOS
CURARE	**URARE**	URARES
CURARES	**URARES**	
CURARI ▪ OURARI	**URARI**	URARIS
CURARIS ▪ OURARIS	**URARIS**	
	URASE	URASES
AURATE ▪ CURATE	**URATE**	URATES
AURATES ▪ CURATES	**URATES**	
BURB ▪ CURB	**URB**	URBS
RURBAN ▪ TURBAN	**URBAN**	URBANE
	URBANE	URBANER
	URBANISE	URBANISED ▪ URBANISES
	URBANISM	URBANISMS
	URBANIST	URBANISTS
	URBANITE	URBANITES
	URBANIZE	URBANIZED ▪ URBANIZES
	URBIA	URBIAS
BURBS ▪ CURBS	**URBS**	
	URCHIN	URCHINS
BURD ▪ CURD ▪ NURD ▪ SURD ▪ TURD	**URD**	URDE ▪ URDS ▪ URDY
	URDE	URDEE
BURDS ▪ CURDS ▪ HURDS ▪ NURDS ▪ SURDS TURDS (offensive)	**URDS**	
CURDY ▪ NURDY	**URDY**	
CURE ▪ DURE ▪ IURE ▪ JURE ▪ LURE ▪ MURE PURE ▪ SURE	**URE**	UREA ▪ URES
	UREA	UREAL ▪ UREAS
	UREAS	UREASE
	UREASE	UREASES
	UREDIA	UREDIAL
	UREDINE	UREDINES
	UREDINIA	UREDINIAL
	UREDO	UREDOS
	UREIDE	UREIDES
	UREMIA	UREMIAS
MURENA	**URENA**	URENAS
MURENAS	**URENAS**	
AURES ▪ CURES ▪ DURES ▪ LURES ▪ MURES PURES ▪ SURES	**URES**	
	URETER	URETERS
	URETHAN	URETHANE ▪ URETHANS
	URETHANE	URETHANES
	URETHRA	URETHRAE ▪ URETHRAL ▪ URETHRAS
GURGE ▪ PURGE ▪ SURGE	**URGE**	URGED ▪ URGER ▪ URGES
GURGED ▪ PURGED ▪ SURGED	**URGED**	
	URGENCE	URGENCES
TURGENCIES	**URGENCIES**	
TURGENCY	**URGENCY**	
SURGENT ▪ TURGENT	**URGENT**	
TURGENTLY	**URGENTLY**	
BURGER ▪ PURGER ▪ SURGER	**URGER**	URGERS
BURGERS ▪ PURGERS ▪ SURGERS	**URGERS**	
GURGES ▪ PURGES ▪ SURGES	**URGES**	
GURGING ▪ PURGING ▪ SURGING	**URGING**	URGINGS
PURGINGS ▪ SURGINGS	**URGINGS**	
BURIAL ▪ CURIAL	**URIAL**	URIALS
BURIALS	**URIALS**	
AURIC	**URIC**	
	URICASE	URICASES
	URIDINE	URIDINES
	URINAL	URINALS
	URINATE	URINATED ▪ URINATES

FRONT HOOK	ROOT WORD	END HOOK
	URINATION	URINATIONS
	URINATOR	URINATORS
MURINE ▪ PURINE	**URINE**	URINED ▪ URINES
	URINEMIA	URINEMIAS
MURINES ▪ PURINES	**URINES**	
CURITE	**URITE**	URITES
CURITES	**URITES**	
	URMAN	URMANS
BURN ▪ CURN ▪ DURN ▪ GURN ▪ OURN ▪ TURN	**URN**	URNS
BURNED ▪ DURNED ▪ GURNED ▪ TURNED	**URNED**	
	URNFIELD	URNFIELDS
	URNFUL	URNFULS
BURNING ▪ DURNING ▪ GURNING ▪ TURNING	**URNING**	URNINGS
BURNINGS ▪ TURNINGS	**URNINGS**	
BURNS ▪ CURNS ▪ DURNS ▪ GURNS ▪ TURNS	**URNS**	
	UROBILIN	UROBILINS
	UROCHORD	UROCHORDS
	UROCHROME	UROCHROMES
	URODELAN	URODELANS
	URODELE	URODELES
	UROKINASE	UROKINASES
	UROLAGNIA	UROLAGNIAS
	UROLITH	UROLITHS
OUROLOGIES	**UROLOGIES**	
	UROLOGIST	UROLOGISTS
OUROLOGY	**UROLOGY**	
	UROMERE	UROMERES
	UROPOD	UROPODS
	UROPYGIA	UROPYGIAL
	UROPYGIUM	UROPYGIUMS
OUROSCOPY	**UROSCOPY**	
	UROSOME	UROSOMES
	UROSTEGE	UROSTEGES
	UROSTYLE	UROSTYLES
BURP ▪ RURP	**URP**	URPS
	URPED	
	URPING	
BURPS ▪ RURPS ▪ TURPS	**URPS**	
BURSA	**URSA**	URSAE
BURSAE	**URSAE**	
	URSID	URSIDS
BURSIFORM	**URSIFORM**	
	URSON	URSONS
	URTEXT	URTEXTS
	URTICA	URTICAS
	URTICANT	URTICANTS
	URTICARIA	URTICARIAL ▪ URTICARIAS
	URTICATE	URTICATED ▪ URTICATES
	URUBU	URUBUS
GURUS ▪ KURUS ▪ RURUS	**URUS**	
	URUSHIOL	URUSHIOLS
MURVA	**URVA**	URVAS
MURVAS	**URVAS**	
BUS ▪ GUS ▪ JUS ▪ MUS ▪ NUS ▪ OUS ▪ PUS ▪ SUS ▪ WUS ▪ YUS	**US**	USE
	USAGE	USAGER ▪ USAGES
	USAGER	USAGERS
	USANCE	USANCES
	USAUNCE	USAUNCES
FUSE ▪ MUSE ▪ RUSE	**USE**	USED ▪ USER ▪ USES
BUSED ▪ FUSED ▪ MUSED	**USED**	
MUSEFUL	**USEFUL**	USEFULS
MUSEFULLY	**USEFULLY**	
FUSELESS	**USELESS**	
LUSER ▪ MUSER	**USER**	USERS
	USERNAME	USERNAMES
LUSERS ▪ MUSERS	**USERS**	
BUSES ▪ FUSES ▪ MUSES ▪ PUSES ▪ RUSES ▪ SUSES ▪ WUSES	**USES**	

FRONT HOOK	ROOT WORD	END HOOK
BUSHER ▪ GUSHER ▪ HUSHER ▪ LUSHER MUSHER ▪ PUSHER ▪ RUSHER	**USHER**	USHERS
HUSHERED	**USHERED**	
	USHERETTE	USHERETTES
HUSHERING	**USHERING**	USHERINGS
BUSHERS ▪ GUSHERS ▪ HUSHERS ▪ LUSHERS MUSHERS ▪ PUSHERS ▪ RUSHERS	**USHERS**	
	USHERSHIP	USHERSHIPS
	USING	
BUSING ▪ FUSING ▪ MUSING	**USNEA**	USNEAS
	USQUABAE	USQUABAES
	USQUE	USQUES
	USQUEBAE	USQUEBAES
	USTION	USTIONS
PUSTULATE	**USTULATE**	
	USUAL	USUALS
	USUCAPION	USUCAPIONS
	USUCAPT	USUCAPTS
	USUFRUCT	USUFRUCTS
	USURE	USURED ▪ USURER ▪ USURES
	USURER	USURERS
	USURES	USURESS
	USURP	USURPS
	USURPER	USURPERS
	USURPING	USURPINGS
	USWARD	USWARDS
BUT ▪ CUT ▪ GUT ▪ HUT ▪ JUT ▪ MUT ▪ NUT OUT ▪ PUT ▪ RUT ▪ TUT	**UT**	UTA ▪ UTE ▪ UTS ▪ UTU
KUTA	**UTA**	UTAS
KUTAS	**UTAS**	
MUTASES	**UTASES**	
BUTE ▪ CUTE ▪ JUTE ▪ LUTE ▪ MUTE	**UTE**	UTES
	UTENSIL	UTENSILS
BUTES ▪ CUTES ▪ JUTES ▪ LUTES ▪ MUTES	**UTES**	
FUTILE ▪ RUTILE ▪ SUTILE	**UTILE**	
	UTILIDOR	UTILIDORS
	UTILISE	UTILISED ▪ UTILISER ▪ UTILISES
	UTILISER	UTILISERS
FUTILITIES	**UTILITIES**	
FUTILITY	**UTILITY**	
	UTILIZE	UTILIZED ▪ UTILIZER ▪ UTILIZES
	UTILIZER	UTILIZERS
CUTIS ▪ KUTIS ▪ MUTIS	**UTIS**	
CUTISES	**UTISES**	
OUTMOST	**UTMOST**	UTMOSTS
	UTOPIA	UTOPIAN ▪ UTOPIAS
	UTOPIAN	UTOPIANS
	UTOPIAS	UTOPIAST
	UTOPIAST	UTOPIASTS
	UTOPISM	UTOPISMS
	UTOPIST	UTOPISTS
	UTRICLE	UTRICLES
BUTS ▪ CUTS ▪ GUTS ▪ HUTS ▪ JUTS ▪ MUTS NUTS ▪ OUTS ▪ PUTS ▪ RUTS ▪ TUTS	**UTS**	
BUTTER ▪ CUTTER ▪ GUTTER ▪ MUTTER NUTTER ▪ PUTTER ▪ RUTTER	**UTTER**	UTTERS
	UTTERANCE	UTTERANCES
BUTTERED ▪ GUTTERED ▪ MUTTERED PUTTERED	**UTTERED**	
MUTTERER ▪ PUTTERER	**UTTERER**	UTTERERS
MUTTERERS ▪ PUTTERERS	**UTTERERS**	
BUTTERING ▪ GUTTERING ▪ MUTTERING PUTTERING	**UTTERING**	UTTERINGS
GUTTERINGS ▪ MUTTERINGS	**UTTERINGS**	
BUTTERLESS	**UTTERLESS**	
	UTTERMOST	UTTERMOSTS
BUTTERS ▪ CUTTERS ▪ GUTTERS ▪ MUTTERS	**UTTERS**	
NUTTERS (offensive) ▪ PUTTERS ▪ RUTTERS KUTU ▪ TUTU	**UTU**	UTUS

FRONT HOOK	ROOT WORD	END HOOK
KUTUS · TUTUS	**UTUS**	
	UVA	UVAE · UVAS
	UVAROVITE	UVAROVITES
	UVEA	UVEAL · UVEAS
	UVULA	UVULAE · UVULAR · UVULAS
	UVULAR	UVULARS
	UXORICIDE	UXORICIDES

V

FRONT HOOK	ROOT WORD	END HOOK
	VAC	VACS
	VACANCE	VACANCES
	VACATE	VACATED · VACATES
	VACATION	VACATIONS
	VACATUR	VACATURS
	VACCINA	VACCINAL · VACCINAS
	VACCINATE	VACCINATED · VACCINATES
	VACCINE	VACCINEE · VACCINES
	VACCINEE	VACCINEES
	VACCINIA	VACCINIAL · VACCINIAS
	VACCINIUM	VACCINIUMS
	VACHERIN	VACHERINS
	VACILLATE	VACILLATED · VACILLATES
EVACUATE	**VACUATE**	VACUATED · VACUATES
EVACUATED	**VACUATED**	
EVACUATES	**VACUATES**	
EVACUATING	**VACUATING**	
EVACUATION	**VACUATION**	VACUATIONS
	VACUIST	VACUISTS
	VACUOLATE	VACUOLATED
	VACUOLE	VACUOLES
	VACUUM	VACUUMS
EVADE	**VADE**	VADED · VADES
EVADED	**VADED**	
EVADES	**VADES**	
EVADING	**VADING**	
UVAE	**VAE**	VAES
	VAG	VAGI · VAGS
	VAGABOND	VAGABONDS
	VAGINA	VAGINAE · VAGINAL · VAGINAS
EVAGINATE	**VAGINATE**	VAGINATED
EVAGINATED	**VAGINATED**	
	VAGINULA	VAGINULAE
	VAGINULE	VAGINULES
	VAGOTONIA	VAGOTONIAS
	VAGRANT	VAGRANTS
	VAGUE	VAGUED · VAGUER · VAGUES
	VAGUES	VAGUEST
	VAHANA	VAHANAS
	VAHINE	VAHINES
AVAIL	**VAIL**	VAILS
AVAILED	**VAILED**	
AVAILING	**VAILING**	
AVAILS	**VAILS**	
	VAINESSE	VAINESSES
	VAIR	VAIRE · VAIRS · VAIRY
	VAIVODE	VAIVODES
	VAKEEL	VAKEELS
	VAKIL	VAKILS
	VALANCE	VALANCED · VALANCES
AVALE	**VALE**	VALES · VALET
	VALENCE	VALENCES
	VALENCIA	VALENCIAS
	VALENTINE	VALENTINES
	VALERATE	VALERATES
	VALERIAN	VALERIANS
AVALES	**VALES**	
	VALET	VALETA · VALETE · VALETS
	VALETA	VALETAS
	VALETE	VALETED · VALETES
	VALETING	VALETINGS
	VALI	VALID · VALIS
	VALIANCE	VALIANCES
	VALIANT	VALIANTS
	VALIDATE	VALIDATED · VALIDATES
	VALINE	VALINES

FRONT HOOK	ROOT WORD	END HOOK
	VALIS	VALISE
	VALISE	VALISES
	VALKYR	VALKYRS
	VALKYRIE	VALKYRIES
	VALLAR	VALLARY
	VALLATION	VALLATIONS
	VALLECULA	VALLECULAE · VALLECULAR
	VALLEY	VALLEYS
	VALLHUND	VALLHUNDS
	VALLONIA	VALLONIAS
	VALLUM	VALLUMS
	VALONEA	VALONEAS
	VALONIA	VALONIAS
	VALOR	VALORS
	VALORISE	VALORISED · VALORISES
	VALORIZE	VALORIZED · VALORIZES
	VALOUR	VALOURS
	VALPROATE	VALPROATES
	VALSE	VALSED · VALSES
EVALUABLE	**VALUABLE**	VALUABLES
EVALUATE	**VALUATE**	VALUATED · VALUATES
EVALUATED	**VALUATED**	
EVALUATES	**VALUATES**	
EVALUATING	**VALUATING**	
EVALUATION	**VALUATION**	VALUATIONS
EVALUATOR	**VALUATOR**	VALUATORS
EVALUATORS	**VALUATORS**	
	VALUE	VALUED · VALUER · VALUES
	VALUER	VALUERS
	VALUTA	VALUTAS
	VALVASSOR	VALVASSORS
	VALVE	VALVED · VALVES
	VALVELET	VALVELETS
	VALVULA	VALVULAE · VALVULAR
	VALVULE	VALVULES
	VAMBRACE	VAMBRACED · VAMBRACES
	VAMOOSE	VAMOOSED · VAMOOSES
	VAMOSE	VAMOSED · VAMOSES
	VAMP	VAMPS · VAMPY
	VAMPER	VAMPERS
	VAMPING	VAMPINGS
	VAMPIRE	VAMPIRED · VAMPIRES
	VAMPIRISE	VAMPIRISED · VAMPIRISES
	VAMPIRISM	VAMPIRISMS
	VAMPIRIZE	VAMPIRIZED · VAMPIRIZES
	VAMPLATE	VAMPLATES
	VAN	VANE · VANG · VANS · VANT
	VANADATE	VANADATES
	VANADIATE	VANADIATES
	VANADIUM	VANADIUMS
	VANASPATI	VANASPATIS
	VANDA	VANDAL · VANDAS
	VANDAL	VANDALS
	VANDALISE	VANDALISED · VANDALISES
	VANDALISM	VANDALISMS
	VANDALIZE	VANDALIZED · VANDALIZES
	VANDYKE	VANDYKED · VANDYKES
	VANE	VANED · VANES
	VANESSA	VANESSAS
	VANESSID	VANESSIDS
	VANG	VANGS
	VANGUARD	VANGUARDS
	VANILLA	VANILLAS
	VANILLIN	VANILLINS
EVANISH	**VANISH**	
EVANISHED	**VANISHED**	
	VANISHER	VANISHERS
EVANISHES	**VANISHES**	
EVANISHING	**VANISHING**	VANISHINGS

FRONT HOOK	ROOT WORD	END HOOK
	VANLOAD	VANLOADS
	VANNER	VANNERS
	VANNING	VANNINGS
	VANPOOL	VANPOOLS
AVANT	**VANT**	VANTS
	VANTAGE	VANTAGED ▪ VANTAGES
	VANTBRACE	VANTBRACES
	VAPOR	VAPORS ▪ VAPORY
EVAPORABLE	**VAPORABLE**	
	VAPORER	VAPORERS
	VAPORETTO	VAPORETTOS
	VAPORING	VAPORINGS
	VAPORISE	VAPORISED ▪ VAPORISER ▪ VAPORISES
	VAPORISER	VAPORISERS
	VAPORIZE	VAPORIZED ▪ VAPORIZER ▪ VAPORIZES
	VAPORIZER	VAPORIZERS
	VAPORWARE	VAPORWARES
	VAPOUR	VAPOURS ▪ VAPOURY
	VAPOURER	VAPOURERS
	VAPOURING	VAPOURINGS
	VAPULATE	VAPULATED ▪ VAPULATES
	VAQUERO	VAQUEROS
	VAR	VARA ▪ VARE ▪ VARS ▪ VARY
	VARA	VARAN ▪ VARAS
	VARACTOR	VARACTORS
	VARAN	VARANS
	VARE	VAREC ▪ VARES
	VAREC	VARECH ▪ VARECS
	VARECH	VARECHS
	VAREUSE	VAREUSES
	VARGUENO	VARGUENOS
	VARIA	VARIAS
	VARIABLE	VARIABLES
	VARIANCE	VARIANCES
	VARIANT	VARIANTS
	VARIATE	VARIATED ▪ VARIATES
	VARIATION	VARIATIONS
	VARICELLA	VARICELLAR ▪ VARICELLAS
AVARICES	**VARICES**	
	VARICOSE	VARICOSED ▪ VARICOSES
	VARIEGATE	VARIEGATED ▪ VARIEGATES
	VARIER	VARIERS
OVARIES	**VARIES**	
	VARIETAL	VARIETALS
	VARIFOCAL	VARIFOCALS
	VARIOLA	VARIOLAR ▪ VARIOLAS
	VARIOLATE	VARIOLATED ▪ VARIOLATES
OVARIOLE	**VARIOLE**	VARIOLES
OVARIOLES	**VARIOLES**	
	VARIOLITE	VARIOLITES
	VARIOLOID	VARIOLOIDS
	VARIORUM	VARIORUMS
OVARIOUS	**VARIOUS**	
	VARISCITE	VARISCITES
	VARISTOR	VARISTORS
	VARITYPE	VARITYPED ▪ VARITYPES
	VARLET	VARLETS
	VARLETTO	VARLETTOS
	VARMENT	VARMENTS
	VARMINT	VARMINTS
	VARNA	VARNAS
	VARNISH	VARNISHY
	VARNISHER	VARNISHERS
	VAROOM	VAROOMS
	VARROA	VARROAS
	VARTABED	VARTABEDS
	VARVE	VARVED ▪ VARVEL ▪ VARVES
	VARVEL	VARVELS
OVARY	**VARY**	

FRONT HOOK	ROOT WORD	END HOOK
	VARYING	VARYINGS
AVAS · KVAS · UVAS	**VAS**	VASA · VASE · VAST
	VASA	VASAL
	VASCULA	VASCULAR
AVASCULAR	**VASCULAR**	
	VASCULUM	VASCULUMS
	VASE	VASES
	VASELINE	VASELINES
KVASES	**VASES**	
	VASOSPASM	VASOSPASMS
	VASOTOCIN	VASOTOCINS
	VASSAIL	VASSAILS
	VASSAL	VASSALS
	VASSALAGE	VASSALAGES
	VASSALISE	VASSALISED · VASSALISES
	VASSALIZE	VASSALIZED · VASSALIZES
AVAST	**VAST**	VASTS · VASTY
	VASTITUDE	VASTITUDES
	VAT	VATS · VATU
	VATFUL	VATFULS
	VATICIDE	VATICIDES
	VATTER	VATTERS
	VATU	VATUS
	VAU	VAUS · VAUT
	VAUDOO	VAUDOOS
	VAULT	VAULTS · VAULTY
	VAULTAGE	VAULTAGES
	VAULTER	VAULTERS
	VAULTING	VAULTINGS
	VAUNCE	VAUNCED · VAUNCES
AVAUNT	**VAUNT**	VAUNTS · VAUNTY
	VAUNTAGE	VAUNTAGES
AVAUNTED	**VAUNTED**	
	VAUNTER	VAUNTERS · VAUNTERY
	VAUNTIE	VAUNTIER
AVAUNTING	**VAUNTING**	VAUNTINGS
AVAUNTS	**VAUNTS**	
	VAURIEN	VAURIENS
	VAUT	VAUTE · VAUTS
	VAUTE	VAUTED · VAUTES
	VAV	VAVS
	VAVASOR	VAVASORS · VAVASORY
	VAVASOUR	VAVASOURS
	VAVASSOR	VAVASSORS
	VAW	VAWS
	VAWARD	VAWARDS
	VAWTE	VAWTED · VAWTES
UVEAL	**VEAL**	VEALE · VEALS · VEALY
	VEALE	VEALED · VEALER · VEALES
	VEALER	VEALERS
	VECTOR	VECTORS
	VECTORING	VECTORINGS
	VECTORISE	VECTORISED · VECTORISES
	VECTORIZE	VECTORIZED · VECTORIZES
	VEDALIA	VEDALIAS
	VEDETTE	VEDETTES
	VEE	VEEP · VEER · VEES
	VEEJAY	VEEJAYS
	VEENA	VEENAS
	VEEP	VEEPS
	VEEPEE	VEEPEES
	VEER	VEERS · VEERY
	VEERING	VEERINGS
	VEG	VEGA · VEGO
	VEGA	VEGAN · VEGAS
	VEGAN	VEGANS
	VEGANISM	VEGANISMS
	VEGELATE	VEGELATES
	VEGEMITE	VEGEMITES

FRONT HOOK	ROOT WORD	END HOOK
	VEGETABLE	VEGETABLES
	VEGETAL	VEGETALS
	VEGETATE	VEGETATED ▪ VEGETATES
	VEGETIST	VEGETISTS
	VEGETIVE	VEGETIVES
	VEGGIE	VEGGIES
	VEGIE	VEGIES
	VEGO	VEGOS
	VEHEMENCE	VEHEMENCES
	VEHICLE	VEHICLES
	VEHM	VEHME
	VEIL	VEILS ▪ VEILY
	VEILER	VEILERS
	VEILING	VEILINGS
	VEILLEUSE	VEILLEUSES
	VEIN	VEINS ▪ VEINY
	VEINER	VEINERS
	VEINING	VEININGS
	VEINLET	VEINLETS
	VEINSTONE	VEINSTONES
	VEINSTUFF	VEINSTUFFS
	VEINULE	VEINULES ▪ VEINULET
	VEINULET	VEINULETS
	VELA	VELAR
	VELAR	VELARS
	VELARISE	VELARISED ▪ VELARISES
	VELARIZE	VELARIZED ▪ VELARIZES
	VELATE	VELATED
	VELATURA	VELATURAS
	VELCRO	VELCROS
	VELD	VELDS ▪ VELDT
	VELDSKOEN	VELDSKOENS
	VELDT	VELDTS
	VELE	VELES
	VELETA	VELETAS
	VELIGER	VELIGERS
KVELL	VELL	VELLS
	VELLENAGE	VELLENAGES
	VELLET	VELLETS
	VELLICATE	VELLICATED ▪ VELLICATES
	VELLON	VELLONS
KVELLS	VELLS	
	VELLUM	VELLUMS
	VELODROME	VELODROMES
	VELOUR	VELOURS
	VELOUTE	VELOUTES
	VELOUTINE	VELOUTINES
	VELSKOEN	VELSKOENS
	VELURE	VELURED ▪ VELURES
	VELVERET	VELVERETS
	VELVET	VELVETS ▪ VELVETY
	VELVETEEN	VELVETEENS
	VELVETING	VELVETINGS
	VENA	VENAE ▪ VENAL
	VENATION	VENATIONS
	VENATOR	VENATORS
	VEND	VENDS
	VENDABLE	VENDABLES
	VENDACE	VENDACES
	VENDAGE	VENDAGES
	VENDANGE	VENDANGES
	VENDEE	VENDEES
	VENDER	VENDERS
	VENDETTA	VENDETTAS
	VENDEUSE	VENDEUSES
	VENDIBLE	VENDIBLES
	VENDING	VENDINGS
	VENDIS	VENDISS
	VENDITION	VENDITIONS

FRONT HOOK	ROOT WORD	END HOOK
	VENDOR	VENDORS
	VENDUE	VENDUES
	VENEER	VENEERS
	VENEERER	VENEERERS
	VENEERING	VENEERINGS
	VENENATE	VENENATED ▪ VENENATES
	VENENE	VENENES
	VENERABLE	VENERABLES
	VENERATE	VENERATED ▪ VENERATES
	VENERATOR	VENERATORS
	VENEREAN	VENEREANS
	VENERER	VENERERS
	VENETIAN	VENETIANS
	VENEWE	VENEWES
	VENEY	VENEYS
AVENGE	**VENGE**	VENGED ▪ VENGER ▪ VENGES
	VENGEANCE	VENGEANCES
AVENGED	**VENGED**	
AVENGEFUL	**VENGEFUL**	
AVENGEMENT	**VENGEMENT**	VENGEMENTS
AVENGER	**VENGER**	VENGERS
AVENGERS	**VENGERS**	
AVENGES	**VENGES**	
AVENGING	**VENGING**	
	VENIDIUM	VENIDIUMS
	VENIN	VENINE ▪ VENINS
	VENINE	VENINES
	VENIRE	VENIRES
	VENISON	VENISONS
	VENITE	VENITES
	VENNEL	VENNELS
	VENOGRAM	VENOGRAMS
	VENOM	VENOMS
	VENOMER	VENOMERS
EVENT	**VENT**	VENTS
	VENTAGE	VENTAGES
AVENTAIL	**VENTAIL**	VENTAILE ▪ VENTAILS
AVENTAILE	**VENTAILE**	VENTAILES
AVENTAILES	**VENTAILES**	
AVENTAILS	**VENTAILS**	
	VENTANA	VENTANAS
	VENTAYLE	VENTAYLES
EVENTED	**VENTED**	
EVENTER	**VENTER**	VENTERS
EVENTERS	**VENTERS**	
	VENTIDUCT	VENTIDUCTS
	VENTIFACT	VENTIFACTS
	VENTIGE	VENTIGES
	VENTIL	VENTILS
	VENTILATE	VENTILATED ▪ VENTILATES
EVENTING	**VENTING**	VENTINGS
EVENTINGS	**VENTINGS**	
EVENTLESS	**VENTLESS**	
	VENTOUSE	VENTOUSES
	VENTRAL	VENTRALS
AVENTRE	**VENTRE**	VENTRED ▪ VENTRES
AVENTRED	**VENTRED**	
AVENTRES	**VENTRES**	
	VENTRICLE	VENTRICLES
AVENTRING	**VENTRING**	VENTRINGS
EVENTS	**VENTS**	
AVENTURE	**VENTURE**	VENTURED ▪ VENTURER ▪ VENTURES
	VENTURER	VENTURERS
AVENTURES	**VENTURES**	
	VENTURI	VENTURIS
	VENTURING	VENTURINGS
AVENUE	**VENUE**	VENUES
AVENUES	**VENUES**	
	VENULE	VENULES

FRONT HOOK	ROOT WORD	END HOOK
	VENVILLE	VENVILLES
	VERANDA	VERANDAH · VERANDAS
	VERANDAH	VERANDAHS
	VERAPAMIL	VERAPAMILS
	VERATRIA	VERATRIAS
	VERATRIN	VERATRINE · VERATRINS
	VERATRINE	VERATRINES
	VERATRUM	VERATRUMS
	VERB	VERBS
	VERBAL	VERBALS
	VERBALISE	VERBALISED · VERBALISER · VERBALISES
	VERBALISM	VERBALISMS
	VERBALIST	VERBALISTS
	VERBALIZE	VERBALIZED · VERBALIZER · VERBALIZES
	VERBARIAN	VERBARIANS
	VERBASCUM	VERBASCUMS
	VERBENA	VERBENAS
	VERBERATE	VERBERATED · VERBERATES
	VERBIAGE	VERBIAGES
	VERBICIDE	VERBICIDES
OVERBID OVERBIDS	**VERBID**	VERBIDS
	VERBIDS	
	VERBILE	VERBILES
	VERBING	VERBINGS
	VERBOSE	VERBOSER
	VERDELHO	VERDELHOS
	VERDERER	VERDERERS
	VERDEROR	VERDERORS
	VERDET	VERDETS
	VERDICT	VERDICTS
	VERDIN	VERDINS
	VERDIT	VERDITE · VERDITS
	VERDITE	VERDITER · VERDITES
	VERDITER	VERDITERS
	VERDURE	VERDURED · VERDURES
	VERGE	VERGED · VERGER · VERGES
	VERGENCE	VERGENCES
	VERGER	VERGERS
	VERIFIER	VERIFIERS
	VERISM	VERISMO · VERISMS
	VERISMO	VERISMOS
	VERIST	VERISTS
	VERITE	VERITES
	VERJUICE	VERJUICED · VERJUICES
	VERLAN	VERLANS
	VERLIGTE	VERLIGTES
	VERMEIL	VERMEILS
	VERMEILLE	VERMEILLED · VERMEILLES
	VERMELL	VERMELLS
	VERMICIDE	VERMICIDES
	VERMICULE	VERMICULES
	VERMIFUGE	VERMIFUGES
	VERMIL	VERMILS · VERMILY
	VERMILION	VERMILIONS
	VERMIN	VERMINS · VERMINY
	VERMINATE	VERMINATED · VERMINATES
OVERMINED	**VERMINED**	
	VERMOUTH	VERMOUTHS
	VERMUTH	VERMUTHS
	VERNACLE	VERNACLES
	VERNALISE	VERNALISED · VERNALISES
	VERNALIZE	VERNALIZED · VERNALIZES
	VERNATION	VERNATIONS
	VERNICLE	VERNICLES
	VERNIER	VERNIERS
	VERONAL	VERONALS
	VERONICA	VERONICAS
	VERQUERE	VERQUERES
	VERQUIRE	VERQUIRES

FRONT HOOK	ROOT WORD	END HOOK
	VERREL	VERRELS
	VERRUCA	VERRUCAE · VERRUCAS
	VERRUGA	VERRUGAS
AVERS · OVERS	**VERS**	VERSE · VERSO · VERST
	VERSAL	VERSALS
	VERSANT	VERSANTS
AVERSE	**VERSE**	VERSED · VERSER · VERSES · VERSET
	VERSELET	VERSELETS
	VERSER	VERSERS
OVERSET	**VERSET**	VERSETS
OVERSETS	**VERSETS**	
	VERSICLE	VERSICLES
	VERSIFIER	VERSIFIERS
	VERSIN	VERSINE · VERSING · VERSINS
	VERSINE	VERSINES
	VERSING	VERSINGS
AVERSION · EVERSION	**VERSION**	VERSIONS
	VERSIONER	VERSIONERS
AVERSIONS · EVERSIONS	**VERSIONS**	
	VERSO	VERSOS
	VERST	VERSTE · VERSTS
	VERSTE	VERSTES
AVERT · EVERT · OVERT	**VERT**	VERTS · VERTU
	VERTEBRA	VERTEBRAE · VERTEBRAL · VERTEBRAS
AVERTED · EVERTED	**VERTED**	
	VERTICAL	VERTICALS
	VERTICIL	VERTICILS
	VERTIGO	VERTIGOS
AVERTING · EVERTING	**VERTING**	
	VERTIPORT	VERTIPORTS
AVERTS · EVERTS	**VERTS**	
	VERTU	VERTUE · VERTUS
	VERTUE	VERTUES
	VERVAIN	VERVAINS
	VERVE	VERVEL · VERVEN · VERVES · VERVET
	VERVEL	VERVELS
	VERVEN	VERVENS
	VERVET	VERVETS
EVERY	**VERY**	
	VESICA	VESICAE · VESICAL
	VESICANT	VESICANTS
	VESICATE	VESICATED · VESICATES
	VESICLE	VESICLES
	VESICULA	VESICULAE · VESICULAR
	VESPA	VESPAS
	VESPER	VESPERS
	VESPERAL	VESPERALS
	VESPID	VESPIDS
	VESSAIL	VESSAILS
	VESSEL	VESSELS
	VEST	VESTA · VESTS
	VESTA	VESTAL · VESTAS
	VESTAL	VESTALS
	VESTEE	VESTEES
	VESTIBULA	VESTIBULAR
	VESTIBULE	VESTIBULED · VESTIBULES
	VESTIGE	VESTIGES
	VESTIGIA	VESTIGIAL
	VESTIMENT	VESTIMENTS
	VESTING	VESTINGS
	VESTITURE	VESTITURES
	VESTMENT	VESTMENTS
	VESTURE	VESTURED · VESTURER · VESTURES
	VESTURER	VESTURERS
	VESUVIAN	VESUVIANS
EVET	**VET**	VETO · VETS
KVETCH	**VETCH**	VETCHY
KVETCHES	**VETCHES**	
KVETCHIER	**VETCHIER**	

FRONT HOOK	ROOT WORD	END HOOK
KVETCHIEST	**VETCHIEST**	
	VETCHLING	VETCHLINGS
KVETCHY	**VETCHY**	
	VETERAN	VETERANS
	VETIVER	VETIVERS ▪ VETIVERT
	VETIVERT	VETIVERTS
	VETKOEK	VETKOEKS
	VETOER	VETOERS
EVETS	**VETS**	
	VETTER	VETTERS
	VETTURA	VETTURAS
	VEX	VEXT
	VEXATION	VEXATIONS
	VEXER	VEXERS
	VEXIL	VEXILS
	VEXILLA	VEXILLAR
	VEXILLAR	VEXILLARY
	VEXING	VEXINGS
	VEZIR	VEZIRS
	VIA	VIAE ▪ VIAL ▪ VIAS
	VIADUCT	VIADUCTS
	VIAL	VIALS
	VIALFUL	VIALFULS
	VIAMETER	VIAMETERS
	VIAND	VIANDS
AVIATIC	**VIATIC**	VIATICA
	VIATICA	VIATICAL
	VIATICAL	VIATICALS
	VIATICUM	VIATICUMS
AVIATOR	**VIATOR**	VIATORS
AVIATORS	**VIATORS**	
	VIBE	VIBES ▪ VIBEX ▪ VIBEY
	VIBIST	VIBISTS
	VIBRACULA	VIBRACULAR
	VIBRAHARP	VIBRAHARPS
	VIBRANCE	VIBRANCES
	VIBRANT	VIBRANTS
	VIBRATE	VIBRATED ▪ VIBRATES
	VIBRATION	VIBRATIONS
	VIBRATO	VIBRATOR ▪ VIBRATOS
	VIBRATOR	VIBRATORS ▪ VIBRATORY
	VIBRIO	VIBRION ▪ VIBRIOS
	VIBRION	VIBRIONS
	VIBRISSA	VIBRISSAE ▪ VIBRISSAL
	VIBURNUM	VIBURNUMS
	VICAR	VICARS ▪ VICARY
	VICARAGE	VICARAGES
	VICARATE	VICARATES
	VICARIANT	VICARIANTS
	VICARIATE	VICARIATES
	VICARSHIP	VICARSHIPS
	VICE	VICED ▪ VICES
	VICEREINE	VICEREINES
	VICEROY	VICEROYS
	VICIATE	VICIATED ▪ VICIATES
	VICINAGE	VICINAGES
	VICOMTE	VICOMTES
	VICTIM	VICTIMS
	VICTIMISE	VICTIMISED ▪ VICTIMISER ▪ VICTIMISES
	VICTIMIZE	VICTIMIZED ▪ VICTIMIZER ▪ VICTIMIZES
EVICTOR	**VICTOR**	VICTORS ▪ VICTORY
	VICTORIA	VICTORIAS
	VICTORINE	VICTORINES
EVICTORS	**VICTORS**	
	VICTROLLA	VICTROLLAS
	VICTUAL	VICTUALS
	VICTUALER	VICTUALERS
	VICUGNA	VICUGNAS
	VICUNA	VICUNAS

FRONT HOOK	ROOT WORD	END HOOK
AVID	**VID**	VIDE · VIDS
	VIDAME	VIDAMES
	VIDE	VIDEO
	VIDEO	VIDEOS
	VIDEODISC	VIDEODISCS
	VIDEODISK	VIDEODISKS
	VIDEOFIT	VIDEOFITS
	VIDEOGRAM	VIDEOGRAMS
	VIDEOLAND	VIDEOLANDS
	VIDEOTAPE	VIDEOTAPED · VIDEOTAPES
	VIDEOTEX	VIDEOTEXT
	VIDEOTEXT	VIDEOTEXTS
	VIDETTE	VIDETTES
	VIDICON	VIDICONS
	VIDUAGE	VIDUAGES
	VIE	VIED · VIER · VIES · VIEW
IVIED	**VIED**	
	VIELLE	VIELLES
	VIER	VIERS
IVIES	**VIES**	
	VIEW	VIEWS · VIEWY
	VIEWDATA	VIEWDATAS
	VIEWER	VIEWERS
	VIEWING	VIEWINGS
	VIEWPHONE	VIEWPHONES
	VIEWPOINT	VIEWPOINTS
	VIFDA	VIFDAS
	VIG	VIGA · VIGS
	VIGA	VIGAS
	VIGIA	VIGIAS
	VIGIL	VIGILS
	VIGILANCE	VIGILANCES
	VIGILANT	VIGILANTE
	VIGILANTE	VIGILANTES
	VIGNERON	VIGNERONS
	VIGNETTE	VIGNETTED · VIGNETTER · VIGNETTES
	VIGNETTER	VIGNETTERS
	VIGOR	VIGORO · VIGORS
	VIGORO	VIGOROS
	VIGOROS	VIGOROSO
	VIGOUR	VIGOURS
	VIHARA	VIHARAS
	VIHUELA	VIHUELAS
	VIKING	VIKINGS
	VIKINGISM	VIKINGISMS
	VILAYET	VILAYETS
	VILD	VILDE
	VILE	VILER
EVILER	**VILER**	
EVILEST	**VILEST**	
	VILIACO	VILIACOS
	VILIAGO	VILIAGOS
	VILIFIER	VILIFIERS
	VILIPEND	VILIPENDS
	VILL	VILLA · VILLI · VILLS
	VILLA	VILLAE · VILLAN · VILLAR · VILLAS
	VILLADOM	VILLADOMS
	VILLAGE	VILLAGER · VILLAGES
	VILLAGER	VILLAGERS · VILLAGERY
	VILLAGIO	VILLAGIOS
	VILLAGREE	VILLAGREES
	VILLAIN	VILLAINS · VILLAINY
	VILLAN	VILLANS · VILLANY
	VILLANAGE	VILLANAGES
	VILLEIN	VILLEINS
	VILLENAGE	VILLENAGES
	VILLIAGO	VILLIAGOS
	VIM	VIMS
	VIMANA	VIMANAS

FRONT HOOK	ROOT WORD	END HOOK
	VIMINA	VIMINAL
	VIN	VINA = VINE = VINO = VINS = VINT = VINY
	VINA	VINAL = VINAS
	VINAL	VINALS
	VINASSE	VINASSES
	VINCA	VINCAS
EVINCIBLE	**VINCIBLE**	
EVINCIBLY	**VINCIBLY**	
	VINCULUM	VINCULUMS
	VINDALOO	VINDALOOS
	VINDICATE	VINDICATED = VINDICATES
AVINE = OVINE	**VINE**	VINED = VINER = VINES = VINEW
	VINEGAR	VINEGARS = VINEGARY
	VINER	VINERS = VINERY
OVINES	**VINES**	
	VINEW	VINEWS
	VINEYARD	VINEYARDS
	VINIFERA	VINIFERAS
	VINO	VINOS
	VINT	VINTS
	VINTAGE	VINTAGED = VINTAGER = VINTAGES
	VINTAGER	VINTAGERS
	VINTAGING	VINTAGINGS
	VINTNER	VINTNERS
	VINY	VINYL
	VINYL	VINYLS
	VIOL	VIOLA = VIOLD = VIOLS
	VIOLA	VIOLAS
	VIOLATE	VIOLATED = VIOLATER = VIOLATES
	VIOLATER	VIOLATERS
	VIOLATION	VIOLATIONS
	VIOLATOR	VIOLATORS
	VIOLENCE	VIOLENCES
	VIOLENT	VIOLENTS
	VIOLER	VIOLERS
	VIOLET	VIOLETS
	VIOLIN	VIOLINS
	VIOLINIST	VIOLINISTS
	VIOLIST	VIOLISTS
	VIOLONE	VIOLONES
	VIOMYCIN	VIOMYCINS
	VIOSTEROL	VIOSTEROLS
	VIPER	VIPERS
	VIRAEMIA	VIRAEMIAS
	VIRAGO	VIRAGOS
	VIRANDA	VIRANDAS
	VIRANDO	VIRANDOS
	VIRE	VIRED = VIREO = VIRES
	VIRELAI	VIRELAIS
	VIRELAY	VIRELAYS
	VIREMENT	VIREMENTS
	VIREMIA	VIREMIAS
	VIREO	VIREOS
	VIREONINE	VIREONINES
	VIRETOT	VIRETOTS
	VIRGA	VIRGAS
	VIRGATE	VIRGATES
	VIRGE	VIRGER = VIRGES
	VIRGER	VIRGERS
	VIRGIN	VIRGINS
	VIRGINAL	VIRGINALS
	VIRGINIA	VIRGINIAS
	VIRGINIUM	VIRGINIUMS
	VIRGULE	VIRGULES
	VIRICIDE	VIRICIDES
	VIRIDIAN	VIRIDIANS
	VIRIDITE	VIRIDITES
	VIRILISE	VIRILISED = VIRILISES
	VIRILISM	VIRILISMS

FRONT HOOK	ROOT WORD	END HOOK
	VIRILIZE	VIRILIZED · VIRILIZES
	VIRINO	VIRINOS
	VIRION	VIRIONS
	VIRL	VIRLS
	VIROGENE	VIROGENES
	VIROID	VIROIDS
	VIROSE	VIROSES
	VIRTU	VIRTUE · VIRTUS
	VIRTUE	VIRTUES
	VIRTUOSA	VIRTUOSAS
	VIRTUOSI	VIRTUOSIC
	VIRTUOSO	VIRTUOSOS
	VIRUCIDE	VIRUCIDES
	VIRULENCE	VIRULENCES
AVIRULENT	**VIRULENT**	
	VIRUSOID	VIRUSOIDS
	VIS	VISA · VISE
	VISA	VISAS
	VISAGE	VISAGED · VISAGES
	VISAGIST	VISAGISTE · VISAGISTS
	VISAGISTE	VISAGISTES
	VISARD	VISARDS
	VISCACHA	VISCACHAS
	VISCARIA	VISCARIAS
	VISCERA	VISCERAL
EVISCERATE	**VISCERATE**	VISCERATED · VISCERATES
	VISCIN	VISCINS
	VISCOSE	VISCOSES
	VISCOUNT	VISCOUNTS · VISCOUNTY
	VISCUM	VISCUMS
AVISE	**VISE**	VISED · VISES
AVISED	**VISED**	
AVISES	**VISES**	
	VISIBLE	VISIBLES
	VISIE	VISIED · VISIER · VISIES
	VISIER	VISIERS
	VISILE	VISILES
AVISING	**VISING**	
	VISION	VISIONS
	VISIONER	VISIONERS
	VISIONING	VISIONINGS
	VISIONIST	VISIONISTS
	VISIT	VISITE · VISITS
	VISITANT	VISITANTS
	VISITATOR	VISITATORS
	VISITE	VISITED · VISITEE · VISITER · VISITES
	VISITEE	VISITEES
	VISITER	VISITERS
	VISITING	VISITINGS
	VISITOR	VISITORS
	VISNE	VISNES
	VISNOMIE	VISNOMIES
	VISON	VISONS
	VISOR	VISORS
	VISTA	VISTAL · VISTAS
	VISTO	VISTOS
	VISUAL	VISUALS
	VISUALISE	VISUALISED · VISUALISER · VISUALISES
	VISUALIST	VISUALISTS
	VISUALIZE	VISUALIZED · VISUALIZER · VISUALIZES
	VITA	VITAE · VITAL · VITAS
AVITAL	**VITAL**	VITALS
	VITALISE	VITALISED · VITALISER · VITALISES
	VITALISER	VITALISERS
	VITALISM	VITALISMS
	VITALIST	VITALISTS
	VITALIZE	VITALIZED · VITALIZER · VITALIZES
	VITALIZER	VITALIZERS
	VITAMER	VITAMERS

FRONT HOOK	ROOT WORD	END HOOK
	VITAMIN	VITAMINE ▪ VITAMINS
	VITAMINE	VITAMINES
	VITASCOPE	VITASCOPES
EVITE	**VITE**	VITEX
	VITELLI	VITELLIN
	VITELLIN	VITELLINE ▪ VITELLINS
	VITELLINE	VITELLINES
	VITESSE	VITESSES
	VITIATE	VITIATED ▪ VITIATES
	VITIATION	VITIATIONS
	VITIATOR	VITIATORS
	VITICETUM	VITICETUMS
	VITICIDE	VITICIDES
	VITILIGO	VITILIGOS
	VITRAGE	VITRAGES
	VITRAIN	VITRAINS
	VITREUM	VITREUMS
	VITRIC	VITRICS
	VITRINE	VITRINES
	VITRIOL	VITRIOLS
	VITTA	VITTAE
	VITTLE	VITTLED ▪ VITTLES
	VIVA	VIVAS ▪ VIVAT
	VIVACE	VIVACES
	VIVANDIER	VIVANDIERE ▪ VIVANDIERS
	VIVARIUM	VIVARIUMS
	VIVAT	VIVATS
	VIVDA	VIVDAS
	VIVE	VIVER ▪ VIVES
	VIVER	VIVERS
	VIVERRA	VIVERRAS
	VIVERRID	VIVERRIDS
	VIVERRINE	VIVERRINES
	VIVIANITE	VIVIANITES
	VIVIFIER	VIVIFIERS
	VIVISECT	VIVISECTS
	VIXEN	VIXENS
	VIZAMENT	VIZAMENTS
	VIZARD	VIZARDS
	VIZCACHA	VIZCACHAS
	VIZIER	VIZIERS
	VIZIERATE	VIZIERATES
	VIZIR	VIZIRS
	VIZIRATE	VIZIRATES
	VIZIRSHIP	VIZIRSHIPS
	VIZOR	VIZORS
	VIZSLA	VIZSLAS
	VIZZIE	VIZZIED ▪ VIZZIES
	VLEI	VLEIS
	VOAR	VOARS
	VOCAB	VOCABS
EVOCABLE	**VOCABLE**	VOCABLES
	VOCABULAR	VOCABULARY
	VOCAL	VOCALS
	VOCALESE	VOCALESES
	VOCALIC	VOCALICS
	VOCALION	VOCALIONS
	VOCALISE	VOCALISED ▪ VOCALISER ▪ VOCALISES
	VOCALISER	VOCALISERS
	VOCALISM	VOCALISMS
	VOCALIST	VOCALISTS
	VOCALIZE	VOCALIZED ▪ VOCALIZER ▪ VOCALIZES
	VOCALIZER	VOCALIZERS
AVOCATION ▪ EVOCATION	**VOCATION**	VOCATIONS
AVOCATIONS ▪ EVOCATIONS	**VOCATIONS**	
EVOCATIVE	**VOCATIVE**	VOCATIVES
	VOCODER	VOCODERS
	VOCULE	VOCULES
	VODKA	VODKAS

FRONT HOOK	ROOT WORD	END HOOK
	VODOU	VODOUN · VODOUS
	VODOUN	VODOUNS
	VODUN	VODUNS
EVOE	**VOE**	VOES
	VOEMA	VOEMAS
	VOGIE	VOGIER
	VOGUE	VOGUED · VOGUER · VOGUES · VOGUEY
	VOGUEING	VOGUEINGS
	VOGUER	VOGUERS
	VOGUING	VOGUINGS
	VOICE	VOICED · VOICER · VOICES
	VOICEMAIL	VOICEMAILS
	VOICEOVER	VOICEOVERS
	VOICER	VOICERS
	VOICING	VOICINGS
AVOID · OVOID	**VOID**	VOIDS
AVOIDABLE	**VOIDABLE**	
AVOIDANCE	**VOIDANCE**	VOIDANCES
AVOIDANCES	**VOIDANCES**	
AVOIDED	**VOIDED**	
	VOIDEE	VOIDEES
AVOIDER	**VOIDER**	VOIDERS
AVOIDERS	**VOIDERS**	
AVOIDING	**VOIDING**	VOIDINGS
AVOIDS · OVOIDS	**VOIDS**	
	VOILE	VOILES
	VOISINAGE	VOISINAGES
	VOITURE	VOITURES
	VOITURIER	VOITURIERS
	VOIVODE	VOIVODES
	VOL	VOLA · VOLE · VOLK · VOLS · VOLT
	VOLA	VOLAE · VOLAR
	VOLANT	VOLANTE
	VOLANTE	VOLANTES
	VOLAR	VOLARY
	VOLATILE	VOLATILES
	VOLCANIC	VOLCANICS
	VOLCANISE	VOLCANISED · VOLCANISES
	VOLCANISM	VOLCANISMS
	VOLCANIST	VOLCANISTS
	VOLCANIZE	VOLCANIZED · VOLCANIZES
	VOLCANO	VOLCANOS
	VOLE	VOLED · VOLES · VOLET
	VOLET	VOLETS
	VOLITATE	VOLITATED · VOLITATES
	VOLITION	VOLITIONS
	VOLITIVE	VOLITIVES
	VOLK	VOLKS
	VOLKSRAAD	VOLKSRAADS
	VOLLEY	VOLLEYS
	VOLLEYER	VOLLEYERS
	VOLOST	VOLOSTS
	VOLPINO	VOLPINOS
	VOLPLANE	VOLPLANED · VOLPLANES
	VOLT	VOLTA · VOLTE · VOLTI · VOLTS
	VOLTAGE	VOLTAGES
	VOLTAISM	VOLTAISMS
	VOLTE	VOLTES
	VOLTIGEUR	VOLTIGEURS
	VOLTINISM	VOLTINISMS
	VOLTMETER	VOLTMETERS
	VOLUME	VOLUMED · VOLUMES
	VOLUMETER	VOLUMETERS
	VOLUMISE	VOLUMISED · VOLUMISES
	VOLUMIST	VOLUMISTS
	VOLUMIZE	VOLUMIZED · VOLUMIZES
	VOLUNTEER	VOLUNTEERS
	VOLUSPA	VOLUSPAS
EVOLUTE	**VOLUTE**	VOLUTED · VOLUTES

FRONT HOOK	ROOT WORD	END HOOK
EVOLUTED	**VOLUTED**	
EVOLUTES	**VOLUTES**	
	VOLUTIN	VOLUTINS
EVOLUTION	**VOLUTION**	VOLUTIONS
EVOLUTIONS	**VOLUTIONS**	
	VOLVA	VOLVAE · VOLVAS
EVOLVE	**VOLVE**	VOLVED · VOLVES
EVOLVED	**VOLVED**	
EVOLVES	**VOLVES**	
EVOLVING	**VOLVING**	
	VOMER	VOMERS
	VOMICA	VOMICAE · VOMICAS
	VOMIT	VOMITO · VOMITS
	VOMITER	VOMITERS
	VOMITING	VOMITINGS
	VOMITIVE	VOMITIVES
	VOMITO	VOMITOS
	VOODOO	VOODOOS
	VOODOOISM	VOODOOISMS
	VOODOOIST	VOODOOISTS
	VOORKAMER	VOORKAMERS
	VOORSKOT	VOORSKOTS
	VOR	VORS
	VORLAGE	VORLAGES
	VORTICISM	VORTICISMS
	VORTICIST	VORTICISTS
	VOTARIST	VOTARISTS
	VOTE	VOTED · VOTER · VOTES
	VOTEEN	VOTEENS
	VOTER	VOTERS
	VOTING	VOTINGS
	VOTIVE	VOTIVES
AVOUCH	**VOUCH**	
AVOUCHED	**VOUCHED**	
	VOUCHEE	VOUCHEES
AVOUCHER	**VOUCHER**	VOUCHERS
AVOUCHERS	**VOUCHERS**	
AVOUCHES	**VOUCHES**	
AVOUCHING	**VOUCHING**	
	VOUCHSAFE	VOUCHSAFED · VOUCHSAFES
	VOUDON	VOUDONS
	VOUDOU	VOUDOUN · VOUDOUS
	VOUDOUN	VOUDOUNS
	VOUGE	VOUGES
	VOULGE	VOULGES
	VOUSSOIR	VOUSSOIRS
	VOUTSAFE	VOUTSAFED · VOUTSAFES
	VOUVRAY	VOUVRAYS
AVOW	**VOW**	VOWS
AVOWED	**VOWED**	
	VOWEL	VOWELS
	VOWELISE	VOWELISED · VOWELISES
	VOWELIZE	VOWELIZED · VOWELIZES
AVOWER	**VOWER**	VOWERS
AVOWERS	**VOWERS**	
AVOWING	**VOWING**	
AVOWS	**VOWS**	
	VOXEL	VOXELS
	VOYAGE	VOYAGED · VOYAGER · VOYAGES
	VOYAGER	VOYAGERS
	VOYAGEUR	VOYAGEURS
	VOYEUR	VOYEURS
	VOYEURISM	VOYEURISMS
	VOZHD	VOZHDS
	VRAIC	VRAICS
	VRAICKER	VRAICKERS
	VRAICKING	VRAICKINGS
	VRIL	VRILS
	VROOM	VROOMS

FRONT HOOK	ROOT WORD	END HOOK
	VROU	VROUS ▪ VROUW
	VROUW	VROUWS
	VROW	VROWS
	VUG	VUGG ▪ VUGH ▪ VUGS
	VUGG	VUGGS ▪ VUGGY
	VUGH	VUGHS ▪ VUGHY
	VULCAN	VULCANS
	VULCANISE	VULCANISED ▪ VULCANISER ▪ VULCANISES
	VULCANISM	VULCANISMS
	VULCANIST	VULCANISTS
	VULCANITE	VULCANITES
	VULCANIZE	VULCANIZED ▪ VULCANIZER ▪ VULCANIZES
	VULGAR	VULGARS
	VULGARIAN	VULGARIANS
	VULGARISE	VULGARISED ▪ VULGARISER ▪ VULGARISES
	VULGARISM	VULGARISMS
	VULGARIZE	VULGARIZED ▪ VULGARIZER ▪ VULGARIZES
EVULGATE	**VULGATE**	VULGATES
EVULGATES	**VULGATES**	
	VULN	VULNS
	VULNERATE	VULNERATED ▪ VULNERATES
	VULPICIDE	VULPICIDES
	VULPINISM	VULPINISMS
	VULPINITE	VULPINITES
	VULSELLA	VULSELLAE
	VULTURE	VULTURES
	VULTURISM	VULTURISMS
	VULTURN	VULTURNS
	VULVA	VULVAE ▪ VULVAL ▪ VULVAR ▪ VULVAS
OVUM	**VUM**	VUMS
	VUVUZELA	VUVUZELAS
	VYING	VYINGS

W

FRONT HOOK	ROOT WORD	END HOOK
	WAAC	WAACS
SWAB	**WAB**	WABS (offensive)
	WABAIN	WABAINS
	WABBLE	WABBLED ▪ WABBLER ▪ WABBLES
	WABBLER	WABBLERS
	WABOOM	WABOOMS
SWABS	**WABS**	
	WABSTER	WABSTERS
SWACK	**WACK**	WACKE ▪ WACKO ▪ WACKS ▪ WACKY
	WACKE	WACKER ▪ WACKES
	WACKER	WACKERS
	WACKES	WACKEST
	WACKO	WACKOS
SWAD	**WAD**	WADD ▪ WADE ▪ WADI ▪ WADS ▪ WADT ▪ WADY
	WADD	WADDS ▪ WADDY
	WADDER	WADDERS
SWADDIE	**WADDIE**	WADDIED ▪ WADDIES
SWADDIES	**WADDIES**	
	WADDING	WADDINGS
SWADDLE ▪ TWADDLE	**WADDLE**	WADDLED ▪ WADDLER ▪ WADDLES
SWADDLED ▪ TWADDLED	**WADDLED**	
SWADDLER ▪ TWADDLER	**WADDLER**	WADDLERS
SWADDLERS ▪ TWADDLERS	**WADDLERS**	
SWADDLES ▪ TWADDLES	**WADDLES**	
TWADDLIER	**WADDLIER**	
TWADDLIEST	**WADDLIEST**	
SWADDLING ▪ TWADDLING	**WADDLING**	
TWADDLY	**WADDLY**	
SWADDY	**WADDY**	
	WADE	WADED ▪ WADER ▪ WADES
	WADER	WADERS
	WADI	WADIS
	WADING	WADINGS
	WADMAAL	WADMAALS
	WADMAL	WADMALS
	WADMEL	WADMELS
	WADMOL	WADMOLL ▪ WADMOLS
	WADMOLL	WADMOLLS
SWADS	**WADS**	
	WADSET	WADSETS ▪ WADSETT
	WADSETT	WADSETTS
	WADSETTER	WADSETTERS
	WADT	WADTS
TWAE	**WAE**	WAES
TWAES	**WAES**	
	WAESUCK	WAESUCKS
	WAFER	WAFERS ▪ WAFERY
	WAFF	WAFFS
	WAFFIE	WAFFIES
	WAFFLE	WAFFLED ▪ WAFFLER ▪ WAFFLES
	WAFFLER	WAFFLERS
	WAFFLING	WAFFLINGS
	WAFT	WAFTS
	WAFTAGE	WAFTAGES
	WAFTER	WAFTERS
	WAFTING	WAFTINGS
	WAFTURE	WAFTURES
SWAG	**WAG**	WAGE ▪ WAGS
SWAGE	**WAGE**	WAGED ▪ WAGER ▪ WAGES
SWAGED	**WAGED**	
	WAGENBOOM	WAGENBOOMS
SWAGER	**WAGER**	WAGERS
	WAGERER	WAGERERS
SWAGERS	**WAGERS**	
SWAGES	**WAGES**	
	WAGGA	WAGGAS

FRONT HOOK	ROOT WORD	END HOOK
SWAGGED	**WAGGED**	
SWAGGER	**WAGGER**	WAGGERS · WAGGERY
SWAGGERS	**WAGGERS**	
SWAGGING	**WAGGING**	
	WAGGLE	WAGGLED · WAGGLER · WAGGLES
	WAGGLER	WAGGLERS
	WAGGON	WAGGONS
	WAGGONER	WAGGONERS
	WAGHALTER	WAGHALTERS
SWAGING	**WAGING**	
	WAGMOIRE	WAGMOIRES
	WAGON	WAGONS
	WAGONAGE	WAGONAGES
	WAGONER	WAGONERS
	WAGONETTE	WAGONETTES
	WAGONFUL	WAGONFULS
	WAGONLOAD	WAGONLOADS
SWAGS	**WAGS**	
	WAGTAIL	WAGTAILS
	WAHCONDA	WAHCONDAS
	WAHINE	WAHINES
	WAHOO	WAHOOS
	WAI	WAID · WAIF · WAIL · WAIN · WAIR WAIS · WAIT
	WAIATA	WAIATAS
	WAID	WAIDE
	WAIF	WAIFS · WAIFT
	WAIFT	WAIFTS
SWAIL	**WAIL**	WAILS
	WAILER	WAILERS
	WAILING	WAILINGS
SWAILS	**WAILS**	
SWAIN · TWAIN	**WAIN**	WAINS
	WAINAGE	WAINAGES
SWAINING	**WAINING**	
SWAINS · TWAINS	**WAINS**	
	WAINSCOT	WAINSCOTS
	WAIR	WAIRS
	WAIRS	WAIRSH
	WAIRUA	WAIRUAS
	WAIS	WAIST
	WAIST	WAISTS
	WAISTBAND	WAISTBANDS
	WAISTBELT	WAISTBELTS
	WAISTCOAT	WAISTCOATS
	WAISTER	WAISTERS
	WAISTING	WAISTINGS
	WAISTLINE	WAISTLINES
AWAIT	**WAIT**	WAITE · WAITS
TWAITE	**WAITE**	WAITED · WAITER · WAITES
AWAITED	**WAITED**	
AWAITER	**WAITER**	WAITERS
	WAITERAGE	WAITERAGES
	WAITERING	WAITERINGS
AWAITERS	**WAITERS**	
TWAITES	**WAITES**	
AWAITING	**WAITING**	WAITINGS
	WAITLIST	WAITLISTS
	WAITRON	WAITRONS
AWAITS	**WAITS**	
	WAITSTAFF	WAITSTAFFS
	WAIVE	WAIVED · WAIVER · WAIVES
	WAIVER	WAIVERS
	WAIVODE	WAIVODES
	WAIWODE	WAIWODES
	WAKA	WAKAS
	WAKAME	WAKAMES
	WAKANDA	WAKANDAS
	WAKANE	WAKANES

FRONT HOOK	ROOT WORD	END HOOK
AWAKE	**WAKE**	WAKED ▪ WAKEN ▪ WAKER ▪ WAKES
	WAKEBOARD	WAKEBOARDS
AWAKED	**WAKED**	
AWAKEN	**WAKEN**	WAKENS
AWAKENED	**WAKENED**	
AWAKENER	**WAKENER**	WAKENERS
AWAKENERS	**WAKENERS**	
AWAKENING	**WAKENING**	WAKENINGS
AWAKENINGS	**WAKENINGS**	
AWAKENS	**WAKENS**	
	WAKER	WAKERS
AWAKES	**WAKES**	
	WAKF	WAKFS
	WAKIKI	WAKIKIS
AWAKING	**WAKING**	WAKINGS
AWAKINGS	**WAKINGS**	
	WALD	WALDO ▪ WALDS
	WALDFLUTE	WALDFLUTES
	WALDGRAVE	WALDGRAVES
	WALDHORN	WALDHORNS
	WALDO	WALDOS
	WALDRAPP	WALDRAPPS
DWALE ▪ SWALE	**WALE**	WALED ▪ WALER ▪ WALES
SWALED	**WALED**	
	WALER	WALERS
DWALES ▪ SWALES	**WALES**	
	WALI	WALIS
SWALIER	**WALIER**	
	WALIES	WALIEST
SWALIEST	**WALIEST**	
SWALING	**WALING**	
	WALIS	WALISE
	WALISE	WALISES
	WALK	WALKS
	WALKABOUT	WALKABOUTS
	WALKATHON	WALKATHONS
	WALKAWAY	WALKAWAYS
	WALKER	WALKERS
	WALKING	WALKINGS
	WALKMILL	WALKMILLS
	WALKOUT	WALKOUTS
	WALKOVER	WALKOVERS
	WALKUP	WALKUPS
	WALKWAY	WALKWAYS
	WALKYRIE	WALKYRIES
	WALL	WALLA ▪ WALLS ▪ WALLY
	WALLA	WALLAH ▪ WALLAS
	WALLABA	WALLABAS
	WALLAH	WALLAHS
	WALLAROO	WALLAROOS
	WALLBOARD	WALLBOARDS
	WALLCHART	WALLCHARTS
	WALLER	WALLERS
SWALLET	**WALLET**	WALLETS
SWALLETS	**WALLETS**	
	WALLEYE	WALLEYED ▪ WALLEYES
	WALLIE	WALLIER ▪ WALLIES
	WALLIES	WALLIEST
	WALLING	WALLINGS
	WALLOP	WALLOPS
	WALLOPER	WALLOPERS
	WALLOPING	WALLOPINGS
SWALLOW	**WALLOW**	WALLOWS
SWALLOWED	**WALLOWED**	
SWALLOWER	**WALLOWER**	WALLOWERS
SWALLOWERS	**WALLOWERS**	
SWALLOWING	**WALLOWING**	WALLOWINGS
SWALLOWS	**WALLOWS**	
	WALLPAPER	WALLPAPERS

FRONT HOOK	ROOT WORD	END HOOK
	WALLSEND	WALLSENDS
	WALLWORT	WALLWORTS
	WALLYBALL	WALLYBALLS
	WALLYDRAG	WALLYDRAGS
	WALNUT	WALNUTS
	WALTZER	WALTZERS
	WALTZING	WALTZINGS
SWALY	**WALY**	
	WAMBENGER	WAMBENGERS
	WAMBLE	WAMBLED ▪ WAMBLES
	WAMBLING	WAMBLINGS
	WAME	WAMED ▪ WAMES
	WAMEFOU	WAMEFOUS
	WAMEFUL	WAMEFULS
	WAMMUL	WAMMULS
	WAMPEE	WAMPEES
SWAMPISH	**WAMPISH**	
	WAMPUM	WAMPUMS
HWAN ▪ SWAN	**WAN**	WAND ▪ WANE ▪ WANG ▪ WANK ▪ WANS WANT ▪ WANY
	WAND	WANDS
	WANDER	WANDERS
	WANDERER	WANDERERS
	WANDERING	WANDERINGS
	WANDEROO	WANDEROOS
	WANDOO	WANDOOS
	WANE	WANED ▪ WANES ▪ WANEY
DWANG ▪ SWANG ▪ TWANG	**WANG**	WANGS
	WANGAN	WANGANS
TWANGLE	**WANGLE**	WANGLED ▪ WANGLER ▪ WANGLES
TWANGLED	**WANGLED**	
TWANGLER	**WANGLER**	WANGLERS
TWANGLERS	**WANGLERS**	
TWANGLES	**WANGLES**	
TWANGLING	**WANGLING**	WANGLINGS
TWANGLINGS	**WANGLINGS**	
DWANGS ▪ TWANGS	**WANGS**	
	WANGUN	WANGUNS
	WANHOPE	WANHOPES
	WANIGAN	WANIGANS
	WANING	WANINGS
	WANION	WANIONS
SWANK ▪ TWANK	**WANK**	WANKS (offensive) ▪ WANKY
SWANKED	**WANKED**	
SWANKER	**WANKER**	WANKERS (offensive)
SWANKERS	**WANKERS**	
SWANKIER	**WANKIER**	
SWANKIEST	**WANKIEST**	
SWANKING	**WANKING**	
SWANKS ▪ TWANKS	**WANKS**	
	WANKSTA	WANKSTAS (offensive)
SWANKY ▪ TWANKY	**WANKY**	
	WANNABE	WANNABEE ▪ WANNABES
	WANNABEE	WANNABEES
SWANNED	**WANNED**	
	WANNIGAN	WANNIGANS
SWANNING	**WANNING**	
SWANS	**WANS**	
	WANT	WANTS ▪ WANTY
	WANTAGE	WANTAGES
	WANTER	WANTERS
	WANTHILL	WANTHILLS
AWANTING	**WANTING**	WANTINGS
	WANTON	WANTONS
	WANTONER	WANTONERS
	WANTONISE	WANTONISED ▪ WANTONISES
	WANTONIZE	WANTONIZED ▪ WANTONIZES
	WANWORTH	WANWORTHS
	WANZE	WANZED ▪ WANZES

FRONT HOOK	ROOT WORD	END HOOK
SWAP	WAP	WAPS
	WAPENSHAW	WAPENSHAWS
	WAPENTAKE	WAPENTAKES
	WAPINSHAW	WAPINSHAWS
	WAPITI	WAPITIS
SWAPPED	WAPPED	
SWAPPER	WAPPER	WAPPERS
SWAPPERS	WAPPERS	
SWAPPING	WAPPING	
SWAPS	WAPS	
	WAQF	WAQFS
	WAR	WARB ▪ WARD ▪ WARE ▪ WARK ▪ WARM
		WARN ▪ WARP ▪ WARS ▪ WART ▪ WARY
	WARAGI	WARAGIS
	WARATAH	WARATAHS
	WARB	WARBS ▪ WARBY
	WARBLE	WARBLED ▪ WARBLER ▪ WARBLES
	WARBLER	WARBLERS
	WARBLING	WARBLINGS
	WARBONNET	WARBONNETS
	WARCRAFT	WARCRAFTS
AWARD ▪ SWARD	WARD	WARDS
	WARDCORN	WARDCORNS
AWARDED ▪ SWARDED	WARDED	
	WARDEN	WARDENS
AWARDER	WARDER	WARDERS
AWARDERS	WARDERS	
AWARDING ▪ SWARDING	WARDING	WARDINGS
	WARDMOTE	WARDMOTES
	WARDOG	WARDOGS
	WARDROBE	WARDROBED ▪ WARDROBER ▪ WARDROBES
	WARDROBER	WARDROBERS
	WARDROOM	WARDROOMS
	WARDROP	WARDROPS
AWARDS ▪ SWARDS	WARDS	
	WARDSHIP	WARDSHIPS
AWARE ▪ SWARE	WARE	WARED ▪ WARES ▪ WAREZ
	WAREHOUSE	WAREHOUSED ▪ WAREHOUSER ▪ WAREHOUSES
	WAREROOM	WAREROOMS
	WARFARE	WARFARED ▪ WARFARER ▪ WARFARES
	WARFARER	WARFARERS
	WARFARIN	WARFARING ▪ WARFARINS
	WARFARING	WARFARINGS
	WARHEAD	WARHEADS
	WARHORSE	WARHORSES
	WARIBASHI	WARIBASHIS
	WARIMENT	WARIMENTS
	WARISON	WARISONS
	WARK	WARKS
	WARLING	WARLINGS
	WARLOCK	WARLOCKS
	WARLORD	WARLORDS
SWARM	WARM	WARMS
	WARMAKER	WARMAKERS
	WARMBLOOD	WARMBLOODS
SWARMED	WARMED	
SWARMER	WARMER	WARMERS
SWARMERS	WARMERS	
SWARMING	WARMING	WARMINGS
SWARMINGS	WARMINGS	
	WARMONGER	WARMONGERS
	WARMOUTH	WARMOUTHS
SWARMS	WARMS	
	WARMTH	WARMTHS
	WARMUP	WARMUPS
AWARN	WARN	WARNS
AWARNED	WARNED	
	WARNER	WARNERS
AWARNING	WARNING	WARNINGS

FRONT HOOK	ROOT WORD	END HOOK
AWARNS	**WARNS**	
	WARP	WARPS
	WARPAGE	WARPAGES
	WARPATH	WARPATHS
	WARPER	WARPERS
	WARPING	WARPINGS
	WARPLANE	WARPLANES
	WARPOWER	WARPOWERS
	WARRAGAL	WARRAGALS
	WARRAGLE	WARRAGLES
	WARRAGUL	WARRAGULS
	WARRAN	WARRAND ▪ WARRANS ▪ WARRANT
	WARRAND	WARRANDS
	WARRANT	WARRANTS ▪ WARRANTY
	WARRANTEE	WARRANTEES
	WARRANTER	WARRANTERS
	WARRANTOR	WARRANTORS
	WARRAY	WARRAYS
	WARRE	WARRED ▪ WARREN ▪ WARREY
	WARREN	WARRENS
	WARRENER	WARRENERS
	WARREY	WARREYS
	WARRIGAL	WARRIGALS
	WARRIOR	WARRIORS
	WARRISON	WARRISONS
	WARS	WARST
	WARSAW	WARSAWS
	WARSHIP	WARSHIPS
	WARSLE	WARSLED ▪ WARSLER ▪ WARSLES
	WARSLER	WARSLERS
	WARSTLE	WARSTLED ▪ WARSTLER ▪ WARSTLES
	WARSTLER	WARSTLERS
SWART	**WART**	WARTS ▪ WARTY
	WARTHOG	WARTHOGS
	WARTIME	WARTIMES
	WARTWEED	WARTWEEDS
	WARTWORT	WARTWORTS
SWARTY	**WARTY**	
	WARWORK	WARWORKS
	WARZONE	WARZONES
TWAS	**WAS**	WASE ▪ WASH ▪ WASM ▪ WASP ▪ WAST
	WASABI	WASABIS
	WASE	WASES
AWASH ▪ SWASH	**WASH**	WASHY
	WASHABLE	WASHABLES
	WASHAWAY	WASHAWAYS
	WASHBALL	WASHBALLS
	WASHBASIN	WASHBASINS
	WASHBOARD	WASHBOARDS
	WASHBOWL	WASHBOWLS
	WASHCLOTH	WASHCLOTHS
	WASHDAY	WASHDAYS
SWASHED	**WASHED**	
SWASHER	**WASHER**	WASHERS ▪ WASHERY
SWASHERS	**WASHERS**	
SWASHES	**WASHES**	
	WASHHOUSE	WASHHOUSES
SWASHIER	**WASHIER**	
SWASHIEST	**WASHIEST**	
	WASHIN	WASHING ▪ WASHINS
SWASHING	**WASHING**	WASHINGS
SWASHINGS	**WASHINGS**	
	WASHLAND	WASHLANDS
	WASHOUT	WASHOUTS
	WASHPOT	WASHPOTS
	WASHRAG	WASHRAGS
	WASHROOM	WASHROOMS
	WASHSTAND	WASHSTANDS
	WASHTUB	WASHTUBS

FRONT HOOK	ROOT WORD	END HOOK
	WASHUP	WASHUPS
	WASHWIPE	WASHWIPES
SWASHY	**WASHY**	
	WASM	WASMS
	WASP	WASPS = WASPY
	WASPIE	WASPIER = WASPIES
	WASPIES	WASPIEST
	WASPNEST	WASPNESTS
	WASSAIL	WASSAILS
	WASSAILER	WASSAILERS
	WAST	WASTE = WASTS
	WASTAGE	WASTAGES
	WASTE	WASTED = WASTEL = WASTER = WASTES
	WASTEL	WASTELS
	WASTELAND	WASTELANDS
	WASTELOT	WASTELOTS
	WASTER	WASTERS = WASTERY
	WASTERIE	WASTERIES
	WASTEWAY	WASTEWAYS
	WASTEWEIR	WASTEWEIRS
	WASTING	WASTINGS
	WASTREL	WASTRELS
	WASTRIE	WASTRIES
	WASTRIFE	WASTRIFES
SWAT = TWAT	**WAT**	WATE = WATS = WATT
	WATAP	WATAPE = WATAPS
	WATAPE	WATAPES
AWATCH = SWATCH	**WATCH**	
	WATCHABLE	WATCHABLES
	WATCHBAND	WATCHBANDS
	WATCHCASE	WATCHCASES
	WATCHDOG	WATCHDOGS
	WATCHER	WATCHERS
SWATCHES	**WATCHES**	
	WATCHET	WATCHETS
	WATCHEYE	WATCHEYES
	WATCHLIST	WATCHLISTS
	WATCHOUT	WATCHOUTS
	WATCHWORD	WATCHWORDS
	WATE	WATER
	WATER	WATERS = WATERY
	WATERAGE	WATERAGES
	WATERBED	WATERBEDS
	WATERBIRD	WATERBIRDS
	WATERBUCK	WATERBUCKS
	WATERDOG	WATERDOGS
	WATERER	WATERERS
	WATERFALL	WATERFALLS
	WATERFOWL	WATERFOWLS
	WATERHEAD	WATERHEADS
	WATERHEN	WATERHENS
	WATERING	WATERINGS
	WATERJET	WATERJETS
	WATERLEAF	WATERLEAFS
	WATERLINE	WATERLINES
	WATERLOG	WATERLOGS
	WATERLOO	WATERLOOS
	WATERMARK	WATERMARKS
	WATERSHED	WATERSHEDS
	WATERSIDE	WATERSIDER = WATERSIDES
	WATERSKI	WATERSKIS
	WATERWAY	WATERWAYS
	WATERWEED	WATERWEEDS
	WATERWORK	WATERWORKS
	WATERZOOI	WATERZOOIS
SWATS = TWATS (offensive)	**WATS**	
	WATT	WATTS
	WATTAGE	WATTAGES
	WATTAPE	WATTAPES

FRONT HOOK	ROOT WORD	END HOOK
SWATTER	WATTER	
	WATTHOUR	WATTHOURS
TWATTLE	WATTLE	WATTLED · WATTLES
TWATTLED	WATTLED	
TWATTLES	WATTLES	WATTLESS
TWATTLING	WATTLING	WATTLINGS
TWATTLINGS	WATTLINGS	
	WATTMETER	WATTMETERS
	WAUCHT	WAUCHTS
	WAUFF	WAUFFS
	WAUGH	WAUGHS · WAUGHT
	WAUGHT	WAUGHTS
	WAUK	WAUKS
	WAUKER	WAUKERS
	WAUKMILL	WAUKMILLS
	WAUL	WAULK · WAULS
	WAULING	WAULINGS
	WAULK	WAULKS
	WAULKER	WAULKERS
	WAULKMILL	WAULKMILLS
	WAUR	WAURS
	WAURS	WAURST
AWAVE	WAVE	WAVED · WAVER · WAVES · WAVEY
	WAVEBAND	WAVEBANDS
	WAVEFORM	WAVEFORMS
	WAVEFRONT	WAVEFRONTS
	WAVEGUIDE	WAVEGUIDES
	WAVELET	WAVELETS
	WAVELLITE	WAVELLITES
	WAVEMETER	WAVEMETERS
	WAVEOFF	WAVEOFFS
	WAVER	WAVERS · WAVERY
	WAVERER	WAVERERS
	WAVERING	WAVERINGS
	WAVESHAPE	WAVESHAPES
	WAVESON	WAVESONS
	WAVEY	WAVEYS
	WAVICLE	WAVICLES
	WAVIES	WAVIEST
	WAVING	WAVINGS
	WAW	WAWA · WAWE · WAWL · WAWS
	WAWA	WAWAS
	WAWE	WAWES
	WAWL	WAWLS
	WAWLING	WAWLINGS
	WAX	WAXY
	WAXBILL	WAXBILLS
	WAXCLOTH	WAXCLOTHS
	WAXER	WAXERS
	WAXEYE	WAXEYES
	WAXFLOWER	WAXFLOWERS
	WAXING	WAXINGS
	WAXPLANT	WAXPLANTS
	WAXWEED	WAXWEEDS
	WAXWING	WAXWINGS
	WAXWORK	WAXWORKS
	WAXWORKER	WAXWORKERS
	WAXWORM	WAXWORMS
AWAY · SWAY · TWAY	WAY	WAYS
	WAYBILL	WAYBILLS
	WAYBOARD	WAYBOARDS
	WAYBREAD	WAYBREADS
SWAYED	WAYED	
	WAYFARE	WAYFARED · WAYFARER · WAYFARES
	WAYFARER	WAYFARERS
	WAYFARING	WAYFARINGS
	WAYGOING	WAYGOINGS
	WAYGOOSE	WAYGOOSES
SWAYING	WAYING	

FRONT HOOK	ROOT WORD	END HOOK
	WAYLAY	WAYLAYS
	WAYLAYER	WAYLAYERS
	WAYLEAVE	WAYLEAVES
	WAYMARK	WAYMARKS
	WAYMENT	WAYMENTS
	WAYPOINT	WAYPOINTS
	WAYPOST	WAYPOSTS
AWAYS · SWAYS · TWAYS	WAYS	
	WAYSIDE	WAYSIDES
	WAYWISER	WAYWISERS
	WAYWODE	WAYWODES
	WAYZGOOSE	WAYZGOOSES
	WAZIR	WAZIRS
	WAZOO	WAZOOS (offensive)
	WAZZOCK	WAZZOCKS
AWE · EWE · OWE	WE	WEB · WED · WEE · WEM · WEN · WET · WEX · WEY
TWEAK	WEAK	
	WEAKEN	WEAKENS
	WEAKENER	WEAKENERS
TWEAKER	WEAKER	
	WEAKLING	WEAKLINGS
	WEAKON	WEAKONS
	WEAKSIDE	WEAKSIDES
SWEAL	WEAL	WEALD · WEALS
	WEALD	WEALDS
SWEALS	WEALS	
	WEALTH	WEALTHS · WEALTHY
	WEAMB	WEAMBS
	WEAN	WEANS
	WEANEL	WEANELS
	WEANER	WEANERS
	WEANING	WEANINGS
	WEANLING	WEANLINGS
	WEAPON	WEAPONS
	WEAPONEER	WEAPONEERS
	WEAPONISE	WEAPONISED · WEAPONISES
	WEAPONIZE	WEAPONIZED · WEAPONIZES
SWEAR	WEAR	WEARS · WEARY
	WEARABLE	WEARABLES
SWEARER	WEARER	WEARERS
SWEARERS	WEARERS	
AWEARIED	WEARIED	
	WEARIES	WEARIEST
SWEARING	WEARING	WEARINGS
SWEARINGS	WEARINGS	
SWEARS	WEARS	
AWEARY	WEARY	
	WEASAND	WEASANDS
	WEASEL	WEASELS · WEASELY
	WEASELER	WEASELERS
	WEASELLER	WEASELLERS
	WEASON	WEASONS
AWEATHER	WEATHER	WEATHERS
	WEATHERER	WEATHERERS
	WEAVE	WEAVED · WEAVER · WEAVES
	WEAVER	WEAVERS
	WEAVING	WEAVINGS
	WEAZAND	WEAZANDS
	WEAZEN	WEAZENS
	WEB	WEBS
	WEBBIE	WEBBIER · WEBBIES
	WEBBIES	WEBBIEST
	WEBBING	WEBBINGS
	WEBCAM	WEBCAMS
	WEBCAST	WEBCASTS
	WEBCASTER	WEBCASTERS
	WEBER	WEBERS
	WEBINAR	WEBINARS

FRONT HOOK	ROOT WORD	END HOOK
	WEBLOG	WEBLOGS
	WEBLOGGER	WEBLOGGERS
	WEBMAIL	WEBMAILS
	WEBMASTER	WEBMASTERS
	WEBPAGE	WEBPAGES
	WEBSITE	WEBSITES
	WEBSTER	WEBSTERS
	WEBWHEEL	WEBWHEELS
	WEBWORK	WEBWORKS
	WEBWORM	WEBWORMS
	WECHT	WECHTS
AWED ▪ OWED	WED	WEDS
	WEDDER	WEDDERS
	WEDDING	WEDDINGS
	WEDEL	WEDELN ▪ WEDELS
	WEDELN	WEDELNS
	WEDGE	WEDGED ▪ WEDGES
	WEDGIE	WEDGIER ▪ WEDGIES
	WEDGIES	WEDGIEST
	WEDGING	WEDGINGS
	WEDLOCK	WEDLOCKS
AWEE ▪ SWEE ▪ TWEE	WEE	WEED ▪ WEEK ▪ WEEL ▪ WEEM ▪ WEEN
		WEEP ▪ WEER ▪ WEES ▪ WEET
SWEED ▪ TWEED	WEED	WEEDS ▪ WEEDY
	WEEDER	WEEDERS ▪ WEEDERY
	WEEDICIDE	WEEDICIDES
TWEEDIER	WEEDIER	
TWEEDIEST	WEEDIEST	
TWEEDINESS	WEEDINESS	
	WEEDING	WEEDINGS
TWEEDS	WEEDS	
TWEEDY	WEEDY	
SWEEING	WEEING	
	WEEK	WEEKE ▪ WEEKS
	WEEKDAY	WEEKDAYS
	WEEKE	WEEKES
	WEEKEND	WEEKENDS
	WEEKENDER	WEEKENDERS
	WEEKNIGHT	WEEKNIGHTS
AWEEL ▪ SWEEL ▪ TWEEL	WEEL	WEELS
SWEELS ▪ TWEELS	WEELS	
	WEEM	WEEMS
TWEEN	WEEN	WEENS ▪ WEENY
TWEENIE	WEENIE	WEENIER ▪ WEENIES
SWEENIES ▪ TWEENIES	WEENIES	WEENIEST
TWEENS	WEENS	WEENSY
SWEENY ▪ TWEENY	WEENY	
SWEEP	WEEP	WEEPS ▪ WEEPY
SWEEPER	WEEPER	WEEPERS
SWEEPERS	WEEPERS	
	WEEPHOLE	WEEPHOLES
	WEEPIE	WEEPIER ▪ WEEPIES
SWEEPIER	WEEPIER	
	WEEPIES	WEEPIEST
SWEEPIEST	WEEPIEST	
SWEEPING	WEEPING	WEEPINGS
SWEEPINGLY	WEEPINGLY	
SWEEPINGS	WEEPINGS	
SWEEPS	WEEPS	
SWEEPY	WEEPY	
SWEER ▪ TWEER	WEER	
SWEES	WEES	WEEST
TWEEST	WEEST	
SWEET ▪ TWEET	WEET	WEETE ▪ WEETS
	WEETE	WEETED ▪ WEETEN ▪ WEETER
SWEETED ▪ TWEETED	WEETED	
SWEETEN	WEETEN	
SWEETER ▪ TWEETER	WEETER	
SWEETEST	WEETEST	

FRONT HOOK	ROOT WORD	END HOOK
SWEETING · TWEETING	**WEETING**	
SWEETS · TWEETS	**WEETS**	
	WEEVER	WEEVERS
	WEEVIL	WEEVILS · WEEVILY
	WEEWEE	WEEWEED · WEEWEES
	WEFT	WEFTE · WEFTS
	WEFTAGE	WEFTAGES
	WEFTE	WEFTED · WEFTES
	WEID	WEIDS
	WEIGELA	WEIGELAS
	WEIGELIA	WEIGELIAS
AWEIGH	**WEIGH**	WEIGHS · WEIGHT
	WEIGHAGE	WEIGHAGES
	WEIGHER	WEIGHERS
	WEIGHING	WEIGHINGS
	WEIGHT	WEIGHTS · WEIGHTY
	WEIGHTER	WEIGHTERS
	WEIGHTING	WEIGHTINGS
	WEIL	WEILS
	WEINER	WEINERS
SWEIR	**WEIR**	WEIRD · WEIRS
	WEIRD	WEIRDO · WEIRDS · WEIRDY
	WEIRDIE	WEIRDIES
	WEIRDO	WEIRDOS
SWEIRED	**WEIRED**	
SWEIRING	**WEIRING**	
SWEIRS	**WEIRS**	
	WEISE	WEISED · WEISES
	WEIZE	WEIZED · WEIZES
	WEKA	WEKAS
	WELCHER	WELCHERS
	WELCOME	WELCOMED · WELCOMER · WELCOMES
	WELCOMER	WELCOMERS
	WELD	WELDS
	WELDER	WELDERS
	WELDING	WELDINGS
	WELDMENT	WELDMENTS
	WELDOR	WELDORS
	WELFARE	WELFARES
	WELFARISM	WELFARISMS
	WELFARIST	WELFARISTS
	WELK	WELKE · WELKS · WELKT
	WELKE	WELKED · WELKES
	WELKIN	WELKING · WELKINS
DWELL · SWELL	**WELL**	WELLS · WELLY
	WELLADAY	WELLADAYS
	WELLAWAY	WELLAWAYS
	WELLBEING	WELLBEINGS
	WELLCURB	WELLCURBS
	WELLDOER	WELLDOERS
DWELLED · SWELLED	**WELLED**	
SWELLHEAD	**WELLHEAD**	WELLHEADS
SWELLHEADS	**WELLHEADS**	
	WELLHOLE	WELLHOLES
	WELLHOUSE	WELLHOUSES
	WELLIE	WELLIES
DWELLING · SWELLING	**WELLING**	WELLINGS
DWELLINGS · SWELLINGS	**WELLINGS**	
DWELLS · SWELLS	**WELLS**	
	WELLSITE	WELLSITES
	WELSHER	WELSHERS
DWELT · SWELT	**WELT**	WELTS
SWELTED	**WELTED**	
SWELTER	**WELTER**	WELTERS
SWELTERED	**WELTERED**	
SWELTERING	**WELTERING**	
SWELTERS	**WELTERS**	
SWELTING	**WELTING**	WELTINGS
SWELTS	**WELTS**	

FRONT HOOK	ROOT WORD	END HOOK
	WEM	WEMB · WEMS
	WEMB	WEMBS
	WEN	WENA · WEND · WENS · WENT
	WENCHER	WENCHERS
	WEND	WENDS
	WENDIGO	WENDIGOS
	WENGE	WENGES
	WENT	WENTS
SWEPT	**WEPT**	
	WEREGILD	WEREGILDS
	WERGELD	WERGELDS
	WERGELT	WERGELTS
	WERGILD	WERGILDS
	WERNERITE	WERNERITES
	WERO	WEROS
	WESAND	WESANDS
	WESKIT	WESKITS
	WESSAND	WESSANDS
EWEST	**WEST**	WESTS
	WESTER	WESTERN · WESTERS
	WESTERING	WESTERINGS
	WESTERN	WESTERNS
	WESTERNER	WESTERNERS
	WESTIE	WESTIES *(offensive)*
	WESTING	WESTINGS
	WESTLIN	WESTLINS
	WESTWARD	WESTWARDS
	WET	WETA · WETS
	WETA	WETAS
	WETBACK	WETBACKS *(offensive)*
	WETHER	WETHERS
	WETLAND	WETLANDS
	WETSUIT	WETSUITS
	WETTER	WETTERS
	WETTIE	WETTIES
	WETTING	WETTINGS
	WETWARE	WETWARES
	WEX	WEXE
	WEXE	WEXED · WEXES
SWEY	**WEY**	WEYS
SWEYS	**WEYS**	
	WEZAND	WEZANDS
	WHA	WHAE · WHAM · WHAP · WHAT
	WHACK	WHACKO · WHACKS · WHACKY
	WHACKER	WHACKERS
	WHACKING	WHACKINGS
	WHACKO	WHACKOS
	WHAISLE	WHAISLED · WHAISLES
	WHAIZLE	WHAIZLED · WHAIZLES
	WHAKAIRO	WHAKAIROS
	WHAKAPAPA	WHAKAPAPAS
	WHALE	WHALED · WHALER · WHALES
	WHALEBACK	WHALEBACKS
	WHALEBOAT	WHALEBOATS
	WHALEBONE	WHALEBONES
	WHALER	WHALERS · WHALERY
	WHALING	WHALINGS
	WHAM	WHAMO · WHAMS
	WHAMMO	WHAMMOS
	WHAMPLE	WHAMPLES
	WHANAU	WHANAUS
	WHANG	WHANGS
	WHANGAM	WHANGAMS
	WHANGEE	WHANGEES
	WHAP	WHAPS
	WHAPPER	WHAPPERS
	WHARE	WHARES
	WHARENUI	WHARENUIS
	WHAREPUNI	WHAREPUNIS

FRONT HOOK	ROOT WORD	END HOOK
	WHARF	WHARFS
	WHARFAGE	WHARFAGES
	WHARFIE	WHARFIES
	WHARFING	WHARFINGS
	WHARVE	WHARVES
	WHAT	WHATA • WHATS
	WHATA	WHATAS
	WHATNOT	WHATNOTS
	WHATS	WHATSO
	WHATSIT	WHATSITS
	WHAUP	WHAUPS
	WHAUR	WHAURS
	WHEAL	WHEALS
	WHEAR	WHEARE
	WHEAT	WHEATS • WHEATY
	WHEATEAR	WHEATEARS
	WHEATEN	WHEATENS
	WHEATLAND	WHEATLANDS
	WHEATMEAL	WHEATMEALS
	WHEATWORM	WHEATWORMS
	WHEE	WHEEL • WHEEN • WHEEP
	WHEECH	WHEECHS
	WHEEDLE	WHEEDLED • WHEEDLER • WHEEDLES
	WHEEDLER	WHEEDLERS
	WHEEDLING	WHEEDLINGS
AWHEEL	WHEEL	WHEELS • WHEELY
	WHEELBASE	WHEELBASES
	WHEELER	WHEELERS
	WHEELIE	WHEELIER • WHEELIES
	WHEELIES	WHEELIEST
	WHEELING	WHEELINGS
AWHEELS	WHEELS	
	WHEELWORK	WHEELWORKS
	WHEEN	WHEENS
	WHEENGE	WHEENGED • WHEENGES
	WHEEP	WHEEPS
	WHEEPLE	WHEEPLED • WHEEPLES
	WHEESH	WHEESHT
	WHEESHT	WHEESHTS
	WHEEZE	WHEEZED • WHEEZER • WHEEZES
	WHEEZER	WHEEZERS
	WHEEZING	WHEEZINGS
	WHEEZLE	WHEEZLED • WHEEZLES
	WHEFT	WHEFTS
	WHELK	WHELKS • WHELKY
	WHELM	WHELMS
	WHELP	WHELPS
	WHEMMLE	WHEMMLED • WHEMMLES
	WHEN	WHENS
	WHENCE	WHENCES
	WHENUA	WHENUAS
	WHENWE	WHENWES
	WHERE	WHERES
	WHEREFOR	WHEREFORE
	WHEREFORE	WHEREFORES
	WHERES	WHERESO
	WHEREWITH	WHEREWITHS
	WHERRET	WHERRETS
	WHERRIT	WHERRITS
	WHERVE	WHERVES
	WHET	WHETS
	WHETSTONE	WHETSTONES
	WHETTER	WHETTERS
	WHEUGH	WHEUGHS
	WHEW	WHEWS
	WHEY	WHEYS
	WHEYFACE	WHEYFACED • WHEYFACES
	WHICKER	WHICKERS
	WHID	WHIDS

FRONT HOOK	ROOT WORD	END HOOK
	WHIDAH	WHIDAHS
	WHIDDER	WHIDDERS
	WHIFF	WHIFFS · WHIFFY
	WHIFFER	WHIFFERS
	WHIFFET	WHIFFETS
	WHIFFING	WHIFFINGS
	WHIFFLE	WHIFFLED · WHIFFLER · WHIFFLES
	WHIFFLER	WHIFFLERS · WHIFFLERY
	WHIFFLING	WHIFFLINGS
	WHIFT	WHIFTS
	WHIG	WHIGS
AWHILE	WHILE	WHILED · WHILES
	WHILLYWHA	WHILLYWHAS · WHILLYWHAW
	WHIM	WHIMS
	WHIMBREL	WHIMBRELS
	WHIMPER	WHIMPERS
	WHIMPERER	WHIMPERERS
	WHIMPLE	WHIMPLED · WHIMPLES
	WHIMS	WHIMSY
	WHIMSEY	WHIMSEYS
	WHIMSIES	WHIMSIEST
	WHIN	WHINE · WHINS · WHINY
	WHINCHAT	WHINCHATS
	WHINE	WHINED · WHINER · WHINES · WHINEY
	WHINER	WHINERS
	WHINGDING	WHINGDINGS
	WHINGE	WHINGED · WHINGER · WHINGES
	WHINGEING	WHINGEINGS
	WHINGER	WHINGERS
	WHINIARD	WHINIARDS
	WHINING	WHININGS
	WHINNIES	WHINNIEST
	WHINSTONE	WHINSTONES
	WHINYARD	WHINYARDS
	WHIP	WHIPS · WHIPT
	WHIPBIRD	WHIPBIRDS
	WHIPCAT	WHIPCATS
	WHIPCORD	WHIPCORDS · WHIPCORDY
	WHIPJACK	WHIPJACKS
	WHIPPER	WHIPPERS
	WHIPPET	WHIPPETS
	WHIPPING	WHIPPINGS
	WHIPRAY	WHIPRAYS
	WHIPSAW	WHIPSAWN · WHIPSAWS
	WHIPSNAKE	WHIPSNAKES
	WHIPSTAFF	WHIPSTAFFS
	WHIPSTALL	WHIPSTALLS
	WHIPSTER	WHIPSTERS
	WHIPSTOCK	WHIPSTOCKS
	WHIPTAIL	WHIPTAILS
	WHIPWORM	WHIPWORMS
	WHIR	WHIRL · WHIRR · WHIRS
AWHIRL	WHIRL	WHIRLS · WHIRLY
	WHIRLBAT	WHIRLBATS
	WHIRLER	WHIRLERS
	WHIRLIES	WHIRLIEST
	WHIRLIGIG	WHIRLIGIGS
	WHIRLING	WHIRLINGS
	WHIRLPOOL	WHIRLPOOLS
	WHIRLWIND	WHIRLWINDS
	WHIRR	WHIRRS · WHIRRY
	WHIRRET	WHIRRETS
	WHIRRING	WHIRRINGS
	WHIRTLE	WHIRTLES
	WHISH	WHISHT
	WHISHT	WHISHTS
	WHISK	WHISKS · WHISKY
	WHISKER	WHISKERS · WHISKERY
	WHISKET	WHISKETS

FRONT HOOK	ROOT WORD	END HOOK
	WHISKEY	WHISKEYS
	WHISPER	WHISPERS · WHISPERY
	WHISPERER	WHISPERERS
	WHIST	WHISTS
	WHISTLE	WHISTLED · WHISTLER · WHISTLES
	WHISTLER	WHISTLERS
	WHISTLING	WHISTLINGS
	WHIT	WHITE · WHITS · WHITY
	WHITE	WHITED · WHITEN · WHITER · WHITES
		WHITEY (offensive)
	WHITEBAIT	WHITEBAITS
	WHITEBEAM	WHITEBEAMS
	WHITECAP	WHITECAPS
	WHITECOAT	WHITECOATS
	WHITECOMB	WHITECOMBS
	WHITEDAMP	WHITEDAMPS
	WHITEFACE	WHITEFACES
	WHITEHEAD	WHITEHEADS
	WHITEN	WHITENS
	WHITENER	WHITENERS
	WHITENING	WHITENINGS
	WHITEOUT	WHITEOUTS
	WHITEPOT	WHITEPOTS
	WHITES	WHITEST
	WHITETAIL	WHITETAILS
	WHITEWALL	WHITEWALLS
	WHITEWARE	WHITEWARES
	WHITEWING	WHITEWINGS
	WHITEWOOD	WHITEWOODS
	WHITEY	WHITEYS (offensive)
	WHITHER	WHITHERS
	WHITIES	WHITIEST (offensive)
	WHITING	WHITINGS
	WHITLING	WHITLINGS
	WHITLOW	WHITLOWS
	WHITRACK	WHITRACKS
	WHITRET	WHITRETS
	WHITRICK	WHITRICKS
	WHITSTER	WHITSTERS
	WHITTAW	WHITTAWS
	WHITTAWER	WHITTAWERS
	WHITTER	WHITTERS
	WHITTLE	WHITTLED · WHITTLER · WHITTLES
	WHITTLER	WHITTLERS
	WHITTLING	WHITTLINGS
	WHITTRET	WHITTRETS
	WHIZ	WHIZZ
	WHIZBANG	WHIZBANGS
	WHIZZ	WHIZZY
	WHIZZBANG	WHIZZBANGS
	WHIZZER	WHIZZERS
	WHIZZING	WHIZZINGS
	WHO	WHOA · WHOM · WHOP · WHOT · WHOW
	WHODUNIT	WHODUNITS
	WHODUNNIT	WHODUNNITS
	WHOLE	WHOLES
	WHOLEFOOD	WHOLEFOODS
	WHOLEMEAL	WHOLEMEALS
	WHOLESALE	WHOLESALED · WHOLESALER · WHOLESALES
	WHOLESOME	WHOLESOMER
	WHOLISM	WHOLISMS
	WHOLIST	WHOLISTS
	WHOM	WHOMP
	WHOMBLE	WHOMBLED · WHOMBLES
	WHOMMLE	WHOMMLED · WHOMMLES
	WHOMP	WHOMPS
	WHOOBUB	WHOOBUBS
	WHOOF	WHOOFS
	WHOOP	WHOOPS

FRONT HOOK	ROOT WORD	END HOOK
	WHOOPEE	WHOOPEES
	WHOOPER	WHOOPERS
	WHOOPIE	WHOOPIES
	WHOOPING	WHOOPINGS
	WHOOPLA	WHOOPLAS
	WHOOPSIE	WHOOPSIES
	WHOOT	WHOOTS
	WHOP	WHOPS
	WHOPPER	WHOPPERS
	WHOPPING	WHOPPINGS
	WHORE	WHORED ▪ WHORES
	WHOREDOM	WHOREDOMS
	WHORESON	WHORESONS
	WHORL	WHORLS
	WHORLBAT	WHORLBATS
	WHORT	WHORTS
	WHORTLE	WHORTLES
EWHOW	**WHOW**	
	WHUMMLE	WHUMMLED ▪ WHUMMLES
	WHUMP	WHUMPS
	WHUNSTANE	WHUNSTANES
	WHUP	WHUPS
	WHY	WHYS
	WHYDAH	WHYDAHS
	WHYDUNIT	WHYDUNITS
	WHYDUNNIT	WHYDUNNITS
	WIBBLE	WIBBLED ▪ WIBBLES
	WICCA	WICCAN ▪ WICCAS
	WICCAN	WICCANS
TWICE	**WICE**	
	WICK	WICKS ▪ WICKY
	WICKAPE	WICKAPES
	WICKED	WICKEDS
	WICKEN	WICKENS
	WICKER	WICKERS
	WICKET	WICKETS
	WICKING	WICKINGS
	WICKIUP	WICKIUPS
	WICKTHING	WICKTHINGS
	WICKYUP	WICKYUPS
	WIDDER	WIDDERS
	WIDDIE	WIDDIES
TWIDDLE	**WIDDLE**	WIDDLED ▪ WIDDLES
TWIDDLED	**WIDDLED**	
TWIDDLES	**WIDDLES**	
TWIDDLING	**WIDDLING**	
	WIDE	WIDEN ▪ WIDER ▪ WIDES
	WIDEAWAKE	WIDEAWAKES
	WIDEN	WIDENS
	WIDENER	WIDENERS
	WIDEOUT	WIDEOUTS
	WIDES	WIDEST
	WIDGEON	WIDGEONS
	WIDGET	WIDGETS
	WIDGIE	WIDGIES
	WIDOW	WIDOWS
	WIDOWBIRD	WIDOWBIRDS
	WIDOWER	WIDOWERS
	WIDOWHOOD	WIDOWHOODS
	WIDTH	WIDTHS
	WIDTHWAY	WIDTHWAYS
	WIEL	WIELD ▪ WIELS
	WIELD	WIELDS ▪ WIELDY
	WIELDER	WIELDERS
	WIENER	WIENERS
	WIENIE	WIENIES
	WIFE	WIFED ▪ WIFES ▪ WIFEY
	WIFEDOM	WIFEDOMS
	WIFEHOOD	WIFEHOODS

FRONT HOOK	ROOT WORD	END HOOK
	WIFEY	WIFEYS
	WIFIE	WIFIES
SWIFTY	WIFTY	
SWIG ▪ TWIG	WIG	WIGS
	WIGAN	WIGANS
	WIGEON	WIGEONS
	WIGGA	WIGGAS (offensive)
SWIGGED ▪ TWIGGED	WIGGED	
SWIGGER ▪ TWIGGER	WIGGER	WIGGERS (offensive) ▪ WIGGERY
SWIGGERS ▪ TWIGGERS	WIGGERS	
TWIGGIER	WIGGIER	
TWIGGIEST	WIGGIEST	
SWIGGING ▪ TWIGGING	WIGGING	WIGGINGS
	WIGGLE	WIGGLED ▪ WIGGLER ▪ WIGGLES
	WIGGLER	WIGGLERS
TWIGGY	WIGGY	
TWIGHT	WIGHT	WIGHTS
TWIGHTED	WIGHTED	
TWIGHTING	WIGHTING	
TWIGHTS	WIGHTS	
TWIGLESS	WIGLESS	
	WIGLET	WIGLETS
TWIGLIKE	WIGLIKE	
	WIGMAKER	WIGMAKERS
SWIGS ▪ TWIGS	WIGS	
	WIGWAG	WIGWAGS
	WIGWAGGER	WIGWAGGERS
	WIGWAM	WIGWAMS
	WIKIUP	WIKIUPS
	WILD	WILDS
	WILDCARD	WILDCARDS
	WILDCAT	WILDCATS
	WILDER	WILDERS
	WILDFIRE	WILDFIRES
	WILDFOWL	WILDFOWLS
	WILDGRAVE	WILDGRAVES
	WILDING	WILDINGS
	WILDLAND	WILDLANDS
	WILDLIFE	WILDLIFES
	WILDLING	WILDLINGS
	WILDWOOD	WILDWOODS
DWILE	WILE	WILED ▪ WILES
DWILES	WILES	
	WILGA	WILGAS
	WILI	WILIS
	WILJA	WILJAS
SWILL ▪ TWILL	WILL	WILLS ▪ WILLY
SWILLED ▪ TWILLED	WILLED	
	WILLEMITE	WILLEMITES
SWILLER	WILLER	WILLERS
SWILLERS	WILLERS	
	WILLET	WILLETS
	WILLEY	WILLEYS
	WILLIAM	WILLIAMS
	WILLIE	WILLIED ▪ WILLIES
TWILLIES	WILLIES	
SWILLING ▪ TWILLING	WILLING	
	WILLIWAU	WILLIWAUS
	WILLIWAW	WILLIWAWS
	WILLOW	WILLOWS ▪ WILLOWY
	WILLOWER	WILLOWERS
	WILLPOWER	WILLPOWERS
SWILLS ▪ TWILLS	WILLS	
TWILLY	WILLY	
	WILLYWAW	WILLYWAWS
TWILT	WILT	WILTS
TWILTED	WILTED	
TWILTING	WILTING	
	WILTJA	WILTJAS

FRONT HOOK	ROOT WORD	END HOOK
TWILTS	**WILTS**	
	WIMBLE	WIMBLED · WIMBLES
	WIMBREL	WIMBRELS
	WIMP	WIMPS · WIMPY
	WIMPLE	WIMPLED · WIMPLES
TWIN	**WIN**	WIND · WINE · WING · WINK · WINN WINO · WINS · WINY
	WINCE	WINCED · WINCER · WINCES · WINCEY
	WINCER	WINCERS
	WINCEY	WINCEYS
	WINCHER	WINCHERS
	WINCING	WINCINGS
	WINCOPIPE	WINCOPIPES
	WIND	WINDS · WINDY
	WINDAC	WINDACS
	WINDAGE	WINDAGES
	WINDBAG	WINDBAGS
	WINDBELL	WINDBELLS
	WINDBILL	WINDBILLS
	WINDBLAST	WINDBLASTS
	WINDBLOW	WINDBLOWN · WINDBLOWS
	WINDBREAK	WINDBREAKS
	WINDBURN	WINDBURNS · WINDBURNT
	WINDCHILL	WINDCHILLS
	WINDER	WINDERS
	WINDFALL	WINDFALLS
	WINDFLAW	WINDFLAWS
	WINDGALL	WINDGALLS
	WINDGUN	WINDGUNS
	WINDHOVER	WINDHOVERS
	WINDIGO	WINDIGOS
	WINDING	WINDINGS
DWINDLE · SWINDLE	**WINDLE**	WINDLED · WINDLES
DWINDLED · SWINDLED	**WINDLED**	
DWINDLES · SWINDLES	**WINDLES**	WINDLESS
DWINDLING · SWINDLING	**WINDLING**	WINDLINGS
SWINDLINGS	**WINDLINGS**	
	WINDMILL	WINDMILLS
	WINDOCK	WINDOCKS
	WINDORE	WINDORES
	WINDOW	WINDOWS · WINDOWY
	WINDOWING	WINDOWINGS
	WINDPIPE	WINDPIPES
	WINDROSE	WINDROSES
	WINDROW	WINDROWS
	WINDROWER	WINDROWERS
	WINDSAIL	WINDSAILS
	WINDSHAKE	WINDSHAKES
	WINDSHIP	WINDSHIPS
	WINDSOCK	WINDSOCKS
	WINDSTORM	WINDSTORMS
	WINDSURF	WINDSURFS
	WINDTHROW	WINDTHROWS
	WINDUP	WINDUPS
	WINDWARD	WINDWARDS
	WINDWAY	WINDWAYS
DWINE · GWINE · SWINE · TWINE	**WINE**	WINED · WINES · WINEY
DWINED · TWINED	**WINED**	
	WINEMAKER	WINEMAKERS
SWINERIES	**WINERIES**	
SWINERY	**WINERY**	
DWINES · SWINES · TWINES	**WINES**	
	WINESAP	WINESAPS
	WINESHOP	WINESHOPS
	WINESKIN	WINESKINS
	WINESOP	WINESOPS
AWING · OWING · SWING	**WING**	WINGE · WINGS · WINGY
	WINGBACK	WINGBACKS
SWINGBEAT	**WINGBEAT**	WINGBEATS

FRONT HOOK	ROOT WORD	END HOOK
SWINGBEATS	**WINGBEATS**	
	WINGBOW	WINGBOWS
	WINGCHAIR	WINGCHAIRS
	WINGDING	WINGDINGS
SWINGE = TWINGE	**WINGE**	WINGED = WINGER = WINGES
SWINGED = TWINGED	**WINGED**	
SWINGEING = TWINGEING	**WINGEING**	
SWINGER	**WINGER**	WINGERS
SWINGERS	**WINGERS**	
SWINGES = TWINGES	**WINGES**	
SWINGIER	**WINGIER**	
SWINGIEST	**WINGIEST**	
SWINGING = TWINGING	**WINGING**	
	WINGLET	WINGLETS
SWINGMAN	**WINGMAN**	
SWINGMEN	**WINGMEN**	
	WINGOVER	WINGOVERS
SWINGS	**WINGS**	
	WINGSPAN	WINGSPANS
	WINGSUIT	WINGSUITS
	WINGTIP	WINGTIPS
SWINGY	**WINGY**	
TWINIER	**WINIER**	
TWINIEST	**WINIEST**	
DWINING = TWINING	**WINING**	
SWINISH	**WINISH**	
SWINK = TWINK	**WINK**	WINKS
SWINKED = TWINKED	**WINKED**	
SWINKER	**WINKER**	WINKERS
SWINKERS	**WINKERS**	
SWINKING = TWINKING	**WINKING**	WINKINGS
TWINKLE	**WINKLE**	WINKLED = WINKLER = WINKLES
TWINKLED	**WINKLED**	
TWINKLER	**WINKLER**	WINKLERS
TWINKLERS	**WINKLERS**	
TWINKLES	**WINKLES**	
TWINKLING	**WINKLING**	
SWINKS = TWINKS	**WINKS**	
	WINN	WINNA = WINNS
	WINNARD	WINNARDS
TWINNED	**WINNED**	
	WINNER	WINNERS
TWINNING	**WINNING**	WINNINGS
TWINNINGS	**WINNINGS**	
	WINNLE	WINNLES
	WINNOCK	WINNOCKS
	WINNOW	WINNOWS
	WINNOWER	WINNOWERS
	WINNOWING	WINNOWINGS
	WINO	WINOS
TWINS	**WINS**	
	WINSEY	WINSEYS
	WINSOME	WINSOMER
TWINTER	**WINTER**	WINTERS = WINTERY
	WINTERER	WINTERERS
	WINTERISE	WINTERISED = WINTERISES
	WINTERIZE	WINTERIZED = WINTERIZES
TWINTERS	**WINTERS**	
	WINTLE	WINTLED = WINTLES
TWINY	**WINY**	
	WINZE	WINZES
SWIPE	**WIPE**	WIPED = WIPER = WIPES
SWIPED	**WIPED**	
	WIPEOUT	WIPEOUTS
SWIPER	**WIPER**	WIPERS
SWIPERS	**WIPERS**	
SWIPES	**WIPES**	
SWIPING	**WIPING**	WIPINGS
	WIPPEN	WIPPENS

FRONT HOOK	ROOT WORD	END HOOK
SWIRE ▪ TWIRE TWIRED	**WIRE**	WIRED ▪ WIRER ▪ WIRES
	WIRED	
	WIREDRAW	WIREDRAWN ▪ WIREDRAWS
	WIREHAIR	WIREHAIRS
	WIREPHOTO	WIREPHOTOS
	WIRER	WIRERS
SWIRES ▪ TWIRES	**WIRES**	
	WIRETAP	WIRETAPS
	WIREWAY	WIREWAYS
	WIREWORK	WIREWORKS
	WIREWORM	WIREWORMS
	WIRILDA	WIRILDAS
TWIRING	**WIRING**	WIRINGS
	WIRRA	WIRRAH
	WIRRAH	WIRRAHS
	WIRRICOW	WIRRICOWS
IWIS ▪ YWIS	**WIS**	WISE ▪ WISH ▪ WISP ▪ WISS ▪ WIST
	WISARD	WISARDS
	WISDOM	WISDOMS
	WISE	WISED ▪ WISER ▪ WISES
	WISEACRE	WISEACRES
	WISECRACK	WISECRACKS
	WISEGUY	WISEGUYS
	WISELING	WISELINGS
	WISENT	WISENTS
	WISES	WISEST
SWISH	**WISH**	WISHA ▪ WISHT
	WISHBONE	WISHBONES
SWISHED	**WISHED**	
SWISHER	**WISHER**	WISHERS
SWISHERS	**WISHERS**	
SWISHES	**WISHES**	
SWISHING	**WISHING**	WISHINGS
SWISHINGS	**WISHINGS**	
	WISKET	WISKETS
	WISP	WISPS ▪ WISPY
SWISS	**WISS**	
SWISSES	**WISSES**	
SWISSING	**WISSING**	
TWIST	**WIST**	WISTS
	WISTARIA	WISTARIAS
TWISTED	**WISTED**	
	WISTERIA	WISTERIAS
TWISTING	**WISTING**	
	WISTITI	WISTITIS
TWISTS	**WISTS**	
TWIT	**WIT**	WITE ▪ WITH ▪ WITS
	WITAN	WITANS
SWITCH ▪ TWITCH	**WITCH**	WITCHY
SWITCHED ▪ TWITCHED	**WITCHED**	
	WITCHEN	WITCHENS
SWITCHES ▪ TWITCHES	**WITCHES**	
	WITCHHOOD	WITCHHOODS
SWITCHIER ▪ TWITCHIER	**WITCHIER**	
SWITCHIEST ▪ TWITCHIEST	**WITCHIEST**	
SWITCHING ▪ TWITCHING	**WITCHING**	WITCHINGS
SWITCHINGS ▪ TWITCHINGS	**WITCHINGS**	
	WITCHKNOT	WITCHKNOTS
SWITCHLIKE	**WITCHLIKE**	
	WITCHWEED	WITCHWEEDS
SWITCHY ▪ TWITCHY	**WITCHY**	
TWITE	**WITE**	WITED ▪ WITES
TWITES	**WITES**	
	WITGAT	WITGATS
SWITH	**WITH**	WITHE ▪ WITHS ▪ WITHY
	WITHDRAW	WITHDRAWN ▪ WITHDRAWS
SWITHE	**WITHE**	WITHED ▪ WITHER ▪ WITHES
SWITHER	**WITHER**	WITHERS
SWITHERED	**WITHERED**	

FRONT HOOK	ROOT WORD	END HOOK
	WITHERER	WITHERERS
SWITHERING	WITHERING	WITHERINGS
	WITHERITE	WITHERITES
	WITHEROD	WITHERODS
SWITHERS	WITHERS	
	WITHHOLD	WITHHOLDS
	WITHIES	WITHIEST
	WITHIN	WITHING ▪ WITHINS
	WITHOUT	WITHOUTS
	WITHSTAND	WITHSTANDS
	WITHWIND	WITHWINDS
	WITHYWIND	WITHYWINDS
	WITLING	WITLINGS
	WITLOOF	WITLOOFS
	WITNESSER	WITNESSERS
	WITNEY	WITNEYS
SWITS ▪ TWITS	WITS	
TWITTED	WITTED	
TWITTER	WITTER	WITTERS
TWITTERED	WITTERED	
TWITTERING	WITTERING	
TWITTERS	WITTERS	
	WITTICISM	WITTICISMS
TWITTING	WITTING	WITTINGS
TWITTINGLY	WITTINGLY	
TWITTINGS	WITTINGS	
	WITTOL	WITTOLS
	WITWALL	WITWALLS
	WITWANTON	WITWANTONS
SWIVE	WIVE	WIVED ▪ WIVER ▪ WIVES
SWIVED	WIVED	
	WIVEHOOD	WIVEHOODS
	WIVER	WIVERN ▪ WIVERS
	WIVERN	WIVERNS
SWIVES	WIVES	
SWIVING	WIVING	
SWIZ	WIZ	
	WIZARD	WIZARDS
	WIZEN	WIZENS
	WIZIER	WIZIERS
	WIZZEN	WIZZENS
SWIZZES	WIZZES	
TWO	WO	WOE ▪ WOF ▪ WOG ▪ WOK ▪ WON ▪ WOO
		WOP (offensive) ▪ WOS ▪ WOT ▪ WOW ▪ WOX
	WOAD	WOADS
	WOADWAXEN	WOADWAXENS
	WOALD	WOALDS
	WOBBEGONG	WOBBEGONGS
	WOBBLE	WOBBLED ▪ WOBBLER ▪ WOBBLES
	WOBBLER	WOBBLERS
	WOBBLIES	WOBBLIEST
	WOBBLING	WOBBLINGS
	WOCK	WOCKS
	WODGE	WODGES
	WOE	WOES
	WOF	WOFS
	WOG	WOGS (offensive)
	WOGGLE	WOGGLES
	WOIWODE	WOIWODES
	WOK	WOKE ▪ WOKS
AWOKE	WOKE	WOKEN
AWOKEN	WOKEN	
	WOLD	WOLDS
	WOLF	WOLFS
	WOLFER	WOLFERS
	WOLFHOUND	WOLFHOUNDS
	WOLFING	WOLFINGS
	WOLFKIN	WOLFKINS
	WOLFLING	WOLFLINGS

FRONT HOOK	ROOT WORD	END HOOK
	WOLFRAM	WOLFRAMS
	WOLFSBANE	WOLFSBANES
	WOLFSKIN	WOLFSKINS
	WOLVE	WOLVED ▪ WOLVER ▪ WOLVES
	WOLVER	WOLVERS
	WOLVERENE	WOLVERENES
	WOLVERINE	WOLVERINES
	WOLVING	WOLVINGS
	WOMAN	WOMANS
	WOMANHOOD	WOMANHOODS
	WOMANISE	WOMANISED ▪ WOMANISER ▪ WOMANISES
	WOMANISER	WOMANISERS
	WOMANISM	WOMANISMS
	WOMANIST	WOMANISTS
	WOMANIZE	WOMANIZED ▪ WOMANIZER ▪ WOMANIZES
	WOMANIZER	WOMANIZERS
	WOMANKIND	WOMANKINDS
	WOMB	WOMBS ▪ WOMBY
	WOMBAT	WOMBATS
	WOMENFOLK	WOMENFOLKS
	WOMENKIND	WOMENKINDS
	WOMERA	WOMERAS
	WOMMERA	WOMMERAS
	WOMMIT	WOMMITS
	WON	WONK ▪ WONS ▪ WONT
	WONDER	WONDERS
	WONDERER	WONDERERS
	WONDERING	WONDERINGS
	WONDERKID	WONDERKIDS
	WONGA	WONGAS
	WONGI	WONGIS
	WONING	WONINGS
	WONK	WONKS ▪ WONKY
	WONNER	WONNERS
	WONNING	WONNINGS
	WONT	WONTS
	WONTON	WONTONS
	WOO	WOOD ▪ WOOF ▪ WOOL ▪ WOON ▪ WOOS ▪ WOOT
	WOOBUT	WOOBUTS
	WOOD	WOODS ▪ WOODY
	WOODBIN	WOODBIND ▪ WOODBINE ▪ WOODBINS
	WOODBIND	WOODBINDS
	WOODBINE	WOODBINES
	WOODBLOCK	WOODBLOCKS
	WOODBORER	WOODBORERS
	WOODCHAT	WOODCHATS
	WOODCHIP	WOODCHIPS
	WOODCHOP	WOODCHOPS
	WOODCHUCK	WOODCHUCKS
	WOODCOCK	WOODCOCKS
	WOODCRAFT	WOODCRAFTS
	WOODCUT	WOODCUTS
	WOODEN	WOODENS
	WOODENTOP	WOODENTOPS
	WOODGRAIN	WOODGRAINS
	WOODHEN	WOODHENS
	WOODHOLE	WOODHOLES
	WOODHORSE	WOODHORSES
	WOODHOUSE	WOODHOUSES
	WOODIE	WOODIER ▪ WOODIES
	WOODIES	WOODIEST
	WOODLAND	WOODLANDS
	WOODLARK	WOODLARKS
	WOODLORE	WOODLORES
	WOODLOT	WOODLOTS
	WOODMEAL	WOODMEALS
	WOODNOTE	WOODNOTES
	WOODPILE	WOODPILES
	WOODPRINT	WOODPRINTS

FRONT HOOK	ROOT WORD	END HOOK
	WOODREEVE	WOODREEVES
	WOODROOF	WOODROOFS
	WOODRUFF	WOODRUFFS
	WOODS	WOODSY
	WOODSCREW	WOODSCREWS
	WOODSHED	WOODSHEDS
	WOODSHOCK	WOODSHOCKS
	WOODSIA	WOODSIAS
	WOODSKIN	WOODSKINS
	WOODSPITE	WOODSPITES
	WOODSTONE	WOODSTONES
	WOODSTOVE	WOODSTOVES
	WOODTONE	WOODTONES
	WOODWALE	WOODWALES
	WOODWARD	WOODWARDS
	WOODWAXEN	WOODWAXENS
	WOODWIND	WOODWINDS
	WOODWORK	WOODWORKS
	WOODWORM	WOODWORMS
	WOODWOSE	WOODWOSES
	WOODYARD	WOODYARDS
	WOOER	WOOERS
	WOOF	WOOFS · WOOFY
	WOOFER	WOOFERS
	WOOFTER	WOOFTERS (offensive)
	WOOING	WOOINGS
	WOOL	WOOLD · WOOLS · WOOLY
	WOOLD	WOOLDS
	WOOLDER	WOOLDERS
	WOOLDING	WOOLDINGS
	WOOLEN	WOOLENS
	WOOLER	WOOLERS
	WOOLFAT	WOOLFATS
	WOOLFELL	WOOLFELLS
	WOOLHAT	WOOLHATS
	WOOLIE	WOOLIER · WOOLIES
	WOOLIES	WOOLIEST
	WOOLLEN	WOOLLENS
	WOOLLIES	WOOLLIEST
	WOOLPACK	WOOLPACKS
	WOOLSACK	WOOLSACKS
	WOOLSEY	WOOLSEYS
	WOOLSHED	WOOLSHEDS
	WOOLSKIN	WOOLSKINS
	WOOLWORK	WOOLWORKS
	WOOMERA	WOOMERAS
	WOOMERANG	WOOMERANGS
SWOON	**WOON**	WOONS
SWOONED	**WOONED**	
SWOONING	**WOONING**	
SWOONS	**WOONS**	
	WOOPIE	WOOPIES
SWOOPS	**WOOPS**	
	WOORALI	WOORALIS
	WOORARA	WOORARAS
	WOORARI	WOORARIS
	WOOS	WOOSE · WOOSH
	WOOSE	WOOSEL · WOOSES
	WOOSEL	WOOSELL · WOOSELS
	WOOSELL	WOOSELLS
SWOOSH	**WOOSH**	
SWOOSHED	**WOOSHED**	
SWOOSHES	**WOOSHES**	
SWOOSHING	**WOOSHING**	
	WOOT	WOOTZ
SWOP	**WOP**	WOPS (offensive)
SWOPPED	**WOPPED**	
SWOPPING	**WOPPING**	
SWOPS	**WOPS**	

935

FRONT HOOK	ROOT WORD	END HOOK
	WORCESTER	WORCESTERS
SWORD	**WORD**	WORDS · WORDY
	WORDAGE	WORDAGES
	WORDBOOK	WORDBOOKS
	WORDBREAK	WORDBREAKS
SWORDED	**WORDED**	
	WORDGAME	WORDGAMES
SWORDING	**WORDING**	WORDINGS
SWORDLESS	**WORDLESS**	
	WORDLORE	WORDLORES
SWORDPLAY	**WORDPLAY**	WORDPLAYS
SWORDPLAYS	**WORDPLAYS**	
SWORDS	**WORDS**	
	WORDSMITH	WORDSMITHS
SWORE	**WORE**	
AWORK	**WORK**	WORKS
	WORKADAY	WORKADAYS
	WORKBAG	WORKBAGS
	WORKBOAT	WORKBOATS
	WORKBOOK	WORKBOOKS
	WORKDAY	WORKDAYS
	WORKER	WORKERS
	WORKERIST	WORKERISTS
	WORKFARE	WORKFARES
	WORKFLOW	WORKFLOWS
	WORKFOLK	WORKFOLKS
	WORKFORCE	WORKFORCES
	WORKGIRL	WORKGIRLS
	WORKGROUP	WORKGROUPS
	WORKHORSE	WORKHORSES
	WORKHOUR	WORKHOURS
	WORKHOUSE	WORKHOUSES
	WORKING	WORKINGS
	WORKLOAD	WORKLOADS
	WORKMATE	WORKMATES
	WORKOUT	WORKOUTS
	WORKPIECE	WORKPIECES
	WORKPLACE	WORKPLACES
	WORKPRINT	WORKPRINTS
	WORKROOM	WORKROOMS
	WORKSHEET	WORKSHEETS
	WORKSHOP	WORKSHOPS
	WORKSPACE	WORKSPACES
	WORKTABLE	WORKTABLES
	WORKTOP	WORKTOPS
	WORKUP	WORKUPS
	WORKWEAR	WORKWEARS
	WORKWEEK	WORKWEEKS
	WORLD	WORLDS
	WORLDBEAT	WORLDBEATS
	WORLDLING	WORLDLINGS
	WORLDVIEW	WORLDVIEWS
	WORM	WORMS · WORMY
	WORMCAST	WORMCASTS
	WORMER	WORMERS · WORMERY
	WORMGEAR	WORMGEARS
	WORMHOLE	WORMHOLED · WORMHOLES
	WORMIL	WORMILS
	WORMROOT	WORMROOTS
	WORMSEED	WORMSEEDS
	WORMWOOD	WORMWOODS
SWORN	**WORN**	
	WORRAL	WORRALS
	WORREL	WORRELS
	WORRICOW	WORRICOWS
	WORRIER	WORRIERS
	WORRIMENT	WORRIMENTS
	WORRIT	WORRITS
	WORRYCOW	WORRYCOWS

FRONT HOOK	ROOT WORD	END HOOK
	WORRYING	WORRYINGS
	WORRYWART	WORRYWARTS
	WORSE	WORSED ▪ WORSEN ▪ WORSER ▪ WORSES
		WORSET
	WORSEN	WORSENS
	WORSET	WORSETS
	WORSHIP	WORSHIPS
	WORSHIPER	WORSHIPERS
	WORST	WORSTS
	WORSTED	WORSTEDS
	WORT	WORTH ▪ WORTS
	WORTH	WORTHS ▪ WORTHY
	WORTHIES	WORTHIEST
	WORTLE	WORTLES
TWOS	**WOS**	WOST
	WOSBIRD	WOSBIRDS
SWOT	**WOT**	WOTS
SWOTS	**WOTS**	
SWOTTED	**WOTTED**	
SWOTTING	**WOTTING**	
	WOUBIT	WOUBITS
	WOULD	WOULDS
	WOULDS	WOULDST
SWOUND	**WOUND**	WOUNDS ▪ WOUNDY
SWOUNDED	**WOUNDED**	
	WOUNDER	WOUNDERS
SWOUNDING	**WOUNDING**	WOUNDINGS
SWOUNDS	**WOUNDS**	
	WOUNDWORT	WOUNDWORTS
	WOURALI	WOURALIS
	WOVE	WOVEN
	WOVEN	WOVENS
	WOW	WOWF ▪ WOWS
	WOWSER	WOWSERS
AWRACK	**WRACK**	WRACKS
	WRAITH	WRAITHS
	WRANG	WRANGS
	WRANGLE	WRANGLED ▪ WRANGLER ▪ WRANGLES
	WRANGLER	WRANGLERS
	WRANGLING	WRANGLINGS
	WRAP	WRAPS ▪ WRAPT
	WRAPOVER	WRAPOVERS
	WRAPPAGE	WRAPPAGES
	WRAPPER	WRAPPERS
	WRAPPING	WRAPPINGS
	WRAPROUND	WRAPROUNDS
	WRASSE	WRASSES
	WRASSLE	WRASSLED ▪ WRASSLES
	WRAST	WRASTS
	WRASTLE	WRASTLED ▪ WRASTLES
	WRATH	WRATHS ▪ WRATHY
	WRAWL	WRAWLS
	WRAXLE	WRAXLED ▪ WRAXLES
	WRAXLING	WRAXLINGS
	WREAK	WREAKS
	WREAKER	WREAKERS
	WREATH	WREATHE ▪ WREATHS ▪ WREATHY
	WREATHE	WREATHED ▪ WREATHEN ▪ WREATHER
		WREATHES
	WREATHER	WREATHERS
	WRECK	WRECKS
	WRECKAGE	WRECKAGES
	WRECKER	WRECKERS
	WRECKING	WRECKINGS
	WREN	WRENS
	WRENCHER	WRENCHERS
	WRENCHING	WRENCHINGS
	WREST	WRESTS
	WRESTER	WRESTERS

FRONT HOOK	ROOT WORD	END HOOK
	WRESTLE	WRESTLED = WRESTLER = WRESTLES
	WRESTLER	WRESTLERS
	WRESTLING	WRESTLINGS
	WRETHE	WRETHED = WRETHES
	WRICK	WRICKS
OWRIER	**WRIER**	
	WRIES	WRIEST
OWRIEST	**WRIEST**	
	WRIGGLE	WRIGGLED = WRIGGLER = WRIGGLES
	WRIGGLER	WRIGGLERS
	WRIGGLING	WRIGGLINGS
	WRIGHT	WRIGHTS
	WRING	WRINGS
	WRINGER	WRINGERS
	WRINGING	WRINGINGS
	WRINKLE	WRINKLED = WRINKLES
	WRINKLIES	WRINKLIEST
	WRIST	WRISTS = WRISTY
	WRISTBAND	WRISTBANDS
	WRISTLET	WRISTLETS
	WRISTLOCK	WRISTLOCKS
	WRIT	WRITE = WRITS
	WRITE	WRITER = WRITES
	WRITER	WRITERS
	WRITHE	WRITHED = WRITHEN = WRITHER = WRITHES
	WRITHER	WRITHERS
	WRITHING	WRITHINGS
	WRITING	WRITINGS
	WROATH	WROATHS
YWROKE	**WROKE**	WROKEN
AWRONG	**WRONG**	WRONGS
	WRONGDOER	WRONGDOERS
	WRONGER	WRONGERS
	WROOT	WROOTS
AWRY	**WRY**	
	WRYBILL	WRYBILLS
	WRYNECK	WRYNECKS
	WUD	WUDS = WUDU
	WUDJULA	WUDJULAS
	WUDU	WUDUS
	WULFENITE	WULFENITES
	WULL	WULLS
	WUNNER	WUNNERS
	WURLEY	WURLEYS
	WURLIE	WURLIES
	WURST	WURSTS
	WURTZITE	WURTZITES
	WURZEL	WURZELS
	WUS	WUSS
	WUSHU	WUSHUS
	WUSS	WUSSY
	WUSSIES	WUSSIEST
	WUTHER	WUTHERS
	WUXIA	WUXIAS
	WUZZLE	WUZZLED = WUZZLES
	WYANDOTTE	WYANDOTTES
	WYE	WYES
	WYLE	WYLED = WYLES
	WYLIECOAT	WYLIECOATS
	WYN	WYND = WYNN = WYNS
	WYND	WYNDS
	WYNN	WYNNS
	WYTE	WYTED = WYTES
	WYVERN	WYVERNS

FRONT HOOK	ROOT WORD	END HOOK
	XANTHAM	XANTHAMS
	XANTHAN	XANTHANS
	XANTHATE	XANTHATES
	XANTHEIN	XANTHEINS
	XANTHENE	XANTHENES
	XANTHIN	XANTHINE ▪ XANTHINS
	XANTHINE	XANTHINES
	XANTHISM	XANTHISMS
	XANTHOMA	XANTHOMAS
	XANTHONE	XANTHONES
	XANTHOXYL	XANTHOXYLS
	XEBEC	XEBECS
	XENIA	XENIAL ▪ XENIAS
AXENIC	**XENIC**	
	XENOBLAST	XENOBLASTS
	XENOCRYST	XENOCRYSTS
	XENOGRAFT	XENOGRAFTS
	XENOLITH	XENOLITHS
	XENOMANIA	XENOMANIAS
	XENOMENIA	XENOMENIAS
	XENON	XENONS
	XENOPHILE	XENOPHILES
	XENOPHOBE	XENOPHOBES
	XENOTIME	XENOTIMES
	XERAFIN	XERAFINS
	XERAPHIM	XERAPHIMS
	XERASIA	XERASIAS
	XERISCAPE	XERISCAPES
	XERODERMA	XERODERMAE ▪ XERODERMAS
	XEROMA	XEROMAS
	XEROMORPH	XEROMORPHS
	XEROPHILE	XEROPHILES
	XEROPHYTE	XEROPHYTES
	XEROSERE	XEROSERES
	XEROSTOMA	XEROSTOMAS
	XI	XIS
	XIPHOID	XIPHOIDS
	XIPHOPAGI	XIPHOPAGIC
AXIS	**XIS**	
	XYLAN	XYLANS
	XYLEM	XYLEMS
	XYLENE	XYLENES
	XYLENOL	XYLENOLS
	XYLIDIN	XYLIDINE ▪ XYLIDINS
	XYLIDINE	XYLIDINES
	XYLITOL	XYLITOLS
	XYLOCARP	XYLOCARPS
	XYLOGEN	XYLOGENS
	XYLOGRAPH	XYLOGRAPHS ▪ XYLOGRAPHY
	XYLOIDIN	XYLOIDINE ▪ XYLOIDINS
	XYLOIDINE	XYLOIDINES
	XYLOL	XYLOLS
	XYLOMA	XYLOMAS
	XYLOMETER	XYLOMETERS
	XYLONITE	XYLONITES
	XYLOPHAGE	XYLOPHAGES
	XYLOPHONE	XYLOPHONES
	XYLORIMBA	XYLORIMBAS
	XYLOSE	XYLOSES
	XYLYL	XYLYLS
	XYST	XYSTI ▪ XYSTS
	XYSTER	XYSTERS

Y

FRONT HOOK	ROOT WORD	END HOOK
PYA · RYA	**YA**	YAD · YAE · YAG · YAH · YAK · YAM · YAP · YAR · YAW · YAY
	YAAR	YAARS
	YABBA	YABBAS
	YABBER	YABBERS
	YABBIE	YABBIED · YABBIES
	YACCA	YACCAS
	YACHT	YACHTS
	YACHTER	YACHTERS
	YACHTIE	YACHTIES
	YACHTING	YACHTINGS
KYACK	**YACK**	YACKA · YACKS
	YACKA	YACKAS
	YACKER	YACKERS
KYACKS	**YACKS**	
DYAD	**YAD**	YADS
DYADS	**YADS**	
NYAFF	**YAFF**	YAFFS
NYAFFED	**YAFFED**	
NYAFFING	**YAFFING**	
	YAFFLE	YAFFLES
NYAFFS	**YAFFS**	
	YAG	YAGI · YAGS
	YAGER	YAGERS
	YAGGER	YAGGERS
	YAGI	YAGIS
AYAH	**YAH**	YAHS
	YAHOO	YAHOOS
	YAHOOISM	YAHOOISMS
	YAHRZEIT	YAHRZEITS
AYAHS	**YAHS**	
	YAIRD	YAIRDS
KYAK	**YAK**	YAKS
	YAKHDAN	YAKHDANS
	YAKIMONO	YAKIMONOS
	YAKITORI	YAKITORIS
	YAKKA	YAKKAS
	YAKKER	YAKKERS
	YAKOW	YAKOWS
KYAKS	**YAKS**	
	YALE	YALES
LYAM	**YAM**	YAMS
	YAMALKA	YAMALKAS
	YAMEN	YAMENS
	YAMMER	YAMMERS
	YAMMERER	YAMMERERS
	YAMMERING	YAMMERINGS
LYAMS	**YAMS**	
	YAMULKA	YAMULKAS
	YAMUN	YAMUNS
KYANG	**YANG**	YANGS
KYANGS	**YANGS**	
	YANK	YANKS
	YANKER	YANKERS
	YANKIE	YANKIES
	YANQUI	YANQUIS
	YANTRA	YANTRAS
	YAOURT	YAOURTS
	YAP	YAPP · YAPS
	YAPOCK	YAPOCKS
	YAPOK	YAPOKS
	YAPON	YAPONS
	YAPP	YAPPS · YAPPY
	YAPPER	YAPPERS
	YAPPIE	YAPPIER · YAPPIES

FRONT HOOK	ROOT WORD	END HOOK
	YAPPIES	YAPPIEST
	YAPSTER	YAPSTERS
	YAQONA	YAQONAS
KYAR	**YAR**	YARD ▪ YARE ▪ YARK ▪ YARN ▪ YARR
	YARCO	YARCOS (*offensive*)
LYARD	**YARD**	YARDS
	YARDAGE	YARDAGES
	YARDANG	YARDANGS
	YARDARM	YARDARMS
	YARDBIRD	YARDBIRDS
	YARDER	YARDERS
	YARDING	YARDINGS
	YARDLAND	YARDLANDS
	YARDSTICK	YARDSTICKS
	YARDWAND	YARDWANDS
	YARDWORK	YARDWORKS
	YARE	YARER
	YARFA	YARFAS
	YARK	YARKS
	YARMELKE	YARMELKES
	YARMULKA	YARMULKAS
	YARMULKE	YARMULKES
	YARN	YARNS
	YARNER	YARNERS
	YARPHA	YARPHAS
	YARR	YARRS
	YARRAMAN	YARRAMANS
	YARRAN	YARRANS
	YARROW	YARROWS
	YARTA	YARTAS
	YARTO	YARTOS
	YASHMAC	YASHMACS
	YASHMAK	YASHMAKS
	YASMAK	YASMAKS
	YATAGAN	YATAGANS
	YATAGHAN	YATAGHANS
	YATE	YATES
	YATTER	YATTERS
	YATTERING	YATTERINGS
	YAUD	YAUDS
	YAUP	YAUPS
	YAUPER	YAUPERS
	YAUPON	YAUPONS
	YAUTIA	YAUTIAS
	YAW	YAWL ▪ YAWN ▪ YAWP ▪ YAWS ▪ YAWY
	YAWL	YAWLS
	YAWMETER	YAWMETERS
	YAWN	YAWNS ▪ YAWNY
	YAWNER	YAWNERS
	YAWNING	YAWNINGS
	YAWP	YAWPS
	YAWPER	YAWPERS
	YAWPING	YAWPINGS
	YAY	YAYS
CYCLED	**YCLED**	
	YCLEEPE	YCLEEPED ▪ YCLEEPES
AYE ▪ BYE ▪ DYE ▪ EYE ▪ HYE ▪ KYE ▪ LYE NYE ▪ OYE ▪ PYE ▪ RYE ▪ SYE ▪ TYE ▪ WYE	**YE**	YEA ▪ YEH ▪ YEN ▪ YEP ▪ YES ▪ YET ▪ YEW YEX
	YEA	YEAD ▪ YEAH ▪ YEAN ▪ YEAR ▪ YEAS
	YEAD	YEADS
	YEAH	YEAHS
	YEALDON	YEALDONS
	YEALING	YEALINGS
	YEALM	YEALMS
	YEAN	YEANS
	YEANLING	YEANLINGS
	YEAR	YEARD ▪ YEARN ▪ YEARS
	YEARBOOK	YEARBOOKS
	YEARD	YEARDS

	FRONT HOOK	ROOT WORD	END HOOK
		YEAREND	YEARENDS
		YEARLING	YEARLINGS
		YEARN	YEARNS
		YEARNER	YEARNERS
		YEARNING	YEARNINGS
		YEAS	YEAST
		YEASAYER	YEASAYERS
		YEAST	YEASTS ▪ YEASTY
		YECCH	YECCHS
		YECH	YECHS ▪ YECHY
		YEDE	YEDES
		YEED	YEEDS
		YEELIN	YEELINS
		YEGG	YEGGS
	GYELD	**YELD**	
		YELDRING	YELDRINGS
		YELDROCK	YELDROCKS
		YELK	YELKS
		YELL	YELLS
		YELLER	YELLERS
		YELLING	YELLINGS
		YELLOCH	YELLOCHS
		YELLOW	YELLOWS ▪ YELLOWY
		YELLOWFIN	YELLOWFINS
		YELM	YELMS
	AYELP	**YELP**	YELPS
		YELPER	YELPERS
		YELPING	YELPINGS
		YELT	YELTS
		YEMMER	YEMMERS
	EYEN ▪ HYEN ▪ SYEN	**YEN**	YENS
	HYENS ▪ SYENS	**YENS**	
		YENTA	YENTAS
		YENTE	YENTES
		YEP	YEPS
		YERBA	YERBAS
		YERD	YERDS
		YERK	YERKS
		YERSINIA	YERSINIAE ▪ YERSINIAS
AYES ▪ BYES ▪ DYES ▪ EYES ▪ HYES ▪ KYES		**YES**	YESK ▪ YEST
LYES ▪ NYES ▪ OYES ▪ PYES ▪ RYES ▪ SYES			
TYES ▪ WYES			
	CYESES ▪ OYESES	**YESES**	
		YESHIVA	YESHIVAH ▪ YESHIVAS
		YESHIVAH	YESHIVAHS
		YESHIVOT	YESHIVOTH
		YESK	YESKS
	OYESSES	**YESSES**	
		YEST	YESTS ▪ YESTY
	DYESTER	**YESTER**	YESTERN
		YESTERDAY	YESTERDAYS
		YESTEREVE	YESTEREVEN ▪ YESTEREVES
		YESTREEN	YESTREENS
	PYET	**YET**	YETI ▪ YETT
		YETI	YETIS
		YETT	YETTS
		YETTIE	YETTIES
		YEUK	YEUKS ▪ YEUKY
		YEVE	YEVEN ▪ YEVES
		YEW	YEWS
		YGO	YGOE
		YICKER	YICKERS
		YID	YIDS *(offensive)*
		YIDAKI	YIDAKIS
		YIELD	YIELDS
		YIELDER	YIELDERS
		YIELDING	YIELDINGS
		YIKE	YIKED ▪ YIKES
		YIKKER	YIKKERS

FRONT HOOK	ROOT WORD	END HOOK
	YILL	YILLS
AYIN ▪ PYIN ▪ TYIN	**YIN**	YINS
AYINS ▪ PYINS	**YINS**	
	YIP	YIPE ▪ YIPS
	YIPE	YIPES
	YIPPER	YIPPERS
	YIPPIE	YIPPIES
	YIRD	YIRDS
	YIRK	YIRKS
	YIRR	YIRRS
	YIRTH	YIRTHS
	YITE	YITES
	YITIE	YITIES
XYLEM	**YLEM**	YLEMS
XYLEMS	**YLEMS**	
	YLKE	YLKES
	YMPE	YMPES
GYMPING (offensive)	**YMPING**	
	YNAMBU	YNAMBUS
	YO	YOB ▪ YOD ▪ YOK ▪ YOM ▪ YON ▪ YOS ▪ YOU ▪ YOW
	YOB	YOBS
	YOBBISM	YOBBISMS
	YOBBO	YOBBOS
	YOCK	YOCKS
	YOD	YODE ▪ YODH ▪ YODS
	YODE	YODEL
	YODEL	YODELS
	YODELER	YODELERS
	YODELLER	YODELLERS
	YODH	YODHS
	YODLE	YODLED ▪ YODLER ▪ YODLES
	YODLER	YODLERS
	YOGA	YOGAS
	YOGEE	YOGEES
	YOGH	YOGHS
	YOGHOURT	YOGHOURTS
	YOGHURT	YOGHURTS
	YOGI	YOGIC ▪ YOGIN ▪ YOGIS
	YOGIN	YOGINI ▪ YOGINS
	YOGINI	YOGINIS
	YOGIS	YOGISM
	YOGISM	YOGISMS
	YOGURT	YOGURTS
	YOHIMBE	YOHIMBES
	YOHIMBINE	YOHIMBINES
	YOICK	YOICKS
	YOJAN	YOJANA ▪ YOJANS
	YOJANA	YOJANAS
	YOK	YOKE ▪ YOKS
	YOKE	YOKED ▪ YOKEL ▪ YOKER ▪ YOKES
	YOKEL	YOKELS (offensive)
	YOKEMATE	YOKEMATES
	YOKER	YOKERS
	YOKING	YOKINGS
	YOKOZUNA	YOKOZUNAS
	YOLDRING	YOLDRINGS
	YOLK	YOLKS ▪ YOLKY
	YOM	YOMP
	YOMP	YOMPS
	YON	YOND ▪ YONI ▪ YONT
	YONDER	YONDERS
	YONI	YONIC ▪ YONIS
	YONKER	YONKERS
	YONNIE	YONNIES
AYONT	**YONT**	
	YOOF	YOOFS
	YOOP	YOOPS
	YOPPER	YOPPERS

	FRONT HOOK	ROOT WORD	END HOOK
		YORE	YORES
		YORK	YORKS
		YORKER	YORKERS
		YORKIE	YORKIES
		YORP	YORPS
		YOTTABYTE	YOTTABYTES
		YOU	YOUK ▪ YOUR ▪ YOUS
		YOUK	YOUKS
		YOUNG	YOUNGS
		YOUNGER	YOUNGERS
		YOUNGLING	YOUNGLINGS
		YOUNGSTER	YOUNGSTERS
		YOUNGTH	YOUNGTHS
		YOUNKER	YOUNKERS
		YOUPON	YOUPONS
		YOUR	YOURN ▪ YOURS ▪ YOURT
		YOURT	YOURTS
		YOUS	YOUSE
		YOUTH	YOUTHS ▪ YOUTHY
		YOUTHEN	YOUTHENS
		YOUTHHEAD	YOUTHHEADS
		YOUTHHOOD	YOUTHHOODS
		YOW	YOWE ▪ YOWL ▪ YOWS
		YOWE	YOWED ▪ YOWES
		YOWIE	YOWIES
		YOWL	YOWLS
		YOWLER	YOWLERS
		YOWLEY	YOWLEYS
		YOWLING	YOWLINGS
		YPERITE	YPERITES
		YPSILON	YPSILONS
		YRNEH	YRNEHS
		YSHEND	YSHENDS
		YTTERBIA	YTTERBIAS
		YTTERBITE	YTTERBITES
		YTTERBIUM	YTTERBIUMS
		YTTRIA	YTTRIAS
		YTTRIUM	YTTRIUMS
	AYU ▪ KYU	YU	YUG ▪ YUK ▪ YUM ▪ YUP ▪ YUS
		YUAN	YUANS
		YUCA	YUCAS
		YUCCA	YUCCAS
		YUCK	YUCKO ▪ YUCKS ▪ YUCKY
		YUCKER	YUCKERS
		YUFT	YUFTS
		YUG	YUGA ▪ YUGS
		YUGA	YUGAS
		YUGARIE	YUGARIES
		YUK	YUKE ▪ YUKO ▪ YUKS ▪ YUKY
		YUKATA	YUKATAS
		YUKE	YUKED ▪ YUKES
		YUKO	YUKOS
		YULAN	YULANS
		YULE	YULES
		YULETIDE	YULETIDES
		YUM	YUMP
		YUMMIES	YUMMIEST
		YUMP	YUMPS
		YUMPIE	YUMPIES
		YUP	YUPS
		YUPON	YUPONS
		YUPPIE	YUPPIES
		YUPPIEDOM	YUPPIEDOMS
		YURT	YURTA ▪ YURTS
		YURTA	YURTAS
	AYUS ▪ KYUS	YUS	
		YUZU	YUZUS

Z

FRONT HOOK	ROOT WORD	END HOOK
	ZA	ZAG ▪ ZAP ▪ ZAS ▪ ZAX
	ZABAIONE	ZABAIONES
	ZABAJONE	ZABAJONES
	ZABETA	ZABETAS
	ZABRA	ZABRAS
	ZABTIEH	ZABTIEHS
	ZACATON	ZACATONS
	ZACK	ZACKS
TZADDIK	**ZADDIK**	ZADDIKS
TZADDIKIM	**ZADDIKIM**	
TZADDIKS	**ZADDIKS**	
	ZAFFAR	ZAFFARS
	ZAFFER	ZAFFERS
	ZAFFIR	ZAFFIRS
	ZAFFRE	ZAFFRES
	ZAG	ZAGS
	ZAIKAI	ZAIKAIS
	ZAIRE	ZAIRES
	ZAITECH	ZAITECHS
	ZAKAT	ZAKATS
	ZAMAN	ZAMANG ▪ ZAMANS
	ZAMANG	ZAMANGS
	ZAMARRA	ZAMARRAS
	ZAMARRO	ZAMARROS
	ZAMBO	ZAMBOS (offensive)
	ZAMBOMBA	ZAMBOMBAS
	ZAMBOORAK	ZAMBOORAKS
	ZAMBUCK	ZAMBUCKS
	ZAMBUK	ZAMBUKS
	ZAMIA	ZAMIAS
	ZAMINDAR	ZAMINDARI ▪ ZAMINDARS ▪ ZAMINDARY
	ZAMINDARI	ZAMINDARIS
	ZAMOUSE	ZAMOUSES
	ZAMPOGNA	ZAMPOGNAS
	ZANANA	ZANANAS
	ZANDER	ZANDERS
	ZANELLA	ZANELLAS
	ZANIES	ZANIEST
	ZANJA	ZANJAS
	ZANJERO	ZANJEROS
	ZANTE	ZANTES
	ZANTHOXYL	ZANTHOXYLS
	ZANYISM	ZANYISMS
	ZANZA	ZANZAS
	ZANZE	ZANZES
	ZAP	ZAPS
	ZAPATEADO	ZAPATEADOS
	ZAPATEO	ZAPATEOS
	ZAPOTILLA	ZAPOTILLAS
	ZAPPER	ZAPPERS
	ZAPTIAH	ZAPTIAHS
	ZAPTIEH	ZAPTIEHS
	ZARAPE	ZARAPES
	ZARATITE	ZARATITES
	ZAREBA	ZAREBAS
	ZAREEBA	ZAREEBAS
	ZARF	ZARFS
	ZARIBA	ZARIBAS
	ZARNEC	ZARNECS
	ZARNICH	ZARNICHS
	ZARZUELA	ZARZUELAS
	ZATI	ZATIS
	ZAYIN	ZAYINS
	ZAZEN	ZAZENS
	ZEA	ZEAL ▪ ZEAS
	ZEAL	ZEALS

FRONT HOOK	ROOT WORD	END HOOK
	ZEALANT	ZEALANTS
	ZEALOT	ZEALOTS
	ZEALOTISM	ZEALOTISMS
	ZEATIN	ZEATINS
	ZEBEC	ZEBECK ▪ ZEBECS
	ZEBECK	ZEBECKS
	ZEBRA	ZEBRAS
	ZEBRANO	ZEBRANOS
	ZEBRAS	ZEBRASS
	ZEBRAWOOD	ZEBRAWOODS
	ZEBRINA	ZEBRINAS
	ZEBRINE	ZEBRINES
	ZEBRULA	ZEBRULAS
	ZEBRULE	ZEBRULES
	ZEBU	ZEBUB ▪ ZEBUS
	ZEBUB	ZEBUBS
	ZECCHIN	ZECCHINE ▪ ZECCHINI ▪ ZECCHINO
		ZECCHINS
	ZECCHINE	ZECCHINES
	ZECCHINO	ZECCHINOS
	ZECHIN	ZECHINS
	ZED	ZEDS
MZEE	**ZEE**	ZEES
MZEES	**ZEES**	
	ZEIN	ZEINS
	ZEITGEBER	ZEITGEBERS
	ZEITGEIST	ZEITGEISTS
	ZEK	ZEKS
	ZEL	ZELS
	ZELANT	ZELANTS
	ZELATOR	ZELATORS
	ZELATRICE	ZELATRICES
	ZELKOVA	ZELKOVAS
	ZELOTYPIA	ZELOTYPIAS
	ZEMINDAR	ZEMINDARI ▪ ZEMINDARS ▪ ZEMINDARY
	ZEMINDARI	ZEMINDARIS
	ZEMSTVO	ZEMSTVOS
	ZENAIDA	ZENAIDAS
	ZENANA	ZENANAS
	ZENDIK	ZENDIKS
	ZENITH	ZENITHS
	ZEOLITE	ZEOLITES
	ZEP	ZEPS
	ZEPHYR	ZEPHYRS
	ZEPPELIN	ZEPPELINS
	ZEPPOLE	ZEPPOLES
	ZERDA	ZERDAS
	ZEREBA	ZEREBAS
	ZERIBA	ZERIBAS
	ZERK	ZERKS
	ZERO	ZEROS
	ZERUMBET	ZERUMBETS
	ZEST	ZESTS ▪ ZESTY
	ZESTER	ZESTERS
	ZETA	ZETAS
	ZETETIC	ZETETICS
	ZETTABYTE	ZETTABYTES
	ZEUGMA	ZEUGMAS
	ZEUXITE	ZEUXITES
	ZEZE	ZEZES
DZHO	**ZHO**	ZHOS
	ZHOMO	ZHOMOS
DZHOS	**ZHOS**	
	ZIBELINE	ZIBELINES
	ZIBELLINE	ZIBELLINES
	ZIBET	ZIBETH ▪ ZIBETS
	ZIBETH	ZIBETHS
	ZIFF	ZIFFS
	ZIG	ZIGS

FRONT HOOK	ROOT WORD	END HOOK
	ZIGAN	ZIGANS
	ZIGANKA	ZIGANKAS
	ZIGGURAT	ZIGGURATS
	ZIGZAG	ZIGZAGS
	ZIGZAGGER	ZIGZAGGERS · ZIGZAGGERY
	ZIKKURAT	ZIKKURATS
	ZIKURAT	ZIKURATS
	ZILA	ZILAS
	ZILL	ZILLA · ZILLS
	ZILLA	ZILLAH · ZILLAS
	ZILLAH	ZILLAHS
	ZILLION	ZILLIONS
	ZILLIONTH	ZILLIONTHS
	ZIMB	ZIMBI · ZIMBS
	ZIMBI	ZIMBIS
	ZIMMER	ZIMMERS
	ZIMOCCA	ZIMOCCAS
	ZIN	ZINC · ZINE · ZING · ZINS
	ZINC	ZINCO · ZINCS · ZINCY
	ZINCATE	ZINCATES
	ZINCITE	ZINCITES
	ZINCO	ZINCOS
	ZINCODE	ZINCODES
AZINE	ZINE	ZINEB · ZINES
	ZINEB	ZINEBS
AZINES	ZINES	
	ZINFANDEL	ZINFANDELS
	ZING	ZINGS · ZINGY
	ZINGEL	ZINGELS
	ZINGER	ZINGERS
	ZINGIBER	ZINGIBERS
	ZINKE	ZINKED · ZINKES
	ZINKENITE	ZINKENITES
	ZINNIA	ZINNIAS
	ZIP	ZIPS
	ZIPPER	ZIPPERS
	ZIPPO	ZIPPOS
	ZIRAM	ZIRAMS
	ZIRCALLOY	ZIRCALLOYS
	ZIRCALOY	ZIRCALOYS
	ZIRCON	ZIRCONS
	ZIRCONIA	ZIRCONIAS
	ZIRCONIUM	ZIRCONIUMS
	ZIT	ZITE · ZITI · ZITS
	ZITHER	ZITHERN · ZITHERS
	ZITHERIST	ZITHERISTS
	ZITHERN	ZITHERNS
	ZITI	ZITIS
	ZIZ	ZIZZ
	ZIZANIA	ZIZANIAS
	ZIZEL	ZIZELS
	ZIZIT	ZIZITH
	ZIZZLE	ZIZZLED · ZIZZLES
	ZLOTY	ZLOTYS
AZO · DZO	ZO	ZOA · ZOL · ZOO · ZOS
	ZOAEA	ZOAEAE · ZOAEAS
	ZOARIA	ZOARIAL
	ZOBO	ZOBOS
	ZOBU	ZOBUS
	ZOCALO	ZOCALOS
	ZOCCO	ZOCCOS
	ZOCCOLO	ZOCCOLOS
	ZODIAC	ZODIACS
	ZOEA	ZOEAE · ZOEAL · ZOEAS
	ZOECHROME	ZOECHROMES
	ZOETROPE	ZOETROPES
	ZOIATRIA	ZOIATRIAS
AZOIC	ZOIC	
	ZOISITE	ZOISITES

FRONT HOOK	ROOT WORD	END HOOK
	ZOISM	ZOISMS
	ZOIST	ZOISTS
	ZOL	ZOLS
	ZOMBI	ZOMBIE ▪ ZOMBIS
	ZOMBIE	ZOMBIES
	ZOMBIISM	ZOMBIISMS
	ZOMBORUK	ZOMBORUKS
	ZONA	ZONAE ▪ ZONAL
AZONAL	**ZONAL**	
OZONATE	**ZONATE**	ZONATED
OZONATED	**ZONATED**	
OZONATION	**ZONATION**	ZONATIONS
OZONATIONS	**ZONATIONS**	
	ZONDA	ZONDAS
OZONE	**ZONE**	ZONED ▪ ZONER ▪ ZONES
	ZONER	ZONERS
OZONES	**ZONES**	
	ZONETIME	ZONETIMES
	ZONING	ZONINGS
	ZONK	ZONKS
	ZONULA	ZONULAE ▪ ZONULAR ▪ ZONULAS
	ZONULE	ZONULES ▪ ZONULET
	ZONULET	ZONULETS
	ZONURE	ZONURES
	ZOO	ZOOM ▪ ZOON ▪ ZOOS ▪ ZOOT
	ZOOBLAST	ZOOBLASTS
	ZOOCHORE	ZOOCHORES
	ZOOEA	ZOOEAE ▪ ZOOEAL ▪ ZOOEAS
	ZOOGAMETE	ZOOGAMETES
	ZOOGLEA	ZOOGLEAE ▪ ZOOGLEAL ▪ ZOOGLEAS
	ZOOGLOEA	ZOOGLOEAE ▪ ZOOGLOEAL ▪ ZOOGLOEAS
	ZOOGRAFT	ZOOGRAFTS
	ZOOID	ZOOIDS
	ZOOKEEPER	ZOOKEEPERS
	ZOOLATER	ZOOLATERS
	ZOOLATRIA	ZOOLATRIAS
	ZOOLITE	ZOOLITES
	ZOOLITH	ZOOLITHS
	ZOOLOGIST	ZOOLOGISTS
	ZOOM	ZOOMS
	ZOOMANIA	ZOOMANIAS
	ZOOMORPH	ZOOMORPHS ▪ ZOOMORPHY
	ZOON	ZOONS
	ZOONITE	ZOONITES
	ZOONOMIA	ZOONOMIAS
	ZOONOMIST	ZOONOMISTS
	ZOOPERIST	ZOOPERISTS
	ZOOPHAGAN	ZOOPHAGANS
	ZOOPHILE	ZOOPHILES
	ZOOPHILIA	ZOOPHILIAS
	ZOOPHOBE	ZOOPHOBES
	ZOOPHOBIA	ZOOPHOBIAS
	ZOOPHORI	ZOOPHORIC
	ZOOPHYTE	ZOOPHYTES
	ZOOSPERM	ZOOSPERMS
	ZOOSPORE	ZOOSPORES
	ZOOSTEROL	ZOOSTEROLS
	ZOOT	ZOOTY
	ZOOTHECIA	ZOOTHECIAL
	ZOOTHEISM	ZOOTHEISMS
	ZOOTHOME	ZOOTHOMES
	ZOOTOMIST	ZOOTOMISTS
	ZOOTOXIN	ZOOTOXINS
	ZOOTROPE	ZOOTROPES
	ZOOTYPE	ZOOTYPES
	ZOOZOO	ZOOZOOS
	ZOPILOTE	ZOPILOTES
	ZORBING	ZORBINGS
	ZORBONAUT	ZORBONAUTS

FRONT HOOK	ROOT WORD	END HOOK
	ZORGITE	ZORGITES
	ZORI	ZORIL ▪ ZORIS
	ZORIL	ZORILS
	ZORILLA	ZORILLAS
	ZORILLE	ZORILLES
	ZORILLO	ZORILLOS
	ZORINO	ZORINOS
	ZORRO	ZORROS
DZOS	**ZOS**	
	ZOSTER	ZOSTERS
	ZOUAVE	ZOUAVES
	ZOUK	ZOUKS
	ZOYSIA	ZOYSIAS
	ZUCCHETTO	ZUCCHETTOS
	ZUCCHINI	ZUCCHINIS
	ZUCHETTA	ZUCHETTAS
	ZUCHETTO	ZUCHETTOS
	ZUGZWANG	ZUGZWANGS
	ZULU	ZULUS
	ZUMBOORUK	ZUMBOORUKS
	ZUPA	ZUPAN ▪ ZUPAS
	ZUPAN	ZUPANS
	ZURF	ZURFS
	ZWIEBACK	ZWIEBACKS
	ZYDECO	ZYDECOS
	ZYGA	ZYGAL
	ZYGANTRUM	ZYGANTRUMS
	ZYGOMA	ZYGOMAS
	ZYGOMATIC	ZYGOMATICS
	ZYGOPHYTE	ZYGOPHYTES
	ZYGOSE	ZYGOSES
AZYGOSES	**ZYGOSES**	
	ZYGOSPERM	ZYGOSPERMS
AZYGOSPORE	**ZYGOSPORE**	ZYGOSPORES
	ZYGOTE	ZYGOTES
	ZYGOTENE	ZYGOTENES
	ZYLONITE	ZYLONITES
	ZYMASE	ZYMASES
AZYME	**ZYME**	ZYMES
AZYMES	**ZYMES**	
AZYMITE	**ZYMITE**	ZYMITES
AZYMITES	**ZYMITES**	
	ZYMOGEN	ZYMOGENE ▪ ZYMOGENS
	ZYMOGENE	ZYMOGENES
	ZYMOGRAM	ZYMOGRAMS
	ZYMOME	ZYMOMES
	ZYMOMETER	ZYMOMETERS
	ZYMOSAN	ZYMOSANS
	ZYMOTIC	ZYMOTICS
	ZYTHUM	ZYTHUMS
	ZYZZYVA	ZYZZYVAS
	ZZZ	ZZZS

TWO AND THREE LETTER WORDS

FRONT HOOK	ROOT WORD	END HOOK
AA · BA · DA · EA · FA · HA · JA · KA · LA · MA · NA · PA · TA · YA · ZA	**A**	AA · AB · AD · AE · AG · AH · AI · AL · AM · AN · AR · AS · AT · AW · AX · AY
AB · OB	**B**	BA · BE · BI · BO · BY
	C	CH
AD · ED · ID · OD	**D**	DA · DE · DI · DO
AE · BE · DE · EE · FE · HE · NE · OE · PE · RE · TE · WE · YE	**E**	EA · ED · EE · EF · EH · EL · EM · EN · ER · ES · ET · EX
EF · IF · OF	**F**	FA · FE · FY
AG · UG	**G**	GI · GO · GU
AH · CH · EH · OH · SH · UH	**H**	HA · HE · HI · HM · HO
AI · BI · DI · GI · HI · KI · LI · MI · OI · PI · QI · SI · TI · XI	**I**	ID · IF · IN · IO · IS · IT
	J	JA · JO
	K	KA · KI · KO · KY
AL · EL	**L**	LA · LI · LO
AM · EM · HM · MM · OM · UM	**M**	MA · ME · MI · MM · MO · MU · MY
AN · EN · IN · ON · UN	**N**	NA · NE · NO · NU · NY
BO · DO · GO · HO · IO · JO · KO · LO · MO · NO · OO · PO · SO · TO · WO · YO · ZO	**O**	OB · OD · OE · OF · OH · OI · OM · ON · OO · OP · OR · OS · OU · OW · OX · OY
OP · UP	**P**	PA · PE · PI · PO
	Q	QI
AR · ER · OR · UR	**R**	RE
AS · ES · IS · OS · US	**S**	SH · SI · SO · ST
AT · ET · IT · ST · UT	**T**	TA · TE · TI · TO
GU · MU · NU · OU · XU · YU	**U**	UG · UH · UM · UN · UP · UR · US · UT
	V	
AW · OW	**W**	WE · WO
AX · EX · OX	**X**	XI · XU
AY · BY · FY · KY · MY · NY · OY	**Y**	YA · YE · YO · YU
	Z	ZA · ZO

FRONT HOOK	ROOT WORD	END HOOK
BAA · CAA · FAA · MAA	**AA**	AAH · AAL · AAS
CAB · DAB · FAB · GAB · JAB · KAB · LAB · NAB · SAB · TAB · WAB	**AB**	ABA · ABB · ABO *(offensive)* · ABS · ABY
BAD · CAD · DAD · FAD · GAD · HAD · LAD · MAD · PAD · RAD · SAD · TAD · WAD · YAD	**AD**	ADD · ADO · ADS · ADZ
DAE · FAE · GAE · HAE · KAE · MAE · NAE · SAE · TAE · VAE · WAE · YAE	**AE**	
BAG · CAG · DAG · FAG · GAG · HAG · JAG · LAG · MAG · NAG · RAG · SAG · TAG · VAG · WAG · YAG · ZAG	**AG**	AGA · AGE · AGO · AGS
AAH · BAH · DAH · FAH · HAH · LAH · NAH · PAH · RAH · YAH	**AH**	AHA · AHI · AHS
JAI · KAI · RAI · SAI · TAI · WAI	**AI**	AIA · AID · AIL · AIM · AIN · AIR · AIS · AIT
AAL · BAL · DAL · GAL · MAL · PAL · SAL	**AL**	ALA · ALB · ALE · ALF · ALL · ALP · ALS · ALT
BAM · CAM · DAM · GAM · HAM · JAM · KAM · LAM · MAM · NAM · PAM · RAM · SAM · TAM · YAM	**AM**	AMA · AMI · AMP · AMU
BAN · CAN · DAN · EAN · FAN · GAN · HAN · MAN · NAN · PAN · RAN · SAN · TAN · VAN · WAN	**AN**	ANA · AND · ANE · ANI · ANN · ANT · ANY
BAR · CAR · EAR · FAR · GAR · JAR · LAR · MAR · OAR · PAR · SAR · TAR · WAR · YAR	**AR**	ARB · ARC · ARD · ARE · ARF · ARK · ARM · ARS · ART · ARY
AAS · BAS · DAS · EAS · FAS · GAS · HAS · KAS · LAS · MAS · NAS · PAS · RAS · TAS · VAS · WAS · ZAS	**AS**	ASH · ASK · ASP · ASS
BAT · CAT · EAT · FAT · GAT · HAT · KAT · LAT · MAT · NAT · OAT · PAT · QAT · RAT · SAT · TAT · VAT · WAT	**AT**	ATE · ATT
CAW · DAW · FAW · HAW · JAW · KAW · LAW · MAW · NAW · PAW · RAW · SAW · TAW · VAW · WAW · YAW	**AW**	AWA · AWE · AWL · AWN
FAX · LAX · MAX · PAX · RAX · SAX · TAX · WAX · ZAX	**AX**	AXE
BAY · CAY · DAY · FAY · GAY · HAY · JAY · KAY · LAY · MAY · NAY · PAY · RAY · SAY · TAY · WAY · YAY	**AY**	AYE · AYS · AYU

FRONT HOOK	ROOT WORD	END HOOK
ABA = OBA	**BA**	BAA = BAC = BAD = BAG = BAH = BAL = BAM BAN = BAP = BAR = BAS = BAT = BAY
OBE	**BE**	BED = BEE = BEG = BEL = BEN = BES = BET BEY = BEZ
OBI	**BI**	BIB = BID = BIG = BIN = BIO = BIS = BIT BIZ
ABO (offensive) = OBO	**BO**	BOA = BOB = BOD = BOG = BOH = BOI = BOK BON = BOO = BOP = BOR = BOS = BOT = BOW BOX = BOY
ABY	**BY**	BYE = BYS
ACH = ECH = ICH = OCH	**CH**	CHA = CHE = CHI
ODA	**DA**	DAB = DAD = DAE = DAG = DAH = DAK = DAL DAM = DAN = DAP = DAS = DAW = DAY
IDE = ODE	**DE**	DEB = DEE = DEF = DEG = DEI = DEL = DEN DEV = DEW = DEX = DEY
	DI	DIB = DID = DIE = DIF = DIG = DIM = DIN DIP = DIS = DIT = DIV
ADO = UDO	**DO**	DOB = DOC = DOD = DOE = DOF = DOG = DOH DOL = DOM = DON = DOO = DOP = DOR = DOS DOT = DOW = DOY
KEA = LEA = PEA = SEA = TEA = YEA = ZEA	**EA**	EAN = EAR = EAS = EAT = EAU
BED = FED = GED = KED = LED = MED = NED PED = RED = SED = TED = WED = ZED	**ED**	EDH = EDS
BEE = CEE = DEE = FEE = GEE = JEE = LEE MEE = NEE = PEE = REE = SEE = TEE = VEE WEE = ZEE	**EE**	EEK = EEL = EEN
DEF = KEF = NEF = REF = TEF	**EF**	EFF = EFS = EFT
FEH = HEH = PEH = REH = YEH	**EH**	EHS
BEL = CEL = DEL = EEL = GEL = MEL = SEL TEL = ZEL	**EL**	ELD = ELF = ELK = ELL = ELM = ELS = ELT
FEM = GEM = HEM = MEM = REM = WEM	**EM**	EME = EMO = EMS = EMU
BEN = DEN = EEN = FEN = GEN = HEN = KEN MEN = PEN = REN = SEN = TEN = WEN = YEN	**EN**	END = ENE = ENG = ENS
FER = HER = PER = SER	**ER**	ERA = ERE = ERF = ERG = ERK = ERN = ERR = ERS
BES = FES = HES = LES (offensive) = MES = OES PES = RES = TES = YES	**ES**	ESS = EST
BET = FET = GET = HET = JET = KET = LET MET = NET = PET = RET = SET = TET = VET WET = YET	**ET**	ETA = ETH
DEX = HEX = KEX = LEX = REX = SEX = TEX VEX = WEX = YEX = ZEX	**EX**	EXO
	FA	FAA = FAB = FAD = FAE = FAG = FAH = FAN FAP = FAR = FAS = FAT = FAW = FAX = FAY
	FE	FED = FEE = FEG = FEH = FEM = FEN = FER FES = FET = FEU = FEW = FEY = FEZ
	GI	GIB = GID = GIE = GIF = GIG = GIN = GIO GIP = GIS = GIT
AGO = EGO = YGO	**GO**	GOA = GOB = GOD = GOE = GON = GOO = GOR GOS = GOT = GOV = GOX = GOY
	GU	GUB = GUE = GUL = GUM = GUN = GUP = GUR GUS = GUT = GUV = GUY
AHA = CHA = SHA = WHA	**HA**	HAD = HAE = HAG = HAH = HAJ = HAM = HAN HAO = HAP = HAS = HAT = HAW = HAY
CHE = SHE = THE	**HE**	HEH = HEM = HEN = HEP = HER = HES = HET HEW = HEX = HEY
AHI = CHI = GHI = KHI = PHI	**HI**	HIC = HID = HIE = HIM = HIN = HIP = HIS HIT
OHM	**HM**	HMM
MHO = OHO = PHO = RHO = THO = WHO = ZHO	**HO**	HOA = HOB = HOC = HOD = HOE = HOG = HOH HOI = HOM = HON = HOO = HOP = HOS (offensive) = HOT = HOW = HOX = HOY
AID = BID = CID = DID = FID = GID = HID KID = LID = MID = NID = RID = TID = VID YID	**ID**	IDE = IDS
DIF = GIF = KIF = RIF = SIF	**IF**	IFF = IFS
AIN = BIN = DIN = FIN = GIN = HIN = JIN KIN = LIN = PIN = RIN = SIN = TIN = VIN WIN = YIN = ZIN	**IN**	INK = INN = INS
BIO = GIO	**IO**	ION = IOS

FRONT HOOK	ROOT WORD	END HOOK
AIS = BIS = CIS = DIS = GIS = HIS = KIS LIS = MIS = NIS = PIS = QIS = SIS = TIS VIS = WIS = XIS	IS	ISH = ISM = ISO
AIT = BIT = CIT = DIT = FIT = GIT = HIT KIT = LIT = NIT = PIT = RIT = SIT = TIT WIT = ZIT	IT	ITA = ITS
	JA	JAB = JAG = JAI = JAK = JAM = JAP = JAR JAW = JAY
	JO	JOB = JOE = JOG = JOL = JOR = JOT = JOW JOY
AKA = OKA = SKA	KA	KAB = KAE = KAF = KAI = KAK = KAM = KAS KAT = KAW = KAY
SKI	KI	
	KO	KOA = KOB = KOI = KON = KOP = KOR = KOS KOW
SKY	KY	KYE = KYU
ALA	LA	LAB = LAC = LAD = LAG = LAH = LAM = LAP LAR = LAS = LAT = LAV = LAW = LAX = LAY
	LI	LIB = LID = LIE = LIG = LIN = LIP = LIS LIT
	LO	LOB = LOD = LOG = LOO = LOP = LOR = LOS LOT = LOU = LOW = LOX = LOY
AMA = SMA	MA	MAA = MAC = MAD = MAE = MAG = MAK = MAL MAM = MAN = MAP = MAR = MAS = MAT = MAW MAX = MAY
EME	ME	MED = MEE = MEG = MEL = MEM = MEN = MES MET = MEU = MEW
AMI	MI	MIB = MIC = MID = MIG = MIL = MIM = MIR MIS = MIX = MIZ
HMM = UMM	MM	
EMO	MO	MOA = MOB = MOC = MOD = MOE = MOG = MOI MOL = MOM = MON = MOO = MOP = MOR = MOS MOT = MOU = MOW = MOY = MOZ
AMU = EMU = UMU	MU	MUD = MUG = MUM = MUN = MUS = MUT = MUX
	MY	MYC
ANA = MNA	NA	NAB = NAE = NAG = NAH = NAM = NAN = NAP NAS = NAT = NAW = NAY
ANE = ENE = ONE	NE	NEB = NED = NEE = NEF = NEG = NEK = NEP NET = NEW
ONO	NO	NOB = NOD = NOG = NOH = NOM = NON = NOO NOR = NOS = NOT = NOW = NOX = NOY
GNU	NU	NUB = NUN = NUR = NUS = NUT
ANY = ONY = SNY	NY	NYE = NYS
BOB = COB = DOB = FOB = GOB = HOB = JOB KOB = LOB = MOB = NOB = ROB = SOB = YOB	OB	OBA = OBE = OBI = OBO = OBS
BOD = COD = DOD = GOD = HOD = LOD = MOD NOD = POD = ROD = SOD = TOD = YOD	OD	ODA = ODD = ODE = ODS
DOE = FOE = GOE = HOE = JOE = MOE = ROE TOE = VOE = WOE	OE	OES
DOF = OOF = WOF	OF	OFF = OFT
BOH = DOH = FOH = HOH = NOH = OOH = POH SOH	OH	OHM = OHO = OHS
BOI = HOI = KOI = MOI = POI	OI	OIK = OIL
DOM = HOM = MOM = NOM = OOM = POM = ROM SOM = TOM = YOM	OM	OMS
BON = CON = DON = EON = FON = GON = HON ION = KON = MON = NON = OON = SON = TON WON = YON	ON	ONE = ONO = ONS = ONY
BOO = COO = DOO = GOO = HOO = LOO = MOO NOO = POO = ROO = TOO = WOO = ZOO	OO	OOF = OOH = OOM = OON = OOP = OOR = OOS OOT
BOP = COP = DOP = FOP = HOP = KOP = LOP MOP = OOP = POP = SOP = TOP = WOP (offensive)	OP	OPE = OPS = OPT
BOR = COR = DOR = FOR = GOR = JOR = KOR LOR = MOR = NOR = OOR = TOR = VOR	OR	ORA = ORB = ORC = ORD = ORE = ORF = ORS ORT
BOS = COS = DOS = GOS = HOS (offensive) = IOS KOS = LOS = MOS = NOS = OOS = POS = SOS WOS = YOS = ZOS	OS	OSE
FOU = LOU = MOU = SOU = YOU	OU	OUD = OUK = OUP = OUR = OUS = OUT

FRONT HOOK	ROOT WORD	END HOOK
BOW · COW · DOW · HOW · JOW · KOW · LOW MOW · NOW · POW · ROW · SOW · TOW · VOW WOW · YOW	OW	OWE · OWL · OWN · OWT
BOX · COX · FOX · GOX · HOX · LOX · NOX POX · SOX · VOX · WOX	OX	OXO · OXY
BOY · COY · DOY · FOY · GOY · HOY · JOY LOY · MOY · NOY · SOY · TOY	OY	OYE · OYS
SPA	PA	PAC · PAD · PAH · PAL · PAM · PAN · PAP PAR · PAS · PAT · PAV · PAW · PAX · PAY
APE · OPE	PE	PEA · PEC · PED · PEE · PEG · PEH · PEN PEP · PER · PES · PET · PEW
	PI	PIA · PIC · PIE · PIG · PIN · PIP · PIR PIS · PIT · PIU · PIX
APO · UPO	PO	POA · POD · POH · POI · POL · POM · POO POP · POS · POT · POW · POX · POZ
	QI	
	QI	QIS
ARE · ERE · IRE · ORE · PRE · URE	RE	REB · REC · RED · REE · REF · REG · REH REI · REN · REM · REO · REP · RES · RET REV · REW · REX · REZ
ASH · ISH	SH	SHA · SHE · SHH · SHY
PSI	SI	SIB · SIC · SIF · SIK · SIM · SIN · SIP SIR · SIS · SIT · SIX
DSO · ISO	SO	SOB · SOC · SOD · SOG · SOH · SOL · SOM SON · SOP · SOS · SOT · SOU · SOV · SOW SOX · SOY
EST · PST	ST	STY
ETA · ITA · UTA	TA	TAB · TAD · TAE · TAG · TAI · TAJ · TAK TAM · TAN · TAO · TAP · TAR · TAS · TAT TAU · TAV · TAW · TAX · TAY
ATE · UTE	TE	TEA · TEC · TED · TEE · TEF · TEG · TEL TEN · TES · TET · TEW · TEX
	TI	TIC · TID · TIE · TIG · TIL · TIN · TIP TIS · TIT · TIX
	TO	TOC · TOD · TOE · TOG · TOM · TON · TOO TOP · TOR · TOT · TOW · TOY
BUG · DUG · FUG · HUG · JUG · LUG · MUG PUG · RUG · TUG · VUG · YUG	UG	UGH · UGS
DUH · HUH · PUH	UH	
BUM · CUM · FUM · GUM · HUM · LUM · MUM RUM · SUM · TUM · VUM · YUM	UM	UMM · UMP · UMU
BUN · DUN · FUN · GUN · HUN · JUN · MUN NUN · PUN · RUN · SUN · TUN	UN	UNI · UNS
CUP · DUP · GUP · HUP · OUP · PUP · SUP TUP · YUP	UP	UPO · UPS
BUR · CUR · FUR · GUR · LUR · NUR · OUR PUR · SUR	UR	URB · URD · URE · URN · URP
BUS · GUS · JUS · MUS · NUS · OUS · PUS SUS · WUS · YUS	US	USE
BUT · CUT · GUT · HUT · JUT · MUT · NUT OUT · PUT · RUT · TUT	UT	UTA · UTE · UTS · UTU
AWE · EWE · OWE	WE	WEB · WED · WEE · WEM · WEN · WET · WEX WEY
TWO	WO	WOE · WOF · WOG · WOK · WON · WOO WOP (offensive) · WOS · WOT · WOW · WOX
	XI	XIS
PYA · RYA	YA	YAD · YAE · YAG · YAH · YAK · YAM · YAP YAR · YAW · YAY
AYE · BYE · DYE · EYE · HYE · KYE · LYE NYE · OYE · PYE · RYE · SYE · TYE · WYE	YE	YEA · YEH · YEN · YEP · YES · YET · YEW YEX
	YO	YOB · YOD · YOK · YOM · YON · YOS · YOU YOW
AYU · KYU	YU	YUG · YUK · YUM · YUP · YUS
	ZA	ZAG · ZAP · ZAS · ZAX
AZO · DZO	ZO	ZOA · ZOL · ZOO · ZOS

SOLUTIONS

See page vi

(U)SABLE allows UNFIT;
(A)VENUE allows FAIN
(U)PLAID allows FUTON;
PRIES(T) allows FAINT
(O)RALLY allows FOUNT;
(S)LANDER allows FIAT